THE DEVELOPMENT OF ENGLISH DRAMA

The
Development of
English
Drama

AN ANTHOLOGY

Edited by

GERALD EADES BENTLEY
Princeton University

. . .

APPLETON–CENTURY–CROFTS, Inc.
New York

Preface

THE PLAYS in this collection have been assembled and edited to fit the needs of under-graduates interested in acquiring some understanding of the course of development of English drama before the twentieth century. They were selected to illustrate as many as possible of the dramatic modes, forms, and conventions which have attained signifi-cance in the dramatic evolution of ten centuries.

Two obvious but generally ignored considerations have governed the preparation of the texts: (1) since they are intended for the use of undergraduates, clarity and not scholarly exactness is the prime consideration; (2) since the works are plays, it is vital that the reader should visualize performance and not simply follow a narrative in dialogue form. These principles have dictated hundreds of alterations in texts which have usually been printed either with all the minute and exact paraphernalia needed by scholars and graduate students, or else with no care at all.

In the interests of clarity, simplicity, and directness of approach to the plays in this volume, and with the sole purpose of helping undergraduates to follow the plays easily, whatever textual variant seems to me nearest to the dramatist's intention has been printed without comment, errors have been silently emended, punctuation has been modernized and regularized, dramatis personae have been completely rewritten and reordered. Annotations have been made with the same intent. All questions of text, source, date, or analogues have been ignored, and the notes have been kept as few as possible and have been designed exclusively to make the plays easier for the undergradu-ate to understand.

The second principle governing the preparation of these texts has led to even more changes. After twenty-five years of discussing plays in the classroom, I am still surprised at the inability of most intelligent undergraduates to visualize scenes—to think of a play as a play. Most of them have been taught to read plays—especially Shakespeare's plays—as if they were either treatises or narratives in dialogue. When asked to visualize a scene either they are baffled completely, or else they go off into the most irrelevant or even contradictory flights of unbridled imagination. To them the art form of Webster and Sheridan has been presented as no different from that of Milton or Richardson. Of course part of the difficulty lies in the frequently-ignored fact that plays are written to be seen, not read, and that the intelligent reading of a play is a far more difficult feat than the reading of a novel or poem of equal subtlety.

In the light of these difficulties I have attempted to help the undergraduate visualize the action by adding hundreds of stage directions to the plays, especially to those before

1600. Most early playwrights gave little consideration to readers, and adequate or even minimal stage directions in their plays are unknown. Clearly they did not hope—except in a few cases like occasional scenes in Ben Jonson's *Devil is an Ass* or *The Tale of a Tub*—to transfer a performance to the printed page. Therefore I have not scrupled to add many stage directions to the early plays printed here. It seems to me far better to risk having the student visualize an action or emphasize an interchange in a fashion occasionally not quite that intended by the dramatist than that he simply follow the original bare dialogue unconscious that any action at all is implied. In the nineteenth century many dramatists adopted the practice of printing frequent explanatory stage directions, and I have therefore added very few to the plays appearing after 1800.

The conventional biographical essay on each author has been here replaced by a list of the principal events in the dramatist's life. I have followed the editors of the Crofts Classics in this device, which seems to me to improve on the biographical essay by increasing the information made available and eliminating dubious personal interpretations. The separate introductions for each play have been designed to demonstrate a variety of approaches, though none of them, I hope, ever loses sight of the fact that a play is primarily a theatrical and only secondarily and occasionally a literary document.

I should like to thank my wife and my research assistant, Mr. Frank Wadsworth, for their unstinted help in preparing the material in this book for publication.

G. E. B.

Contents

❧❧❧❧❧

Quem Quaeritis

The drama of the Western world—as distinguished from the still older drama of India and China—began in Greece in the sixth century B.C. and flourished in the fifth and fourth. From Greece it was carried to Rome and greatly modified during the centuries of Roman ascendency. The great classic drama degenerated in the later centuries of the Roman Empire into grossly immoral performances closely associated with the spectacles of the Coliseum and the other great amphitheatres of the Roman Empire. This degenerate Roman drama earned the hatred and fear of the early church fathers, of most of the Roman moralists, and even of a number of the emperors. Its hold on the people was so great, however, that neither the power of the government nor the threats of the early church—including excommunication—could stamp it out. For centuries the bishops preached against it and accomplished nothing. It was finally obliterated in the barbarian invasions, by the effective device of destroying the financial backing, tearing down the theatres, and murdering the actors—the rude and violent Lombards succeeded where the sermons and edicts of the church had failed for five centuries. Nonetheless the effect of the long and unsuccessful opposition by the moralists and by the church to the popular theatre has not even yet entirely disappeared, and in the time of Marlowe and Shakespeare the ancient tendency to think of the theatre and of actors as immoral was common.

Under the circumstances it is not strange that when drama appeared again in the Western world it developed slowly from the most rudimentary beginnings as if it had never before been known. It is ironic that it arose in the Christian church, but it is not surprising, for all the known drama of the world, in whatever civilization, has always developed as a part of religious rites. The religious observance from which modern English and American drama derives is the mass of the Roman Catholic church as sung in the great monastic churches of Western Europe during the ninth and tenth centuries.

In these monastic communities the climax of the year was, of course, Holy Week. The entire life of the community during this week was devoted to contemplation of the suffering, crucifixion, burial, and resurrection of Jesus, and the brothers developed many observances to vivify their devotions. On Good Friday the cross at the high altar was reverently taken down, as if it were the body of Jesus, and concealed, as if in a tomb. At the tenebrae services in the latter days of the week the lights of the great church were extinguished one by one to symbolize the gathering darkness of the death of Jesus and the apparent doom of mankind. The Easter services marked the boundless joy at the resurrection of Jesus, and more mimetic actions were developed to recall vividly all the details of the greatest event in Christian history. These mimetic actions gradually became drama.

From the dramatic point of view the fundamental development was the evolution of simple musical dialogues called tropes. At first the tropes appeared to differ little from other parts of the service: they were sung by the brothers of the choir, they were invariably in Latin (like the rest of the service), they involved no more action than any anthem, and they were sung antiphonally (that is, first one part of the choir sang and then the other answered). The important trope for the Easter service consisted of three lines of the dialogue at the tomb of Jesus on the first Easter morning as recorded in the Bible; one part of the choir was given the lines of the three Marys who had come to the tomb to annoint the body of Jesus, and the other part was given the lines of the angel at the door of the tomb. They sang:

Quem quaeritis in sepulchro, O Christicolae?
[Whom do you seek in the tomb, O Christians?]
Jhesum Nazarenum crucifixum, O coelicolae.
[Jesus of Nazareth who was crucified, O heavenly one.]
Non est hic, surrexit sicut praedixerat; ite, nuntiate quia surrexit de sepulchro.
[He is not here, he is risen as foretold; go announce that he has risen from the tomb.]

As the great religious communities which were scattered over Western Europe tried to make their Easter services more moving and more vivid, it was inevitable that they gradually, over the course of centuries, combined and elaborated these features of the liturgy until they had evolved, as part of the Easter matins service, a rudimentary little playlet. The development took place in many great churches, but most of the records, like other medieval documents, have been lost or destroyed through centuries of fires, wars, and riots. One of the records preserved is a document prepared by St. Ethelwold, who became Bishop of Winchester in 963, which gives instructions for the service of Easter matins. The instructions seem to have been composed about 970, and they are thought to record the practice at Winchester Cathedral about this time. Bishop Ethelwold's instructions are written in Latin, but they may be translated as follows:

While the third lesson [of the Easter matins service] is being chanted, let four brethren vest themselves. Let one of these, vested in an alb [a white tunic which would suggest the angel] enter as though to take part in the service, and let him without being observed approach the place of the sepulchre and there sit quietly, holding a palm in his hand. While the third responsory is being sung, let the remaining three follow, all three vested in copes [vestments like long cloaks] and carrying in their hands censers filled with incense, and, stepping hesitantly in the manner of those seeking something, come before the place of the sepulchre. These things are done in imitation of the angel seated at the monument and of the women coming with spices to anoint the body of Jesus. When, therefore, he who sits there shall see the three approach like folk straying and seeking something,

let him begin in a dulcet voice of medium pitch to sing *Quem quaeritis in sepulchro, O Christicolae?* When he has sung it to the end, let the three respond in unison, *Jhesum Nazarenum crucifixum, O coelicolae.* To whom he replies, *Non est hic; surrexit sicut praedixerat. Ite, nuntiate quia surrexit a mortuis.* At the word of this command let those three turn to the choir and say, *Alleluia! resurrexit Dominus!* This said, let the former again seating himself, as if recalling them, sing the anthem, *Venite et videte locum ubi positus erat Dominus, alleluia, alleluia* [Come and see the place where the Lord was laid, Alleluia, Alleluia]. Saying this, let him rise and lift the veil and show them the place bare of the cross, but only the cloths in which the cross was wrapped laid there. Seeing this, let them set down the censers which they carried to the same sepulchre and take up the cloth and hold it out before the clergy, and as if to show that the Lord has risen and is no longer wrapped therein, let them sing this anthem, *Surrexit Dominus de sepulchro* [The Lord is risen from the sepulchre]. And let them lay the cloth upon the altar. When the anthem is finished, let the Prior, rejoicing with them at the triumph of our King, in that having conquered death, He arose, begin the hymn *Te Deum laudamus* [We praise thee, O God]. This begun, all the bells are rung together.

This rudimentary playlet, with impersonation, dialogue, action, faint suggestions of costume, and properties, must have been highly effective when combined with the solemn music of the cathedral and the impressive background of the great stone church, and played before a devout medieval congregation whose emotions had already been stirred by constant reminders of Christ's passion and the glorious resurrection whose anniversary the playlet was designed to commemorate. The *Te Deum* and the joyous clangor of all the great bells rung out together marked an emotional climax beyond the scope of most secular playwrights.

Medieval churchmen did not neglect the great possibilities which the *Quem Quaeritis* made apparent. Other episodes of the Biblical narrative were dramatized in a similar fashion and attached to appropriate occasions in the church calendar, especially Christmas, and episodes were elaborated by attaching to them preceding and succeeding events, like the Annunciation, the Flight into Egypt, and the Slaughter of the Innocents.

As the development went on and the presentations became more lengthy and elaborate, the plays became detached from the mass, passages in the vernacular instead of Latin were introduced, laymen were added to the actors, and finally the plays were acted entirely outside the church itself. The transition was a slow and laborious process of three or four hundred years, but eventually the plays were no longer in the hands of churchmen, but were acted entirely by laymen and in the language of the people.

In England several of these great collections of plays became the responsibility of local guilds and were performed all together in one long series on a specified religious holiday, like Corpus Christi day or Whitsuntide. Such cycles of religious plays—often called mystery plays because they dealt with the mysteries of the Christian religion—mark another stage of dramatic development in England well beyond the tropes of the great cathedrals and monastic churches.

The Deluge or Noah's Flood

INTRODUCTION

This little play is the third in the religious cycle of twenty-five which was given annually in the fourteenth, fifteenth, and sixteenth centuries in the medieval city of Chester, on the river Dee near the west coast of England. This cycle of plays—whose purpose was largely religious—like others of the time dramatized principal events of the Biblical narrative, from the Fall of Lucifer and the Creation of the World to the day of the Last Judgment. The performance of the entire cycle, which took three days, was a municipal enterprise in the hands of the local craft gilds; this particular play was performed by "the water leaders and drawers of the Dee." No charge was made to the spectators, who stood at open-air "stations" in the streets of the city to watch the performances on pageant wagons drawn up before them.

The most apparent characteristic of *The Deluge,* as of most medieval mystery plays, is its naiveté. A simple narrative is set forth in dialogue, with little attempt at emphasis or characterization in the speeches, little attempt to build up effective scenes, and only a very slight attempt to adapt the action of the narrative to the possibilities and the limitations of the stage. All these shortcomings are a natural result of the break in dramatic tradition in the Dark Ages and of the amateur character of the authorship and production of medieval plays.

In spite of his serious handicaps, however, it is clear that the Chester dramatist, who may have been Randall Higden, a monk of Chester Abbey, had learned something of the possibilities of the drama. His purpose is to make the Biblical story real and convincing for the people of Chester, and to do this he must make Noah and his family as much like Chester folk as possible. Therefore they swear by Christ and by St. John, they build their ark like one of the medieval ships which sailed up the Dee to Chester, and they fill it with the familiar birds and beasts of Cheshire, together with a few of the better known heraldic animals, like lions and leopards. The whole organization of the play, furthermore, shows a certain amount of skill in handling the attention of the audience. First God speaks solemnly of the state of the world and the righteousness of Noah; then Noah and family dutifully carry out their orders; then, lest the attention of the audience stray, Noah and his wife—a shrewish favorite of the audience—stage a family row; then God appears again with more orders and further obedient response by the family, followed by a picture show of the animals; and then comes the hilarious drinking scene of Mrs. Noah and her gossips, another family fight, and from then on a straight account of the voyage of the ark up to its successful conclusion. At the end, to remind the audience of the sacred significance of what they have seen, there is a final address by God on the faithfulness of Noah and a solemn promise of no more floods. Such a mingling of secular entertainment and sacred doctrine is deliberate; it bears some resemblance to Bernard Shaw's adroit mixture of farce with political and social analysis.

It takes only the most cursory examination of the account of the flood in Genesis to see that the Chester dramatist has made a shrewd and not wholly unskilled attempt to adapt the story for the stage and for his audience. The whole matter of Noah's difficulties with his wife is an addition for the entertainment of the medieval audience, and

4

while it is not highly developed, there is enough of it to show that the Chester playwright was not confining his interest solely to religious instruction but was feeling his way toward dramatic effectiveness. Though the Chester play of *The Deluge* is by no means a great play, it is an interesting example of the recrudescence of dramatic skill in the Middle Ages.

The text printed here has been modernized, and stage directions have been added.

THE DELUGE OR NOAH'S FLOOD

Dramatis personae

In order of first appearance

GOD

NOAH, An old man who has found favor in the sight of God.

SHEM, Noah's eldest son.

HAM, Noah's second son.

JAPHETH, Noah's third son.

NOAH'S WIFE, A scolding old woman, fond of her drinking cronies.

SHEM'S WIFE

HAM'S WIFE

JAPHETH'S WIFE

GOSSIPS, Alehouse drinking companions of Noah's Wife.

(*When the pageant wagon stops before the crowd, the spectators see at one end of its stage the Ark. Near the Ark* SHEM, HAM, JAPHETH, *their wives, and* NOAH'S WIFE *stand talking. Apart from them stands* NOAH, *looking up to* GOD. GOD *stands on an upper level of the pageant among painted clouds, and begins the action by speaking down to* NOAH.)

GOD. (*Solemnly*) I, God, that all the world have wrought,
Heaven and earth, and all of nought,
I see my people, in deed and thought,
Are set foul in sin.

My ghost shall not lenge[1] in man,
That through fleshly liking is my fone,[2]
But till six score years be gone,
To look if they will blynne.[3]

Man that I made I will destroy,
Beast, worm, and fowl to fly;
For on earth they do me nye,[4]
The folk that are thereon.

It harms me so hurtfully,
The malice that now doth multiply,
That sore it grieveth me inwardly
That ever I made man.

Therefore, Noah, my servant free,
That righteous man art, as I see,
A ship soon thou shalt make thee
Of trees dry and light.

Little chambers therein thou make;
And binding slich[5] also thou take,
Within and out thou never slake
To anoint it through all thy might.

300 Cubits it shall be long,
And 50 of breadth, to make it strong,
Of height 50. The mete[6] thou fonge,[7]
Thus measure it about.

One window work through thy wit,
One cubit of length and breadth make it.
Upon the side a door shall sit
For to come in and out.

Eating places thou make also;
Three-roofed chambers, one or two;
For with water I think to flow[8]
Man that I did make.

---

[1] Remain.   [2] Foe.   [3] Cease.   [4] Annoy.   [5] Slime, pitch.   [6] Dimensions.   [7] Take.   [8] Deluge.

Destroyed all the world shall be,
Save thou; thy wife, thy sons three,
And all their wives also with thee
Shall saved be, for thy sake.

NOAH. (*Raising his arms to* GOD) Ah!
 Lord, I thank Thee loud and still,
That to me are in such will,
And spares me and my house to spill,[9]
As now I soothly find.

Thy bidding, Lord, I shall fulfill,
And never more Thee grieve nor grill,[10]
That such grace hast sent me till
Among all mankind.

(NOAH *turns and calls to his family*)

Have done, you men and women all!
Help, for ought that may befall,
To work this ship, chamber and hall,
As God hath bidden us do.

SHEM. Father, I am already bowne.[11]
An axe I have, by my crown,
As sharp as any in all this town,
For to go thereto.

HAM. I have a hatchet wonder-keen
To bite well, as may be seen;
A better sharpened, as I ween,
Is not in all this town.

JAPHETH. And I can well make a pin,
And with this hammer knock it in;
Go and work without more din,
And I am ready bowne.

NOAH'S WIFE. And we shall bring timber
 too,
For we may nothing else do;
Women be weak to undergo
Any great travail.

SHEM'S WIFE. Here is a good hackstock;[12]
On this you may hew and knock;
Shall none be idle in this flock,
Nor now may no man fail.

HAM'S WIFE. And I will go to gather
 sliche,
The ship for to caulk and pitch;

Anointed it must be every stitch,
Board, tree, and pin.

JAPHETH'S WIFE. And I will gather chips
 here
To make a fire for you in feere,[13]
And for to dight [14] your dinner,
Against you come in.

(*They work at the Ark with their tools*)

NOAH. Now in the name of God I will
 begin
To make the ship that we shall in,
That we be ready for to swim
At the coming of the flood.

These boards I join here together,
To keep us safe from the weather,
That we may row both hither and thither,
And safe be from this flood.

Of this tree will I make the mast
Tied with cables that will last,
With a sail-yard for each blast,
And each thing in their kind.

With topcastle and bowsprit,
With cords and ropes I have all meet,
To sail forth at the next weete.[15]
This ship is at an end.

(NOAH *with all his family works
 at the Ark*)

Wife, in this castle we shall be keped,[16]
My childer and thou, I would, in leaped.
 NOAH'S WIFE. In faith, Noah, I had as
 lief thou slept.
For all thy frankish fare [17]

I will not do after thy red.[18]
 NOAH. Good wife, do now as I thee bid.
 NOAH'S WIFE. By Christ! not or I see
 more need,
Though thou stand all the day and stare.

(*She rages about the stage*)

NOAH. (*Turning to the audience*) Lord,
 that women be crabbed aye,
And never are meek, that dare I say.

---

[9] Destroy. [11] Ready. [13] Likewise. [15] Rainy weather. [17] Frantic behavior.
[10] Vex. [12] Chopping-block. [14] Prepare. [16] Preserved. [18] Advice.

This is well seen by me today,
In witness of you each one.

(NOAH *turns back to his wife*)

Good wife, let be all this beere [19]
That thou makes in this place here;
For all they wene [20] thou art master,—
(NOAH'S WIFE *threatens him*)
And so thou art, by St. John!

(GOD *speaks above*)

GOD. Noah, take thou thy meanye, [21]
And in the ship hie that you be;
For none so righteous man to me
Is now on earth living.

Of clean beasts with thee thou take
Seven and seven, ere thou slake, [22]
He and she, mate to mate,
Be-lyve [23] in that thou bring;

Of beasts unclean two and two,
Male and female, without moe;
Of clean fowls seven also,
The he and she together;

Of fowls unclean two and no more,
As I of beasts said before;
That shall be saved through my lore,
Against I send the weather.

Of all meats that must be eaten
Into the ship look there be getten;
For that no way may be forgotten,
And do all this bydeen, [24]

To sustain man and beast therein,
Aye till the water cease and blyn.
This world is filled full of sin,
And that is now well seen.

Seven days be yet coming,
You shall have space them in to bring;
After that is my liking
Mankind for to noye. [25]

40 days and 40 nights
Rain shall fall for their unrights;

And that I have made through my mights
Now think I to destroy.

NOAH. Lord, at Your bidding I am bayne, [26]
Since no other grace will gain,
It will I fulfill fain,
For gracious I Thee find.

A 100 winters and 20
This ship making tarried have I,
If through amendment any mercy
Would fall unto mankind.

(NOAH *calls to his family*)

Have done, you men and women all!
Hie you lest this water fall,
That each beast were in his stall,
And into the ship brought.

Of clean beasts seven shall be,
Of unclean two; this God bade me.
This flood is nigh, well may we see,
Therefore tarry you nought.

(*Then* NOAH *shall go into the Ark with all
his family, his wife excepted, and the
Ark must be boarded round about, and
on the boards all the beasts and fowls
received must be painted that these
words may agree with the pictures*)

SHEM. (*As he mentions each animal he
points to its picture painted on the
boards about the Ark*)

Sir, here are lions, leopards in;
Horses, mares, oxen, and swine,
Goats, calves, sheep and kine
Here sitten thou may see.

HAM. (*Pointing*) Camels, asses men may
find,
Buck, doe, hart, and hind,
And beasts of all manner kind
Here be, as thinkes me.

JAPHETH. Take here cats and dogs too,
Otter, fox, polecat also;

---

[19] Tumult. [21] Household. [23] Quickly. [25] Annoy.
[20] Think. [22] Slacken, stop. [24] At once. [26] Ready.

Hares hopping gaily can go
Have cowle [27] here for to eat.

NOAH'S WIFE. And here are bears, wolves
    set,
Apes, owls, marmoset,
Weasels, squirrels, and ferret;
Here they eaten their meat.

(NOAH'S WIFE *leaves the Ark*)

SHEM'S WIFE. Yet more beasts are in this
    house:
Here cats make it full crowse,[28]
Here a rotten,[29] here a mouse,
They stand nigh together.

HAM'S WIFE. And here are fowls, less and
    more:
Herns, cranes, and byttour,
Swans, peacocks; and them before
Meat for this weather.

JAPHETH'S WIFE. Here are cocks, kites,
    crows,
Rooks, ravens, many rowes,
Ducks, curlews. Who ever knows
Each one in his kind?

And here are doves, diggs, drakes,
Redshanks running through the lakes;
And each fowl that ledden [30] makes
In this ship men may find.

(NOAH *leaves the Ark and goes to his wife*)

NOAH. Wife, come in! Why stands thou
    here?
Thou art ever froward, that dare I swear.
Come in, on God's half! Time it were,
For fear lest that we drown.

NOAH'S WIFE. Yea, sir, set up your sail
And row forth with evil heale! [31]
For, without any fail,
I will not out of this town.

But [32] I have my gossips every one,
One foot further I will not gone;
They shall not drown, by St. John,
And [33] I may save their life!

They loved me full well, by Christ;
But thou wilt let them in thy chist,
Else row forth, Noah, whither thou list,
And get thee a new wife!

(NOAH *returns to the Ark*)

NOAH. Shem, son, lo, thy mother is
    wraw.[34]
For sooth such another I do not know.
    SHEM. Father, I shall fetch her in, I trow,
Without any fail.

(SHEM *leaves the Ark and crosses
    over to his mother*)

Mother, my father after thee send,
And bids thee into yonder ship wend.
Look up and see the wind,
For we be ready to sail.

NOAH'S WIFE. Son, go again to him and
    say:
I will not come therein today.
    NOAH. (*Calling from the Ark*) Come in,
    wife, in 20 devil's way!
Or else stand there without.

HAM. Shall we all fetch her in?
    NOAH. Yea, sons, in Christ's blessing and
    mine:
I would you hied you betime,
For of this flood I am in doubt.

(*The* WIFE'S GOSSIPS *enter with a large
    pot of malmsey wine*)

THE GOOD GOSSIPS. The flood comes in,
    full fleeting fast,
On every side it spreadeth full far.
For fear of drowning I am aghast;
Good gossip, let us draw near.

And let us drink ere we depart,
For often times we have done so;
For at a draught thou drinks a quart,
And so will I do, ere I go.

(*They sing*)

---

[27] A general name for various cruciferous
plants, as cabbage or turnips.
    [28] Frolic.

[29] Rat.   [32] Unless.
[30] Song.   [33] If.
[31] Fortune.   [34] Angry, fierce.

Here is a pottle of malmsey, good and strong,
It will rejoice both heart and tongue;
Though Noah think us never so long
Yet we will drink alike.

(NOAH's *three sons approach their*
mother and her gossips)

JAPHETH. Mother, we pray you al-
together—
For we are here your own childer—
Come into the ship for fear of the weather,
For His love that you bought.

NOAH'S WIFE. That will I not for all your
call,
But I have my gossips all.
SHEM. In faith, mother, yet you shall,
Whether you will or not.

(*They drag her struggling into the Ark*)

NOAH. (*Obsequiously*) Welcome, wife,
into this boat.
NOAH'S WIFE. And have thou that for
thy mote! [35]
(*She hits him*)
NOAH. Ah! ha! this is hote!
(*He turns to the audience*)
It is good to be still.

Ah! children, me thinks my boat removes;
Our tarrying here hugely me grieves.
Over the land the water spreads. [36]
God do as He will.

Ah! great God that art so good!
Who works not Thy will is wood. [37]
Now all this world is on a flood,
As I see well in sight.

This window I will shut anon,
And into my chamber will I gone
Till this water, so great one,
Be slaked through Thy might.

(*Then* NOAH *shall close the window of the*
Ark, and for a short while within let
them sing the Psalm "Save me, O God";

[35] Talking, prating.
[36] In the Middle English original, removes,
grieves, and spreads are good rhymes.

and opening the window and looking
around, NOAH *says:*)

Now 40 days are fully gone.
Send a raven I will anon
If ought-where earth, tree, or stone
Be dry in any place.

And if this fowl come not again,
It is a sign, sooth to sayne,
That dry it is on hill or plain,
And God hath done some grace.

(*Then he shall send out the raven; and tak-*
ing a dove in his hand let him say:)

Ah! Lord, wherever this raven be,
Somewhere is dry, well I see.
But yet a dove, by my lewtye, [38]
After I will send.

Thou wilt turn again to me
.   .   .   .   .
For of all fowls that may fly,
Thou are most meek and hend. [39]

(*Then he shall send out the dove; and there*
shalt be in the ship another dove bear-
ing an olive branch in its mouth, which
NOAH *shall let down from the mast by*
a string in his hand; and afterwards let
NOAH *say:*)

Ah! Lord, blessed be Thou aye,
That me hast comfort thus today;
By this sight I may well say
This flood begins to cease.

My sweet dove to me brought has
A branch of olive from some place;
This betokeneth God has done us some grace,
And is a sign of peace.

Ah! Lord, honored must Thou be!
All earth dries now, I see,
But yet, till Thou command me,
Hence will I not hie.

All this water is away,
Therefore as soon as I may

[37] Insane.
[38] Loyalty.
[39] Obedient.

Sacrifice I shall do in faye
To Thee devoutly.

           (GOD *speaks above*)

    GOD. Noah, take thy wife anon,
And thy children every one;
Out of the ship thou shalt gone,
And they all with thee.

Beasts and all that can fly
Out anon they shall hie,
On earth to grow and multiply.
I will that it be so.

      NOAH. Lord, I thank Thee through Thy
        might;
Thy bidding shall be done in height.[40]
And as fast as I may dighte [41]
I will do Thee honor,

And to Thee offer sacrifice;
Therefore comes in all wise,
For of these beasts that be His,
Offer I will this store.

(Then going out of the Ark with all his fam-
ily he shall take his animals and birds,
and shall offer them and make sacrifice)

Lord, God in majesty,
That such grace hast granted me,
Where all was lost, saved to be;
Therefore now I am bowne,[42]

My wife, my childer, my meanye [43]
With sacrifice to honor Thee
With beasts, fowls, as Thou may see,
·I offer here right soon.

           (GOD *speaks above*)

    GOD. Noah, to me thou art full able,
And thy sacrifice acceptable,
For I have found thee true and stable,
On thee now must I myn: [44]

Warry [45] Earth will I no more
For man's sin that grieves me sore;

For of youth man full yore
Has been inclined to sin.

You shall now grow and multiply,
And earth again you edify;
Each beast and fowl that may fly,
Shall be afraid of you.

And fish in sea that may flit,
Shall sustain you, I you behite; [46]
To eat of them you ne let,[47]
That clean be you may know.

Thereas you have eaten before
Grass and roots, since you were bore,[48]
Of clean beasts now, less and more,
I give you leave to eat;

Save blood and flesh both in fear
Of wrong-dead carrion that is here,
Eat not of that in no manner;
For that aye you shall let.

Manslaughter also you shall flee;
For that is not pleasant to me.
Who sheds blood, he or she,
Ought-where amongst mankind,

That blood foul shed shall be
And vengeance have, that men shall see;
Therefore beware now, all ye,
You fall not in that sin.

A forwarde [49] now with thee I make,
And all thy seed for thy sake,
Of such vengeance for to slake,
For now I have my will.

Here I behet thee a heaste,[50]
That man, woman, fowl nor beast,
With water, while the world shall last,
I will no more spill.[51]

My bow between you and me
In the firmament shall be,
By very token that you may see
That such vengeance shall cease,

That man nor woman shall never more
Be wasted by water as is before;

[40] With speed.   [43] Household.
[41] Get ready.   [44] Remember kindly.
[42] Ready.   [45] Curse.

[46] Promise.   [49] Covenant.
[47] Do not hesitate.   [50] Here I make thee a promise.
[48] Born.   [51] Destroy.

But for sin that grieveth me sore,
Therefore this vengeance was.

Where clouds in the welkin been,
That ilke [52] bow shall be seen,
In tokening that my wrath and tene [53]
Shall never this wroken be. [54]

The string is turned toward you,
And toward me is bent the bow,

That such weather shall never show;
And this behett [55] I thee.

My blessing now I give thee here,
To thee, Noah, my servant dear,
For vengeance shall no more appear.
And now, farewell, my darling dear.

(*The pageant wagon moves on to
the next station*)

[52] Same.   [53] Vexation.   [54] Shall never be given vent.   [55] Promise.

Abraham and Isaac

〜〜〜〜〜〜〜〜〜〜〜〜〜

INTRODUCTION

Each of the extant English mystery cycles contains one play devoted to the story of Abraham's preparation to sacrifice his son Isaac at God's command. The particular version of the play given here does not, however, come from any of the cycles; it is extant in a manuscript which contains no other mystery plays. This manuscript is preserved in the library of Brome Manor; hence the play is generally called the Brome *Abraham and Isaac*. Whether the play ever belonged to a complete cycle is unknown, but it was written during the same general period as other cycle plays, and it was evidently intended to be acted similarly.

Like *The Deluge or Noah's Flood* from the Chester cycle, this play at first glance may seem naive, but a closer examination reveals considerably more literary and dramatic skill than can be found in *The Deluge;* indeed, the unknown author of *Abraham and Isaac* was a man of great talent. An adequate appreciation of his poetic skill requires a study of his original text, where modernized spelling and vocabulary do not obscure or spoil his subtle meter and rhyme and where his adroit allusiveness can be more fully realized, but even in a modernized text such as this his dramatic effectiveness can be seen. As all successful writers of one-act plays must, he concentrates on the traits of his characters which are essential for his story and for the effect he wants to secure in his audience—Abraham's God-fearing piety in cruel conflict with his love for his cherished youngest son, and Isaac's childish sweetness and trust in his father. All the words and actions of these two characters are nicely conceived to develop the audience's perception of their essential qualities. There is none of the usual blurring of effect by the introduction of irrelevancies which may have interested or amused the dramatist. The first lines of the play, Abraham's opening prayer, set forth his two essential characteristics, upon which the ensuing action must depend, and the very act of prayer helps to induce in the audience the proper mood for the play. After the prayer, Isaac's gentle submissiveness is suggested in three lines, and the dramatist then proceeds at once to the central conflict of his play with God's solemn announcement of his proposed trial of Abraham and of the terms of the trial, which are clearly fitted to the two essential traits of Abraham's character just set forth. Such an assured handling of the opening situation in a mere forty-five lines makes the problem look easy, as it always looks when handled by a master.

The scene of the sacrifice on the mount is equally skillful in its development. The playwright's problem is to make the audience feel the agony of the conflict in Abraham's soul. The force of God's commandment was, of course, easier to suggest to a devout medieval audience than to a modern one, and the mere presence of God and his angels on the stage would accomplish it, but a feeling of the power of the father's love was not so easy to convey. The dramatist elected to rely on the childish helplessness and unselfishness of Isaac to pull at the heart strings of his audience. The progression from Isaac's initial terror, to his wish for his mother, to his attempt to comfort his distraught father, and finally to his childish thoughtfulness for his grieving mother, is skillfully interspersed with his fear of the sword, his reluctance to be bound, and his request to be blindfolded. In making the audience pity the child, the dramatist has brought them closer to a real-

12

ization of Abraham's love for him and consequently to an appreciation of his agony of soul in obeying God at the sacrifice of his beloved son.

For the modern audience, the appearance of the Doctor-Epilogue with his little sermon on the obvious is an excrescence. It serves as a reminder, however, that the purpose of these plays was primarily religious. Though the unknown dramatist displayed no little mastery of the art of Sophocles and Shakespeare, his purpose was the purpose of the preacher.

❧

ABRAHAM AND ISAAC

Dramatis personae

In order of first appearance

GOD

ANGEL, A messenger and agent of GOD.

ABRAHAM, A devout old man who has frequently received commands from GOD, has generally obeyed them, and has been made to prosper.

ISAAC, A boy, ABRAHAM's favorite child, and the delight of his old age.

DOCTOR, A learned religious man who delivers the epilogue applying the lesson of the play for the audience.

(*There are two stages, one above the other. On the upper stage sit* GOD *and his angels; on the lower all the action involving* ABRAHAM *and* ISAAC *takes place. On one side of the stage a slight eminence with a rough altar has been built. This is the mount or hill on which the sacrifice takes place. As the play opens* ABRAHAM *enters with his young son* ISAAC; *they walk to the side of the stage opposite the mount and kneel to pray.*)

ABRAHAM. Father of Heaven, omnipotent,
　With all my heart to Thee I call.
Thou hast given me both land and rent,
And my livelihood Thou hast me sent.
　I thank Thee highly evermore for all.

First of the earth Thou madest Adam,
　And Eve also to be his wife;
All other creatures of them two came.

And now Thou hast granted to me, Abraham,
　Here in this land to lead my life.

In my age Thou hast granted me this,
　That this young child with me shall wone.[1]
I love nothing so much, ywis,
Except Thine own self, dear Father of bliss,
　As Isaac here, my own sweet son.

I have divers children mo,
　The which I love not half so well.
This fair sweet child, he cheers me so
In every place where that I go,
　That no disease[2] here may I feel.

And therefore, Father of Heaven, I Thee pray
　For his health and also for his grace.
Now, Lord, keep him both night and day,
That never disease nor no fray
　Come to my child in no place.
　　　(*He rises from his knees and turns to* ISAAC)

Now come on, Isaac, my own sweet child;
　Go we home and take our rest.
　ISAAC. Abraham, mine own father so mild,
To follow you I am full pressed,
　Both early and late.

　ABRAHAM. Come on, sweet child; I love thee best
　　Of all the children that ever I begat.

[1] Dwell.　　　　[2] Trouble or discomfort.

(They move to another part of the stage and stand quietly while the action continues on the upper stage)

GOD. *(To an* ANGEL*)* Mine angel, fast hie
 thee thy way,
And on to middle-earth [3] anon thou go;
Abraham's heart now will I assay,
 Whether that he be steadfast or no.

Say I commanded him for to take
 Isaac, his young son, that he loves so
 well,
And with his blood sacrifice he make,
 If any of my friendship he will feel.

Show him the way on to the hill
 Where that his sacrifice shall be.
I shall assay now his good will,
 Whether he loveth better his child or
 me.

All men shall take example by him
 My commandments how they shall
 keep.
(Exit ANGEL *from the upper stage.* ABRA-
HAM *leaves* ISAAC, *who kneels to pray,
and comes to the center of the lower
stage)*

ABRAHAM. *(Kneeling)* Now, Father of
 Heaven, that formed all thing,
My prayers I make to Thee again,
For this day my tender-offering
 Here must I give to Thee, certain.
Ah! Lord God, Almighty King,
 What manner [4] best will make Thee
 most fain?
If I had thereof true knowing,
 It should be done with all my main,
 Full soon anon.
 To do Thy pleasing on a hill,
 Verily, it is my will,
 Dear Father, God in Trinity.

(Enter ANGEL *on lower stage)*

ANGEL. Abraham! Abraham! will thou
 rest!
Our Lord commandeth thee for to take

Isaac, thy young son, that thou lovest best,
 And with his blood sacrifice that thou
 make.

Into the Land of Vision thou go,
 And offer thy child unto thy Lord;
I shall thee lead and show also.
 Unto God's hest, [5] Abraham, accord,

And follow me upon this green.
 ABRAHAM. Welcome to me be my Lord's
 sand, [6]
 And his hest I will not withstand.
Yet Isaac, my young son in land,
A full dear child to me hath been.

I had liefer, if God had been pleased,
 For to have forborne all the goods that
 I have,
Than Isaac my son should be diseased,
 So God in Heaven my soul may save!

I loved never thing so much on earth,
 And now I must the child go kill.
Ah, Lord God, my conscience is strongly
 stirred!
And yet, my dear Lord, I am sore afraid
 To begrudge anything against Your
 will.

I love my child as my life,
 But yet I love my God much more.
For though my heart would make any strife,
Yet will I not spare for child nor wife,
 But do after my Lord's lore. [7]

Though I love my son never so well,
 Yet smite off his head soon I shall.
(Raising his arms to heaven) Ah! Father of
 Heaven, to Thee I kneel;
A hard death my son shall feel,
 For to honor Thee, Lord, withal!

 ANGEL. Abraham! Abraham! This is well
 said,

 And all these commandments look that
 thou keep.
But in thy heart be nothing dismayed.
 ABRAHAM. Nay, nay, forsooth, I hold me
 well paid

[3] The world.   [4] Kind of offering.   [5] Command.   [6] Message.   [7] Bidding.

To please my God to the best that I
   have.

For though my heart be heavily set
   To see the blood of my own dear son,
Yet for all this I will not let,
But Isaac, my son, I will go fet,[8]
   And come as fast as ever we can.
               (*Exit* ANGEL)

Now, Isaac, my own son dear!
(*Calling, almost in panic*) Where art thou,
      child? Speak to me.
   ISAAC. (*Quietly*) My father, sweet father,
     I am here,
And make my prayers to the Trinity.

ABRAHAM. Rise up, my child, and fast
   come hither,
My gentle bairn that art so wise,
For we two, child, must go together
And unto my Lord make sacrifice.

ISAAC. I am full ready, my father. Lo!
   Given at your hands, I stand right here,
And whatsoever ye bid me do,
   It shall be done with glad cheer,
   Full well and fine.
ABRAHAM. Ah! Isaac, my own son so dear,
   God's blessing I give thee, and mine.

(*He gives* ISAAC *a bundle of wood*) Hold
      this faggot upon thy back,
And here myself fire shall bring.
   ISAAC. Father, all this here will I pack,
I am full fain to do your bidding.
   ABRAHAM. (*Aside*) Ah! Lord of Heaven,
     my hands I wring,
   This child's words all do wound my
     heart.

Now, Isaac, son, go we our way
   Unto yon mount with all our main.
     (*They walk about the stage as if
      going to the Mount*)
   ISAAC. Go we, my dear father, as fast as
     I may;
To follow you I am full fain,
Although I be slender.
   ABRAHAM. (*Aside*) Ah! Lord, my heart
     breaketh in twain,
   This child's words, they be so tender.

Ah, Isaac, son, anon lay it down,
   No longer upon thy back it hold,
For I must make ready full soon
   To honor my Lord God as I should.
              (*Draws his sword*)

ISAAC. Lo, my dear father, where it is.
     (*Lays down the bundle of wood*)
   To cheer you always I draw me near.
But, father, I marvel sore of this,
   Why that ye make this heavy cheer;

And also, father, evermore dread I:
   Where is your quick beast that ye
     should kill?
Both fire and wood we have ready,
   But quick beast have we none on this
     hill.

A quick beast, I wot well, must be dead
   Your sacrifice for to make.
   ABRAHAM. Dread thee naught, my child,
     I thee red,[9]
Our Lord will send me one to this stead[10]
   Some manner of beast for to take
     Through his sweet sond.[11]
   ISAAC. Yea, father, but my heart begin-
     neth to quake
   To see that sharp sword in your hand.

Why bear ye your sword drawn so?
   Of your countenance I have much
     wonder.
   ABRAHAM. (*Aside*) Ah! Father of Heaven,
     so I am woe!
   This child here breaks my heart
     asunder.

ISAAC. Tell me, my dear father, ere that
     ye cease,
   Bear ye your sword drawn for me?
   ABRAHAM. Ah, Isaac, sweet son, peace,
     peace!
   For ywis thou break my heart in three.

ISAAC. Now truly, somewhat, father, ye
     think,
   That ye mourn thus more and more.
   ABRAHAM. (*Aside*) Ah! Lord of Heaven,
     thy grace let sink,
   For my heart was never half so sore.

[8] Fetch.   [9] Counsel.

[10] Place.   [11] Messenger.

IsAAC. I pray you, father, that ye will let
    me that wit,[12]
Whether shall I have any harm or no.
ABRAHAM. Ywis, sweet son, I may not tell
    thee yet,
My heart is now so full of woe.

IsAAC. Dear father, I pray you, hide it not
    from me,
But some of your thought that ye tell me.
    ABRAHAM. Ah! Isaac, Isaac, I must kill
        thee!
IsAAC. Kill me, father? Alas! what have I
    done?

If I have trespassed against you ought,
    With a rod ye may make me full mild;
And with your sharp sword kill me nought,
    For ywis, father, I am but a child.

    ABRAHAM. I am full sorry, son, thy blood
        for to spill,
        But truly, my child, I may not choose.
    IsAAC. Now I would to God my mother
        were here on this hill!

    She would kneel for me on both her
        knees
        To save my life.
And since that my mother is not here,
I pray you, father, change your cheer,
    And kill me not with your knife.

    ABRAHAM. Forsooth, son, unless I thee
        kill,
    I should grieve God right sore, I dread.
It is His commandment and also His will,
    That I should do this same deed.

He commanded me, son, for certain,
    To make my sacrifice with thy blood.
    IsAAC. And is it God's will that I should
        be slain?
    ABRAHAM. Yea, truly, Isaac, my son so
        good,
    And therefore my hands I wring.

IsAAC. Now, father, against my Lord's will
I will never grudge, loud nor still.
    He might have sent me a better destiny
If it had been His pleasure.

[12] Know.

ABRAHAM. Forsooth, son, but if I did this
    deed,
Grievously displeased our Lord will be.
IsAAC. Nay, nay, father, God forbid
    That ever ye should grieve Him for me.

Ye have other children, one or two,
    The which ye should love well by
        kind.[13]
I pray you, father, make ye no woe;
For, be I once dead, and from you go,
    I shall be soon out of your mind.

Therefore do our Lord's bidding,
    And when I am dead, then pray for me.
But, good father, tell ye my mother nothing;
Say that I am in another country dwelling.
    ABRAHAM. Ah, Isaac, Isaac, blessèd may
        thou be!

My heart beginneth strongly to rise,
    To see the blood of thy blessèd body.
    IsAAC. Father, since it may be no other
        wise,
        Let it pass over, as well as I.

But, father, ere I go unto my death,
    I pray you bless me with your hand.
                        (IsAAC kneels)
    ABRAHAM. Now, Isaac, with all my breath
        My blessing I give thee upon this land,
        And God's also thereto, ywis.
    Isaac, Isaac, son, up thou stand,
        Thy fair sweet mouth that I may
            kiss.

    IsAAC. Now farewell, my own father so
        fine;
        And greet well my mother on earth.
But I pray you, father, to hide my eyne,
    That I see not the stroke of your sharp
        sword,
        That my flesh shall defile.
    ABRAHAM. Son, thy words make me to
        weep full sore;
Now, my dear son Isaac, speak no more.
    IsAAC. Ah! my own dear father, where-
        fore?
        We shall speak together here but a
            while.

[13] I.e., naturally.

And since that I must needs be dead,
Yet, my dear father, to you I pray,
Smite but few strokes at my head,
And make an end as soon as ye may,
And tarry not too long.
ABRAHAM. Thy meek words, child, make
me afraid;
So "Welaway!" [14] may be my song,

Except alone God's will.
Ah! Isaac, my own sweet child,
Yet kiss me again upon this hill!
In all this world is none so mild.

ISAAC. Now truly, father, all this tarrying
It doth my heart but harm;
I pray you, father, make an ending.
ABRAHAM. Come up, sweet son, into my
arm. (*Begins to bind him*)

I must bind thy hands two,
Although thou be never so mild.
ISAAC. Ah! mercy, father! Why should ye
do so?
ABRAHAM. That thou should'st not let [15]
me, my child.

ISAAC. Nay, ywis, father, I will not let you.
Do on, for me, your will;
And on the purpose that ye have set you,
For God's love, keep it for thee still.

I am full sorry this day to die,
But yet I want not my God to grieve.
Do on your list for me hardily;
My fair sweet father, I give you leave.

But, father, I pray you evermore,
Tell ye my mother no deal; [16]
If she wist it, she would weep full sore,
For ywis, father, she loveth me full
well.
God's blessing may she have!

Now farewell, my mother so sweet!
We two be like no more to meet.
ABRAHAM. Ah, Isaac, Isaac, son, thou
makest me to greet,
And with thy words thou distemperest
me.

ISAAC. Ywis, sweet father, I am sorry to
grieve you.
I cry you mercy of that I have done,
And of all trespass that ever I did move you;
Now, dear father, forgive me that I
have done.
God of Heaven be with me!

ABRAHAM. Ah! dear child, leave off thy
moans;
In all thy life thou grieved me never once.
Now blessèd be thou, body and bones,
That ever thou were bred and born!
Thou hast been to me child full good.
But ywis, child, though I mourn never
so fast,
Yet must I needs here at the last
In this place shed all thy blood.

Therefore, my dear son, here shall thou lie.
(*Places him on the altar*)
Unto my work I must me stead.
Ywis, I had as lief myself to die,
If God will be pleased with my deed,
And mine own body for to offer.
ISAAC. Ah, mercy, father, mourn ye no
more!
Your weeping maketh my heart sore,
As my own death that I shall suffer.

Your kerchief, father, about my eyes ye wind.
ABRAHAM. So I shall, my sweetest child
on earth.
ISAAC. Now yet, good father, have this in
mind,
And smite me not often with your
sharp sword,
But hastily that it be sped.
(ABRAHAM *blindfolds him*)
ABRAHAM. Now farewell, my child so full
of grace.
ISAAC. Ah! father, father, turn downward
my face,
For of your sharp sword I am ever
adread.

ABRAHAM. (*Aside*) To do this deed I am
full sorry,
But, Lord, Thy behest I will not withstand.

[14] A common exclamation of grief or sadness.

[15] Hinder, interfere with.   [16] Nothing.

Isaac. Ah! Father of Heaven, to Thee I cry;
Lord, receive me into Thy hand.

Abraham. Lo! now is the time come, certain,
That my sword in his neck shall bite.
Ah, Lord, my heart riseth there against;
I may not find it in my heart to smite;
My heart will not now thereto.
Yet fain I would work my Lord's will,
But this young innocent lieth so still,
I may not find it in my heart him to kill.
Oh! Father of Heaven, what shall I do?

Isaac. Ah, mercy, father, why tarry ye so,
And let me lie thus long on this heath?
Now I would to God the stroke were do!
Father, I pray you heartily, short me of my woe,
And let me not look thus after my death.

Abraham. Now, heart, why would'st not thou break in three?
Yet shall thou not make me to my God unmild.
I will no longer let for thee,
For that my God aggrieved would be.
Now hold [17] the stroke, my own dear child.

(As Abraham raises his arm to strike, the Angel enters behind him and seizes his sword)

Angel. I am an angel, thou mayest see blithe,
That from heaven to thee is sent.
Our Lord thanketh thee an hundred sythe [18]
For the keeping of His commandment.

He knoweth thy will, and also thy heart,
That thou dreadest Him above all things;
And some of thy heaviness for to depart
A fair ram yonder I did bring.

He standeth tied, lo, among the briars.
Now, Abraham, amend thy mood,
For Isaac, thy young son that here is,
This day shall not shed his blood.

[17] Receive.

Go, make thy sacrifice with yon ram.
Now farewell, blessèd Abraham,
For unto heaven I go now home;
The way is full straight.
Take up thy son so free.
(Exit Angel)

Abraham. Ah! Lord, I thank Thee of Thy great grace,
Now am I eased in divers wise.
Arise up, Isaac, my dear son, arise;
Arise up, sweet child, and come to me.

Isaac. Ah! mercy, father, why smite ye not?
Ah! smite on, father, once with your knife.
Abraham. (Removing the blindfold and helping him up) Peace, my sweet son, and take no thought,
For our Lord of Heaven hath granted thy life
By His angel now,

That thou shalt not die this day, son, truly.
Isaac. Ah, father, full glad then were I;
Ywis—father—I say—ywis—
If this tale were true!
Abraham. An hundred times, my son fair of hue,
For joy thy mouth now will I kiss.

Isaac. Ah! my dear father, Abraham,
Will not God be wroth that we do thus?
Abraham. No, no, hardily, my sweet son,
For yon same ram He hath us sent
Hither down to us.

Yon beast shall die here in thy stead,
In the worship of our Lord alone.
Go, fetch him hither, my child, indeed.
Isaac. Father, I will go seize him by the head,
And bring yon beast with me anon.
(Isaac unties the ram)

Ah, sheep, sheep, blessèd may thou be,
That ever thou were sent down hither!
Thou shall this day die for me
In the worship of the Holy Trinity.

[18] Times.

Now come fast and go we together
To my Father of Heaven.
Though thou be never so gentle and good,
Yet had I liefer thou sheddest thy blood
Ywis, sheep, than I.
(*Leads the ram to his father*)

Lo, father, I have brought here full smart
This gentle sheep, and him to you I
give.
But, Lord God, I thank Thee with all my
heart,
For I am glad that I shall live,
And kiss once my dear mother.
ABRAHAM. Now be right merry, my sweet
child,
For this quick beast, that is so mild,
Here I shall present before all other.

ISAAC. And I will fast begin to blow;
This fire shall burn a full good speed.
But father, while I stoop down low,
Ye will not kill me with your sword, I trow?
ABRAHAM. No, hardily, sweet son; have
no dread;
My mourning is past.
ISAAC. Yea! but I would that sword were
in a gleed,[19]
For, ywis, father, it makes me full ill
aghast.
(ABRAHAM *makes his offering, and he and*
ISAAC *kneel*)

ABRAHAM. Now, Lord God of Heaven in
Trinity,
Almighty God omnipotent,
My offering I make in the worship of Thee,
And with this quick beast I Thee pre-
sent.
Lord, receive Thou mine intent,
As [Thou] art God and ground of
our grace.

GOD. (*Speaking from the upper stage*) Ab-
raham, Abraham, well may thou
speed,
And Isaac, thy young son, thee by!
Truly, Abraham, for this deed
I shall multiply both your seed,
As thick as stars be in the sky,
Both more and less,
And as thick as gravel in the sea,

So thick multiplied your seed shall be.
This grant I you for your goodness.

Of you shall come fruits great [won],[20]
And ever be in bliss without end,
For ye dread Me as God alone
And keep My commandments every one;
My blessing I give, wheresoever ye
wend.
(ABRAHAM *and* ISAAC *rise from their
knees*)

ABRAHAM. Lo, Isaac, my son, how think
ye
Of this work that we have wrought?
Full glad and blithe we may be,
Against the will of God that we
grudged naught,
Upon this fair heath.
ISAAC. Ah! father, I thank our Lord every
deal,
That my wit served me so well
For to dread God more than my
death.

ABRAHAM. Why, dear worthy son, wert
thou adread?
Heartily, child, tell me thy lore.[21]
ISAAC. Yea, by my faith, father, now have
I rede,[22]
I was never so afraid before
As I have been on yon hill.
But, by my faith, father, I swear
I will nevermore come there
But it be against my will.

ABRAHAM. Yea! come on with me, my
own sweet son,
And homeward fast now let us go.
ISAAC. By my faith, father, thereto I grant;
I had never so good will to go home,
And to speak with my dear mother.
ABRAHAM. Ah! Lord of Heaven, I thank
Thee,
For now may I lead home with me
Isaac, my young son so free,
The gentlest child above all other,
This may I well avow.

Now go we forth, my blessèd son.
ISAAC. I grant, father, and let us go;
For, by my troth, were I at home,
I would never go out under that form.[23]

___

[19] Fire.   [20] Number.   [21] Thinking.   [22] Judgment.   [23] In that manner.

I pray God give us grace evermore,
And all those that we be beholden to.
(Exeunt)

(Enter the DOCTOR, robed. He addresses the
audience as an epilogue)

DOCTOR. Lo, sovereigns and sirs, now
have we showed
This solemn story to great and small.
It is good learning to learnéd and lewd[24]
And the wisest of us all,
Without any barring.
For this story showeth you [here]
How we should keep, to our power,
God's commandments without grudg-
ing.

Think ye, sirs, and[25] God sent an angel
And commanded you your child be
slain,
By your troth, is there any of you
That either would grudge or strive there
again?
How think ye now, sirs, thereby?

I think there be three or four or more.
And these women, that weep so sorrowfully
When that their children die them fro,
As nature will and kind,
It is but folly, I may well avow,
To grudge against God or to grieve you,
For ye shall never see him mischiefed,
well I know,
By land nor water, have this in mind.

And grudge not against our Lord God
In wealth or woe, whether[26] that He
you send,
Though ye be never so hard bestead;
For when He will, He may it amend,
His commandments truly if ye keep with
good heart,
As this story hath now showed you
before,
And faithfully serve Him while ye be quart,[27]
That ye may please God both even and
morn.
Now Jesu, that wore the crown of
thorn,
Bring us all to heavenly bliss!

[24] Unlettered.   [25] If.   [26] Whichever.   [27] Safe and sound.

The Second Shepherds' Play

This play comes from another of the great cycles of mystery plays which are the most conspicuous phase of dramatic development in medieval England. The cycle, sometimes called the Towneley Plays, was acted in the fifteenth and early sixteenth centuries, probably at the town of Wakefield, some thirty to forty miles southwest of the great ecclesiastical center of the north, York. Since the Wakefield cycle contains two different plays about the visit of the shepherds to the Christ-child, this one is called *Secunda Pastorum,* or *The Second Shepherds' Play.*

In all the great mystery cycles, plays were rewritten or added to the series from time to time as changing local conditions altered the requirements for performances. Several plays in the Wakefield cycle were composed or elaborated by an unknown dramatist who was so skillful in achieving comic and satiric effects that he has come to be known as "the Wakefield Master." One of the plays which he wrote is *The Second Shepherds' Play.*

Among medieval religious plays this one is unique, for in no other does the secular interest of the playwright seem so completely to overshadow the religious function of the cycle: 636 lines are given to the farce of Mak and the shepherds, and only 116 to the Nativity. But it is not the dramatist's apparent neglect of the usual religious didacticism, however commendable that may seem to some unsympathetic modern readers, which has made *The Second Shepherds' Play* the most widely read and the most frequently acted of English medieval plays. The Wakefield Master had great talent for dialogue and characterization, and the farce of Mak the sheep thief displays his talent most effectively. The opening speech of the First Shepherd demonstrates the abilities of the unknown dramatist and the distinctive character of his approach. Instead of the usual solemn opening of mystery plays (a speech by God or Jesus, or a prayer by one of the characters), the Wakefield Master opens with the completely secular grumbling of the surly First Shepherd, a vivid Yorkshire countryman, soured and depressed by his poverty, his hard life, and his hopeless grievances against the weather, his employer, and the government. The other shepherds and Mak are also realized as rough local country folk with shrewish wives and hungry children. Mak is a beautiful characterization of the small-time country thief, an imaginative liar, impudent and persuasive, but stupidly short-sighted. The sheep-in-the-cradle hoax is fitted to the characters of these men with masterly skill, the final revelation growing amusingly out of the very effectiveness of Mak and his wife in perpetrating the fraud, an effectiveness which makes the simple shepherds a little ashamed that they have left no gift for the poor baby.

Violently disparate as the sheep-stealing story and the Nativity story seem to us, the Wakefield Master has made them fit easily together. Medieval man often demonstrated in his church carvings and paintings as well as in his literature that earthy, every-day affairs and laughter were to him much more easily compatible with deep religious devotion than they are to twentieth-century man. The three shepherds who admire the angels' song and kneel in simple adoration at the manger differ not at all from the three sheep herders of the moor who tossed Mak in a blanket. Furthermore, shocking as it may seem to modern readers, the Wakefield Master was well aware that, like so much medieval religious art, the first part of his play closely paralleled the last. Both involve three shepherds watching their flocks at night who are disturbed and distracted by a visitor, who make a visit to a humble couple, and who pay their respects to a newborn child. To medieval man it was funny but not sacrilegious that in the first instance the babe was a stolen sheep and in the second the Christ-child.

THE SECOND SHEPHERDS' PLAY

Dramatis personae

In order of first appearance

FIRST SHEPHERD, COLL, A hired shepherd. He is a rough Yorkshire countryman with grievances against his employers and the government.

SECOND SHEPHERD, GIB, Another hired shepherd, much like Coll, with additional grievances against his wife and the marital state.

THIRD SHEPHERD, DAW, A youth, their helper.

MAK, A local neer-do-well and thief. He has a thief's short-sighted cunning and whining persuasiveness, but still a merry rogue.

MAK'S WIFE, JILL, A scolding slattern, a worthy accomplice for Mak.

ANGEL, One of the heavenly choir which sings at the Nativity.

VIRGIN MARY

CHRIST CHILD

(The stage of the pageant wagon must represent three places, the open fields, the hut of MAK and his WIFE, and the stable where Jesus was born. The only properties necessary are a bed and a cradle.)

(Enter FIRST SHEPHERD, slapping his arms with the cold. He walks to the edge of the stage and addresses the audience.)

FIRST SHEPHERD. Lord, what these weathers are cold, and I am ill happed.[1]
I am near-hand dold,[2] so long have I napped.
My legs they fold, my fingers are chapped;

It is not as I would, for I am all lapped
  In sorrow.
In storms and tempest,
Now in the east, now in the west,
Woe is him has never rest
  Midday nor morrow!

But we silly[3] shepherds that walk on the moor,
In faith, we are near-hands out of the door.
No wonder, as it stands, if we be poor,
For the tilth of our lands lies fallow as the floor,
  As ye ken.
We are so hamyd,
For-taxed and ramyd,[4]
We are made hand-tamed
  With these gentlery-men.

Thus they reave us of our rest; Our Lady them wary![5]
These men that are lord-fast, they cause the plough tarry.
That, men say, is for the best; we find it contrary.
Thus are husbandmen oppressed, in point to miscarry,
  In life.
Thus hold they us under;
Thus they bring us in blunder!
It were great wonder
  And ever should we thrive.

There shall come a swain as proud as a po,[6]
He must borrow my wain, my plough also;

---

[1] Clothed.   [2] Nearly dumb.   [3] Poor, simple.   [4] Over-taxed and crushed.   [5] Curse.   [6] Peacock.

Then I am full fain to grant ere he go.
Thus live we in pain, anger, and woe
    By night and day.
He must have if he langéd,
If I should forgang[7] it.
I were better be hangéd
    Than once say him nay.

For may he get a painted sleeve, or a brooch,
    now-a-days,
Woe to him that him grieves, or one word
    against says!
Dare no man him reprove, what mastery he
    displays.
And yet may no man believe one word that
    he says,
    No letter.
He can make purveyance,
With boast and bragance;
And all is through maintenance
    Of men that are greater.

It does me good, as I walk thus by mine own,
Of this world for to talk in manner of moan.
To my sheep will I stalk and hearken anon;
There abide on a balk,[8] or sit on a stone,
    Full soon.
For I trow, pardie,
True men if they be,
We get more company
    Ere it be noon.
      (*He retires to a corner of the stage,
        still grumbling.*)

(*Enter* SECOND SHEPHERD. *Without seeing*
FIRST SHEPHERD, *he walks to the edge of
the stage and addresses the audience.*)

  SECOND SHEP. Benste[9] and Dominus!
    What may this bemean?
Why fares this world thus? Oft have we not
    seen!
Lord, these weathers are spytus, and the
    winds full keen;
And the frosts so hideous, they water my
    eyne;
    No lie.
Now in dry, now in wet,
Now in snow, now in sleet,
When my shoes freeze to my feet,
    It is not all easy.

But, as far as I ken, or yet as I go,
We silly wedded men suffer mickle woe;
We have sorrow then and then, it falls oft so.
Silly Capel, our hen, both to and fro
    She cackles;
But begin she to croak,
To grumble or cluck,
Woe is him our cock,
    For he is in the shackles.

These men that are wed have not all their
    will.
When they are full hard bestead, they sigh
    full still.
God knows they are led full hard and full ill;
In bower nor in bed they say nought theretill.
    This tide,
My part have I found,
I know my lesson!
Woe is him that is bound,
    For he must abide.

But now late in our lives,—a marvel to me,
That I think my heart rives such wonders
    to see,
What that destiny drives, it should so be!—
Some men will have two wives, and some
    men three
    In store.
Some are woe that has any!
But so far ken I—
Woe is him that has many,
    For he feels sore.

But, young men, of wooing, for God that you
    bought,
Be well ware of wedding, and think in your
    thought,
"Had I wist"[10] is a thing it serves of naught.
Mickle still mourning has wedding home
    brought,
    And griefs,
With many a sharp shower;
For thou may catch in an hour
That shall [savor] full sour
    As long as thou lives.

For, as ever read I epistle,[11] I have one to
    my fere,[12]
As sharp as a thistle, as rough as a briar;
She is browed like a bristle, with a sour-
    looking cheer;

---

[7] Forego.   [8] Ridge.   [9] Benedicite.   [10] Had I only known.   [11] *I.e.* The New Testament.   [12] Wife

Had she once wet her whistle, she could sing
  full clear
    Her paternoster.
She is as great as a whale;
She has a gallon of gall;
By him that died for us all,
    I would I had run till I had lost her!

(FIRST SHEPHERD *walks up to him*)

FIRST SHEP. (*Jeering*) God! look over the
  raw! Full deafly ye stand.
SECOND SHEP. Yea, the devil in thy maw
  —so tarrying!
Sawest thou aught of Daw?
FIRST SHEP. Yea, on a lea-land
Heard I him blow. He comes here at hand
  Not far.
Stand still.
SECOND SHEP. Why?
FIRST SHEP. For he comes, hope I.
SECOND SHEP. He will make us both a lie
Unless we beware. (*They walk aside*)

(*Enter* THIRD SHEPHERD *who, without seeing the others, addresses the audience as
they have done*)

THIRD SHEP. Christ's cross me speed, and
  Saint Nicholas! [13]
Thereof had I need; it is worse than it was.
Whoso knows, take heed, and let the world
  pass,
It is ever in dread and brittle as glass,
    And slithers.
This world fared never so,
With marvels moe and moe,
Now in weal, now in woe,
    And all things writhes.

Was never since Noah's flood such floods
  seen,
Winds and rains so rude, and storms so keen!
Some stammered, some stood in doubt, as
  I ween.
Now God turn all to good! I say as I mean.
    For ponder:
These floods so they drown,
Both in fields and in town,

[13] Patron saint of children—and of thieves.
[14] Heath.
[15] After.

And bear all down;
    And that is a wonder.

We that walk in the nights our cattle to keep,
We see sudden sights when other men sleep.

(*Seeing the others, but still addressing the
  audience*)

Yet methinks my heart lights; I see rascals
  peep.
Ye are two tall wights! I will give my sheep
  A turn.
But full ill have I meant;
As I walk on this bent, [14]
I may lightly repent,
    My toes if I spurn.

(FIRST SHEPHERD *and* SECOND SHEPHERD
  walk up to him)

Ah, sir, God you save and master mine!
A drink fain would I have, and somewhat
  to dine.
    FIRST SHEP. Christ's curse, my knave,
      thou art a worthless hind!
    SECOND SHEP. What! the boy lists to rave!
      Abide unto syne [15]
    We have made it.
Ill thrift on thy pate!
Though the rascal came late,
Yet is he in state
    To dine—if he had it.

THIRD SHEP. Such servants as I, that
  sweats and swinks, [16]
Eat our bread full dry, and that me for-
  thinks. [17]
We are oft wet and weary when master men
  winks;
Yet come full lately both dinners and drinks.
    But neatly
Both our dame and our sire,
When we have run in the mire,
They can nip at our hire,
    And pay us full lately.

But hear my truth, master: for the fare that
  ye make
I shall do hereafter—work as I take; [18]

[16] Toils.
[17] Displeases.
[18] Work as I am paid.

I shall do a little, sir, and among ever lake; [19]
For yet lay my supper never on my stomache
   In the fields.
Whereto should I threap? [20]
With my staff can I leap;
And men say "Light cheap
   Badly for-yields." [21]

    First Shep. Thou were an ill lad, to ride
      on wooing
With a man that had but little of spending.
    Second Shep. Peace, boy, I bade! No
      more jangling,
Or I shall make thee full 'fraid, by the
      Heaven's King,
    With thy gawds.
Where are our sheep, boy? We scorn.
    Third Shep. Sir, this same day at morn
I them left in the corn,
    When they rang lauds. [22]

They have pasture good, they cannot go
    wrong.
    First Shep. That is right. By the rood,
    these nights are long!
Yet I would, ere we yode, [23] one gave us a
    song.
    Second Shep. So I thought as I stood, to
    mirth us among.
    Third Shep. I grant.

    First Shep. Let me sing the tenory.
    Second Shep. And I the treble so high.
    Third Shep. Then the mean falls to me.
Let see how ye chant.   (They sing)

(Enter Mak, muffled in a cloak)

    Mak. Now, Lord, for thy names seven,
    that made both moon and starns,
Well more than I can name; thy will, Lord,
    of me tharns. [24]
I am all uneven; that moves oft my harnes. [25]
Now would to God I were in heaven, for
    there weep no bairns
    So still. [26]
    First Shep. Who is that pipes so poor?
    Mak. Would God ye knew how I fare!

Lo, a man that walks on the moor,
    And has not all his will!

    Second Shep. Mak, where hast thou
    gone? Tell us tidings.
    Third Shep. Is he come? Then every-
    one take heed to his things.
      (Snatches the cloak from him)
    Mak. (Speaking in a southern dialect to
    conceal his identity) What! Ich be a
    yeoman, ich tell you, of the king;
The self and the same, sent from a great
    lording,
    And such.
Fie on you! Go hence!
Out of my presence!
Ich must have reverence.
    Why, who be ich?

    First Shep. Why make ye it so quaint?
    Mak, ye do wrong.
    Second Shep. But Mak, list, ye saint?
    I trow for that you long.
    Third Shep. I trow the shrew can paint!
    The devil might him hang!
    Mak. Ich shall make complaint, and make
    you all to thwang. [27]
    At a word,
And tell even how ye doth.
    First Shep. But, Mak, is that truth?
Now take out that southern tooth,
    And set in a tord.

    Second Shep. Mak, the devil in your eye!
    A stroke would I lend you.
      (Strikes him)
    Third Shep. Mak, know ye not me?
    By God, I could teen you.
    Mak. God, look you all three! Methought
    I had seen you. Ye are a fair com-
    pany.
    First Shep. Can ye now mean you? [28]
    Second Shep. Shrewd jape!
Thus late as thou goes,
What will men suppose?
And thou hast an ill noise [29]
    Of stealing of sheep.

[19] And play now and then.
[20] Argue.
[21] "A cheap bargain yields little."
[22] I.e. Rang the bell for lauds, the first service
of the day.
[23] Went.

[24] Leaves something to be desired.
[25] Disturbs me.
[26] Constantly.
[27] Be beaten.
[28] Remember yourself.
[29] Ill reputation.

Mak. And I am true as steel! all men wot!
But a sickness I feel that holds me full hot;
My belly fares not well, it is out of its state.
Third Shep. Seldom lies the devil dead
    by the gate!

Mak. Therefore
Full sore am I and ill;
If I stand stone still,
I eat not a nedyll
    This month and more.

    First Shep. How fares thy wife? By my
      hood, how fares she?
    Mak. Lies weltering! by the rood! by the
      fire, lo!
And a house full of brood.[30] She drinks well,
    too;
Ill speed other good that she will do
    But so!
Eats as fast as she can;
And every year that comes to man
She bring forth a lakan—[31]
    And some years two.

But were I not more gracious and richer by
    far,
I were eaten out of house and of harbor.
Yet is she a foul slut if ye come near;
There is none that trows nor knows a war[32]
    Than ken I.
Now will ye see what I proffer?
To give all in my coffer
Tomorrow at next to offer
    Her head-mass[33] penny.

    Second Shep. (Yawning) I wot so for-
      waked[34] is none in this shire.
I would sleep, if I takéd less to my hire.
    Third Shep. I am cold and naked,
      and would have a fire.
    First Shep. I am weary, for-rakéd,[34] and
      run in the mire.
    Stay awake, thou!
    Second Shep. Nay, I will lie down by,
For I must sleep, truly.
    Third Shep. As good a man's son was I
    As any of you.
But, Mak, come hither! Between shalt thou
    lie down.

[30] Children.
[31] Baby.
[32] Worse.
[33] Funeral.

Mak. Then might I hinder you, bedene,
    of that ye would rown,[35]
.   .   .   .   .   .
.   .   . (They lie down, making Mak
      lie between them)
Mak. No dread.
From my top to my toe,
Manus tuas commendo,
Pontio Pilato,
    Christ's cross me speed!

(They lie quietly for a minute or two, and
    then Mak looks up)

Now were time for a man that lacks what
    he would
To stalk privily then unto a fold,
And nimbly to work then, and be not too
    bold,
For he might pay sore for the bargain, if it
    were told,
    At the ending.
(Mak rises stealthily) Now were time for
    to revel;
But he needs good counsel
That fain would fare well,
    And has but little spending.
(Mak, pretending to be a magician, draws a
    magic circle about the sleeping Shep-
    herds)

But about you a circle as round as a moon,
Till I have done that I will, till that it be
    noon,
That ye lie stone still till that I have done.
And I shall say thereto of good words a foyn[36]
    On height.
(Making magic passes over them) Over your
    heads my hand I lift:
Out go your eyes! Fore-do your sight!
But yet I must make better shift
    And it be right.
               (The Shepherds snore)
Lord, what! They sleep hard, that may ye
    all hear.
Was I never a shepherd, but now will I lere.[37]
If the flock be scared, yet shall I nip near.
            (Approaches the sheep)

[34] Worn out, tired.
[35] Whisper. The two lines which should follow are missing in the manuscript.
[36] Few.   [37] Learn.

How! Draw hitherward! Now mends our
    cheer
      From sorrow.
A fat sheep, I dare say!
A good fleece, dare I lay!
Repay when I may,
      But this will I borrow.
(MAK *takes a sheep, and crosses the stage to
his hut*)

How, Gill, art thou in? Get us some light.
    WIFE. Who makes such din this time of
      the night?
I am set for to spin; I hope not I might
Rise a penny to win. I curse them on height
    So fares!
A housewife that has been
To be raised thus between!
Here may no work be seen
    For such small chares.[38]

    MAK. Good wife, open the hek![39] Seest
    thou not what I bring?
    WIFE. I may let thee draw the sneck.[40]
    Ah, come in, my sweeting!
    MAK. Yea, thou dost not reck of my long
    standing.
    WIFE. By the naked neck art thou like
    for to hang!
    MAK. Go away:
I am worthy of my meat;
For in a strait can I get
More than they that swink and sweat
All the long day.

Thus it fell to my lot, Gill! I had such grace.
                (*Shows her the sheep*)
    WIFE. It were a foul blot to be hanged
    for the case.
    MAK. I have escaped, Gilott, often as
    hard a glase.[41]
    WIFE. But so long goes the pot to the
    water, men say,
    At last
Comes it home broken.
    MAK. Well know I the token,
But let it never be spoken;
    But come and help fast.

I would he were slain; I list well eat.

This twelvemonth was I not so fain of one
    sheep's meat.
    WIFE. Should they come ere he be slain,
    and hear the sheep bleat—
    MAK. (*Frightened*) Then might I be ta'en!
    That were a cold sweat!
    Go bar
The gate door.
    WIFE. Yes, Mak,
For and they come at thy back—
    MAK. Then might I pay for all the pack!
    The devil of the war.[42]

    WIFE. A good trick have I spied, since
    thou can none.
Here shall we him hide till they be gone—
In my cradle abide—let me alone,
And I shall lie beside in childbed, and groan.
    MAK. Thou red![43]
And I shall say thou was light
Of a male child this night.
    WIFE. Now well is me! Day bright
    That ever was I bred.

This is a good disguise and a far cast!
Yet a woman's advice helps at the last!
I wot never who spies. Again go thou fast.
    MAK. But I come ere they rise, else blows
    a cold blast!
    I will go sleep. (MAK *returns to the
    *SHEPHERDS, *and lies down in his
    place*)
Yet sleeps all this company;
And I shall go stalk privily,
As it had never been I
    That carried their sheep. (FIRST *and*
    SECOND SHEPHERDS *awake*)

    FIRST SHEP. *Resurrex a mortuis!*[44] Take
    hold of my hand.
Judas carnas dominus! I may not well stand.
My foot sleeps, by Jesus; and I water fast
    stand.
I thought that we laid us full near England.
    SECOND SHEP. Ah, yea!
Lord, but I have slept well!
As fresh as an eel,
As light I me feel
    As leaf on a tree.
                (THIRD SHEPHERD *awakes*)

---

[38] Chores. [39] Door. [40] Draw the latch. [41] Blow or difficulty. [42] Worse. [43] Advise well. [44] Mock Latin.

THIRD SHEP. (*Still half-dreaming*) Benste
    be herein! So my [body] quakes,
My heart is out of skin what-so it makes.
Who makes all this din? So my head grows
    black.
To the door will I win. Hark, fellows, wake!
    We were four:
See ye aught of Mak now?
    FIRST SHEP. We were up ere thou.
    SECOND SHEP. Man, I give God a vow,
    Yet went he nowhere.

    THIRD SHEP. Methought he was lapped
    in a wolf's skin.
    FIRST SHEP. So are many happed now—
    namely, within.
    THIRD SHEP. When we had long napped,
    methought with a gin [45]
A fat sheep he trapped; but he made no din.
    SECOND SHEP. Be still!
Thy dream makes thee mad;
It is but phantasy, by the rood.
    FIRST SHEP. Now God turn all to good,
    If it be his will! (*They awaken* MAK)

    SECOND SHEP. Rise, Mak! For shame!
    Thou liest right long.
    MAK. Now Christ's holy name be us
    among!
What is this, by Saint James! I may not well
    gang!
I trow I be the same. Ah! my neck has lain
    wrong
    Enough. (*They help* MAK *to his feet*)
Many thanks! Since yester even,
Now, by Saint Stephen,
I was flayed with a sweven
    My heart out of slough. [46]

I thought Gill began to croak and travail full
    sad,
Well nigh at the first cock, of a young lad
For to mend our flock. Then be I never glad;
I have tow on my rock [47] more than ever I
    had.
    Ah, my head!
A house full of young tharnes! [48]
The devil knock out their harnes! [49]

Woe is him has many bairns,
    And thereto little bread!

I must go home, by your leave, to Gill, as I
    thought.
I pray you look in my sleeve that I steal
    naught;
I am loath you to grieve or from you take
    aught. (MAK *leaves*)
    THIRD SHEP. Go forth; ill might thou
    chefe! [50] Now would I we sought,
    This morn,
That we had all our store.
    FIRST SHEP. But I will go before;
Let us meet.
    SECOND SHEP. Where?
    THIRD SHEP. At the crooked thorn.
        (*Exeunt* SHEPHERDS)

(MAK *crosses the stage to his hut*)

    MAK. Undo this door! Who is here? How
    long shall I stand?
    WIFE. Who makes such a stir? Now walk
    in the wenyand! [51]
    MAK. Ah, Gill, what cheer? It is I, Mak,
    your husband.
    WIFE. Then may we see here the devil in
    a band,
    Sir Guile.
Lo, he comes with a lote [52]
As he were holden in the throat.
I may not sit at my note [53]
    A hand-long while.

    MAK. Will ye hear what fare she makes
    to get her an excuse?
She does naught but lakes, [54] and claws her
    toes.
    WIFE. Why, who wanders? Who wakes?
    Who comes? Who goes?
Who brews? Who bakes? Who makes me
    this hose?
    And then,
It is ruth to behold,
Now in hot, now in cold,
Full woeful is the household
    That wants a woman.

---

[45] Trick.
[46] Nightmare.
[47] *I.e.* More to provide for.
[48] Bellies.
[49] Brains.

[50] Prosper.
[51] Waning of the moon—an unlucky time.
[52] Noise.
[53] Work.
[54] Plays.

But what end hast thou made with the herds-
 men, Mak?
 MAK. The last word that they said, when
  I turned my back,
They would look that they had all their
 sheep in the pack.
I hope they will not be well paid when they
 their sheep lack.
  Perdie.
But how so the game goes,
To me they will suppose,
And make a foul noise,
  And cry out upon me.

But thou must do as thou hight.[55]
 WIFE. I accord me theretill;
I shall swaddle him right in my cradle.
If it were a greater slight, yet could I help till.
I will lie down straight. Come, cover me.
 MAK. I will. (*Tucks her in bed*)
 WIFE. Behind!
Come Coll and his marrow,[56]
They will nip us full narrow.
 MAK. But I may cry "Out, harrow!"[57]
  The sheep if they find.

 WIFE. Hearken aye when they call; they
  will come anon.
Come and make ready all; and sing by thine
 own;
Sing lullaby thou shall, for I must groan
And cry out by the wall on Mary and John,
 For sore.
Sing Lullaby on fast
When thou hears at the last;
And but I play a false cast,
  Trust me no more!

(*The* SHEPHERDS *return and speak at the
 other end of the pageant*)
 THIRD SHEP. Ah, Coll, good morn! Why
  sleep thou not?
 FIRST SHEP. Alas, that ever was I born!
  We have a foul blot.
A fat wether have we lorn.
 THIRD SHEP. Marry, God forbot![58]
 SECOND SHEP. Who should do us that
  scorn? That were a foul spot.
 FIRST SHEP. Some shrew.
I have sought with my dogs

[55] Promised.
[56] Mate.
[57] "Help."
[58] Forbid.

All Horbury Shrogs,[59]
And of fifteen hogs
 Found I but one ewe.

 THIRD SHEP. Now trust me if ye will; by
  Saint Thomas of Kent,
Either Mak or Gill was at that assent.
 FIRST SHEP. Peace, man! Be still! I saw
  when he went.
Thou slanders him ill. Thou ought to repent,
 Good speed.
 SECOND SHEP. Now as ever might I
  thrive,
If I should even here die,
I would say it were he
  That did that same deed.

 THIRD SHEP. Go we thither, I rede, and
  run on our feet.
I shall never eat bread the truth till I wit.
 FIRST SHEP. Nor drink in my heed with
  him till I meet.
 SECOND SHEP. I will rest in no stead till
  that I him greet,
  My brother!
One I will hight:[60]
Till I see him in sight
Shall I never sleep one night
  There I do another.

(*They cross to* MAK's *hut. His* WIFE *begins
 to groan and* MAK, *sitting by the cradle,
 begins to sing a lullaby*)
 THIRD SHEP. Will ye hear how they hack?
  Our sire tries to croon.
 FIRST SHEP. Heard I never one crack so
  clear out of tune!
Call on him.
 SECOND SHEP. Mak! Undo your door
  soon.
 MAK. Who is it that spake as it were noon
  On loft?
Who is that, I say?
 THIRD SHEP. Good fellows, were it day.
 MAK. (*Opens door*) As far as ye may,
  Good, speak soft,

Over a sick woman's head that is at malaise;
I had liefer be dead or she had any disease.[61]

[59] Horbury thickets—about four miles from
Wakefield.
[60] One thing I will swear.
[61] Annoyance.

WIFE. Go to another stead! I may not
  well gueasse.[62]
Each foot that ye tread goes through my nose
  So high!
FIRST SHEP. Tell us, Mak, if ye may,
How fare ye, I say?
  MAK. But are ye in this town today?
    Now how fare ye?

Ye have run in the mire, and are wet yet.
I shall make you a fire if ye will sit.
A nurse would I hire, think ye on it.
Well quit is my hire; my dream—this is it,
  (Points to cradle)
  A season.
I have bairns, if ye knew,
Well more than enow.
But we must drink as we brew,
  And that is but reason.

I would ye dined ere ye yode.[63] Methinks
  that ye sweat.
  SECOND SHEP. Nay, neither mends our
    mood, drink nor meat.
  MAK. Why, sir, ails you aught but good?
  THIRD SHEP. Yea, our sheep that we get
Are stolen as they yode. Our loss is great.
  MAK. Sirs, drink!
Had I been there,
Some should have bought it full sore.
  FIRST SHEP. Marry, some men think that
    ye were;
And that makes us think.

  SECOND SHEP. Mak, some men trows that
    it should be ye.
  THIRD SHEP. Either ye or your spouse, so
    say we.
  MAK. Now, if ye have suspicion on Gill
    or on me,
Come search our house, and then ye may see
  Who had her.
If I any sheep got,
Any cow or stott,[64]
And Gill, my wife, rose not
  Since here she laid her;

As I am true and leal, to God here I pray
That this be the first meal that I shall eat
  this day. (Points to cradle)

FIRST SHEP. Mak, as have I weal, advise
  thee, I say;
He learned timely to steal that could not
  say nay. (The SHEPHERDS begin to
  search the hut)
  WIFE. I swelt! [65]
Out, thieves, from my wonys! [66]
Ye come to rob us, for the nonce.
  MAK. Hear ye not how she groans?
    Your hearts should melt.

  WIFE. Out, thieves, from my bairn! Go
    not nigh him there!
  MAK. Knew ye how she had farne,[67] your
    hearts would be sore.
Ye do wrong, I you warn, that thus come
  before
To a woman that has farne. But I say no
  more!
  WIFE. Ah, my middle!
I pray to God so mild,
If ever I you beguiled,
That I eat this child
  That lies in this cradle.

  MAK. Peace, woman, for God's pain! And
    cry not so!
Thou spills thy brain, and makes me full of
  woe.
  SECOND SHEP. I trow our sheep be slain.
    What find ye two?
  THIRD SHEP. All work we in vain; as well
    may we go.
But, hatters,[68]
I can find no flesh,
Hard nor nesh,
Salt nor fresh,
  But two empty platters.

Living cattle but this, tame nor wild,
None, as have I bliss, as loud as he smelled.
  WIFE. No, so God me bless, and give me
    joy of my child!
  FIRST SHEP. We have marked amiss; I
    hold us beguiled.
  SECOND SHEP. Sir, done!
              (To MAK at the cradle)
Sir, Our Lady him save!

---

[62] Breathe.   [63] Went.   [64] Bullock.   [65] Faint.   [66] House.   [67] Suffered.   [68] A mild oath.

Is your child a knave? [69]
MAK. Any lord might him have,
  This child as his son.

When he wakens he kips,[70] that joy is to see.
  THIRD SHEP. In good time to his hips,
    and in cele! [71]
But who were his gossips,[72] so soon ready?
  MAK. So fair fall their lips!
  FIRST SHEP. (*Aside*) Hark now, a lie!
  MAK. So God them thank,
Parkin and Gibbon Waller, I say,
And gentle John Horn, in good faith,
He made all the garray [73]
  With his great shank.

  SECOND SHEP. Mak, friends will we be,
    for we are all one.
  MAK. Whee! Now I hold for me, for
    amends get I none.
Farewell, all three! All glad were ye gone!
    (SHEPHERDS *leave the hut*)
  THIRD SHEP. Fair words may there be, but
    love is there none
    This year.
  FIRST SHEP. Gave ye the child anything?
  SECOND SHEP. I trow, not one farthing!
  THIRD SHEP. Fast back will I fling;
    Abide ye me here. (THIRD SHEPHERD
    goes back into the hut)

Mak, take it to no grief, if I come to thy
  bairn.
  MAK. Nay, thou does me great reproof,
    and foul has thou farne.
  THIRD SHEP. The child will it not grieve,
    that little day-star.
Mak, with your leave, let me give your bairn
  But sixpence.
  MAK. Nay, do 'way! He sleeps.
  THIRD SHEP. Methinks he peeps.
  MAK. When he wakens he weeps!
    I pray you go hence!

  THIRD SHEP. Give me leave him to kiss,
    and lift up the clout.
(*Lifts the cover and starts back, thinking the
  baby deformed*)
What the devil is this? He has a long snout!

[69] A boy.
[70] Snatches.
[71] Happiness.
[72] Sponsors at baptism.

(*The other* SHEPHERDS *come in and crowd
  around the cradle*)
  FIRST SHEP. He is marked amiss. We wait
    ill about.
  SECOND SHEP. An ill spun woof, ywis,
    aye comes foul out.[74]
(*Looks more closely and sees that it is a
  sheep*)
    Aye, so!
He is like to our sheep!
  THIRD SHEP. How, Gib, may I peep?
  FIRST SHEP. I trow, nature will creep
    Where it may not go!
    (*They lift the sheep out of the cradle*)

  SECOND SHEP. This was a quaint gawd
    and a far cast!
It was a high fraud!
  THIRD SHEP. Yea, sirs, was't.
Let burn this bawd, and bind her fast.
Ah! false scold, hang at the last,
  So shall thou!
Will ye see how they swaddle
His four feet in the middle?
Saw I never in a cradle
  A hornéd lad ere now!

  MAK. Peace, bid I! What! Let be your
    fare!
I am he that him begot, and yon woman him
  bare.
  FIRST SHEP. After what devil shall he be
    hatt? [75] "Mak"? Lo, God, Mak's heir!
  SECOND SHEP. Let be all that. Now God
    give him care,
    I say.
  WIFE. A pretty child is he
As sits on a woman's knee;
A dilly-downe, perdie,
  To make a man laugh.

  THIRD SHEP. I know him by the ear-mark;
    that is a good token!
  MAK. I tell you, sirs, hark! His nose was
    broken;
Later told me a clerk that he was fore-
  spoken.[76]
  FIRST SHEP. This is a false work; I would
    fain be wroken.[77]

[73] Commotion.
[74] An old proverb.
[75] Be named.
[76] Bewitched.   [77] Avenged.

Get a weapon!

WIFE. He was taken by an elf,[78]
I saw it myself;
When the clock struck twelve
   Was he misshapen.

FIRST SHEP. Ye two are well feoffed—
   same in a stead.[79]
THIRD SHEP. Since they maintain their
   theft, let's do them to dead.
MAK. If I trespass eft, gird off my head!
With you will I be left.
FIRST SHEP. Sirs, do my rede: [80]
   For this trespass
We will neither ban ne flyte,[81]
Fight nor chide,
But have done as tight,
   And cast him in canvas.
(*They toss* MAK *in a blanket and then go
back to the fields*)

FIRST SHEP. Lord, what! I am sore in
   point for to burst.
In faith, I may no more; therefore will I
   rest.
SECOND SHEP. As a sheep of seven score
   he weighed in my fist.
For to sleep anywhere methinks that I list.
THIRD SHEP. Now I pray you,
Lie down on this green.
FIRST SHEP. On these thieves yet I mean.[82]
THIRD SHEP. Whereto should ye tene? [83]
   Do as I say you!
      (*They lie down and fall asleep*)

(*An* ANGEL *enters and sings "Gloria
in excelsis"*)

ANGEL. Rise, herd-men heynd! [84] For now
   is he born
That shall take from the fiend that Adam
   had lorn:
That warlock to sheynd [85] this night is he
   born;
God is made your friend now at this morn.
   He behests
At Bethlehem go see,
There lies that free [86]

In a crib full poorly
   Between two beasts.   (*Exit* ANGEL)

FIRST SHEP. This was a quaint steven [87]
   that ever yet I heard.
It is a marvel to name, thus to be scared.
SECOND SHEP. Of God's son of heaven he
   spake upward;
All the wood in a levin [88] methought that he
   gard [89]
   Appear.
THIRD SHEP. He spake of a bairn
In Bethlehem, I you warn.
FIRST SHEP. (*Pointing to the sky*) That
   betokens yon starn;
   Let us seek him there.

SECOND SHEP. Say, what was his song?
   Heard ye not how he cracked it,
Three briefs to a long?
THIRD SHEP. Yea, marry, he hacked it;
Was no crotchet wrong, nor nothing that
   lacked it.
FIRST SHEP. For to sing us among, right
   as he knacked it,
   I can.
SECOND SHEP. Let's see how ye croon.
Can ye bark at the moon?
THIRD SHEP. Hold your tongues! Have
   done!
FIRST SHEP. Hark after, then!

SECOND SHEP. To Bethlehem he bade that
   we should gang;
I am full 'fraid that we tarry too long.
THIRD SHEP. Be merry and not sad; of
   mirth is our song;
Everlastingly glad our reward may we fang [90]
   Without noise.
FIRST SHEP. Hie we thither, fore-thy,[91]
If we be wet and weary,
To that Child and that Lady!
   We have it not to lose.

SECOND SHEP. We find by the prophecy—
   let be your din!—
Of David and Isaiah and more than I mind,
They prophesied by clergy that in a virgin

---

[78] Exchanged by a fairy.
[79] Agreed in your story.
[80] Suggestion.
[81] Curse nor quarrel.
[82] Ponder.
[83] Worry.
[84] Gracious.
[85] Fiend to destroy.
[86] Noble child.
[87] Voice.
[88] Flash of lightning.
[89] Made.
[90] Take.
[91] Therefore.

Should he light and lie, to quench our sin
    And slake it,
Our kind from woe.
For Isaiah said so:
Ecce virgo
    Concipet a child that is naked.

THIRD SHEP. Full glad may we be, and
    abide that day
That lovely to see, that One almighty.
Lord, well were me, for once and for aye,
Might I kneel on my knee some word for
    to say
    To that child.
But the angel said,
In a crib was he laid;
He was poorly arrayed,
    Both meek and mild.

FIRST SHEP. Patriarchs that have been,
    and prophets beforne,
They desired to have seen this child that is
    born.
They are gone full clean; that have they lorn.
We shall see him, I ween, ere it be morn,
    To token.
When I see him and feel,
Then wot I full well
It is true as steel
    That prophets have spoken:

To so poor as we are that he would appear,
First find, and declare by his messenger.
    SECOND SHEP. Go we now, let us fare;
      the place is us near.
    THIRD SHEP. I am ready and yare; go we
      in fear[92]
    To that bright.
Lord, if thy will it be—
We are lewd[93] all three—
Grant us some kind of glee
    To comfort thy wight.

(*They enter the stable.* FIRST SHEPHERD
    kneels before the Christ-child)
    FIRST SHEP. Hail, comely and clean! Hail,
      young Child!
Hail, Maker, as I mean! Of a maiden so mild!

[92] Together.
[93] Unlettered.
[94] Evil deceiver.
[95] Kept my promise.

Thou has cursed, I ween, the devil so wild;
The false guiler of teen,[94] now goes he
    beguiled.
    Lo, he merry is!
Lo, he laughs, my sweeting!
A welfare meeting!
I have holden my heting.[95]
    Have a bob of cherries!
      (SECOND SHEPHERD *kneels*)

SECOND SHEP. Hail, sovereign Savior, for
    thou hast us sought!
Hail! noble child and flower, that all things
    has wrought!
Hail, full of favor, that made all of nought!
Hail! I kneel and I cower. A bird have I
    brought
    To my bairn.
Hail, little tiny mop!
Of our creed thou art crop.
I would drink of thy cup,
    Little day-star!
      (THIRD SHEPHERD *kneels*)

THIRD SHEP. Hail, darling dear, full of
    Godhead!
I pray thee be near when that I have need.
Hail! Sweet is thy cheer! My heart would
    bleed
To see thee sit here in so poor weed,
    With no pennies.
Hail! Put forth thy dall[96]
I bring thee but a ball:
Have and play thee withal,
    And go to the tennis.

MARY. The Father of Heaven, God
    omnipotent,
That set all on seven,[97] his Son has he sent.
My name could he neven[98] and light ere he
    went.
I conceived him full even, through might
    as he meant;
    And now he is born.
He keep you from woe!
I shall pray him so.
Tell it, forth as ye go,
    And mind on this morn.

[96] Fist.
[97] Created the world in seven days.
[98] Name.

FIRST SHEP. Farewell, lady, so fair to
  behold,
With thy child on thy knee!
  SECOND SHEP. But he lies full cold.
Lord, well is me! Now we go, thou behold.
  THIRD SHEP. Forsooth, already it seems to
    be told
  Full oft.

[60] Let it ring on high.

FIRST SHEP. What grace we have found!
SECOND SHEP. Come forth; now are we
  won!
THIRD SHEP. To sing are we bound:
  Let take on loft! [60]

                    (*They go out singing*)

EXPLICIT PAGINA PASTORUM

The Summoning of Everyman

INTRODUCTION

The great cycles of mystery plays, represented here by *The Deluge, Abraham and Isaac,* and *The Second Shepherds' Play,* were not the only kind of dramatic production in medieval England. Equally characteristic were the morality plays, of which *The Summoning of Everyman* (commonly abbreviated to *Everyman*) is the best known example. Like the mysteries, these plays are evidence of the vast importance of religion to medieval man: as the mysteries concentrated on Christian myth, the moralities concentrated on Christian dogma and precept.

In method, the morality plays operated on a principle very popular in medieval thought, but less congenial today, that is, instead of using individuals as characters, they used symbols or personifications. In the mystery plays the characters are Mak and Noah's Wife and Pontius Pilate and Judas Iscariot; in modern plays they are Lord Darlington and Lavinia Mannon and Patrick Murphy; but in the morality plays they are Charity, Lechery, Good Deeds, Pride, Covetousness, Death, Meekness, and Fellowship. The writers of the morality plays were not seeking individuality in characterization or originality in plot; they always wrote about the salvation of man's soul and the familiar helps and hindrances to salvation. Some of the episodes may differ, the emphasis may vary, and the characters may be regrouped or increased in number from play to play, but the end is always the same, and the characters, whatever their names, are simply reminders of the temptations and the guides in the life of the Christian. The purpose of the morality playwright was to make the message of the preacher more vivid and compelling; he had nothing new to say.

Neither the message nor the method is a popular one in the theatre of the twentieth century; indeed, it often seems to the modern playwright that the writer of morality plays deliberately discarded the essential advantages of the drama over other literary forms—the vivid individualization made possible by the actual sight of costume and action and features and by the sound of tones of voice, instead of the descriptions of them to which novels, stories, and poems are limited. Considering all these disadvantages of mode and method, the number of successful stage presentations of *The Summoning of Everyman* in twentieth-century theatres is astonishing. Again and again the play has impressed audiences in hundreds of little theatres all over England and America, and in commercial presentations in London and New York as well.

There seem to be two principal factors at the root of the successful appeal of *Everyman* to audiences of our time; one is the universality of the theme, and the other is the deep sincerity with which it is presented. The theme is man's preparation for death, a favorite subject in the thought and art of the Middle Ages, but one which, as a rule, is timidly ignored in popular literature of the twentieth century. To the anonymous writer of *The Summoning of Everyman,* as to many of his contemporaries, this was the most important subject conceivable; to him, man's life on earth was transitory and insignificant when compared with his life everlasting, earthly rewards and sufferings petty and illusory. The life to come was the only worthy goal for man's striving. Man's concern with clothes and property and friends and pleasures was the pitiful dallying of a thoughtless child; they must be rejected and abandoned,

35

as they abandon Everyman, at the inevitable summons of Death.

The deep sincerity with which this theme is presented has moved hundreds of audiences, often including people who had hastily read the play and thought it dull. There is no deviation into humor, or grisly horrors, or the delightful trivialities which have always been popular in the theatre, but an unwavering concentration on Everyman's slow realization of the realities of death and his relief as he seizes, one by one, the aids and comforts prescribed for the medieval Christian abandoning life on earth and entering into life everlasting. Each character is presented not as an individual or a separate appeal to the audience, but as he appears to Everyman, about to die. Such sincerity and single-mindedness are rare in the theatre, where it is common to sacrifice everything to entertainment; *The Summoning of Everyman* is one of the few successful plays in which all devices to entertain have been sacrificed, and the dramatist strives only to teach.

THE SUMMONING OF EVERYMAN

Dramatis personae

In order of first appearance

MESSENGER, The Speaker of the Prologue.

GOD, Called also Adonai and Messias. He does not appear, but speaks off stage.

DEATH

EVERYMAN, The personification of all men, short-sighted, thoughtless, and self-centered. He is proud of his financial status and not given to charity.

FELLOWSHIP, The boon companion of Everyman's frivolous hours.

KINDRED } Everyman's relatives.
COUSIN }

GOODS, Everyman's property, one of his principal liabilities as he faces God's final judgment.

GOOD DEEDS, The pious and charitable deeds Everyman has accomplished in his life.

KNOWLEDGE, Not knowledge in the modern sense, but understanding of the orthodox dogma of the medieval church and of the basic duties of the Christian life.

CONFESSION

BEAUTY, The physical beauty of man.

STRENGTH, Everyman's physical strength.

DISCRETION

FIVE WITS, Everyman's senses—sight, taste, smell, hearing, feeling.

ANGEL, He does not appear, but speaks from off stage.

DOCTOR, The learned religious man who delivers the epilogue applying the lesson of the play, as in *Abraham and Isaac*.

(*In one corner of the stage is an inconspicuous grave into which* EVERYMAN *must descend at the end of the play. In the opposite corner* GOOD DEEDS *lies so quietly as to be forgotten until* EVERYMAN *calls her in the middle of the play.*)

(*Enter* MESSENGER)

MESSENGER. I pray you all give your audience,
And hear this matter with reverence,
By figure a moral play.
The *Summoning of Everyman* called it is,
That of our lives and ending shows
How transitory we be all day.
This matter is wondrous precious,
But the intent of it is more gracious,
And sweet to bear away.
The story saith:—Man, in the beginning
Look well, and take good heed to the ending,
Be you never so gay!
Ye think sin in the beginning full sweet,
Which in the end causeth thy soul to weep,
When the body lieth in clay.

Here shall you see how *Fellowship* and *Jollity*,
Both *Strength, Pleasure,* and *Beauty,*
Will fade from thee as flower in May.
For ye shall hear how our Heaven King
Calleth Everyman to a general reckoning.
Give audience, and hear what he doth say.
(*Exit*)
GOD. (*Speaking solemnly from off stage*)
 I perceive, here in my majesty,
How that all creatures be to me unkind,
Living without dread in worldly prosperity:
Of ghostly sight[1] the people be so blind,
Drowned in sin, they know me not for their God.
In worldly riches is all their mind;
They fear not my righteousness, the sharp rod;
My love that I showed when I for them died
They forget clean, and shedding of my blood red;
I hanged between two, it cannot be denied;
To get them life I suffered to be dead;
I healed their feet, with thorns hurt was my head.
I could do no more than I did, truly;
And now I see the people do clean forsake me.
They use the seven deadly sins damnable,
As pride, covetise, wrath, and lechery,
Now in the world be made commendable;
And thus they leave of angels, the heavenly company.
Everyman liveth so after his own pleasure,
And yet of their life they be nothing sure.
I see the more that I them forbear
The worse they be from year to year;
All that liveth appaireth[2] fast.
Therefore I will, in all the haste,
Have a reckoning of Everyman's person;
For and I leave the people thus alone
In their life and wicked tempests,
Verily they will become much worse than beasts;
For now one would by envy another up eat;
Charity they all do clean forget.
I hoped well that Everyman
In my glory should make his mansion,
And thereto I had them all elect;
But now I see, like traitors deject,
They thank me not for the pleasure that I to them meant,

Nor yet for their being that I them have lent.
I proffered the people great multitude of mercy,
And few there be that asketh it heartily.
They be so cumbered with worldly riches,
That needs on them I must do justice,
On Everyman living, without fear.
Where art thou, Death, thou mighty messenger?

(*Enter* DEATH)

DEATH. Almighty God, I am here at Your will,
Your commandment to fulfil.
GOD. Go thou to Everyman,
And show him, in my name,
A pilgrimage he must on him take,
Which he in no wise may escape;
And that he bring with him a sure reckoning
Without delay or any tarrying.
DEATH. Lord, I will in the world go run over all,
And cruelly out search both great and small.
Every man will I beset that liveth beastly
Out of God's laws, and dreadeth not folly.
He that loveth riches I will strike with my dart,
His sight to blind, and from heaven to depart—
Except that alms be his good friend—
In hell for to dwell, world without end.

(*Enter* EVERYMAN *at the opposite end of the stage, walking jauntily*)

Lo, yonder I see Everyman walking;
Full little he thinketh on my coming;
His mind is on fleshly lusts and his treasure,
And great pain it shall cause him to endure
Before the Lord, Heaven's King.
(*Calling*) Everyman, stand still! (EVERYMAN *stops*) Whither art thou going
Thus gaily? Hast thou thy Maker forgot?
EVERYMAN. Why askest thou?
Wouldest thou wete?[3]
DEATH. Yea, sir, I will show you;
In great haste I am sent to thee
From God out of His Majesty.
EVERYMAN. What, sent to me?
DEATH. Yea, certainly.
Though thou have forgot Him here,

---

[1] Spiritual insight.   [2] Degenerates.

[3] Know.

He thinketh on thee in the heavenly sphere,
As, or we depart, thou shalt know.
EVERYMAN. What desireth God of me?
DEATH. That shall I show thee:
A reckoning He will needs have
Without any longer respite.
EVERYMAN. To give a reckoning longer
leisure I crave;
This blind matter troubleth my wit.
DEATH. On thee thou must take a long
journey;
Therefore thy book of count with thee thou
bring;
For turn again thou can not by no way.
And look thou be sure of thy reckoning,
For before God thou shalt answer and show
Thy many bad deeds, and good but a few,
How thou hast spent thy life, and in what
wise,
Before the Chief Lord of paradise.
Have ado⁴ that we were in that way,
For, know thou well, thou shalt make none
attournay.
EVERYMAN. Full unready I am such reck-
oning to give.
I know thee not. What messenger art thou?
DEATH. I am Death, that no man dread-
eth.⁵
For every man I rest, and no man spareth;
For it is God's commandment
That all to me should be obedient.
EVERYMAN. (Ingratiatingly) O Death!
thou comest when I had thee least in
mind!
In thy power it lieth me to save;
Yet of my goods will I give thee, if thou
will be kind,
Yea, a thousand pound shalt thou have,
And defer this matter till another day.
DEATH. Everyman, it may not be, by no
way.
I set not by gold, silver, nor riches,
Nor by pope, emperor, king, duke, nor
princes.
For, and I would receive gifts great,
All the world I might get;
But my custom is clean contrary.
I give thee no respite. Come hence, and not
tarry!
EVERYMAN. Alas! shall I have no longer
respite?

I may say Death giveth no warning.
To think on thee, it maketh my heart sick,
For all unready is my book of reckoning.
But twelve year and I might have abiding,
My counting-book I would make so clear,
That my reckoning I should not need to
fear.
(Pleading) Wherefore, Death, I pray thee,
for God's mercy,
Spare me till I be provided of remedy.
DEATH. Thee availeth not to cry, weep,
and pray;
But haste thee lightly that thou wert gone
that journey,
And prove thy friends if thou can.
For wete thou well the tide abideth no man;
And in the world each living creature
For Adam's sin must die of nature.
EVERYMAN. Death, if I should this pil-
grimage take,
And my reckoning surely make,
Show me, for Saint Charity,
Should I not come again shortly?
DEATH. No, Everyman; and thou be once
there,
Thou mayst never more come here,
Trust me verily.
EVERYMAN. O gracious God, in the high
seat celestial,
Have mercy on me in this most need!
Shall I have no company from this vale
terrestrial
Of mine acquaintance that way me to lead?
DEATH. Yea, if any be so hardy,
That would go with thee and bear thee
company.
Hie thee that thou wert gone to God's mag-
nificence,
Thy reckoning to give before His presence.
What! weenest⁶ thou thy life is given thee,
And thy worldly goods also?
EVERYMAN. I had weened so, verily.
DEATH. Nay, nay; it was but lent thee;
For, as soon as thou art gone,
Another a while shall have it, and then go
therefrom,
Even as thou hast done.
Everyman, thou art mad! Thou hast thy wits
five,
And here on earth will not amend thy life;
For suddenly I do come.

⁴ Hasten.　　　⁵ That respects no man.　　　⁶ Thinkest.

EVERYMAN. O wretched caitiff! whither shall I flee,
That I might 'scape this endless sorrow?
Now, gentle Death, spare me till tomorrow,
That I may amend me
With good advisement.

DEATH. Nay; thereto I will not consent,
Nor no man will I respite;
But to the heart suddenly I shall smite
Without any advisement.
And now out of thy sight I will me hie.
See thou make thee ready shortly,
For thou mayst say this is the day
That no man living may 'scape away.

(*Exit* DEATH)

EVERYMAN. Alas! I may well weep with sighs deep!
Now have I no manner of company
To help me in my journey and me to keep;
And also my writing is full unready.
How shall I do now for to excuse me?
I would to God I had never been gete! [7]
To my soul a full great profit it had be;
For now I fear pains huge and great.
The time passeth. Lord, help, that all wrought!
For though I mourn, it availeth naught.
The day passeth, and is almost a-go;
I wot not well what for to do.
To whom were I best my complaint to make?
What and I to Fellowship thereof spake,
And showed him of this sudden chance?
For in him is all mine affiance; [8]
We have in the world so many a day
Been good friends in sport and play.
(*Looking off stage*) I see him yonder, certainly;
I trust that he will bear me company;
Therefore to him will I speak to ease my sorrow.

(*Enter* FELLOWSHIP *fashionably dressed*)

Well met, good Fellowship, and good morrow!

FELLOWSHIP. Everyman, good morrow! By this day,
Sir, why lookest thou so piteously?
If any thing be amiss, I pray thee me say,
That I may help to remedy.

EVERYMAN. Yea, good Fellowship, yea;
I am in great jeopardy.

FELLOWSHIP. My true friend, show to me your mind;
I will not forsake thee unto my life's end
In the way of good company.

EVERYMAN. That was well spoken, and lovingly.

FELLOWSHIP. Sir, I must needs know your heaviness;
I have pity to see you in any distress.
If any have you wronged, ye shall revenged be,
Though I on the ground be slain for thee,
Though that I know before that I should die.

EVERYMAN. Verily, Fellowship, gramercy.

FELLOWSHIP. Tush! by thy thanks I set not a straw!
Show me your grief, and say no more.

EVERYMAN. If I my heart should to you break,
And then you to turn your mind from me,
And would not me comfort when you hear me speak,
Then should I ten times sorrier be.

FELLOWSHIP. Sir, I say as I will do, indeed.

EVERYMAN. Then be you a good friend at need;
I have found you true here before.

FELLOWSHIP. And so ye shall evermore;
For, in faith, and thou go to hell
I will not forsake thee by the way!

EVERYMAN. Ye speak like a good friend; I believe you well.
I shall deserve it, and I may.

FELLOWSHIP. I speak of no deserving, by this day.
For he that will say, and nothing do,
Is not worthy with good company to go.
Therefore show me the grief of your mind,
As to your friend most loving and kind.

EVERYMAN. I shall show you how it is:
Commanded I am to go a journey—
A long way, hard and dangerous—
And give a strait count without delay
Before the high judge, Adonai. [9]
Wherefore, I pray you, bear me company,
As ye have promised, in this journey.

FELLOWSHIP. That is matter indeed!
Promise is duty;

---

[7] Begotten. [8] Trust. [9] God. An Old Testament name.

But, and I should take such a voyage on me,
I know it well, it should be to my pain.
Also it maketh me afeared, certain.
But let us take counsel here as well as we can,
For your words would fear a strong man.

EVERYMAN. Why, ye said if I had need,
Ye would me never forsake, quick nor dead,
Though it were to hell, truly.

FELLOWSHIP. So I said, certainly.
But such pleasures be set aside, the sooth to
say.
And also, if we took such a journey,
When should we come again?

EVERYMAN. Nay, never again till the day
of doom.

FELLOWSHIP. In faith, then will not I
come there!
Who hath you these tidings brought?

EVERYMAN. Indeed, Death was with me
here.

FELLOWSHIP. Now, by God that all hath
bought,
If Death were the messenger,
For no man that is living today
I will not go that loath journey—
Not for the father that begat me!

EVERYMAN. Ye promised otherwise,
pardie.[10]

FELLOWSHIP. I wot well I said so, truly.
And yet if thou wilt eat, and drink, and
make good cheer,
Or haunt to women the lusty company,
I would not forsake you while the day is
clear,
Trust me verily!

EVERYMAN. Yea, thereto ye would be
ready;
To go to mirth, solace, and play,
Your mind will sooner apply
Than to bear me company in my long jour-
ney.

FELLOWSHIP. Now, in good faith, I will
not that way.
But and thou wilt murder, or any man kill,
In that I will help thee with a good will!

EVERYMAN. O, that is a simple advice
indeed!
Gentle Fellow, help me in my necessity!
We have loved long, and now I need,
And now, gentle Fellowship, remember me!

FELLOWSHIP. Whether ye have loved me
or no,

[10] A mild oath.

By Saint John, I will not with thee go!

EVERYMAN. Yet, I pray thee, take the
labor, and do so much for me
To bring me forward, for Saint Charity,
And comfort me till I come without the
town.

FELLOWSHIP. Nay, and thou would give
me a new gown,
I will not a foot with thee go;
But, and thou had tarried, I would not have
left thee so.
And as now God speed thee in thy journey,
For from thee I will depart as fast as I may.

EVERYMAN. Whither away, Fellowship?
Will you forsake me?

FELLOWSHIP. Yea, by my fay! To God I
betake thee.

EVERYMAN. Farewell, good Fellowship!
For thee my heart is sore.
Adieu for ever! I shall see thee no more.

FELLOWSHIP. In faith, Everyman, farewell now at the end;
For you I will remember that parting is
mourning.

(*Exit* FELLOWSHIP)

EVERYMAN. Alack! shall we thus depart
indeed
(Ah, Lady, help!) without any more com-
fort?
Lo, Fellowship forsaketh me in my most
need.
For help in this world whither shall I resort?
Fellowship herebefore with me would merry
make,
And now little sorrow for me doth he take.
It is said, "In prosperity men friends may
find,
Which in adversity be full unkind."
Now whither for succor shall I flee,
Sith that Fellowship hath forsaken me?
To my kinsmen I will, truly,
Praying them to help me in my necessity.
I believe that they will do so,
For "kind will creep where it may not go."
(*Looking off stage*) I will go say,[11] for yon-
der I see them go.
Where be ye now, my friends and kinsmen?

(*Enter* KINDRED *and* COUSIN)

KINDRED. Here be we now, at your commandment.

[11] Assay, or try.

Cousin, I pray you show us your intent
In any wise, and do not spare.

COUSIN. Yea, Everyman, and to us declare
If ye be disposed to go any whither,
For, wete you well, we will live and die
together.

KINDRED. In wealth and woe we will with
you hold,
For over his kin a man may be bold.

EVERYMAN. Gramercy, my friends and
kinsmen kind.
Now shall I show you the grief of my mind.
I was commanded by a messenger
That is an high king's chief officer:
He bade me go a pilgrimage, to my pain,
And I know well I shall never come again.
Also I must give a reckoning straight,
For I have a great enemy that hath me in
wait,
Which intendeth me for to hinder.

KINDRED. What account is that which ye
must render?
That would I know.

EVERYMAN. Of all my works I must show
How I have lived, and my days spent;
Also of ill deeds that I have used
In my time, sith life was me lent;
And of all virtues that I have refused.
Therefore, I pray you, go thither with me,
To help to make mine account, for Saint
Charity.

COUSIN. What, to go thither? Is that the
matter?
Nay, Everyman, I had liefer fast bread and
water
All this five year and more.

EVERYMAN. Alas, that ever I was bore!
For now shall I never be merry
If that you forsake me.

KINDRED. Ah, sir; what, ye be a merry
man!
Take good heart to you, and make no moan.
But one thing I warn you, by Saint Anne—
As for me, ye shall go alone.

EVERYMAN. My Cousin, will you not with
me go?

COUSIN. No, by Our Lady! (*Casting
about for an excuse*) I have the cramp
in my toe.
Trust not to me; for, so God me speed,
I will deceive you in your most need.

KINDRED. It availeth not us to tice.[12]

[12] Entice.

Ye shall have my maid with all my heart;
She loveth to go to feasts, there to be nice,
And to dance, and abroad to start;
I will give her leave to help you in that
journey,
If that you and she may agree.

EVERYMAN. Now show me the very effect
of your mind.
Will you go with me, or abide behind?

KINDRED. Abide behind? Yea, that will I,
and I may!
Therefore farewell till another day.

(*Exit* KINDRED)

EVERYMAN. How should I be merry or
glad?
For fair promises men to me make,
But when I have most need, they me forsake.
I am deceived; that maketh me sad.

COUSIN. Cousin Everyman, farewell now,
For verily I will not go with you.
Also of mine own life an unready reckoning
I have to account; therefore I make tarrying.
Now, God keep thee, for now I go.

(*Exit* COUSIN)

EVERYMAN. Ah, Jesus! is all come hereto?
Lo, fair words maketh fools fain;
They promise and nothing will do certain.
My kinsmen promised me faithfully
For to abide with me steadfastly,
And now fast away do they flee:
Even so Fellowship promised me.
What friend were best me of to provide?
I lose my time here longer to abide.
Yet in my mind a thing there is—
All my life I have loved riches;
If that my Goods now help me might,
He would make my heart full light.
I will speak to him in this distress.
(*Calling*) Where art thou, my Goods and
riches?

GOODS. (*From within*) Who calleth me?
Everyman? What! hast thou haste?
I lie here in corners, trussed and piled so
high,
And in chests I am locked so fast,
Also sacked in bags—thou mayst see with
thine eye—
I cannot stir; in packs low I lie.
What would ye have? Lightly me say.

EVERYMAN. Come hither, Goods, in all
the haste thou may,
For of counsel I must desire thee.

(Enter Goods)

Goods. Sir, and ye in the world have sorrow or adversity,
That can I help you to remedy shortly.
Everyman. It is another disease that grieveth me;
In this world it is not, I tell thee so.
I am sent for another way to go,
To give a strait count general
Before the highest Jupiter of all;
And all my life I have had joy and pleasure in thee.
Therefore I pray thee go with me,
For, peradventure, thou mayst before God Almighty
My reckoning help to clean and purify;
For it is said ever among,
That "money maketh all right that is wrong."
Goods. Nay, Everyman; I sing another song!
I follow no man in such voyages;
For, and I went with thee,
Thou shouldst fare much the worse for me;
For because on me thou did set thy mind,
Thy reckoning I have made blotted and blind,
That thine account thou cannot make truly;
And that hast thou for the love of me.
Everyman. That would grieve me full sore,
When I should come to that fearful answer.
Up, let us go thither together.
Goods. Nay, not so! I am too brittle, I may not endure;
I will follow no man one foot, be ye sure.
Everyman. Alas! I have thee loved, and had great pleasure
All my life-days on goods and treasure.
Goods. That is to thy damnation, without lesing! [13]
For my love is contrary to the love everlasting.
But if thou had me loved moderately during,
As to the poor to give part of me,
Then shouldst thou not in this dolor be,
Nor in this great sorrow and care.
Everyman. Lo, now was I deceived ere I was ware,
And all I may wyte my spending [14] of time.
Goods. What, weenest thou that I am thine?

[13] Lying.   [14] Charge to misspending.

Everyman. I had weened so.
Goods. Nay, Everyman, I say no.
As for a while I was lent thee,
A season thou hast had me in prosperity.
My condition is man's soul to kill;
If I save one, a thousand I do spill.
Weenest thou that I will follow thee?
Nay, not from this world verily.
Everyman. I had weened otherwise.
Goods. Therefore to thy soul Goods is a thief;
For when thou art dead, this is my guise—
Another to deceive in the same wise
As I have done thee, and all to his soul's reprief.
Everyman. O false Goods, curséd thou be!
Thou traitor to God, that hast deceived me
And caught me in thy snare.
Goods. *(Laughing at* Everyman) Mary! thou brought thyself in care;
Whereof I am right glad.
I must needs laugh, I cannot be sad.
Everyman. Ah, Goods, thou hast had long my hearty love;
I gave thee that which should be the Lord's above.
But wilt thou not go with me indeed?
I pray thee truth to say.
Goods. No, so God me speed!
Therefore farewell, and have good day.
(Exit Goods)
Everyman. O, to whom shall I make my moan
For to go with me in that heavy journey?
First Fellowship said he would with me gone;
His words were very pleasant and gay,
But afterward he left me alone.
Then spake I to my kinsmen, all in despair,
And also they gave me words fair—
They lacked no fair speaking,
But all forsook me in the ending.
Then went I to my Goods, that I loved best,
In hope to have comfort, but there had I least;
For my Goods sharply did me tell
That he bringeth many into hell.
Then of my self I was ashamed,
And so I am worthy to be blamed;
Thus may I well my self hate.
Of whom shall I now counsel take?
I think that I shall never speed

Till that I go to my Good Deed.
But alas! she is so weak
That she can neither go nor speak.
Yet will I venture on her now.
(*Calling*) My Good Deeds, where be you?

(GOOD DEEDS, *lying in one corner of the
stage, feebly raises her head and speaks*)

GOOD DEEDS. Here I lie, cold in the
ground.
Thy sins hath me sore bound,
That I cannot stir.
EVERYMAN. O Good Deeds! I stand in
fear!
I must you pray of counsel,
For help now should come right well.
GOOD DEEDS. Everyman, I have under-
standing
That ye be summoned account to make
Before Messias, of Jerusalem King;
And you do by me,[15] that journey with you
will I take.
EVERYMAN. Therefore I come to you my
moan to make;
I pray you that ye will go with me.
GOOD DEEDS. I would full fain, but I
cannot stand, verily.
EVERYMAN. Why, is there anything on
you fallen?
GOOD DEEDS. Yea, sir, I may thank you
of all;
If ye had perfectly cheered me,
Your book of count full ready had be.
(GOOD DEEDS *shows him a large
account book*)
Look, the books of your works and deeds eke!
Ah, see how they lie under the feet,
To your soul's heaviness.
EVERYMAN. Our Lord Jesus help me!
For one letter here I can not see.
GOOD DEEDS. There is a blind reckoning
in time of distress!
EVERYMAN. Good Deeds, I pray you, help
me in this need,
Or else I am for ever damned indeed.
Therefore help me to make my reckoning
Before the Redeemer of all thing,
That King is, and was, and ever shall.
GOOD DEEDS. (*Trying unsuccessfully to
rise*) Everyman, I am sorry of your fall,

And fain would I help you, and I were able.
EVERYMAN. Good Deeds, your counsel I
pray you give me.
GOOD DEEDS. That shall I do verily;
Though that on my feet I may not go,
I have a sister that shall with you also,
Called Knowledge, which shall with you
abide,
To help you to make that dreadful reckon-
ing.

(*Enter* KNOWLEDGE)

KNOWLEDGE. Everyman, I will go with
thee, and be thy guide,
In thy most need to go by thy side.
EVERYMAN. (*With great relief*) In good
condition I am now in every thing,
And am wholly content with this good thing;
Thanked be God my Creator!
GOOD DEEDS. And when he hath brought
thee there,
Where thou shalt heal thee of thy smart,
Then go you with your reckoning and your
Good Deeds together
For to make you joyful at heart
Before the blessèd Trinity.
EVERYMAN. My Goods Deeds, gramercy!
I am well content, certainly,
With your words sweet.
KNOWLEDGE. Now go we together lov-
ingly
To Confession, that cleansing river.
EVERYMAN. For joy I weep; I would we
were there!
But, I pray you, give me cognition
Where dwelleth that holy man, Confession.
KNOWLEDGE. In the house of salvation;
We shall find him in that place,
That shall us comfort, by God's grace.

(*Enter* CONFESSION *dressed as a priest.*
KNOWLEDGE *leads* EVERYMAN *to him.*)

Lo, this is Confession. Kneel down and ask
mercy,
For he is in good conceit[16] with God Almighty.
EVERYMAN. (*Kneeling*) O glorious fountain, that all uncleanness doth clarify,
Wash from me the spots of vice unclean,

---

[15] If you will take my advice.   [16] High esteem.

That on me no sin may be seen.
I come, with Knowledge, for my redemption,
Redempt with hearty and full contrition;
For I am commanded a pilgrimage to take,
And great accounts before God to make.
Now, I pray you, Shrift, mother of salvation,
Help my Good Deeds for my piteous ex-
  clamation.
CONFESSION. I know your sorrow well,
  Everyman.
Because with Knowledge ye come to me,
I will you comfort as well as I can,
And a precious jewel I will give thee,
Called penance, voider of adversity;
Therewith shall your body chastised be
With abstinence and perseverance in God's
  service.
Here shall you receive that scourge of me,
        (*Gives* EVERYMAN *a scourge*)
Which is penance strong, that ye must en-
  dure
To remember thy Savior was scourged for
  thee
With sharp scourges, and suffered it
  patiently;
So must thou, or thou 'scape that painful
  pilgrimage.
Knowledge, keep him in this voyage,
And by that time Good Deeds will be with
  thee.
But in any wise be seeker of mercy,
For your time draweth fast; and ye will saved
  be,
Ask God mercy, and He will grant truly;
When with the scourge of penance man doth
  him bind,
The oil of forgiveness then shall he find.
        (*Exit* CONFESSION)
EVERYMAN. Thanked be God for His
  gracious work!
For now I will my penance begin;
This hath rejoiced and lighted my heart,
Though the knots be painful and hard
  within.
KNOWLEDGE. Everyman, look your pen-
  ance that ye fulfil,
What pain that ever it to you be,
And Knowledge shall give you counsel at
  will
How your account ye shall make clearly.

(EVERYMAN *hands the scourge to* KNOWL-
EDGE *and kneels to pray*)

EVERYMAN. O eternal God! O heavenly
  figure!
O way of righteousness! O goodly vision!
Which descended down in a virgin pure
Because He would Everyman redeem,
Which Adam forfeited by his disobedience.
O blessèd Godhead! elect and high divine,
Forgive me my grievous offence.
Here I cry Thee mercy in this presence.
O ghostly treasure! O ransomer and re-
  deemer!
Of all the world hope and conductor,
Mirror of joy, and founder of mercy,
Which illumineth heaven and earth thereby,
Hear my clamorous complaint, though it
  late be!
Receive my prayers; unworthy of thy
  benignity.
Though I be a sinner most abominable,
Yet let my name be written in Moses' table.
O Mary! pray to the Maker of all thing
Me for to help at my ending,
And save me from the power of my enemy,
For Death assaileth me strongly.
And, Lady, that I may by means of thy
  prayer
Of your Son's glory to be partner,
By the means of His passion I it crave;
I beseech you, help my soul to save.
        (*He rises and turns to* KNOWLEDGE)
Knowledge, give me the scourge of penance.
        (KNOWLEDGE *hands him the scourge*)
My flesh therewith shall give a quittance.
I will now begin, if God give me grace.
    KNOWLEDGE. Everyman, God give you
      time and space.
Thus I bequeath you in the hands of our
  Savior,
Now may you make your reckoning sure.
    EVERYMAN. In the name of the Holy
      Trinity,
My body sore punished shall be.
        (*Scourges himself*)
Take this, body, for the sin of the flesh!
Also thou delightest to go gay and fresh,
And in the way of damnation thou did me
  bring;
Therefore suffer now strokes of punishing.
Now of penance I will wade the water clear,
To save me from purgatory, that sharp fire.

(GOOD DEEDS *rises from the floor*)

GOOD DEEDS. I thank God, now I can walk and go,
And am delivered of my sickness and woe.
Therefore with Everyman I will go, and not spare;
His good works I will help him to declare.
KNOWLEDGE. Now, Everyman, be merry and glad;
Your Good Deeds cometh now, ye may not be sad;
Now is your Good Deeds whole and sound,
Going upright upon the ground.
EVERYMAN. My heart is light, and shall be evermore.
Now will I smite faster than I did before.
GOOD DEEDS. Everyman, pilgrim, my special friend,
Blessèd be thou without end;
For thee is prepared the eternal glory.
Ye have me made whole and sound,
Therefore I will bide by thee in every stound.[17]
EVERYMAN. Welcome, my Good Deeds! Now I hear thy voice,
I weep for very sweetness of love.
KNOWLEDGE. Be no more sad, but ever rejoice;
God seeth thy living in His throne above.
(*Holding up a black robe*) Put on this garment to thy behoof,[18]
Which is wet with your tears,
Or else before God you may it miss,
When you to your journey's end come shall.
EVERYMAN. Gentle Knowledge, what do ye it call?
KNOWLEDGE. It is the garment of sorrow;
From pain it will you borrow;
Contrition it is
That getteth forgiveness;
It pleaseth God passing well.
GOOD DEEDS. Everyman, will you wear it for your heal?

(EVERYMAN *puts on the robe of contrition*)

EVERYMAN. Now blessèd be Jesu, Mary's Son!
For now have I on true contrition.
And let us go now without tarrying.
Good Deeds, have we clear our reckoning?
GOOD DEEDS. Yea, indeed I have [it] here.

EVERYMAN. Then I trust we need not fear.
Now, friends, let us not part in twain.
KNOWLEDGE. Nay, Everyman, that will we not, certain.
GOOD DEEDS. Yet must thou lead with thee
Three persons of great might.
EVERYMAN. Who should they be?
GOOD DEEDS. Discretion and Strength they hight,[19]
And thy Beauty may not abide behind.
KNOWLEDGE. Also ye must call to mind
Your Five Wits[20] as for your counselors.
GOOD DEEDS. You must have them ready at all hours.
EVERYMAN. How shall I get them hither?
KNOWLEDGE. You must call them all together,
And they will hear you incontinent.
EVERYMAN. (*Calling*) My friends, come hither and be present,
Discretion, Strength, my Five Wits, and Beauty.

(*Enter* DISCRETION, STRENGTH, FIVE WITS, *and* BEAUTY)

BEAUTY. Here at your will we be all ready.
What will ye that we should do?
GOOD DEEDS. That ye would with Everyman go,
And help him in his pilgrimage.
Advise you, will ye with him or not in that voyage?
STRENGTH. We will bring him all thither,
To his help and comfort, ye may believe me.
DISCRETION. So will we go with him all together.
EVERYMAN. (*Lifting his arms to Heaven*) Almighty God, lovèd may Thou be,
I give Thee laud that I have hither brought
Strength, Discretion, Beauty, and Five Wits.
Lack I naught;
And my Good Deeds, with Knowledge clear,
All be in company at my will here.
I desire no more to my business.
STRENGTH. And I, Strength, will by you stand in distress,
Though thou would in battle fight on the ground.
FIVE WITS. And though it were through the world round,

---

[17] Attack.   [18] Benefit.

[19] Are called.   [20] *I.e.* Five senses.

We will not depart for sweet nor sour.

BEAUTY. No more will I, unto death's hour,
Whatsoever thereof befall.

DISCRETION. Everyman, advise you first of all;
Go with a good advisement and deliberation.
We all give you virtuous monition
That all shall be well.

EVERYMAN. My friends, hearken what I will tell—
I pray God reward you in His heavenly sphere.
Now hearken, all that be here,
For I will make my testament
Here before you all present:
In alms half my goods I will give with my hands twain
In the way of charity, with good intent,
And the other half still shall remain,
I it bequeath to be returned there it ought to be.
This I do in despite of the fiend of hell,
To go quite out of his peril
Ever after and this day.

KNOWLEDGE. Everyman, hearken what I say:
Go to Priesthood, I you advise,
And receive of him in any wise
The holy sacrament and ointment together;
Then shortly see ye turn again hither;
We will all abide you here.

FIVE WITS. Yea, Everyman, hie you that ye ready were.
There is no emperor, king, duke, nor baron,
That of God hath commission
As hath the least priest in the world being;
For of the blessèd sacraments pure and benign
He beareth the keys, and thereof hath the cure
For man's redemption—it is ever sure—
Which God for our soul's medicine
Gave us out of His heart with great pain.
Here in this transitory life, for thee and me
The blessèd sacraments seven there be:
Baptism, confirmation, with priesthood good,
And the sacrament of God's precious flesh and blood,
Marriage, the holy extreme unction, and penance.

[21] Spiritual.

These seven be good to have in remembrance,
Gracious sacraments of high divinity.

EVERYMAN. Fain would I receive that holy body
And meekly to my ghostly [21] father I will go.

FIVE WITS. Everyman, that is the best that ye can do.
God will you to salvation bring,
For priesthood exceedeth all other thing;
To us Holy Scripture they do teach,
And converteth man from sin heaven to reach;
God hath to them more power given
Than to any angel that is in heaven.
With five words he may consecrate
God's body in flesh and blood to make,
And handleth his Maker between his hands.
The priest bindeth and unbindeth all bands,
Both in earth and in heaven.
Thou ministers all the sacraments seven;
Though we kissed thy feet, thou wert worthy;
Thou art the surgeon that cureth sin deadly;
No remedy we find under God
But all only priesthood.
Everyman, God gave priests that dignity,
And setteth them in His stead among us to be;
Thus be they above angels in degree.

(EVERYMAN *walks solemnly out to receive the last rites of the church*)

KNOWLEDGE. If priests be good, it is so, surely.[22]
But when Jesus hanged on the cross with great smart,
There He gave out of His blessèd heart
The same sacrament in great torment.
He sold them not to us, that Lord omnipotent.
Therefore Saint Peter the Apostle doth say
That Jesus' curse hath all they
Which God their Savior do buy or sell,
Or they for any money do take or tell.
Sinful priests giveth the sinners example bad;
Their children sitteth by other men's fires, I have heard;
And some haunteth women's company
With unclean life, as lusts of lechery.

[22] Replying to the last line. He goes on to talk about bad priests.

These be with sin made blind.

FIVE WITS. I trust to God no such may
we find.

Therefore let us priesthood honor,

And follow their doctrine for our souls'
succor.

We be their sheep, and they shepherds be,

By whom we all be kept in surety.

Peace! for yonder I see Everyman come,

Which hath made true satisfaction.

GOOD DEEDS. Methinketh it is he indeed.

(*Re-enter* EVERYMAN)

EVERYMAN. Now Jesu be your alder
speed.[23]

I have received the sacrament for my
redemption,

And then mine extreme unction.

Blesséd be all they that counseled me to
take it!

And now, friends, let us go without longer
respite;

I thank God that ye have tarried so long.

Now set each of you on this rod your hand,

And shortly follow me.

I go before, there I would be. God be our
guide!

STRENGTH. Everyman, we will not from
you go

Till ye have gone this voyage long.

DISCRETION. I, Discretion, will bide by
you also.

KNOWLEDGE. And though this pilgrimage
be never so strong,[24]

I will never part you fro.

Everyman, I will be as sure by thee

As ever I did by Judas Maccabee.

(*They proceed together to the grave*)

EVERYMAN. Alas! I am so faint I may
not stand,

My limbs under me do fold.

Friends, let us not turn again to this land,

Not for all the world's gold;

For into this cave must I creep

And turn to earth, and there to sleep.

BEAUTY. What, into this grave? Alas!

EVERYMAN. Yea, there shall you consume,
more and less.[25]

BEAUTY. And what! should I smother
here?

EVERYMAN. Yea, by my faith, and never
more appear.

In this world live no more we shall,

But in heaven before the highest Lord of all.

BEAUTY. I cross out all this! Adieu, by
Saint John!

I take my cap in my lap and am gone.

EVERYMAN. What, Beauty, whither will
ye?

BEAUTY. Peace! I am deaf. I look not
behind me,

Not and thou would give me all the gold
in thy chest. (*Exit* BEAUTY)

EVERYMAN. Alas, whereto may I trust?

Beauty goeth fast away from me;

She promised with me to live and die.

STRENGTH. Everyman, I will thee also
forsake and deny;

Thy game liketh me not at all.

EVERYMAN. Why then, ye will forsake
me all!

Sweet Strength, tarry a little space.

STRENGTH. Nay, sir, by the rood of grace!

I will hie me from thee fast,

Though thou weep till thy heart to-brast.[26]

EVERYMAN. Ye would ever bide by me,
ye said.

STRENGTH. Yea, I have you far enough
conveyed;

Ye be old enough, I understand,

Your pilgrimage to take on hand.

I repent me that I hither came.

EVERYMAN. Strength, you to displease I
am to blame;

Will you break promise that is debt?

STRENGTH. In faith, I care not!

Thou are but a fool to complain;

You spend your speech and waste your brain.

Go, thrust thee into the ground!

(*Exit* STRENGTH)

EVERYMAN. Had I thought surer, I should
you have found.

He that trusteth in his Strength,

She him deceiveth at the length.

Both Strength and Beauty forsake me,

Yet they promised me fair and lovingly.

DISCRETION. Everyman, I will after
Strength be gone;

As for me I will leave you alone.

EVERYMAN. Why, Discretion! Will ye
forsake me?

[23] The help of you all.   [24] Hard.   [25] Men of high and low degree.   [26] Break in pieces.

DISCRETION. Yea, in faith, I will go from thee;
For when Strength goeth before,
I follow after evermore.

EVERYMAN. Yet, I pray thee, for the love of the Trinity,
Look in my grave once piteously.

DISCRETION. Nay, so nigh will I not come.
Farewell, every one!   (*Exit* DISCRETION)

EVERYMAN. Oh, all thing faileth, save God alone—
Beauty, Strength, and Discretion;
For when Death bloweth his blast,
They all run from me full fast.

FIVE WITS. Everyman, my leave now of thee I take;
I will follow the other, for here I thee forsake.

EVERYMAN. Alas! Then may I wail and weep,
For I took you for my best friend.

FIVE WITS. I will no longer thee keep.
Now farewell, and there an end.
    (*Exit* FIVE WITS)

EVERYMAN. O Jesu, help! All hath forsaken me!

GOOD DEEDS. Nay, Everyman, I will bide with thee;
I will not forsake thee indeed;
Thou shalt find me a good friend at need.

EVERYMAN. Gramercy, Good Deeds! Now may I true friends see.
They have forsaken me, every one;
I loved them better than my Good Deeds alone.
Knowledge, will ye forsake me also?

KNOWLEDGE. Yea, Everyman, when ye to death shall go;
But not yet, for no manner of danger.

EVERYMAN. Gramercy, Knowledge, with all my heart!

KNOWLEDGE. Nay, yet I will not from hence depart
Till I see where ye shall be come.

EVERYMAN. Methink, alas, that I must be gone
To make my reckoning and my debts pay,
For I see my time is nigh spent away.
Take example, all ye that this do hear or see,
How they that I loved best do forsake me,
Except my Good Deeds, that bideth truly.

[27] *Into thy hands, most mighty,*
    For ever I commend my spirit.

GOOD DEEDS. All earthly things is but vanity.
Beauty, Strength, and Discretion do man forsake,
Foolish friends, and kinsmen that fair spake—
All fleeth save Good Deeds, and that am I.

EVERYMAN. Have mercy on me, God most mighty;
And stand by me, thou Mother and Maid, holy Mary!

GOOD DEEDS. Fear not, I will speak for thee.

EVERYMAN. Here I cry God mercy!

GOOD DEEDS. Short our end, and minish our pain.
Let us go, and never come again.

EVERYMAN. Into Thy hands, Lord, my soul I commend.
Receive it, Lord, that it be not lost.
As Thou me boughtest, so me defend,
And save me from the fiend's boast,
That I may appear with that blessèd host
That shall be saved at the day of doom.
In manus tuas, of might most,
For ever *commendo spiritum meum.*[27]
    (EVERYMAN *and* GOOD DEEDS *descend into the grave*)

KNOWLEDGE. (*Speaking over the grave*)
Now hath he suffered that we all shall endure;
The Good Deeds shall make all sure.
Now hath he made ending.
Methinketh that I hear angels sing
And make great joy and melody
Where Everyman's soul received shall be.

ANGEL. (*Within*) Come, excellent elect spouse to Jesu!
Here above thou shalt go
Because of thy singular virtue.
Now the soul is taken the body fro,
Thy reckoning is crystal-clear.
Now shalt thou in to the heavenly sphere,
Unto the which all ye shall come
That liveth well before the day of doom.
    (*Exit* KNOWLEDGE)

(*Enter* DOCTOR *as Epilogue*)

DOCTOR. This moral, men may have in mind:

Ye hearers, take it of worth, old and young,
And forsake pride, for he deceiveth you in
    the end,
And remember Beauty, Five Wits, Strength,
    and Discretion,
They all at the last do Everyman forsake,
Save his Good Deeds there doth he take.
But beware, and they be small,
Before God he hath no help at all.
None excuse may be there for Everyman.
Alas, how shall he do then?
For, after death, amends may no man make,
For then mercy and pity do him forsake.

[28] "Go, ye accursed, into everlasting fire."

If his reckoning be not clear when he do
    come,
God will say—"*ite, maledicti, in ignem æter-
num.*"[28]
And he that hath his account whole and
    sound,
High in heaven he shall be crowned.
Unto which place God bring us all thither,
That we may live body and soul together.
Thereto help, the Trinity!
Amen, say ye, for Saint Charity.

THUS ENDETH THIS MORAL PLAY OF
EVERYMAN.

ROBERT GREENE

Friar Bacon and Friar Bungay

PRINCIPAL EVENTS IN GREENE'S LIFE

1558, July, Born at Norwich.

1575, Nov., Entered St. John's College, Cambridge.

1578, B.A. from Cambridge.

1578?-1579?, Greene says he travelled in Italy, Spain, France, Germany, Denmark, and Poland.

1580, His romance, *Mamilia,* entered in the Stationers' Register; published three years later.

1583, M.A. from Cambridge.

c. 1585, He married, but shortly after deserted his wife.

1586-90, He published several tales and romances, including *Penelope's Web, Perimedes the Blacksmith,* and *Menaphon,* and attained popularity as a writer.

c. 1587, Alphonsus, King of Arragon, acted.

1588, July, M.A. from Oxford.

c. 1589, Friar Bacon and Friar Bungay acted by the Queen's players.

c. 1589, He became associated with a London gangster named Ball and took Ball's sister as his mistress.

c. 1590, A Looking Glass for London and England, written in collaboration with Thomas Lodge, acted.

c. 1591, Orlando Furioso acted.

c. 1591, James IV acted.

1590-92, Greene published a number of popular exposés of the criminal world, called coney-catching pamphlets, including *A Notable Discovery of Cosenage, The Second Part of Coney-Catching,* and *The Black Book's Messenger.*

1592, Sept., Just before his death Greene wrote a pamphlet called *A Groatsworth of Wit Bought with a Million of Repentance* in which he made a jealous attack on Shakespeare.

1592, 3 Sept., Greene died of a surfeit in squalid lodgings.

INTRODUCTION

Friar Bacon and Friar Bungay is our earliest example of romantic comedy, a type of comedy made familiar to us by Shakespeare's *As You Like It* and *A Midsummer Night's Dream.* In their general treatment of dramatic material—though not in their literary distinction—such plays are more like our musical comedies than any other modern form. Usually they are given a romantically remote setting, distant in time or place, like the Forest of Arden, or ancient Athens, or thirteenth-century Oxford, or Illyria. Romantic love between persons who would almost never marry in real life—like a great nobleman and a country girl, or a princess and a poor gentleman, or a duke and a shipwrecked daughter of a merchant—constitute an important part of the plot of such plays. The romantic and the unfamiliar are the major elements in their appeal.

In *Friar Bacon and Friar Bungay*, Greene relies primarily on the appeal of the romantic love affair between Margaret, the country-bred daughter of a gamekeeper, and the Earl of Lincoln, one of the great nobles of the realm and a favorite companion of the Prince of Wales, and on the spectacular magic feats of Friar Bacon, Friar Bungay, and Jaques Vandermast. Romantic love in improbable circumstances is such a standard ingredient in modern plays and movies that it requires no comment; it is much more commonly exploited in the twentieth century than it was in the sixteenth. Magic is less hackneyed.

The precise boundary between science and magic is never very clear in the popular mind. Even after more than a century of unprecedented concentration on scientific research and scientific education, fortunes are still made by exploiting the popular confusion of science and magic—witness the advertisements of perfumes or patent medicines, to say nothing of numerology and astrology. In the time of Greene and Marlowe this confusion was much greater; even the scientists who were doing the basic research in physics and chemistry were also investigating alchemy and magic powders and salves. Men of unusual scientific attainments, like Friar Bacon in the play, were popularly thought to have acquired such masses of obscure and occult knowledge that they could call up devils from Hell and force them to exercise their supernatural powers in any manner dictated by the scientist. This is what Friar Bacon does in Act I, scene 2, and Act V, scene 2, and Friar Bungay and Jaques Vandermast in III, 2. In other episodes, such as the scene with the brass head or the television scenes, Friar Bacon uses his vast knowledge and his years of research to create machines not beyond human powers—though the methods and the amount of knowledge and research involved are not what Greene and his audience imagined.

❧

FRIAR BACON AND FRIAR BUNGAY

Dramatis personae

In order of first appearance

PRINCE EDWARD, Prince of Wales, son of Henry III, lover of Margaret; eventually married to Princess Elinor of Castile.

LACY, EARL OF LINCOLN, Companion and attendant of Prince Edward, in love with Margaret.

WARREN, EARL OF SUSSEX, Companion and attendant of Prince Edward.

WILLIAM ERMSBY, A gentleman of the Court. Another companion and attendant of the Prince.

RALPH SIMNELL, The professional Court Fool, who exercises the usual licence of the Court comedian.

FRIAR BACON, A Fellow of Brasenose College, Oxford, the most learned scientist of his time. He practises magic.

MILES, An impoverished Oxford student who acts as Bacon's servant and research assistant. He is clownish, blundering, and credulous, but devoted to Friar Bacon. He is the second comedian of the play.

DOCTOR BURDEN	Three learned professors of Oxford. They represent the administration of the University.
DOCTOR MASON	
DOCTOR CLEMENT	

HOSTESS, The proprietress of the Bell Tavern at Henley, near Oxford.

A DEVIL, Conjured up by Friar Bacon to do his bidding.

MARGARET, A country girl, the acknowledged beauty of her district, called the Fair Maid of Fressingfield. Daughter of the Keeper.

JOAN, A country girl, friend of Margaret.

THOMAS, A country fellow, friend of Margaret and Joan.

RICHARD, Another country fellow, friend of Margaret and Joan.

HENRY III, King of England 1216-1272; father of Prince Edward.

EMPEROR, Historically he was Fredrick II, Emperor of the Romans and King of Germany, but in the play he is given no particular identity. He is visiting at the court of Henry III.

KING OF CASTILE, Father of Princess Elinor. Like the Emperor, he is unidentified, but historically he was Ferdinand III, King of Castile 1217-1252.

ELINOR, PRINCESS OF CASTILE, Daughter of the King of Castile. She has been brought to England by her father, who wishes to arrange a royal match with Prince Edward.

JAQUES VANDERMAST, A German scholar and magician in the train of the Emperor.

FRIAR BUNGAY, An English scholar and magician.

CONSTABLE, An Oxford policeman.

HERCULES, Really a devil in the person of the demi-god Hercules, conjured up by Vandermast.

LAMBERT, A country landowner, suitor for the hand of Margaret.

SERLSBY, The Keeper's landlord, a well-to-do squire, and suitor for the hand of Margaret.

KEEPER, The head gamekeeper of the royal hunting preserve and father of Margaret.

POST, A messenger.

FIRST SCHOLAR, An Oxford undergraduate, son of Lambert.

SECOND SCHOLAR, An Oxford undergraduate, son of Serlsby.

FRIEND, A friend of Margaret and the Keeper, her father.

Several country bumpkins, lords, and attendants of King Henry's court.

SCENE: *The action takes place successively at the village of Framlingham, at Oxford, at Harleston Fair, Hampton Court, Fressingfield, and London*

Act I

SCENE I. *A Room at Framlingham.*

(*Enter* PRINCE EDWARD, *silent and moody, followed by three gentlemen of his court:* LACY, EARL OF LINCOLN, WARREN, EARL OF SUSSEX, *and* WILL ERMSBY. *After them comes* RALPH SIMNELL, *the Court Fool, dressed in motley, and wearing a fool's cap and a wooden dagger.* PRINCE EDWARD *walks apart, preoccupied, and the others discuss his melancholy*)

LACY. Why looks my lord like to a troubled sky
When heaven's bright shine is shadowed with a fog?
Alate we ran the deer, and through the lawns
'Stripped with our nags the lofty frolic bucks
That scudded 'fore the teasers [1] like the wind.
Ne'er was the deer of merry Fressingfield

So lustily pulled down by jolly mates,
Nor shared the farmers such fat venison,
So frankly dealt, this hundred years before;
Nor have I seen my lord more frolic in the chase,
And now changed to a melancholy dump.
    WAR. After the prince got to the Keeper's lodge,
And had been jocund in the house awhile,
Tossing off ale and milk in country cans,
Whether it was the country's sweet content,
Or else the bonny damsel filled us drink
That seemed so stately in her stammel [2] red,
Or that a qualm did cross his stomach then,
But straight he fell into his passions.
    ERMS. (*To the Fool*) Sirrah Ralph, what say you to your master,

[1] Hounds.

[2] Coarse woolen cloth used for making petticoats.

Shall he thus all amort[3] live malcontent?

RALPH. (*To* PRINCE EDWARD) Hearest thou, Ned?—(*Aside to the others*) Nay, look if he will speak to me!

P. EDW. What say'st thou to me, fool?

RALPH. I prithee, tell me, Ned, art thou in love with the Keeper's daughter?

P. EDW. How if I be, what then?

RALPH. Why, then, sirrah, I'll teach thee how to deceive Love.

P. EDW. (*Indulgently*) How, Ralph?

RALPH. Marry, Sirrah Ned, thou shalt put on my cap and my coat and my dagger, and I will put on thy clothes and thy sword; and so thou shalt be my fool.

P. EDW. And what of this?

RALPH. Why, so thou shall beguile Love; for Love is such a proud scab, that he will never meddle with fools nor children. (*Capering about*) Is not Ralph's counsel good, Ned?

P. EDW. Tell me, Ned Lacy, didst thou mark the maid,
How lively in her country-weeds she looked?
A bonnier wench all Suffolk cannot yield:—
All Suffolk! nay, all England holds none such.

RALPH. Sirrah Will Ermsby, Ned is deceived.

ERMS. Why, Ralph?

RALPH. He says all England hath no such, and I say, and I'll stand to it, there is one better in Warwickshire.

WAR. How provest thou that, Ralph?

RALPH. Why, is not the abbot a learned man, and hath read many books, and thinkest thou he hath not more learning than thou to choose a bonny wench? Yes, I warrant thee, by his whole grammar.

ERMS. A good reason, Ralph.

P. EDW. I tell thee, Lacy, that her sparkling eyes
Do lighten forth sweet love's alluring fire;
And in her tresses she doth fold the looks
Of such as gaze upon her golden hair;
Her bashful white, mixed with the morning's red,
Luna doth boast upon her lovely cheeks;
Her front is beauty's table, where she paints
The glories of her gorgeous excellence;
Her teeth are shelves of precious marguerites,[4]

Richly enclosed with ruddy coral cliffs.
Tush, Lacy, she is beauty's over-match,
If thou survey'st her curious imagery.

LACY. I grant, my lord, the damsel is as fair
As simple Suffolk's homely towns can yield;
But in the court be quainter dames than she,
Whose faces are enriched with honor's taint,[5]
Whose beauties stand upon the stage of Fame,
And vaunt their trophies in the courts of love.

P. EDW. Ah, Ned, but hadst thou watched her as myself,
And seen the secret beauties of the maid,
Their courtly coyness were but foolery.

ERMS. Why, how watched you her, my lord?

P. EDW. Whenas she swept like Venus through the house,
And in her shape fast folded up my thoughts,
Into the milk-house went I with the maid,
And there amongst the cream-bowls she did shine
As Pallas 'mongst her princely huswifery.
She turned her smock over her lily arms,
And dived them into milk to run her cheese;
But whiter than the milk her crystal skin,
Checkéd with lines of azure, made her blush[6]
That art or nature durst bring for compare.
Ermsby, if thou hadst seen, as I did note it well,
How beauty played the huswife, how this girl,
Like Lucrece, laid her fingers to the work,
Thou wouldst, with Tarquin, hazard Rome and all
To win the lovely maid of Fressingfield.

RALPH. Sirrah Ned, would'st fain have her?

P. EDW. Ay, Ralph.

RALPH. Why, Ned, I have laid the plot in my head; thou shalt have her already.

P. EDW. I'll give thee a new coat, an learn me that.

RALPH. Why Sirrah Ned, we'll ride to Oxford to Friar Bacon. O, he is a brave scholar, sirrah; they say he is a brave necromancer, that he can make women of devils, and he can juggle cats into costermongers.

P. EDW. And how then, Ralph?

[3] Disconsolate.   [4] Pearls.

[5] Tint.

[6] Would have made that woman blush whom art . . .

RALPH. Marry, sirrah, thou shalt go to him; and because thy father Harry shall not miss thee, he shall turn me into thee; and I'll to the court, and I'll prince it out (*strutting before them*); and he shall make thee either a silken purse full of gold, or else a fine wrought smock.

P. EDW. But how shall I have the maid?

RALPH. Marry, sirrah, if thou be'st a silken purse full of gold, then on Sundays she'll hang thee by her side, and you must not say a word. Now, sir, when she comes into a great press of people, for fear of the cutpurse, on a sudden she'll swap thee into her plackerd; [7] then, sirrah, being there, you may plead for yourself.

ERMS. Excellent policy!

P. EDW. But how if I be a wrought smock?

RALPH. Then she'll put thee into her chest and lay thee into lavender, and upon some good day she'll put thee on; and at night when you go to bed, then being turned from a smock to a man, you may make up the match.

LACY. Wonderfully, wisely counseled, Ralph.

P. EDW. Ralph shall have a new coat.

RALPH. God thank you when I have it on my back, Ned.

P. EDW. Lacy, the fool hath laid a perfect plot;
For why our country Margaret is so coy,
And stands so much upon her honest points,
That marriage or no market with the maid.
Ermsby, it must be necromantic spells
And charms of art that must enchain her love,
Or else shall Edward never win the girl.
Therefore, my wags, we'll horse us in the morn,
And post to Oxford to this jolly friar:
Bacon shall by his magic do this deed.

WAR. Content, my lord; and that's a speedy way
To wean these headstrong puppies from the teat.

P. EDW. I am unknown, not taken for the prince;
They only deem us frolic courtiers,
That revel thus among our liege's game;
Therefore I have devised a policy.

[7] A slit in a woman's skirt.

Lacy, thou know'st next Friday is Saint James',[8]
And then the country flocks to Harleston Fair;
Then will the Keeper's daughter frolic there,
And over-shine the troop of all the maids
That come to see and to be seen that day.
Haunt thee disguised among the country-swains,
Feign thou'rt a farmer's son, not far from thence,
Espy her loves, and who she liketh best;
Cote[9] him, and court her to control the clown;
Say that the courtier 'tiréd all in green,
That helped her handsomely to run her cheese,
And filled her father's lodge with venison,
Commends him, and sends fairings to herself.
Buy something worthy of her parentage,
Not worth her beauty; for, Lacy, then the fair
Affords no jewel fitting for the maid.
And when thou talk'st of me, note if she blush;
O, then she loves; but if her cheeks wax pale,
Disdain it is. Lacy, send how she fares,
And spare no time nor cost to win her loves.

LACY. I will, my lord, so execute this charge
As if that Lacy were in love with her.

P. EDW. Send letters speedily to Oxford of the news.

RALPH. And, Sirrah Lacy, buy me a thousand thousand million of fine bells.

LACY. What wilt thou do with them, Ralph?

RALPH. Marry, every time that Ned sighs for the Keeper's daughter, I'll tie a bell about him, and so within three or four days I will send word to his father Harry, that his son and my master Ned is become Love's morris-dance.

P. EDW. Well, Lacy, look with care unto thy charge,
And I will haste to Oxford to the friar,
That he by art and thou by secret gifts
Mayst make me lord of merry Fressingfield.

LACY. God send your honor your heart's desire.   (*Exeunt*)

[8] St. James' Day, July 25.
[9] Overtake.

SCENE II. FRIAR BACON'S *study in Brasenose College, Oxford.*

(*Enter* FRIAR BACON *with three Oxford dons,* BURDON, MASON, *and* CLEMENT, *dressed in their doctor's gowns. They are followed by* MILES *wearing a ragged undergraduate's gown and carrying an arm load of books*)

BACON. Miles, where are you?

MILES. *Hic sum, doctissime et reverendissime doctor.*

BACON. *Attulisti nos libros meos de necromantia?*

MILES. *Ecce quam bonum et quam jucundum habitare libros in unum!* [10]

BACON. Now, masters of our academic state,
That rule in Oxford, viceroys in your place,
Whose heads contain maps of the liberal arts,
Spending your time in depth of learnéd skill,
Why flock you thus to Bacon's secret cell,
A friar newly stalled in Brazen-nose?
Say what's your mind, that I may make reply.

BURD. Bacon, we hear that long we have suspect,
That thou art read in magic's mystery;
In pyromancy, to divine by flames;
To tell, by hydromatic, ebbs and tides;
By aeromancy to discover doubts,
To plain out questions, as Apollo did.

BACON. Well, Master Burden, what of all this?

MILES. (*Ridiculing the Doctors*) Marry, sir, he doth but fulfil, by rehearsing of these names, the fable of the Fox and the Grapes; that which is above us pertains nothing to us.

BURD. I tell thee, Bacon, Oxford makes report,
Nay, England, and the court of Henry says,
Thou'rt making of a brazen head by art,
Which shall unfold strange doubts and aphorisms,

And read a lecture in philosophy;
And, by the help of devils and ghastly fiends,
Thou mean'st, ere many years or days be past,
To compass England with a wall of brass.

BACON. And what of this?

MILES. What of this, master! Why, he doth speak mystically; for he knows, if your skill fail to make a brazen head, yet Mother Waters' strong ale will fit his turn to make him have a copper nose.

CLEM. Bacon, we come not grieving at thy skill,
But joying that our académy yields
A man supposed the wonder of the world;
For if thy cunning work these miracles,
England and Europe shall admire thy fame,
And Oxford shall in characters of brass,
And statues, such as were built up in Rome,
Etérnize Friar Bacon for his art.

MASON. Then, gentle friar, tell us thy intent.

BACON. Seeing you come as friends unto the friar,
Resolve you, doctors, Bacon can by books
Make storming Boreas thunder from his cave,
And dim fair Luna to a dark eclipse.
The great arch-ruler, potentate of hell,
Trembles when Bacon bids him or his fiends,
Bow to the force of his pentaganon. [11]
What art can work, the frolic friar knows;
And therefore will I turn my magic books,
And strain out necromancy to the deep.
I have contrived and framed a head of brass
(I made Belcephon hammer out the stuff),
And that by art shall read philosophy;
And I will strengthen England by my skill,
That if ten Cæsars lived and reigned in Rome,
With all the legions Europe doth contain,
They should not touch a grass of English ground.
The work that Ninus reared at Babylon,
The brazen walls framed by Semiramis,
Carved out like to the portal of the sun,
Shall not be such as rings the English strand
From Dover to the market-place of Rye.

BURD. (*Sceptically*) Is this possible?

[10] "Here I am, most erudite and learned doctor."

"Have you brought us my books on necromancy?"

"See how good and pleasant it is to have books together in one place." In the universities of the time students and faculty were required to converse in Latin.

[11] A five pointed figure affording magical influence over supernatural beings.

MILES. I'll bring ye two or three witnesses.

BURD. What be these?

MILES. Marry, sir, three or four as honest devils and good companions as any be in hell.

MASON. No doubt but magic may do much in this;
For he that reads but mathematic rules
Shall find conclusions that avail to work
Wonders that pass the common sense of men.

BURD. (Scornfully) But Bacon roves a bow beyond his reach,
And tells of more than magic can perform,
Thinking to get a fame by fooleries.
Have I not passed as far in state of schools,
And read of many secrets? Yet to think
That heads of brass can utter any voice,
Or more, to tell of deep philosophy,
This is a fable Æsop had forgot.

BACON. Burden, thou wrong'st me in detracting thus;
Bacon loves not to stuff himself with lies.
But tell me 'fore these doctors, if thou dare,
Of certain questions I shall move to thee.

BURD. I will; ask what thou can.

MILES. Marry, sir, he'll straight be on your pick-pack,[12] to know whether the feminine or the masculine gender be most worthy.

BACON. Were you not yesterday, Master Burden, at Henley upon the Thames?

BURD. (Defiantly) I was; what then?

BACON. What book studied you thereon all night?

BURD. (Obviously shaken but still defiant) I! none at all; I read not there a line.

BACON. Then, doctors, Friar Bacon's art knows naught.

CLEM. What say you to this, Master Burden? Doth he not touch you?

BURD. (Scornfully) I pass not of his frivolous speeches.

MILES. Nay, Master Burden, my master, ere he hath done with you, will turn you from a doctor to a dunce, and shake you so small, that he will leave no more learning in you than is in Balaam's ass.

BACON. Masters, for that learnéd Burden's skill is deep,
And sore he doubts of Bacon's cabalism,
I'll show you why he haunts to Henley oft:
Not, doctors, for to taste the fragrant air,
But there to spend the night in alchemy,

[12] Shoulders.

To multiply with secret spells of art;
Thus private steals he learning from us all.
To prove my sayings true, I'll show you straight
The book he keeps at Henley for himself.

MILES. (Showing childish delight mingled with awe) Nay, now my master goes to conjuration, take heed.

BACON. Masters, stand still, fear not, I'll show you but his book.

(BACON solemnly draws a circle about himself on the floor, makes conjuring passes in the air, and mutters incantations)

Per omnes deos infernales, Belcephon!

(Enter HOSTESS, walking in a daze, carrying a half-roasted shoulder of mutton skewered on a spit. She is followed by a DEVIL as if he were driving her)

MILES. O, master, cease your conjuration, or you spoil all; for here's a she-devil come with a shoulder of mutton on a spit. You have marred the devil's supper; but no doubt he thinks our college fare is slender, and so hath sent you his cook with a shoulder of mutton, to make it exceed.

HOSTESS. (Completely bewildered) O, where am I, or what's become of me?

BACON. What art thou?

HOSTESS. Hostess at Henley, mistress of the Bell.

BACON. How camest thou here?

HOSTESS. As I was in the kitchen 'mongst the maids,
Spitting the meat 'gainst supper for my guests,
A motion[13] moved me to look forth of door:
No sooner had I pried into the yard,
But straight a whirlwind hoisted me from thence,
And mounted me aloft unto the clouds.
As in a trance, I thought nor feared naught,
Nor know I where or whither I was ta'en,
Nor where I am nor what these persons be.

BACON. No? Know you not Master Burden?

HOSTESS. (Recognizing BURDEN with relief) O, yes, good sir, he is my daily guest.—

[13] Whim.

What, Master Burden! 'twas but yesternight
That you and I at Henley played at cards.

BURD. (*Chagrined and annoyed*) I know
not what we did.—A pox of all conjuring
friars!

CLEM. Now, jolly friar, tell us, is this the
book
That Burden is so careful to look on?

BACON. It is.—But, Burden, tell me now,
Think'st thou that Bacon's necromantic
skill
Cannot perform his head and wall of brass,
When he can fetch thine hostess in such
post?

MILES. I'll warrant you, master, if Master
Burden could conjure as well as you, he
would have his book every night from Henley to study on at Oxford.

MASON. (*Amused at* BURDEN's *sulks*)
Burden, what, are you mated [14] by this
frolic friar?—
Look how he droops! His guilty conscience
Drives him to 'bash, and makes his hostess
blush.

BACON. Well, mistress, for I will not have
you missed,
You shall to Henley to cheer up your guests

'Fore supper 'gin.—(*Taunting* BURDEN)
Burden, bid her adieu.
Say farewell to your hostess 'fore she goes.—
Sirrah, away, and set her safe at home.

HOSTESS. Master Burden, when shall we
see you at Henley?

BURD. (*Bursting out angrily*) The devil
take thee and Henley too.
(*Exeunt* HOSTESS *and* DEVIL)

MILES. Master, shall I make a good motion?

BACON. What's that?

MILES. Marry, sir, now that my hostess
is gone to provide supper, conjure up another
spirit, and send Doctor Burden flying after.

BACON. (*Ignoring* MILES) Thus, rulers of
our academic state,
You have seen the friar frame his art by
proof;
And as the college callèd Brazen-nose
Is under him, and he the master there,
So surely shall this head of brass be framed,
And yield forth strange and uncouth apho-
risms;
And hell and Hecate shall fail the friar,
But I will circle England round with brass.

MILES. So be it *et nunc et semper*; amen.
(*Exeunt*)

SCENE III. *Harleston Fair.*

(*Enter* MARGARET, *a beautiful girl in country dress;* JOAN, *a country girl dressed up for
the fair;* THOMAS *and* RICHARD, *country
bumpkins; and* LACY, *disguised as a farmer,
followed by several other country bumpkins*)

THOM. By my troth, Margaret, here's a
weather is able to make a man call his father
"whoreson"; if this weather hold, we shall
have hay good cheap, and butter and cheese
at Harleston will bear no price.

MAR. Thomas, maids when they come to
see the fair
Count not to make a cope [15] for dearth of hay;
When we have turned our butter to the salt,
And set our cheese safely upon the racks,
Then let our fathers price it as they please.
We country sluts of merry Fressingfield

Come to buy needless naughts to make us
fine,
And look that young men should be frank
this day,
And court us with such fairings [16] as they can.
Phœbus is blithe, and frolic looks from
heaven,
As when he courted lovely Semele,
Swearing the pedlers shall have empty packs,
If that fair weather may make chapmen buy.

LACY. But, lovely Peggy, Semele is dead,
And therefore Phœbus from his palace pries,
And, seeing such a sweet and seemly saint,
Shows all his glories for to court yourself.

MAR. This is a fairing, gentle sir, indeed,
To soothe me up with such smooth flattery;
But learn of me, your scoff's too broad
before.—

[14] Checkmated. [15] Bargain. [16] Presents from the fair.

Well, Joan, our beauties must abide their
    jests;
We serve the turn in jolly Fressingfield.
    JOAN. Margaret, a farmer's daughter for a
    farmer's son;
I warrant you, the meanest of us both
Shall have a mate to lead us from the church.
    (All this while LACY whispers MARGARET
    in the ear)
But, Thomas, what's the news? (Teasing
    him) What, in a dump?
Give me your hand, we are near a pedler's
    shop;
Out with your purse, we must have fairings
    now.
    THOM. Faith, Joan, and shall. I'll bestow
a fairing on you, and then we will to the
tavern, and snap off a pint of wine or two.
    MAR. (To Lacy) Whence are you, sir?
    Of Suffolk? For your terms
Are finer than the common sort of men.
    LACY. Faith, lovely girl, I am of Beccles
    by,
Your neighbor, not above six miles from
    hence,
A farmer's son, that never was so quaint
But that he could do courtesy to such dames.
But trust me, Margaret, I am sent in charge
From him that reveled in your father's house,
And filled his lodge with cheer and venison,
'Tired in green. (Taking out an embroidered
    purse) He sent you this rich purse,
His token that he helped you run your
    cheese,
And in the milkhouse chatted with yourself.
    MAR. To me?
    LACY. You forget yourself;
Women are often weak in memory.
    MAR. O, pardon, sir, I call to mind the
    man.
(Hesitating) 'Twere little manners to refuse
    his gift,
And yet I hope he sends it not for love;
For we have little leisure to debate of that.
    JOAN. What, Margaret! blush not; maids
must have their loves.

[17] A base, worthless wretch.

    THOM. Nay, by the mass, she looks pale
as if she were angry.
    RICH. Sirrah, are you of Beccles? I pray,
how doth Goodman Cob? My father bought
a horse of him.—I'll tell you, Margaret, 'a
were good to be a gentleman's jade, for of
all things the foul hilding [17] could not abide
a dung-cart.
    MAR. (Walking aside while the others
    talk, and speaking to herself) How dif-
    ferent is this farmer from the rest
That erst as yet have pleased my wandering
    sight!
His words are witty, quickened with a smile,
His courtesy gentle, smelling of the court;
Facile and debonair in all his deeds;
Proportioned as was Paris, when, in gray, [18]
He courted Œnon in the vale by Troy.
Great lords have come and pleaded for my
    love;
Who but the Keeper's lass of Fressingfield?
And yet methinks this farmer's jolly son
Passeth the proudest that hath pleased mine
    eye.
But, Peg, disclose not that thou art in love,
And show as yet no sign of love to him,
Although thou well wouldst wish him for
    thy love;
Keep that to thee till time doth serve thy
    turn,
To show the grief wherein thy heart doth
    burn.—
(Returning to the others) Come, Joan and
    Thomas, shall we to the fair?—
You, Beccles man, will not forsake us now?
    LACY. Not whilst I may have such quaint
    girls as you.
    MAR. Well, if you chance to come by
    Fressingfield,
Make but a step into the Keeper's lodge,
And such poor fare as woodmen can afford,
Butter and cheese, cream and fat venison,
You shall have store, and welcome there-
    withal.
    LACY. Gramercies, Peggy; look for me ere
    long.   (Exeunt)

[18] I.e., a shepherd's costume.

Act II

SCENE I. *Hampton Court Palace.*

(*Enter* HENRY III, *King of England, the*
EMPEROR, *and the* KING OF CASTILE, *all
dressed in regal robes and wearing crowns.
After them* ELINOR, *Princess of Castile, and*
JAQUES VANDERMAST, *a German scholar and
magician, wearing a doctor's gown*)

K. HEN. Great men of Europe, monarchs
    of the west,
Ringed with the walls of old Oceanus,
Whose lofty surge is like the battlements
That compassed high-built Babel in with
    towers,
Welcome, my lords, welcome, brave western
    kings,
To England's shore, whose promontory cliffs
Show Albion is another little world;
Welcome, says English Henry to you all;
Chiefly unto the lovely Elinor,
Who dared for Edward's sake cut through
    the seas,
And venture as Agenor's damsel through the
    deep,
To get the love of Henry's wanton son.
   K. OF CAST. England's rich monarch,
    brave Plantagenet,
The Pyren Mounts swelling above the
    clouds,
That ward the wealthy Castile in with walls,
Could not detain the beauteous Elinor;
But, hearing of the fame of Edward's youth,
She dared to brook Neptunus' haughty pride,
And bide the brunt of froward Æolus.
Then may fair England welcome her the
    more.
   ELIN. After that English Henry by his
    lords
Had sent Prince Edward's lovely counterfeit,
A present to the Castile Elinor,
The comely portrait of so brave a man,
The virtuous fame discourséd of his deeds,
Edward's courageous resolution,
Done at the Holy Land 'fore Damas' walls,
Led both mine eye and thoughts in equal
    links

To like so of the English monarch's son,
That I attempted perils for his sake.
   EMP. Where is the prince, my lord?
   K. HEN. He posted down, not long since,
    from the court,
To Suffolk side, to merry Framlingham,
To sport himself amongst my fallow deer;
From thence, by packets sent to Hampton-
    house,
We hear the prince is ridden with his lords,
To Oxford, in the académy there
To hear dispute amongst the learnéd men.
But we will send forth letters for my son,
To will him come from Oxford to the court.
   EMP. Nay, rather, Henry, let us, as we be,
Ride for to visit Oxford with our train.
Fain would I see your universities,
And what learned men your académy yields.
From Hapsburg have I brought a learnéd
    clerk
To hold dispute with English orators.
This doctor, surnamed Jaques Vandermast,
A German born, passed into Padua,
To Florence and to fair Bologna,
To Paris, Rheims, and stately Orleans,
And, talking there with men of art, put down
The chiefest of them all in aphorisms,[19]
In magic, and the mathematic rules.
Now let us, Henry, try him in your schools.
   K. HEN. He shall, my lord; this motion
    likes me well.
We'll progress straight to Oxford with our
    trains,
And see what men our académy brings.—
And, wonder Vandermast, welcome to me.
In Oxford shalt thou find a jolly friar,
Called Friar Bacon, England's only flower;
Set him but nonplus in his magic spells,
And make him yield in mathematic rules,
And for thy glory I will bind thy brows,
Not with a poet's garland made of bays,
But with a coronet of choicest gold.
Whilst then we set to Oxford with our troops,
Let's in and banquet in our English court.
                   (*Exeunt*)

---

[19] Statements of scientific principles.

SCENE II. *A Street in Oxford.*

(*Enter* RALPH SIMNELL *in* PRINCE ED-
WARD'S *apparel; and* EDWARD, WARREN, *and*
ERMSBY, *disguised*)

RALPH. (*Strutting and burlesquing the
manner of the Prince*) Where be these vagabond knaves, that they attend no better on
their master?

P. EDW. (*Very obsequious*) If it please
your honor, we are all ready at an inch.[20]

RALPH. Sirrah Ned, I'll have no more
post-horse to ride on. I'll have another fetch.[21]

ERMS. I pray you, how is that, my lord?

RALPH. Marry, sir, I'll send to the Isle of
Ely for four or five dozen of geese, and I'll
have them tied six and six together with
whip-cord. Now upon their backs will I have
a fair field-bed with a canopy; and so, when
it is my pleasure, I'll flee into what place I
please. This will be easy.

WAR. (*With a solemn bow*) Your honor
hath said well; but shall we to Brazen-nose
College before we pull off our boots?

ERMS. Warren, well motioned; we will
to the friar
Before we revel it within the town.—
Ralph, see you keep your countenance like
a prince.

RALPH. Wherefore have I such a company
of cutting[22] knaves to wait upon me, but to
keep and defend my countenance against all
mine enemies? Have you not good swords
and bucklers?

ERMS. Stay, who comes here?

WAR. Some scholar; and we'll ask him
where Friar Bacon is.

(*Enter* FRIAR BACON *and* MILES *absorbed
in their conversation*)

BACON. Why, thou arrant dunce, shall I
never make thee a good scholar? Doth not
all the town cry out and say, Friar Bacon's
subsizer[23] is the greatest blockhead in all

[20] At a moment's notice.
[21] Device.
[22] Swaggering.
[23] A poor student who worked for the college
in lieu of fees.

Oxford? Why, thou canst not speak one
word of true Latin.

MILES. (*Indignantly*) No, sir? Yes, what
is this else? *Ego sum tuus homo,* "I am your
man": I warrant you, sir, as good Tully's
phrase as any is in Oxford.

BACON. Come on, sirrah; what part of
speech is *Ego?*

MILES. *Ego,* that is "I"; marry, *nomen
substantivo.*

BACON. How prove you that?

MILES. Why, sir, let him prove himself
an 'a will; I can be heard, felt, and understood.

BACON. O gross dunce!

(FRIAR BACON *beats* MILES)

P. EDW. Come, let us break off this dispute between these two.—
Sirrah, where is Brazen-nose College?

MILES. Not far from Coppersmith's Hall.

P. EDW. What, dost thou mock me?

MILES. Not I, sir; but what would you at
Brazen-nose?

ERMS. Marry, we would speak with Friar
Bacon.

MILES. Whose men be you?

ERMS. Marry, scholar, here's our master.

RALPH. Sirrah, I am the master of these
good fellows; mayst thou not know me to
be a lord by my reparrel?

MILES. Then here's good game for the
hawk; for here's the master-fool and a covey
of coxcombs. One wise man, I think, would
spring you all.

P. EDW. Gog's wounds! Warren, kill him.
(PRINCE EDWARD, WARREN, *and* ERMSBY
*try to draw their weapons, but they stick
in the scabbards*)

WAR. (*Amazed*) Why, Ned, I think the
devil be in my sheath; I cannot get out my
dagger.

ERMS. Nor I mine. 'Swounds, Ned, I
think I am bewitched.

MILES. A company of scabs! The proudest
of you all draw your weapon, if he can.—
(*Aside*) See how boldly I speak, now my
master is by.

P. EDW. I strive in vain; but if my sword
be shut

And conjured fast by magic in my sheath,
Villain, here is my fist.

(*Strikes* MILES *a box on the ear*)

MILES. O, I beseech you conjure his hands
too, that he may not lift his arms to his head,
for he is light-fingered!

RALPH. (*Keeping at a safe distance*) Ned,
strike him; I'll warrant thee by mine honor.

BACON. What means the English prince
to wrong my man?

P. EDW. To whom speak'st thou?

BACON. To thee.

P. EDW. (*In astonishment*) Who art thou?

BACON. Could you not judge when all
your swords grew fast,
That Friar Bacon was not far from hence?
Edward, King Henry's son and Prince of
Wales,
Thy fool disguised cannot conceal thyself.
I know both Ermsby and the Sussex Earl,
Else Friar Bacon had but little skill.
Thou com'st in post from merry Fressingfield,
Fast-fancied to the Keeper's bonny lass,
To crave some succor of the jolly friar;
And Lacy, Earl of Lincoln, hast thou left
To treat fair Margaret to allow thy loves;
But friends are men, and love can baffle lords;
The earl both woos and courts her for him-
self.

WAR. Ned, this is strange; the friar
knoweth all.

ERMS. Apollo could not utter more than
this.

P. EDW. (*Aside*) I stand amazed to hear
this jolly friar
Tell even the very secrets of my thoughts.—
But, learnèd Bacon, since thou know'st the
cause
Why I did post so fast from Fressingfield,

Help, Friar, at a pinch, that I may have
The love of lovely Margaret to myself,
And, as I am true Prince of Wales, I'll give
Living and lands to strength thy college state.

WAR. Good friar, help the prince in this.

RALPH. Why, servant Ned, will not the
friar do it? Were not my sword glued to my
scabbard by conjuration, I would cut off his
head, and make him do it by force.

MILES. In faith, my lord, your manhood
and your sword is all alike; they are so fast
conjured that we shall never see them.

ERMS. What, doctor, in a dump! Tush,
help the prince,
And thou shalt see how liberal he will prove.

BACON. Crave not such actions greater
dumps than these?
I will, my lord, strain out my magic spells;
For this day comes the earl to Fressingfield,
And 'fore that night shuts in the day with
dark,
They'll be betrothèd each to other fast.
But come with me; we'll to my study straight,
And in a glass prospective I will show
What's done this day in merry Fressingfield.

P. EDW. Gramercies, Bacon; I will 'quite
thy pain.

BACON. But send your train, my lord, into
the town;
My scholar shall go bring them to their inn;
Meanwhile we'll see the knavery of the earl.

P. EDW. Warren, leave me;—and, Ermsby,
take the fool;
Let him be master, and go revel it,
Till I and Friar Bacon talk awhile.

WAR. We will, my lord.

RALPH. Faith, Ned, and I'll lord it out till
thou comest. I'll be Prince of Wales over all
the black-pots [24] in Oxford. (*Exeunt*)

SCENE III. FRIAR BACON'S *Study*.

(*Enter* FRIAR BACON *and* PRINCE EDWARD)

BACON. Now, frolic Edward, welcome to
my cell;
Here tempers Friar Bacon many toys,
And holds this place his consistory-court,
Wherein the devils plead homage to his
words.

[24] Leathern wine jugs.

(*Shows him a crystal ball*) Within this glass
prospective thou shalt see
This day what's done in merry Fressingfield
'Twixt lovely Peggy and the Lincoln Earl.

P. EDW. Friar, thou glad'st me. Now shall
Edward try
How Lacy meaneth to his sovereign Lord.

BACON. Stand there and look directly in
the glass.

(PRINCE EDWARD *continues to gaze into the crystal ball during the following scene between* MARGARET, FRIAR BUNGAY, *and* LACY. *The scene takes place on the upper stage, out of the range of* PRINCE EDWARD'S *vision. He sees everything in the crystal, but he hears nothing. Only* FRIAR BACON *and the audience hear what* MARGARET, BUNGAY, *and* LACY *say*)

(*Enter* MARGARET *and* FRIAR BUNGAY *on the upper stage*)

BACON. What sees my lord?
P. EDW. I see the Keeper's lovely lass appear,
As brightsome as the paramour of Mars,
Only attended by a jolly friar.
BACON. Sit still, and keep the crystal in your eye.
MAR. But tell me, Friar Bungay, is it true
That this fair courteous country swain,
Who says his father is a farmer nigh,
Can be Lord Lacy, Earl of Lincolnshire?
BUN. Peggy, 'tis true, 'tis Lacy for my life,
(Or else mine art and cunning both do fail)
Left by Prince Edward to procure his loves.
For he in green, that holp you run your cheese,
Is son to Henry, and the Prince of Wales.
MAR. Be what he will, *his* lure is but for lust.
But did Lord Lacy like poor Margaret,
Or would he deign to wed a country lass,
Friar, I would his humble handmaid be,
And for great wealth 'quite him with courtesy.
BUN. Why, Margaret, dost thou love him?
MAR. His personage, like the pride of vaunting Troy,
Might well avouch to shadow Helen's rape;
His wit is quick and ready in conceit,
As Greece afforded in her chiefest prime.
Courteous, ah friar, full of pleasing smiles!
Trust me, I love too much to tell thee more;
Suffice to me he's England's paramour.[25]
BUN. Hath not each eye that viewed thy pleasing face
Surnaméd thee Fair Maid of Fressingfield?
MAR. Yes, Bungay; and would God the lovely earl

[25] Paragon (?).

Had that in *esse* that so many sought.
BUN. (*Patting her shoulder*) Fear not, the friar will not be behind
To show his cunning to entangle love.
P. EDW. I think the friar courts the bonny wench;
Bacon, methinks he is a lusty churl.
BACON. Now look, my lord.

(*Enter* LACY *on the upper stage in his farmer's disguise*)

P. EDW. Gog's wounds, Bacon, here comes Lacy!
BACON. Sit still, my lord, and mark the comedy.
BUN. Here's Lacy, Margaret; step aside awhile.
(*They move to the back of the upper stage*)
LACY. (*Talking to himself*) Daphne, the damsel that caught Phœbus fast,
And locked him in the brightness of her looks,
Was not so beauteous in Apollo's eyes
As is fair Margaret to the Lincoln Earl.
Recant thee, Lacy, thou art put in trust.
Edward, thy sovereign's son, hath chosen thee,
A secret friend, to court her for himself,
And dar'st thou wrong thy prince with treachery?
Lacy, love makes no exception of a friend,
Nor deems it of a prince but as a man.
Honor bids thee control him in his lust;
His wooing is not for to wed the girl,
But to entrap her and beguile the lass.
Lacy, thou lov'st, then brook not such abuse,
But wed her, and abide thy prince's frown;
For better die than see her live disgraced.
MAR. Come, friar, I will shake him from his dumps.—   (*Comes forward*)
How cheer you, sir? A penny for your thought.
You're early up, pray God it be the near.[26]
What, come from Beccles in a morn so soon?
LACY. Thus watchful are such men as live in love,
Whose eyes brook broken slumbers for their sleep.
I tell thee, Peggy, since last Harleston Fair
My mind hath felt a heap of passions.

[26] The nearer (to your intent).

MAR. A trusty man, that court it for your
friend.
Woo you still for the courtier all in green?
I marvel that he sues not for himself.

LACY. Peggy, I pleaded first to get your
grace for him;
But when mine eyes surveyed your beauteous
looks,
Love, like a wag, straight dived into my
heart,
And there did shrine the idea of yourself.
Pity me, though I be a farmer's son,
And measure not my riches, but my love.

MAR. You are very hasty; for to garden
well,
Seeds must have time to sprout before they
spring:
Love ought to creep as doth the dial's shade,
For timely [27] ripe is rotten too-too soon.

BUN. (Coming forward) Deus hic; room
for a merry friar!
What, youth of Beccles, with the Keeper's
lass?
'Tis well; but tell me, hear you any news?

LACY. No, friar. What news?

BUN. Hear you not how the pursuivants
do post
With proclamations through each country-
town?

LACY. For what, gentle friar? Tell the
news.

BUN. Dwell'st thou in Beccles, and hear'st
not of these news?
Lacy, the Earl of Lincoln, is late fled
From Windsor court, disguiséd like a swain,
And lurks about the country here unknown.
Henry suspects him of some treachery,
And therefore doth proclaim in every way,
That who can take the Lincoln Earl shall
have,
Paid in the Exchequer, twenty thousand
crowns.

LACY. The Earl of Lincoln! Friar, thou
art mad.
It was some other; thou mistak'st the man.
The Earl of Lincoln! why, it cannot be.

MAR. Yes, very well, my lord, for you are
he.
The Keeper's daughter took you prisoner.
Lord Lacy, yield, I'll be your jailer once.

P. EDW. How familiar they be, Bacon!

BACON. Sit still, and mark the sequel of
their loves.

LACY. Then am I double prisoner to thyself.
Peggy, I yield. But are these news in jest?

MAR. In jest with you, but earnest unto
me;
For-why these wrongs do wring me at the
heart.
Ah, how these earls and noblemen of birth
Flatter and feign to forge poor women's ill!

LACY. Believe me, lass, I am the Lincoln
Earl.
I not deny, but, 'tiréd thus in rags,
I lived disguised to win fair Peggy's love.

MAR. What love is there where wedding
ends not love?

LACY. I mean, fair girl, to make thee Lacy's
wife.

MAR. I little think that earls will stoop so
low.

LACY. Say, shall I make thee countess ere
I sleep?

MAR. Handmaid unto the earl, so please
himself;
A wife in name, but servant in obedience.

LACY. The Lincoln Countess, for it shall
be so;
I'll plight the bands, and seal it with a kiss.

P. EDW. (Enraged) Gog's wounds, Bacon,
they kiss! I'll stab them.

BACON. O, hold your hands, my lord, it is
the glass!

P. EDW. Choler to see the traitors 'gree so
well
Made me think the shadows substances.

BACON. 'Twere a long poniard, my lord,
to reach between
Oxford and Fressingfield; but sit still and
see more.

BUN. Well, Lord of Lincoln, if your loves
be knit,
And that your tongues and thoughts do both
agree,
To avoid ensuing jars, I'll hamper up the
match.
I'll take my portace [28] forth and wed you here,
Then go to bed and seal up your desires.

LACY. Friar, content.—Peggy, how like
you this?

[27] Untimely, prematurely.

[28] Pocket breviary.

MAR. What likes my lord is pleasing unto
me.

BUN. Then hand-fast hand, and I will to
my book.

BACON. What sees my lord now?

P. EDW. Bacon, I see the lovers hand in
hand,

The friar ready with his portace there

To wed them both; then am I quite undone.

Bacon, help now, if e'er thy magic served;

Help, Bacon; stop the marriage now,

If devils or necromancy may suffice,

And I will give thee forty thousand crowns.

BACON. Fear not, my lord, I'll stop the jolly
friar

For [29] mumbling up his orisons this day.

LACY. Why speak'st not, Bungay? Friar,
to thy book.

(BUNGAY *is struck dumb. He struggles and
utters inarticulate sounds.*)

MAR. (*With concern*) How look'st thou,
friar, as a man distraught?

Reft of thy senses, Bungay? Show by signs,

If thou be dumb, what passion holdeth thee.

LACY. He's dumb indeed. Bacon hath
with his devils

Enchanted him, or else some strange disease

Or apoplexy hath possessed his lungs.

But, Peggy, what he cannot with his book,

We'll 'twixt us both unite it up in heart.

MAR. Else let me die, my lord, a miscreant.

P. EDW. Why stands Friar Bungay so
amazed?

BACON. I have struck him dumb, my lord;
and, if your honor please,

I'll fetch this Bungay straightway from
Fressingfield,

And he shall dine with us in Oxford here.

P. EDW. Bacon, do that, and thou content-
est me.

LACY. Of courtesy, Margaret, let us lead
the friar

Unto thy father's lodge, to comfort him

With broths, to bring him from this hapless
trance.

MAR. Or else, my lord, we were passing
unkind

To leave the friar so in his distress.

(*Enter a Devil, who carries off* BUNGAY *on
his back*)

O, help, my lord! a devil, a devil, my lord!

Look how he carries Bungay on his back!

Let's hence, for Bacon's spirits be abroad.

(*Exit with* LACY)

P. EDW. Bacon, I laugh to see the jolly
friar

Mounted upon the devil, and how the earl

Flees with his bonny lass for fear.

As soon as Bungay is at Brazen-nose,

And I have chatted with the merry friar,

I will in post hie me to Fressingfield,

And 'quite these wrongs on Lacy ere 't be
long.

BACON. So be it, my lord; but let us to our
dinner;

For ere we have taken our repast awhile,

We shall have Bungay brought to Brazen-
nose.   (*Exeunt*)

SCENE IV. *The Regent-house of Oxford University.*

(*Enter* DOCTORS BURDEN, MASON, *and*
CLEMENT)

MASON. Now that we are gathered in the
Regent-house,

It fits us talk about the king's repair,[30]

For he, troopéd with all the western kings,

That lie alongst the Dantzic seas by east,

North by the clime of frosty Germany,

The Almain [31] monarch, and the Saxon duke,

Castile and lovely Elinor with him,

Have in their jests resolved for Oxford town.

BURD. We must lay plots of stately
tragedies,

Strange comic shows, such as proud Roscius

Vaunted before the Roman emperors,

To welcome all the western potentates.

CLEM. But more; the king by letters hath
foretold

That Frederick, the Almain emperor,

Hath brought with him a German of esteem,

Whose surname is Don Jaques Vandermast,

Skilful in magic and those secret arts.

MASON. Then must we all make suit unto
the friar,

[29] From.   [30] Visit.   [31] German.

To Friar Bacon, that he vouch this task,
And undertake to countervail in skill
The German; else there's none in Oxford can
Match and dispute with learnéd Vandermast.

BURD. Bacon, if he will hold the German
play,
Will teach him what an English friar can do.
The devil, I think, dare not dispute with
him.

CLEM. Indeed, Mas doctor, he displeas-
ured you,
In that he brought your hostess with her spit,
From Henley, posting unto Brazen-nose.

BURD. A vengeance on the friar for his
pains!
But leaving that, let's hie to Bacon straight,
To see if he will take this task in hand.

(*Shouting and commotion off stage*)

CLEM. Stay, what rumor is this? The
town is up in a mutiny.
What hurly-burly is this?

(*Enter* RALPH SIMNELL, WARREN, *and*
ERMSBY, *all disguised as before, and* MILES,
protesting and arguing with the CONSTABLE)

CONS. Nay, masters, if you were ne'er so
good, you shall before the doctors to answer
your misdemeanor.

BURD. What's the matter, fellow?

CONS. Marry, sir, here's a company of ruf-
flers, that, drinking in the tavern, have made
a great brawl and almost killed the vintner.

MILES. *Salve*, Doctor Burden!
This lubberly lurden [32]
Ill-shaped and ill-faced,
Disdained and disgraced,
What he tells unto *vobis*
Mentitur de nobis.

BURD. Who is the master and chief of this
crew?

MILES. (*Pointing to* RALPH)
Ecce asinum mundi
Figura rotundi,
Neat, sheat, [33] and fine,
As brisk as a cup of wine.

BURD. What are you?

RALPH. I am, father doctor, as a man
would say, the bell-wether of this company;
these are my lords, and I the Prince of Wales.

CLEM. Are you Edward, the king's son?

RALPH. Sirrah Miles, bring hither the tapster that drew the wine, and, I warrant, when
they see how soundly I have broke his head,
they'll say 'twas done by no less man than
a prince.

MASON. I cannot believe that this is the
Prince of Wales.

WAR. And why so, sir?

MASON. For they say the prince is a brave
and a wise gentleman.

WAR. Why, and think'st thou, doctor,
that he is not so?
Dar'st thou detract and derogate from him,
Being so lovely and so brave a youth?

ERMS. Whose face, shining with many a
sugared smile,
Bewrays that he is bred of princely race.

MILES. And yet, master doctor,
To speak like a proctor,
And tell unto you
What is veriment and true;
To cease of this quarrel,
Look but on his apparel;
Then mark but my talis,
He is great Prince of Walis,
The chief of our *gregis*,
And *filius regis*;
Then 'ware what is done,
For he is Henry's white son. [34]

RALPH. Doctors, whose doting night-caps
are not capable of my ingenious dignity,
know that I am Edward Plantagenet, whom
if you displease will make a ship that shall
hold all your colleges, and so carry away the
university with a fair wind to the Bankside in
Southwark—How sayest thou, Ned Warren,
shall I not do it?

WAR. Yes, my good lord; and, if it please
your lordship, I will gather up all your old
pantofles, [35] and with the cork make you a
pinnace of five-hundred ton, that shall serve
the turn marvelous well, my lord.

ERMS. And I, my lord, will have pioneers [36]
to undermine the town, that the very gardens
and orchards be carried away for your sum-
mer-walks.

MILES. And I, with *scientia*
And great *diligentia*,
Will conjure and charm,
To keep you from harm;
That *utrum horum mavis,*

---

[32] Lazy heavy fellow. [33] Nimble. [34] Darling son. [35] Slippers. [36] Mine layers.

Your very great *navis*,
Like Barclay's ship,[37]
From Oxford do skip
With colleges and schools,
Full-loaden with fools.
Quid dicis ad hoc,
Worshipful *Domine* Dawcock?[38]

CLEM. Why, hair-brained courtiers, are
you drunk or mad,
To taunt us up with such scurrility?
Deem you us men of base and light esteem,
To bring us such a fop for Henry's son?—
Call out the beadles and convey them hence
Straight to Bocardo;[39] let the roisters lie
Close clapt in bolts, until their wits be tame.

ERMS. Why, shall we to prison, my lord?

RALPH. What sayest, Miles, shall I honor
the prison with my presence?

MILES. No, no; out with your blades,
And hamper these jades;
Have a flurt and a crash,
Now play revel-dash,
And teach these sacerdos
That the Bocardos,
Like peasants and elves,
Are meet for themselves.

MASON. To the prison with them, constable.

WAR. Well, doctors, seeing I have sported
me
With laughing at these mad and merry wags,
Know that Prince Edward is at Brazen-nose,
And this, attiréd like the Prince of Wales,
Is Ralph, King Henry's only lovéd fool;
I, Earl of Sussex, and this Ermsby,
One of the privy-chamber to the king;
Who, while the prince with Friar Bacon
stays,
Have reveled it in Oxford as you see.

MASON. My lord, pardon us, we knew not
what you were;
But courtiers may make greater scapes than
these.
Wilt please your honor dine with me today?

WAR. I will, Master doctor, and satisfy the
vintner for his hurt; only I must desire you
to imagine him (*pointing to* RALPH) all this
forenoon the Prince of Wales.

MASON. I will, sir.

RALPH. And upon that I will lead the
way; only I will have Miles go before me,
because I have heard Henry say that wisdom
must go before majesty.   (*Exeunt*)

Act III

SCENE I. *A Room at Fressingfield.*

(*Enter* PRINCE EDWARD, *very angry, with
his poniard in his hand. He is followed by*
LACY *and* MARGARET)

P. EDW. Lacy, thou canst not shroud thy
traitorous thoughts,
Nor cover, as did Cassius, all his wiles;
For Edward hath an eye that looks as far
As Lynceus from the shores of Græcia.
Did not I sit in Oxford by the friar,
And see thee court the maid of Fressingfield,
Sealing thy flattering fancies with a kiss?
Did not proud Bungay draw his portace
forth,
And joining hand in hand had married you,
If Friar Bacon had not struck him dumb,
And mounted him upon a spirit's back,

That we might chat at Oxford with the friar?
Traitor, what answer'st? Is not all this true?

LACY. Truth all, my lord; and thus I make
reply:
At Harleston Fair, there courting for your
grace,
Whenas mine eye surveyed her curious
shape,
And drew the beauteous glory of her looks
To dive into the center of my heart,
Love taught me that your honor did but jest,
That princes were in fancy but as men;
How that the lovely maid of Fressingfield
Was fitter to be Lacy's wedded wife
Than concubine unto the Prince of Wales.

P. EDW. Injurious Lacy, did I love thee
more

---

[37] Barclay's *The Ship of Fools.*   [38] Simpleton.   [39] An Oxford prison.

Than Alexander his Hephæstion?
Did I unfold the passions of my love,
And lock them in the closet of thy thoughts?
Wert thou to Edward second to himself,
Sole friend, and partner of his secret loves?
And could a glance of fading beauty break
Th' enchainéd fetters of such private friends?
Base coward, false, and too effeminate
To be corrival with a prince in thoughts!
From Oxford have I posted since I dined,
To 'quite a traitor 'fore that Edward sleep.

MAR. 'Twas I, my lord, not Lacy stept
    awry;
For oft he sued and courted for yourself,
And still wooed for the courtier all in green;
But I, whom fancy made but over-fond,
Pleaded myself with looks as if I loved;
I fed mine eye with gazing on his face,
And still bewitched loved Lacy with my
    looks;
My heart with sighs, mine eyes pleaded with
    tears,
My face held pity and content at once,
And more I could not cipher-out by signs,
But that I loved Lord Lacy with my heart.
Then, worthy Edward, measure with thy
    mind
If women's favors will not force men fall,
If beauty, and if darts of piercing love,
Are not of force to bury thoughts of friends.

P. EDW. I tell thee, Peggy, I will have thy
    loves;
Edward or none shall conquer Margaret.
In frigates bottomed with rich Sethin planks,
Topt with the lofty firs of Lebanon,
Stemmed and incased with burnished ivory,
And over-laid with plates of Persian wealth,
Like Thetis shalt thou wanton on the waves,
And draw the dolphins to thy lovely eyes,
To dance lavoltas in the purple streams;
Sirens, with harps and silver psalteries,
Shall wait with music at thy frigate's stem,
And entertain fair Margaret with their lays.
England and England's wealth shall wait on
    thee;
Britain shall bend unto her prince's love,
And do due homage to thine excellence,
If thou wilt be but Edward's Margaret.

MAR. Pardon, my lord; if Jove's great
    royalty
Sent me such presents as to Danaë;
If Phœbus, 'tiréd in Latona's webs,
Came courting from the beauty of his lodge;

The dulcet tunes of frolic Mercury,
Nor all the wealth heaven's treasury affords,
Should make me leave Lord Lacy or his love.

P. EDW. I have learned at Oxford, then,
    this point of schools,—
Ablata causa, tollitur effectus: [40]
(*Turning to* LACY) Lacy, the cause that
    Margaret cannot love
Nor fix her liking on the English prince,
Take him away, and then th' effects will fail.
Villain, prepare thyself; for I will bathe
My poniard in the bosom of an earl.

LACY. (*Kneeling*) Rather than live, and
    miss fair Margaret's love,
Prince Edward, stop not at the fatal doom,
But stab it home; end both my loves and life.

MAR. (*Kneeling beside* LACY) Brave
    Prince of Wales, honored for royal
    deeds,
'Twere sin to stain fair Venus' courts with
    blood;
Love's conquest ends, my lord, in courtesy.
Spare Lacy, gentle Edward; let me die,
For so both you and he do cease your loves.

P. EDW. Lacy shall die as traitor to his lord.

LACY. I have deserved it, Edward; act it
well.

MAR. What hopes the prince to gain by
    Lacy's death?

P. EDW. To end the loves 'twixt him and
Margaret.

MAR. Why, thinks King Henry's son that
    Margaret's love
Hangs in th' uncertain balance of proud
    time?
That death shall make a discord of our
    thoughts?
No, stab the earl, and, 'fore the morning sun
Shall vaunt him thrice over the lofty east,
Margaret will meet her Lacy in the heavens.

LACY. If aught betides to lovely Margaret
That wrongs or wrings her honor from con-
    tent,
Europe's rich wealth nor England's monarchy
Should not allure Lacy to over-live.
Then, Edward, short my life, and end her
    loves.

MAR. Rid me, and keep a friend worth
many loves.

[40] "When the cause is removed, the effect is
removed."

Lacy. Nay, Edward, keep a love worth many friends.

Mar. An if thy mind be such as fame hath blazed,
Then, princely Edward, let us both abide
The fatal resolution of thy rage.
Banish thou fancy, and embrace revenge,
And in one tomb knit both our carcasses,
Whose hearts were linkéd in one perfect love.

P. Edw. (*Aside*) Edward, art thou that famous Prince of Wales,
Who at Damasco beat the Saracens,
And brought'st home triumph on thy lance's point?
And shall thy plumes be pulled by Venus down?
Is't princely to dissever lovers' leagues,
To part such friends as glory in their loves?
Leave, Ned, and make a virtue of this fault,
And further Peg and Lacy in their loves;
So in subduing fancy's passion,
Conquering thyself, thou gett'st the richest spoil.—

Lacy, rise up. (Lacy *rises*. Prince Edward *assists* Margaret *to rise*.) Fair Peggy, here's my hand.
The Prince of Wales hath conquered all his thoughts,
And all his loves he yields unto the earl.
Lacy, enjoy the maid of Fressingfield;
Make her thy Lincoln Countess at the church,
And Ned, as he is true Plantagenet,
Will give her to thee frankly for thy wife.
(*He places* Margaret's *hand in* Lacy's)

Lacy. Humbly I take her of my sovereign,
As if that Edward gave me England's right,
And riched me with the Albion diadem.

Mar. And doth the English prince mean true?
Will he vouchsafe to cease his former loves,
And yield the title of a country maid
Unto Lord Lacy?

P. Edw. I will, fair Peggy, as I am true lord.

Mar. Then, lordly sir, whose conquest is as great,
In conquering love, as Cæsar's victories,
Margaret, as mild and humble in her thoughts
As was Aspasia unto Cyrus self,
Yields thanks, and, next Lord Lacy, doth enshrine
Edward the second secret in her heart.

P. Edw. Gramercy, Peggy. Now that vows are past,
And that your loves are not to be revolt,
Once, Lacy, friends again. Come, we will post
To Oxford; for this day the king is there,
And brings for Edward Castile Elinor.
Peggy, I must go see and view my wife;
I pray God I like her as I loved thee.
Beside, Lord Lincoln, we shall hear dispute
'Twixt Friar Bacon and learnéd Vandermast.
Peggy, we'll leave you for a week or two.

Mar. As it please Lord Lacy; but love's foolish looks
Think footsteps miles and minutes to be hours.

Lacy. I'll hasten, Peggy, to make short return.—
But please your honor go unto the lodge,
We shall have butter, cheese, and venison;
And yesterday I brought for Margaret
A lusty bottle of neat claret-wine;
Thus can we feast and entertain your grace.

P. Edw. 'Tis cheer, Lord Lacy, for an emperor,
If he respect the person and the place.
Come, let us in; for I will all this night
Ride post until I come to Bacon's cell.
(*Exeunt*)

Scene II. *Brasenose College, Oxford.*

(*Enter* King Henry, *the* Emperor, *the* King of Castile, Elinor, Vandermast, *and* Bungay)

Emp. Trust me, Plantagenet, these Oxford schools
Are richly seated near the river-side;
The mountains full of fat and fallow deer,
The battling [41] pastures lade with kine and flocks,

[41] Fattening or battening.

The town gorgeous with high-built colleges,
And scholars seemly in their grave attire,
Learnéd in searching principles of art.—
What is thy judgment, Jaques Vandermast?
    VAN. That lordly are the buildings of the
       town,
Spacious the rooms, and full of pleasant
    walks;
But for the doctors, how that they be learnéd,
It may be meanly, for aught I can hear.
    BUN. I tell thee, German, Hapsburg holds
      none such,
None read so deep as Oxenford contains.
There are within our academic state
Men that may lecture it in Germany
To all the doctors of your Belgic schools.
    K. HEN. Stand to him, Bungay, charm
      this Vandermast,
And I will use thee as a royal king.
    VAN. Wherein dar'st thou dispute with
me?
    BUN. In what a doctor and a friar can.
    VAN. Before rich Europe's worthies put
      thou forth
The doubtful question unto Vandermast.
    BUN. Let it be this,—Whether the spirits
of pyromancy or geomancy be most predomi-
nant in magic?
    VAN. I say, of pyromancy.
    BUN. And I, of geomancy.
    VAN. The cabalists that write of magic
spells,
As Hermes, Melchie, and Pythagoras,
Affirm that, 'mongst the quadruplicity
Of elemental essence, *terra* is but thought
To be a *punctum* squared [42] to the rest;
And that the compass of ascending elements
Exceed in bigness as they do in height;
Judging the concave circle of the sun
To hold the rest in his circumference.
If, then, as Hermes says, the fire be greatest,
Purest, and only giveth shape to spirits,
Then must these dæmones that haunt that
    place
Be every way superior to the rest.
    BUN. I reason not of elemental shapes,
Nor tell I of the concave latitudes,
Noting their essence nor their quality,
But of the spirits that pyromancy calls,
And of the vigor of the geomantic fiends.
I tell thee, German, magic haunts the
    ground,

[42] An atom compared.

And those strange necromantic spells,
That work such shows and wondering in
    the world,
Are acted by those geomantic spirits
That Hermes calleth *terræ filii*.
The fiery spirits are but transparent shades,
That lightly pass as heralds to bear news;
But earthly fiends, closed in the lowest deep,
Dissever mountains, if they be but charged,
Being more gross and massy in their power.
    VAN. Rather these earthly geomantic
    spirits
Are dull and like the place where they re-
    main;
For when proud Lucifer fell from the
    heavens,
The spirits and angels that did sin with him,
Retained their local essence as their faults,
All subject under Luna's continent.
They which offended less hung in the fire,
And second faults did rest within the air;
But Lucifer and his proud-hearted fiends
Were thown into the center of the earth,
Having less understanding than the rest,
As having greater sin and lesser grace.
Therefore such gross and earthly spirits do
    serve
For jugglers, witches, and vile sorcerers;
Whereas the pyromantic genii
Are mighty, swift, and of far-reaching power.
But grant that geomancy hath most force;
Bungay, to please these mighty potentates,
Prove by some instance what thy art can do.
    BUN. I will.
    EMP. Now, English Harry, here begins
      the game;
We shall see sport between these learnéd
    men.
    VAN. What wilt thou do?
    BUN. Show thee the tree, leaved with re-
    finéd gold,
Whereon the fearful dragon held his seat,
That watched the garden called Hesperides,
Subdued and won by conquering Hercules.

(BUNGAY *draws a circle about himself, makes*
    signs, and mutters incantations. A tree
    comes up through the stage with a
    dragon beside it, shooting fire.)

VAN. Well done!
    K. HEN. What say you, royal lordings, to
    my friar?

Hath he not done a point of cunning skill?
VAN. Each scholar in the necromantic
    spells
Can do as much as Bungay hath performed.
But as Alcmena's bastard razed this tree,
So will I raise him up as when he lived,
And cause him pull the dragon from his seat,
And tear the branches piecemeal from the
    root.—
        (*He makes his circle and conjures*)
Hercules! *Prodi, prodi,*[43] Hercules!

(HERCULES *rises up through the stage,
    dressed in his lion's skin*)

    HER. *Quis me vult?* [44]
VAN. Jove's bastard son, thou Libyan Her-
    cules,
Pull off the sprigs from off th' Hesperian
    tree,
As once thou didst to win the golden fruit.
    HER. *Fiat.*[45]
        (*He begins to break the branches*)
VAN. Now Bungay, if thou canst by magic
    charm
The fiend, appearing like great Hercules,
From pulling down the branches of the tree,
Then art thou worthy to be counted learnéd.
    BUN. (*Amazed and chagrined*) I cannot.
VAN. Cease, Hercules, until I give thee
    charge.—(HERCULES *desists and stands
    quietly beside the tree*)
(*Turning to* KING HENRY) Mighty com-
    mander of this English isle,
Henry, come from the stout Plantagenets,
Bungay is learnéd enough to be a friar;
But to compare with Jaques Vandermast,
Oxford and Cambridge must go seek their
    cells
To find a man to match him in his art.
I have given non-plus to the Paduans,
To them of Sien, Florence, and Bologna,
Rheims, Louvain, and fair Rotterdam,
Frankfort, Lutetia,[46] and Orleans;
And now must Henry, if he do me right,
Crown me with laurel, as they all have done.

        (*Enter* BACON)

    BACON. (*Bowing to the three monarchs*)
    All hail to this royal company,

That sit to hear and see this strange dispute!—
        (*Turning to* FRIAR BUNGAY)
Bungay, how stand'st thou as a man amazed?
What, hath the German acted more than
    thou?
    VAN. What art thou that question'st thus?
    BACON. Men call me Bacon.
    VAN. (*Cautiously*) Lordly thou look'st, as
        if that thou were learned;
Thy countenance as if science held her seat
Between the circled arches of thy brows.
    K. HEN. (*Eagerly anticipating an English
    triumph*) Now, monarchs, hath the German
    found his match.
    EMP. Bestir thee, Jaques, take not now the
        foil,
Lest thou dost lose what foretime thou didst
    gain.
    VAN. Bacon, wilt thou dispute?
    BACON. (*Disdainfully*) No,
Unless he were more learnéd than Vander-
    mast;
For yet, tell me, what has thou done?
    VAN. Raised Hercules to ruinate that tree
That Bungay mounted by his magic spells.
    BACON. Set Hercules to work.
    VAN. Now Hercules, I charge thee to thy
        task;
Pull off the golden branches from the root.
    HER. (*Continues to stand motionless*) I
        dare not. See'st thou not great Bacon
        here,
Whose frown doth act more than my magic
    can?
    VAN. (*Desperately*) By all the thrones,
        and dominations,
Virtues, powers, and mighty hierarchies,
I charge thee to obey to Vandermast.
    HER. Bacon, that bridles headstrong Bel-
        cephon,
And rules Asmenoth, guider of the north,
Binds me from yielding unto Vandermast.
    K. HEN. (*Triumphantly*) How now, Van-
        dermast! Have you met with your
        match?
    VAN. (*Fearfully*) Never before was't
        known to Vandermast
That men held devils in such obedient awe.
Bacon doth more than art, or else I fail.
    EMP. Why, Vandermast, art thou over-
        come?—

[43] "Come forth."   [44] "Who wants me?"   [45] "Let it be done."   [46] Paris (?).

Bacon, dispute with him, and try his skill.

BACON. I came not, monarchs, for to hold
dispute
With such a novice as is Vandermast;
I came to have your royalties to dine
With Friar Bacon here in Brazen-nose;
And, for this German troubles but the place,
And holds this audience with a long sus-
pense,
I'll send him to his académy hence.—

(*Turning from the monarchs to*
HERCULES)

Thou Hercules, whom Vandermast did raise,
Transport the German unto Hapsburg
straight,
That he may learn by travail, 'gainst the
spring,
More secret dooms and aphorisms of art.
Vanish the tree, and thou away with him!

(HERCULES *leaves the tree, seizes the terrified* VANDERMAST, *and carries him back
to the tree, and all three disappear beneath the stage*)

EMP. (*Amazed and somewhat frightened*)
Why, Bacon, whither dost thou send him?

BACON. To Hapsburg; there your highness
at return
Shall find the German in his study safe.

K. HEN. Bacon, thou hast honored Eng-
land with thy skill,
And made fair Oxford famous by thine art;
I will be English Henry to thyself.
But tell me, shall we dine with thee today?

BACON. With me, my lord; and while I fit
my cheer,
See where Prince Edward comes to welcome
you,
Gracious as the morning-star of Heaven.

(*Exit*)

(*Enter* PRINCE EDWARD, LACY, WARREN,
ERMSBY, *in their proper dress*)

EMP. Is this Prince Edward, Henry's
royal son?
How martial is the figure of his face!
Yet lovely and beset with amorets.[47]

K. HEN. Ned, where hast thou been?

P. EDW. At Framlingham, my lord, to try
your bucks
If they could 'scape the teasers or the toil.
But hearing of these lordly potentates

[47] Love-kindling glances.   [48] Waiter.

Landed, and progressed up to Oxford town,
I posted to give entertain to them;

(*Bowing to the monarchs in turn*) Chief to
the Almain monarch; next to him,
And joint with him, Castile and Saxony
Are welcome as they may be to the English
court. (*Gazing at* PRINCESS ELINOR)
Thus for the men: but see, Venus appears,
Or one that overmatcheth Venus in her
shape!
Sweet Elinor, beauty's high-swelling pride,
Rich nature's glory and her wealth at once,
Fair of all fairs, welcome to Albion;
Welcome to me, and welcome to thine own,
If thou that deign'st the welcome from
myself.

ELIN. Martial Plantagenet, Henry's high-
minded son,
The mark that Elinor did count her aim,
I liked thee 'fore I saw thee; now I love,
And so as in so short a time I may;
Yet so as time shall never break that so,
And therefore so accept of Elinor.

K. OF CAST. Fear not, my lord, this couple
will agree,
If love may creep into their wanton eyes:—
And therefore, Edward, I accept thee here,
Without suspense, as my adopted son.

K. HEN. Let me that joy in these consort-
ing greets,
And glory in these honors done to Ned,
Yield thanks for all these favors to my son,
And rest a true Plantagenet to all.

(*Enter* MILES *with a cloth and trenchers and
salt*)

MILES. (*Bowing awkwardly to the mon-
archs*) Salvete, omnes reges,
That govern your greges
In Saxony and Spain,
In England and in Almain!
For all this frolic rabble
Must I cover the table
With trenchers, salt, and cloth;
And then look for your broth.

(*He sets the table clumsily, making a spectacle of himself*)

EMP. What pleasant fellow is this?

K. HEN. 'Tis, my lord, Doctor Bacon's
poor scholar.

MILES. (*Aside*) My master hath made me
sewer [48] of these great lords; and, God knows,

I am as serviceable at a table as a sow is under
an apple-tree. 'Tis no matter; their cheer
shall not be great, and therefore what skills
where the salt stand, before or behind? [49]
                                          (*Exit*)

K. OF CAST. These scholars know more
    skill in axioms,
How to use quips and sleights of sophistry,
Than for to cover courtly for a king.

(*Re-enter* MILES *with a mess of pottage and
broth, followed by* FRIAR BACON *admonish-
ing him*)

    MILES. (*Tilting the dishes precariously*)
        Spill, sir? why, do you think I never
        carried two-penny chop before in my
        life?—
By your leave, *nobile decus,*
For here comes Doctor Bacon's *pecus,*
Being in his full age
To carry a mess of pottage.
    BACON. (*As* MILES *puts the dishes on the
        table*) Lordings, admire not if your
        cheer be this,
For we must keep our academic fare;
No riot where philosophy doth reign:
And therefore, Henry, place these potentates,
And bid them fall unto their frugal cates.
    EMP. (*With regal disapproval*) Presump-
        tuous friar! What, scoff'st thou at a
        king?
What, dost thou taunt us with thy peasants'
    fare,
And give us cates fit for country swains?—
Henry, proceeds this jest of thy consent,
To twit us with a pittance of such price?
Tell me, and Frederick will not grieve thee
    long.
    K. HEN. By Henry's honor, and the royal
        faith

The English monarch beareth to his friend,
I knew not of the friar's feeble fare,
Nor am I pleased he entertains you thus.
    BACON. (*Unperturbed by the royal dis-
        pleasure*) Content thee, Frederick, for
        I showed these cates,
To let thee see how scholars used to feed;
How little meat refines our English wits.—
Miles, take away, and let it be thy dinner.
    MILES. Marry, sir, I will. (*Hastily clear-
        ing the table*)
This day shall be a festival-day with me;
For I shall exceed in the highest degree.
                                    (*Exit* MILES)
    BACON. I tell three, monarch, all the
        German peers
Could not afford thy entertainment such,
So royal and so full of majesty,
As Bacon will present to Frederick.
The basest waiter that attends thy cups
Shall be in honors greater than thyself;
And for thy cates, rich Alexandria drugs,
Fetched by carvels [50] from Ægypt's richest
    straits,
Found in the wealthy strand of Africa,
Shall royalize the table of my king;
Wines richer than th' Ægyptian courtesan
Quaffed to Augustus' kingly countermatch,
Shall be caroused in English Henry's feast;
Candy [51] shall yield the richest of her canes;
Persia, down her Volga by canoes,
Send down the secrets of her spicery;
The Afric dates, mirabolans [52] of Spain,
Conserves and suckets [53] from Tiberias,
Cates from Judæa, choicer than the lamp [54]
That firéd Rome with sparks of gluttony,
Shall beautify the board for Frederick:
And therefore grudge not at a friar's feast.
    (*Exeunt,* BACON *ushering them to his
        banquet*)

SCENE III. *Near the* KEEPER'S *Lodge at Fressingfield.*

(*Enter two gentlemen,* LAMBERT *and*
SERLSBY, *with the* KEEPER)

    LAM. Come, frolic Keeper of our liege's
        game,

[49] The ornate salt cellar always stood in the
center of the table as a point of social demarca-
tion for seating guests.
[50] Light and fast ships.

Whose table spread hath ever venison
And jacks [55] of wine to welcome passengers,
Know I'm in love with jolly Margaret,
That overshines our damsels as the moon
Darkeneth the brightest sparkles of the night.

[51] Candia.   [52] Dried plums.
[53] Sweetmeats.
[54] Lamprey, a variety of eel (?).
[55] Leather jugs.

In Laxfield here my land and living lies;
I'll make thy daughter jointer of it all,
So thou consent to give her to my wife;
And I can spend five hundred marks a-year.

SER. I am the lands-lord, Keeper, of thy holds,
By copy all thy living lies in me;
Laxfield did never see me raise my due;
I will enfeoff fair Margaret in all,
So she will take her to a lusty squire.

KEEP. Now, courteous gentles, if the Keeper's girl
Hath pleased the liking fancy of you both,
And with her beauty hath subdued your thoughts,
'Tis doubtful to decide the question.
It joys me that such men of great esteem
Should lay their liking on this base estate,
And that her state should grow so fortunate
To be a wife to meaner men than you.
But sith such squires will stoop to keeper's fee,[56]
I will, to avoid displeasure of you both,
Call Margaret forth, and she shall make her choice.

LAM. Content, Keeper; send her unto us.
(*Exit* KEEPER)
(*Offensively to* SERLSBY) Why, Serlsby, is thy wife so lately dead,
Are all thy loves so lightly passéd over,
As thou canst wed before the year be out?

SER. I live not, Lambert, to content the dead,
Nor was I wedded but for life to her;
The grave ends and begins a married state.

(*Enter* MARGARET)

LAM. Peggy, the lovely flower of all towns,
Suffolk's fair Helen, and rich England's star,
Whose beauty, tempered with her huswifery,
Makes England talk of merry Fressingfield!

SER. I cannot trick it up with poesies,
Nor paint my passions with comparisons,
Nor tell a tale of Phœbus and his loves;
But this believe me,—Laxfield here is mine,
Of ancient rent seven hundred pounds a-year,
And if thou canst but love a country squire,
I will enfeoff thee, Margaret, in all.
I cannot flatter; try me, if thou please.

MAR. Brave neighboring squires, the stay of Suffolk's clime,
A keeper's daughter is too base in 'gree[57]
To match with men accounted of such worth;
But might I not displease, I would reply.

LAM. Say, Peggy; naught shall make us discontent.

MAR. Then, gentles, note that love hath little stay,
Nor can the flames that Venus sets on fire
Be kindled but by fancy's motion.
Then pardon, gentles, if a maid's reply
Be doubtful, while I have debated with myself,
Who, or of whom, love shall constrain me like.

SER. Let it be me; and trust me, Margaret,
The meads environed with the silver streams,
Whose battling pastures fatten all my flocks,
Yielding forth fleeces stapled with such wool
As Lempster cannot yield more finer stuff,
And forty kine with fair and burnished heads,
With strouting dugs that paggle to the ground,
Shall serve thy dairy, if thou wed with me.

LAM. Let pass the country wealth, as flocks and kine,
And lands that wave with Ceres' golden sheaves,
Filling my barns with plenty of the fields;
But, Peggy, if thou wed thyself to me,
Thou shalt have garments of embroidered silk,
Lawns, and rich net-works for thy head-attire.
Costly shall be thy fair habiliments,
If thou wilt be but Lambert's loving wife.

MAR. Content you, gentles, you have proffered fair,
And more than fits a country maid's degree;
But give me leave to counsel me a time,
For fancy blooms not at the first assault;
Give me but ten days' respite, and I will reply,
Which or to whom myself affectionates.

SER. (*Disdainfully*) Lambert, I tell thee, thou'rt importunate;
Such beauty fits not such a base esquire;
It is for Serlsby to have Margaret.

LAM. Think'st thou with wealth to over-reach me?
Serlsby, I scorn to brook thy country braves;

---

[56] Estate.   [57] Degree.

(*He strikes* Serlsby *in the face with his glove*)

I dare thee, coward, to maintain this wrong,
At dint of rapier, single in the field.

Ser. I'll answer, Lambert, what I have
  avouched.—
Margaret, farewell; another time shall serve.
          (*Exit* Serlsby)

Lam. I'll follow.—Peggy, farewell to thyself;
Listen how well I'll answer for thy love.
          (*Exit* Lambert)

Mar. (*Sadly*) How fortune tempers lucky
  haps with frowns,
And wrongs me with the sweets of my
  delight!
Love is my bliss, and love is now my bale.
Shall I be Helen in my froward fates,
As I am Helen in my matchless hue,
And set rich Suffolk with my face afire?
If lovely Lacy were but with his Peggy,
The cloudy darkness of his bitter frown
Would check the pride of these aspiring
  squires.
Before the term of ten days be expired,
Whenas they look for answer of their loves,
My lord will come to merry Fressingfield,
And end their fancies and their follies both.
Till when, Peggy, be blithe and of good
  cheer.

(*Enter a* Post *dressed in riding clothes and
  carrying a letter and a leather bag*)

Post. Fair lovely damsel, which way leads
  this path?
How might I post me unto Fressingfield?
Which footpath leadeth to the Keeper's
  lodge?

Mar. Your way is ready, and this path is
  right;
Myself do dwell hereby in Fressingfield;
And if the Keeper be the man you seek,
I am his daughter: may I know the cause?

Post. Lovely, and once belovéd of my
  lord,—
(*Aside*) No marvel if his eye was lodged so
  low,
When brighter beauty is not in the
  heavens,—
The Lincoln Earl hath sent you letters here,
And, with them, just an hundred pounds
  in gold.

Sweet, bonny wench, read them, and make
  reply.

Mar. The scrolls that Jove sent Danaë,
Wrapt in rich closures of fine burnished gold,
Were not more welcome than these lines
  to me.
Tell me, whilst that I do unrip the seals,
Lives Lacy well? How fares my lovely lord?

Post. Well, if that wealth may make men
  to live well.
          (*Gives the letter, and* Margaret
          reads it)

Mar. The blooms of the almond-tree grow
in a night, and vanish in a morn; the flies
hæmeræ,[58] fair Peggy, take life with the sun,
and die with the dew; fancy that slippeth in
with a gaze, goeth out with a wink; and too
timely loves have ever the shortest length.
I write this as thy grief, and my folly, who
at Fressingfield loved that which time hath
taught me to be but mean dainties. Eyes are
dissemblers, and fancy is but queasy; therefore know, Margaret, I have chosen a Spanish lady to be my wife, chief waiting-woman
to the Princess Elinor; a lady fair, and no
less fair than thyself, honorable and wealthy.
In that I forsake thee, I leave thee to thine
own liking; and for thy dowry I have sent
thee an hundred pounds; and ever assure
thee of my favor, which shall avail thee and
thine much.
  Farewell.

                    Not thine, nor his own,
                        Edward Lacy.

Fond Até, doomer of bad-boding fates,
That wrapp'st proud fortune in thy snaky
  locks,
Didst thou enchant my birthday with such
  stars
As lightened mischief from their infancy?
If heavens had vowed, if stars had made
  decree,
To show on me their froward influence,
If Lacy had but loved, heavens, hell, and all,
Could not have wronged the patience of my
  mind.

Post. It grieves me, damsel; but the earl
  is forced
To love the lady by the king's command.

[58] Short-lived insects.

MAR. The wealth combined within the English shelves,
Europe's commander, nor the English king,
Should not have moved the love of Peggy from her lord.
POST. What answer shall I return to my lord?
MAR. First, for thou cam'st from Lacy whom I loved,—
Ah, give me leave to sigh at every thought!
Take thou, my friend, the hundred pound he sent;
For Margaret's resolution craves no dower.
The world shall be to her as vanity;
Wealth, trash; love, hate; pleasure, despair—
For I will straight to stately Framlingham,
And in the abbey there be shorn a nun,
And yield my loves and liberty to God.
Fellow, I give thee this, not for the news,
For those be hateful unto Margaret,
But for thou'rt Lacy's man, once Margaret's love.
POST. What I have heard, what passions I have seen,
I'll make report of them unto the earl.
MAR. Say that she joys his fancies be at rest,
And prays that his misfortunes may be hers.
(*Exeunt*)

Act IV

SCENE I. FRIAR BACON'S *Study.*

(FRIAR BACON *sits with a white wand in one hand and an open book in the other. Beside him a lamp burns. In the center of the stage is a large head made of brass. Nearby is a curtained bed.* MILES *sits in one corner surrounded by swords, daggers, two pistols, and a pike*)

BACON. Miles, where are you?
MILES. Here, sir.
BACON. How chance you tarry so long?
MILES. Think you that the watching of the Brazen Head craves no furniture? (*Fondling his weapons*) I warrant you, sir, I have so armed myself that if all your devils come, I will not fear them an inch.
BACON. Miles, thou know's that I have divéd into hell,
And sought the darkest palaces of fiends;
That with my magic spells great Belcephon
Hath left his lodge and kneeléd at my cell;
The rafters of the earth rent from the poles,
And three-formed Luna hid her silver looks,
Trembling upon her concave continent,
When Bacon read upon his magic book.
With seven years' tossing necromantic charms,
Poring upon dark Hecat's principles,
I have framed out a monstrous head of brass,
That, by the enchanting forces of the devil,
Shall tell out strange and uncouth aphorisms,
And girt fair England with a wall of brass.
Bungay and I have watched these threescore days,
And now our vital spirits crave some rest.
If Argus lived, and had his hundred eyes,
They could not over-watch Phobetor's night.
Now, Miles, in thee rests Friar Bacon's weal:
The honor and renown of all his life
Hangs in the watching of this Brazen Head;
Therefore I charge thee by the immortal God,
That holds the souls of men within his fist,
This night thou watch; (*He lays aside his book and wand and goes to the bed*) for ere the morning-star
Sends out his glorious glister on the north,
The head will speak: then, Miles, upon thy life,
Wake me; for then by magic art I'll work
To end my seven years' task with excellence.
If that a wink but shut thy watchful eye,
Then farewell Bacon's glory and his fame!
(*He gets into the bed*)
Draw close the curtains, Miles: now, for thy life,
Be watchful, and— (BACON *falls asleep*)
MILES. (*Closing the bed curtains*) So; I thought you would talk yourself asleep anon; and 'tis no marvel, for Bungay on the days, and he on the nights, have watched just these ten and fifty days; now this is the night, and

'tis my task, and no more. (*He examines the head fearfully*) Now, Jesus bless me, what a goodly head it is! and a nose! you talk of *nos autem glorificare*; but here's a nose that I warrant may be called *nos autem populare* for the people of the parish. Well, I am furnished with weapons; now, sir, I will set me down by a post, and make it as good as a watchman to wake me, if I chance to slumber. (*He sits quiet a moment, peering at the head*) I thought, Goodman Head, I would call you out of your *memento*. (*He goes to sleep and falls over, hitting his head*) Passion o' God, I have almost broke my pate! (*He scrambles for his weapons*) Up, Miles, to your task; take your brown-bill [59] in your hand; here's some of your master's hobgoblins abroad.

(THE HEAD *speaks. A loud noise off stage.*)

THE BRAZEN HEAD. Time is!
MILES. (*Relieved*) Time is! Why, Master Brazen-head, have you such a capital nose, and answer you with syllables, "Time is"? Is this all my master's cunning, to spend seven years' study about "Time is"? Well, sir, it may be we shall have some better orations of it anon. Well, I'll watch you as narrowly as ever you were watched, and I'll play with you as the nightingale with the slow-worm. (*He sits down again and props the pike with its point against his chest*) I'll set a prick against my breast. Now rest there, Miles. (*He dozes off again and leans against the point of the pike*) Lord have mercy upon me, I have almost killed myself! (*A great noise off stage*) Up, Miles; list how they rumble.
THE BRAZEN HEAD. Time was!
MILES. Well, Friar Bacon, you have spent your seven-years' study well, that can make your head speak but two words at once, "Time was." Yea, marry, time was when my master was a wise man, but that was before he began to make the Brazen Head. You shall lie while your arse ache, an your head speak no better. Well, I will watch, and walk up and down, and be a peripatetian and a philosopher of Aristotle's stamp. (*Another loud noise off stage.* MILES *seizes his*

weapons.) What, a fresh noise? Take thy pistols in hand, Miles.

(*Here* THE HEAD *speaks, and a lightning flashes forth, and a hand appears that breaks down* THE HEAD *with a hammer*)

THE BRAZEN HEAD. Time is past!
MILES. (*Dashing in terror to* BACON's *bed*) Master, master, up! Hell's broken loose; your head speaks; and there's such a thunder and lightning, that I warrant all Oxford is up in arms. Out of your bed, and take a brown-bill in your hand; the latter day is come.
BACON. Miles, I come. (*Getting out of bed, dazed with sleep. He does not see the head.*) O, passing warily watched! Bacon will make thee next himself in love. When spake the head?
MILES. When spake the head! Did not you say that he should tell strange principles of philosophy? Why, sir, it speaks but two words at a time.
BACON. Why, villain, hath it spoken oft?
MILES. Oft! ay, marry, hath it, thrice; but in all those three times it hath uttered but seven words.
BACON. As how?
MILES. Marry, sir, the first time he said "Time is," as if Fabius Commentator [60] should have pronounced a sentence; the second time he said "Time was"; and the third time, with thunder and lightning, as in great choler, he said, "Time is past."
BACON. (*He sees the broken head for the first time*) 'Tis past indeed. Ah, villain! time is past.
My life, my fame, my glory, all are past.—
Bacon, the turrets of thy hope are ruined down,
Thy seven years' study lieth in the dust;
Thy Brazen Head lies broken through a slave
That watched, and would not when the head did will.—
What said the head first?
MILES. Even, sir, "Time is."
BACON. Villain, if thou hadst called to Bacon then,
If thou hadst watched, and waked the sleepy friar,
The Brazen Head had uttered aphorisms,

---

[59] Pike.

[60] Miles' blunder for Fabius Cunctator (Delayer).

And England had been circled round with
　　brass;
But proud Asmenoth, ruler of the north,
And Demogorgon, master of the fates,
Grudge that a mortal man should work so
　　much.
Hell trembled at my deep-commanding spells,
Fiends frowned to see a man their over-
　　match;
Bacon might boast more than a man might
　　boast.
(Sadly) But now the braves of Bacon have
　　an end,
Europe's conceit of Bacon hath an end,
His seven years' practice sorteth to ill end:
And, villain, sith my glory hath an end,
I will appoint thee to some fatal end.
Villain, avoid! get thee from Bacon's sight!
Vagrant, go roam and range about the world,
And perish as a vagabond on earth!

MILES. Why, then, sir, you forbid me your
　　service?
BACON. My service, villain! with a fatal
　　curse,
That direful plagues and mischief fall on
　　thee.
MILES. 'Tis no matter, I am against you
with the old proverb,—The more the fox is
cursed,[61] the better he fares. God be with
you, sir. I'll take but a book in my hand, a
wide-sleeved gown on my back, and a
crowned cap on my head, and see if I can
want promotion.
BACON. Some fiend or ghost haunt on thy
　　weary steps,
Until they do transport thee quick to hell;
For Bacon shall have never merry day,
To lose the fame and honor of his head.
　　　　　　　　　　　　　　　(Exeunt)

SCENE II. KING HENRY'S *Palace at London*

(*Enter the* EMPEROR, *the* KING OF CASTILE,
KING HENRY, ELINOR, PRINCE EDWARD,
LACY, *and* RALPH SIMNELL)

　EMP. Now, lovely prince, the prime of
　　Albion's wealth,
How fare the Lady Elinor and you?
What, have you courted and found Castile
　fit
To answer England in equivalence?
Will't be a match 'twixt bonny Nell and
　thee?
　P. EDW. Should Paris enter in the courts
　　of Greece,
And not lie fettered in fair Helen's looks?
Or Phœbus 'scape those piercing amorets
That Daphne glancéd at his deity?
Can Edward, then, sit by a flame and freeze,
Whose heat puts Helen and fair Daphne
　down?
Now, monarchs, ask the lady if we 'gree.
　K. HEN. What, madam, hath my son
found grace or no?
　ELIN. Seeing, my lord, his lovely counter-
feit,
And hearing how his mind and shape agreed,

I came not, trooped with all this warlike
　train,
Doubting of love, but so affectionate
As Edward hath in England what he won in
　Spain.
　K. OF CAST. A match, my lord; these
　　wantons needs must love;
Men must have wives, and women will be
　wed.
Let's haste the day to honor up the rites.
　RALPH. Sirrah Harry, shall Ned marry
Nell?
　K. HEN. Ay, Ralph; how then?
　RALPH. Marry, Harry, follow my counsel.
Send for Friar Bacon to marry them, for he'll
so conjure him and her with his necromancy,
that they shall love together like pig and
lamb whilst they live.
　K. OF CAST. But hearest thou, Ralph, art
thou content to have Elinor to thy lady?
　RALPH. Ay, so she will promise me two
things.
　K. OF CAST. What's that, Ralph?
　RALPH. That she will never scold with
Ned, nor fight with me.—Sirrah Harry, I
have put her down with a thing unpossible.
　K. HEN. What's that, Ralph?
　RALPH. Why, Harry, didst thou ever see

[61] Pun on coursed.

that a woman could both hold her tongue
and her hands? No; but when egg-pies grow
on apple-trees, then will thy gray mare prove
a bag-piper.

EMP. What say the Lord of Castile and
the Earl of Lincoln, that they are in such
earnest and secret talk?

K. OF CAST. I stand, my lord, amazéd at
his talk,
How he discourseth of the constancy
Of one surnamed, for beauty's excellence,
The Fair Maid of merry Fressingfield.

K. HEN. 'Tis true, my lord, 'tis wondrous
    for to hear;
Her beauty passing Mars's paramour,
Her virgin's right as rich as Vesta's was.
Lacy and Ned have told me miracles.

K. OF CAST. What says Lord Lacy? Shall
she be his wife?

LACY. Or else Lord Lacy is unfit to live.—
May it please your highness give me leave
    to post
To Fressingfield, I'll fetch the bonny girl,
And prove, in true appearance at the court,
What I have vouchéd often with my tongue.

K. HEN. Lacy, go to the 'querry of my
    stable,
And take such coursers as shall fit thy turn;
Hie thee to Fressingfield, and bring home
    the lass;
And, for her fame flies through the English
    coast,

If it may please the Lady Elinor,
One day shall match your excellence and her.

ELIN. We Castile ladies are not very coy;
Your highness may command a greater boon;
And glad were I to grace the Lincoln Earl
With being partner of his marriage-day.

P. EDW. Gramercy, Nell, for I do love
    the lord,
As he that's second to thyself in love.

RALPH. You love her?—Madame Nell,
never believe him you, though he swears he
loves you.

ELIN. Why, Ralph?

RALPH. Why, his love is like unto a
tapster's glass that is broken with every
touch; for he loved the fair maid of Fressingfield once out of all ho.[62]—Nay, Ned, never
wink upon me; I care not, I.

K. HEN. Ralph tells all; you shall have
    a good secretary of him.—
But, Lacy, haste thee post to Fressingfield;
For ere thou hast fitted all things for her
    state,
The solemn marriage-day will be at hand.

LACY. I go, my lord.   (Exit)

EMP. How shall we pass this day, my
lord?

K. HEN. To horse, my lord; the day is
    passing fair,
We'll fly the partridge, or go rouse the deer.
Follow, my lords; you shall not want for
    sport.   (Exeunt)

SCENE III. FRIAR BACON'S *Study*.

(*Enter* FRIAR BACON *with* FRIAR BUNGAY)

BUN. What means the friar that frolicked
    it of late,
To sit as melancholy in his cell
As if he had neither lost nor won today?

BACON. Ah, Bungay, my Brazen Head is
    spoiled,
My glory gone, my seven years' study lost!
The fame of Bacon, bruited through the
    world,
Shall end and perish with this deep disgrace.

BUN. Bacon hath built foundation of his
    fame
So surely on the wings of true report,

    [62] Immeasurably.

With acting strange and uncouth miracles,
As this cannot infringe what he deserves.

BACON. Bungay, sit down, for by pros-
    pective skill
I find this day shall fall out ominous;
Some deadly act shall 'tide me ere I sleep;
But what and wherein little can I guess.

BUN. My mind is heavy, whatsoe'er shall
hap. (*Knocking off stage*)

BACON. Who's that knocks?

BUN. (*Goes to the door*) Two scholars that
desire to speak with you.

BACON. Bid them come in.

(*Enter two* OXFORD UNDERGRADUATES, *sons
of* LAMBERT *and* SERLSBY)

Now, my youths, what would you have?

FIRST SCHOL. Sir, we are Suffolk-men and
  neighboring friends;
Our fathers in their countries lusty squires;
Their lands adjoin; in Cratfield mine doth
  dwell,
And his in Laxfield. We are college-mates,
Sworn brothers, as our fathers live as friends.

BACON. To what end is all this?

SECOND SCHOL. Hearing your worship
  kept within your cell
A glass prospective, wherein men might see
Whatso their thoughts or hearts' desire could
  wish,
We come to know how that our fathers fare.

BACON. My glass is free for every honest
  man.
Sit down, and you shall see ere long, how
Or in what state your friendly fathers live.
Meanwhile, tell me your names.

FIRST SCHOL. Mine Lambert.

SECOND SCHOL. And mine Serlsby.

BACON. (Aside to BUNGAY) Bungay, I
smell there will be a tragedy.

(The two UNDERGRADUATES gaze into
BACON's crystal. What they see is enacted on
the upper stage, as in II, 3.)

(Enter on the upper stage LAMBERT and
SERLSBY with rapiers and daggers)

LAM. Serlsby, thou hast kept thine hour
  like a man;
Thou'rt worthy of the title of a squire,
That durst, for proof of thy affection
And for thy mistress' favor, prize [63] thy blood.
Thou know'st what words did pass at
  Fressingfield,
Such shameless braves as manhood cannot
  brook.
Ay, for I scorn to bear such piercing taunts,
Prepare thee, Serlsby; one of us will die.

SER. Thou see'st I single meet thee in the
  field,
And what I spake, I'll maintain with my
  sword.
Stand on thy guard, I cannot scold it out.
An if thou kill me, think I have a son,
That lives in Oxford in the Broadgates-hall,
Who will revenge his father's blood with
  blood.

[63] Risk.   [64] Bout.   [65] Doomed.

LAM. And, Serlsby, I have there a lusty
  boy,
That dares at weapon buckle with thy son,
And lives in Broadgates too, as well as thine.
But draw thy rapier, for we'll have a bout.

BACON. Now, lusty younkers, look within
  the glass,
And tell me if you can discern your sires.

FIRST SCHOL. Serlsby, 'tis hard; thy father
  offers wrong,
To combat with my father in the field.

SECOND SCHOL. Lambert, thou liest, my
  father's is th' abuse,
And thou shalt find it, if my father harm.

BUN. How goes it, sirs?

FIRST SCHOL. Our fathers are in combat
hard by Fressingfield.

BACON. Sit still, my friends, and see the
event.

LAM. Why stand'st thou, Serlsby? Doubt-
  'st thou of thy life?
A veney,[64] man! fair Margaret craves so
  much.

SER. Then this for her. (They fight)

FIRST SCHOL. Ah, well thrust!

SECOND SCHOL. But mark the ward.

  (LAMBERT and SERLSBY kill each other)

LAM. O, I am slain!   (Dies)

SER. And I,—Lord have mercy on me!
                                    (Dies)

FIRST SCHOL. My father slain!—Serlsby,
ward that.   (Stabs him)

SECOND SCHOL. And so is mine!—Lam-
bert, I'll 'quite thee well. (Stabs in return)
                    (The Two SCHOLARS die)

BUN. O strange stratagem!

BACON. See, friar, where the fathers both
  lie dead!—
Bacon, thy magic doth effect this massacre.
This glass prospective worketh many woes;
And therefore seeing these brave lusty
  Brutes,
These friendly youths, did perish by thine
  art,
End all thy magic and thine art at once.
The poniard that did end their fatal [65] lives,
Shall break the cause efficient of their woes.
                    (He breaks the glass)
So fade the glass, and end with it the shows
That necromancy did infuse the crystal with.

BUN. What means learned Bacon thus to
break his glass?

BACON. I tell thee, Bungay, it repents me
    sore
That ever Bacon meddled in this art.
The hours I have spent in pyromantic spells,
The fearful tossing in the latest night
Of papers full of necromantic charms,
Conjuring and adjuring devils and fiends,
With stole and alb and strong pentageron;
The wresting of the holy name of God,
As Sother, Eloim, and Adonai,
Alpha, Manoth, and Tetragrammaton,
With praying to the five-fold powers of
    heaven,
Are instances that Bacon must be damned
For using devils to countervail his God.—
Yet, Bacon, cheer thee, drown not in despair;

Sins have their salves, repentance can do
    much.
Think Mercy sits where Justice holds her
    seat,
And from those wounds those bloody Jews
    did pierce,
Which by thy magic oft did bleed afresh,
From thence for thee the dew of mercy
    drops,
To wash the wrath of high Jehovah's ire,
And make thee as a new-born babe from sin.
Bungay, I'll spend the remnant of my life
In pure devotion, praying to my God
That he would save what Bacon vainly lost.
                        (*Exeunt*)

Act V

SCENE I. *Near the* KEEPER'S *Lodge at Fressingfield.*

(*Enter* MARGARET *dressed as a nun, with her father, the* KEEPER, *and a* FRIEND)

KEEPER. Margaret, be not so headstrong
    in these vows;
O, bury not such beauty in a cell,
That England hath held famous for the hue!
Thy father's hair, like to the silver blooms
That beautify the shrubs of Africa,
Shall fall before the dated time of death,
Thus to forego his lovely Margaret.
    MAR. (*Sadly*) Ah, father, when the har-
    mony of heaven
Soundeth the measures of a lively faith,
The vain illusions of this flattering world
Seem odious to the thoughts of Margaret.
I lovéd once,—Lord Lacy was my love,
And now I hate myself for that I loved,
And doted more on him than on my God;
For this I scourge myself with sharp repents.
But now the touch of such aspiring sins
Tells me all love is lust but love of heaven;
That beauty used for love is vanity.
The world contains naught but alluring baits,
Pride, flattery, and inconstant thoughts.
To shun the pricks of death, I leave the
    world,
And vow to meditate on heavenly bliss,
To live in Framlingham a holy nun,
Holy and pure in conscience and in deed;

And for to wish all maids to learn of me
To seek heaven's joy before earth's vanity.
    FRIEND. And will you, then, Margaret, be
shorn a nun, and so leave us all?
    MAR. Now farewell world, the engine of
    all woe!
Farewell to friends and father! Welcome
    Christ!
Adieu to dainty robes! This base attire
Better befits an humble mind to God
Than all the show of rich habiliments.
Farewell, O love! and, with fond love, fare-
    well
Sweet Lacy, whom I lovéd once so dear!
Ever be well, but never in my thoughts,
Lest I offend to think on Lacy's love:
But even to that, as to the rest, farewell!

(*Enter* LACY, *speaking over his shoulder to*
WARREN *and* ERMSBY, *who follow him. All
three are booted and spurred as if newly
dismounted*)

LACY. Come on, my wags, we're near the
    Keeper's lodge.
Here have I oft walked in the watery meads,
And chatted with my lovely Margaret.
    WAR. Sirrah Ned, is not this the Keeper?
    LACY. 'Tis the same.

ERMS. The old lecher hath gotten holy mutton[66] to him; a nun, my lord.

LACY. (*Gaily*) Keeper, how far'st thou? Holla, man, what cheer?

How doth Peggy, thy daughter and my love?

KEEPER. Ah, good my lord! O, woe is me for Peggy!

See where she stands clad in her nun's attire,

Ready for to be shorn in Framlingham;

She leaves the world because she left your love.

O, good my lord, persuade her if you can!

LACY. (*Recognizing her with amazement*) Why, how now, Margaret! what, a malcontent?

A nun? What holy father taught you this,

To task yourself to such a tedious life

As die a maid? 'Twere injury to me,

To smother up such beauty in a cell.

MAR. Lord Lacy, thinking of my former 'miss,[67]

How fond the prime of wanton years were spent

In love (O, fie upon that fond conceit,

Whose hap and essence hangeth in the eye!),

I leave both love and love's content at once,

Betaking me to Him that is true love,

And leaving all the world for love of Him.

LACY. Whence, Peggy, comes this metamorphosis?

What, shorn a nun, and I have from the court

Posted with coursers to convey thee hence

To Windsor, where our marriage shall be kept!

Thy wedding-robes are in the tailor's hands.

Come, Peggy, leave these peremptory vows.

MAR. Did not my lord resign his interest,

And make divorce 'twixt Margaret and him?

LACY. 'Twas but to try sweet Peggy's constancy.

But will fair Margaret leave her love and lord?

MAR. Is not heaven's joy before earth's fading bliss,

And life above sweeter than life in love?

LACY. Why, then, Margaret will be shorn a nun?

[66] Slang for lewd woman.
[67] Fault.

MAR. Margaret hath made a vow which may not be revoked.

WAR. We cannot stay, my lord; an if she be so strict,

Our leisure grants us not to woo afresh.

ERMS. Choose you, fair damsel, yet the choice is yours,—

Either a solemn nunnery or the court,

God or Lord Lacy. Which contents you best,

To be a nun or else Lord Lacy's wife?

LACY. A good motion.—Peggy, your answer must be short.

MAR. The flesh is frail; my lord doth know it well

That when he comes with his enchanting face,

Whate'er betide, I cannot say him nay.

Off goes the habit of a maiden's heart,

And, seeing fortune will, fair Framlingham,

And all the show of holy nuns, farewell!

Lacy for me, if he will be my lord.

LACY. Peggy, thy lord, thy love, thy husband.

Trust me, by truth of knighthood, that the king

Stays for to marry matchless Elinor,

Until I bring thee richly to the court,

That one day may both marry her and thee.—

How say'st thou, Keeper? Art thou glad of this?

KEEP. As if the English king had given

The park and deer of Fressingfield to me.

ERMS. I pray thee, my Lord of Sussex, why art thou in a brown study?

WAR. To see the nature of women; that be they never so near

God, yet they love to die in a man's arms.

LACY. What have you fit for breakfast? We have hied

And posted all this night to Fressingfield.

MAR. Butter and cheese, and umbles[68] of a deer,

Such as poor keepers have within their lodge.

LACY. And not a bottle of wine?

MAR. We'll find one for my lord.

LACY. Come, Sussex, let us in; we shall have more,

For she speaks least, to hold her promise sure.

(*Exeunt*)

[68] Liver, kidneys, etc.

Scene II. Friar Bacon's *Study*.

(*Enter a* Devil, *grumbling*)

Devil. How restless are the ghosts of hell-
  ish spirits,
When every charmer with his magic spells
Calls us from nine-fold-trenchéd Phlegethon,
To scud and over-scour the earth in post
Upon the speedy wings of swiftest winds!
Now Bacon hath raised me from the darkest
  deep,
To search about the world for Miles his man,
For Miles, and to torment his lazy bones
For careless watching of his Brazen Head.
                    (*Looking off stage*)
See where he comes. O, he is mine.

(*Enter* Miles *with a scholar's cap
and gown*)

Miles. (*Holding up his cap and gown in
disgust*) A scholar, quoth you! marry, sir, I
would I had been a bottle-maker when I was
made a scholar; for I can get neither to be
a deacon, reader, nor schoolmaster, no, not
the clerk of a parish. Some call me a dunce;
another saith, my head is as full of Latin as
an egg's full of oatmeal. Thus I am tormented, that the devil and Friar Bacon
haunt me.—Good Lord, here's one of my
master's devils! I'll go speak to him.—What,
master Plutus, how cheer you?

Dev. Dost thou know me?

Miles. Know you, sir! Why, are not you
one of my master's devils, that were wont to
come to my master, Doctor Bacon, at Brazen-
nose?

Dev. Yes, marry, am I.

Miles. Good Lord, Master Plutus, I have
seen you a thousand times at my master's,
and yet I had never the manners to make
you drink. But, sir, I am glad to see how con-
formable you are to the statute.—(*To the
audience*) I warrant you, he's as yeomanly a
man as you shall see; mark you, masters,
here's a plain, honest man, without welt or

guard.[60]—But I pray you, sir, do you come
lately from hell?

Dev. Ay, marry; how then?

Miles. Faith, 'tis a place I have desired
long to see. Have you not good tippling-
houses there? May not a man have a lusty
fire there, a pot of good ale, a pair of cards,
a swinging piece of chalk,[70] and a brown
toast that will clap a white waistcoat[71] on a
cup of good drink?

Dev. All this you may have there.

Miles. You are for me, friend, and I am
for you. But I pray you, may I not have an
office there?

Dev. Yes, a thousand. What wouldst thou
be?

Miles. By my troth, sir, in a place where
I may profit myself. I know hell is a hot
place, and men are marvelous dry, and much
drink is spent there; I would be a tapster.

Dev. Thou shalt.

Miles. There's nothing lets me from going with you, but that 'tis a long journey,
and I have never a horse.

Dev. Thou shalt ride on my back.

Miles. Now surely here's a courteous
devil, that, for to pleasure his friend, will not
stick to make a jade of himself.—But I pray
you, goodman friend, let me move a question
to you.

Dev. What's that?

Miles. I pray you, whether is your pace
a trot or an amble?

Dev. An amble.

Miles. 'Tis well; but take heed it be not
a trot: but 'tis no matter, I'll prevent it.
                    (*He buckles on a pair of spurs*)

Dev. What dost?

Miles. Marry, friend, I put on my spurs;
for if I find your pace either a trot or else
uneasy, I'll put you to a false gallop; I'll make
you feel the benefit of my spurs.

Dev. Get up upon my back. (Miles
  mounts on the Devil's *back*)

Miles. O Lord, here's even a goodly marvel, when a man rides to hell on the devil's
back! (*They caper about the stage and
exeunt roaring*)

[60] Trimmings or facings.
[70] For credit.
[71] Froth.

Scene III. *The Royal Palace.*

(*Enter a royal procession carrying symbolic devices: the* Emperor *with a pointless sword;* [72] *next the* King of Castile *carrying a sword with a point;* Lacy *carrying the* Globe; Prince Edward; Warren *carrying a rod of gold with a dove on it;* Ermsby *with a crown and scepter;* Princess Elinor *with* Margaret, *now Countess of Lincoln, on her left hand;* King Henry; Bacon; *with other* Lords *attending*)

P. Edw. Great potentates, earth's miracles
  for state,
Think that Prince Edward humbles at your
  feet,
And, for these favors, on his martial sword
He vows perpetual homage to yourselves,
Yielding these honors unto Elinor.
  K. Hen. Gramercies, lordings; old Plan-
    tagenet,
That rules and sways the Albion diadem,
With tears discovers these conceivéd joys,
And vows requital, if his men-at-arms,
The wealth of England, or due honors done
To Elinor, may 'quite his favorites.
But all this while what say you to the dames
That shine like to the crystal lamps of
  heaven?
  Emp. If but a third were added to these
    two,
They did surpass those gorgeous images [73]
That gloried Ida with rich beauty's wealth.
  Mar. 'Tis I, my lords, who humbly on my
    knee
Must yield her orisons to mighty Jove
For lifting up his handmaid to this state;
Brought from her homely cottage to the
  court,
And graced with kings, princes, and em-
  perors,
To whom (next to the noble Lincoln Earl)
I vow obedience, and such humble love
As may a handmaid to such mighty men.
  P. Elin. Thou martial man that wears the
    Almain crown,
And you the western potentates of might,

The Albion princess, English Edward's wife,
Proud that the lovely star of Fressingfield,
Fair Margaret, Countess to the Lincoln Earl,
Attends on Elinor,—gramercies, lord, for
  her,—
'Tis I give thanks for Margaret to you all,
And rest for her due bounden to yourselves.
  K. Hen. Seeing the marriage is solém-
    nized,
Let's march in triumph to the royal feast.—
But why stands Friar Bacon here so mute?
  Bacon. Repentant for the follies of my
    youth,
That magic's secret mysteries misled,
And joyful that this royal marriage
Portends such bliss unto this matchless realm.
  K. Hen. Why, Bacon,
What strange event shall happen to this
  land?
Or what shall grow from Edward and his
  queen?
  Bacon. I find by deep prescience of mine
    art, [74]
Which once I tempered in my secret cell,
That here where Brute did build his Troyno-
  vant, [75]
From forth the royal garden of a king
Shall flourish out so rich and fair a bud,
Whose brightness shall deface proud Phœ-
  bus' flower,
And over-shadow Albion with her leaves.
Till then Mars shall be master of the field,
But then the stormy threats of wars shall
  cease;
The horse shall stamp as careless of the pike,
Drums shall be turned to timbrels of delight;
With wealthy favors plenty shall enrich
The strand that gladded wandering Brute to
  see,
And peace from heaven shall harbor in these
  leaves
That gorgeous beautify this matchless flower;
Apollo's heliotropion then shall stoop,

---

[72] The pointless sword for mercy, the pointed for justice, and the rod of gold for equity.
[73] Minerva, Juno, and Venus.

[74] The audience was expected to recognize the following prophecy of Queen Elizabeth and her reign.
[75] There was a popular legend that the Trojan, Brutus, had founded London and first called it Troynovant.

And Venus' hyacinth shall vail her top;
Juno shall shut her gilliflowers up,
And Pallas' bay shall 'bash her brightest
     green;
Ceres' carnation, in consort with those,
Shall stoop and wonder at Diana's rose.
    K. HEN. This prophecy is mystical.—
But, glorious commanders of Europa's love,
That make fair England like that wealthy
     isle
Circled with Gihon and swift Euphrates,[76]
In royalizing Henry's Albion

[76] Paradise was supposedly circled by four rivers.

With presence of your princely mightiness,—
Let's march: the tables all are spread,
And viands, such as England's wealth affords,
Are ready set to furnish out the boards.
You shall have welcome, mighty potentates;
It rests to furnish up this royal feast,
Only your hearts be frolic; for the time
Craves that we taste of naught but jouissance.
Thus glories England over all the west.
                    (*Exeunt omnes*)

Omne tulit punctum qui miscuit utile dulci [77]

[77] "He has won every vote who has mingled profit with pleasure."—Greene's favorite motto.

CHRISTOPHER MARLOWE

Doctor Faustus

~~~~~~~~~~~~~~~~~~~~~~~~~

PRINCIPAL EVENTS IN MARLOWE'S LIFE

1564, 6 Feb., Christopher Marlowe, son of John Marlowe, a shoemaker, was born in Canterbury.

1576, The first commercial theatre, called *The Theatre,* built in London.

1579, 14 Jan., Christopher Marlowe entered King's School, Canterbury, on a scholarship.

1580, Autumn, He entered Corpus Christi College, Cambridge, and was elected to an Archbishop Parker Scholarship, which he held for seven years.

1584, Feb., Granted an A.B. degree by Cambridge University. Stayed on for his M.A.

1586-87, At some time in these years, according to a letter of the Privy Council to the University authorities, Marlowe rendered valuable service to the government. The character of the service is unknown, but the letter indicates that it was secret and important.

1587, Tamburlaine, Part I and Part II, acted in London with great success.

1589, 18 Sept., Marlowe fought a duel in London. His opponent was killed by Marlowe's friend William Watson, and Marlowe was imprisoned for a time.

c. 1589, The Jew of Malta acted.

c. 1592, Doctor Faustus acted with great success.

1592, 9 May, Marlowe was put under bond to keep the peace. Cause unknown.

c. 1592, Edward II acted.

1593, Jan., The Massacre at Paris acted at the Rose theatre.

1593, 12 May, Thomas Kyd charged that sensational free-thinking notes on religious matters found among his papers actually belonged to Marlowe.

1593, 20 May, Marlowe appeared before the Privy Council to answer Kyd's charges. He was freed on bail (an indication that the Privy Council did not think him particularly dangerous) and ordered to remain in or near London for further questioning.

1593, 30 May, Marlowe was killed by Ingram Frizer in a tavern fight at Deptford, a village near London.

1593, 28 June, A pardon was issued to Ingram Frizer on the grounds that he had killed Marlowe in self-defense.

1593, 28 Sept., Lucan's *Civil War,* Book I, translated by Marlowe, was entered for publication in the Stationers' Register. The only extant edition is dated 1600.

1594, Marlowe's *The Tragedy of Dido, Queen of Carthage,* printed. It had been acted by a boys' company at an unknown date.

c. 1595, Ovid's Elegies, translated by Marlowe, printed.

1598, Marlowe's *Hero and Leander,* completed by George Chapman, published.

INTRODUCTION

Doctor Faustus was first acted in London some time around 1592. The play was very popular for thirty years both in London and, as acted by English touring companies, in the provinces and in Germany, and for nearly two hundred years, in one form and another, it continued to be performed with some frequency. The great Elizabethan actor, Edward Alleyn, was famous for his performance in the leading rôle and may well have created the part.

This play is a mutilated masterpiece. The earliest extant edition was not published until eleven years after Marlowe's death, and in the meantime the play had been cut and revised and added to until the padding and miscellaneous horse play obscured the grand design which Marlowe had conceived. The reader is forced to wade through a great deal of slap-stick in order to follow the tragic progress of the learned doctor from great eminence to damnation. Yet, in spite of the scenes of crude farce, the tragedy of *Doctor Faustus* is an epochal one, deeply moving for all who can sift out the weak comedy and grasp the fundamental conceptions upon which Marlowe based his play.

Witchcraft was a very real thing for the people in Marlowe's audience; popular literature was full of accounts of witches and their practices, learned men were not infrequently accused of commerce with the devil, and the trials of witches often occupied the attention of the courts. A witch (that is, a man or woman who practised black magic) was supposed to obtain his spectacular powers from the devil and eventually to pay for them with his immortal soul. Men and women alleged to be witches were feared and hated by the people; Marlowe's account of the temptation of Doctor Faustus, his practice of the black arts, and his final payment of the inevitable penalty of damnation is not unusual in its subject matter, but it is unusual in the poet's sympathetic treatment of the great scholar and his intense realization of the human motives and the human suffering involved.

Marlowe has conceived a man exalted far above his fellows by his intense desire for knowledge in all fields of learning, a man who, at the opening of the play, has already extended his knowledge to the limits of human possibility. It is inevitable that such a man should hesitate only momentarily at the limits of human achievement when he could go so much further with diabolical assistance. It is likewise inevitable, according to the ideas of the time, that Faustus should pay, with his immortal soul, for the diabolical aid he had accepted. So much of the Faust story was current knowledge in the sixteenth century. Marlowe's great achievement is the intensity with which he has conceived and the effectiveness with which he has portrayed, through the medium of his *dramatic* blank verse, the exalted aspiration of Doctor Faustus, the supreme satisfaction which his diabolically attained knowledge brought him, the improbability that such a man could ever honestly repent having attained such powers, and the terrifying acceptance of his own damnation. Never before had an English play so vividly conveyed to an audience the essential realities of a human soul in terrible conflict with universal law. And in spite of the change in our conception of universal laws, in spite of the vulgarizing by the play's revisers of many of the scenes of Faustus' temptation and Faustus' power, in spite of the disappearance of much of Marlowe's original work, the mutilated tragedy still has for the perceptive reader those elements of universal tragic significance which made it four-centuries ago an epochal play.

DOCTOR FAUSTUS

Dramatis personae

In order of first appearance

CHORUS, The speaker of the prologue, or chorus.

DOCTOR JOHN FAUSTUS, A learned scholar and scientist of the University of Wittenberg.

WAGNER, His servant. Wagner has picked up a smattering of learning from his master, but he is essentially naive and uneducated.

GOOD ANGEL, Really a personification of Faustus' good impulses. He appears only to Faustus.

EVIL ANGEL, A personification of Faustus' bad impulses.

VALDES, A German scholar and friend of Faustus.

CORNELIUS, Another German scholar and friend of Faustus.

FIRST SCHOLAR, A student of Faustus' at Wittenberg.

SECOND SCHOLAR, Another student of Faustus'.

MEPHISTOPHILIS, A Prince of Hell who conducts the negotiations for Faustus' soul and who, in payment of his part of the bargain, acts as Faustus' supernatural servant.

CLOWN, A stupid country fellow.

DEVILS

LUCIFER ⎫ Princes of Hell.
BELZEBUB ⎭

SEVEN DEADLY SINS, Personifications of Pride, Covetousness, Wrath, Envy, Gluttony, Sloth, and Lechery.

THE POPE

CARDINAL OF LORRAIN

FRIARS, Attendants of the Pope.

ROBIN, The hostler at an inn.

RALPH, A fellow servant at the inn.

VINTNER, Keeper of a tavern.

EMPEROR, Charles V, Emperor of Germany.

KNIGHT, One of the Emperor's court.

ALEXANDER THE GREAT, Really a spirit who appears as Alexander.

ALEXANDER'S PARAMOUR, A spirit in her likeness.

HORSE-COURSER, A horse dealer.

DUKE OF VANHOLT

DUCHESS OF VANHOLT

THIRD SCHOLAR, A student of Faustus' at Wittenberg.

HELEN OF TROY, A spirit in the image of Helen.

OLD MAN

SCENE: *Wittenberg, Rome, Court of Charles V, and Vanholt (i.e. Anholt)*

(*Enter* CHORUS)

CHORUS. Not marching now in fields of Thrasimene,
Where Mars did mate the warlike Carthagens;
Nor sporting in the dalliance of love,
In courts of kings where state is overturn'd;
Nor in the pomp of proud audacious deeds,
Intends our Muse to vaunt his heavenly verse:
Only this, gentles,—we must now perform
The form of Faustus' fortunes, good or bad.
And now to patient judgments we appeal,
And speak for Faustus in his infancy.
Now is he born, of parents base of stock,
In Germany, within a town call'd Rhodes;
At riper years to Wittenberg he went,
Whereas his kinsmen chiefly brought him up.
So much he profits in divinity,
The fruitful plot of scholarism grac'd,
That shortly he was grac'd with Doctor's name,

Excelling all whose sweet delight disputes
In heavenly matters of theology;
Till swoll'n with cunning, of a self-conceit,
His waxen wings did mount above his reach,
And, melting, Heavens conspir'd his over-
    throw;
For, falling to a devilish exercise,

And glutted now with learning's golden gifts,
He surfeits upon cursed necromancy;
Nothing so sweet as magic is to him,
Which he prefers before his chiefest bliss.
And this the man that in his study sits!
(*He pulls aside the curtain to the inner stage
    to reveal* FAUSTUS *in his study. Exit*)

Act I

SCENE I. FAUSTUS' *Study.*

(FAUSTUS *is seated before a table piled with
    books and manuscripts*)

FAUST. Settle thy studies, Faustus, and
    begin
To sound the depth of that thou wilt profess;
Having commenc'd, be a divine in show,
Yet level [1] at the end of every art,
And live and die in Aristotle's works.
Sweet Analytics, 'tis thou hast ravish'd me,
Bene disserere est finis logices.
Is to dispute well logic's chiefest end?
Affords this art no greater miracle?
Then read no more, thou hast attain'd that
    end;
A greater subject fitteth Faustus' wit.
Bid ὂν καὶ μὴ ὄν farewell; Galen come,
Seeing *Ubi desinit Philosophus, ibi incipit
    Medicus;* [2]
Be a physician, Faustus, heap up gold,
And be eternis'd for some wondrous cure.
Summum bonum medicinæ sanitas,
"The end of physic is our body's health."
Why, Faustus, hast thou not attain'd that
    end?
Is not thy common talk sound Aphorisms?
Are not thy bills hung up as monuments,
Whereby whole cities have escap'd the
    plague,
And thousand desperate maladies been eas'd?
Yet art thou still but Faustus and a man.
Couldst thou make men to live eternally,
Or, being dead, raise them to life again?
Then this profession were to be esteem'd.
Physic, farewell. Where is Justinian?
       (*He picks up a book and reads*)

[1] Aim.
[2] Where the philosopher ends, there the physician begins.

*Si una eademque res legatur duobus, alter
    rem, alter valorem rei,* [3]
A pretty case of paltry legacies!   (*Reads*)
Exhæreditare filium non potest pater nisi [4]—
Such is the subject of the Institute
And universal body of the law.
His study fits a mercenary drudge,
Who aims at nothing but external trash;
Too servile and illiberal for me. (*He puts
    down the book and takes another*)
When all is done, divinity is best;
Jerome's Bible, Faustus, view it well.
                   (*Reads*)
Stipendium peccati mors est. Ha! *Stipen-
    dium—&.*
"The reward of sin is death." That's hard.
                   (*Reads*)
*Si peccasse negamus, fallimur, et nulla est
    in nobis veritas.*
"If we say that we have no sin we deceive
ourselves, and there's no truth in us." Why
then, belike we must sin and so consequently
die.
Ay, we must die an everlasting death.
What doctrine call you this, *Che sera, sera,*
"What will be shall be"? Divinity, adieu!
    (*Puts down the book and takes a third*)
These metaphysics of magicians
And necromantic books are heavenly;
Lines, circles, scenes, letters, and characters,
Ay, these are those that Faustus most desires.
O what a world of profit and delight,
Of power, of honor, of omnipotence
Is promis'd to the studious artisan!

[3] If one and the same thing is willed to two
people, one shall take the thing and the other
its value.
[4] A father cannot disinherit his son, unless. . . .

All things that move between the quiet poles
Shall be at my command. Emperors and
  kings
Are but obeyed in their several provinces,
Nor can they raise the wind or rend the
  clouds;
But his dominion that exceeds in this,
Stretcheth as far as doth the mind of man.
A sound magician is a demi-god:
Here, Faustus, try thy brains to gain a deity.
(*Calling*) Wagner!

(*Enter* WAGNER)

Wagner, commend me to my dearest friends,
The German Valdes and Cornelius;
Request them earnestly to visit me.
  WAG. I will, sir.   (*Exit*)
  FAUST. Their conference will be a greater
  help to me
Than all my labors, plod I ne'er so fast.

(*Enter* GOOD ANGEL *and* EVIL ANGEL)

  G. ANG. O Faustus! lay that damned book
  aside,
And gaze not on it lest it tempt thy soul,
And heap God's heavy wrath upon thy head.
Read, read the Scriptures: that is blasphemy.
  E. ANG. Go forward, Faustus, in that
  famous art,
Wherein all Nature's treasure is contain'd:
Be thou on earth as Jove is in the sky,
Lord and commander of these elements.
               (*Exeunt* ANGELS)
  FAUST. How am I glutted with conceit
  of this!
Shall I make spirits fetch me what I please,
Resolve me of all ambiguities,
Perform what desperate enterprise I will?
I'll have them fly to India for gold,
Ransack the ocean for orient pearl,
And search all corners of the new-found
  world
For pleasant fruits and princely delicates;
I'll have them read me strange philosophy
And tell the secrets of all foreign kings;
I'll have them wall all Germany with brass,
And make swift Rhine circle fair Wittenberg;
I'll have them fill the public schools with
  [silk],
Wherewith the students shall be bravely
  clad;

I'll levy soldiers with the coin they bring,
And chase the Prince of Parma from our
  land,
And reign sole king of all the provinces;
Yea, stranger engines for the brunt of war
Than was the fiery keel at Antwerp's bridge,
I'll make my servile spirits to invent.
               (*He calls*)
Come, German Valdes and Cornelius,
And make me blest with your sage confer-
  ence.

(*Enter* VALDES *and* CORNELIUS)

Valdes, sweet Valdes, and Cornelius,
Know that your words have won me at the
  last
To practise magic and concealed arts:
Yet not your words only, but mine own
  fantasy,
That will receive no object; for my head
But ruminates on necromantic skill.
Philosophy is odious and obscure;
Both law and physic are for petty wits;
Divinity is basest of the three,
Unpleasant, harsh, contemptible, and vile:
'Tis magic, magic, that hath ravish'd me.
Then, gentle friends, aid me in this attempt;
And I, that have with subtle syllogisms
Gravell'd the pastors of the German church,
And made the flow'ring pride of Wittenberg
Swarm to my problems, as the infernal spirits
On sweet Musæus, when he came to hell,
Will be as cunning as Agrippa was,
Whose shadows made all Europe honor him.
  VALD. Faustus, these books, thy wit, and
  our experience
Shall make all nations to canónise us.
As Indian Moors obey their Spanish lords,
So shall the spirits of every element
Be always serviceable to us three;
Like lions shall they guard us when we
  please;
Like Almain rutters with their horsemen's
  staves,
Or Lapland giants, trotting by our sides;
Sometimes like women or unwedded maids,
Shadowing more beauty in their airy brows
Than have the white breasts of the Queen of
  Love.
From Venice shall they drag huge argosies,
And from America the golden fleece
That yearly stuffs old Philip's treasury;

If learned Faustus will be resolute.

FAUST. Valdes, as resolute am I in this
As thou to live; therefore object it not.

CORN. The miracles that magic will per-
form
Will make thee vow to study nothing else.
He that is grounded in astrology,
Enrich'd with tongues, well seen in minerals,
Hath all the principles magic doth require.
Then doubt not, Faustus, but to be renown'd,
And more frequented for this mystery
Than heretofore the Delphian oracle.
The spirits tell me they can dry the sea,
And fetch the treasure of all foreign wrecks,
Yea, all the wealth that our forefathers hid
Within the massy entrails of the earth.
Then tell me, Faustus, what shall we three
want?

FAUST. Nothing, Cornelius! O this cheers
my soul!
Come, show me some demonstrations magical,

That I may conjure in some bushy grove,
And have these joys in full possession.

VALD. Then haste thee to some solitary
grove,
And bear wise Bacon's and Albanus's works,
The Hebrew Psalter and New Testament;
And whatsoever else is requisite
We will inform thee ere our conference cease.

CORN. Valdes, first let him know the words
of art;
And then, all other ceremonies learn'd,
Faustus may try his cunning by himself.

VALD. First I'll instruct thee in the rudiments,
And then wilt thou be perfecter than I.

FAUST. Then come and dine with me, and
after meat,
We'll canvass every quiddity⁵ thereof;
For ere I sleep I'll try what I can do.
This night I'll conjure though I die therefore.
(*Exeunt*)

SCENE II. *Before* FAUSTUS' *House.*

(*Enter two* SCHOLARS)

1 SCHOL. I wonder what's become of
Faustus that was wont to make our schools
ring with *sic probo?*

(*Enter* WAGNER *carrying wine*)

2 SCHOL. That shall we know, for see here
comes his boy.

1 SCHOL. How now, sirrah! Where's thy
master?

WAG. God in heaven knows!

2 SCHOL. Why, dost not thou know?

WAG. Yes, I know; but that follows not.

1 SCHOL. Go to, sirrah! Leave your jesting,
and tell us where he is.

WAG. That follows not necessary by force
of argument, that you, being licentiate,
should stand upon't: therefore, acknowledge
your error and be attentive.

2 SCHOL. Why, didst thou not say thou
knew'st?

WAG. Have you any witness on't?

1 SCHOL. Yes, sirrah, I heard you.

WAG. Ask my fellow if I be a thief.

2 SCHOL. Well, you will not tell us?

WAG. Yes, sir, I will tell you; yet if you
were not dunces, you would never ask me
such a question; for is not he *corpus naturale?*
and is not that *mobile?* Then wherefore
should you ask me such a question? But that
I am by nature phlegmatic, slow to wrath,
and prone to lechery (to love, I would say),
it were not for you to come within forty foot
of the place of execution, although I do not
doubt but to see you both hang'd the next
sessions. Thus having triumph'd over you,
I will set my countenance like a precisian,⁶
and begin to speak thus:—Truly, my dear
brethren, my master is within at dinner, with
Valdes and Cornelius, as this wine, if it could
speak, would inform your worships; and so
the Lord bless you, preserve you, and keep
you, my dear brethren, my dear brethren.
(*Exit*)

1 SCHOL. O Faustus! Then I fear that
which I have long suspected, that thou art
fallen into that damned Art, for which they
two are infamous through the world.

2 SCHOL. Were he a stranger, and not

⁵ Essential point.   ⁶ Puritan.

allied to me, yet should I grieve for him. But come, let us go and inform the Rector, and see if he by his grave counsel can reclaim him.

1 SCHOL. Oh, but I fear me nothing can reclaim him.

2 SCHOL. Yet let us try what we can do.

(*Exeunt*)

SCENE III. *A Grove.*

(*Enter* FAUSTUS *in a long robe and carrying a wand to begin his magic conjurations*)

FAUST. Now that the gloomy shadow of the night,
Longing to view Orion's drizzling look,
Leaps from th' antarctic world unto the sky,
And dims the welkin with her pitchy breath,
Faustus, begin thine incantations,
And try if devils will obey thy hest,
Seeing thou hast pray'd and sacrific'd to
    them. (*He draws a circle about him on
    the ground and writes the magic words
    in it as he speaks*)
Within this circle is Jehovah's name,
Forward and backward anagrammatis'd,
The breviated names of holy saints,
Figures of every adjunct to the Heavens,
And characters of signs and erring stars,
By which the spirits are enforc'd to rise.
Then fear not, Faustus, but be resolute,
And try the utmost magic can perform.

(*Thunder*)

*Sint mihi Dei Acherontis propitii! Valeat
numen triplex Jehovae! Ignei, aerii, aquatani
spiritus, salvete! Orientis princeps Belzebub,
inferni ardentis monarcha, et Demogorgon,
propitiamus vos, ut appareat et surgat Mephistophilis. Quid tu moraris? Per Jehovam,
Gehennam, et consecratum aquam quam
nunc spargo, signumque crucis quod nunc
facio, et per vota nostra, ipse nunc surgat
nobis dicatus Mephistophilis!*[7]

(*Enter* [MEPHISTOPHILIS] *a hideous Devil*)

[7] Be propitious to me, Gods of Acheron! May the triple name of Jehovah prevail! Spirits of fire, air, and water hail! Belzebub, Prince of the East, Sovereign of Burning Hell, and Demogorgon, we propitiate you, that Mephistophilis may appear and rise. Why delayest thou? By Jehovah, Gehenna, and the holy water which now I sprinkle, and the sign of the cross which now I make, and by our prayer, may Mephistophilis, summoned by us, now arise!

(*Startled*) I charge thee to return and change
    thy shape;
Thou art too ugly to attend on me.
Go, and return an old Franciscan friar;
That holy shape becomes a devil best.

(*Exit* DEVIL)

I see there's virtue in my heavenly words;
Who would not be proficient in this art?
How pliant is this Mephistophilis,
Full of obedience and humility!
Such is the force of magic and my spells.
[Now,] Faustus, thou art conjuror laureate,
Thou canst command great Mephistophilis:
Quin redis Mephistophilis fratris imagine.[8]

(*Re-enter* MEPHISTOPHILIS *in the shape of
    a Franciscan Friar*)

MEPH. Now, Faustus, what would'st thou have me do?

FAUST. I charge thee wait upon me whilst I live,
To do whatever Faustus shall command,
Be it to make the moon drop from her sphere,
Or the ocean to overwhelm the world.

MEPH. I am a servant to great Lucifer,
And may not follow thee without his leave;
No more than he commands must we per-
    form.

FAUST. Did he not charge thee to appear to me?

MEPH. No, I came hither of mine own accord.

FAUST. Did not my conjuring speeches raise thee? Speak!

MEPH. That was the cause, but yet *per
    accidens*;
For when we hear one rack[8a] the name of
    God,
Abjure the Scriptures and his Savior Christ,
We fly, in hope to get his glorious soul;

[8] Why do you not return, Mephistophilis, in the image of a friar?

[8a] Torture into anagrams.

Nor will we come, unless he use such means
Whereby he is in danger to be damn'd.
Therefore the shortest cut for conjuring
Is stoutly to abjure the Trinity,
And pray devoutly to the Prince of Hell.

FAUST. So Faustus hath
Already done; and holds this principle,
There is no chief but only Belzebub,
To whom Faustus doth dedicate himself.
This word "damnation" terrifies not him,
For he confounds hell in Elysium;
His ghost be with the old philosophers!
But, leaving these vain trifles of men's souls,
Tell me what is that Lucifer thy lord?

MEPH. Arch-regent and commander of
all spirits.

FAUST. Was not that Lucifer an angel
once?

MEPH. Yes, Faustus, and most dearly lov'd
of God.

FAUST. How comes it then that he is
prince of devils?

MEPH. O, by aspiring pride and insolence;
For which God threw him from the face of
Heaven.

FAUST. And what are you that you live
with Lucifer?

MEPH. Unhappy spirits that fell with
Lucifer,
Conspir'd against our God with Lucifer,
And are for ever damn'd with Lucifer.

FAUST. Where are you damn'd?

MEPH. In hell.

FAUST. How comes it then that thou art
out of hell?

MEPH. Why this is hell, nor am I out of it.
Think'st thou that I, who saw the face of
God,
And tasted the eternal joys of Heaven,

Am not tormented with ten thousand hells,
In being depriv'd of everlasting bliss?
O Faustus! leave these frivolous demands,
Which strike a terror to my fainting soul!

FAUST. What, is great Mephistophilis so
passionate
For being depriv'd of the joys of Heaven?
Learn thou of Faustus manly fortitude,
And scorn those joys thou never shalt possess.
Go, bear these tidings to great Lucifer:
Seeing Faustus hath incurr'd eternal death
By desperate thoughts against Jove's deity,
Say he surrenders up to him his soul,
So he will spare him four and twenty years,
Letting him live in all voluptuousness;
Having thee ever to attend on me;
To give me whatsoever I shall ask,
To tell me whatsoever I demand,
To slay mine enemies, and aid my friends,
And always be obedient to my will.
Go, and return to mighty Lucifer,
And meet me in my study at midnight,
And then resolve me of thy master's mind.

MEPH. I will, Faustus.   (*Exit*)

FAUST. (*Exultantly*) Had I as many souls
as there be stars,
I'd give them all for Mephistophilis.
By him I'll be great emperor of the world,
And make a bridge through the moving air,
To pass the ocean with a band of men;
I'll join the hills that bind the Afric shore,
And make that country continent to Spain,
And both contributory to my crown.
The Emperor shall not live but by my leave,
Nor any potentate of Germany.
Now that I have obtain'd what I desire,
I'll live in speculation of this art
Till Mephistophilis return again.   (*Exit*)

SCENE IV. *A field near Wittenberg.*

(*Enter* WAGNER *and the* CLOWN)

WAG. Sirrah, boy, come hither.

CLOWN. How, "boy"! Swowns, "boy"! I
hope you have seen many boys with such
pickadevaunts° as I have. "Boy," quotha!

WAG. Tell me, sirrah, hast thou any com-
ings in?

° Pointed beards.

CLOWN. Ay, and goings out too. You may
see else.

WAG. Alas, poor slave! See how poverty
jesteth in his nakedness! The villain is bare
and out of service, and so hungry that I know
he would give his soul to the devil for a shoulder of mutton, though it were blood-raw.

CLOWN. How? My soul to the Devil for
a shoulder of mutton, though 'twere blood-
raw! Not so, good friend. By'r Lady, I had

need have it well roasted and good sauce to it, if I pay so dear.

WAG. Well, wilt thou serve me, and I'll make thee go like *Qui mihi discipulus?* [10]

CLOWN. How, in verse?

WAG. No, sirrah; in beaten silk and stavesacre. [11]

CLOWN. How, how, Knave's acre! Ay, I thought that was all the land his father left him. Do you hear? I would be sorry to rob you of your living.

WAG. Sirrah, I say in stavesacre.

CLOWN. Oho! Oho! Stavesacre! Why, then, belike if I were your man I should be full of vermin.

WAG. So thou shalt, whether thou beest with me or no. But, sirrah, leave your jesting, and bind yourself presently unto me for seven years, or I'll turn all the lice about thee into familiars, and they shall tear thee in pieces.

CLOWN. Do you hear, sir? You may save that labor; they are too familiar with me already. Swowns! they are as bold with my flesh as if they had paid for my meat and drink.

WAG. Well, do you hear, sirrah? Hold, take these guilders.   (*Gives money*)

CLOWN. Gridirons! what be they?

WAG. Why, French crowns.

CLOWN. Mass, but for the name of French crowns, a man were as good have as many English counters. And what should I do with these?

WAG. Why, now, sirrah, thou art at an hour's warning, whensoever or wheresoever the Devil shall fetch thee.

CLOWN. No, no. Here, take your gridirons again.

WAG. Truly I'll none of them.

CLOWN. Truly but you shall.

WAG. Bear witness I gave them him.

CLOWN. Bear witness I give them you again.

WAG. Well, I will cause two devils pres-

ently to fetch thee away—(*calling*) Baliol and Belcher.

CLOWN. Let your Baliol and your Belcher come here, and I'll knock them, they were never so knockt since they were devils. Say I should kill one of them, what would folks say? "Do you see yonder tall fellow in the round slop?—he has kill'd the devil." So I should be call'd Kill-devil all the parish over.

WAG. (*Calling again*) Baliol and Belcher! (*Enter two Devils: the* CLOWN *runs up and down crying*) Spirits, away!

(*Exeunt Devils*)

CLOWN. What, are they gone? A vengeance on them, they have vile long nails! There was a he-devil, and a she-devil! I'll tell you how you shall know them: all he-devils has horns, and all she-devils has clifts and cloven feet.

WAG. Well, sirrah, follow me.

CLOWN. But, do you hear—if I should serve you, would you teach me to raise up Banios and Belcheos?

WAG. I will teach thee to turn thyself to anything; to a dog, or a cat, or a mouse, or a rat, or anything.

CLOWN. How! a Christian fellow to a dog or a cat, a mouse or a rat! No, no, sir. If you turn me into anything, let it be in the likeness of a little pretty frisking flea, that I may be here and there and everywhere. Oh, I'll tickle the pretty wenches' plackets; I'll be amongst them, i' faith.

WAG. Well, sirrah, come.

CLOWN. But, do you hear, Wagner?

WAG. How!—Baliol and Belcher!

CLOWN. O Lord! I pray, sir, let Banio and Belcher go sleep.

WAG. Villain—call me Master Wagner, and let thy left eye be diametarily fixt upon my right heel, with *quasi vestigias nostras insistere.* [12]   (*Exit*)

CLOWN. God forgive me, he speaks Dutch fustian. Well, I'll follow him; I'll serve him, that's flat.   (*Exit*)

[10] *I.e.* a model scholar.   [11] A lice repellent.   [12] As if to tread in our tracks.

Act II

Scene I. Faustus' *Study*.

(*The curtains of the inner stage are drawn aside to reveal* Faustus *in his study as in* I, 1)

Faust. Now, Faustus, must
Thou needs be damn'd, and canst thou not
be sav'd:
What boots it then to think of God or
Heaven?
Away with such vain fancies, and despair:
Despair in God, and trust in Belzebub.
Now go not backward: no, Faustus, be reso-
lute.
Why waverest thou? O, something soundeth
in mine ears
"Abjure this magic, turn to God again!"
Ay, and Faustus will turn to God again.
To God? He loves thee not;
The God thou serv'st is thine own appetite,
Wherein is fix'd the love of Belzebub;
To him I'll build an altar and a church,
And offer lukewarm blood of new-born
babes.

(*Enter* Good Angel *and* Evil Angel)

E. Ang. Go forward, Faustus, in that fa-
mous art.
G. Ang. Sweet Faustus, leave that ex-
ecrable art.
Faust. Contrition, prayer, repentance!
What of them?
G. Ang. O, they are means to bring thee
unto Heaven.
E. Ang. Rather illusions, fruits of lunacy,
That make them foolish that do use them
most.
G. Ang. Sweet Faustus, think of Heaven,
and heavenly things.
E. Ang. No, Faustus; think of honor and
of wealth.   (*Exeunt* Angels)
Faust. Of wealth!
Why, the signiory of Emden shall be mine.
When Mephistophilis shall stand by me,
What God can hurt me? Faustus, thou art
safe;
Cast no more doubts. Come, Mephistophilis,

And bring glad tidings from great Lucifer!—
Is't not midnight? Come, Mephistophilis;
Veni, veni, Mephistophile!

(*Enter* Mephistophilis)

Now tell me, what says Lucifer thy lord?
  Meph. That I shall wait on Faustus whilst
    he lives,
So he will buy my service with his soul.
  Faust. Already Faustus hath hazarded
that for thee.
  Meph. But now thou must bequeath it
    solemnly,
And write a deed of gift with thine own
blood,
For that security craves Lucifer.
If thou deny it, I must back to hell.
  Faust. Stay, Mephistophilis! and tell me
    what good
Will my soul do thy lord.
  Meph. Enlarge his kingdom.
  Faust. Is that the reason why he tempts
us thus?
  Meph. *Solamen miseris socios habuisse
doloris.*[13]
  Faust. Why, have you any pain that
torture others?
  Meph. As great as have the human souls
    of men.
But tell me, Faustus, shall I have thy soul?
And I will be thy slave, and wait on thee,
And give thee more than thou hast wit to ask.
  Faust. Ay, Mephistophilis, I give it thee.
  Meph. Then Faustus, stab thine arm
    courageously,
And bind thy soul that at some certain day
Great Lucifer may claim it as his own;
And then be thou as great as Lucifer.
  Faust. (*Takes up a knife and stabs his
    arm*) Lo, Mephistophilis, for love of
    thee,
I cut mine arm, and with my proper blood
Assure my soul to be great Lucifer's,
Chief lord and regent of perpetual night!

[13] Misery loves company.

View here this blood that trickles from mine arm,
And let it be propitious for my wish.

MEPH. But, Faustus, thou must
Write it in manner of a deed of gift.

FAUST. Ay, so I will. (*Dips a pen in his blood and writes*) But, Mephistophilis,
My blood congeals, and I can write no more.

MEPH. I'll fetch thee fire to dissolve it straight. (*Exit*)

FAUST. What might the staying of my blood portend?
Is it unwilling I should write this bill?
Why streams it not that I may write afresh?
"Faustus gives to thee his soul." Ah, there it stay'd.
Why should'st thou not? Is not thy soul thine own?
Then write again, "Faustus gives to thee his soul."

(*Re-enter* MEPHISTOPHILIS *with a chafer of coals*)

MEPH. Here's fire. Come, Faustus, set it on.

FAUST. So, now the blood begins to clear again;
Now will I make an end immediately. (*Writes*)

MEPH. (*Aside*) O what will not I do to obtain his soul.

FAUST. *Consummatum est:* this bill is ended,
And Faustus hath bequeath'd his soul to Lucifer.
But what is this inscription on mine arm?
Homo, fuge! Whither should I fly?
If unto God, he'll throw me down to hell.
My senses are deceiv'd; here's nothing writ:—
O yes, I see it plain; even here is writ,
Homo fuge! Yet shall not Faustus fly.

MEPH. (*Aside*) I'll fetch him somewhat to delight his mind. (*Exit*)

(*Re-enter* MEPHISTOPHILIS *with* DEVILS, *who give crowns and rich apparel to* FAUSTUS, *and dance, and then depart*)

FAUST. Speak, Mephistophilis, what means this show?

MEPH. Nothing, Faustus, but to delight thy mind,
And let thee see what magic can perform.

FAUST. But may I raise up spirits when I please?

MEPH. Ay, Faustus, and do greater things than these.

FAUST. Then there's enough for a thousand souls.
Here, Mephistophilis, receive this scroll,
A deed of gift of body and of soul:
But yet conditionally that thou perform
All articles prescrib'd between us both.

MEPH. Faustus, I swear by hell and Lucifer
To effect all promises between us made.

FAUST. Then hear me read them:
On these conditions following. First, that Faustus may be a spirit in form and substance. Secondly, that Mephistophilis shall be his servant, and at his command. Thirdly, that Mephistophilis shall do for him and bring him whatsoever [he desires]. Fourthly, that he shall be in his chamber or house invisible. Lastly, that he shall appear to the said John Faustus, at all times, in what form or shape soever he please. I, John Faustus, of Wittenberg, Doctor, by these presents do give both body and soul to Lucifer, Prince of the East, and his minister, Mephistophilis; and furthermore grant unto them that, twenty-four years being expired, the articles above written being inviolate, full power to fetch or carry the said John Faustus, body and soul, flesh, blood, or goods, into their habitation wheresoever. By me, JOHN FAUSTUS.

MEPH. Speak, Faustus, do you deliver this as your deed?

FAUST. Ay, take it, and the Devil give thee good on't.

MEPH. Now, Faustus, ask what thou wilt.

FAUST. First will I question with thee about hell.
Tell me, where is the place that men call hell?

MEPH. Under the heavens.

FAUST. Ay, but whereabout?

MEPH. Within the bowels of these elements,
Where we are tortur'd and remain for ever.
Hell hath no limits, nor is circumscrib'd
In one self place; for where we are is hell,
And where hell is, there must we ever be:

And, to conclude, when all the world dis-
    solves,
And every creature shall be purified,
All places shall be hell that is not Heaven.
    FAUST. Come, I think hell's a fable.
    MEPH. Ay, think so, till experience change
thy mind.
    FAUST. Why, think'st thou then that Faus-
tus shall be damn'd?
    MEPH. Ay, of necessity, for here's the
    scroll
Wherein thou hast given thy soul to Lucifer.
    FAUST. Ay, and body too; but what of
    that?
Think'st thou that Faustus is so fond to
    imagine
That, after this life, there is any pain?
Tush! these are trifles, and mere old wives'
    tales.
    MEPH. But, Faustus, I am an instance to
    prove the contrary,
For I am damned, and am now in hell.
    FAUST. How! now in hell!
Nay, an this be hell, I'll willingly be damn'd
    here.
What! Sleeping, eating, walking, and dis-
    puting?
But, leaving off this, let me have a wife,
The fairest maid in Germany;
For I am wanton and lascivious,
And cannot live without a wife.
    MEPH. How—a wife?
I prithee, Faustus, talk not of a wife.
    FAUST. Nay, sweet Mephistophilis, fetch
me one, for I will have one.

    MEPH. Well, thou wilt have one. Sit there
    till I come:
I'll fetch thee a wife in the Devil's name.
                                    (*Exit*)

(*Re-enter* MEPHISTOPHILIS *with a Devil
dressed like a woman. Fireworks shoot from
her*)

    FAUST. (*Startled*) What sight is this?
    MEPH. Now, Faustus, wilt thou have a
wife?
    FAUST. A plague on her for a hot whore!
    MEPH. Tut, Faustus,
Marriage is but a ceremonial toy;
And if thou lovest me, think no more of it.
I'll cull thee out the fairest courtesans,
And bring them every morning to thy bed;
She whom thine eye shall like, thy heart
    shall have,
Be she as chaste as was Penelope,
As wise as Saba, or as beautiful
As was bright Lucifer before his fall. (*Gives*
    FAUSTUS *a book*)
Here, take this book, peruse it thoroughly:
(*Pointing out passages in the book*) The iter-
    ating of these lines brings gold;
The framing of this circle on the ground
Brings whirlwinds, tempests, thunder and
    lightning;
Pronounce this thrice devoutly to thyself,
And men in armor shall appear to thee,
Ready to execute what thou desir'st.
    FAUST. Thanks, Mephistophilis, for this
sweet book. This will I keep as chary as my
life.   (*Exeunt*)

SCENE II. FAUSTUS' *Study.*

(*Enter* FAUSTUS *and* MEPHISTOPHILIS)

    FAUST. When I behold the heavens, then
    I repent,
And curse thee, wicked Mephistophilis,
Because thou hast depriv'd me of those joys.
    MEPH. Why, Faustus,
Think'st thou Heaven is such a glorious
    thing?
I tell thee 'tis not half so fair as thou,
Or any man that breathes on earth.
    FAUST. How prov'st thou that?
    MEPH. 'Twas made for man, therefore is
    man more excellent.

    FAUST. If it were made for man, 'twas
    made for me;
I will renounce this magic and repent.

(*Enter* GOOD ANGEL *and* EVIL ANGEL)

    G. ANG. Faustus, repent; yet God will pity
thee.
    E. ANG. Thou art a spirit; God cannot
pity thee.
    FAUST. Who buzzeth in mine ears, I am
    a spirit?
Be I a devil, yet God may pity me;
Ay, God will pity me if I repent.

E. Ang. Ay, but Faustus never shall repent.   (*Exeunt* Angels)

Faust. My heart's so hard'ned I cannot repent.
Scarce can I name salvation, faith, or heaven,
But fearful echoes thunder in mine ears
"Faustus, thou art damn'd!" Then swords and knives,
Poison, guns, halters, and envenom'd steel
Are laid before me to despatch myself;
And long ere this I should have slain myself,
Had not sweet pleasure conquer'd deep despair.
Have I not made blind Homer sing to me
Of Alexander's love and Œnon's death?
And hath not he that built the walls of Thebes
With ravishing sound of his melodious harp,
Made music with my Mephistophilis?
Why should I die then, or basely despair?
I am resolv'd: Faustus shall ne'er repent.
Come, Mephistophilis, let us dispute again,
And reason of divine astrology.
Speak, are there many heavens above the moon?
Are all celestial bodies but one globe,
As is the substance of this centric earth?

Meph. As are the elements, such are the spheres
Mutually folded in each other's orb,
And, Faustus,
All jointly move upon one axletree
Whose terminine is term'd the world's wide pole;
Nor are the names of Saturn, Mars, or Jupiter
Feign'd, but are erring stars.

Faust. But tell me, have they all one motion, both *situ et tempore?* [14]

Meph. All jointly move from east to west in four-and-twenty hours upon the poles of the world; but differ in their motion upon the poles of the zodiac.

Faust. Tush!
These slender trifles Wagner can decide.
Hath Mephistophilis no greater skill?
Who knows not the double motion of the planets?
The first is finish'd in a natural day;
The second thus: Saturn in thirty years;
Jupiter in twelve; Mars in four; the Sun,
Venus, and Mercury in a year; the moon in

[14] In space and time.

twenty-eight days. Tush, these are freshmen's questions. But tell me, hath every sphere a dominion or *intelligentia?* [15]

Meph. Ay.

Faust. How many heavens, or spheres, are there?

Meph. Nine: the seven planets, the firmament, and the empyreal heaven.

Faust. Well, resolve me in this question: Why have we not conjunctions, oppositions, aspects, eclipses, all at one time, but in some years we have more, in some less?

Meph. *Per inæqualem motum respecta totius.* [16]

Faust. Well, I am answer'd. Tell me who made the world.

Meph. I will not.

Faust. Sweet Mephistophilis, tell me.

Meph. Move me not, for I will not tell thee.

Faust. Villain, have I not bound thee to tell me anything?

Meph. Ay, that is not against our kingdom; but this is.
Think thou on hell, Faustus, for thou art damn'd.

Faust. Think, Faustus, upon God that made the world.

Meph. Remember this.   (*Exit*)

Faust. Ay, go, accursed spirit, to ugly hell!
(*Fearfully*) 'Tis thou hast damn'd distressed Faustus' soul.
Is't not too late?

(*Re-enter* Good Angel *and* Evil Angel)

E. Ang. Too late.

G. Ang. Never too late, if Faustus can repent.

E. Ang. If thou repent, devils shall tear thee in pieces.

G. Ang. Repent, and they shall never raze thy skin.   (*Exeunt* Angels)

Faust. (*Terrified*) Ah, Christ, my Savior, my Savior,
Help to save distressed Faustus' soul.

(*Enter* Lucifer, Belzebub, *and* Mephistophilis)

[15] Ruling spirit.
[16] Because of their unequal motion in relation to the whole.

Luc. Christ cannot save thy soul, for he
   is just;
There's none but I have interest in the same.
Faust. O what art thou that look'st so
terrible?
Luc. I am Lucifer,
And this is my companion-prince in hell.
Faust. O Faustus! they are come to fetch
away thy soul!
Belz. We come to tell thee thou dost
injure us.
Luc. Thou call'st on Christ contrary to
thy promise.
Belz. Thou should'st not think on God.
Luc. Think of the Devil.
Belz. And of his dam, too.
Faust. Nor will I henceforth: pardon me
   in this,
And Faustus vows never to look to Heaven,
Never to name God, or to pray to him,
To burn his Scriptures, slay his ministers,
And make my spirits pull his churches down.
Luc. Do so, and we will highly gratify
thee. Faustus, we are come from hell to show
thee some pastime. Sit down, and thou shalt
see all the Seven Deadly Sins appear in their
proper shapes.
Faust. That sight will be as pleasing unto
   me,
As Paradise was to Adam the first day
Of his creation.
Luc. Talk not of Paradise nor creation,
but mark this show. Go, Mephistophilis,
fetch them in.

(*Enter the* Seven Deadly Sins *appropri-
ately costumed*)

Belz. Now, Faustus, examine them of
their several names and dispositions.
Faust. What art thou—the first?
Pride. I am Pride. I disdain to have any
parents. I am like to Ovid's flea; I can creep
into every corner of a wench; sometimes, like
a periwig, I sit upon her brow; or like a fan
of feathers, I kiss her lips; indeed I do—what
do I not? But, fie, what a smell is here! I'll
not speak another word, except the ground
be perfum'd, and covered with cloth of arras.
Faust. Thou art a proud knave, indeed!
What art thou—the second?
Covet. I am Covetousness, begotten of
an old churl in an old leather bag; and

might I have my wish I would desire that
this house and all the people in it were
turn'd to gold, that I might lock you up in
my good chest. O, my sweet gold!
Faust. What art thou—the third?
Wrath. I am Wrath. I had neither father
nor mother: I leapt out of a lion's mouth
when I was scarce half an hour old; and ever
since I have run up and down the world
with this case of rapiers wounding myself
when I had nobody to fight withal. I was
born in hell; and look to it, for some of you
shall be my father.
Faust. What art thou—the fourth?
Envy. I am Envy, begotten of a chimney
sweeper and an oyster-wife. I cannot read,
and therefore wish all books were burnt. I
am lean with seeing others eat. O that there
would come a famine through all the world,
that all might die, and I live alone! then
thou should'st see how fat I would be. But
must thou sit and I stand! Come down with
a vengeance!
Faust. Away, envious rascal! What art
thou—the fifth?
Glut. Who, I, sir? I am Gluttony. My
parents are all dead, and the devil a penny
they have left me, but a bare pension, and
that is thirty meals a day and ten bevers [17]—
a small trifle to suffice nature. O, I come of
a royal parentage! My grandfather was a
Gammon of Bacon, my grandmother a Hogs-
head of Claret-wine; my godfathers were
these, Peter Pickle-herring, and Martin Mar-
lemas-beef. O, but my godmother, she was
a jolly gentlewoman, and well beloved in
every good town and city; her name was
Mistress Margery Marchbeer. Now, Faustus,
thou hast heard all my progeny, wilt thou
bid me to supper?
Faust. No, I'll see thee hanged: thou
wilt eat up all my victuals.
Glut. Then the Devil choke thee!
Faust. Choke thyself, glutton! Who art
thou—the sixth?
Sloth. (*Yawning*) Heigh ho! I am Sloth.
I was begotten on a sunny bank, where I
have lain ever since; and you have done me
great injury to bring me from thence: let me
be carried thither again by Gluttony and
Lechery. Heigh ho! I'll not speak another
word for a king's ransom.

[17] Snacks.

FAUST. What are you, Mistress Minx, the seventh and last?

LECH. Who, I, sir? I am one that loves an inch of raw mutton better than an ell of fried stockfish; and the first letter of my name begins with Lechery.

LUC. Away to hell, to hell! (*Exeunt the* SINS)—Now, Faustus, how dost thou like this?

FAUST. O, this feeds my soul!

LUC. Tut, Faustus, in hell is all manner of delight.

FAUST. O might I see hell, and return again, safe,

How happy were I then!

LUC. Thou shalt; I will send for thee at midnight.
In meantime take this book; peruse it throughly,
And thou shalt turn thyself into what shape thou wilt.

FAUST. Great thanks, mighty Lucifer!
This will I keep as chary as my life.

LUC. Farewell, Faustus, and think on the Devil.

FAUST. Farewell, great Lucifer! Come, Mephistophilis.   (*Exeunt omnes*)

Act III

(*Enter* CHORUS)

CHOR. Learned Faustus,
To find the secrets of astronomy,
Graven in the book of Jove's high firmament,
Did mount him up to scale Olympus' top,
Being seated in a chariot burning bright,
Drawn by the strength of yoked dragons' necks.
He now is gone to prove cosmography,
And, as I guess, will first arrive at Rome,
To see the Pope and manner of his court,
And take some part of holy Peter's feast,
The which this day is highly solemnis'd.
                              (*Exit*)

SCENE I. *The* POPE'S *Privy Chamber. A banquet table set out.*

(*Enter* FAUSTUS *and* MEPHISTOPHILIS)

FAUST. Having now, my good Mephistophilis,
Pass'd with delight the stately town of Trier,
Environ'd round with airy mountain-tops,
With walls of flint, and deep entrenched lakes,
Not to be won by any conquering prince;
From Paris next, coasting the realm of France,
We saw the river Maine fall into Rhine,
Whose banks are set with groves of fruitful vines;
Then up to Naples, rich Campania,
Whose buildings fair and gorgeous to the eye,
The streets straight forth, and pav'd with finest brick,
Quarter the town in four equivalents.
There saw we learned Maro's [18] golden tomb,
The way he cut, an English mile in length,

[18] Virgil.

Thorough a rock of stone in one night's space;
From thence to Venice, Padua, and the rest,
In one of which a sumptuous temple stands,
That threats the stars with her aspiring top,
Whose frame is paved with sundry colored stones,
And roof'd aloft with curious work in gold.
Thus hitherto has Faustus spent his time:
But tell me, now, what resting-place is this?
Hast thou, as erst I did command,
Conducted me within the walls of Rome?

MEPH. I have, my Faustus, and for proof thereof
This is the goodly Palace of the Pope;
And 'cause we are no common guests
I choose his privy-chamber for our use.

FAUST. I hope his Holiness will bid us welcome.

MEPH. Tut, 'tis no matter, man, we'll be bold with his good cheer.
And now, my Faustus, that thou may'st perceive

What Rome containeth to delight thee with,
Know that this city stands upon seven hills
That underprop the groundwork of the same.
Just through the midst runs flowing Tiber's
    stream,
With winding banks that cut it in two parts:
Over the which four stately bridges lean,
That make safe passage to each part of Rome.
Upon the bridge call'd Ponto Angelo
Erected is a castle passing strong,
Within whose walls such store of ordnance
    are,
And double cannons, fram'd of carved brass,
As match the days within one cómplete year;
Besides the gates and high pyramides,
Which Julius Cæsar brought from Africa.

    FAUST. Now by the kingdoms of infernal
      rule,
Of Styx, of Acheron, and the fiery lake
Of ever-burning Phlegethon, I swear
That I do long to see the monuments
And situation of bright-splendent Rome:
Come therefore, let's away.

    MEPH. Nay, Faustus, stay; I know you'd
      see the Pope,
And take some part of holy Peter's feast,
Where thou shalt see a troop of bald-pate
    friars,
Whose *summum bonum* is in belly-cheer.

    FAUST. Well, I'm content to compass then
      some sport,
And by their folly make us merriment.
Then charm me, Mephistophilis, that I
May be invisible, to do what I please
Unseen of any whilst I stay in Rome.

             (MEPHISTOPHILIS *charms him*)
    MEPH. So, Faustus, now
Do what thou wilt, thou shalt not be dis-
    cern'd.

(*A fanfare of trumpets. Enter the* POPE *and
the* CARDINAL OF LORRAIN *to the banquet,
with* FRIARS *attending*)

    POPE. My Lord of Lorrain, wilt please you
draw near?
    FAUST. Fall to, and the devil choke you
an you spare!
    POPE. How now! Who's that which spake?
—Friars, look about.
    1 FRIAR. Here's nobody, if it like your
Holiness.

    POPE. My lord, here is a dainty dish was
sent me from the Bishop of Milan.
    FAUST. I thank you, sir.
             (*Snatches the dish*)
    POPE. How now! Who's that which
snatch'd the meat from me? Will no man
look? My Lord, this dish was sent me from
the Cardinal of Florence.
    FAUST. You say true; I'll ha't.
             (*Snatches the dish*)
    POPE. What, again! My lord, I'll drink to
your Grace.
    FAUST. I'll pledge your Grace.
             (*Snatches the cup*)
    C. OF LOR. My Lord, it may be some ghost
newly crept out of purgatory, come to beg
a pardon of your Holiness.
    POPE. It may be so. Friars, prepare a dirge
to lay the fury of this ghost. Once again, my
lord, fall to.   (*The* POPE *crosses himself*)
    FAUST. What, are you crossing of yourself?
Well, use that trick no more I would advise
    you.
        (*The* POPE *crosses himself again*)
Well, there's the second time. Aware the
    third,
I give you fair warning.
(*The* POPE *crosses himself again, and*
    FAUSTUS *hits him a box on the ear. The*
    POPE, CARDINAL, *and* FRIARS *run
    away*)
Come on, Mephistophilis, what shall we do?
    MEPH. Nay, I know not. We shall be
curs'd with bell, book, and candle.
    FAUST. How! bell, book, and candle,—
      candle, book, and bell,
Forward and backward to curse Faustus to
    hell!
Anon you shall hear a hog grunt, a calf bleat,
    and an ass bray,
Because it is Saint Peter's holiday.

(*Re-enter all the* FRIARS *to sing the Dirge*)

    1 FRIAR. Come, brethren, let's about our
business with good devotion.

(*The* FRIARS *sing*)

*Cursed be he that stole away his Holiness'
    meat from the table! Maledicat Domi-
    nus!* [19]

[19] The Lord curse him.

Cursed be he that struck his Holiness a blow
    on the face! Maledicat Dominus!
Cursed be he that took Friar Sandelo a blow
    on the pate! Maledicat Dominus!
Cursed be he that disturbeth our holy dirge!
    Maledicat Dominus!

Cursed be he that took away his Holiness'
    wine! Maledicat Dominus! Et omnes
    sancti! Amen!

(MEPHISTOPHILIS and FAUSTUS beat the
    FRIARS, and fling fireworks among
    them, and so exeunt)

SCENE II. An Innyard.

(Enter ROBIN THE OSTLER with a book in
    his hand)

ROBIN. O, this is admirable! here I ha'
stolen one of Dr. Faustus' conjuring books,
and i' faith I mean to search some circles for
my own use. Now will I make all the maidens in our parish dance at my pleasure, stark
naked before me; and so by that means I
shall see more than e'er I felt or saw yet.

(Enter RALPH calling ROBIN)

RALPH. Robin, prithee come away; there's
a gentleman tarries to have his horse, and
he would have his things rubb'd and made
clean. He keeps such a chafing with my mistress about it; and she has sent me to look
thee out. Prithee come away.

ROBIN. Keep out, keep out, or else you
are blown up; you are dismemb'red, Ralph:
keep out, for I am about a roaring piece of
work.

RALPH. Come, what dost thou with that
same book? Thou canst not read.

ROBIN. Yes, my master and mistress shall

find that I can read, he for his forehead, she
for her private study; she's born to bear with
me, or else my art fails.

RALPH. Why, Robin, what book is that?

ROBIN. What book! Why, the most intolerable book for conjuring that e'er was
invented by any brimstone devil.

RALPH. Canst thou conjure with it?

ROBIN. I can do all these things easily with
it: first, I can make thee drunk with ippocras
at any tavern in Europe for nothing; that's
one of my conjuring works.

RALPH. Our Master Parson says that's
nothing.

ROBIN. True, Ralph; and more, Ralph, if
thou hast any mind to Nan Spit, our kitchen-
maid, then turn her and wind her to thy own
use as often as thou wilt, and at midnight.

RALPH. O brave Robin, shall I have Nan
Spit, and to mine own use? On that condition I'll feed thy devil with horsebread as
long as he lives, of free cost.

ROBIN. No more, sweet Ralph: let's go
and make clean our boots, which lie foul
upon our hands, and then to our conjuring
in the Devil's name.   (Exeunt)

SCENE III. The Same.

(Enter ROBIN and RALPH with a silver
    goblet)

ROBIN. Come, Ralph, did not I tell thee
we were for ever made by this Doctor Faustus' book? Ecce signum, here's a simple purchase for horsekeepers; our horses shall eat
no hay as long as this lasts.

(Enter the VINTNER)

RALPH. But, Robin, here comes the vintner.

ROBIN. Hush! I'll gull him supernaturally.
Drawer, I hope all is paid: God be with you.
Come, Ralph.

VINT. Soft, sir; a word with you. I must
yet have a goblet paid from you, ere you go.

ROBIN. I, a goblet, Ralph; I, a goblet! I
scorn you, and you are but a &c.[20] I, a goblet!
search me.

VINT. I mean so, sir, with your favor.
    (Searches him)

[20] Gag to be added by the actor ad lib.

ROBIN. How say you now?

VINT. I must say somewhat to your fellow. You, sir!

RALPH. Me, sir! me, sir! search your fill. (VINTER *searches him*) Now, sir, you may be ashamed to burden honest men with a matter of truth.

VINT. Well, t' one of you hath this goblet about you.

ROBIN. (*Aside*) You lie, drawer, 'tis afore me.—Sirrah you, I'll teach ye to impeach honest men; stand by;—I'll scour you for a goblet!—stand aside you had best, I charge you in the name of Belzebub. (*Aside to* RALPH) Look to the goblet, Ralph.

VINT. What mean you, sirrah?

ROBIN. I'll tell you what I mean. (*Reads from a book*) Sanctobulorum, Periphrasticon—Nay, I'll tickle you, vintner. (*Aside to* RALPH) Look to the goblet, Ralph. (*Reads*) Polypragmos Belseborams framanto pacostiphos tostu, Mephistophilis, &c.[21]

(*Enter* MEPHISTOPHILIS, *sets squibs at their backs, and then exit. They run about*)

VINT. O nomine Domini! what meanest thou, Robin? Thou hast no goblet.

RALPH. Peccatum peccatorum! Here's thy goblet, good vintner.

(*Gives the goblet to* VINTNER. *Exit* VINTNER)

ROBIN. *Misericordia pro nobis!* What shall I do? Good Devil, forgive me now, and I'll never rob thy library more.

(*Re-enter to them* MEPHISTOPHILIS)

MEPH. Monarch of hell, under whose black survey
Great potentates do kneel with awful fear,
Upon whose altars thousand souls do lie,
How am I vexed with these villains' charms?
From Constantinople am I hither come
Only for pleasure of these damned slaves.

ROBIN. How, from Constantinople? You have had a great journey. Will you take sixpence in your purse to pay for your supper, and begone?

MEPH. Well, villains, for your presumption, I transform thee into an ape, and thee into a dog; and so begone. (*Exit*)

ROBIN. How, into an ape? That's brave! I'll have fine sport with the boys. I'll get nuts and apples enow.

RALPH. And I must be a dog.

ROBIN. I' faith thy head will never be out of the pottage pot. (*Exeunt*)

Act IV

(*Enter* CHORUS)

CHORUS. When Faustus had with pleasure ta'en the view
Of rarest things, and royal courts of kings,
He stay'd his course, and so returned home;
Where such as bear his absence but with grief,
I mean his friends, and near'st companions,
Did gratulate his safety with kind words,
And in their conference of what befell,
Touching his journey through the world and air,
They put forth questions of Astrology,
Which Faustus answer'd with such learned skill,
As they admir'd and wond'red at his wit.
Now is his fame spread forth in every land;
Amongst the rest the Emperor is one,
Carolus the Fifth, at whose palace now
Faustus is feasted 'mongst his noblemen.
What there he did in trial of his art,
I leave untold—your eyes shall see perform'd.
(*Exit*)

SCENE I. *The German Court.*

(*Enter* EMPEROR, FAUSTUS, MEPHISTOPHILIS *and a* KNIGHT *with attendants*)

EMP. Master Doctor Faustus, I have heard

[21] Latin and Greek gibberish.

strange report of thy knowledge in the black art, how that none in my empire nor in the whole world can compare with thee for the rare effects of magic; they say thou hast a familiar spirit, by whom thou canst accomplish what thou list. This, therefore, is my request, that thou let me see some proof of thy skill, that mine eyes may be witnesses to confirm what mine ears have heard reported; and here I swear to thee by the honor of mine imperial crown, that, whatever thou doest, thou shalt be no ways prejudiced or endamaged.

KNIGHT. (*Aside*) I' faith he looks much like a conjuror.

FAUST. My gracious sovereign, though I must confess myself far inferior to the report men have published, and nothing answerable to the honor of your imperial majesty, yet for that love and duty binds me thereunto, I am content to do whatsoever your majesty shall command me.

EMP. Then, Doctor Faustus, mark what I shall say.

As I was sometime solitary set
Within my closet, sundry thoughts arose
About the honor of mine ancestors,
How they had won by prowess such exploits,
Got such riches, subdued so many kingdoms,
As we that do succeed, or they that shall
Hereafter possess our throne, shall
(I fear me) ne'er attain to that degree
Of high renown and great authority;
Amongst which kings is Alexander the Great,
Chief spectacle of the world's pre-eminence,
The bright shining of whose glorious acts
Lightens the world with his reflecting beams,
As, when I heard your motion made of him,
It grieves my soul I never saw the man.
If, therefore, thou by cunning of thine art
Canst raise this man from hollow vaults below,
Where lies entomb'd this famous conqueror,
And bring with him his beauteous paramour,
Both in their right shapes, gesture, and attire
They us'd to wear during their time of life,
Thou shalt both satisfy my just desire,
And give me cause to praise thee whilst I live.

FAUST. My gracious lord, I am ready to accomplish your request so far forth as by art, and power of my Spirit, I am able to perform.

KNIGHT. (*Aside*) I' faith that's just nothing at all.

FAUST. But, if it like your Grace, it is not in my ability to present before your eyes the true substantial bodies of those two deceased princes, which long since are consumed to dust.

KNIGHT. (*Aside*) Ay, marry, Master Doctor, now there's a sign of grace in you, when you will confess the truth.

FAUST. But such spirits as can lively resemble Alexander and his paramour shall appear before your Grace in that manner that they best liv'd in, in their most flourishing estate, which I doubt not shall sufficiently content your imperial majesty.

EMP. Go to, Master Doctor, let me see them presently.

KNIGHT. Do you hear, Master Doctor? You bring Alexander and his paramour before the Emperor!

FAUST. How then, sir?

KNIGHT. I' faith, that's as true as Diana turn'd me to a stag!

FAUST. No, sir, but when Actæon died, he left the horns for you. Mephistophilis, begone.

(*Exit* MEPHISTOPHILIS)

KNIGHT. Nay, an you go to conjuring, I'll begone. (*Exit*)

FAUST. I'll meet with you anon for interrupting me so. Here they are, my gracious lord.

(*Re-enter* MEPHISTOPHILIS *with Spirits in the shape of* ALEXANDER *and his Paramour*)

EMP. Master Doctor, I heard this lady while she liv'd had a wart or mole in her neck: how shall I know whether it be so or no?

FAUST. Your Highness may boldly go and see. (EMPEROR *examines her*)

EMP. Sure these are no spirits, but the true substantial bodies of those two deceased princes. (*Exeunt Spirits*)

FAUST. Will't please your Highness now to send for the knight that was so pleasant with me here of late?

EMP. One of you call him forth.

(*Exit Attendant*)

(*Re-enter the* KNIGHT *with a pair of horns on his head*)

How now, Sir Knight! why I had thought

thou had'st been a bachelor, but now I see
thou hast a wife, that not only gives thee
horns, but makes thee wear them. Feel on
thy head.

KNIGHT. Thou damned wretch and ex-
    ecrable dog,
Bred in the concave of some monstrous rock,
How darest thou thus abuse a gentleman?
Villain, I say, undo what thou hast done!

FAUST. Oh, not so fast, sir; there's no
haste. But, good, are you rememb'red how
you crossed me in my conference with the
Emperor? I think I have met with you for it.

EMP. Good Master Doctor, at my entreaty
release him; he hath done penance sufficient.

FAUST. My gracious lord, not so much for
the injury he off'red me here in your presence, as to delight you with some mirth, hath
Faustus worthily requited this injurious
knight, which being all I desire, I am content to release him of his horns. And, Sir
Knight, hereinafter speak well of scholars.
Mephistophilis, transform him straight.
(MEPHISTOPHILIS *removes the horns*) Now,
my good lord, having done my duty I humbly take my leave.

EMP. Farewell, Master Doctor; yet, ere
    you go,
Expect from me a bounteous reward.

                                    (*Exeunt*)

SCENE II. *A Common.*

(*Enter* FAUSTUS *and* MEPHISTOPHILIS)

FAUST. Now, Mephistophilis, the restless
    course
That Time doth run with calm and silent
    foot,
Short'ning my days and thread of vital life,
Calls for the payment of my latest years;
Therefore, sweet Mephistophilis, let us
Make haste to Wittenberg.

MEPH. What, will you go on horseback
or on foot?

FAUST. Nay, till I'm past this fair and
    pleasant green,
I'll walk on foot.

(*Enter a* HORSE-COURSER)

HORSE-C. I have been all this day seeking
one Master Fustian. Mass, see where he is!
God save you, Master Doctor!

FAUST. What, horse-courser! You are well
met.

HORSE-C. Do you hear, sir? I have brought
you forty dollars for your horse.

FAUST. I cannot sell him so. If thou likest
him for fifty, take him.

HORSE-C. Alas, sir, I have no more.—I
pray you speak for me.

MEPH. I pray you let him have him. He
is an honest fellow, and he has a great charge,
neither wife nor child.

                (*Exit* MEPHISTOPHILIS)

FAUST. Well, come, give me your
money. (HORSE-COURSER *gives* FAUSTUS *the
money*) My boy will deliver him to you.
But I must tell you one thing before you
have him; ride him not into the water at
any hand.

HORSE-C. Why, sir, will he not drink of
all waters?

FAUST. O yes, he will drink of all waters,
but ride him not into the water. Ride him
over hedge or ditch, or where thou wilt, but
not into the water.

HORSE-C. Well, sir.—(*Aside*) Now I am
made man for ever. I'll not leave my horse
for forty. If he had but the quality of hey-
ding-ding, hey-ding-ding, I'd make a brave
living on him. He has a buttock as slick as
an eel. (*To* FAUSTUS) Well, God b' wi' ye,
sir. Your boy will deliver him me. But hark
ye, sir; if my horse be sick or ill at ease, if
I bring his water to you, you'll tell me what
it is?   (*Exit* HORSE-COURSER)

FAUST. Away, you villain. What, dost
think I am a horse-doctor?

                    (*Retires to his study*)
What art thou, Faustus, but a man con-
    demn'd to die?
Thy fatal time doth draw to final end;
Despair doth drive distrust unto my
    thoughts;
Confound these passions with a quiet sleep.
Tush, Christ did call the thief upon the
    cross;

Then rest thee, Faustus, quiet in conceit.
(Sleeps in his chair)

(Re-enter Horse-Courser, *all wet, crying)*

Horse-C. Alas, alas! Doctor Fustian,
quotha? Mass, Doctor Lopus was never
such a doctor. Has given me a purgation has
purg'd me of forty dollars; I shall never see
them more. But yet, like an ass as I was, I
would not be ruled by him, for he bade me
I should ride him into no water. Now I,
thinking my horse had had some rare quality
that he would not have had me know of,
I, like a venturous youth, rid him into the
deep pond at the town's end. I was no sooner
in the middle of the pond, but my horse
vanish'd away, and I sat upon a bottle of
hay, never so near drowning in my life. But
I'll seek out my Doctŏr, and have my forty
dollars again, or I'll make it the dearest horse!
—*(Enter* Mephistophilis) O, yonder is his
snipper-snapper.—Do you hear? You hey-
pass, where's your master?

Meph. Why, sir, what would you? You
cannot speak with him.

Horse-C. But I will speak with him.

Meph. Why, he's fast asleep. Come some
other time.

Horse-C. I'll speak with him now, or I'll
break his glass windows about his ears.

Meph. I tell thee he has not slept this
eight nights.

Horse-C. An he have not slept this eight
weeks,
I'll speak with him.

Meph. See where he is, fast asleep.

Horse-C. Ay, this is he. God save you,
Master Doctor! Master Doctor, Master Doctor
Fustian!—Forty dollars, forty dollars for a
bottle of hay!

Meph. Why, thou seest he hears thee not.

Horse-C. So ho, ho!—so ho, ho! *(Hollas
in his ear)* No, will you not wake? I'll make
you wake ere I go. *(Pulls* Faustus *by the
leg, and pulls it away)* Alas, I am undone!
What shall I do?

Faust. O my leg, my leg! Help, Mephistophilis! Call the officers. My leg, my leg!

Meph. Come, villain, to the constable.

Horse-C. O lord, sir, let me go, and I'll
give you forty dollars more.

Meph. Where be they?

Horse-C. I have none about me. Come
to my ostry [22] and I'll give them you.

Meph. Begone quickly!
*(*Horse-Courser *runs away)*

Faust. What, is he gone? Farewell he!
Faustus has his leg again, and the horse-
courser, I take it, a bottle of hay for his labor.
Well, this trick shall cost him forty dollars
more.

(Enter Wagner)

How now, Wagner, what's the news with
thee?

Wag. Sir, the Duke of Vanholt doth
earnestly entreat your company.

Faust. The Duke of Vanholt! an honorable gentleman, to whom I must be no nig-
gard of my cunning. Come, Mephistophilis,
let's away to him.   *(Exeunt)*

Scene III. *Court of the* Duke *of* Vanholt.

(Enter the Duke of Vanholt, *the* Duchess, Faustus, *and* Mephistophilis)

Duke. Believe me, Master Doctor, this
merriment hath much pleased me.

Faust. My gracious lord, I am glad it contents you so well.—But it may be, madam,
you take no delight in this. I have heard
that great-bellied women do long for some
dainties or other. What is it, madam? Tell
me, and you shall have it.

Duchess. Thanks, good Master Doctor;
and, for I see your courteous intent to pleasure me, I will not hide from you the thing
my heart desires. An were it now summer,
as it is January and the dead time of the
winter, I would desire no better meat than
a dish of ripe grapes.

Faust. Alas, madam, that's nothing!
Mephistophilis, begone. *(Exit* Mephistophilis) Were it a greater thing than this, so
it would content you, you should have it.

---

[22] Hostelry, inn.

(*Re-enter* MEPHISTOPHILIS *with the grapes*)

Here they be, madam. Wilt please you taste on them?

DUKE. Believe me, Master Doctor, this makes me wonder above the rest, that being in the dead time of winter, and in the month of January, how you should come by these grapes.

FAUST. If it like your Grace, the year is divided into two circles over the whole world, that, when it is here winter with us, in the contrary circle it is summer with them, as in India, Saba,[23] and farther countries in the East; and by means of a swift spirit that I have, I had them brought hither, as ye see.—How do you like them, madam; be they good?

DUCHESS. Believe me, Master Doctor, they be the best grapes that I e'er tasted in my life before.

FAUST. I am glad they content you so, madam.

DUKE. Come, madam, let us in, where you must well reward this learned man for the great kindness he hath show'd to you.

DUCHESS. And so I will, my lord; and whilst I live, rest beholding for this courtesy.

FAUST. I humbly thank your Grace.

DUKE. Come, Master Doctor, follow us and receive your reward.   (*Exeunt*)

SCENE IV. FAUSTUS' *Study.*

(*Enter* WAGNER)

WAG. I think my master means to die
    shortly,
For he hath given to me all his goods;
And yet, methinks, if that death were near,
He would not banquet and carouse and swill
Amongst the students, as even now he doth,
Who are at supper with such belly-cheer
As Wagner ne'er beheld in all his life.
See where they come! Belike the feast is
    ended.

(*Enter* FAUSTUS, *with two or three* SCHOLARS
and MEPHISTOPHILIS)

1 SCHOLAR. Master Doctor Faustus, since our conference about fair ladies, which was the beautifullest in all the world, we have determined with ourselves that Helen of Greece was the admirablest lady that ever lived: therefore, Master Doctor, if you will do us that favor, as to let us see that peerless dame of Greece, whom all the world admires for majesty, we should think ourselves much beholding unto you.

FAUST. Gentlemen,
For that I know your friendship is unfeigned,
And Faustus' custom is not to deny
The just requests of those that wish him
    well,

You shall behold that peerless dame of
    Greece,
No otherways for pomp and majesty
Than when Sir Paris cross'd the seas with
    her,
And brought the spoils to rich Dardania.
Be silent, then, for danger is in words.
        (*Music sounds, and* HELEN *passeth
            over the stage*)
    2 SCHOL. Too simple is my wit to tell her
        praise,
Whom all the world admires for majesty.
    3 SCHOL. No marvel though the angry
        Greeks pursu'd
With ten years' war the rape of such a queen,
Whose heavenly beauty passeth all compare.
    1 SCHOL. Since we have seen the pride of
        Nature's works,
And only paragon of excellence,

(*Enter an* OLD MAN)

Let us depart; and for this glorious deed
Happy and blest be Faustus evermore.
    FAUSTUS. Gentlemen, farewell—the same
        I wish to you.
        (*Exeunt* SCHOLARS *and* WAGNER)
    OLD MAN. Ah, Doctor Faustus, that I
        might prevail
To guide thy steps unto the way of life,
By which sweet path thou may'st attain the
    goal

[23] Arabia.

That shalt conduct thee to celestial rest!
Break heart, drop blood, and mingle it with
    tears,
Tears falling from repentant heaviness
Of thy most vile and loathsome filthiness,
The stench whereof corrupts the inward soul
With such flagitious crimes of heinous sins
As no commiseration may expel,
But mercy, Faustus, of thy Savior sweet,
Whose blood alone must wash away thy guilt.
    Faust. Where art thou, Faustus? Wretch,
    what hast thou done?
Damn'd art thou, Faustus, damn'd; despair
    and die!
Hell calls for right, and with a roaring voice
Says "Faustus! come! thine hour is almost
    come!"
And Faustus now will come to do thee right.
    (Mephistophilis gives him a dagger)
    Old Man. Ah stay, good Faustus, stay thy
    desperate steps!
I see an angel hovers o'er thy head,
And, with a vial full of precious grace,
Offers to pour the same into thy soul.
Then call for mercy, and avoid despair.
    Faust. Ah, my sweet friend, I feel
Thy words do comfort my distressed soul.
Leave me a while to ponder on my sins.
    Old Man. I go, sweet Faustus, but with
    heavy cheer,
Fearing the ruin of thy hopeless soul.
                                    (Exit)
    Faust. Accursed Faustus, where is mercy
    now?
I do repent; and yet I do despair;
Hell strives with grace for conquest in my
    breast.
What shall I do to shun the snares of death?
    Meph. Thou traitor, Faustus, I arrest thy
    soul
For disobedience to my sovereign lord;
Revolt, or I'll in piecemeal tear thy flesh.
    Faust. Sweet Mephistophilis, entreat thy
    lord
To pardon my unjust presumption,
And with my blood again I will confirm
My former vow I made to Lucifer.
    Meph. Do it now then quickly, with un-
    feigned heart,
Lest greater danger do attend thy drift.
    (Faustus stabs his arm and writes on a
    paper with his blood)

    Faust. Torment, sweet friend, that base
    and crooked age,[24]
That durst dissuade me from thy Lucifer,
With greatest torments that our hell affords.
    Meph. His faith is great, I cannot touch
    his soul;
But what I may afflict his body with
I will attempt, which is but little worth.
    Faust. One thing, good servant, let me
    crave of thee,
To glut the longing of my heart's desire,—
That I might have unto my paramour
That heavenly Helen, which I saw of late,
Whose sweet embracings may extinguish
    clean
These thoughts that do dissuade me from my
    vow,
And keep mine oath I made to Lucifer.
    Meph. Faustus, this or what else thou
    shalt desire
Shall be perform'd in twinkling of an eye.

                (Enter Helen)

    Faust. Was this the face that launch'd a
    thousand ships,
And burnt the topless towers of Ilium?
Sweet Helen, make me immortal with a kiss.
                                (Kisses her)
Her lips suck forth my soul; see where it
    flies!—
Come, Helen, come, give me my soul again.
                                (Kisses her)
Here will I dwell, for Heaven be in these lips,
And all is dross that is not Helena.

                (Enter Old Man)

I will be Paris, and for love of thee,
Instead of Troy, shall Wittenberg be sack'd;
And I will combat with weak Menelaus,
And wear thy colors on my plumed crest;
Yea, I will wound Achilles in the heel,
And then return to Helen for a kiss.
Oh, thou art fairer than the evening air
Clad in the beauty of a thousand stars;
Brighter art thou than flaming Jupiter
When he appear'd to hapless Semele:
More lovely than the monarch of the sky
In wanton Arethusa's azur'd arms:
And none but thou shalt be my paramour.
                (Exeunt all except Old Man)

[24] I.e. the Old Man.

OLD MAN. Accursed Faustus, miserable man,
That from thy soul exclud'st the grace of Heaven,
And fly'st the throne of his tribunal seat!

(*Enter Devils to torture him*)

Satan begins to sift me with his pride.

As in this furnace God shall try my faith,
(*Defiantly*) My faith, vile hell, shall triumph over thee.
(*Triumphantly to the Devils*) Ambitious fiends! see how the heavens smile
At your repulse, and laugh your state to scorn!
Hence, hell! for hence I fly unto my God!
(*Exeunt*)

SCENE V. FAUSTUS' *Study. The night of the expiration of* FAUSTUS' *contract.*

(*Enter* FAUSTUS *with the* SCHOLARS)

FAUST. Ah, gentlemen!
1 SCHOL. What ails Faustus?
FAUST. Ah, my sweet chamber-fellow, had I lived with thee, then had I lived still! But now I die eternally. (*Stares in panic*) Look, comes he not, comes he not?
2 SCHOL. (*Amazed*) What means Faustus?
3 SCHOL. Belike he is grown into some sickness by being over solitary.
1 SCHOL. If it be so, we'll have physicians to cure him. 'Tis but a surfeit. Never fear, man.
FAUST. (*With despair*) A surfeit of deadly sin that hath damn'd both body and soul.
2 SCHOL. Yet, Faustus, look up to Heaven; remember God's mercies are infinite.
FAUST. But Faustus' offences can ne'er be pardoned. The serpent that tempted Eve may be sav'd, but not Faustus. Ah, gentlemen, hear me with patience, and tremble not at my speeches! Though my heart pants and quivers to remember that I have been a student here these thirty years, oh, would I had never seen Wittenberg, never read book! And what wonders I have done, all Germany can witness, yea, all the world; for which Faustus hath lost both Germany and the world, yea Heaven itself, Heaven, the seat of God, the throne of the blessed, the kingdom of joy, and must remain in hell for ever, hell, ah, hell, for ever! Sweet friends! what shall become of Faustus being in hell for ever?
3 SCHOL. Yet, Faustus, call on God.
FAUST. On God, whom Faustus hath abjur'd! On God, whom Faustus hath blasphemed! Ah, my God, I would weep, but the Devil draws in my tears. Gush forth blood instead of tears! Yea, life and soul! Oh, he stays my tongue! I would lift up my hands, but see, they hold them, they hold them!
ALL. Who, Faustus?
FAUST. Lucifer and Mephistophilis. Ah, gentlemen, I gave them my soul for my cunning!
ALL. (*In horror*) God forbid!
FAUST. God forbade it indeed; but Faustus hath done it. For vain pleasure of four-and-twenty years hath Faustus lost eternal joy and felicity. I writ them a bill with mine own blood. The date is expired; the time will come, and he will fetch me.
1 SCHOL. Why did not Faustus tell us of this before, that divines might have prayed for thee?
FAUST. Oft have I thought to have done so; but the Devil threat'ned to tear me in pieces if I nam'd God; to fetch both body and soul if I once gave ear to divinity. And now 'tis too late. Gentlemen, away, lest you perish with me!
2 SCHOL. Oh, what shall we do to save Faustus?
FAUST. Talk not of me, but save yourselves, and depart.
3 SCHOL. God will strengthen me. I will stay with Faustus.
1 SCHOL. Tempt not God, sweet friend; but let us into the next room, and there pray for him.
FAUST. Ay, pray for me, pray for me! And what noise soever ye hear, come not unto me, for nothing can rescue me.
2 SCHOL. Pray thou, and we will pray that God may have mercy upon thee.
FAUST. Gentlemen, farewell! If I live till

morning, I'll visit you. If not—Faustus is gone to hell.

ALL. Faustus, farewell!

(*Exeunt* SCHOLARS. *The clock strikes eleven*)

FAUST. Ah, Faustus,
Now hast thou but one bare hour to live,
And then thou must be damn'd perpetually!
Stand still, you ever-moving spheres of Heaven,
That time may cease, and midnight never come!
Fair Nature's eye, rise, rise again and make
Perpetual day; or let this hour be but
A year, a month, a week, a natural day,
That Faustus may repent and save his soul!
O lente, lente, currite noctis equi! [25]
The stars move still, time runs, the clock will strike,
The Devil will come, and Faustus must be damn'd.
O, I'll leap up to my God! Who pulls me down?
See, see where Christ's blood streams in the firmament!
One drop would save my soul—half a drop: ah, my Christ!
Ah, rend not my heart for naming of my Christ!
Yet will I call on him! O spare me, Lucifer!—
Where is it now? 'Tis gone; and see where God
Stretcheth out his arm, and bends his ireful brows!
Mountain and hills come, come and fall on me,
And hide me from the heavy wrath of God!
No! no!
Then will I headlong run into the earth.
Earth gape! O no, it will not harbor me!
You stars that reign'd at my nativity,
Whose influence hath allotted death and hell,
Now draw up Faustus like a foggy mist
Into the entrails of yon lab'ring clouds,
That when they vomit forth into the air,
My limbs may issue from their smoky mouths,
So that my soul may but ascend to Heaven.

(*The clock strikes the half hour*)

Ah, half the hour is past! 'Twill all be past anon!

[25] Run slowly, slowly, Horses of the Night.

O God!
If thou wilt not have mercy on my soul,
Yet for Christ's sake whose blood hath ransom'd me,
Impose some end to my incessant pain.
Let Faustus live in hell a thousand years—
A hundred thousand, and at last be sav'd!
O, no end is limited to damnéd souls!
Why wert thou not a creature wanting soul?
Or why is this immortal that thou hast?
Ah, Pythagoras' metempsychosis! were that true,
This soul should fly from me, and I be chang'd
Unto some brutish beast! All beasts are happy,
For, when they die,
Their souls are soon dissolv'd in elements;
But mine must live, still to be plagu'd in hell.
Curst be the parents that engend'red me!
No, Faustus, curse thyself; curse Lucifer
That hath depriv'd thee of the joys of Heaven.

(*The clock strikes twelve*)

O, it strikes, it strikes! Now, body, turn to air,
Or Lucifer will bear thee quick to hell.

(*Thunder and lightning*)

O soul, be chang'd into little water-drops,
And fall into the ocean—ne'er be found.
My God! my God! look not so fierce on me!

(*Enter Devils*)

Adders and serpents, let me breathe awhile!
Ugly hell, gape not! come not, Lucifer!
I'll burn my books!—Ah Mephistophilis!

(*Exeunt Devils with* FAUSTUS)

(*Enter* CHORUS)

CHO. Cut is the branch that might have grown full straight,
And burnéd is Apollo's laurel bough,
That sometime grew within this learned man.
Faustus is gone; regard his hellish fall,
Whose fiendful fortune may exhort the wise
Only to wonder at unlawful things,
Whose deepness doth entice such forward wits
To practise more than heavenly power permits.

(*Exit*)

THOMAS DEKKER

The Shoemakers' Holiday

~~~~~~

PRINCIPAL EVENTS IN DEKKER'S LIFE

c. 1572, Dekker was born about this time in London.

1590-97, He probably did some play writing in these years, but there are no extant records.

1598, 15 Jan., Dekker was paid by the theatrical magnate, Philip Henslowe, for work on a play called *Phaethon,* now lost.

1598-1602, Henslowe paid Dekker for writing or collaborating on over thirty plays in these years; most of them are now lost.

1599, 15 July, Henslowe paid him £3 for writing *The Shoemakers' Holiday.*

1600, 1 Jan., The Shoemakers' Holiday was acted at court before Queen Elizabeth by the Lord Admiral's players.

1601, Satiromastix, a collaboration with John Marston attacking Ben Jonson, was acted by the Lord Chamberlain's men, Shakespeare's company.

1604, Dekker's *The Magnificent Entertainment,* a description of the pageantry for the coronation of James I, was published. Part of the speeches in the pageant were written by Dekker himself.

1604, The Honest Whore, Part 1, acted by Prince Henry's players.

1604, Westward Ho, a collaboration with John Webster, acted.

1604, The Wonderful Year, a pamphlet describing the terrible London plague of 1603, published.

1605, Northward Ho, a collaboration with John Webster, acted.

1606, News from Hell published.

1608, The Bellman of London and *Lanthorn and Candlelight,* popular low life exposés, published.

1609, The Gull's Hornbook, a satirical pamphlet containing much about the theatres, published.

c. 1610, The Roaring Girl, a collaboration with Thomas Middleton, acted by Prince Henry's players.

1612, 29 Oct., Dekker's pageant, *Troja-Nova Triumphans,* was performed at the inauguration of John Swinerton, a Merchant Taylor, as Lord Mayor of London.

1613-1619, Dekker appears to have spent these years in prison for debt.

1621, The Witch of Edmonton, a collaboration with Thomas Middleton, acted by Prince Charles's players.

1624, The Sun's Darling, a collaboration with John Ford, was acted by the Princess Elizabeth's players at the Cockpit theatre.

1624, On order for the manager of the Red Bull theatre, Dekker wrote, in collaboration with John Ford, William Rowley, and John Webster, a play called *A Late Murder of the Son upon the Mother, or Keep the Widow Waking,* based upon two current London scandals.

1628, 29 Oct., Dekker's pageant, *Britannia's Honor,* was performed at the inauguration of Richard Deane, a Skinner, as Lord Mayor of London.

1629, 29 Oct., Dekker's pageant, *London's Tempe,* performed at the inauguration of James Campbell, an Ironmonger, as Lord Mayor of London.

1632, 25 Aug., The "Thomas Decker, Householder," who was buried at St. James, Clerkenwell, in London, was probably the dramatist.

The titles of more than fifty plays written in whole or in part by Thomas Dekker are known. Most of them have been lost; probably he wrote many others of which even the titles are lost.

INTRODUCTION

In *The Shoemakers' Holiday,* Dekker has recorded one of our best pictures of middle-class life in Elizabethan London. He wrote the play for Philip Henslowe, the principal theatrical magnate of the time; Henslowe's account books (generally called Henslowe's Diary; the best edition is by W. W. Greg, 2 volumes, London, 1904 and 1908) record that Dekker was paid £3 for the play on 15 July 1599. One of Henslowe's theatrical companies, the Lord Admiral's Men, acted the play at court before Queen Elizabeth the following New Year's night.

Most previous plays for the Elizabethan theatres had dealt with fabulous events in distant places or times—*Romeo and Juliet* with Italy, *Tamburlaine* with the Near East, *Doctor Faustus* with Germany, *Edward II* with the fourteenth century—and the London audience was accustomed to the exotic and romantic in the theatre. Just the year before Dekker wrote his play, however, Ben Jonson had had a hit performed by the Lord Chamberlain's company with William Shakespeare in the cast. This play was called *Every Man in His Humour,* and it dealt with contemporary types and fads and customs in Elizabethan London. Though in his original version Jonson had given the characters Italian names and called the city Florence, the characters were so unmistakably Londoners and their haunts so clearly London and its environs that it was a simple matter later to substitute London and English names.

Dekker followed Jonson in exploiting not the strange and remote but the immediate and familiar. The places mentioned in the play were known to every Londoner, and the character types could be seen on the street any day; the scenes of the shoemakers, for instance, at work in their open-fronted shop, as in Act IV, Scene 2, were familiar sights of the city. Dekker has, moreover, presented his story from the point of view of middle-class London citizens: the guilds in his play are noble institutions; the jolly shoemakers are as good as knights and nobles; the Earl of Lincoln is haughty and proud and unsympathetic to lovers and has to be put in his place by the King; the King himself is a "good fellow" and properly appreciative of the noble guild members of London.

Indeed the whole story of the play is based on one of the local half-historical legends of the rise of a middle-class man, like Dick Whittington. The allusions to the history of the Shoemakers' Guild or the Gentle Craft were familiar to cockneys and the special pride of the Shoemakers, or Cordwainers, all of whom knew the legend that St. Hugh, a Christian martyr, had in his wanderings learned the shoemaker's trade and when in prison had been befriended by shoemakers. Because of their kindness, St. Hugh had called them members of the gentle craft and had bequeathed them his skeleton. From his bones the shoemakers had made a set of shoemaker's tools, and afterwards the shoemakers called their tools "St. Hugh's bones." The central figure of Dekker's play is based on a fifteenth-century Lord Mayor of London named Simon Eyre who had been a great civic benefactor. His story, mostly imaginary, was written up by Thomas Deloney in a piece of popular fiction called *The Gentle Craft.*

All this historic and legendary material Dekker has built into a fine lusty play, vulgar and sentimental in spots, but so skillful in its presentation of the merry, vigorous, and irrepressible Simon Eyre, the coarse and bumbling Margery, the naive, hearty camaraderie of the shoemaker's shop, that it has long been a favorite. Though the Elizabethan dramatic conventions and staging methods which Dekker takes for granted are so far from the modern ones, the play has often been performed in English and American university and experimental theatres. For many persons, Orson Welles' production of the play at the Mercury Theatre in New York in 1938 is still a cherished memory.

THE SHOEMAKERS' HOLIDAY

Dramatis personae

In order of their first appearance

LORD MAYOR, Sir Roger Oteley. Like all Lord Mayors of London, a wealthy guild member, elected by the guilds for a one year term and knighted by the King after his election.

EARL OF LINCOLN, A great nobleman and uncle of Rowland Lacy.

LOVELL, A gentleman of the court.

ROWLAND LACY, Nephew and heir of the Earl of Lincoln, in love with Rose Oteley. In Acts II, III, and IV, disguised as Hans Meulter, a Dutch shoemaker.

ASKEW, Another nephew of the Earl of Lincoln.

SIMON EYRE, An ebullient and eccentric shoemaker, proud of his guild and his class. Owner of a small shoe factory in London

ROGER or HODGE. Foreman of Eyre's shop. Later master of his own shop.

FIRK, An irrepressible shoemaker in Eyre's shop.

MARGERY EYRE, Simon Eyre's wife. A vulgar, garrulous, grumbling, and abusive woman, but essentially kind-hearted.

JANE, Recent bride of Ralph. At the opening of the play employed in Eyre's household.

RALPH, Another shoemaker in Eyre's shop, who has just been drafted as the play opens.

DODGER, A retainer of the Earl of Lincoln.

ROSE OTELEY, Daughter of Sir Roger, in love with Lacy.

SYBIL, Her impudent and flirtatious maid.

BOY, A helper in Eyre's shop.

MASTER HAMMON, A well-to-do London gentleman.

MASTER WARNER, His friend.

BOY, A country boy.

HUNTSMAN

SKIPPER, A Dutch sea captain.

MASTER SCOTT, A friend of Sir Roger Oteley.

PRENTICE, A London apprentice attending the Lord Mayor.

KING, Historically Henry V, but in the play simply the ruler of England, with almost no historical traits.

UNNAMED NOBLEMAN

EARL OF CORNWALL

Huntsmen, Officers, Soldiers, Shoemakers, Apprentices, and Attendants.

SCENE: *London and Nearby Countryside*

The Prologue

Addressed to Queen Elizabeth at a command performance

As wretches in a storm (expecting day),
With trembling hands and eyes cast up to heaven,
Make prayers the anchor of their conquered hopes,
So we, dear goddess, wonder of all eyes,
Your meanest vassals, through mistrust and fear
To sink into the bottom of disgrace
By our imperfect pastimes, prostrate thus
On bended knees, our sails of hope do strike,
Dreading the bitter storms of your dislike.
Since then, unhappy men, our hap is such,
That to ourselves ourselves no help can bring,
But needs must perish, if your saint-like ears
(Locking the temple where all mercy sits)
Refuse the tribute of our begging tongues:
Oh grant, bright mirror of true chastity,
From those life-breathing stars, your sun-like eyes
One gracious smile: for your celestial breath
Must send us life, or sentence us to death.

Act I

Scene I. *A Street in London.*

(*Enter the* Lord Mayor *and the* Earl of Lincoln)

Lincoln. My lord mayor, you have sun-
    dry times
Feasted myself and many courtiers more:
Seldom or never can we be so kind
To make requital of your courtesy.
But leaving this, I hear my cousin [1] Lacy
Is much affected to your daughter Rose.
    Lord Mayor. True, my good lord, and
    she loves him so well
That I mislike her boldness in the chase.
    Lincoln. Why, my lord mayor, think you
    it then a shame,
To join a Lacy with an Oteley's name?
    Lord Mayor. Too mean is my poor girl
    for his high birth;
Poor citizens must not with courtiers wed,
Who will in silks and gay apparel spend
More in one year than I am worth, by far:
Therefore your honor need not doubt my
    girl.
    Lincoln. Take heed, my lord, advise you
    what you do;
A verier unthrift lives not in the world,
Than is my cousin; for I'll tell you what:
'Tis now almost a year since he requested
To travel countries for experience;
I furnished him with coin, bills of exchange,
Letters of credit, men to wait on him,
Solicited my friends in Italy
Well to respect him. But to see the end!
Scant had he journeyed through half Ger-
    many,
But all his coin was spent, his men cast off,
His bills embezzled,[2] and my jolly coz,
Ashamed to show his bankrupt presence here,
Became a shoemaker in Wittenberg.
A goodly science for a gentleman
Of such descent! Now judge the rest by this:
Suppose your daughter have a thousand
    pound,

He did consume me more in one half year;
And make him heir to all the wealth you
    have,
One twelvemonth's rioting will waste it all.
Then seek, my lord, some honest citizen
To wed your daughter to.
    Lord Mayor. I thank your lordship.
(*Aside*) Well, fox, I understand your sub-
    tilty.—
As for your nephew, let your lordship's eye
But watch his actions, and you need not fear,
For I have sent my daughter far enough.
And yet your cousin Rowland might do well,
Now he hath learned an occupation;
And yet I scorn to call him son-in-law.
    Lincoln. Ay, but I have a better trade
    for him:
I thank his grace, he hath appointed him
Chief colonel of all those companies
Mustered in London and the shires about,
To serve his highness in those wars of France.
See where he comes!—

(*Enter* Lovell, Lacy, *and* Askew)

Lovell, what news with you?
    Lovell. My Lord of Lincoln, 'tis his
    highness' will,
That presently your cousin ship for France
With all his powers; he would not for a
    million,
But they should land at Dieppe within four
    days.
    Lincoln. Go certify his grace, it shall be
    done.   (*Exit* Lovell)
Now, cousin Lacy, in what forwardness
Are all your companies?
    Lacy. All well prepared.
The men of Hertfordshire lie at Mile-end,
Suffolk and Essex train in Tothill-fields,
The Londoners and those of Middlesex,
All gallantly prepared in Finsbury,
With frolic spirits long for their parting hour.
    Lord Mayor. They have their imprest,[3]
    coats, and furniture;[4]

---

[1] In Elizabethan times used for any relative not of the immediate family.
[2] Squandered.
[3] Advance pay.   [4] Equipment.

And, if it please your cousin Lacy come
To the Guildhall, he shall receive his pay;
And twenty pounds besides my brethren
Will freely give him, to approve our loves
We bear unto my lord, your uncle here.

LACY. I thank your honor.

LINCOLN. Thanks, my good lord mayor.

LORD MAYOR. At the Guildhall we will
expect your coming.   (*Exit*)

LINCOLN. (*Sarcastically*) To approve your
loves to me! No subtilty!
Nephew, that twenty pound he doth bestow
For joy to rid you from his daughter Rose.
But, cousins both, now here are none but
friends,
I would not have you cast an amorous eye
Upon so mean a project as the love
Of a gay, wanton, painted citizen.
I know, this churl even in the height of scorn
Doth hate the mixture of his blood with
thine.
I pray thee, do thou so! Remember, coz,
What honorable fortunes wait on thee:
Increase the king's love, which so brightly
shines,
And gilds thy hopes. I have no heir but
thee,—
And yet not thee, if with a wayward spirit
Thou start from the true bias of my love.

LACY. My lord, I will for honor, not
desire
Of land or livings, or to be your heir,
So guide my actions in pursuit of France,
As shall add glory to the Lacys' name.

LINCOLN. Coz, for those words here's
thirty Portuguese,[5]
And, Nephew Askew, there a few for you.
Fair Honor, in her loftiest eminence,
Stays in France for you, till you fetch her
thence.
Then, nephews, clap swift wings on your
designs:
Begone, begone, make haste to the Guildhall;
There presently I'll meet you. Do not stay:
Where honor beckons, shame attends delay.
                                      (*Exit*)

ASKEW. How gladly would your uncle
have you gone!

LACY. True, coz, but I'll o'erreach his
policies.
I have some serious business for three days,

[5] A gold coin, varying in value from £3 5s to
£4 10s.

Which nothing but my presence can dis-
patch.
You, therefore, cousin, with the companies,
Shall haste to Dover; there I'll meet with
you:
Or, if I stay past my prefixéd time,
Away for France; we'll meet in Normandy.
The twenty pounds my lord mayor gives to
me
You shall receive, and these ten Portuguese,
Part of mine uncle's thirty. Gentle coz,
Have care to our great charge; I know your
wisdom
Hath tried itself in higher consequence.

ASKEW. Coz, all myself am yours: yet
have this care,
To lodge in London with all secrecy;
Our uncle Lincoln hath, besides his own,
Many a jealous eye that in your face
Stares only to watch means for your disgrace.

LACY. Stay, cousin, who be these?

(*Enter* SIMON EYRE, *his wife* MARGERY
EYRE, JANE, HODGE, FIRK, *and* RALPH, *carrying a pair of women's shoes, just finished.
All are in working clothes, as if they had just
run out of the shop. The men are talking
excitedly, and the women are crying*)

EYRE. Leave whining, leave whining!
Away with this whimpering, this puling,
these blubbering tears, and these wet eyes!
I'll get thy husband discharged, I warrant
thee, sweet Jane; go to!

HODGE. Master, here be the captains.

EYRE. Peace, Hodge; husht, ye knave,
husht!

FIRK. Here be the cavaliers and the colonels, master.

EYRE. Peace, Firk; peace, my fine Firk!
Stand by with your pishery-pashery, away!
I am a man of the best presence; I'll speak to
them, an they were Popes.—Gentlemen, captains, colonels, commanders! Brave men,
brave leaders, may it please you to give me
audience. I am Simon Eyre, the mad shoemaker of Tower Street; this wench with the
mealy mouth that will never tire is my wife,
I can tell you; here's Hodge, my man and
my foreman; here's Firk, my fine firking[6]
journeyman, and this is blubbered Jane. All

[6] Frisking.

we come to be suitors for this honest Ralph.
Keep him at home, and as I am a true shoemaker and a gentleman of the Gentle Craft,
buy spurs yourselves, and I'll find ye boots
these seven years.

MARGERY. Seven years, husband?

EYRE. Peace, midriff, peace! I know what
I do. Peace!

FIRK. Truly, master cormorant, you shall
do God good service to let Ralph and his
wife stay together. She's a young new-married woman; if you take her husband away
from her a night, you undo her; she may beg
in the daytime; for he's as good a workman
at a prick and an awl, as any is in our trade.

JANE. O let him stay, else I shall be undone.

FIRK. Ay, truly, she shall be laid at one
side like a pair of old shoes else, and be
occupied for no use.

LACY. Truly, my friends, it lies not in
my power:
The Londoners are pressed, paid, and set
forth
By the lord mayor, I cannot change a man.

HODGE. Why, then you were as good be
a corporal as a colonel, if you cannot discharge one good fellow; and I tell you true,
I think you do more than you can answer,
to press a man within a year and a day of his
marriage.

EYRE. Well said, melancholy Hodge;
gramercy, my fine foreman.

MARGERY. Truly, gentlemen, it were ill
done for such as you, to stand so stiffly against
a poor young wife; considering her case, she
is new-married, but let that pass: I pray, deal
not roughly with her; her husband is a young
man, and but newly entered, but let that
pass.

EYRE. Away with your pishery-pashery,
your pols and your edipols![7] Peace, midriff;
silence, Cicely Bumtrinket! Let your head
speak.

FIRK. Yea, and the horns too, master.

EYRE. Too soon, my fine Firk, too soon!
Peace, scoundrels! See you this man? Captains, you will not release him? (LACY *and*
ASKEW *shake their heads*) Well, let him go;
he's a proper shot; let him vanish! Peace,
Jane, dry up thy tears, they'll make his powder dankish. Take him, brave men; Hector

of Troy was an hackney[8] to him, Hercules
and Termagant[9] scoundrels, Prince Arthur's
Round-table—by the Lord of Ludgate—ne'er
fed such a tall, such a dapper swordsman; by
the life of Pharaoh, a brave resolute swordsman! Peace, Jane! I say no more, mad knaves.

FIRK. See, see, Hodge, how my master
raves in commendation of Ralph!

HODGE. Ralph, th' art a gull, by this hand,
an thou goest not.

ASKEW. I am glad, good Master Eyre, it
is my hap
To meet so resolute a soldier.
Trust me, for your report and love to him,
A common slight regard shall not respect him.

LACY. Is thy name Ralph?

RALPH. Yes, sir.

LACY. Give me thy hand;
Thou shalt not want, as I am a gentleman.
Woman, be patient; God, no doubt, will send
Thy husband safe again; but he must go,
His country's quarrel says it shall be so.

HODGE. Th' art a gull, by my stirrup, if
thou dost not go. I will not have thee strike
thy gimlet into these weak vessels (*pointing
to the shoes* RALPH *is carrying*); prick thine
enemies, Ralph.

(*Enter* DODGER)

DODGER. My lord, your uncle on the
Tower-hill
Stays with the lord mayor and the aldermen,
And doth request you with all speed you
may,
To hasten thither.

ASKEW. Cousin, come let's go.

LACY. Dodger, run you before, tell them
we come.—   (*Exit* DODGER)
This Dodger is mine uncle's parasite.
The arrant'st varlet that e'er breathed on
earth;
He sets more discord in a noble house
By one day's broaching of his pickthank tales,
Than can be salved again in twenty years,
And he, I fear, shall go with us to France,
To pry into our actions.

ASKEW. Therefore, coz,

[7] Various forms of asseveration.

[8] *I.e.* a common drudge.

[9] An imaginary deity whom the Mohamme-
dans were supposed to worship. Popularly presented in the old mystery plays as a violent,
overbearing personage.

It shall behove you to be circumspect.

LACY. Fear not, good cousin.—Ralph, hie to your colors.   (*Exeunt* LACY *and* ASKEW)

RALPH. I must, because there is no remedy;
But, gentle master and my loving dame,
As you have always been a friend to me,
So in my absence think upon my wife.

JANE. Alas, my Ralph.

MARGERY. She cannot speak for weeping.

EYRE. Peace, you cracked groats,[10] you mustard tokens,[11] disquiet not the brave soldier. Go thy ways, Ralph!

JANE. Ay, ay, you bid him go; what shall I do
When he is gone?

FIRK. Why, be doing with me or my fellow Hodge; be not idle.

EYRE. Let me see thy hand, Jane. This fine hand, this white hand, these pretty fingers must spin, must card, must work; work, you bombast-cotton-candle-quean;[12] work for your living, with a pox to you.— Hold thee, Ralph, here's five sixpences for thee; fight for the honor of the Gentle Craft, for the gentlemen shoemakers, the courageous cordwainers, the flower of St. Martin's, the mad knaves of Bedlam, Fleet Street, Tower Street and Whitechapel; crack me the crowns of the French knaves; a pox on them, crack them; fight, by the Lord of Ludgate; fight, my fine boy!

FIRK. Here, Ralph, here's three twopences: two carry into France, the third shall wash our souls at parting, for sorrow is dry.

For my sake, firk the *Basa mon cues.*

HODGE. Ralph, I am heavy at parting; but here's a shilling for thee. God send thee to cram thy slops[13] with French crowns, and thy enemies' bellies with bullets.

RALPH. I thank you, master, and I thank you all.

Now, gentle wife, my loving lovely Jane,
Rich men, at parting, give their wives rich gifts,
Jewels and rings, to grace their lily hands.
Thou know'st our trade makes rings for women's heels:
Here take this pair of shoes, cut out by Hodge,
Stitched by my fellow Firk, seamed by myself,
Made up and pinked[14] with letters for thy name.
Wear them, my dear Jane, for thy husband's sake,
And every morning, when thou pull'st them on,
Remember me, and pray for my return.
Make much of them; for I have made them so,
That I can know them from a thousand mo.

(*Drum sounds. Enter the* LORD MAYOR, *the* EARL OF LINCOLN, LACY, ASKEW, DODGER, *and Soldiers. They pass over the stage;* RALPH *falls in amongst them;* FIRK *and the rest cry "Farewell,"* &c., *and so exeunt.*)

Act II

SCENE I. *The Garden of the* LORD MAYOR's *Country House at Old Ford, near London.*

(*Enter* ROSE, *alone, making a garland*)

ROSE. Here sit thou down upon this flow'ry bank,
And make a garland for thy Lacy's head.
These pinks, these roses, and these violets,
These blushing gilliflowers, these marigolds,
The fair embroidery of his coronet,
Carry not half such beauty in their cheeks,

As the sweet countenance of my Lacy doth.
O my most unkind father! O my stars,
Why lowered you so at my nativity,
To make me love, yet live robbed of my love?
Here as a thief am I imprisonèd
For my dear Lacy's sake within those walls,
Which by my father's cost were builded up
For better purposes; here must I languish

[10] Worthless coins.
[11] Coupons given to purchasers of mustard.

[12] Bombast is another name for cotton; a cotton candle is one with a cotton wick.
[13] Baggy breeches.   [14] Punched.

For him that doth as much lament, I know,
Mine absence, as for him I pine in woe.

(*Enter* SYBIL *in travelling dress, having just returned from London*)

SYBIL. (*Gaily*) Good morrow, young mistress. I am sure you make that garland for me; against I shall be Lady of the Harvest.

ROSE. Sybil, what news at London?

SYBIL. None but good; my lord mayor, your father, and master Philpot, your uncle, and Master Scott, your cousin, and Mistress Frigbottom by Doctors' Commons, do all, by my troth, send you most hearty commendations.

ROSE. Did Lacy send kind greetings to his love?

SYBIL. O yes, out of cry,[15] by my troth. I scant knew him; here 'a wore a scarf; and here a scarf, here a bunch of feathers, and here precious stones and jewels, and a pair of garters,—O, monstrous! like one of our yellow silk curtains at home here in Old Ford house, here in Master Bellymount's chamber. I stood at our door in Cornhill, looked at him, he at me indeed, spake to him, but he not to me, not a word; marry go-up, thought I, with a wanion![16] He passed by me as proud—Marry foh! are you grown humorous, thought I; and so shut the door, and in I came.

ROSE. O Sybil, how dost thou my Lacy wrong!
My Rowland is as gentle as a lamb,
No dove was ever half so mild as he.

SYBIL. Mild? (*Sarcastically*) yea, as a bushel of stamped crabs.[17] He looked upon me as sour as verjuice. Go thy ways, thought I; thou may'st be much in thy gaskins, but nothing in thy nether-stocks.[18] This is your fault, mistress, to love him that loves not you; he thinks scorn to do as he's done to; but if
I were as you, I'd cry: Go by, Jeronimo, go by![19]
I'd set mine old debts against my new driblets,
And the hare's foot against the goose giblets,[20]
For if ever I sigh, when sleep I should take,
Pray God I may lose my maidenhead when I wake.

ROSE. Will my love leave me then, and go to France?

SYBIL. I know not that, but I am sure I see him stalk before the soldiers. By my troth, he is a proper man; but he is proper that proper doth. Let him go snick up,[20a] young mistress.

ROSE. Get thee to London, and learn perfectly
Whether my Lacy go to France, or no.
Do this, and I will give thee for thy pains
My cambric apron and my Romish gloves,
My purple stockings and a stomacher.
Say, wilt thou do this, Sybil, for my sake?

SYBIL. Will I, quoth a? At whose suit? By my troth, yes I'll go. A cambric apron, gloves, a pair of purple stockings, and a stomacher! I'll sweat in purple, mistress, for you; I'll take anything that comes a God's name. O rich! a cambric apron! Faith, then have at "up tails all." I'll go jiggy-joggy to London, and be here in a trice, young mistress. (*Exit*)

ROSE. Do so, good Sybil. Meantime wretched I
Will sit and sigh for his lost company. (*Exit*)

SCENE II. *A Street in London.*

(*Enter* ROWLAND LACY, *disguised like a Dutch Shoemaker and carrying a kit of shoemakers' tools*)

LACY. How many shapes have gods and kings devised,
Thereby to compass their desired loves!
It is no shame for Rowland Lacy, then,
To clothe his cunning with the Gentle Craft,
That, thus disguised, I may unknown possess
The only happy presence of my Rose.
For her have I forsook my charge in France,

[15] Beyond measure.   [16] Vengeance.
[17] Crushed crab-apples.

[18] "You may be superior in that fine costume, but you're no better than any one else in your underclothes."
[19] A misquotation from *The Spanish Tragedy*, which most dramatists ridiculed at this time.
[20] A proverbial phrase for setting one thing off against another.
[20a] Go and be hanged!

Incurred the king's displeasure, and stirred up
Rough hatred in mine uncle Lincoln's breast.
O love, how powerful art thou, that canst change
High birth to baseness, and a noble mind
To the mean semblance of a shoemaker!
But thus it must be. For her cruel father,
·Hating the single union of our souls,
Hath secretly conveyed my Rose from London,
To bar me of her presence; but I trust,
Fortune and this disguise will further me
Once more to view her beauty, gain her sight.
Here in Tower Street with Eyre the shoemaker
Mean I a while to work; I know the trade,
I learnt it when I was in Wittenberg.
Then cheer thy hoping spirits, be not dismayed,
Thou canst not want: do Fortune what she can,
The Gentle Craft is living for a man. (*Exit*)

SCENE III. *The Street before* SIMON EYRE'S *combined shop and house, and the open work shop behind it.*

(*Enter* SIMON EYRE, *finishing dressing as he walks*)

EYRE. Where be these boys, these girls, these drabs, these scoundrels? They wallow in the fat brewis [21] of my bounty, and lick up the crumbs of my table, yet will not rise to see my walks cleansed. (*Shouting back into the house at the top of his voice*) Come out, you powder-beef [22] queans! What, Nan! what, Madge Mumble-crust! Come out, you fat midriff-swag-belly-whores, and sweep me these kennels that the noisome stench offend not the noses of my neighbors. What, Firk, I say; what, Hodge! Open my shop-windows! What, Firk, I say!

(*Enter* FIRK *half dressed, yawning and scratching*)

FIRK. O master, is't you that speak bandog [23] and Bedlam this morning? I was in a dream, and mused what madman was got into the street so early; have you drunk this morning that your throat is so clear?

EYRE (*Laughing and bustling about*) Ah, well said, Firk; well said, Firk. To work, my fine knave, to work! Wash thy face, and thou'lt be more blest.

FIRK. Let them wash my face that will eat it. Good master, send for a souse-wife, [24] if you will have my face cleaner.

[21] Bread soaked in broth.
[22] Salt beef.
[23] A dog kept tied up.
[24] Woman who pickled pigs' faces.

(*Enter* HODGE)

EYRE. Away, sloven! avaunt, scoundrel! —Good-morrow, Hodge; good-morrow, my fine foreman.

HODGE. O master, good-morrow; y'are an early stirrer. Here's a fair morning.—Good-morrow, Firk, I could have slept this hour. Here's a brave day towards.

EYRE. Oh, haste to work, my fine foreman, haste to work.

FIRK. Master, I am dry as dust to hear my fellow Roger talk of fair weather; let us pray for good leather, and let clowns and plough-boys and those that work in the fields pray for brave days. We work in a dry shop; what care I if it rain?

(*Enter* MARGERY *sleepily rubbing her eyes*)

EYRE. How now, Dame Margery, can you see to rise? Trip and go, call up the drabs, your maids.

MARGERY. See to rise? I hope 'tis time enough, 'tis early enough for any woman to be seen abroad. I marvel how many wives in Tower Street are up so soon. Gods me, 'tis not noon,—here's a yowling!

EYRE. Peace, Margery, peace! Where's Cicely Bumtrinket, your maid? She has a privy fault, she farts in her sleep. Call the quean up; if my men want shoe-thread, I'll swinge her in a stirrup. [25]

[25] *I.e.* "I'll whip her with a stirrup if she doesn't keep the men supplied with shoe-thread fast enough."

FIRK. Yet, that's but a dry beating; here's still a sign of drought.

(*Enter* LACY, *in his disguise as* HANS MEULTER, *Dutch shoemaker, singing*)

HANS. *Der was een bore van Gelderland*
Frolick sie byen;
He was als dronck he cold nyet
stand,
Upsolce sie byen.
Tap eens de canneken,
Drincke, schone mannekin.[26]

FIRK. Master, for my life, yonder's a brother of the Gentle Craft; if he bear not Saint Hugh's bones,[27] I'll forfeit my bones; he's some uplandish[28] workman: hire him, good master, that I may learn some gibble-gabble; 'twill make us work the faster.

EYRE. Peace, Firk! A hard world! Let him pass, let him vanish; we have journeymen enow. Peace, my fine Firk!

MARGERY. (*Sarcastically*) Nay, nay, y' are best follow your man's counsel; you shall see what will come on't: we have not men enow, but we must entertain every butter-box;[29] but let that pass.

HODGE. Dame, 'fore God, if my master follow your counsel, he'll consume little beef. He shall[30] be glad of men, an he can catch them.

FIRK. Ay, that he shall.

HODGE. 'Fore God, a proper man, and I warrant, a fine workman. Master, farewell; dame, adieu; if such a man as he cannot find work, Hodge is not for you.
(*Starts to pack up his tools and leave the shop*)

EYRE. Stay, my fine Hodge.

FIRK. Faith, an your foreman go, dame, you must take a journey to seek a new journeyman; if Roger remove, Firk follows.

---

[26] There was a boor from Gelderland,
Jolly they be;
He was so drunk he could not stand,
Half-seas-over (?) they be:
Tap once the cannikin,
Drink, pretty mannikin!
[27] Affectionate name for shoemakers' tools.
[28] Country.
[29] A contemptuous name for a Dutchman.
[30] Ought to.

If Saint Hugh's bones shall not be set a-work, I may prick mine awl in the walls, and go play. Fare ye well, master; good-bye, dame.

EYRE. Tarry, my fine Hodge, my brisk foreman! Stay, Firk!—Peace, pudding-broth! By the Lord of Ludgate, I love my men as my life. Peace, you gallimafry!—Hodge, if he want work, I'll hire him. One of you to him; stay,—he comes to us.

HANS. Goeden dach, meester, ende u vro oak.[31]

FIRK. Nails, if I should speak after him without drinking, I should choke. And you, friend Oake, are you of the Gentle Craft?

HANS. Yaw, yaw, ik bin den skomawker.[32]

FIRK. Den skomaker, quoth a! And hark you, skomaker, have you all your tools, a good rubbing-pin, a good stopper, a good dresser, your four sorts of awls, and your two balls of wax, your paring knife, your hand- and thumb-leathers, and good St. Hugh's bones to smooth up your work?

HANS. Yaw, yaw; be niet vorveard. Ik hab all de dingen voour mack skooes groot and cleane.[33]

FIRK. Ha, ha! Good master, hire him; he'll make me laugh so that I shall work more in mirth than I can in earnest.

EYRE. Hear ye, friend, have ye any skill in the mystery of cordwainers?

HANS. Ik weet niet wat yow seg; ich verstaw you niet.[34]

FIRK. Why, thus, man: (*He goes through a pantomime of a shoemaker at work*) Ich verste u niet, quoth a.

HANS. Yaw, yaw, yaw; ick can dat wel doen.[35]

FIRK. Yaw yaw! He speaks yawing like a jackdaw that gapes to be fed with cheese-curds. Oh, he'll give a villanous pull at a can of double-beer; but Hodge and I have the vantage, we must drink first, because we are the eldest journeymen.

EYRE. What is thy name?

HANS. Hans—Hans Meulter.

EYRE. Give me thy hand; th' art welcome.

---

[31] Good day, master, and you, mistress, too.
[32] Yes, yes, I am a shoemaker.
[33] Yes, yes; be not afraid. I have everything to make shoes big and little.
[34] I know not what you say; I understand you not.
[35] Yes, yes, yes; I can do that well.

—Hodge, entertain him; Firk, bid him welcome; come, Hans. Run, wife, bid your maids, your trullibubs,[36] make ready my fine men's breakfasts. To him, Hodge!

HODGE. Hans, th' art welcome; use thyself friendly, for we are good fellows; if not, thou shalt be fought with, wert thou bigger than a giant.

FIRK. Yea, and drunk with, wert thou Gargantua. My master keeps no cowards, I tell thee.—Ho, boy, bring him an heel-block, here's a new journeyman.

(*Enter Boy*)

HANS. O, ich wersto you; ich moet een halve dossen cans betaelen; here, boy, nempt dis skilling, tap eens freelicke.[37]

(*Exit Boy*)

EYRE. Quick, snipper-snapper, away! Firk, scour thy throat, thou shalt wash it with Castilian liquor.

(*Enter Boy with tankards of beer*)

Come, my last of the fives,[38] give me a can. Have to thee, Hans; here, Hodge; here, Firk; drink, you mad Greeks, and work like true Trojans, and pray for Simon Eyre, the shoemaker.—Here, Hans, and th' art welcome.

FIRK. Lo, dame, you would have lost a good fellow that will teach us to laugh. This beer came hopping in well.

MARGERY. Simon, it is almost seven.

EYRE. Is't so, Dame Clapper-dudgeon? Is't seven a clock, and my men's breakfast not ready? Trip and go, you soused conger, away! Come, you mad hyperboreans; follow me, Hodge; follow me, Hans; come after, my fine Firk; to work, to work a while, and then to breakfast! (*Exit SIMON EYRE*)

FIRK. Soft! Yaw, yaw, good Hans, (*pulling HANS back and stepping in front of him*) though my master have no more wit but to call you afore me, I am not so foolish to go behind you, I being the elder journeyman.

(*Exeunt*)

SCENE IV. *A Field near Old Ford.*

(*Hunters calling off stage. Then enter Master WARNER and Master HAMMON, attired as Hunters*)

HAMMON. Cousin, beat every brake, the game's not far.
This way with wingèd feet he fled from death,
Whilst the pursuing hounds, scenting his steps,
Find out his highway to destruction.
Besides, the miller's boy told me even now,
He saw him take soil,[39] and he halloaed him,
Affirming him to have been so embost[40]
That long he could not hold.

WARNER. If it be so,

'Tis best we trace these meadows by Old Ford.

(*Sounds of hunters and dogs off stage. Enter a BOY*)

HAMMON. How now, boy? Where's the deer? speak, saw'st thou him?

BOY. O yea; I saw him leap through a hedge, and then over a ditch, then at my lord mayor's pale. Over he skipped me, and in he went me, and "holla" the hunters cried, and "there, boy; there, boy!" But there he is, 'a mine honesty.

HAMMON. Boy, God amercy. Cousin, let's away;
I hope we shall find better sport to-day.

(*Exeunt*)

[36] A cant term for anything very trifling.
[37] O, I understand you; I must pay for a half-dozen cans; here, boy, take this shilling, tap once freely.
[38] A small size of last.
[39] Take to the water.
[40] Exhausted.

SCENE V. *Another Part of the Field.*

(Sounds of hunters and dogs off stage again.
Enter ROSE *and* SYBIL)

ROSE. Why, Sybil, wilt thou prove a
forester?

SYBIL. Upon some, no; [41] forester, go by;
no, faith, mistress. The deer came running
into the barn through the orchard and over
the pale; I wot well, I looked as pale as a
new cheese to see him. But whip, says goodman Pinclose, up with his flail, and our Nick
with a prong, and down he fell, and they
upon him, and I upon them. By my troth,
we had such sport; and in the end we ended
him; his throat we cut, flayed him, unhorned
him, and my lord mayor shall eat of him
anon, when he comes.

          (Hunting horns off stage)
ROSE. Hark, hark, the hunters come; y'
    are best take heed,
They'll have a saying to you for this deed.

(Enter Master HAMMON, Master WARNER,
Huntsmen, and BOY)

HAMMON. God save you, fair ladies.
SYBIL. Ladies! O gross! [42]
WARNER. Came not a buck this way?
ROSE. No, but two does.
HAMMON. And which way went they?
Faith, we'll hunt at those.
SYBIL. *(Coquettishly)* At those? upon
some, no: when, can you tell?
WARNER. Upon some, ay.
SYBIL. Good Lord!
WARNER. Wounds! Then farewell!
HAMMON. Boy, which way went he?
BOY. This way, sir, he ran.
HAMMON. This way he ran indeed, fair
    Mistress Rose;
Our game was lately in your orchard seen.
WARNER. Can you advise, which way he
took his flight?
SYBIL. *(Impudently)* Follow your nose;
his horns will guide you right.
WARNER. Th' art a mad wench.
SYBIL. O, rich!
ROSE. Trust me, not I.

[41] No indeed.   [42] Stupid.

It is not like that the wild forest-deer
Would come so near to places of resort;
You are deceived, he fled some other way.
WARNER. *(to* SYBIL) Which way, my
sugar-candy, can you shew?
SYBIL. *(Flirting with him)* Come up,
good honeysops, upon some, no.
ROSE. Why do you stay, and not pursue
your game?
SYBIL. I'll hold my life, their hunting-nags
be lame.
HAMMON. A deer more dear is found
within this place.
ROSE. But not the deer, sir, which you
had in chase.
HAMMON. I chased the deer, but this dear
chaseth me.
ROSE. The strangest hunting that ever I
    see.
But where's your park?
          (She offers to go away)
HAMMON. My park? 'Tis here: O stay!
ROSE. Impale me in't, and then I will not
stray.
WARNER. They wrangle, wench; we are
more kind than they.
SYBIL. What kind of hart is that dear
heart, you seek?
WARNER. A hart, dear heart.
SYBIL. Who ever saw the like?
ROSE. To lose your heart, is't possible you
can?
HAMMON. My heart is lost.
ROSE. *(Mockingly)* Alack, good gentle-
man!
HAMMON. This poor lost heart would I
wish you might find.
ROSE. You, by such luck, might prove
your hart a hind.
HAMMON. Why, Luck had horns, so have
I heard some say.
ROSE. Now, God, an't be his will, send
Luck into your way.

(Enter the LORD MAYOR *and Servants)*

LORD MAYOR. What, Master Hammon?
Welcome to Old Ford!
SYBIL. Gods pittikins, hands off, sir!
Here's my lord.

LORD MAYOR. I hear you had ill luck, and lost your game.

HAMMON. 'Tis true, my lord.

LORD MAYOR. I am sorry for the same. What gentleman is this?

HAMMON. My brother-in-law.

LORD MAYOR. Y' are welcome both; sith Fortune offers you
Into my hands, you shall not part from hence,
Until you have refreshed your wearied limbs.—
Go, Sybil, cover the board!—You shall be guest

To no good cheer, but even a hunter's feast.

HAMMON. I thank your lordship.—(To WARNER) Cousin, on my life,
For our lost venison I shall find a wife.
(*Exeunt*)

LORD MAYOR. In, gentlemen; I'll not be absent long.—
This Hammon is a proper gentleman.
A citizen by birth, fairly allied;
How fit an husband were he for my girl!
Well, I will in, and do the best I can,
To match my daughter to this gentleman.
(*Exit*)

Act III

SCENE I. SIMON EYRE'S *Shop.*

(*Enter* LACY *still disguised as* HANS, SKIPPER, HODGE, *and* FIRK)

SKIPPER. Ick sal yow wat seggen, Hans; dis skip, dat comen from Candy, is al vol, by Got's sacrament, van sugar, civet, almonds, cambrick, end alle dingen, towsand towsand ding. Nempt it, Hans, nempt it vor v meester. Daer be de bils van laden. Your meester Simon Eyre sal hae good copen. Wat seggen yow, Hans? [43]

FIRK. Wat seggen de reggen, de copen slopen—laugh, Hodge, laugh!

HANS. Mine liever broder Firk, bringt Meester Eyre tot det signe vn Swannekin; daer sal yow finde dis skipper end me. Wat seggen yow, broder Firk? Doot it, Hodge. [44] Come, skipper.

(*Exeunt* HANS *and* SKIPPER)

FIRK. Bring him, quoth you? Here's no knavery, to bring my master to buy a ship worth of lading of two or three hundred thousand pounds. Alas, that's nothing; a trifle, a bauble, Hodge.

[43] I'll tell you what, Hans; this ship that comes from Candia, is all full, by God's sacrament, of sugar, civet, almonds, cambric, and all things, a thousand, thousand things. Take it, Hans, take it for your master. There are the bills of lading. Your master, Simon Eyre, shall have a good bargain. What say you, Hans?

[44] My dear brother Firk, bring Master Eyre to the sign of the Swan; there shall you find this skipper and me. What say you, brother Firk? Do it, Hodge.

HODGE. The truth is, Firk, that the merchant owner of the ship dares not shew his head, and therefore this skipper that deals for him, for the love he bears to Hans, offers my master Eyre a bargain in the commodities. He shall have a reasonable day of payment; he may sell the wares by that time, and be an huge gainer himself.

FIRK. Yea, but can my fellow Hans lend my master twenty porpentines as an earnest penny?

HODGE. Portegues, [45] thou wouldst say; here they be, Firk; hark, they jingle in my pocket like St. Mary Overy's bells.

(*Enter* EYRE *and* MARGERY *followed by* BOY)

FIRK. Mum, here comes my dame and my master. She'll scold, on my life, for loitering this Monday; but all's one, let them all say what they can, Monday's our holiday.
(*He sings*)

MARGERY. You sing, Sir Sauce, but I beshrew your heart, I fear, for this your singing we shall smart.

FIRK. Smart for me, dame; why, dame, why?

HODGE. Master, I hope you'll not suffer my dame to take down your journeymen.

FIRK. If she take me down, I'll take her up; yea, and take her down too, a button-hole lower.

[45] I.e. Portuguese, see note on p. 114.

EYRE. Peace, Firk; not I, Hodge; by the life of Pharaoh, by the Lord of Ludgate, by this beard, every hair whereof I value at a king's ransom, she shall not meddle with you. —Peace, you bombast-cotton-candle-quean; away, queen of clubs; quarrel not with me and my men, with me and my fine Firk; I'll firk you, if you do.

MARGERY. Yea, yea, man, you may use me as you please; but let that pass.

EYRE. Let it pass, let it vanish away; peace! Am I not Simon Eyre? Are not these my brave men, brave shoemakers, all gentlemen of the Gentle Craft? Prince am I none, yet am I nobly born, as being the sole son of a shoemaker. Away, rubbish! vanish, melt; melt like kitchen-stuff.

MARGERY. Yea, yea, 'tis well; I must be called rubbish kitchen-stuff, for a sort[46] of knaves.

FIRK. Nay, dame, you shall not weep and wail in woe for me. Master, I'll stay no longer; here's an inventory of my shop-tools. Adieu, master; Hodge, farewell.

HODGE. Nay, stay, Firk, thou shalt not go alone.

MARGERY. I pray, let them go; there be more maids than Mawkin, more men than Hodge, and more fools than Firk.

FIRK. Fools? Nails! if I tarry now, I would my guts might be turned to shoe-thread.

HODGE. And if I stay, I pray God I may be turned to a Turk, and set in Finsbury[47] for boys to shoot at.—Come, Firk.

EYRE. Stay, my fine knaves, you arms of my trade, you pillars of my profession. What, shall a tittle-tattle's words make you forsake Simon Eyre?—Avaunt, kitchen-stuff! Rip, you brown-bread Tannikin; out of my sight! Move me not! Have not I ta'en you from selling tripes in Eastcheap, and set you in my shop, and made you hail-fellow with Simon Eyre, the shoemaker? And now do you deal thus with my journeymen? Look, you powder-beef-quean, on the face of Hodge, here's a face for a lord.

FIRK. (Pointing at MARGERY, mockingly) And here's a face for any lady in Christendom.

EYRE. Rip, you chitterling, avaunt! Boy,

bid the tapster of the Boar's Head fill me a dozen cans of beer for my journeymen.

FIRK. A dozen cans? O brave! Hodge, now I'll stay.

EYRE. (Aside to the BOY) An the knave fills any more than two, he pays for them. (Exit BOY. Aloud) A dozen cans of beer for my journeymen. (Re-enter BOY) Here, you mad Mesopotamians, wash your livers with this liquor. Where be the odd ten? (Aside) No more, Madge, no more.—Well said. Drink and to work!—What work dost thou, Hodge? what work?

HODGE. I am a-making a pair of shoes for my lord mayor's daughter, Mistress Rose.

FIRK. And I a pair of shoes for Sybil, my lord's maid. I deal with her.

EYRE. Sybil? Fie, defile not thy fine workmanly fingers with the feet of kitchen-stuff and basting-ladles. Ladies of the court, fine ladies, my lads, commit their feet to our apparelling; put gross work to Hans. Yark[48] and seam, yark and seam!

FIRK. For yarking and seaming let me alone, an I come to 't.

HODGE. Well, Master, all this is from the bias.[49] Do you remember the ship my fellow Hans told you of? The Skipper and he are both drinking at the Swan. Here be the Portegues to give earnest. If you go through with it, you cannot choose but be a lord at least.

FIRK. Nay, dame, if my master prove not a lord, and you a lady, hang me.

MARGERY. Yea, like enough, if you may loiter and tipple thus.

FIRK. Tipple, dame? No, we have been bargaining with Skellum Skanderbag: can you Dutch spreaken for a ship of silk Cyprus, laden with sugar-candy?

(Enter the BOY with a velvet coat and an Alderman's gown. EYRE puts them on)

EYRE. Peace, Firk; silence, Tittle-tattle! Hodge, I'll go through with it. Here's a seal-ring, and I have sent for a guarded gown[50] and a damask cassock. See where it comes; look here, Maggy; help me, Firk; apparel me,

[46] Set.
[47] A famous practising ground for archery.
[48] Thrust, i.e., push the awl through the leather.
[49] Off the point.
[50] A gown with guards or facings.

Hodge; silk and satin, you mad Philistines, silk and satin.

Firk. Ha, ha, my master will be as proud as a dog in a doublet, all in beaten [51] damask and velvet.

Eyre. Softly, Firk, for rearing of the nap, and wearing threadbare my garments. How dost thou like me, Firk? How do I look, my fine Hodge?

Hodge. Why, now you look like yourself, master. I warrant you, there's few in the city, but will give you the wall, and come upon you with the right worshipful.

Firk. Nails, my master looks like a threadbare cloak new turned and dressed. Lord, Lord, to see what good raiment doth! Dame, dame, are you not enamored?

Eyre. How say'st thou, Maggy, am I not brisk? Am I not fine?

Margery. Fine? By my troth, sweetheart, very fine! By my troth, I never liked thee so well in my life, sweetheart; but let that pass. I warrant, there be many women in the city have not such handsome husbands, but only for their apparel; but let that pass too.

(*Re-enter* Hans *and* Skipper)

Hans. Godden day, mester. Dis be de skipper dat heb de skip van marchandice; de commodity ben good; nempt it, master, nempt it. [52]

Eyre. Godamercy, Hans; welcome, skipper. Where lies this ship of merchandise?

Skipper. De skip ben in revere; dor be van Sugar, cyvet, almonds, cambrick, and a towsand towsand tings, gotz sacrament; nempt it, mester: ye sal heb good copen. [53]

Firk. To him, master! O sweet master! O sweet wares! Prunes, almonds, sugar-candy, carrot-roots, turnips, O brave fatting meat! Let not a man buy a nutmeg but yourself.

Eyre. Peace, Firk! Come, skipper, I'll go aboard with you.—Hans, have you made him drink?

Skipper. Yaw, yaw, ic heb veale gedrunck. [54]

Eyre. Come, Hans, follow me. Skipper, thou shalt have my countenance in the city.

(*Exeunt* Eyre, Hans *and* Skipper)

Firk. Yaw, heb veale gedrunck, quoth a. They may well be called butter-boxes, when they drink fat veal and thick beer too. But come, dame, I hope you'll chide us no more.

Margery. No, faith, Firk; no, perdy, Hodge. I do feel honor creep upon me, and which is more, a certain rising in my flesh; but let that pass.

Firk. Rising in your flesh do you feel, say you? Ay, you may be with child, but why should not my master feel a rising in his flesh, having a gown and a gold ring on? But you are such a shrew, you'll soon pull him down.

Margery. Ha, ha! prithee, peace! Thou mak'st my worship laugh; but let that pass. Come, I'll go in; Hodge, prithee, go before me; Firk, follow me.

Firk. Firk doth follow: Hodge, pass out in state.

(*Exeunt*)

Scene II. *A Room in the* Earl of Lincoln's *London House.*

(*Enter the* Earl of Lincoln *and* Dodger)

Lincoln. How now, good Dodger, what's the news in France?

Dodger. My lord, upon the eighteenth day of May
The French and English were prepared to fight;

Each side with eager fury gave the sign
Of a most hot encounter. Five long hours
Both armies fought together; at the length
The lot of victory fell on our sides.
Twelve thousand of the Frenchmen that day died,
Four thousand English, and no man of name

[51] Embroidered.
[52] Good day, master. This is the skipper that has the ship of merchandise; the commodity is good; take it, master, take it.
[53] The ship is in the river; there are sugar, civet, almonds, cambric, and a thousand thousand things, God's sacrament! take it, master; you shall have a good bargain.
[54] Yes, yes, I have drunk well.

But Captain Hyam and young Ardington,
Two gallant gentlemen, I knew them well.
    LINCOLN. But, Dodger, prithee, tell me, in
    this fight
How did my cousin Lacy bear himself?
    DODGER. My lord, your cousin Lacy was
not there.
    LINCOLN. Not there?
    DODGER. No, my good lord.
    LINCOLN. Sure, thou mistakest.
I saw him shipped, and a thousand eyes be-
    side
Were witnesses of the farewells which he
    gave,
When I, with weeping eyes, bid him adieu.
Dodger, take heed.
    DODGER. My lord, I am advised,
That what I spake is true: to prove it so,
His cousin Askew, that supplied his place,
Sent me for him from France, that secretly
He might convey himself thither.
    LINCOLN. Is't even so?
Dares he so carelessly venture his life
Upon the indignation of a king?
Has he despised my love, and spurned those
    favors
Which I with prodigal hand poured on his
    head?
He shall repent his rashness with his soul;
Since of my love he makes no estimate,
I'll make him wish he had not known my
    hate.
Thou hast no other news?
    DODGER. None else, my lord.

    LINCOLN. None worse I know thou hast.—
(*Fuming*) Procure the king
To crown his giddy brows with ample
    honors,
Send him chief colonel, and all my hope
Thus to be dashed! But 'tis in vain to grieve,
One evil cannot a worse one relieve.
Upon my life, I have found out his plot;
That old dog, Love, that fawned upon him so,
Love to that puling girl, his fair-cheeked
    Rose,
The lord mayor's daughter, hath distracted
    him,
And in the fire of that love's lunacy
Hath he burnt up himself, consumed his
    credit.
Lost the king's love, yea, and I fear, his life,
Only to get a wanton to his wife.
Dodger, it is so.
    DODGER. I fear so, my good lord.
    LINCOLN. It is so—nay, sure it cannot be!
I am at my wits' end. Dodger!
    DODGER. Yea, my lord.
    LINCOLN. Thou art acquainted with my
    nephew's haunts; (*Giving him money*)
Spend this gold for thy pains; go seek him
    out;
Watch at my lord mayor's—there if he live,
Dodger, thou shalt be sure to meet with him.
Prithee, be diligent.—Lacy, thy name
Lived once in honor, now 'tis dead in
    shame.—
Be circumspect.   (*Exit*)
    DODGER. I warrant you, my lord.   (*Exit*)

SCENE III. *A Room in the* LORD MAYOR's *London House.*

(*Enter the* LORD MAYOR *and* Master SCOTT)

    LORD MAYOR. Good Master Scott, I have
    been bold with you,
To be a witness to a wedding-knot
Betwixt young Master Hammon and my
    daughter.
O, stand aside; see where the lovers come.

(*Enter* Master HAMMON *and* ROSE)

    ROSE. Can it be possible you love me so?
No, no, within those eyeballs I espy
Apparent likelihoods of flattery.

Pray now, let go my hand.
    HAMMON. Sweet Mistress Rose,
Misconstrue not my words, nor misconceive
Of my affection, whose devoted soul
Swears that I love thee dearer than my heart.
    ROSE. As dear as your own heart? I judge
    it right,
Men love their hearts best when th' are out
    of sight.
    HAMMON. I love you, by this hand.
    ROSE. Yet hands off now!
If flesh be frail, how weak and frail's your
    vow!
    HAMMON. Then by my life I swear.

Rose. Then do not brawl;
One quarrel loseth wife and life and all.
Is not your meaning thus?

Hammon. In faith, you jest.

Rose. Love loves to sport; therefore leave
    love, y' are best.

Lord Mayor. What? square they, Master
Scott?

Scott. Sir, never doubt,
Lovers are quickly in, and quickly out.

Hammon. Sweet Rose, be not so strange
    in fancying me.
Nay, never turn aside, shun not my sight:
I am not grown so fond, to fond [55] my love
On any that shall quit it with disdain;
If you will love me, so—if not, farewell.

Lord Mayor. Why, how now, lovers, are
you both agreed?

Hammon. Yes, faith, my lord.

Lord Mayor. 'Tis well, give me your
    hand.
Give me yours, daughter. (Rose and Ham-
    mon both step back and refuse)—How
    now, both pull back?
What means this, girl?

Rose. I mean to live a maid.

Hammon. (Aside) But not to die one;
pause, ere that be said.

Lord Mayor. Will you still cross me, still
be obstinate?

Hammon. Nay, chide her not, my lord,
    for doing well;
If she can live an happy virgin's life,
'Tis far more blessed than to be a wife.

Rose. Say, sir, I cannot: I have made a
    vow,
Whoever be my husband, 'tis not you.

Lord Mayor. Your tongue is quick; but
    Master Hammon, know,
I bade you welcome to another end.

Hammon. What, would you have me pule
    and pine and pray,
        With "lovely lady," "mistress of
            my heart,"
        "Pardon your servant," and the
            rhymer play,
            Railing on Cupid and his tyrant's-
                dart;
Or shall I undertake some martial spoil,
Wearing your glove at tourney and at tilt,
And tell how many gallants I unhorsed—
Sweet, will this pleasure you?

[55] Another spelling of "found."

Rose. Yea, when wilt begin?
What, love rhymes, man? Fie on that deadly
    sin!

Lord Mayor. If you will have her, I'll
make her agree.

Hammond. Enforced love is worse than
    hate to me.
(Aside) There is a wench keeps shop in the
    Old Change.
To her will I; it is not wealth I seek,
I have enough, and will prefer her love
Before the world.—(Aloud) My good lord
    mayor, adieu.
Old love for me, I have no luck with new.
                                    (Exit)

Lord Mayor. Now, mammet, [56] you have
    well behaved yourself,
But you shall curse your coyness if I live.
    —(Calling)
Who's within there? See you convey your
    mistress
Straight to th' Old Ford! I'll keep you straight
    enough.
'Fore God, I would have sworn the puling
    girl
Would willingly accept of Hammon's love;
But banish him, my thoughts!—Go, minion,
    in!   (Exit Rose)
Now tell me, Master Scott, would you have
    thought
That Master Simon Eyre, the shoemaker,
Had been of wealth to buy such merchan-
    dise?

Scott. 'Twas well, my lord, your honor
    and myself
Grew partners with him; for your bills of
    lading
Shew that Eyre's gains in one commodity
Rise at the least to full three thousand pound
Besides like gain in other merchandise.

Lord Mayor. Well, he shall spend some
    of his thousands now.
For I have sent for him to the Guildhall.

(Enter Eyre)

See, where he comes. Good morrow, Master
    Eyre.

Eyre. Poor Simon Eyre, my lord, your
shoemaker.

Lord Mayor. Well, well, it likes yourself
to term you so.

[56] Doll, puppet.

(*Enter* DODGER)

Now, Master Dodger, what's the news with
  you?

DODGER. I'd gladly speak in private to
your honor.

LORD MAYOR. You shall, you shall.—Master Eyre and Master Scott,
I have some business with this gentleman;
I pray, let me entreat you to walk before
To the Guildhall; I'll follow presently.
Master Eyre, I hope ere noon to call you
  sheriff.

EYRE. I would not care, my lord, if you
might call me King of Spain.—Come, Master
Scott.   (*Exeunt* EYRE *and* SCOTT)

LORD MAYOR. Now, Master Dodger,
what's the news you bring?

DODGER. The Earl of Lincoln by me greets
  your lordship,
And earnestly requests you, if you can,
Inform him, where his nephew Lacy keeps.

LORD MAYOR. Is not his nephew Lacy
now in France?

DODGER. No, I assure your lordship, but
  disguised

Lurks here in London.

LORD MAYOR. London? is't even so?
It may be; but upon my faith and soul,
I know not where he lives, or whether he
  lives:
So tell my Lord of Lincoln.—Lurks in London?
Well, Master Dodger, you perhaps may start
  him;
Be but the means to rid him into France,
I'll give you a dozen angels for your pains:
So much I love his honor, hate his nephew.
And, prithee, so inform thy lord from me.

DODGER. I take my leave. (*Exit* DODGER)

LORD MAYOR. Farewell, good Master
  Dodger.
Lacy in London? I dare pawn my life,
My daughter knows thereof, and for that
  cause
Denied young Master Hammon in his love.
Well, I am glad I sent her to Old Ford.
Gods Lord, 'tis late; to Guildhall I must hie;
I know my brethren stay my company.
                                        (*Exit*)

SCENE IV. EYRE'S *Shop.*

(*Enter* FIRK, MARGERY, HANS, *and* HODGE)

MARGERY. Thou goest too fast for me,
Roger. O, Firk!

FIRK. Ay, forsooth.

MARGERY. I pray thee, run—do you hear?
—run to Guildhall, and learn if my husband,
Master Eyre, will take that worshipful vocation of Master Sheriff upon him. Hie thee,
good Firk.

FIRK. Take it? Well, I go; an he should
not take it, Firk swears to forswear him. Yes,
forsooth, I go to Guildhall.

MARGERY. Nay, when? thou art too compendious and tedious.

FIRK. O rare, your excellence is full of
eloquence. (*Aside*) How like a new cartwheel my dame speaks, and she looks like
an old musty ale-bottle going to scalding.

MARGERY. (*Impatiently. To* FIRK) Nay,
when? thou wilt make me melancholy.

FIRK. God forbid your worship should fall
into that humor;—I run.   (*Exit*)

MARGERY. Let me see now, Roger and
Hans.

HODGE. Ay, forsooth, dame—mistress I
should say, but the old term so sticks to the
roof of my mouth, I can hardly lick it off.

MARGERY. Even what thou wilt, good
Roger; dame is a fair name for any honest
Christian; but let that pass. How dost thou,
Hans?

HANS. Mee tanck you, vro.[57]

MARGERY. Well, Hans and Roger, you
see, God hath blest your master, and, perdy,
if ever he comes to be Master Sheriff of London—as we are all mortal—you shall see, I
will have some odd thing or other in a corner
for you: I will not be your back-friend;[58]
but let that pass. Hans, pray thee, tie my
shoe.

HANS. Yaw, ic sal, vro.[59]

MARGERY. Roger, thou know'st the length
of my foot; as it is none of the biggest, so I
thank God, it is handsome enough; prithee,
let me have a pair of shoes made, cork, good

---

[57] I thank you, mistress.   [58] False friend.

[59] Yes, I will, mistress.

Roger, wooden heel too.

HODGE. You shall.

MARGERY. Art thou acquainted with never a farthingale-maker, nor a French hood-maker? I must enlarge my bum, ha, ha! How shall I look in a hood, I wonder! Perdy, oddly, I think.

HODGE. (*Aside*) As a cat out of a pillory. —Very well, I warrant you, mistress.

MARGERY. Indeed, all flesh is grass; and, Roger, canst thou tell where I may buy a good hair?

HODGE. Yes, forsooth, at the poulterer's in Gracious Street.

MARGERY. Thou art an ungracious wag; perdy, I mean a false hair for my periwig.

HODGE. Why, mistress, the next time I cut my beard, you shall have the shavings of it; but they are all true hairs.

MARGERY. It is very hot, I must get me a fan or else a mask.

HODGE. (*Aside*) So you had need, to hide your wicked face.

MARGERY. Fie upon it, how costly this world's calling is; perdy, but that it is one of the wonderful works of God, I would not deal with it. Is not Firk come yet? Hans, be not so sad, let it pass and vanish, as my husband's worship says.

HANS. Ick bin vrolicke, lot see yow soo.[60]

HODGE. Mistress, will you drink a pipe of tobacco?

MARGERY. Oh, fie upon it, Roger, perdy! These filthy tobacco-pipes are the most idle slavering baubles that ever I felt. Out upon it! God bless us, men look not like men that use them.

(*Enter* RALPH, *hobbling with a crutch*)

HODGE. What, fellow Ralph? Mistress, look here, Jane's husband! Why, how now, lame? Hans, make much of him, he's a brother of our trade, a good workman, and a tall soldier.

HANS. You be welcome, broder.

MARGERY. Perdy, I knew him not. How dost thou, good Ralph? I am glad to see thee well.

RALPH. I would to God you saw me, dame, as well
As when I went from London into France.

[60] I am merry; let's see you so.

MARGERY. Trust me, I am sorry, Ralph, to see thee impotent. Lord, how the wars have made him sunburnt! The left leg is not well; 'twas a fair gift of God the infirmity took not hold a little higher, considering thou camest from France; but let that pass.

RALPH. I am glad to see you well, and I rejoice
To hear that God hath blest my master so
Since my departure.

MARGERY. Yea, truly, Ralph, I thank my Maker; but let that pass.

HODGE. And, sirrah Ralph, what news, what news in France?

RALPH. Tell me, good Roger, first, what news in England?
How does my Jane? When didst thou see my wife?
Where lives my poor heart? She'll be poor indeed,
Now I want limbs to get whereon to feed.

HODGE. Limbs? Hast thou not hands, man?
Thou shalt never see a shoemaker want bread,
though he have but three fingers on a hand.

RALPH. Yet all this while I hear not of my Jane.

MARGERY. O Ralph, your wife,—perdy, we know not what's become of her. She was here a while, and because she was married, grew more stately than became her, I checked her, and so forth; away she flung, never returned, nor said bye nor bah; and, Ralph, you know, "ka me, ka thee." [60a] And so, as I tell ye— Roger, is not Firk come yet?

HODGE. No, forsooth.

MARGERY. And so, indeed, we heard not of her, but I hear she lives in London; but let that pass. If she had wanted, she might have opened her case to me or my husband, or to any of my men; I am sure, there's not any of them, perdy, but would have done her good to his power. Hans, look if Firk be come.

HANS. Yaw, ik sal, vro.   (*Exit* HANS)

MARGERY. And so, as I said—but, Ralph, why dost thou weep? Thou knowest that naked we came out of our mother's womb, and naked we must return; and, therefore, thank God for all things.

HODGE. No, faith, Jane is a stranger here;

[60a] You serve me, and I'll serve thee.

but, Ralph, pull up a good heart, I know thou hast one. Thy wife, man, is in London; one told me, he saw her awhile ago very brave and neat; we'll ferret her out, an London hold her.

MARGERY. Alas, poor soul, he's overcome with sorrow; he does but as I do, weep for the loss of any good thing. But, Ralph, get thee in, call for some meat and drink, thou shalt find me worshipful towards thee.

RALPH. I thank you, dame; since I want limbs and lands,
I'll trust to God, my good friends and my hands. (*Exit*)

(*Enter* HANS *and* FIRK *running*)

FIRK. Run, good Hans! O Hodge, O mistress! Hodge, heave up thine ears; mistress, smug up[61] your looks; on with your best apparel; my master is chosen, my master is called, nay, condemned by the cry of the country to be sheriff of the city for this famous year now to come. And time now being, a great many men in black gowns were asked for their voices and their hands, and my master had all their fists about his ears presently, and they cried "Ay, ay, ay, ay,"—and so I came away—

Wherefore without all other grieve
I do salute you, Mistress Shrieve.[62]

HANS. Yaw, my mester is de groot man, de shrieve.

HODGE. Did not I tell you, mistress? Now I may boldly say: Good-morrow to your worship.

MARGERY. Good-morrow, good Roger. I thank you, my good people all.—Firk, hold up thy hand: here's a three-penny piece for thy tidings.

FIRK. 'Tis but three-half-pence, I think. Yes, 'tis three-pence, I smell the rose.

HODGE. But, mistress, be ruled by me, and do not speak so pulingly.

FIRK. 'Tis her worship speaks so, and not she. No, faith, mistress, speak me in the old key: "To it, Firk," "there, good Firk," "ply your business, Hodge," "Hodge, with a full mouth," "I'll fill your bellies with good cheer, till they cry twang."

(*Enter* EYRE *wearing a gold chain, the insignia of a sheriff*)

HANS. See, myn liever broder, heer compt my meester.

MARGERY. Welcome home, Master Shrieve; I pray God continue you in health and wealth.

EYRE. See here, my Maggy, a chain, a gold chain for Simon Eyre. I shall make thee a lady; here's a French hood for thee; on with it, on with it! dress thy brows with this flap of a shoulder of mutton,[63] to make thee look lovely. Where be my fine men? Roger, I'll make over my shop and tools to thee; Firk, thou shalt be the foreman; Hans, thou shalt have an hundred for twenty.[64] Be as mad knaves as your master Sim Eyre hath been, and you shall live to be Sheriffs of London. —How dost thou like me, Margery? Prince am I none, yet am I princely born. Firk, Hodge, and Hans!

ALL THREE. Ay, forsooth, what says your worship, Master Sheriff?

EYRE. Worship and honor, you Babylonian knaves, for the Gentle Craft. But I forgot myself; I am bidden by my lord mayor to dinner to Old Ford; he's gone before, I must after. Come, Madge, on with your trinkets! No, my true Trojans, my fine Firk, my dapper Hodge, my honest Hans, some device, some odd crotchets, some morris, or such like, for the honor of the gentlemen shoemakers. Meet me at Old Ford, you know my mind. Come, Madge, away. Shut up the shop, knaves, and make holiday. (*Exeunt*)

FIRK. O rare! O brave! Come, Hodge; follow me, Hans;
We'll be with them for a morris-dance.
(*Exeunt*)

[61] Smarten up.
[62] Sheriff.

[63] A hood.
[64] *I.e.* For the twenty Portuguese previously lent.

SCENE V. *A Room in the* LORD MAYOR'S *Country House at Old Ford.*

(*Enter the* LORD MAYOR, ROSE, EYRE, MARGERY *in a French hood,* SYBIL, *and other Servants*)

LORD MAYOR. Trust me, you are as welcome to Old Ford
As I myself.
MARGERY. Truly, I thank your lordship.
LORD MAYOR. Would our bad cheer were worth the thanks you give.
EYRE. Good cheer, my lord mayor, fine cheer! A fine house, fine walls, all fine and neat.
LORD MAYOR. Now, by my troth, I'll tell thee, Master Eyre,
It does me good, and all my brethren,
That such a madcap fellow as thyself
Is entered into our society.
MARGERY. Ay, but, my lord, he must learn now to put on gravity.
EYRE. Peace, Maggy, a fig for gravity! When I go to Guildhall in my scarlet gown, I'll look as demurely as a saint, and speak as gravely as a justice of peace; but now I am here at Old Ford, at my good lord mayor's house, let it go by, vanish, Maggy, I'll be merry; away with flip-flap, these fooleries, these gulleries. What, honey? Prince am I none, yet am I princely born. What says my lord mayor?
LORD MAYOR. Ha, ha, ha! I had rather than a thousand pound,
I had an heart but half so light as yours.
EYRE. Why, what should I do, my lord? A pound of care pays not a dram of debt. Hum, let's be merry, whiles we are young; old age, sack and sugar will steal upon us, ere we be aware.
LORD MAYOR. It's well done; Mistress Eyre, pray, give good counsel
To my daughter.
MARGERY. I hope, Mistress Rose will have the grace to take nothing that's bad.
LORD MAYOR. Pray God she do; for i' faith, Mistress Eyre,
I would bestow upon that peevish girl
A thousand marks more than I mean to give her
Upon condition she'd be ruled by me.

The ape still crosseth me. There came of late
A proper gentleman of fair revenues,
Whom gladly I would call a son-in-law:
But my fine cockney would have none of him.
(*Turning to Rose*) You'll prove a coxcomb for it, ere you die:
A courtier, or no man must please your eye.
EYRE. Be ruled, sweet Rose: th' art ripe for a man. Marry not with a boy that has no more hair on his face than thou hast on thy cheeks. A courtier? wash, go by! stand not upon pishery-pashery: those silken fellows are but painted images, outsides, outsides, Rose; their inner linings are torn. No, my fine mouse, marry me with a gentleman grocer like my lord mayor, your father; a grocer is a sweet trade: plums, plums. Had I a son or daughter should marry out of the generation and blood of the shoemakers, he should pack; what, the Gentle Trade is a living for a man through Europe, through the world.
(*Sound of a tabor and pipe playing off stage*)
LORD MAYOR. What noise is this?
EYRE. O my lord mayor, a crew of good fellows that for love to your honor are come hither with a morris-dance. Come in, my Mesopotamians, cheerily.

(*Enter* HODGE, HANS, RALPH, FIRK, *and other* SHOEMAKERS, *in a morris; after a little dancing the* LORD MAYOR *speaks*)

LORD MAYOR. Master Eyre, are all these shoemakers?
EYRE. All cordwainers, my good lord mayor.
ROSE. (*Aside*) How like my Lacy looks yond' shoemaker!
HANS. (*Aside*) O that I durst but speak unto my love!
LORD MAYOR. Sybil, go fetch some wine to make these drink.
You are all welcome.
ALL. We thank your lordship.
(ROSE *takes a cup of wine and goes to* HANS)

Rose. For his sake whose fair shape thou
represent'st,
Good friend, I drink to thee.

Hans. Ic bedancke, good frister.[65]

Margery. I see, Mistress Rose, you do
not want judgment; you have drunk to the
properest man I keep.

Firk. Here be some have done their parts
to be as proper as he.

Lord Mayor. Well, urgent business calls
me back to London:
Good fellows, first go in and taste our cheer;
And to make merry as you homeward go,
Spend these two angels in beer at Stratford-
Bow.

Eyre. To these two, my mad lads, Sim
Eyre adds another; then cheerily, Firk; tickle
it, Hans, and all for the honor of shoemakers.
(*All go dancing out*)

Lord Mayor. Come, Master Eyre, let's
have your company. (*Exeunt*)

Rose. Sybil, what shall I do?

Sybil. Why, what's the matter?

Rose. That Hans the shoemaker is my
love Lacy,
Disguised in that attire to find me out.
How should I find the means to speak with
him?

Sybil. What, mistress, never fear; I dare
venture my maidenhead to nothing, and
that's great odds, that Hans the Dutchman,
when we come to London, shall not only see
and speak with you, but in spite of all your
father's policies[66] steal you away and marry
you. Will not this please you?

Rose. Do this, and ever be assured of my
love.

Sybil. Away, then, and follow your father
to London, lest your absence cause him to
suspect something:
To-morrow, if my counsel be obeyed,
I'll bind you prentice to the Gentle
Trade. (*Exeunt*)

Act IV

Scene I. *A Street before an Open Shop Front in London.*

(Jane *in a Seamster's shop, working. Enter*
Master Hammon, *with a hat pulled over
his eyes and his cloak up over his face. He
stands aloof.*)

Hammon. Yonder's the shop, and there
my fair love sits.
She's fair and lovely, but she is not mine.
O, would she were! Thrice have I courted
her,
Thrice hath my hand been moistened with
her hand,
Whilst my poor famished eyes do feed on
that
Which made them famish. I am infortunate:
I still love one, yet nobody loves me.
I muse, in other men what women see,
That I so want! Fine Mistress Rose was coy,
And this too curious![67] Oh, no, she is chaste,
And for she thinks me wanton, she denies
To cheer my cold heart with her sunny eyes.
How prettily she works, oh pretty hand!
Oh happy work! It doth me good to stand
Unseen to see her. Thus I oft have stood

In frosty evenings, a light burning by her,
Enduring biting cold, only to eye her.
One only look hath seemed as rich to me
As a king's crown; such is love's lunacy.
Muffled I'll pass along, and by that try
Whether she know me.

Jane. Sir, what is't you buy?
What is't you lack, sir, calico, or lawn,
Fine cambric shirts, or bands, what will you
buy?

Hammon. (*Aside*) That which thou wilt
not sell.
Faith, yet I'll try.—
How do you sell this handkercher?

Jane. Good cheap.

Hammon. And how these ruffs?

Jane. Cheap too.

Hammon. And how this band?

Jane. Cheap too.

Hammon. All cheap; how sell you then
this hand?

Jane. (*Drawing back*) My hands are not
to be sold.

Hammon. To be given then!

---

[65] I thank you, good maid. [66] Devices.

[67] Fastidious.

Nay, faith, I come to buy.

JANE. But none knows when.

HAMMON. Good sweet, leave work a little
while; let's play.

JANE. I cannot live by keeping holiday.

HAMMON. I'll pay you for the time which
shall be lost.

JANE. With me you shall not be at so much
cost.

HAMMON. Look how you wound this
cloth, so you wound me.

JANE. It may be so.

HAMMON. 'Tis so.

JANE. What remedy?

HAMMON. Nay, faith, you are too coy.

JANE. Let go my hand.

HAMMON. I will do any task at your com-
mand;
I would let go this beauty, were I not
In mind to disobey you by a power
That controls kings: I love you!

JANE. So, now part.

HAMMON. With hands I may, but never
with my heart.
In faith, I love you.

JANE. (Sadly) I believe you do.

HAMMON. Shall a true love in me breed
hate in you?

JANE. I hate you not.

HAMMON. Then you must love?

JANE. I do.
What are you better now? I love not you.

HAMMON. All this, I hope, is but a wom-
an's fray,
That means: come to me, when she cries:
away!
In earnest, mistress, I do not jest,
A true chaste love hath entered in my breast.
I love you dearly, as I love my life,
I love you as a husband loves a wife;
That, and no other love, my love requires.
Thy wealth, I know, is little; my desires
Thirst not for gold. Sweet, beauteous Jane,
what's mine
Shall, if thou make myself thine, all be thine.
Say, judge, what is thy sentence, life or
death?
Mercy or cruelty lies in thy breath.

JANE. Good sir, I do believe you love me
well;
For 'tis a silly conquest, silly pride
For one like you—I mean a gentleman—

To boast that by his love-tricks he hath
brought
Such and such women to his amorous lure;
I think you do not so, yet many do,
And make it even a very trade to woo.
I could be coy, as many women be,
Feed you with sunshine smiles and wanton
looks,
But I detest witchcraft; say that I
Do constantly believe you, constant have——

HAMMON. Why dost thou not believe me?

JANE. I believe you;
But yet, good sir, because I will not grieve
you
With hopes to taste fruit which will never
fall,
In simple truth this is the sum of all:
My husband lives, at least, I hope he lives.
Pressed was he to these bitter wars in France;
Bitter they are to me by wanting him.
I have but one heart, and that heart's his due.
How can I then bestow the same on you?
Whilst he lives, his I live, be it ne'er so poor,
And rather be his wife than a king's whore.

HAMMON. Chaste and dear woman, I will
not abuse thee,
Although it cost my life, if thou refuse me.
Thy husband, pressed for France, what was
his name?

JANE. Ralph Damport.

HAMMON. Damport?—Here's a letter sent
From France to me, from a dear friend of
mine,
A gentleman of place; here he doth write
Their names that have been slain in every
fight.

JANE. I hope death's scroll contains not
my love's name.

HAMMON. Cannot you read?

JANE. I can.

HAMMON. Peruse the same.
To my remembrance such a name I read
Amongst the rest. See here.

JANE. Ay me, he's dead!
He's dead! if this be true, my dear heart's
slain!

HAMMON. Have patience, dear love.

JANE. Hence, hence!

HAMMON. Nay, sweet Jane,
Make not poor sorrow proud with these rich
tears.
I mourn thy husband's death, because thou
mourn'st.

JANE. (*Wildly*) That bill is forged; 'tis signed by forgery.

HAMMON. I'll bring thee letters sent besides to many,
Carrying the like report: Jane, 'tis too true.
Come, weep not: mourning, though it rise from love,
Helps not the mournéd, yet hurts them that mourn.

JANE. For God's sake, leave me.

HAMMON. Whither dost thou turn?
Forget the dead, love them that are alive:
His love is faded, try how mine will thrive.

JANE. 'Tis now no time for me to think on love.

HAMMON. 'Tis now best time for you to think on love,
Because your love lives not.

JANE. Though he be dead,
My love to him shall not be buried;
For God's sake, leave me to myself alone.

HAMMON. 'Twould kill my soul, to leave thee drowned in moan.
Answer me to my suit, and I am gone;
Say to me yea or no.

JANE. No.

HAMMON. Then farewell!
One farewell will not serve, I come again;
Come, dry these wet cheeks; tell me, faith, sweet Jane,
Yea or no, once more.

JANE. Once more I say, no;
Once more be gone, I pray; else will I go.

HAMMON. Nay, then I will grow rude, by this white hand,
Until you change that cold "no"; here I'll stand
Till by your hard heart——

JANE. Nay, for God's love, peace!
My sorrows by your presence more increase.
Not that you thus are present, but all grief
Desires to be alone; therefore in brief
Thus much I say, and saying bid adieu:
If ever I wed man, it shall be you.

HAMMON. O blessed voice! Dear Jane, I'll urge no more;
Thy breath hath made me rich.

JANE. Death makes me poor.   (*Exeunt*)

SCENE II. *A Street before* SIMON EYRE's *Shop, now* HODGE's, *and the Interior of the Shop.*

(HODGE, *at his shop-board,* RALPH, FIRK, HANS, *and a Boy at work*)

ALL. (*Singing*) *Hey, down a down, derry.*

HODGE. Well said, my hearts; ply your work to-day, we loitered yesterday; to it pell-mell, that we may live to be lord mayors, or aldermen at least.

FIRK. *Hey, down a down, derry.*

HODGE. Well said, i' faith! How say'st thou, Hans, doth not Firk tickle it?

HANS. Yaw, mester.

FIRK. Not so neither, my organ-pipe squeaks this morning for want of liquoring. *Hey, down a down, derry!*

HANS. Forward, Firk, tow best un jolly yongster. Hort, ay, mester, ic bid yo, cut me un pair vampres vor Mester Jeffre's boots.[68]

HODGE. Thou shalt, Hans.

FIRK. Master!

HODGE. How now, boy?

FIRK. Pray, now you are in the cutting vein, cut me out a pair of counterfeits, or else my work will not pass current; *hey, down a down!*

HODGE. Tell me, sirs, are my cousin Mistress Priscilla's shoes done?

FIRK. Your cousin? No, master; one of your aunts,[69] hang her; let them alone.

RALPH. I am in hand with them; she gave charge that none but I should do them for her.

FIRK. Thou do for her? then 'twill be a lame doing, and that she loves not. Ralph, thou might'st have sent her to me, in faith, I would have yearked and firked your Priscilla. *Hey, down a down, derry.* This gear will not hold.

HODGE. How say'st thou, Firk, were we not merry at Old Ford?

[68] Forward, Firk, thou art a jolly youngster. Hark, ay, master, I bid you, cut me a pair of vamps for Master Jeffrey's boots. "Vamps," upper leathers of a shoe.

[69] A cant term for a prostitute or procuress.

FIRK. How, merry? why, our buttocks went jiggy-joggy like a quagmire. Well, Sir Roger Oatmeal, if I thought all meal of that nature, I would eat nothing but bagpuddings.

RALPH. Of all good fortunes my fellow Hans had the best.

FIRK. 'Tis true, because Mistress Rose drank to him.

HODGE. Well, well, work apace. They say, seven of the aldermen be dead, or very sick.

FIRK. I care not, I'll be none.

RALPH. No, nor I; but then my Master Eyre will come quickly to be lord mayor.

(*Enter* SYBIL)

FIRK. Whoop, yonder comes Sybil.

HODGE. Sybil, welcome, i' faith; and how dost thou, mad wench?

FIRK. Syb-whore, welcome to London.

SYBIL. Godamercy, sweet Firk; good lord, Hodge, what a delicious shop you have got! You tickle it, i' faith.

RALPH. Godamercy, Sybil, for our good cheer at Old Ford.

SYBIL. That you shall have, Ralph.

FIRK. Nay, by the mass, we had tickling cheer, Sybil; and how the plague dost thou and Mistress Rose and my lord mayor? I put the women in first.

SYBIL. Well, Godamercy; but God's me, I forget myself, where's Hans the Fleming?

FIRK. Hark, butter-box, now you must yelp out some spreken.

HANS. Wat begaie you? Vat vod you, Frister? [70]

SYBIL. Marry, you must come to my young mistress, to pull on her shoes you made last.

HANS. Vare ben your egle fro, vare ben your mistris? [71]

SYBIL. Marry, here at our London house in Cornhill.

FIRK. Will nobody serve her turn but Hans?

SYBIL. No, sir. Come, Hans, I stand upon needles.

HODGE. Why then, Sybil, take heed of pricking.

SYBIL. For that let me alone. I have a trick in my budget. Come, Hans.

[70] What do you want? what would you, girl?
[71] Where is your noble lady, where is your mistress?

HANS. Yaw, yaw, ic sall meete yo gane. [72]
(*Exeunt* HANS *and* SYBIL)

HODGE. Go, Hans, make haste again. Come, who lacks work?

FIRK. I, master, for I lack my breakfast; 'tis munching-time and past.

HODGE. Is't so? why, then leave work, Ralph. To breakfast! Boy, look to the tools. Come, Ralph; come, Firk.   (*Exeunt*)

(*Enter a* SERVING-MAN *dressed in livery*)

SERVING-MAN. Let me see now, the sign of the Last in Tower Street. Mass, yonder's the house. (*Calling*) What, haw! Who's within?

(*Enter* RALPH)

RALPH. Who calls there? What want you, sir?

SERVING-MAN. Marry, I would have a pair of shoes made for a gentlewoman against to-morrow morning. What, can you do them?

RALPH. Yes, sir, you shall have them. But what's length her foot?

SERVING-MAN. Why, you must make them in all parts like this shoe; but, at any hand, fail not to do them, for the gentlewoman is to be married very early in the morning.

RALPH. (*Looking at the shoe in amazement*) How? by this shoe must it be made? by this? Are you sure, sir, by this?

SERVING-MAN. (*Impatiently*) How, by this? Am I sure, by this? Art thou in thy wits? I tell thee, I must have a pair of shoes, dost thou mark me? a pair of shoes, two shoes, made by this very shoe, this same shoe, against to-morrow morning by four a clock. Dost understand me? Canst thou do 't?

RALPH. Yes, sir, yes—ay, ay!—I can do 't. By this shoe, you say? I should know this shoe. Yes, sir, yes, by this shoe, I can do't. Four a clock, well. Whither shall I bring them?

SERVING-MAN. To the sign of the Golden Ball in Watling Street; enquire for one Master Hammon, a gentleman, my master.

RALPH. Yea, sir, by this shoe, you say?

SERVING-MAN. I say, Master Hammon at the Golden Ball; he's the bridegroom, and those shoes are for his bride.

[72] Yes, yes, I will go with you.

RALPH. They shall be done by this shoe; well, well, Master Hammon at the Golden Shoe—I would say, the Golden Ball; very well, very well. But I pray you, sir, where must Master Hammon be married?

SERVING-MAN. At Saint Faith's Church, under Paul's.[73] But what's that to thee? Prithee, dispatch those shoes, and so farewell.

(Exit)

RALPH. By this shoe, said he. How am I amazed
At this strange accident! Upon my life,
This was the very shoe I gave my wife,
When I was pressed for France; since when, alas!
I never could hear of her: 'tis the same,
And Hammon's bride no other but my Jane.

(Enter FIRK)

FIRK. 'Snails, Ralph, thou hast lost thy part of three pots, a countryman of mine gave me to breakfast.

RALPH. I care not; I have found a better thing.

FIRK. A thing? away! Is it a man's thing, or a woman's thing?

RALPH. Firk, dost thou know this shoe?

FIRK. No, by my troth; neither doth that know me! I have no acquaintance with it, 'tis a mere stranger to me.

RALPH. Why, then I do; this shoe, I durst be sworn,
Once covered the instep of my Jane.
This is her size, her breadth, thus trod my love;
These true-love knots I pricked; I hold my life,
By this old shoe I shall find out my wife.

FIRK. Ha, ha! Old shoe, that wert new! How a murrain came this ague-fit of foolishness upon thee?

RALPH. Thus, Firk: even now here came a serving-man;
By this shoe would he have a new pair made
Against to-morrow morning for his mistress,
That's to be married to a gentleman.
And why may not this be my sweet Jane?

FIRK. And why may'st not thou be my sweet ass? Ha, ha!

RALPH. Well, laugh and spare not! But the truth is this:
Against to-morrow morning I'll provide
A lusty crew of honest shoemakers,
To watch the going of the bride to church.
If she prove Jane, I'll take her in despite
From Hammon and the devil, were he by.
If it be not my Jane, what remedy?
Hereof I am sure, I shall live till I die,
Although I never with a woman lie. *(Exit)*

FIRK. Thou lie with a woman, to build nothing but Cripple-gates! Well, God sends fools fortune, and it may be, he may light upon his matrimony by such a device; for wedding and hanging goes by destiny.

(Exit)

SCENE III. *A Room in the* LORD MAYOR's *London House in Cornhill.*

(Enter HANS and ROSE, arm in arm)

HANS. How happy am I by embracing thee!
Oh, I did fear such cross mishaps did reign,
That I should never see my Rose again.

ROSE. Sweet Lacy, since fair opportunity
Offers herself to further our escape,
Let not too over-fond esteem of me
Hinder that happy hour. Invent the means,
And Rose will follow thee through all the world.

HANS. Oh, how I surfeit with excess of joy,
Made happy by thy rich perfection!
But since thou pay'st sweet interest to my hopes,
Redoubling love on love, let me once more
Like to a bold-faced debtor crave of thee,
This night to steal abroad, and at Eyre's house,
Who now by death of certain aldermen
Is mayor of London, and my master once,
Meet thou thy Lacy, where in spite of change,
Your father's anger, and mine uncle's hate,
Our happy nuptials will we consummate.

(Enter SYBIL running)

[73] Next door to St. Paul's Cathedral.

SYBIL. Oh God, what will you do, mistress? Shift for yourself, your father is at hand! He's coming, he's coming! Master Lacy, hide yourself in my mistress! For God's sake, shift for yourselves!

HANS. Your father come, sweet Rose—what shall I do?
Where shall I hide me? How shall I escape?

ROSE. A man, and want wit in extremity?
Come, come, be Hans still, play the shoemaker,
Pull on my shoe.

HANS. Mass, and that's well remembered.

SYBIL. Here comes your father.

(Enter the LORD MAYOR*)*

HANS. Forware, metresse, 'tis un good skow, it sal vel dute, or ye sal neit betallen.[74]

ROSE. Oh God, it pincheth me; what will you do?

HANS. *(Aside)* Your father's presence pincheth, not the shoe.

LORD MAYOR. Well done; fit my daughter well, and she shall please thee well.

HANS. Yaw, yaw, ick weit dat well; forware, 'tis un good skoo, 'tis gimait van neits leither; see euer, mine here.[75]

(Enter a London APPRENTICE*)*

LORD MAYOR. I do believe it.—*(To the* APPRENTICE*)* What's the news with you?

PRENTICE. Please you, the Earl of Lincoln at the gate
Is newly 'lighted, and would speak with you.

LORD MAYOR. The Earl of Lincoln come to speak with me?
Well, well, I know his errand. Daughter Rose,
Send hence your shoemaker, dispatch, have done!
Syb, make things handsome! Sir boy, follow me.
(Exeunt LORD MAYOR *and* APPRENTICE*)*

HANS. Mine uncle come! Oh, what may this portend?
Sweet Rose, this of our love threatens an end.

ROSE. Be not dismayed at this; whate'er befall,
Rose is thine own. To witness I speak truth,
Where thou appoint'st the place, I'll meet with thee.
I will not fix a day to follow thee,
But presently steal hence. Do not reply:
Love which gave strength to bear my father's hate,
Shall now add wings to further our escape.
(Exeunt)

SCENE IV. *Another Room in the same House.*

(Enter the LORD MAYOR *and the* EARL OF LINCOLN*)*

LORD MAYOR. Believe me, on my credit, I speak truth:
Since first your nephew Lacy went to France,
I have not seen him. It seemed strange to me,
When Dodger told me that he stayed behind,
Neglecting the high charge the king imposed.

LINCOLN. Trust me, Sir Roger Oteley, I did think
Your counsel had given head to this attempt,
Drawn to it by the love he bears your child.
Here I did hope to find him in your house;
But now I see mine error, and confess,
My judgment wronged you by conceiving so.

LORD MAYOR. Lodge in my house, say you? Trust me, my lord,
I love your nephew Lacy too too dearly,
So much to wrong his honor; and he hath done so,
That first gave him advice to stay from France.
To witness I speak truth, I let you know,
How careful I have been to keep my daughter
Free from all conference or speech of him;
Not that I scorn your nephew, but in love
I bear your honor, lest your noble blood
Should by my mean worth be dishonored.

---

[74] In truth, mistress, 'tis a good shoe, it shall do well, or you shall not pay.

[75] Yes, yes, I know that well; in truth, 'tis a good shoe, 'tis made of neat's leather; only look, sir!

LINCOLN. (*Aside*) How far the churl's tongue wanders from his heart!
—Well, well, Sir Roger Oteley, I believe you,
With more than many thanks for the kind love
So much you seem to bear me. But, my lord,
Let me request your help to seek my nephew,
Whom if I find, I'll straight embark for France.
So shall your Rose be free, my thoughts at rest,
And much care die which now lies in my breast.

(*Enter* SYBIL *in great excitement*)

SYBIL. Oh Lord! Help, for God's sake! my mistress; oh, my young mistress!

LORD MAYOR. Where is thy mistress? What's become of her?

SYBIL. She's gone, she's fled!

LORD MAYOR. Gone! Whither is she fled?

SYBIL. I know not, forsooth; she's fled out of doors with Hans the shoemaker; I saw them scud, scud, scud, apace, apace!

LORD MAYOR. Which way? (*Calling*) What, John! Where be my men? Which way?

SYBIL. I know not, an it please your worship.

LORD MAYOR. Fled with a shoemaker? Can this be true?

SYBIL. Oh Lord, sir, as true as God's in Heaven.

LINCOLN. (*Aside*) Her love turned shoemaker? I am glad of this.

LORD MAYOR. A Fleming butter-box, a shoemaker!
Will she forget her birth, requite my care
With such ingratitude? Scorned she young Hammon
To love a honnikin,[76] a needy knave?
Well, let her fly, I'll not fly after her,
Let her starve, if she will; she's none of mine.

LINCOLN. Be not so cruel, sir.

(*Enter* FIRK *with shoes*)

SYBIL. (*Aside*) I am glad she's 'scaped.

LORD MAYOR. I'll not account of her as of my child.
Was there no better object for her eyes

But a foul drunken lubber, swill-belly,
A shoemaker? That's brave!

FIRK. Yea, forsooth; 'tis a very brave shoe, and as fit as a pudding.

LORD MAYOR. How now, what knave is this? From whence comest thou?

FIRK. No knave, sir. I am Firk the shoemaker, lusty Roger's chief lusty journeyman, and I come hither to take up the pretty leg of sweet Mistress Rose, and thus hoping your worship is in as good health, as I was at the making hereof, I bid you farewell, yours, Firk.

LORD MAYOR. Stay, stay, Sir Knave!

LINCOLN. Come hither, shoemaker!

FIRK. 'Tis happy the knave is put before the shoemaker, or else I would not have vouchsafed to come back to you. I am moved, for I stir.

LORD MAYOR. My lord, this villain calls us knaves by craft.

FIRK. Then 'tis by the Gentle Craft, and to call one knave gently, is no harm. Sit your worship merry! (*Aside to* SYBIL) Syb, your young mistress—I'll so bob them, now my Master Eyre is lord mayor of London.

LORD MAYOR. Tell me, sirrah, whose man are you?

FIRK. I am glad to see your worship so merry. I have no maw to this gear, no stomach as yet to a red petticoat.
                              (*Pointing to* SYBIL)

LINCOLN. He means not, sir, to woo you to his maid,
But only doth demand whose man you are.

FIRK. I sing now to the tune of Rogero. Roger, my fellow, is now my master.

LINCOLN. Sirrah, know'st thou one Hans, a shoemaker?

FIRK. Hans, shoemaker? Oh yes, stay, yes, I have him. (*Speaking confidentially to the* LORD MAYOR) I tell you what, I speak it in secret: Mistress Rose and he are by this time —no, not so, but shortly are to come over one another with "Can you dance the shaking of the sheets?" It is that Hans—(*Aside*) I'll so gull these diggers![77]

LORD MAYOR. Know'st thou, then, where he is?

FIRK. Yes, forsooth; yea, marry!

LINCOLN. Canst[78] thou, in sadness?

[76] A term of abuse.

[77] *I.e.* Diggers for information.
[78] Knowest.

FIRK. No, forsooth; no marry!

LORD MAYOR. Tell me, good honest fellow, where he is,

And thou shalt see what I'll bestow of thee.

FIRK. Honest fellow? No, sir; not so, sir;
my profession is the Gentle Craft; I care not
for seeing, I love feeling; let me feel it here;
aurium tenus, ten pieces of gold; genuum
tenus, ten pieces of silver; and then Firk is
your man—(*Aside*) in a new pair of stretch-
ers.[79]

LORD MAYOR. Here is an angel, part of
thy reward,

Which I will give thee; tell me where he is.

FIRK. No point![80] Shall I betray my
brother? No! Shall I prove Judas to Hans?
No! Shall I cry treason to my corporation?
No, I shall be firked and yerked then. But
give me your angel; your angel shall tell you.

LINCOLN. Do so, good fellow; 'tis no hurt
to thee.

FIRK. Send simpering Syb away.

LORD MAYOR. Huswife, get you in.

(*Exit* SYBIL)

FIRK. Pitchers have ears, and maids have
wide mouths; but for Hauns-prauns, upon
my word, to-morrow morning he and young
Mistress Rose go to this gear, they shall be
married together, by this rush, or else turn
Firk to a firkin of butter, to tan leather
withal.

LORD MAYOR. But art thou sure of this?

FIRK. Am I sure that Paul's steeple is a
handful higher than London Stone[81] or that
the Pissing-Conduit[82] leaks nothing but pure
Mother Bunch?[83] Am I sure I am lusty Firk?
God's nails, do you think I am so base to
gull you?

LINCOLN. Where are they married? Dost
thou know the church?

FIRK. I never go to church, but I know
the name of it; it is a swearing church—stay
a while, 'tis—Ay, by the mass, no, no,—'tis—
Ay, by my troth, no, nor that; 'tis—Ay, by

my faith, that, that, 'tis, Ay, by my Faith's
Church under Paul's Cross. There they shall
be knit like a pair of stockings in matrimony;
there they'll be inconie.

LINCOLN. Upon my life, my nephew Lacy
walks

In the disguise of this Dutch shoemaker.

FIRK. Yes, forsooth.

LINCOLN. Doth he not, honest fellow?

FIRK. No, forsooth; I think Hans is nobody but Hans, no spirit.

LORD MAYOR. My mind misgives me now,
'tis so, indeed.

LINCOLN. My cousin speaks the language,
knows the trade.

LORD MAYOR. Let me request your company, my lord;

Your honorable presence may, no doubt,

Refrain their headstrong rashness, when myself

Going alone perchance may be o'erborne.

Shall I request this favor?

LINCOLN. This, or what else.

FIRK. Then you must rise betimes, for they
mean to fall to their "hey-pass and repass,"[84]
"pindy-pandy, which hand will you have,"[85]
very early.

LORD MAYOR. My care shall every way
equal their haste.

This night accept your lodging in my house,

The earlier shall we stir, and at Saint Faith's

Prevent this giddy hare-brained nuptial.

This traffic of hot love shall yield cold gains:

They ban our loves, and we'll forbid their
banns.   (*Exit*)

LINCOLN. At Saint Faith's Church thou
say'st?

FIRK. Yes, by my troth.

LINCOLN. Be secret, on thy life.   (*Exit*)

FIRK. Yes, when I kiss your wife! Ha, ha,
here's no craft in the Gentle Craft. I came
hither of purpose with shoes to Sir Roger's
worship, whilst Rose, his daughter, be cony-
catched by Hans. Soft now; these two gulls
will be at Saint Faith's Church to-morrow
morning, to take Master Bridegroom and Mistress Bride napping, and they, in the meantime, shall chop up the matter at the Savoy.
But the best sport is, Sir Roger Oteley will

[79] Lies.

[80] Not a bit!

[81] A stone which marked the center from
which the old Roman-roads radiated.

[82] A small conduit erected about 1500 near the
Stocks Market where the Mansion House now
stands.

[83] Here evidently used for water—why is not
apparent.

[84] A juggler's formula.

[85] A term used in a children's game, a small
object being hidden in one of two closed hands.

find my fellow lame Ralph's wife going to marry a gentleman, and then he'll stop her instead of his daughter. Oh, brave! there will be fine tickling sport. Soft now, what have I to do? Oh, I know; now a mess of shoemakers meet at the Woolsack in Ivy Lane, to cozen my gentlemen of lame Ralph's wife, that's true.

Alack, alack!
Girls, hold out tack! [86]
For now smocks for this jumbling
Shall go to wrack.   (*Exit*)

Act V

Scene I. *A Room in* Eyre's *House.*

(*Enter* Eyre, *in his Lord Mayor's robes and official gold chain,* Margery, *elaborately dressed in a farthingale and French hood,* Hans, *and* Rose)

Eyre. This is the morning, then, say, my bully, my honest Hans, is it not?

Hans. This is the morning, that must make us two happy or miserable; therefore, if you——

Eyre. Away with these ifs and ans, Hans, and these et caeteras! By mine honor, Rowland Lacy, none but the king shall wrong thee. Come, fear nothing, am not I Sim Eyre? Is not Sim Eyre lord mayor of London? Fear nothing, Rose: let them all say what they can; dainty, come thou to me—laughest thou?

Margery. Good my lord, stand her friend in what thing you may.

Eyre. Why, my sweet Lady Madgy, think you Simon Eyre can forget his fine Dutch journeyman? No, vah! Fie, I scorn it, it shall never be cast in my teeth, that I was unthankful. Lady Madgy, thou had'st never covered thy Saracen's head with this French flap, nor loaden thy bum with this farthingale ('tis trash, trumpery, vanity); Simon Eyre had never walked in a red petticoat, nor wore a chain of gold, but for my fine journeyman's Portigues.—And shall I leave him? No! Prince am I none, yet bear a princely mind.

Hans. My lord, 'tis time for us to part from hence.

Eyre. Lady Madgy, Lady Madgy, take two or three of my pie-crust-eaters, my buff-jerkin varlets, that do walk in black gowns at Simon Eyre's heels; take them, good Lady Madgy; trip and go, my brown queen of peri-wigs, with my delicate Rose and my jolly Rowland to the Savoy; see them linked, countenance the marriage; and when it is done, cling, cling together, you Hamborow turtle-doves. I'll bear you out, come to Simon Eyre; come, dwell with me, Hans, thou shalt eat minced-pies and marchpane.[87] Rose, away, cricket; trip and go, my Lady Madgy, to the Savoy; Hans, wed, and to bed; kiss, and away! Go, vanish!

Margery. Farewell, my lord.

Rose. Make haste, sweet love.

Margery. She'd fain the deed were done.

Hans. Come, my sweet Rose; faster than deer we'll run.

(*Exeunt all but* Eyre)

Eyre. Go, vanish, vanish! Avaunt, I say! By the Lord of Ludgate, it's a mad life to be a lord mayor; it's a stirring life, a fine life, a velvet life, a careful life. Well, Simon Eyre, yet set a good face on it, in the honor of Saint Hugh. Soft, the king this day comes to dine with me, to see my new buildings; his majesty is welcome, he shall have good cheer, delicate cheer, princely cheer. This day, my fellow prentices of London come to dine with me too; they shall have fine cheer, gentlemanlike cheer. I promised the mad Cappadocians, when we all served at the Conduit together,[88] that if ever I came to be mayor of London, I would feast them all, and I'll do 't, I'll do 't, by the life of Pharaoh; by this beard, Sim Eyre will be no flincher. Besides, I have procured that upon every Shrove Tuesday, at the sound of the pancake

---

[86] (?) Stand at bay.

[87] Marzipan.

[88] One of the duties of apprentices was to fetch water for the household from the conduits.

bell,[89] my fine dapper Assyrian lads shall clap up their shop windows, and away. This is the day, and this day they shall do 't, they shall do 't.

Boys, that day are you free, let masters care,
And prentices shall pray for Simon Eyre. (*Exit*)

Scene II. *A Street near St. Faith's Church.*

(*Enter* Hodge, Firk, Ralph, *and five or six* Shoemakers, *all with cudgels or such weapons*)

Hodge. Come, Ralph; stand to it, Firk. My masters, as we are the brave bloods of the shoemakers, heirs apparent to Saint Hugh, and perpetual benefactors to all good fellows, thou shalt have no wrong; were Hammon a king of spades, he should not delve in thy close without thy sufferance. But tell me, Ralph, art thou sure 'tis thy wife?

Ralph. Am I sure this is Firk? This morning, when I stroked[90] on her shoes, I looked upon her, and she upon me, and sighed, asked me if ever I knew one Ralph. Yes, said I. For his sake, said she—tears standing in her eyes—and for thou are somewhat like him, spend this piece of gold. I took it; my lame leg and my travel beyond sea made me unknown. All is one for that: I know she's mine.

Firk. Did she give thee this gold? O glorious glittering gold! She's thine own, 'tis thy wife, and she loves thee; for I'll stand to 't, there's no woman will give gold to any man, but she thinks better of him, than she thinks of them she gives silver to. And for Hammon, neither Hammon nor hangman shall wrong thee in London. Is not our old master Eyre, lord mayor? Speak, my hearts.

All. Yes, and Hammon shall know it to his cost.

(*Enter* Hammon, *his* Serving-man, Jane, *and wedding guests*)

Hodge. Peace, my bullies; yonder they come.

Ralph. Stand to 't, my hearts. Firk, let me speak first.

Hodge. No, Ralph, let me.—(*Barring* Hammon's *way*) Hammon, whither away so early?

Hammon. Unmannerly, rude slave, what's that to thee?

Firk. To him, sir? Yes, sir, and to me, and others. Good-morrow, Jane, how dost thou? Good Lord, how the world is changed with you! God be thanked!

Hammon. Villains, hands off! How dare you touch my love?

All the Shoemakers. Villains? Down with them! Cry "clubs!" for prentices!

Hodge. Hold, my hearts! Touch her, Hammon? Yea, and more than that: we'll carry her away with us. My masters and gentlemen, never draw your bird-spits; shoemakers are steel to the back, men every inch of them, all spirit.

Those of Hammon's Side. Well, and what of all this?

Hodge. I'll show you.—Jane, dost thou know this man? 'Tis Ralph, I can tell thee; nay, 'tis he in faith, though he be lamed by the wars. Yet look not strange, but run to him, fold him about the neck and kiss him.

Jane. Lives then my husband? Oh God, let me go,
Let me embrace my Ralph.

Hammon. What means my Jane?

Jane. Nay, what meant you, to tell me he was slain?

Hammon. O pardon me, dear love, for being misled.
(*To* Ralph) 'Twas rumored here in London, thou wert dead.

Firk. Thou seest he lives. Lass, go, pack home with him. Now, Master Hammon, where's your mistress, your wife?

Serving-man. 'Swounds, master, fight for her! Will you thus lose her?

Shoemakers. Down with that creature! Clubs! Down with him!

Hodge. Hold, hold!

[89] Rung about 11 a.m. originally to call people to confession, later as a sign that the holiday had begun. [90] Fitted.

HAMMON. Hold, fool! Sirs, he shall do no wrong. Will my Jane leave me thus, and break her faith?

FIRK. (*Taunting* HAMMON) Yea, sir! She must, sir! She shall, sir! What then? Mend it!

HODGE. Hark, fellow Ralph, follow my counsel: set the wench in the midst, and let her choose her man, and let her be his woman.

JANE. Whom should I choose? Whom should my thoughts affect
But him whom Heaven hath made to be my love?
Thou art my husband, and these humble weeds
Make thee more beautiful than all his wealth.
Therefore, I will but put off his attire,
Returning it into the owner's hand,
And after ever be thy constant wife.

HODGE. Not a rag, Jane! The law's on our side; he that sows in another man's ground, forfeits his harvest. Get thee home, Ralph; follow him, Jane; he shall not have so much as a busk-point from thee.

FIRK. Stand to that, Ralph; the appurtenances are thine own. Hammon, look not at her!

SERVING-MAN. O, 'swounds, no!

FIRK. Blue coat, be quiet, we'll give you a new livery else; we'll make Shrove Tuesday Saint George's Day [91] for you. Look not, Hammon, leer not! I'll firk you! For thy head now, not one glance, one sheep's eye, anything, at her! Touch not a rag, lest I and my brethren beat you to clouts.

SERVING-MAN. Come, Master Hammon, there's no striving here.

HAMMON. Good fellows, hear me speak; and, honest Ralph,
Whom I have injured most by loving Jane,
Mark what I offer thee: here in fair gold
Is twenty pound, I'll give it for thy Jane;
If this content thee not, thou shalt have more.

HODGE. Sell not thy wife, Ralph; make her not a whore.

HAMMON. Say, wilt thou freely cease thy claim in her,
And let her be my wife?

ALL THE SHOEMAKERS. No, do not, Ralph.

[91] On which day a festival attended by bluecoats, or serving-men was held at St. Paul's.

RALPH. Sirrah Hammon, Hammon, dost thou think a shoemaker is so base to be a bawd to his own wife for commodity? Take thy gold, choke with it! Were I not lame, I would make thee eat thy words.

FIRK. A shoemaker sell his flesh and blood? Oh, indignity!

HODGE. Sirrah, take up your pelf, and be packing.

HAMMON. I will not touch one penny, but in lieu
Of that great wrong I offeréd thy Jane,
To Jane and thee I give that twenty pound.
Since I have failed of her, during my life,
I vow, no woman else shall be my wife.
Farewell, good fellows of the Gentle Trade:
Your morning mirth my mourning day hath made. (*Exit*)

FIRK. (*To the* SERVING-MAN, *who reaches for the money*) Touch the gold, creature, if you dare! Y 're best be trudging. Here, Jane, take thou it. (*Exeunt* SERVING-MAN *and wedding guests*) Now let's home, my hearts.

HODGE. Stay! Who comes here? Jane, on again with thy mask!

(*Enter the* EARL OF LINCOLN, *the* LORD MAYOR, *and Servants*)

LINCOLN. Yonder's the lying varlet mocked us so.

LORD MAYOR. Come hither, sirrah!

FIRK. I, sir? I am sirrah? You mean me, do you not?

LINCOLN. Where is my nephew married?

FIRK. Is he married? God give him joy, I am glad of it. They have a fair day, and the sign is in a good planet, Mars in Venus.

LORD MAYOR. Villain, thou toldst me that my daughter Rose
This morning should be married at Saint Faith's;
We have watched there these three hours at the least,
Yet see we no such thing.

FIRK. Truly, I am sorry for 't; a bride's a pretty thing.

HODGE. Come to the purpose. Yonder's the bride and bridegroom you look for, I hope. Though you be lords, you are not to bar by your authority men from women, are you?

LORD MAYOR. See, see, my daughter's masked.

LINCOLN. True, and my nephew,
To hide his guilt, now counterfeits him lame.

FIRK. Yea, truly; God help the poor couple,
they are lame and blind.

LORD MAYOR. I'll ease her blindness.

LINCOLN. I'll his lameness cure.

FIRK. (*Aside to the* SHOEMAKERS) Lie
down, sirs, and laugh! My fellow Ralph is
taken for Rowland Lacy, and Jane for Mistress Damask Rose. This is all my knavery.

LORD MAYOR. What, have I found you,
minion?

LINCOLN. O base wretch!
Nay, hide thy face, the horror of thy guilt
Can hardly be washed off. Where are thy
        powers?
What battles have you made? O yes, I see,
Thou fought'st with Shame, and Shame hath
        conquered thee.
This lameness will not serve.

LORD MAYOR. Unmask yourself.

LINCOLN. Lead home your daughter.

LORD MAYOR. Take your nephew hence.

RALPH. Hence! 'Swounds, what mean
you? Are you mad? I hope you cannot enforce
my wife from me. Where's Hammon?

LORD MAYOR. Your wife?

LINCOLN. What Hammon?

RALPH. Yea, my wife; and, therefore, the
proudest of you that lays hands on her first,
I'll lay my crutch 'cross his pate.

FIRK. To him, lame Ralph! Here's brave
sport!

RALPH. Rose call you her? Why, her name
is Jane. Look here else; do you know her
now?   (*Unmasking* JANE)

LINCOLN. Is this your daughter?

LORD MAYOR. No, nor this your nephew.
My Lord of Lincoln, we are both abused
By this base, crafty varlet.

FIRK. Yea, forsooth, no varlet; forsooth,
no base; forsooth, I am but mean; no crafty
neither, but of the Gentle Craft.

LORD MAYOR. Where is my daughter
Rose? Where is my child?

LINCOLN. Where is my nephew Lacy married?

FIRK. Why, here is good laced mutton, as
I promised you.

LINCOLN. Villain, I'll have thee punished
for this wrong.

FIRK. Punish the journeyman villain, but
not the journeyman shoemaker.

(*Enter* DODGER)

DODGER. My lord, I come to bring unwelcome news.
Your nephew Lacy and your daughter Rose
Early this morning wedded at the Savoy,
None being present but the lady mayoress.
Besides, I learnt among the officers,
The lord mayor vows to stand in their
        defence
'Gainst any that shall seek to cross the match.

LINCOLN. Dares Eyre the shoemaker uphold the deed?

FIRK. Yes, sir, shoemakers dare stand in
a woman's quarrel, I warrant you, as deep as
another, and deeper too.

DODGER. Besides, his grace to-day dines
with the mayor;
Who on his knees humbly intends to fall
And beg a pardon for your nephew's fault.

LINCOLN. But I'll prevent him! Come, Sir
Roger Oteley;
The king will do us justice in this cause.
Howe'er their hands have made them man
        and wife,
I will disjoin the match, or lose my life.
                                    (*Exeunt*)

FIRK. Adieu, Monsieur Dodger! Farewell,
fools! Ha, ha! Oh, if they had stayed, I would
have so lambed [92] them with flouts! O heart,
my codpiece-point is ready to fly in pieces
every time I think upon Mistress Rose; but
let that pass, as my lady mayoress says.

HODGE. This matter is answered. Come,
Ralph; home with thy wife. Come, my fine
shoemakers, let's to our master's, the new
lord mayor, and there swagger this Shrove
Tuesday. I'll promise you wine enough, for
Madge keeps the cellar.

ALL. O rare! Madge is a good wench.

FIRK. And I'll promise you meat enough,
for simp'ring Susan keeps the larder. I'll lead
you to victuals, my brave soldiers; follow
your captain. O brave! Hark, hark!
                                    (*Bell rings*)

ALL. The pancake-bell rings, the pancakebell! Trilill, my hearts!

FIRK. O brave! O sweet bell! O delicate
pancakes! Open the doors, my hearts, and
shut up the windows! keep in the house,
let out the pancakes! Oh, rare, my hearts!

---

[92] Whipped.

Let's march together for the honor of Saint Hugh to the great new hall [93] in Gracious Street-corner, which our master, the new lord mayor, hath built.

RALPH. O the crew of good fellows that will dine at my lord mayor's cost to-day!

HODGE. By the Lord, my lord mayor is a most brave man. How shall prentices be bound to pray for him and the honor of the gentlemen shoemakers! Let's feed and be fat with my lord's bounty.

FIRK. O musical bell, still! O Hodge, O my brethren! There's cheer for the heavens: venison-pasties walk up and down piping hot, like sergeants; beef and brewis comes marching in dry-fats,[94] fritters and pancakes come trowling in in wheel-barrows; hens and oranges hopping in porters'-baskets, collops and eggs in scuttles, and tarts and custards come quavering in in malt-shovels.

(*Enter more* PRENTICES)

ALL. Whoop, look here, look here!

HODGE. How now, mad lads, whither away so fast?

FIRST PRENTICE. Whither? Why, to the great new hall, know you not why? The lord mayor hath bidden all the prentices in London to breakfast this morning.

ALL. Oh, brave shoemaker, oh, brave lord of incomprehensible good fellowship! Whoo! Hark you! The pancake-bell rings.

(*Cast up caps*)

FIRK. Nay, more, my hearts! Every Shrove Tuesday is our year of jubilee; and when the pancake-bell rings, we are as free as my lord mayor; we may shut up our shops, and make holiday. I'll have it called Saint Hugh's Holiday.

ALL. Agreed, agreed! Saint Hugh's Holiday.

HODGE. And this shall continue for ever.

ALL. Oh, brave! Come, come, my hearts! Away, away!

FIRK. O eternal credit to us of the Gentle Craft! March fair, my hearts! Oh, rare! (*Exeunt*)

SCENE III. *A Street in London.*

(*Enter the* KING *and his Train over the stage*)

KING. Is our lord mayor of London such a gallant?

NOBLEMAN. One of the merriest madcaps in your land.
Your grace will think, when you behold the man,
He's rather a wild ruffian than a mayor.
Yet thus much I'll ensure your majesty.
In all his actions that concern his state,
He is as serious, provident, and wise,
As full of gravity amongst the grave,

As any mayor hath been these many years.

KING. I am with child,[95] till I behold this huffcap.[96]
But all my doubt is, when we come in presence,
His madness will be dashed clean out of countenance.

NOBLEMAN. It may be so, my liege.

KING. Which to prevent
Let some one give him notice, 'tis our pleasure
That he put on his wonted merriment.
Set forward!

ALL. On afore! (*Exeunt*)

SCENE IV. *A Great Hall.*

(*Enter* EYRE, HODGE, FIRK, RALPH, *and other* Shoemakers, *all with napkins on their shoulders*)

EYRE. Come, my fine Hodge, my jolly gentlemen shoemakers; soft, where be these cannibals, these varlets, my officers? Let them all walk and wait upon my brethren; for my meaning is, that none but shoemakers,

[93] "Simon Eyre, Draper, Mayor 1446, builded the Leaden hall for a common garner of corn to the use of this City."—*Stow.*   [94] Barrels.

[95] *I.e.* In suspense.   [96] Swaggerer.

none but the livery of my company shall in their satin hoods wait upon the trencher of my sovereign.

FIRK. O my lord, it will be rare!

EYRE. No more, Firk; come, lively! Let your fellow prentices want no cheer; let wine be plentiful as beer, and beer as water. Hang these penny-pinching fathers, that cram wealth in innocent lambskins. Rip, knaves, avaunt! Look to my guests!

HODGE. My lord, we are at our wits' end for room; those hundred tables will not feast the fourth part of them.

EYRE. Then cover me those hundred tables again, and again, till all my jolly prentices be feasted. Avoid, Hodge! Run, Ralph! Frisk about, my nimble Firk! Carouse me fathom-healths to the honor of the shoemakers. Do they drink lively, Hodge? Do they tickle it, Firk?

FIRK. Tickle it? Some of them have taken their liquor standing so long that they can stand no longer; but for meat, they would eat it, an they had it.

EYRE. Want they meat? Where's this swag-belly, this greasy kitchenstuff cook? Call the varlet to me! Want meat? Firk, Hodge, lame Ralph, run, my tall men, beleaguer the shambles, beggar all Eastcheap, serve me whole oxen in chargers, and let sheep whine upon the tables like pigs for want of good fellows to eat them. Want meat? Vanish, Firk! Avaunt, Hodge!

HODGE. Your lordship mistakes my man Firk; he means, their bellies want meat, not the boards; for they have drunk so much, they can eat nothing.

(*Enter* HANS, ROSE, *and* MARGERY)

MARGERY. Where is my lord?

EYRE. How now, Lady Madgy?

MARGERY. The king's most excellent majesty is new come; he sends me for thy honor; one of his most worshipful peers bade me tell thou must be merry, and so forth; but let that pass.

EYRE. Is my sovereign come? Vanish, my tall shoemakers, my nimble brethren; look to my guests, the prentices. Yet stay a little! How now, Hans? How looks my little Rose?

HANS. Let me request you to remember me.
I know, your honor easily may obtain
Free pardon of the king for me and Rose,
And reconcile me to my uncle's grace.

EYRE. Have done, my good Hans, my honest journeyman; look cheerily! I'll fall upon both my knees, till they be as hard as horn, but I'll get thy pardon.

MARGERY. Good my lord, have a care what you speak to his grace.

EYRE. Away, you Islington whitepot![97] hence, you hopperarse! you barley-pudding, full of maggots! you broiled carbonado![98] avaunt, avaunt, avoid, Mephistophilus! Shall Sim Eyre learn to speak of you, Lady Madgy? Vanish, Mother Miniver-cap;[99] vanish, go, trip and go; meddle with your partlets[100] and your pishery-pashery, your flewes[101] and your whirligigs; go, rub, out of mine alley! Sim Eyre knows how to speak to a Pope, to Sultan Soliman, to Tamburlaine, an he were here, and shall I melt, shall I droop before my sovereign? No, come, my Lady Madgy! Follow me, Hans! About your business, my frolic free-booters! Firk, frisk about, and about, and about, for the honor of mad Simon Eyre, lord mayor of London.

FIRK. Hey, for the honor of the shoemakers. (*Exeunt*)

SCENE V. *An Open Yard before the Hall.*

(*A long flourish, or two. Enter the* KING, NOBLES, EYRE, MARGERY, LACY, ROSE. LACY *and* ROSE *kneel*)

KING. Well, Lacy, though the fact was very foul
Of your revolting from our kingly love
And your own duty, yet we pardon you.

Rise both, and, Mistress Lacy, thank my lord mayor

[97] A dish, made of milk, eggs, and sugar, baked in a pot.
[98] A piece of meat scored across for broiling.
[99] Fur-cap. [100] Bands or collars.
[101] Properly the chaps of a hound; here perhaps the flaps of a hood.

For your young bridegroom here.

EYRE. So, my dear liege, Sim Eyre and my brethren, the gentlemen shoemakers, shall set your sweet majesty's image cheek by jowl by Saint Hugh for this honor you have done poor Simon Eyre. I beseech your grace, pardon my rude behavior; I am a handicraftsman, yet my heart is without craft; I would be sorry at my soul, that my boldness should offend my king.

KING. Nay, I pray thee, good lord mayor,
    be even as merry
As if thou wert among thy shoemakers;
It does me good to see thee in this humor.

EYRE. Say'st thou me so, my sweet Dioclesian? Then, humph! Prince am I none, yet am I princely born. By the Lord of Ludgate, my liege, I'll be as merry as a pie.[102]

KING. Tell me, in faith, mad Eyre, how old thou art.

EYRE. My liege, a very boy, a stripling, a younker; you see not a white hair on my head, not a grey in this beard. Every hair, I assure thy majesty, that sticks in this beard, Sim Eyre values at the King of Babylon's ransom, Tamar Cham's beard was a rubbing brush to 't: yet I'll shave it off, and stuff tennis-balls with it, to please my bully king.

KING. But all this while I do not know your age.

EYRE. My liege, I am six and fifty year old, yet I can cry humph! with a sound heart for the honor of Saint Hugh. Mark this old wench, my king: I danced the shaking of the sheets with her six and thirty years ago, and yet I hope to get two or three young lord mayors, ere I die. I am lusty still, Sim Eyre still. Care and cold lodging brings white hairs. My sweet Majesty, let care vanish, cast it upon thy nobles, it will make thee look always young like Apollo, and cry humph! Prince am I none, yet am I princely born.

KING. Ha, ha!
Say, Cornwall, didst thou ever see his like?

CORNWALL. Not I, my lord.

(*Enter the* EARL OF LINCOLN *and the*
    LORD MAYOR)

KING. Lincoln, what news with you?

LINCOLN. My gracious lord, have care unto yourself,

[102] Magpie.

For there are traitors here.

ALL. Traitors? Where? Who?

EYRE. Traitors in my house? God forbid! Where be my officers? I'll spend my soul, ere my king feel harm.

KING. Where is the traitor, Lincoln?

LINCOLN. Here he stands.

KING. Cornwall, lay hold on Lacy!—Lincoln, speak,
What canst thou lay unto thy nephew's
    charge?

LINCOLN. This, my dear liege: your Grace,
    to do me honor,
Heaped on the head of this degenerous boy
Desertless favors; you made choice of him,
To be commander over powers in France.
But he——

KING. Good Lincoln, prithee, pause a
    while!
Even in thine eyes I read what thou wouldst
    speak.
I know how Lacy did neglect our love,
Ran himself deeply, in the highest degree,
Into vile treason——

LINCOLN. Is he not a traitor?

KING. Lincoln, he was; now have we pardoned him.
'Twas not a base want of true valor's fire,
That held him out of France, but love's
    desire.

LINCOLN. I will not bear his shame upon my back.

KING. Nor shalt thou, Lincoln; I forgive you both.

LINCOLN. Then, good my liege, forbid the
    boy to wed
One whose mean birth will much disgrace his bed.

KING. Are they not married?

LINCOLN. No, my liege.

BOTH. We are.

KING. Shall I divorce them then? O be
    it far,
That any hand on earth should dare untie
The sacred knot, knit by God's majesty;
I would not for my crown disjoin their hands,
That are conjoined in holy nuptial bands.
How say'st thou, Lacy, wouldst thou lose thy
    Rose?

LACY. Not for all India's wealth, my sovereign.

KING. But Rose, I am sure, her Lacy would forego?

Rose. If Rose were asked that question, she'd say no.

King. You hear them, Lincoln?

Lincoln. Yea, my liege, I do.

King. Yet canst thou find i' th' heart to part these two?
Who seeks, besides you, to divorce these lovers?

Lord Mayor. I do, my gracious lord. I am her father.

King. Sir Roger Oteley, our last mayor, I think?

Nobleman. The same, my liege.

King. Would you offend Love's laws?
Well, you shall have your wills. You sue to me,
To prohibit the match. Soft, let me see—
You both are married, Lacy, art thou not?

Lacy. I am, dread sovereign.

King. Then, upon thy life,
I charge thee not to call this woman wife.

Lord Mayor. I thank your grace.

Rose. O my most gracious lord! (*Kneels*)

King. Nay, Rose, never woo me; I tell you true,
Although as yet I am a bachelor,
Yet I believe, I shall not marry you.

Rose. Can you divide the body from the soul,
Yet make the body live?

King. Yea, so profound?
I cannot, Rose, but you I must divide.
This fair maid, bridegroom, cannot be your bride.
Are you pleased, Lincoln? Oteley, are you pleased?

Both. Yes, my lord.

King. Then must my heart be eased;
For, credit me, my conscience lives in pain,
Till these whom I divorced, be joined again.
Lacy, give me thy hand; Rose, lend me thine!
Be what you would be! Kiss now? So, that's fine.
At night, lovers, to bed!—Now, let me see,
Which of you all mislikes this harmony.

Lord Mayor. Will you then take from me my child perforce?

King. Why, tell me, Oteley: shines not Lacy's name
As bright in the world's eye as the gay beams
Of any citizen?

Lincoln. Yea, but, my gracious lord,
I do mislike the match far more than he;

Her blood is too too base.

King. Lincoln, no more.
Dost thou not know that love respects no blood,
Cares not for difference of birth or state?
The maid is young, well born, fair, virtuous,
A worthy bride for any gentleman.
Besides, your nephew for her sake did stoop
To bare necessity, and, as I hear,
Forgetting honors and all courtly pleasures,
To gain her love, became a shoemaker.
As for the honor which he lost in France,
Thus I redeem it: Lacy, kneel thee down!—
   (*Touches* Lacy *on the shoulder with his sword*)
Arise, Sir Rowland Lacy! Tell me now,
Tell me in earnest, Oteley, canst thou chide,
Seeing thy Rose a lady and a bride?

Lord Mayor. I am content with what your grace hath done.

Lincoln. And I, my liege, since there's no remedy.

King. Come on, then, all shake hands:
   I'll have you friends;
Where there is much love, all discord ends.
What says my mad lord mayor to all this love?

Eyre. O my liege, this honor you have done to my fine journeyman here, Rowland Lacy, and all these favors which you have shown to me this day in my poor house, will make Simon Eyre live longer by one dozen of warm summers more than he should.

King. Nay, my mad lord mayor, that shall be thy name,
If any grace of mine can length thy life,
One honor more I'll do thee: that new building,
Which at thy cost in Cornhill is erected,
Shall take a name from us; we'll have it called
The Leadenhall, because in digging it
You found the lead that covereth the same.

Eyre. I thank your majesty.

Margery. God bless your grace!

King. Lincoln, a word with you!
   (*The* King *and the* Earl of Lincoln *confer aside*)

(*Enter* Hodge, Firk, Ralph, *and more* Shoemakers)

Eyre. How now, my mad knaves? Peace,

speak softly, yonder is the king.

KING. With the old troop which there we
    keep in pay,
We will incorporate a new supply;
Before one summer more pass o'er my head,
France shall repent England was injured.
(Sees SHOEMAKERS) What are all those?

LACY. All shoemakers, my liege,
Sometime my fellows; in their companies
I lived as merry as an emperor.

KING. My mad lord mayor, are all these
shoemakers?

EYRE. All shoemakers, my liege; all gentlemen of the Gentle Craft, true Trojans, courageous cordwainers; they all kneel to the
shrine of holy Saint Hugh.

ALL THE SHOEMAKERS. God save your
majesty!

KING. Mad Simon, would they anything
with us?

EYRE. Mum, mad knaves! Not a word!
I'll do 't; I warrant you.—They are all beggars, my liege; all for themselves, and I for
them all, on both my knees do entreat, that
for the honor of poor Simon Eyre and the
good of his brethren, these mad knaves, your
grace would vouchsafe some privilege to my
new Leadenhall, that it may be lawful for us
to buy and sell leather there two days a week.

KING. Mad Sim, I grant your suit, you
    shall have patent
To hold two market-days in Leadenhall,
Mondays and Fridays, those shall be the
    times.
Will this content you?

ALL. Jesus bless your grace!

EYRE. In the name of these my poor brethren shoemakers, I most humbly thank your
grace. But before I rise, seeing you are in
the giving vein and we in the begging, grant
Sim Eyre one boon more.

KING. What is it, my lord mayor?

EYRE. Vouchsafe to taste of a poor banquet that stands sweetly waiting for your
sweet presence.

KING. I shall undo thee, Eyre, only with
    feasts;
Already have I been too troublesome;
Say, have I not?

EYRE. O my dear King, Sim Eyre was
taken unawares upon a day of shroving,
which I promised long ago to the prentices
of London. For, an 't please your highness, in

time past, I bare the water-tankard, and my
coat sits not a whit the worse upon my back;
and then, upon a morning, some mad boys,
it was Shrove Tuesday, even as 'tis now,
gave me my breakfast, and I swore then by
the stopple of my tankard, if ever I came to
be lord mayor of London, I would feast all
the prentices. This day, my liege, I did it,
and the slaves had an hundred tables five
times covered; they are gone home and vanished;

    Yet add more honor to the Gentle Trade,
    Taste of Eyre's banquet, Simon's happy
      made.

KING. Eyre, I will taste of thy banquet,
    and will say,
I have not met more pleasure on a day.
Friends of the Gentle Craft, thanks to you
    all,
Thanks, my kind lady mayoress, for our
    cheer.—
Come, lords, a while let 's revel it at home!
When all our sports and banquetings are
    done,
Wars must right wrongs which Frenchmen
    have begun.   (Exeunt)

THE FIRST THREE-MAN'S SONG

O the month of May, the merry month of
    May,
    So frolic, so gay, and so green, so green,
      so green!
O, and then did I unto my true love say:
    "Sweet Peg, thou shalt be my summer's
      queen!

"Now the nightingale, the pretty nightingale,
    The sweetest singer in all the forest's
      choir,
Entreats thee, sweet Peggy, to hear thy true
    love's tale;
    Lo, yonder she sitteth, her breast against
      a brier.

"But O, I spy the cuckoo, the cuckoo, the
    cuckoo;
    See where she sitteth: come away, my joy;
Come away, I prithee: I do not like the
    cuckoo
    Should sing where my Peggy and I kiss
      and toy."

O the month of May, the merry month of
    May,
  So frolic, so gay, and so green, so green,
    so green!
And then did I unto my true love say:
  "Sweet Peg, thou shalt be my summer's
    queen!"

THE SECOND THREE-MAN'S SONG

(This is to be sung at the latter end)

Cold's the wind, and wet's the rain,
  Saint Hugh be our good speed:
Ill is the weather that bringeth no gain,
  Nor helps good hearts in need.
Trowl [103] the bowl, the jolly nut-brown bowl,
  And here, kind mate, to thee:

[103] Send round.

Let's sing a dirge for Saint Hugh's soul,
  And down it merrily.

Down a down heydown a down,
            (Close with the tenor boy)
  Hey derry derry, down a down!
Ho, well done; to me let come!
  Ring compass,[104] gentle joy.

Trowl the bowl, the nut-brown bowl,
  And here, kind mate, to thee: &c.
(Repeat as often as there be men to drink; and
    at last when all have drunk, this verse:)

Cold's the wind, and wet's the rain,
  Saint Hugh be our good speed:
Ill is the weather that bringeth no gain,
  Nor helps good hearts in need.

[104] (?) Come full circle.

FRANCIS BEAUMONT
JOHN FLETCHER

The Knight of the Burning Pestle

PRINCIPAL EVENTS IN BEAUMONT'S LIFE

1584 or 1585, Francis Beaumont was born on his father's estates at Grace Dieu Priory. His father later became Justice of the Court of Common Pleas.

1597, Entered Broadgates Hall, Oxford.

1600, Entered the Middle Temple.

1605, 5 Nov., Several of Beaumont's relatives and friends were involved or suspected in the notorious Gunpowder Plot.

c. 1606, Beaumont's play, *The Woman Hater*, was acted by a boy company.

1607, Beaumont and Fletcher both wrote verses in praise of Jonson's *Volpone*.

1607, The Knight of the Burning Pestle, by Beaumont and Fletcher, was produced by a boy company at Blackfriars Theatre.

1609, Beaumont and Ben Jonson wrote verses in praise of Fletcher's *Faithful Shepherdess*.

c. 1609, Philaster, by Beaumont and Fletcher, produced by the King's men.

c. 1609, Beaumont wrote a famous verse letter to Ben Jonson about their merry meetings at the Mermaid Tavern.

c. 1609, The Coxcomb, by Beaumont and Fletcher, produced by a boy company.

c. 1610, The Maid's Tragedy, by Beaumont and Fletcher, produced by the King's men.

1611, A King and No King, by Beaumont and Fletcher, produced by the King's men.

1611, Beaumont and Fletcher wrote verses in praise of Jonson's *Catiline*.

1612, Beaumont's *Masque of the Inner Temple and Gray's Inn* was presented by the lawyers of these societies before the King, Queen, and Court.

1612 or 1613, He married Ursula Isley, a Kentish heiress, and probably spent the remaining years of his life as a country gentleman at Sundridge, Kent.

1614 or 1615, His daughter Elizabeth was born.

1616, 6 March, He died and was buried in Westminster Abbey.

1647, A large folio volume entitled *Comedies and Tragedies written by Francis Beaumont and John Fletcher, Gentlemen*, containing thirty-four plays and a masque, was published. A number of the plays in the volume cannot possibly contain any work of Beaumont, since they were written after his death.

1679, The second folio of Beaumont and Fletcher, containing fifty-two plays and a masque, was published. As in the previous volume, most of the plays are not Beaumont's.

PRINCIPAL EVENTS IN FLETCHER'S LIFE

1579, Dec., Born in Rye, the son of a clergyman who later became Lord Bishop of London and a favorite of Queen Elizabeth.

1591, Oct., Probably the John Fletcher who entered Corpus Christi College, Cambridge.

1595, Fletcher's father lost the favor of Queen Elizabeth and died the next year.

1607, The Knight of the Burning Pestle, by Beaumont and Fletcher, was produced by a boy company at Blackfriars Theatre.

1608 or 1609, The Faithful Shepherdess, by Fletcher alone, produced by a boy company at Blackfriars.

c. 1609, Philaster, by Beaumont and Fletcher, produced by Shakespeare's company, the King's men.

c. 1610, The Maid's Tragedy, by Beaumont and Fletcher, produced by the King's men.

1611, A King and No King, by Beaumont and Fletcher, produced by the King's men.

1613, The Two Noble Kinsmen, by Shakespeare and Fletcher, produced by the King's men.

1616, Francis Beaumont died.

1616, The Mad Lover acted by the King's men.

1618, The Loyal Subject acted by the King's men.

1621, The Wild Goose Chase acted by the King's men.

1621, The Pilgrim acted by the King's men.

1622, The Spanish Curate acted by the King's men.

1623, The Lover's Progress acted by the King's men.

1624, Rule a Wife and Have a Wife acted by the King's men.

1625, 29 Aug., Fletcher was buried in the parish of St. Saviour's, Southwark, where he had died in the great plague of 1625.

1647, A large folio volume entitled *Comedies and Tragedies written by Francis Beaumont and John Fletcher, Gentlemen* was published. It contained thirty-four plays and a masque.

1679, The second folio of Beaumont and Fletcher was published. It contained fifty-two plays and a masque.

INTRODUCTION

The Knight of the Burning Pestle, like *The Shoemakers' Holiday,* is a play written to please a particular social class, but a class quite different from the one for which Dekker wrote his comedy. The two plays focus on the same stratum of society, but whereas Dekker glorified middle-class Londoners and displayed their sturdy independence, Beaumont and Fletcher ridiculed them by dwelling on their pretentious ignorance and gullibility. Obviously the two plays were not prepared with the same audience in mind. Dekker's play, in fact, was written to be performed by an adult company, the Lord Admiral's men, at a large public theatre on the Bankside, the Rose, while *The Knight of the Burning Pestle* was written eight years later to be performed by a boy company at a small, exclusive private theatre, the Blackfriars.

These two types of theatre were standard in the time, and experienced dramatists then, as in all ages, wrote with particular attention to the type of theatre and stage for which their productions were intended. The problems posed for the dramatist by these two types of theatre were very different. The public theatres were large—most of them seem to have had a capacity of two thousand or more—and their general admission price was low. The private theatres were very much smaller; their general admission price was six times that of the public theatres; they had seats for all members of the audience. One consequence of these differences was that the middle and poorer classes tended to patronize the public theatres, where they could get in for a penny at the time *The Shoemakers' Holiday* was written. The private theatres, like the Blackfriars, tended more and more to cater to people who could afford to pay for comfort and exclusiveness. In London, at the time *The Knight of the Burning Pestle* was written, these people were chiefly the gentry, the courtiers, and the law students and lawyers at the Inns of Court. Such an audience was likely to find Beaumont and Fletcher's attitude toward the London guilds and the middle-class shop keepers much more congenial than Dekker's.

Beaumont and Fletcher took advantage of another feature of the production in their play. The acting company for which they wrote was not an adult company like the Lord Admiral's men or Shakespeare's company, the Lord Chamberlain-King's men, but a boy company, a troupe made up entirely of boys from about eight to seventeen years of age. Such troupes were popular in London; up to this time, performances at private theatres were always by boy companies. In such a company, as Beaumont and Fletcher knew, it would be easy to cast parts for small boys, so they included little fellows like Michael and George, and gave the name of several minor roles and walk-on parts as simply "Boy."

The prime objects of Beaumont and Fletcher's ridicule in this play are certain characteristics of middle-class Londoners as represented by Citizen, Citizen's Wife, and the Citizen's apprentice, Ralph—their naiveté, their pride in the London guilds, especially their own company of the Grocers, and their taste for the grossly improbable romances of chivalry, like *Palmerin of England,* and the romantic melodramas, like *The Spanish Tragedy.* These pieces with their high-flown language and their ridiculous situations represent the literary ideals of the three citizens, and most of Ralph's speeches and actions burlesque them or are directly quoted from them.

The pride of Citizen, Wife, and Ralph in the Grocers' guild is quite like that of the shoemakers in their guild as presented in *The Shoemakers' Holiday,* but Dekker presented it sympathetically, while Beaumont and Fletcher burlesqued it. When *The Knight of the Burning Pestle* was written, the Grocers' Company of London still included the apothecaries or druggists, and from various remarks in the play it is clear that Citizen's business dealt mostly in drugs and spices. The selection of the pestle as Ralph's knightly insignia and his use of a large pestle as a mace or a lance is an amusing adaptation of the burlesque to Ralph's particular loyalties.

Like some other burlesques, this one is a little confusing for the reader, for it combines into one action, *a,* the play originally intended for performance at the theatre (the story of Luce, Jasper, Humphrey, and the Merrythoughts); *b,* the various stories hastily invented by Citizen and Citizen's Wife to show off Ralph; and *c,* the actions and comments of people outside all the plots—Citizen, Citizen's Wife, and several of the boy actors. The very incoherence of it all is deliberate; the finest achievements of the dramatists are in the superb Citizen and Citizen's Wife who are really not in any plot at all, and the confusion is wholly a result of their lusty, impromptu stage management. Some of their inventions were evidently suggested to Beaumont and Fletcher by *Don Quixote,* but as characters the Citizen and his wife are among the immortal originals of the English drama.

THE KNIGHT OF THE BURNING PESTLE

Dramatis personae

In order of their first appearance

PROLOGUE, A boy actor who has been designated to deliver the prologue of the original play.

CITIZEN, A middle-aged London business man, a member of the Grocers' Guild, *i.e.*, the trade organization of wholesale and retail grocers, druggists, and spice importers. He is very much of a Babbitt—blustering, naive, sentimental, credulous, proud of his class and his hometown, and resentful of the gentry and his more sophisticated contemporaries.

CITIZEN'S WIFE, His wife, an ignorant, garrulous, uninhibited woman, extremely naive but kind-hearted and enthusiastic. Like many respectable middle-class London women of the time, she has never been in a theatre. In the course of the play she misunderstands almost everything she sees on the stage.

RALPH, Citizen's apprentice; that is, he not only works for Citizen, learning the business, but lives as a member of his family. Ralph is an amateur actor, and his performances are enthusiastically admired by his master and mistress. Like them, he is a great admirer of the improbably romantic tales of chivalry, and he believes every word of them.

VENTUREWELL, A well-to-do London merchant, father of Luce.

JASPER MERRYTHOUGHT, Venturewell's apprentice until dismissed. A handsome, intelligent young man, in love with Luce.

BOY, One of the boy actors at the theatre where the play is presented.

LUCE, Daughter of Venturewell, in love with Jasper but pursued by her father's favorite, Humphrey.

HUMPHREY, A silly, almost half-witted young man, rather like Sir Andrew Aguecheek in *Twelfth Night*. He fancies himself in love with Luce and acts as he thinks a lover is supposed to.

TIM, First Ralph's apprentice and then his squire after Ralph becomes the Knight of the Burning Pestle.

GEORGE, A bright little boy who becomes Ralph's page.

MISTRESS MERRYTHOUGHT, A vigorous and garrulous woman, wife of Merrythought and mother of Jasper and Michael.

MICHAEL MERRYTHOUGHT, Her younger son and favorite. An unnaturally sweet child who plays up to his mother on all occasions.

MERRYTHOUGHT, A merry old man, her husband. He refuses to worry about anything, to his wife's great annoyance. He has a great repertory of popular songs which he sings on any and every occasion, often with amusing appropriateness.

BOY, A boy dancer who entertains in the intermissions after the first and third acts.

TAPSTER }
HOST   } Of the Bell Inn at Waltham.

BARBER, Of Waltham, who pretends to be a cruel giant.

FIRST MAN } Customers at the Waltham
SECOND MAN } barber shop who pretend to
THIRD MAN } be knights and ladies in dis-
WOMAN   } tress.

BOY, A London boy who runs errands and helps Jasper in his scheme.

POMPIONA, The beauteous daughter of the King of Cracovia.

BOY, A servant in Venturewell's house.

SERVANT, Another servant in Venturewell's house.

SERGEANT, A sergeant in the London train bands, *i.e.*, militia.

WILLIAM HAMMERTON, A London pewterer, a stupid and incompetent member of the train bands.

GEORGE GREENGOOSE, A London poulterer, also a member of the train bands and similarly accomplished.

FIRST SOLDIER } Other members of the
SECOND SOLDIER } London train bands.

Induction

(The setting for the induction is the actual stage on which the play was intended to be performed. When the play begins, several well dressed gentlemen are seated on stools on the stage itself, as was customary. They are the well-to-do young men about town who would be there at any performance. Their stools would be at the edge of the stage where they would interfere as little as possible with the actors and the view of the rest of the audience. The CITIZEN, *the* CITIZEN'S WIFE, *and* RALPH *are seated with the other spectators in the pit. At first they would be indistinguishable as actors.*

The PROLOGUE *is one of the regular boy actors of the company. He is dressed in the costume he will wear later in the play, but over his costume he wears the customary long black cloak of the prologue speaker. He wears a black hat. He walks clear down stage, removes his hat, bows deeply to the audience, and begins the prologue.)*

PROL. "From all that's near the court, from
    all that's great,
Within the compass of the city-walls—
We now have brought our scene——"
CIT. (*Calling from the audience*) Hold your peace, goodman boy!
PROL. What do you mean, sir?
CIT. (*Making his way to the stage*) That you have no good meaning: this seven years there hath been plays at this house, (*climbs up on the stage*) I have observed it, you have still girds at citizens; and now you call your play "The London Merchant." Down with your title,[1] boy! down with your title!
PROL. Are you a member of the noble city?
CIT. I am.
PROL. (*With mock respect*) And a free-man?
CIT. Yea, and a grocer.[2]
PROL. So, grocer, then, by your sweet favor, we intend no abuse to the city.
CIT. No, sir! yes, sir: if you were not

resolved to play the Jacks,[3] what need you study for new subjects, purposely to abuse your betters? why could not you be contented, as well as others, with "The legend of Whittington," or "The Life and Death of Sir Thomas Gresham, with the building of the Royal Exchange," or "The story of Queen Eleanor, with the rearing of London Bridge upon woolsacks?"[4]
PROL. (*With mock admiration*) You seem to be an understanding man: what would you have us do, sir?
CIT. Why, present something notably in honor of the commons of the city.
PROL. (*With exaggerated seriousness*) Why, what do you say to "The Life and Death of Fat Drake, or the Repairing of Fleet-privies?"
CIT. I do not like that; but I will have a citizen, and he shall be of my own trade.
PROL. Oh, you should have told us your mind a month since; our play is ready to begin now.
CIT. 'Tis all one for that; I will have a grocer, and he shall do admirable things.
PROL. What will you have him do?
CIT. Marry, I will have him——
WIFE. (*Calling from the audience*) Husband, husband!
RALPH. (*Trying to quiet her*) Peace, mistress.
WIFE. Hold thy peace, Ralph; I know what I do, I warrant ye.—Husband, husband!
CIT. What sayest thou, cony?
WIFE. Let him kill a lion with a pestle, husband! let him kill a lion with a pestle!
CIT. So he shall.—I'll have him kill a lion with a pestle.
WIFE. Husband! shall I come up, husband?
CIT. Ay, cony.—Ralph, help your mistress this way.—(*to the audience*) Pray, gentlemen, make her a little room.—(*to a gentleman seated on the stage*) I pray you, sir, lend me your hand to help up my wife. (WIFE *is hauled up by* CITIZEN *and a gentle-*

[1] The board on which the title of the day's play was displayed.
[2] One of the twelve powerful guilds which controlled the government of London.

[3] Mock us.
[4] All three titles refer to popular London stories glorifying citizens.

man and boosted by RALPH) I thank you, sir.—So.

WIFE. By your leave, gentlemen all; I'm something troublesome: I'm a stranger here; I was ne'er at one of these plays, as they say, before; but I should have seen "Jane Shore" once; and my husband hath promised me, any time this twelvemonth, to carry me to "The Bold Beauchamps," but in truth he did not. I pray you, bear with me.

CIT. Boy, let my wife and I have a couple of stools and then begin; and let the grocer do rare things. *(Stools are brought)*

PROL. But, sir, we have never a boy to play him: every one hath a part already.

WIFE. *(Struck by a brilliant idea)* Husband, husband, for God's sake, let Ralph play him! beshrew me, if I do not think he will go beyond them all.

CIT. Well remembered, wife.—*(calling down)* Come up, Ralph.—I'll tell you, gentlemen; let them but lend him a suit of reparel and necessaries, and, by gad, if any of them all blow wind in the tail on him, I'll be hanged.

(RALPH comes on the stage)

WIFE. *(To* PROLOGUE) I pray you, youth, let him have a suit of reparel!—I'll be sworn, gentlemen, my husband tells you true: he will act you sometimes at our house, that all the neighbors cry out on him; he will fetch you up a couraging part so in the garret, that we are all as feared, I warrant you, that we quake again: we'll fear our children with him; if they be never so unruly, do but cry, "Ralph comes, Ralph comes!" to them, and they'll be as quiet as lambs.—Hold up thy head, Ralph; show the gentlemen what thou canst do; speak a huffing part; I warrant you, the gentlemen will accept of it.

CIT. Do, Ralph, do.

RALPH. *(He strikes an attitude and recites with violent gestures)* "By Heaven, methinks, it were an easy leap
To pluck bright honor from the pale-faced moon;
Or dive into the bottom of the sea,
Where never fathom-line touched any ground,
And pluck up drowned honor from the lake of hell." [5]

CIT. *(Proudly)* How say you, gentlemen,

is it not as I told you? *(The gentlemen on the stage wink at each other and pretend to be impressed)*

WIFE. Nay, gentlemen, he hath played before, my husband says, Mucedorus, before the wardens of our company.

CIT. Ay, and he should have played Jeronimo [6] with a shoemaker for a wager.

PROL. He shall have a suit of apparel, if he will go in.

CIT. In, Ralph, in, Ralph; and set out the grocery in their kind, if thou lovest me.

(Exit RALPH)

WIFE. I warrant, our Ralph will look finely when he's dressed.

PROL. But what will you have it called?

CIT. *(After deep thought)* "The Grocer's Honor."

PROL. *(Baiting him)* Methinks "The Knight of the Burning Pestle" were better.

WIFE. I'll be sworn, husband, that's as good a name as can be.

CIT. Let it be so.—Begin, begin; my wife and I will sit down.

PROL. I pray you, do.

CIT. What stately music have you? you have shawms? [7]

PROL. Shawms! no.

CIT. No! I'm a thief, if my mind did not give me so. Ralph plays a stately part, and he must needs have shawms: I'll be at the charge of them myself, rather than we'll be without them.

PROL. So you are like to be.

CIT. Why, and so I will be: there's two shillings;—*(Gives money)*—let's have the waits of Southwark; they are as rare fellows as any are in England; and that will fetch them all o'er the water with a vengeance, as if they were mad.

PROL. You shall have them. Will you sit down, then?

CIT. Ay.—Come, wife.

WIFE. Sit you merry all, gentlemen; I'm bold to sit amongst you for my ease.

(CITIZEN and WIFE *sit down)*

PROL. *(He walks down stage and delivers his prologue to the audience)* "From all that's near the court, from all that's great,

[5] *Henry IV*, Part 1, I, iii, 201-205.

[6] The leading role in *The Spanish Tragedy*, by this time ridiculed by sophisticated people.

[7] Primitive oboes.

Within the compass of the city-walls,
We now have brought our scene. Fly far
   from hence
All private taxes, immodest phrases,
Whatever may but show like vicious!
For wicked mirth never true pleasure brings,
But honest minds are pleased with honest
   things."—

(*Turning to the* CITIZEN) Thus much for
that we do; but for Ralph's part you must
answer for yourself.

   CIT. Take you no care for Ralph; he'll
discharge himself, I warrant you.
               (*Exit* PROLOGUE)
   WIFE. I'faith, gentlemen, I'll give my
word for Ralph.

Act I

SCENE I. *A Room in the House of* VENTUREWELL.

(*Enter* VENTUREWELL *talking angrily to*
JASPER)

   VENT. Sirrah, I'll make you know you are
   my prentice,
And whom my charitable love redeemed
Even from the fall of fortune; gave thee heat
And growth, to be what now thou art, new-
   cast thee;
Adding the trust of all I have, at home,
In foreign staples, or upon the sea,
To thy direction; tied the good opinions
Both of myself and friends to thy endeavors;
So fair were thy beginnings. But with these,
As I remember, you had never charge
To love your master's daughter, and even
   then
When I had found a wealthy husband for
   her—
I take it, sir, you had not. But, however,
I'll break the neck of that commission,
And make you know you are but a merchant's
   factor.[8]
   JASP. Sir, I do liberally confess I am yours,
Bound both by love and duty to your service,
In which my labor hath been all my profit:
I have not lost in bargain, nor delighted
To wear your honest gains upon my back;
Nor have I given a pension to my blood,
Or lavishly in play consumed your stock;
These, and the miseries that do attend them,
I dare with innocence proclaim are strangers
To all my temperate actions. For your
   daughter,
If there be any love to my deservings
Borne by her virtuous self, I cannot stop it;
Nor am I able to refrain her wishes,

   [8] Agent.

She's private to herself, and best of knowl-
   edge
Whom she will make so happy as to sigh for:
Besides, I cannot think you mean to match
   her
Unto a fellow of so lame a presence,
One that hath little left of nature in him.
   VENT. 'Tis very well, sir: I can tell your
   wisdom
How all this shall be cured.
   JASP. Your care becomes you.
   VENT. And thus it shall be, sir: I here
   discharge you
My house and service; take your liberty;
And when I want a son, I'll send for you.
               (*Exit*)
   JASP. These be the fair rewards of them
   that love!
Oh, you that live in freedom, never prove
The travail of a mind led by desire!

(*Enter* LUCE)

   LUCE. Why, how now, friend? struck
with my father's thunder!
   JASP. Struck, and struck dead, unless the
   remedy
Be full of speed and virtue; I am now,
What I expected long, no more your father's.
   LUCE. But mine.
   JASP. But yours, and only yours, I am;
That's all I have to keep me from the statute.[9]
You dare be constant still?
   LUCE. O, fear me not!
In this I dare be better than a woman:
Nor shall his anger nor his offers move me,

   [9] The law providing punishment for apprentices who left their masters.

Were they both equal to a prince's power.
　Jasp. You know my rival!
　Luce. Yes, and love him dearly;
Even as I love an ague or foul weather:
I prithee, Jasper, fear him not.
　Jasp. Oh, no!
I do not mean to do him so much kindness.
But to our own desires: you know the plot
We both agreed on?
　Luce. Yes, and will perform
My part exactly.
　Jasp. I desire no more.
Farewell, and keep my heart; 'tis yours.
　Luce. I take it;
He must do miracles makes me forsake it.
　　　　　　　　　　　　　(Exeunt)
　Cit. Fie upon 'em, little infidels! what a

matter's here now! Well, I'll be hanged for
a halfpenny, if there be not some abomination knavery in this play. Well; let 'em look
to't; Ralph must come, and if there be any
tricks a-brewing——
　Wife. Let 'em brew and bake too, husband, a' God's name; Ralph will find all out,
I warrant you, an they were older than they
are.—(Enter Boy)—I pray, my pretty youth,
is Ralph ready?
　Boy. He will be presently.
　Wife. Now, I pray you, make my commendations unto him, and withal carry him
this stick of liquorice: tell him his mistress
sent it to him; and bid him bite a piece; 'twill
open his pipes the better, say.　(Exit Boy)

SCENE II. *Another Room in the House of* VENTUREWELL.

(*Enter* VENTUREWELL *and* HUMPHREY)

　Vent. Come, sir, she's yours; upon my
　　faith, she's yours;
You have my hand: for other idle lets
Between your hopes and her, thus with a
　wind
They are scattered and no more. My wanton
　prentice,
That like a bladder blew himself with love,
I have let out, and sent him to discover
New masters yet unknown.
　Hum. I thank you, sir,
Indeed, I thank you, sir; and, ere I stir,
It shall be known, however you do deem,
I am of gentle blood, and gentle seem.
　Vent. Oh, sir, I know it certain.
　Hum. Sir, my friend,
Although, as writers say, all things have end,
And that we call a pudding hath his two,
Oh, let it not seem strange, I pray, to you,
If in this bloody simile I put
My love, more endless than frail things or
　gut!
　Wife. (*Interrupting the performance*)
Husband, I prithee, sweet lamb, tell me one
thing; but tell me truly.—Stay, youths, I
beseech you, till I question my husband.
　Cit. What is it, mouse?
　Wife. Sirrah, didst thou ever see a prettier
child? how it behaves itself, I warrant ye,

and speaks and looks, and perts up the head!
—I pray you, brother, with your favor, were
you never none of Master Moncaster's
scholars?
　Cit. Chicken, I prithee heartily, contain
thyself: the childer are pretty childer; but
when Ralph comes, lamb——
　Wife. Ay, when Ralph comes, cony!—
Well, my youth, you may proceed.
　Vent. Well, sir, you know my love, and
rest, I hope,
Assured of my consent; get but my daugh-
　ter's,
And wed her when you please. You must be
　bold,
And clap in close unto her: come, I know
You have language good enough to win a
　wench.
　Wife. (*In a loud whisper*) A whoreson
tyrant! h'as been an old stringer [10] in's days,
I warrant him.
　Hum. I take your gentle offer, and withal
Yield love again for love reciprocal.
　Vent. (*Calling*) What, Luce! within
there!

(*Enter* LUCE)

　Luce. Called you, sir?
　Vent. I did:

[10] Libertine.

Give entertainment to this gentleman;
And see you be not froward.—To her, sir:
My presence will but be an eye-sore to you.
(*Exit*)

HUM. (*Simpering foolishly*) Fair Mistress
     Luce, how do you? Are you well?
Give me your hand, and then I pray you tell
How doth your little sister and your brother;
And whether you love me or any other.

LUCE. Sir, these are quickly answered.
HUM. So they are,
Where women are not cruel. But how far
Is it now distant from the place we are in,
Unto that blessèd place, your father's war-
     ren?

LUCE. What makes you think of that, sir?
HUM. Even that face;
For, stealing rabbits whilom in that place,
God Cupid, or the keeper, I know not
     whether,
Unto my cost and charges brought you
     thither,
And there began——

LUCE. Your game, sir.
HUM. Let no game,
Or any thing that tendeth to the same,
Be ever more remembered, thou fair killer,
For whom I sate me down, and brake my
     tiller.[11]

WIFE. There's a kind gentleman, I warrant you: (*coquettishly*) when will you do
as much for me, George?

LUCE. (*Concealing her amusement*) Be-
     shrew me, sir, I am sorry for your losses,
But, as the proverb says, I cannot cry:
I would you had not seen me!

HUM. So would I,
Unless you had more maw [12] to do me good.

LUCE. Why, cannot this strange passion
     be withstood;
Send for a constable, and raise the town.

HUM. Oh, no! my valiant love will batter
     down
Millions of constables, and put to flight
Even that great watch of Midsummer-day at
     night.[13]

LUCE. Beshrew me, sir, 'twere good I
     yielded, then;
Weak women cannot hope, where valiant
     men

[11] Crossbow.
[12] Desire.
[13] The annual London military muster.

Have no resistance.
HUM. Yield, then; I am full
Of pity, though I say it, and can pull
Out of my pocket thus a pair of gloves.
(*Eagerly pointing out the beauties of his
     gift*)
Look, Lucé, look; the dog's tooth nor the
     dove's
Are not so white as these; (*smelling them*)
     and sweet they be,
And whipt about with silk, as you may see.
If you desire the price, shoot from your eye
A beam to this place, and you shall espy
F S, which is to say, my sweetest honey,
They cost me three and twopence, or no
     money.

LUCE. Well, sir, I take them kindly, and
     I thank you. (*She pauses.* HUMPHREY
     looks foolish.)
What would you more?
HUM. Nothing.
LUCE. Why, then, farewell.
HUM. Nor so, nor so; for, lady, I must tell,
Before we part, for what we met together:
God grant me time and patience and fair
     weather!

LUCE. Speak, and declare your mind in
terms so brief.

HUM. I shall. Then, first and foremost,
     for relief
I call to you, if that you can afford it;
I care not at what price, for, on my word, it
Shall be repaid again, although it cost me
More than I'll speak of now; for love hath
     tost me
In furious blanket like a tennis-ball,
And now I rise aloft, and now I fall.

LUCE. Alas, good gentleman, alas the day!
HUM. I thank you heartily; and, as I say,
Thus do I still continue without rest,
I' the morning like a man, at night a beast,
Roaring and bellowing mine own disquiet,
That much I fear, forsaking of my diet
Will bring me presently to that quandary,
I shall bid all adieu.

LUCE. Now, by St. Mary,
That were great pity!
HUM. So it were, beshrew me;
Then, ease me, lusty Luce, and pity show
     me.

LUCE. Why, sir, you know my will is
     nothing worth
Without my father's grant; get his consent,

And then you may with assurance try me.

Hum. The worshipful your sire will not
   deny me;
For I have asked him, and he hath replied,
"Sweet Master Humphrey, Luce shall be thy
   bride."

Luce. Sweet Master Humphrey, then I
am content.

Hum. And so am I, in truth.

Luce. Yet take me with you; [14]
There is another clause must be annexed,
And this it is: I swore, and will perform it,
No man shall ever joy me as his wife
But he that stole me hence. If you dare ven-
   ture,
I am yours (you need not fear; my father
   loves you);
If not, farewell for ever! (*She walks toward
   the door*)

Hum. Stay, nymph, stay:
I have a double gelding, colored bay,
Sprung by his father from Barbarian kind;
Another for myself, though somewhat blind,
Yet true as trusty tree.

Luce. I am satisfied;
And so I give my hand. Our course must lie
Through Waltham forest, where I have a
   friend
Will entertain us. So, farewell, Sir Hum-
   phrey,
And think upon your business.   (*Exit*)

Hum. Though I die,
I am resolved to venture life and limb
For one so young, so fair, so kind, so trim.
                                    (*Exit*)

Wife. By my faith and troth, George, and
as I am virtuous, it is e'en the kindest young
man that ever trod on shoe-leather.—Well,
go thy ways; if thou hast her not, 'tis not thy
fault, i'faith.

Cit. I prithee, mouse, be patient; 'a shall
have her, or I'll make some of 'em smoke for't.

Wife. That's my good lamb, George.—
(*Looking at the gentlemen seated on the
stage who are smoking pipes*) Fie, this stinking tobacco kills me! would there were none
in England!—Now, I pray, gentlemen, what
good does this stinking tobacco do you?
nothing, I warrant you: make chimneys o'
your faces!

Scene III. *A Grocer's Shop.*

(*The curtain of the inner stage is drawn
back to reveal* Ralph, *dressed as a grocer,
reading aloud* "Palmerin of England," *a
popular romance. Listening to him are* Tim,
dressed as an apprentice, and George, *a
small boy*)

Wife. Oh, husband, husband, now, now!
there's Ralph, there's Ralph.

Cit. Peace, fool! let Ralph alone.—Hark
you, Ralph; do not strain yourself too much
at the first.—Peace!—Begin, Ralph.

Ralph. (*Reads*) Then Palmerin and
Trineus, snatching their lances from their
dwarfs, and clasping their helmets, galloped
amain after the giant; and Palmerin, having
gotten a sight of him, came posting amain,
saying, "Stay, traitorous thief! for thou mayst
not so carry away her, that is worth the greatest lord in the world;" and, with these words,
gave him a blow on the shoulder, that he
struck him besides his elephant. And

[14] Understand me.

Trineus, coming to the knight that had Agric-
ola behind him, set him soon besides his
horse, with his neck broken in the fall; so
that the princess, getting out of the throng,
between joy and grief, said, "All happy
knight, the mirror of all such as follow arms,
now may I be well assured of the love thou
bearest me." (Ralph *closes the book and
speculates sagely*) I wonder why the kings
do not raise an army of fourteen or fifteen
hundred thousand men, as big as the army
that the Prince of Portigo brought against
Rosicleer, and destroy these giants; they do
much hurt to wandering damsels, that go in
quest of their knights.

Wife. Faith, husband, and Ralph says
true; for they say the King of Portugal cannot sit at his meat, but the giants and the
ettins will come and snatch it from him.

Cit. Hold thy tongue.—On, Ralph!

Ralph. And certainly those knights are
much to be commended, who, neglecting
their possessions, wander with a squire and

a dwarf through the deserts to relieve poor ladies.

WIFE. Ay, by my faith, are they, Ralph; let 'em say what they will, they are indeed. Our knights neglect their possessions well enough, but they do not the rest.

RALPH. There are no such courteous and fair well-spoken knights in this age: they will call one "the son of a whore," that Palmerin of England would have called "fair sir;" and one that Rosicleer would have called "right beauteous damsel," they will call "damned bitch."

WIFE. I'll be sworn will they, Ralph; they have called me so an hundred times about a scurvy pipe of tobacco.

RALPH. But what brave spirit could be content to sit in his shop, with a flappet of wood, and a blue apron before him, selling mithridatum and dragon's-water to visited houses, that might pursue feats of arms, and, through his noble achievements, procure such a famous history to be written of his heroic prowess?

CIT. Well said, Ralph; some more of those words, Ralph!

WIFE. They go finely, by my troth.

RALPH. Why should not I, then, pursue this course, both for the credit of myself and our Company? For amongst all the worthy books of achievements, I do not call to mind that I yet read of a grocer-errant: I will be the said knight.—Have you heard of any that hath wandered unfurnished of his squire and dwarf? My elder prentice Tim shall be my trusty squire, and little George my dwarf. (*Taking off his apron and throwing it aside*) Hence, my blue apron! Yet, in remembrance of my former trade, upon my shield shall be portrayed a Burning Pestle, and I will be called the Knight of the Burning Pestle.

WIFE. Nay, I dare swear thou wilt not forget thy old trade; thou wert ever meek.

RALPH. Tim!

TIM. Anon.

RALPH. My beloved squire, and George my dwarf, I charge you that from henceforth you never call me by any other name but "the right courteous and valiant Knight of the Burning Pestle;" and that you never call any female by the name of a woman or wench, but "fair lady," if she have her desires, if not, "distressed damsel;" that you call all forests and heaths "deserts," and all horses "palfreys."

WIFE. This is very fine, faith.—Do the gentlemen like Ralph, think you, husband?

CIT. Ay, I warrant thee; the players would give all the shoes in their shop for him.

RALPH. My beloved squire Tim, stand out. Admit this were a desert, and over it a knight-errant pricking, and I should bid you inquire of his intents, what would you say?

TIM. Sir, my master sent me to know whither you are riding?

RALPH. No, thus: "Fair sir, the right courteous and valiant Knight of the Burning Pestle commanded me to inquire upon what adventure you are bound, whether to relieve some distressed damsel, or otherwise."

CIT. Whoreson blockhead, cannot remember!

WIFE. I'faith, and Ralph told him on't before: all the gentlemen heard him.—Did he not, gentlemen? did not Ralph tell him on't?

GEORGE. Right courteous and valiant Knight of the Burning Pestle, here is a distressed damsel to have a halfpenny-worth of pepper.

WIFE. That's a good boy! see, the little boy can hit it; by my troth, it's a fine child.

RALPH. Relieve her, with all courteous language. Now shut up shop; no more my prentices, but my trusty squire and dwarf. I must bespeak my shield and arming pestle. (*Exeunt* TIM *and* GEORGE)

CIT. Go thy ways, Ralph! As I'm a true man, thou art the best on 'em all.

WIFE. Ralph, Ralph!

RALPH. What say you, mistress?

WIFE. I prithee, come again quickly, sweet Ralph.

RALPH. By and by. (*Exit*)

SCENE IV. *A Room in* MERRYTHOUGHT'S *House.*

(*Enter* MISTRESS MERRYTHOUGHT *violently scolding* JASPER)

MIST. MER. Give thee my blessing? No, I'll ne'er give thee my blessing; I'll see thee hanged first; it shall ne'er be said I gave thee my blessing. Thou art thy father's own son, of the right blood of the Merrythoughts. I may curse the time that e'er I knew thy father; he hath spent all his own and mine too; and when I tell him of it, he laughs, and dances, and sings, and cries, "A merry heart lives long-a." And thou art a waste-thrift, and art run away from thy master that loved thee well, and art come to me; and I have laid up a little for my younger son Michael, and thou thinkest to bezzle that, but thou shalt never be able to do it.—(*calling*) Come hither, Michael!

(*Enter* MICHAEL)

Come, Michael, down on thy knees; thou shalt have my blessing.
MICH. (*He kneels and speaks with af-fected sweetness*) I pray you, mother, pray to God to bless me.
MIST. MER. God bless thee! (MICHAEL *rises*) But Jasper shall never have my bless-ing; he shall be hanged first: shall he not, Michael? how sayest thou?
MICH. Yes, forsooth, mother, and grace of God.
MIST. MER. That's a good boy!
WIFE. I'faith, it's a fine-spoken child.
JASP. Mother, though you forget a parent's love
I must preserve the duty of a child.
I ran not from my master, nor return
To have your stock maintain my idleness.
WIFE. Ungracious child, I warrant him; hark, how he chops logic [15] with his mother!—Thou hadst best tell her she lies; do, tell her she lies.
CIT. If he were my son, I would hang him up by the heels, and flay him, and salt him, whoreson haltersack.
JASP. My coming only is to beg your love,

[15] Argues.

Which I must ever, though I never gain it;
And, howsoever you esteem of me,
There is no drop of blood hid in these veins
But, I remember well, belongs to you
That brought me forth, and would be glad for you
To rip them all again, and let it out.
MIST. MER. I'faith, I had sorrow enough for thee, God knows; but I'll hamper thee well enough. Get thee in, thou vagabond, get thee in, and learn of thy brother Michael.
(*Exeunt* JASPER *and* MICHAEL)
MER. (*Singing off stage*)

Nose, nose, jolly red nose,
And who gave thee this jolly red nose?

MIST. MER. Hark, my husband! he's sing-ing and hoiting; and I'm fain to cark and care, and all little enough.—(*calling shrilly*) Husband! Charles! Charles Merrythought!

(*Enter* MERRYTHOUGHT)

MER. (*Singing*)

Nutmegs and ginger, cinnamon and cloves;
And they gave me this jolly red nose.

MIST. MER. If you would consider your state, you would have little list to sing, i-wis.
MER. It should never be considered, while it were an estate, if I thought it would spoil my singing.
MIST. MER. But how wilt thou do, Charles? Thou art an old man, and thou canst not work, and thou hast not forty shill-ings left, and thou eatest good meat, and drinkest good drink, and laughest.
MER. And will do.
MIST. MER. But how wilt thou come by it, Charles?
MER. How? Why, how have I done hitherto these forty years? I never came into my dining room, but, at eleven and six o'clock, I found excellent meat and drink o' the table; my clothes were never worn out, but next morning a tailor brought me a new suit: and without question it will be so ever;

use makes perfectness. If all should fail, it
is but a little straining myself extraordinary,
and laugh myself to death.

WIFE. (*Somewhat uncertainly*) It's a
foolish old man this; is not he, George?

CIT. Yes, cony.

WIFE. Give me a penny i' the purse while
I live, George.

CIT. Ay, by lady, cony, hold thee there.

MIST. MER. Well, Charles; you promised
to provide for Jasper, and I have laid up for
Michael. I pray you, pay Jasper his portion:
he's come home, and he shall not consume
Michael's stock; he says his master turned
him away, but, I promise you truly, I think
he ran away.

WIFE. (*Very earnestly*) No, indeed, Mistress Merrythought; though he be a notable
gallows, yet I'll assure you his master did
turn him away, even in this place; 'twas,
i'faith, within this half-hour, about his
daughter; my husband was by.

CIT. Hang him, rogue! he served him well
enough: love his master's daughter! By my
troth, cony, if there were a thousand boys,
thou wouldst spoil them all with taking their
parts; let his mother alone with him.

WIFE. Ay, George; but yet truth is truth.

MER. Where is Jasper? He's welcome,
however. Call him in; he shall have his portion. Is he merry?

MIST. MER. Ah, foul chive him,[16] he is
too merry!—Jasper! Michael!

(*Re-enter* JASPER *and* MICHAEL)

MER. Welcome, Jasper! though thou run-
nest away, welcome! God bless thee! 'Tis thy
mother's mind thou shouldst receive thy portion; thou hast been abroad, and I hope hast
learned experience enough to govern it; thou
art of sufficient years; hold thy hand—(*counting out shillings*) one, two, three, four, five,
six, seven, eight, nine, there is ten shillings
for thee. Thrust thyself into the world with
that, and take some settled course. If fortune
cross thee, thou hast a retiring place; come
home to me; I have twenty shillings left. Be
a good husband; that is, wear ordinary
clothes, eat the best meat, and drink the best
drink; be merry, and give to the poor, and,

[16] Bad luck to him.

believe me, thou hast no end of thy goods.

JASP. (*Affectionately*) Long may you live
free from all thought of ill,
And long have cause to be thus merry still!
But, father——

MER. No more words, Jasper; get thee
gone.
Thou hast my blessing; thy father's spirit
upon thee! Farewell, Jasper! (*singing*)

But yet, or ere you part (*oh, cruel!*)
Kiss me, kiss me, sweeting, mine own dear
jewel!

So, now begone; no words. (*Exit* JASPER)

MIST. MER. So, Michael, now get thee
gone too.

MICH. Yes, forsooth, mother; but I'll have
my father's blessing first.

MIST. MER. No, Michael; 'tis no matter
for his blessing; thou hast my blessing; begone. I'll fetch my money and jewels, and
follow thee. I'll stay no longer with him, I
warrant thee. (*Exit* MICHAEL)—Truly,
Charles, I'll be gone too.

MER. What! you will not?

MIST. MER. Yes, indeed will I.

MER. (*Sings*)

Heigh-ho, farewell, Nan,
I'll never trust wench more again, if I can.

MIST. MER. (*Spitefully*) You shall not
think, when all your own is gone, to spend
that I have been scraping up for Michael.

MER. Farewell, good wife; I expect it not.
All I have to do in this world, is to be merry;
which I shall, if the ground be not taken
from me; and if it be, (*sings*)

When earth and seas from me are reft,
The skies aloft for me are left.

(MERRYTHOUGHT *goes out one door singing,
and* MISTRESS MERRYTHOUGHT
marches sternly out the other)

WIFE. I'll be sworn he's a merry old
gentleman for all that. (*Music off stage*)
Hark, hark, husband, hark! fiddles, fiddles!
now surely they go finely. They say 'tis present death for these fiddlers, to tune their

rebecks before the great Turk's grace; it's not, George? (*Enter a Boy who dances during the intermission to the off stage music*) But, look, look! here's a youth dances!—Now, good youth, do a turn o' the toe.—Sweetheart, i'faith, I'll have Ralph come and do some of his gambols.—He'll ride the wild mare, gentlemen, 'twould do your hearts good to see him.—I thank you, kind youth; pray, bid Ralph come.

CIT. (*Annoyed at the dancing which he cannot understand*) Peace, cony!—Sirrah, you scurvy boy, bid the players send Ralph; or, by God's——an they do not, I'll tear some of their periwigs beside their heads: this is all riff-raff. (*Exit Boy*)

Act II

SCENE I. *A Room in the House of* VENTUREWELL.

(*Enter* VENTUREWELL *and* HUMPHREY)

VENT. And how, faith, how goes it now, son Humphrey?

HUM. Right worshipful, and my belovéd friend
And father dear, this matter's at an end.

VENT. 'Tis well: it should be so: I'm glad the girl
Is found so tractable.

HUM. Nay, she must whirl
From hence (and you must wink; for so, I say,
The story tells,) to-morrow before day.

WIFE. George, dost thou think in thy conscience now 'twill be a match? tell me but what thou thinkest, sweet rogue. Thou seest the poor gentleman, dear heart, how it labors and throbs, I warrant you, to be at rest! I'll go move the father for't.

CIT. No, no; I prithee, sit still, honeysuckle; thou'lt spoil all. If he deny him, I'll bring half-a-dozen good fellows myself, and in the shutting of an evening, knock't up, and there's an end.

WIFE. I'll buss thee for that, i'faith, boy. Well, George, well, you have been a wag in your days, I warrant you; but God forgive you, and I do with all my heart.

VENT. How was it, son? you told me that to-morrow
Before day-break, you must convey her hence.

HUM. I must, I must; and thus it is agreed:
Your daughter rides upon a brown-bay steed,
I on a sorrel, which I bought of Brian,
The honest host of the Red roaring Lion,
In Waltham situate. Then, if you may,
Consent in seemly sort; lest, by delay,

The Fatal Sisters come, and do the office,
And then you'll sing another song.

VENT. Alas,
Why should you be thus full of grief to me,
That do as willing as yourself agree
To any thing, so it be good and fair?
Then, steal her when you will, if such a pleasure
Content you both; I'll sleep and never see it,
To make your joys more full. But tell me why
You may not here perform your marriage?

WIFE. God's blessing o' thy soul, old man! i'faith, thou art loath to part true hearts. I see 'a has her, George; and I'm as glad on't! —Well, go thy ways, Humphrey, for a fair-spoken man; I believe thou hast not thy fellow within the walls of London; an I should say the suburbs too, I should not lie.—Why dost not rejoice with me, George?

CIT. If I but could see Ralph again, I were as merry as mine host, i'faith.

HUM. The cause you seem to ask, I thus declare—
Help me, O Muses nine! Your daughter sware
A foolish oath, and more it was the pity;
Yet no one but myself within this city
Shall dare to say so, but a bold defiance
Shall meet him, were he of the noble science; [17]
And yet she sware, and yet why did she sware?
Truly, I cannot tell, unless it were
For her own ease; for, sure, sometimes an oath,
Being sworn thereafter, is like cordial broth;
And this it was she swore, never to marry

[17] A fencer.

But such a one whose mighty arm could carry
(As meaning me, for I am such a one)
Her bodily away, through stick and stone,
Till both of us arrive, at her request,
Some ten miles off, in the wild Waltham
   forest.
   VENT. If this be all, you shall not need
   to fear

Any denial in your love: proceed;
I'll neither follow, nor repent the deed.
   HUM. Good night, twenty good nights,
   and twenty more,
And twenty more good nights,—(*looking
   foolishly about*) that makes three-score!
                     (*Exeunt*)

SCENE II. *Waltham Forest.*

(*Enter* MISTRESS MERRYTHOUGHT *carrying
a jewel casket and a purse, followed by*
MICHAEL)

MIST. MER. Come, Michael; art thou not
weary, boy?
   MICH. No, forsooth, mother, not I.
   MIST. MER. Where be we now, child?
   MICH. Indeed, forsooth, mother, I cannot
tell, unless we be at Mile-End. Is not all the
world Mile-End, mother?
   MIST. MER. No, Michael, not all the
world, boy; but I can assure thee, Michael,
Mile End is a goodly matter: there has been
a pitchfield, my child, between the naughty
Spaniels and the Englishmen; and the Spaniels ran away, Michael, and the Englishmen
followed. My neighbor Coxstone was there,
boy, and killed them all with a birding-piece.
   MICH. Mother, forsooth——
   MIST. MER. What says my white boy? [18]
   MICH. Shall not my father go with us too?
   MIST. MER. No, Michael, let thy father
go snick-up; he shall never come between
a pair of sheets with me again while he lives;
let him stay at home, and sing for his supper,
boy. Come, child, sit down, and I'll show my
boy fine knacks, indeed. (*They sit down; she
opens the jewel casket and shows* MICHAEL
the contents one by one) Look, here, Michael; here's a ring, and here's a brooch, and
here's a bracelet, and here's two rings more,
and here's money and gold by th'eye, my boy.
   MICH. Shall I have all this, mother?
   MIST. MER. Ay, Michael, thou shalt have
all, Michael.
   CIT. How likest thou this, wench?
   WIFE. I cannot tell; I would have Ralph,
George; I'll see no more else, indeed, la; and
I pray you, let the youths understand so much

by word of mouth; for, I tell you truly, I'm
afraid o' my boy. Come, come, George, let's
be merry and wise: the child's a fatherless
child; and say they should put him into a
strait pair of gaskins,[19] 'twere worse than knot-
grass; he would never grow after it.

(*Enter* RALPH, *ridiculously tricked out as a
knight-errant, carrying a pestle. He is followed by* TIM *and by* GEORGE *who carries
his shield*)

CIT. Here's Ralph, here's Ralph!
   WIFE. How do you do, Ralph? You are
welcome, Ralph, as I may say; it's a good
boy, hold up thy head, and be not afraid;
we are thy friends, Ralph; the gentlemen
will praise thee, Ralph, if thou playest thy
part with audacity. Begin, Ralph, a' God's
name!
   RALPH. My trusty squire, unlace my helm:
   give me my hat.
Where are we, or what desert may this be?
   GEORGE. Mirror of knighthood, this is, as
I take it, the perilous Waltham-down; in
whose bottom stands the enchanted valley.
   MIST. MER. Oh, Michael, we are betrayed,
we are betrayed! here be giants! Fly, boy! fly,
boy, fly!
(*She runs off dragging* MICHAEL *and for-
getting her casket of jewels and her
purse*)
   RALPH. Lace on my helm again. What
   noise is this?
A gentle lady, flying the embrace
Of some uncourteous knight! I will relieve
   her.
Go, squire, and say, the Knight that wears
   this Pestle
In honor of all ladies, swears revenge
Upon that recreant coward that pursues her;
Go, comfort her, and that same gentle squire

---

[18] Darling.   [19] Tight breeches.

That bears her company.

TIM. I go, brave knight.   (*Exit*)

RALPH. My trusty dwarf and friend, reach
    me my shield;
And hold it while I swear. First, by my
    knighthood;
Then by the soul of Amadis de Gaul,
My famous ancestor; then by my sword
The beauteous Brionella girt about me;
By this bright burning Pestle, of mine honor
The living trophy; and by all respect
Due to distressèd damsels; here I vow
Never to end the quest of this fair lady
And that forsaken squire till by my valor
I gain their liberty!

GEORGE. Heaven bless the knight
That thus relieves poor errant gentlewomen!
                                        (*Exeunt*)

WIFE. Ay, marry, Ralph, this has some
savor in't; I would see the proudest of them
all offer to carry his books after him. But,
George, I will not have him go away so soon;
I shall be sick if he go away, that I shall: call
Ralph again, George, call Ralph again; I
prithee, sweetheart, let him come fight before me, and let's ha' some drums and some
trumpets, and let him kill all that comes
near him, an thou lovest me, George!

CIT. Peace a little, bird: he shall kill them
all, an they were twenty more on 'em than
there are.

(*Enter* JASPER)

JASP. Now, Fortune, if thou be'st not
    only ill,
Show me thy better face, and bring about
Thy desperate wheel, that I may climb at
    length,

And stand. This is our place of meeting,
If love have any constancy. Oh, age,
Where only wealthy men are counted happy!
How shall I please thee, how deserve thy
    smiles,
When I am only rich in misery? (*Taking out
    the ten shillings his father gave him*)
My father's blessing and this little coin
Is my inheritance; a strong revénue!
From earth thou art, and to the earth I give
    thee: (*Throws away the money*)
There grow and multiply, whilst fresher air
Breeds me a fresher fortune.—(*Sees the for-
    gotten purse and casket*) How! illusion?
What, hath the devil coined himself before
    me?   (*Opens the casket*)
'Tis metal good, it rings well; I am waking,
And taking too, I hope. Now, God's dear
    blessing
Upon his heart that left it here! 'Tis mine;
These pearls, I take it, were not left for
    swine.

                (*Exit with the casket and purse*)

WIFE. I do not like that this unthrifty
youth should embezzle away the money; the
poor gentlewoman his mother will have a
heavy heart for it, God knows.

CIT. And reason good, sweetheart.

WIFE. But let him go; I'll tell Ralph a
tale in's ear shall fetch him again with a
wanion, I warrant him, if he be above
ground; and besides, George, here are a
number of sufficient gentlemen can witness,
and myself, and yourself, and the musicians,
if we be called in question. But here comes
Ralph, George; thou shalt hear him speak
as he were an emperal.

SCENE III. *Another Part of the Forest.*

(*Enter* RALPH *and* GEORGE)

RALPH. Comes not sir squire again?

GEORGE. Right courteous knight,
Your squire doth come, and with him comes
    the lady,
For and the Squire of Damsels, as I take it.

(*Enter* TIM, MISTRESS MERRYTHOUGHT,
    and MICHAEL, *weeping*)

RALPH. Madam, if any service or devoir
Of a poor errant knight may right your
    wrongs,
Command it; I am prest to give you succor;
For to that holy end I bear my armor.

MIST. MER. Alas, sir, I am a poor gentlewoman, and I have lost my money in this
forest!

RALPH. Desert, you would say, lady; and
    not lost

Whilst I have sword and lance. Dry up your
    tears,
Which ill befit the beauty of that face,
And tell the story, if I may request it,
Of your disastrous fortune.
    Mist. Mer. Out, alas! I left a thousand
pound, a thousand pound, e'en all the money
I had laid up for this youth, upon the sight
of your mastership; you looked so grim, and,
as I may say it, saving your presence, more
like a giant than a mortal man.
    Ralph. (*Condescendingly*) I am as you
    are, lady; so are they;
All mortal. But why weeps this gentle squire?
    Mist. Mer. Has he not cause to weep,
do you think, when he hath lost his inheritance?
    Ralph. Young hope of valor, weep not;
    I am here
That will confound thy foe, and pay it dear
Upon his coward head, that dares deny

Distresséd squires and ladies equity.
I have but one horse, on which shall ride
This fair lady behind me, and before
This courteous squire: fortune will give us
    more
Upon our next adventure. Fairly speed
Beside us, squire and dwarf, to do us need!
                                    (*Exeunt*)
    Cit. Did not I tell you, Nell, what your
man would do? By the faith of my body,
wench, for clean action and good delivery,
they may all cast their caps at him.
    Wife. And so they may, i'faith; for I dare
speak it boldly, the twelve companies of London cannot match him, timber for timber.
Well, George, an he be not inveigled by
some of these paltry players, I ha' much
marvel: but, George, we ha' done our parts,
if the boy have any grace to be thankful.
    Cit. Yes, I warrant thee, duckling.

Scene IV. *Another Part of the Forest.*

(*Enter* Humphrey *and* Luce)

    Hum. Good Mistress Luce, however I in
    fault am
For your lame horse, you're welcome unto
    Waltham;
But which way now to go, or what to say,
I know not truly, till it be broad day.
    Luce. Oh, fear not, Master Humphrey;
    I am guide
For this place good enough.
    Hum. Then, up and ride;
Or, if it please you, walk, for your repose,
Or sit, or, if you will, go pluck a rose;
Either of which shall be indifferent
To your good friend and Humphrey, whose
    consent
Is so entangled ever to your will,
As the poor harmless horse is to the mill.
    Luce. Faith, an you say the word, we'll
    e'en sit down,
And take a nap.
    Hum. 'Tis better in the town,
Where we may nap together; for, believe me,
To sleep without a snatch [20] would mickle
    grieve me.

[20] Snack.

    Luce. You're merry, Master Humphrey.
    Hum. So I am,
And have been ever merry from my dam.
    Luce. Your nurse had the less labor.
    Hum. Faith, it may be,
Unless it were by chance I did beray me.

(*Enter* Jasper)

    Jasp. (*Calling*) Luce! dear friend Luce!
    Luce. (*Running to him*) Here, Jasper.
    Jasp. You are mine.
    Hum. If it be so, my friend, you use me
    fine:
What do you think I am?
    Jasp. An errant noddy.
    Hum. A word of obloquy! Now, by God's
    body,
I'll tell thy master; for I know thee well.
    Jasp. Nay, an you be so forward for to tell,
                            (*beating* Humphrey)
Take that, and that; and tell him, sir, I gave
    it:
And say, I paid you well.
    Hum. Oh, sir, I have it,
And do confess the payment! Pray, be quiet.
    Jasp. Go, get you to your night-cap and
    the diet,

To cure your beaten bones.

Luce. Alas, poor Humphrey;
Get thee some wholesome broth, with sage
    and comfrey;
A little oil of roses and a feather
To 'noint thy back withal.

Hum. When I came hither,
Would I had gone to Paris with John Dory!

Luce. Farewell, my pretty nump; I am
very sorry I cannot bear thee company.

Hum. Farewell:
The devil's dam was ne'er so banged in hell.

(*Exeunt* Luce *and* Jasper; Humphrey
    *stands about rubbing his head and
    shoulders*)

Wife. This young Jasper will prove me
another thing, o' my conscience, an he may
be suffered. George, dost not see, George,
how 'a swaggers, and flies at the very heads
o' folks, as he were a dragon? Well, if I do
not do his lesson for wronging the poor gentleman, I am no true woman. His friends
that brought him up might have been better
occupied, i-wis, than have taught him these
fegaries: he's e'en in the high way to the
gallows, God bless him!

Cit. You're too bitter, cony; the young
man may do well enough for all this.

Wife. Come hither, Master Humphrey;

has he hurt you? Now, beshrew his fingers
for't! Here, sweetheart, here's some green
ginger for thee. Now, beshrew my heart, but
'a has peppernel in's head, as big as a pullet's
egg! Alas, sweet lamb, how thy temples beat!
Take the peace on him, sweetheart, take the
peace on him.

(*Enter a* Boy)

Cit. No, no; you talk like a foolish
woman: I'll ha' Ralph fight with him, and
swinge him up well-favoredly.—(*calling*)
Sirrah boy, come hither. Let Ralph come in
and fight with Jasper.

Wife. Ay, and beat him well; he's an
unhappy boy.

Boy. Sir, you must pardon; the plot of our
play lies contrary; and 'twill hazard the spoiling of our play.

Cit. Plot me no plots! I'll ha' Ralph come
out; I'll make your house too hot for you else.

Boy. Why, sir, he shall; but if any thing
fall out of order, the gentlemen must pardon
us.

Cit. Go your ways, goodman boy! (*Exit*
Boy) I'll hold him a penny, he shall have
his bellyful of fighting now. Ho, here comes
Ralph! no more!

Scene V. *The Same.*

(*Enter* Ralph, Mistress Merrythought,
    Michael, Tim, *and* George)

Ralph. (*Seeing* Humphrey) What
    knight is that, squire? Ask him if he keep
The passage, bound by love of lady fair,
Or else but prickant.

Hum. Sir, I am no knight,
But a poor gentleman, that this same night
Had stolen from me, on yonder green,
My lovely wife, and suffered (to be seen
Yet extant on my shoulders) such a greeting,
That whilst I live I shall think of that meet-
    ing.

Wife. Ay, Ralph, he beat him unmercifully, Ralph; an thou sparest him, Ralph, I
would thou wert hanged.

Cit. No more, wife, no more.

Ralph. Where is the caitiff-wretch hath
done this deed?

Lady, your pardon; that I may proceed
Upon the quest of this injurious knight.—
And thou, fair squire, repute me not the
    worse,
In leaving the great venture of the purse
And the rich casket, till some better leisure.

Hum. (*Pointing off stage*) Here comes
the broker hath purloined my treasure.

(*Enter* Jasper *and* Luce)

Ralph. Go, squire, and tell him I am here,
An errant knight-at-arms, to crave delivery
Of that fair lady to her own knight's arms.
If he deny, bid him take choice of ground,
And so defy him.

Tim. From the Knight that bears
The Golden Pestle, I defy thee, knight,
Unless thou make fair restitution
Of that bright lady.

Jasp. Tell the knight that sent thee,
He is an ass; and I will keep the wench,
And knock his head-piece.

Ralph. Knight, thou art but dead,
If thou recall not thy uncourteous terms.

Wife. Break 's pate, Ralph; break 's pate,
Ralph, soundly!

Jasp. Come, knight; I am ready for you.
(Jasper *snatches* Ralph's *pestle away
from him*) Now your Pestle
Shall try what temper, sir, your mortar's of.
With that he stood upright in his stirrups,
and gave the Knight of the calf-skin such a
knock (*He knocks* Ralph *down with the
pestle*) that he forsook his horse, and down
he fell; and then he leaped upon him, and
plucking off his helmet——

Hum. Nay, an my noble knight be down
     so soon,
Though I can scarcely go, I needs must run.
                              (*Exit hurriedly*)

Wife. Run, Ralph, run, Ralph; run for
     thy life, boy;
Jasper comes, Jasper comes!   (*Exit* Ralph)

Jasp. Come, Luce, we must have other
     arms for you:
Humphrey, and Golden Pestle, both adieu!
                              (*Exeunt*)

Wife. Sure the devil (God bless us!) is
in this springald! Why, George, didst ever
see such a fire-drake? I am afraid my boy's
miscarried: if he be, though he were Master
Merrythought's son a thousand times, if
there be any law in England, I'll make some
of them smart for't.

Cit. No, no; I have found out the matter,
sweetheart; as sure as we are here, he is
enchanted: he could no more have stood in
Ralph's hands than I can in my Lord Mayor's.
I'll have a ring to discover all enchantments,
and Ralph shall beat him yet. Be no more
vexed, for it shall be so.

Scene VI. *Before the Bell Inn, Waltham.*

(*Enter* Ralph, Mistress Merrythought,
     Michael, Tim, *and* George)

Wife. Oh, husband, here's Ralph again!
—Stay, Ralph again, let me speak with thee.
How dost thou, Ralph? Art thou not
shrewdly hurt? The foul great lungies laid
unmercifully on thee. There's some sugar-
candy for thee. Proceed; thou shalt have another bout with him.

Cit. If Ralph had him at the fencing-
school, if he did not make a puppy of him,
and drive him up and down the school, he
should ne'er come in my shop more.

Mist. Mer. Truly, Master Knight of the
Burning Pestle, I am weary.

Mich. Indeed, la, mother, and I am very
hungry.

Ralph. Take comfort, gentle dame, and
     you, fair squire;
For in this desert there must needs be placed
Many strong castles, held by courteous
     knights;
And till I bring you safe to one of those,
I swear by this my order ne'er to leave you.

Wife. Well said, Ralph!—George, Ralph
was ever comfortable, was he not?

Cit. Yes, duck.

Wife. I shall ne'er forget him. When we
had lost our child, (you know it was strayed
almost alone to Puddle Wharf, and the criers
were abroad for it, and there it had drowned
itself but for a sculler,) Ralph was the most
comfortablest to me: "Peace, mistress," says
he, "let it go; I'll get you another as good."
Did he not, George, did he not say so?

Cit. Yes, indeed did he, mouse.

George. I would we had a mess of pottage
and a pot of drink, squire, and were going
to bed!

Tim. Why, we are at Waltham town's
end, and that's the Bell Inn.

George. Take courage, valiant knight,
     damsel, and squire!
I have discovered, not a stone's cast off,
An ancient castle, held by the old knight
Of the most holy order of the Bell,
Who gives to all knights-errant entertain.
There plenty is of food, and all prepared
By the white hands of his own lady dear.
He hath three squires that welcome all his
     guests;
The first, hight Chamberlino, who will see

Our beds prepared, and bring us snowy
  sheets,
Where never footman stretched his buttered
  hams;
The second, hight Tapstero, who will see
Our pots full filled, and no froth therein;
The third, a gentle squire, Ostlero hight,
Who will our palfreys slick with wisps of
  straw,
And in the manger put them oats enough,
And never grease their teeth with candle-
  snuff.

WIFE. That same dwarf's a pretty boy, but
the squire's a groutnol.[21]

RALPH. Knock at the gates, my squire,
with stately lance.

(TIM *knocks at the door*)

(*Enter* TAPSTER)

TAP. Who's there?— You're welcome, gentlemen: will you see a room?

GEORGE. Right courteous and valiant
Knight of the Burning Pestle, this is the
Squire Tapstero.

RALPH. Fair Squire Tapstero, I a wander-
  ing knight,
Hight of the Burning Pestle, in the quest
Of this fair lady's casket and wrought purse,
Losing myself in this vast wilderness,
Am to this castle well by fortune brought;
Where, hearing of the goodly entertain
Your knight of holy order of the Bell
Gives to all damsels and all errant knights,
I thought to knock, and now am bold to enter.

TAP. An't please you see a chamber, you
are very welcome. (*Exeunt*)

WIFE. George, I would have something
done, and I cannot tell what it is.

CIT. What is it, Nell?

WIFE. Why, George, shall Ralph beat
nobody again? Prithee, sweetheart, let him.

CIT. So he shall, Nell; and if I join with
him, we'll knock them all.

SCENE VII. *A Room in the House of* VENTUREWELL.

(*Enter* HUMPHREY *and* VENTUREWELL)

WIFE. Oh, George, here's Master Humphrey again now that lost Mistress Luce, and
Mistress Luce's father. Master Humphrey
will do somebody's errand, I warrant him.

HUM. Father, it's true in arms I ne'er shall
clasp her;
For she is stoln away by your man Jasper.

WIFE. I thought he would tell him.

VENT. Unhappy that I am, to lose my
child!
Now I begin to think on Jasper's words,
Who oft hath urged to me thy foolishness.
Why didst thou let her go? Thou lov'st her
  not,
That wouldst bring home thy life, and not
  bring her.

HUM. Father, forgive me. Shall I tell you
true?
Look on my shoulders, they are black and
  blue:
Whilst to and fro fair Luce and I were
  winding,

[21] Blockhead.

He came and basted me with a hedge-bind-
  ing.

VENT. Get men and horses straight: we
  will be there
Within this hour. You know the place
  again?

HUM. I know the place where he my
  loins did swaddle;
I'll get six horses, and to each a saddle.

VENT. Meantime I will go talk with Jasper's father. (*Exeunt*)

WIFE. George, what wilt thou lay with
me now, that Master Humphrey has not
Mistress Luce yet? Speak, George, what wilt
thou lay with me?

CIT. No, Nell; I warrant thee, Jasper is
at Puckeridge with her by this.

WIFE. Nay, George, you must consider
Mistress Luce's feet are tender; and besides
'tis dark; and, I promise you truly, I do not
see how he should get out of Waltham forest
with her yet.

CIT. Nay, cony, what wilt thou lay with
me, that Ralph has her not yet?

WIFE. I will not lay against Ralph, honey,
because I have not spoken with him.

Scene VIII. *A Room in* Merrythought's *House.*

(*Enter* Merrythought)

Wife. But look, George, peace! here comes the merry old gentleman again.

Mer. (*Sings*)

> When it was grown to dark midnight,
>   And all were fast asleep,
> In came Margaret's grimly ghost,
>   And stood at William's feet.

I have money, and meat, and drink beforehand, till to-morrow at noon; why should I be sad? Methinks I have half-a-dozen jovial spirits within me!   (*Sings*)

I am three merry men, and three merry men!

To what end should any man be sad in this world? Give me a man that when he goes to hanging cries,

> Troll the black bowl to me!

and a woman that will sing a catch in her travail! I have seen a man come by my door with a serious face, in a black cloak, without a hat-band, carrying his head as if he looked for pins in the street; I have looked out of my window half a year after, and have spied that man's head upon London Bridge. 'Tis vile: never trust a tailor that does not sing at his work; his mind is of nothing but filching.

Wife. Mark this, George; 'tis worth noting; Godfrey my tailor, you know, never sings, and he had fourteen yards to make this gown: and I'll be sworn, Mistress Penistone the draper's wife had one made with twelve.

Mer. (*Sings*)

> 'Tis mirth that fills the veins with blood,
> More than wine, or sleep, or food;
> Let each man keep his heart at ease,
> No man dies of that disease.
> He that would his body keep
> From diseases, must not weep;
> But whoever laughs and sings,

> Never he his body brings
> Into fevers, gouts, or rheums,
> Or lingeringly his lungs consumes,
> Or meets with achés in the bone,
> Or catarrhs or griping stone;
> But contented lives for aye;
> The more he laughs, the more he may.

Wife. Look, George; how sayst thou by this, George? Is't not a fine old man?—Now, God's blessing o' thy sweet lips!—When wilt thou be so merry, George? Faith, thou art the frowningest little thing, when thou art angry, in a country.

Cit. Peace, cony; thou shalt see him taken down too, I warrant thee.

(*Enter* Venturewell)

Here's Luce's father come now.

Mer. (*Sings*)

> As you came from Walsingham,
>   From that holy land,
> There met you not with my true love
>   By the way as you came?

Vent. Oh, Master Merrythought, my daughter's gone! This mirth becomes you not; my daughter's gone!

Mer. (*Sings*)

> Why, an if she be, what care I?
> Or let her come, or go, or tarry.

Vent. Mock not my misery; it is your son (Whom I have made my own, when all forsook him) Has stoln my only joy, my child, away.

Mer. (*Sings*)

> He set her on a milk-white steed,
>   And himself upon a grey;
> He never turned his face again,
>   But he bore her quite away.

Vent. Unworthy of the kindness I have shown To thee and thine! too late I well perceive

Thou art consenting to my daughter's loss.

MER. Your daughter! what a stir's here wi' your daughter? Let her go, think no more on her, but sing loud. If both my sons were on the gallows, I would sing,   (*Sings*)

Down, down, down they fall;
Down, and arise they never shall.

VENT. Oh, might I behold her once again, And she once more embrace her aged sire!

MER. Fie, how scurvily this goes! (*whining*) "And she once more embrace her aged sire?" You'll make a dog on her, will ye? She cares much for her aged sire, I warrant you.   (*Sings*)

She cares not for her daddy, nor
She cares not for her mammy,
For she is, she is, she is, she is
My lord of Lowgave's lassy.

VENT. For this thy scorn I will pursue that son
Of thine to death.

MER. Do; and when you ha' killed him,
    (*Sings*)

Give him flowers enow, palmer, give him
flowers enow.
Give him red, and white, and blue, green,
and yellow.

VENT. I'll fetch my daughter——

MER. I'll hear no more o' your daughter; it spoils my mirth.

VENT. I say, I'll fetch my daughter.

MER. (*Sings*)

Was never man for lady's sake,
    Down, down,
Tormented as I poor Sir Guy,
    De derry down,
For Lucy's sake, that lady bright,
    Down, down,
As ever men beheld with eye,
    De derry down.

VENT. I'll be revenged, by Heaven!
    (*Exeunt severally*)

WIFE. How dost thou like this, George?

CIT. Why, this is well, cony; but if Ralph were hot once, thou shouldst see more.
    (*Music off stage*)

WIFE. The fiddlers go again, husband.

CIT. Ay, Nell; but this is scurvy music. I gave the whoreson gallows money, and I think he has not got me the waits of South-wark. If I hear 'em not anon, I'll twinge him by the ears.—(*Calling*) You musicians, play Baloo!

WIFE. No, good George, let's ha' Lach-rymæ!

CIT. Why, this is it, cony.

WIFE. It's all the better, George. (*Pointing to the tapestry hanging at the back of the stage*) Now, sweet lamb, what story is that painted upon the cloth? The Confutation of St. Paul?

CIT. No, lamb; that's Ralph and Lucrece.

WIFE. Ralph and Lucrece! which Ralph? Our Ralph?

CIT. No, mouse, that was a Tartarian.

WIFE. A Tartarian! Well, I would the fiddlers had done, that we might see our Ralph again!

Act III

SCENE I. *Waltham Forest.*

(*Enter* JASPER *and* LUCE)

JASP. Come, my dear dear; though we have lost our way
We have not lost ourselves. Are you not weary
With this night's wandering, broken from your rest,
And frighted with the terror that attends

The darkness of this wild unpeopled place?

LUCE. No, my best friend; I cannot either fear,
Or entertain a weary thought, whilst you (The end of all my full desires) stand by me.
Let them that lose their hopes, and live to languish
Amongst the number of forsaken lovers,
Tell the long weary steps, and number time,

Start at a shadow, and shrink up their blood,
Whilst I (possessed with all content and
    quiet)
Thus take my pretty love, and thus embrace
    him.

    JASP. You have caught me, Luce, so fast,
    that, whilst I live,
I shall become your faithful prisoner,
And wear these chains for ever. Come, sit
    down,
And rest your body, too, too delicate
For these disturbances.—(*They sit down*)
    So: will you sleep?
Come, do not be more able than you are;
I know you are not skilful in these watches,
For women are no soldiers: be not nice,
But take it; sleep, I say.

    LUCE. I cannot sleep;
Indeed, I cannot, friend.

    JASP. Why, then, we'll sing,
And try how that will work upon our senses.

    LUCE. I'll sing, or say, or any thing but
sleep.

    JASP. Come, little mermaid, rob me of my
    heart
With that enchanting voice.

    LUCE. You mock me, Jasper. (*They sing*)

    JASP. *Tell me, dearest, what is love?*
    LUCE. *'Tis a lightning from above;*
       'Tis an arrow, 'tis a fire,
       'Tis a boy they call Desire;
         'Tis a smile
         Doth beguile
    JASP. *The poor hearts of men that prove.*[22]
       Tell me more, are women true?
    LUCE. *Some love change, and so do you.*
    JASP.   *Are they fair and never kind?*
    LUCE.   *Yes, when men turn with the*
       wind.
    JASP.   *Are they froward?*
    LUCE.   *Ever toward*
       Those that love, to love anew.

    JASP. Dissemble it no more; I see the god
Of heavy sleep lay on his heavy mace
Upon your eyelids.

    LUCE. (*Sleepily*) I am very heavy.

    JASP. Sleep, sleep; and quiet rest crown thy
    sweet thoughts!
Keep from her fair blood distempers, start-
    ings,

[22] Experience it.

Horrors, and fearful shapes! Let all her
    dreams
Be joys, and chaste delights, embraces,
    wishes,
And such new pleasures as the ravished soul
Gives to the senses!—(*sees she is asleep*) So;
    my charms have took.—
Keep her, you powers divine, whilst I con-
    template
Upon the wealth and beauty of her mind!
She is only fair and constant, only kind,
And only to thee, Jasper. Oh, my joys!
Whither will you transport me? Let not ful-
    ness
Of my poor buried hopes come up together
And overcharge my spirits! I am weak.
Some say (however ill) the sea and women
Are governed by the moon; both ebb and
    flow,
Both full of changes; yet to them that know,
And truly judge, these but opinions are,
And heresies, to bring on pleasing war
Between our tempers, that without these were
Both void of after-love and present fear,
Which are the best of Cupid. Oh, thou child
Bred from despair, I dare not entertain thee,
Having a love without the faults of women,
And greater in her perfect goods than men!
Which to make good, and please myself the
    stronger,
Though certainly I am certain of her love,
I'll try her, that the world and memory
May sing to after-times her constancy.—
          (*Draws his sword*)
Luce! Luce! awake!

    LUCE. (*Starting up*) Why do you fright
    me, friend,
With those distempered looks? What makes
    your sword
Drawn in your hand? Who hath offended
    you?
I prithee, Jasper, sleep; thou art wild with
    watching.

    JASP. (*Threatening her with his sword*)
    Come, make your way to Heaven, and
    bid the world,
With all the villanies that stick upon it,
Farewell; you're for another life.

    LUCE. Oh, Jasper,
How have my tender years committed evil,
Especially against the man I love,
Thus to be cropped untimely?

    JASP. Foolish girl,

Canst thou imagine I could love his daughter
That flung me from my fortune into nothing?
Dischargéd me his service, shut the doors
Upon my poverty, and scorned my prayers,
Sending me, like a boat without a mast,
To sink or swim? Come; by this hand you
   die;
I must have life and blood, to satisfy
Your father's wrongs.

   WIFE. Away, George, away! raise the
watch at Ludgate, and bring a mittimus from
the justice for this desperate villain!—Now,
I charge you, gentlemen, see the king's peace
kept!—Oh, my heart, what a varlet's this, to
offer manslaughter upon the harmless gentlewoman!

   CIT. I warrant thee, sweetheart, we'll have
him hampered.

   LUCE. Oh, Jasper, be not cruel!
If thou wilt kill me, smile, and do it quickly,
And let not many deaths appear before me.
I am a woman, made of fear and love,
A weak, weak woman; kill not with thy eyes,
They shoot me through and through. Strike,
   I am ready;
And, dying, still I love thee.

(*Enter* VENTUREWELL, HUMPHREY, *and*
   his MEN)

   VENT. Whereabouts?

   JASP. (*Aside*) No more of this; now to myself again.

   HUM. There, there he stands, with sword,
like martial knight,
Drawn in his hand; therefore beware the
   fight,
You that be wise; for, were I good Sir Bevis,
I would not stay his coming, by your leavés.

   VENT. Sirrah, restore my daughter!

   JASP. Sirrah, no.

   VENT. Upon him, then!

(*The* MEN *beat down* JASPER'S *sword,
slightly wounding him. Then they seize
and hold him while* VENTUREWELL
tears LUCE *away from him*)

   WIFE. (*Highly excited*) So; down with
him, down with him, down with him! cut
him i' the leg, boys, cut him i' the leg!

   VENT. Come your ways, minion: I'll provide a cage
For you, you're grown so tame.—Horse her
   away.

   HUM. Truly, I'm glad your forces have
the day.   (*Exeunt all except* JASPER)

   JASP. They are gone, and I am hurt; my
   love is lost,
Never to get again. Oh, me unhappy!
Bleed, bleed and die! I cannot. Oh, my folly,
Thou hast betrayed me! Hope, where art
   thou fled?
Tell me, if thou be'st anywhere remaining,
Shall I but see my love again? Oh, no!
She will not deign to look upon her butcher,
Nor is it fit she should; yet I must venture.
Oh, Chance, or Fortune, or whate'er thou
   art,
That men adore for powerful, hear my cry,
And let me loving live, or losing die! (*Exit*)

   WIFE. Is 'a gone, George?

   CIT. Ay, cony.

   WIFE. Marry, and let him go, sweetheart.
By the faith o' my body, 'a has put me into
such a fright, that I tremble (as they say)
as 'twere an aspen-leaf. Look o' my little
finger, George, how it shakes. Now, in truth,
every member of my body is the worse for't.

   CIT. (*Taking her in his arms*) Come, hug
in mine arms, sweet mouse; he shall not fright
thee any more. Alas, mine own dear heart,
how it quivers!

SCENE II. *A Room in the Bell Inn, Waltham.*

(*Enter* MISTRESS MERRYTHOUGHT, RALPH,
MICHAEL, TIM, GEORGE, HOST, *and* TAP-
   STER)

   WIFE. Oh, Ralph! how dost thou, Ralph?
How hast thou slept to-night? Has the knight
used thee well?

   CIT. Peace, Nell; let Ralph alone.

   TAP. Master, the reckoning is not paid.

   RALPH. Right courteous knight, who, for
the order's sake
Which thou hast ta'en, hang'st out the holy
   Bell,
As I this flaming Pestle bear about,
We render thanks to your puissant self,
Your beauteous lady, and your gentle squires,

For thus refreshing of our wearied limbs,
Stiffened with hard achievements in wild
    desert.
  TAP. Sir, there is twelve shillings to pay.
  RALPH. Thou merry Squire Tapstero,
    thanks to thee
For comforting our souls with double jug:
And, if adventurous fortune prick thee forth,
Thou jovial squire, to follow feats of arms,
Take heed thou tender every lady's cause,
Every true knight, and every damsel fair;
But spill the blood of treacherous Saracens,
And false enchanters that with magic spells
Have done to death full many a noble
    knight.
  HOST. Thou valiant Knight of the Burn-
ing Pestle, give ear to me; there is twelve
shillings to pay, and, as I am a true knight,
I will not bate a penny.
  WIFE. George, I prithee, tell me, must
Ralph pay twelve shillings now?
  CIT. No, Nell, no; nothing but the old
knight is merry with Ralph.
  WIFE. Oh, is't nothing else? Ralph will
be as merry as he.
  RALPH. Sir Knight, this mirth of yours be-
    comes you well;
But, to requite this liberal courtesy,
If any of your squires will follow arms,
He shall receive from my heroic hand
A knighthood, by the virtue of this Pestle.
  HOST. Fair knight, I thank you for your
    noble offer:
Therefore, gentle knight,
Twelve shillings you must pay, or I must
    cap [23] you.
  WIFE. Look, George! did not I tell thee as
much? The knight of the Bell is in earnest.
Ralph shall not be beholding to him: give
him his money, George, and let him go snick
up.
  CIT. Cap Ralph! no.—(He marches across
the stage to HOST) Hold your hand, Sir
Knight of the Bell; there's your money (gives
money): have you anything to say to Ralph
now? (indignantly) Cap Ralph!
  WIFE. I would you should know it, Ralph
has friends that will not suffer him to be
capt for ten times so much, and ten times to
the end of that.—Now take thy course, Ralph.
  MIST. MER. Come, Michael; thou and I
will go home to thy father; he hath enough

left to keep us a day or two, and we'll set
fellows abroad to cry our purse and our
casket: shall we, Michael?
  MICH. Ay, I pray, mother; in truth my
feet are full of chilblains with travelling.
  WIFE. Faith, and those chilblains are a
foul trouble. Mistress Merrythought, when
your youth comes home, let him rub all the
soles of his feet, and his heels, and his ankles
with a mouse-skin; or, if none of your people
can catch a mouse, when he goes to bed, let
him roll his feet in the warm embers, and, I
warrant you, he shall be well; and you may
make him put his fingers between his toes,
and smell to them; it's very sovereign for his
head, if he be costive.
  MIST. MER. Master Knight of the Burning
Pestle, my son Michael and I bid you farewell. I thank your worship heartily for your
kindness.
  RALPH. Farewell, fair lady, and your
    tender squire.
If pricking through these deserts, I do hear
Of any traitorous knight, who through his
    guile
Hath light upon your casket and your purse,
I will despoil him of them, and restore them.
  MIST. MER. I thank your worship.
               (Exit with MICHAEL)
  RALPH. Dwarf, bear my shield; squire,
    elevate my lance:—
And now farewell, you Knight of holy Bell.
  CIT. Ay, ay, Ralph, all is paid.
  RALPH. But yet, before I go, speak, worthy
    knight,
Of aught you do of sad adventures know,
Where errant knight may through his
    prowess win
Eternal fame, and free some gentle souls
From endless bonds of steel and lingering
    pain.
  HOST. (Aside to TAPSTER) Sirrah, go to
Nick the barber, and bid him prepare him-
self, as I told you before, quickly.
  TAP. I am gone, sir.   (Exit)
  HOST. Sir Knight, this wilderness afford-
eth none
But the great venture, where full many a
    knight
Hath tried his prowess, and come off with
    shame;
And where I would not have you lose your
    life

Against no man, but furious fiend of hell.
    RALPH. Speak on, Sir Knight; tell what he
        is and where;
For here I vow, upon my blazing badge,
Never to blaze a day in quietness,
But bread and water will I only eat,
And the green herb and rock shall be my
    couch,
Till I have quelled that man, or beast, or
    fiend,
That works such damage to all errant knights.
    HOST. Not far from hence, near to a craggy
        cliff,
At the north end of this distresséd town,
There doth stand a lowly house,
Ruggedly builded, and in it a cave
In which an ugly giant now doth wone,[24]
Ycleped Barbarossa. In his hand
He shakes a naked lance of purest steel,
With sleeves turned up; and him before he
    wears
A motley garment, to preserve his clothes
From blood of those knights which he mas-
    sacres
And ladies gent. Without his door doth hang
A copper basin on a prickant spear;[25]
At which no sooner gentle knights can knock,
But the shrill sound fierce Barbarossa hears,
And rushing forth, brings in the errant
    knight,
And sets him down in an enchanted chair;
Then with an engine, which he hath pre-
    pared,
With forty teeth, he claws his courtly crown;
Next makes him wink, and underneath his
    chin
He plants a brazen piece of mighty bord,[26]
And knocks his bullets round about his
    cheeks;
Whilst with his fingers, and an instrument
With which he snaps his hair off, he doth fill

The wretch's ears with a most hideous noise:
Thus every knight-adventurer he doth trim,
And now no creature dares encounter him.
    RALPH. In God's name, I will fight with
        him. Kind sir,
Go but before me to this dismal cave,
Where this huge giant Barbarossa dwells,
And, by that virtue that brave Rosicleer
That damnéd brood of ugly giants slew,
And Palmerin Frannarco overthrew,
I doubt not but to curb this traitor foul,
And to the devil send his guilty soul.
    HOST. Brave-sprighted knight, thus far I
        will perform
This your request; I'll bring you within sight
Of this most loathsome place, inhabited
By a more loathsome man; but dare not stay,
For his main force swoops all he sees away.
    RALPH. Saint George, set on before!
        march, squire and page!   (Exeunt)
    WIFE. George, dost think Ralph will con-
found the giant?
    CIT. I hold my cap to a farthing he does:
why, Nell, I saw him wrestle with the great
Dutchman, and hurl him.
    WIFE. Faith, and that Dutchman was a
goodly man, if all things were answerable
to his bigness. And yet they say there was a
Scotchman higher than he, and that they two
and a knight met, and saw one another for
nothing. But of all the sights that ever were
in London, since I was married, methinks
the little child that was so fair grown about
the members was the prettiest; that and the
hermaphrodite.
    CIT. Nay, by your leave, Nell, Ninivie[27]
was better.
    WIFE. Ninivie! oh, that was the story of
Jone and the wall,[28] was it not, George?
    CIT. Yes, lamb.

SCENE III. *The Street before* MERRYTHOUGHT'S *House.*

(*Enter* MISTRESS MERRYTHOUGHT)

    WIFE. Look, George, here comes Mistress
Merrythought again! and I would have
Ralph come and fight with the giant; I tell
you true, I long to see't.

    [24] Dwell.
    [25] Elizabethan barber shops had both a barber
pole and a basin for their sign.

    CIT. Good Mistress Merrythought, be-
gone, I pray you, for my sake; I pray you,
forbear a little; you shall have audience
presently; I have a little business.
    WIFE. Mistress Merrythought, if it please

    [26] I.e., the barber's brass basin.
    [27] Ninevah, a puppet show.
    [28] Jonah and the whale.

you to refrain your passion a little, till Ralph have despatched the giant out of the way, we shall think ourselves much bound to you. (*Exit* MISTRESS MERRYTHOUGHT. *Enter* BOY) I thank you, good Mistress Merrythought.

CIT. Boy, come hither. Send away Ralph and this whoreson giant quickly.

BOY. In good faith, sir, we cannot; you'll utterly spoil our play, and make it to be hissed; and it cost money; you will not suffer us to go on with our plot.—(*To the gentlemen seated on the stage*) I pray, gentlemen, rule him.

CIT. Let him come now and despatch this, and I'll trouble you no more.

BOY. Will you give me your hand of that?

WIFE. Give him thy hand, George, do; and I'll kiss him. I warrant thee, the youth means plainly.

BOY. I'll send him to you presently.

WIFE. (*Kissing him*) I thank you, little youth. (*Exit* BOY) Faith, the child hath a sweet breath, George; but I think it be troubled with the worms; carduus benedictus and mare's milk were the only thing in the world for't.

SCENE IV. *Before a* BARBER'S *Shop, Waltham. The shop is indicated as usual by a striped barber's pole and a copper basin with a piece cut out of the rim to fit the customer's neck. Beside them hangs a string of human teeth, for barbers also practised dentistry.*

(*Enter* RALPH, HOST, TIM, *and* GEORGE)

WIFE. Oh, Ralph's here, George!—God send thee good luck, Ralph!

HOST. Puissant knight, yonder his mansion is.

Lo, where the spear and copper basin are!

Behold that string, on which hangs many a tooth,

Drawn from the gentle jaw of wandering knights!

I dare not stay to sound; he will appear.
                                          (*Exit*)

RALPH. Oh, faint not, heart! Susan, my lady dear,

The cobbler's maid in Milk Street, for whose sake

I take these arms, oh, let the thought of thee

Carry thy knight through all adventurous deeds;

And, in the honor of thy beauteous self,

May I destroy this monster Barbarossa!—

Knock, squire, upon the basin, till it break

With the shrill strokes, or till the giant speak.
                        (TIM *knocks upon the basin*)

(*Enter* BARBER)

WIFE. Oh, George, the giant, the giant!—Now, Ralph, for thy life!

BAR. What fond unknowing wight is this, that dares

So rudely knock at Barbarossa's cell,

Where no man comes but leaves his fleece behind?

RALPH. I, traitorous caitiff, who am sent by fate

To punish all the sad enormities

Thou hast committed against ladies gent

And errant knights. Traitor to God and men,

Prepare thyself; this is the dismal hour

Appointed for thee to give strict account

Of all thy beastly treacherous villanies.

BAR. Fool-hardy knight, full soon thou shalt aby [29]

This fond reproach: thy body will I bang;
                              (*Takes down his pole*)

And, lo, upon that string thy teeth shall hang!

Prepare thyself, for dead soon shalt thou be.

RALPH. Saint George for me!

    (*They fight ludicrously with the pestle and the barber's pole*)

BAR. Gargantua for me!

WIFE. (*In great excitement*) To him, Ralph, to him! hold up the giant; set out thy leg before, Ralph!

CIT. Falsify a blow, Ralph, falsify a blow! the giant lies open on the left side.

WIFE. Bear't off, bear't off still! there, boy!—

    (RALPH *slips and falls to one knee*)

Oh, Ralph's almost down, Ralph's almost down!

[29] Pay for.

RALPH. Susan, inspire me! now have up again.

WIFE. Up, up, up, up, up! so, Ralph! down with him, down with him, Ralph!

CIT. Fetch him o'er the hip, boy!

(RALPH *knocks down the* BARBER)

WIFE. There, boy! kill, kill, kill, kill, kill, Ralph!

CIT. No, Ralph; get all out of him first.

RALPH. (*Posing with his foot on the* BARBER'S *chest*) Presumptuous man, see to what desperate end
Thy treachery hath brought thee! The just gods,
Who never prosper those that do despise them,
For all the villanies which thou hast done
To knights and ladies, now have paid thee home
By my stiff arm, a knight adventurous.
But say, vile wretch, before I send thy soul
To sad Avernus, (whither it must go)
What captives holdst thou in thy sable cave?

BAR. Go in, and free them all; thou hast the day.

RALPH. Go, squire and dwarf, search in this dreadful cave,
And free the wretched prisoners from their bonds. (*Exeunt* TIM *and* GEORGE)

BAR. I crave for mercy, as thou art a knight,
And scorn'st to spill the blood of those that beg.

RALPH. Thou show'd'st no mercy, nor shalt thou have any;
Prepare thyself, for thou shalt surely die.

(*Re-enter* TIM *leading a* MAN *whose face is lathered, whose eyes are closed, and who holds a barber's basin under his chin*)

TIM. Behold, brave knight, here is one prisoner,
Whom this vile man hath uséd as you see.

WIFE. This is the first wise word I heard the squire speak.

RALPH. Speak what thou art, and how thou hast been used,
That I may give him condign punishment.

MAN. I am a knight that took my journey post
Northward from London; and in courteous-wise
This giant trained me to his loathsome den,
Under pretence of killing of the itch;
And all my body with a powder strewed,
That smarts and stings; and cut away my beard,
And my curled locks wherein were ribands tied;
And with a water washed my tender eyes,
(Whilst up and down about me still he skipt,)
Whose virtue is, that, till my eyes be wiped
With a dry cloth, for this my foul disgrace,
I shall not dare to look a dog i' the face.

WIFE. Alas, poor knight!—Relieve him, Ralph; relieve poor knights, whilst you live.

RALPH. My trusty squire, convey him to the town,
Where he may find relief.—Adieu, fair knight.

(*Exeunt* MAN *with* TIM, *who presently re-enters*)

(*Re-enter* GEORGE, *leading a second* MAN, *with a patch over his nose*)

GEORGE. Puissant Knight, of the Burning Pestle hight,
See here another wretch, whom this foul beast
Hath scotched and scored in this inhuman wise.

RALPH. Speak me thy name, and eke thy place of birth,
And what hath been thy usage in this cave.

2ND MAN. I am a knight, Sir Pockhole is my name,
And by my birth I am a Londoner,
Free by my copy, but my ancestors
Were Frenchmen all; and riding hard this way
Upon a trotting horse, my bones did ache;
And I, faint knight, to ease my weary limbs,
Light at this cave; when straight this furious fiend,
With sharpest instrument of purest steel,
Did cut the gristle of my nose away,
And in the place this velvet plaster stands:
Relieve me, gentle knight, out of his hands!

WIFE. Good Ralph, relieve Sir Pockhole, and send him away; for in truth his breath stinks.

RALPH. Convey him straight after the other knight.—Sir Pockhole, fare you well.

2ND MAN. Kind sir, good night.

(*Exit with* George, *who presently re-enters*)

3RD MAN. (*Within*) Deliver us!
                    (*Cries within*)
WOMAN. (*Within*) Deliver us!
WIFE. Hark, George, what a woeful cry there is! I think some woman lies-in there.
3RD MAN. (*Within*) Deliver us!
WOMAN. (*Within*) Deliver us!
RALPH. What ghastly noise is this? Speak, Barbarossa,
Or, by this blazing steel, thy head goes off!
BAR. Prisoners of mine, whom I in diet keep.
Send lower down into the cave,
And in a tub that's heated smoking hot,[30]
There may they find them, and deliver them.
RALPH. Run, squire and dwarf; deliver them with speed.
                    (*Exeunt* TIM *and* GEORGE)
WIFE. But will not Ralph kill this giant? Surely I am afraid, if he let him go, he will do as much hurt as ever he did.
CIT. Not so, mouse, neither, if he could convert him.
WIFE. Ay, George, if he could convert him; but a giant is not so soon converted as one of us ordinary people. There's a pretty tale of a witch, that had the devil's mark about her, (God bless us!) that had a giant to her son, that was called Lob-lie-by-the-fire; didst never hear it, George?
CIT. Peace, Nell, here comes the prisoners.

(*Re-enter* TIM, *leading a third* MAN, *with a glass of lotion in his hand, and* GEORGE *leading a* WOMAN, *with diet-bread and drink in her hand*)

GEORGE. Here be these pinéd wretches, manful knight,
That for this six weeks have not seen a wight.
RALPH. Deliver what you are, and how you came
To this sad cave, and what your usage was?
3RD MAN. I am an errant knight that followed arms
With spear and shield; and in my tender years
I stricken was with Cupid's fiery shaft,
And fell in love with this my lady dear,

And stole her from her friends in Turnbull Street,[31]
And bore her up and down from town to town,
Where we did eat and drink, and music hear;
Till at the length at this unhappy town
We did arrive, and coming to this cave,
This beast us caught, and put us in a tub,
Where we this two months sweat, and should have done
Another month, if you had not relieved us.
WOMAN. This bread and water hath our diet been,
Together with a rib cut from a neck
Of burned mutton; hard hath been our fare:
Release us from this ugly giant's snare!
3RD MAN. This hath been all the food we have received;
But only twice a-day, for novelty,
He gave a spoonful of this hearty broth
To each of us, through this same slender quill.   (*Pulls out a syringe*)
RALPH. From this infernal monster you shall go,
That useth knights and gentle ladies so!—
Convey them hence.

(3RD MAN *and* WOMAN *are led off by* TIM *and* GEORGE, *who presently re-enter*)

CIT. Cony, I can tell thee, the gentlemen like Ralph.
WIFE. Ay, George, I see it well enough.—Gentlemen, I thank you all heartily for gracing my man Ralph; and I promise you, you shall see him oftener.
BAR. Mercy, great knight! I do recant my ill,
And henceforth never gentle blood will spill.
RALPH. I give thee mercy; but yet shalt thou swear,
Upon my Burning Pestle, to perform
Thy promise utteréd.
BAR. (*Kisses the pestle*) I swear and kiss.
RALPH. Depart, then and amend.—
                    (*Exit* BARBER)
Come, squire and dwarf; the sun grows towards his set,
And we have many more adventures yet.
                    (*Exeunt*)
CIT. Now Ralph is in this humor, I know

[30] Barbers treated patients for syphilis by soaking them in tubs of hot water.

[31] A London street notorious for its prostitutes.

he would ha' beaten all the boys in the house, if they had been set on him.

WIFE. Ay, George, but it is well as it is.

SCENE V. *The Street before* MERRYTHOUGHT's *House.*

(*Enter* MISTRESS MERRYTHOUGHT *and* MICHAEL)

WIFE. But, look, George; here comes Mistress Merrythought, and her son Michael. —Now you are welcome, Mistress Merrythought; now Ralph has done, you may go on.

MIST. MER. Mick, my boy——

MICH. Ay, forsooth, mother.

MIST. MER. Be merry, Mick; we are at home now; where, I warrant you, you shall find the house flung out of the windows. (*Music within*) Hark! hey, dogs, hey! this is the old world, i'faith, with my husband. If I get in among them, I'll play them such a lesson, that they shall have little list to come scraping hither again—(*calling shrilly*) Why, Master Merrythought! husband! Charles Merrythought!

(MERRYTHOUGHT *looks out an upper window, singing*)

If you will sing, and dance, and laugh,
  And hollow, and laugh again,
And then cry, "there, boys, there!" why, then,
  One, two, three, and four,
  We shall be merry within this hour.

MIST. MER. (*Pleading*) Why, Charles, do you not know your own natural wife? I say, open the door, and turn me out those mangy companions; 'tis more than time that they were fellow and fellow-like with you. You are a gentleman, Charles, and an old man, and father of two children; and I myself, (though I say it) by my mother's side niece to a worshipful gentleman and a conductor; he has been three times in his majesty's service at Chester, and is now the fourth time, God bless him and his charge, upon his journey.

MER. (*Sings*)

Go from my window, love, go;
Go from my window, my dear!

(*Very solemnly*) I warrant you, the gentlemen do consider what it is to overthrow a giant.

The wind and the rain
Will drive you back again;
You cannot be lodged here.

Hark you, Mistress Merrythought, you that walk upon adventures, and forsake your husband, because he sings with never a penny in his purse; what, shall I think myself the worse? Faith, no, I'll be merry. You come not here. Here's none but lads of mettle, lives of a hundred years and upwards; care never drunk their bloods, nor want made them warble "Heigh-ho, my heart is heavy."

MIST. MER. (*Whining*) Why, Master Merrythought, what am I, that you should laugh me to scorn thus abruptly? Am I not your fellow-feeler, as we may say, in all our miseries? your comforter in health and sickness? Have I not brought you children? are they not like you, Charles? look upon thine own image, hard-hearted man! and yet for all this——

MER. (*Singing*)

Begone, begone, my juggy, my puggy,
Begone, my love, my dear!
  The weather is warm,
  'Twill do thee no harm:
Thou canst not be lodged here.—

(*To those inside*) Be merry, boys! some light music, and more wine!   (*Exit above*)

WIFE. He's not in earnest, I hope, George, is he?

CIT. What if he be, sweetheart?

WIFE. Marry, if he be, George, I'll make bold to tell him he's an ingrant old man to use his bedfellow so scurvily.

CIT. What! how does he use her, honey?

WIFE. (*Turning on him*) Marry, come up, sir saucebox! I think you'll take his part, will you not? (*Scornfully*) Lord, how hot you have grown! You are a fine man, an' you had a fine dog; it becomes you sweetly!

CIT. Nay, prithee, Nell, chide not; for,

as I am an honest man and a true Christian grocer, I do not like his doings.

WIFE. I cry you mercy, then, George! you know we are all frail and full of infirmities. —(*Calling*) D'ye hear, Master Merrythought? may I crave a word with you?

MER. (*Appearing above*) Strike up lively, lads!

WIFE. I had not thought, in truth, Master Merrythought, that a man of your age and discretion, as I may say, being a gentleman, and therefore known by your gentle conditions, could have used so little respect to the weakness of his wife; (*shaking her finger at him*) for your wife is your own flesh, the staff of your age, your yoke-fellow, with whose help you draw through the mire of this transitory world; nay, she's your own rib: and again——

MER. (*Singing at* WIFE)

I came not hither for thee to teach,
I have no pulpit for thee to preach,
I would thou hadst kissed me under the
        breech,
    As thou art a lady gay.

WIFE. (*Fidgeting with indignation*) Marry, with a vengeance! I am heartily sorry for the poor gentlewoman: but if I were thy wife, i'faith, greybeard, i'faith——

CIT. I prithee, sweet honeysuckle, be content.

WIFE. Give me such words, that am a gentlewoman born! hang him, hoary rascal! Get me some drink, George; I am almost molten with fretting. Now, beshrew his knave's heart for it!   (*Exit* CITIZEN)

MER. Play me a light lavolta. Come, be frolic. Fill the good fellows wine.

MIST. MER. Why, Master Merrythought, are you disposed to make me wait here? You'll open, I hope; I'll fetch them that shall open else.

MER. Good woman, if you will sing, I'll give you something, if not—— (*Sings*)

You are no love for me, Margaret.
    I am no love for you.—

(*Calling to those inside the house*) Come aloft, boys, aloft!   (*Exit above*)

MIST. MER. Now a churl's fart in your teeth, sir!—Come, Mick, we'll not trouble him; 'a shall not ding us i' the teeth with his bread and his broth, that he shall not. Come, boy; I'll provide for thee, I warrant thee. We'll go to Master Venturewell's, the merchant: I'll get his letter to mine host of the Bell in Waltham; there I'll place thee with the tapster: will not that do well for thee, Mick? And let me alone for that old cuckoldly knave your father; I'll use him in his kind, I warrant ye.   (*Exeunt*)

(*Re-enter* CITIZEN *carrying a tankard of
        beer and mugs*)

WIFE. Come, George, where's the beer?

CIT. Here, love.

WIFE. This old fornicating fellow will not out of my mind yet.—(*Raising her mug to the gentlemen on the stage*) Gentlemen, I'll begin to you all; and I desire more of your acquaintance with all my heart. (*Drinks*) Fill the gentlemen some beer, George.

(*Enter a* BOY *who dances during the intermission to off stage music, as at the end of
        Act I*)

WIFE. Look, George, the little boy's come again. Methinks he looks something like the Prince of Orange in his long stocking, if he had a little harness [32] about his neck.— George, I will have him dance "Fading."— (*to the gentlemen on the stage*) "Fading" is a fine jig, I'll assure you, gentlemen.— Begin brother.
(*The* BOY *stops dancing, looks at her despairingly; the music changes and he
        begins another dance*)

WIFE. Now 'a capers, sweetheart!—Now a turn o' the toe. And then a tumble. (*Boy stops dancing*) Cannot you tumble, youth?

BOY. (*With some annoyance*) No, indeed, forsooth.

WIFE. Nor eat fire?

BOY. Neither.

WIFE. Why, then, I thank you heartily; there's twopence to buy you points withal.
        (*Exit* BOY)

[32] Armor.

Act IV

SCENE I. *A Street in London.*

(*Enter* JASPER *and* BOY)

JASP. (*Giving him a letter*) There, boy,
deliver this; but do it well.
Hast thou provided me four lusty fellows,
Able to carry me? and art thou perfect
In all thy business?

BOY. Sir, you need not fear;
I have my lesson here, and cannot miss it:
The men are ready for you, and what else
Pertains to this employment.

JASP. (*Giving him a penny*) There, my
boy;
Take it, but buy no land.

BOY. Faith, sir, 'twere rare
To see so young a purchaser. I fly,
And on my wings carry your destiny.

JASP. Go, and be happy! (*Exit* BOY) Now,
my latest hope,
Forsake me not, but fling thy anchor out,
And let it hold! Stand fixed, thou rolling
stone,
Till I enjoy my dearest! Hear me, all
You powers, that rule in men, celestial!
(*Exit*)

WIFE. Go thy ways; thou art as crooked
a sprig as ever grew in London. I warrant
him, he'll come to some naughty end or
other; for his looks say no less. Besides, his
father (you know, George) is none of the
best; you heard him take me up like a flirt-
gill, and sing bawdy songs upon me; but,
i'faith, if I live, George,——

CIT. Let me alone, sweetheart; I have a
trick in my head shall lodge him in the
Arches for one year, and make him sing
peccavi ere I leave him; and yet he shall
never know who hurt him neither.

(*Enter a* BOY *actor*)

WIFE. Do, my good George, do!

CIT. What shall we have Ralph do now,
boy?

BOY. (*Resignedly*) You shall have what
you will, sir.

CIT. Why, so, sir; go and fetch me him
then, and let the Sophy of Persia come and
christen him a child.

BOY. Believe me, sir, that will not do so
well; 'tis stale; it has been had before at the
Red Bull. [33]

WIFE. (*Eagerly*) George, let Ralph travel
over great hills, and let him be very weary,
and come to the King of Cracovia's house,
covered with black velvet; and there let the
king's daughter stand in her window, all in
beaten gold, combing her golden locks with
a comb of ivory; and let her spy Ralph, and
fall in love with him, and come down to him,
and carry him into her father's house; and
then let Ralph talk with her.

CIT. Well said, Nell; it shall be so.—Boy,
let's ha't done quickly.

BOY. (*Wearily*) Sir, if you will imagine
all this to be done already, you shall hear
them talk together; but we cannot present
a house covered with black velvet, and a
lady in beaten gold.

CIT. Sir boy, let's ha't as you can, then.

BOY. Besides, it will show ill-favoredly
to have a grocer's prentice to court a king's
daughter.

CIT. (*With great indignation*) Will it so,
sir? (*Sarcastically*) you are well read in histories! I pray you, what was Sir Dagonet?
Was not he prentice to a grocer in London?
Read the play of "The Four Prentices of London," where they toss their pikes so. I pray
you, fetch him in, sir, fetch him in.

BOY. It shall be done.—(*Shrugging his
shoulders to the gentlemen*) It is not our
fault, gentlemen. (*Exit*)

WIFE. Now we shall see fine doings, I
warrant ye, George.

[33] A large public theatre with a low reputation.

SCENE II. *A Hall in the King of Moldavia's Court.*

(*Enter* POMPIONA, *ridiculously over-dressed,* RALPH, TIM, *and* GEORGE)

WIFE. Oh, here they come! how prettily the King of Cracovia's daughter is dressed!

CIT. Ay, Nell, it is the fashion of that country, I warrant ye.

POMP. Welcome, Sir Knight, unto my father's court,
King of Moldavia; unto me Pompiona,
His daughter dear! But, sure, you do not like
Your entertainment, that will stay with us
No longer but a night.

RALPH. Damsel right fair,
I am on many sad adventures bound,
That call me forth into the wilderness;
Besides, my horse's back is something galled,
Which will enforce me ride a sober pace.
But many thanks, fair lady, be to you
For using errant knight with courtesy!

POMP. But say, brave knight, what is your name and birth?

RALPH. My name is Ralph; I am an Englishman
(As true as steel, a hearty Englishman),
And prentice to a grocer in the Strand
By deed indent, of which I have one part:
But fortune calling me to follow arms,
On me this only order I did take
Of Burning Pestle, which in all men's eyes
I bear, confounding ladies' enemies.

POMP. Oft have I heard of your brave countrymen,
And fertile soil and store of wholesome food;
My father oft will tell me of a drink
In England found, and nipitato called,
Which driveth all the sorrow from your hearts.

RALPH. Lady, 'tis true; you need not lay your lips
To better nipitato than there is.

POMP. And of a wild fowl he will often speak,
Which powdered-beef-and-mustard calléd is:
For there have been great wars 'twixt us and you;
But truly, Ralph, it was not 'long of me.

Tell me then, Ralph, could you contented be
To wear a lady's favor in your shield?

RALPH. (*Smugly*) I am a knight of a religious order,
And will not wear a favor of a lady
That trusts in Antichrist and false traditions.

CIT. Well said, Ralph! convert her, if thou canst.

RALPH. Besides, I have a lady of my own
In merry England, for whose virtuous sake
I took these arms; and Susan is her name,
A cobbler's maid in Milk Street; whom I vow
Ne'er to forsake whilst life and Pestle last.

POMP. Happy that cobbling dame, whoe'er she be,
That for her own, dear Ralph, hath gotten thee!
Unhappy I, that ne'er shall see the day
To see thee more, that bear'st my heart away!

RALPH. Lady, farewell; I needs must take my leave.

POMP. Hard-hearted Ralph, that ladies dost deceive!

CIT. Hark thee, Ralph: (*giving him money*) there's money for thee; give something in the King of Cracovia's house; be not beholding to him.

RALPH. Lady, before I go, I must remember
Your father's officers, who truth to tell,
Have been about me very diligent.
Hold up thy snowy hand, thou princely maid!
There's twelve-pence for your father's chamberlain;
And another shilling for his cook,
For, by my troth, the goose was roasted well;
And twelve-pence for your father's horse-keeper,
For 'nointing my horse-back, and for his butter
There is another shilling; to the maid
That washed my boot-hose there's an English groat
And two-pence to the boy that wiped my boots;

And last, fair lady, there is for yourself
Three-pence, to buy you pins at Bumbo-fair.
    POMP. Full many thanks; and I will keep
      them safe
Till all the heads be off, for thy sake, Ralph.
    RALPH. Advance, my squire and dwarf!

I cannot stay.
    POMP. Thou kill'st my heart in passing
thus away.   (*Exeunt*)
    WIFE. I commend Ralph yet, that he will
not stoop to a Cracovian; there's properer
women in London than any are there, I-wis.

SCENE III. *A Room in the House of* VENTUREWELL.

(*Enter* VENTUREWELL, HUMPHREY, LUCE,
and Boy)

    WIFE. But here comes Master Humphrey
and his love again now, George.
    CIT. Ay, cony; peace.
    VENT. Go, get you up; I will not be
entreated;
And, gossip mine, I'll keep you sure hereafter
From gadding out again with boys and un-
thrifts.
Come, they are women's tears; I know your
fashion.—
(*To the Boy*) Go, sirrah, lock her in, and
keep the key
Safe as you love your life.
              (*Exeunt* LUCE *and Boy*)
Now, my son Humphrey,
You may both rest assuréd of my love
In this, and reap your own desire.
    HUM. I see this love you speak of, through
      your daughter,
Although the hole be little; and hereafter
Will yield the like in all I may or can,
Fitting a Christian and a gentleman.
    VENT. I do believe you, my good son,
      and thank you;
For 'twere an impudence to think you
flattered.
    HUM. It were, indeed; but shall I tell you
why?
I have been beaten twice about the lie.
    VENT. Well, son, no more of compliment.
      My daughter
Is yours again: appoint the time and take her;
We'll have no stealing for it; I myself
And some few of our friends will see you
    married.
    HUM. I would you would, i'faith! for, be
it known,
I ever was afraid to lie alone.
    VENT. Some three days hence, then.

    HUM. Three days! let me see:
'Tis somewhat of the most; yet I agree,
Because I mean against the appointed day
To visit all my friends in new array.

(*Enter* SERVANT)

    SERV. Sir, there's a gentlewoman without
would speak with your worship.
    VENT. What is she?
    SERV. Sir, I asked her not.
    VENT. Bid her come in.
              (*Exit* SERVANT)

(*Enter* MISTRESS MERRYTHOUGHT *and*
MICHAEL)

    MIST. MER. Peace be to your worship!
I come as a poor suitor to you, sir, in the
behalf of this child.
    VENT. Are you not wife to Merrythought?
    MIST. MER. Yes, truly. Would I had ne'er
seen his eyes! He has undone me and himself
and his children; and there he lives at home,
and sings and hoits and revels among his
drunken companions! but, I warrant you,
where to get a penny to put bread in his
mouth he knows not: and therefore, if it
like your worship, I would entreat your letter to the honest host of the Bell in Waltham, that I may place my child under the
protection of his tapster, in some settled
course of life.
    VENT. I'm glad the heavens have heard
      my prayers. Thy husband,
When I was ripe in sorrows, laughed at me;
Thy son, like an unthankful wretch, I
    having
Redeemed him from his fall, and made him
    mine,
To show his love again, first stole my
    daughter,

Then wronged this gentleman, and, last of
    all,
Gave me that grief had almost brought me
    down
Unto my grave, had not a stronger hand
Relieved my sorrows. Go, and weep as I did,
And be unpitied; for I here profess
An everlasting hate to all thy name.

    Mist. Mer. Will you so, sir? how say
you by that?—Come, Mick; let him keep
his wind to cool his pottage. We'll go to
thy nurse's, Mick: she knits silk stockings,
boy; and we'll knit too, boy, and be beholding to none of them all.

                 (*Exit with* Michael)

(*Enter the London* Boy *with* Jasper's
             letter)

    Boy. Sir, I take it you are the master of
this house.

    Vent. How then, boy!

    Boy. (*Giving him the letter*) Then to
yourself, sir, comes this letter.

    Vent. From whom, my pretty boy?

    Boy. From him that was your servant;
        but no more
Shall that name ever be, for he is dead:

Grief of your purchased anger broke his
    heart.
I saw him die, and from his hand received
This paper, with a charge to bring it hither:
Read it, and satisfy yourself in all.

    Vent. (*Reads*) Sir, that I have wronged
your love I must confess; in which I have
purchased to myself, besides mine own undoing, the ill opinion of my friends. Let not
your anger, good sir, outlive me, but suffer
me to rest in peace with your forgiveness:
let my body (if a dying man may so much
prevail with you) be brought to your daughter, that she may truly know my hot flames
are now buried, and withal receive a testimony of the zeal I bore her virtue. Farewell
for ever, and be ever happy!   Jasper.

    (*Solemnly*) God's hand is great in this:
        I do forgive him;
Yet I am glad he's quiet, where I hope
He will not bite again.—Boy, bring the body,
And let him have his will, if that be all.

    Boy. 'Tis here without, sir.

    Vent. So, sir; if you please,
You may conduct it in; I do not fear it.

    Hum. I'll be your usher, boy; for, though
        I say it,
He owed me something once, and well did
        pay it.   (*Exeunt*)

Scene IV. *Another Room in the House of* Venturewell.

(*Enter* Luce)

    Luce. If there be any punishment in-
    flicted
Upon the miserable, more than yet I feel,
Let it together seize me, and at once
Press down my soul! I cannot bear the pain
Of these delaying tortures.—Thou that art
The end of all, and the sweet rest of all,
Come, come, oh, Death! bring me to thy
    peace,
And blot out all the memory I nourish
Both of my father and my cruel friend!—
Oh, wretched maid, still living to be
    wretched,
To be a say to Fortune in her changes,
And grow to number times and woes together!
How happy had I been, if, being born,
My grave had been my cradle!

(*Enter* Servant)

    Serv. By your leave,
Young mistress; here's a boy hath brought
    a coffin.
What 'a would say, I know not; but your
    father
Charged me to give you notice. Here they
    come.   (*Exit*)

(*Enter* Boy, *and two Men bearing a coffin
covered with a black pall*)

    Luce. For me I hope 'tis come, and 'tis
most welcome.

    Boy. (*They set down the coffin*) Fair mis-
    tress, let me not add greater grief
To that great store you have already. Jasper
(That whilst he lived was yours, now dead

And here enclosed) commanded me to bring
His body hither, and to crave a tear
From those fair eyes (though he deserved
    not pity),
To deck his funeral; for so he bid me
Tell her for whom he died.

    Luce. He shall have many.—
Good friends, depart a little, whilst I take
My leave of this dead man, that once I loved.
        (Exeunt Boy *and Men)*
Hold yet a little, life! and then I give thee
To thy first heavenly being. Oh, my friend!
Hast thou deceived me thus, and got before
    me?
I shall not long be after. But, believe me,
Thou wert too cruel, Jasper, 'gainst thyself,
In punishing the fault I could have pardoned,
With so untimely death: thou didst not
    wrong me,
But ever wert most kind, most true, most
    loving;
And I the most unkind, most false, most
    cruel!
Didst thou but ask a tear? I'll give thee all,
Even all my eyes can pour down, all my
    sighs,
And all myself, before thou goest from me.
These are but sparing rights; but if thy soul
Be yet about this place, and can behold
And see what I prepare to deck thee with,
It shall go up, borne on the wings of peace,
And satisfied. First will I sing thy dirge,
Then kiss thy pale lips, and then die myself,
And fill one coffin and one grave together.
        (Sings)

   Come, you whose loves are dead,
     And, whiles I sing,
     Weep, and wring
   Every hand, and every head
   Bind with cypress and sad yew;
   Ribands black and candles blue
   For him that was of men most true!

   Come with heavy moaning,
     And on his grave
     Let him have
   Sacrifice of sighs and groaning;
   Let him have fair flowers enow,
   White and purple, green and yellow,
   For him that was of men most true!

Thou sable cloth, sad cover of my joys,
I lift thee up, and thus I meet with death.

    (Removes the pall, and Jasper *rises out
      of the coffin)*
    Jasp. And thus you meet the living.
    Luce. Save me, Heaven!
    Jasp. Nay, do not fly me, fair; I am no
    spirit:
Look better on me; do you know me yet?
    Luce. Oh, thou dear shadow of my friend!
    Jasp. Dear substance;
I swear I am no shadow. Feel my hand,
It is the same it was; I am your Jasper,
Your Jasper that's yet living, and yet loving.
Pardon my rash attempt, my foolish proof
I put in practice of your constancy;
For sooner should my sword have drunk my
    blood,
And set my soul at liberty, than drawn
The least drop from that body: for which
    boldness
Doom me to anything; if death, I take it,
And willingly.
    Luce. *(Kisses him)* This death I'll give
    you for it.
So, now I am satisfied you are no spirit,
But my own truest, truest, truest friend.
Why do you come thus to me?
    Jasp. First, to see you;
Then to convey you hence.
    Luce. It cannot be;
For I am locked up here, and watched at all
    hours,
That 'tis impossible for me to scape.
    Jasp. Nothing more possible. Within this
    coffin
Do you convey yourself. Let me alone,
I have the wits of twenty men about me;
Only I crave the shelter of your closet
A little, and then fear me not. Creep in,
That they may presently convey you hence:
Fear nothing, dearest love; I'll be your
    second;
    *(*Luce *lies down in the coffin, and* Jasper
      covers her with the cloth)*
Lie close: so; all goes well yet.—Boy!

    (Re-enter Boy *and Men)*

    Boy. At hand, sir.
    Jasp. Convey away the coffin, and be wary.
    Boy. 'Tis done already.
        (Exeunt Men with the coffin)
    Jasp. Now must I go conjure.
        (Exit into a closet)

(*Enter* VENTUREWELL)

VENT. Boy, boy!

BOY. Your servant, sir.

VENT. Do me this kindness, boy; hold,
    (*giving him a coin*) here's a crown;
Before thou bury the body of this fellow,
Carry it to his old merry father, and salute
    him

From me, and bid him sing; he hath cause.

BOY. I will, sir.

VENT. (*Vindictively*) And then bring me
    word what tune he is in,
And have another crown; but do it truly.—
I have fitted him a bargain now will vex him.

BOY. God bless your worship's health, sir!

VENT. Farewell, boy!

(*Exeunt severally*)

SCENE V. *A Street before* MERRYTHOUGHT's *House.*

(*Enter* MERRYTHOUGHT)

WIFE. Ah, old Merrythought, art thou
there again? let's hear some of thy songs.

MER. (*Sings*)

Who can sing a merrier note
Than he that cannot change a groat?

Not a denier left, and yet my heart leaps:
I do wonder yet, as old as I am, that any
man will follow a trade, or serve, that may
sing and laugh, and walk the streets. My
wife and both my sons are I know not where;
I have nothing left, nor know I how to come
by meat to supper; yet am I merry still, for
I know I shall find it upon the table at six
o'clock; therefore, hang thought!   (*Sings*)

I would not be a serving-man
    To carry the cloak-bag still,
Nor would I be a falconer
    The greedy hawks to fill;
But I would be in a good house,
    And have a good master too;
But I would eat and drink of the best,
    And no work would I do.

This it is that keeps life and soul together,
mirth; this is the philosopher's stone that
they write so much on, that keeps a man ever
young.

(*Enter a* BOY)

BOY. Sir, they say they know all your
money is gone, and they will trust you for
no more drink.

MER. Will they not? let 'em choose! The

best is, I have mirth at home, and need not
send abroad for that; let them keep their
drink to themselves.   (*Sings*)

For Julian of Berry, she dwells on a hill,
And she hath good beer and ale to sell,
And of good fellows she thinks no ill;
    And thither will we go now, now, now,
    And thither will we go now.

And when you have made a little stay,
You need not ask what is to pay,
But kiss your hostess, and go your way;
    And thither will we go now, now, now,
    And thither will we go now.

(*Enter another* BOY)

2ND BOY. Sir, I can get no bread for supper.

MER. Hang bread and supper! let's preserve our mirth, and we shall never feel
hunger, I'll warrant you. Let's have a catch,
boys; follow me, come.   (*They sing*)

Ho, ho, nobody at home!
Meat, nor drink, nor money ha' we none.
Fill the pot, Eedy,
Never more need I.

MER. So, boys; enough. Follow me: Let's
change our place, and we shall laugh afresh.

(*Exeunt*)

WIFE. Let him go, George; 'a shall not
have any countenance from us, nor a good
word from any i' the company, if I may strike
stroke in't.

CIT. No more 'a sha'not, love. But, Nell,
I will have Ralph do a very notable matter

now, to the eternal honor and glory of all grocers.—(*calling*) Sirrah! you there, boy! Can none of you hear?

(*Enter a* Boy *actor*)

Boy. Sir, your pleasure?

Cit. Let Ralph come out on May-day in the morning, and speak upon a conduit, with all his scarfs about him, and his feathers, and his rings, and his knacks.

Boy. Why, sir, you do not think of our plot; what will become of that, then?

Cit. Why, sir, I care not what become on't: I'll have him come out, or I'll fetch him out myself; I'll have something done in honor of the city. Besides, he hath been long enough upon adventures. Bring him out quickly; or, if I come in amongst you——

Boy. Well, sir, he shall come out, but if our play miscarry, sir, you are like to pay for't.

Cit. Bring him away then!   (*Exit* Boy)

Wife. This will be brave, i'faith! George, shall not he dance the morris too, for the credit of the Strand?

Cit. No, sweetheart, it will be too much for the boy. Oh, there he is, Nell! he's reasonable well in reparel: but he has not rings enough.

(*Enter* Ralph, *dressed as a May-lord*)

Ralph. London, to thee I do present the
     merry month of May;
Let each true subject be content to hear me
     what I say:
For from the top of conduit-head, as plainly
     may appear,
I will both tell my name to you, and where-
     fore I came here.
My name is Ralph, by due descent though
     not ignoble I
Yet far inferior to the stock of gracious
     grocery;
And by the common counsel of my fellows
     in the Strand,
With gilded staff and crosséd scarf, the May-
     lord here I stand.
Rejoice, oh, English hearts, rejoice! rejoice,
     oh, lovers dear!
Rejoice, oh, city, town, and country! rejoice,
     eke every shire!

For now the fragrant flowers do spring and
     sprout in seemly sort,
The little birds do sit and sing, the lambs do
     make fine sport;
And now the birchen-tree doth bud, that
     makes the schoolboy cry;
The morris rings, while hobby-horse doth
     foot it feateously;
The lords and ladies now abroad, for their
     disport and play,
Do kiss sometimes upon the grass, and some-
     times in the hay;
Now butter with a leaf of sage is good to
     purge the blood;
Fly Venus and phlebotomy, for they are
     neither good;
Now little fish on tender stone begin to cast
     their bellies,
And sluggish snails, that erst were mewed,
     do creep out of their shellies;
The rumbling rivers now do warm, for little
     boys to paddle;
The sturdy steed now goes to grass, and up
     they hang his saddle;
The heavy hart, the bellowing buck, the
     rascal, and the pricket,
Are now among the yeoman's peas, and leave
     the fearful thicket:
And be like them, oh, you, I say, of this
     same noble town,
And lift aloft your velvet heads, and slipping
     off your gown,
With bells on legs, and napkins clean unto
     your shoulders tied,
With scarfs and garters as you please, and
     "Hey for our town!" cried,
March out, and show your willing minds, by
     twenty and by twenty,
To Hogsdon or to Newington, where ale and
     cakes are plenty;
And let it ne'er be said for shame, that we
     the youths of London
Lay thrumming of our caps at home, and
     left our custom undone.
Up, then, I say, both young and old, both
     man and maid a-maying,
With drums, and guns that bounce aloud,
     and merry tabor playing!
Which to prolong, God save our king, and
     send his country peace,
And root out treason from the land! and so,
     my friends, I cease.   (*Exit*)

Act V

SCENE I. *A Room in the House of* VENTUREWELL.

(*Enter* VENTUREWELL)

VENT. I will have no great store of company at the wedding; a couple of neighbors and their wives; and we will have a capon in stewed broth, with marrow, and a good piece of beef stuck with rosemary.

(*Enter* JASPER, *from the closet. His face is whitened with flour, and he glides along like a ghost*)

JASP. (*In a deep hollow voice*) Forbear thy pains, fond man! it is too late.
VENT. Heaven bless me! Jasper!
JASP. Ay, I am his ghost,
Whom thou hast injured for his constant love;
Fond worldly wretch! who dost not understand
In death that true hearts cannot parted be.
First know, thy daughter is quite borne away
On wings of angels, through the liquid air,
To far out of thy reach, and never more
Shalt thou behold her face. But she and I
Will in another world enjoy our loves;
Where neither father's anger, poverty,
Nor any cross that troubles earthly men,
Shall make us sever our united hearts.
And never shalt thou sit or be alone
In any place, but I will visit thee
With ghastly looks, and put into thy mind
The great offences which thou didst to me.
When thou art at thy table with thy friends,
Merry in heart, and filled with swelling wine,
I'll come in midst of all thy pride and mirth,
Invisible to all men but thyself,
And whisper such a sad tale in thine ear
Shall make thee let the cup fall from thy hand,
And stand as mute and pale as death itself.
VENT. (*Thoroughly terrified*) Forgive me, Jasper! Oh, what might I do,
Tell me, to satisfy thy troubled ghost?
JASP. There is no means; too late thou think'st of this.

VENT. But tell me what were best for me to do?
JASP. Repent thy deed, and satisfy my father,
And beat fond Humphrey out of thy doors.
(*Exit*)
WIFE. Look, George; his very ghost would have folks beaten.

(*Enter* HUMPHREY)

HUM. Father, my bride is gone, fair Mistress Luce:
My soul's the fount of vengeance, mischief's sluice.
VENT. Hence, fool, out of my sight with thy fond passion!
Thou hast undone me.   (*Beats him*)
HUM. Hold, my father dear,
For Luce thy daughter's sake, that had no peer!
VENT. Thy father, fool! there's some blows more; begone.—   (*Beats him*)
(*Aside*) Jasper, I hope thy ghost be well appeased
To see thy will performed. Now will I go
To satisfy thy father for thy wrongs. (*Exit*)
HUM. What shall I do? I have been beaten twice,
And Mistress Luce is gone. Help me, device!
Since my true love is gone, I never more,
Whilst I do live, upon the sky will pore;
But in the dark will wear out my shoe-soles
In passion in Saint Faith's church under Paul's.   (*Exit*)
WIFE. George, call Ralph hither; if you love me, call Ralph hither: I have the bravest thing for him to do, George; prithee, call him quickly.
CIT. Ralph! why, Ralph, boy!

(*Enter* RALPH)

RALPH. Here, sir.
CIT. Come hither, Ralph; come to thy mistress, boy.

WIFE. Ralph, I would have thee call all the youths together in battle-ray, with drums, and guns, and flags, and march to Mile-End in pompous fashion, and there exhort your soldiers to be merry and wise, and to keep their beards from burning, Ralph; and then skirmish, and let your flags fly, and cry, "Kill, kill, kill!" My husband shall lend you his jerkin, Ralph, and there's a scarf; for the rest, the house shall furnish you, and we'll pay for't. Do it bravely, Ralph; and think before whom you perform, and what person you represent.[34]

RALPH. I warrant you, mistress; if I do it not, for the honor of the city and the credit of my master, let me never hope for freedom!

WIFE. 'Tis well spoken, i'faith. Go thy ways; thou art a spark indeed.

CIT. Ralph, Ralph, double your files bravely, Ralph!

RALPH. I warrant you, sir.   (*Exit*)

CIT. Let him look narrowly to his service; I shall take him else. I was there myself a pikeman once, in the hottest of the day, wench; had my feather shot sheer away, the fringe of my pike burnt off with powder, my pate broken with a scouring-stick, and yet, I thank God, I am here.

(*Drums beat off stage*)

WIFE. Hark, George, the drums!

CIT. Ran, tan, tan, tan, tan, tan! Oh, wench, an thou hadst but seen little Ned of Aldgate, Drum-Ned, how he made it roar again, and laid on like a tyrant, and then struck softly till the ward came up, and then thundered again, and together we go! "Sa, sa, sa, bounce!" quoth the guns; "Courage, my hearts!" quoth the captains; "Saint George!" quoth the pikemen; and withal, here they lay: and there they lay: and yet for all this I am here, wench.

WIFE. Be thankful for it, George; for indeed 'tis wonderful.

SCENE II. *A Street (and afterwards Mile End).*

(*Enter* RALPH *commanding a company which marches in with drums and colors. The* TROOPS *are London shop keepers playing soldiers. They are ridiculously got up and constantly get tangled up with their swords, muskets, and pikes*)

RALPH. (*Calling orders and advice as they march about the stage*) March fair, my hearts! Lieutenant, beat the rear up.— Ancient, let your colors fly; but have a great care of the butcher's hooks at Whitechapel; they have been the death of many a fair ancient.—Open your files, that I may take a view both of your persons and munition.— Sergeant, call a muster.

SERG. A stand! (*They halt. When their names are called the men step out for inspection*)—William Hammerton, pewterer!

HAM. Here, captain!

RALPH. A corselet and a Spanish pike; 'tis well: can you shake it with a terror?

HAM. I hope so, captain.

RALPH. Charge upon me. (*He charges on*

RALPH)—'Tis with the weakest: but more strength, William Hammerton, more strength. As you were again!—Proceed, Sergeant.

SERG. George Greengoose, poulterer!

GREEN. Here!

RALPH. Let me see your piece, neighbor Greengoose. (*Inspecting his musket*) When was she shot in?

GREEN. An't like you, master captain, I made a shot even now, partly to scour her, and partly for audacity.

RALPH. It should seem so certainly, for her breath is yet inflamed; besides, there is a main fault in the touch-hole, it runs and stinketh; and I tell you moreover, and believe it, ten such touch-holes would breed the pox in the army. Get you a feather, neighbor, get you a feather, sweet oil, and paper, and your piece may do well enough yet. Where's your powder?

GREEN. Here.

RALPH. What, in a paper! As I am a soldier and a gentleman, it craves a martial court! You ought to die for't. Where's your horn? Answer me to that.

[34] She is asking for the annual muster of the London militia.

GREEN. An't like you, sir, I was oblivious.

RALPH. It likes me not you should be so; 'tis a shame for you, and a scandal to all our neighbors, being a man of worth and estimation, to leave your horn behind you: I am afraid 'twill breed example. But let me tell you no more on't.—Stand, till I view you all. —What's become o' the nose of your flask?

1ST SOLD. Indeed, la, captain, 'twas blown away with powder.

RALPH. Put on a new one at the city's charge.—Where's the stone of this piece?

2ND SOLD. The drummer took it out to light tobacco.

RALPH. 'Tis a fault, my friend; put it in again.—You want a nose,—and you a stone.— Sergeant, take a note on't, for I mean to stop it in the pay.—Remove, and march! (*They march and* RALPH *drills them on the stage*) Soft and fair, gentlemen, soft and fair! Double your files! As you were! Faces about! Now, you with the sodden face, keep in there! Look to your match, sirrah, it will be in your fellow's flask anon. So. Make a crescent now! Advance your pikes! Stand and give ear!—Gentlemen, countrymen, friends, and my fellow-soldiers, I have brought you this day, from the shops of security and the counters of content, to measure out in these furious fields honor by the ell, and prowess by the pound. Let it not, oh, let it not, I say, be told hereafter, the noble issue of this city fainted; but bear yourselves in this fair action like men, valiant men, and free men! Fear not the face of the enemy, nor the noise of the guns, for, believe me, brethren, the rude rumbling of a brewer's cart is far more terrible, of which you have a daily experience; neither let the stink of powder offend you, since a more valiant stink is nightly with you. To a resolvéd mind his home is everywhere: I speak not this to take away the hope of your return; for you shall see (I do not doubt it) and that very shortly your loving wives again and your sweet children, whose care doth bear you company in baskets. Remember, then, whose cause you have in hand, and, like a sort of true-born scavengers, scour me this famous realm of enemies. I have no more to say but this: stand to your tacklings, lads, and show to the world you can as well brandish a sword as shake an apron. Saint George, and on, my hearts!

ALL. Saint George, Saint George!

(RALPH *marches them off the stage*)

WIFE. 'Twas well done, Ralph! I'll send thee a cold capon a-field and a bottle of March beer; and, it may be, come myself to see thee.

CIT. Nell, the boy hath deceived me much; I did not think it had been in him. He has performed such a matter, wench, that, if I live, next year I'll have him captain of the galley-foist, or I'll want my will.

SCENE III. *A Room in* MERRYTHOUGHT's *House.*

(*Enter* MERRYTHOUGHT)

MER. Yet, I thank God, I break not a wrinkle more than I had. Not a stoop, boys? Care, live with cats: I defy thee! My heart is as sound as an oak; and though I want drink to wet my whistle, I can sing;　　(*Sings*)

Come no more there, boys, come no more there;
For we shall never whilst we live come any more there.

(*Enter* BOY, *and two* MEN *bearing the coffin*)

BOY. God save you, sir!

MER. It's a brave boy. Canst thou sing?

BOY. Yes, sir, I can sing; but 'tis not so necessary at this time.

MER. (*Sings*)

Sing we, and chant it;
Whilst love doth grant it.

BOY. Sir, sir, if you knew what I have brought you, you would have little list to sing.

MER. (*Sings*)

Oh, the Mimon round,
Full long I have thee sought,
And now I have thee found,
And what hast thou here brought?

Boy. A coffin, sir, and your dead son Jasper in it.　　　　　　　(*Exit with* Men)

Mer. Dead! (*Sings*)

> Why, farewell he!
> Thou wast a bonny boy,
> And I did love thee.

(*Enter* Jasper)

Jasp. Then, I pray you, sir, do so still.

Mer. Jasper's ghost!　　　　　(*Sings*)

> Thou art welcome from Stygian lake so soon;
> Declare to me what wondrous things in
>   Pluto's court are done.

Jasp. By my troth, sir, I ne'er came there; 'tis too hot for me, sir.

Mer. A merry ghost, a very merry ghost!
　　　　　　　　　　　　　　(*Sings*)

> And where is your true love? Oh, where is
>   yours?

Jasp. Marry, look you, sir!
　　(*Removes the pall, and* Luce *rises out
　　　　of the coffin*)

Mer. Ah, ha! art thou good at that, i'faith?
　　　　　　　　　　　　　　(*Sings*)

> With hey, trixy, terlery-whiskin,
>   The world it runs on wheels;
> When the young man's ——,
>   Up goes the maiden's heels.

Mist. Mer. (*Calling off stage and knocking*) What, Master Merrythought! will you not let's in? what do you think shall become of us?

Mer. (*Sings*)

> What voice is that that calleth at our door?

Mist. Mer. (*Within*) You know me well enough; I am sure I have not been such a stranger to you.

Mer. (*Sings*)

> And some they whistled, and some they sung,
>   Hey, down, down!
> And some did loudly say,

> Ever as the Lord Barnet's horn blew,
>   Away, Musgrave, away!

Mist. Mer. (*Within*) You will not have us starve here, will you, Master Merrythought?

Jasp. Nay, good sir, be persuaded; she is my mother.
If her offences have been great against you,
Let your own love remember she is yours,
And so forgive her.

Luce. Good Master Merrythought,
Let me entreat you; I will not be denied.

Mist. Mer. (*Within*) Why, Master Merrythought, will you be a vexed thing still?

Mer. Woman, I take you to my love again; but you shall sing before you enter; therefore despatch your song and so come in.

Mist. Mer. (*Within*) Well, you must have your will, when all's done.—Mick, what song canst thou sing, boy?

Mich. (*Within*) I can sing none, forsooth, but "A Lady's Daughter, of Paris" properly,
　　　　　　　　(Michael *sings off stage*)

> It was a lady's daughter, etc.

(Merrythought *opens the door; enter* Mistress Merrythought *and* Michael)

Mer. Come, you're welcome home again.
　　　　　　　　　　　　　　(*Sings*)

> If such danger be in playing,
>   And jest must to earnest turn,
> You shall go no more a-maying——

Vent. (*Calling off stage*) Are you within, sir? Master Merrythought!

Jasp. It is my master's voice! Good sir, go hold him
In talk, whilst we convey ourselves into
Some inward room.　　　(*Exit with* Luce)

Mer. What are you? are you merry?
You must be very merry, if you enter.

Vent. (*Within*) I am, sir.

Mer. Sing, then.

Vent. (*Within*) Nay, good sir, open to me.

Mer. Sing, I say,
Or, by the merry heart, you come not in!

Vent. (*Within*) Well, sir, I'll sing.
　　　　　　　　(*He sings dolefully*)

Fortune, my foe, etc.

(MERRYTHOUGHT *opens the door; enter* VENTUREWELL)

MER. You are welcome, sir, you are welcome. You see your entertainment; pray you, be merry.

VENT. Oh, Master Merrythought, I'm
come to ask you
Forgiveness for the wrongs I offered you,
And your most virtuous son! They're infinite;
Yet my contrition shall be more than they:
I do confess my hardness broke his heart,
For which just Heaven hath given me punishment
More than my age can carry. His wandering spirit,
Nor yet at rest, pursues me everywhere,
Crying, "I'll haunt thee for thy cruelty."
My daughter, she is gone, I know not how,
Taken invisible, and whether living
Or in the grave, 'tis yet uncertain to me.
Oh, Master Merrythought, these are the weights
Will sink me to my grave! Forgive me, sir.

MER. Why, sir, I do forgive you; and be merry.
And if the wag in's lifetime played the knave,
Can you forgive him too?

VENT. With all my heart, sir.

MER. Speak it again, and heartily.

VENT. I do, sir;
Now, by my soul, I do.

(*Re-enter* LUCE *and* JASPER)

MER. (*Sings*)

With that came out his paramour;
She was as white as the lily flower:
Hey, troll, trolly, lolly!
With that came out her own dear knight;
He was as true as ever did fight, etc.

Sir, if you will forgive 'em, clap their hands together; there's no more to be said i' the matter.

VENT. I do, I do.

CIT. I do not like this. (*Calling to the actors*) Peace, boys! Hear me, one of you! Everybody's part is come to an end but Ralph's, and he's left out.

BOY. 'Tis 'long of yourself, sir; we have nothing to do with his part.

CIT. Ralph, come away!—Make an end on him, as you have done of the rest, boys; come.

WIFE. Now, good husband, let him come out and die.

CIT. He shall, Nell.—Ralph, come away quickly, and die, boy!

BOY. 'Twill be very unfit he should die, sir, upon no occasion—and in a comedy, too.

CIT. Take you no care of that, Sir Boy; is not his part at an end, think you, when he's dead?—Come away, Ralph!

(*Enter* RALPH, *with a forked arrow through his head*)

RALPH.[35] When I was mortal, this my costive corpse
Did lap up figs and raisins in the Strand;
Where sitting, I espied a lovely dame,
Whose master wrought with lingel and with awl,
And underground he vampéd many a boot.
Straight did her love prick forth me, tender sprig,
To follow feats of arms in warlike wise
Through Waltham desert; where I did perform
Many achievements, and did lay on ground
Huge Barbarossa, that insulting giant,
And all his captives soon set at liberty.
Then honor pricked me from my native soil
Into Moldavia, where I gained the love
Of Pompiona, his belovéd daughter;
But yet proved constant to the black thumbed maid
Susan, and scornéd Pompiona's love;
Yet liberal I was, and gave her pins,
And money for her father's officers.
I then returnéd home, and thrust myself
In action, and by all men chosen was
Lord of the May, where I did flourish it,
With scarfs and rings, and posy in my hand.
After this action I preferréd was,
And chosen city-captain at Mile End,
With hat and feather, and with leading-staff,
And trained my men, and brought them all off clear,

[35] Various parts of this speech parody the lines of the ghost in the popular melodrama *The Spanish Tragedy.*

Save one man that berayed him with the
    noise.
But all these things I Ralph did undertake
Only for my belovéd Susan's sake.
Then coming home, and sitting in my shop
With apron blue, Death came into my stall
To cheapen *aquavitæ*; but ere I
Could take the bottle down and fill a taste,
Death caught a pound of pepper in his hand,
And sprinkled all my face and body o'er
And in an instant vanishéd away.

    CIT. 'Tis a pretty fiction, i'faith.

    RALPH. Then took I up my bow and shaft
    in hand,
And walked into Moorfields to cool myself:
But there grim cruel Death met me again,
And shot this forkéd arrow through my head;
And now I faint. Therefore be warned by me,
My fellows every one, of forkéd heads!
Farewell, all you good boys in merry London!
Ne'er shall we more upon Shrove Tuesday
    meet,
And pluck down houses of iniquity;—
My pain increaseth;—I shall never more
Hold open, whilst another pumps both legs,
Nor daub a satin gown with rotten eggs;
Set up a stake, oh, never more I shall!
I die! fly, fly, my soul, to Grocers' Hall!
Oh, oh, oh, etc.

    WIFE. (*Applauding*) Well said, Ralph!
do your obeisance to the gentlemen, and go
your ways: well said, Ralph!

        (RALPH *rises, bows, and exit*)

    MER. Methinks all we, thus kindly and
unexpectedly reconciled, should not depart
without a song.

    VENT. A good motion.

    MER. Strike up, then! (*The music begins
and they all sing*)

SONG

*Better music ne'er was known
Than a quire of hearts in one.
Let each other, that hath been
Troubled with the gall or spleen,
Learn of us to keep his brow
Smooth and plain, as ours are now:
Sing, though before the hour of dying;
He shall rise, and then be crying,
"Hey, ho, 'tis nought but mirth
That keeps the body from the earth!"*

        (*Exeunt*)

    CIT. Come, Nell, shall we go? The play's
done.

    WIFE. Nay, by my faith, George, I have
more manners than so; I'll speak to these
gentlemen first.—I thank you all, gentlemen,
for your patience and countenance to Ralph,
a poor fatherless child; and if I might see you
at my house, it should go hard but I would
have a bottle of wine and a pipe of tobacco
for you: for, truly, I hope you do like the
youth, but I would be glad to know the
truth; I refer it to your own discretions,
whether you will applaud him or no; for I
will wink, and whilst you shall do what you
will. (*She closes her eyes, and the gentlemen
on the stage applaud*) I thank you with all
my heart. God give you good night!—Come,
George.   (*Exeunt*)

BEN JONSON

The Alchemist

~~~~~~~~~~

PRINCIPAL EVENTS IN JONSON'S LIFE

1572, Jonson was born, probably in London.

c. 1583-c. 1589, He was a student at Westminster School, London.

c. 1589, He was apprentice bricklayer to his stepfather.

c. 1594, Served as a soldier against the Spaniards in Flanders.

1598, Sept. 22, Killed the actor, Gabriel Spencer, in a duel.

1598, Sept., Every Man in His Humour performed by the Lord Chamberlain's company with William Shakespeare in the cast.

1601, Jonson's satiric comedy *Poetaster* attacking his enemies, John Marston and Thomas Dekker and others, performed by the Children of the Chapel at Blackfriars theatre.

1601, Thomas Dekker's play *Satiromastix,* ridiculing Jonson, acted by the Lord Chamberlain's company at the Globe a few weeks after *Poetaster.* These two plays are the principal dramatic documents in the "War of the Theatres."

1603, March 25, James I, a learned man and an admirer of Jonson's work, proclaimed King of England.

1603, Sejanus, Jonson's learned tragedy of Roman history, performed by the King's Men at the Globe theatre with William Shakespeare in the cast.

c. 1603, The famous society of Jonson's admirers and friends called "The Tribe of Ben" began meeting at the Mermaid Tavern.

1605, Jan. 6, The Masque of Blackness, the first of Jonson's spectacular entertainments, presented before the King and court at Whitehall palace with Queen Anne as one of the performers.

1605, Jonson, Chapman, and Marston jailed for satire of the Scots and of King James himself, in their play *Eastward Ho.*

1606, Volpone or the Fox acted by the King's Men at the Globe theatre.

1608, Feb. 9, Lord Haddington's Masque, sometimes called *The Hue and Cry after Cupid,* written for the wedding of Viscount Haddington and Lady Elizabeth Radcliffe, presented before the King and court.

1609, Epicoene or the Silent Woman acted by the Children of the Queen's Revels.

1610, Autumn, The Alchemist acted by the King's Men at the Blackfriars theatre.

1611, Catiline, the second of Jonson's learned tragedies of Roman history, acted by the King's Men.

1612, Jan. 6, Love Restored, a masque, presented at Whitehall palace before the King and court.

1612-1613, In France as tutor to the son of Sir Walter Raleigh.

1614, Oct. 31, Bartholomew Fair acted at the Hope theatre on the Bankside by the Lady Elizabeth's Men.

1616, Feb., King James granted a pension to Jonson.

1616, A collection of Jonson's plays, masques, and poems published under the title *The Works of Benjamin Jonson.*

1618, Summer and Autumn, Jonson went on a walking tour to Edinburgh, where he was made an honorary burgess of the city. For two or three weeks he was the guest of William Drummond, of Hawthornden, who kept notes of his conversations.

1619, July, Jonson formally inducted as honorary Master of Arts by Oxford University.

1621, Aug. 3 and 5, and Sept., The Gypsies Metamorphosed, Jonson's humorous masque, presented at the country houses of the Marquis of Buckingham and the Earl of Rutland and at Windsor Castle.

1625, Death of Jonson's admirer, King James I, and accession of Charles I.

1626, The Staple of News performed by the King's Men.

1628, Made City Chronologer for London.

1632, Jonson's last comedy, *The Magnetic Lady,* performed by the King's Men at Blackfriars.

1637, Died Aug. 6; buried Aug. 9 in Westminster Abbey.

1638, Jonsonus Virbius, a collection of poems in praise of Jonson by thirty-one of the leading literary men of the time, published.

INTRODUCTION

When *The Alchemist* was first performed by Shakespeare's company, the King's Men, at the Blackfriars theatre in London in the autumn or winter of 1610, Jonson was already widely known as one of the leading English men of letters. He had written or collaborated in a dozen or more plays; he had been recognized as the best writer of court masques, those spectacular entertainments at the court of King James about which all London talked; he was widely admired as the most learned poet and critic of the time.

Jonson's reputation was due in part to the fact that he was the most articulate dramatic critic of his day. He pointed again and again to the shortcomings of contemporary plays, as he saw them; he stated repeatedly what he thought plays ought to be; and he had the temerity to announce that his plays were "such as other plays should be." He thought that comedies should not be like Shakespeare's *As You Like It* and *Twelfth Night* or Robert Greene's *Scottish History of James IV* and *Friar Bacon and Friar Bungay.* Such plays, set in the Forest of Arden or Illyria or thirteenth-century Oxford, were too far removed from everyday London life. Jonson thought that comedy should contribute to the improvement of society and therefore should depict contemporary Londoners as they really lived in his day. He objected therefore to the unnatural mixture of classes which characterized romantic comedies—a countess in love with a page, as in *Twelfth Night,* a king's son in love with a gamekeeper's daughter, as in *Friar Bacon and Friar Bungay,* or two princesses wandering about in a forest with a clown, as in *As You Like It.*

Jonson also objected to the romantic plots and the highly idealized language of many Elizabethan plays. Characters in comedies, he thought, should undergo experiences common in London, and they should speak, not like Viola and Orsino in *Twelfth Night,* but like the people one met on the streets and in the shops of the town. As he phrased it, comedy should deal with "deeds and language such as men do use." The purpose of comedy should not be mere entertainment, but a picture of contemporary follies so presented that, by laughing at its own vices seen on the stage, the audience might be led to more rational conduct.

Elizabethan plays in general were too sprawling in their structure and too romantic in their characterization to suit Jonson. He agreed with the classic critics that the action of a play should be confined to one city and if possible to a period of less than twenty-four hours. Characters should consistently display their dominant characteristics or humors: the jealous man should exhibit his jealousy on all occasions, the greedy man his greed, the gullible man his credulity, the vain man his vanity. No human being, of course, ever succeeds in living up to his own principles at all times, and Jonson, like others, sometimes produced plays which did not measure up to his own standards. His best comedies, however, are remarkable applications of the principles which he advocated. None of them more fully exemplifies the type of comedy which Jonson thought London should have than *The Alchemist*.

Not only is this play set in contemporary London, but Jonson has carefully indicated the precise district in London—the very one in which the theatre in which it was first given is located. The time is not the distant past nor even the approximate present; it is the very year of the first performance. Jonson repeatedly indicates that the action takes place during a London epidemic of the plague. This fatal and terrifying disease was one of the great horrors of Jacobean London. When the epidemic was raging, thousands died, often on the streets, and the terrified citizens lived in dread, or, if they were well-to-do like Lovewit in the play, fled the town and left their houses in the hands of servants like Jeremy, *alias* Face, *alias* Lungs. Such epidemics of the plague occurred in 1609 and 1610, and probably a number of well-to-do people in the Blackfriars audience at the first performance of *The Alchemist* had, like Lovewit, recently returned to their London houses after the plague of 1610.

The Alchemist further exemplifies Jonson's standards of play-writing in its avoidance of the unusual mixture of classes which characterizes romantic comedies like *Mucedorus, George-a-Greene*, or *As You Like It*. In the *dramatis personae* of *The Alchemist* there are, on the one hand, no kings or queens, princes or nobles, and on the other no beggars or dairy maids. The characters are representative of the upper and lower middle classes commonly found in social or business contact in Jacobean London—a tobacconist, a gambler, a butler, a foolish young country gentleman and his sister, a prostitute, a confidence man, a Puritan minister. In the play these ordinary London characters undergo experiences which might take place in the English capital any day. They are the victims or the perpetrators of swindles like those reported daily in modern metropolitan police courts. Of course the crooks use specific Jacobean tricks and not the tricks of twentieth-century confidence men, but the characters, the motives, and the general methods of swindlers and swindled are much the same in the seventeenth century and the twentieth.

The particular type of swindle which Jonson has Face and Subtle use most extensively on their victims is that of the fake alchemist. Today we are familiar with swindles like palmistry, astrology, numerology, the badger game, marked cards, loaded dice, bogus companies, rubber checks, "protection," fraudulent advertising, spiritualism—several of which Face, Subtle, and Dol use—but the fake alchemist rarely appears in modern police court news. It was a favorite device of London crooks in Jonson's time because most people then were confused and uncertain about the possibilities of chemistry and physics. For centuries the natural scientists had believed in the essential unity of all matter, and that matter might be transmuted from one state to another. The transmutation of baser metals to gold was only one of many possibilities, but it was the one most appealing to avaricious men. Hundreds of alchemists, many of them men of great learning and no little laboratory experience, had worked in Europe in the middle ages and the Renaissance. They had tried many experiments, but most often they had attempted to develop the philosopher's stone (sometimes called the magisterium or the elixir or the quintessence), the perfect universal essence of all matter which because of its perfection and universality might do all things for all men. These experiments of the alchemists were widely but ignorantly discussed. What a chance for clever crooks! Many of them seized the opportunity and practised vigorously. A few of the cleverest, like John Dee and Edward Kelley, whom Jonson mentions in his play, had practised on kings and queens and great nobles. The pretensions of Subtle in *The Alchemist* are no greater than those of Edward Kelley; Jonson simply makes Subtle's true character clearer to the audience than Kelley's character was to his victims. This is a familiar difference between swindling in plays and swindling in real life.

Jonson's Subtle is by no means an ignorant crook. He shows a wide and accurate knowledge of the many books on alchemy; he is familiar with all the current scientific terms and methods; he presents a scientific argument for the theory of alchemy which even the sceptical Surly cannot answer. Subtle is certainly a crook and not a scientist, but like many crooks he has studied long and painstakingly in his profession. Probably none of the members of Jonson's audience understood all the learned terms that Subtle used, but they knew a few, and, having heard many of the others in a scientific context, they took their scientific accuracy on faith, just as most modern patients do when listening to the doctor.

Jonson has thus selected for his play characters from everyday London life, and he shows them engaged in swindles which were common enough in London in 1610. Their deeds are "such as men do use," and their language is too. This further fidelity of Jonson to his realistic principles causes one of the chief difficulties of the play for modern readers. People like those depicted in *The Alchemist* are not noted for the purity of their speech. They resort constantly to slang, vulgarisms, and colloquialisms, types of language which soon pass out of fashion. Today some of this accurately transcribed speech of the Londoners of three hundred years ago is as difficult to understand as "Jeez, that hep cat sure can send me!" will be three hundred years from now. Many of the expressions must be explained in footnotes, and some of them are unintelligible even to the scholars who write the footnotes.

The characters of *The Alchemist* are not only familiar types of Londoners of the year 1610, but they are set forth in such a way that the audience may be edified as well as amused by their conduct. Jonson had said that comedies ought to "show an image of the times and sport with human follies." The follies of the gullible Dapper, the greedy, sensual Mammon, the childish Drugger, and the silly, bumptious Kastril are made plain enough and ridiculous enough in the play for any spectator to understand and to profit by if he himself had any such tendencies. The Puritan minister, Tribulation Wholesome, and the deacon of his congregation, Ananias, are of a different order. These religious hypocrites are portrayed by Jonson as more vicious than the other gulls. In Act II, Scene 5, they are ready to cheat orphans if their parents have not been Puritans; they preach nonsense about the imaginary sins of other people; in III, 2, and IV, 7, they are willing to engage in counterfeiting for the profit of the congregation. To Jonson these Puritans seemed more contemptible and less amusing than the other gulls of Face and Subtle. His portrayal of the sect, and even of some of the congregations, which furnished the passenger list for the ship Mayflower in 1620 may well be contrasted with some of the New England Puritans' writings about themselves.

With all his care to adhere to the principles he thinks fitting for comedy, Jonson never allows *The Alchemist* to become pedantic. Though the play is constructed with such exquisite skill that Coleridge once said it had one of the three best plots in all literature, it is boisterous and rollicking from beginning to end. When the comedy is performed, the audience is always struck by the rapid pace of the action and the masculine virility of the scenes. In his life Jonson was a hearty and violent man; much of his own gusto appears in *The Alchemist*.

THE ALCHEMIST

Dramatis personae

In order of first appearance

FACE, Really Jeremy, butler to Lovewit, who has grown a beard and who disguises himself throughout the action of the play, sometimes as an army captain and sometimes as Lungs, laboratory assistant to the alchemist Subtle.

SUBTLE, A rogue who poses as an alchemist.

DOL COMMON, A prostitute who acts as accomplice to Face and Subtle.

DAPPER, A gullible lawyer's clerk.

ABEL DRUGGER, Proprietor of a small tobacco shop.

SIR EPICURE MAMMON, A swaggering, avaricious knight.

PERTINAX SURLY, A gambler and friend of Mammon.

ANANIAS, Deacon of a congregation of zealous English Puritans who have emigrated to Amsterdam; a violent fanatic, formerly a tailor.

TRIBULATION WHOLESOME, Pastor of the congregation.

KASTRIL, A gullible, well-to-do youth, come up to London from the country to learn how to be a city brawler.

DAME PLIANT, His sister, an attractive but stupid young widow of nineteen.

LOVEWIT, A prosperous London gentleman, master of Jeremy (alias Face) and owner of the house in Blackfriars where all the action takes place.

Neighbors, officers of the law, a parson.

SCENE: LOVEWIT's house in the Blackfriars district of London. Autumn, 1610.

The Argument

T he sickness hot,[1] a master quit, for fear,
H is house in town, and left one servant there.
E ase him corrupted, and gave means to know
A Cheater and his punk,[2] who now brought low,
L eaving their narrow practice, were become
C oz'ners[3] at large; and only wanting some
H ouse to set up, with him they here contract,
E ach for a share, and all begin to act.
M uch company they draw, and much abuse,
I n casting figures,[4] telling fortunes, news,
S elling of flies,[5] flat bawdry, with the stone;[6]
T ill it, and they, and all in fume[7] are gone.

Prologue

FORTUNE, that favors fools, these two short hours
We wish away, both for your sakes and ours,
Judging spectators; and desire in place,
To th' author justice, to ourselves but grace.
Our scene is London, 'cause we would make known,
No country's mirth is better than our own.

[1] Raging.
[2] Mistress, whore.
[3] Swindlers.
[4] Calculating horoscopes.
[5] Familiar spirits.
[6] Philosopher's stone.
[7] Smoke.

No clime breeds better matter for your whore,
  Bawd, squire,[8] imposter, many persons
    more,
Whose manners, now call'd humors, feed the
    stage;
  And which have still been subject for the
    rage
Or spleen of comic writers. Though this pen
  Did never aim to grieve, but better men,
Howe'er the age he lives in doth endure
  The vices that she breeds, above their cure.
But when the wholesome remedies are
  sweet,

And, in their working gain and profit
  meet,
He hopes to find no spirit so much diseas'd,
  But will with such fair correctives be
    pleas'd.
For here he doth not fear who can apply.
  If there be any that will sit so nigh
Unto the stream, to look what it doth run,
  They shall find things, they'd think, or
    wish, were done;
They are so natural follies, but so shown,
  As even the doers may see, and yet not
    own.

Act I

Scene I. *A Room in* Lovewit's *House.*

(*Enter* Face, *wearing a captain's uniform and* Subtle, *carrying a vial of chemical. They are quarreling violently.* Dol Common *follows them in*)

Face. Believe 't, I will.
Subtle. Thy worst. I fart at thee.
Dol Common. Ha' you your wits? Why, gentlemen! for love—
Face. Sirrah, I'll strip you—
Subtle. What to do? Lick figs
Out at my—
Face. Rogue, rogue!—out of all your sleights.[9]
Dol Common. Nay, look ye, sovereign, general, are you madmen?
Subtle. O, let the wild sheep loose. I'll gum your silks
With good strong water, an you come.
Dol Common. Will you have
The neighbors hear you? Will you betray all?
Hark! I hear somebody.
Face. Sirrah—
Subtle. I shall mar
All that the tailor has made, if you approach.
Face. You most notorious whelp, you insolent slave,
Dare you do this?
Subtle. Yes, faith; yes, faith.
Face. Why, who

Am I, my mongrel, who am I?
Subtle. I'll tell you,
Since you know not yourself.
Face. Speak lower, rogue.
Subtle. Yes. You were once (time's not long past) the good,
Honest, plain, livery-three-pound-thrum,[10] that kept
Your master's worship's house here in the Friars,
For the vacations—
Face. Will you be so loud?
Subtle. Since, by my means, translated suburb-captain.[11]
Face. By your means, doctor dog!
Subtle. Within man's memory,
All this I speak of.
Face. Why, I pray you, have I
Been countenanc'd by you, or you by me?
Do but 'collect, sir, where I met you first.
Subtle. I do not hear well.
Face. Not of this, I think it.
But I shall put you in mind, sir;—at Pie-corner,
Taking your meal of steam in, from cooks' stalls,
Where, like the father of hunger, you did walk
Piteously costive, with your pinch'd-horn-nose,
And your complexion of the Roman wash,

---

[8] Pander.   [9] Tricks.   [10] Under-paid drudge.   [11] Suburbs were low districts.

Stuck full of black and melancholic worms,
Like powder-corns shot at th' artillery-yard.

SUBTLE. I wish you could advance your
voice a little.

FACE. When you went pinn'd up in the
several rags
Y' had rak'd and pick'd from dunghills, be-
fore day;
Your feet in moldy slippers, for your kibes; [12]
A felt of rug, [13] and a thin threaden cloak,
That scarce would cover your no-buttocks—

SUBTLE. So, sir!

FACE. When all your alchemy, and your
algebra,
Your minerals, vegetals, and animals,
Your conjuring, coz'ning, and your dozen of
trades,
Could not relieve your corpse with so much
linen
Would make you tinder, but to see a fire;
I ga' you count'nance, credit for your coals,
Your stills, your glasses, your materials;
Built you a furnace, drew you customers,
Advanc'd all your black arts; lent you, beside,
A house to practise in—

SUBTLE. Your master's house!

FACE. Where you have studied the more
thriving skill
Of bawdry since.

SUBTLE. Yes, in your master's house.
You and the rats here kept possession.
Make it not strange. [14] I know you were one
could keep
The buttery-hatch still lock'd, and save the
chippings,
Sell the dole beer to aqua vitae men, [15]
The which, together with your Christmas
vails [16]
At post-and-pair, [17] your letting out of coun-
ters,
Made you a pretty stock, some twenty marks,
And gave you credit to converse with cob-
webs
Here, since your mistress' death hath broke
up house.

[12] Chilblains.
[13] Hat of coarse material.
[14] Do not pretend to forget.
[15] Doles of waste bread, or "chippings," and
beer were distributed to the poor from great
houses. Subtle accuses Face of selling the beer
to liquor-dealers.
[16] Tips.   [17] A card game.

FACE. You might talk softlier, rascal.

SUBTLE. No, you scarab,
I'll thunder you in pieces. I will teach you
How to beware to tempt a Fury again
That carries tempest in his hand and voice.

FACE. The place has made you valiant.

SUBTLE. No, your clothes.
Thou vermin, have I ta'en thee out of dung,
So poor, so wretched, when no living thing
Would keep thee company, but a spider or
worse?
Rais'd thee from brooms and dust and
wat'ring-pots?
Sublim'd thee, and exalted thee, and fix'd
thee
I' the third region, call'd our state of grace?
Wrought thee to spirit, to quintessence, [18]
with pains
Would twice have won me the philosopher's
work?
Put thee in words and fashion? made thee fit
For more than ordinary fellowships?
Giv'n thee thy oaths, thy quarrelling dimen-
sions? [19]
Thy rules to cheat at horse-race, cock-pit,
cards,
Dice, or whatever gallant tincture [20] else?
Made thee a second in mine own great art?
And have I this for thanks! Do you rebel?
Do you fly out i' the projection? [21]
Would you be gone now?

DOL COMMON. Gentlemen, what mean
you?
Will you mar all?

SUBTLE. Slave, thou hadst had no name—

DOL COMMON. Will you undo yourselves
with civil war?

SUBTLE. Never been known, past *equi
clibanum*,
The heat of horse-dung, under ground, in
cellars,
Or an ale-house darker than deaf John's;
been lost
To all mankind, but laundresses and tapsters,
Had not I been.

DOL COMMON. Do you know who hears
you, sovereign?

FACE. Sirrah—

[18] Technical terms in alchemy.
[19] Rules for conducting a quarrel.
[20] Accomplishment.
[21] When success is near.

DOL COMMON. Nay, general, I thought you were civil.

FACE. I shall turn desperate, if you grow thus loud.

SUBTLE. And hang thyself, I care not.

FACE. Hang thee, collier,
And all thy pots and pans, in picture I will,
Since thou hast mov'd me—

DOL COMMON. (Aside) O, this'll o'erthrow all.

FACE. Write thee up bawd in Paul's;[22] have all thy tricks
Of coz'ning with a hollow coal, dust, scrapings,
Searching for things lost, with a sieve and shears,
Erecting figures in your rows of houses,
And taking in of shadows with a glass,
Told in red letters; and a face cut for thee,
Worse than Gamaliel Ratsey's.[23]

DOL COMMON. Are you sound?
Ha' you your senses, masters?

FACE. I will have
A book, but barely reckoning thy impostures,
Shall prove a true philosopher's stone to printers.

SUBTLE. Away, you trencher-rascal!

FACE. Out, you dog-leech!
The vomit of all prisons—

DOL COMMON. Will you be
Your own destructions, gentlemen?

FACE. Still spew'd out
For lying too heavy o' the basket.[24]

SUBTLE. Cheater!

FACE. Bawd!

SUBTLE. Cow-herd!

FACE. Conjurer!

SUBTLE. Cutpurse!

FACE. Witch!

DOL COMMON. O me!
We are ruin'd! lost! Ha' you no more regard
To your reputations? Where's your judgment? 'Slight,
Have yet some care of me, o' your republic—

FACE. Away this brach! I'll bring thee, rogue, within
The statute of sorcery, tricesimo tertio

Of Harry the Eight:[25] ay, and perhaps thy neck
Within a noose, for laund'ring gold and barbing it.[26]

DOL COMMON. You'll bring your head within a coxcomb,[27] will you?
        (She catcheth out FACE his sword, and
                breaks SUBTLE's glass)
And you, sir, with your menstrue![28]—Gather it up.
'Sdeath, you abominable pair of stinkards,
Leave off your barking, and grow one again,
Or, by the light that shines, I'll cut your throats.
I'll not be made a prey unto the marshal
For ne'er a snarling dog-bolt o' you both.
Ha' you together cozen'd all this while,
And all the world, and shall it now be said,
You've made most courteous shift to cozen yourselves?
(To FACE) You will accuse him! You will "bring him in
Within the statute!" Who shall take your word?
A whoreson, upstart, apocryphal captain,
Whom not a Puritan in Blackfriars will trust
So much as for a feather! (To SUBTLE) And you, too,
Will give the cause, forsooth? You will insult,
And claim a primacy[29] in the divisions?
You must be chief? As if you only had
The powder to project with, and the work
Were not begun out of equality!
The venter tripartite![30] All things in common!
Without priority! 'Sdeath! you perpetual curs,
Fall to your couples again, and cozen kindly,
And heartily, and lovingly, as you should,
And lose not the beginning of a term,[31]
Or, by this hand, I shall grow factious too,
And take my part, and quit you.

[22] St. Paul's Cathedral, a place of resort for business and pleasure, where notices were often posted.

[23] A notorious highwayman, executed 1605, who wore a hideous mask.

[24] Eating more than his share of prison rations.

[25] The first law against witchcraft, 33 Henry VIII (i.e., 1541).

[26] Washing gold in acid; chipping coins.

[27] Fool's cap.

[28] A liquid which dissolves solids.

[29] First choice.

[30] Threefold agreement.

[31] I.e., one of the terms of the law courts, when ignorant country people came to town and the social season was at its height.

FACE. 'T is his fault;
He ever murmurs, and objects his pains,
And says the weight of all lies upon him.
SUBTLE. Why, so it does.
DOL COMMON. How does it? Do not we
Sustain our parts?
SUBTLE. Yes, but they are not equal.
DOL COMMON. Why, if your part exceed
to-day, I hope
Ours may to-morrow match it.
SUBTLE. Ay, they may.
DOL COMMON. May, murmuring mastiff?
Ay, and do.
Death on me! Help me to throttle him.
(Seizes SUBTLE by the throat)
SUBTLE. Dorothy! Mistress Dorothy!
'Ods precious, I'll do anything. What do you
mean?
DOL COMMON. Because o' your fermenta-
tion and cibation? [32]
SUBTLE. Not I, by heaven—
DOL COMMON. Your Sol and Luna [33]—
(To FACE) Help me.
SUBTLE. Would I were hang'd then! I'll
conform myself.
DOL COMMON. Will you, sir? Do so then,
and quickly: swear.
SUBTLE. What should I swear?
DOL COMMON. To leave your faction, sir,
And labor kindly in the common work.
SUBTLE. Let me not breathe if I meant
aught beside.
I only used those speeches as a spur
To him.
DOL COMMON. I hope we need no spurs,
sir. Do we?
FACE. 'Slid, prove to-day who shall shark
best.
SUBTLE. Agreed.
DOL COMMON. Yes, and work close and
friendly.
SUBTLE. 'Slight, the knot
Shall grow the stronger for this breach, with
me. (They shake hands)
DOL COMMON. Why, so, my good ba-
boons! Shall we go make
A sort of sober, scurvy, precise neighbors,
That scarce have smil'd twice sin' the king
came in,
A feast of laughter at our follies? Rascals,

Would run themselves from breath, to see
me ride, [34]
Or you t' have but a hole to thrust your heads
in, [35]
For which you should pay ear-rent? [36] No,
agree.
And may Don Provost [37] ride a-feasting long,
In his old velvet jerkin and stain'd scarfs,
My noble sovereign, and worthy general,
Ere we contribute a new crewel garter
To his most worsted worship.
SUBTLE. Royal Dol!
Spoken like Claridiana, and thyself.
FACE. For which, at supper, thou shalt sit
in triumph,
And not be styl'd Dol Common, but Dol
Proper,
Dol Singular; the longest cut at night
Shall draw thee for his Dol Particular.
(Bell rings without)
SUBTLE. Who's that? One rings. To the
window, Dol!—
Pray heav'n
The master do not trouble us this quarter.
FACE. O, fear not him. While there dies
one a week
O' the plague, he's safe from thinking toward
London.
Beside, he's busy at his hop-yards now;
I had a letter from him. If he do,
He'll send such word, for airing o' the house,
As you shall have sufficient time to quit it.
Though we break up a fortnight, 't is no
matter.
SUBTLE. Who is it, Dol?
DOL COMMON. A fine young quodling.
FACE. O,
My lawyer's clerk, I lighted on last night,
In Holborn, at the Dagger. He would have
(I told you of him) a familiar, [38]
To rifle [39] with at horses, and win cups.
DOL COMMON. O, let him in.
SUBTLE. Stay. Who shall do 't?
FACE. Get you
Your robes on; I will meet him, as going out.

[32] Processes in alchemy.
[33] Gold and silver.
[34] I.e., on a cart, a punishment for whores.
[35] The pillory.
[36] Have your ears cut off; a police court punishment.
[37] The hangman, who got the clothes of executed criminals.
[38] Familiar spirit, "fly."
[39] Gamble.

Dol Common. And what shall I do?
Face. Not be seen; away!

(*Exit* Dol Common)

Seem you very reserv'd.
   Subtle. Enough.   (*Exit*)

Face. (*In a loud voice as he goes to the door*) God be wi' you, sir.
I pray you, let him know that I was here:
His name is Dapper. I would gladly have
stay'd, but—

SCENE II. *The Same.*

Dapper. (*Within*) Captain, I am here.
Face. Who's that?—He's come, I think,
   Doctor.   (Face *admits* Dapper)
Good faith, sir, I was going away.
   Dapper. In truth,
I'm very sorry, Captain.
   Face. But I thought
Sure I should meet you.
   Dapper. Ay, I'm very glad.
I had a scurvy writ or two to make,
And I had lent my watch last night to one
That dines to-day at the shrieve's,[40] and so
      was robbed
Of my pass-time.

(*Re-enter* Subtle *in his velvet cap and
         gown*)

Is this the cunning-man?
   Face. This is his worship.
   Dapper. Is he a doctor?
   Face. Yes.
   Dapper. And ha' you broke[41] with him,
Captain?
   Face. Ay.
   Dapper. And how?
   Face. Faith, he does make the matter, sir,
      so dainty,
I know not what to say.
   Dapper. Not so, good Captain.
   Face. Would I were fairly rid on 't,
believe me.
   Dapper. Nay, now you grieve me, sir.
      Why should you wish so?
I dare assure you, I'll not be ungrateful.
   Face. I cannot think you will, sir. But the
      law
Is such a thing—and then he says, Read's[42]
      matter
Falling so lately—

Dapper. Read! he was an ass,
And dealt, sir, with a fool.
   Face. It was a clerk,[43] sir.
   Dapper. A clerk!
   Face. Nay, hear me, sir. You know the
      law
Better, I think—
   Dapper. I should, sir, and the danger:
You know, I show'd the statute to you.
   Face. You did so.
   Dapper. And will I tell then! By this hand
      of flesh,
Would it might never write good courthand
      more,
If I discover. What do you think of me,
That I am a chiaus?
   Face. What's that?
   Dapper. The Turk was here.
As one would say, do you think I am a Turk?
   Face. I'll tell the Doctor so.
   Dapper. Do, good sweet Captain.
   Face. Come, noble Doctor, pray thee, let's
      prevail;
This is the gentleman, and he is no chiaus.
   Subtle. Captain, I have return'd you all
      my answer.
I would do much, sir, for your love—But
      this
I neither may, nor can.
   Face. Tut, do not say so.
You deal now with a noble fellow, Doctor,
One that will thank you richly; and he's no
      chiaus.
Let that, sir, move you.
   Subtle. Pray you, forbear—
   Face. He has
Four angels[44] here.
   Subtle. You do me wrong, good sir.
   Face. Doctor, wherein? To tempt you
with these spirits?

---

[40] Sheriff's.
[41] Broached the subject.
[42] A magician indicted in 1608.

[43] Read had dealt with a law clerk (like Dapper) named Tobias Matthews.
[44] Gold coins.

SUBTLE. To tempt my art and love, sir,
  to my peril.
'Fore heav'n, I scarce can think you are my
  friend,
That so would draw me to apparent danger.
  FACE. I draw you! A horse draw you, and
  a halter,
You, and your flies together—
  DAPPER. Nay, good Captain.
  FACE. That know no difference of men.
  SUBTLE. Good words, sir.
  FACE. Good deeds, sir, Doctor Dogs'-meat.
  'Slight, I bring you
No cheating Clim o' the Cloughs or Claribels,
That look as big as five-and-fifty, and flush; [45]
And spit out secrets like hot custard—
  DAPPER. Captain!
  FACE. Nor any melancholic underscribe,
Shall tell the vicar; but a special gentle, [46]
That is the heir to forty marks a year,
Consorts with the small poets of the time,
Is the sole hope of his old grandmother;
That knows the law, and writes you six fair
  hands, [47]
Is a fine clerk, and has his ciph'ring perfect;
Will take his oath o' the Greek Xenophon,
If need be, in his pocket; and can court
His mistress out of Ovid.
  DAPPER. Nay, dear Captain—
  FACE. Did you not tell me so?
  DAPPER. Yes; but I'd ha' you
Use Master Doctor with some more respect.
  FACE. Hang him, proud stag, with his
  broad velvet head!—
But for your sake, I'd choke ere I would
  change
An article of breath with such a puck-fist!
Come, let's be gone.   (Going)
  SUBTLE. Pray you, le' me speak with you.
  DAPPER. His worship calls you, Captain.
  FACE. I am sorry
I e'er embark'd myself in such a business.
  DAPPER. Nay, good sir; he did call you.
  FACE. Will he take then?
  SUBTLE. First, hear me—
  FACE. Not a syllable, 'less you take.
  SUBTLE. Pray ye, sir—

  FACE. Upon no terms but an *assumpsit.* [48]
  SUBTLE. Your humor must be law.
                  (He takes the money)
  FACE. Why now, sir, talk.
Now I dare hear you with mine honor.
  Speak.
So may this gentleman too.
  SUBTLE. Why, sir—
          (Offering to whisper to FACE)
  FACE. No whisp'ring.
  SUBTLE. 'Fore heav'n, you do not appre-
  hend the loss
You do yourself in this.
  FACE. Wherein? for what?
  SUBTLE. Marry, to be so importunate for
  one
That, when he has it, will undo you all:
He'll win up all the money i' the town.
  FACE. How!
  SUBTLE. Yes, and blow up gamester after
  gamester,
As they do crackers in a puppet-play.
If I do give him a familiar,
Give you him all you play for; never set
  him, [49]
For he will have it.
  FACE. You're mistaken, Doctor.
Why, he does ask one but for cups and horses,
A rifling fly; none o' your great familiars.
  DAPPER. Yes, Captain, I would have it for
all games.
  SUBTLE. I told you so.
  FACE. (Taking DAPPER aside) 'Slight,
  that's a new business!
I understood you, a tame bird, to fly
Twice in a term, or so, on Friday nights,
When you had left the office, for a nag
Of forty or fifty shillings.
  DAPPER. Ay, 'tis true, sir;
But I do think, now, I shall leave the law,
And therefore—
  FACE. Why, this changes quite the case!
D' you think that I dare move him?
  DAPPER. If you please, sir;
All's one to him, I see.
  FACE. What! for that money?
I cannot with my conscience; nor should you
Make the request, methinks.
  DAPPER. No, sir, I mean

---

[45] Winning hands in the game of primero.
[46] Gentleman.
[47] Professional scribes like Dapper cultivated
several different handwritings for use in various
types of documents.

[48] He has taken the money and undertaken
the affair (legal term).
[49] Bet against him.

To add consideration.

FACE. Why, then, sir,

I'll try. (*Goes to* SUBTLE) Say that it were
    for all games, Doctor?

SUBTLE. I say then, not a mouth shall eat
    for him

At any ordinary, but o' the score,[50]

That is a gaming mouth, conceive me.

FACE. Indeed!

SUBTLE. He'll draw you all the treasure
    of the realm,

If it be set him.

FACE. Speak you this from art?

SUBTLE. Ay, sir, and reason too, the
    ground of art.

He's o' the only best complexion,

The queen of Faery loves.

FACE. What! Is he?

SUBTLE. Peace.

He'll overhear you. Sir, should she but see
    him—

FACE. What?

SUBTLE. Do not you tell him.

FACE. Will he win at cards too?

SUBTLE. The spirits of dead Holland,
    living Isaac,

You'd swear, were in him; such a vigorous
    luck

As cannot be resisted. 'Slight, he'll put

Six o' your gallants to a cloak, indeed.

FACE. A strange success, that some man
    shall be born to!

SUBTLE. He hears you, man—

DAPPER. Sir, I'll not be ingrateful.

FACE. Faith, I have a confidence in his
    good nature:

You hear, he says he will not be ingrateful.

SUBTLE. Why, as you please; my venture
follows yours.

FACE. Troth, do it, Doctor; think him
    trusty, and make him.

He may make us both happy in an hour;

Win some five thousand pound, and send
    us two on't.

DAPPER. Believe it, and I will, sir.

FACE. And you shall, sir.

You have heard all? (FACE *takes him aside*)

DAPPER. No, what was't? Nothing, I, sir.

FACE. Nothing?

DAPPER. A little, sir.

FACE. Well, a rare star

Reign'd at your birth.

[50] On credit.

DAPPER. At mine, sir! No.

FACE. The Doctor

Swears that you are—

SUBTLE. Nay, Captain, you'll tell all now.

FACE. Allied to the queen of Faery.

DAPPER. Who! That I am?

Believe it, no such matter—

FACE. Yes, and that

You were born with a caul o' your head.

DAPPER. Who says so?

FACE. Come,

You know it well enough, though you dissemble it.

DAPPER. I' fac, I do not; you are mistaken.

FACE. How!

Swear by your fac, and in a thing so known

Unto the Doctor? How shall we, sir, trust
    you

I' the other matter? Can we ever think,

When you have won five or six thousand
    pound,

You'll send us shares in 't, by this rate?

DAPPER. By Jove, sir,

I'll win ten thousand pound, and send you
    half.

I' fac's no oath.

SUBTLE. No, no, he did but jest.

FACE. Go to. Go thank the Doctor. He's
    your friend,

To take it so.

DAPPER. I thank his worship.

FACE. So!

Another angel.

DAPPER. Must I?

FACE. Must you! 'Slight,

What else is thanks? Will you be trivial?—

(DAPPER *gives him the money*) Doctor,

When must he come for his familiar?

DAPPER. Shall I not ha' it with me?

SUBTLE. O, good sir!

There must a world of ceremonies pass;

You must be bath'd and fumigated first;

Besides, the queen of Faery does not rise

Till it be noon.

FACE. Not if she danc'd to-night.

SUBTLE. And she must bless it.

FACE. Did you never see

Her Royal Grace yet?

DAPPER. Whom?

FACE. Your aunt of Faery?

SUBTLE. Not since she kiss'd him in the
cradle, Captain; I can resolve you that.

FACE. Well, see her Grace,

Whate'er it cost you, for a thing that I know.
It will be somewhat hard to compass; but
However, see her. You are made, believe it,
If you can see her. Her Grace is a lone
  woman,
And very rich; and if she take a fancy,
She will do strange things. See her, at any
  hand.
'Slid, she may hap to leave you all she has!
It is the Doctor's fear.
  DAPPER. How will't be done, then?
  FACE. Let me alone, take you no thought.
  Do you
But say to me, "Captain, I'll see her Grace."
  DAPPER. "Captain. I'll see her Grace."
  FACE. Enough.   (One knocks without)
  SUBTLE. Who's there?
Anon!—(Aside to FACE) Conduct him forth
  by the back way.—

Sir, against one o'clock prepare yourself;
Till when, you must be fasting; only, take
Three drops of vinegar in at your nose,
Two at your mouth, and one at either ear;
Then bathe your fingers' ends and wash your
  eyes,
To sharpen your five senses, and cry "hum"
Thrice, and then "buz" as often; and then
  come.   (Exit)
  FACE. Can you remember this?
  DAPPER. I warrant you.
  FACE. Well then, away. 'Tis but your
  bestowing
Some twenty nobles [51] 'mong her Grace's
  servants,
And put on a clean shirt. You do not know
What grace her Grace may do you in clean
  linen.   (Exeunt FACE and DAPPER)

SCENE III. *The Same.*

SUBTLE. (*Within, as if to other clients*)
  Come in! Good wives, I pray you, for-
  bear me now;
Troth, I can do you no good till afternoon.—

(*Enter* SUBTLE, *followed by* DRUGGER)

What is your name, say you? Abel Drugger?
  DRUGGER. Yes, sir.
  SUBTLE. A seller of tobacco?
  DRUGGER. Yes, sir.
  SUBTLE. Umph!
Free [52] of the Grocers?
  DRUGGER. Ay, an't please you.
  SUBTLE. Well—
Your business, Abel?
  DRUGGER. This, an't please your worship:
I am a young beginner, and am building
Of a new shop, an't like your worship, just
At corner of a street.—Here's the plot on 't—
And I would know by art, sir, of your
  worship,
Which way I should make my door, by
  necromancy,
And where my shelves; and which should
  be for boxes,
And which for pots. I would be glad to
  thrive, sir;

And I was wish'd to your worship by a gentle-
  man,
One Captain Face, that says you know men's
  planets,
And their good angels, and their bad.
  SUBTLE. I do,
If I do see 'em—

(*Enter* FACE)

  FACE. What! my honest Abel?
Thou art well met here.
  DRUGGER. Troth, sir, I was speaking,
Just as your worship came here, of your wor-
  ship.
I pray you, speak for me to Master Doctor.
  FACE. He shall do anything. Doctor, do
  you hear?
This is my friend, Abel, an honest fellow;
He lets me have good tobacco, and he does
  not
Sophisticate it with sack-lees or oil,
Nor washes it in muscadel and grains, [53]
Nor buries it in gravel, under ground,
Wrapp'd up in greasy leather, or piss'd clouts,
But keeps it in fine lily pots that, open'd,
Smell like conserve of roses, or French beans.
He has his maple block, his silver tongs,
Winchester pipes, and fire of juniper:

[51] Coins worth 6s. 8d.   [52] A member of the Grocers' Company.   [53] A kind of spice.

A neat, spruce, honest fellow, and no gold-
    smith.[54]

Subtle. He's a fortunate fellow, that I
am sure on.

Face. Already, sir, ha' you found it? Lo
thee, Abel!

Subtle. And in right way toward riches—

Face. Sir!

Subtle. This summer
He will be of the clothing[55] of his company,
And next spring call'd to the scarlet,[56] spend
what he can.

Face. What, and so little beard?

Subtle. Sir, you must think,
He may have a receipt to make hair come.
But he'll be wise, preserve his youth, and
    fine[57] for 't;
His fortune looks for him another way.

Face. 'Slid, Doctor, how canst thou know
    this so soon?
I am amus'd[58] at that.

Subtle. By a rule, Captain,
In metoposcopy,[59] which I do work by;
A certain star i' the forehead, which you see
    not.
Your chestnut or your olive-color'd face
Does never fail, and your long ear doth
    promise.
I knew 't by certain spots, too, in his teeth,
And on the nail of his mercurial finger.

Face. Which finger's that?

Subtle. His little finger. Look.
You were born upon a Wednesday?

Drugger. Yes, indeed, sir.

Subtle. The thumb, in chiromancy, we
    give Venus;
The forefinger to Jove; the midst to Saturn;
The ring to Sol; the least to Mercury,
Who was the lord, sir, of his horoscope,
His house of life being Libra; which fore-
    show'd
He should be a merchant, and should trade
    with balance.

Face. Why, this is strange! Is't not, honest
Nab?

Subtle. There is a ship now coming from
    Ormus,

That shall yield him such a commodity
Of drugs—This is the west, and this the
    south?

                    (*Pointing to the plan*)

Drugger. Yes, sir.

Subtle. And those are your two sides?

Drugger. Ay, sir.

Subtle. Make me your door then, south;
    your broad side, west;
And on the east side of your shop, aloft,
Write Mathlai, Tarmiel, and Baraborat;
Upon the north part, Rael, Velel, Thiel.
They are the names of those Mercurial spirits
That do fright flies from boxes.

Drugger. Yes, sir.

Subtle. And
Beneath your threshold, bury me a loadstone
To draw in gallants that wear spurs; the rest,
They'll seem[60] to follow.

Face. That's a secret, Nab!

Subtle. And, on your stall, a puppet,
    with a vice,[61]
And a court-fucus,[62] to call city-dames.
You shall deal much with minerals.

Drugger. Sir, I have,
At home, already—

Subtle. Ay, I know, you've arsenic,
Vitriol, sal-tartar, argaile, alkali,
Cinoper: I know all.—This fellow, Captain,
Will come, in time, to be a great distiller,
And give a say[63]—I will not say directly,
But very fair—at the philosopher's stone.

Face. Why, how now, Abel! is this true?

Drugger. (*Aside to* Face) Good Captain,
What must I give?

Face. Nay, I'll not counsel thee.
Thou hear'st what wealth (he says, spend
    what thou canst)
Th' art like to come to.

Drugger. I would gi' him a crown.

Face. A crown! and toward such a for-
    tune? Heart,
Thou shalt rather gi' him thy shop. No gold
    about thee?

Drugger. Yes, I have a portague, I ha'
kept this half-year.

Face. Out on thee, Nab! 'Slight, there
    was such an offer—

---

[54] Usurer.
[55] Wear the livery.
[56] Made sheriff.
[57] Pay the fine for declining to serve as sheriff.
[58] Amazed, made to muse.
[59] A branch of physiognomy.

[60] Think it seemly.
[61] Mechanical figure.
[62] Cosmetic.
[63] Make an attempt.

Shalt keep 't no longer, I'll gi' it him for thee.
Doctor,
Nab prays your worship to drink this, and
swears
He will appear more grateful, as your skill
Does raise him in the world.
DRUGGER. I would entreat
Another favor of his worship.
FACE. What is't, Nab?
DRUGGER. But to look over, sir, my al-
manac,
And cross out my ill-days, that I may neither
Bargain, nor trust upon them.
FACE. That he shall, Nab.
Leave it, it shall be done, 'gainst afternoon.
SUBTLE. And a direction for his shelves.
FACE. Now, Nab,
Art thou well pleas'd, Nab?

DRUGGER. 'Thank, sir, both your worships.
FACE. Away. (*Exit* DRUGGER)
Why, now, you smoky persecutor of nature!
Now do you see, that something's to be done,
Beside your beech-coal, and your cor'sive
waters,
Your crosslets, crucibles, and cucurbites? [64]
You must have stuff brought home to you,
to work on!
And yet you think I am at no expense
In searching out these veins, then following
'em,
Then trying 'em out. 'Fore God, my intelli-
gence
Costs me more money than my share oft
comes to,
In these rare works.
SUBTLE. You're pleasant, sir.—How now!

SCENE IV. *The Same.*

(*Enter* DOL COMMON)

SUBTLE. What says my dainty Dolkin?
DOL COMMON. Yonder fish-wife
Will not away. And there's your giantess,
The bawd of Lambeth.
SUBTLE. Heart, I cannot speak with 'em.
DOL COMMON. Not afore night, I have
told 'em in a voice,
Thorough the trunk,[65] like one of your
familiars.
But I have spied Sir Epicure Mammon—
SUBTLE. Where?
DOL COMMON. Coming along, at far end
of the lane,
Slow of his feet, but earnest of his tongue
To one that's with him.
SUBTLE. Face, go you and shift.
Dol, you must presently make ready too.
(*Exit* FACE)
DOL COMMON. Why, what's the matter?
SUBTLE. O, I did look for him
With the sun's rising: marvel he could sleep!

This is the day I am to perfect for him
The magisterium, our great work, the stone;
And yield it, made, into his hands; of which
He has, this month, talk'd as he were pos-
sess'd.
And now he's dealing pieces on 't away.
Methinks I see him ent'ring ordinaries,
Dispensing for the pox, and plaguy houses,
Reaching his dose, walking Moorfields for
lepers,
And off'ring citizens' wives pomander-brace-
lets [66]
As his preservative, made of the elixir;
Searching the 'spital, to make old bawds
young;
And the highways, for beggars to make rich.
I see no end of his labors. He will make
Nature asham'd of her long sleep; when art,
Who's but a step-dame, shall do more than
she,
In her best love to mankind, ever could.
If his dream last, he'll turn the age to gold.
(*Exeunt*)

[64] Glass vessels used in alchemy.
[65] Speaking-tube.

[66] A perfume ball supposed to protect the
wearer from infection.

Act II

Scene I. *A Room in* Lovewit's *House.*

(*Enter* Sir Epicure Mammon *and* Surly)

Mammon. Come on, sir. Now you set
    your foot on shore
In *Novo Orbe;* here's the rich Peru,
And there within, sir, are the golden mines,
Great Solomon's Ophir! He was sailing to 't
Three years, but we have reach'd it in ten
    months.
This is the day wherein, to all my friends,
I will pronounce the happy word, *Be rich;*
This day you shall be spectatissimi.
You shall no more deal with the hollow die,[67]
Or the frail card; no more be at charge of
    keeping
The livery-punk [68] for the young heir, that
    must
Seal,[69] at all hours, in his shirt: no more,
If he deny, ha' him beaten to 't, as he is
That brings him the commodity; [70] no more
Shall thirst of satin, or the covetous hunger
Of velvet entrails [71] for a rude-spun cloak,
To be display'd at Madam Augusta's, make
The sons of Sword and Hazard fall before
The golden calf, and on their knees, whole
    nights,
Commit idolatry with wine and trumpets,
Or go a-feasting after drum and ensign.
No more of this. You shall start up young
    viceroys,
And have your punks and punkettees, my
    Surly.
And unto thee I speak it first, *be rich.*
Where is my Subtle there? Within, ho!
    Face. (*Within*) Sir,
He'll come to you by and by.
    Mammon. That's his fire-drake,
His Lungs, his Zephyrus, he that puffs his
    coals,

[67] Loaded dice.
[68] Prostitute-accomplice of a swindler.
[69] Seal a bond, in favor of the swindlers.
[70] Elizabethan loan sharks often gave borrowers merchandise, or "commodity," instead of cash. The borrower then found that he must sell the goods at a heavy loss.
[71] Lining.

Till he firk nature up, in her own center.
You are not faithful,[72] sir. This night I'll
    change
All that is metal in my house to gold,
And, early in the morning, will I send
To all the plumbers and the pewterers
And buy their tin and lead up; and to Loth-
    bury
For all the copper.
    Surly. What, and turn that, too?
    Mammon. Yes, and I'll purchase Devon-
    shire and Cornwall,
And make them perfect Indies! You admire [73]
    now?
    Surly. No, faith.
    Mammon. But when you see th' effects of
    the Great Med'cine,
Of which one part projected on a hundred
Of Mercury, or Venus,[74] or the Moon,[75]
Shall turn it to as many of the Sun; [76]
Nay, to a thousand, so *ad infinitum:*
You will believe me.
    Surly. Yes, when I see 't, I will.
But if my eyes do cozen me so, and I
Giving 'em no occasion, sure I'll have
A whore, shall piss 'em out next day.
    Mammon. Ha! why?
Do you think I fable with you? I assure you,
He that has once the flower of the sun,
The perfect ruby, which we call elixir,
Not only can do that, but by its virtue,
Can confer honor, love, respect, long life;
Give safety, valor, yea, and victory,
To whom he will. In eight-and-twenty days,
I'll make an old man of fourscore a child.
    Surly. No doubt: he's that already.
    Mammon. Nay, I mean,
Restore his years, renew him, like an eagle,
To the fifth age; make him get sons and
    daughters,
Young giants; as our philosophers have done,

[72] A believer.
[73] Wonder.
[74] Copper.
[75] Silver.
[76] Gold.

The ancient patriarchs, afore the flood,
But taking, once a week, on a knife's point,
The quantity of a grain of mustard of it;
Become stout Marses, and beget young
    Cupids.
    SURLY. The decay'd vestals of Pickt-
    hatch [77] would thank you,
That keep the fire alive there.
    MAMMON. 'Tis the secret
Of nature naturiz'd 'gainst all infections,
Cures all diseases coming of all causes;
A month's grief in a day, a year's in twelve;
And, of what age soever, in a month,
Past all the doses of your drugging doctors.
I'll undertake, withal, to fright the plague
Out o' the kingdom in three months.
    SURLY. And I'll
Be bound, the players [78] shall sing your
    praises then,
Without their poets.
    MAMMON. Sir, I'll do 't. Meantime,
I'll give away so much unto my man,
Shall serve th' whole city with preservative
Weekly; each house his dose, and at the
    rate—
    SURLY. As he that built the Water-work
does with water?
    MAMMON. You are incredulous.
    SURLY. Faith, I have a humor,
I would not willingly be gull'd. Your stone
Cannot transmute me.
    MAMMON. Pertinax Surly,
Will you believe antiquity? Records?
I'll show you a book where Moses, and his
    sister,
And Solomon have written of the art;

Ay, and a treatise penn'd by Adam—
    SURLY. How!
    MAMMON. O' the philosopher's stone, and
in High Dutch. [79]
    SURLY. Did Adam write, sir, in High
Dutch?
    MAMMON. He did;
Which proves it was the primitive tongue.
    SURLY. What paper?
    MAMMON. On cedar board.
    SURLY. O that, indeed, they say,
Will last 'gainst worms.
    MAMMON. 'Tis like your Irish wood
'Gainst cobwebs. I have a piece of Jason's
    fleece too,
Which was no other than a book of alchemy,
Writ in large sheepskin, a good fat ram-
    vellum.
Such was Pythagoras' thigh, Pandora's tub,
And all that fable of Medea's charms,
The manner of our work; the bulls, our
    furnace,
Still breathing fire; our *argent-vive,* [80] the
    dragon;
The dragon's teeth, mercury sublimate,
That keeps the whiteness, hardness, and the
    biting;
And they are gather'd into Jason's helm,
Th' alembic, and then sow'd in Mars his field,
And thence sublim'd so often, till they're
    fix'd.
Both this, th' Hesperian garden, Cadmus'
    story,
Jove's shower, the boon of Midas, Argus' eyes,
Boccace his Demogorgon, thousands more,
All abstract riddles of our stone.—How now!

SCENE II. *The Same.*

(*Enter* FACE, *now disguised as* SUBTLE's
laboratory assistant and called LUNGS *or*
ULEN SPIEGEL)

    MAMMON. Do we succeed? Is our day
come? And holds it?
    FACE. The evening will set red upon you,
    sir;

You have color for it, crimson: the red fer-
    ment
Has done his office; three hours hence pre-
    pare you
To see projection.
    MAMMON. Pertinax, my Surly,
Again I say to thee, aloud, *be rich.*
This day thou shalt have ingots; and tomor-
    row

---

[77] A resort of prostitutes and pick-pockets.
[78] Since the theatres were closed by law during visitations of the plague, the players lost
their livelihood. They were therefore especially
concerned about the plague.

[79] These and most of the following absurdities
can be found in the crack-pot literature of the
time. Jonson satirizes; he does not invent.
[80] Quicksilver.

Give lords th' affront.—Is it, my Zephyrus,
   right?
Blushes the bolt's-head? [81]
   FACE. Like a wench with child, sir,
That were but now discover'd to her master.
   MAMMON. Excellent witty Lungs!—My
      only care is
Where to get stuff enough now, to project on;
This town will not half serve me.
   FACE. No, sir? Buy
The covering off o' churches.
   MAMMON. That's true.
   FACE. Yes.
Let 'em stand bare, as do their auditory;
Or cap 'em new with shingles.
   MAMMON. No, good thatch:
Thatch will lie light upo' the rafters, Lungs.
Lungs, I will manumit thee from the furnace;
I will restore thee thy complexion, Puff,
Lost in the embers; and repair this brain,
Hurt wi' the fume o' the metals.
   FACE. I have blown, sir,
Hard, for your worship; thrown by many a
   coal,
When 't was not beech; weigh'd those I put
   in, just,
To keep your heat still even. These blear'd
   eyes
Have wak'd to read your several colors, sir,
Of the pale citron, the green lion, the crow,
The peacock's tail, the plumed swan.
   MAMMON. And lastly,
Thou hast descried the flower, the *sanguis
   agni?*
   FACE. Yes, sir.
   MAMMON. Where's master?
   FACE. At's prayers, sir, he;
Good man, he's doing his devotions
For the success.
   MAMMON. Lungs, I will set a period
To all thy labors; thou shalt be the master
Of my seraglio.
   FACE. Good, sir.
   MAMMON. But do you hear?
I'll geld you, Lungs.
   FACE. Yes, sir.
   MAMMON. For I do mean
To have a list of wives and concubines
Equal with Solomon, who had the stone
Alike with me; and I will make me a back
With the elixir, that shall be as tough

[81] A kind of flask.

As Hercules, to encounter fifty a night.—
Th'art sure thou saw'st it blood?
   FACE. Both blood and spirit, sir.
   MAMMON. I will have all my beds blown
      up, not stuff'd:
Down is too hard; and then, mine oval room
Fill'd with such pictures as Tiberius took
From Elephantis, and dull Aretine
But coldly imitated. Then, my glasses
Cut in more subtle angles, to disperse
And multiply the figures, as I walk
Naked between my succubæ. My mists
I'll have of perfume, vapor'd 'bout the room,
To lose our selves in; and my baths, like pits
To fall into; from whence we will come forth,
And roll us dry in gossamer and roses.—
Is it arrived at ruby?—Where I spy
A wealthy citizen, or rich lawyer,
Have a sublim'd pure wife, unto that fellow
I'll send a thousand pound to be my cuckold.
   FACE. And I shall carry it?
   MAMMON. No, I'll ha' no bawds
But fathers and mothers: they will do it best,
Best of all others. And my flatterers
Shall be the pure, and gravest of divines
That I can get for money. My mere fools,
Eloquent burgesses, and then my poets
The same that writ so subtly of the fart,
Whom I will entertain still for that subject.
The few that would give out themselves to
   be
Court- and town-stallions, and, each-where,
   bely
Ladies who are known most innocent, for
   them,—
These will I beg, to make me eunuchs of,
And they shall fan me with ten estrich tails
Apiece, made in a plume to gather wind.
We will be brave, Puff, now we ha' the
   med'cine.
My meat shall all come in, in Indian shells,
Dishes of agate set in gold, and studded
With emeralds, sapphires, hyacinths, and
   rubies.
The tongues of carps, dormice, and camels'
   heels,
Boil'd i' the spirit of Sol, and dissolv'd pearl
(Apicius' diet, 'gainst the epilepsy):
And I will eat these broths with spoons of
   amber,
Headed with diamond and carbuncle.
My foot-boy shall eat pheasants, calver'd
   salmons,

Knots,[82] godwits,[83] lampreys. I myself will have
The beards of barbels[84] serv'd instead of salads;
Oil'd mushrooms; and the swelling unctuous paps
Of a fat pregnant sow, newly cut off,
Dress'd with an exquisite and poignant sauce;
For which, I'll say unto my cook, *There's gold;*
Go forth, and be a knight.[85]

FACE. Sir, I'll go look
A little, how it heightens.   (*Exit*)

MAMMON. Do.—My shirts
I'll have of taffeta-sarsnet, soft and light
As cobwebs; and for all my other raiment,
It shall be such as might provoke the Persian,
Were he to teach the world riot anew.
My gloves of fishes and birds' skins, perfum'd
With gums of paradise, and Eastern air—

SURLY. And do you think to have the stone with this?

MAMMON. No, I do think t' have all this with the stone.

SURLY. Why, I have heard he must be *homo frugi,*
A pious, holy, and religious man,
One free from mortal sin, a very virgin.

MAMMON. That makes it, sir; he is so.
But I buy it;
My venture brings it me. He, honest wretch,
A notable, superstitious, good soul,
Has worn his knees bare and his slippers bald
With prayer and fasting for it. And, sir, let him
Do it alone, for me, still. Here he comes.
Not a profane word afore him; 't is poison.—

SCENE III. *The Same.*

(*Enter* SUBTLE)

MAMMON. Good morrow, father.

SUBTLE. Gentle son, good morrow,
And to your friend there. What is he is with you?

MAMMON. An heretic, that I did bring along,
In hope, sir, to convert him.

SUBTLE. Son, I doubt[86]
You're covetous, that thus you meet your time
I' the just point, prevent[87] your day at morning.
This argues something worthy of a fear
Of importune and carnal appetite.
Take heed you do not cause the blessing leave you,
With your ungovern'd haste. I should be sorry
To see my labors, now e'en at perfection,
Got by long watching and large patience,

Not prosper where my love and zeal hath plac'd 'em:
Which (heaven I call to witness, with your self,
To whom I have pour'd my thoughts) in all my ends,
Have look'd no way, but unto public good,
To pious uses, and dear charity,
Now grown a prodigy with men. Wherein
If you, my son, should now prevaricate,
And to your own particular lusts employ
So great and catholic a bliss, be sure
A curse will follow, yea, and overtake
Your subtle and most secret ways.

MAMMON. I know, sir;
You shall not need to fear me; I but come
To ha' you confute this gentleman.

SURLY. Who is,
Indeed, sir, somewhat costive of belief
Toward your stone; would not be gull'd.

SUBTLE. Well, son,
All that I can convince him in, is this,
The work is done, bright Sol is in his robe.
We have a med'cine of the triple soul,
The glorified spirit.[88] Thanks be to heaven,
And make us worthy of it!—
                              (*Calling to* FACE)

---

[82] A kind of snipe.

[83] Marsh birds.

[84] Fresh-water fish.

[85] A sly dig at King James' wholesale creation of undeserving knights.

[86] Fear.

[87] Anticipate.

[88] *I.e.*, the philosopher's stone.

Ulen Spiegel![89]

FACE. (*Within*) Anon, sir.

SUBTLE. Look well to the register,
And let your heat still lessen by degrees,
To the aludels.[90]

FACE. (*Within*) Yes, sir.

SUBTLE. Did you look
O' the bolt's-head yet?

FACE. (*Within*) Which? On D, sir?

SUBTLE. Ay;
What's the complexion?

FACE. (*Within*) Whitish.

SUBTLE. Infuse vinegar,
To draw his volatile substance and his tinc-
ture,
And let the water in glass E be filt'red,
And put into the gripe's egg. Lute him well;
And leave him clos'd *in balneo.*

FACE. (*Within*) I will, sir.

SURLY. (*Aside*) What a brave language
here is! next to canting![91]

SUBTLE. I have another work you never
saw, son,
That three days since passed the philosopher's
wheel,
In the lent heat of Athanor; and 's become
Sulphur o' Nature.

MAMMON. But 'tis for me?

SUBTLE. What need you?
You have enough, in that is, perfect.

MAMMON. O, but—

SUBTLE. Why, this is covetise![92]

MAMMON. No, I assure you,
I shall employ it all in pious uses,
Founding of colleges and grammar schools,
Marrying young virgins, building hospitals,
And, now and then, a church.

(*Enter* FACE)

SUBTLE. How now!

FACE. Sir, please you,

[89] Owl Glass, the rogue-hero of an old German
jest-book.

[90] Here and in the lines following Jonson uses
correctly the highly technical jargon of the alchemists to give the effect of authenticity. The
original audience probably did not understand
the exact meaning of the terms, but the words
at least had a more familiar sound then than
now.

[91] Thieves' slang.

[92] Covetousness.

Shall I not change the filter?

SUBTLE. Marry, yes;
And bring me the complexion of glass B.

(*Exit* FACE)

MAMMON. Ha' you another?

SUBTLE. Yes, son; were I assur'd
Your piety were firm, we would not want
The means to glorify it: but I hope the best.
I mean to tinct C in sand-heat to-morrow,
And give him imbibition.

MAMMON. Of white oil?

SUBTLE. No, sir, of red. F is come over
the helm too,
I thank my maker, in St. Mary's bath,
And shows *lac virginis.* Blessed be heaven!
I sent you of his fæces there calcin'd;
Out of that calx, I ha' won the salt of mer-
cury.

MAMMON. By pouring on your rectified
water?

SUBTLE. Yes, and reverberating in Athanor.

(*Re-enter* FACE)

How now! what color says it?

FACE. The ground black, sir.

MAMMON. That's your crow's head?

SURLY. (*Aside*) Your cock's comb's,[93] is it
not?

SUBTLE. No, 'tis not perfect. Would it
were the crow!
That work wants something.

SURLY. (*Aside*) O, I look'd for this,
The hay is a-pitching.

SUBTLE. Are you sure you loos'd 'em
I' their own menstrue?

FACE. Yes, sir, and then married 'em,
And put 'em in a bolt's-head nipp'd to diges-
tion,
According as you bade me, when I set
The liquor of Mars to circulation
In the same heat.

SUBTLE. The process then was right.

FACE. Yes, by the token, sir, the retort
brake,
And what was sav'd was put into the pelican,
And sign'd with Hermes' seal.

SUBTLE. I think 't was so.
We should have a new amalgama.

SURLY. (*Aside*) O, this ferret

[93] *I.e.,* coxcomb's, fool's.

Is rank as any polecat.

SUBTLE. But I care not;
Let him e'en die; we have enough beside,
In embrion. H has his white shirt on?

FACE. Yes, sir,
He's ripe for inceration, he stands warm,
In his ash-fire. I would not you should let
Any die now, if I might counsel, sir,
For luck's sake to the rest: it is not good.

MAMMON. He says right.

SURLY. (Aside) Ay, are you bolted? [94]

FACE. Nay, I know 't, sir,
I've seen th' ill fortune. What is some three
      ounces
Of fresh materials?

MAMMON. Is 't no more?

FACE. No more, sir,
Of gold, t' amalgam with some six of mer-
      cury.

MAMMON. Away, here's money. What
will serve?

FACE. Ask him, sir.

MAMMON. How much?

SUBTLE. Give him nine pound; you may
gi' him ten.

SURLY. (Aside) Yes, twenty, and be
cozen'd; do.

MAMMON. There 't is.
                    (Gives FACE the money)

SUBTLE. This needs not; but that you will
      have it so,
To see conclusions of all: for two
Of our inferior works are at fixation,
A third is in ascension. Go your ways.
Ha' you set the oil of Luna in kemia?

FACE. Yes, sir.

SUBTLE. And the philosopher's vinegar?

FACE. Ay.   (Exit)

SURLY. (Aside) We shall have a salad!

MAMMON. When do you make projection?

SUBTLE. Son, be not hasty, I exalt our
      med'cine,
By hanging him in balneo vaporoso,
And giving him solution; then congeal him;
And then dissolve him; then again congeal
      him;
For look, how oft I iterate the work,
So many times I add unto his virtue.
As, if at first one ounce convert a hundred,
After his second loose, he'll turn a thousand;
His third solution, ten; his fourth, a hundred;

[94] Driven by the ferret into the net.

After his fifth, a thousand thousand ounces
Of any imperfect metal, into pure
Silver or gold, in all examinations
As good as any of the natural mine.
Get you your stuff here against afternoon,
Your brass, your pewter, and your andirons.

MAMMON. Not those of iron?

SUBTLE. Yes, you may bring them too;
We'll change all metals.

SURLY. (Aside) I believe you in that.

MAMMON. Then I may send my spits?

SUBTLE. Yes, and your racks.

SURLY. And dripping-pans, and pot-hang-
      ers, and hooks?
Shall he not?

SUBTLE. If he please.

SURLY. —To be an ass.

SUBTLE. How, sir!

MAMMON. This gent'man you must bear
      withal.
I told you he had no faith.

SURLY. And little hope, sir;
But much less charity, should I gull myself.

SUBTLE. Why, what have you observ'd,
      sir, in our art,
Seems so impossible?

SURLY. But your whole work, no more.
That you should hatch gold in a furnace, sir,
As they do eggs in Egypt!

SUBTLE. Sir, do you
Believe that eggs are hatch'd so?

SURLY. If I should?

SUBTLE. Why, I think that the greater
      miracle.
No egg but differs from a chicken more
Than metals in themselves.

SURLY. That cannot be.
The egg's ordain'd by nature to that end,
And is a chicken in potentia.

SUBTLE. The same we say of lead and
      other metals,
Which would be gold if they had time.

MAMMON. And that
Our art doth furder.

SUBTLE. Ay, for 't were absurd
To think that nature in the earth bred gold
Perfect i' the instant: something went before.
There must be remote matter.

SURLY. Ay, what is that?

SUBTLE. Marry, we say—

MAMMON. Ay, now it heats: stand, father,
Pound him to dust.

SUBTLE. It is, of the one part,

A humid exhalation, which we call
Materia liquida, or the unctuous water;
On th' other part, a certain crass and viscous
Portion of earth; both which, concorporate,
Do make the elementary matter of gold;
Which is not yet *propria materia,*
But common to all metals and all stones.
For, where it is forsaken of that moisture,
And hath more dryness, it becomes a stone;
Where it retains more of the humid fatness,
It turns to sulphur, or to quicksilver,
Who are the parents of all other metals.
Nor can this remote matter suddenly
Progress so from extreme unto extreme,
As to grow gold, and leap o'er all the means.[95]
Nature doth first beget th' imperfect, then
Proceeds she to the perfect. Of that airy
And oily water, mercury is engend'red;
Sulphur o' the fat and earthy part; the one,
Which is the last, supplying the place of
     male,
The other of the female, in all metals.
Some do believe hermaphrodeity
That both do act and suffer. But these two
Make the rest ductile, malleable, extensive.
And even in gold they are; for we do find
Seeds of them by our fire, and gold in them;
And can produce the species of each metal
More perfect thence, than nature doth in
     earth.
Beside, who doth not see in daily practice
Art can beget bees, hornets, beetles, wasps,
Out of the carcases and dung of creatures;
Yea, scorpions of an herb, being rightly
     plac'd?
And these are living creatures, far more per-
     fect
And excellent than metals.
     MAMMON. Well said, father!
Nay, if he take you in hand, sir, with an
     argument,
He'll bray you in a mortar.
     SURLY. Pray you, sir, stay.
Rather than I'll be bray'd, sir, I'll believe
That Alchemy is a pretty kind of game,
Somewhat like tricks o' the cards, to cheat a
     man
With charming.
     SUBTLE. Sir?
     SURLY. What else are all your terms,
Whereon no one o' your writers 'grees with
     other?

[95] Intermediate stages.

Of your elixir, your *lac virginis,*
Your stone, your med'cine, and your chryso-
     sperm,
Your sal, your sulphur, and your mercury,
Your oil of height, your tree of life, your
     blood,
Your marchesite, your tutie, your magnesia,
Your toad, your crow, your dragon, and your
     panther,
Your sun, your moon, your firmament, your
     adrop,
Your lato, azoch, zernich, chibrit, heautarit,
And then your red man, and your white
     woman,
With all your broths, your menstrues, and
     materials
Of piss and egg-shells, women's terms, man's
     blood,
Hair o' the head, burnt clouts, chalk, merds,
     and clay,
Powder of bones, scalings of iron, glass,
And worlds of other strange ingredients,
Would burst a man to name?
     SUBTLE. And all these, nam'd,
Intending but one thing; which art our writ-
     ers
Us'd to obscure their art.
     MAMMON. Sir, so I told him—
Because the simple idiot should not learn it,
And make it vulgar.
     SUBTLE. Was not all the knowledge
Of the Egyptians writ in mystic symbols?
Speak not the Scriptures oft in parables?
Are not the choicest fables of the poets,
That were the fountains and first springs of
     wisdom,
Wrapp'd in perplexed allegories?
     MAMMON. I urg'd that,
And clear'd to him, that Sisyphus was
     damn'd
To roll the ceaseless stone, only because
He would have made ours common.

(DOL *appears at the door*)

Who is this?
     SUBTLE. God's precious!—What do you
          mean? Go in, good lady,
Let me entreat you. (DOL *retires*)—(*Call-
     ing*) Where's this varlet?

(*Re-enter* FACE)

FACE. Sir.

SUBTLE. You very knave! do you use me thus?

FACE. Wherein, sir?

SUBTLE. Go in and see, you traitor. Go!
(*Exit* FACE)

MAMMON. Who is it, sir?

SUBTLE. Nothing, sir; nothing.

MAMMON. What's the matter, good sir?
I have not seen you thus distemp'red: who is 't?

SUBTLE. All arts have still had, sir, their adversaries;
But ours the most ignorant.—

(FACE *returns*)

What now?

FACE. 'T was not my fault, sir; she would speak with you.

SUBTLE. Would she, sir! Follow me.
(*Exit*)

MAMMON. (*Stopping him*) Stay, Lungs.

FACE. I dare not, sir.

MAMMON. How! pray thee, stay.

FACE. She's mad, sir, and sent hither—

MAMMON. Stay, man; what is she?

FACE. A lord's sister, sir.
He'll be mad too—

MAMMON. I warrant thee.—Why sent hither?

FACE. Sir, to be cur'd.

SUBTLE. (*Within*) Why, rascal!

FACE. Lo, you!—here, sir! (*He goes out*)

MAMMON. 'Fore God, a Bradamante,[96] a brave piece.

SURLY. Heart, this is a bawdy-house! I'll be burnt else.

MAMMON. O, by this light, no! Do not wrong him. He's
Too scrupulous that way; it is his vice.
No, he's a rare physician, do him right,
An excellent Paracelsian,[97] and has done
Strange cures with mineral physic. He deals all
With spirits, he; he will not hear a word
Of Galen, or his tedious recipes.—

(*Re-enter* FACE)

How now, Lungs!

FACE. Softly, sir; speak softly. I meant
To ha' told your worship all. This[98] must not hear.

MAMMON. No, he will not be gull'd; let him alone.

FACE. Y'are very right, sir; she is a most rare scholar,
And is gone mad with studying Broughton's works.
If you but name a word touching the Hebrew,
She falls into her fit, and will discourse
So learnedly of genealogies,
As you would run mad too, to hear her, sir.

MAMMON. How might one do t' have conference with her, Lungs?

FACE. O, divers have run mad upon the conference.
I do not know, sir: I am sent in haste
To fetch a vial.

SURLY. Be not gull'd, Sir Mammon.

MAMMON. Wherein? Pray ye, be patient.

SURLY. Yes, as you are,
And trust confederate knaves and bawds and whores.

MAMMON. You are too foul, believe it.—
Come here, Ulen,
One word.

FACE. I dare not, in good faith. (*Going*)

MAMMON. Stay, knave.

FACE. He's extreme angry that you saw her, sir.

MAMMON. Drink that. (*Gives him money*) What is she when she's out of her fit?

FACE. O, the most affablest creature, sir! so merry!
So pleasant! She'll mount you up, like quicksilver,
Over the helm; and circulate like oil,
A very vegetal:[99] discourse of state,
Of mathematics, bawdry, anything—

MAMMON. Is she no way accessible? no means,
No trick to give a man a taste of her—wit—
Or so?—Ulen?

FACE. I'll come to you again, sir. (*Exit*)

MAMMON. Surly, I did not think one o' your breeding
Would traduce personages of worth.

[96] A heroine in Ariosto's *Orlando Furioso*.
[97] *I.e.*, a physician who uses the mineral remedies of Paracelsus, instead of the vegetable remedies of Galen.

[98] Surly.   [99] Animated person.

SURLY. Sir Epicure,
Your friend to use; yet still loath to be gull'd:
I do not like your philosophical bawds.
Their stone is lechery enough to pay for,
Without this bait.
MAMMON. Heart, you abuse yourself.
I know the lady, and her friends, and means,
The original of this disaster. Her brother
Has told me all.
SURLY. And yet you ne'er saw her
Till now!
MAMMON. O yes, but I forgot. I have,
    believe it,
One o' the treacherous'st memories, I do
    think,
Of all mankind.
SURLY. What call you her brother?
MAMMON. My lord—
He wi' not have his name known, now I
    think on't.
SURLY. A very treacherous memory!
MAMMON. O' my faith—
SURLY. Tut, if you ha' it not about you,
    pass it
Till we meet next.
MAMMON. Nay, by this hand, 'tis true.
He's one I honor, and my noble friend;
And I respect his house.
SURLY. Heart! can it be
That a grave sir, a rich, that has no need,
A wise sir, too, at other times, should thus,
With his own oaths and arguments make
    hard means
To gull himself? An this be your elixir,
Your *lapis mineralis,* and your lunary,
Give me your honest trick yet at primero,
Or gleek,[100] and take your *lutum sapientis,*
Your *menstruum simplex!* I'll have gold be-
    fore you,
And with less danger of the quicksilver,
Or the hot sulphur.[101]

(Re-enter FACE)

FACE. Here's one from Captain Face,[102] sir,
                        (To SURLY)
Desires you meet him i' the Temple-church,
Some half-hour hence, and upon earnest
    business.—   *(He whispers MAMMON)*
Sir, if you please to quit us now, and come
Again within two hours, you shall have

My master busy examining o' the works;
And I will steal you in unto the party,
That you may see her converse.—*(To
    SURLY)* Sir, shall I say
You'll meet the captain's worship?
    SURLY. Sir, I will.—   *(Aside)*
But, by attorney,[103] and to a second purpose.
Now I am sure it is a bawdy-house;
I'll swear it, were the marshal here to thank
    me:
The naming this commander doth confirm
    it.
Don Face! why he's the most authentic dealer
I' these commodities, the superintendent
To all the quainter traffickers in town!
He is the visitor, and does appoint
Who lies with whom, and at what hour;
    what price;
Which gown, and in what smock; what
    fall;[104] what tire.[105]
Him will I prove, by a third person, to find
The subtleties of this dark labyrinth:
Which if I do discover, dear Sir Mammon,
You'll give your poor friend leave, though
    no philosopher,
To laugh; for you that are, 't is thought, shall
    weep.
    FACE. Sir, he does pray you'll not forget.
    SURLY. I will not, sir.
Sir Epicure, I shall leave you?   *(Exit)*
    MAMMON. I follow you straight.
    FACE. But do so, good sir, to avoid
    suspicion.
This gent'man has a parlous head.
    MAMMON. But wilt thou, Ulen,
Be constant to thy promise?
    FACE. As my life, sir.
    MAMMON. And wilt thou insinuate what
    I am, and praise me,
And say I am a noble fellow?
    FACE. O, what else, sir?
And that you'll make her royal with the
    stone,
An empress; you yourself king of Bantam.
    MAMMON. Wilt thou do this?
    FACE. Will I, sir!
    MAMMON. Lungs, my Lungs!
I love thee.

---

[100] Card games.
[101] The usual treatments for venereal disease.
[102] Surly has failed to recognize Face, the laboratory assistant, as the same man he has seen
elsewhere called Captain Face.
[103] In disguise.   [104] Veil.   [105] Headdress.

FACE. Send your stuff, sir, that my master
May busy himself about projection.
MAMMON. Thou'st witch'd me, rogue:
take, go.   (Gives him money)
FACE. Your jack,[106] and all, sir.
MAMMON. (Hilariously) Thou art a vil-
lain—I will send my jack,
And the weights too. Slave, I could bite thine
ear.
Away, thou dost not care for me.
FACE. Not I, sir?

MAMMON. Come, I was born to make
thee, my good weasel,
Set thee on a bench, and ha' thee twirl a
chain
With the best lord's vermin of 'em all.
FACE. Away, sir.
MAMMON. A count, nay, a count pala-
tine—
FACE. Good sir, go.
MAMMON. Shall not advance thee better:
no, nor faster.   (Exit)

SCENE IV. *The Same.*

(*Enter* SUBTLE *and* DOL)

SUBTLE. Has he bit? has he bit?
FACE. And swallow'd, too, my Subtle.
I ha' given him line, and now he plays,
i' faith.
SUBTLE. And shall we twitch him?
FACE. Thorough both the gills.
A wench is a rare bait, with which a man
No sooner's taken, but he straight firks mad.
SUBTLE. Dol, my Lord What's-hum's
sister, you must now
Bear yourself *statelich.*
DOL COMMON. O, let me alone,
I'll not forget my race, I warrant you.
I'll keep my distance, laugh and talk aloud;
Have all the tricks of a proud scurvy lady,
And be as rude's her women.
FACE. Well said, sanguine! [107]
SUBTLE. But will he send his andirons?
FACE. His jack too,
And 's iron shoeing-horn; I ha' spoke to him.
Well,
I must not lose my wary gamester yonder.
SUBTLE. O, Monsieur Caution, that will
not be gull'd?
FACE. Ay,
If I can strike a fine hook into him, now!—
The Temple-church, there I have cast mine
angle.
Well, pray for me. I'll about it.
                    (One knocks)

SUBTLE. What, more gudgeons! [108]
Dol, scout, scout!
                    (DOL goes to the window)
Stay, Face, you must go to the door;
'Pray God it be my Anabaptist—Who is 't,
Dol?
DOL COMMON. I know him not: he looks
like a gold-end-man.[109]
SUBTLE. Gods so! 'tis he, he said he would
send—what call you him?
The sanctified elder, that should deal
For Mammon's jack and andirons. Let him
in.
Stay, help me off, first, with my gown. (Exit
FACE *with the gown*) Away,
Madam, to your withdrawing chamber. Now,
                    (Exit DOL)
In a new tune, new gesture, but old lan-
guage.—
This fellow is sent from one negotiates with
me
About the stone too, for the holy brethren
Of Amsterdam, the exil'd saints,[110] that hope
To raise their discipline [111] by it. I must use
him
In some strange fashion now, to make him
admire me.

[108] Small fish, *i.e.,* suckers.
[109] One who buys odds and ends of gold.
[110] A congregation of English Puritans whose
zeal had led them to migrate to Holland where
the church was more congenial to their fanati-
cism. Jonson uses "saints" satirically.
[111] Puritan form of church government.

[106] A mechanical device for turning a spit.
[107] Modern equivalent: Blondie.

Scene V. *The Same.*

(*Enter* Ananias)

Subtle. (*Calling*) Where is my drudge?

(*Enter* Face)

Face. Sir!
Subtle. Take away the recipient,
And rectify your menstrue from the phlegma.
Then pour it o' the Sol, in the cucurbite,
And let 'em macerate together.
Face. Yes, sir.
And save the ground?
Subtle. No: *terra damnata*
Must not have entrance in the work.—Who
    are you?
Ananias. A faithful brother,[112] if it please
you.
Subtle. What's that?
A Lullianist? a Ripley? *Filius artis?*
Can you sublime and dulcify? Calcine?
Know you the sapor pontic? Sapor stiptic?
Or what is homogene, or heterogene?
Ananias. I understand no heathen lan-
guage, truly.
Subtle. Heathen! You Knipperdoling![113]
    Is Ars sacra,
Or chrysopoeia, or spagyrica,
Or the pamphysic, or panarchic knowledge,
A heathen language?
Ananias. Heathen Greek, I take it.
Subtle. How! Heathen Greek?
Ananias. All's heathen but the Hebrew.
Subtle. Sirrah my varlet, stand you forth
    and speak to him
Like a philosopher; answer i' the language.
Name the vexations, and the martyrizations
Of metals in the work.
Face. Sir, putrefaction,
Solution, ablution, sublimation,
Cohobation, calcination, ceration, and
Fixation.
Subtle. This is heathen Greek, to you,
    now?—
And when comes vivification?
Face. After mortification.

[112] So the Puritans called themselves. Subtle
pretends to think he means a fellow alchemist.
[113] A leader of the Anabaptists.

Subtle. What's cohobation?
Face. 'Tis the pouring on
Your *aqua regis,* and then drawing him off,
To the trine circle of the seven spheres.
Subtle. What's the proper passion of
metals?
Face. Malleation.
Subtle. What's your *ultimum supplicium
auri?*
Face. Antimonium.
Subtle. This's heathen Greek to you?—
And what's your mercury?
Face. A very fugitive, he will be gone, sir.
Subtle. How know you him?
Face. By his viscosity,
His oleosity, and his suscitability.
Subtle. How do you sublime him?
Face. With the calce of egg-shells,
White marble, talc.
Subtle. Your magisterium now,
What's that?
Face. Shifting, sir, your elements,
Dry into cold, cold into moist, moist into hot,
Hot into dry.
Subtle. This's heathen Greek to you
    still?—
Your *lapis philosophicus?*
Face. 'Tis a stone,
And not a stone; a spirit, a soul, and a body,
Which if you do dissolve, it is dissolv'd;
If you coagulate, it is coagulated;
If you make it to fly, it flieth.
Subtle. Enough.   (*Exit* Face)
This's heathen Greek to you? What are you,
    sir?
Ananias. Please you, a servant of the
    exil'd brethren,
That deal with widows' and with orphans'
    goods,
And make a just account unto the saints:
A deacon.
Subtle. O, you are sent from Master
    Wholesome,
Your teacher?
Ananias. From Tribulation Wholesome,
Our very zealous pastor.
Subtle. Good! I have
Some orphans' goods to come here.

ANANIAS. Of what kind, sir?

SUBTLE. Pewter and brass, andirons and
kitchen-ware;

Metals, that we must use our med'cine on:
Wherein the brethren may have a penn'orth
For ready money.

ANANIAS. Were the orphans' parents
Sincere professors? [114]

SUBTLE. Why do you ask?

ANANIAS. Because
We then are to deal justly, and give, in truth,
Their utmost value.

SUBTLE. 'Slid, you'd cozen else,
An if their parents were not of the faithful?—
I will not trust you, now I think on't,
Till I ha' talk'd with your pastor. Ha' you
    brought money
To buy more coals?

ANANIAS. No, surely.

SUBTLE. No? How so?

ANANIAS. The brethren bid me say unto
    you, sir,
Surely, they will not venter any more
Till they may see projection.

SUBTLE. How!

ANANIAS. You've had
For the instruments, as bricks, and loam, and
    glasses,
Already thirty pound; and for materials,

They say, some ninety more. And they have
    heard since,
That one at Heidelberg, made it of an egg,
And a small paper of pin-dust.

SUBTLE. What's your name?

ANANIAS. My name is Ananias.

SUBTLE. Out, the varlet
That cozen'd the apostles! Hence, away!
Flee, mischief! had your holy consistory
No name to send me, of another sound
Than wicked Ananias? Send your elders
Hither to make atonement for you, quickly,
And gi' me satisfaction; or out goes
The fire; and down th' alembics, and the
    furnace,
Piger Henricus, or what not. Thou wretch!
Both *sericon* and *bufo* shall be lost,
Tell 'em. All hope of rooting out the bishops,
Or th' anti-Christian hierarchy shall perish,
If they stay threescore minutes; the aqueity,
Terreity, and sulphureity
Shall run together again, and all be annull'd,
Thou wicked Ananias! (*Exit* ANANIAS) This
    will fetch 'em,
And make 'em haste towards their gulling
    more.
A man must deal like a rough nurse, and
    fright
Those that are froward to an appetite.

SCENE VI. *The Same.*

(*Enter* FACE, *in his Captain's uniform, fol-
    lowed by* ABEL DRUGGER)

FACE. He's busy with his spirits, but we'll
upon him.

SUBTLE. How now! What mates, what
Bayards ha' we here?

FACE. I told you he would be furious.—
Sir, here's Nab
Has brought you another piece of gold to
    look on;   (*Aside to* DRUGGER)
—We must appease him. Give it me,—and
    prays you,
You would devise—what is it, Nab?

DRUGGER. A sign, sir.

FACE. Ay, a good lucky one, a thriving
sign, Doctor.

SUBTLE. I was devising now.

FACE. (*Aside to* SUBTLE) 'Slight, do not
    say so,
He will repent he ga' you any more.—
What say you to his constellation, Doctor,
The Balance?

SUBTLE. No, that way is stale and
    common.
A townsman born in Taurus, gives [115] the bull,
Or the bull's head; in Aries, the ram,—
A poor device! No, I will have his name
Form'd in some mystic character, whose *radii,*
Striking the senses of the passers-by,
Shall, by a virtual influence, breed affections,
That may result upon the party owns it:
As thus—

FACE. Nab!

[114] *I.e.,* subscribers to the Puritan faith.

[115] Uses as the sign for his shop.

SUBTLE. He first shall have *a bell*, that's
   Abel;
And by it standing one whose name is *Dee*,[116]
In a *rug*[117] gown, there's D, and *Rug*, that's
   drug;
And right anenst him a dog snarling *er*;
There's Drugger, Abel Drugger. That's his
   sign.
And here's now mystery and hieroglyphic!
   FACE. Abel, thou art made.
   DRUGGER. Sir, I do thank his worship.
   FACE. Six o' thy legs[118] more will not do
   it, Nab.
He has brought you a pipe of tobacco, Doctor.
   DRUGGER. Yes, sir.
I have another thing I would impart—
   FACE. Out with it, Nab.
   DRUGGER. Sir, there is lodg'd, hard by me,
A rich young widow—
   FACE. Good! a bona roba?[119]
   DRUGGER. But nineteen at the most.
   FACE. Very good, Abel.
   DRUGGER. Marry, she's not in fashion yet;
   she wears
A hood, but 't stands a cop.[120]
   FACE. No matter, Abel.
   DRUGGER. And I do now and then give
her a fucus[121]—
   FACE. What! dost thou deal, Nab?
   SUBTLE. I did tell you, Captain.
   DRUGGER. And physic too, sometime, sir;
   for which she trusts me
With all her mind. She's come up here of
   purpose
To learn the fashion.
   FACE. Good (his match too!)—On, Nab.
   DRUGGER. And she does strangely long
to know her fortune.
   FACE. God's lid, Nab, send her to the
doctor, hither.
   DRUGGER. Yes, I have spoke to her of his
   worship already;
But she's afraid it will be blown abroad,
And hurt her marriage.
   FACE. Hurt it! 'tis the way
To heal it, if 'twere hurt; to make it more
Follow'd and sought. Nab, thou shalt tell her
   this.
She'll be more known, more talk'd of; and
   your widows

Are ne'er of any price till they be famous;
Their honor is their multitude of suitors.
Send her! it may be thy good fortune. What!
Thou dost not know?
   DRUGGER. No, sir, she'll never marry
Under a knight; her brother has made a vow.
   FACE. What! and dost thou despair, my
   little Nab,
Knowing what the doctor has set down for
   thee,
And seeing so many o' the city dubb'd?
One glass o' thy water, with a madam I know,
Will have it done, Nab. What's her brother?
   a knight?
   DRUGGER. No, sir, a gentleman newly
   warm in's land, sir,
Scarce cold in his one-and-twenty, that does
   govern
His sister here; and is a man himself
Of some three thousand a year, and is come
   up
To learn to quarrel, and to live by his wits,
And will go down again, and die i' the
   country.
   FACE. How! to quarrel?
   DRUGGER. Yes, sir, to carry quarrels,
As gallants do; to manage 'em by line.
   FACE. 'Slid, Nab! The doctor is the only
   man
In Christendom for him. He has made a
   table,
With mathematical demonstrations,
Touching the art of quarrels. He will give
   him
An instrument to quarrel by. Go, bring 'em
   both,
Him and his sister. And, for thee, with her
The doctor happ'ly may persuade. Go to!
'Shalt give his worship a new damask suit
Upon the premises.
   SUBTLE. O, good Captain!
   FACE. He shall;
He is the honestest fellow, Doctor. Stay not,
No offers; bring the damask, and the parties.
   DRUGGER. I'll try my power, sir.
   FACE. And thy will too, Nab.
   SUBTLE. 'Tis good tobacco, this! What
is't an ounce?
   FACE. He'll send you a pound, Doctor.
   SUBTLE. O no.

[116] Dr. John Dee, a famous astrologer (d.
1608).
[117] Of coarse frieze.   [118] Bows.

[119] Handsome wench.
[120] High on her head.
[121] Cosmetic.

FACE. He will do't.
It is the goodest soul!—Abel, about it.
Thou shalt know more anon. Away, be gone.
                              (*Exit* ABEL)
A miserable rogue, and lives with cheese,
And has the worms. That was the cause,
    indeed,
Why he came now: he dealt with me in
    private,
To get a med'cine for 'em.
    SUBTLE. And shall, sir. This works.
    FACE. A wife, a wife for one on's, my dear
Subtle!
We'll e'en draw lots, and he that fails shall
    have

The more in goods, the other has in tail.
    SUBTLE. Rather the less; for she may be
        so light
She may want grains.[122]
    FACE. Ay, or be such a burden,
A man would scarce endure her for the
    whole.
    SUBTLE. Faith, best let's see her first,
and then determine.
    FACE. Content. But Dol must ha' no
breath on't.
    SUBTLE. Mum.
Away you, to your Surly yonder, catch him.
    FACE. Pray God I ha' not stay'd too long.
    SUBTLE. I fear it.   (*Exeunt*)

Act III

SCENE I. *Before* LOVEWIT's *House.*

(*Enter* PARSON TRIBULATION WHOLESOME
        and DEACON ANANIAS)

TRIBULATION. These chastisements are
    common to the saints,
And such rebukes we of the separation
Must bear with willing shoulders, as the trials
Sent forth to tempt our frailties.
    ANANIAS. In pure zeal,
I do not like the man; he is a heathen,
And speaks the language of Canaan, truly.
    TRIBULATION. I think him a profane per-
son indeed.
    ANANIAS. He bears
The visible mark of the beast in his forehead.
And for his stone, it is a work of darkness,
And with philosophy blinds the eyes of man.
    TRIBULATION. Good brother, we must
    bend unto all means
That may give furtherance to the holy cause.
    ANANIAS. Which his cannot: the sanctified
cause
Should have a sanctified course.
    TRIBULATION. Not always necessary.
The children of perdition are oft times
Made instruments even of the greatest works.
Besides, we should give somewhat to man's
    nature,
The place he lives in, still about the fire,
And fume of metals, that intoxicate
The brain of man, and make him prone to
    passion.

Where have you greater atheists than your
    cooks?
Or more profane, or choleric, than your
    glass-men?
More anti-Christian than your bell-founders?
What makes the devil so devilish, I would
    ask you,
Sathan, our common enemy, but his being
Perpetually about the fire, and boiling
Brimstone and arsenic? We must give, I say,
Unto the motives, and the stirrers up
Of humors in the blood. It may be so,
Whenas the work is done, the stone is made,
This heat of his may turn into a zeal,
And stand up for the beauteous discipline
Against the menstruous cloth and rag of
    Rome.
We must await his calling, and the coming
Of the good spirit. You did fault, t' upbraid
    him
With the brethren's blessing of Heidelberg,
    weighing
What need we have to hasten on the work,
For the restoring of the silenc'd[123] saints,
Which ne'er will be but by the philosopher's
    stone.
And so a learned elder, one of Scotland,
Assur'd me; *aurum potabile*[124] being
The only med'cine for the civil magistrate,

[122] Weight.
[123] Dissenting ministers who were not allowed
to preach in English churches.
[124] A sovereign remedy, *i.e.,* bribery.

T' incline him to a feeling of the cause;
And must be daily us'd in the disease.
    ANANIAS. I have not edified more, truly,
      by man,
Not since the beautiful light first shone on
    me,

And I am sad my zeal hath so offended.
    TRIBULATION. Let us call on him then.
    ANANIAS. The motion's good,
And of the spirit; I will knock first. (*Knocks*)
    Peace be within.

SCENE II. *A Room in* LOVEWIT'S *House.*

(SUBTLE *admits* TRIBULATION *and*
ANANIAS)

SUBTLE. O, are you come? 'Twas time.
    Your threescore minutes
Were at the last thread, you see; and down
    had gone
Furnus acediæ, turris circulatorius: [125]
Limbec, bolt's-head, retort, and pelican
Had all been cinders. Wicked Ananias!
Art thou return'd? Nay, then, it goes down
    yet.
    TRIBULATION. Sir, be appeased; he is come
      to humble
Himself in spirit, and to ask your patience,
If too much zeal hath carried him aside
From the due path.
    SUBTLE. Why, this doth qualify! [126]
    TRIBULATION. The brethren had no pur-
      pose, verily,
To give you the least grievance; but are ready
To lend their willing hands to any project
The spirit and you direct.
    SUBTLE. This qualifies more!
    TRIBULATION. And for the orphans' goods,
      let them be valu'd,
Or what is needful else to the holy work,
It shall be numb'red, here, by me, the saints
Throw down their purse before you.
    SUBTLE. This qualifies most!
Why, thus it should be, now you understand.
Have I discours'd so unto you of our stone,
And of the good that it shall bring your
    cause?
Show'd you (beside the main of hiring forces
Abroad, drawing the Hollanders, your
    friends,
From th' Indies, to serve you, with all their
    fleet)

That even the med'cinal use shall make you
    a faction
And party in the realm? As, put the case,
That some great man in state, he have the
    gout,
Why, you but send three drops of your elixir,
You help him straight: there you have made
    a friend.
Another has the palsy or the dropsy,
He takes of your incombustible stuff,
He's young again: there you have made a
    friend.
A lady that is past the feat of body,
Though not of mind, and hath her face de-
    cay'd
Beyond all cure of paintings, you restore
With the oil of talc: there you have made
    a friend;
And all her friends. A lord that is a leper,
A knight that has the bone-ache, or a squire
That hath both these, you make 'em smooth
    and sound
With a bare fricace of your med'cine; still
You increase your friends.
    TRIBULATION. Ay, 'tis very pregnant.
    SUBTLE. And then the turning of this
      làwyer's pewter
To plate at Christmas—
    ANANIAS. Christ-tide,[127] I pray you.
    SUBTLE. Yet, Ananias!
    ANANIAS. I have done.
    SUBTLE. Or changing
His parcel gilt[128] to massy gold. You cannot
But raise your friends withal, to be of power
To pay an army in the field, to buy
The King of France out of his realms, or
    Spain
Out of his Indies. What can you not do
Against lords spiritual or temporal,

[125] The compound furnace and glass still.
[126] Modifies the situation.

[127] The Puritans avoided *mass* as a Popish
word.   [128] Partly gilded silverware.

That shall oppose you?

TRIBULATION. Verily, 'tis true.
We may be temporal lords ourselves, I take it.

SUBTLE. You may be anything, and leave off to make
Long-winded exercises; or suck up
Your *ha!* and *hum!* in a tune. I not deny,
But such as are not graced in a state,
May, for their ends, be adverse in religion,
And get a tune to call the flock together.
For, to say sooth, a tune does much with women
And other phlegmatic people; it is your bell.

ANANIAS. Bells are profane; a tune may be religious.

SUBTLE. No warning with you? Then farewell my patience.
'Slight, it shall down; I will not be thus tortur'd.

TRIBULATION. I pray you, sir.

SUBTLE. All shall perish. I have spoke it.

TRIBULATION. Let me find grace, sir, in your eyes; the man,
He stands corrected: neither did his zeal,
But as yourself, allow a tune somewhere,
Which now, being tow'rd[129] the stone, we shall not need.

SUBTLE. No, nor your holy vizard, to win widows
To give you legacies; or make zealous wives
To rob their husbands for the common cause;
Nor take the start of bonds broke but one day,
And say they were forfeited by providence.
Nor shall you need o'er night to eat huge meals,
To celebrate your next day's fast the better;
The whilst the brethren and the sisters humbled,
Abate the stiffness of the flesh. Nor cast
Before your hungry hearers scrupulous bones;
As whether a Christian may hawk or hunt,
Or whether matrons of the holy assembly
May lay their hair out, or wear doublets,
Or have that idol, starch, about their linen.

ANANIAS. It is indeed an idol.

TRIBULATION. Mind him not, sir.
I do commend thee, spirit (of zeal, but trouble),
To peace within him! Pray you, sir, go on.

SUBTLE. Nor shall you need to libel 'gainst the prelates,

And shorten[130] so your ears against the hearing
Of the next wire-drawn grace. Nor of necessity
Rail against plays, to please the alderman
Whose daily custard you devour; nor lie
With zealous rage till you are hoarse. Not one
Of these so singular arts. Nor call yourselves
By names of Tribulation, Persecution,
Restraint, Long-patience, and such like, affected
By the whole family or wood[131] of you,
Only for glory, and to catch the ear
Of the disciple.

TRIBULATION. Truly, sir, they are
Ways that the godly brethren have invented,
For propagation of the glorious cause,
As very notable means, and whereby also
Themselves grow soon, and profitably, famous.

SUBTLE. O, but the stone, all's idle to't! Nothing!
The art of angels, nature's miracle,
The divine secret that doth fly in clouds
From east to west, and whose tradition
Is not from men, but spirits.

ANANIAS. I hate traditions;
I do not trust them—

TRIBULATION. Peace!

ANANIAS. They are popish all.
I will not peace! I will not—

TRIBULATION. Ananias!

ANANIAS. Please the profane, to grieve the godly!
I may not.

SUBTLE. Well, Ananias, thou shalt overcome.

TRIBULATION. It is an ignorant zeal that haunts him, sir,
But truly else a very faithful brother,
A botcher,[132] and a man by revelation
That hath a competent knowledge of the truth.

SUBTLE. Has he a competent sum there i' the bag
To buy the goods within? I am made guardian,
And must, for charity and conscience' sake,

[130] Have them cut off in the pillory as punishment.

[131] Assemblage.

[132] Mender, petty tailor.

[129] Near possession of.

Now see the most be made for my poor
   orphan,
Though I desire the brethren, too, good
   gainers;
There they are within. When you have
   view'd and bought 'em,
And ta'en the inventory of what they are,
They are ready for projection; there's no more
To do: cast on the med'cine, so much silver
As there is tin there, so much gold as brass,
I'll gi' it you in by weight.
   TRIBULATION. But how long time,
Sir, must the saints expect yet?
   SUBTLE. Let me see,
How's the moon now? Eight, nine, ten days
   hence,
He will be silver potate; then three days
Before he citronize. Some fifteen days,
The magisterium will be perfected.
   ANANIAS. About the second day of the
      third week,
In the ninth month?
   SUBTLE. Yes, my good Ananias.
   TRIBULATION. What will the orphans'
goods arise to, think you?
   SUBTLE. Some hundred marks, as much
      as fill'd three cars,
Unladed now: you'll make six millions of
   'em—
But I must ha' more coals laid in.
   TRIBULATION. How?
   SUBTLE. Another load,
And then we ha' finish'd. We must now
   increase
Our fire to *ignis ardens;* we are past
Fimus equinus, balnei, cineris,
And all those lenter heats. If the holy purse
Should with this draught fall low, and that
   the saints

Do need a present sum, I have a trick
To melt the pewter, you shall buy now
   instantly,
And with a tincture make you as good Dutch
   dollars
As any are in Holland.
   TRIBULATION. Can you so?
   SUBTLE. Ay, and shall bide the third ex-
amination.
   ANANIAS. It will be joyful tidings to the
brethren.
   SUBTLE. But you must carry it secret.
   TRIBULATION. Ay; but stay,
This act of coining, is it lawful?
   ANANIAS. Lawful!
We know no magistrate; or, if we did,
This's foreign coin.
   SUBTLE. It is no coining, sir.
It is but casting.
   TRIBULATION. Ha! you distinguish well;
Casting of money may be lawful.
   ANANIAS. 'Tis, sir.
   TRIBULATION. Truly, I take it so.
   SUBTLE. There is no scruple,
Sir, to be made of it; believe Ananias;
This case of conscience he is studied in.
   TRIBULATION. I'll make a question of it to
the brethren.
   ANANIAS. The brethren shall approve it
      lawful, doubt not.
Where shall't be done?
   SUBTLE. For that we'll talk anon.
                           (*Knock without*)
There's some to speak with me. Go in, I
   pray you,
And view the parcels. That's the inventory.
I'll come to you straight.
        (*Exeunt* TRIBULATION *and* ANANIAS)
Who is it?—Face! appear.

SCENE III. *The Same.*

(*Enter* FACE *in his captain's uniform*)

   SUBTLE. How now! good prize?
   FACE. Good pox! Yond' costive cheater [133]
Never came on.
   SUBTLE. How then?
   FACE. I ha' walk'd the round
Till now, and no such thing.
   [133] Surly.

   SUBTLE. And ha' you quit him?
   FACE. Quit him! An hell would quit him
      too, he were happy.
'Slight! would you have me stalk like a mill-
jade,
All day, for one that will not yield us grains?
I know him of old.
   SUBTLE. O, but to ha' gull'd him,
Had been a mastery.

FACE. Let him go, black boy!
And turn thee, that some fresh news may
    possess thee.
A noble count, a don of Spain (my dear
Delicious compeer, and my party-bawd),
Who is come hither private for his conscience
And brought munition with him, six great
    slops,
Bigger than three Dutch hoys, beside round
    trunks,
Furnish'd with pistolets, and pieces of eight,
Will straight be here, my rogue, to have thy
    bath,
(That is the color [134]) and to make his batt'ry
Upon our Dol, our castle, our cinqueport,
Our Dover pier, [135] our what thou wilt. Where
    is she?
She must prepare perfumes, delicate linen,
The bath in chief, a banquet, and her wit,
For she must milk his epididymis.
Where is the doxy?
    SUBTLE. I'll send her to thee;
And but despatch my brace of little John
    Leydens [136]
And come again myself.
    FACE. Are they within then?
    SUBTLE. Numb'ring the sum.
    FACE. How much?
    SUBTLE. A hundred marks, boy. (Exit)
    FACE. Why, this's a lucky day. Ten
        pounds of Mammon!
Three o' my clerk! A portague o' my grocer!
This o' the brethren! Beside reversions
And states to come, i' the widow, and my
    count!
My share to-day will not be bought for
    forty—

(Enter DOL)

DOL COMMON. What?
FACE. Pounds, dainty Dorothy! Art thou
so near?
DOL COMMON. Yes. Say, lord general,
how fares our camp?
    FACE. As with the few that had entrench'd
        themselves
Safe, by their discipline, against a world, Dol,
And laugh'd within those trenches, and grew
    fat

With thinking on the booties, Dol, brought
    in
Daily by their small parties. This dear hour,
A doughty don is taken with my Dol;
And thou mayst make his ransom what thou
    wilt,
My Dowsabel; he shall be brought here,
    fetter'd
With thy fair looks, before he sees thee; and
    thrown
In a down-bed, as dark as any dungeon;
Where thou shalt keep him waking with thy
    drum;
Thy drum, my Dol, thy drum; till he be tame
As the poor blackbirds were i' the great
    frost, [137]
Or bees are with a basin; and so hive him
I' the swan-skin coverlid and cambric sheets,
Till he work honey and wax, my little God's-
    gift. [138]
    DOL COMMON. What is he, General?
    FACE. An adalantado, [139]
A grandee, girl. Was not my Dapper here
    yet?
    DOL COMMON. No.
    FACE. Nor my Drugger?
    DOL COMMON. Neither.
    FACE. A pox on 'em,
They are so long a furnishing! such
    stinkards
Would not be seen upon these festival days.—

(Re-enter SUBTLE)

How now! ha' you done?
    SUBTLE. Done. They are gone; the sum
Is here in bank, my Face. I would we knew
Another chapman now would buy 'em out-
    right.
    FACE. 'Slid, Nab shall do't against he ha'
        the widow,
To furnish household.
    SUBTLE. Excellent, well thought on.
Pray God he come.
    FACE. I pray he keep away
Till our new business be o'erpast.
    SUBTLE. But, Face,
How cam'st thou by this secret don?
    FACE. A spirit
Brought me th' intelligence in a paper here,

---

[134] Pretext.
[135] English ports of entry on the Channel.
[136] Puritans.
[137] The great frost of 1608.
[138] Greek meaning of Dorothea.
[139] A Spanish governor of a province.

As I was conjuring yonder in my circle
For Surly; I ha' my flies abroad. Your bath
Is famous, Subtle, by my means. Sweet Dol,
You must go tune your virginal, no losing
O' the least time. And—do you hear?—good
    action!
Firk like a flounder; kiss like a scallop, close;
And tickle him with thy mother-tongue. His
    great
Verdugoship [140] has not a jot of language;
So much the easier to be cozen'd, my Dolly.
He will come here in a hir'd coach, obscure,
And our own coachman, whom I have sent
    as guide,
No creature else.—Who's that?
            (*One knocks. DOL goes to the window*)
    SUBTLE. It is not he?
    FACE. O no, not yet this hour.

SUBTLE. Who is't?
DOL COMMON. Dapper,
Your clerk.
    FACE. God's will then, Queen of Faery,
On with your tire; (*Exit* DOL) and, Doctor,
    with your robes.
Let's despatch him for God's sake.
    SUBTLE. 'Twill be long.
    FACE. I warrant you, take but the cues
    I give you,
It shall be brief enough.
                        (*Goes to the window*)
'Slight, here are more!
Abel, and, I think, the angry boy, the heir,
That fain would quarrel.
    SUBTLE. And the widow?
    FACE. No,
Not that I see. Away!   (*Exit* SUBTLE)

SCENE IV. *The Same.*

(FACE *admits* DAPPER)

FACE. O, sir, you are welcome.
The doctor is within a-moving for you.—
I have had the most ado to win him to it!—
He swears you'll be the darling o' the dice;
He never heard her Highness dote till now,
    he says.
Your aunt has giv'n you the most gracious
    words
That can be thought on.
    DAPPER. Shall I see her Grace?
    FACE. See her, and kiss her too.—

(*Enter* ABEL DRUGGER, *followed by*
    KASTRIL)

What, honest Nab!
Hast brought the damask?
    DRUGGER. No, sir; here's tobacco.
    FACE. 'Tis well done, Nab; thou'lt bring
    the damask too?
    DRUGGER. Yes. Here's the gentleman,
    Captain, Master Kastril,
I have brought to see the doctor.
    FACE. Where's the widow?
    DRUGGER. Sir, as he likes, his sister, he
says, shall come.
    FACE. O, is it so? Good time. Is your name
Kastril, sir?

[140] The Spanish word means "executioner."
[141] Riotous youths, sports.

KASTRIL. Ay, and the best o' the Kastrils,
    I'd be sorry else,
By fifteen hundred a year. Where is this
    doctor?
My mad tobacco-boy here tells me of one
That can do things. Has he any skill?
    FACE. Wherein, sir?
    KASTRIL. To carry a business, manage a
    quarrel fairly,
Upon fit terms.
    FACE. It seems, sir, y' are but young
About the town, that can make that a
    question.
    KASTRIL. Sir, not so young but I have
    heard some speech
Of the angry boys, [141] and seen 'em take
    tobacco;
And in his shop; and I can take it too.
And I would fain be one of 'em, and go
    down
And practise i' the country.
    FACE. Sir, for the duello,
The doctor, I assure you, shall inform you,
To the least shadow of a hair; and show you
An instrument he has of his own making,
Wherewith, no sooner shall you make report
Of any quarrel, but he will take the height
    on't
Most instantly, and tell in what degree
Of safety it lies in, or mortality.

And how it may be borne, whether in a right
line,
Or a half circle; or may else be cast
Into an angle blunt, if not acute:
All this he will demonstrate. And then, rules
To give and take the lie by.
    KASTRIL. How! to take it?
    FACE. Yes, in oblique he'll show you, or
in circle; [142]
But never in diameter. [143] The whole town
Study his theorems, and dispute them ordi-
narily
At the eating academies.
    KASTRIL. But does he teach
Living by the wits too?
    FACE. Anything whatever.
You cannot think that subtlety but he reads
it.
He made me a captain. I was a stark pimp,
Just o' your standing, 'fore I met with him;
It's not two months since. I'll tell you his
method:
First, he will enter you at some ordinary.
    KASTRIL. No, I'll not come there; you shall
pardon me.
    FACE. For why, sir?
    KASTRIL. There's gaming there, and tricks.
    FACE. Why, would you be
A gallant, and not game?
    KASTRIL. Ay, 'twill spend a man.
    FACE. Spend you! It will repair you when
you are spent.
How do they live by their wits there, that
have vented
Six times your fortunes?
    KASTRIL. What, three thousand a year!
    FACE. Ay, forty thousand.
    KASTRIL. Are there such?
    FACE. Ay, sir,
And gallants yet. Here's a young gentleman
Is born to nothing,—(Points to DAPPER)
forty marks a year,
Which I count nothing—he's to be initiated,
And have a fly o' the doctor. He will win you
By unresistible luck, within this fortnight,
Enough to buy a barony. They will set him
Upmost, at the groom porter's, [144] all the
Christmas;

[142] The lie circumstantial.   [143] The lie direct.
[144] An officer of the royal household in charge
of gaming. He provided materials, settled disputes, and had the privilege of keeping a free
table at Christmas.

And for the whole year through at every place
Where there is play, present him with the
chair,
The best attendance, the best drink, some-
times
Two glasses of Canary, and pay nothing;
The purest linen and the sharpest knife,
The partridge next his trencher, and some-
where
The dainty bed, in private, with the dainty.
You shall ha' your ordinaries bid for him,
As playhouses for a poet; and the master
Pray him aloud to name what dish he affects,
Which must be butter'd shrimps; and those
that drink
To no mouth else, will drink to his, as being
The goodly president mouth of all the board.
    KASTRIL. Do you not gull one?
    FACE. 'Ods my life! Do you think it?
You shall have a cast commander, (can but
get
In credit with a glover, or a spurrier,
For some two pair of either's ware aforehand)
Will, by most swift posts, dealing with him,
Arrive at competent means to keep himself,
His punk, and naked boy, in excellent
fashion,
And be admir'd for 't.
    KASTRIL. Will the doctor teach this?
    FACE. He will do more, sir. When your
land is gone,
(As men of spirit hate to keep earth long),
In a vacation, when small money is stirring,
And ordinaries suspended till the term,
He'll show a perspective, [145] where on one side
You shall behold the faces and the persons
Of all sufficient young heirs in town,
Whose bonds are current for commodity;
On th' other side, the merchants' forms, and
others,
That without help of any second broker,
Who would expect a share, will trust such
parcels;
In the third square, the very street and sign
Where the commodity dwells, and does but
wait
To be deliver'd, be it pepper, soap,

[145] An ingeniously made picture, the appearance of which changes with the spectator's point
of view or which looks distorted unless seen from
a certain angle. Another form could be properly
seen only through a small hole in a piece of
paper.

Hops, or tobacco, oatmeal, woad, or cheeses.
All which you may so handle, to enjoy
To your own use, and never stand oblig'd.
    KASTRIL. I' faith! is he such a fellow?
    FACE. Why, Nab here knows him.
And then for making matches for rich
    widows,
Young gentlewomen, heirs, the fortunat'st
    man!
He's sent to, far and near, all over England,
To have his counsel, and to know their
    fortunes.
    KASTRIL. God's will, my suster shall see
him.
    FACE. I'll tell you, sir,
What he did tell me of Nab. It's a strange
    thing—
(By the way, you must eat no cheese, Nab,
    it breeds melancholy,
And that same melancholy breeds worms)
    but pass it—
He told me this honest Nab here was ne'er at
    tavern
But once in's life.
    DRUGGER. Truth, and no more I was not.
    FACE. And then he was so sick—
    DRUGGER. Could he tell you that too?
    FACE. How should I know it?
    DRUGGER. In troth, we had been a-shoot-
    ing,
And had a piece of fat ram-mutton to supper,
That lay so heavy o' my stomach—
    FACE. And he has no head
To bear any wine; for what with the noise
    o' the fiddlers,
And care of his shop, for he dares keep no
    servants—
    DRUGGER. My head did so ache—
    FACE. As he was fain to be brought home.
The doctor told me. And then a good old
    woman—
    DRUGGER. Yes, faith, she dwells in Sea-
    coal-lane,—did cure me,
With sodden ale, and pellitory o' the wall;
Cost me but twopence. I had another sickness
Was worse than that.
    FACE. Ay, that was with the grief
Thou took'st for being 'cess'd [146] at eighteeen-
    pence

[146] Assessed, taxed.

For the waterwork.
    DRUGGER. In truth, and it was like
T' have cost me almost my life.
    FACE. Thy hair went off?
    DRUGGER. Yes, sir; 'twas done for spite.
    FACE. Nay, so says the doctor.
    KASTRIL. Pray thee, tobacco-boy, go fetch
    my suster;
I'll see this learned boy before I go;
And so shall she.
    FACE. Sir, he is busy now,
But if you have a sister to fetch hither,
Perhaps your own pains may command her
    sooner;
And he by that time will be free.
    KASTRIL. I go.   (Exit)
    FACE. Drugger, she's thine! The damask!
                (Exit ABEL)
(Aside) Subtle and I
Must wrastle for her.—Come on, Master
    Dapper,
You see how I turn clients here away,
To give your cause dispatch. Ha' you per-
    form'd
The ceremonies were enjoin'd you?
    DAPPER. Yes, o' the vinegar,
And the clean shirt.
    FACE. 'Tis well; that shirt may do you
More worship than you think. Your aunt's
    afire,
But that she will not show it, t' have a sight
    on you.
Ha' you provided for her Grace's servants?
    DAPPER. Yes, here are six score Edward
shillings.
    FACE. Good!
    DAPPER. And an old Harry's sovereign.
    FACE. Very good!
    DAPPER. And three James shillings, and
    an Elizabeth groat,
Just twenty nobles.
    FACE. O, you are too just.
I would you had had the other noble in
    Maries.[147]
    DAPPER. I have some Philip and Maries.
    FACE. Ay, those same
Are best of all; where are they? Hark, the
    doctor.

[147] Coins of the reign of Queen Mary.

Scene V. *The Same.*

(*Enter* Subtle, *dressed like a priest of Faery and carrying a robe for* Drugger *and a blindfold*)

Subtle. (*In a disguised voice*) Is yet her Grace's cousin come?

Face. He is come.

Subtle. And is he fasting?

Face. Yes.

Subtle. And hath cried "hum"?

Face. Thrice, you must answer.

Dapper. Thrice.

Subtle. And as oft "buz"?

Face. If you have, say.

Dapper. I have.

Subtle. Then, to her cuz,
Hoping that he hath vinegar'd his senses,
As he was bid, the Faery Queen dispenses,
By me, this robe, the petticoat of Fortune;
Which that he straight put on, she doth
    importune.
And though to Fortune near be her petticoat,
Yet nearer is her smock, the Queen doth
    note,
And therefore, even of that a piece she hath
    sent,
Which, being a child, to wrap him in was
    rent;
And prays him for a scarf he now will wear it,
With as much love as then her Grace did
    tear it,
About his eyes, to show he is fortunate;
        (*They blindfold him with a rag*)
And, trusting unto her to make his state,
He'll throw away all worldly pelf about him;
Which that he will perform, she doth not
    doubt him.

Face. She need not doubt him, sir. Alas,
    he has nothing
But what he will part withal as willingly,
Upon her Grace's word—throw away your
    purse—
As she would ask it—handkerchiefs and all—
She cannot bid that thing but he'll obey.—
If you have a ring about you, cast it off,
Or a silver seal at your wrist; her Grace will
    send
        (*He throws away, as they bid him*)
Her fairies here to search you, therefore deal

Directly with her Highness. If they find
That you conceal a mite, you are undone.

Dapper. Truly, there's all.

Face. All what?

Dapper. My money; truly.

Face. Keep nothing that is transitory
    about you.
(*Aside to* Subtle) Bid Dol play music.—
    Look, the elves are come
        (Dol *enters with a cittern* [148])
To pinch you, if you tell not truth. Advise
    you.   (*They pinch him*)

Dapper. O! I have a paper with a spur-
ryal [149] in't.

Face. *Ti, ti.*
They knew't, they say.

Subtle. *Ti, ti, ti, ti.* He has more yet.

Face. *Ti, ti-ti-ti.* I' the tother pocket?

Subtle. *Titi, titi, titi, titi.*
They must pinch him or he will never con-
    fess, they say. (*They pinch him again*)

Dapper. O, O!

Face. Nay, pray you, hold; he is her
    Grace's nephew!
Ti, ti, ti? What care you? Good faith, you
    shall care.—
Deal plainly, sir, and shame the fairies. Show
You are an innocent.

Dapper. By this good light, I ha' nothing.

Subtle. *Ti ti, ti ti to ta.* He does equivo-
cate, she says:
Ti, ti do ti, ti ti do, ti da; and swears by the
    light when he is blinded.

Dapper. By this good dark, I ha' nothing
    but a half-crown
Of gold about my wrist, that my love gave me;
And a leaden heart I wore sin' she forsook me.

Face. I thought 'twas something. And
    would you incur
Your aunt's displeasure for these trifles?
    Come,
I had rather you had thrown away twenty
    half-crowns.   (*Takes it off*)
You may wear your leaden heart still.—
    (*Aside to* Dol, *who has come from the
    window*) How now!

---

[148] A stringed instrument somewhat like a modern guitar.
[149] A gold coin of Edward IV.

SUBTLE. (*Aside*) What news, Dol?

DOL COMMON. (*Aside*) Yonder's your knight, Sir Mammon.

FACE. (*Aside*) God's lid, we never thought of him till now!
Where is he?

DOL COMMON. (*Aside*) Here, hard by. He's at the door.

SUBTLE. (*Aside*) And you are not ready now! Dol, get his suit.[150] (*Exit* DOL)
He must not be sent back.

FACE. (*Aside*) O, by no means.
What shall we do with this same puffin here,
Now he's o' the spit?

SUBTLE. (*Aside*) Why, lay him back awhile,
With some device.

(*Re-enter* DOL *with* FACE's *clothes*)

—*Ti, ti ti, ti ti ti.* Would her Grace speak with me?
I come.—(*Aside*) Help, Dol![151]

FACE. —Who's there? Sir Epicure,
(*He speaks through the keyhole, the other knocking*)
My master's i' the way. Please you to walk
Three or four turns, but till his back be turn'd,
And I am for you.—(*Aside*) Quickly, Dol!

SUBTLE. Her Grace
Commends her kindly to you, Master Dapper.

DAPPER. I long to see her Grace.

SUBTLE. She now is set
At dinner in her bed, and she has sent you
From her own private trencher, a dead mouse

And a piece of gingerbread, to be merry withal
And stay your stomach, lest you faint with fasting.
Yet if you could hold out till she saw you, she says,
It would be better for you.

FACE. Sir, he shall
Hold out, an't were this two hours, for her Highness;
I can assure you that. We will not lose
All we ha' done.—

SUBTLE. He must nor see, nor speak
To anybody, till then.

FACE. For that we'll put, sir,
A stay in's mouth.

SUBTLE. Of what?

FACE. Of gingerbread.
Make you it fit. He that hath pleas'd her Grace
Thus far, shall not now crinkle[152] for a little.—
Gape, sir, and let him fit you.
(*They thrust a gag of gingerbread into his mouth*)

SUBTLE. (*Aside*) —Where shall we now Bestow him?

DOL COMMON. (*Aside*) I' the privy.—

SUBTLE. Come along, sir,
I now must show you Fortune's privy lodgings.

FACE. Are they perfum'd, and his bath ready?

SUBTLE. All;
Only the fumigation's somewhat strong.

FACE. (*Speaking through the keyhole*)
Sir Epicure, I am yours, sir, by and by.
(*Exeunt with* DAPPER)

Act IV

SCENE I. *A Room in* LOVEWIT's *House.*

(FACE, *dressed as a laboratory assistant, admits* MAMMON)

FACE. O, sir, y' are come i' the only finest time.—

MAMMON. Where's Master?

FACE. Now preparing for projection, sir.
Your stuff will be all chang'd shortly.

MAMMON. Into gold?

FACE. To gold and silver, sir.

MAMMON. Silver I care not for.

FACE. Yes, sir, a little to give beggars.

[150] *I.e.*, Face's laboratory assistant's clothes.
[151] *I.e.*, Face wants Dol to help him get out of his uniform and into his laboratory assistant's clothes to receive Mammon.
[152] Turn aside from his purpose.

MAMMON. Where's the lady?

FACE. At hand here. I ha' told her such
brave things o' you,
Touching your bounty and your noble spirit—

MAMMON. Hast thou?

FACE. As she is almost in her fit to see you.
But, good sir, no divinity i' your conference,
For fear of putting her in rage.

MAMMON. I warrant thee.

FACE. Six men will not hold her down.
And then,
If the old man should hear or see you—

MAMMON. Fear not.

FACE. The very house, sir, would run mad.
You know it,
How scrupulous he is, and violent,
'Gainst the least act of sin. Physic or mathe-
matics,
Poetry, state, or bawdry, as I told you,
She will endure, and never startle; but
No word of controversy.

MAMMON. I am school'd, good *Ulen*.

FACE. And you must praise her house, remember that,
And her nobility.

MAMMON. Let me alone:
No herald, no, nor antiquary, Lungs,
Shall do it better. Go.

FACE. (*Aside*) Why, this is yet
A kind of modern happiness, to have
Dol Common for a great lady.   (*Exit*)

MAMMON. Now, Epicure,
Heighten thyself, talk to her all in gold;
Rain her as many showers as Jove did drops
Unto his Danaë; show the god a miser,
Compar'd with Mammon. What! the stone
will do't.
She shall feel gold, taste gold, hear gold,
sleep gold;
Nay, we will *concumbere* [153] gold. I will be
puissant
And mighty in my talk to her.—

(*Re-enter* FACE *with* DOL *richly dressed*)

Here she comes.

FACE. (*Aside*) To him, Dol, suckle him.—
This is the noble knight
I told your ladyship—

MAMMON. Madam, with your pardon,
I kiss your vesture.

[153] Fornicate.

DOL COMMON. Sir, I were uncivil
If I would suffer that; my lip to you, sir.

MAMMON. I hope my lord your brother be
in health, lady.

DOL COMMON. My lord my brother is,
though I no lady, sir.

FACE. (*Aside*) Well said, my Guinea
bird. [154]

MAMMON. Right noble madam—

FACE. (*Aside*) O, we shall have most fierce
idolatry.

MAMMON. 'Tis your prerogative.

DOL COMMON. Rather your courtesy.

MAMMON. Were there nought else t' enlarge your virtues to me,
These answers speak your breeding and your
blood.

DOL COMMON. Blood we boast none, sir;
a poor baron's daughter.

MAMMON. Poor! and gat you? Profane not.
Had your father
Slept all the happy remnant of his life
After the act, lien but there still, and panted,
He'd done enough to make himself, his issue,
And his posterity noble.

DOL COMMON. Sir, although
We may be said to want the gilt and trap-
pings,
The dress of honor, yet we strive to keep
The seeds and the materials.

MAMMON. I do see
The old ingredient, virtue, was not lost,
Nor the drug, money, us'd to make your
compound.
There is a strange nobility i' your eye,
This lip, that chin! Methinks you do re-
semble
One o' the Austriac princes.

FACE. (*Aside*) Very like!
Her father was an Irish costermonger.

MAMMON. The house of Valois, just, had
such a nose,
And such a forehead yet the Medici
Of Florence boast.

DOL COMMON. Troth, and I have been
lik'ned
To all these princes.

FACE. (*Aside*) I'll be sworn, I heard it.

MAMMON. I know not how! it is not any
one,
But e'en the very choice of all their features.

[154] Slang for prostitute.

FACE. (*Aside*) I'll in, and laugh. (*Exit*)

MAMMON. A certain touch, or air,
That sparkles a divinity beyond
An earthly beauty!

DOL COMMON. O, you play the courtier.

MAMMON. Good lady, gi' me leave—

DOL COMMON. In faith, I may not,
To mock me, sir.

MAMMON. To burn i' this sweet flame;
The phœnix never knew a nobler death.

DOL COMMON. Nay, now you court the
courtier, and destroy
What you would build. This art, sir, i' your
words,
Calls your whole faith in question.

MAMMON. By my soul—

DOL COMMON. Nay, oaths are made o' the
same air, sir.

MAMMON. Nature
Never bestow'd upon mortality
A more unblam'd, a more harmonious
feature;
She play'd the step-dame in all faces else.
Sweet madam, le' me be particular [155]—

DOL COMMON. Particular, sir! I pray you,
know your distance.

MAMMON. In no ill sense, sweet lady, but
to ask
How your fair graces pass the hours? I see
Y' are lodg'd here, i' the house of a rare man,
An excellent artist; but what's that to you?

DOL COMMON. Yes, sir. I study here the
mathematics,
And distillation.

MAMMON. O, I cry your pardon.
He's a divine instructor! can extract
The souls of all things by his art; call all
The virtues and the miracles of the sun
Into a temperate furnace; teach dull nature
What her own forces are. A man, the emp'ror
Has courted above Kelley; [156] sent his medals
And chains t' invite him.

DOL COMMON. Ay, and for his physic,
sir—

MAMMON. Above the art of Æsculapius,
That drew the envy of the thunderer!
I know all this, and more.

DOL COMMON. Troth, I am taken, sir,

Whole with these studies that contemplate
nature.

MAMMON. It is a noble humor; but this
form
Was not intended to so dark a use.
Had you been crooked, foul, of some coarse
mold,
A cloister had done well; but such a feature,
That might stand up the glory of a kingdom,
To live recluse is a mere solecism,
Though in a nunnery. It must not be.
I muse, my lord your brother will permit it!
You should spend half my land first, were
I he.
Does not this diamond better on my finger
Than i' the quarry?

DOL COMMON. Yes.

MAMMON. Why, you are like it.
You were created, lady, for the light.
Here, you shall wear it; take it, the first
pledge
Of what I speak, to bind you to believe me.

DOL COMMON. In chains of adamant?

MAMMON. Yes, the strongest bands.
And take a secret too.—Here, by your side,
Doth stand this hour the happiest man in
Europe.

DOL COMMON. You are contented, sir?

MAMMON. Nay, in true being,
The envy of princes and the fear of states.

DOL COMMON. Say you so, Sir Epicure?

MAMMON. Yes, and thou shalt prove it,
Daughter of honor. I have cast mine eye
Upon thy form, and I will rear this beauty
Above all styles.

DOL COMMON. You mean no treason, sir?

MAMMON. No, I will take away that
jealousy.
I am the lord of the philosopher's stone,
And thou the lady.

DOL COMMON. How, sir! ha' you that?

MAMMON. I am the master of the mas-
tery.[157]
This day the good old wretch here o' the
house
Has made it for us. Now he's at projection.
Think therefore thy first wish now, let me
hear it;
And it shall rain into thy lap, no shower,
But floods of gold, whole cataracts, a deluge,
To get a nation on thee.

---

[155] Familiar.
[156] An alchemist (d. 1595), associate of Dr.
Dee. Rudolph II of Germany was one of his
dupes.

[157] Art of transmutation, magisterium.

Dol Common. You are pleas'd, sir,
To work on the ambition of our sex.
  Mammon. I'm pleas'd the glory of her sex
    should know,
This nook here of the Friars [158] is no climate
For her to live obscurely in, to learn
Physic and surgery, for the constable's wife
Of some odd hundred [159] in Essex; but come
    forth,
And taste the air of palaces; eat, drink
The toils of emp'rics, and their boasted prac-
    tice;
Tincture of pearl, and coral, gold, and amber;
Be seen at feasts and triumphs; have it ask'd,
What miracle she is; set all the eyes
Of court a-fire, like a burning glass,
And work 'em into cinders, when the jewels
Of twenty states adorn thee, and the light
Strikes out the stars; that, when thy name
    is mention'd,
Queens may look pale; and, we but showing
    our love,
Nero's Poppæa may be lost in story!
Thus will we have it.
  Dol Common. I could well consent, sir.
But in a monarchy, how will this be?
The prince will soon take notice, and both
    seize
You and your stone, it being a wealth unfit
For any private subject.
  Mammon. If he knew it.
  Dol Common. Yourself do boast it, sir.
  Mammon. To thee, my life.
  Dol Common. O, but beware, sir! you
    may come to end
The remnant of your days in a loath'd prison,
By speaking of it.

  Mammon. 'Tis no idle fear!
We'll therefore go with all, my girl, and live
In a free state, where we will eat our mullets,
Sous'd in high-country wines, sup pheasants'
    eggs,
And have our cockles boil'd in silver shells;
Our shrimps to swim again, as when they
    liv'd,
In a rare butter made of dolphins' milk,
Whose cream does look like opals; and with
    these
Delicate meats set ourselves high for pleasure,
And take us down again, and then renew
Our youth and strength with drinking the
    elixir;
And so enjoy a perpetuity
Of life and lust! And thou shalt ha' thy
    wardrobe
Richer than Nature's, still to change thyself,
And vary oft'ner for thy pride than she,
Or Art, her wise and almost-equal servant.

  (*Re-enter* Face)

  Face. Sir, you are too loud. I hear you
    every word
Into the laboratory. Some fitter place;
The garden, or great chamber above. (*Aside*)
    How like you her?
  Mammon. Excellent, Lungs! There's for
thee.   (*Gives him money*)
  Face. But do you hear?
Good sir, beware, no mention of the rabbins.
  Mammon. We think not on 'em.
  Face. O, it is well, sir.
                (*Exeunt* Mammon *and* Dol)
—Subtle!

SCENE II. *The Same.*

(*Enter* Subtle)

Dost thou not laugh?
  Subtle. Yes; are they gone?
  Face. All's clear.
  Subtle. The widow is come.

[158] Blackfriars, the district of London in which
Lovewit's house is located and which also contained the theatre in which the play was probably first performed.
[159] Subdivision of a county.

  Face. And your quarreling disciple?
  Subtle. Ay.
  Face. I must to my captainship again then.
  Subtle. Stay, bring 'em in first.
  Face. So I meant. What is she?
A bonnibel?
  Subtle. I know not.
  Face. We'll draw lots;
You'll stand to that?
  Subtle. What else?
  Face. O, for a suit,

To fall now like a curtain, flap![160]

SUBTLE. To th' door, man.

FACE. You'll ha' the first kiss, 'cause I am not ready.   (*Exit*)

SUBTLE. Yes, and perhaps hit you through both the nostrils.

FACE. (*Within*) Who would you speak with?

KASTRIL. (*Within*) Where's the Captain?

FACE. (*Within*) Gone, sir,
About some business.

KASTRIL. (*Within*) Gone!

FACE. (*Within*) He'll return straight.
But Master Doctor, his lieutenant, is here.

(*Enter* KASTRIL, *followed by* DAME PLIANT)

SUBTLE. Come near, my worshipful boy,
    my *terræ fili*,
That is, my boy of land; make thy approaches.
Welcome; I know thy lusts and thy desires,
And I will serve and satisfy 'em. Begin,
Charge me from thence, or thence, or in this
    line;
Here is my centre: ground thy quarrel.

KASTRIL. You lie.

SUBTLE. How, child of wrath and anger!
  the loud lie?
For what, my sudden boy?

KASTRIL. Nay, that look you to,
I am aforehand.

SUBTLE. O, this's no true grammar,
And as ill logic! You must render causes,[161]
    child,
Your first and second intentions, know your
    canons
And your divisions, moods, degrees, and dif-
    ferences,
Your predicaments, substance, and accident,
Series extern and intern, with their causes
Efficient, material, formal, final,
And ha' your elements perfect—

KASTRIL. What is this?
The angry[162] tongue he talks in?

SUBTLE. That false precept,

---

[160] *I.e.*, so that he could change his suit without leaving Subtle alone with the girl.

[161] Subtle's language in this passage, derived
from the jargon of scholastic logic and philosophy, is designed to confuse Kastril. There were
books on the etiquette of quarrelling for the gallants of the time.

[162] Swaggering.

Of being aforehand, has deceiv'd a number,
And made 'em enter quarrels oftentimes
Before they were aware; and afterward,
Against their wills.

KASTRIL. How must I do then, sir?

SUBTLE. I cry this lady mercy; she should
    first
Have been saluted. I do call you lady,
Because you are to be one ere't be long,
My soft and buxom widow.   (*He kisses her*)

KASTRIL. Is she, i' faith?

SUBTLE. Yes, or my art is an egregious
liar.

KASTRIL. How know you?

SUBTLE. By inspection on her forehead,
And subtlety of her lip, which must be
    tasted
Often to make a judgment.
                        (*He kisses her again*)
'Slight, she melts
Like a myrobolane.[163] Here is yet a line,
In *rivo frontis*,[164] tells me he is no knight.

DAME PLIANT. What is he then, sir?

SUBTLE. Let me see your hand.
O, your *linea fortunæ* makes it plain;
And *stella* here *in monte veneris*.
But, most of all, *junctura annularis*.[165]
He is a soldier, or a man of art, lady,
But shall have some great honor shortly.

DAME PLIANT. Brother,
He's a rare man, believe me!

(*Re-enter* FACE, *in his uniform*)

KASTRIL. Hold your peace.
Here comes the tother rare man.—'Save you,
    Captain.

FACE. Good master Kastril! Is this your
sister?

KASTRIL. Ay, sir.
Please you to kuss her, and be proud to know
    her.

FACE. I shall be proud to know you, lady.
                              (*Kisses her*)

DAME PLIANT. Brother,
He calls me lady, too.

KASTRIL. Ay, peace; I heard it.
                         (*Takes her aside*)

FACE. The count is come.

SUBTLE. Where is he?

---

[163] Sugar plum.
[164] Frontal vein.
[165] Terms in palmistry.

FACE. At the door.

SUBTLE. Why, you must entertain him.

FACE. What'll you do
With these the while?

SUBTLE. Why, have 'em up, and show 'em
Some fustian book, or the dark glass.

FACE. 'Fore God,
She is a delicate dabchick! I must have her.
                              (Exit)

SUBTLE. (Aside) Must you! Ay, if your
    fortune will, you must.—
Come, sir, the Captain will come to us pres-
    ently.
I'll ha' you to my chamber of demonstrations,
Where I'll show you both the grammar and
    logic
And rhetoric of quarreling; my whole method
Drawn out in tables; and my instrument,
That hath the several scale upon't shall make
    you
Able to quarrel at a straw's-breadth by moon-
    light.
And, lady, I'll have you look in a glass,
Some half an hour, but to clear your eyesight,
Against you see your fortune; which is
    greater
Than I may judge upon the sudden, trust me.
                              (Exeunt)

SCENE III. *The Same.*

(*Enter* FACE)

FACE. Where are you, Doctor?

SUBTLE. (*Within*) I'll come to you pres-
    ently.

FACE. I will ha' this same widow, now I
    ha' seen her,
On any composition.

(*Enter* SUBTLE)

SUBTLE. What do you say?

FACE. Ha' you dispos'd of them?

SUBTLE. I ha' sent 'em up.

FACE. Subtle, in troth, I needs must have
this widow.

SUBTLE. Is that the matter?

FACE. Nay, but hear me.

SUBTLE. Go to.
If you rebel once, Dol shall know it all.
Therefore be quiet, and obey your chance.

FACE. Nay, thou art so violent now. Do
but conceive,
Thou art old, and canst not serve—

SUBTLE. Who cannot? I?
'Slight, I will serve her with thee, for a—

FACE. Nay,
But understand; I'll gi' you composition.

SUBTLE. I will not treat with thee. What!
    sell my fortune?
'Tis better than my birthright. Do not mur-
    mur.
Win her, and carry her. If you grumble, Dol
Knows it directly.

FACE. Well, sir, I am silent.
Will you go help to fetch in Don in state?
                              (Exit)

SUBTLE. I follow you, sir. We must keep
    Face in awe,
Or he will overlook us like a tyrant.

(*Re-enter* FACE, *ushering in* SURLY, *who is
    disguised in the elaborate costume of a
    Spanish nobleman*)

Brain of a tailor! who comes here? Don John!

SURLY. Señores, beso las manos à vuestras
mercedes.[166]

SUBTLE. Would you had stopp'd a little,
and kiss'd our *anos.*

FACE. Peace, Subtle!

SUBTLE. Stab me; I shall never hold, man.
He looks in that deep ruff like a head in a
    platter,
Serv'd in by a short cloak upon two trestles.

FACE. Or what do you say to a collar of
    brawn, cut down

Beneath the souse, and wriggled with a
    knife?

SUBTLE. 'Slud, he does look too fat to be
a Spaniard.

FACE. Perhaps some Fleming or some Hol-
    lander got him
In d'Alva's time; Count Egmont's bastard.

SUBTLE. Don,
Your scurvy, yellow, Madrid face is welcome.

SURLY. *Gratia.*

[166] Gentlemen, I kiss your worships' hands.

SUBTLE. He speaks out of a fortification.
Pray God he ha' no squibs in those deeps
   sets.[167]
SURLY. *Por dios, señores, muy linda
casa!* [168]
SUBTLE. What says he?
FACE. Praises the house, I think;
I know no more but's action.
SUBTLE. Yes, the *casa*,
My precious Diego, will prove fair enough
To cozen you in. Do you mark? You shall
Be cozened, Diego.
FACE. Cozened, do you see,
My worthy Donzel, cozened.
SURLY. *Entiendo.*[169]
SUBTLE. Do you intend it? So do we, dear
   Don.
Have you brought pistolets or portagues,
My solemn Don? (*To* FACE) Dost thou feel
   any?   (*He feels his pockets*)
FACE. Full.
SUBTLE. You shall be emptied, Don,
   pumped and drawn
Dry, as they say.
FACE. Milked, in troth, sweet Don.
SUBTLE. See all the monsters; the great
lion of all, Don.
SURLY. *Con licencia, se puede ver à esta
señora?* [170]
SUBTLE. What talks he now?
FACE. O' the señora.
SUBTLE. O, Don,
That is the lioness, which you shall see
Also, my Don.
FACE. 'Slid, Subtle, how shall we do?
SUBTLE. For what?
FACE. Why, Dol's employ'd, you know.
SUBTLE. That's true.
'Fore heav'n I know not: he must stay, that's
all.
FACE. Stay! that he must not by no means.
SUBTLE. No! why?
FACE. Unless you'll mar all. 'Slight, he'll
   suspect it;
And then he will not pay, not half so well.
This is a travell'd punk-master, and does
   know
All the delays; a notable hot rascal,
And looks already rampant.

[167] Plaits of his ruff.
[168] By God, sirs, a very pretty house.
[169] I understand.
[170] If you please, may I see the lady?

SUBTLE. 'Sdeath, and Mammon
Must not be troubled.
FACE. Mammon! in no case.
SUBTLE. What shall we do then?
FACE. Think: you must be sudden.
SURLY. *Entiendo que la señora es tan
hermosa, que codìcio tan à verla como la bien
aventuránça de mi vida.*[171]
FACE. *Mi vida!* 'Slid, Subtle, he puts me
   in mind o' the widow.
What dost thou say to draw her to 't, ha!
And tell her it is her fortune? All our venter
Now lies upon't. It is but one man more,
Which on's chance to have her: and beside,
There is no maidenhead to be fear'd or lost.
What dost thou think on't, Subtle?
SUBTLE. Who, I? why—
FACE. The credit of our house, too, is en-
gag'd.
SUBTLE. You made me an offer for my
   share erewhile.
What wilt thou gi' me, i'faith?
FACE. O, by that light,
I'll not buy now. You know your doom [172]
   to me.
E'en take your lot, obey your chance, sir; win
   her,
And wear her—out for me.
SUBTLE. 'Slight, I'll not work her then.
FACE. It is the common cause; therefore
   bethink you.
Dol else must know it, as you said.
SUBTLE. I care not.
SURLY. *Señores, porque se tarda tanto?* [173]
SUBTLE. Faith, I am not fit, I am old.
FACE. That's now no reason, sir.
SURLY. *Puede ser de hazer burla de mi
amor?* [174]
FACE. You hear the Don too? By this air,
   I call,
And loose the hinges. Dol!
SUBTLE. A plague of hell—
FACE. Will you then do?
SUBTLE. Y'are a terrible rogue!
I'll think of this. Will you, sir, call the
   widow?
FACE. Yes, and I'll take her, too, with all
   her faults,

[171] I understand that the lady is so beautiful
that I am as anxious about seeing her as about
the good fortune of my life.
[172] Decision.   [173] Sirs, why so much delay?
[174] Can it be to make fun of my love?

Now I do think on't better.

SUBTLE. With all my heart, sir;
Am I discharg'd o' the lot?

FACE. As you please.

SUBTLE. Hands.   (*They shake hands*)

FACE. Remember now, that upon any
change
You never claim her.

SUBTLE. Much good joy and health to you,
sir.

Marry a whore! Fate, let me wed a witch
first.

SURLY. *Por estas honradas barbas—*[175]

SUBTLE. He swears by his beard.
Dispatch, and call the brother, too.
                    (*Exit* FACE)

SURLY. *Tengo duda, señores' que no me
hágan alguna traycion.*[176]

SUBTLE. How, issue on? Yes, *præsto,
señor.* Please you

Enthratha the *chambratha,* worthy Don,
Where if you please the fates, in your
bathada,
You shall be soak'd, and strok'd, and tubb'd,
and rubb'd,
And scrubb'd, and fubb'd, dear Don, before
you go.
You shall in faith, my scurvy baboon Don,
Be curried, claw'd, and flaw'd, and taw'd,
indeed.
I will the heartilier go about it now,
And make the widow a punk so much the
sooner,
To be reveng'd on this impetuous Face:
The quickly doing of it is the grace.
                    (*Exeunt* SUBTLE *and* SURLY)

SCENE IV. *The Same.*

(*Re-enter* FACE, *accompanied by* KASTRIL
and his sister, DAME PLIANT)

FACE. Come, lady. (*To* KASTRIL) I knew
the Doctor would not leave
Till he had found the very nick of her fortune.

KASTRIL. To be a countess, say you?

FACE. A Spanish countess, sir.

DAME PLIANT. Why, is that better than
an English countess?

FACE. Better! 'Slight, make you that a
question, lady?

KASTRIL. Nay, she is a fool, Captain, you
must pardon her.

FACE. Ask him from your courtier to your
inns-of-court-man,
To your mere milliner; they will tell you all,
Your Spanish jennet is the best horse; your
Spanish
Stoop is the best garb;[177] your Spanish beard
Is the best cut; your Spanish ruffs are the best
Wear; your Spanish pavin the best dance;
Your Spanish titillation in a glove
The best perfume; and for your Spanish pike
And Spanish blade, let your poor captain
speak.—
Here comes the Doctor.

(*Enter* SUBTLE *with a paper*)

SUBTLE. My most honor'd lady,
For so I am now to style you, having found
By this my scheme,[178] you are to undergo
An honorable fortune very shortly,
What will you say now, if some—

FACE. I ha' told her all, sir,
And her right worshipful brother here, that
she shall be
A countess; do not delay 'em, sir; a Spanish
countess.

SUBTLE. Still, my scarce-worshipful captain, you can keep
No secret! Well, since he has told you,
madam,
Do you forgive him, and I do.

KASTRIL. She shall do that, sir;
I'll look to't; 'tis my charge.

SUBTLE. Well, then, nought rests
But that she fit her love now to her fortune.

DAME PLIANT. Truly I shall never brook
a Spaniard.

SUBTLE. No?

DAME PLIANT. Never sin' eighty-eight
could I abide 'em,
And that was some three year afore I was
born, in truth.

SUBTLE. Come, you must love him, or be
miserable;

[175] By this honored beard.
[176] I fear, sirs, you are playing me some foul
trick.   [177] Bodily carriage.

[178] Horoscope.

Choose which you will.

FACE. By this good rush,[179] persuade her.
She will cry [180] strawberries else within this
twelvemonth.

SUBTLE. Nay, shads and mackerel, which
is worse.

FACE. Indeed, sir!

KASTRIL. God's lid, you shall love him,
or I'll kick you.

DAME PLIANT. Why,
I'll do as you will ha' me, brother.

KASTRIL. Do,
Or by this hand I'll maul you.

FACE. Nay, good sir,
Be not so fierce.

SUBTLE. No, my enraged child;
She will be rul'd. What, when she comes
to taste
The pleasures of a countess! to be courted—

FACE. And kiss'd and ruffled!

SUBTLE. Ay, behind the hangings.

FACE. And then come forth in pomp!

SUBTLE. And know her state!

FACE. Of keeping all th' idolators o' the
chamber
Barer to her, than at their prayers!

SUBTLE. Is serv'd
Upon the knee!

FACE. And has her pages, ushers,
Footmen, and coaches—

SUBTLE. Her six mares—

FACE. Nay, eight!

SUBTLE. To hurry her through London,
to th' Exchange,
Bet'lem, the China-houses—

FACE. Yes, and have
The citizens gape at her, and praise her tires,
And my lord's goose-turd [181] bands, that rides
with her!

KASTRIL. Most brave! By this hand, you
are not my suster
If you refuse.

DAME PLIANT. I will not refuse, brother.

(*Enter* SURLY)

SURLY. *Que es esto, señores, que non se
venga?
Esta tardanza me mata!* [182]

[179] The floor of the stage was covered with
rushes.
[180] Hawk on the street.   [181] Greenish-yellow.
[182] Why does she not come, sirs? This delay
is killing me.

FACE. It is the count come!
The Doctor knew he would be here, by his
art.

SUBTLE. (*Introducing* DAME PLIANT) *En
gallanta madama, Don! gallantissima!*

SURLY. *Por todos los dioses, la mas acabada
Hermosura, que he visto en mi vida!* [183]

FACE. Is't not a gallant language that they
speak?

KASTRIL. An admirable language! Is't not
French?

FACE. No, Spanish, sir.

KASTRIL. It goes like law French,
And that, they say, is the courtliest language.

FACE. List, sir.

SURLY. *El sol ha perdido su lumbre, con el
Resplandor que tràe esta dama! Valga me
dios!* [184]

FACE. H'admires your sister.

KASTRIL. Must not she make curt'sy?

SUBTLE. 'Ods will, she must go to him,
man, and kiss him!
It is the Spanish fashion, for the women
To make first court.

FACE. 'Tis true he tells you, sir;
His art knows all.

SURLY. *Porque no se acùde?* [185]

KASTRIL. He speaks to her, I think.

FACE. That he does, sir.

SURLY. *Por el amor de dios, que es esto
que se tàrda?* [186]

KASTRIL. Nay, see: she will not understand him! Gull, noddy!

DAME PLIANT. What say you, brother?

KASTRIL. Ass, my suster,
Go kuss him, as the cunning man would ha'
you;
I'll thrust a pin i' your buttocks else.

FACE. O no, sir.

SURLY. *Señora mia, mi persona muy
indigna està
Allegar à tanta hermosura.* [187]

FACE. Does he not use her bravely?

KASTRIL. Bravely, i' faith!

FACE. Nay, he will use her better.

[183] By all the gods, the most perfect beauty
that I have seen in my life!
[184] The sun has lost his light with the splendor
this lady brings, so help me God.
[185] Why do you not draw near?
[186] For the love of God, why this delay?
[187] My lady, my person is most unworthy to
approach such beauty.

KASTRIL. Do you think so?
SURLY. *Señora, si sera servida, entremos.*[188]
        (*Exit with* DAME PLIANT)
KASTRIL. Where does he carry her?
FACE. Into the garden, sir;
Take you no thought. I must interpret for
    her.
SUBTLE. (*Aside to* FACE) Give Dol the
    word.   (*Exit* FACE)
—Come, my fierce child, advance,
We'll to our quarrelling lesson again.
KASTRIL. Agreed.
I love a Spanish boy with all my heart.
SUBTLE. Nay, and by this means, sir, you
    shall be brother
To a great count.
KASTRIL. Ay, I knew that at first.

This match will advance the house of the
    Kastrils.
SUBTLE. 'Pray God your sister prove but
pliant!
KASTRIL. Why,
Her name is so, by her other husband.
SUBTLE. How!
KASTRIL. The Widow Pliant. Knew you
not that?
SUBTLE. No, faith, sir;
Yet, by the erection of her figure,[189] I guess'd
it.
Come, let's go practise.
KASTRIL. Yes, but do you think, Doctor,
I e'er shall quarrel well?
SUBTLE. I warrant you.   (*Exeunt*)

SCENE V. *The Same.*

(*Enter* DOL, *in her fit of violent talking,*[190] *followed by* MAMMON)

DOL COMMON. For, after Alexander's
death—
MAMMON. Good lady—
DOL COMMON. That Perdiccas and An-
tigonus were slain,
The two that stood, Seleuc' and Ptolemy—
MAMMON. Madam—
DOL COMMON. Made up the two legs,
    and the fourth beast,
That was Gog-north and Egypt-south: which
    after
Was call'd Gog-iron-leg and South-iron-leg—
MAMMON. Lady—
DOL COMMON. And then Gog-horned.
    So was Egypt, too:
Then Egypt-clay-leg, and Gog-clay-leg—
MAMMON. Sweet madam—
DOL COMMON. And last Gog-dust, and
    Egypt-dust, which fall
In the last link of the fourth chain. And these
Be stars in story, which none see, or look at—

MAMMON. What shall I do?
DOL COMMON. For, as he says, except
We call the rabbins, and the heathen
    Greeks—
MAMMON. Dear lady—
DOL COMMON. To come from Salem, and
    from Athens,
And teach the people of Great Britain—

(*Enter* FACE *hastily, in his laboratory assistant's dress*)

FACE. What's the matter, sir?
DOL COMMON. To speak the tongue of
Eber and Javan—
MAMMON. O,
She's in her fit.
DOL COMMON. We shall know nothing—
FACE. Death, sir,
We are undone!
DOL COMMON. Where then a learned
    linguist
Shall see the ancient us'd communion
Of vowels and consonants—
FACE. My master will hear!
DOL COMMON. A wisdom, which Pythag-
oras held most high—
MAMMON. Sweet honorable lady!
DOL COMMON. To comprise
All sounds of voices, in few marks of letters.

[188] Madam, if you please, let us go in.
[189] Horoscope (with an obvious pun).
[190] Face had told Mammon (II, 3, 251-56) that Dol was being treated for madness. She raves whenever anything touching the Hebrew scriptures is mentioned.

FACE. Nay, you must never hope to lay her now.

(*They speak together* [191])

DOL COMMON. And so we may arrive by Talmud skill,
And profane Greek, to raise the building up
Of Helen's house against the Ismaelite,
King of Thogarma, and his habergions
Brimstony, blue, and fiery; and the force
Of king Abaddon, and the beast of Cittim:
Which rabbi David Kimchi, Onkelos,
And Aben Ezra do interpret Rome.

FACE. How did you put her into't?

MAMMON. Alas, I talk'd
Of a fift monarchy I would erect
With the philosopher's stone, by chance, and she
Falls on the other four straight.

FACE. Out of Broughton!
I told you so. 'Slid, stop her mouth.

MAMMON. Is't best?

FACE. She'll never leave else. If the old man hear her,
We are but *fæces*, ashes.

SUBTLE. (*Within*) What's to do there?

FACE. O, we are lost! Now she hears him, she is quiet.

(*Enter* SUBTLE. MAMMON *stands aghast. Exeunt* FACE *and* DOL)

MAMMON. Where shall I hide me!

SUBTLE. How! What sight is here?
Close deeds of darkness, and that shun the light!
Bring him again. Who is he? What, my son!
O, I have liv'd too long.

MAMMON. Nay, good, dear father,
There was no unchaste purpose.

SUBTLE. Not? and flee me
When I come in?

MAMMON. That was my error.

SUBTLE. Error?
Guilt, guilt, my son; give it the right name. No marvel
If I found check in our great work within,
When such affairs as these were managing!

MAMMON. Why, have you so?

SUBTLE. It has stood still this half hour,
And all the rest of our less works gone back.
Where is the instrument of wickedness,

My lewd false drudge?

MAMMON. Nay, good sir, blame not him;
Believe me, 'twas against his will or knowledge.
I saw her by chance.

SUBTLE. Will you commit more sin,
T'excuse a varlet?

MAMMON. By my hope, 'tis true, sir.

SUBTLE. Nay, then I wonder less, if you, for whom
The blessing was prepar'd, would so tempt heaven,
And lose your fortunes.

MAMMON. Why, sir?

SUBTLE. This'll retard
The work a month at least.

MAMMON. Why, if it do,
What remedy? But think it not, good father;
Our purposes were honest. [192]

SUBTLE. As they were,
So the reward will prove.

(*A great crack and noise within*)
How now! ay me!
God and all saints be good to us.—

(*Re-enter* FACE)

What's that?

FACE. O, sir, we are defeated! All the works
Are flown *in fumo*, every glass is burst!
Furnace and all rent down, as if a bolt
Of thunder had been driven through the house.
Retorts, receivers, pelicans, bolt-heads,
All struck in shivers!

(SUBTLE *falls down, as in a swoon*)
Help, good sir! alas,
Coldness and death invades him. Nay, Sir Mammon,
Do the fair offices of a man! You stand,
As you were readier to depart than he.

(*One knocks*)
Who's there? My lord her brother is come.

MAMMON. Ha, Lungs!

FACE. His coach is at the door. Avoid his sight,
For he's as furious as his sister is mad.

MAMMON. Alas!

FACE. My brain is quite undone with the fume, sir,
I ne'er must hope to be mine own man again.

---

[191] *I.e.,* Dol continues to rave while Mammon and Face speak.

[192] Chaste.

MAMMON. Is all lost, Lungs? Will nothing
  be preserv'd
Of all our cost?
FACE. Faith, very little, sir;
A peck of coals or so, which is cold comfort,
  sir.
MAMMON. O, my voluptuous mind! I am
  justly punish'd.
FACE. And so am I, sir.
MAMMON. Cast from all my hopes—
FACE. Nay, certainties, sir.
MAMMON. By mine own base affections.
        (SUBTLE *seems come to himself*)
SUBTLE. O, the curst fruits of vice and
lust!
MAMMON. Good father,
It was my sin. Forgive it.
SUBTLE. Hangs my roof
Over us still, and will not fall, O Justice,
Upon us, for this wicked man!
FACE. Nay, look, sir,
You grieve him now with staying in his sight.
Good sir, the nobleman will come too, and
  take you,
And that may breed a tragedy.
MAMMON. I'll go.
FACE. Ay, and repent at home, sir. It may
  be,
For some good penance you may ha' it yet;
A hundred pound to the box at Bet'lem—
MAMMON. Yes.
FACE. For the restoring such as ha' their
wits.
MAMMON. I'll do't.
FACE. I'll send one to you to receive it.
MAMMON. Do.
Is no projection left?
FACE. All flown, or stinks, sir.
MAMMON. Will nought be sav'd that's
good for med'cine, think'st thou?

FACE. I cannot tell, sir. There will be
  perhaps
Something about the scraping of the shards,
Will cure the itch,—though not your itch
  of mind, sir.
It shall be sav'd for you, and sent home.
  Good sir,
This way, for fear the lord should meet you.
                (*Exit* MAMMON)
SUBTLE. (*Raising his head*) Face!
FACE. Ay.
SUBTLE. Is he gone?
FACE. Yes, and as heavily
As all the gold he hop'd for were in his blood.
Let us be light though.
SUBTLE. (*Leaping up*) Ay, as balls, and
  bound
And hit our heads against the roof for joy:
There's so much of our care now cast away.
FACE. Now to our Don.
SUBTLE. Yes, your young widow by this
  time
Is made a countess, Face; she's been in
  travail
Of a young heir for you.
FACE. Good, sir.
SUBTLE. Off with your case,[193]
And greet her kindly, as a bridegroom should,
After these common hazards.
FACE. Very well, sir.
Will you go fetch Don Diego off the while?
SUBTLE. And fetch him over too, if you'll
  be pleas'd, sir.
Would Dol were in her place, to pick his
  pockets now!
FACE. Why, you can do it as well, if you
  would set to't.
I pray you prove your virtue.
SUBTLE. For your sake, sir.   (*Exeunt*)

SCENE VI. *The Same.*

(*Enter* SURLY, *still in his Spanish nobleman's costume, and* DAME PLIANT)

SURLY. Lady, you see into what hands you
  are fall'n;
'Mongst what a nest of villains! and how near
Your honor was t'have catch'd a certain clap,
Through your credulity, had I but been

So punctually forward, as place, time,
And other circumstance would ha' made a
  man;
For y'are a handsome woman: would you
  were wise too!
I am a gentleman come here disguis'd,

---

[193] His laboratory assistant's costume.

Only to find the knaveries of this citadel;
And where I might have wrong'd your honor,
　　and have not,
I claim some interest in your love. You are,
They say, a widow, rich; and I'm a bachelor,
Worth nought. Your fortunes may make me
　　a man,
As mine ha' preserv'd you a woman. Think
　　upon it,
And whether I have deserv'd you or no.
　　DAME PLIANT. I will, sir.
　　SURLY. And for these household-rogues,
　　let me alone
To treat with them.

(Enter SUBTLE*)*

SUBTLE. How doth my noble Diego,
And my dear madam Countess? Hath the
　　Count
Been courteous, lady? liberal and open?
Donzel, methinks you look melancholic,
After your *coitum,* and scurvy! Truly,
I do not like the dulness of your eye;
It hath a heavy cast, 'tis upsee Dutch,
And says you are a lumpish whore-master.
Be lighter, I will make your pockets so.
　　　　　　(He falls to picking of them)
　　SURLY. Will you, Don Bawd and Pick-
　　purse?
(Knocks him down) How now! Reel you?
Stand up, sir, you shall find, since I am so
　　heavy,
I'll gi' you equal weight.
　　SUBTLE. Help! murder!
　　SURLY. No, sir,
There's no such thing intended. A good cart
And a clean whip [194] shall ease you of that
　　fear.
I am the Spanish Don that should be cozened,
Do you see? Cozened? Where's your Captain
　　Face,

That parcel-broker, and whole-bawd, all
　　rascal?

(Enter FACE *in his uniform)*

　　FACE. How, Surly!
　　SURLY. O, make your approach, good
　　Captain.
I've found from whence your copper rings
　　and spoons
Come now, wherewith you cheat abroad in
　　taverns.
'Twas here you learn'd t'anoint your boot
　　with brimstone,
Then rub men's gold on't for a kind of touch,
And say 'twas naught, when you had chang'd
　　the color,
That you might ha't for nothing. And this
　　Doctor,
Your sooty, smoky-bearded compeer, he
Will close you so much gold, in a bolt's-head,
And, on a turn, convey i' the stead another
With sublim'd mercury, that shall burst i'
　　the heat,
And fly out all *in fumo!* Then weeps Mam-
　　mon;
Then swoons his worship. Or, *(*FACE *slips
　　out)* he is the Faustus,
That casteth figures and can conjure, cures
Plagues, piles, and pox, by the ephemerides,
And holds intelligence with all the bawds
And midwives of three shires; while you
　　send in—
Captain!—What! is he gone?—damsels with
　　child,
Wives that are barren, or the waiting-maid
With the green sickness.
　　　　　　(Seizes SUBTLE *as he is retiring)*
—Nay, sir, you must tarry,
Though he be scap'd; and answer by the ears,
　　sir.

SCENE VII. *The Same.*

(Re-enter FACE *with* KASTRIL*)*

　　FACE. Why, now's the time, if ever you
　　will quarrel
Well, as they say, and be a true-born child.

[194] Bawds were whipped through town at the
tail of a cart.

The Doctor and your sister both are abus'd.
　　KASTRIL. Where is he? Which is he?
　　He is a slave,
Whate'er he is, and the son of a whore.—
　　Are you
The man, sir, I would know?
　　SURLY. I should be loth, sir,

To confess so much.

Kastril. Then you lie i' your throat.

Surly. How!

Face. (*To* Kastril) A very arrant rogue, sir, and a cheater,

Employ'd here by another conjurer

That does not love the Doctor, and would cross him,

If he knew how.

Surly. Sir, you are abus'd.

Kastril. You lie:

And 'tis no matter.

Face. Well said, sir! He is

The impudent'st rascal—

Surly. You are indeed. Will you hear me, sir?

Face. By no means. Bid him be gone.

Kastril. Begone, sir, quickly.

Surly. This's strange! Lady, do you inform your brother.

Face. There is not such a foist [195] in all the town.

The Doctor had him presently; and finds yet

The Spanish Count will come here.— (*Aside*) Bear up, Subtle.

Subtle. Yes, sir, he must appear within this hour.

Face. And yet this rogue would come in a disguise,

By the temptation of another spirit,

To trouble our art, though he could not hurt it.

Kastril. Ay,

I know—(*To his sister*) Away, you talk like a foolish mauther. [196]

Surly. Sir, all is truth she says.

Face. Do not believe him, sir.

He is the lying'st swabber! Come your ways, sir.

Surly. You are valiant out of company!

Kastril. Yes, how then, sir?

(*Enter* Drugger *with a piece of damask*)

Face. Nay, here's an honest fellow too that knows him,

And all his tricks.—(*Aside to* Drugger) Make good what I say, Abel;

This cheater would ha' cozen'd thee o' the widow.—

He owes this honest Drugger here seven pound,

He has had on him in twopenny'orths of tobacco.

Drugger. Yes, sir. And's damn'd himself three terms to pay me.

Face. And what does he owe for lotium?

Drugger. Thirty shillings, sir;

And for six syringes.

Surly. Hydra of villainy!

Face. Nay, sir, you must quarrel him out o' the house.

Kastril. I will.

—Sir, if you get not out o' doors, you lie;

And you are a pimp.

Surly. Why, this is madness, sir,

Not valor in you. I must laugh at this.

Kastril. It is my humor; you are a pimp and a trig, [197]

And an Amadis de Gaul, or a Don Quixote.

Drugger. Or a knight o' the curious coxcomb, do you see?

(*Enter* Ananias)

Ananias. Peace to the household!

Kastril. I'll keep peace for no man.

Ananias. Casting of dollars is concluded lawful.

Kastril. Is he the constable?

Subtle. Peace, Ananias.

Face. No, sir.

Kastril. Then you are an otter, and a shad, a whit,

A very tim.

Surly. You'll hear me, sir?

Kastril. I will not.

Ananias. What is the motive?

Subtle. Zeal in the young gentleman,

Against his Spanish slops.

Ananias. They are profane,

Lewd, superstitious, and idolatrous breeches.

Surly. New rascals!

Kastril. Will you be gone, sir?

Ananias. Avoid, Sathan!

Thou art not of the light! That ruff of pride

About thy neck betrays thee, and is the same

With that which the unclean birds, in seventy-seven,

Were seen to prank it with on divers coasts:

Thou look'st like Antichrist, in that lewd hat.

Surly. I must give way.

Kastril. Be gone, sir.

---

[195] Crook. [196] Wench.

[197] Coxcomb.

Surly. But I'll take
A course with you—
　Ananias. Depart, proud Spanish fiend!
　Surly. Captain and Doctor—
　Ananias. Child of perdition!
　Kastril. Hence, sir!—　　(Exit Surly)
Did I not quarrel bravely?
　Face. Yes, indeed, sir.
　Kastril. Nay, an I give my mind to't,
I shall do't.
　Face. O, you must follow, sir, and threaten
　　him tame.
He'll turn again else.
　Kastril. I'll re-turn him then.　　(Exit)
　Face. Drugger, this rogue prevented us,
　　for thee.
We had determin'd that thou should'st ha'
　　come
In a Spanish suit, and ha' carried her so;
　　and he,
A brokerly slave, goes, puts it on himself.
Hast brought the damask?
　Drugger. Yes, sir.
　Face. Thou must borrow
A Spanish suit. Hast thou no credit with
　　the players?
　Drugger. Yes, sir; did you never see me
play the Fool?
　Face. I know not, Nab.—(Aside) Thou
　　shalt, if I can help it.—
Hieronimo's [198] old cloak, ruff, and hat will
　　serve;
I'll tell thee more when thou bring'st 'em.
　　　　　　　　　　(Exit Drugger)
　Ananias. (Subtle hath whisper'd with
　　him this while)
Sir, I know
The Spaniard hates the Brethren, and hath
　　spies
Upon their actions; and that this was one
I make no scruple.—But the Holy Synod
Have been in prayer and meditation for it;
And 'tis reveal'd no less to them than me,
That casting of money is most lawful.
　Subtle. True.
But here I cannot do it; if the house
Should chance to be suspected, all would out,
And we be lock'd up in the Tower for ever,
To make gold there for th' state, never come
　　out.
And then are you defeated.
　Ananias. I will tell

[198] Character in Kyd's Spanish Tragedy.

This to the elders and the weaker Brethren,
That the whole company of the Separation
May join in humble prayer again.
　Subtle. And fasting.
　Ananias. Yea, for some fitter place. The
　　peace of mind
Rest with these walls!
　Subtle. Thanks, courteous Ananias.
　　　　　　　　　　(Exit Ananias)
　Face. What did he come for?
　Subtle. About casting dollars,
Presently, out of hand. And so I told him,
A Spanish minister came here to spy
Against the faithful—
　Face. I conceive. Come, Subtle,
Thou art so down upon the least disaster!
How wouldst thou ha' done, if I had not
　　help'd thee out?
　Subtle. I thank thee, Face, for the angry
boy, i' faith.
　Face. Who would ha' look'd it should ha'
　　been that rascal
Surly? He had dy'd his beard and all. Well,
　　sir,
Here's damask come to make you a suit.
　Subtle. Where's Drugger?
　Face. He is gone to borrow me a Spanish
　　habit;
I'll be the count now.
　Subtle. But where's the widow?
　Face. Within, with my lord's sister;
　　Madam Dol
Is entertaining her.
　Subtle. By your favor, Face,
Now she is honest, I will stand again.
　Face. You will not offer it!
　Subtle. Why?
　Face. Stand to your word,
Or—here comes Dol!—she knows—
　Subtle. Y'are tyrannous still.

　　　　　　(Enter Dol hastily)

　Face. —Strict for my right.—How now,
　　Dol! Hast told her
The Spanish Count will come?
　Dol Common. Yes, but another is come,
You little look'd for!
　Face. Who's that?
　Dol Common. Your master—
The master of the house.
　Subtle. How, Dol!
　Face. She lies,

This is some trick. Come, leave your quiblins,
   Dorothy.
DOL COMMON. Look out and see.
            (FACE *goes to the window*)
SUBTLE. Art thou in earnest?
DOL COMMON. 'Slight,
Forty o' the neighbors are about him, talking.
  FACE. 'Tis he, by this good day.
DOL COMMON. 'Twill prove ill day
For some on us.
  FACE. We are undone, and taken.
DOL COMMON. Lost, I'm afraid.
SUBTLE. You said he would not come,
While there died one a week within the
   liberties.[199]
  FACE. No: 'twas within the walls.
SUBTLE. Was't so? Cry you mercy.
I thought the liberties. What shall we do
  now, Face?
  FACE. Be silent: not a word, if he call or
   knock.
I'll into mine old shape again and meet him,

Of Jeremy, the butler. I' the meantime,
Do you two pack up all the goods and
  purchase[200]
That we can carry i' the two trunks. I'll
  keep him
Off for to-day, if I cannot longer, and then
At night, I'll ship you both away to Ratcliff,
Where we will meet to-morrow, and there
  we'll share.
Let Mammon's brass and pewter keep the
  cellar;
We'll have another time for that. But, Dol,
'Pray thee go heat a little water quickly;
Subtle must shave me. All my captain's beard
Must off, to make me appear smooth Jeremy.
You'll do't?
  SUBTLE. Yes, I'll shave you as well as I
can.
  FACE. And not cut my throat, but trim
me?
  SUBTLE. You shall see, sir. ·   (*Exeunt*)

Act V

SCENE I. *Before* LOVEWIT'S *House.*

(*Enter* LOVEWIT *with a Crowd of*
      NEIGHBORS)

LOVEWIT. Has there been such resort, say
you?
  1 NEIGHBOR. Daily, sir.
  2 NEIGHBOR. And nightly, too.
  3 NEIGHBOR. Ay, some as brave as lords.
  4 NEIGHBOR. Ladies and gentlewomen.
  5 NEIGHBOR. Citizens' wives.
  1 NEIGHBOR. And knights.
  6 NEIGHBOR. In coaches.
  2 NEIGHBOR. Yes, and oyster-women.
  1 NEIGHBOR. Beside other gallants.
  3 NEIGHBOR. Sailors' wives.
  4 NEIGHBOR. Tobacco men.
  5 NEIGHBOR. Another Pimlico.[201]
LOVEWIT. What should my knave advance,
To draw this company? He hung out no
  banners

Of a strange calf with five legs to be seen,
Or a huge lobster with six claws?
  6 NEIGHBOR. No, sir.
  3 NEIGHBOR. We had gone in then, sir.
LOVEWIT. He has no gift
Of teaching i' the nose[202] that e'er I knew of.
You saw no bills[203] set up that promis'd cure
Of agues or the tooth-ache?
  2 NEIGHBOR. No such thing, sir!
LOVEWIT. Nor heard a drum struck for
baboons or puppets?
  5 NEIGHBOR. Neither, sir.
LOVEWIT. What device should he bring
  forth now?
I love a teeming wit as I love my nourish-
  ment.
'Pray God he ha' not kept such open house,
That he hath sold my hangings, and my
  bedding!
I left him nothing else. If he have eat 'em,
A plague o' the moth, say I! Sure he has got

---

[199] Suburban slum districts of London.
[200] Loot.   [201] A popular resort.

[202] *I.e.*, preaching with a nasal whine like a
Puritan.   [203] Posters.

Some bawdy pictures to call all this ging: [204]
The Friar and the Nun; or the new motion
Of the knight's courser covering the parson's
　　mare;
The boy of six year old, with the great thing;
Or 't may be, he has the fleas that run at tilt
Upon a table, or some dog to dance.
When saw you him?
　　1 Neighbor. Who, sir, Jeremy?
　　2 Neighbor. Jeremy butler?
We saw him not this month.
　　Lovewit. How!
　　4 Neighbor. Not these five weeks, sir.
　　6 Neighbor. These six weeks, at the least.
　　Lovewit. You amaze me, neighbors!
　　5 Neighbor. Sure, if your worship know
　　not where he is,
He's slipp'd away.
　　6 Neighbor. Pray God he be not made
away.
　　Lovewit. Ha! It's no time to question,
then.　　　　　　　　　　　　(He knocks)
　　6 Neighbor. About
Some three weeks since I heard a doleful cry,
As I sat up a-mending my wife's stockings.

[204] Gang.

　　Lovewit. This's strange that none will
　　answer! Did'st thou hear
A cry, sayst thou?
　　6 Neighbor. Yes, sir, like unto a man
That had been strangled an hour, and could
　　not speak.
　　2 Neighbor. I heard it, too, just this day
　　three weeks, at two o'clock
Next morning.
　　Lovewit. These be miracles, or you make
　　'em so!
A man an hour strangled, and could not
　　speak,
And both you heard him cry?
　　3 Neighbor. Yes, downward, sir.
　　Lovewit. Thou art a wise fellow. Give me
　　thy hand, I pray thee.
What trade art thou on?
　　3 Neighbor. A smith, an't please your
worship.
　　Lovewit. A smith! Then lend me thy
help to get this door open.
　　3 Neighbor. That I will presently, sir,
but fetch my tools—　　　　　　　(Exit)
　　1 Neighbor. Sir, best to knock again afore
you break it.

Scene II. *The Same.*

(Lovewit knocks again) I will.

　　(Enter Face in his butler's livery)

Face. What mean you, sir?
1, 2, 4 Neighbor. O, here's Jeremy!
Face. Good sir, come from the door.
Lovewit. Why, what's the matter?
Face. Yet farder, you are too near yet.
Lovewit. I' the name of wonder,
What means the fellow!
Face. The house, sir, has been visited.
　　Lovewit. What, with the plague? Stand
thou then farder.
　　Face. No, sir,
I had it not.
　　Lovewit. Who had it then? I left
None else but thee i' the house.
　　Face. Yes, sir, my fellow,
The cat that kept the buttery, had it on her

A week before I spied it; but I got her
Convey'd away i' the night; and so I shut
The house up for a month—
　　Lovewit. How!
　　Face. Purposing then, sir,
T'have burnt rose-vinegar, treacle, and tar,
And ha' made it sweet, that you should ne'er
　　ha' known it;
Because I knew the news would but afflict
　　you, sir.
　　Lovewit. Breathe less, and farder off!

　　(He moves hastily away from the door.
　　The rest follow.)

　　Why this is stranger:
The neighbors tell me all here that the doors
Have still been open—
　　Face. How, sir!
　　Lovewit. Gallants, men and women,
And of all sorts, tag-rag, been seen to flock
　　here

In threaves,[205] these ten weeks, as to a second
    Hogsden,
In days of Pimlico and Eye-bright.
    FACE. Sir,
Their wisdoms will not say so.
    LOVEWIT. To-day they speak
Of coaches and gallants; one in a French
    hood
Went in, they tell me; and another was seen
In a velvet gown at the windore; divers more
Pass in and out.
    FACE. They did pass through the doors
    then,
Or walls, I assure their eye-sights, and their
    spectacles;
For here, sir, are the keys, and here have
    been,
In this my pocket, now above twenty days!
And for before, I kept the fort alone there.
But that 'tis yet not deep i' the afternoon,
I should believe my neighbors had seen
    double
Through the black pot,[206] and made these
    apparitions!
For, on my faith to your worship, for these
    three weeks
And upwards, the door has not been open'd.
    LOVEWIT. Strange!
    1 NEIGHBOR. Good faith, I think I saw a
coach.
    2 NEIGHBOR. And I too,

I'd ha' been sworn.
    LOVEWIT. Do you but think it now?
And but one coach?
    4 NEIGHBOR. We cannot tell, sir; Jeremy
Is a very honest fellow.
    FACE. Did you see me at all?
    1 NEIGHBOR. No; that we are sure on.
    2 NEIGHBOR. I'll be sworn o'that.
    LOVEWIT. Fine rogues to have your testi-
monies built on!

(Re-enter THIRD NEIGHBOR, with his tools)

    3 NEIGHBOR. Is Jeremy come!
    1 NEIGHBOR. O yes; you may leave your
    tools;
We were deceiv'd, he says.
    2 NEIGHBOR. He's had the keys,
And the door has been shut these three
    weeks.
    3 NEIGHBOR. Like enough.
    LOVEWIT. Peace, and get hence, you
changelings.

(Enter SURLY and MAMMON)

    FACE. (Aside) Surly come!
And Mammon made acquainted! They'll tell
all.
How shall I beat them off? What shall I do?
Nothing's more wretched than a guilty
    conscience.

SCENE III. *The Same.*

SURLY. No, sir, he was a great physician.
    This,
It was no bawdy-house, but a mere chancel!
You knew the lord and his sister.
    MAMMON. Nay, good Surly.
    SURLY. The happy word, *be rich—*
    MAMMON. Play not the tyrant.
    SURLY. Should be to-day pronounc'd to
    all your friends.
And where be your andirons now? And your
    brass pots,
That should ha' been golden flagons, and
    great wedges?
    MAMMON. Let me but breathe. What,
    they ha' shut their doors,

Methinks!   (MAMMON *and* SURLY *knock*)
    SURLY. Ay, now 'tis holiday with them.
    MAMMON. Rogues,
Cozeners, impostors, bawds!
    FACE. What mean you, sir?
    MAMMON. To enter if we can.
    FACE. Another man's house!
Here is the owner, sir; turn you to him,
And speak your business.
    MAMMON. Are you, sir, the owner?
    LOVEWIT. Yes, sir.
    MAMMON. And are those knaves, within,
your cheaters?
    LOVEWIT. What knaves, what cheaters?
    MAMMON. Subtle and his Lungs.
    FACE. The gentleman is distracted, sir!
    No lungs

[205] Droves.   [206] From drinking too much.

Nor lights ha' been seen here these three weeks, sir,
Within these doors, upon my word.
   SURLY. Your word,
Groom arrogant!
   FACE. Yes, sir. I am the housekeeper,
And know the keys ha' not been out o' my hands.
   SURLY. This's a new Face.
   FACE. You do mistake the house, sir.
What sign was't at?
   SURLY. You rascal! This is one
O' the confederacy. Come, let's get officers,
And force the door.
   LOVEWIT. Pray you stay, gentlemen.
   SURLY. No, sir, we'll come with warrant.
   MAMMON. Ay, and then
We shall ha' your doors open.
      (*Exeunt* MAMMON *and* SURLY)
   LOVEWIT. What means this?
   FACE. I cannot tell, sir.
   1 NEIGHBOR. These are two o' the gallants
That we do think we saw.
   FACE. Two o' the fools!
You talk as idly as they. Good faith, sir,
I think the moon has craz'd 'em all.
      (*Enter* KASTRIL)
(*Aside*) O me,
The angry boy come too! He'll make a noise,
And ne'er away till he have betray'd us all.
      (KASTRIL *knocks*)
   KASTRIL. What, rogues, bawds, slaves, you'll open the door anon!
Punk, cockatrice, my suster! By this light,
I'll fetch the marshal to you. You are a whore
To keep your castle—
   FACE. Who would you speak with, sir?
   KASTRIL. The bawdy Doctor, and the cozening Captain,
And puss my suster.
   LOVEWIT. This is something, sure.
   FACE. Upon my trust, the doors were never open, sir.
   KASTRIL. I have heard all their tricks told me twice over,
By the fat knight and the lean gentleman.
   LOVEWIT. Here comes another.

(*Enter* ANANIAS *and* TRIBULATION)

   FACE. Ananias too!
And his pastor!

   TRIBULATION. The doors are shut against us.
      (*They beat, too, at the door*)
   ANANIAS. Come forth, you seed of sulphur, sons of fire!
Your stench it is broke forth; abomination
Is in the house.
   KASTRIL. Ay, my suster's there.
   ANANIAS. The place,
It is become a cage of unclean birds.
   KASTRIL. Yes, I will fetch the scavenger, and the constable.
   TRIBULATION. You shall do well.
   ANANIAS. We'll join to weed them out.
   KASTRIL. You will not come then, punk devise,[207] my suster!
   ANANIAS. Call her not sister; she is a harlot verily.
   KASTRIL. I'll raise the street.
   LOVEWIT. Good gentlemen, a word.
   ANANIAS. Sathan, avoid, and hinder not our zeal!
      (*Exeunt* ANANIAS, TRIBULATION, *and* KASTRIL)
   LOVEWIT. The world's turn'd Bet'lem.
   FACE. These are all broke loose,
Out of St. Katherine's, where they use to keep
The better sort of mad-folks.
   1 NEIGHBOR. All these persons
We saw go in and out here.
   2 NEIGHBOR. Yes, indeed, sir.
   3 NEIGHBOR. These were the parties.
   FACE. Peace, you drunkards! Sir,
I wonder at it. Please you to give me leave
To touch the door; I'll try an the lock be chang'd.
   LOVEWIT. It mazes me!
   FACE. (*Goes to the door*) Good faith, sir, I believe
There's no such thing; 'tis all *deceptio visus*—
(*Aside*) Would I could get him away.
      (DAPPER *cries out within*)
   DAPPER. Master Captain! Master Doctor!
   LOVEWIT. Who's that?
   FACE. (*Aside*) Our clerk within, that I forgot!—
I know not, sir.
   DAPPER. (*Within*) For God's sake, when will her Grace be at leisure?
   FACE. Ha! (*With feigned amazement*)

---

[207] Perfect harlot.

Illusions, some spirit o' the air!—(*Aside*) His
   gag is melted,
And now he sets out the throat.
   DAPPER. (*Within*) I am almost stifled—
   FACE. (*Aside*) Would you were alto-
gether.
   LOVEWIT. 'Tis i' the house.
Ha! list.
   FACE. Believe it, sir, i' the air.
   LOVEWIT. Peace, you.
   DAPPER. (*Within*) Mine aunt's grace does
not use me well.
   SUBTLE. (*Within*) You fool,
Peace, you'll mar all.
   FACE. (*Speaks through the keyhole, un-
aware that* LOVEWIT *has tiptoed up behind
him and overhears*) Or you will else, you
rogue.
   LOVEWIT. O, is it so? Then you converse
   with spirits!—
Come, sir. No more o' your tricks, good
   Jeremy.
The truth, the shortest way.
   FACE. Dismiss this rabble, sir.—
(*Aside*) What shall I do? I am catch'd.
   LOVEWIT. Good neighbors,
I thank you all. You may depart. (*Exeunt*
   NEIGHBORS)—

Come, sir,
You know that I am an indulgent master;
And therefore conceal nothing. What's your
   med'cine,
To draw so many several sorts of wild fowl?
   FACE. Sir, you were wont to affect mirth
   and wit—
But here's no place to talk on't i' the street.
Give me but leave to make the best of my
   fortune,
And only pardon me th' abuse of your house:
It's all I beg. I'll help you to a widow,
In recompense, that you shall gi' me thanks
   for,
Will make you seven years younger, and a
   rich one.
'Tis but your putting on a Spanish cloak;
I have her within. You need not fear the
   house;
It was not visited.
   LOVEWIT. But by me, who came
Sooner than you expected.
   FACE. It is true, sir.
'Pray you forgive me.
   LOVEWIT. Well, let's see your widow.
                           (*Exeunt*)

SCENE IV. *A Room in* LOVEWIT'S *House.*

(*Enter* SUBTLE, *leading in* DAPPER, *with his
   eyes bound as before*)

   SUBTLE. How! ha' you eaten your gag?
   DAPPER. Yes, faith, it crumbled
Away i' my mouth.
   SUBTLE. You ha' spoil'd all then.
   DAPPER. No!
I hope my aunt of Faery will forgive me.
   SUBTLE. Your aunt's a gracious lady; but
   in troth
You were to blame.
   DAPPER. The fume did overcome me,
And I did do't to stay my stomach. 'Pray you
So satisfy her Grace.

(*Enter* FACE *in his uniform*)

Here comes the Captain.
   FACE. How now! Is his mouth down?

   SUBTLE. Ay, he has spoken!
   FACE. (*Aside*) A pox, I heard him, and
   you too.
(*Aloud*) He's undone then.—
(*Aside to* SUBTLE) I have been fain to say,
   the house is haunted
With spirits, to keep churl back.
   SUBTLE. (*Aside*) And hast thou done it?
   FACE. (*Aside*) Sure, for this night.
   SUBTLE. (*Aside*) Why, then triumph and
   sing
Of Face so famous, the precious king
Of present wits.
   FACE. (*Aside*) Did you not hear the coil
About the door?
   SUBTLE. (*Aside*) Yes, and I dwindled
with it.
   FACE. (*Aside*) Show him his aunt, and
   let him be dispatch'd:
I'll send her to you.   (*Exit* FACE)

SUBTLE. Well, sir, your aunt her Grace
Will give you audience presently, on my suit,
And the Captain's word that you did not
    eat your gag
In any contempt of her Highness.
               (*Unbinds his eyes*)
DAPPER. Not I, in troth, sir.

(*Enter* DOL *like the Queen of Faery*)

SUBTLE. Here she is come. Down o' your
    knees and wriggle:
She has a stately presence. (DAPPER *kneels
    and shuffles toward her*) Good! Yet
    nearer,
And bid, God save you!
    DAPPER. Madam!
    SUBTLE. And your aunt.
    DAPPER. And my most gracious aunt, God
save your Grace.
    DOL COMMON. Nephew, we thought to
    have been angry with you;
But that sweet face of yours hath turn'd the
    tide,
And made it flow with joy, that ebb'd of love.
Arise, and touch our velvet gown.
    SUBTLE. The skirts,
And kiss 'em. So!
    DOL COMMON. Let me now stroke that
    head.
*Much, nephew, shalt thou win, much shalt
    thou spend;*
*Much shalt thou give away; much shalt thou
    lend.*
    SUBTLE. (*Aside*) Ay, much indeed!—Why
do you not thank her Grace?
    DAPPER. I cannot speak for joy.
    SUBTLE. See, the kind wretch!
Your Grace's kinsman right.
    DOL COMMON. Give me the bird.—
Here is your fly in a purse, about your neck,
    cousin;
Wear it, and feed it about this day sev'n-
    night,
On your right wrist—
    SUBTLE. Open a vein with a pin
And let it suck but once a week; till then,
You must not look on't.
    DOL COMMON. No. And, kinsman,
Bear yourself worthy of the blood you come
    on.
    SUBTLE. Her Grace would ha' you eat no
more Woolsack[208] pies,
Nor Dagger frume'ty.[209]
    DOL COMMON. Nor break his fast
In Heaven and Hell.[210]
    SUBTLE. She's with you everywhere!
Nor play with costermongers, at mumchance,
    traytrip,
God-make-you-rich (when as your aunt has
    done it); but keep
The gallant'st company, and the best games—
    DAPPER. Yes, sir.
    SUBTLE. Gleek and primero; and what
you get, be true to us.
    DAPPER. By this hand, I will.
    SUBTLE. You may bring's a thousand
    pound
Before to-morrow night, if but three thou-
    sand
Be stirring, an you will.
    DAPPER. I swear I will then.
    SUBTLE. Your fly will learn you all games.
    FACE. (*Within*) Ha' you done there?
    SUBTLE. Your Grace will command him
no more duties?
    DOL COMMON. No;
But come and see me often. I may chance
To leave him three or four hundred chests
    of treasure,
And some twelve thousand acres of fairy land,
If he game well and comely with good
    gamesters.
    SUBTLE. There's a kind aunt; kiss her
    departing part.—
But you must sell your forty mark a year now.
    DAPPER. Ay, sir, I mean.
    SUBTLE. Or, gi't away; pox on't!
    DAPPER. I'll gi't mine aunt. I'll go and
fetch the writings.
    SUBTLE. 'Tis well; away. (*Exit* DAPPER)

(*Re-enter* FACE)

    FACE. Where's Subtle?
    SUBTLE. Here. What news?
    FACE. Drugger is at the door; go take his
    suit,
And bid him fetch a parson presently.
Say he shall marry the widow. Thou shalt
    spend

[208] A tavern.
[209] Wheat boiled in milk.
[210] Taverns.

A hundred pound by the service!

(Exit SUBTLE)

Now, Queen Dol,

Have you pack'd up all?

DOL COMMON. Yes.

FACE. And how do you like

The Lady Pliant?

DOL COMMON. A good dull innocent.

(Re-enter SUBTLE)

SUBTLE. Here's your Hieronimo's cloak
and hat.

FACE. Give me 'em.

SUBTLE. And the ruff too?

FACE. Yes; I'll come to you presently.

(Exit)

SUBTLE. Now he is gone about his project,
Dol,

I told you of, for the widow.

DOL COMMON. 'Tis direct

Against our articles.

SUBTLE. Well, we'll fit him, wench.

Hast thou gull'd her of her jewels or her
bracelets?

DOL COMMON. No; but I will do't.

SUBTLE. Soon at night, my Dolly,

When we are shipp'd and all our goods
aboard,

Eastward for Ratcliff, we will turn our course

To Brainford, westward, if thou sayst the
word,

And take our leaves of this o'erweening rascal,

This peremptory Face.

DOL COMMON. Content; I'm weary of him.

SUBTLE. Thou'st cause, when the slave
will run a-wiving, Dol,

Against the instrument that was drawn between us.

DOL COMMON. I'll pluck his bird as bare
as I can.

SUBTLE. Yes, tell her

She must by any means address some present
To th' cunning man, make him amends for
wronging

His art with her suspicion; send a ring

Or chain of pearl; she will be tortur'd else

Extremely in her sleep, say, and ha' strange
things

Come to her. Wilt thou?

DOL COMMON. Yes.

SUBTLE. My fine flitter-mouse,

My bird o' the night! We'll tickle it at the
Pigeons,[211]

When we have all, and may unlock the
trunks,

And say, this's mine, and thine; and thine,
and mine.   *(They kiss)*

(Re-enter FACE)

FACE. What now! a-billing?

SUBTLE. Yes, a little exalted

In the good passage of our stock-affairs.

FACE. Drugger has brought his parson;
take him in, Subtle,

And send Nab back again to wash his face.

SUBTLE. I will. And shave himself?

FACE. If you can get him. *(Exit* SUBTLE)

DOL COMMON. You are hot upon it, Face,
whate'er it is!

FACE. A trick that Dol shall spend ten
pound a month by.

(Re-enter SUBTLE)

Is he gone?

SUBTLE. The chaplain waits you i' the
hall, sir.

FACE. I'll go bestow him.   *(Exit)*

DOL COMMON. He'll now marry her instantly.

SUBTLE. He cannot yet, he is not ready.
Dear Dol,

Cozen her of all thou canst. To deceive him

Is no deceit, but justice, that would break

Such an inextricable tie as ours was.

DOL COMMON. Let me alone to fit him.

(Re-enter FACE)

FACE. Come, my venturers,

You ha' pack'd up all? Where be the trunks?
Bring forth.

SUBTLE. Here.

FACE. Let's see 'em. Where's the money?

SUBTLE. Here,

In this.

FACE. Mammon's ten pound; eight score
before.

The Brethren's money this. Drugger's and
Dapper's?

What paper's that?

[211] An inn at Brainford.

DOL COMMON. The jewel of the waiting
    maid's,
That stole it from her lady, to know certain—
FACE. If she should have precedence of
her mistress?
DOL COMMON. Yes.
FACE. What box is that?
SUBTLE. The fish-wives' rings, I think,
And th'ale-wives' single money.[212] Is't not,
    Dol?
DOL COMMON. Yes, and the whistle that
    the sailor's wife
Brought you to know an her husband were
    with Ward.[213]
FACE. We'll wet it to-morrow; and our
    silver beakers
And tavern cups. Where be the French petti-
coats
And girdles and hangers?
SUBTLE. Here, i' the trunk,
And the bolts of lawn.
FACE. Is Drugger's damask there,
And the tobacco?
SUBTLE. Yes.
FACE. Give me the keys.
DOL COMMON. Why you the keys?
SUBTLE. No matter, Dol; because
We shall not open 'em before he comes.
FACE. 'Tis true, you shall not open them,
    indeed;
Nor have 'em forth, do you see? Not forth,
    Dol.
DOL COMMON. No!
FACE. No, my smock-rampant. The right
    is, my master
Knows all, has pardon'd me, and he will keep
    'em.

Doctor, 'tis true—you look—for all your
    figures!
I sent for him, indeed. Wherefore, good
    partners,
Both he and she, be satisfied; for here
Determines[214] the indenture tripartite
'Twixt Subtle, Dol, and Face. All I can do
Is to help you over the wall, o' the back-side,
Or lend you a sheet to save your velvet gown,
    Dol.
Here will be officers presently; bethink you
Of some course suddenly to scape the dock;
For thither you'll come else.
        (*Violent knocking at the door*)
Hark you, thunder.
SUBTLE. You are a precious fiend!
OFFICERS. (*Without*) Open the door.
FACE. Dol, I am sorry for thee, i' faith;
    but hear'st thou?
It shall go hard but I will place thee some-
where.
Thou shalt ha' my letter to Mistress Amo—
DOL COMMON. Hang you!
FACE. Or Madam Cæsarean.
DOL COMMON. Pox upon you, rogue,
Would I had but time to beat thee!
FACE. Subtle,
Let's know where you set up next; I'll send
    you
A customer now and then, for old acquaint-
ance.
What new course ha' you?
SUBTLE. Rogue, I'll hang myself,
That I may walk a greater devil than thou,
And haunt thee i' the flock-bed and the
    buttery.   (*Exeunt*)

SCENE V. *Another Room.*

(*Enter* LOVEWIT *in a Spanish costume, with
the Parson. Knocking at the door continues*)

LOVEWIT. What do you mean, my mas-
ters?
MAMMON. (*Without*) Open your door,
Cheaters, bawds, conjurers.
OFFICER. (*Without*) Or we'll break it
open.

LOVEWIT. What warrant have you?
OFFICER. (*Without*) Warrant enough,
    sir, doubt not,
If you'll not open it.
LOVEWIT. Is there an officer there?
OFFICER. (*Without*) Yes, two or three for
failing.
LOVEWIT. Have but patience,
And I will open it straight.

---

[212] Small change.   [213] A famous pirate.   [214] Terminates.

(*Enter* FACE *in his butler's livery*)

FACE. Sir, ha' you done?
Is it a marriage? Perfect?
LOVEWIT. Yes, my brain.
FACE. Off with your ruff and cloak then;
be yourself, sir.
SURLY. (*Without*) Down with the door.
KASTRIL. (*Without*) 'Slight, ding it open.
LOVEWIT. (*Opening the door*) Hold,
Hold, gentlemen, what means this violence?

(MAMMON, SURLY, KASTRIL, ANANIAS,
TRIBULATION, *and* OFFICERS *rush in*)

MAMMON. Where is this collier?
SURLY. And my Captain Face?
MAMMON. These day-owls.
SURLY. That are birding[215] in men's
purses.
MAMMON. Madam Suppository.
KASTRIL. Doxy, my suster.
ANANIAS. Locusts
Of the foul pit.
TRIBULATION. Profane as Bel and the
Dragon.
ANANIAS. Worse than the grasshoppers,
or the lice of Egypt.
LOVEWIT. Good gentlemen, hear me. Are
you officers,
And cannot stay this violence?
OFFICER. Keep the peace.
LOVEWIT. Gentlemen, what is the matter?
Whom do you seek?
MAMMON. The chemical cozener.
SURLY. And the captain pandar.
KASTRIL. The nun my suster.
MAMMON. Madam Rabbi.
ANANIAS. Scorpions,
And caterpillars.
LOVEWIT. Fewer at once, I pray you.
OFFICER. One after another, gentlemen,
I charge you,
By virtue of my staff.
ANANIAS. They are the vessels
Of pride, lust, and the cart.
LOVEWIT. Good zeal, lie still
A little while.
TRIBULATION. Peace, Deacon Ananias.
LOVEWIT. The house is mine here, and
the doors are open;
If there be any such persons as you seek for,

Use your authority, search on, o'God's name.
I am but newly come to town, and finding
This tumult 'bout my door, to tell you true,
It somewhat maz'd me; till my man here,
fearing
My more displeasure, told me he had done
Somewhat an insolent part, let out my house
(Belike presuming on my known aversion
From any air o' the town while there was
sickness),
To a doctor and a captain; who, what they are
Or where they be, he knows not.
MAMMON. Are they gone?
LOVEWIT. You may go in and search, sir.
(*They enter*)
Here, I find
The empty walls worse than I left 'em,
smok'd,
A few crack'd pots, and glasses, and a
furnace;
The ceiling fill'd with poesies of the candle,
And "Madam with a dildo"[216] writ o' the
walls.
Only one gentlewoman I met here,
That is within, that said she was a widow—
KASTRIL. Ay, that's my suster; I'll go
thump her. Where is she?   (*Goes in*)
LOVEWIT. And should ha' married a Span-
ish count, but he,
When he came to't, neglected her so grossly,
That I, a widower, am gone through with her.
SURLY. How! have I lost her, then?
LOVEWIT. Were you the don, sir?
Good faith, now, she does blame you
extremely, and says
You swore, and told her you had ta'en the
pains
To dye your beard, and umber o'er your face,
Borrow'd a suit and ruff, all for her love;
And then did nothing. What an oversight
And want of putting forward, sir, was this!
Well fare an old harquebusier[217] yet,
Could prime his powder, and give fire, and
hit,
All in a twinkling!
(MAMMON *comes forth*)
MAMMON. The whole nest are fled!
LOVEWIT. What sort of birds were they?
MAMMON. A kind of choughs,
Or thievish daws, sir, that have pick'd my
purse

---

[215] Pilfering.   [216] Refrain of a popular ballad.   [217] Musketeer.

Of eight score and ten pounds within these
five weeks,
Beside my first materials; and my goods,
That lie i' the cellar, which I am glad they
ha' left,
I may have home yet.
LOVEWIT. Think you so, sir?
MAMMON. Ay.
LOVEWIT. By order of law, sir, but not
otherwise.
MAMMON. Not mine own stuff?
LOVEWIT. Sir, I can take no knowledge
That they are yours, but by public means.
If you can bring certificate that you were
gull'd of 'em,
Or any formal writ out of a court,
That you did cozen yourself, I will not hold
them.
MAMMON. I'll rather lose 'em.
LOVEWIT. That you shall not, sir,
By me, in troth. Upon these terms, they're
yours.
What, should they ha' been, sir, turn'd into
gold, all?
MAMMON. No.
I cannot tell.—It may be they should.—What
then?
LOVEWIT. What a great loss in hope have
you sustain'd!
MAMMON. Not I; the commonwealth has.
FACE. Ay, he would ha' built
The city new; and made a ditch about it
Of silver, should have run with cream from
Hogsden;
That every Sunday in Moorfields the
younkers
And tits and tom-boys should have fed on,
gratis.
MAMMON. I will go mount a turnip-cart,
and preach
The end o' the world within these two
months.—Surly,
What! in a dream?
SURLY. Must I needs cheat myself
With that same foolish vice of honesty!
Come, let us go and hearken out the rogues.
That Face I'll mark for mine, if e'er I meet
him.
FACE. If I can hear of him, sir, I'll bring
you word
Unto your lodging; for in troth, they were
strangers

To me; I thought 'em honest as myself, sir.
(*Exeunt* SURLY *and* MAMMON)

(*Re-enter* ANANIAS *and* TRIBULATION)

TRIBULATION. 'Tis well, the saints shall
not lose all yet. Go
And get some carts—
LOVEWIT. For what, my zealous friends?
ANANIAS. To bear away the portion of the
righteous
Out of this den of thieves.
LOVEWIT. What is that portion?
ANANIAS. The goods, sometimes the
orphans', that the
Brethren bought with their silver pence.
LOVEWIT. What, those i' the cellar,
The knight Sir Mammon claims?
ANANIAS. I do defy
The wicked Mammon, so do all the Brethren.
Thou profane man! I ask thee with what
conscience
Thou canst advance that idol against us
That have the seal? [218] Were not the shillings
numb'red
That made the pounds; were not the pounds
told out
Upon the second day of the fourth week,
In the eight month, upon the table dormant,
The year of the last patience of the saints,
Six hundred and ten?
LOVEWIT. Mine earnest vehement botcher,
And deacon also, I cannot dispute with you;
But if you get you not away the sooner,
I shall confute you with a cudgel.
ANANIAS. Sir!
TRIBULATION. Be patient, Ananias.
ANANIAS. I am strong,
And will stand up, well girt, against an host
That threaten Gad in exile.
LOVEWIT. I shall send you
To Amsterdam, to your cellar.
ANANIAS. I will pray there,
Against thy house. May dogs defile thy walls,
And wasps and hornets breed beneath thy
roof,
This seat of falsehood, and this cave of
coz'nage!
(*Exeunt* ANANIAS *and* TRIBULATION)

(DRUGGER *enters*)

[218] Are sealed as God's people.

LOVEWIT. Another too?

DRUGGER. Not I, sir, I am no Brother.

LOVEWIT. Away, you Harry Nicholas! [219]
do you talk?   (He beats him away)

FACE. No, this was Abel Drugger. (To
the PARSON [220]) Good sir, go,

And satisfy him; tell him all is done.

He stay'd too long a-washing of his face.

The Doctor, he shall hear of him at West-
chester;

And of the Captain, tell him, at Yarmouth,
or

Some good port-town else, lying for a wind.
          (Exit PARSON)

If you get off the angry child now, sir—

(Enter KASTRIL, dragging in his sister
DAME PLIANT)

KASTRIL. Come on, you ewe, you have
match'd most sweetly, ha' you not?

Did not I say, I would never ha' you tupp'd

But by a dubb'd boy, [221] to make you a lady-
tom?

'Slight, you are a mammet! [222] O, I could
touse you now.

Death, mun [223] you marry with a pox!

LOVEWIT. You lie, boy;

As sound as you; and I'm aforehand with you.

KASTRIL. Anon?

LOVEWIT. Come, will you quarrel? I will
feize [224] you, sirrah;

Why do you not buckle to your tools?

KASTRIL. God's light,

This is a fine old boy as e'er I saw!

LOVEWIT. What, do you change your copy
now? Proceed;

Here stands my dove: stoop [225] at her if you
dare.

KASTRIL. 'Slight, I must love him! I cannot
choose, i' faith,

An I should be hang'd for't! Suster, I protest,

I honor thee for this match.

[219] A notorious religious fanatic.

[220] I.e., the local parson who came in with
Lovewit, but who has said nothing.

[221] Knight.

[222] Puppet.

[223] Must.

[224] Beat.

[225] Swoop (a term in falconry).

LOVEWIT. O, do you so, sir?

KASTRIL. Yes, an thou canst take tobacco
and drink, old boy,

I'll give her five hundred pound more to her
marriage,

Than her own state.

LOVEWIT. Fill a pipe full, Jeremy.

FACE. Yes; but go in and take it, sir.

LOVEWIT. We will.

I will be rul'd by thee in anything, Jeremy.

KASTRIL. 'Slight, thou art not hide-bound,
thou art a jovy boy!

Come, let's in, I pray thee, and take our
whiffs.

LOVEWIT. Whiff in with your sister,
brother boy.

          (Exeunt KASTRIL and DAME PLIANT)

That master

That had receiv'd such happiness by a
servant,

In such a widow, and with so much wealth,

Were very ungrateful, if he would not be

A little indulgent to that servant's wit,

And help his fortune, though with some
small strain

Of his own candor.

          (Advancing for the epilogue and ad-
          dressing the audience)

Therefore, gentlemen,

And kind spectators, if I have outstripp'd

An old man's gravity, or strict canon, think

What a young wife and a good brain may do:

Stretch age's truth sometimes, and crack it
too.

Speak for thyself, knave.

FACE. So I will, sir.

          (Advancing to the front of the stage)

Gentlemen,

My part a little fell in this last scene,

Yet 'twas decorum. [226] And though I am clean

Got off from Subtle, Surly, Mammon, Dol,

Hot Ananias, Dapper, Drugger, all

With whom I traded; yet I put myself

On you, that are my country; [227] and this pelf

Which I have got, if you do quit [228] me, rests,

To feast you often, and invite new guests.

          (Exeunt)

[226] Dramatic propriety.

[227] Jury (legal term).

[228] Acquit.

JOHN WEBSTER

The White Devil

~~~~~~~~~~~~

PRINCIPAL EVENTS IN WEBSTER'S LIFE

c. 1580?, There is no record of Webster's birth, but it must have been about this date.

1598, 1 Aug., He may be the John Webster admitted to the Middle Temple.

1602, May, Webster, Drayton, Middleton, Dekker, and Munday collaborated on a play, now lost, called *Caesar's Fall, or The Two Shapes*. They wrote it to be acted by the Lord Admiral's company.

1602, Oct., Webster collaborated with Dekker, Heywood, and Smith on a play called *Lady Jane*, written for the Earl of Worcester's company. It was perhaps the same as the play later published under the title *Sir Thomas Wyat*.

1602, Nov., He collaborated with Chettle, Dekker, and Heywood on a play, now lost, called *Christmas Comes but Once a Year*.

1604, He wrote for the King's company an Induction to Marston's play *The Malcontent*.

1604, He collaborated with Thomas Dekker on *Westward Ho*, written for the boy company called the Children of Paul's.

1605, He collaborated with Dekker on *Northward Ho*, for the same company.

c. 1608, Probably about this time he wrote *Appius and Virginia*, not published until 1654.

c. 1610-11, He wrote *The White Devil*, for performance by Queen Anne's company.

1612, He wrote commendatory verses for Thomas Heywood's *Apology for Actors*.

1613-1614, He wrote *The Duchess of Malfi* for performance by the King's company at the Globe and Blackfriars theatres.

1615, The sixth edition of Sir Thomas Overbury's *Characters* contains a number of new characters probably written by Webster.

c. 1619-20, He wrote *The Devil's Law Case* for Queen Anne's company.

1624, Sept., He collaborated with Dekker, Ford, and Rowley on a catchpenny play, now lost, called *The Late Murder of the Son upon the Mother, or Keep the Widow Waking*. It was acted at the Red Bull theatre.

1624, 29 Oct., Webster's show, written for the occasion and entitled *Monuments of Honor*, was acted at the inauguration of the new Lord Mayor of London.

c. 1624-25, About this time Webster collaborated with William Rowley on a play called *A Cure for a Cuckold*.

1635, The date of Webster's death is unknown, but a book by his friend Thomas Heywood, published in 1635, speaks of Webster in the past tense.

INTRODUCTION

The White Devil is one of the most "Elizabethan" of the tragedies of Shakespeare's time. That is, it partakes more of the peculiar methods of dramatic statement conventional in an Elizabethan theatre and is less like the modern "well-made" play than most of the compositions of Marlowe, Greene, Dekker, Fletcher, Shakespeare, and Ford. Though there is a connected narrative which runs through Webster's tragedies, he is not much concerned to build up the probability of the events or to give explicit motivations to the actions of his characters. He is more concerned with flashes of insight into the minds and emotions of his characters, with an understanding of tortured individuals struggling in an evil world.

Many of the Jacobean dramatists were preoccupied with this conception of an evil world—a world in which dishonesty, ingratitude, hypocrisy, corruption, lechery, and cruelty seemed to dominate the actions of men. Probably the most familiar presentation of it is in *King Lear,* but the contemporary plays of Tourneur, Webster, Chapman, and Marston exhibit the same revulsion, often more unrelieved than Shakespeare's. In this world Webster's characters move, most of them in *The White Devil* exhibiting in themselves the vices from which they suffer in others. No characters in the play are made to display great moral virtue, but some have resolution and courage of heroic proportions even though coupled with cruelty and lust. Vittoria herself is the best example. The first two acts leave no doubt of her lustful and murderous propensities, yet her magnificent courage and defiance in the trial scene and in her death scene show the strength of heroes. Her defiance of the Cardinal and the whole court at her trial is memorable:

> You are deceived!
> For know that all your strict-combinèd heads

Which strike against this mine of diamonds
Shall prove but glassen hammers—they shall break.
These are but feignèd shadows of my evils.
Terrify babes, my lord, with painted devils;
I am past such needless palsy. For your names
Of whore and murderess, they proceed from you,
As if a man should spit against the wind;
The filth returns in's face.

And at her death, after defying and taunting her murderers, she dies without a word of fear or repentance.

> My soul, like to a ship in a black storm,
> Is driven, I know not whither.

Webster was one of the greatest of the many fine poets of his time, and he makes his poet's gifts serve his dramatic ends as effectively as Marlowe did, though in a different way. His most impressive lines are usually in the form of condensed observations about human affairs uttered under stress of emotion by characters who seem to have sudden perceptions of new values or of the true significance of their own deeds, like Flamineo's

> We cease to grieve, cease to be fortune's slaves,
> Nay, cease to die, by dying.

Webster's full stature as a tragic dramatist is difficult to perceive at a first reading by one not accustomed to the conventions of the Elizabethan stage. When one learns to grant easily the "willing suspension of unbelief," his thoughtful scenes can be profoundly moving and illuminating.

❧

THE WHITE DEVIL

Dramatis personae

In order of first appearance

LODOVICO, A profligate Italian count who has squandered his fortune, committed murders, and consequently been banished from Rome.

ANTONELLI ⎱ His friends, like-minded, dependents of Francisco, Duke of
GASPARO ⎰ Florence.

BRACHIANO—Paulo Giordano Orsini, Duke of Brachiano—A ruthless, proud, intemperate man, accustomed to the magnificence of wealth and the tools of power. He is married to the meek Isabella (sister of Francisco de Medicis, the powerful Duke of Florence) and violently in love with Vittoria Corombona.

VITTORIA CORAMBONA, Wife of Camillo and

later of Brachiano. A beautiful, imperious woman—the White Devil of the title.

FLAMINEO, Brother of Vittoria, secretary to Brachiano; crafty, clever, heartless, without scruple or fear, possessed of a gay, cruel wit and the cool courage of a man without remorse.

CAMILLO, Husband of Vittoria and nephew of the great Cardinal Monticelso, a stupid, gullible, pompous man of small fortune.

ZANCHE, A Moor, servant to Vittoria.

CORNELIA, Mother of Vittoria, Flamineo, and Marcello, who provides the contrast of piety, tenderness, and moral tone for these darkly passionate characters.

FRANCISCO DE MEDICIS, DUKE OF FLORENCE, Brother of Isabella, burning to revenge the wrong done him through her with all the craft, cruelty, and power at his command.

ISABELLA, Brachiano's wife and Francisco's sister, a meek, devoted, ruined woman.

GIOVANNI, The son of Isabella and Brachiano, a witty, spirited boy, tender-hearted and courageous.

MARCELLO, Brother of Vittoria and Flamineo.

CARDINAL MONTICELSO, afterwards POPE PAUL IV, a lawyer-prelate, jealous of power, and cunning and unscrupulous in using it.

JAQUES, A Moor, servant to Giovanni.

DOCTOR JULIO, A corrupt physician willing to administer poison for a fee.

CONJURER
CHRISTOPHERO ⎫
GUIDANTONIO ⎬ Figures in the dumb show
CAPTAINS ⎭ of Act II.

CHANCELLOR ⎫
REGISTER ⎬ In the employ of Francisco
LAWYER ⎭ and Monticelso.

SAVOY AMBASSADOR ⎫
FRENCH AMBASSADOR ⎪
ENGLISH AMBASSADOR ⎬ Resident in
SPANISH AMBASSADOR ⎪ Rome.
TWO OTHER AMBASSADORS ⎭

MATRON of the House of Convertites.

CARDINAL OF ARRAGON

HORTENSIO, One of Brachiano's officers.

Guards, spectators, servants, officers, cardinals, armorer, two physicians, courtiers, etc.

SCENE: *Italy*

Act I

SCENE I. *A Street in Rome.*

(*Enter* COUNT LODOVICO, ANTONELLI, *and* GASPARO)

LODOVICO. Banished?

ANTONELLI. It grieved me much to hear the sentence.

LODOVICO. Ha, ha! O Democritus, thy gods
That govern the whole world—courtly reward
And punishment! Fortune's a right whore:
If she give aught, she deals it in small parcels,
That she may take away all at one swoop.
This 'tis to have great enemies—God quit them!
Your wolf no longer seems to be a wolf
Than when she's hungry.

GASPARO. You term those enemies

Are men of princely rank.

LODOVICO. O, I pray for them.
The violent thunder is adored by those
Are pashed in pieces by it.

ANTONELLI. Come, my lord,
You are justly doomed. Look but a little back
Into your former life; you have in three years
Ruined the noblest earldom.

GASPARO. Your followers
Have swallowed you like mummia [1] and, being sick
With such unnatural and horrid physic,
Vomit you up i' the kennel. [2]

ANTONELLI. All the damnable degrees

[1] Pieces of mummied flesh.
[2] Channel or gutter.

Of drinkings have you staggered through;
one citizen
Is lord of two fair manors called you master
Only for caviare.

GASPARO. Those noblemen
Which were invited to your prodigal feasts
(Wherein the phœnix scarce could scape
your throats)
Laugh at your misery; as fore-deeming you
An idle meteor, which, drawn forth the earth,
Would be soon lost i' the air;—

ANTONELLI. Jest upon you,
And say you were begotten in an earthquake,
You have ruined such fair lordships.

LODOVICO. Very good.
This well goes with two buckets; I must tend
The pouring out of either.

GASPARO. Worse than these;
You have acted certain murders here in
Rome,
Bloody and full of horror.

LODOVICO. 'Las,—they were flea-bitings.
Why took they not my head, then?

GASPARO. Oh, my lord,
The law doth sometimes mediate, thinks it
good
Not ever to steep violent sins in blood;
This gentle penance may both end your
crimes,
And in the example better these bad times.

LODOVICO. So; but I wonder, then, some
great men scape
This banishment. There's Paulo Giordano
Ursini,
The Duke of Brachiano, now lives in Rome,
And by close panderism seeks to prostitute
The honor of Vittoria Corombona;
Vittoria, she that might have got my pardon
For one kiss to the duke.

ANTONELLI. Have a full man within you.[3]
We see that trees bear no such pleasant fruit
There where they grew first, as where they
are new set;
Perfumes, the more they are chafed, the more
they render
Their pleasing scents; and so affliction
Expresseth virtue fully, whether true
Or else adulterate.

LODOVICO. Leave your painted comforts.
I'll make Italian cut-works in their guts,
If ever I return.

GASPARO. O, sir!

LODOVICO. I am patient.
I have seen some ready to be executed
Give pleasant looks and money, and grown
familiar
With the knave hangman: so do I, I thank
them,
And would account them nobly merciful,
Would they dispatch me quickly.

ANTONELLI. Fare you well.
We shall find time, I doubt not, to repeal
Your banishment.

LODOVICO. I am ever bound to you.
This is the world's alms; pray, make use of it.
Great men sell sheep thus, to be cut in pieces,
When first they have shorn them bare and
sold their fleeces.   (*Exeunt*)

SCENE II. *Rome.* CAMILLO's *House.*

(*Sennet.*[4] *Enter* BRACHIANO, CAMILLO,
FLAMINEO, VITTORIA COROMBONA, *and*
Attendants)

BRACHIANO. Your best of rest!
VITTORIA. Unto my lord the duke
The best of welcome!—More lights! attend
the duke.
          (*Exeunt* CAMILLO *and* VITTORIA)
BRACHIANO. Flamineo—
FLAMINEO. My lord?
BRACHIANO. Quite lost, Flamineo!

FLAMINEO. Pursue your noble wishes; I
am prompt
As lightning to your service, O my lord!
(*Whispers*) The fair Vittoria, my happy sis-
ter,
Shall give you present audience.—(*To At-*
tendants) Gentlemen,
Let the caroche[5] go on; and 'tis his pleasure
You put out all your torches and depart.
          (*Exeunt Attendants*)
BRACHIANO. Are we so happy?
FLAMINEO. Can't[6] be otherwise?

---

[3] Keep up your courage.   [4] A flourish of trumpets.   [5] Coach.   [6] Can it.

Observed you not to-night, my honored lord,
Which way soe'er you went, she threw her
　　eyes?
I have dealt already with her chambermaid,
Zanche the Moor, and she is wondrous proud
To be the agent for so high a spirit.

BRACHIANO. We are happy above thought,
because 'bove merit.

FLAMINEO. 'Bove merit!—we may now talk
freely—'bove merit! What is 't you doubt?
her coyness? that's but the superficies of lust
most women have; yet why should ladies
blush to hear that named which they do not
fear to handle? Oh, they are politic: they
know our desire is increased by the difficulty
of enjoying, where a satiety is a blunt, weary,
and drowsy passion. If the buttery-hatch[7] at
court stood continually open, there would be
nothing so passionate crowding, nor hot suit
after the beverage.

BRACHIANO. Oh, but her jealous husband!

FLAMINEO. Hang him! a gilder that hath
his brains perished with quicksilver[8] is not
more cold in the liver; the great barriers
molted not more feathers than he hath shed
hairs, by the confession of his doctor; an
Irish gamester that will play himself naked,
and then wage all downward at hazard, is
not more venturous; so unable to please a
woman, that, like a Dutch doublet, all his
back is shrunk into his breeches.

Shrowd you within this closet, good my lord.
Some trick now must be thought on to divide
My brother-in-law from his fair bedfellow.

BRACHIANO. Oh, should she fail to come!

FLAMINEO. I must not have your lordship
thus unwisely amorous. I myself have loved
a lady, and pursued her with a great deal of
under-age protestation, whom some three or
four gallants that have enjoyed would with
all their hearts have been glad to have been
rid of. 'Tis just like a summer birdcage in a
garden; the birds that are without despair to
get in, and the birds that are within despair
and are in a consumption for fear they shall
never get out.
Away, away, my lord!

　　[7] Wine room door.
　　[8] Mercurial poisoning, caused by absorption of
the vapors of mercury, used in gilding, resulting
in symptoms ranging from tremors to acute
mania.

See, here he comes. (*Exit* BRACHIANO) This
　　fellow by his apparel
Some men would judge a politician;
But call his wit in question—you shall find it
Merely an ass in 's foot-cloth.

(*Re-enter* CAMILLO)

How now, brother?
What, travelling to bed to your kind wife?

　　CAMILLO. I assure you, brother, no; my
　　　　voyage lies
More northerly, in a far colder clime.
I do not well remember, I protest,
When I last lay with her.

　　FLAMINEO. Strange you should lose your
count.

　　CAMILLO. We never lay together but ere
　　　　morning
There grew a flaw between us.

　　FLAMINEO. 'T had been your part
To have made up that flaw.

　　CAMILLO. True, but she loathes
I should be seen in 't.

　　FLAMINEO. Why, sir, what's the matter?

　　CAMILLO. The duke, your master, visits
　　　　me, I thank him;
And I perceive how, like an earnest bowler,
He very passionately leans that way
He should have his bowl run.

　　FLAMINEO. I hope you do not think—

　　CAMILLO. That noblemen bowl booty?[9]
　　　　faith, his cheek
Hath a most excellent bias; it would fain
Jump with my mistress.

　　FLAMINEO. Will you be an ass,
Despite your Aristotle? or a cuckold,
Contrary to your Ephemerides,[10]
Which shows you under what a smiling
　　planet
You were first swaddled?

　　CAMILLO. Pew-wew, sir, tell not me
Of planets nor of Ephemerides;
A man may be made cuckold in the day-time,
When the stars' eyes are out.

　　FLAMINEO. Sir, God b' wi' you.
I do commit you to your pitiful pillow
Stuffed with horn-shavings.

　　CAMILLO. Brother—

　　[9] Cheat by bowling in collusion with others.
　　[10] Astrological tables giving positions of the
planets for every day of the year.

FLAMINEO. God refuse me!
Might I advise you now, your only course
Were to lock up your wife—
CAMILLO. 'Twere very good.
FLAMINEO. Bar her the sight of revels—
CAMILLO. Excellent.
FLAMINEO. Let her not go to church, but
like a hound
In lyam [11] at your heels—
CAMILLO. 'Twere for her honor.
FLAMINEO. And so you should be certain
in one fortnight,
Despite her chastity or innocence,
To be cuckolded, which yet is in suspense.
This is my counsel, and I ask no fee for 't.
CAMILLO. Come, you know not where my
nightcap wrings me.
FLAMINEO. Wear it o' the old fashion; let
your large ears come through, it will be more
easy:—nay, I will be bitter. Bar your wife of
her entertainment? Women are more willing
and more gloriously chaste when they are
least restrained of their liberty. It seems you
would be a fine, capricious, mathematically
jealous coxcomb, take the height of your own
horns with a Jacob's staff afore they are up.
These politic inclosures for paltry mutton [12]
make more rebellion in the flesh than all the
provocative electuaries [13] doctors have uttered
since last jubilee.
CAMILLO. This doth not physic me.
FLAMINEO. It seems you are jealous; I'll
show you the error of it by a familiar example. I have seen a pair of spectacles fashioned
with such perspective art that, lay down but
one twelve pence o' the board, 'twill appear
as if there were twenty; now, should you
wear a pair of these spectacles and see your
wife tying her shoe, you would imagine
twenty hands were taking up of your wife's
clothes, and this would put you into a horrible causeless fury.
CAMILLO. The fault there, sir, is not in the
eyesight.
FLAMINEO. True; but they that have the
yellow jaundice think all objects they look
on to be yellow. Jealousy is worser; her fits
present to a man, like so many bubbles in a
basin of water, twenty several crabbed faces;

[11] Leash.
[12] Elizabethan slang for loose women.
[13] Medicated syrup; here, aphrodisiac.

many times makes his own shadow his
cuckold-maker. See, she comes.

(Re-enter VITTORIA)

What reason have you to be jealous of this
creature? what an ignorant ass or fluttering
knave might he be counted, that should write
sonnets to her eyes, or call her brow the snow
of Ida or ivory of Corinth, or compare her
hair to the blackbird's bill, when 'tis liker
the blackbird's feather! This is all. Be wise;
I will make you friends, and you shall go
to bed together. Marry, look you, it shall not
be your seeking; do you stand upon that by
any means. Walk you aloof; I would not
have you seen in 't. (CAMILLO retires to the
back of the stage and watches them) Sister
—(whispers to her) my lord attends you in
the banqueting-house—your husband is wondrous discontented.
VITTORIA. I did nothing to displease him:
I carved to him at suppertime.
FLAMINEO. (Aside to her) You need not
have carved him, in faith; they say he is a
capon already. I must now seemingly fall out
with you.—Shall a gentleman so well descended as Camillo—(whispers to her) a
lousy slave, that within this twenty years
rode with the black guard in the duke's carriage, 'mongst spits and dripping-pans—
CAMILLO. Now he begins to tickle her.
FLAMINEO. An excellent scholar,—(whispers) one that hath a head filled with calves'
brains without any sage in them—come
crouching in the hams to you for a night's
lodging?—(whispers) that hath an itch in's
hams, which like the fire at the glass-house
hath not gone out this seven years.—Is he not
a courtly gentleman?—(whispers) when he
wears white satin, one would take him by his
black muzzle to be no other creature than a
maggot.—You are a goodly foil, [14] I confess,
well set out—(whispers) but covered with a
false stone, yon counterfeit diamond.
CAMILLO. He will make her know what
is in me.
FLAMINEO. (Whispers) Come, my lord attends you; thou shalt go to bed to my lord—
CAMILLO. Now he comes to 't.
FLAMINEO. (Whispers) With a relish as
curious as a vintner going to taste new wine.

[14] Thin leaf of metal—hence, jewel-setting.

—(*To* CAMILLO) I am opening your case hard.

CAMILLO. A virtuous brother, o' my credit!

FLAMINEO. He will give thee a ring with a philosopher's stone[15] in it.

CAMILLO. Indeed, I am studying alchemy.

FLAMINEO. Thou shalt lie in a bed stuffed with turtles' feathers; swoon in perfumed linen, like the fellow was smothered in roses. So perfect shall be thy happiness, that as men at sea think land and trees and ships go that way they go, so both heaven and earth shall seem to go your voyage.—(*whispers*) Shalt meet him; 'tis fixed with nails of diamonds to inevitable necessity.

VITTORIA. (*Whispers*) How shall 's rid him hence?

FLAMINEO. (*Whispers*) I will put the brees[16] in 's tail—set him gadding presently. —(*Leaves her and steps back to* CAMILLO) I have almost wrought her to it, I find her coming: but, might I advise you now, for this night I would not lie with her; I would cross her humor to make her more humble.

CAMILLO. Shall I, shall I?

FLAMINEO. It will show in you a supremacy of judgement.

CAMILLO. True, and a mind differing from the tumultuary opinion; for, *quae negata, grata.*[17]

FLAMINEO. Right; you are the adamant[18] shall draw her to you, though you keep distance off.

CAMILLO. A philosophical reason.

FLAMINEO. Walk by her o' the nobleman's fashion, and tell her you will lie with her at the end of the progress.

CAMILLO. (*Coming forward*) Vittoria, I cannot be induced, or, as a man would say, incited—

VITTORIA. To do what, sir?

CAMILLO. To lie with you to-night. Your silk-worm useth to fast every third day, and the next following spins the better. To-morrow at night I am for you.

VITTORIA. You'll spin a fair thread, trust to 't.

FLAMINEO. (*Aside to* CAMILLO) But, do you hear, I shall have you steal to her chamber about midnight.

[15] Which changed base metals into gold.

[16] Gadflies.

[17] "What is refused, is desired."　　[18] Magnet.

CAMILLO. Do you think so? Why, look you, brother, because you shall not think I'll gull you, take the key, lock me into the chamber, and say you shall be sure of me. (*Gives key*)

FLAMINEO. In troth, I will; I'll be your jailer once. But have you ne'er a false door?

CAMILLO. A pox on 't, as I am a Christian! Tell me to-morrow how scurvily she takes my unkind parting.

FLAMINEO. I will.

CAMILLO. Didst thou not mark the jest of the silkworm? Good-night. In faith, I will use this trick often.

FLAMINEO. Do, do, do. (*Exit* CAMILLO, *and* FLAMINEO *locks the door on him*) So, now you are safe. Ha, ha, ha! thou entanglest thyself in thine own work like a silkworm. (*Turns to* VITTORIA) Come, sister; darkness hides your blush. Women are like curst dogs: civility keeps them tied all daytime, but they are let loose at midnight; then they do most good, or most mischief.—(*Calls softly*) My lord, my lord!

(*Re-enter* BRACHIANO. ZANCHE *brings out a carpet, spreads it, and lays on it two fair cushions*)

BRACHIANO. Give credit, I could wish time
　　　　would stand still,
And never end this interview, this hour:
But all delight doth itself soon'st devour.

(FLAMINEO *and* ZANCHE *withdraw to one
　　side. Enter* CORNELIA *on the other. She
　　listens unobserved*)

Let me into your bosom, happy lady,
Pour out, instead of eloquence, my vows;
Loose me not, madam, for if you forgo me,
I am lost eternally.

VITTORIA. Sir, in the way of pity
I wish you heart-whole.

BRACHIANO. You are a sweet physician.

VITTORIA. Sure, sir, a loathèd cruelty in
　　ladies
Is as to doctors many funerals;
It takes away their credit.

BRACHIANO. Excellent creature!
We call the cruel fair: what name for you
That are so merciful?　　　　(*They kiss*)

ZANCHE. (*Aside*) See, now they close.

FLAMINEO. (*Aside*) Most happy union!

CORNELIA. (*Aside*) My fears are fall'n upon me. O my heart!
My son the pander! Now I find our house
Sinking to ruin. Earthquakes leave behind,
Where they have tyrannized, iron, or lead, or stone;
But, woe to ruin, violent lust leaves none!
BRACHIANO. What value is this jewel?
VITTORIA. 'Tis the ornament
Of a weak fortune.
BRACHIANO. In sooth, I'll have it; nay, I will but change
My jewel for your jewel.
(*They exchange brooches*)
FLAMINEO. (*Aside*) Excellent!
His jewel for her jewel!—well put in, duke.
BRACHIANO. Nay, let me see you wear it.
VITTORIA. Here, sir?
BRACHIANO. Nay, lower, you shall wear my jewel lower.
FLAMINEO. (*Aside*) That's better; she must wear his jewel lower.
VITTORIA. To pass away the time, I'll tell your grace
A dream I had last night.
BRACHIANO. Most wishedly.
VITTORIA. A foolish idle dream.
Methought I walked about the mid of night
Into a churchyard, where a goodly yew-tree
Spread her large root in ground. Under that yew,
As I sate sadly leaning on a grave
Chequered with cross sticks, there came stealing in
Your duchess and my husband; one of them
A pickaxe bore, the other a rusty spade,
And in rough terms they 'gan to challenge me
About this yew.
BRACHIANO. That tree?
VITTORIA. This harmless yew.
They told me my intent was to root up
That well-grown yew, and plant i' the stead of it
A withered blackthorn; and for that they vowed
To bury me alive. My husband straight
With pickaxe 'gan to dig, and your fell duchess
With shovel, like a Fury, voided out
The earth and scattered bones. Lord, how, methought,
I trembled! and yet, for all this terror,
I could not pray.

FLAMINEO. (*Aside*) No, the devil was in your dream.
VITTORIA. When to my rescue there arose, methought,
A whirlwind, which let fall a massy arm
From that strong plant,
And both were struck dead by that sacred yew,
In that base shallow grave that was their due.
FLAMINEO. (*Aside*) Excellent devil! She hath taught him in a dream
To make away his duchess and her husband.
BRACHIANO. Sweetly shall I interpret this your dream.
You are lodged within his arms who shall protect you
From all the fevers of a jealous husband,
From the poor envy of our phlegmatic duchess.
I'll seat you above law and above scandal,
Give to your thoughts the invention of delight,
And the fruition; nor shall government
Divide me from you longer than a care
To keep you great. You shall to me at once
Be dukedom, health, wife, children, friends, and all.
CORNELIA. (*Coming forward*) Woe to light hearts, they still forerun our fall!
FLAMINEO. What Fury raised thee up?—
Away, away! (*Exit* ZANCHE)
CORNELIA. (*To* BRACHIANO) What make you here, my lord, this dead of night?
Never dropped mildew on a flower here
Till now.
FLAMINEO. I pray, will you go to bed, then,
Lest you be blasted?
CORNELIA. O, that this fair garden
Had with all poisoned herbs of Thessaly
At first been planted, made a nursery
For witchcraft, rather than a burial plot
For both your honors!
VITTORIA. Dearest mother, hear me.
CORNELIA. O, thou dost make my brow bend to the earth
Sooner than nature! See, the curse of children!
In life they keep us frequently in tears,
And in the cold grave leave us in pale fears.
BRACHIANO. Come, come, I will not hear you.
VITTORIA. Dear my lord—

CORNELIA. Where is thy duchess now,
   adulterous duke?
Thou little dreamd'st this night she is come
   to Rome.
FLAMINEO. How! Come to Rome!
VITTORIA. The duchess!
BRACHIANO. She had been better—
CORNELIA. The lives of princes should
   like dials [19] move,
Whose regular example is so strong,
They make the times by them go right or
   wrong.
FLAMINEO. So, have you done?
CORNELIA. Unfortunate Camillo!
VITTORIA. I do protest, if any chaste denial,
In anything but blood could have allayed
His long suit to me—
CORNELIA. I will join with thee,
To the most woeful end e'er mother kneeled.
If thou dishonor thus thy husband's bed,
Be thy life short as are the funeral tears
In great men's.
BRACHIANO. Fie, fie, the woman's mad.
CORNELIA. Be thy act Judas-like—betray
   in kissing!
Mayst thou be envied during his short breath,
And pitied like a wretch after his death!
VITTORIA. O me accurst! (Exit VITTORIA)
FLAMINEO. Are you out of your wits, my
   lord?
I'll fetch her back again?
BRACHIANO. No, I'll to bed:
Send Doctor Julio to me presently.—
Uncharitable woman! thy rash tongue
Hath raised a fearful and prodigious storm.
Be thou the cause of all ensuing harm.
                    (Exit BRACHIANO)
FLAMINEO. Now, you that stand so much
   upon your honor,
Is this a fitting time o' night, think you,
To send a duke home without e'er a man?
I would fain know where lies the mass of
   wealth
Which you have hoarded for my main-
   tenance,
That I may bear my beard out of the level
Of my lord's stirrup. [20]
CORNELIA. What! because we are poor
Shall we be vicious?

[19] Sundials.
[20] Cease to walk at my Lord's stirrup like a
footman.

FLAMINEO. Pray, what means have you
To keep me from the galleys or the gallows?
My father proved himself a gentleman,
Sold all 's land, and, like a fortunate fellow,
Died ere the money was spent. You brought
   me up
At Padua, I confess, where, I protest,
For want of means (the university judge me)
I have been fain to heel my tutor's stock-
   ings, [21]
At least seven years: conspiring with a beard
Made me a graduate; then to this duke's
   service.
I visited the court, whence I returned
More courteous, more lecherous by far,
But not a suit the richer; and shall I,
Having a path so open and so free
To my preferment, still retain your milk
In my pale forehead? No, this face of mine
I'll arm and fortify with lusty wine
'Gainst shame and blushing.
CORNELIA. O, that I ne'er had borne thee!
FLAMINEO. So would I;
I would the common'st courtezan in Rome
Had been my mother, rather than thyself.
Nature is very pitiful to whores,
To give them but few children, yet those
   children
Plurality of fathers; they are sure
They shall not want. Go, go,
Complain unto my great lord cardinal;
Yet maybe he will justify the act.
Lycurgus wondered much men would pro-
   vide
Good stallions for their mares, and yet would
   suffer
Their fair wives to be barren.
CORNELIA. Misery of miseries!
                    (Exit CORNELIA)
FLAMINEO. The duchess come to court! I
   like not that.
We are engaged to mischief, and must on.
As rivers to find out the ocean
Flow with the crook bendings beneath forcèd
   banks,
Or as we see, to aspire some mountain's top,
The way ascends not straight, but imitates
The subtle foldings of a winter's snake,
So who knows policy and her true aspèct,
Shall find her ways winding and indirect.
                    (Exit)

[21] Act as servant to a tutor.

Act II

Scene I. *Rome.* Francisco's *Palace.*

(*Enter* Francisco de Medicis, Cardinal Monticelso, Marcello, Isabella, *young* Giovanni, *with little Jaques the Moor*)

Francisco. Have you not seen your husband since you arrived?

Isabella. Not yet, sir.

Francisco. Surely he is wondrous kind.
If I had such a dove-house as Camillo's,
I would set fire on 't, were 't but to destroy
The pole-cats that haunt to it.—(*To* Giovanni) My sweet cousin!

Giovanni. Lord uncle, you did promise me a horse
And armor.

Francisco. That I did, my pretty cousin.—
Marcello, see it fitted.

Marcello. My lord, the duke is here.

Francisco. Sister, away! you must not yet be seen.

Isabella. I do beseech you,
Entreat him mildly; let not your rough tongue
Set us at louder variance. All my wrongs
Are freely pardoned; and I do not doubt,
As men to try the precious unicorn's horn,[22]
Make of the powder a preservative circle
And in it put a spider, so these arms
Shall charm his poison, force it to obeying,
And keep him chaste from an infected straying.

Francisco. I wish it may. Be gone. Void the chamber.

(*Exeunt* Isabella, *followed by* Marcello, Giovanni, *and* Jaques)

(*Enter* Brachiano *and* Flamineo)

You are welcome; will you sit?—I pray, my lord,
Be you my orator, my heart's too full;
I'll second you anon.

Monticelso. Ere I begin,
Let me entreat your grace forgo all passion

Which may be raisèd by my free discourse.

Brachiano. As silent as i' the church;
you may proceed.

Monticelso. It is a wonder to your noble friends,
That you, who have, as 'twere, entered the world
With a free sceptre in your able hand,
And have to th' use of nature well applied
High gifts of learning, should in your prime age
Neglect your awful throne for the soft down
Of an insatiate bed. O, my lord,
The drunkard after all his lavish cups
Is dry, and then is sober; so at length,
When you awake from this lascivious dream,
Repentance then will follow, like the sting
Placed in the adder's tail. Wretched are princes
When fortune blasteth but a petty flower
Of their unwieldy crowns, or ravisheth
But one pearl from their sceptres, but, alas,
When they to wilful shipwreck loose good fame,
All princely titles perish with their name!

Brachiano. You have said, my lord.

Monticelso. Enough to give you taste
How far I am from flattering your greatness.

Brachiano. Now you that are his second, what say you?
Do not like young hawks fetch a course about;
Your game flies fair and for you.

Francisco. Do not fear it!
I'll answer you in your own hawking phrase.
Some eagles that should gaze upon the sun
Seldom soar high, but take their lustful ease,
Since they from dunghill birds their prey can seize.
You know Vittoria?

Brachiano. Yes.

Francisco. You shift your shirt there,
When you retire from tennis?

Brachiano. Happily.

Francisco. Her husband is lord of a poor fortune,

---

[22] From ancient times on, the mere presence of the unicorn's horn was believed to counter-act poison in food or drink.

Yet she wears cloth of tissue.[23]

BRACHIANO. What of this?—
Will you urge that, my good lord cardinal,
As part of her confession at next shrift,
And know from whence it sails?

FRANCISCO. She is your strumpet.

BRACHIANO. Uncivil sir, there's hemlock
    in thy breath,
And that black slander. Were she a whore
    of mine,
All thy loud cannons and thy borrowed
    Switzers,[24]
Thy galleys, nor thy sworn confederates,
Durst not supplant her.

FRANCISCO. Let's not talk on thunder.
Thou hast a wife, our sister. Would I had
    given
Both her white hands to death, bound and
    locked fast
In her last winding-sheet, when I gave thee
But one!

BRACHIANO. Thou hadst given a soul to
God then.

FRANCISCO. True!
Thy ghostly father, with all's absolution,
Shall ne'er do so by thee.

BRACHIANO. Spit thy poison!

FRANCISCO. I shall not need; lust carries
    her sharp whip
At her own girdle. Look to 't, for our anger
Is making thunder-bolts.

BRACHIANO. Thunder? in faith,
They are but crackers.

FRANCISCO. We'll end this with the cannon.

BRACHIANO. Thou'lt get naught by it but
    iron in thy wounds,
And gunpowder in thy nostrils.

FRANCISCO. Better that
Than change perfumes for plasters.

BRACHIANO. Pity on thee!
'Twere good you'd show your slaves or men
    condemned
Your new-ploughed forehead-defiance![25] and
    I'll meet thee,
Even in a thicket of thy ablest men.

MONTICELSO. My lords, you shall not
    word it any further
Without a milder limit.

FRANCISCO. Willingly.

[23] Rich material, woven with gold or silver
thread.   [24] Swiss mercenaries.
[25] Forehead wrinkled in anger.

BRACHIANO. Have you proclaimed a
    triumph, that you bait
A lion thus?

MONTICELSO. My lord!

BRACHIANO. I am tame, I am tame, sir.

FRANCISCO. We send unto the duke[26] for
    conference
'Bout levies 'gainst the pirates; my lord duke
Is not at home. We come ourself in person;
Still my lord duke is busied. But we fear
When Tiber to each prowling passenger
Discovers flocks of wild ducks, then, my lord,
'Bout molting time I mean, we shall be cer-
tain
To find you sure enough, and speak with you.

BRACHIANO. Ha!

FRANCISCO. A mere tale of a tub,[27] my
    words are idle;
But to express the sonnet by natural reason—
When stags grow melancholic, you'll find the
    season.

MONTICELSO. No more, my lord; here
    comes a champion
Shall end the difference between you both,—

(Re-enter GIOVANNI clad in his new armor)

Your son, the Prince Giovanni. See, my lords,
What hopes you store in him; this is a casket
For both your crowns, and should be held
    like dear.
Now is he apt for knowledge; therefore know,
It is a more direct and even way
To train to virtue those of princely blood
By examples than by precepts. If by examples,
Whom should he rather strive to imitate
Than his own father? Be his pattern, then;
Leave him a stock of virtue that may last,
Should fortune rend his sails and split his
    mast.

BRACHIANO. Your hand, boy. Growing to
a soldier?

GIOVANNI. Give me a pike.

FRANCISCO. What, practising your pike so
young, fair coz?

GIOVANNI. Suppose me one of Homer's
    frogs, my lord,
Tossing my bullrush thus. Pray, sir, tell me,
Might not a child of good discretion
Be leader to an army?

FRANCISCO. Yes, cousin, a young prince

[26] I.e., Brachiano.
[27] A cock-and-bull story.

Of good discretion might.
GIOVANNI. So you say?
Indeed, I have heard 'tis fit a general
Should not endanger his own person oft,
So that he make a noise when he's o' horse-
    back,
Like a Dansk [28] drummer, O, 'tis excellent!
He need not fight—methinks his horse as well
Might lead an army for him. If I live,
I'll charge the French foe in the very front
Of all my troops, the foremost man.
    FRANCISCO. What, what!
    GIOVANNI. And will not bid my soldiers
        up and follow,
But bid them follow me.
    BRACHIANO. Forward lapwing! [29]
He flies with the shell on 's head.
    FRANCISCO. Pretty cousin!
    GIOVANNI. The first year, uncle, that I go
        to war,
All prisoners that I take I will set free
Without their ransom.
    FRANCISCO. Ha, without their ransom?
How, then, will you reward your soldiers
That took those prisoners for you?
    GIOVANNI. Thus, my lord;
I'll marry them to all the wealthy widows
That fall that year.
    FRANCISCO. Why, then, the next year fol-
        lowing,
You'll have no men to go with you to war.
    GIOVANNI. Why, then, I'll press the
        women to the war,
And then the men will follow.
    MONTICELSO. Witty prince!
    FRANCISCO. See, a good habit makes a
        child a man,
Whereas a bad one makes a man a beast.
(To BRACHIANO) Come, you and I are
    friends.
    BRACHIANO. Most wishedly;
Like bones which, broke in sunder and well
    set,
Knit the more strongly.
    FRANCISCO. (To FLAMINEO) Call Camillo
        hither.   (Exit FLAMINEO)
You have received the rumor how Count
    Lodowick
Is turned a pirate?

[28] Danish.
[29] Favorite Elizabethan comparison for a pre-
cocious child. The lapwing begins to run about
as soon as it is hatched.

BRACHIANO. Yes.
FRANCISCO. We are now preparing
Some ships to fetch him in.

(*Re-enter* ISABELLA)

Behold your duchess.
We now will leave you, and expect from you
Nothing but kind entreaty.
    BRACHIANO. You have charmed me.
        (*Exeunt* FRANCISCO, MONTICELSO, *and*
            GIOVANNI)
You are in health, we see,—
    ISABELLA. And above health,
To see my lord well.
    BRACHIANO. So! I wonder much
What amorous whirlwind hurried you to
    Rome.
    ISABELLA. Devotion, my lord.
    BRACHIANO. Devotion?
Is your soul charged with any grievous sin?
    ISABELLA. 'Tis burdened with too many;
        and I think
The oftener that we cast our reckonings up,
Our sleeps will be the sounder.
    BRACHIANO. Take your chamber.
    ISABELLA. Nay, my dear lord, I will not
        have you angry.
Doth not my absence from you, now two
    months,
Merit one kiss?
    BRACHIANO. I do not use to kiss.
If that will dispossess your jealousy,
I'll swear it to you.
    ISABELLA. O my loved lord,
I do not come to chide. My jealousy?
I am to learn what that Italian means.
You are as welcome to these longing arms
As I to you a virgin.
    BRACHIANO. Oh, your breath!
Out upon sweetmeats and continued physic—
The plague is in them!
    ISABELLA. You have oft for these two lips
Neglected cassia [30] or the natural sweets
Of the spring-violet; they are not yet much
    withered.
My lord, I should be merry. These your
    frowns
Show in a helmet lovely; but on me,
In such a peaceful interview, methinks
They are too, too roughly knit.

[30] Chinese cinnamon.

BRACHIANO. O dissemblance!
Do you bandy factions 'gainst me? Have you learnt
The trick of impudent baseness, to complain
Unto your kindred?
　　ISABELLA. Never, my dear lord.
　　BRACHIANO. Must I be hunted out? Or was 't your trick
To meet some amorous gallant here in Rome
That must supply our discontinuance?
　　ISABELLA. I pray, sir, burst my heart, and in my death
Turn to your ancient pity, though not love.
　　BRACHIANO. Because your brother is the corpulent duke,
That is, the great duke, 'sdeath, I shall not shortly
Racket away five hundred crowns at tennis
But it shall rest upon record! I scorn him!
Like a shaved Polack, all his reverend wit
Lies in his wardrobe; he's a discreet fellow
When he is made up in his robes of state.
Your brother, the great duke, because h'as galleys
And now and then ransacks a Turkish fly-boat
(Now all the hellish Furies take his soul!),
First made this match. Accursèd be the priest
That sang the wedding mass, and even my issue!
　　ISABELLA. Oh, too, too far you have cursed!
　　BRACHIANO. Your hand I'll kiss;
This is the lastest ceremony of my love.
Henceforth I'll never lie with thee; by this,
This wedding-ring, I'll ne'er more lie with thee,
And this divorce shall be as truly kept
As if the judge had doomed it. Fare you well!
Our sleeps are severed.
　　ISABELLA. Forbid it, the sweet union
Of all things blessèd! Why, the saints in Heaven
Will knit their brows at that.
　　BRACHIANO. Let not thy love
Make thee an unbeliever; this my vow
Shall never, on my soul, be satisfied
With my repentance; let thy brother rage
Beyond a horrid tempest or sea-fight,
My vow is fixed.
　　ISABELLA. O my winding-sheet!
Now shall I need thee shortly.—Dear my lord,

Let me hear once more what I would not hear:
Never?
　　BRACHIANO. Never.
　　ISABELLA. O my unkind lord! may your sins find mercy,
As I upon a woeful widowed bed
Shall pray for you, if not to turn your eyes
Upon your wretched wife and hopeful son,
Yet that in time you'll fix them upon Heaven!
　　BRACHIANO. No more. Go, go complain to the great duke.
　　ISABELLA. No, my dear lord; you shall have present witness
How I'll work peace between you. I will make
Myself the author of your cursèd vow;
I have some cause to do it, you have none.
Conceal it, I beseech you, for the weal
Of both your dukedoms, that you wrought the means
Of such a separation; let the fault
Remain with my supposèd jealousy,
And think with what a piteous and rent heart
I shall perform this sad ensuing part.
　　　　　　　　　　　　　(She weeps)

(Re-enter FRANCISCO, FLAMINEO, MONTI-
　　　　CELSO, MARCELLO)

　　BRACHIANO. Well, take your course.—My honorable brother!
　　FRANCISCO. Sister!—This is not well, my lord.—Why, sister!—
She merits not this welcome.
　　BRACHIANO. Welcome, say?
She hath given a sharp welcome.
　　FRANCISCO. Are you foolish?
Come, dry your tears. Is this a modest course
To better what is naught, to rail and weep?
Grow to a reconcilement, or, by Heaven,
I'll ne'er more deal between you.
　　ISABELLA. Sir, you shall not;
No, though Vittoria, upon that condition,
Would become honest.
　　FRANCISCO. Was your husband loud
Since we departed?
　　ISABELLA. By my life, sir, no;
I swear by that I do not care to lose.
Are all these ruins of my former beauty
Laid out for a whore's triumph?
　　FRANCISCO. Do you hear?

Look upon other women, with what patience
They suffer these slight wrongs, with what
    justice
They study to requite them; take that course.
    ISABELLA. O, that I were a man, or that
        I had power
To execute my apprehended wishes!
I would whip some with scorpions.
    FRANCISCO. What, turned Fury?
    ISABELLA. To dig the strumpet's eyes out,
        let her lie
Some twenty months a dying, to cut off
Her nose and lips, pull out her rotten teeth,
Preserve her flesh like mummia,[31] for trophies
Of my just anger! Hell to my affliction
Is mere snow-water. By your favor, sir—
Brother, draw near, and my lord cardinal—
Sir, let me borrow of you but one kiss;
Henceforth I'll never lie with you, by this,
This wedding-ring.
    FRANCISCO. How? ne'er more lie with
        him?
    ISABELLA. And this divorce shall be as
        truly kept
As if in throngèd court a thousand ears
Had heard it, and a thousand lawyers' hands
Sealed to the separation.
    BRACHIANO. Ne'er lie with me?
    ISABELLA. Let not my former dotage
Make thee an unbeliever. This my vow
Shall never, on my soul, be satisfied
With my repentance; *manet alta mente
    repostum.*[32]
    FRANCISCO. Now, by my birth, you are a
        foolish, mad,
And jealous woman.
    BRACHIANO. You see 'tis not my seeking.
    FRANCISCO. Was this your circle of pure
        unicorn's horn
You said should charm your lord? Now, horns
    upon thee,
For jealousy deserves them! Keep your vow,
And take your chamber.
    ISABELLA. No, sir, I'll presently to Padua;
I will not stay a minute.
    MONTICELSO. O good madam!
    BRACHIANO. 'Twere best to let her have
        her humor.
Some half-day's journey will bring down her
    stomach,

And then she'll turn in post.[33]
    FRANCISCO. To see her come
To my lord cardinal for a dispensation
Of her rash vow will beget excellent laughter.
    ISABELLA. (*Aside*) Unkindness, do thy
        office; poor heart, break.
Those are the killing griefs which dare not
    speak.   (*Exit*)

(*Enter* CAMILLO)

    MARCELLO. Camillo's come, my lord.
    FRANCISCO. Where's the commission?
    MARCELLO. 'Tis here.
    FRANCISCO. Give me the signet.
    (*Exeunt* FRANCISCO, MONTICELSO, CAMIL-
        LO, *and* MARCELLO *two by two, con-
        versing*)
    FLAMINEO. My lord, do you mark their
whispering? I will compound a medicine out
of their two heads stronger than garlic, dead-
lier than stibium.[34] The cantharides,[35] which
are scarce seen to stick upon the flesh when
they work to the heart, shall not do it with
more silence or invisible cunning.
    BRACHIANO. About the murder?
    FLAMINEO. They are sending him to
Naples, but I'll send him to Candy.[36]

(*Enter* DOCTOR)

Here's another property too.
    BRACHIANO. Oh, the doctor!
    FLAMINEO. A poor quack-salving knave,
my lord; one that should have been lashed
for 's lechery, but that he confessed a judgement, had an execution laid upon him, and
so put the whip to a non plus.[37]
    DOCTOR. And was cozened, my lord, by an
arranter knave than myself, and made pay
all the colorable execution.
    FLAMINEO. He will shoot pills into a man's
guts shall make them have more ventages
than a cornet or a lamprey;[38] he will poison
a kiss; and was once minded, for his masterpiece, because Ireland breeds no poison, to

[31] Mummied flesh used as medicine.
[32] "It lies deep buried in my heart."
[33] Return post-haste.
[34] Antimony, similar in symptoms to arsenic.
[35] A drug violently irritating to the skin.
[36] Perdition.
[37] Escaped flogging for lechery by pretending
he was guilty of another charge.
[38] Wind instruments with a number of holes.

have prepared a deadly vapor in a Spaniard's fart that should have poisoned all Dublin.

BRACHIANO. Oh, Saint Anthony's fire! [39]

DOCTOR. Your secretary is merry, my lord.

FLAMINEO. O thou cursed antipathy to nature!—Look, his eye's bloodshed,[40] like a needle a chirurgeon stitcheth a wound with. —Let me embrace thee, toad, and love thee, O thou abominable loathsome gargarism,[41] that will fetch up lungs, lights, heart, and liver, by scruples!

BRACHIANO. No more.—I must employ thee, honest doctor.
You must to Padua, and by the way
Use some of your skill for us.

DOCTOR. Sir, I shall.

BRACHIANO. But for Camillo?

FLAMINEO. He dies this night by such a politic strain
Men shall suppose him by 's own engine [42] slain.
But for your duchess' death—

DOCTOR. I'll make her sure.

BRACHIANO. Small mischiefs are by greater made secure.

FLAMINEO. Remember this, you slave; when knaves come to preferment, they rise as gallowses [43] are raised i' the Low Countries, one upon another's shoulders.   (*Exeunt*)

(*Re-enter* FRANCISCO, MONTICELSO, CAMILLO, *and* MARCELLO)

MONTICELSO. Here is an emblem,[44] nephew, pray peruse it;
'Twas thrown in at your window.

CAMILLO. At my window?
Here is a stag, my lord, hath shed his horns,
And for the loss of them the poor beast weeps.
The word, *Inopem me copia fecit.*[45]

MONTICELSO. That is,
Plenty of horns hath made him poor of horns.

CAMILLO. What should this mean?

MONTICELSO. I'll tell you: 'tis given out You are a cuckold.

CAMILLO. Is it given out so?
I had rather such report as that, my lord,
Should keep within doors.

[39] Erysipelas.   [40] Blood-shot.
[41] Gargle.   [42] Device.
[43] Criminals condemned to the gallows.
[44] Symbolic picture.
[45] "Plenty makes me poor."

FRANCISCO. Have you any children?

CAMILLO. None, my lord.

FRANCISCO. You are the happier.
I'll tell you a tale.

CAMILLO. Pray, my lord.

FRANCISCO. An old tale.
Upon a time Phœbus, the god of light,
Or him we call the Sun, would needs be married.
The gods gave their consent, and Mercury
Was sent to voice it to the general world.
But what a piteous cry there straight arose
Amongst smiths and felt-makers, brewers and cooks,
Reapers and butterwomen, amongst fish-mongers,
And thousand other trades, which are annoyed
By his excessive heat! 'Twas lamentable.
They came to Jupiter all in a sweat,
And do forbid the banns. A great fat cook
Was made their speaker, who entreats of Jove
That Phœbus might be gelded; for if now,
When there was but one sun, so many men
Were like to perish by his violent heat,
What should they do if he were married
And should beget more, and those children
Make fireworks like their father? So say I,
Only I will apply it to your wife;
Her issue, should not Providence prevent it,
Would make both nature, time, and man repent it.

MONTICELSO. Look you, cousin,
Go, change the air, for shame; see if your absence
Will blast your cornucopia. Marcello
Is chosen with you joint commissioner
For the relieving our Italian coast
From pirates.

MARCELLO. I am much honored in 't.

CAMILLO. But, sir,
Ere I return the stag's horns may be sprouted
Greater than those are shed.

MONTICELSO. Do not fear it;
I'll be your ranger.

CAMILLO. You must watch i' the nights;
Then's the most danger.

FRANCISCO. Farewell, good Marcello.
All the best fortunes of a soldier's wish
Bring you a-ship-board!

CAMILLO. Were I not best, now I am turned soldier,

Ere that I leave my wife, sell all she hath
And then take leave of her?
  MONTICELSO. I expect good from you,
Your parting is so merry.
  CAMILLO. Merry, my lord! O' the captain's
    humor right;
I am resolved to be drunk this night.
      (*Exeunt* CAMILLO *and* MARCELLO)
  FRANCISCO. So, 'twas well fitted. Now
    shall we discern
How his wished absence will give violent
    way
To Duke Brachiano's lust.
  MONTICELSO. Why, that was it;
To what scorned purpose else should we
    make choice
Of him for a sea-captain? And besides,
Count Lodowick, which was rumored for a
    pirate,
Is now in Padua.
  FRANCISCO. Is 't true?
  MONTICELSO. Most certain.
I have letters from him which are suppliant

To work his quick repeal from banishment.
He means to address himself for pension
Unto our sister duchess.
  FRANCISCO. Oh, 'twas well;
We shall not want his absence past six days.
I fain would have the Duke Brachiano run
Into notorious scandal; for there's naught
In such cursed dotage to repair his name,
Only the deep sense of some deathless shame.
  MONTICELSO. It may be objected, I am
    dishonorable
To play thus with my kinsman; but I answer,
For my revenge I'd stake a brother's life,
That, being wronged, durst not avenge him-
    self.
  FRANCISCO. Come, to observe this strum-
pet.
  MONTICELSO. Curse of greatness!
Sure he'll not leave her?
  FRANCISCO. There's small pity in 't.
Like mistletoe on sear elms spent by weather,
Let him cleave to her, and both rot together.
                              (*Exeunt*)

SCENE II. *Rome.* CAMILLO's *House.*

(*Enter* BRACHIANO, *with a* CONJURER)

BRACHIANO. Now, sir, I claim your prom-
    ise. 'Tis dead midnight,
The time prefixed to show me, by your art,
How the intended murder of Camillo
And our loathed duchess grow to action.
  CONJURER. You have won me by your
    bounty to a deed
I do not often practise. Some there are
Which by sophistic tricks aspire that name,
Which I would gladly lose, of necromancer;
As some that use to juggle upon cards,
Seeming to conjure when indeed they cheat;
Others that raise up their confederate spirits
'Bout windmills, and endanger their own
    necks
For making of a squib; and some there are
Will keep a curtal [46] to show juggling tricks,
And give out 'tis a spirit; besides these,
Such a whole realm of almanac-makers,
    figure-flingers,

—fellows, indeed, that only live by stealth,
Since they do merely lie about stol'n goods—
They'd make men think the devil were fast
    and loose,
With speaking fustian Latin. [47] Pray sit down.
Put on this night-cap, sir, 'tis charmed. And
    now
I'll show you, by my strong commanding art,
The circumstance that breaks your duchess'
    heart.

A DUMB SHOW

(*Enter suspiciously* JULIO *and* CHRISTO-
PHERO. *They draw the curtain from before*
BRACHIANO'S *picture, put on spectacles of
glass which cover their eyes and noses, and
then burn perfumes afore the picture, and
wash the lips of the picture; that done,
quenching the fire, and putting off their
spectacles, they depart laughing.*

Enter ISABELLA *in her nightgown, as to bed,
with lights after her,* COUNT LODOVICO,

[46] A docked horse; a reference to Morocco, a
performing horse frequently referred to in Elizabethan literature.

[47] Gibberish.

GIOVANNI, GUIDANTONIO, *and others wait-*
ing on her; she kneels down as to prayers,
then draws the curtain of the picture, does
three reverences to it, and kisses it thrice;
she faints, and will not suffer them to come
near it; dies; sorrow expressed in GIOVANNI
and in COUNT LODOVICO; *she is conveyed out*
solemnly)

BRACHIANO. Excellent! then she's dead?
CONJURER. She's poisoned
By the fumed [48] picture. 'Twas her custom
    nightly
Before she went to bed to go and visit
Your picture, and to feed her eyes and lips
On the dead shadow. Doctor Julio,
Observing this, infects it with an oil
And other poisoned stuff, which presently
Did suffocate her spirits.
BRACHIANO. Methought I saw
Count Lodowick there.
CONJURER. He was, and by my art
I find he did most passionately dote
Upon your duchess. Now turn another way,
And view Camillo's far more politic fate.
Strike louder, music, from this charmèd
    ground,
To yield, as fits the act, a tragic sound!

THE SECOND DUMB SHOW

(*Enter* FLAMINEO, MARCELLO, CAMILLO,
with four more, as Captains; they drink
healths, and dance. A vaulting-horse is
brought into the room. MARCELLO *and two*
more whispered out of the room, while
FLAMINEO *and* CAMILLO *strip themselves*
to their shirts, as to vault; they compliment
who shall begin. As CAMILLO *is about to*
vault, FLAMINEO *pitcheth him upon his*
neck, and with the help of the rest, writhes
his neck about; seems to see if it be broke,

and lays him folded double, as 'twere, under
the horse; makes shows to call for help.
MARCELLO *comes in, laments; sends for the*
Cardinal and Duke, who come forth with
armed men; wonder at the act; command
the body to be carried home; apprehend
FLAMINEO, MARCELLO, *and the rest, and go,*
as 't were, to apprehend VITTORIA)

BRACHIANO. 'Twas quaintly done; but yet
    each circumstance
I taste not fully.
CONJURER. O, 'twas most apparent.
You saw them enter, charged with their
    deep healths
To their bon voyage, and to second that,
Flamineo calls to have a vaulting-horse
Maintain their sport; the virtuous Marcello
Is innocently plotted forth the room;
Whilst your eyes saw the rest, and can in-
    form you
The engine of all.
BRACHIANO. It seems Marcello and Fla-
    mineo
Are both committed.
CONJURER. Yes, you saw them guarded,
And now they are come with purpose to
    apprehend
Your mistress, fair Vittoria. We are now
Beneath her roof; 'twere fit we instantly
Make out by some back-postern.
BRACHIANO. Noble friend,
You bind me ever to you: this [49] shall stand
As the firm seal annexèd to my hand;
It shall enforce a payment.
CONJURER. Sir, I thank you.
                          (*Exit* BRACHIANO)
Both flowers and weeds spring when the sun
    is warm,
And great men do great good or else great
    harm.   (*Exit*)

Act III

SCENE I. *Ante-chamber of Court of Justice.*

(*Enter* FRANCISCO *and* MONTICELSO, *their*
CHANCELLOR *and* REGISTER)

FRANCISCO. You have dealt discreetly to
    obtain the presence

Of the grave lieger ambassadors, [50]
To hear Vittoria's trial.
MONTICELSO. 'Twas not ill,

[48] *I.e.,* perfumed, with the poisonous vapors.

[49] This service, that is, the conjuring.
[50] Resident ambassadors, as contrasted with
special envoys.

For, sir, you know we have naught but cir-
cumstances
To charge her with about her husband's
death;
Their approbation, therefore, to the proofs
Of her black lust shall make her infamous
To all our neighboring kingdoms. I wonder
If Brachiano will be here.

FRANCISCO. Oh fie!
'Twere impudence too palpable.   (*Exeunt*)

(*Enter* FLAMINEO *and* MARCELLO *guarded,
and a* LAWYER)

LAWYER. What, are you in by the week?
so,
I will try now whether thy wit be close
prisoner.
Methinks none should sit upon thy sister but
old whore-masters.

FLAMINEO. Or cuckolds; for your cuckold
is your most terrible tickler of lechery.
Whore-masters would serve; for none are
judges at tilting but those that have been old
tilters.

LAWYER. My lord duke and she have been
very private.

FLAMINEO. You are a dull ass; 'tis threatened they have been very public.

LAWYER. If it can be proved they have but
kissed one another—

FLAMINEO. What then?

LAWYER. My lord cardinal will ferret
them.

FLAMINEO. A cardinal, I hope, will not
catch conies.[51]

LAWYER. For to sow kisses (mark what I
say), to sow kisses is to reap lechery; and I
am sure a woman that will endure kissing
is half won.

FLAMINEO. True, her upper part, by that
rule; if you will win her nether part, too, you
know what follows.

LAWYER. Hark! the ambassadors are
lighted.   (*He goes to the door*)

FLAMINEO. (*Aside*) I do put on this
feignèd garb of mirth
To gull[52] suspicion.

MARCELLO. O my unfortunate sister!
I would my dagger-point had cleft her heart

[51] Rabbits. A *double-entendre*, for to catch
conies was to swindle.
[52] Deceive.

When she first saw Brachiano. You, 'tis said,
Were made his engine and his stalking-horse
To undo my sister.

FLAMINEO. I made a kind of path
To her and mine own preferment.

MARCELLO. Your ruin.

FLAMINEO. Hum! Thou art a soldier,
Follow'st the great duke, feed'st his victories,
As witches do their serviceable spirits,
Even with thy prodigal blood. What hast got
But, like the wealth of captains, a poor hand-
ful,
Which in thy palm thou bear'st as men hold
water?
Seeking to grip it fast, the frail reward
Steals through thy fingers.

MARCELLO. Sir!

FLAMINEO. Thou hast scarce maintenance
To keep thee in fresh chamois.[53]

MARCELLO. Brother!

FLAMINEO. Hear me!—
And thus, when we have even poured our-
selves
Into great fights for their ambition
Or idle spleen, how shall we find reward?
But as we seldom find the mistletoe,
Sacred to physic, on the builder oak
Without a mandrake by it,[54] so in our quest
of gain,
Alas, the poorest of their forced dislikes
At a limb proffers, but at heart it strikes!
This is lamented doctrine.

MARCELLO. Come, come.

FLAMINEO. When age shall turn thee
White as a blooming hawthorn—

MARCELLO. I'll interrupt you.—
For love of virtue bear an honest heart
And stride o'er every politic respect,
Which, where they most advance, they most
infect.
Were I your father, as I am your brother,
I should not be ambitious to leave you
A better patrimony.

FLAMINEO. I'll think on 't.—
The lord ambassadors.

(*Here there is a passage of the lieger* AM-
BASSADORS *over the stage severally*)

LAWYER. O my sprightly Frenchman!

[53] Chamois jerkin worn under armor.
[54] *I.e.*, the healing mistletoe is always near the
fatal mandrake.

(*Bows*)—Do you know him? He's an admirable tilter.

FLAMINEO. I saw him at last tilting; he showed like a pewter candlestick fashioned like a man in armor, holding a tilting-staff in his hand little bigger than a candle of twelve i' the pound.

LAWYER. O, but he's an excellent horseman.

FLAMINEO. A lame one in his lofty tricks; he sleeps a-horseback, like a poulter.[55]

LAWYER. (*Bows*) Lo you, my Spaniard!

FLAMINEO. He carries his face in 's ruff, as I have seen a serving man carry glasses in a cypress[56] hatband, monstrous steady, for fear of breaking; he looks like the claw of a blackbird, first salted, then broiled in a candle.   (*Exeunt*)

SCENE II. *A Court of Justice.*

(*Enter* FRANCISCO, MONTICELSO, *the six lieger* AMBASSADORS, BRACHIANO, VITTORIA, FLAMINEO, MARCELLO, LAWYER, *a Guard, Attendants, and Spectators*)

MONTICELSO. (*To* BRACHIANO) Forbear, my lord; here is no place assigned you.
This business by his holiness is left
To our examination.

BRACHIANO. May it thrive with you!
(*Lays a rich gown on the floor and sits on it*)

FRANCISCO. A chair there for his lordship!

BRACHIANO. Forbear your kindness. An unbidden guest
Should travel as Dutchwomen go to church,
Bear their stools with them.

MONTICELSO. At your pleasure, sir.—
Stand to the table, gentlewoman.—Now, signior,
Fall to your plea.

LAWYER. *Domine judex, converte oculos in hanc pestem, mulierum corruptissimam.*[57]

VITTORIA. What's he?

FRANCISCO. A lawyer that pleads against you.

VITTORIA. Pray, my lord, let him speak his usual tongue;
I'll make no answer else.

FRANCISCO. Why? You understand Latin.

VITTORIA. I do, sir, but amongst this auditory
Which come to hear my cause, the half or more
May be ignorant in 't.

MONTICELSO. Go on, sir.

VITTORIA. By your favor,
I will not have my accusation clouded
In a strange tongue; all this assembly
Shall hear what you can charge me with.

FRANCISCO. Signior,
You need not stand on 't much; pray, change your language.

MONTICELSO. Oh, for God's sake!—Gentlewoman, your credit
Shall be more famous by it.

LAWYER. Well, then, have at you!

VITTORIA. I am at the mark, sir; I'll give aim to you,
And tell you how near you shoot.

LAWYER. (*Pompously*) Most literated judges, please your lordships
So to connive your judgements to the view
Of this debauched and diversivolent[58] woman;
Who such a black concatenation
Of mischief hath effected, that to extirp
The memory of 't must be the consummation
Of her and her projections—

VITTORIA. What's all this?

LAWYER. Hold your peace!
Exorbitant sins must have exulceration.

VITTORIA. Surely, my lords, this lawyer here hath swallowed
Some 'pothecaries' bills, or proclamations,
And now the hard and undigestible words
Come up, like stones we use give hawks for physic.
Why, this is Welsh to Latin.

LAWYER. My lords, the woman

---

[55] A dealer in poultry, who rode early to market.

[56] Very sheer fabric.

[57] "My Lord, turn your eyes upon this plague, this worst of women."

[58] Given to stirring up discord.

Knows not her tropes nor figures, nor is perfect
In the academic derivation
Of grammatical elocution.

FRANCISCO. Sir, your pains
Shall be well spared, and your deep eloquence
Be worthily applauded amongst those
Which understand you.

LAWYER. My good lord—

FRANCISCO. Sir,
Put up your papers in your fustian bag—
    (FRANCISCO speaks this as in scorn)
Cry mercy, sir, 'tis buckram—and accept
My notion of your learned verbosity.

LAWYER. I most graduatically thank your lordship;
I shall have use for them elsewhere.
                    (Exit LAWYER)

MONTICELSO. I shall be plainer with you, and paint out
Your follies in more natural red and white
Than that upon your cheek.

VITTORIA. Oh, you mistake!
You raise a blood as noble in this cheek
As ever was your mother's.

MONTICELSO. I must spare you till proof cry "whore" to that.—
Observe this creature here, my honored lords,
A woman of a most prodigious spirit,
In her effected.

VITTORIA. Honorable my lord,
It doth not suit a reverend cardinal
To play the lawyer thus.

MONTICELSO. Oh, your trade
Instructs your language.—
You see, my lords, what goodly fruit she seems;
Yet, like those apples travellers report
To grow where Sodom and Gomorrah stood,
I will but touch her, and you straight shall see
She'll fall to soot and ashes.

VITTORIA. Your envenomed
'Pothecary should do 't.

MONTICELSO. I am resolved
Were there a second Paradise to lose,
This devil would betray it.

VITTORIA. O poor charity,
Thou art seldom found in scarlet.[59]

MONTICELSO. Who knows not how, when several night by night

[59] The cardinal, of course, is magnificently robed in scarlet.

Her gates were choked with coaches and her rooms
Outbraved the stars with several kind of lights,
When she did counterfeit a prince's court
In music, banquets, and most riotous surfeits,
This whore, forsooth, was holy?

VITTORIA. Ha! Whore? What's that?

MONTICELSO. Shall I expound whore to you? Sure, I shall;
I'll give their perfect character. They are, first,
Sweetmeats which rot the eater, in man's nostril
Poisoned perfumes; they are cozening alchymy,
Shipwrecks in calmest weather. What are whores?
Cold Russian winters, that appear so barren
As if that nature had forgot the spring.
They are the true material fire of hell,
Worse than those tributes i' the Low Countries paid,
Exactions upon meat, drink, garments, sleep,
Ay, even on man's perdition, his sin.
They are those brittle evidences of law
Which forfeit all a wretched man's estate
For leaving out one syllable. What are whores?
They are those flattering bells have all one tune,
At weddings and at funerals. Your rich whores
Are only treasuries by extortion filled,
And emptied by cursed riot. They are worse,
Worse than dead bodies which are begged at gallows
And wrought upon by surgeons to teach man
Wherein he is imperfect. What's a whore?
She's like the guilty counterfeited coin
Which, whosoe'er first stamps it, brings in trouble
All that receive it.

VITTORIA. This character 'scapes me.

MONTICELSO. You, gentlewoman!
Take from all beasts and from all minerals
Their deadly poison—

VITTORIA. Well, what then?

MONTICELSO. I'll tell thee:
I'll find in thee a 'pothecary's shop,
To sample them all.

FRENCH AMBASSADOR. She hath lived ill.

ENGLISH AMBASSADOR. True; but the cardinal's too bitter.

MONTICELSO. You know what whore is.
  Next the devil adultery,
Enters the devil murder.

FRANCISCO. Your unhappy
Husband is dead.

VITTORIA. O, he's a happy husband;
Now he owes nature nothing.

FRANCISCO. And by a vaulting-engine.

MONTICELSO. An active plot;
He jumped into his grave.

FRANCISCO. What a prodigy was 't
That from some two yards' height a slender man
Should break his neck!

MONTICELSO. I' the rushes!

FRANCISCO. And what's more,
Upon the instant lose all use of speech,
All vital motion, like a man had lain
Wound up [60] three days. Now mark each circumstance.

MONTICELSO. And look upon this creature was his wife.
She comes not like a widow; she comes armed
With scorn and impudence. Is this a mourning-habit?

VITTORIA. Had I foreknown his death, as you suggest,
I would have bespoke my mourning.

MONTICELSO. O, you are cunning.

VITTORIA. You shame your wit and judgement
To call it so. What, is my just defence
By him that is my judge called impudence?
Let me appeal, then, from this Christian court
To the uncivil Tartar.

MONTICELSO. See, my lords,
She scandals our proceedings.

VITTORIA. Humbly thus,
Thus low, to the most worthy and respected
Lieger ambassadors, my modesty
And womanhood I tender; but withal
So entangled in a cursèd accusation
That my defence of force,[61] like Perseus,
Must personate masculine virtue. To the point!
Find me but guilty, sever head from body,
We'll part good friends; I scorn to hold my life

At yours or any man's entreaty, sir.

ENGLISH AMBASSADOR. She hath a brave spirit.

MONTICELSO. Well, well, such counterfeit jewels
Make true ones oft suspected.

VITTORIA. You are deceived!
For know that all your strict-combinèd heads
Which strike against this mine of diamonds
Shall prove but glassen hammers—they shall break.
These are but feignèd shadows of my evils.
Terrify babes, my lord, with painted devils;
I am past such needless palsy. For your names
Of whore and murderess, they proceed from you,
As if a man should spit against the wind;
The filth returns in 's face.

MONTICELSO. Pray you, mistress, satisfy me one question:
Who lodged beneath your roof that fatal night
Your husband brake his neck?

BRACHIANO. (Leaping to his feet) That question
Enforceth me break silence. I was there.

MONTICELSO. Your business?

BRACHIANO. Why, I came to comfort her
And take some course for settling her estate,
Because I heard her husband was in debt
To you, my lord.

MONTICELSO. He was.

BRACHIANO. And 'twas strangely feared
That you would cozen [62] her.

MONTICELSO. Who made you overseer?

BRACHIANO. Why, my charity, my charity, which should flow
From every generous and noble spirit
To orphans and to widows.

MONTICELSO. Your lust!

BRACHIANO. Cowardly dogs bark loudest.
  Sirrah priest,
I'll talk with you hereafter. Do you hear?
The sword you frame of such an excellent temper
I'll sheathe in your own bowels.
There are a number of thy coat resemble
Your common post-boys—

MONTICELSO. Ha!

BRACHIANO. —your mercenary post-boys.
Your letters carry truth, but 'tis your guise

---

[60] In his winding sheet.   [61] Perforce.   [62] Cheat.

To fill your mouths with gross and impudent
  lies.   (*Moves towards the door*)
SERVANT. My lord, your gown.
BRACHIANO. Thou liest, 'twas my stool.
Bestow 't upon thy master, that will challenge
The rest o' the household-stuff; for Brachiano
Was ne'er so beggarly to take a stool
Out of another's lodging. Let him make
Valance [63] for his bed on 't, or a demi-foot-
  cloth
For his most reverent moil.[64] Monticelso,
Nemo me impune lacessit.[65]
                    (*Exit* BRACHIANO)
MONTICELSO. Your champion's gone.
VITTORIA. The wolf may prey the better.
FRANCISCO. My lord, there's great sus-
  picion of the murder,
But no sound proof who did it. For my part,
I do not think she hath a soul so black
To act a deed so bloody. If she have,
As in cold countries husbandmen plant vines
And with warm blood manure them, even so
One summer she will bear unsavory fruit,
And ere next spring wither both branch and
  root.
The act of blood let pass; only descend
To matter of incontinence.
VITTORIA. I discern poison under your
gilded pills.
MONTICELSO. Now the duke's gone, I will
  produce a letter
Wherein 'twas plotted he and you should
  meet
At an apothecary's summer-house
Down by the river Tiber—view 't, my lords—
Where, after wanton bathing and the heat
Of a lascivious banquet—I pray read it,
I shame to speak the rest.
VITTORIA. Grant I was tempted;
Temptation to lust proves not the act:
Casta est quam nemo rogavit.[66]
You read his hot love to me, but you want
My frosty answer.
MONTICELSO. Frost i' the dog-days?
Strange!
VITTORIA. Condemn you me for that the
  duke did love me?
So may you blame some fair and crystal river
For that some melancholic distracted man
Hath drowned himself in 't.

----

[63] Hangings.   [64] Mule.
[65] "No man attacks me with impunity."
[66] "She is chaste whom no one has solicited."

MONTICELSO. Truly drowned, indeed.
VITTORIA. Sum up my faults, I pray, and
  you shall find
That beauty and gay clothes, a merry heart,
And a good stomach to a feast are all,
All the poor crimes that you can charge me
  with.
In faith, my lord, you might go pistol flies;
The sport would be more noble.
MONTICELSO. Very good.
VITTORIA. But take your course. It seems
  you have beggared me first,
And now would fain undo me. I have houses,
Jewels, and a poor remnant of crusadoes; [67]
Would those would make you charitable!
MONTICELSO. If the devil
Did ever take good shape, behold his picture.
VITTORIA. You have one virtue left—you
will not flatter me.
FRANCISCO. Who brought this letter?
VITTORIA. I am not compelled to tell
you.
MONTICELSO. My lord duke sent to you
  a thousand ducats
The twelfth of August.
VITTORIA. 'Twas to keep your cousin
From prison; I paid use for 't.
MONTICELSO. I rather think
'Twas interest for his lust.
VITTORIA. Who says so
But yourself? If you be my accuser,
Pray cease to be my judge. Come from the
  bench,
Give in your evidence 'gainst me, and let
  these
Be moderators. My lord cardinal,
Were your intelligencing ears as loving
As to my thoughts, had you an honest tongue,
I would not care though you proclaimed
  them all.
MONTICELSO. Go to, go to.
After your goodly and vainglorious banquet,
I'll give you a choke-pear.[68]
VITTORIA. O' your own grafting?
MONTICELSO. You were born in Venice,
  honorably descended
From the Vittelli. 'Twas my cousin's fate—
Ill may I name the hour—to marry you;
He bought you of your father.
VITTORIA. Ha!

----

[67] Portuguese gold or silver coins.
[68] A bitter pear.

MONTICELSO. He spent there in six months
Twelve thousand ducats and (to my acquaintance)
Received in dowry with you not one julio.[69]
'Twas a hard pennyworth, the ware being so light.
I yet but draw the curtain; now to your picture.
You came from thence a most notorious strumpet,
And so you have continued.
VITTORIA. My lord—
MONTICELSO. Nay, hear me;
You shall have time to prate. My lord Brachiano—
Alas, I make but repetition
Of what is ordinary and Rialto talk,
And ballated, and would be played o' the stage,
But that vice many times finds such loud friends
That preachers are charmed silent.—
You gentlemen, Flamineo and Marcello,
The court hath nothing now to charge you with,
Only you must remain upon your sureties
For your appearance.
FRANCISCO. I stand for Marcello.
FLAMINEO. And my lord duke for me.
MONTICELSO. For you, Vittoria, your public fault,
Joined to the condition of the present time,
Takes from you all the fruits of noble pity,
Such a corrupted trial have you made
Both of your life and beauty, and been styled
No less an ominous fate than blazing stars
To princes, here's your sentence: you are confined
Unto a house of convertites, and your bawd—
FLAMINEO. (Aside) Who, I?
MONTICELSO. The Moor.
FLAMINEO. (Aside) O, I am a sound man again.
VITTORIA. A house of convertites! what's that?
MONTICELSO. A house
Of penitent whores.
VITTORIA. Do the noblemen in Rome
Erect it for their wives, that I am sent
To lodge there?

[69] Italian coin of small value.

FRANCISCO. You must have patience.
VITTORIA. I must first have vengeance.
I fain would know if you have your salvation
By patent, that you proceed thus.
MONTICELSO. Away with her!
Take her hence.
VITTORIA. A rape! A rape!
MONTICELSO. How?
VITTORIA. Yes, you have ravished justice,
Forced her to do your pleasure.
MONTICELSO. Fie, she's mad!
VITTORIA. Die with those pills in your most cursèd maw
Should bring you health! Or while you sit o' the bench
Let your own spittle choke you!—
MONTICELSO. She's turned Fury.
VITTORIA. That the last day of judgement may so find you,
And leave you the same devil you were before!
Instruct me, some good horse-leech, to speak treason;
For since you cannot take my life for deeds,
Take it for words! O woman's poor revenge,
Which dwells but in the tongue! I will not weep;
No, I do scorn to call up one poor tear
To fawn on your injustice; bear me hence
Unto this house of—what's your mitigating title?
MONTICELSO. Of convertites.
VITTORIA. It shall not be a house of convertites;
My mind shall make it honester to me
Than the Pope's palace, and more peaceable
Than thy soul, though thou art a cardinal.
Know this, and let it somewhat raise your spite,
Through darkness diamonds spread their richest light.
(Exit VITTORIA with Guards, followed by Spectators)

(Re-enter BRACHIANO)

BRACHIANO. Now you and I are friends, sir, we'll shake hands
In a friend's grave together; a fit place,
Being the emblem of soft peace, to atone our hatred.
FRANCISCO. Sir, what's the matter?
BRACHIANO. I will not chase more blood from that loved cheek;

You have lost too much already. Fare you
    well.   (*Exit*)

FRANCISCO. How strange these words
sound! What's the interpretation?

FLAMINEO. (*Aside*) Good; this is a preface
to the discovery of the duchess' death: he
carries it well. Because now I cannot counterfeit a whining passion for the death of
my lady, I will feign a mad humor for the
disgrace of my sister, and that will keep off
idle questions. Treason's tongue hath a villainous palsy in 't. I will talk to any man,
hear no man, and for a time appear a politic
madman.   (*Exit*)

(*Enter* GIOVANNI, COUNT LODOVICO)

FRANCISCO. How now, my noble cousin?
What, in black?

GIOVANNI. Yes, uncle, I was taught to
    imitate you
In virtue, and you now must imitate me
In colors of your garments. My sweet mother
Is—

FRANCISCO. How! Where?

GIOVANNI. Is there; no, yonder. Indeed,
    sir, I'll not tell you,
For I shall make you weep.

FRANCISCO. Is dead?

GIOVANNI. Do not blame me now;
I did not tell you so.

LODOVICO. She's dead, my lord.

FRANCISCO. Dead?

MONTICELSO. Blessed lady, thou art now
    above thy woes!—
Will 't please your lordships to withdraw a
    little?   (*Exeunt* AMBASSADORS)

GIOVANNI. What do the dead do, uncle?
    do they eat,
Hear music, go a-hunting, and be merry,
As we that live?

FRANCISCO. No, coz; they sleep.

GIOVANNI. Lord, Lord, that I were dead!
I have not slept these six nights.—When do
    they wake?

FRANCISCO. When God shall please.

GIOVANNI. Good God, let her sleep ever!
For I have known her wake an hundred
    nights,
When all the pillow where she laid her head
Was brine-wet with her tears. I am to com-
    plain to you, sir;
I'll tell you how they have used her now
    she's dead:
They wrapped her in a cruel fold of lead,
And would not let me kiss her.

FRANCISCO. Thou didst love her.

GIOVANNI. I have often heard her say she
    gave me suck,
And it should seem by that she dearly loved
    me,
Since princes seldom do it.

FRANCISCO Oh, all of my poor sister that
    remains!—
Take him away, for God's sake!
            (LODOVICO *and* MARCELLO *lead off*
                GIOVANNI)

MONTICELSO. How now, my lord?

FRANCISCO. Believe me, I am nothing but
    her grave,
And I shall keep her blessèd memory
Longer than thousand epitaphs.
        (*Exeunt* FRANCISCO *and* MONTICELSO)

SCENE III. *The Ante-Chamber.*

(*Enter* FLAMINEO *counterfeiting madness*)

FLAMINEO. We endure the strokes like
    anvils or hard steel,
Till pain itself make us no pain to feel.
Who shall do me right now? Is this the end
of service? I'd rather go weed garlic; travel
through France and be mine own ostler; wear
sheepskin linings, or shoes that stink of
blacking; be entered into the list of the forty
thousand pedlars in Poland.

(*Enter* AMBASSADORS *of* Savoy, France, *and*
England, *followed by* LODOVICO *and* MAR-
    CELLO)

Would I had rotted in some surgeon's house
at Venice, built upon the pox as well as on
piles, ere I had served Brachiano!

SAVOY AMBASSADOR. You must have comfort.

FLAMINEO. Your comfortable words are
like honey; they relish well in your mouth

that's whole, but in mine that's wounded they go down as if the sting of the bee were in them. Oh, they have wrought their purpose cunningly, as if they would not seem to do it of malice! In this a politician imitates the devil, as the devil imitates a cannon; wheresoever he comes to do mischief, he comes with his backside towards you.

FRENCH AMBASSADOR. The proofs are evident.

FLAMINEO. Proof! 'Twas corruption. O gold, what a god art thou! and O man, what a devil art thou to be tempted by that cursed mineral! Your diversivolent lawyer, mark him: knaves turn informers, as maggots turn to flies; you may catch gudgeons[70] with either. A cardinal! I would he would hear me; there's nothing so holy but money will corrupt and putrify it, like victual under the line.[71] You are happy in England, my lord; here they sell justice with those weights they press men to death with. O horrible salary!

ENGLISH AMBASSADOR. Fie, fie, Flamineo!
(*Exeunt* Ambassadors)

FLAMINEO. Bells ne'er ring well till they are at their full pitch, and I hope yon cardinal shall never have the grace to pray well till he come to the scaffold. If they were racked now to know the confederacy—but your noblemen are privileged from the rack; and well may, for a little thing would pull some of them a-pieces afore they came to their arraignment. Religion, oh, how it is commedled with policy! The first bloodshed in the world happened about religion. Would I were a Jew!

MARCELLO. Oh, there are too many.

FLAMINEO. You are deceived; there are not Jews enough, priests enough, nor gentlemen enough.

MARCELLO. How?

FLAMINEO. I'll prove it. For if there were Jews enough, so many Christians would not turn usurers; if priests enough, one should not have six benefices; and if gentlemen enough, so many early mushrooms, whose best growth sprang from a dunghill, should not aspire to gentility. Farewell! Let others live by begging; be thou one of them practise

[70] Small fish.
[71] At the equator.

the art of Wolner[72] in England, to swallow all's given thee; and yet let one purgation make thee as hungry again as fellows that work in a saw-pit. I'll go hear the screechowl.   (*Exit*)

LODOVICO. (*Aside*) This was Brachiano's pander and 'tis strange
That, in such open and apparent guilt
Of his adulterous sister, he dare utter
So scandalous a passion. I must wind him.[73]

(*Re-enter* FLAMINEO)

FLAMINEO. (*Aside*) How dares this banished count return to Rome,
His pardon not yet purchased? I have heard
The deceased duchess gave him pension,
And that he came along from Padua
I' the train of the young prince. There's somewhat in 't.
Physicians, that cure poisons, still do work
With counter-poisons.

MARCELLO. Mark this strange encounter.

FLAMINEO. (*To* LODOVICO) The god of melancholy turn thy gall to poison,
And let the stigmatic[74] wrinkles in thy face,
Like to the boisterous waves in a rough tide,
One still overtake another.

LODOVICO. I do thank thee,
And I do wish ingeniously for thy sake
The dog-days[75] all year long.

FLAMINEO. How croaks the raven?
Is our good duchess dead?

LODOVICO. Dead.

FLAMINEO. O fate!
Misfortune comes, like the coroner's business,
Huddle upon huddle.

LODOVICO. Shalt thou and I join housekeeping?

FLAMINEO. Yes, content.
Let's be unsociably sociable—

LODOVICO. Sit some three days together, and discourse—

FLAMINEO. Only with making faces. Lie in our clothes—

LODOVICO. With faggots for our pillows—

FLAMINEO. And be lousy—

[72] Richard Wolner, a freak of the mid-sixteenth century, who could reputedly digest iron and glass.
[73] Follow his scent.
[74] Literally, branded; hence hideous.
[75] Days of calamity.

LODOVICO. In taffata linings; that's genteel
melancholy.
Sleep all day—
FLAMINEO. Yes, and, like your melan-
cholic hare,
Feed after midnight.—

(*Enter at the back* ANTONELLI *and*
GASPARO, *laughing*)

We are observed. See how yon couple grieve!
LODOVICO. What a strange creature is a
laughing fool!
As if man were created to no use
But only to show his teeth.
FLAMINEO. I'll tell thee what—
It would do well, instead of looking-glasses,
To set one's face each morning by a saucer
Of a witch's congealed blood.
LODOVICO. Precious rogue!
We'll never part.
FLAMINEO. Never, till the beggary of cour-
tiers,
The discontent of churchmen, want of sol-
diers,
And all the creatures that hang manacled,
Worse than strappadoed, on the lowest felly [76]
Of Fortune's wheel, be taught, in our two
lives,
To scorn that world which life of means
deprives.
ANTONELLI. (*Coming forward*) My lord,
I bring good news. The Pope, on 's
deathbed,
At the earnest suit of the Great Duke of
Florence
Hath signed your pardon and restored unto
you—
LODOVICO. I thank you for your news.—
Look up again,
Flamineo; see my pardon.
FLAMINEO. Why do you laugh?
There was no such condition in our covenant.
LODOVICO. Why?
FLAMINEO. You shall not seem a happier
man than I.
You know our vow, sir; if you will be merry,
Do it i' the like posture as if some great man
Sate while his enemy were executed;
Though it be very lechery unto thee,
Do 't with a crabbèd politician's face.

[76] Strappado: a form of torture; felly: rim of a
wheel.

LODOVICO. Your sister is a damnable
whore.
FLAMINEO. Ha!
LODOVICO. Look you, I spake that laugh-
ing.
FLAMINEO. Dost ever think to speak
again?
LODOVICO. Do you hear?
Wilt sell me forty ounces of her blood
To water a mandrake? [77]
FLAMINEO. Poor lord, you did vow
To live a lousy creature.
LODOVICO. Yes.
FLAMINEO. Like one
That had for ever forfeited the daylight
By being in debt.
LODOVICO. Ha, ha!
FLAMINEO. I do not greatly wonder you
do break;
Your lordship learned it long since. But I'll
tell you—
LODOVICO. What?
FLAMINEO. And 't shall stick by you—
LODOVICO. I long for it.
FLAMINEO. This laughter scurvily becomes
your face.
If you will not be melancholy, be angry.
(*Strikes him*)
See, now I laugh too.
MARCELLO. You are to blame; I'll force
you hence.
(*Seizes* FLAMINEO. LODOVICO *draws his
sword, but* MARCELLO *catches his arm*)
LODOVICO. Unhand me.
(*Exeunt* MARCELLO *with* FLAMINEO)
That e'er I should be forced to right myself
Upon a pander!
ANTONELLI. My lord,—
LODOVICO. H'ad been as good
Met with his fist a thunderbolt.
GASPARO. How this shows!
LODOVICO. Ud's death, how did my sword
miss him? These rogues
That are most weary of their lives still 'scape
The greatest dangers.
A pox upon him! all his reputation,
Nay, all the goodness of his family,
Is not worth half this earthquake.
I learned it of no fencer to shake thus.
Come, I'll forget him, and go drink some
wine. (*Exeunt*)

[77] The mandrake was supposed to thrive especially under the rotting bodies on the gallows.

Act IV

Scene I. *Rome.* Francisco's *Palace.*

(*Enter* Francisco *and* Monticelso)

Monticelso. Come, come, my lord, untie
      your folded thoughts,
And let them dangle loose as a bride's hair.[78]
Your sister's poisoned.
      Francisco. Far be it from my thoughts
To seek revenge.
      Monticelso. What, are you turned all
      marble?
      Francisco. Shall I defy him, and impose
      a war
Most burdensome on my poor subjects' necks
Which at my will I have not power to end?
You know, for all the murders, rapes, and
      thefts
Committed in the horrid lust of war,
He that unjustly caused it first proceed
Shall find it in his grave and in his seed.
      Monticelso. That's not the course I'd
      wish you; pray, observe me.
We see that undermining more prevails
Than doth the cannon. Bear your wrongs
      concealed,
And, patient as the tortoise, let this camel
Stalk o'er your back unbruised; sleep with
      the lion
And let this brood of secure foolish mice
Play with your nostrils till the time be ripe
For the bloody audit and the fatal gripe.
Aim like a cunning fowler, close one eye
That you the better may your game espy.
      Francisco. Free me, my innocence, from
      treacherous acts!
I know there's thunder yonder; and I'll stand
Like a safe valley which low bends the knee
To some aspiring mountain, since I know
Treason, like spiders weaving nets for flies,
By her foul work is found, and in it dies.
To pass away these thoughts, my honored
      lord,
It is reported you possess a book
Wherein you have quoted, by intelligence,[79]
The names of all notorious offenders
Lurking about the city.

[78] Virgin brides customarily wore their hair
down at their weddings.
[79] Noted down from information received.
[80] Informers.

Monticelso. Sir, I do,
And some there are which call it my black
      book.
Well may the title hold, for though it teach
      not
The art of conjuring, yet in it lurk
The names of many devils.
      Francisco. Pray, let's see it.
      Monticelso. I'll fetch it to your lordship.
                              (*Exit* Monticelso)
      Francisco. Monticelso,
I will not trust thee, but in all my plots
I'll rest as jealous as a town besieged.
Thou canst not reach what I intend to act.
Your flax soon kindles, soon is out again,
But gold slow heats, and long will hot re-
      main.

(*Re-enter* Monticelso, *and presents* Fran-
      cisco *with a book*)

Monticelso. 'Tis here, my lord.
      Francisco. First, your intelligencers,[80]
pray, let's see.
      Monticelso. Their number rises strange-
      ly, and some of them
You'd take for honest men. Next are
      panders—
These are your pirates—and these following
      leaves
For base rogues that undo young gentlemen
By taking up commodities,[81] for politic bank-
      rupts;
For fellows that are bawds to their own wives,
Only to put off horses, and slight jewels,
Clocks, defaced plate, and such commodities,
At birth of their first children.[82]
      Francisco. Are there such?
      Monticelso. These are for impudent
      bawds
That go in men's apparel; for usurers
That share with scriveners for their good
      reportage;
For lawyers that will antedate their writs.

[81] That is, usurers who loaned not money but
grossly over-valued goods which could be sold
only at a loss.
[82] *I.e.* they blackmailed their wives' lovers into
buying worthless goods.

And some divines you might find folded there,
But that I slip them o'er for conscience' sake.
Here is a general catalogue of knaves;
A man might study all the prisons o'er,
Yet never attain this knowledge.
    FRANCISCO. Murderers!
Fold down the leaf, I pray.
Good my lord, let me borrow this strange doctrine.
    MONTICELSO. Pray, use 't, my lord.
    FRANCISCO. I do assure your lordship
You are a worthy member of the state,
And have done infinite good in your dis-
covery
Of these offenders.
    MONTICELSO. Somewhat, sir.
    FRANCISCO. O God!
Better than tribute of wolves paid in Eng-
land.
'Twill hang their skins o' the hedge.
    MONTICELSO. I must make bold
To leave your lordship.
    FRANCISCO. Dearly, sir, I thank you.
If any ask for me at court, report
You have left me in the company of knaves.
                 (*Exit* MONTICELSO)
I gather now by this, some cunning fellow
That's my lord's officer, one that lately skipped
From a clerk's desk up to a justice' chair,
Hath made this knavish summons and in-
tends,
As the Irish rebels wont were to sell heads,
So to make prize of these. And thus it hap-
pens
Your poor rogues pay for 't which have not the means
To present bribe in fist; the rest o' the band
Are razed out of the knaves' record, or else
My lord he winks at them with easy will;
His man grows rich, the knaves are the knaves still.
But to the use I'll make of it: it shall serve
To point me out a list of murderers,
Agents for any villainy. Did I want
Ten leash [53] of courtezans, it would furnish me;
Nay, laundress three armies. That in so little paper
Should lie the undoing of so many men!

[53] Sporting term for a set of three.

'Tis not so big as twenty declarations.
See the corrupted use some make of books:
Divinity, wrested by some factious blood,
Draws swords, swells battles, and o'erthrows all good.
To fashion my revenge more seriously,
Let me remember my dead sister's face.
Call for her picture? No, I'll close mine eyes,
And in a melancholic thought I'll frame

        (*Enter Isabella's Ghost*)

Her figure 'fore me. Now I ha't.—How strong
Imagination works! How she can frame
Things which are not! Methinks she stands afore me,
And by the quick idea of my mind,
Were my skill pregnant, I could draw her picture.
Thought, as a subtle juggler, makes us deem
Things supernatural which yet have cause
Common as sickness. 'Tis my melancholy.—
How cam'st thou by thy death?—How idle am I
To question mine own idleness! Did ever
Man dream awake till now? Remove this object;
Out of my brain with 't! What have I to do
With tombs, or death-beds, funerals, or tears,
That have to meditate upon revenge?
                  (*Exit Ghost*)
So, now 'tis ended, like an old wives' story;
Statesmen think often they see stranger sights
Than madmen. Come, to this weighty busi-
ness.
My tragedy must have some idle mirth in 't,
Else it will never pass. I am in love,
In love with Corombona, and my suit
Thus halts to her in verse.[54]—   (*He writes*)
I have done it rarely. Oh, the fate of princes!
I am so used to frequent flattery
That, being alone, I now flatter myself.
But it will serve; 'tis sealed.

        (*Enter Servant*)

Bear this
To the house of convertites and watch your leisure
To give it to the hands of Corombona,
Or to the matron, when some followers

[54] An ironical statement, designed to let the audience know the purport of the letter.

Of Brachiano may be by. Away!
                              (*Exit Servant*)
He that deals all by strength, his wit is
    shallow;
When a man's head goes through, each limb
    will follow.
The engine for my business, bold Count
Lodowick.

'Tis gold must such an instrument procure;
With empty fist no man doth falcons lure.
Brachiano, I am now fit for thy encounter;
Like the wild Irish, I'll ne'er think thee dead
Till I can play at football with thy head.
Flectere si nequeo superos, Acheronta
    movebo.[85]   (*Exit*)

SCENE II. *A Room in the House of Convertites.*

(*Enter the* MATRON *and* FLAMINEO)

MATRON. Should it be known the duke
    hath such recourse
To your imprisoned sister, I were like
To incur much damage by it.
    FLAMINEO. Not a scruple!
The Pope lies on his death-bed, and their
    heads
Are troubled now with other business
Than guarding of a lady.

(*Enter* SERVANT)

SERVANT. (*Aside*) Yonder's Flamineo in
    conference
With the matrona.—Let me speak with you;
I would entreat you to deliver for me
This letter to the fair Vittoria—
    MATRON. I shall, sir. (*Enter* BRACHIANO)
    SERVANT. —with all care and secrecy.
Hereafter you shall know me, and receive
Thanks for this courtesy.   (*Exit* SERVANT)
    FLAMINEO. How now? What's that?
    MATRON. A letter.
    FLAMINEO. To my sister? (*Takes letter*)
I'll see't delivered.   (*Exit* MATRON)
    BRACHIANO. What's that you read, Flami-
neo?
    FLAMINEO. Look.
    BRACHIANO. Ha!   (*Reads*)
"To the most unfortunate, his best respected
    Vittoria."—
Who was the messenger?
    FLAMINEO. I know not.
    BRACHIANO. No?
Who sent it?
    FLAMINEO. Ud's foot, you speak as if a
    man
Should know what fowl is coffined[86] in a
    baked meat

Afore you cut it up.
    BRACHIANO. I'll open 't, were 't her heart.
What's here subscribed?
"Florence!" This juggling is gross and palpa-
    ble.
I have found out the conveyance.—Read it,
    read it!
    FLAMINEO. (*Reads the letter*) "*Your tears*
        I'll turn to triumphs, be but mine.
Your prop is fall'n; I pity that a vine
Which princes heretofore have longed to
        gather,
Wanting supporters, now should fade and
        wither."
Wine, i' faith, my lord, with lees would serve
    his turn.
"*Your sad imprisonment I'll soon uncharm,*
And with a princely uncontrollèd arm
Lead you to Florence, where my love and care
Shall hang your wishes in my silver hair."—
A halter on his strange equivocation!
"*Nor for my years return me the sad willow;*[87]
Who prefer blossoms before fruit that's
        mellow?"—
Rotten, on my knowledge, with lying too
    long i' the bed-straw.
"*And all the lines of age this line convinces,*
The gods never wax old, no more do
        princes."—
A pox on 't, tear it; let's have no more atheists,
    for God's sake.
    BRACHIANO. Ud's death, I'll cut her into
        atomies,
And let th' irregular north wind sweep her
    up
And blow her into his nostrils! Where's this
    whore?

[85] Virgil, *Aeneid:* "If I cannot move the Gods
above, I shall move hell."
    [86] Baked in a pie.
    [87] Traditional symbol of unsuccessful lovers.

FLAMINEO. That—what do you call her?

BRACHIANO. Oh, I could be mad,
Prevent the cursed disease she'll bring me to,
And tear my hair off! Where's this change-
    able stuff?

FLAMINEO. O'er head and ears in water,
    I assure you;
She is not for your wearing.

BRACHIANO. In, you pander!

FLAMINEO. What, me, my lord? Am I
    your dog?

BRACHIANO. A blood-hound!
Do you brave, do you stand me?

FLAMINEO. Stand you! Let those that have
    diseases run;
I need no plasters.

BRACHIANO. Would you be kicked?

FLAMINEO. Would you have your neck
    broke?
I tell you, duke, I am not in Russia; [88]
My shins must be kept whole.

BRACHIANO. Do you know me?

FLAMINEO. Oh, my lord, methodically.
As in this world there are degrees of evils,
So in this world there are degrees of devils.
You're a great duke, I your poor secretary.
I do look now for a Spanish fig or an Italian
salad [89] daily.

BRACHIANO. Pander, ply your convoy, and
leave your prating.

FLAMINEO. All your kindness to me is
like that miserable courtesy of Polyphemus
to Ulysses: you reserve me to be devoured
last. You would dig turfs out of my grave to
feed your larks; that would be music to you.
Come, I'll lead you to her.

            (FLAMINEO retreats before him)

BRACHIANO. Do you face me?

FLAMINEO. Oh, sir, I would not go before
a politic enemy with my back towards him,
though there were behind me a whirlpool.

            (Enter VITTORIA)

BRACHIANO. Can you read, mistress? Look
    upon that letter.
There are no characters nor hieroglyphics;

You need no comment. I am grown your
    receiver. [90]
God's precious! You shall be a brave great
    lady,
A stately and advancèd whore.

VITTORIA. Say, sir?

BRACHIANO. Come, come, let's see your
    cabinet, discover
Your treasury of love-letters. Death and
    Furies!
I'll see them all.

VITTORIA. Sir, upon my soul,
I have not any. Whence was this directed?

BRACHIANO. Confusion on your politic
    ignorance!   (Gives her the letter)
You are reclaimed, [91] are you? I'll give you the
    bells [92]
And let you fly to the devil.

FLAMINEO. 'Ware hawk, my lord!

VITTORIA. "Florence"! This is some treach-
    erous plot, my lord!
To me he ne'er was lovely, I protest,
So much as in my sleep.

BRACHIANO. Right! They are plots.
Your beauty! Oh, ten thousand curses on 't!
How long have I beheld the devil in crystal?
Thou hast led me, like an heathen sacrifice,
With music and with fatal yokes of flowers,
To my eternal ruin. Woman to man
Is either a god or a wolf.

VITTORIA. My lord—

BRACHIANO. Away!
We'll be as differing as two adamants; [93]
The one shall shun the other. What, dost
    weep?
Procure but ten of thy dissembling trade,
Ye'd furnish all the Irish funerals
With howling past wild Irish.

FLAMINEO. Fie, my lord!

BRACHIANO. That hand, that cursèd hand,
    which I have wearied
With doting kisses!—O my sweetest duchess,
How lovely art thou now!—(To VITTORIA)
    Thy loose thoughts
Scatter like quicksilver. I was bewitched,
For all the world speaks ill of thee.

VITTORIA. No matter.

[90] Your pimp to receive and deliver your
lover's letter.

[91] Hawking term: tamed.

[92] Bells were fastened to a hawk's legs to make
her easier to find.

[93] Magnets.

[88] Thomas Dekker, Seven Deadly Sins: "The
Russians have an excellent custom; they beat
them on the shins, that have money, and will
not pay their debts."

[89] Notoriously used for administering poison.

I'll live so now, I'll make that world recant
And change her speeches. You did name your
    duchess.
    BRACHIANO. Whose death God pardon!
    VITTORIA. Whose death God revenge
On thee, most godless duke!
    FLAMINEO. (*Aside*) Now for two whirl-
winds!
    VITTORIA. What have I gained by thee but
    infamy?
Thou hast stained the spotless honor of my
    house
And frighted thence noble society,
Like those which, sick o' the palsy and re-
    taining
Ill-scenting foxes 'bout them, are still
    shunned
By those of choicer nostrils. What do you
    call this house?
Is this your palace? Did not the judge style it
A house of penitent whores? Who sent me
    to it?
Who hath the honor to advance Vittoria
To this incontinent college? Is 't not you?
Is 't not your high preferment? Go, go, brag
How many ladies you have undone like me.
Fare you well, sir; let me hear no more of
    you.
I had a limb corrupted to an ulcer,
But I have cut it off; and now I'll go
Weeping to Heaven on crutches. For your
    gifts,
I will return them all; and I do wish
That I could make you full executor
To all my sins. Oh, that I could toss myself
Into a grave as quickly! For all thou art
    worth
I'll not shed one tear more—I'll burst first.
            (*She throws herself upon a bed*)
    BRACHIANO. I have drunk Lethe.—Vit-
    toria!
My dearest happiness! Vittoria!
What do you ail, my love? Why do you
    weep?
    VITTORIA. Yes, I now weep poniards, do
you see?
    BRACHIANO. Are not those matchless eyes
mine?
    VITTORIA. I had rather
They were not matches!
    BRACHIANO. Is not this lip mine?
    VITTORIA. Yes; thus to bite it off, rather
than give it thee.

    FLAMINEO. Turn to my lord, good sister.
    VITTORIA. Hence, you pander!
    FLAMINEO. Pander! Am I the author of
your sin?
    VITTORIA. Yes; he's a base thief that a thief
lets in.
    FLAMINEO. We're blown up, my lord.
    BRACHIANO. Wilt thou hear me?
Once to be jealous of thee, is to express
That I will love thee everlastingly
And never more be jealous.
    VITTORIA. O thou fool,
Whose greatness hath by much o'ergrown
    thy wit!
What dar'st thou do that I not dare to suffer,
Excepting to be still thy whore? For that,
In the sea's bottom sooner thou shalt make
A bonfire.
    FLAMINEO. Oh, no oaths, for God's sake!
    BRACHIANO. Will you hear me!
    VITTORIA. Never.
    FLAMINEO. What a damned imposthume [94]
    is a woman's will!
Can nothing break it?—Fie, fie, my lord,
Women are caught as you take tortoises;
She must be turned on her back.—Sister, by
    this hand,
I am on your side.—Come, come, you have
    wronged her.
What a strange credulous man were you, my
    lord,
To think the Duke of Florence would love
    her!
Will any mercer take another's ware
When once 'tis toused and sullied?—And yet,
    sister,
How scurvily this frowardness becomes you!
Young leverets stand not long,[95] and women's
    anger
Should, like their flight, procure a little sport;
A full cry for a quarter of an hour,
And then be put to the dead quat.[96]
    BRACHIANO. Shall these eyes,
Which have so long time dwelt upon your
    face,
Be now put out?
    FLAMINEO. No cruel landlady i' th' world,
    which lends forth groats
To broom-men and takes use for them, would
    do 't.—

[94] Abscess.
[95] Young rabbits do not hold out for long.
[96] Squat—especially of a rabbit.

Hand her, my lord, and kiss her; be not like
A ferret, to let go your hold with blowing.
    BRACHIANO. Let us renew right hands.
    VITTORIA. Hence!
    BRACHIANO. Never shall rage
Or the forgetful wine make me commit
Like fault.
    FLAMINEO. Now you are i' the way on 't,
follow 't hard.
    BRACHIANO. Be thou at peace with me,
let all the world
Threaten the cannon.
    FLAMINEO. Mark his penitence.
Best natures do commit the grossest faults
When they're given o'er to jealousy, as best
wine,
Dying, makes strongest vinegar. I'll tell you—
The sea's more rough and raging than calm
rivers,
But not so sweet nor wholesome. A quiet
woman
Is a still water under a great bridge;
A man may shoot her safely.
    VITTORIA. Oh, ye dissembling men!—
    FLAMINEO. We sucked that, sister,
From women's breasts, in our first infancy.
    VITTORIA. To add misery to misery!
    BRACHIANO. Sweetest—
    VITTORIA. Am I not low enough?
Aye, aye, your good heart gathers like a
snowball,
Now your affection's cold.
    FLAMINEO. Ud's foot, it shall melt
To a heart again, or all the wine in Rome
Shall run o' the lees for 't.
    VITTORIA. Your dog or hawk should be
rewarded better
Than I have been. I'll speak not one word
more.
    FLAMINEO. Stop her mouth with a sweet
kiss, my lord. So,
Now the tide's turned, the vessel's come
about.
He's a sweet armful. Oh, we curled-haired
men
Are still most kind to women! This is well.
    BRACHIANO. That you should chide thus!
    FLAMINEO. O, sir, your little chimneys
Do ever cast most smoke! I sweat for you.
Couple together with as deep a silence
As did the Grecians in their wooden horse.
My lord, supply your promises with deeds;
You know that painted meat no hunger feeds.

    BRACHIANO. Stay! Ingrateful Rome—[97]
    FLAMINEO. Rome! It deserves
To be called Barbary for our villainous
usage.
    BRACHIANO. Soft! The same project which
the Duke of Florence
(Whether in love or gullery I know not)
Laid down for her escape, will I pursue.
    FLAMINEO. And no time fitter than this
night, my lord.
The Pope being dead and all the cardinals
entered
The conclave for the electing a new Pope,
The city in a great confusion,
We may attire her in a page's suit,
Lay her post horses,[98] take shipping, and
amain
For Padua.
    BRACHIANO. I'll instantly steal forth the
Prince Giovanni
And make for Padua. You two with your old
mother
And young Marcello that attends on Flor-
ence,
If you can work him to it, follow me.
I will advance you all.—For you, Vittoria,
Think of a duchess' title.
    FLAMINEO. Lo, you, sister!—
Stay, my lord; I'll tell you a tale. The crocodile, which lives in the river Nilus, hath a
worm breeds i' the teeth of 't, which puts it
to extreme anguish; a little bird no bigger
than a wren is barbar-surgeon to this crocodile, flies into the jaws of 't, picks out the
worm, and brings present remedy. The fish,
glad of ease but ingrateful to her that did it,
that the bird may not talk largely of her
abroad for non-payment, closeth her chaps,
intending to swallow her and so put her to
perpetual silence. But nature, loathing such
ingratitude, hath armed this bird with a quill
or prick on the top o' th' head, which wounds
the crocodile i' the mouth, forceth her open
her bloody prison, and away flies the pretty
tooth-picker from her cruel patient.
    BRACHIANO. Your application is, I have
not rewarded
The service you have done me.
    FLAMINEO. No, my lord.—

[97] Brachiano suddenly recalls their peril in
Rome.
[98] Order relays of post horses.

You, sister, are the crocodile. You are blem-
ished in your fame, my lord cures it; and
though the comparison hold not in every
particle, yet observe, remember what good
the bird with the prick i' the head hath done
you, and scorn ingratitude.—(*Aside*) It may
appear to some ridiculous

Thus to talk knave and madman, and some-
    times
Come in with a dried sentence, stuft with
    sage:
But this allows my varying of shapes;
Knaves do grow great by being great men's
    apes.   (*Exeunt*)

Scene III. *Before the Vatican.*

(*Enter* Lodovico, Gasparo, *and six* Ambassadors. *At another door* Francisco,
Duke of Florence)

Francisco. So, my lord, I commend your
    diligence.
Guard well the conclave; and, as the order is,
Let none have conference with the cardinals.
    Lodovico. I shall, my lord.—Room for the
ambassadors!
    Gasparo. They're wondrous brave [99] to-
    day. Why do they wear
These several habits?
    Lodovico. Oh, sir, they're knights
Of several orders. That lord i' the black cloak
With the silver cross is Knight of Rhodes;
    the next,
Knight of St. Michael; that, of the Golden
    Fleece;
The Frenchman, there, Knight of the Holy
    Ghost;
My lord of Savoy, Knight of the Annuncia-
    tion;
The Englishman is Knight of the honored
    Garter,
Dedicated unto their saint, St. George. I
    could
Describe to you their several institutions,
With the laws annexed to their orders, but
    that time
Permits not such discovery.
    Francisco. Where's Count Lodowick?
    Lodovico. Here, my lord.
    Francisco. 'Tis o' the point of dinner
    time.
Marshal the cardinals' service.
    Lodovico. Sir, I shall.

(*Enter* Servants, *with several dishes*
covered)

[99] Gorgeously dressed.

Stand, let me search your dish. Who's this
    for?
    Servant. For my Lord Cardinal Monti-
celso.
    Lodovico. Whose this?
    Servant. For my Lord Cardinal of Bour-
bon.
    French Ambassador. Why doth he
    search the dishes? To observe
What meat is drest?
    English Ambassador. No, sir, but to pre-
    vent
Lest any letters should be conveyed in,
To bribe or to solicit the advancement
Of any cardinal. When first they enter,
'Tis lawful for the ambassador of princes
To enter with them, and to make their suit
For any man their prince affecteth best;
But after, till a general election,
No man may speak with them.
    Lodovico. You that attend on the lord
    cardinals,
Open the window and receive their viands!
    An Officer. (*At the window*) You must
    return the service. The lord cardinals
Are busied 'bout electing of the Pope;
They have given o'er scrutiny and are fall'n
To admiration. [100]
    Lodovico. Away, away!
                        (*Exeunt* Servants)
    Francisco. I'll lay a thousand ducats you
    hear news
Of a Pope presently. Hark! sure, he's elected!
    (*A* Cardinal *appears on the balcony*)
Behold, my Lord of Arragon appears
On the church battlements.
    Arragon. *Denuntio vobis gaudium mag-*

[100] The cardinals were locked in and denied
communication with the world until by secret
ballot (schutinium) they had elected a new
pope.

num. Reverendissimus cardinalis Lorenzo
de Monticelso *electus est in sedem apostoli-*
cam, et elegit sibi nomen Paulum *Quartum.*
OMNES. *Vivat sanctus pater Paulus Quar-*
tus! [101]

(*Enter* SERVANT)

SERVANT. Vittoria, my lord,—
FRANCISCO. Well, what of her?
SERVANT. Is fled the city—
FRANCISCO. Ha?
SERVANT. With Duke Brachiano.
FRANCISCO. Fled? Where's the Prince
Giovanni?
SERVANT. Gone with his father.
FRANCISCO. Let the matrona of the con-
vertites
Be apprehended.—Fled! Oh, damnable!
(*Exit* SERVANT)
(*Aside*) How fortunate are my wishes! Why,
'twas this
I only labored. I did send the letter
To instruct him what to do. Thy fame, fond
duke,
I first have poisoned; directed thee the way
To marry a whore. What can be worse? This
follows—
The hand must act to drown the passionate
tongue.
I scorn to wear a sword and prate of wrong.

(*Enter* MONTICELSO *in state*)

MONTICELSO. *Concedimus vobis apostoli-*
cam benedictionem et remissionem pecca-
torum. [102]
My lord reports Vittoria Corombona
Is stol'n from forth the house of convertites
By Brachiano, and they're fled the city.
Now, though this be the first day of our state,
We cannot better please the divine power
Than to sequester from the holy Church
These cursed persons. Make it therefore
known,
We do denounce excommunication

[101] "I announce to you tidings of great joy.
The Most Reverend Cardinal Lorenzo di Monticelso has been elected to the Papal throne and
has taken the name of Paul the Fourth."
"*All.* Long live the Holy Father, Paul the
Fourth."
[102] "We grant to you the apostolic benediction
and remission of sins."

Against them both. All that are theirs in
Rome
We likewise banish. Set on.
(*Exeunt* MONTICELSO, *his train,*
AMBASSADORS, *&c.*)
FRANCISCO. (*Privately to* LODOVICO)
Come, dear Lodovico;
You have ta'en the sacrament to prosecute
The intended murder.
LODOVICO. With all constancy.
But, sir, I wonder you'll engage yourself
In person, being a great prince.
FRANCISCO. Divert me not.
Most of his court are of my faction,
And some are of my council. Noble friend,
Our danger shall be like in this design;
Give leave, part of the glory may be mine.
(*Exit, sweeping off his hat in farewell.*
GASPARO *follows*)

(*Re-enter* MONTICELSO *by another door*)

MONTICELSO. Why did the Duke of
Florence with such care
Labor your pardon? Say.
LODOVICO. Italian beggars will resolve you
that,
Who, begging of an alms, bid those they beg
of,
Do good for their own sakes; or 't may be,
He spreads his bounty with a sowing hand,
Like kings, who many times give out of
measure,
Not for desert so much, as for their pleasure.
MONTICELSO. I know you're cunning.
Come, what devil was that
That you were raising?
LODOVICO. Devil, my lord?
MONTICELSO. I ask you
How doth the duke employ you, that his
bonnet
Fell with such compliment unto his knee
When he departed from you?
LODOVICO. Why, my lord,
He told me of a resty Barbary horse
Which he would fain have brought to the
career,
The sault, and the ring-galliard; [103] now, my
lord,
I have a rare French rider.
MONTICELSO. Take you heed

[103] Technical terms for formalized exercises in
the riding academies.

Lest the jade break your neck. Do you put
me off
With your wild horse-tricks? Sirrah, you do
lie.
Oh, thou'rt a foul black cloud, and thou dost
threat
A violent storm!
    Lodovico. Storms are i' the air, my lord;
I am too low to storm.
    Monticelso. Wretched creature!
I know that thou are fashioned for all ill,
Like dogs that once get blood, they'll ever
kill.
About some murder, was 't not?
    Lodovico. I'll not tell you,
And yet I care not greatly if I do.
Marry, with this preparation. Holy father,
I come not to you as an intelligencer
But as a penitent sinner. What I utter
Is in confession merely, which you know
Must never be revealed.
    Monticelso. You have o'erta'en me.
    Lodovico. Sir, I did love Brachiano's
duchess dearly,
Or rather I pursued her with hot lust,
Though she ne'er knew on 't. She was
poisoned;
Upon my soul, she was; for which I have
sworn
To avenge her murder.
    Monticelso. To the Duke of Florence?
    Lodovico. To him I have.
    Monticelso. Miserable creature!
If thou persist in this, 'tis damnable.
Dost thou imagine thou canst slide on blood,
And not be tainted with a shameful fall?
Or, like the black and melancholic yew-tree,
Dost think to root thyself in dead men's
graves
And yet to prosper? Instruction to thee
Comes like sweet showers to over-hardened
ground;
They wet, but pierce not deep. And so I
leave thee,
With all the Furies hanging 'bout thy neck,
Till by thy penitence thou remove this evil
In conjuring from thy breast that cruel devil.
                  (*Exit* Monticelso)

    Lodovico. I'll give it o'er; he says 'tis
damnable;
Besides I did expect his suffrage
By reason of Camillo's death.

    (*Re-enter at the rear* Francisco *with a*
Servant)

    Francisco. (*To* Servant) Do you know
that count?
    Servant. Yes, my lord.
    Francisco. Bear him these thousand
ducats to his lodging;
Tell him the Pope hath sent them.—(*Aside*)
Happily
That will confirm him more than all the rest.
                  (*Exit*)
    Servant. (*Coming up to* Lodovico)
Sir—
    Lodovico. To me, sir?
    Servant. His Holiness hath sent you
A thousand crowns, and wills you, if you
travel,
To make him your patron for intelligence.
    Lodovico. His creature ever to be com-
manded.   (*Exit* Servant)
Why, now 'tis come about. He railed upon
me,
And yet these crowns were told out and laid
ready
Before he knew my voyage. O the art,
The modest form of greatness! that do sit,
Like brides at wedding-dinners, with their
looks turned
From the least wanton jest, their puling
stomach
Sick of the modesty, when their thoughts are
loose,
Even acting of those hot and lustful sports
Are to ensue about midnight: such his cun-
ning.
He sounds my depth thus with a golden
plummet.
I am doubly armed now. Now to the act of
blood.
There's but three Furies found in spacious
hell,
But in a great man's breast three thousand
dwell.   (*Exit*)

Act V

Scene I. *Padua.* Brachiano's *Palace.*

(*A procession across the stage of* Brachiano, Flamineo, Marcello, Hortensio, Vittoria, Cornelia, Zanche, *and others. Then re-enter* Flamineo *and* Hortensio)

Flamineo. In all the weary minutes of my life,
Day ne'er broke up till now. This marriage
Confirms me happy.
Hortensio. 'Tis a good assurance.
Saw you not yet the Moor that's come to court?
Flamineo. Yes, and conferred with him i' the duke's closet.
I have not seen a goodlier personage,
Nor ever talked with man better experienced
In state affairs or rudiments of war.
He hath, by report, served the Venetian
In Candy these twice seven years, and been chief
In many a bold design.
Hortensio. What are those two
That bear him company?
Flamineo. Two noblemen of Hungary
that, living in the emperor's service as commanders, eight years since, contrary to the expectation of all the court, entered into religion, into the strict order of Capuchins, but being not well settled in their undertaking, they left their order and returned to court; for which, being after troubled in conscience, they vowed their service against the enemies of Christ, went to Malta, were there knighted, and in their return back, at this great solemnity, they are resolved for ever to forsake the world and settle themselves here in a house of Capuchins in Padua.
Hortensio. 'Tis strange.
Flamineo. One thing makes it so: they have vowed for ever to wear, next their bare bodies, those coats of mail they serve in.
Hortensio. Hard penance! Is the Moor a Christian?
Flamineo. He is.
Hortensio. Why proffers he his service to our duke?
Flamineo. Because he understands there's like to grow
Some wars between us and the Duke of Florence,
In which he hopes employment.
I never saw one in a stern bold look
Wear more command, nor in a lofty phrase
Express more knowing or more deep contempt
Of our slight airy courtiers. He talks
As if he had travelled all the princes' courts
Of Christendom, in all things strives to express,
That all that should dispute with him may know,
Glories, like glow-worms, afar off shine bright,
But looked to near, have neither heat nor light.—
The duke!

(*Re-enter* Brachiano, *with* Francisco *disguised like* Mulinassar, Lodovico *disguised as* Carlo, Antonelli, Gasparo *disguised as* Pedro; *an officer bearing their swords and helmets; and* Marcello)

Brachiano. You are nobly welcome. We have heard at full
Your honorable service 'gainst the Turk.
To you, brave Mulinassar, we assign
A competent pension, and are inly sorry
The vows of those two worthy gentlemen
Make them incapable of our proffered bounty.
Your wish is, you may leave your warlike swords
For monuments in our chapel. I accept it
As a great honor done me, and must crave
Your leave to furnish out our duchess' revels.
Only one thing, as the last vanity
You e'er shall view, deny me not to stay
To see a barriers prepared to-night;
You shall have private standings. It hath pleased
The great ambassadors of several princes,

In their return from Rome to their own
countries,
To grace our marriage and to honor me
With such a kind of sport.

FRANCISCO. I shall persuade them
To stay, my lord.

BRACHIANO. Set on there to the presence!

(*Exeunt* BRACHIANO, FLAMINEO, MAR-
CELLO, *and* HORTENSIO)

LODOVICO. Noble my lord, most fortunately welcome!

(*The Conspirators here embrace*)

You have our vows, sealed with the sacrament,
To second your attempts.

GASPARO. And all things ready.
He could not have invented his own ruin,
Had he despaired, with more propriety.

LODOVICO. You would not take my way.

FRANCISCO. 'Tis better ordered.

LODOVICO. T' have poisoned his prayer-
book, or a pair [104] of beads,
The pummel of his saddle, his looking-glass,
Or th' handle of his racket—Oh, that, that!
That while he had been bandying at tennis,
He might have sworn himself to hell and
strook
His soul into the hazard! Oh, my lord,
I would have our plot be ingenious,
And have it hereafter recorded for example,
Rather than borrow example.

FRANCISCO. There's no way
More speeding than this thought on.

LODOVICO. On, then.

FRANCISCO. And yet methinks that this
revenge is poor,
Because it steals upon him like a thief.
To have ta'en him by the casque in a pitched
field,
Led him to Florence!—

LODOVICO. It had been rare. And there
Have crowned him with a wreath of stinking
garlic,
T' have shown the sharpness of his govern-
ment
And rankness of his lust.—Flamineo comes.

(*Exeunt* LODOVICO, ANTONELLI, *and*
GASPARO)

(*Re-enter* FLAMINEO, MARCELLO *and*
ZANCHE)

[104] A set. These were common methods of
poisoning.

MARCELLO. Why doth this devil haunt
you, say?

FLAMINEO. I know not;
For, by this light, I do not conjure for her.
'Tis not so great a cunning as men think,
To raise the devil; for here's one up already;
The greatest cunning were to lay him down.

MARCELLO. She is your shame.

FLAMINEO. I prithee, pardon her.
In faith, you see, women are like to burrs;
Where their affection throws them, there
they'll stick.

ZANCHE. That is my countryman, a goodly
person.
When he's at leisure, I'll discourse with him
In our own language.

FLAMINEO. I beseech you do.

(*Exit* ZANCHE)

(*To the disguised* FRANCISCO) How is 't,
brave soldier? Oh, that I had seen
Some of your iron days! I pray, relate
Some of your service to us.

FRANCISCO. 'Tis a ridiculous thing for a
man to be his own chronicle. I did never
wash my mouth with mine own praise for
fear of getting a stinking breath.

MARCELLO. You're too stoical. The duke
will expect other discourse from you.

FRANCISCO. I shall never flatter him; I
have studied man too much to do that. What
difference is between the duke and I? No
more than between two bricks, all made of
one clay; only 't may be one is placed on the
top of a turret, the other in the bottom of a
well, by mere chance. If I were placed as
high as the duke, I should stick as fast, make
as fair a show, and bear out weather equally.

FLAMINEO. (*Aside*) If this soldier had a
patent to beg in churches, then he would
tell them stories.

MARCELLO. I have been a soldier too.

FRANCISCO. How have you thrived?

MARCELLO. Faith, poorly.

FRANCISCO. That's the misery of peace;
only outsides are then respected. As ships
seem very great upon the river which show
very little upon the seas, so some men i' the
court seem colossuses in a chamber, who, if
they came into the field, would appear pitiful pigmies.

FLAMINEO. Give me a fair room yet hung
with arras,[105] and some great cardinal to lug

[105] Behind which to hide.

me by the ears as his endeared minion.

FRANCISCO. And thou mayst do the devil knows what villainy.

FLAMINEO. And safely.

FRANCISCO. Right. You shall see in the country in harvest-time, pigeons, though they destroy never so much corn, the farmer dare not present the fowling-piece to them. Why? Because they belong to the lord of the manor; whilst your poor sparrows, that belong to the Lord of Heaven, they go to the pot for 't.

FLAMINEO. I will now give you some politic instructions. The duke says he will give you a pension. That's but bare promise; get it under his hand. For I have known men that have come from serving against the Turk, for three or four months they have had pension to buy them new wooden legs and fresh plasters, but, after, 'twas not to be had. And this miserable courtesy shows as if a tormentor should give hot cordial drinks to one three-quarters dead o' the rack, only to fetch the miserable soul again to endure more dog-days.   (*Exit* FRANCISCO)

(*Re-enter* HORTENSIO *and* ZANCHE, *with a Young Lord and two more*)

How now, gallants! What, are they ready for the barriers?

YOUNG LORD. Yes; the lords are putting on their armor.

HORTENSIO. (*Walking aside with* FLAMINEO) What's he?

FLAMINEO. A new upstart; one that swears like a falconer and will lie in the duke's ear day by day, like a maker of almanacs, and yet I knew him, since he came to the court, smell worse of sweat than an under tennis-court-keeper.

HORTENSIO. Look you, yonder's your sweet mistress.

FLAMINEO. Thou art my sworn brother. I'll tell thee, I do love that Moor, that witch, very constrainedly. She knows some of my villainy. I do love her just as a man holds a wolf by the ears: but for fear of turning upon me and pulling out my throat, I would let her go to the devil.

HORTENSIO. I hear she claims marriage of thee.

FLAMINEO. Faith, I made to her some such dark promise; and, in seeking to fly from 't,

I run on, like a frighted dog with a bottle at 's tail, that fain would bite it off, and yet dares not look behind him.—Now, my precious gipsy.

ZANCHE. Aye, your love to me rather cools than heats.

FLAMINEO. Marry, I am the sounder lover. We have many wenches about the town heat too fast.

HORTENSIO. What do you think of these perfumed gallants, then?

FLAMINEO. Their satin cannot save them; I am confident
They have a certain spice of the disease;
For they that sleep with dogs shall rise with fleas.

ZANCHE. Believe it! A little painting and gay clothes
Make you loathe me.

FLAMINEO. How? Love a lady for painting or gay apparel? I'll unkennel one example more for thee. Æsop had a foolish dog that let go the flesh to catch the shadow: I would have courtiers be better diners.

ZANCHE. You remember your oaths?

FLAMINEO. Lovers' oaths are like mariners' prayers, uttered in extremity; but when the tempest is o'er, and that the vessel leaves tumbling, they fall from protesting to drinking. And yet amongst gentlemen, protesting and drinking go together, and agree as well as shoemakers and Westphalia bacon. They are both drawers on; for drink draws on protestation and protestation draws on more drink. Is not this discourse better now than the morality of your sunburnt gentleman?

(*Re-enter* CORNELIA)

CORNELIA. Is this your perch, you haggard? [106] Fly to the stews. (*Striking* ZANCHE)

FLAMINEO. You should be clapt by the heels now:
Strike i' the court! [107]   (*Exit* CORNELIA)

ZANCHE. She's good for nothing but to make her maids
Catch cold a-nights; they dare not use a bed-staff
For fear of her light fingers.

---

[106] Literally a partially trained hawk; figuratively a wanton.

[107] Put in the stocks. Striking anyone at court was a strictly punished offense.

MARCELLO. You're a strumpet,
An impudent one.   (*Kicking* ZANCHE)
FLAMINEO. Why do you kick her? Say!
Do you think that she's like a walnut-tree? [108]
Must she be cudgelled ere she bear good
       fruit?
MARCELLO. She brags that you shall marry
her.
FLAMINEO. What then?
MARCELLO. I had rather she were pitched
       upon a stake
In some new-seeded garden, to affright
Her fellow crows thence.
FLAMINEO. You're a boy, a fool.
Be guardian to your hound; I am of age.
MARCELLO. If I take her near you, I'll cut
her throat.
FLAMINEO. With a fan of feathers?
MARCELLO. And for you, I'll whip
This folly from you.
FLAMINEO. Are you choleric?
I'll purge 't with rhubarb.
                    (*Threatens to strike him*)
HORTENSIO. Oh! your brother?
FLAMINEO. Hang him!
He wrongs me most that ought to offend me
       least.—
I do suspect my mother played foul play
When she conceived thee.
MARCELLO. Now, by all my hopes,
Like the two slaughtered sons of Œdipus, [109]
The very flames of our affection
Shall turn two ways. Those words I'll make
       thee answer
With thy heart-blood.
FLAMINEO. Do, like the geese in the
       progress.
You know where you shall find me.

MARCELLO. Very good. (*Exit* FLAMINEO)
An thou be'st a noble, friend, bear him my
       sword,
And bid him fit the length on 't.
YOUNG LORD. Sir, I shall.
                    (*Exeunt all but* ZANCHE)
ZANCHE. He comes. Hence, petty thoughts
of my disgrace!

(*Re-enter* FRANCISCO, *the Duke of Florence*)

(*To him*) I ne'er loved my complexion till
       now,
'Cause I may boldly say, without a blush,
I love you.
FRANCISCO. Your love is untimely sown;
there's a spring at Michaelmas, [110] but 'tis but
a faint one. I am sunk in years, and I have
vowed never to marry.
ZANCHE. Alas, poor maids get more lovers
than husbands. Yet you may mistake my
wealth. For, as when ambassadors are sent
to congratulate princes, there's commonly
sent along with them a rich present, so that,
though the prince like not the ambassador's
person nor words, yet he likes well of the
presentment; so I may come to you in the
same manner, and be better loved for my
dowry than my virtue.
FRANCISCO. I'll think on the motion.
ZANCHE. Do. I'll now
Detain you no longer. At your better leisure
I'll tell you things shall startle your blood.
Nor blame me that this passion I reveal;
Lovers die inward that their flames conceal.
FRANCISCO. (*Aside*) Of all intelligence
       this may prove the best;
Sure, I shall draw strange fowl from this foul
       nest.   (*Exeunt*)

SCENE II. *Another Room in* BRACHIANO's *Palace.*

(*Enter* MARCELLO *and* CORNELIA)

CORNELIA. I hear a whispering all about
the court

[108] Old proverb:
A spaniel, a woman, and a walnut-tree,
The more they're beaten, the better they be.
[109] The sons of Œdipus killed each other. According to legend, when men sacrificed to them,
the flame and smoke went in two directions, for
their hate endured after death.

You are to fight. Who is your opposite?
What is the quarrel?
MARCELLO. 'Tis an idle rumor.
CORNELIA. Will you dissemble? Sure, you
do not well
To fright me thus; you never look thus pale
But when you are most angry. I do charge
you

[110] Indian summer. Michaelmas is September
29th.

Upon my blessing—nay, I'll call the duke,
And he shall school you.

MARCELLO. Publish not a fear
Which would convert to laughter; 'tis not so.
Was not this crucifix my father's?

CORNELIA. Yes.

MARCELLO. I have heard you say, giving
my brother suck,
He took the crucifix between his hands
And broke a limb off.

CORNELIA. Yes; but 'tis mended.

(*Enter* FLAMINEO)

FLAMINEO. I have brought your weapon
back.

(FLAMINEO *runs* MARCELLO *through*)

CORNELIA. Ha! Oh, my horror!

MARCELLO. You have brought it home,
indeed.   (*He falls*)

CORNELIA. Help! Oh, he's murdered!

FLAMINEO. Do you turn your gall up? I'll
to sanctuary
And send a surgeon to you.   (*Exit*)

(*Enter* HORTENSIO)

HORTENSIO. How? O' th' ground?

MARCELLO. O mother, now remember
what I told
Of breaking of the crucifix! Farewell.
There are some sins which Heaven doth duly
punish
In a whole family. This it is to rise
By all dishonest means! Let all men know,
That tree shall long time keep a steady foot
Whose branches spread no wider than the
root.   (*Dies*)

CORNELIA. O! My perpetual sorrow!

HORTENSIO. Virtuous Marcello!
He's dead.—Pray, leave him, lady; come, you
shall.

CORNELIA. Alas! he is not dead; he's in a
trance. Why, here's nobody shall get anything by his death. Let me call him again,
for God's sake!

HORTENSIO. I would you were deceived.

CORNELIA. Oh, you abuse me, you abuse
me, you abuse me! How many have gone
away thus, for lack of tendance! Rear up 's
head, rear up 's head; his bleeding inward
will kill him.

HORTENSIO. You see he is departed.

CORNELIA. Let me come to him; give me
him as he is. If he be turned to earth, let me
but give him one hearty kiss, and you shall
put us both into one coffin. Fetch a looking-
glass, see if his breath will not stain it; or
pull out some feathers from my pillow and
lay them to his lips. Will you lose him for
a little painstaking?

HORTENSIO. Your kindest office is to pray
for him.

CORNELIA. Alas! I would not pray for him
yet. He may live to lay me i' the ground and
pray for me, if you'll let me come to him.

(*Enter* BRACHIANO *all armed, save the
beaver,*[111] *with* FLAMINEO, FRANCISCO,
LODOVICO, *and* PAGE *carrying the beaver*)

BRACHIANO. Was this your handiwork?

FLAMINEO. It was my misfortune.

CORNELIA. He lies, he lies! He did not
kill him; these have killed him that would
not let him be better looked to.

BRACHIANO. Have comfort, my grieved
mother.

CORNELIA. Oh, you screech-owl!

HORTENSIO. Forbear, good madam.

CORNELIA. Let me go, let me go.
(*She runs to* FLAMINEO *with her knife
drawn, and, coming to him, lets it fall*)
The God of Heaven forgive thee! Dost not
wonder
I pray for thee? I'll tell thee what's the
reason:
I have scarce breath to number twenty min-
utes;
I'd not spend that in cursing. Fare thee well.
Half of thyself lies there, and mayst thou
live
To fill an hour-glass with his moldered
ashes,
To tell how thou shouldst spend the time to
come
In blest repentance!

BRACHIANO. Mother, pray tell me
How came he by his death? What was the
quarrel?

CORNELIA. Indeed, my younger boy pre-
sumed too much
Upon his manhood, gave him bitter words,
Drew his sword first; and so, I know not how,

[111] Helmet.

For I was out of my wits, he fell with 's head
Just in my bosom.
    PAGE. This is not true, madam.
    CORNELIA. I pray thee, peace.
One arrow's grassed already; [112] it were vain
T' lose this for that will ne'er be found again.
    BRACHIANO. Go, bear the body to Cor-
    nelia's lodging,
And we command that none acquaint our
    duchess
With this sad accident. For you, Flamineo,
Hark you, I will not grant your pardon.
    FLAMINEO. No?
    BRACHIANO. Only a lease of your life, and
    that shall last
But for one day; thou shalt be forced each
    evening

To renew it or be hanged.
    FLAMINEO. At your pleasure.
        (LODOVICO *sprinkles* BRACHIANO'S
          beaver with a poison)
Your will is law now, I'll not meddle with it.
    BRACHIANO. You once did brave me in
    your sister's lodging;
I'll now keep you in awe for 't.—Where's our
    beaver?
    FRANCISCO. (*Aside*) He calls for his de-
    struction. Noble youth,
I pity thy sad fate! Now to the barriers.
This shall his passage to the black lake
    further:
The last good deed he did, he pardoned
    murther.   (*Exeunt*)

SCENE III. *The Lists at Padua.*

(*Charges and shouts. They fight at bar-
riers;* [113] *first single pairs, then three to three*)

(*Enter* BRACHIANO, FRANCISCO, *and* FLA-
MINEO, *with others*)

    BRACHIANO. An armorer! Ud's death, an
armorer!
    FLAMINEO. Armorer! Where's the ar-
morer?
    BRACHIANO. Tear off my beaver.
    FLAMINEO. Are you hurt, my lord?

(*Enter* ARMORER)

    BRACHIANO. Oh, my brain's on fire! The
helmet is poisoned.
    ARMORER. My lord,
Upon my soul—
    BRACHIANO. Away with him to torture!
There are some great ones that have hand in
    this,
And near about me.

(*Enter* VITTORIA)

    VITTORIA. Oh, my loved lord! Poisoned?
    FLAMINEO. Remove the bar. [114] Here's un-
    fortunate revels!
Call the physicians.

[112] Lost in the grass.
[113] Waist high barriers across which the con-
testants fought.
[114] Probably the bar of the helmet.

(*Enter two* PHYSICIANS)

A plague upon you!
We have too much of your cunning here
    already.
I fear the ambassadors are likewise poisoned.
    BRACHIANO. Oh, I am gone already! The
    infection
Flies to the brain and heart. O thou strong
    heart!
There's such a covenant 'tween the world
    and it,
They're loth to break.

(*Enter* GIOVANNI)

    GIOVANNI. O my most loved father!
    BRACHIANO. Remove the boy away.—
Where's this good woman?—Had I infinite
    worlds,
They were too little for thee; must I leave
    thee?—
What say you, screech-owls, is the venom
    mortal?
    FIRST PHYSICIAN. Most deadly.
    BRACHIANO. Most corrupted politic hang-
    man,
You kill without book; but your art to save
Fails you as oft as great men's needy friends.
I that have given life to offending slaves
And wretched murderers, have I not power
To lengthen mine own a twelvemonth?—

Do not kiss me, for I shall poison thee.
This unction's sent from the great Duke of
    Florence.
    FRANCISCO. Sir, be of comfort.
    BRACHIANO. O thou soft natural death,
        that art joint-twin
To sweeter slumber! No rough-bearded
    comet
Stares on thy mild departure; the dull owl
Beats not against thy casement; the hoarse
    wolf
Scents not thy carrion. Pity winds thy corse,
Whilst horror waits on princes.
    VITTORIA. I am lost for ever.
    BRACHIANO. How miserable a thing it is
        to die
'Mongst women howling!

(*Enter* LODOVICO *and* GASPARO, *in the habit
        of Capuchins*)

What are those?
    FLAMINEO. Franciscans.[115]
They have brought the extreme unction.
    BRACHIANO. On pain of death, let no man
        name death to me;
It is a word infinitely terrible.
Withdraw into our cabinet.
(*Exeunt all but* FRANCISCO *and* FLAMINEO,
    BRACHIANO *being carried out*)
    FLAMINEO. To see what solitariness is
about dying princes! As heretofore they have
unpeopled towns, divorced friends, and made
great houses unhospitable, so now, O justice!
where are their flatterers now? Flatterers are
but the shadows of princes' bodies; the least
thick cloud makes them invisible.
    FRANCISCO. There's great moan made for
him.
    FLAMINEO. Faith, for some few hours salt
water will run most plentifully in every office
o' the court, but, believe it, most of them
do but weep as over their stepmothers' graves.
    FRANCISCO. How mean you?
    FLAMINEO. Why, they dissemble, as some
men do that live within compass o' the verge.
    FRANCISCO. Come, you have thrived well
under him.
    FLAMINEO. Faith, like a wolf in a wom-
an's breast; I have been fed with poultry. But,
for money, understand me, I had as good

[115] Until 1619 the Capuchins were a subdivision of the Franciscan order.

a will to cozen him as e'er an officer of them
all, but I had not cunning enough to do it.
    FRANCISCO. What didst thou think of
him? Faith, speak freely.
    FLAMINEO. He was a kind of statesman
that would sooner have reckoned how many
cannon-bullets he had discharged against a
town, to count his expense that way, than
how many of his valiant and deserving subjects he lost before it.
    FRANCISCO. Oh, speak well of the duke.
    FLAMINEO. I have done. Wilt hear some
of my court-wisdom? To reprehend princes
is dangerous; and to over-commend some of
them is palpable lying.

(*Re-enter* LODOVICO)

    FRANCISCO. How is it with the duke?
    LODOVICO. Most deadly ill.
He's fall'n into a strange distraction;
He talks of battle and monopolies,
Levying of taxes, and from that descends
To the most brain-sick language. His mind
    fastens
On twenty several objects, which confound
Deep sense with folly. Such a fearful end
May teach some men that bear too lofty crest,
Though they live happiest, yet they die not
    best.
He hath conferred the whole state of the
    dukedom
Upon your sister, till the prince arrive
At mature age.
    FLAMINEO. There's some good luck in
that yet.
    FRANCISCO. See, here he comes.

(*Enter* BRACHIANO, *carried in a bed,*
    VITTORIA, *and others*)

There's death in 's face already.
    VITTORIA. O my good lord!
    BRACHIANO. Away! you have abused me:
    (*These speeches are several kinds of dis-
        tractions, and in the action should
        appear so*)
You have conveyed coin forth our territories,
Bought and sold offices, oppressed the poor,
And I ne'er dreamt on 't. Make up your
    accounts;
I'll now be mine own steward.

FLAMINEO. Sir, have patience.

BRACHIANO. Indeed, I am to blame,
For did you ever hear the dusky raven
Chide blackness? Or was 't ever known the devil
Railed against cloven creatures?

VITTORIA. O my lord!

BRACHIANO. Let me have some quails to supper.

FLAMINEO. Sir, you shall.

BRACHIANO. No, some fried dog-fish; your quails feed on poison.[116]
That old dog-fox, that politician, Florence!
I'll forswear hunting and turn dog-killer.
Rare! I'll be friends with him; for, mark you, sir,
One dog still sets another a-barking. Peace,
Peace! Yonder's a fine slave come in now.

FLAMINEO. Where?

BRACHIANO. Why, there, in a blue bonnet, and a pair
Of breeches with a great cod-piece. Ha, ha, ha!
Look you, his cod-piece is stuck full of pins,
With pearls o' the head of them. Do not you know him?

FLAMINEO. No, my lord.

BRACHIANO. Why, 'tis the devil;
I know him by a great rose he wears on 's shoe
To hide his cloven foot. I'll dispute with him;
He's a rare linguist.

VITTORIA. My lord, here's nothing.

BRACHIANO. Nothing? Rare! Nothing! When I want money,
Our treasury is empty, there is nothing.
I'll not be used thus.

VITTORIA. Oh, lie still, my lord!

BRACHIANO. See, see Flamineo, that killed his brother,
Is dancing on the ropes there, and he carries
A money-bag in each hand, to keep him even,
For fear of breaking 's neck. And there's a lawyer
In a gown whipt with velvet, stares and gapes
When the money will fall. How the rogue cuts capers!
It should have been a halter. 'Tis there. What's she?

FLAMINEO. Vittoria, my lord.

BRACHIANO. Ha, ha, ha! Her hair

Is sprinkled with arras-powder,[117] that makes her look
As if she had sinned in the pastry.—What's he?

FLAMINEO. A divine, my lord.

(BRACHIANO *seems here near his end.* LODO-VICO *and* GASPARO, *in the habit of Capuchins, present him in his bed with a crucifix and hallowed candle*)

BRACHIANO. He will be drunk; avoid him.
T' argument is fearful, when churchmen stagger in 't.
Look you, six grey rats that have lost their tails
Crawl up the pillow: send for a rat-catcher.
I'll do a miracle, I'll free the court
From all foul vermin. Where's Flamineo?

FLAMINEO. (*Aside*) I do not like that he names me so often,
Especially on 's death-bed; 'tis sign
I shall not live long.—See, he's near his end.

LODOVICO. Pray, give us leave.—*Attende, domine Brachiane.*[118]

FLAMINEO. See, see how firmly he doth fix his eye
Upon the crucifix.

VITTORIA. Oh, hold it constant!
It settles his wild spirits; and so his eyes
Melt into tears.

LODOVICO. *Domine Brachiane, solebas in bello tutus esse tuo clypeo; nunc hunc clypeum hosti tuo opponas infernali.*

GASPARO. *Olim hasta valuisti in bello; nunc hanc sacram hastam vibrabis contra hostem animarum.*

LODOVICO. *Attende, domine Brachiane; si nunc quoque probas ea quae acta sunt inter nos, flecte caput in dextrum.*

GASPARO. *Esto securus, domine Brachiane; cogita quantum habeas meritorum; denique memineris meam animam pro tua oppignoratam si quid esset periculi.*

LODOVICO. *Si nunc quoque probas ea quae acta sunt inter nos, flecte caput in leavum.*—[119]

---

[116] *Double-entendre:* in Elizabethan slang, quails also meant loose women.

[117] A violet-scented powder made from orris root.

[118] "Give heed, Lord Brachiano."

[119] "Lord Brachiano, thou wast wont to be guarded in battle by thy shield; *this* shield thou shalt now oppose to thine infernal enemy."
"Once with thy spear thou didst prevail in battle; *this* sacred spear thou shalt now wield against the enemy of souls."
"Give heed, Lord Brachiano; if now also

He is departing. Pray, stand all apart,
And let us only whisper in his ears
Some private meditations, which our order
Permits you not to hear.
(*Here, the rest being departed,* LODOVICO
and GASPARO *throw back their cowls;*
BRACHIANO *partly raises himself in hor-
ror and then falls back*)
GASPARO. Brachiano—
LODOVICO. Devil,
Brachiano, thou art damned.
GASPARO. Perpetually.
LODOVICO. A slave condemned and given
up to the gallows
Is thy great lord and master.
GASPARO. True; for thou
Art given up to the devil.
LODOVICO. O you slave!
You that were held the famous politician,
Whose art was poison—
GASPARO. And whose conscience, murder!
LODOVICO. That would have broke your
wife's neck down the stairs,
Ere she was poisoned!
GASPARO. That had your villainous
salads—
LODOVICO. And fine embroidered bottles
and perfumes,
Equally mortal with a winter-plague!
GASPARO. Now there's mercury—
LODOVICO. And copperas—
GASPARO. And quicksilver—
LODOVICO. With other devilish 'pothecary
stuff,
A-melting in your politic brains. Dost hear?
GASPARO. This is Count Lodovico.
LODOVICO. This, Gasparo.
And thou shalt die like a poor rogue.
GASPARO. And stink
Like a dead fly-blown dog.
LODOVICO. And be forgotten
Before thy funeral sermon.
BRACHIANO. Vittoria! Vittoria!
LODOVICO. Oh, the cursèd devil
Comes to himself again! We are undone.

thou approvest what hath been done betwixt
us, bow thine head to the right."
"Be of good cheer, Lord Brachiano; think how
many good deeds thou hast done; lastly be mind-
ful that my soul stands pledged for thine, if any
peril there should be."
"If now also thou approvest what hath been
done betwixt us, bow thine head to the left."

GASPARO. Strangle him in private.
(*They hastily pull forward their cowls*)

(*Enter* VITTORIA, *running, followed by* Attendants. *She is checked by* GASPARO, *who
sternly waves her back while* LODOVICO
stands before BRACHIANO's *bed, hiding him
from* VITTORIA's *sight*)

(*To* VITTORIA) What, will you call him
again
To live in treble torments? For charity,
For Christian charity, avoid the chamber.
(*Exeunt* VITTORIA *and Attendants*)
LODOVICO. You would prate, sir? This is
a true-love-knot
Sent from the Duke of Florence.
(*He strangles* BRACHIANO)
GASPARO. What, is it done?
LODOVICO. The snuff is out.[120] No woman-
keeper i' th' world,
Though she had practised seven year at the
pest-house,
Could have done 't quaintlier.

(*Re-enter* VITTORIA, FRANCISCO, FLAMINEO,
and Attendants)

My lords, he's dead.
OMNES. Rest to his soul.
VITTORIA. Oh me! This place is hell.
(*Exit*)
FRANCISCO. How heavily she takes it!
FLAMINEO. Oh, yes, yes;
Had women navigable rivers in their eyes,
They would dispend them all. Surely, I
wonder
Why we should wish more rivers to the city,
When they sell water so good cheap. I'll tell
thee,
These are but moonish[121] shades of griefs
or fears;
There's nothing sooner dry than women's
tears.
Why, here's an end of all my harvest; he
has given me nothing.
Court-promises! Let wise men count them
cursed,

[120] The candle is snuffed—life is gone. The
following passage refers to a common belief that
nurses sometimes hastened the death of patients.
[121] Changeable as the moon.

For while you live, he that scores best pays
　　worst.

FRANCISCO. Sure, this was Florence' doing.

FLAMINEO. Very likely.

Those are found weighty strokes which come
　　from th' hand,
But those are killing strokes which come
　　from th' head.
Oh, the rare tricks of a Machiavellian!
He doth not come, like a gross plodding slave
And buffet you to death; no, my quaint
　　knave,
He tickles you to death, makes you die
　　laughing,
As if you had swallowed down a pound of
　　saffron.
You see the feat, 'tis practised in a trice;
To teach court-honesty, it jumps on ice.

FRANCISCO. Now have the people liberty
　　to talk
And descant on his vices.

FLAMINEO. Misery of princes,
That must of force be censured by their
　　slaves!
Not only blamed for doing things are ill,
But for not doing all that all men will.
One were better be a thresher.—Ud's death,
I would fain speak with this duke yet.

FRANCISCO. Now he's dead.

FLAMINEO. I cannot conjure; but if
　　prayers or oaths
Will get to the speech of him, though forty
　　devils
Wait on him in his livery of flames,
I'll speak to him and shake him by the hand,
Though I be blasted.　　(Exit FLAMINEO)

FRANCISCO. Excellent Lodovico!
What, did you terrify him at the last gasp?

LODOVICO. Yes, and so idly, that the duke
　　had like
To have terrified us.

FRANCISCO. How?

LODOVICO. You shall hear that hereafter.

(Enter the Moor ZANCHE)

See, yon's the infernal that would make up
　　sport.
Now to the revelation of that secret
She promised when she fell in love with you.

FRANCISCO. (To ZANCHE) You're passionately met in this sad world.

ZANCHE. I would have you look up, sir;
　　these court-tears
Claim not your tribute to them. Let those
　　weep
That guiltily partake in the sad cause.
I knew last night, by a sad dream I had,
Some mischief would ensue; yet, to say truth,
My dream most concerned you.

LODOVICO. (Aside to FRANCISCO) Shall's
fall a-dreaming?

FRANCISCO. Yes, and for fashion sake I'll
dream with her.

ZANCHE. Methought, sir, you came stealing to my bed.

FRANCISCO. Wilt thou believe me, sweet-
ing? By this light,
I was a-dreamt on thee too; for methought
I saw thee naked.

ZANCHE. Fie, sir! As I told you,
Methought you lay down by me.

FRANCISCO. So dreamt I;
And lest thou shouldst take cold, I covered
　　thee
With this Irish mantle.

ZANCHE. Verily, I did dream
You were somewhat bold with me. But to
　　come to 't—

LODOVICO. (Aside) How, how! I hope
you will not go to 't here.

FRANCISCO. Nay, you must hear my dream
out.

ZANCHE. Well, sir, forth!

FRANCISCO. When I threw the mantle
　　o'er thee, thou didst laugh
Exceedingly, methought.

ZANCHE. Laugh?

FRANCISCO. And cried'st out,
The hair did tickle thee.

ZANCHE. There was a dream indeed!

LODOVICO. (Aside) Mark her, I prithee;
　　she simpers like the suds
A collier hath been washed in.

ZANCHE. Come, sir, good fortune tends
　　you. I did tell you
I would reveal a secret: Isabella,
The Duke of Florence' sister, was im-
poisoned
By a fumed picture, and Camillo's neck
Was broke by damned Flamineo, the mis-
chance
Laid on a vaulting-horse.

FRANCISCO. Most strange!

ZANCHE. Most true.

Lodovico. (*Aside*) The bed of snakes is broke.

Zanche. I sadly do confess I had a hand
In the black deed.

Francisco. Thou kept'st their counsel?

Zanche. Right.
For which, urged with contrition, I intend
This night to rob Vittoria.

Lodovico. (*Aside*) Excellent penitence!
Usurers dream on 't while they sleep out
    sermons.

Zanche. To further our escape, I have
    entreated
Leave to retire me, till the funeral,
Unto a friend i' the country. That excuse
Will further our escape. In coin and jewels
I shall at least make good unto your use
An hundred thousand crowns.

Francisco. O noble wench!

Lodovico. Those crowns we'll share.

Zanche. It is a dowry,
Methinks, should make that sun-burnt
    proverb false,

And wash the Æthiop white.

Francisco. It shall. Away!

Zanche. Be ready for our flight.

Francisco. An hour 'fore day.
                (*Exit the Moor* Zanche)
O strange discovery! Why, till now we knew
    not
The circumstance of either of their deaths.

(*Re-enter* Zanche)

Zanche. You'll wait about midnight in
the chapel?

Francisco. There.   (*Exit* Zanche)

Lodovico. Why, now our action's justified.

Francisco. Tush for justice!
What harms it justice? We now, like the
    partridge,
Purge the disease with laurel; for the fame
Shall crown the enterprise and quit the
    shame.   (*Exeunt*)

Scene IV. *A Room in the Palace at Padua.*

(*Enter* Flamineo *and* Gasparo *at one door;
    another way,* Giovanni, *attended*)

Gasparo. The young duke: did you e'er
see a sweeter prince?

Flamineo. I have known a poor woman's
bastard better favored; this is behind him;
now, to his face, all comparisons were hateful. Wise was the courtly peacock that, being
a great minion, and being compared for
beauty by some dottrels [122] that stood by to
the kingly eagle, said the eagle was a far
fairer bird than herself, not in respect of her
feathers, but in respect of her long talons:
his will grow out in time.—My gracious lord!

Giovanni. I pray, leave me, sir.

Flamineo. Your grace must be merry; 'tis
I have cause to mourn. For, wot you, what
said the little boy that rode behind his father
on horseback?

Giovanni. Why, what said he?

Flamineo. "When you are dead, father,"
said he, "I hope then I shall ride in the saddle." Oh, 'tis a brave thing for a man to
sit by himself! He may stretch himself in the

stirrups, look about and see the whole compass of the hemisphere. You're now, my lord,
i' th' saddle.

Giovanni. Study your prayers, sir, and be
penitent.
'Twere fit you'd think on what hath former
    been;
I have heard grief named the eldest child
    of sin.   (*Exit*)

Flamineo. Study my prayers! He threatens me divinely.
I am falling to pieces already. I care not
though, like Anacharsis, [123] I were pounded
to death in a mortar. And yet that death were
fitter for usurers, gold and themselves to be
beaten together, to make a most cordial
cullis [124] for the devil.
He hath his uncle's villainous look already,
In decimo sexto. [125]

[123] Anaxarchus, a philosopher of Thrace, who,
having spoken harshly of the Cyprian tyrant
Nicrocreon, was later seized by him and put to
death in the manner indicated.

[124] Broth.

[125] Lit., a very small book, one whose page is
1/16th of a full page. A common Elizabethan expression for a small person.

[122] A kind of plover, a stupid bird.

(*Enter* Courtier)

Now, sir, what are you?

Courtier. It is the pleasure, sir, of the
young duke,
That you forbear the presence, and all rooms
That owe him reverence.

Flamineo. So, the wolf and the raven
Are very pretty fools when they are young.
Is it your office, sir, to keep me out?

Courtier. So the duke wills.

Flamineo. Verily, master courtier, extremity is not to be used in all offices. Say that
a gentlewoman were taken out of her bed
about midnight and committed to Castle
Angelo, or to the Tower yonder, with nothing about her but her smock, would it not
show a cruel part in the gentleman-porter to
lay claim to her upper garment, pull it o'er
her head and ears, and put her in naked?

Courtier. Very good. You are merry.
(*Exit*)

Flamineo. Doth he make a court-eject-
ment of me? A flaming fire-brand casts more
smoke without a chimney than within 't. I'll
smoor [126] some of them.

(*Enter* Francisco)

How now! thou art sad.

Francisco. I met even now with the most
piteous sight.

Flamineo. Thou meet'st another here, a
pitiful
Degraded courtier.

Francisco. Your reverend mother
Is grown a very old woman in two hours.
I found them winding of Marcello's corse;
And there is such a solemn melody,
'Tween doleful songs, tears, and sad elegies—
Such as old grandams watching by the dead
Were wont to outwear the nights with—that,
believe me,
I had no eyes to guide me forth the room,
They were so o'ercharged with water.

Flamineo. I will see them.

Francisco. 'Twere much uncharity in
you, for your sight
Will add unto their tears.

Flamineo. I will see them.
They are behind the traverse; I'll discover

Their superstitious howling.
(*Draws the curtain*)
(Cornelia, Zanche, *and three other*
Ladies *discovered winding* Marcello's
corse. A Song.)

Cornelia. This rosemary is withered;
pray get fresh.
I would have these herbs grow up in his
grave,
When I am dead and rotten. Reach the bays,
I'll tie a garland here about his head;
'Twill keep my boy from lightning. This
sheet [127]
I have kept this twenty year, and every day
Hallowed it with my prayers: I did not think
He should have wore it.

Zanche. Look you who are yonder.

Cornelia. Oh, reach me the flowers.

Zanche. Her ladyship's foolish.

Lady. Alas! her grief
Hath turned her child again!

Cornelia. You're very welcome:
There's rosemary for you—and rue for you—
(*To* Flamineo)
Heart's-ease for you; I pray make much of it.
I have left more for myself.

Francisco. Lady, who's this?

Cornelia. You are, I take it, the grave-
maker.

Flamineo. So.

Zanche. 'Tis Flamineo.

Cornelia. Will you make me such a fool?
Here's a white hand:
Can blood so soon be washed out? Let me see;
When screech-owls croak upon the chimney-
tops,
And the strange cricket i' the oven sings and
hops,
When yellow spots do on your hands appear,
Be certain then you of a corse shall hear.
Out upon 't, how 'tis speckled! H'as handled
a toad, sure.
Cowslip-water is good for the memory; pray,
buy me three ounces of 't.

Flamineo. I would I were from hence.

Cornelia. Do you hear, sir? I'll give you
a saying which my grandmother was wont,
when she heard the bell toll, to sing o'er unto
her lute.

Flamineo. Do, an you will, do.

---

[126] Smother.

[127] Winding-sheet.

CORNELIA. *Call for the robin-red-breast and the wren,*[128]

(CORNELIA *doth this in several forms of distraction*)

Since o'er shady groves they hover,
And with leaves and flowers do cover
The friendless bodies of unburied men.
Call unto his funeral dole
The ant, the field-mouse, and the mole,
To rear him hillocks that shall keep him warm,
And (when gay tombs are robbed) sustain no harm.
But keep the wolf far thence, that's foe to men,
For with his nails he'll dig them up again.[129]

They would not bury him 'cause he died in a quarrel,
But I have an answer for them:
Let holy Church receive him duly,
Since he paid the church-tithes truly.
His wealth is summed, and this is all his store;
This poor men get, and great men get no more.
Now the wares are gone, we may shut up shop.
Bless you all, good people.

(*Exeunt* CORNELIA *and* LADIES)

FLAMINEO. I have a strange thing in me, to the which
I cannot give a name, without it be
Compassion. I pray, leave me.

(*Exit* FRANCISCO)

This night I'll know the utmost of my fate;
I'll be resolved what my rich sister means
To assign me for my service. I have lived
Riotously ill, like some that live in court,
And sometimes when my face was full of smiles
Have felt the maze of conscience in my breast.

[128] The robin was popularly supposed to care for the dead, covering the face of an unattended body with moss. The wren was believed to be the robin's wife.

[129] According to popular belief, murdered bodies were thus dug up.

Oft gay and honored robes those tortures try;
We think caged birds sing, when indeed they cry.

(*Enter* BRACHIANO's *Ghost, in his leather cassock and breeches, boots and cowl; in his hand a pot of lily-flowers, with a skull in it*)

Ha! I can stand thee: nearer, nearer yet!
What a mockery hath death made of thee!
Thou look'st sad.
In what place art thou? In yon starry gallery?
Or in the cursèd dungeon?—No? Not speak?
Pray, sir, resolve me, what religion's best
For a man to die in? Or is it in your knowledge
To answer me how long I have to live?
That's the most necessary question.
Not answer? Are you still like some great men
That only walk like shadows up and down,
And to no purpose? Say!—

(*The Ghost throws earth upon him, and shows him the skull*)

What's that? O, fatal! he throws earth upon me!
A dead man's skull beneath the roots of flowers!—
I pray, speak, sir. Our Italian churchmen
Make us believe dead men hold conference
With their familiars, and many times
Will come to bed to them, and eat with them.

(*Exit Ghost*)

He's gone; and see, the skull and earth are vanished.
This is beyond melancholy.[130] I do dare my fate
To do its worst. Now to my sister's lodging,
And sum up all these horrors: the disgrace
The prince threw on me; next the piteous sight
Of my dead brother; and my mother's dotage;
And last this terrible vision. All these
Shall with Vittoria's bounty turn to good,
Or I will drown this weapon in her blood.

(*Exit*)

[130] Hallucination.

Scene V. *A Street in Padua.*

(*Enter* Francisco *and* Lodovico. Hortensio *enters by another door and, unobserved,
listens to their conversation*)

Lodovico. My lord, upon my soul, you
   shall no further;
You have most ridiculously engaged yourself
Too far already. For my part, I have paid
All my debts; so, if I should chance to fall,
My creditors fall not with me; and I vow
To quit all in this bold assembly
To the meanest follower. My lord, leave the
   city,
Or I'll forswear the murder.   (*Exit*)

Francisco. Farewell, Lodovico.
If thou dost perish in this glorious act,
I'll rear unto thy memory that fame
Shall in the ashes keep alive thy name.
   (*Exit*)
Hortensio. There's some black deed on
   foot.
I'll presently
Down to the citadel, and raise some force.
These strong court-factions, that do brook no
   checks,
In the career oft break the riders' necks.
   (*Exit*)

Scene VI. *A Room in the Palace.*

(*Enter* Vittoria *with a book in her hand,
and* Zanche; Flamineo *following them*)

Flamineo. What, are you at your prayers?
Give o'er.
Vittoria. How, ruffian?
Flamineo. I come to you 'bout worldly
   business.
Sit down, sit down! (*To* Zanche) Nay, stay,
   blowze, you may hear it;
The doors are fast enough.
Vittoria. Ha! Are you drunk?
Flamineo. Yes, yes, with wormwood-
   water; you shall taste
Some of it presently.
Vittoria. What intends the Fury?
Flamineo. You are my lord's executrix,
   and I claim
Reward for my long service.
Vittoria. For your service?
Flamineo. Come, therefore, here is pen
   and ink; set down
What you will give me.   (*She writes*)
Vittoria. There.
Flamineo. Ha! Have you done already?
'Tis a most short conveyance.
Vittoria. I will read it.
"I give that portion to thee, and no other,
Which Cain groaned under, having slain his
   brother."

Flamineo. A most courtly patent to beg
by!
Vittoria. You are a villain.
Flamineo. Is 't come to this? They say,
   affrights cure agues.
Thou hast a devil in thee; I will try
If I can scare him from thee. Nay, sit still.
My lord hath left me yet two case of jewels
Shall make me scorn your bounty; you shall
   see them.   (*Exit*)
Vittoria. Sure, he's distracted.
Zanche. Oh, he's desperate!
For your own safety give him gentle lan-
   guage.

(*Re-enter* Flamineo *with two pairs of
pistols*)

Flamineo. Look, these are better far at
   a dead lift [131]
Than all your jewel-house.
Vittoria. And yet, methinks
These stones have no fair lustre, they are ill
   set.
Flamineo. I'll turn the right side towards
   you; you shall see
How they will sparkle.
Vittoria. Turn this horror from me!

[131] In a tight corner.

What do you want? What would you have
  me do?
Is not all mine yours? Have I any children?

FLAMINEO. Pray thee, good woman, do
  not trouble me
With this vain worldly business; say your
  prayers.
I made a vow to my deceasèd lord,
Neither yourself nor I should outlive him
The numbering of four hours.

VITTORIA. Did he enjoin it?

FLAMINEO. He did; and 'twas a deadly
  jealousy,
Lest any should enjoy thee after him,
That urged him vow me to it. For my death,
I did propound it voluntarily, knowing,
If he could not be safe in his own court,
Being a great duke, what hope, then, for us?

VITTORIA. This is your melancholy and
despair.

FLAMINEO. Away!
Fool that thou art to think that politicians
Do use to kill the effects of injuries
And let the cause live. Shall we groan in
  irons,
Or be a shameful and a weighty burden
To a public scaffold? This is my resolve;
I would not live at any man's entreaty,
Nor die at any's bidding.

VITTORIA. Will you hear me?

FLAMINEO. My life hath done service to
  other men;
My death shall serve mine own turn. Make
  you ready.

VITTORIA. Do you mean to die indeed?

FLAMINEO. With as much pleasure
As e'er my father gat me.

VITTORIA. Are the doors locked?

ZANCHE. Yes, madam.

VITTORIA. Are you grown an atheist?
Will you turn your body,
Which is the goodly palace of the soul,
To the soul's slaughter-house? Oh, the cursèd
  devil,
—Which doth present us with all other sins
Thrice-candied o'er, despair with gall and
  stibium;
Yet we carouse it off;—(*Aside to* ZANCHE)
  Cry out for help!—
Makes us forsake that which was made for
  man,
The world, to sink to that was made for
  devils,

Eternal darkness!

ZANCHE. Help! help!

FLAMINEO. I'll stop your throat
With winter-plums.

VITTORIA. I prithee, yet remember,
Millions are now in graves, which at last day
Like mandrakes shall rise shrieking.[132]

FLAMINEO. Leave your prating,
For these are but grammatical laments,
Feminine arguments, and they move me,
As some in pul███████████eir auditory,
More with th█████████████ sense
Of reason or █████doctrine.

ZANCHE. (*Aside to* VITTORIA) Gentle
  madam,
Seem to consent, only persuade him teach
The way to death; let him die first.

VITTORIA. 'Tis good.
I apprehend it.
—To kill one's self is meat that we must take
Like pills, not chew 't, but quickly swallow it;
The smart o' the wound, or weakness of the
  hand,
May else bring treble torments.

FLAMINEO. I have held it
A wretched and most miserable life
Which is not able to die.

VITTORIA. O, but frailty!
Yet I am now resolved: farewell, affliction!
Behold, Brachiano, I that while you lived
Did make a flaming altar of my heart
To sacrifice unto you, now am ready
To sacrifice heart and all.—Farewell, Zanche!

ZANCHE. How, madam! Do you think that
  I'll outlive you;
Especially when my best self, Flamineo,
Goes the same voyage?

FLAMINEO. O, most loved Moor!

ZANCHE. Only by all my love let me en-
  treat you—
Since it is most necessary one of us
Do violence on ourselves—let you or I
Be her sad taster, teach her how to die.

FLAMINEO. Thou dost instruct me nobly.
  Take these pistols,
Because my hand is stained with blood al-
  ready.
Two of these you shall level at my breast,
The other 'gainst your own, and so we'll die
Most equally contented. But first swear
Not to outlive me.

[132] One of the popular beliefs about this plant
was that it shrieked when pulled up.

VITTORIA AND ZANCHE. Most religiously.
FLAMINEO. Then here's an end of me;
    farewell, daylight!
And, O contemptible physic, that dost take
So long a study, only to preserve
So short a life, I take my leave of thee!—
                (*Showing the pistols*)
These are two cupping-glasses that shall draw
All my infected blood out. Are you ready?
VITTORIA AND ZANCHE. Ready.
FLAMINEO. ~~What~~ ~~place~~ ~~is~~ ~~this~~ now? O
Lucian, ~~thy~~ ~~ridiculous~~ ~~purgatory!~~ To find
Alexander ~~the~~ ~~Great~~ ~~cobbling~~ ~~shoes,~~ Pompey
ta~~nning~~ ~~leather,~~ ~~and~~ ~~Julius~~ ~~Cæsa~~r making
hair-buttons! Hannibal selling blacking, and
Augustus crying garlic! Charlemagne selling
lists by the dozen, and King Pepin crying
apples in a cart drawn with one horse!
Whether I resolve to fire, earth, water, air,
Or all the elements by scruples, I know not,
Nor greatly care.—Shoot, shoot!
Of all deaths the violent death is best;
For from ourselves it steals ourselves so fast,
The pain, once apprehended, is quite past.
        (*They shoot; he falls; and they run to
            him, and tread upon him*)
VITTORIA. What, are you dropt?
FLAMINEO. I am mixed with earth already.
    As you are noble,
Perform your vows, and bravely follow me.
VITTORIA. Whither? To hell?
ZANCHE. To most assured damnation?
VITTORIA. O thou most cursèd devil!
ZANCHE. Thou art caught—
VITTORIA. In thine own engine. I tread the
    fire out
That would have been my ruin.
FLAMINEO. Will you be perjured? What
a religious oath was Styx, that the gods never
durst swear by and violate! Oh, that we had
such an oath to minister, and to be so well
kept in our courts of justice!
VITTORIA. Think whither thou art go-
ing.
ZANCHE. And remember
What villainies thou hast acted.
VITTORIA. This thy death
Shall make me like a blazing ominous star.
Look up and tremble.
FLAMINEO. O, I am caught with a springe!
VITTORIA. You see the fox comes many
    times short home;
'Tis here proved true.

FLAMINEO. Killed with a couple of
braches! [133]
VITTORIA. No fitter offering for the in-
fernal Furies
Than one in whom they reigned while he
    was living.
FLAMINEO. Oh, the way's dark and horrid!
    I cannot see.
Shall I have no company?
VITTORIA. Oh, yes, thy sins
Do run before thee to fetch fire from hell,
To light thee thither.
FLAMINEO. Oh, I smell soot,
Most stinking soot! The chimney is a-fire!
My liver's parboiled, like Scotch holly-bread;
There's a plumber laying pipes in my guts,
    it scalds.—
Wilt thou outlive me?
ZANCHE. Yes, and drive a stake
Through thy body; [134] for we'll give it out
Thou didst this violence upon thyself.
FLAMINEO. O cunning devils! now I have
    tried your love,
And doubled all your reaches.[135]—I am not
    wounded;   (FLAMINEO *rises*)
The pistols held no bullets; 'twas a plot
To prove your kindness to me, and I live
To punish your ingratitude. I knew,
One time or other, you would find a way
To give me a strong potion.—O men
That lie upon your death-beds and are
    haunted
With howling wives, ne'er trust them!
    They'll re-marry
Ere the worm pierce your winding-sheet, ere
    the spider
Make a thin curtain for your epitaphs.—
How cunning you were to discharge! Do you
practise at the Artillery-yard?—Trust a
woman? Never, never! Brachiano be my
precedent. We lay our souls to pawn to the
devil for a little pleasure, and a woman makes
the bill of sale. That ever man should marry!
For one Hypermnestra [136] that saved her lord

[133] Bitches.
[134] Suicides were traditionally buried at a cross-
road with a stake through the body to prevent
their ghosts from wandering.
[135] Escaped your plots.
[136] The only merciful one of the fifty daughters of Danaus who, forced to marry their cousins, on the advice of their father killed their
husbands on the bridal night.

and husband, forty-nine of her sisters cut their husbands' throats all in one night: there was a shoal of virtuous horse leeches!— Here are two other instruments.

(*Showing pistols*)

VITTORIA. Help, help!

(*Enter* LODOVICO *and* GASPARO, *disguised, with other* CONSPIRATORS)

FLAMINEO. What noise is that? Ha! False keys i' the court!

LODOVICO. We have brought you a masque.

FLAMINEO. A matachin,[137] it seems by your drawn swords.

Churchmen turned revellers!

CONSPIRATORS. Isabella! Isabella!

LODOVICO. Do you know us now?

(*They throw off their disguise*)

FLAMINEO. Lodovico! And Gasparo!

LODOVICO. Yes; and that Moor the duke gave pension to

Was the great Duke of Florence.

VITTORIA. Oh, we are lost!

FLAMINEO. You shall not take justice from forth my hands—

Oh, let me kill her!—I'll cut my safety

Through your coats of steel. Fate's a spaniel,

We cannot beat it from us. What remains now?

Let all that do ill, take this precedent:

Man may his fate foresee, but not prevent.

And of all axioms this shall win the prize—

'Tis better to be fortunate than wise.

GASPARO. Bind him to the pillar.

VITTORIA. Oh, your gentle pity!

I have seen a blackbird that would sooner fly

To a man's bosom, than to stay the gripe

Of the fierce sparrowhawk.

GASPARO. Your hope deceives you.

VITTORIA. If Florence be i' the court, would he would kill me!

GASPARO. Fool! Princes give rewards with their own hands,

But death or punishment by the hands of others.

LODOVICO. Sirrah, you once did strike me; I'll strike you

Into the center.

FLAMINEO. Thou'lt do it like a hangman,

[137] A sword dance.

A base hangman, not like a noble fellow;

For thou see'st I cannot strike again.

LODOVICO. Dost laugh?

FLAMINEO. Would'st have me die, as I was born, in whining?

GASPARO. Recommend yourself to Heaven.

FLAMINEO. No, I will carry

Mine own commendations thither.

LODOVICO. Oh ... I kill you forty times a day ...

And use ... together, 'twere too little!

Naught ... that you are too few to feed

The famine of our vengeance. What dost think on?

FLAMINEO. Nothing; of nothing. Leave thy idle questions.

I am i' th' way to study a long silence;

To prate were idle. I remember nothing.

There's nothing of so infinite vexation

As man's own thoughts.

LODOVICO. (*To* VITTORIA) O thou glorious strumpet!

Could I divide thy breath from this pure air

When 't leaves thy body, I would suck it up

And breathe 't upon some dunghill.

VITTORIA. You, my death's-man!

Methinks thou dost not look horrid enough;

Thou hast too good a face to be a hangman.

If thou be, do thy office in right form;

Fall down upon thy knees, and ask forgiveness.[138]

LODOVICO. Oh, thou hast been a most prodigious comet.

But I'll cut off your train—kill the Moor first.

VITTORIA. You shall not kill her first; behold my breast.

I will be waited on in death; my servant

Shall never go before me.

GASPARO. Are you so brave?

VITTORIA. Yes, I shall welcome death

As princes do some great ambassadors;

I'll meet thy weapon half way.

LODOVICO. Thou dost tremble.

Methinks fear should dissolve thee into air.

VITTORIA. Oh, thou art deceived, I am too true a woman;

Conceit can never kill me. I'll tell thee what,

I will not in my death shed one base tear;

Or if look pale, for want of blood, not fear.

[138] The executioner customarily asked forgiveness of his victim before carrying out his duty.

GASPARO. (*To* ZANCHE) Thou art my task, black Fury.

ZANCHE. I have blood
As red as either of theirs; wilt drink some?
'Tis good for the falling-sickness. I am proud
Death cannot alter my complexion,
For I shall ne'er look pale.

LODOVICO. Strike, strike,
With a joint motion!

(*They stab* VITTORIA, ZANCHE, *and*
FLAMINEO)

VITTORIA. 'Twas a manly blow!
The next thou giv'st, murder some sucking infant,
And then thou wilt be famous.

FLAMINEO. Oh, what blade is 't?
A Toledo, or an English fox? [139]
I ever thought a cutler should distinguish
The cause of my death, rather than a doctor.
Search my wound deeper; tent it with the steel
That made it.

VITTORIA. Oh, my greatest sin lay in my blood;
Now my blood pays for 't.

FLAMINEO. Thou 'rt a noble sister!
I love thee now. If woman do breed man,
She ought to teach him manhood. Fare thee well.
Know, many glorious women that are famed
For masculine virtue have been vicious,
Only a happier silence did betide them.
She hath no faults who hath the art to hide them.

VITTORIA. My soul, like to a ship in a black storm,
Is driven, I know not whither.

FLAMINEO. Then cast anchor.
Prosperity doth bewitch men, seeming clear;
But seas do laugh, show white, when rocks are near.
We cease to grieve, cease to be fortune's slaves,
Nay, cease to die, by dying. Art thou gone?
And thou so near the bottom? False report,
Which says that women vie with the nine Muses
For nine tough durable lives! I do not look
Who went before, nor who shall follow me.
No, at myself I will begin and end.
While we look up to Heaven, we confound

Knowledge with knowledge. Oh, I am in a mist!

VITTORIA. Oh, happy they that never saw the court,
Nor ever knew great man but by report!

(VITTORIA *dies*)

FLAMINEO. I recover like a spent taper, for a flash,
And instantly go out.
Let all that belong to great men remember th' old wives' tradition, to be like the lions i' th' Tower on Candlemas-day: to mourn if the sun shine, for fear of the pitiful remainder of winter to come.
'Tis well yet there's some goodness in my death;
My life was a black charnel. I have caught
An everlasting cold; I have lost my voice
Most irrecoverably. Farewell, glorious villains!
This busy trade of life appears most vain,
Since rest breeds rest, where all seek pain by pain.
Let no harsh flattering bells resound my knell;
Strike, thunder, and strike loud, to my farewell!   (*Dies*)

ENGLISH AMBASSADOR. (*Within*) This way, this way! Break ope the doors! This way!

LODOVICO. Ha! Are we betrayed?
Why, then let's constantly die all together;
And having finished this most noble deed,
Defy the worst of fate, not fear to bleed.

(*Enter* AMBASSADORS *and* GIOVANNI)

ENGLISH AMBASSADOR. Keep back the prince! Shoot, shoot!

(*They shoot, and* LODOVICO *falls*)

LODOVICO. Oh, I am wounded!
I fear I shall be ta'en.

GIOVANNI. You bloody villains,
By what authority have you committed
This massacre?

LODOVICO. By thine.

GIOVANNI. Mine?

LODOVICO. Yes; thy uncle,
Which is a part of thee, enjoined us to 't.
Thou know'st me, I am sure; I am Count Lodowick,
And thy most noble uncle in disguise
Was last night in thy court.

[139] Slang for sword.

GIOVANNI. Ha!

GASPARO. Yes, that Moor

Thy father chose his pensioner.

GIOVANNI. He turned murderer?—

Away with them to prison and to torture!

All that have hands in this shall taste our
justice,

As I hope Heaven.

LODOVICO. I do glory yet

That I can call this act mine own. For my
part,

The rack, the gallows, and the torturing
wheel,

Shall be but sound sleeps to me. Here's my
rest;

I limned this night-piece, and it was my best.

GIOVANNI. Remove the bodies.—See, my
honored lord,

What use you ought make of their punishment.

Let guilty men remember, their black deeds

Do lean on crutches made of slender reeds.

(*Exeunt*)

JOHN FLETCHER *

The Wild-Goose Chase

INTRODUCTION

Fletcher's *Wild-Goose Chase* is one of the best sophisticated comedies of its time, a comedy of manners with most of the characteristics which make the Restoration comedies of a later period by Wycherley, Etherege, and Congreve the finest examples of the type in English. Fletcher's wit is not so highly refined as theirs, but the situations, the character types, the basic motives, and the assumption of the audience's detached amusement at the "war of the sexes" are much the same.

Though the locale of the comedy is Paris and the characters are given French names, Fletcher is really writing about London and Englishmen of the upper classes. He makes no attempt at Parisian local color, and he gives his characters none of the traits popularly thought to characterize Frenchmen. Young Englishmen of wealthy families did everything Mirabel, Pinac, and Belleur do, and Nantolet and La Castre are really prosperous English fathers with marriageable sons and daughters. Fletcher obviously expected his sophisticated audience at the Blackfriars to ignore the stated locale of the play and recognize themselves and their friends on the

* See p. 150 for biographical details.

stage. The fact that the play continued in active repertory at London theatres for more than a hundred years indicates that he succeeded.

In its type of appeal, *The Wild-Goose Chase* contrasts sharply with comedies like *Friar Bacon and Friar Bungay* or *The Shoemakers' Holiday*. Those plays were planned for the popular audiences of the great public theatres whose naiveté and insatiable appetite for the romantic (ridiculed in *The Knight of the Burning Pestle*) were not unlike that of the popular movie audiences of today. Such an audience would disapprove of *The Wild-Goose Chase*, and Fletcher, one of the most theatre-wise of dramatists, did not intend it for them. He wrote it for the small, sophisticated audience at the Blackfriars Theatre whose interest in the happy termination of the love affairs would be only incidental, but who would be connoisseurs of the technique of the chase. To them, Mirabel's attitude toward women would be a familiar one, more amusing than shocking, and Oriana's campaign highly entertaining. A similar campaign became the subject, three hundred years later, of one of G. B. Shaw's masterpieces, *Man and Superman*.

THE WILD-GOOSE CHASE

Dramatis personae

In order of their first appearance

DE GARD, A serious-minded young man, newly returned from foreign travel. Brother of Oriana.

FOOTBOY, An attendant of De Gard's who runs beside his master's horse.

LA CASTRE, A well-to-do old man, the indulgent father of Mirabel. Anxious for his son to marry and settle down.

ORIANA, A young lady, sister of De Gard, who has been the guest of La Castre while her brother was abroad. She is in love with Mirabel, and was engaged to him when he set out on his travels, three years before.

MIRABEL, An attractive but wild and irresponsible young man who has returned from three years of foreign travel. Only son of La Castre. He is the wild-goose.

PINAC, Mirabel's friend and travelling companion.

BELLEUR, Another friend and travelling companion of Mirabel. A big burly young man, rather literal minded, who is ridiculously bashful in the presence of gentlewomen.

NANTOLET, A gentleman of good estate, father of the beautiful Rosalura and Lillia Bianca. He is anxious to arrange good marriages for his daughters.

ROSALURA, Daughter of Nantolet. A merry and forthright young woman who has no use for maidenly modesty.

LILLIA BIANCA, Her sister, more quiet and studious. She has a caustic tongue, but is equally interested in getting herself a husband.

LUGIER, Tutor to Rosalura and Lillia Bianca. A bustling, officious, and outspoken little man, with many very positive ideas of how a young lady should acquire a husband.

SERVANT, An impudent man-servant to Lillia Bianca.

PETELLA, Lillia Bianca's maid.

SINGING BOY, A child musician employed in the household of Nantolet.

BOY, A page in the household of Nantolet.

MARIANA, An Englishwoman who is presented as a great lady.

FIRST GENTLEMAN

SECOND GENTLEMAN

PRIEST

FIRST WOMAN

SECOND WOMAN } Friends of Rosalura

THIRD WOMAN } and Lillia Bianca.

FOURTH WOMAN

YOUNG MAN, The pretended Italian representative of a French firm.

SERVANTS AND ATTENDANTS

TWO MEN, Pretended French merchants.

SCENE: *Paris*

Act I

SCENE I. *A Hall in the House of* LA CASTRE.

(*Enter* DE GARD *in dusty riding clothes followed by his* FOOTBOY)

DE GARD. Sirrah, you know I have rid hard; stir my horse well,
And let him want no litter.

F. BOY. (*Grumbling*) I am sure I have run hard;

Would somebody would walk me, and see me littered,
For I think my fellow-horse cannot in reason
Desire more rest, nor take up his chamber before me:
But we are the beasts now, and the beasts are our masters.

DE GARD. When you have done, step to the ten-crown ordinary——

F. BOY. (*With sudden enthusiasm*) With all my heart, sir; for I have a twenty-crown stomach.

DE GARD. And there bespeak a dinner.

F. BOY. (*Running off*) Yes, sir, presently.

DE GARD. For whom, I beseech you, sir?

F. BOY. For myself, I take it, sir.

DE GARD. In truth, you shall not take it; 'tis not meant for you:—

There's for your provender (*Gives money*):
—bespeak a dinner

For Monsieur Mirabel and his companions;

They'll be in town within this hour. When you have done, sirrah,

Make ready all things at my lodgings for me,

And wait me there.

F. BOY. The ten-crown ordinary?

DE GARD. Yes, sir, if you have not forgot it.

F. BOY. I'll forget my feet first:

'Tis the best part of a footman's faith.

(*Exit*)

DE GARD. These youths,

For all they have been in Italy to learn thrift,

And seem to wonder at men's lavish ways,

Yet they cannot rub off old friends, their French itches;

They must meet sometimes to disport their bodies

With good wine and good women, and good store too:

Let 'em be what they will, they are armed at all points,

And then hang saving, let the sea grow high!

This ordinary can fit 'em of all sizes.

They must salute their country with old customs.

(*Enter* LA CASTRE *and* ORIANA)

ORI. Brother! (*Running to* DE GARD)

DE GARD. (*Embracing her*) My dearest sister!

ORI. Welcome, welcome!

Indeed, you are welcome home, most welcome!

DE GARD. Thank you. (*Holding her off*)

You are grown a handsome woman, Oriana

(Blush at your faults): I am wondrous glad to see you.—

Monsieur La Castre, let not my affection

To my fair sister make me held unmannerly:

I am glad to see you well, to see you lusty,

Good health about you, and in fair company;

Believe me, I am proud——

LA CAST. Fair sir, I thank you.

Monsieur De Gard, you are welcome from your journey;

Good men have still good welcome: give me your hand, sir:

Once more, you are welcome home. You look still younger.

DE GARD. (*Laughing*) Time has no leisure to look after us;

We wander every where; age cannot find us.

LA CAST. And how does all?

DE GARD. All well, sir, and all lusty.

LA CAST. I hope my son be so: I doubt not, sir,

But you have often seen him in your journeys,

And bring me some fair news.

DE GARD. Your son is well, sir,

And grown a proper gentleman; he is well and lusty.

Within this eight hours I took leave of him,

And over-hied him, having some slight business

That forced me out o' the way: I can assure you,

He will be here to-night.

LA CAST. You make me glad, sir,

For, o' my faith, I almost long to see him:

Methinks, he has been away—

DE GARD. 'Tis but your tenderness;

What are three years? a love-sick wench will allow it.

His friends, that went out with him, are come back too,

Belleur and young Pinac. He bid me say little,

Because he means to be his own glad messenger.

LA CAST. I thank you for this news, sir: he shall be welcome,

And his friends too: indeed, I thank you heartily:

And how (for I dare say you will not flatter him)

Has Italy wrought on him? Has he mewed [1] yet

His wild fantastic toys? They say that climate

[1] Molted, cast off.

Is a great purger of those humorous fluxes:
How is he improved, I pray you?

DE GARD. (*Hesitating*) No doubt, sir,
well;
H'as borne himself a full and noble gentleman:
To speak him farther is beyond my charter.

LA CAST. I am glad to hear so much good.
Come, I see
You long to enjoy your sister; yet I must en-
treat you,
Before I go, to sup with me to-night,
And must not be denied.

DE GARD. (*Bowing*) I am your servant.

LA CAST. Where you shall meet fair,
merry, and noble company;
My neighbor Nantolet and his two fair
daughters.

DE GARD. Your supper's seasoned well,
sir: I shall wait upon you.

LA CAST. Till then I'll leave ye: and you're
once more welcome.

DE GARD. I thank you, noble sir!
(*Exit* LA CASTRE)
Now, Oriana,
How have you done since I went? have ye
had your health well?
And your mind free?

ORI. You see, I am not bated;
Merry, and eat my meat.

DE GARD. A good preservative.
And how have you been used? You know,
Oriana,
Upon my going out, at your request,
I left your portion in La Castre's hands,
The main means you must stick to: for that
reason,
And 'tis no little one, I ask you, sister,
With what humanity he entertains you,
And how you find his courtesy?

ORI. Most ready:
I can assure you, sir, I am used most nobly.

DE GARD. I am glad to hear it: but I
prithee, tell me,
And tell me true, what end had you, Oriana,
In trusting your money here? He is no kins-
man,
Nor any tie upon him of a guardian;
Nor dare I think you doubt my prodigality.

ORI. No, certain, sir; none of all this provoked [2] me;

[2] Prompted.

(*Embarrassed*) Another private reason.

DE GARD. (*Severely*) 'Tis not private,
Nor carried so; 'tis common, my fair sister;
Your love to Mirabel: your blushes tell it:
'Tis too much known, and spoken of too
largely;
And with no little shame I wonder at it.

ORI. Is it a shame to love?

DE GARD. To love undiscreetly:
A virgin should be tender of her honor,
Close, and secure.

ORI. I am as close as can be,
And stand upon as strong and honest guards
too;
Unless this warlike age need a portcullis:
Yet, I confess, I love him.

DE GARD. Hear the people.

ORI. (*Indignantly*) Now, I say, hang the
people! he, that dares
Believe what they say, dares be mad, and
give
His mother, nay, his own wife, up to rumor:
All grounds of truth they build on is a tavern,
And their best censure's sack, sack in abun-
dance;
For, as they drink, they think: they ne'er
speak modestly
Unless the wine be poor, or they want
money:
(*Scornfully*) Believe them! believe Amadis
de Gaul,
The Knight o' the Sun, or Palmerin of Eng-
land;
For these, to them, are modest and true
stories.
Pray, understand me; if their tongues be
truth,
And if *in vino veritas* be an oracle,
What woman is, or has been ever, honest?
Give 'em but ten round cups, they'll swear
Lucretia
Died not for want of power to resist Tarquin,
But want of pleasure, that he stayed no
longer;
And Portia, that was famous for her piety
To her loved lord, they'll face you out, died
o' the pox.

DE GARD. (*Persisting*) Well, there is
something, sister.

ORI. If there be, brother,
'Tis none of their things; 'tis not yet so
monstrous:
My thing is marriage; and, at his return,

I hope to put their squint eyes right again.

DE GARD. (*Doubtingly*) Marriage? 'tis
  true his father is a rich man,
Rich both in land and money; he his heir,
A young and handsome man, I must confess,
  too;
But of such qualities, and such wild flings,
Such admirable imperfections, sister,
(For all his travel and bought experience,)
I should be loth to own him for my brother:
Methinks, a rich mind in a state indifferent
Would prove the better fortune.

  ORI. If he be wild,
The reclaiming him to good and honest,
  brother,
Will make much for my honor; which, if I
  prosper,
Shall be the study of my love, and life too.

  DE GARD. You say well; would he
  thought as well, and loved too!
He marry! he'll be hanged first; he knows
  no more
What the conditions and the ties of love are,
The honest purposes and grounds of marriage,
Nor will know, nor ever be brought to
  endeavor,

Than I do how to build a church: he was ever
A loose and strong defier of all order;
His loves are wanderers, they knock at each
  door,
And taste each dish, but are no residents.
Or say, he may be brought to think of mar-
  riage,
(As 'twill be no small labor), thy hopes are
  strangers:
I know there is a labored match now fol-
  lowed,
Now at this time, for which he was sent for
  home too:
Be not abused; Nantolet has two fair daugh-
  ters,
And he must take his choice.

  ORI. Let him take freely:
For all this I despair not; my mind tells
  me
That I, and only I, must make him perfect;
And in that hope I rest.

  DE GARD. Since you're so confident,
Prosper your hope! I'll be no adversary;
Keep yourself fair and right, he shall not
  wrong you.

  ORI. (*Sturdily*) When I forget my virtue,
no man know me!   (*Exeunt*)

SCENE II. *Before* LA CASTRE's *House.*

(*Enter* MIRABEL, PINAC, BELLEUR, *and*
Servants)

  MIR. (*Expansively*) Welcome to Paris,
  once more, gentlemen!
We have had a merry and a lusty ordinary,
And wine, and good meat, and a bouncing
  reckoning;
And let it go for once; 'tis a good physic:
Only the wenches are not for my diet;
They are too lean and thin, their embraces
  brawn-fallen.[3]
Give me the plump Venetian, fat and lusty,
That meets me soft and supple; smiles upon
  me,
As if a cup of full wine leaped to kiss me:
These slight things I affect not.

  PIN. They are ill-built;
Pin-buttocked, like your dainty Barbaries,

[3] Feeble.

And weak i' the pasterns; they'll endure no
  hardness.

  MIR. There's nothing good or handsome
  bred amongst us:
Till we are travelled, and live abroad, we are
  coxcombs.
(*Scornfully*) You talk of France—a slight
  unseasoned country,
Abundance of gross food, which makes us
  blockheads;
We are fair set out indeed, and so are fore-
  horses:
Men say, we are great courtiers,—men abuse
  us;
We are wise, and valiant too,—*non credo,*
  signor;
Our women the best linguists,—they are parrots;
O' this side the Alps they are nothing but
  mere drolleries.[4]

[4] Puppets.

Ha! *Roma la Santa,* Italy for my money!
Their policies, their customs, their frugalities,
Their courtesies so open, yet so reserved too,
As, when you think you are known best,
    you're a stranger;
Their very pick-teeth speak more man than
    we do,
And season of more salt.
    PIN. 'Tis a brave country;
Not pestered with your stubborn precise
    puppies,
That turn all useful and allowed content-
    ments
To scabs and scruples—hang 'em, capon-
    worshippers.
    BEL. I like that freedom well, and like
    their women too,
And would fain do as others do; but I am so
    bashful,
So naturally an ass! Look ye, I can look upon
    'em,
And very willingly I go to see 'em,
(There's no man willinger), and I can kiss
    'em,
And make a shift——
    MIR. But, if they chance to flout you,
Or say, (*mimicking a coquette*) "You are too
    bold! fie, sir, remember!
I pray, sit farther off——"
    BEL. 'Tis true—I am humbled,
I am gone; I confess ingenuously, I am
    silenced;
The spirit of amber [5] cannot force me answer.
    PIN. Then would I sing and dance——
    BEL. You have wherewithal, sir.
    PIN. And charge her up again.
    BEL. I can be hanged first:
Yet, where I fasten well, I am a tyrant.
    MIR. Why, thou dar'st fight?
    BEL. Yes, certainly, I dare fight,
And fight with any man at any weapon.
Would the other were no more! but, a pox
    on't!
When I am sometimes in my height of hope,
And reasonable valiant that way, my heart
    hardened,
Some scornful jest or other chops between me
And my desire. What would you have me
    to do, then, gentlemen?
    MIR. Belleur, you must be bolder: (*accus-
    ingly*) travel three years,

    [5] Amber was considered to be a strong pro-
vocative.

And bring home such a baby to betray you
As bashfulness! a great fellow, and a soldier!
    BEL. You have the gift of impudence; be
    thankful;
Every man has not the like talent. I will
    study,
And, if it may be revealed to me——
    MIR. Learn of me,
And of Pinac: no doubt, you'll find employ-
    ment;
Ladies will look for courtship.
    PIN. 'Tis but fleshing,
But standing one good brunt or two. Hast
    thou any mind to marriage?
We'll provide thee some soft-natured wench,
    that's dumb too.
    MIR. Or an old woman that cannot refuse
thee in charity.
    BEL. A dumb woman, or an old woman,
    that were eager,
And cared not for discourse, I were excellent
    at.
    MIR. You must now put on boldness
    (there's no avoiding it),
And stand all hazards, fly at all games
    bravely;
They'll say you went out like an ox, and
    returned like an ass, else.
    BEL. I shall make danger, sure.
    MIR. I am sent for home now;
I know it is to marry; but my father shall
    pardon me.
Although it be a weighty ceremony,
And may concern me hereafter in my gravity,
I will not lose the freedom of a traveller:
A new strong lusty bark cannot ride at one
    anchor.
Shall I make divers suits to show to the same
    eyes?
'Tis dull and homespun;—study several
    pleasures,
And want employments for 'em? I'll be
    hanged first.
Tie me to one smock? make my travels fruit-
    less?
I'll none of that; for every fresh behavior,
By your leave, father, (*bowing with mock
    solemnity*) I must have a fresh mistress,
And a fresh favor too.
    BEL. I like that passingly;
As many as you will, so they be willing,
Willing, and gentle, gentle.
    PIN. There's no reason

A gentleman, and a traveller, should be clapt
    up,
(For 'tis a kind of bilboes [6] to be married),
Before he manifest to the world his good
    parts:
Tug ever, like a rascal, at one oar?

Give me the Italian liberty!
    MIR. That I study,
And that I will enjoy. Come, go in, gentle-
    men;
There mark how I behave myself, and fol-
    low.   (*Exeunt*)

SCENE III. *A Room in the House of* LA CASTRE.

(*Enter* LA CASTRE, NANTOLET, ROSALURA, *and* LILLIA BIANCA *followed by* LUGIER)

LA CAST. You and your beauteous daugh-
ters are most welcome:
Beshrew my blood, they are fair ones!—Wel-
come, beauties,
Welcome, sweet birds. (*The two girls curtsy*)
    NANT. They are bound much to your
courtesies.
    LA CAST. I hope we shall be nearer ac-
quainted.
    NANT. That's my hope too:
For, certain, sir, I much desire your alliance.
You see 'em; they are no gypsies: for their
    breeding,
It has not been so coarse but they are able
To rank themselves with women of fair
    fashion;
Indeed, they have been trained well.
    LUG. (*Smirking*) Thank me.
    NANT. Fit for the heirs of that state I shall
leave 'em:
To say more, is to sell 'em. They say your
    son,
Now he has travelled, must be wondrous
    curious
And choice in what he takes; these are no
    coarse ones.
Sir, (*indicating* ROSALURA) here's a merry
wench—let him look to himself—
All heart, i' faith—may chance to startle him;
For all his care, and travelled caution,
May creep into his eye: if he love gravity,
Affect a solemn face, (*indicating* LILLIA
    BIANCA) there's one will fit him.
    LA CAST. So young and so demure?
    NANT. She is my daughter,
Else I would tell you, sir, she is a mistress
Both of those manners, and that modesty,

You would wonder at: she is no often-
    speaker,
But, when she does, she speaks well; nor
    no reveller,
Yet she can dance, and has studied the court
    elements,
And sings, as some say, handsomely; if a
    woman,
With the decency of her sex, may be a
    scholar,
I can assure you, sir, she understands too.
    LA CAST. These are fit garments, sir.
    LUG. (*Thrusting himself forward offi-
ciously*) Thank them that cut 'em:
Yes, they are handsome women; they have
    handsome parts too,
Pretty becoming parts.
    LA CAST. (*Trying to ignore* LUGIER) 'Tis
like they have, sir.
    LUG. Yes, yes, and handsome education
    they have had too,
Had it abundantly; they need not blush at
    it:
I taught it, I'll avouch it.
    LA CAST. You say well, sir.
    LUG. (*Belligerently insisting on attention*)
    I know what I say, sir, and I say but
    right, sir:
I am no trumpet of their commendations
Before their father; else I should say farther.
    LA CAST. (*To* NANTOLET *with some an-
noyance*) Pray you, what's this gentle-
man?
    NANT. One that lives with me, sir;
A man well bred and learned, but blunt and
    bitter;
Yet it offends no wise man; I take pleasure
    in't.
Many fair gifts he has, in some of which,
That lie most easy to their understandings
H'as handsomely bred up my girls, I thank
    him.

[6] Fetters.

Lug. I have put it to 'em, that's my part,
  I have urged it;
It seems, they are of years now to take hold
  on't.
Nant. He's wond'rous blunt.
La Cast. By my faith, I was afraid of him:
Does he not fall out with the gentlewomen
  sometimes?
Nant. No, no; he's that way moderate and
discreet, sir.
Ros. If he did, we should be too hard for
him.
Lug. (*Delighted*) Well said, sulphur!
Too hard for thy husband's head, if he wear
  not armor.
Nant. (*Amused at them*) Many of these
bickerings, sir.
La Cast. I am glad they are no oracles.
(*Gazing at* Lugier) Sure as I live, he beats
  them, he's so puissant.

(*Enter* Mirabel *and* Oriana, *arguing intently. They are followed by* Pinac, Belleur, *and* De Gard)

Ori. (*Indignantly*) Well, if you do for-
get——
Mir. Prithee, hold thy peace:
I know thou art a pretty wench; I know thou
  lov'st me;
Preserve it till we have a fit time to discourse
  on't,
And a fit place; I'll ease thy heart, I warrant
  thee:
Thou seest I have much to do now.
Ori. (*Offended*) I am answered, sir:
With me you shall have nothing on these
  conditions.
De Gard. (*Calling* Mirabel's *attention
to the others*) Your father and your friends.
La Cast. (*To* Mirabel) You are wel-
come home, sir;
Bless you, you are very welcome! (*Introduc-
ing* Nantolet, Rosalura, *and* Lillia
Bianca) Pray, know this gentleman,
And these fair ladies.
Nant. Monsieur Mirabel,
I am much affected with your fair return, sir;
You bring a general joy.
Mir. I bring you service,
And these bright beauties, sir.
Nant. (*Turning to* Pinac *and* Belleur)
Welcome home, gentlemen,

Welcome with all my heart!
Bel. & Pin. We thank you, sir.
La Cast. Your friends will have their
share too.
Bel. Sir, we hope
They'll look upon us, though we show like
  strangers.
Nant. Monsieur De Gard; I must salute
  you also,
(*To* Oriana) And this fair gentlewoman:
  you are welcome from your travel too;—
All welcome, all.
De Gard. We render you our loves, sir,
The best wealth we bring home.—(*Bowing
  to* Rosalura *and* Lillia Bianca) By
  your favors, beauties.—
    (*The party breaks up into groups*)
(*Aside to* Oriana) One of these two: you
  know my meaning.
Ori. (*Aside to her brother*) Well, sir;
They are fair and handsome, I must needs
  confess it,
And, let it prove the worst, I shall live after
  it:
Whilst I have meat and drink, love cannot
  starve me;
For, if I die o' the first fit, I am unhappy,
And worthy to be buried with my heels
  upward.
Mir. (*To his father, with astonishment*)
To marry, sir?
La Cast. You know I am an old man,
And every hour declining to my grave,
One foot already in; more sons I have not,
Nor more I dare not seek whilst you are
  worthy;
In you lies all my hope, and all my name,
The making good or wretched of my memory,
The safety of my state.
Mir. And you have provided,
Out of this tenderness, these handsome
  gentlewomen,
Daughters to this rich man, to take my choice
  of?
La Cast. I have, dear son.
Mir. (*Affectionately*) 'Tis true, you are
  old and feebled;
Would you were young again, and in full
  vigor!
I love a bounteous father's life, a long one;
I am none of those that, when they shoot
  to ripeness,

Do what they can to break the boughs they grew on;
I wish you many years, and many riches,
And pleasures to enjoy 'em: but, for marriage,
I neither yet believe in't, nor affect it,
Nor think it fit.

LA CAST. You will render me your reasons?

MIR. Yes, sir, both short and pithy, and these they are:—
You would have me marry a maid?

LA CAST. A maid! what else?

MIR. Yes, there be things called widows, dead men's wills,
I never loved to prove those; nor never longed yet
To be buried alive in another man's cold monument.
And there be maids appearing, and maids being;
The appearing are fantastic things, mere shadows;
And, if you mark 'em well, they want their heads too;
Only the world, to cozen misty eyes,
Has clapt 'em on new faces. The maids being,
A man may venture on, if he be so mad to marry,
If he have neither fear before his eyes, nor fortune;
And let him take heed how he gather these too.
For, look you, father, they are just like melons,
Musk-melons are the emblems of these maids;
Now they are ripe, now cut 'em, they taste pleasantly,
And are a dainty fruit, digested easily;
Neglect this present time, and come to-morrow,
They are so ripe they are rotten gone, their sweetness
Run into humor, and their taste to surfeit.

LA CAST. Why, these are now ripe, son.

MIR. I'll try them presently,
And, if I like their taste——

LA CAST. 'Pray you, please yourself, sir.

MIR. That liberty is my due, and I'll maintain it.—(*Turning from his father and addressing* ROSALURA)

Lady, what think you of a handsome man now?

Ros. (*Pertly*) A wholesome too, sir?

MIR. That's as you make your bargain.
A handsome, wholesome man, then, and a kind man,
To cheer your heart up, to rejoice you, lady?

Ros. Yes, sir, I love rejoicing.

MIR. To lie close to you?
Close as a cockle? keep the cold nights from you?

Ros. That will be looked for too; our bodies ask it.

MIR. (*Hoping to shock her*) And get two boys at every birth?

Ros. That's nothing;
I have known a cobbler do it, a poor thin cobbler,
A cobbler out of moldy cheese perform it,
Cabbage, and coarse black bread: methinks, a gentleman
Should take foul scorn to have a nawl[7] outname him.
Two at a birth! why, every house-dove has it:
That man that feeds well, promises as well too,
I should expect indeed something of worth from.
You talk of two!

MIR. (*Pretending astonishment*) She would have me get two dozen,
Like buttons, at a birth.

Ros. You love to brag, sir:
If you proclaim these offers at your marriage,
(You are a pretty-timbered man, take heed,)
They may be taken hold of, and expected,
Yes, if not hoped for at a higher rate too.

MIR. I will take heed, and thank you for your counsel.
Father, what think you?

LA CAST. (*Laughing*) 'Tis a merry gentlewoman:
Will make, no doubt, a good wife.

MIR. Not for me:
I marry her, and, happily, get nothing.
In what a state am I then, father? I shall suffer,
For any thing I hear to the contrary, *more majorum;*
I were as sure to be a cuckold, father,
A gentleman of antler——

---

[7] Awl.

LA CAST. (*Half amused, half annoyed*)
Away, away, fool!
MIR. As I am sure to fail her expectation,
I had rather get the pox than get her babies.
    LA CAST. You are much to blame: if this
      do not affect you,
Pray, try the other; she's of a more demure
    way.
    BEL. (*Aside, admiringly*) That I had but
    the audacity to talk thus!
I love that plain-spoken gentlewoman admirably;
And, certain, I could go as near to please her,
If down-right doing—she has a per'lous countenance—
If I could meet one that would believe me,
And take my honest meaning without circumstance——
    MIR. You shall have your will, sir; I will
    try the other;
But 'twill be to small use.—(*Addressing* LIL-
    LIA BIANCA) I hope, fair lady,
(For, methinks, in your eyes I see more
    mercy,)
You will enjoin your lover a less penance;
And though I'll promise much, as men are
    liberal,
And vow an ample sacrifice of service,
Yet your discretion, and your tenderness,
And thriftiness in love, good huswife's carefulness
To keep the stock entire——
    LIL. (*Disdainfully*) Good sir, speak louder,
That these may witness, too, you talk of
    nothing:
I should be loath alone to bear the burthen
Of so much indiscretion.
                (*She turns away from him*)
    MIR. Hark you, hark you;
'Ods-bobs, you are angry, lady.
    LIL. (*Coldly*) Angry! no, sir;
I never owned an anger to lose poorly.
    MIR. But you can love, for all this; and
    delight too,
For all your set austerity, to hear
Of a good husband, lady?
    LIL. You say true, sir;
For, by my troth, I have heard of none these
    ten years,
They are so rare; and there are so many, sir,
So many longing women on their knees too,

That pray the dropping-down of these good
    husbands—
The dropping-down from Heaven; for they
    are not bred here—
That you may guess at all my hope, but
    hearing——
    MIR. Why may not I be one?
    LIL. You were near 'em once, sir,
When you came o'er the Alps; those are near
    Heaven:
But since you missed that happiness, there's
    no hope of you.
    MIR. Can you love a man?
    LIL. Yes, if the man be lovely,
That is, be honest, modest: I would have him
    valiant,
His anger slow, but certain for his honor;
Travelled he should be, but through himself
    exactly,
For 'tis fairer to know manners well than
    countries;
He must be no vain talker, nor no lover
To hear himself talk; they are brags of a
    wanderer,
Of one finds no retreat for fair behavior.
(*Surveying him coolly*) Would you learn
    more?
    MIR. Yes.
    LIL. Learn to hold your peace, then.
Fond [8] girls are got with tongues, women
    with tempers.
    MIR. Women, with I know what; but let
    that vanish.
Go thy way, good-wife Bias! Sure, thy husband
Must have a strong philosopher's stone, he
    will ne'er please thee else.—
Here's a starched piece of austerity!—Do you
    hear, father?
Do you hear this moral lecture?
    LA CAST. Yes, and like it.
    MIR. Why, there's your judgment now;
    there's an old bolt shot!
This thing must have the strangest observation,
(Do you mark me, father?) when she is married once,
The strangest custom too of admiration
On all she does and speaks, 'twill be past
    sufferance.
I must not lie with her in common language,

[8] Foolish.

Nor cry, "Have at thee, Kate!" I shall be
hissed then;
Nor eat my meat without the sauce of sen-
tences,[9]
Your powdered beef and problems, a rare
diet!
My first son, Monsieur Aristotle, I know it,
Great master of the metaphysics, or so;
The second, Solon, and the best law-setter;
And I must look [10] Egyptian god-fathers,
Which will be no small trouble: my eldest
daughter,
Sappho, or such a fiddling kind of poetess,
And brought up, *invitâ Minervâ*, at her
needle!
My dogs must look their names too, and all
Spartan,
Lelaps, Melampus; no more Fox and Bawdy-
face.
I married to a sullen set of sentences!
To one that weighs her words and her be-
haviors
In the gold-weights of discretion! I'll be
hanged first.
  La Cast. Prithee, reclaim thyself.
  Mir. Pray you, give me time, then:
If they can set me any thing to play at,

That seems fit for a gamester, have at the
fairest,
Till I see more, and try more!
  La Cast. Take your time, then;
I'll bar you no fair liberty.—Come, gentle-
men;
And, ladies, come; to all, once more, a wel-
come!
And now let's in to supper.
  (*Exeunt* La Castre, Nantolet, Rosalura,
    Lillia Bianca, *and* Lugier)
  Mir. How dost like 'em?
  Pin. They are fair enough, but of so
strange behaviors——
  Mir. Too strange for me: I must have
those have mettle,
And mettle to my mind. Come, let's be
merry.
  Bel. Bless me from this woman! I would
stand the cannon,
Before ten words of hers.
  (*Exeunt* Mirabel, Pinac, *and* Belleur)
  De Gard. (*Hoping his sister has seen
enough of* Mirabel) Do you find him
now?
Do you think he will be ever firm?
  Ori. (*Undaunted*) I fear not. (*Exeunt*)

Act II

Scene I. *A Garden belonging to the House of* La Castre.

(*Enter* Mirabel *protesting to* Pinac *and*
Belleur)

  Mir. Ne'er tell me of this happiness; 'tis
nothing;
The state they bring with being sought-to,[11]
scurvy:
I had rather make mine own play, and I will
do.
My happiness is in mine own content,
And the despising of such glorious [12] trifles,
As I have done a thousand more. For my
humor,
Give me a good free fellow, that sticks to me,
A jovial fair companion; there's a beauty!
For women, I can have too many of them;
Good women too, as the age reckons 'em,

More than I have employment for.
  Pin. You are happy.
  Mir. My only fear is, that I must be
forced,
Against my nature, to conceal myself:
Health and an able body are two jewels.
  Pin. If either of these two women were
offered to me now,
I would think otherwise, and do accordingly;
Yes, and recant my heresies; I would, sir;
And be more tender of opinion,
And put a little of my travelled liberty
Out of the way, and look upon 'em seriously.
Methinks, this grave-carried wench——
  Bel. (*Earnestly*) Methinks, the other,
The home-spoken gentlewoman, that desires
to be fruitful,

---

[9] Moral observations.   [10] Seek out.

[11] *I.e.* Sought after.   [12] Vain-glorious.

That treats of the full manage of the matter,
(For there lies all my aim,) that wench, me-
thinks,
If I were but well set on, for she is affable,
If I were but hounded right, and one to teach
me—
She speaks to the matter, and comes home to
the point—
Now do I know I have such a body to please
her
As all the kingdom cannot fit her with, I
am sure on't,
If I could but talk myself into her favor.
    MIR. That's easily done.
    BEL. That's easily said; would 'twere
done!
You should see then how I would lay about
me.
If I were virtuous, it would never grieve me,
Or any thing that might justify my modesty;
But when my nature is prone to do a charity,
And my calf's tongue will not help me——
    MIR. Will ye go to 'em?
They cannot but take it courteously.
    PIN. I'll do my part,
Though I am sure 'twill be the hardest I e'er
played yet,
A way I never tried too, which will stagger
me;
And, if it do not shame me, I am happy.
    MIR. Win 'em and wear 'em; I give up
my interest.
    PIN. What say you, Monsieur Belleur?
    BEL. Would I could say,
Or sing, or any thing that were but hand-
some!
I would be with her presently!
    PIN. Yours is no venture;
A merry ready wench.
    BEL. A vengeance squibber;
She'll fleer me out of faith too.
    MIR. I'll be near thee;
Pluck up thy heart; I'll second thee at all
brunts.
Be angry, if she abuse thee, and beat her a
little;
Some women are won that way.
    BEL. Pray, be quiet,
And let me think. (Making up his mind)
    I am resolved to go on;
But how I shall get off again——
    MIR. I am persuaded

Thou wilt so please her, she will go near to
ravish thee.
    BEL. I would 'twere come to that once!
Let me pray a little.
    MIR. Now, for thine honor, Pinac, board
me this modesty;
Warm but this frozen snow-ball, 'twill be a
conquest
(Although I know thou art a fortunate
wencher,
And hast done rarely in thy days) above all
thy ventures.
    BEL. (Cautiously) You will be ever near?
    MIR. At all necessities;
And take thee off, and set thee on again, boy,
And cherish thee, and stroke thee.
    BEL. Help me out too;
For I know I shall stick i' the mire. If you
see us close once,
Be gone, and leave me to my fortune, sud-
denly,
For I am then determined to do wonders.
Farewell, and fling an old shoe. How my
heart throbs!
Would I were drunk! Farewell, Pinac:
Heaven send us
A joyful and a merry meeting, man!
    PIN. Farewell,
And cheer thy heart up; and remember,
Belleur,
They are but women.
    BEL. I had rather they were lions.
    MIR. About it; I'll be with you instantly.—
            (Exeunt BELLEUR and PINAC)

(Enter ORIANA)

(Groaning as he sees ORIANA) Shall I ne'er
be at rest? no peace of conscience?
No quiet for these creatures? Am I ordained
To be devoured quick [13] by these she-canni-
bals?
Here's another they call handsome; I care
not for her,
I ne'er look after her: when I am half-tippled,
It may be I should turn her, and peruse her;
Or, in my want of women, I might call for
her;
But to be haunted when I have no fancy,
No maw to the matter—(To ORIANA, petu-
lantly) Now, why do you follow me?

[13] Alive.

Ori. I hope, sir, 'tis no blemish to my
  virtue;
Nor need you, out of scruple, ask that ques-
  tion,
If you remember you, before your travel,
The contract you tied to me: 'tis my love, sir,
That makes me seek you, to confirm your
  memory;
And, that being fair and good, I cannot suffer.
I come to give you thanks too.
  Mir. For what, prithee?
  Ori. For that fair piece of honesty you
  showed, sir,
That constant nobleness.
  Mir. (*Puzzled*) How? for I am short-
headed.
  Ori. I'll tell you then; for refusing that
  free offer
Of Monsieur Nantolet's, those handsome
  beauties,
Those two prime ladies, that might well have
  pressed you
If not to have broken, yet to have bowed
  your promise.
I know it was for my sake, for your faith-sake,
You slipt 'em off; your honesty compelled
  you;
And let me tell ye, sir, it showed most hand-
  somely.
  Mir. And let me tell thee, there was no
  such matter;
Nothing intended that way, of that nature:
I have more to do with my honesty than
  to fool it,
Or venture it in such leak barks as women.
I put 'em off because I loved 'em not,
Because they are too queasy for my temper,
And not for thy sake, nor the contract sake,
Nor vows, nor oaths; I have made a thousand
  of 'em;
They are things indifferent, whether kept
  or broken;
Mere venial slips, that grow not near the
  conscience;
Nothing concerns those tender parts; they
  are trifles;
For, as I think, there was never man yet
  hoped for
Either constancy or secrecy from a woman,
Unless it were an ass ordained for sufferance;
Nor to contract with such can be a tie-all;
So let them know again; for 'tis a justice,
And a main point of civil policy,

Whate'er we say or swear, they being repro-
  bates,
Out of the state of faith, we are clear of all
  sides,
And 'tis a curious blindness to believe us.
  Ori. You do not mean this, sure?
  Mir. Yes, sure, and certain;
And hold it positively, as a principle,
As ye are strange things, and made of strange
  fires and fluxes,
So we are allowed as strange ways to obtain
  ye,
But not to hold; we are all created errant.
  Ori. You told me other tales.
  Mir. I not deny it;
I have tales of all sorts for all sorts of women,
And protestations likewise of all sizes,
As they have vanities to make us coxcombs.
If I obtain a good turn, so it is,
I am thankful for it; if I be made an ass,
The 'mends are in mine own hands—or the
  surgeon's,
And there's an end on 't.
  Ori. (*Plaintively*) Do not you love me,
then?
  Mir. As I love others; heartily I love thee;
When I am high and lusty, I love thee
  cruelly:
After I have made a plenteous meal, and
  satisfied
My senses with all delicates, come to me,
And thou shalt see how I love thee.
  Ori. (*Despairingly*) Will not you marry
me?
  Mir. No, certain, no, for any thing I know
  yet:
I must not lose my liberty, dear lady,
And, like a wanton slave, cry for more
  shackles.
What should I marry for? do I want any
  thing?
Am I an inch the farther from my pleasure?
Why should I be at charge to keep a wife
  of mine own,
When other honest married men will ease
  me,
And thank me too, and be beholding to me?
Thou think'st I am mad for a maidenhead;
  thou art cozened.
Or, if I were addicted to that diet,
Can you tell me where I should have one?
  Thou art eighteen now,
And, if thou hast thy maidenhead yet extant,

Sure, 'tis as big as cods-head; and those grave
    dishes
I never love to deal withal. (*Takes a note
    book from his pocket*) Dost thou see
    this book here?
Look over all these ranks. (*Turning pages*)
    All these are women,
Maids, and pretenders to maidenheads; these
    are my conquests;
All these I swore to marry, as I swore to thee,
With the same reservation, and most
    righteously—
Which I need not have done neither; for,
    alas, they made no scruple,
And I enjoyed 'em at my will, and left 'em.
Some of 'em are married since, and were as
    pure maids again,
Nay, o' my conscience, better than they were
    bred for;
The rest, fine sober women.
    Ori. (*Ready to weep with vexation*) Are
you not ashamed, sir?
    Mir. No, by my troth, sir; there's no
    shame belongs to it.
I hold it as commendable to be wealthy in
    pleasure,
As others do in rotten sheep and pasture.

(*Enter* De Gard)

    Ori. (*Weeping*) Are all my hopes come to
    this? Is there no faith,
No truth, nor modesty, in men?
    De Gard. How now, sister?
Why weeping thus? Did I not prophesy?
Come, tell me why——
    Ori. I am not well; pray you pardon me.
                  (*Runs out*)
    De Gard. (*Half seriously*) Now, Mon-
    sieur Mirabel, what ails my sister?
You have been playing the wag with her.
    Mir. As I take it,
She is crying for a cod-piece. Is she gone?
Lord, what an age is this! I was calling for
    you;
For, as I live, I thought she would have
    ravished me.
    De Gard. You are merry, sir.
    Mir. Thou know'st this book, De Gard,
this inventory?
    De Gard. The debt-book of your mis-
tresses; I remember it.

    Mir. Why, this was it that angered her;
    she was stark mad
She found not her name here; and cried
    downright
Because I would not pity her immediately,
And put her in my list.
    De Gard. Sure, she had more modesty.
    Mir. Their modesty is anger to be over-
done;
They'll quarrel sooner for precedence here,
And take it in more dudgeon to be slighted,
Than they will in public meetings; 'tis their
    natures.
And, alas, I have so many to despatch yet,
And to provide myself for my affairs too,
That, in good faith——
    De Gard. (*Annoyed*) Be not too glorious
    foolish;
Sum not your travels up with vanities;
It ill becomes your expectation.[14]
(*Solemnly*) Temper your speech, sir:
    whether your loose story
Be true or false, (for you are so free, I fear
    it,)
Name not my sister in't, I must not hear it.
(*With rising anger*) Upon your danger,
    name her not! I hold her
A gentlewoman of those happy parts and
    carriage,
A good man's tongue may be right proud to
    speak her.
    Mir. (*Surprised at his anger, and an-
    noyed*) Your sister, sir! Do you blench
    at that? Do you cavil?
Do you hold her such a piece she may not be
    played withal?
I have had an hundred handsomer and nobler
Have sued to me, too, for such a courtesy;
Your sister comes i' the rear. Since you are
    so angry,
And hold your sister such a strong recusant,
I tell you, I may do it; and, it may be, will too.
It may be, have too; there's my free confes-
    sion;
Work upon that now!
    De Gard. If I thought you had, I would
    work,
And work such stubborn work should make
    your heart ache:
But I believe you, as I ever knew you,
A glorious talker, and a legend-maker

[14] *I.e.* What is expected of you.

Of idle tales and trifles; a depraver
Of your own truth: their honors fly about
    you!
And so, I take my leave; but with this
    caution,
Your sword be surer than your tongue; you'll
    smart else.
    Mir. I laugh at thee, so little I respect
    thee;
And I'll talk louder, and despise thy sister;
Set up a chamber-maid that shall outshine
    her,

And carry her in my coach too—and that will
    kill her.
Go, get thy rents up, go!
    De Gard. (*Sarcastically*) You are a fine
gentleman!   (*Exit*)
    Mir. Now, have at my two youths! I'll
    see how they do;
How they behave themselves; and then I'll
    study
What wench shall love me next, and when
    I'll lose her.[15]   (*Exit*)

Scene II. *Room in the House of* Nantolet.

(*Enter* Pinac *and* Servant)

    Pin. Art thou her servant, sayest thou?
    Serv. Her poor creature;
But servant to her horse, sir.
    Pin. Canst thou show me
The way to her chamber, or where I may
    conveniently
See her, or come to talk to her?
    Serv. That I can, sir;
But the question is, whether I will or no.
    Pin. Why, I'll content thee.
                  (*Opening his purse*)
    Serv. Why, I'll content thee, then; now
you come to me.
    Pin. There's for your diligence.
                    (*Gives money*)
    Serv. (*Pointing to a door*) There's her
chamber, sir,
And this way she comes out; stand you but
    here, sir,
You have her at your prospect or your
    pleasure.
    Pin. (*Cautiously*) Is she not very angry?
    Serv. You'll find that quickly:
May be, she'll call you saucy, scurvy fellow,
Or some such familiar name; may be, she
    knows you,
And will fling a piss-pot at you, or a pantofle,[16]
According as you are in acquaintance. If she
    like you,
May be she'll look upon you; may be no;
And two months hence call for you.
    Pin. This is fine.
She is monstrous proud, then?
    Serv. She is a little haughty;

Of a small body, she has a mind well
    mounted.
Can you speak Greek?
    Pin. No, certain.
    Serv. Get you gone, then!—
And talk of stars, and firmaments, and fire-
    drakes?
Do you remember who was Adam's school-
    master,
And who taught Eve to spin? She knows
    all these,
And will run you over the beginning o' the
    world
As familiar as a fiddler.
Can you sit seven hours together, and say
    nothing?
Which she will do, and, when she speaks,
    speak oracles,
Speak things that no man understands—nor
    herself neither.
    Pin. Thou mak'st me wonder.
    Serv. Can you smile?
    Pin. Yes, willingly;
For naturally I bear a mirth about me.
    Serv. She'll ne'er endure you, then; she
    is never merry;
If she see one laugh, she'll swoon past *aqua
    vitæ.*
Never come near her, sir; if you chance to
    venture,
And talk not like a doctor, you are damned
    too.
I have told you enough for your crown, and
    so, good speed you!   (*Exit*)
    Pin. (*Worried*) I have a pretty task, if
    she be thus curious,
As, sure, it seems she is! If I fall off now,

---

[15] Get rid of her.   [16] Slipper.

I shall be laughed at fearfully; if I go for-
ward,
I can but be abused, and that I look for.
And yet I may hit right, but 'tis unlikely.
   (*Paces up and down*)
Stay: in what mood and figure shall I attempt
 her?
A careless way? No, no, that will not waken
 her;
Besides, her gravity will give me line still,
And let me lose myself; yet this way often
Has hit, and handsomely. A wanton method?
Ay, if she give it leave to sink into her con-
 sideration;
But there's the doubt: if it but stir her blood
 once,
And creep into the crannies of her fancy,
Set her a-gog—but, if she chance to slight
 it,
And by the power of her modesty fling it
 back,
I shall appear the arrant'st rascal to her,
The most licentious knave! for I shall talk
 lewdly.
To bear myself austerely? rate my words?
And fling a general gravity about me,
As if I meant to give laws? But this I cannot
 do.
This is a way above my understanding;
Or, if I could, 'tis odds she'll think I mock
 her;
For serious and sad things are ever still
 suspicious.
Well, I'll say something:
But learning I have none, and less good
 manners,
Especially for ladies. Well, I'll set my best
 face.
(*Agitated*) I hear some coming. This is the
 first woman
I ever feared yet, the first face that shakes me.
  (*Retires to a corner of the stage and hides
  behind a chair*)

(*Enter* LILLIA BIANCA *and* PETELLA)

LIL. (*Abandoning her cold, formal manner*) Give me my hat, Petella; take this
 veil off,
This sullen cloud; it darkens my delights.
Come, wench, be free, and let the music
 warble:—(*calling back through the
 door*)

Play me some lusty measure.
  (*Lively dance music within, to which
  presently* LILLIA *dances*)
PIN. (*Amazed*) This is she, sure,
The very same I saw, the very woman,
The gravity I wondered at. Stay, stay;
Let me be sure. (*He rubs his eyes*) Ne'er
 trust me, but she danceth!
Summer is in her face now, and she
 skippeth!
I'll go a little nearer.
  (*He steps cautiously from behind the
  furniture*)
LIL. (*Calling to the musicians*) Quicker
 time, fellows!
I cannot find my legs yet.—Now, Petella!

(*Enter* MIRABEL, *who stops just inside the
 door and stares*)

PIN. (*Aside*) I am amazed; I am foundered
 in my fancy!
MIR. (*Aside*) Ha! say you so? is this your
 gravity?
This the austerity you put upon you?
I'll see more o' this sport.
LIL. (*Calls*) A song now!

(*Enter a* SINGING-BOY)

Call in for a merry and a light song;
And sing it with a liberal spirit.
S. BOY. Yes, madam.
LIL. And be not amazed, sirrah, but take
 us for your own company.—(*The* BOY
 sings a song, bows, and exit)
(*To Petella*) Let's walk ourselves: come,
 wench: would we had a man or two!
PIN. (*Aside*) Sure, she has spied me, and
 will abuse me dreadfully:
She has put on this for the purpose: yet I
 will try her.—
  (*He walks timidly across the stage and
  speaks to* LILLIA)
Madam, I would be loth my rude intrusion,
Which I must crave a pardon for——
LIL. (*Heartily*) Oh, you are welcome,
You are very welcome, sir! we want such a
 one.
(*Calling to the musicians*) Strike up again!—
 I dare presume you dance well:
(*Seizes him*) Quick, quick, sir, quick! the
 time steals on.

Pin. I would talk with you.

Lil. Talk as you dance.

(*They dance violently,* Lillia *dragging* Pinac *along*)

Mir. (*Aside*) She'll beat him off his legs first.

This is the finest masque!

Lil. Now, how do you, sir?

Pin. (*Panting*) You have given me a shrewd heat.

Lil. I'll give you a hundred.

Come, sing now, sing: for I know you sing well;

I see you have a singing face.

Pin. (*Aside*) A fine modesty!

If I could, she'd never give me breath—

Madam, would

I might sit and recover!

Lil. Sit here, and sing now;

Let's do things quickly, sir, and hand-somely.—

Sit close, wench, close. (Lillia *and* Petella *crowd up close to the embarrassed* Pinac)—Begin, begin.

Pin. I am lessoned.

(Pinac *feebly sings a song*)

Lil. 'Tis very pretty, i' faith. (*shouting*)

Give me some wine now.

Pin. I would fain speak to you.

(*A servant brings them wine*)

Lil. You shall drink first, believe me.

Here's to you a lusty health.   (*They drink*)

Pin. I thank you, lady.—

(*aside*) Would I were off again! I smell my misery;

I was never put to this rack: I shall be drunk too.

Mir. (*Aside*) If thou be'st not a right one, I have lost mine aim much:

I thank Heaven that I have 'scaped thee. To her, Pinac!

For thou art as sure to have her, and to groan for her—

I'll see how my other youth does. This speeds trimly:

A fine grave gentlewoman, and worth much honor!   (*Exit*)

Lil. Now, how do you like me, sir?

Pin. (*Weakly*) I like you rarely.

Lil. (*Jumps up and strides about*) You see, sir, though sometimes we are grave and silent,

And put on sadder dispositions,

Yet we are compounded of free parts, and sometimes too

Our lighter, airy, and our fiery mettles

Break out, and show themselves: and what think you of that, sir?

Pin. Good lady, sit (for I am very weary),

And then I'll tell you.

Lil. Fie! a young man idle! (*Jerks him to his feet and drags him about the stage*)

Up, and walk; be still in action;

The motions of the body are fair beauties;

Besides, 'tis cold. 'Ods me, sir, let's walk faster!

What think you now of the Lady Felicia?

And Bellafronte, the duke's fair daughter? ha!

Are they not handsome things? There is Duarta,

And brown Olivia——

Pin. (*Miserably*) I know none of 'em.

Lil. But brown must not be cast away, sir. If young Lelia

Had kept herself till this day from a husband,

Why, what a beauty, sir! You know Ismena,

The fair gem of Saint-Germains?

Pin. By my troth, I do not.

Lil. And, then, I know, you must hear of Brisac,

How unlike a gentleman——

Pin. As I live, I have heard nothing.

Lil. (*Calls to musicians*) Strike me an-other galliard! [17]

Pin. By this light, I cannot!

(*Desperately*) In troth, I have sprained my leg, madam.

Lil. Now sit you down, sir,

And tell me why you came hither? why you chose me out?

What is your business? your errand? des-patch, despatch.

(*Peering at him*) May be, you are some gen-tleman's man, (and I mistook you,)

That have brought me a letter, or a haunch of venison,

Sent me from some friend of mine.

Pin. Do I look like a carrier?

You might allow me, what I am, a gentle-man.

Lil. Cry you mercy, sir! I saw you yester-day;

You are new-come out of travel; I mistook you:

[17] A lively dance.

And how do all our impudent friends in Italy?

PIN. Madam, I came with duty, and fair courtesy,

Service, and honor to you.

LIL. You came to jeer me.

You see I am merry, sir; I have changed my copy;

None of the sages now: and, pray you, proclaim it.

Fling on me what aspersion you shall please, sir,

Of wantonness or wildness; I look for it;

And tell the world I am an hypocrite,

Mask in a forced and borrowed shape; I expect it.

But not to have you believed: for, mark you, sir,

I have won a nobler estimation,

A stronger tie, by my discretion,

Upon opinion (howe'er you think I forced it)

Than either tongue or act of yours can slubber,

And, when I please, I will be what I please, sir,

So I exceed not mean; [18] and none shall brand it,

Either with scorn or shame, but shall be slighted.

PIN. (Overwhelmed) Lady, I come to love you.

LIL. Love yourself, sir;

And, when I want observers,[19] I'll send for you.

Heigh-ho! my fit's almost off; for we do all by fits, sir:

If you be weary, sit till I come again to you.

(She marches off, followed by PETELLA)

PIN. This is a wench of a dainty spirit; but

Hang me, if I know yet either what to think

Or make of her. She had her will of me,

And baited me abundantly, I thank her;

And, I confess, I never was so blurted,[20]

Nor never so abused: I must bear mine own sins.

You talk of travels; here's a curious country!

Yet I will find her out, or forswear my faculty.

(Exit)

SCENE III. *A Garden belonging to the House of NANTOLET, with a Summer-house in the back-ground.*

(*Enter ROSALURA and ORIANA followed by a maid*)

ROS. Ne'er vex yourself, nor grieve; you are a fool, then.

ORI. I am sure I am made so: yet, before I suffer

Thus like a girl, and give him leave to triumph——

ROS. You say right; for, as long as he perceives you

Sink under his proud scornings, he'll laugh at you.

For me, secure yourself; and, for my sister,

I partly know her mind too; howsoever,

To obey my father, we have made a tender

Of our poor beauties to the travelled monsieur;

Yet two words to a bargain. He slights us

As skittish things, and we shun him as curious.[21]

May be my free behavior turns his stomach,

And makes him seem to doubt a loose opinion: [22]

I must be so sometimes, though all the world saw it.

ORI. Why should not you? Are our minds only measured?

As long as here you stand secure——

ROS. You say true;

As long as mine own conscience makes no question,

What care I for report? That woman's miserable,

That's good or bad for their tongues' sake. Come, let's retire.

(*To the maid*) And get my veil, wench.

(*Exit maid*)

By my troth, your sorrow,

[18] Moderation.

[19] Admirers.

[20] Contemptuously treated.

[21] Fastidious.

[22] Suspect an unchaste reputation.

And the consideration of men's humorous
    maddings,
Have put me into a serious contemplation.
       (*The maid returns with her veil
          which* Rosalura *puts on*)
   Ori. Come, faith, let's sit and think.
   Ros. That's all my business.
       (*They go into the summer-house,
         and sit down*)

(Belleur *tiptoes in and peers fearfully
   about. He is followed by* Mirabel)

   Mir. Why stand'st thou peeping here?
(*Pushing him*) Thou great slug, forward!
   Bel. (*Whispering*) She is there; peace!
   Mir. Why stand'st thou here, then,
Sneaking and peeking as thou wouldst steal
    linen?
Hast thou not place and time?
   Bel. I had a rare speech
Studied, and almost ready; and your violence
Has beat it out of my brains.
   Mir. Hang your rare speeches!
Go me on like a man.
   Bel. (*Hanging back and smoothing his
    hair and beard*) Let me set my beard
    up.
How has Pinac performed?
   Mir. He has won already;
He stands not thrumming of caps thus.
   Bel. Lord, what should I ail!
What a cold I have over my stomach! would
    I had some hum! [23]
Certain I have a great mind to be at her,
A mighty mind.
   Mir. On, fool!
   Bel. Good words, I beseech you;
For I will not be abused by both.
   Mir. Adieu, then (*walking toward the
    door*)
(I will not trouble you; I see you are valiant);
And work your own way.
   Bel. Hist, hist! (*catching* Mirabel *and
    pulling him back*) I will be ruled;
I will, i' faith; I will go presently:
Will you forsake me now, and leave me i' the
    suds?
You know I am false-hearted this way. I be-
    seech you,
Good sweet Mirabel—(*suddenly threaten-
    ing*) I'll cut your throat, if you leave me,

[23] Very strong ale.

Indeed I will—(*pleading*) sweet-heart—
   Mir. (*Laughing at him*) I will be ready,
Still at thine elbow. Take a man's heart to
    thee,
And speak thy mind; the plainer still the
    better:
She is a woman of that free behavior,
Indeed, that common courtesy, she cannot
    deny thee;
Go bravely on.
   Bel. (*Calling timidly*) Madam—keep
    close about me,
Still at my back—Madam, sweet madam—
   Ros. Ha! (*Very lady-like*)
What noise is that? what saucy sound to
    trouble me?
   Mir. What said she?
   Bel. I am saucy.
       (Rosalura *and* Oriana *rise and
         come forward*)
   Mir. 'Tis the better.
   Bel. She comes; must I be saucy still?
   Mir. More saucy.
   Ros. (*With dignity*) Still troubled with
    these vanities? Heaven bless us!
What are we born to?—Would you speak
    with any of my people?
Go in, sir; I am busy.
   Bel. (*Amazed at her dignity*) This is not
    she, sure:
Is this two children at a birth? I'll be hanged,
    then:
Mine was a merry gentlewoman, talked
    daintily,
Talked of those matters that befitted
    women;
This is a parcel prayer-book. I'm served
    sweetly!
And now I am to look to; I was prepared for
    th' other way.
   Ros. Do you know that man?
   Ori. Sure, I have seen him, lady.
   Ros. (*Slowly looking Belleur up and
    down*) Methinks 'tis pity such a lusty
    fellow
Should wander up and down, and want em-
    ployment.
   Bel. She takes me for a rogue!—You may
    do well, madam,
To stay this wanderer, and set him a-work,
    forsooth;
He can do something that may please your
    ladyship:

I have heard of women that desire good
    breedings,
Two at a birth, or so.
    Ros. The fellow's impudent.
    Ori. Sure, he is crazed.
    Ros. I have heard of men too that have
    had good manners;
Sure, this is want of grace: indeed, 'tis great
    pity
The young man has been bred so ill; but this
    lewd age
Is full of such examples.
    Bel. I am foundered,
And some shall rue the setting of me on.
    Mir. (*Mocking* Rosalura) Ha! so book-
    ish, lady? is it possible?
Turned holy at the heart too? I'll be hanged
    then.
Why, this is such a feat, such an activity,
Such fast and loose! [24] a veil too for your
    knavery?
O *Dio, Dio!*
    Ros. What do you take me for, sir?
    Mir. An hypocrite, a wanton, a dissembler,
Howe'er you seem; and thus you are to be
    handled!—(*snatches her veil*)
Mark me, Belleur;—and this you love, I know
    it. (*Puts his arm around her*)
    Ros. Stand off, bold sir!
    Mir. You wear good clothes to this end,
Jewels; love feasts and masques.
    Ros. You are monstrous saucy.
    Mir. All this to draw on fools: and thus,
    thus, lady,   (*seizes and kisses her*)
You are to be lulled.
    Bel. (*Pulling* Mirabel *away from her*)
    Let her alone, I'll swinge you else,
I will, i' faith! for, though I cannot skill o'
    this matter
Myself, I will not see another do it before me,
And do it worse.
    Ros. Away! you are a vain thing:
You have travelled far, sir, to return again
A windy and poor bladder. You talk of
    women,
That are not worth the favor of a common
    one,
The grace of her grew in an hospital!
Against a thousand such blown fooleries
I am able to maintain good women's honors,
Their freedoms, and their fames, and I will
    do it—

[24] A cheating game.

Mir. (*Puzzled*) She has almost struck me
dumb too.
    Ros. And declaim
Against your base malicious tongues, your
    noises,
For they are nothing else. You teach be-
    haviors!
Or touch us for our freedoms! Teach your-
    selves manners,
Truth, and sobriety, and live so clearly
That our lives may shine in ye; and then task
    us.
It seems ye are hot; the suburbs will supply
    ye:
Good women scorn such gamesters.[25] So, I'll
    leave ye.
I am sorry to see this: faith, sir, live fairly.
             (*Exit with* Oriana)
    Mir. This woman, if she hold on, may be
    virtuous;
'Tis almost possible: we'll have a new day.
    Bel. You brought me on, you forced me
    to this foolery;
I am ashamed, I am scorned, I am flurted;
    yes, I am so.
Though I cannot talk to a woman like your
    worship,
And use my phrases and my learnèd figures,
Yet I can fight with any man.
    Mir. Fie!
    Bel. I can, sir;
And I will fight.
    Mir. With whom?
    Bel. With you; with any man;
For all men now will laugh at me.
    Mir. Prithee, be moderate.
    Bel. And I'll beat all men. Come.
    Mir. I love thee dearly.
    Bel. I will beat all that love; love has un-
    done me:
Never tell me; I will not be a history.
    Mir. Thou art not.
    Bel. 'Sfoot, I will not! Give me room,
And let me see the proudest of ye jeer me;
    (*advancing on* Mirabel)
And I'll begin with you first.
    Mir. (*Retreating*) Prithee, Belleur—
If I do not satisfy thee——
    Bel. Well, look you do.
But, now I think on't better, 'tis impossible:
I must beat somebody; I am mauled myself,

[25] Dissolute fellows.

And I ought in justice——

MIR. No, no, no; you are cozened:
But walk, and let me talk to thee.

BEL. Talk wisely,
And see that no man laugh, upon no occasion;
For I shall think then 'tis at me.

MIR. I warrant thee.

BEL. Nor no more talk of this.

MIR. Dost think I am maddish?

BEL. I must needs fight yet; for I find it concerns me:
A pox on't: I must fight.

MIR. I' faith, thou shalt not.

(*Exeunt*, MIRABEL *trying to soothe* BELLEUR)

Act III

SCENE I. *A Public Walk.*

(*Enter* DE GARD *and* LUGIER)

DE GARD. I know you are a scholar, and can do wonders.

LUG. There's no great scholarship belongs to this, sir;
What I am, I am. I pity your poor sister,
And heartily I hate these travellers,
These gim-cracks, made of mops and motions:
There's nothing in their houses here but hummings;
A bee has more brains. I grieve and vex too
The insolent licentious carriage
Of this out-facing fellow Mirabel;
And I am mad to see him prick his plumes up.

DE GARD. His wrongs you partly know.

LUG. Do not you stir, sir;
Since he has begun with wit, let wit revenge it:
Keep your sword close; we'll cut his throat a new way.
I am ashamed the gentlewoman should suffer
Such base lewd wrongs.

DE GARD. I will be ruled; he shall live,
And left to your revenge.

LUG. Ay, ay, I'll fit him:
He makes a common scorn of handsome women.
Modesty and good manners are his May-games;
He takes up maidenheads with a new commission,—
The church-warrant's out of date. Follow my counsel,
For I am zealous in the cause.

DE GARD. I will, sir.
And will be still directed; for the truth is,

My sword will make my sister seem more monstrous—
Besides, there is no honor won on reprobates.

LUG. You are i' the right. The slight he has showed my pupils
Sets me a-fire too. Go; I'll prepare your sister,
And as I told you——

DE GARD. Yes; all shall be fit, sir.

LUG. And seriously, and handsomely.

DE GARD. I warrant you.

LUG. A little counsel more.

(*He whispers to* DE GARD *at some length*)

DE GARD. 'Tis well.

LUG. Most stately:
See that observed; and then——

(*Whispers again*)

DE GARD. I have you every way.

LUG. Away, then, and be ready.

DE GARD. With all speed, sir.

LUG. We'll learn to travel too, may be, beyond him.

(*Exit* DE GARD)

(*Enter* LILLIA BIANCA, ROSALURA, *and* ORIANA)

LUG. Good day, fair beauties!

LIL. (*Ironically*) You have beautified us,
We thank you, sir; you have set us off most gallantly
With your grave precepts.

ROS. We expected husbands
Out of your documents and taught behaviors,
Excellent husbands; thought men would run stark mad on us,
Men of all ages and all states. We expected
An inundation of desires and offers,

A torrent of trim suitors; all we did,
Or said, or purposed, to be spells about us,
Spells to provoke.
    LIL. You have provoked us finely!
We followed your directions, we did rarely,
We were stately, coy, demure, careless, light,
    giddy,
And played at all points: this, you swore,
    would carry.
    ROS. We made love, and contemned love;
    now seemed holy,
With such a reverent put-on reservation
Which could not miss, according to your
    principles;
Now gave more hope again; now close, now
    public,
Still up and down we beat it like a billow;
And ever those behaviors you read to us,
Subtle and new: but all this will not help us.
    LIL. (*Almost tearfully*) They help to
    hinder us of all acquaintance,
They have frighted off all friends. What am
    I better
For all my learning, if I love a dunce,
A handsome dunce? To what use serves my
    reading?
You should have taught me what belongs to
    horses,
Dogs, dice, hawks, banquets, masques, free
    and fair meetings,
To have studied gowns and dressings.
    LUG. (*Looking from one to the other with
    amazement*) Ye are not mad, sure!
    ROS. We shall be, if we follow your en-
    couragements:
I'll take mine own way now.
    LIL. And I my fortune;
We may live maids else till the moon drop
    millstones.
I see, your modest women are taken for
    monsters;
A dowry of good breeding is worth nothing.
    LUG. Since ye take it so to th' heart, pray
    ye, give me leave yet,
And ye shall see how I'll convert this heretic:
Mark how this Mirabel——
    LIL. Name him no more;
For, though I long for a husband, I hate him,
And would be married sooner to a monkey,
Or to a Jack of Straw, than such a juggler.
    ROS. I am of that mind too: he is too
    nimble,

And plays at fast and loose too learnedly,
For a plain-meaning woman; that's the truth
    on't.
Here's one too, (*indicating* ORIANA) that we
    love well, would be angry;
And reason why. No, no, we will not trouble
    you,
Nor him at this time: may he make you
    happy!
We'll turn ourselves loose now to our fair
    fortunes;
And the downright way——
    LIL. The winning way we'll follow;
We'll bait that men may bite fair, and not be
    frighted.
Yet we'll not be carried so cheap neither; we'll
    have some sport,
Some mad-morris or other for our money,
    tutor.
    LUG. 'Tis like enough: prosper your own
    devices!
Ye are old enough to choose. But, for this
    gentlewoman,
So please her give me leave——
    ORI. I shall be glad, sir,
To find a friend whose pity may direct me.
    LUG. I'll do my best, and faithfully deal
    for you;
But then you must be ruled.
    ORI. In all, I vow to you.
    ROS. Do, do: he has a lucky hand some-
    times, I'll assure you,
And hunts the recovery of a lost lover deadly.
    LUG. You must away straight.
    ORI. Yes.
    LUG. And I'll instruct you:
Here you can know no more.
    ORI. By your leave, sweet ladies;
And all our fortunes arrive at our own wishes!
    LIL. Amen, amen!
    LUG. I must borrow your man.
    LIL. Pray, take him;
He is within: to do her good, take any thing,
Take us and all.
    LUG. No doubt, ye may find takers;
And so, we'll leave ye to your own disposes.
        (*Exeunt* LUGIER *and* ORIANA)
    LIL. Now, which way, wench?
    ROS. We'll go a brave way, fear not;
A safe and sure way too; and yet a by-way.
I must confess I have a great mind to be
    married.

LIL. So have I too a grudging [26] of good-
will that way,
And would as fain be despatched. But this
Monsieur Quicksilver——
Ros. No, no; we'll bar him, bye and main:
let him trample;
There is no safety in his surquedry: [27]
An army-royal of women are too few for him;
He keeps a journal of his gentleness,
And will go near to print his fair despatches,
And call it his "Triumph over time and
women:"
Let him pass out of memory! What think you
Of his two companions?
LIL. Pinac, methinks, is reasonable.
A little modesty he has brought home with
him,
And might be taught, in time, some hand-
some duty.
Ros. They say, he is a wencher too.
LIL. I like him better;
A free light touch or two becomes a gentle-
man,
And sets him seemly off: so he exceed not,
But keep his compass clear, he may be looked
at.
I would not marry a man that must be taught,
And conjured up with kisses; the best game
Is played still by the best gamesters.
Ros. (*Pretending to be shocked*) Fie upon
thee!
What talk hast thou!
LIL. Are not we alone, and merry?
Why should we be ashamed to speak what
we think? Thy gentleman,
The tall fat fellow, he that came to see
thee——
Ros. Is't not a goodly man?
LIL. (*Teasing her*) A wondrous goodly!
H'as weight enough, I warrant thee: mercy
upon me,
What a serpent wilt thou seem under such a
St. George.
Ros. Thou art a fool! give me a man brings
mettle,
Brings substance with him, needs no broths
to lare [28] him.
These little fellows shew like fleas in boxes,
Hop up and down, and keep a stir to vex us:

[26] Secret inclination.
[27] Conceit.
[28] To fatten.

Give me the puissant pike; take you the small
shot.
LIL. Of a great thing, I have not seen a
duller;
Therefore, methinks, sweet sister——
Ros. Peace, he's modest;
A bashfulness; which is a point of grace,
wench:
But, when these fellows come to molding,
sister,
To heat, and handling—As I live, I like him;
And, methinks, I could form him.
LIL. (*Seeing* MIRABEL *approach*) Peace;
the fire-drake.

(*Enter* MIRABEL)

MIR. Bless ye, sweet beauties, sweet in-
comparable ladies,
(*mocking them*) Sweet wits, sweet humors!
bless you, learnèd lady!
And you, most holy nun, bless your devo-
tions!
LIL. And bless your brains, sir, your most
pregnant brains, sir!
They are in travel; may they be delivered
Of a most hopeful wild-goose!
Ros. Bless your manhood!
They say you are a gentleman of action,
A fair accomplished man, and a rare engineer;
You have a trick to blow up maidenheads,
A subtle trick, they say abroad.
MIR. I have, lady.
Ros. And often glory in their ruins.
MIR. Yes, forsooth;
I have a speedy trick, please you to try it;
My engine will despatch you instantly.
Ros. (*Primly*) I would I were a woman,
sir, fit for you!
As there be such, no doubt, may engine you
too;
May, with a counter-mine, blow up your
valor.
But, in good faith, sir, we are both too honest;
And, the plague is, we cannot be persuaded;
For, look you, if we thought it were a glory
To be the last of all your lovely ladies——
MIR. Come, come, leave prating: this has
spoiled your market!
This pride and puft-up heart will make ye
fast, ladies,
Fast when ye are hungry too.
Ros. The more our pain, sir.

LIL. The more our health, I hope too.

MIR. Your behaviors
Have made men stand amazed; those men
  that loved ye,
Men of fair states[29] and parts. Your strange
  conversions
Into I know not what, nor how, nor where-
  fore;
Your scorns of those that came to visit ye;
Your studied whim-whams, and your fine set
  faces,
What have these got ye? Proud and harsh
  opinions.
A travelled monsieur was the strangest crea-
  ture,
The wildest monster to be wondered at;
His person made a public scoff, his knowl-
  edge
(As if he had been bred 'mongst bears or
  bandogs[30])
Shunned and avoided; his conversation
  snuffed at;—
What harvest brings all this?

ROS. (Suppressing her annoyance) I pray
  you, proceed, sir.

MIR. Now ye shall see in what esteem a
  traveller,
An understanding gentleman, and a mon-
  sieur,
Is to be held; and, to your griefs, confess it,
Both to your griefs and galls.

LIL. In what, I pray you, sir?
We would be glad to understand your excellence.

MIR. Go on, sweet ladies; it becomes ye
  rarely!
For me, I have blest me from ye; scoff on
  seriously;
And note the man ye mocked. You, Lady
  Learning,
Note the poor traveller that came to visit you,
That flat unfurnished fellow; note him
  throughly;
You may chance to see him anon.

LIL. 'Tis very likely.

MIR. And see him courted by a travelled
  lady,
Held dear and honored by a virtuous virgin;
May be, a beauty not far short of yours
  neither;

[29] Estates.
[30] Dogs kept chained up to increase their
fierceness.

It may be, clearer.

LIL. Not unlikely.

MIR. Younger: (pauses to let this shot
  take effect)
As killing eyes as yours, a wit as poignant;
May be, a state to that may top your fortune.
Inquire how she thinks of him, how she holds
  him;
His good parts, in what precious price al-
  ready;
Being a stranger to him, how she courts him;
A stranger to his nation too, how she dotes
  on him.
Inquire of this; be sick to know. Curse, lady,
And keep your chamber; cry, and curse! A
  sweet one,
A thousand in yearly land, well bred, well
  friended,
Travelled, and highly followed for her
  fashions.

LIL. (Pretending indifference) Bless his
good fortune, sir!

MIR. This scurvy fellow,
I think they call his name Pinac, this serving-
  man
That brought you venison, as I take it,
  madam,
Note but this scab: 'tis strange that this coarse
  creature,
That has no more set-off but his jugglings,
His travelled tricks——

LIL. Good sir, I grieve not at him,
Nor envy not his fortune. Yet I wonder:
He's handsome; yet I see no such perfection.

MIR. Would I had his fortune! for 'tis a
  woman
Of that sweet-tempered nature, and that
  judgment,
Besides her state, that care, clear understanding,
And such a wife to bless him——

ROS. Pray you, whence is she?

MIR. Of England, and a most accom-
  plished lady;
So modest that men's eyes are frighted at her,
And such a noble carriage—

(Enter a BOY)

How now, sirrah?

BOY. Sir, the great English lady——

MIR. What of her, sir?

BOY. Has newly left her coach, and coming this way,

Where you may see her plain: Monsieur
  Pinac
The only man that leads her.
  MIR. He is much honored;
Would I had such a favor!

(*Exit* BOY)

(*Enter* MARIANA, *elaborately dressed and
followed by Attendants and* PINAC. MARIANA
*is presumably unable to speak or understand
the language, and only bows and smiles in
the ensuing scene*)

Now vex, ladies,
Envy, and vex, and rail!
  Ros. You are short of us, sir.
  MIR. Bless your fair fortune, sir!
  PIN. I nobly thank you.
  MIR. Is she married, friend?
  PIN. No, no.
  MIR. A goodly lady;
A sweet and delicate aspéct!—Mark, mark,
  and wonder!—
Hast thou any hope of her?
  PIN. A little.
  MIR. Follow close, then;
Lose not that hope.
              (MARIANA *curtsies to* MIRABEL)
  PIN. To you, sir.
  MIR. Gentle lady!
  Ros. (*To* LILLIA, *uneasily*) She is fair,
indeed.
  LIL. I have seen a fairer; yet
She is well.
  Ros. Her clothes sit handsome too.
  LIL. She dresses prettily.
  Ros. And, by my faith, she is rich; she
  looks still sweeter:
A well-bred woman, I warrant her.
  LIL. (*To* PINAC) Do you hear, sir?
May I crave this gentlewoman's name?
  PIN. Mariana, lady.
  LIL. (*Hesitant but desperate*) I will not
  say I owe you a quarrel, monsieur,
For making me your stale: [31] a noble gentle-
  man
Would have had more courtesy, at least more
  faith,
Than to turn off his mistress at first trial.
You know not what respect I might have
  showed you;
I find you have worth.

[31] Stalking-horse.

  PIN. I cannot stay to answer you;
You see my charge. I am beholding to you
For all your merry tricks you put upon me,
Your bobs,[32] and base accounts. I came to love
  you,
To woo you, and to serve you; I am much
  indebted to you
For dancing me off my legs, and then for
  walking me;
For telling me strange tales I never heard of,
More to abuse me; for mistaking me,
When you both knew I was a gentleman,
And one deserved as rich a match as you are.
  LIL. Be not so bitter, sir.
  PIN. You see this lady:
She is young enough and fair enough to
  please me;
A woman of a loving mind, a quiet,
And one that weighs the worth of him that
  loves her.
I am content with this, and bless my fortune:
Your curious wits, and beauties——
  LIL. Faith, see me once more.
  PIN. I dare not trouble you.
  LIL. May I speak to your lady?
  PIN. I pray you, content yourself. I know
  you are bitter,
And, in your bitterness, you may abuse her;
Which if she comes to know (for she under-
  stands you not),
It may breed such a quarrel to your kindred,
And such an indiscretion fling on you too
(For she is nobly friended)——
  LIL. (*Aside, with suppressed rage*) I could
eat her.
  PIN. Rest as you are, a modest noble
  gentlewoman,
And afford your honest neighbors some of
  your prayers.
              (*Exeunt* PINAC, MARIANA, *and
              Attendants*)
  MIR. (*Taunting them*) What think you
now?
  LIL. (*Controlling herself and pretending
  indifference*) Faith, she's a pretty whit-
  ing;
She has got a pretty catch too.
  MIR. You are angry,
Monstrous angry now, grievously angry;
And the pretty heart does swell now.
  LIL. No, in troth, sir.

[32] Sneers.

MIR. And it will cry anon, "A pox upon
    it!"
And it will curse itself, and eat no meat,
    lady;
And it will sigh.
    LIL. Indeed, you are mistaken;
It will be very merry.
    Ros. Why, sir, do you think
There are no more men living, nor no hand-
    somer,
Than he or you? By this light, there be ten
    thousand,
Ten thousand thousand! Comfort yourself,
    dear monsieur;
Faces, and bodies, wits, and all abiliments [33]—
There are so many we regard 'em not.
    MIR. That such a noble lady—(*shouting
    with laughter*) I could burst now!—
So far above such trifles——

(*Enter* BELLEUR *driving before him two*
GENTLEMEN *who are trying to mollify him*)

    BEL. You did laugh at me;
And I know why ye laughed.
    1ST GENT. (*Terrified*) I pray you, be sat-
isfied:
If we did laugh, we had some private reason,
And not at you.
    2ND GENT. Alas, we know you not, sir!
    BEL. (*Threatening them*) I'll make you
    know me. Set your faces soberly;
Stand this way, and look sad; I'll be no May-
    game. (*The* GENTLEMEN *try to look
    mournful*)
Sadder! Demurer yet.
    Ros. What is the matter?
What ails this gentleman?
    BEL. Go off now backward, that I may
    behold ye.
And not a simper, on your lives!
        (*Exeunt* GENTLEMEN, *walking back-
        wards and trying to look sad*)
    LIL. He's mad, sure.
    BEL. (*Advancing on* MIRABEL) Do you
observe me too?
    MIR. I may look on you.
    BEL. Why do you grin? I know your mind.
    MIR. You do not.
You are strangely humorous: is there no
    mirth nor pleasure

[33] Accomplishments.

But you must be the object?
    BEL. Mark, and observe me. Wherever I
    am named,
The very word shall raise a general sadness,
For the disgrace this scurvy woman did me,
This proud pert thing. (*Threatening again*)
    Take heed you laugh not at me,
Provoke me not; take heed.
    Ros. I would fain please you;
Do any thing to keep you quiet.   •
    BEL. Hear me.
Till I receive a satisfaction
Equal to the disgrace and scorn you gave
    me,
You are a wretched woman; till thou woo'st
    me,
And I scorn thee as much, as seriously
Jeer and abuse thee; ask what gill [34] thou art,
Or any baser name; I will proclaim thee,
I will so sing thy virtue, so be-paint thee——
    Ros. Nay, good sir, be more modest.
    BEL. Do you laugh again?—
Because you are a woman, you are lawless,
And out of compass of an honest anger.
    Ros. (*Pleading*) Good sir, have a better
belief of me.
    LIL. Away, dear sister!
            (*She flees with* ROSALURA)
    MIR. (*Laughing and clapping* BELLEUR
    on the back) Is not this better now, this
    seeming madness,
Than falling out with your friends?
    BEL. Have I not frighted her?
    MIR. Into her right wits, I warrant thee:
    follow this humor,
And thou shalt see how prosperously 'twill
    guide thee.
    BEL. I am glad I have found a way to woo
    yet. I was afraid once
I never should have made a civil suitor.
Well, I'll about it still.
    MIR. Do, do, and prosper.
                (*Exit* BELLEUR)
What sport do I make with these fools! what
    pleasure
Feeds me, and fats my sides at their poor
    innocence!
Wooing and wiving—hang it! give me mirth,
Witty and dainty mirth! I shall grow in love,
    sure,
With mine own happy head.

[34] A wanton wench.

(*Enter* LUGIER, *disguised as a well dressed*
Italian gentleman)

(*Aside*) Who's this?—(*As* LUGIER *approach-*
es him) To me, sir?—
(*Aside*) What youth is this?
  LUG. Yes, sir, I would speak with you,
If your name be Monsieur Mirabel.
  MIR. You have hit it:
Your business, I beseech you?
  LUG. This it is, sir;
There is a gentlewoman hath long time af-
fected you,
And loved you dearly.
  MIR. Turn over, and end that story;
'Tis long enough. I have no faith in women,
sir.
  LUG. It seems so, sir. I do not come to woo
for her,
Or sing her praises, though she well deserve
'em.
I come to tell you, you have been cruel to her,
Unkind and cruel, false of faith, and careless;
Taking more pleasure in abusing her,
Wresting her honor to your wild disposes,
Than noble in requiting her affection:
Which, as you are a man, I must desire you
(A gentleman of rank) not to persist in,
No more to load her fair name with your
injuries.
  MIR. Why, I beseech you, sir?
  LUG. Good sir, I'll tell you.
And I'll be short; I'll tell you because I love
you,
Because I would have you shun the shame
may follow.
There is a nobleman, new come to town, sir,
A noble and a great man, that affects her,
(A countryman of mine, a brave Savoyan,
Nephew to the duke) and so much honors
her,
That 'twill be dangerous to pursue your old
way,
To touch at any thing concerns her honor,
Believe, most dangerous. Her name is Oriana,
And this great man will marry her. Take
heed, sir;
For howsoe'er her brother, a staid gentleman,
Lets things pass upon better hopes, this lord,
sir,
Is of that fiery and that poignant metal,
(Especially provoked on by affection)
That 'twill be hard—but you are wise.

  MIR. (*Impressed*) A lord, sir?
  LUG. Yes, and a noble lord.
  MIR. Send her good fortune!
This will not stir her lord. A Baroness!
(*Musing*) Say you so? say you so? By'r lady,
a brave title!
Top and top-gallant now! save her great lady-
ship!
I was a poor servant of hers, I must confess,
sir,
And in those days I thought I might be jovy,[35]
And make a little bold to call in to her;
But, *basta;*[36] now I know my rules and dis-
tance.
Yet, if she want an usher, such an implement,
One that is throughly paced, a clean-made
gentleman,
Can hold a hanging up with approbation,
Plant his hat formally, and wait with pa-
tience,
I do beseech you, sir——
  LUG. Sir, leave your scoffing,
And, as you are a gentleman, deal fairly:
I have given you a friend's counsel. So, I'll
leave you.
  MIR. But, hark you, hark you, sir; is't
possible
I may believe what you say?
  LUG. You may choose, sir.
  MIR. No baits? no fish-hooks, sir? no gins?
no nooses?
No pitfalls to catch puppies?
  LUG. I tell you certain:
You may believe; if not, stand to the danger!
                                    (*Exit*)
  MIR. A lord of Savoy, says he? the duke's
nephew?
A man so mighty? by lady, a fair marriage!
By my faith, a handsome fortune! I must
leave prating:
For, to confess the truth, I have abused her,
For which I should be sorry, but that will
seem scurvy.
I must confess she was, ever since I knew her,
As modest as she was fair. I am sure she loved
me;
Her means good, and her breeding excellent;
And for my sake she has refused fair matches:
I may play the fool finely.—Stay: who are
these?

[35] Jovial.
[36] *Ital.* Enough.

(*Enter* DE GARD, *disguised as an Italian nobleman, with* ORIANA, *elaborately dressed. They are followed by Attendants*)

MIR. (*Aside*) 'Tis she, I am sure; and that the lord, it should seem;
He carries a fair port, is a handsome man too.
(*Ruefully*) I do begin to feel I am a coxcomb.
ORI. Good my lord, choose a nobler; for I know
I am so far below your rank and honor,
That what you can say this way I must credit
But spoken to beget yourself sport. Alas, sir,
I am so far off from deserving you,
My beauty so unfit for your affection,
That I am grown the scorn of common railers,
Of such injurious things that, when they cannot
Reach at my person, lie with my reputation!
I am poor, besides.
DE GARD. You are all wealth and goodness;
And none but such as are the scum of men,
The ulcers of an honest state, spite-weavers,
That live on poison only, like swoln spiders,
Dare once profane such excellence, such sweetness.
MIR. (*Aside*) This man speaks loud indeed.
DE GARD. Name but the men, lady;
Let me but know these poor and base depravers,
Lay but to my revenge their persons open,
And you shall see how suddenly, how fully,
For your most beauteous sake, how direfully,
I'll handle their despites. (*Looking indignantly at* MIRABEL) Is this thing one?
Be what he will——
MIR. Sir?
DE GARD. Dare your malicious tongue, sir——
MIR. I know you not, nor what you mean.
ORI. Good my lord——
DE GARD. If he, or any he——
ORI. I beseech your honor—
This gentleman's a stranger to my knowledge;
And, no doubt, sir, a worthy man.
DE GARD. Your mercy!—
But, had he been a tainter of your honor,
A blaster of those beauties reign within you—
But we shall find a fitter time. Dear lady,

As soon as I have freed you from your guardian,
And done some honored offices unto you,
I'll take you with those faults the world flings on you,
And dearer than the whole world I'll esteem you!
(*Exit with* ORIANA *and Attendants*)
MIR. This is a thundering lord: I am glad I 'scaped him.
How lovingly the wench disclaimed my villany!
I am vexed now heartily that he shall have her;
Nor that I care to marry, or to lose her,
But that this bilbo-lord [37] shall reap that maidenhead
That was my due; that he shall rig and top her:
I'd give a thousand crowns now, he might miss her.

(*Enter* LILLIA BIANCA's SERVANT, *rubbing his shoulder and grumbling*)

SERV. Nay, if I bear your blows, and keep your counsel,
(*To* MIRABEL) You have good luck, sir
(*Aside*) I teach you to strike lighter.
MIR. Come hither, honest fellow: canst thou tell me
Where this great lord lies? this Savoy lord?
Thou met'st him;
He now went by thee, certain.
SERV. Yes, he did, sir. (*Speaking confidentially*)
I know him, and I know you are fooled.
MIR. Come hither: (*gives him money*)
Here's all this, give me truth.
SERV. Not for your money,
(And yet that may do much) but I have been beaten,
And by the worshipful contrivers beaten, and I'll tell you:
This is no lord, no Savoy lord.
MIR. (*Delighted*) Go forward.
SERV. This is a trick, and put upon you grossly
By one Lugier. The lord is Monsieur De Gard, sir,
An honest gentleman, and a neighbor here:

[37] A blustering or swaggering lord.

Their ends you understand better than I,
sure.

MIR. Now I know him; know him now
plain.

SERV. I have discharged my colors; so,
God b' wi' you, sir!   (*Exit*)

MIR. What a purblind puppy was I! Now
I remember him;

All the whole cast on's face, though it were
umbered,

And masked with patches. What a dunder-
whelp,

To let him domineer thus! how he strutted,

And what a load of lord he clapt upon him!

Would I had him here again! I would so
bounce him,

I would so thank his lordship for his lewd
plot!

Do they think to carry it away, with a great
band made of bird-pots,

And a pair of pin-buttocked breeches?—(*Seeing them approach off stage*) Ha! 'tis
he again!

(MIRABEL *sings*)

He comes, he comes, he comes! have at him!

(*Re-enter* DE GARD, ORIANA, *and
Attendants*)

(*Elaborately deferential*) *My Savoy lord,
why dost thou frown on me?*

And will that favor never sweeter be?
Wilt thou, I say, for ever play the fool?
(*Laughing at him*) *De Gard, be wise, and,
Savoy, go to school!*
*My lord De Gard, I thank you for your
antic;*
*My lady bright, that will be sometimes
frantic;*
You worthy train, that wait upon this pair,
*Send you more wit, and them a bouncing
bair!* [38]

And so I take my humble leave of your
honors!   (*Exit*)

DE GARD. (*Sadly*) We are discovered;
there's no remedy.

Lillia Bianca's man, upon my life,

In stubbornness, because Lugier corrected
him—

A shameless slave! plague on him for a rascal!

ORI. (*In despair*) I was in a perfect hope.
The bane on't is now,

He will make mirth on mirth, to persecute us.

DE GARD. We must be patient: I am
vexed to the proof too.

I'll try once more; then, if I fail, here's one
speaks.

                    (*Puts his hand on his sword*)

ORI. Let me be lost and scorned first!

DE GARD. Well, we'll consider.

Away, and let me shift; I shall be hooted
else.   (*Exeunt*)

Act IV

SCENE I. *A Street before the Lodging of* PINAC.

(*Enter* LUGIER, LILLIA BIANCA, *and her
SERVANT, carrying a willow garland*)

LUG. Faint not, but do as I direct you:
trust me;

Believe me too; for what I have told you,
lady,

As true as you are Lillia, is authentic.

I know it, I have found it: 'tis a poor courage

Flies off for one repulse. These travellers

Shall find, before we have done, a homespun wit,

A plain French understanding, may cope
with 'em.

They have had the better yet, (*with a with-
ering look at the SERVANT*) thank your
sweet squire here!

And let 'em brag. You would be revenged?

LIL. Yes, surely.

LUG. And married too.

LIL. I think so.

LUG. Then be counselled;

You know how to proceed. I have other irons

Heating as well as yours, and I will strike

Three blows with one stone home. Be ruled,
and happy.

And so, I leave you: now is the time.

LIL. I am ready,

[38] Bairn.

If he do come to dor [39] me. (*Exit* Lugier)
  Serv. Will you stand here,
And let the people think you are God knows
  what, mistress?
Let boys and prentices presume upon you?
  Lil. Prithee, hold thy peace.
  Serv. Stand at his door that hates you?
  Lil. Prithee, leave prating.
  Serv. Pray you, go to the tavern: I'll give
  you a pint of wine there.
If any of the mad-cap gentlemen should come
  by,
That take up women upon special warrant,
You were in a wise case now.
  Lil. Give me the garland;
And wait you here.
(*Takes the garland from* Servant, *who goes
to a far corner of the stage and waits*)

(*Enter* Mirabel, Pinac, Mariana, Priest,
and Attendants)

  Mir. (*He sees* Lillia *with her mourning
garland and turns gleefully to* Pinac)
  She is here to seek thee, sirrah:
I told thee what would follow; she is mad
  for thee:
Show, and advance.—(*To* Lillia) So early
  stirring, lady?
It shows a busy mind, a fancy troubled:
A willow garland too? is't possible?
'Tis pity so much beauty should lie musty;
But 'tis not to be helped now.
  Lil. (*Mournfully*) The more's my mis-
  ery.—
(*To* Mariana) Good fortune to you,
  lady! you deserve it;
To me, too-late repentance! I have sought it.
I do not envy, though I grieve a little,
You are mistress of that happiness, those joys,
That might have been, had I been wise—
  but fortune—
  Pin. She understands you not; pray you,
  do not trouble her:
And do not cross me like a hare thus; 'tis as
  ominous.
  Lil. I come not to upbraid your levity
(Though you made show of love, and though
  I liked you),
To claim an interest (we are yet both
  strangers;

[39] Mock.

But what we might have been, had you per-
  sèvered, sir!)
To be an eye-sore to your loving lady:
This garland shows I give myself forsaken
(Yet, she must pardon me, 'tis most un-
  willingly;)
And all the power and interest I had in you
(As, I persuade myself, somewhat you loved
  me)
Thus patiently I render up, I offer
To her that must enjoy you, and so bless you.
Only, I heartily desire this courtesy,
And would not be denied, to wait upon you
This day, to see you tied, then no more
  trouble you.
  Pin. It needs not, lady.
  Lil. Good sir, grant me so much.
  Pin. 'Tis private, and we make no invi-
tation.
  Lil. My presence, sir, shall not proclaim
it public.
  Pin. May be, 'tis not in town.
  Lil. I have a coach, sir,
And a most ready will to do you service.
  Mir. (*Aside to* Pinac) Strike now or
  never; make it sure: I tell thee,
She will hang herself, if she have thee not.
  Pin. (*Aloud to* Mirabel) Pray you, sir,
Entertain my noble mistress. Only a word
  or two
With this importunate woman, and I'll re-
  lieve you.—
(*To* Lillia) Now you see what your flings
  are, and your fancies,
Your states, and your wild stubbornness; now
  you find
What 'tis to gird and kick at men's fair
  services,
To raise your pride to such a pitch and glory
That goodness shows like gnats, scorned
  under you.
'Tis ugly, naught! A self-will in a woman,
Chained to an overweening thought, is
  pestilent,
Murders fair fortune first, then fair opinion. [40]
(*Indicating* Mariana) There stands a pat-
  tern, a true patient pattern,
Humble and sweet.
  Lil. I can but grieve my ignorance.
Repentance, some say too, is the best sacri-
  fice;
[40] Reputation.

For, sure, sir, if my chance had been so
    happy
(As I confess I was mine own destroyer)
As to have arrived at you, I will not prophesy,
But certain, as I think, I should have pleased
    you;
Have made you as much wonder at my
    courtesy,
My love, and duty, as I have disheartened
    you.
(*Sighing*) Some hours we have of youth,
    and some of folly;
And being free-born maids, we take a liberty,
And, to maintain that, sometimes we strain
    highly.
    PIN. Now you talk reason.
    LIL. But, being yoked and governed,
Married, and those light vanities purged
    from us,
How fair we grow! How gentle, and how
    tender,
We twine about those loves that shoot up
    with us!
A sullen woman fear, that talks not to you;
She has a sad and darkened soul, loves dully:
A merry and a free wench, give her liberty,
Believe her, in the lightest form she appears
    to you,
Believe her excellent, though she despise
    you;
Let but these fits and flashes pass, she will
    show to you
As jewels rubbed from dust, or gold new
    burnished.
Such had I been, had you believed.
    PIN. Is't possible?
    LIL. And to your happiness, I dare assure
    you,
If true love be accounted so: your pleasure,
Your will, and your command, had tied my
    motions.
But that hope's gone. I know you are young
    and giddy,
And, till you have a wife can govern with
    you,
You sail upon this world's sea light and
    empty,
Your bark in danger daily. 'Tis not the name
    neither
Of wife can steer you, but the noble nature,
The diligence, the care, the love, the
    patience:

She makes the pilot, and preserves the hus-
    band,
That knows and reckons every rib he is built
    on.
But this I tell you, to my shame.
    PIN. I admire you;
And now am sorry that I aim beyond you.
    MIR. (*Aside to* PINAC) So, so, so: fair and
    softly! she is thine own, boy;
She comes now without lure.
    PIN. But that it must needs
Be reckoned to me as a wantonness,
Or worse, a madness, to forsake a blessing,
A blessing of that hope——
    LIL. I dare not urge you;
And yet, dear sir——
    PIN. 'Tis most certain, I had rather,
If 'twere in mine own choice—for you are
    my country-woman,
A neighbor here, born by me; she a stranger,
And who knows how her friends——
    LIL. Do as you please, sir;
If you be fast, not all the world—(*sadly*) I
    love you.
It is most true, and clear I would persuade
    you;
And I shall love you still.
    PIN. (*Eagerly*) Go, get before me—
So much you have won upon me—do it
    presently:
Here's a priest ready—I'll have you.
    LIL. (*Her manner changes completely and
    she taunts him*) Not now, sir;
No, you shall pardon me. Advance your lady;
I dare not hinder your most high preferment:
'Tis honor enough for me I have unmasked
    you.
    PIN. How's that?
    LIL. (*Triumphantly*) I have caught you,
    sir! Alas, I am no states-woman,
Nor no great traveller! yet I have found you:
I have found your lady too, (*scornfully*)
    your beauteous lady!
I have found her birth and breeding too, her
    discipline,
Who brought her over, and who kept your
    lady,
And, when he laid her by, what virtuous
    nunnery
Received her in. I have found all these.
    (*Laughing at them*) Are you blank
    now?

Methinks, such travelled wisdoms should not
  fool thus,—
Such excellent indiscretions!
  MIR. (*Surprised and annoyed*) How could
she know this?
  LIL. 'Tis true she is English-born; but
  most part French now,
And so I hope you will find her to your com-
  fort.
Alas, I am ignorant of what she cost you!
The price of these hired clothes I do not
  know, gentlemen!
Those jewels are the broker's, how you stand
  bound for 'em!
  PIN. Will you make this good?
  LIL. Yes, yes; and to her face, sir,
That she is an English whore, a kind of
  fling-dust,
One of your London light-o'-loves, a right
  one;
Came over in thin pumps and half a petti-
  coat,
One faith, and one smock, with a broken
  haberdasher.
I know all this without a conjurer:
Her name is Jumping Joan, an ancient sin-
  weaver;
She was first a lady's chambermaid, there
  slipped,
And broke her leg above the knee; departed,
And set up shop herself; stood the fierce con-
  flicts
Of many a furious term; there lost her colors,
And last shipped over hither.
  MIR. We are betrayed!
  LIL. Do you come to fright me with this
  mystery?

To stir me with a stink none can endure,
  sir?
I pray you, proceed; the wedding will be-
  come you.
Who gives the lady? (*To* MIRABEL) You? an
  excellent father!
A careful man, and one that knows a beauty!
Send you fair shipping, sir! and so, I'll leave
  you:
Be wise and manly; then I may chance to
  love you!
(*She laughs at them and trips off the stage
  followed by her grinning* SERVANT)
  MIR. As I live, I am ashamed this wench
  has reached me,
Monstrous ashamed; but there's no remedy.
This skewed-eyed carrion——
  PIN. This I suspected ever.—
(*Harshly to* MARIANA) Come, come, uncase;
  we have no more use of you;
Your clothes must back again.
  MARI. (*Abandoning her elegant airs*) Sir,
  you shall pardon me;
'Tis not our English use to be degraded.
If you will visit me, and take your venture,
You shall have pleasure for your properties:
And so, sweetheart——
(*She laughs mockingly at them and exit*)
  MIR. (*As* PINAC *starts angrily after her*)
  Let her go, and the devil go with her!
We have never better luck with these pre-
  ludiums.
Come, be not daunted; think she is but a
  woman,
And, let her have the devil's wit, we'll reach
  her!   (*Exeunt*)

SCENE II. *A Public Walk.*

(*Enter* ROSALURA *and* LUGIER)

  ROS. You have now redeemed my good
  opinion, tutor,
And you stand fair again.
  LUG. I can but labor,
And sweat in your affairs. I am sure Belleur
Will be here instantly, and use his anger,
His wonted harshness.
  ROS. I hope he will not beat me.
  LUG. No, sure, he has more manners. Be
you ready.

  ROS. Yes, yes, I am; and am resolved to fit
  him,
With patience to outdo all he can offer.
But how does Oriana?
  LUG. Worse and worse still;
There is a sad house for her; she is now,
Poor lady, utterly distracted.
  ROS. Pity,
Infinite pity! 'tis a handsome lady.
That Mirabel's a beast, worse than a mon-
  ster,
If this affliction work not.

(*Enter* Lillia Bianca *gaily*)

Lil. Are you ready?
Belleur is coming on here, hard behind me:
I have no leisure to relate my fortune;
Only I wish you may come off as handsomely.
Upon the sign, you know what.
    Ros. Well, well; leave me.
    (*Exeunt* Lillia Bianca *and* Lugier *at
    one door as* Belleur *enters at another*)
    Bel. How now?
    Ros. (*Curtsying demurely to him*) You
are welcome, sir.
    Bel. 'Tis well you have manners.
That court'sy again, (*She curtsies obedient-
ly*) and hold your countenance staidly.
That look's too light; take heed: (*She looks
more demure*) so. Sit you down now;
And, to confirm me that your gall is gone,
Your bitterness dispersed, (for so I'll have
it)
Look on me steadfastly, and, whatsoe'er I say
to you,
Move not, nor alter in your face; you are
gone, then;
For, if you do express the least distaste,
Or show an angry wrinkle, (mark me,
woman!
We are now alone,) I will so conjure thee,
The third part of my execution
Cannot be spoke.
    Ros. I am at your dispose, sir. (*In what
follows she dutifully accepts his every
suggestion*)
    Bel. Now rise, and woo me a little; let me
hear that faculty:
But touch me not; nor do not lie, I charge
you.
Begin now.
    Ros. If so mean and poor a beauty
May ever hope the grace——
    Bel. You cog,[41] you flatter;
Like a lewd thing, you lie: "May hope that
grace!"
Why, what grace canst thou hope for?
Answer not;
For, if thou dost, and liest again, I'll swinge
thee.
Do not I know thee for a pestilent woman?
A proud at both ends? Be not angry,
Nor stir not, o' your life.
    Ros. I am counselled, sir.
    [41] Cheat, cajole.

    Bel. Art thou not now (confess, for I'll
have the truth out)
As much unworthy of a man of merit,
Or any of ye all, nay, of mere man,
Though he were crooked, cold, all wants
upon him,
Nay, of any dishonest thing that bears that
figure,
As devils are of mercy?
    Ros. We are unworthy.
    Bel. Stick to that truth, and it may chance
to save thee.
And is it not our bounty that we take ye?
That we are troubled, vexed, or tortured
with ye,
Our mere and special bounty?
    Ros. Yes.
    Bel. Our pity,
That for your wickedness we swinge ye
soundly;
Your stubbornness and stout hearts, we be-
labor ye?
Answer to that!
    Ros. I do confess your pity.
    Bel. And dost not thou deserve in thine
own person,
Thou impudent, thou pert (*She suppresses a
giggle*)—Do not change countenance.
    Ros. I dare not, sir.
    Bel. For, if you do——
    Ros. I am settled.
    Bel. Thou wagtail, peacock, puppy, look
on me:
I am a gentleman.
    Ros. It seems no less, sir.
    Bel. And dar'st thou in thy sur-
quedry [42]——
    Ros. I beseech you!—
It was my weakness, sir, I did not view you,
I took not notice of your noble parts,
Nor called your person nor your fashion
proper.
    Bel. This is some amends yet.
    Ros. I shall mend, sir, daily,
And study to deserve.
    Bel. Come a little nearer:
Canst thou repent thy villany?
    Ros. Most seriously.
    Bel. And be ashamed?
    Ros. I am ashamed.
    Bel. Cry.
    Ros. It will be hard to do, sir.
    [42] Presumption.

BEL. Cry now instantly;
Cry monstrously, that all the town may hear
thee.
Cry seriously, as if thou hadst lost thy
monkey;
And, as I like thy tears——
Ros. (*Unable to restrain her laughter any
longer, she calls out*) Now!
BEL. How! how! do you jeer me?
Have you broke your bounds again, dame?

(*Enter* LILLIA BIANCA, *with four* WOMEN,
laughing. They dance about BELLEUR)

Ros. Yes, and laugh at you,
And laugh most heartily.
BEL. What are these? whirlwinds?
Is hell broke loose, and all the Furies flut-
tered?
Am I greased once again?
Ros. Yes, indeed are you;
And once again you shall be, if you quarrel.
Do you come to vent your fury on a virgin?
Is this your manhood, sir?
1ST WOM. Let him do his best;
Let's see the utmost of his indignation;
I long to see him angry.—Come, proceed,
sir.—   (*The women draw knives*)
Hang him, he dares not stir; a man of timber!
2ND WOM. Come hither to fright maids
with thy bull-faces!
To threaten gentlewomen! Thou a man! a
Maypole,
A great dry pudding.
3RD WOM. Come, come, do your worst,
sir;
Be angry, if thou dar'st.
BEL. The Lord deliver me!
4TH WOM. Do but look scurvily upon this
lady,
Or give us one foul word!—We are all mis-
taken;
This is some mighty dairy-maid in man's
clothes.
LIL. I am of that mind too.
BEL. (*Aside*) What will they do to me?
LIL. And hired to come and abuse us:—
a man has manners;
A gentleman, civility and breeding:—
Some tinker's trull, with a beard glued on.
1ST WOM. Let's search him,
And, as we find him——
BEL. Let me but depart from ye,

Sweet Christian women!
LIL. Hear the thing speak, neighbors.
BEL. 'Tis but a small request: if e'er I
trouble ye,
If e'er I talk again of beating women,
Or beating any thing that can but turn to me;
Of ever thinking of a handsome lady
But virtuously and well; of ever speaking
But to her honor,—this I'll promise ye,
I will take rhubarb, and purge choler[43]
mainly,
Abundantly I'll purge.
LIL. I'll send you broths, sir.
BEL. I will be laughed at, and endure it
patiently;
I will do any thing.
Ros. I'll be your bail, then.
When you come next to woo, pray you, come
not boisterously,
And furnished like a bear-ward.
BEL. No, in truth, forsooth.
Ros. I scented you long since.
BEL. I was to blame, sure:
I will appear a gentleman.
Ros. 'Tis the best for you,
For a true noble gentleman's a brave thing.
Upon that hope, we quit you. (*Threatening
him*) You fear seriously?
BEL. Yes, truly do I; I confess I fear you,
And honor you, and any thing.
Ros. Farewell, then.
WOM. And, when you come to woo next,
bring more mercy.
          (*Exeunt all except* BELLEUR)
BEL. A dairy-maid! a tinker's trull! Heaven
bless me!
Sure, if I had provoked 'em, they had quar-
tered me.

(*Enter the two* GENTLEMEN *whom* BEL-
LEUR *bullied in III,* 1)

I am a most ridiculous ass, now I perceive it;
A coward, and a knave too.
1ST GENT. 'Tis the mad gentleman;
Let's set our faces right.
BEL. No, no; laugh at me,
And laugh aloud.
2ND GENT. (*Terrified*) We are better
mannered, sir.

[43] Bile, the supposed cause of anger and other
passions.

BEL. I do deserve it; call me patch and puppy,
And beat me, if you please.
1ST GENT. No, indeed; we know you.
BEL. (*Roaring at them*) 'Death, do as I would have ye!
2ND GENT. You are an ass, then,
A coxcomb, and a calf!
BEL. I am a great calf.

Kick me a little now: why, when? (*They kick him*) Sufficient.
Now laugh aloud, and scorn me. So good b' wi' ye!
And ever, when ye meet me, laugh.
GENTLEMEN. We will, sir.
(*Exeunt on one side, the two* GENTLE-MEN; *on the other,* BELLEUR)

SCENE III. *A Room in the House of* LA CASTRE.

(*Enter* NANTOLET, LA CASTRE, DE GARD, *and* LUGIER, *all upbraiding* MIRABEL)

MIR. Your patience, gentlemen; why do ye bait me?
NANT. Is't not a shame you are so stubborn-hearted,
So stony and so dull, to such a lady,
Of her perfections and her misery?
LUG. Does she not love you? does not her distraction
For your sake only, her most pitied lunacy
Of all but you, show ye? does it not compel you?
MIR. Soft and fair, gentlemen; pray ye, proceed temperately.
LUG. If you have any feeling, any sense in you,
The least touch of a noble heart——
LA CAST. Let him alone:
It is his glory that he can kill beauty.—
You bear my stamp, but not my tenderness;
Your wild unsavory courses let [44] that in you!
For shame, be sorry, though you cannot cure her;
Show something of a man, of a fair nature.
MIR. Ye make me mad!
DE GARD. Let me pronounce this to you;
You take a strange felicity in slighting
And wronging women, which my poor sister feels now;
Heaven's hand be gentle on her! Mark me, sir;
That very hour she dies (there's small hope otherwise),
That minute, you and I must grapple for it;
Either your life or mine.
MIR. Be not so hot, sir;

I am not to be wrought on by these policies,
In truth, I am not; nor do I fear the tricks,
Or the high-sounding threats, of a Savoyan.
I glory not in cruelty, (ye wrong me,)
Nor grow up watered with the tears of women.
This let me tell ye, howsoe'er I show to ye,
Wild, as ye please to call it, or self-willed,
When I see cause, I can both do and suffer,
Freely and feelingly, as a true gentleman.

(*Enter* ROSALURA *and* LILLIA BIANÇA *weeping*)

Ros. Oh, pity, pity! thousand, thousand pities!
LIL. Alas, poor soul, she will die! she is grown senseless;
She will not know nor speak now.
Ros. Die for love!
And love of such a youth! I would die for a dog first:
He that kills me, I'll give him leave to eat me;
I'll know men better, ere I sigh for any of 'em.
LIL. You have done a worthy act, sir, a most famous;
You have killed a maid the wrong way; you are a conqueror.
Ros. A conqueror! a cobbler! hang him, sowter! [45]
Go hide thyself, for shame! go lose thy memory!
Live not 'mongst men; thou art a beast, a monster,
A blatant beast!
LIL. If you have yet any honesty,
Or ever heard of any, take my counsel;

[44] *I.e.* Suppress.

[45] Cobbler.

Off with your garters, and seek out a bough,—
A handsome bough, for I would have you
    hang like a gentleman;
And write some doleful matter to the world,
A warning to hard-hearted men.

MIR. Out, kittlings!
What caterwauling's here! what gibing!
Do you think my heart is softened with a
    black santis? [46]
Show me some reason.

ROS. Here then, here is a reason. (*She
pulls aside the curtains of the inner stage
to reveal* ORIANA *lying on a couch, apparently demented*)

NANT. Now, if you be a man, let this sight
shake you!

LA CAST. Alas, poor gentlewoman!—Do
you know me, lady?

LUG. How she looks up, and stares!

ORI. I know you very well;
You are my godfather: and that's the mon-
    sieur.

DE GARD. And who am I?

ORI. You are Amadis de Gaul, sir.—
Oh, oh, my heart!—Were you never in love,
    sweet lady?
And do you never dream of flowers and
    gardens?
I dream of walking fires: take heed; it comes
    now.
(*Pointing at* MIRABEL) Who's that? Pray,
    stand away. I have seen that face,
    sure.—
How light my head is!

ROS. Take some rest.

ORI. I cannot;
For I must be up to-morrow to go to church,
And I must dress me, put my new gown on,
And be as fine to meet my love! Heigh-ho!
Will not you tell me where my love lies
    buried?

MIR. (*Feebly*) He is not dead.—(*Aside*)
Beshrew my heart, she stirs me!

ORI. He is dead to me.

MIR. (*Aside*) Is't possible my nature
Should be so damnable to let her suffer?—
(*To* ORIANA) Give me your hand.

ORI. How soft you feel, how gentle!
I'll tell you your fortune, friend.

MIR. How she stares on me!

[46] A black mass, performed with howling and
beating on pans.

ORI. You have a flattering face, but 'tis
    a fine one;
I warrant you may have a hundred sweet-
    hearts.
Will you pray for me? I shall die to-morrow;
And will you ring the bells?

MIR. I am most unworthy,
I do confess, unhappy. Do you know me?

ORI. I would I did!

MIR. Oh, fair tears, how ye take me!

ORI. Do you weep too? you have not lost
    your lover?
You mock me: I'll go home and pray.

MIR. Pray you, pardon me;
Or, if it please you to consider justly,
Scorn me, for I deserve it; scorn and shame
    me,
Sweet Oriana!

LIL. Let her alone; she trembles:
Her fits will grow more strong, if you provoke
    her.

LA CAST. Certain she knows you not, yet
    loves to see you.
How she smiles now!

(*Enter* BELLEUR)

BEL. Where are you? Oh, why do not you
    laugh? come, laugh at me:
Why a devil art thou sad, and such a subject,
Such a ridiculous subject, as I am,
Before thy face?

MIR. (*Solemnly*) Prithee, put off this
    lightness;
This is no time for mirth, nor place; I have
    used too much on't:
I have undone myself and a sweet lady,
By being too indulgent to my foolery,
Which truly I repent. Look here.

BEL. What ails she?

MIR. Alas, she is mad!

BEL. Mad!

MIR. Yes, too sure; for me too.

BEL. Dost thou wonder at that? by this
    good light, they are all so;
They are cozening-mad, they are brawling-
    mad, they are proud-mad;
They are all, all mad: I came from a world
    of mad women,
Mad as March hares: get 'em in chains, then
    deal with 'em.
(*Pointing to* ROSALURA) There's one that's
    mad; she seems well, but she is dog-
    mad.

(*Looking at* ORIANA) Is she dead, dost think?
  MIR. Dead! Heaven forbid!
  BEL. Heaven further it!
For, till they be key-cold dead, there's no
  trusting of 'em:
Whate'er they seem, or howsoe'er they carry
  it,
Till they be chap-faln, and their tongues at
  peace,
Nailed in their coffins sure: I'll ne'er believe
  'em.
Shall I talk with her?
  MIR. No, dear friend, be quiet,
And be at peace a while.
  BEL. I'll walk aside,
And come again anon. But take heed to her:
You say she is a woman?
  MIR. Yes.
  BEL. Take great heed;
For, if she do not cozen thee, then hang me:
Let her be mad, or what she will, she'll cheat
  thee!
  MIR. Away, wild fool!   (*Exit* BELLEUR)
How vile this shows in him now!—
Now take my faith, (before ye all I speak
  it,)
And with it my repentant love.
  LA CAST. This seems well.
  MIR. Were but this lady clear again, whose
  sorrows
My very heart melts for, were she but per-
  fect,
(For thus to marry her would be two
  miseries,)
Before the richest and the noblest beauty,
France or the world could show me, I would
  take her:
As she is now, my tears and prayers shall
  wed her.
  DE GARD. This makes some small amends.
    (ORIANA *beckons to* MIRABEL *and*
    motions the others to leave)
  Ros. She beckons to you;
To us, too, to go off.
  NANT. Let's draw aside all.
(*Exeunt all except* ORIANA *and* MIRABEL)
  ORI. Oh, my best friend! I would fain——
  MIR. What! (*aside, suspiciously*) she
  speaks well,
And with another voice.
  ORI. (*Hesitantly*) But I am fearful,
And shame a little stops my tongue——
  MIR. Speak boldly.

  ORI. Tell you, I am well. I am perfect well
  (pray you, mock not)
And that I did this to provoke your nature;
Out of my infinite and restless love,
To win your pity. Pardon me!
  MIR. Go forward:
Who set you on?
  ORI. None, as I live, no creature;
Not any knew or ever dreamed what I meant.
Will you be mine?
  MIR. 'Tis true, I pity you;
But, when I marry you, you must be wiser.
(*With rising indignation*) Nothing but
  tricks? devices?
  ORI. Will you shame me?
  MIR. Yes, marry, will I.—(*Calling out*)
  Come near, come near! a miracle!
The woman's well; she was only mad for
  marriage,
Stark mad to be stoned to death: give her
  good counsel.—
Will this world never mend?—Are you
  caught, damsel?

(*Re-enter* BELLEUR, NANTOLET, LA CASTRE,
  DE GARD, LUGIER, ROSALURA, *and* LILLIA
    BIANCA)

  BEL. How goes it now?
  MIR. Thou art a kind of prophet;
The woman's well again, and would have
  gulled me;
Well, excellent well, and not a taint upon
  her.
  BEL. Did not I tell you? let 'em be what
  can be,
Saints, devils, any thing, they will abuse us.
Thou wert an ass to believe her so long, a
  coxcomb:
Give 'em a minute, they'll abuse whole mil-
  lions.
  MIR. And am not I a rare physician, gentle-
  men,
That can cure desperate mad minds?
  DE GARD. Be not insolent.
  MIR. Well, go thy ways: from this hour
  I disclaim thee,
Unless thou hast a trick above this; then I'll
  love thee.
You owe me for your cure.—(*Pretending*
  solicitude) Pray, have a care of her,
For fear she fall into relapse.—Come, Bel-
  leur;
We'll set up bills to cure diseasèd virgins.

Bel. Shall we be merry?

Mir. Yes.

Bel. But I'll no more projects:
If we could make 'em mad, it were some
mastery.

(*Exeunt* Mirabel *and* Belleur)

Lil. I am glad she is well again.

Ros. So am I, certain.—
Be not ashamed.

Ori. (*Hiding her face*) I shall never see
a man more.

De Gard. Come, you are a fool: had you
but told me this trick,

He should not have gloried thus.

Lug. He shall not long, neither.

La Cast. Be ruled, and be at peace. You
have my consent,
And what power I can work with.

Nant. Come, leave blushing;
We are your friends; an honest way com-
pelled you;
Heaven will not see so true a love unrecom-
pensed.
Come in, and slight him too.

Lug. The next shall hit him. (*Exeunt*)

Act V

Scene I. *A Street, before the House of* La Castre.

(*Enter* De Gard *and* Lugier)

De Gard. (*Shaking his head*) 'Twill be
discovered.

Lug. That's the worst can happen:
If there be any way to reach, and work upon
him,
Upon his nature suddenly, and catch him—
That he loves,
Though he dissemble it, and would show
contrary,
And will at length relent, I'll lay my fortune;
Nay, more, my life.

De Gard. Is she won?

Lug. Yes, and ready,
And my designments set.

De Gard. They are now for travel;
All for that game again; they have forgot
wooing.

Lug. Let 'em; we'll travel with 'em.

De Gard. Where's his father?

Lug. Within; he knows my mind too, and
allows it,
Pities your sister's fortune most sincerely,

And has appointed, for our more assistance,
Some of his secret friends.

De Gard. Speed the plough!

Lug. Well said!
And be you serious too.

De Gard. I shall be diligent.

Lug. Let's break the ice for one, the rest
will drink too
(Believe me, sir) of the same cup. My young
gentlewomen
Wait but who sets the game a-foot. Though
they seem stubborn,
Reserved, and proud now, yet I know their
hearts,
Their pulses how they beat, and for what
cause, sir,
And how they long to venture their abilities
In a true quarrel; husbands they must and
will have,
Or nunneries and thin collations
To cool their bloods. Let's all about our busi-
ness;
And, if this fail, let nature work.

De Gard. You have armed me. (*Exeunt*)

Scene II. *A Public Walk.*

(*Enter* La Castre, *protesting to his son*
Mirabel. *They are followed by* Nantolet)

La Cast. Will you be wilful, then?

Mir. Pray, sir, your pardon;
For I must travel. Lie lazy here,

Bound to a wife! Chained to her subleties,
Her humors, and her wills, which are mere
fetters!
To have her to-day pleased, to-morrow
peevish,
The third day mad, the fourth rebellious!

You see before they are married, what moris-
coes,[47]

What masques and mummeries they put
upon us:

To be tied here, and suffer their lavoltas![48]

NANT. 'Tis your own seeking.

MIR. Yes, to get my freedom.
Were they as I could wish 'em——

LA CAST. Fools and meacocks,[49]

To endure what you think fit to put upon
'em.

Come, change your mind.

MIR. Not before I have changed air,
father.

When I know women worthy of my company,

I will return again, and wait upon 'em.

Till then, dear sir, I'll amble all the world
over,

And run all hazards, misery, and poverty,

So I escape the dangerous bay of matrimony.

(*Enter* PINAC *and* BELLEUR)

PIN. Are you resolved?

MIR. Yes, certain; I will out again.

PIN. We are for you, sir; we are your servants once more:

Once more we'll seek our fortune in strange
countries;

Ours is too scornful for us.

BEL. Is there ne'er a land

That you have read or heard of (for I care
not how far it be,

Nor under what pestiferous star it lies),

A happy kingdom, where there are no
women?

Nor have been ever? nor no mention

Of any such lewd things with lewder qualities?

For thither would I travel; where 'tis felony

To confess he had a mother; a mistress, treason.

LA CAST. Are you for travel too?

BEL. For any thing,

For living in the moon, and stopping hedges,

Ere I stay here to be abused and baffled.

NANT. Why did ye not break your minds
to me? They are my daughters;

And, sure, I think I should have that command over 'em,

To see 'em well bestowed. I know ye are
gentlemen,

Men of fair parts and states;[50] I know your
parents:

And, had ye told me of your fair affections—

Make but one trial more, and let me second
ye.

BEL. No; I'll make hob-nails first, and
mend old kettles.

Can you lend me an armor of high proof, to
appear in,

And two or three field-pieces to defend me?

The king's guard are mere pigmies.

NANT. They will not eat you.

BEL. Yes, and you too, and twenty fatter
monsieurs,

If their high stomachs hold. They came with
chopping-knives,

To cut me into rands and sirloins, and so
powder me.—

Come, shall we go?

NANT. You cannot be so discourteous,

If ye intend to go, as not to visit 'em,

And take your leaves.

MIR. That we dare do, and civilly,

And thank 'em too.

PIN. Yes, sir, we know that honesty.

BEL. I'll come i' the rear, forty foot off,
I'll assure you,

With a good gun in my hand. I'll no more
Amazons,

I mean, no more of their frights: I'll make
my three legs,[51]

Kiss my hand twice, and, if I smell no danger,

If the interview be clear, may be I'll speak
to her.

I'll wear a privy coat too, and behind me,

To make those parts secure, a bandog.

LA CAST. You are a merry gentleman.

BEL. A wary gentleman, I do assure you;

I have been warned; and must be armed.

LA CAST. Well, son,

These are your hasty thoughts. When I see
you are bent to it,

Then I'll believe, and join with you: so,
we'll leave you.—

(*Aside*) There's a trick will make you stay.

NANT. (*Aside*) I hope so.

(*Exeunt* LA CASTRE *and* NANTOLET)

MIR. We have won immortal fame now,
if we leave 'em.

---

[47] Morris-dances.   [48] Bounding waltzes.   [49] Cowardly creatures.   [50] Estates.   [51] Bows.

PIN. You have; but we have lost.

MIR. Pinac, thou art cozened:
I know they love ye; and to gain ye handsomely,
Not to be thought to yield, they would give
 millions.
Their father's willingness, that must needs
 show ye.

PIN. If I thought so——

MIR. You shall be hanged, you recreant!
Would you turn renegado now?

BEL. No; let's away, boys,
Out of the air and tumult of their villanies.
Though I were married to that grasshopper,
And had her fast by the legs, I should think
 she would cozen me.

(*Enter a* YOUNG MAN, *disguised as a Factor*)

Y. MAN. Monsieur Mirabel, I take it?

MIR. You're i' the right, sir.

Y. MAN. I am come to seek you, sir; I have
 been at your father's,
And, understanding you were here——

MIR. You are welcome.
May I crave your name?

Y. MAN. Fosse, sir, and your servant.
That you may know me better, I am factor
To your old merchant, Leverdure.

MIR. How does he?

Y. MAN. Well, sir, I hope; he is now at
 Orleans,
About some business.

MIR. You are once more welcome.
Your master's a right honest man, and one
I am much beholding to, and must very
 shortly
Trouble his love again.

Y. MAN. You may be bold, sir.

MIR. Your business, if you please now?

Y. MAN. This, it is, sir.
I know you well remember in your travel
A Genoa merchant——

MIR. I remember many.

Y. MAN. But this man, sir, particularly;
 your own benefit
Must needs imprint him in you; one Alberto,
A gentleman you saved from being murdered
A little from Bologna.
I was then myself in Italy, and supplied you;
Though happily you have forgot me now.

MIR. No, I remember you,
And that Alberto too; a noble gentleman:

More to remember were to thank myself, sir.
What of that gentleman?

Y. MAN. He is dead.

MIR. I am sorry.

Y. MAN. But on his death-bed, leaving to
 his sister
All that he had, beside some certain jewels,
Which, with a ceremony, he bequeathed to
 you,
In grateful memory, he commanded strictly
His sister, as she loved him and his peace,
To see those jewels safe and true delivered,
And, with them, his last love. She, as tender
 to
Observe his will, not trusting friend nor
 servant
With such a weight, is come herself to Paris,
And at my master's house.

MIR. You tell me a wonder.

Y. MAN. I tell you a truth, sir. She is young
 and handsome,
And well attended; of much state and riches;
So loving and obedient to her brother,
That, on my conscience, if he had given her
 also,
She would most willingly have made her
 tender.

MIR. May not I see her?

Y. MAN. She desires it heartily.

MIR. And presently?

Y. MAN. She is now about some business,
Passing accounts of some few debts here
 owing,
And buying jewels of a merchant.

MIR. Is she wealthy?

Y. MAN. I would you had her, sir, at all
 adventure!
Her brother had a main state.

MIR. And fair too?

Y. MAN. The prime of all those parts of
 Italy,
For beauty and for courtesy.

MIR. I must needs see her.

Y. MAN. 'Tis all her business, sir. You may
 now see her;
But to-morrow will be fitter for your visita-
 tion,
For she is not yet prepared.

MIR. Only her sight, sir:
And, when you shall think fit, for further
 visit.

Y. MAN. Sir, you may see her, and I'll wait
your coming.

Mir. And I'll be with you instantly;—I
know the house;—
Meantime, my love and thanks, sir.
Y. Man. Your poor servant.   (*Exit*)
Pin. Thou hast the strangest luck! what
was that Alberto?
Mir. An honest noble merchant, 'twas my
chance
To rescue from some rogues had almost slain
him.
And he in kindness to remember this!
Bel. Now we shall have you
For all your protestations and your forward-
ness,
Find out strange fortunes in this lady's eyes,
And new enticements to put off your journey;
And who shall have honor then?
Mir. No, no, never fear it:
I must needs see her to receive my legacy.
Bel. If it be tied up in her smock, Heaven
help thee!
May not we see too?
Mir. Yes, afore we go:
I must be known myself, ere I be able
To make thee welcome. Wouldst thou see
more women?
I thought you had been out of love with all.

Bel. I may be
(I find that), with the least encouragement;
Yet I desire to see whether all countries
Are naturally possessed with the same spirits,
For, if they be, I'll take a monastery,
And never travel: for I had rather be a
friar,
And live mewed up, than be a fool, and
flouted.
Mir. Well, well, I'll meet ye anon, then
tell you more, boys.
However, stand prepared, prest [52] for our
journey;
For certain we shall go, I think, when I have
seen her,
And viewed her well.
Pin. Go, go, and we'll wait for you;
Your fortune directs ours.
Bel. You shall find us i' the tavern,
Lamenting in sack and sugar for our losses.
If she be right Italian, and want servants, [53]
You may prefer the properest man. How I
could
Worry a woman now!
Pin. Come, come, leave prating:
You may have enough to do, without this
boasting.   (*Exeunt*)

Scene III. *A Room in the House of* Nantolet.

(*Enter* Lugier, De Gard, Rosalura, *and*
Lillia Bianca)

Lug. This is the last adventure.
De Gard. And the happiest,
As we hope, too.
Ros. (*Wearily*) We should be glad to find
it.
Lil. Who shall conduct us thither?
Lug. Your man is ready,
For I must not be seen; no, nor this gentle-
man;
That may beget suspicion; all the rest
Are people of no doubt. I would have ye,
ladies,
Keep your old liberties, and as we instruct ye.
Come, look not pale; you shall not lose your
wishes,
Nor beg 'em neither; but be yourselves and
happy.
Ros. I tell you true, I cannot hold off
longer,

Nor give no more hard language.
De Gard. You shall not need.
Ros. I love the gentleman, and must now
show it:
Shall I beat a proper man out of heart?
Lug. There's none advises you.
Lil. Faith, I repent me too.
Lug. Repent, and spoil all;
Tell what you know, you had best!
Lil. I'll tell what I think;
For, if he ask me now, if I can love him,
I'll tell him, yes, I can. The man's a kind man,
And out of his true honesty affects me:
Although he played the fool, which I re-
quited,
Must I still hold him at the staff's end?
Lug. You are two strange women.
Ros. We may be, if we fool still.
Lug. Dare ye believe me?
Follow but this advice I have set you in now,

[52] Ready.   [53] Lovers.

And if ye lose—Would ye yield now so
    basely?
Give up without your honors saved?
  De Gard. Fie, ladies!
Preserve your freedom still.
    Lil. Well, well, for this time.
    Lug. And carry that full state—
    Ros. That's as the wind stands;

If it begin to chop about, and scant us,
Hang me, but I know what I'll do! Come,
    direct us;
I make no doubt we shall do handsomely.
    De Gard. Some part o' the way we'll wait
    upon ye, ladies;
The rest your man supplies.
    Lug. Do well, I'll honor ye.   (Exeunt)

Scene IV. A Room in a neighboring House, with a Gallery.

(Enter on the upper stage Oriana in a gorgeous costume and elaborately made up as an Italian lady. With her are two persons disguised as Merchants. They are examining jewels and appear to converse. Enter, below, the Young Man disguised as a Factor, and Mirabel)

Y. Man. Look you, sir, there she is; you see
    how busy.
Methinks you are infinitely bound to her for
    her journey.
    Mir. How gloriously she shows! she is a
tall woman.
    Y. Man. Of a fair size, sir. My master not
being at home,
I have been so out of my wits to get her company!
I mean, sir, of her own fair sex and fashion—
    Mir. Afar off, she is most fair too.
    Y. Man. Near, most excellent—
At length, I have entreated two fair ladies
(And happily you know 'em), the young
    daughters
Of Monsieur Nantolet.
    Mir. I know 'em well, sir.
What are those? Jewels?
    Y. Man. All.
    Mir. They make a rich show.
    Y. Man. There is a matter of ten thousand
    pounds too
Was owing here. You see those merchants
    with her;
They have brought it in now.
    Mir. How handsomely her shape shows!
    Y. Man. Those are still neat; your Italians
    are most curious.
Now she looks this way.
    Mir. She has a goodly presence;
How full of courtesy!—Well, sir, I'll leave
you;

And, if I may be bold to bring a friend or two,
Good noble gentlemen——
    Y. Man. No doubt, you may, sir;
For you have most command.
    Mir. I have seen a wonder!   (Exit)
    Ori. (Peering down and calling) Is he
gone?
    Y. Man. Yes.
    Ori. How?
    Y. Man. Taken to the utmost:
A wonder dwells about him.
    Ori. He did not guess at me?
    Y. Man. No, be secure; you show another
    woman.
He is gone to fetch his friends.
    Ori. Where are the gentlewomen?
    Y. Man. Here, here: now they are come,
Sit still, and let them see you.

(Enter, below, Rosalura, Lillia Bianca,
and Servant)

    Ros. Pray you, where's my friend, sir?
    Y. Man. She is within, ladies; but here's
    another gentlewoman,
A stranger to this town: so please you visit
    her,
'Twill be well taken.
    Lil. Where is she?
    Y. Man. There, above, ladies.
    Serv. (Astonished at Oriana's exotic costume) Bless me, what thing is this?
Two pinnacles
Upon her pate! Is't not a glade to catch woodcocks?
    Ros. Peace, you rude knave!
    Serv. What a bouncing bum she has too!
There's sail enough for a carrack.[54]
    Ros. What is this lady?

[54] A large ship of burden.

For, as I live, she is a goodly woman.

Y. MAN. Guess, guess.

LIL. I have not seen a nobler presence.

SERV. 'Tis a lusty wench; now could I
spend my forty-pence,
With all my heart, to have but one fling at
her,
To give her but one swashing blow.

LIL. You rascal!

SERV. Ay, that's all a man has for's good
will: 'twill be long enough
Before you cry, "Come, Anthony, and kiss
me."

LIL. I'll have you whipt.

Ros. Has my friend seen this lady?

Y. MAN. Yes, yes, and is well known to
her.

Ros. I much admire her presence.

LIL. So do I too;
For, I protest, she is the handsomest,
The rarest, and the newest to mine eye,
That ever I saw yet.

Ros. I long to know her;
My friend shall do that kindness.

ORI. (*Laughing and calling down*) So she
shall, ladies:

Come, pray ye, come up.

Ros. Oh me!

LIL. Hang me, if I knew her!—
Were I a man myself, I should now love
you;
Nay, I should dote.

Ros. I dare not trust mine eyes;
For, as I live, you are the strangest
altered!
I must come up to know the truth.

SERV. So must I, lady:
For I'm a kind of unbeliever too.

LIL. Get you gone, sirrah;
And what you have seen be secret in; you are
paid else!
No more of your long tongue.

Y. MAN. Will ye go in, ladies,
And talk with her? These venturers will
come straight.
Away with this fellow!

LIL. (*Giving* SERVANT *money*) There, sirrah; go, disport you.

SERV. I would the trunk-hosed woman
would go with me.

(*Exeunt, the ladies at one door, the
men at another*)

SCENE V. *The Street, before the same House.*

(*Enter* MIRABEL, PINAC, *and* BELLEUR)

PIN. Is she so glorious handsome?

MIR. You would wonder;
Our women look like gipsies, like gills [55] to
her;
Their clothes and fashions beggarly, and
bankrupt,
Base, old, and scurvy.

BEL. How looks her face?

MIR. Most heavenly;
And the becoming motion of her body
So sets her off!

BEL. Why then, we shall stay.

MIR. Pardon me,
That's more than I know; if she be that
woman
She appears to be–

BEL. As 'tis impossible.

MIR. I shall then tell ye more.

PIN. Did you speak to her?

[55] Sluts.

MIR. No, no, I only saw her; she was
busy.
Now I go for that end; and mark her, gentle-
men,
If she appear not to ye one of the sweetest,
The handsomest, the fairest in behavior!
We shall meet the two wenches there too;
they come to visit her,
To wonder, as we do.

PIN. Then we shall meet 'em.

BEL. I had rather meet two bears.

MIR. There you may take your leaves,
despatch that business,
And, as ye find their humors——

PIN. Is your love there too?

MIR. No, certain; she has no great heart
to set out again.
This is the house; I'll usher ye.

BEL. I'll bless me,
And take a good-heart, if I can.

MIR. Come, nobly.

(*Exeunt into the house*)

Scene VI. *A Room in the same House.*

(Enter the Young Man *disguised as a Factor,* Rosalura, Lillia Bianca, *and* Oriana *disguised as before)*

Y. Man. They are come in. Sit you two off, as strangers.—(Lillia Bianca *and* Rosalura *seat themselves at the far side of the stage)*
(Seating Oriana*)* There, lady.—Where's the boy?

(Enter Boy)

Be ready, sirrah,
And clear your pipes.—The music now; they
    enter.   *(Music within)*

(Enter Mirabel, Pinac, *and* Belleur*)*

Pin. *(Impressed)* What a state she keeps!
    How far off they sit from her!
How rich she is! Ay, marry, this shows
    bravely!
Bel. She is a lusty wench, and may allure
    a good man;
But, if she have a tongue, I'll not give two-
    pence for her.
There sits my Fury; how I shake to see her!
Y. Man. Madam, this is the gentleman.
Mir. *(He kisses* Oriana *in the customary formal greeting)* How sweet she kisses!
She has a spring dwells on her lips, a para-
    dise!
This is the legacy.

(Song by the Boy, while he presents a jewel casket to Mirabel*)*

> *From the honored dead I bring*
> *Thus his love and last offering.*
> *Take it nobly, 'tis your due,*
> *From a friendship ever true;*
> *From a faith, &c.*

Ori. *(Speaking with an Italian accent)*
    Most noble sir,
This from my now-dead brother, as his love,
And grateful memory of your great benefit;
From me my thanks, my wishes, and my
    service.

Till I am more acquainted, I am silent;
Only I dare say this,—you are truly noble.
Mir. What should I think?
Pin. Think you have a handsome fortune:
Would I had such another!
Ros. Ye are well met, gentlemen;
We hear ye are for travel.
Pin. You hear true, lady;
And come to take our leaves.
Lil. We'll along with ye:
We see you are grown so witty by your
    journey,
We cannot choose but step out too. This lady
We mean to wait upon as far as Italy.
Bel. *(Aside)* I'll travel into Wales,
    amongst the mountains,
In hope they cannot find me.
Ros. If you go further,
So good and free society we hold ye,
We'll jog along too.
Pin. Are you so valiant, lady?
Lil. And we'll be merry, sir, and laugh.
Pin. It may be
We'll go by sea.
Lil. Why, 'tis the only voyage:
I love a sea-voyage, and a blustering tempest;
(Imitating a sailor) And let all split!
Pin. *(Aside)* This is a dainty damosel!—
I think 'twill tame you. Can you ride post?
Lil. Oh, excellently! I am never weary
    that way:
A hundred mile a-day is nothing with me.
Bel. I'll travel under ground. Do you
    hear, sweet lady?
I find it will be dangerous for a woman.
Ros. No danger, sir, I warrant; I love to
be under.
Bel. I see she will abuse me all the world
    over.—
But say we pass through Germany, and drink
    hard?
Ros. We'll learn to drink, and swagger too.
Bel. *(Aside)* She'll beat me!—
Lady, I'll live at home.
Ros. And I'll live with thee;
And we'll keep house together.
Bel. *(Aside)* I'll keep hounds first;
And those I hate right heartily.
Pin. I go for Turkey;

And so, it may be, up into Persia.

LIL. We cannot know too much; I'll travel with you.

PIN. And you'll abuse me?

LIL. Like enough.

PIN. 'Tis dainty!

BEL. I will live in a bawdy-house.

Ros. I dare come to you.

BEL. Say I am disposed to hang myself?

Ros. There I'll leave you.

BEL. I am glad I know how to avoid you.

MIR. May I speak yet?

Y. MAN. She beckons to you.

MIR. Lady, I could wish I knew to recompense,

Even with the service of my life, those pains,

And those high favors you have thrown upon me.

Till I be more desertful in your eye,

And till my duty shall make known I honor you,

Noblest of women, do me but this favor,

To accept this back again, as a poor testimony.
                    (Offering the casket)

ORI. (Banteringly) I must have you too with 'em; else the will,

That says they must rest with you, is infringed, sir;

Which, pardon me, I dare not do.

MIR. Take me then,

And take me with the truest love.

ORI. 'Tis certain

My brother loved you dearly, and I ought

As dearly to preserve that love. But, sir,

Though I were willing, these are but your ceremonies.[56]

MIR. As I have life, I speak my soul!

ORI. I like you:

But how you can like me, without I have testimony,

A stranger to you——

MIR. I'll marry you immediately;

A fair state I dare promise you.

BEL. Yet she'll cozen thee.

ORI. Would some fair gentleman durst promise for you!

MIR. By all that's good——

(Enter LA CASTRE, NANTOLET, LUGIER, and DE GARD)

[56] Polite forms.

LA CAST., NANT., &c., And we'll make up the rest, lady.

ORI. (Dropping her Italian accent) Then Oriana takes you. Nay, she has caught you:

If you start now, let all the world cry shame on you!

I have out-travelled you.

BEL. Did not I say she would cheat thee?

MIR. I thank you; I am pleased you have deceived me,

And willingly I swallow it, and joy in't.

And yet, perhaps, I knew you. Whose plot was this?

LUG. He is not ashamed that cast it; he that executed,

Followed your father's will.

MIR. (With mock despair) What a world's this!

Nothing but craft and cozenage!

ORI. Who begun, sir?

MIR. Well; I do take thee upon mere compassion;

And I do think I shall love thee. As a testimony,

I'll burn my book, and turn a new leaf over.

But these fine clothes you shall wear still.

ORI. (Curtsying) I obey you, sir, in all.

NANT. And how, how, daughters? What say you to these gentlemen?—

What say ye, gentlemen, to the girls?

PIN. By my troth—if she can love me—

LIL. How long?

PIN. Nay, if once you love——

LIL. Then take me,

And take your chance.

PIN. Most willingly: you are mine, lady;

And, if I use you not, that you may love me——

LIL. A match, i' faith.

PIN. Why, now you travel with me.

Ros. How that thing stands!

BEL. It will, if you urge it:

Bless your five wits! (Starting to leave)

Ros. Nay, prithee, stay; I'll have thee.

BEL. You must ask me leave first.

Ros. Wilt thou use me kindly,

And beat me but once a week?

BEL. If you deserve no more.

Ros. And wilt thou get me with child?

BEL. Dost thou ask me seriously?

Ros. Yes, indeed do I.

Bel. Yes, I will get thee with child. Come,
   presently,
An't be but in revenge, I'll do thee that
   courtesy.
Well, if thou wilt fear God and me, have
   at thee!
Ros. I'll love you, and I'll honor you.
Bel. I am pleased, then.

Mir. This *Wild-Goose Chase* is done; we
   have won o' both sides.
(*To* De Gard) Brother, your love. And now
   to church of all hands;
Let's lose no time.
   Pin. Our travelling lay by.
   Bel. No more for Italy; for the Low Coun-
      tries, I.   (*Exeunt*)

JOHN FORD

'Tis Pity She's a Whore

~~~~~~~~~~~~~~~~~~~~~~~~~~~~~~~~~~~

PRINCIPAL EVENTS IN FORD'S LIFE

1586, 17 April, Baptized at Islington, Devonshire. Son of a well established family of landed gentry.

1601, 21 March, Perhaps he was the John Ford who matriculated at Exeter College, Oxford.

1602, 16 Nov., Admitted to the Inner Temple, but apparently never called to the bar.

1606, Published *Fame's Memorial,* an elegy on the Earl of Devonshire; a tract, *Honor Triumphant;* and verses, *The Monarchs' Meeting.*

1621, Ford collaborated with Thomas Dekker and William Rowley on *The Witch of Edmonton,* acted by Prince Charles' company at the Phoenix theatre and later before the King and Queen at court.

1624, 3 March, The Sun's Darling, a masque written by Ford and Dekker, was licensed for performance at the Phoenix theatre.

1624, 11 June, His lost play, *The Fairy Knight,* written with Thomas Dekker, was licensed for performance.

1624, He collaborated with Dekker, Webster, and Rowley on a tragedy called *The Late Murder of the Son upon the Mother or Keep the Widow Waking,* based upon contemporary events. It was acted at the Red Bull theatre.

1624, 22 Oct., The lost play, *The Bristow*

Merchant, written by Ford and Dekker, was licensed for performance by the Palsgrave's company at the Fortune theatre.

1628, 24 Nov., The Lovers' Melancholy was licensed and later performed by the King's company at the Blackfriars theatre.

1625-1633,* {
  'Tis Pity She's a Whore was acted by Queen Henrietta's company at the Phoenix theatre.

  The Broken Heart was acted by the King's company at the Blackfriars theatre.

  Love's Sacrifice was acted by Queen Henrietta's company at the Phoenix theatre.

  Perkin Warbeck was acted by Queen Henrietta's company at the Phoenix.
}

1635-1636, The Fancies Chaste and Noble was acted by Queen Henrietta's company at the Phoenix.

1638, 3 May, The Lady's Trial was licensed for performance by Their Majesties' Young Company at the Phoenix theatre.

1639, After the publication of *The Lady's Trial* in this year, nothing is known about Ford—not even the date of his death.

INTRODUCTION

'Tis Pity She's a Whore is one of the more strange and exotic of the plays of Shakespeare's age. It presents attitudes and values

* Precise dates unknown.

more familiar in nineteenth- and twentieth-century literature than in seventeenth. Other dramatists of the time, however violent and bloody the action of their plays, however depraved their villains, however bitterly disillusioned their pictures of contemporary society, however lonely and persecuted their good characters, nevertheless clearly accepted conventional standards of Christian morality. In their plays murder may be common, but it is not condoned; adultery may be flaunted before the audience, but it is not excused; and adulterers are usually punished at the close of the play. This is not to say that poetic justice regularly triumphs at the end of Elizabethan tragedies, as every reader of *Othello* and *King Lear, The White Devil* and *The Duchess of Malfi* knows, but the playwrights themselves do not suggest any questioning of the moral code of their fathers.

John Ford was different. He did not advocate the general violation of the accepted moral code, but in his serious plays he repeatedly presented an individual who did violate that code, and he presented him in a sympathetic light. He was a passionate advocate of the individual against society, usually an individual driven by a violent and irresistible love. His predecessors had dealt with the power of love often enough, but they treated it sympathetically when the parties were free to love, as in *Romeo and Juliet,* or unsympathetically when one of the parties was married to another, as in *A Woman Killed with Kindness*. Ford insisted that the terrible power of love was the same whatever society and its moral code said about the eligibility of the lovers. His lovers are frustrated not by surmountable barriers, like the opposition of parents, or differences of social class, but by inviolable social taboos like the universal condemnation of adultery or of incest. In his presentation of such love affairs he concentrates on the violence and beauty of the passion just as Shakespeare does in the more innocent affair of Juliet and Romeo.

'Tis Pity She's a Whore presents this problem of an irresistible love doomed by an inalterable social taboo more successfully than any of Ford's other plays because he succeeds in making the sincerity of the love and the overwhelming nature of the opposition equally convincing. Though Annabella is crushed by her sense of sin, she never wavers in her love for her brother; Giovanni exults in his love even as he dies. To Ford, love was a beautiful thing, but it was always terrible in its power; the climax of *'Tis Pity She's a Whore* dramatized this terrible power.

The other threads of the play are handled less effectively. The fatal entanglements of Hippolita in the toils of love are not equally clear and persuasive; the corruption of the Cardinal and Soranzo and Vasques are not made so relevant as Webster's similar pictures of corruption in *The White Devil;* Bergetto and Poggio might be more amusing in another play but they add little here. The play is Giovanni and Annabella and their tragic passion.

❧

'TIS PITY SHE'S A WHORE

Dramatis personae

In order of first appearance

FRIAR BONAVENTURA, Giovanni's confessor, tutor, and friend.

GIOVANNI,* The handsome, brilliant son of Florio.

GRIMALDI, A Roman military man of good family, nephew of the Cardinal, suitor to Annabella.

* Pronounced Jo-van-i.

VASQUES, The devoted and trusted but unscrupulous old servant of Soranzo, as formerly of Soranzo's father.

FLORIO, A wealthy citizen of Parma, father of Annabella and Giovanni.

DONADO, His friend, of like age and fortune, uncle of the foolish Bergetto.

SORANZO, A handsome, rich, hot-blooded

young nobleman, in love with Annabella.

ANNABELLA, The beautiful, spirited daughter of Florio.

PUTANA, Her aged duenna, one-time nurse, vulgar, crafty, and devoted.

BERGETTO, A silly, almost half-witted young man, the nephew and heir of Donado, and at his instance suitor to Annabella.

POGGIO, His slightly more intelligent servant.

RICHARDETTO, The betrayed and vengeful husband of Hippolita, supposed lost at sea. During most of the play he is disguised as a physician from Padua.

PHILOTIS, His niece.

HIPPOLITA, Richardetto's wife, violently revengeful toward Soranzo, for whom she plotted her husband's death, only to be jilted.

CARDINAL, Papal nuncio at Parma and uncle of Grimaldi.

Officers, masked dancers, banditti, attendants, servants.

SCENE: *Parma*

Act I

SCENE I. FRIAR BONAVENTURA's *Cell.*

(*Enter* FRIAR *and* GIOVANNI, *talking earnestly*)

FRIAR. Dispute no more in this; for know, young man,
These are no school points; nice philosophy
May tolerate unlikely arguments,
But Heaven admits no jest: wits that presumed
On wit too much, by striving how to prove
There was no God, with foolish grounds of art,
Discovered first the nearest way to hell;
And filled the world with devilish atheism.
Such questions, youth, are fond:[1] far better 'tis
To bless the sun, than reason why it shines;
Yet He thou talk'st of, is above the sun.—
No more! I may not hear it.
  GIO. Gentle father,
To you I have unclasped my burdened soul,
Emptied the storehouse of my thoughts and heart,
Made myself poor of secrets; have not left
Another word untold, which hath not spoke
All what I ever durst, or think, or know;
And yet is here the comfort I shall have?
Must I not do what all men else may,—love?
  FRIAR. Yes, you may love, fair son.
  GIO. Must I not praise
That beauty, which, if framed anew, the gods

[1] Vain.

Would make a god of, if they had it there;
And kneel to it, as I do kneel to them?
  FRIAR. Why, foolish madman!—
  GIO. Shall a peevish sound,
A customary form, from man to man,
Of brother and of sister, be a bar
'Twixt my perpetual happiness and me?
Say that we had one father, say one womb
(Curse to my joys!) gave both us life and birth;
Are we not, therefore, each to other bound
So much the more by nature? by the links
Of blood, of reason? nay, if you will have it,
Even of religion, to be ever one,
One soul, one flesh, one love, one heart, one all?
  FRIAR. Have done, unhappy youth! for thou art lost.
  GIO. Shall, then, for that I am her brother born,
My joys be ever banished from her bed?
No, father; in your eyes I see the change
Of pity and compassion; from your age,
As from a sacred oracle, distils
The life of counsel: tell me, holy man,
What cure shall give me ease in these extremes?
  FRIAR. Repentance, son, and sorrow for this sin:
For thou hast moved a Majesty above,
With thy unranged almost blasphemy.
  GIO. O do not speak of that, dear confessor!

FRIAR. Art thou, my son, that miracle of wit,
Who once, within these three months, wert esteemed
A wonder of thine age, throughout Bononia?[2]
How did the University applaud
Thy government, behavior, learning, speech,
Sweetness, and all that could make up a man!
I was proud of my tutelage, and chose
Rather to leave my books, than part with thee;
I did so:—but the fruits of all my hopes
Are lost in thee, as thou art in thyself.
O Giovanni! hast thou left the schools
Of knowledge, to converse with lust and death?
For death waits on thy lust. Look through the world,
And thou shalt see a thousand faces shine
More glorious than this idol thou ador'st:
Leave her, and take thy choice, 'tis much less sin;
Though in such games as those, they lose that win.
GIO. It were more ease to stop the ocean
From floats and ebbs, than to dissuade my vows.

FRIAR. Then I have done, and in thy wilful flames
Already see thy ruin; Heaven is just.—
Yet hear my counsel.
GIO. As a voice of life.
FRIAR. Hie to thy father's house, there lock thee fast
Alone within thy chamber; then fall down
On both thy knees, and grovel on the ground;
Cry to thy heart; wash every word thou utter'st
In tears (and if't be possible) of blood.
Beg Heaven to cleanse the leprosy of lust
That rots thy soul; acknowledge what thou art,
A wretch, a worm, a nothing; weep, sigh, pray
Three times a-day, and three times every night.
For seven days space do this; then, if thou find'st
No change in thy desires, return to me;
I'll think on remedy. Pray for thyself
At home, whilst I pray for thee here.—Away!
My blessing with thee! We have need to pray.
GIO. All this I'll do, to free me from the rod
Of vengeance; else I'll swear my fate's my god.   (*Exeunt*)

SCENE II. *The Street before* FLORIO'S *House.*

(*Enter* GRIMALDI *and* VASQUES, *ready to fight*)

VAS. Come, sir, stand to your tackling;[3] if you prove craven, I'll make you run quickly.
GRIM. Thou art no equal match for me.
VAS. Indeed I never went to the wars to bring home news; nor I cannot play the mountebank for a meal's meat, and swear I got my wounds in the field. See you these grey hairs? they'll not flinch for a bloody nose. Wilt thou to this gear?
GRIM. Why, slave, think'st thou I'll balance my reputation with a cast-suit?[4] Call thy master, he shall know that I dare—

VAS. Scold like a cot-quean;[5]—that's your profession. Thou poor shadow of a soldier, I will make thee know my master keeps servants, thy betters in quality and performance. Com'st thou to fight or prate?
GRIM. Neither, with thee. I am a Roman and a gentleman; one that have got mine honor with expense of blood.
VAS. You are a lying coward, and a fool. Fight, or by these hills I'll kill thee.—Brave my lord! You'll fight?
GRIM. Provoke me not, for if thou dost—
VAS. Have at you.
(*They fight,* GRIMALDI *hath the worst*)

(*Enter* FLORIO, DONADO, *and* SORANZO, *from opposite sides*)

[2] Latin name of Bologna, seat of the oldest university in Europe.
[3] Defend yourself.
[4] One who wears cast-off clothes.

[5] A vulgar, scolding woman.

FLO. What mean these sudden broils so
   near my doors?
Have you not other places, but my house,
To vent the spleen of your disordered bloods?
Must I be haunted still with such unrest,
As not to eat, or sleep in peace at home?
Is this your love, Grimaldi? Fie, 'tis naught!
   DON. And, Vasques, I may tell thee, 'tis
   not well
To broach these quarrels; you are ever for-
   ward
In seconding contentions.

(*Enter* ANNABELLA *and* PUTANA *on the
   balcony above*)

FLO. What's the ground?
SOR. That, with your patience, signiors,
   I'll resolve.
This gentleman, whom fame reports a soldier,
(For else I know not) rivals me in love
To Signior Florio's daughter; to whose ears
He still prefers his suit, to my disgrace,
Thinking the way to recommend himself
Is to disparage me in his report.—
But know, Grimaldi, though may be thou art
My equal in thy blood, yet this bewrays
A lowness in thy mind; which, wert thou
   noble,
Thou would'st as much disdain as I do thee
For this unworthiness; and on this ground
I willed my servant to correct his tongue,
Holding a man so base no match for me.
VAS. And had not your sudden coming
prevented us, I had let my gentleman blood
under the gills; I should have wormed you,
sir, for running mad.[6]
GRIM. I'll be revenged, Soranzo.
VAS. On a dish of warm broth to stay your
stomach—do, honest innocence, do! Spoon-
meat is a wholesomer diet than a Spanish
blade.
   GRIM. Remember this! (*Exit* GRIMALDI)
SOR. I fear thee not, Grimaldi.
FLO. My lord Soranzo, this is strange to
me.
Why you should storm, having my word
   engaged;
Owning her heart, what need you doubt
   her ear?

[6] "The allusion is to the practice of cutting
what is called the *worm* from under a dog's
tongue, as a *preventive* of madness."—Gifford.

Losers may talk, by law of any game.
   VAS. Yet the villainy of words, Signior
Florio, may be such as would make any
unspleened dove choleric. Blame not my lord
in this.
   FLO. Be you more silent.
I would not, for my wealth, my daughter's
   love
Should cause the spilling of one drop of
   blood.
Vasques, put up; let's end this fray in wine.
                                 (*Exeunt*)
   PUT. (*Above*) How like you this, child?
Here's threatening, challenging, quarrelling,
and fighting, on every side, and all is for your
sake; you had need look to yourself, charge,
you'll be stolen away sleeping else shortly.
   ANN. But, tutoress, such a life gives no
   content
To me; my thoughts are fixed on other ends.
Would you would leave me!
   PUT. Leave you! No marvel else. Leave
me no leaving, charge; this is love outright.
Indeed, I blame you not; you have choice
fit for the best lady in Italy.
   ANN. Pray do not talk so much.
   PUT. Take the worst with the best, there's
Grimaldi the soldier, a very well-timbered
fellow. They say he's a Roman, nephew to
the Duke Montferrato; they say he did good
service in the wars against the Milanese; but,
'faith, charge, I do not like him, an't be for
nothing but for being a soldier. Not one
amongst twenty of your skirmishing captains
but have some privy maim or other that mars
their standing upright. I like him the worse,
he crinkles so much in the hams; though he
might serve if there were no more men, yet
he's not the man I would choose.
   ANN. Fie, how thou prat'st!
   PUT. As I am a very woman, I like Signior
Soranzo well; he is wise, and what is more,
rich; and what is more than that, kind; and
what is more than all this, a nobleman. Such
a one, were I the fair Annabella myself, I
would wish and pray for. Then he is bountiful; besides, he is handsome, and by my
troth, I think, wholesome,[7] and that's news
in a gallant of three-and-twenty. Liberal, that
I know; loving, that you know; and a man
sure, else he could never have purchased
such a good name with Hippolita, the lusty

[7] Free from venereal disease.

widow, in her husband's lifetime. An 'twere but for that report, sweetheart, would he were thine! Commend a man for his qualities, but take a husband as he is a plain, sufficient, naked man; such a one is for your bed, and such a one is Signior Soranzo, my life for't.

Ann. (Annoyed) Sure the woman took her morning's draught too soon.

(Enter Bergetto and Poggio)

Put. But look, sweetheart, look what thing comes now! Here's another of your ciphers to fill up the number. Oh, brave old ape in a silken coat! Observe.

Ber. Didst thou think, Poggio, that I would spoil my new clothes, and leave my dinner, to fight!

Pog. No, sir, I did not take you for so arrant a baby.

Ber. I am wiser than so; for I hope, Poggio, thou never heardst of an elder brother that was a coxcomb; didst, Poggio?

Pog. Never indeed, sir, as long as they had either land or money left them to inherit.

Ber. Is it possible, Poggio? Oh, monstrous! Why, I'll undertake, with a handful of silver, to buy a headful of wit at any time. But, sirrah, I have another purchase in hand: I shall have the wench, mine uncle says. I will but wash my face and shift socks, and then have at her, i'faith.—Mark my pace, Poggio! (Struts across the stage)

Pog. Sir,—I have seen an ass and a mule trot the Spanish pavin[8] with a better grace, I know not how often. (Exeunt)

Ann. (Above) This idiot haunts me too.

Put. Ay, ay, he needs no description. The rich magnifico that is below with your father, charge, Signior Donado, his uncle, for that he means to make this, his cousin,[9] a golden calf, thinks that you will be right Israelite and fall down to him presently, but I hope I have tutored you better. They say a fool's bauble is a lady's play-fellow; yet you, having wealth enough, you need not cast upon the dearth of flesh, at any rate. Hang him, innocent![10]

(Giovanni passes over the stage)

Ann. But see, Putana, see what blessed shape
Of some celestial creature now appears!—
What man is he, that with such sad aspéct
Walks careless of himself?

Put. Where?

Ann. Look below.

Put. Oh, 'tis your brother, sweet.

Ann. Ha!

Put. 'Tis your brother.

Ann. Sure 'tis not he; this is some woeful thing
Wrapped up in grief, some shadow of a man.
Alas, he beats his breast and wipes his eyes,
Drowned all in tears; methinks I hear him sigh.
Let's down, Putana, and partake the cause.
I know my brother, in the love he bears me,
Will not deny me partage in his sadness.
My soul is full of heaviness and fear. (Exeunt)

Scene III. A Hall in Florio's House.

Gio. Lost! I am lost! My fates have doomed my death.
The more I strive, I love; the more I love,
The less I hope: I see my ruin certain.
What judgment or endeavors could apply
To my incurable and restless wounds,
I thoroughly have examined, but in vain.
O, that it were not in religion sin
To make our love a god and worship it!
I have even wearied heaven with prayers, dried up

The springs of my continual tears, even starved
My veins with daily fasts; what wit or art
Could counsel, I have practised, but, alas!
I find all these but dreams and old men's tales
To fright unsteady youth; I am still the same:
Or I must speak, or burst. 'Tis not, I know,
My lust, but 'tis my fate, that leads me on.
Keep fear and low faint-hearted shame with slaves!

[8] A stately ceremonial dance.

[9] His nephew. Cousin was a general term of address among relatives. [10] Idiot.

I'll tell her that I love her, though my heart
Were rated at the price of that attempt.
Oh me! she comes.

(*Enter* ANNABELLA *and* PUTANA)

ANN. Brother!
GIO. (*Aside*) If such a thing
As courage dwell in men, ye heavenly powers,
Now double all that virtue in my tongue!
ANN. Why, brother,
Will you not speak to me?
GIO. Yes; how do you, sister?
ANN. Howe'er I am, methinks you are not
well.
PUT. Bless us! Why are you so sad, sir?
GIO. Let me entreat you, leave us a while,
Putana.
Sister, I would be private with you.
ANN. Withdraw, Putana.
PUT. I will.—(*Aside*) If this were any
other company for her, I should think my
absence an office of some credit; but I will
leave them together. (*Exit* PUTANA)
GIO. Come, sister, lend your hand; let's
walk together.
I hope you need not blush to walk with me;
Here's none but you and I.
ANN. How's this?
GIO. Faith,
I mean no harm.
ANN. Harm?
GIO. No, good faith.
How is it with thee?
ANN. (*Aside*) I trust he be not frantic.—
I am very well, brother.
GIO. Trust me, but I am sick; I fear so
sick,
'Twill cost my life.
ANN. Mercy forbid it! 'Tis not so, I hope.
GIO. I think you love me, sister.
ANN. Yes, you know
I do.
GIO. I know it, indeed.— You are very fair.
ANN. Nay, then I see you have a merry
sickness.
GIO. That's as it proves. The poets feign,
I read,
That Juno for her forehead did exceed
All other goddesses; but I durst swear
Your forehead exceeds hers, as hers did
theirs.
ANN. 'Troth, this is pretty.

GIO. Such a pair of stars
As are thine eyes, would, like Promethean
fire,
If gently glanced, give life to senseless stones.
ANN. Fie upon you!
GIO. The lily and the rose, most sweetly
strange,
Upon your dimple cheeks do strive for
change;
Such lips would tempt a saint; such hands as
those
Would make an anchorite lascivious.
ANN. Do you mock me, or flatter me?
GIO. If you would see a beauty more exact
Than art can counterfeit, or nature frame,
Look in your glass, and there behold your
own.
ANN. O, you are a trim youth!
GIO. Here! (*Offers his dagger to her*)
ANN. What to do?
GIO. And here's my breast; strike home!
Rip up my bosom, there thou shalt behold
A heart in which is writ the truth I speak.—
Why stand you?
ANN. Are you earnest?
GIO. Yes, most earnest.
You cannot love?
ANN. Whom?
GIO. Me! My tortured soul
Hath felt affliction in the heat of death.
O, Annabella, I am quite undone!
The love of thee, my sister, and the view
Of thy immortal beauty have untuned
All harmony both of my rest and life.
Why do you not strike?
ANN. Forbid it, my just fears!
If this be true, 'twere fitter I were dead.
GIO. True, Annabella! 'Tis no time to
jest.
I have too long suppressed my hidden flames,
That almost have consumed me; I have spent
Many a silent night in sighs and groans;
Ran over all my thoughts, despised my fate,
Reasoned against the reasons of my love,
Done all that smooth-cheeked virtue could
advise,
But found all bootless; 'tis my destiny
That you must either love, or I must die.
ANN. Comes this in sadness [11] from you?
GIO. Let some mischief
Befall me soon, if I dissemble aught.
ANN. You are my brother Giovanni.

[11] Earnest.

GIO. You
My sister Annabella; I know this
And could afford you instance why to love
So much the more for this; to which intent
Wise nature first in your creation meant
To make you mine; else't had been sin and
    foul
To share one beauty to a double soul.
Nearness in birth and blood doth but per-
    suade
A nearer nearness in affection.
I have asked counsel of the holy church,
Who tells me I may love you; and 'tis just
That, since I may, I should; and will, yes will!
Must I now live, or die?
    ANN. Live; thou hast won
The field, and never fought. What thou hast
    urged
My captive heart had long ago resolved.
I blush to tell thee,—but I'll tell thee now—
For every sigh that thou hast spent for me,
I have sighed ten; for every tear, shed twenty,
And not so much for that I loved, as that
I durst not say I loved, nor scarcely think it.
    GIO. Let not this music be a dream, ye
    gods,

For pity's sake, I beg you!
    ANN. On my knees,   (*She kneels*)
Brother, even by our mother's dust, I charge
    you,
Do not betray me to your mirth or hate;
Love me, or kill me, brother.
    GIO. On my knees,   (*He kneels*)
Sister, even by my mother's dust I charge
    you,
Do not betray me to your mirth or hate;
Love me, or kill me, sister.
    ANN. You mean good sooth, then?
    GIO. In good troth, I do;
And so do you, I hope. Say, I'm in
    earnest.
    ANN. I'll swear it, I.
    GIO. And I; and by this kiss, (*Kisses her*)
Once more, yet once more; now let's rise.
    (*They rise*) By this,
I would not change this minute for Elysium.
What must we now do?
    ANN. What you will.
    GIO. Come then;
After so many tears as we have wept,
Let's learn to court in smiles, to kiss, and
    sleep.   (*Exeunt*)

SCENE IV. *A Street.*

(*Enter* FLORIO *and* DONADO)

    FLO. Signior Donado, you have said
    enough,
I understand you; but would have you know
I will not force my daughter 'gainst her will.
You see I have but two, a son and her;
And he is so devoted to his book,
As I must tell you true, I doubt his health.
Should he miscarry, all my hopes rely
Upon my girl.[12] As for worldly fortune,
I am, I thank my stars, blessed with enough.
My care is, how to match her to her liking;
I would not have her marry wealth, but love,
And if she like your nephew, let him have
    her;
Here's all that I can say.
    DON. Sir, you say well,
Like a true father; and, for my part, I,
If the young folks can like, ('twixt you and
    me)

[12] Pronounced here and elsewhere as a dis-
syllable.

Will promise to assure my nephew presently
Three thousand florins yearly, during life,
And after I am dead my whole estate.
    FLO. 'Tis a fair proffer, sir; meantime your
    nephew
Shall have free passage to commence his suit.
If he can thrive, he shall have my consent.
So for this time I'll leave you, Signior.
    (*Exit*)
    DON. Well,
Here's hope yet, if my nephew would have
    wit;
But he is such another dunce, I fear
He'll never win the wench. When I was
    young,
I could have done 't, i'faith, and so shall he,
If he will learn of me. And in good time
He comes himself.

(*Enter* BERGETTO *and* POGGIO)

How now, Bergetto, whither away so fast?
    BER. O uncle! I have heard the strangest

news that ever came out of the mint; have I not, Poggio?

Pog. Yes, indeed, sir.

Don. What news, Bergetto?

Ber. Why, look ye, uncle, my barber told me just now that there is a fellow come to town who undertakes to make a mill go without the mortal help of any water or wind, only with sand-bags; and this fellow hath a strange horse, a most excellent beast, I'll assure you, uncle, my barber says; whose head, to the head, to the wonder of all Christian people, stands just behind where his tail is. Is't not true, Poggio?

Pog. So the barber swore, forsooth.

Don. And you are running thither?

Ber. Ay, forsooth, uncle.

Don. Wilt thou be a fool still? Come, sir, you shall not go; you have more mind of a puppet-play than on the business I told you. Why, thou great baby, wilt never have wit? Wilt make thyself a May-game[13] to all the world?

Pog. Answer for yourself, master.

Ber. Why, uncle, should I sit at home still, and not go abroad to see fashions like other gallants?

Don. To see hobby-horses! What wise talk, I pray, had you with Annabella, when you were at Signior Florio's house?

Ber. Oh, the wench!—Uds sa'me, uncle, I tickled her with a rare speech, that I made her almost burst her belly with laughing.

Don. Nay, I think so; and what speech was't?

Ber. What did I say, Poggio?

Pog. Forsooth, my master said that he loved her almost as well as he loved parmasent,[14] and swore (I'll be sworn for him) that she wanted but such a nose as his was, to be as pretty a young woman as any was in Parma.

Don. Oh gross!

Ber. Nay, uncle.—Then she asked me whether my father had more children than myself? and I said no; 'twere better he should have had his brains knocked out first.

Don. This is intolerable.

Ber. Then said she, will Signior Donado, your uncle, leave you all his wealth?

Don. Ha! That was good; did she harp upon that string?

Ber. Did she harp upon that string! Ay, that she did. I answered, "Leave me all his wealth? Why, woman, he hath no other wit; if he had, he should hear on't to his everlasting glory and confusion. I know, quoth I, I am his white boy,[15] and will not be gulled," and with that she fell into a great smile and went away. Nay, I did fit her.

Don. Ah, sirrah, then I see there's no changing of nature. Well, Bergetto, I fear thou wilt be a very ass still.

Ber. I should be sorry for that, uncle.

Don. Come, come you home with me; since you are no better a speaker, I'll have you write to her after some courtly manner and enclose some rich jewel in the letter.

Ber. Ay marry, that will be excellent.

Don. Peace, innocent!
Once in my time I'll set my wits to school;
If all fail, 'tis but the fortune of a fool.

Ber. Poggio, 'twill do, Poggio! (*Exeunt*)

Act II

Scene I. *An Apartment in* Florio's *House.*

(*Enter* Giovanni *and* Annabella *as from their chamber*)

Gio. Come, Annabella,—no more Sister now,
But Love, a name more gracious. Do not blush,
Beauty's sweet wonder, but be proud to know

That yielding thou hast conquered, and inflamed
A heart whose tribute is thy brother's life.

Ann. And mine is his. Oh, how these stolen contents
Would print a modest crimson on my cheeks,
Had any but my heart's delight prevailed!

[13] A laughing-stock.

[14] Parmesan cheese.

[15] Favorite, "fair-haired boy."

Gio. I marvel why the chaster of your sex
Should think this pretty toy called maiden-
    head
So strange a loss; when, being lost, 'tis noth-
    ing,
And you are still the same.
    Ann. 'Tis well for you;
Now you can talk.
    Gio. Music as well consists
In th' ear, as in the playing.
    Ann. Oh, you are wanton!—
Tell on't, you were best; do.
    Gio. Thou wilt chide me, then.
Kiss me—so! Thus hung Jove on Leda's
    neck
And sucked divine ambrosia from her lips.
I envy not the mightiest man alive,
But hold myself, in being king of thee,
More great than were I king of all the
    world.—
But I shall lose you, sweetheart.
    Ann. But you shall not.
    Gio. You must be married, mistress.
    Ann. Yes, to whom?
    Gio. Some one must have you.
    Ann. You must.
    Gio. Nay, some other.
    Ann. Now prithee do not speak so; with-
    out jesting,
You'll make me weep in earnest.
    Gio. What, you will not!
But tell me, sweet, canst thou be dared to
    swear
That thou wilt live to me, and to no other?
    Ann. By both our loves I dare; for didst
        thou know,
My Giovanni, how all suitors seem
To my eyes hateful, thou would'st trust me
    then.
    Gio. Enough, I take thy word. Sweet, we
        must part.
Remember what thou vow'st; keep well my
    heart.
    Ann. Will you be gone?
    Gio. I must.
    Ann. When to return?
    Gio. Soon.
    Ann. Look you do.
    Gio. Farewell.   (Exit)
    Ann. Go where thou wilt, in mind I'll
        keep thee here,
And where thou art, I know I shall be there.
Guardian!

(*Enter* Putana)

    Put. Child, how is't, child? Well, thank
heaven, ha?
    Ann. O guardian, what a paradise of joy
Have I past over!
    Put. Nay, what a paradise of joy have you
past under! Why, now I commend thee,
charge. Fear nothing, sweet-heart; what
though he be your brother? Your brother's a
man, I hope; and I say still, if a young wench
feel the fit upon her, let her take any body,
father or brother, all is one.
    Ann. I would not have it known for all the
world.
    Put. Nor I indeed, for the speech of the
people; else 'twere nothing.
    Flo. (*Within*) Daughter Annabella!
    Ann. O me, my father!—Here, sir!—Reach
my work.
    Flo. (*Within*) What are you doing?
    Ann. So; let him come now.

(*Enter* Florio, *followed by* Richardetto *as
a Doctor of Physic and* Philotis *with a lute
in her hand*)

    Flo. So hard at work! That's well; you lose
        no time.
Look, I have brought you company; here's
    one,
A learned doctor, lately come from Padua,
Much skilled in physic; and for that I see
You have of late been sickly, I entreated
This reverend man to visit you some time.
    Ann. You are very welcome, sir.
    Rich. I thank you, mistress.
Loud fame in large report hath spoke your
    praise,
As well for virtue as perfection; [16]
For which I have been bold to bring with me
A kinswoman of mine, a maid, for song
And music, one perhaps will give content;
Please you to know her.
    Ann. They are parts I love,
And she for them most welcome.
    Phi. Thank you, lady.
    Flo. Sir, now you know my house, pray
        make not strange;
And if you find my daughter need your art,
I'll be your pay-master.
    Rich. Sir, what I am
She shall command.

[16] Beauty.

FLO. You shall bind me to you.
Daughter, I must have conference with you
About some matters that concern us both.
Good master doctor, please you but walk in,
We'll crave a little of your cousin's cunning;

I think my girl hath not quite forgot
To touch an instrument; she could have
    done't;
We'll hear them both.
    RICH. I'll wait upon you, sir.   (*Exeunt*)

SCENE II. *A Room in* SORANZO'S *House.*

(*Enter* SORANZO *in his study reading a book*)

Love's measure is extreme, the comfort pain;
The life unrest, and the reward disdain.

What's here? Look't o'er again.—'Tis so; so
    writes
This smooth licentious poet in his rhymes.
But, Sannazar,[17] thou lyest; for had thy bosom
Felt such oppression as is laid on mine,
Thou wouldst have kissed the rod that made
    thee smart.
To work then, happy Muse, and contradict
What Sannazar hath in his envy writ.
                                        (*Writes*)

Love's measure is the mean, sweet his annoys;
His pleasures life, and his reward all joys.

Had Annabella lived when Sannazar
Did in his brief Encomium celebrate
Venice, that queen of cities, he had left
That verse which gained him such a sum of
    gold,
And for one only look from Annabel
Had writ of her and her diviner cheeks.
O, how my thoughts are—
    VAS. (*Within*) Pray forbear; in rules of
civility, let me give notice on't. I shall be
taxed of my neglect of duty and service.
    SOR. What rude intrusion interrupts my
    peace?
Can I be no where private?
    VAS. (*Within*) Troth, you wrong your
modesty.
    SOR. What's the matter, Vasques? Who
is't?

(*Enter* HIPPOLITA *and* VASQUES)

HIP. 'Tis I;
Do you know me now? Look, perjured man,
    on her

[17] Jacopo Sannazaro, a Neapolitan poet (1458-
1530).

Whom thou and thy distracted lust have
    wronged.
Thy sensual rage of blood hath made my
    youth
A scorn to men and angels; and shall I
Be now a foil to thy unsated change?[18]
Thou knowst, false wanton, when my modest
    fame
Stood free from stain or scandal, all the
    charms
Of hell or sorcery could not prevail
Against the honor of my chaster bosom.
Thine eyes did plead in tears, thy tongue in
    oaths,
Such and so many that a heart of steel
Would have been wrought to pity, as was
    mine;
And shall the conquest of my lawful bed,
My husband's death, urged on by his disgrace,
My loss of womanhood, be ill-rewarded
With hatred and contempt? No! Know, Sor-
    anzo,
I have a spirit doth as much distaste
The slavery of fearing thee, as thou
Dost loath the memory of what hath past.
    SOR. Nay, dear Hippolita—
    HIP. Call me not dear,
Nor think with supple words to smooth the
    grossness
Of my abuses. 'Tis not your new mistress,
Your goodly Madam Merchant, shall
    triúmph
On my dejection. Tell her thus from me,
My birth was nobler, and by much more free.
    SOR. You are too violent.
    HIP. You are too double
In your dissimulation. Seest thou this,
This habit, these black mourning weeds of
    care?
'Tis thou art cause of this, and hast divorced
My husband from his life and me from him,
And made me widow in my widowhood.

[18] Insatiable lust.

Sor. Will you yet hear?

Hip. More of thy perjuries?
Thy soul is drowned too deeply in those sins;
Thou need'st not add to the number.

Sor. Then I'll leave you;
You are past all rules of sense.

Hip. And thou of grace.

Vas. Fie, mistress, you are not near the limits of reason. If my lord had a resolution as noble as virtue itself, you take the course to unedge it all. Sir, I beseech you do not perplex her; griefs, alas, will have a vent. I dare undertake madam Hippolita will now freely hear you.

Sor. Talk to a woman frantic!—Are these the fruits of your love?

Hip. They are the fruits of thy untruth, false man!
Did'st thou not swear, whilst yet my husband lived,
That thou would'st wish no happiness on earth
More than to call me wife? Did'st thou not vow
When he should die to marry me? For which
The devil in my blood, and thy protests,
Caused me to counsel him to undertake
A voyage to Ligorne, for that we heard
His brother there was dead and left a daughter
Young and unfriended, whom, with much ado,
I wished him to bring hither. He did so,
And went; and, as thou know'st, died on the way.
Unhappy man, to buy his death so dear,
With my advice! Yet thou, for whom I did it,
Forget'st thy vows and leav'st me to my shame.

Sor. Who could help this?

Hip. Who? Perjured man, thou could'st,
If thou had'st faith or love.

Sor. You are deceived.
The vows I made, if you remember well,
Were wicked and unlawful; 'twere more sin
To keep them than to break them. As for me,
I cannot mask my penitence. Think thou
How much thou hast digressed from honest shame
In bringing of a gentleman to death
Who was thy husband; such a one as he,
So noble in his quality, condition,
Learning, behavior, entertainment, love,
As Parma could not show a braver man.

Vas. You do not well; this was not your promise.

Sor. I care not; let her know her monstrous life.
Ere I'll be servile to so black a sin,
I'll be a curse.—Woman, come here no more;
Learn to repent, and die; for by my honor
I hate thee and thy lust. You have been too foul. (Exit)

Vas. This part has been scurvily played.

Hip. How foolishly this beast contemns his fate
And shuns the use of that, which I more scorn
Than I once loved, his love! But let him go,
My vengeance shall give comfort to his woe.[19]
(She offers to go away)

Vas. Mistress, mistress, madam Hippolita! Pray, a word or two.

Hip. With me, sir?

Vas. With you, if you please.

Hip. What is't?

Vas. I know you are infinitely moved now, and you think you have cause; some I confess you have, but sure not so much as you imagine.

Hip. Indeed!

Vas. O you were miserably bitter, which you followed even to the last syllable; 'faith, you were somewhat too shrewd.[20] By my life, you could not have took my lord in a worse time since I first knew him; to-morrow, you shall find him a new man.

Hip. Well, I shall wait his leisure.

Vas. Fie, this is not a hearty patience; it comes sourly from you; 'troth, let me persuade you for once.

Hip. (Aside) I have it, and it shall be so; thanks, opportunity!—Persuade me! To what?

Vas. Visit him in some milder temper. O, if you could but master a little your female spleen, how might you win him!

Hip. He will never love me. Vasques, thou hast been a too trusty servant to such a master, and I believe thy reward in the end will fall out like mine.

Vas. So perhaps too.

Hip. Resolve thyself it will. Had I one so true, so truly honest, so secret to my counsels,

[19] The woe occasioned by his lie.
[20] Shrewish.

as thou hast been to him and his, I should think it a slight acquaintance not only to make him master of all I have, but even of myself.

Vas. O you are a noble gentlewoman!

Hip. Wilt thou feed always upon hopes? Well, I know thou art wise and seest the reward of an old servant daily, what it is.

Vas. Beggary and neglect.

Hip. True; but, Vasques, wert thou mine and would'st be private to me and my designs, I here protest, myself and all what I can else call mine should be at thy dispose.

Vas. (Aside) Work you that way, old mole? then I have the wind of you.—I were not worthy of it by any desert that could lie —within my compass; if I could—

Hip. What then?

Vas. I should then hope to live in these my old years with rest and security.

Hip. Give me thy hand. Now promise but thy silence,
And help to bring to pass a plot I have;
And here, in sight of Heaven, that being done,
I make thee lord of me and mine estate.

Vas. Come, you are merry; this is such a happiness that I can neither think or believe.

Hip. Promise thy secrecy, and 'tis confirmed.

Vas. Then here I call our good genii for witnesses, whatsoever your designs are, or against whomsoever, I will not only be a special actor therein, but never disclose it till it be effected.

Hip. I take thy word and, with that, thee for mine;
Come then, let's more confer of this anon.—
On this delicious bane my thoughts shall banquet,
Revenge shall sweeten what my griefs have tasted.   (Exeunt)

Scene III. *The Street.*

(*Enter* Richardetto *and* Philotis)

Rich. Thou see'st, my lovely niece, these strange mishaps,
How all my fortunes turn to my disgrace,
Wherein I am but as a looker-on
Whilst others act my shame, and I am silent.

Phi. But, uncle, wherein can this borrowed shape [21]
Give you content?

Rich. I'll tell thee, gentle niece.
Thy wanton aunt in her lascivious riots
Lives now secure, thinks I am surely dead
In my late journey to Ligorne for you,—
As I have caused it to be rumored out.—
Now would I see with what an impudence
She gives scope to her loose adultery,
And how the common voice allows hereof;
Thus far I have prevailed.

Phi. Alas, I fear
You mean some strange revenge.

Rich. O be not troubled;
Your ignorance shall plead for you in all.—
But to our business.—What! You learned for certain,

[21] His disguise as physician.

How Signior Florio means to give his daughter
In marriage to Soranzo?

Phi. Yes, for certain.

Rich. But how find you young Annabella's love
Inclined to him?

Phi. For aught I could perceive,
She neither fancies him or any else.

Rich. There's mystery in that, which time must show.
She used you kindly?

Phi. Yes.

Rich. And craved your company?

Phi. Often.

Rich. 'Tis well; it goes as I could wish.
I am the doctor now, and as for you,
None knows you; if all fail not, we shall thrive.

(*Enter* Grimaldi)

But who comes here?—I know him; 'tis Grimaldi,
A Roman and a soldier, near allied
Unto the Duke of Montferrato, one

Attending on the nuncio of the pope
That now resides in Parma; by which means
He hopes to get the love of Annabella.

GRIM. Save you, sir.

RICH. And you, sir.

GRIM. I have heard
Of your approved skill, which through the city
Is freely talked of, and would crave your aid.

RICH. For what, sir?

GRIM. Marry, sir, for this—
But I would speak in private.

RICH. Leave us, cousin.   (*Exit* PHI.)

GRIM. I love fair Annabella, and would know
Whether in arts there may not be receipts [22]
To move affection.

RICH. Sir, perhaps there may,
But these will nothing profit you.

GRIM. Not me?

RICH. Unless I be mistook, you are a man
Greatly in favor with the cardinal.

GRIM. What of that?

RICH. In duty to his grace,
I will be bold to tell you, if you seek
To marry Florio's daughter, you must first
Remove a bar 'twixt you and her.

GRIM. Who's that?

RICH. Soranzo is the man that hath her heart,
And while he lives, be sure you cannot speed.

GRIM. Soranzo! What, mine enemy? Is't he?

RICH. Is he your enemy?

GRIM. The man I hate
Worse than confusion; I'll tell him straight.

RICH. Nay, then take my advice,
Even for his grace's sake the cardinal.
I'll find a time when he and she do meet,
Of which I'll give you notice, and to be sure
He shall not 'scape you, I'll provide a poison
To dip your rapier's point in. If he had
As many heads as Hydra had, he dies.

GRIM. But shall I trust thee, doctor?

RICH. As yourself;
Doubt not in aught. (*Exit* GRIMALDI) Thus shall the fates decree,
By me Soranzo falls, that ruined me.
          (*Exit*)

SCENE IV. *Another Part of the Street.*

(*Enter* DONADO *with a letter,* BERGETTO, *and* POGGIO)

DON. Well, sir, I must be content to be both your secretary and your messenger myself. I cannot tell what this letter may work; but, as sure as I am alive, if thou come once to talk with her, I fear thou wilt mar whatsoever I make.

BER. You make, uncle! Why, am not I big enough to carry mine own letter, I pray?

DON. Ay, ay, carry a fool's head o' thy own! Why, thou dunce, would'st thou write a letter, and carry it thyself?

BER. Yes, that I would, and read it to her with mine own mouth; for you must think, if she will not believe me myself when she hears me speak, she will not believe another's hand-writing. Oh, you think I am a blockhead, uncle. No, sir, Poggio knows I have indited a letter myself; so I have.

POG. Yes, truly, sir, I have it in my pocket.

DON. A sweet one, no doubt; pray let's see 't.

BER. I cannot read my own hand very well, Poggio; read it, Poggio.

DON. Begin.

POG. (*Reads*) *Most dainty and honey-sweet mistress, I could call you fair, and lie as fast as any that loves you; but my uncle being the elder man, I leave it to him, as more fit for his age, and the color of his beard. I am wise enough to tell you I can bourd* [23] *where I see occasion; or if you like my uncle's wit better than mine, you shall marry me; if you like mine better than his, I will marry you, in spite of your teeth. So, commending my best parts to you, I rest*
          Yours, upwards and downwards, or
          you may choose.
                    BERGETTO.

BER. Ah, ha! here's stuff, uncle!

DON. Here's stuff indeed—to shame us all. Pray whose advice did you take in this learned letter?

[22] Charms, love-potions, etc.   [23] Jest.

Pog. None, upon my word, but mine own.

Ber. And mine, uncle, believe it, nobody's else; 'twas mine own brain, I thank a good wit for't.

Don. Get you home, sir, and look you keep within doors till I return.

Ber. How? That were a jest indeed! I scorn it, i'faith.

Don. What! You do not?

Ber. Judge me, but I do now.

Pog. Indeed, sir, 'tis very unhealthy.

Don. Well, sir, if I hear any of your apish running to motions [24] and fopperies till I come back, you were as good not; look to't.

(*Exit* Don.)

Ber. Poggio, shall's steal to see this horse with the head in's tail?

Pog. Ay, but you must take heed of whipping.

Ber. Dost take me for a child, Poggio? Come, honest Poggio.　　　　(*Exeunt*)

Scene V. Friar Bonaventura's *Cell.*

(*Enter* Friar *and* Giovanni)

Friar. Peace! Thou hast told a tale whose every word
Threatens eternal slaughter to the soul.
I'm sorry I have heard it; would mine ears
Had been one minute deaf before the hour
That thou cam'st to me! O young man, castaway,
By the religious number of mine order,
I day and night have waked my aged eyes
Above my strength, to weep on thy behalf;
But Heaven is angry, and be thou resolved,
Thou art a man remarked [25] to taste a mischief.
Look for't; though it come late, it will come sure.

Gio. Father, in this you are uncharitable.
What I have done, I'll prove both fit and good.
It is a principle which you have taught,
When I was yet your scholar, that the frame
And composition of the mind doth follow
The frame and composition of body.
So, where the body's furniture is beauty,
The mind's must needs be virtue; which allowed,
Virtue itself is reason but refined,
And love the quintessence of that. This proves
My sister's beauty, being rarely fair,
Is rarely virtuous; chiefly in her love,
And chiefly, in that love, her love to me.
If her's to me, then so is mine to her,
Since in like causes are effects alike.

Friar. O ignorance in knowledge! Long ago,
How often have I warned thee this before!
Indeed, if we were sure there were no Deity,
Nor heaven nor hell, then to be led alone
By nature's light—as were philosophers
Of elder times—might instance some defence.
But 'tis not so. Then, madman, thou wilt find
That nature is in Heaven's positions blind. [26]

Gio. Your age o'errules you. Had you youth like mine,
You'd make her love your heaven, and her divine.

Friar. Nay, then I see thou'rt too far sold to hell;
It lies not in the compass of any prayers
To call thee back. Yet let me counsel thee:
Persuade thy sister to some marriage.

Gio. Marriage! Why that's to damn her; that's to prove
Her greedy of variety of lust.

Friar. O fearful! If thou wilt not, give me leave
To shrive her, lest she should die unabsolved.

Gio. At your best leisure, father. Then she'll tell you
How dearly she doth prize my matchless love;
Then you will know what pity 'twere we two
Should have been sundered from each other's arms.
View well her face, and in that little round
You may observe a world's variety;
For color, lips; for sweet perfumes, her breath;

---

[24] Puppet-shows.　　　[25] Marked out.　　　[26] Nature ignores divine law.

For jewels, eyes; for threads of purest gold,
Hair; for delicious choice of flowers, cheeks;
Wonder in every portion of that throne.
Hear her but speak, and you will swear the
    spheres
Make music to the citizens in heaven.
But father, what is else for pleasure framed,
Lest I offend your ears, shall go unnamed.
    Friar. The more I hear, I pity thee the
    more,
That one so excellent should give those parts
All to a second death.[27] What I can do,
Is but to pray; and yet I could advise thee,

Wouldst thou be ruled.
    Gio. In what?
    Friar. Why, leave her yet.
The throne of mercy is above your trespass;
Yet time is left you both—
    Gio. To embrace each other,
Else let all time be struck quite out of
    number.
She is like me, and I like her, resolved.
    Friar. No more! I'll visit her. This grieves
    me most,
Things being thus, a pair of souls are lost.
                   (Exeunt)

Scene VI. *A Room in* Florio's *House.*

(*Enter* Florio, Donado, Annabella, *and*
    Putana)

Flo. Where's Giovanni?
    Ann. Newly walked abroad,
And, as I heard him say, gone to the friar,
His reverend tutor.
    Flo. That's a blessed man,
A man made up of holiness; I hope
He'll teach him how to gain another world.
    Don. Fair gentlewoman, here's a letter
    sent
To you from my young cousin. I dare swear
He loves you in his soul. Would you could
    hear
Sometimes, what I see daily, sighs and tears,
As if his breast were prison to his heart.
    Flo. Receive it, Annabella.
    Ann. Alas, good man! (*Takes the letter*)
    Don. What's that she said?
    Put. And please you, sir, she said, "Alas,
good man!" Truly I do commend him to her
every night before her first sleep, because I
would have her dream of him; and she heark-
ens to that most religiously.
    Don. Say'st so? God a' mercy, Putana!
There's something for thee. (*Gives her
money*) And prithee do what thou canst
on his behalf; sha' not be lost labor, take my
word for 't.
    Put. Thank you most heartily, sir; now
I have a feeling of your mind, let me alone
to work.
    Ann. Guardian!

[27] *I.e.*, the soul's.

Put. Did you call?
    Ann. Keep this letter.
    Don. Signior Florio, in any case bid her
read it instantly.
    Flo. Keep it! For what? Pray read it me
here right.
    Ann. I shall, sir. (*She reads*)
    Don. How d' you find her inclined,
signior?
    Flo. Troth, sir, I know not how; not all
so well
As I could wish.
    Ann. Sir, I am bound to rest your cousin's
    debtor.
The jewel I'll return; for if he love,
I'll count that love a jewel.
    Don. Mark you that?
Nay, keep them both, sweet maid.
    Ann. You must excuse me,
Indeed I will not keep it.
    Flo. Where's the ring,
That which your mother in her will be-
    queathed,
And charged you on her blessing not to
    give 't
To any but your husband? Send back that.
    Ann. I have it not.
    Flo. Ha! Have it not! where is 't?
    Ann. My brother in the morning took it
    from me,
Said he would wear 't to-day.
    Flo. Well, what do you say
To young Bergetto's love! Are you content
To match with him? Speak.
    Don. There's the point, indeed.

ANN. (*Aside*) What shall I do? I must say
something now.

FLO. What say? Why d' you not speak?

ANN. Sir, with your leave,
Please you to give me freedom?

FLO. Yes, you have it.

ANN. Signior Donado, if your nephew
    mean
To raise his better fortunes in his match,
The hope of me will hinder such a hope.
Sir, if you love him, as I know you do,
Find one more worthy of his choice than me;
In short, I'm sure I sha' not be his wife.

DON. Why, here's plain dealing; I com-
    mend thee for't;
And all the worst I wish thee, is, heaven
    bless thee!
Your father yet and I will still be friends—
Shall we not, Signior Florio?

FLO. Yes; why not?
Look, here your cousin comes.

(*Enter* BERGETTO *and* POGGIO)

DON. (*Aside*) Oh coxcomb! What doth he
make here?

BER. Where is my uncle, sirs?

DON. What's the news now?

BER. Save you, uncle, save you! You must
not think I come for nothing, masters; and
how, and how is 't! What, you have read my
letter? Ah, there I—tickled you, i'faith.

POG. (*Aside to* BER.) But 'twere better
you had tickled her in another place.

BER. Sirrah sweetheart, I'll tell thee a good
jest, and riddle what 'tis.

ANN. You say you'll tell me.

BER. As I was walking just now in the
street, I met a swaggering fellow would needs
take the wall of me;[28] and because he did
thrust me, I very valiantly called him rogue;
he hereupon bade me draw, I told him I had
more wit than so, but when he saw that I
would not, he did so maul me with the hilt
of his rapier that my head sung whilst my
feet capered in the kennel.

DON. Was ever the like ass seen!

ANN. And what did you all this while?

BER. Laugh at him for a gull, till I saw
the blood run about mine ears, and then I
could not choose but find in my heart to cry;

[28] Push me into the gutter (kennel).

till a fellow with a broad beard—they say
he is a new-come doctor—called me into his
house and gave me a plaster; look you, here
'tis. And, sir, there was a young wench
washed my face and hands most excellently;
i'faith I shall love her as long as I live for 't—
did she not, Poggio?

POG. Yes, and kissed him too.

BER. Why, la, now, you think I tell a lie,
uncle, I warrant.

DON. Would he that beat thy blood out of
thy head, had beaten some wit into it, for I
fear thou never wilt have any.

BER. Oh uncle, but there was a wench
would have done a man's heart good to have
looked on her. By this light, she had a face
methinks worth twenty of you, Mistress Annabella.

DON. Was ever such a fool born?

ANN. I am glad she liked[29] you, sir.

BER. Are you so? By my troth I thank you,
forsooth.

FLO. Sure 'twas the doctor's niece, that
was last day with us here.

BER. 'Twas she! 'Twas she!

DON. How do you know that, Simplicity?

BER. Why does not he say so? If I should
have said no, I should have given him the
lie, uncle, and so have deserved a dry beating
again; I'll none of that.

FLO. A very modest well-behaved young
    maid,
As I have seen.

DON. Is she indeed?

FLO. Indeed
She is, if I have any judgment.

DON. Well, sir, now you are free. You
need not care for sending letters now, you
are dismissed; your mistress here will none of
you.

BER. No! Why what care I for that! I can
have wenches enough in Parma for half a
crown a-piece—cannot I, Poggio?

POG. I'll warrant you, sir.

DON. Signior Florio,
I thank you for your free recourse you gave
For my admittance; and to you, fair maid,
That jewel I will give you 'gainst your mar-
    riage.
Come, will you go, sir?

BER. Ay, marry, will I. Mistress, farewell,

[29] Pleased.

mistress; I'll come again to-morrow—farewell, mistress.

(*Exeunt* DONADO, BERGETTO, *and* POGGIO)

(*Enter* GIOVANNI)

FLO. Son, where have you been? What alone, alone, still, still?
I would not have it so; you must forsake
This over-bookish humor. Well, your sister
Hath shook the fool off.

GIO. 'Twas no match for her.

FLO. 'Twas not indeed; I meant it nothing less.
Soranzo is the man I only like;
Look on him, Annabella.—Come, 'tis supper-time,
And it grows late. (*Exit*)

GIO. Whose jewel's that?

ANN. Some sweetheart's.

GIO. So I think.

ANN. A lusty youth,
Signior Donado, gave it me to wear
Against my marriage.

GIO. But you shall not wear it;
Send it him back again.

ANN. What, you are jealous?

GIO. That you shall know anon, at better leisure.
Welcome, sweet night! the evening crowns the day. (*Exeunt*)

Act III

SCENE I. *A Room in* DONADO's *House.*

(*Enter* BERGETTO *and* POGGIO)

BER. Does my uncle think to make me a baby still? No, Poggio; he shall know I have a sconce[30] now.

POG. Ay, let him not bob[31] you off like an ape with an apple.

BER. 'Sfoot, I will have the wench, if he were ten uncles, in despite of his nose, Poggio.

POG. Hold him to the grindstone, and give not a jot of ground; she hath in a manner promised you already.

BER. True, Poggio; and her uncle, the doctor, swore I should marry her.

POG. He swore; I remember.

BER. And I will have her, that's more. Did'st see the codpiece-point she gave me, and the box of marmalade?

POG. Very well; and kissed you, that my chops watered at the sight on't. There is no way but to clap up a marriage in hugger-mugger.[32]

BER. I will do 't; for I tell thee, Poggio, I begin to grow valiant methinks, and my courage begins to rise.

POG. Should you be afraid of your uncle?

BER. Hang him, old doating rascal! No, I say I will have her.

POG. Lose no time then.

BER. I will beget a race of wise men and constables that shall cart whores[33] at their own charges; and break the duke's peace ere I have done, myself.—Come away. (*Exeunt*)

SCENE II. *A Room in* FLORIO's *House.*

(*Enter* FLORIO, GIOVANNI, SORANZO, ANNABELLA, PUTANA, *and* VASQUES)

FLO. My lord Soranzo, though I must confess
The proffers that are made me have been great
In marriage of my daughter, yet the hope
Of your still rising honors has prevailed
Above all other jointures. Here she is;
She knows my mind; speak for yourself to her.—

[32] With haste and secrecy.

[33] Whores were often carried through town in a cart, then whipped afterwards.

[30] Head.   [31] Cheat.

And hear you, daughter, see you use him
    nobly.
For any private speech, I'll give you time.—
Come, son, and you the rest; let them alone;
Agree they as they may.
    Sor. I thank you, sir.
    Gio. (*Aside to* Ann.) Sister, be not all
woman; think on me.
    Sor. Vasques!
    Vas. My lord.
    Sor. Attend me without.
(*Exeunt all but* Soranzo *and* Annabella)
    Ann. Sir, what's your will with me?
    Sor. Do you not know
What I should tell you?
    Ann. Yes; you'll say you love me.
    Sor. And I will swear it too; will you
believe it?
    Ann. 'Tis not point of faith.

(*Enter* Giovanni *in the gallery above*)

    Sor. Have you not will to love?
    Ann. Not you.
    Sor. Whom then?
    Ann. That's as the fates infer.
    Gio. (*Aside*) Of those I'm regent now.
    Sor. What mean you, sweet?
    Ann. To live and die a maid.
    Sor. Oh, that's unfit.
    Gio. (*Aside*) Here's one can say that's but
a woman's note.
    Sor. Did you but see my heart, then would
you swear—
    Ann. That you were dead!
    Gio. (*Aside*) That's true, or somewhat
near it.
    Sor. See you these true love's tears?
    Ann. No.
    Gio. (*Aside*) Now she winks.
    Sor. They plead to you for grace.
    Ann. Yet nothing speak.
    Sor. Oh, grant my suit.
    Ann. What is't?
    Sor. To let me live—
    Ann. Take it.
    Sor. Still yours.
    Ann. That is not mine to give.
    Gio. (*Aside*) One such another word
would kill his hopes.
    Sor. Mistress, to leave those fruitless
    strifes of wit,

Know I have loved you long, and loved you
    truly;
Not hope of what you have, but what you
    are,
Hath drawn me on; then let me not in vain
Still feel the rigor of your chaste disdain.
I'm sick, and sick to the heart.
    Ann. Help! Aqua vitæ!
    Sor. What mean you?
    Ann. Why, I thought you had been sick.
    Sor. Do you mock my love?
    Gio. (*Aside*) There, sir, she was too
nimble.
    Sor. (*Aside*) 'Tis plain; she laughs at me.
    —These scornful taunts
Neither become your modesty or years.
    Ann. You are no looking-glass; or if you
    were,
I'd dress my language by you.
    Gio. (*Aside*) I'm confirmed.
    Ann. To put you out of doubt, my lord,
    methinks
Your common sense should make you under-
    stand
That if I loved you, or desired your love,
Some way I should have given you better
    tastes.
But since you are a nobleman, and one
I would not wish should spend his youth in
    hopes,
Let me advise you to forbear your suit,
And think I wish you well, I tell you this.
    Sor. Is't you speak this?
    Ann. Yes, I myself; yet know,—
Thus far I give you comfort,—if mine eyes
Could have picked out a man amongst all
    those
That sued to me to make a husband of,
You should have been that man. Let this
    suffice;
Be noble in your secrecy, and wise.
    Gio. (*Aside*) Why, now I see she loves
me.
    Ann. One word more.
As ever virtue lived within your mind,
As ever noble courses were your guide,
As ever you would have me know you loved
    me,
Let not my father know hereof by you.
If I hereafter find that I must marry,
It shall be you or none.
    Sor. I take that promise.
    Ann. Oh, oh, my head!

Sor. What's the matter, not well?

Ann. Oh, I begin to sicken.

Gio. (*Aside*) Heaven forbid!

(*Exit from above*)

Sor. Help, help, within there, ho!
Look to your daughter, Signior Florio.

(*Enter* Florio, Giovanni, *and* Putana)

Flo. Hold her up, she swoons.

Gio. Sister, how d'you?

Ann. Sick,—brother, are you there?

Flo. Convey her to bed instantly, whilst I
send for a physician; quickly I say.

Put. Alas, poor child!

(*Exeunt all but* Sor.)

(*Re-enter* Vasques)

Vas. My lord.

Sor. Oh, Vasques! Now I doubly am un-
done,
Both in my present and my future hopes.
She plainly told me that she could not love,
And thereupon soon sickened; and I fear
Her life's in danger.

Vas. (*Aside*) By'r lady, sir, and so is
yours, if you knew all.—'Las, sir, I am sorry
for that; may be, 'tis but the maids-sickness,
an over-flux of youth; and then, sir, there is
no such present remedy as present marriage.
But hath she given you an absolute denial?

Sor. She hath, and she hath not; I'm full
of grief.
But what she said, I'll tell thee as we go.

(*Exeunt*)

Scene III. *Another Room in the Same.*

(*Enter* Giovanni *and* Putana)

Put. Oh, sir, we are all undone, quite undone, utterly undone, and shamed for ever!
Your sister, oh your sister!

Gio. What of her? For heaven's sake,
speak; how does she?

Put. Oh that ever I was born to see this
day!

Gio. She is not dead, ha? Is she?

Put. Dead! No, she is quick; 'tis worse,
she is with child. You know what you have
done; heaven forgive you! 'Tis too late to
repent now, heaven help us!

Gio. With child? How dost thou know't?

Put. How do I know't? Am I at these
years ignorant what the meanings of qualms
and water-pangs be? Of changing of colors,
queasiness of stomachs, pukings, and another thing that I could name? Do not, for
her and your credit's sake, spend the time in
asking how, and which way. 'Tis so; she is
quick, upon my word. If you let a physician
see her water, y' are undone.

Gio. But in what case is she?

Put. Prettily amended. 'Twas but a fit,
which I soon espied, and she must look for
often henceforward.

Gio. Commend me to her, bid her take
no care.[34]
Let not the doctor visit her, I charge you;
Make some excuse, till I return.—Oh me!
I have a world of business in my head.
Do not discomfort her—
How do these news perplex me!—If my
father
Come to her, tell him she's recovered well;
Say 'twas but some ill diet; d'ye hear,
woman?
Look you to 't.

Put. I will, sir. (*Exeunt*)

Scene IV. *Another Room in the Same.*

(*Enter* Florio *and* Richardetto)

Flo. And how d'you find her, sir?

Rich. Indifferent well;
I see no danger, scarce perceive she's sick,
But that she told me she had lately eaten
Melons, and, as she thought, those disagreed
With her young stomach.

Flo. Did you give her aught?

[34] Do not worry.

Rich. An easy surfeit-water, nothing else.
You need not doubt her health. I rather
think
Her sickness is a fulness of her blood,—
You understand me?

Flo. I do—you counsel well—
And once, within these few days, will so
order 't
She shall be married ere she know the time.

Rich. Yet let not haste, sir, make unworthy choice;
That were dishonor.

Flo. Master doctor, no;
I will not do so neither. In plain words,
My lord Soranzo is the man I mean.

Rich. A noble and a virtuous gentleman.

Flo. As any is in Parma. Not far hence
Dwells Father Bonaventure, a grave friar,
Once tutor to my son; now at his cell
I'll have 'em married.

Rich. You have plotted wisely.

Flo. I'll send one straight to speak with
him to-night.

Rich. Soranzo's wise; he will delay no
time.

Flo. It shall be so.

(*Enter* Friar *and* Giovanni)

Friar. Good peace be here, and love!

Flo. Welcome, religious friar; you are one
That still bring blessing to the place you
come to.

Gio. Sir, with what speed I could, I did
my best
To draw this holy man from forth his cell
To visit my sick sister, that with words
Of ghostly [35] comfort in this time of need
He might absolve her whether she live or die.

Flo. 'Twas well done, Giovanni; thou
herein
Hast shewed a Christian's care, a brother's
love.
Come, father, I'll conduct you to her chamber,
And one thing would entreat you.

Friar. Say on, sir.

Flo. I have a father's dear impression,
And wish before I fall into my grave
That I might see her married, as 'tis fit.
A word from you, grave man, will win her
more
Than all our best persuasions.

Friar. Gentle sir,
All this I'll say, that Heaven may prosper
her. (*Exeunt*)

Scene V. *A Room in* Richardetto's *House.*

(*Enter* Grimaldi)

Grim. Now if the doctor keep his word,
Soranzo,
Twenty to one you miss your bride. I know
'Tis an unnoble act and not becomes
A soldier's valor; but in terms of love,
Where merit cannot sway, policy must.
I am resolved; if this physician
Play not on both hands, then Soranzo falls.

(*Enter* Richardetto)

Rich. You are come as I could wish; this
very night
Soranzo, 'tis ordained, must be affied [36]
To Annabella and, for aught I know,
Married.

Grim. How!

[35] Spiritual.   [36] Affianced.

Rich. Yet your patience.—
The place, 'tis friar Bonaventure's cell.
Now I would wish you to bestow this night
In watching thereabouts; 'tis but a night.—
If you miss now, to-morrow I'll know all.

Grim. Have you the poison?

Rich. Here 'tis, in this box;
Doubt nothing, this will do 't; in any case,
As you respect your life, be quick and sure.

Grim. I'll speed him.

Rich. Do. Away, for 'tis not safe
You should be seen much here. Ever my
love!

Grim. And mine to you. (*Exit* Grim.)

Rich. So! If this hit, I'll laugh and hug
revenge,
And they that now dream of a wedding-feast
May chance to mourn the lusty bridegroom's
ruin.
But to my other business. Niece Philotis!

(*Enter* PHILOTIS)

PHI. Uncle.

RICH. My lovely niece,
You have bethought you?

PHI. Yes, and, as you counselled,
Fashioned my heart to love him; but he swears
He will to-night be married; for he fears
His uncle else, if he should know the drift,
Will hinder all, and call his coz to shrift.

RICH. To-night? Why, best of all! But let me see—
I—ha!—yes,—so it shall be. In disguise
We'll early to the friar's—I have thought on 't.

(*Enter* BERGETTO *and* POGGIO)

PHI. Uncle, he comes.

RICH. Welcome, my worthy coz.

BER. Lass, pretty lass, come buss, lass!
A-ha, Poggio!   (*Kisses her*)

RICH. (*Aside*) There's hope of this yet.—
You shall have time enough. Withdraw a little;
We must confer at large.

BER. Have you not sweetmeats or dainty devices for me?

PHI. You shall have enough, sweetheart.

BER. Sweetheart! Mark that, Poggio. By my troth I cannot choose but kiss thee once more for that word, *sweetheart.* Poggio, I have a monstrous swelling about my stomach, whatsoever the matter be.

POG. You shall have physic for 't, sir.

RICH. Time runs apace.

BER. Time's a blockhead.

RICH. Be ruled; when we have done what's fit to do,
Then you may kiss your fill, and bed her too.
(*Exeunt*)

SCENE VI. ANNABELLA's *Chamber.*

(*A table with wax lights;* ANNABELLA *at confession before the* FRIAR; *she weeps and wrings her hands*)

FRIAR. I am glad to see this penance; for, believe me,
You have unripped a soul so foul and guilty,
As I must tell you true, I marvel how
The earth hath borne you up; but weep, weep on,
These tears may do you good; weep faster yet,
Whilst I do read a lecture.

ANN. Wretched creature!

FRIAR. Ay, you are wretched, miserably wretched,
Almost condemned alive. There is a place,—
List, daughter,—in a black and hollow vault,
Where day is never seen; there shines no sun,
But flaming horror of consuming fires,
A lightless sulphur, choked with smoky fogs
Of an infected darkness; in this place
Dwell many thousand thousand sundry sorts
Of never-dying deaths; there damned souls
Roar without pity; there are gluttons fed
With toads and adders; there is burning oil
Poured down the drunkard's throat; the usurer
Is forced to sup whole draughts of molten gold;
There is the murderer for ever stabbed,
Yet can he never die; there lies the wanton
On racks of burning steel, whilst in his soul
He feels the torment of his raging lust.—

ANN. Mercy! Oh mercy!

FRIAR. There stand these wretched things,
Who have dreamed out whole years in lawless sheets
And secret incests, cursing one another;
Then you will wish each kiss your brother gave
Had been a dagger's point; then you shall hear
How he will cry, "Oh, would my wicked sister
Had first been damned, when she did yield to lust!"—
But soft, methinks I see repentance work
New motions in your heart; say, how is 't with you?

ANN. Is there no way left to redeem my miseries?

FRIAR. There is, despair not; Heaven is merciful
And offers grace even now. 'Tis thus agreed:
First, for your honor's safety, that you marry
My lord Soranzo; next, to save your soul,
Leave off this life, and henceforth live to him.

ANN. Ay me!

FRIAR. Sigh not; I know the baits of sin
Are hard to leave; oh, 'tis a death to do 't.
Remember what must come. Are you content?

ANN. I am.

FRIAR. I like it well; we'll take the time.—
Who's near us there?

(*Enter* FLORIO *and* GIOVANNI)

FLO. Did you call, father?

FRIAR. Is Lord Soranzo come?

FLO. He stays below.

FRIAR. Have you acquainted him at full?

FLO. I have,

And he is overjoyed.

FRIAR. And so are we.
Bid him come near.

GIO. (*Aside*) My sister weeping?—Ha!
I fear this friar's falsehood.—I will call him.
(*Exit*)

FLO. Daughter, are you resolved?

ANN. Father, I am.

(*Re-enter* GIOVANNI, *with* SORANZO
and VASQUES)

FLO. My lord Soranzo, here
Give me your hand; for that, I give you this.
(*Joins their hands*)

SOR. Lady, say you so too?

ANN. I do, and vow
To live with you and yours.

FRIAR. Timely resolved;
My blessing rest on both! More to be done,
You may perform it on the morning-sun.
(*Exeunt*)

SCENE VII. *The Street before the Monastery.*

(*Enter* GRIMALDI *with his rapier drawn and
a dark lantern*)

GRIM. 'Tis early night as yet, and yet too soon
To finish such a work; here I will lie
To listen who comes next. (*He lies down*)

(*Enter* BERGETTO *and* PHILOTIS *disguised,
followed by* RICHARDETTO *and* POGGIO)

BER. We are almost at the place, I hope, sweetheart.

GRIM. (*Aside*) I hear them near, and heard one say "sweetheart."
'Tis he; now guide my hand, some angry justice,
Home to his bosom!—Now have at you, sir!
(*Stabs* BERGETTO, *and exit*)

BER. Oh help, help! here's a stitch fallen in my guts; oh for a flesh-tailor quickly!—Poggio!

PHI. What ails my love?

BER. I am sure I cannot piss forward and backward, and yet I am wet before and behind.—Lights! lights! ho, lights!

PHI. Alas, some villain here has slain my love.

RICH. O Heaven forbid it! Raise up the next neighbors
Instantly, Poggio, and bring lights.
(*Exit* POG.)
How is 't, Bergetto? Slain? It cannot be;
Are you sure y'are hurt?

BER. O my belly seethes like a porridge-pot! Some cold water, I shall boil over else. My whole body is in a sweat, that you may wring my shirt; feel here—why, Poggio!

(*Re-enter* POGGIO, *with* OFFICERS *and
lights and halberts*)

POG. Here. Alas! how do you?

RICH. Give me a light. What's here? All blood! O sirs,
Signior Donado's nephew now is slain.
Follow the murderer with all the haste
Up to the city. He cannot be far hence.
Follow, I beseech you.

OFFICERS. Follow, follow, follow.
(*Exeunt* OFFICERS)

RICH. Tear off thy linen, coz, to stop his wounds;
Be of good comfort, man.

BER. Is all this mine own blood? Nay, then, good night with me. Poggio, commend me to my uncle, dost hear? Bid him, for my sake, make much of this wench—Oh!—I am going the wrong way sure, my belly aches so —oh farewell, Poggio!—oh!—oh!— (Dies)

PHI. O, he is dead.

POG. How! Dead!

RICH. He's dead indeed;
'Tis now too late to weep. Let's have him home,
And, with what speed we may, find out the murderer.

POG. Oh my master! my master! my master! (Exeunt)

SCENE VIII. *A Room in* HIPPOLITA'S *House.*

(*Enter* VASQUES *and* HIPPOLITA)

HIP. Betrothed?

VAS. I saw it.

HIP. And when's the marriage-day?

VAS. Some two days hence.

HIP. Two days! Why man, I would but wish two hours
To send him to his last and lasting sleep;
And, Vasques, thou shalt see I'll do it bravely.

VAS. I do not doubt your wisdom, nor, I trust, you my secrecy; I am infinitely yours.

HIP. I will be thine in spite of my disgrace.—

So soon? O wicked man! I durst be sworn,
He'd laugh to see me weep.

VAS. And that's a villainous fault in him.

HIP. No, let him laugh; I am armed in my resolves.
Be thou still true.

VAS. I should get little by treachery against so hopeful a preferment, as I am like to climb to—

HIP. Even to—my bosom, Vasques. Let my youth
Revel in these new pleasures; if we thrive,
He now hath but a pair of days to live. (Exeunt)

SCENE IX. *The Street before the* CARDINAL'S *Gates.*

(*Enter* FLORIO, DONADO, RICHARDETTO, POGGIO, *and* OFFICERS)

FLO. 'Tis bootless now to shew yourself a child.
Signior Donado, what is done, is done;
Spend not the time in tears, but seek for justice.

RICH. I must confess, somewhat I was in fault,
That had not first acquainted you what love
Past 'twixt him and my niece; but, as I live,
His fortune grieves me as it were mine own.

DON. Alas, poor creature, he meant no man harm,
That I am sure of.

FLO. I believe that too.
But stay, my masters are you sure you saw
The murderer pass here?

FIRST OFFICER. An it please you, sir, we are sure we saw a ruffian, with a naked weapon in his hand all bloody, get into my lord Cardinal's grace's gate; that we are sure of; but for fear of his grace (bless us!) we durst go no farther.

DON. Know you what manner of man he was?

SECOND OFFICER. Yes sure, I know the man; they say he is a soldier—he that loved your daughter, sir, an 't please ye; 'twas he for certain.

FLO. Grimaldi, on my life.

SECOND OFFICER. Ay, ay, the same.

RICH. The Cardinal is noble; he no doubt
Will give true justice.

DON. Knock, some one, at the gate.

POG. I'll knock, sir. (Knocks)

SERV. (Within) What would ye?

FLO. We require speech with the lord Cardinal

About some present business; pray inform
His grace that we are here.

(*Enter* CARDINAL, *followed by* GRIMALDI)

CAR. Why, how now, friends! What saucy
   mates are you
That know nor duty nor civility?
Are we a person fit to be your host;
Or is our house become your common inn,
To beat our doors at pleasure? What such
   haste
Is yours, as that it cannot wait fit times?
Are you the masters of this commonwealth,
And know no more discretion? Oh, your
   news
Is here before you; you have lost a nephew,
Donado, last night by Grimaldi slain.
Is that your business? Well, sir, we have
   knowledge on 't,
Let that suffice.
   GRIM. In presence of your grace,
In thought I never meant Bergetto harm.
But, Florio, you can tell with how much
   scorn
Soranzo, backed with his confederates,
Hath often wronged me; I to be revenged,—
For that I could not win him else to fight—
Had thought, by way of ambush, to have
   killed him,
But was, unluckily, therein mistook;

Else he had felt what late Bergetto did.
And though my fault to him were merely
   chance,
Yet humbly I submit me to your grace,
                          (*Kneeling*)
To do with me as you please.
   CAR. Rise up, Grimaldi.   (*He rises*)
You citizens of Parma, if you seek
For justice, know, as Nuncio from the pope,
For this offence I here receive Grimaldi
Into his Holiness' protection.
He is no common man, but nobly born,
Of princes' blood, though you, sir Florio,
Thought him too mean a husband for your
   daughter.
If more you seek for, you must go to Rome,
For he shall thither; learn more wit for
   shame.
Bury your dead.—Away, Grimaldi; leave 'em!
            (*Exeunt* CARDINAL *and* GRIMALDI)
   DON. Is this a churchman's voice? Dwells
justice here?
   FLO. Justice is fled to heaven and comes
   no nearer.
Soranzo!—was 't for him? O impudence!
Had he the face to speak it, and not blush?
Come, come, Donado, there's no help in this,
When cardinals think murder's not amiss.
Great men may do their wills, we must obey,
But Heaven will judge them for 't another
   day.   (*Exeunt*)

Act IV

SCENE I. *A Room in* FLORIO'S *House. A Banquet set out. Hautboys play.*

(*Enter the* FRIAR, GIOVANNI, ANNABELLA,
PHILOTIS, SORANZO, DONADO, FLORIO, RICH-
ARDETTO, PUTANA, *and* VASQUES)

   FRIAR. These holy rites performed, now
   take your times
To spend the remnant of the day in feast;
Such fit repasts are pleasing to the saints,
Who are your guests, though not with mortal
   eyes
To be beheld.—Long prosper in this day,
You happy couple, to each other's joy!
   SOR. Father, your prayer is heard; the
   hand of goodness
Hath been a shield for me against my death;

And, more to bless me, hath enriched my life
With this most precious jewel; such a prize
As earth hath not another like to this.—
Cheer up, my love.—And, gentlemen, my
   friends,
Rejoice with me in mirth; this day we'll
   crown
With lusty cups to Annabella's health.
   GIO. (*Aside*) Oh torture! Were the mar-
   riage yet undone,
Ere I'd endure this sight, to see my love
Clipt [37] by another, I would dare confusion,
And stand the horror of ten thousand deaths.
   VAS. Are you not well, sir?

   [37] Embraced.

Gio. Prithee, fellow, wait;
I need not thy officious diligence.

Flo. Signior Donado, come, you must forget
Your late mishaps, and drown your cares in wine.

Sor. Vasques!

Vas. My lord.

Sor. Reach me that weighty bowl.
Here, brother Giovanni, here's to you;
Your turn comes next, though now a bachelor.
Here's to your sister's happiness, and mine!
(*Drinks and offers him the bowl*)

Gio. I cannot drink.

Sor. What!

Gio. 'Twill indeed offend me.

Ann. Pray do not urge him, if he be not willing.   (*Hautboys play off stage*)

Flo. How now! What noise is this?

Vas. O sir, I had forgot to tell you. Certain young maidens of Parma, in honor to madam Annabella's marriage, have sent their loves to her in a masque, for which they humbly crave your patience and silence.

Sor. We are much bound to them; so much the more,
As it comes unexpected. Guide them in.

(*Enter* Hippolita, *followed by* Ladies *in white robes, with garlands of willows, all masked. Music and a dance*)

Sor. Thanks, lovely virgins! Now might we but know
To whom we have been beholding for this love,
We shall acknowledge it.

Hip. Yes, you shall know.   (*Unmasks*)
What think you now?

Omnes. Hippolita!

Hip. 'Tis she.
Be not amazed, nor blush, young lovely bride;
I come not to defraud you of your man.
'Tis now no time to reckon up the talk
What Parma long hath rumored of us both;
Let rash report run on! The breath that vents it
Will, like a bubble, break itself at last.
But now to you, sweet creature.—Lend your hand.—
Perhaps it hath been said that I would claim
Some interest in Soranzo, now your lord;
What I have right to do, his soul knows best,
But in my duty to your noble worth,
Sweet Annabella, and my care of you,
Here, take Soranzo, take this hand from me;
I'll once more join what by the holy church
Is finished and allowed.—Have I done well?

Sor. You have too much engaged us.

Hip. One thing more.
That you may know my single[38] charity,
Freely I here remit all interest
I e'er could claim, and give you back your vows;
And to confirm 't,—reach me a cup of wine—
My lord Soranzo, in this draught I drink
Long rest t' ye!—(*Aside to* Vasques)—Look to it, Vasques.

Vas. Fear nothing—(*He gives her a poisoned cup; she drinks*)

Sor. Hippolita, I thank you, and will pledge
This happy union as another life.—
Wine, there!

Vas. You shall have none; neither shall you pledge her.

Hip. How!

Vas. Know now, mistress she-devil, your own mischievous treachery hath killed you;
I must not marry you.

Hip. Villain!

Omnes. What's the matter?

Vas. Foolish woman, thou art now like a firebrand that hath kindled others and burnt thyself.—*Troppo sperar, inganna*,[39]—thy vain hope hath deceived thee. Thou art but dead; if thou hast any grace, pray.

Hip. Monster!

Vas. Die in charity, for shame.—This thing of malice, this woman, hath privately corrupted me with promise of marriage, under this politic reconciliation, to poison my lord, whilst she might laugh at his confusion on his marriage-day. I promised her fair; but I knew what my reward should have been, and would willingly have spared her life, but that I was acquainted with the danger of her disposition; and now have fitted her a just payment in her own coin. There she is, she hath yet[40]—and end thy days in peace, vile

[38] Single-minded.
[39] "Excessive hope is deceitful."
[40] Original editions omit something here.

woman. As for life, there's no hope, think
not on 't.
    OMNES. Wonderful justice!
    RICH. Heaven, thou art righteous.
    HIP. O 'tis true,
I feel my minute coming. Had that slave
Kept promise,—O my torment!—thou this
    hour
Hadst died, Soranzo,—heat above hell-fire!—
Yet, ere I pass away,—cruel, cruel flames!—
Take here my curse amongst you. May thy
    bed
Of marriage be a rack unto thy heart,
Burn blood, and boil in vengeance—O my
    heart,
My flame's intolerable!—May'st thou live
To father bastards; may her womb bring forth
Monsters; and die together in your sins,
Hated, scorned and unpitied!—oh!—oh!—
                    (*Dies*)

    FLO. Was e'er so vile a creature!
    RICH. Here's the end
Of lust and pride.
    ANN. It is a fearful sight.
    SOR. Vasques, I know thee now a trusty
    servant,
And never will forget thee.—Come, my love,
We'll home and thank the heavens for this
    escape.
Father and friends, we must break up this
    mirth;
It is too sad a feast.
    DON. Bear hence the body.
    FRIAR. (*Aside to* GIO.) Here's an omi-
    nous change!
Mark this, my Giovanni, and take heed!
I fear the event; that marriage seldom's good,
Where the bride-banquet so begins in blood.
                  (*Exeunt*)

SCENE II. *A Room in* RICHARDETTO'*s House.*

(*Enter* RICHARDETTO *and* PHILOTIS)

    RICH. My wretched wife, more wretched
    in her shame
Than in her wrongs to me, hath paid too
    soon
The forfeit of her modesty and life.
And I am sure, my niece, though vengeance
    hover,
Keeping aloof yet from Soranzo's fall,
Yet he will fall, and sink with his own
    weight.
I need not now (my heart persuades me so,)
To further his confusion; there is One
Above begins to work. For as I hear,
Debates already 'twixt his wife and him
Thicken and run to head; she, as 'tis said,
Slightens his love, and he abandons hers.
Much talk I hear. Since things go thus, my
    niece,
In tender love and pity of your youth,

My counsel is that you should free your years
From hazard of these woes by flying hence
To fair Cremona, there to vow your soul
In holiness, a holy votaress;
Leave me to see the end of these extremes.
All human worldly courses are uneven,
No life is blessed but the way to heaven.
    PHI. Uncle, shall I resolve to be a nun?
    RICH. Ay, gentle niece; and in your hourly
    prayers
Remember me, your poor unhappy uncle.
Hie to Cremona now, as fortune leads,
Your home your cloister, your best friends
    your beads.
Your chaste and single life shall crown your
    birth;
Who dies a virgin, lives a saint on earth.
    PHI. Then farewell, world, and worldly
    thoughts, adieu!
Welcome, chaste vows, myself I yield to you.
                  (*Exeunt*)

SCENE III. *A Chamber in* SORANZO'S *House.*

(*Enter* SORANZO *unbraced, and dragging in*
ANNABELLA)

SOR. Come, strumpet, famous whore! were
    every drop
Of blood that runs in thy adulterous veins
A life, this sword (dost see 't?) should in one
    blow
Confound them all. Harlot, rare, notable
    harlot,
That with thy brazen face maintain'st thy
    sin,
Was there no man in Parma to be bawd
To your loose cunning whoredom else but I?
Must your hot itch and pleurisy of lust,
The heyday of your luxury,[41] be fed
Up to a surfeit, and could none but I
Be picked out to be cloak to your close tricks,
Your belly-sports?—Now I must be the dad
To all that gallimaufry [42] that is stuffed
In thy corrupted bastard-bearing womb!—
Say, must I?
    ANN. Beastly man! Why 'tis thy fate.
I sued not to thee; for, but that I thought
Your over-loving lordship would have run
Mad on denial, had you lent me time
I would have told you in what case I was.
But you would needs be doing.
    SOR. Whore of whores!
Darest thou tell me this?
    ANN. O yes; why not?
You were deceived in me; 'twas not for love
I chose you, but for honor. Yet know this,
Would you be patient yet and hide your
    shame,
I'd see whether I could love you.
    SOR. Excellent quean! [43]
Why, art thou not with child?
    ANN. What needs all this,
When 'tis superfluous? I confess I am.
    SOR. Tell me by whom.
    ANN. Soft, 'twas not in my bargain.
Yet somewhat, sir, to stay your longing
    stomach,
I'm content t' acquaint you with. The man,
The more than man, that got this sprightly
    boy,—
For 'tis a boy, that for glory, sir,

Your heir shall be a son—
    SOR. Damnable monster!
    ANN. Nay, an you will not hear, I'll speak
no more.
    SOR. Yes speak, and speak thy last.
    ANN. A match, a match!—
This noble creature was in every part
So angel-like, so glorious, that a woman
Who had not been but human, as was I,
Would have kneeled to him and have begged
    for love.—
You! Why you are not worthy once to name
His name without true worship, or, indeed,
Unless you kneeled, to hear another name
    him.
    SOR. What was he called?
    ANN. We are not come to that.
Let it suffice that you shall have the glory
To father what so brave a father got.
In brief, had not this chance fallen out as
    it doth,
I never had been troubled with a thought
That you had been a creature;—but for mar-
    riage,
I scarce dream yet of that.
    SOR. Tell me his name.
    ANN. Alas, alas, there's all! Will you be-
lieve?
    SOR. What?
    ANN. You shall never know.
    SOR. How!
    ANN. Never.
If you do, let me be cursed.
    SOR. Not know it, strumpet! I'll rip up
    thy heart
And find it there.
    ANN. Do, do.
    SOR. And with my teeth
Tear the prodigious lecher joint by joint.
    ANN. Ha, ha, ha! The man's merry.
    SOR. Dost thou laugh?
Come, whore, tell me your lover, or by truth
I'll hew thy flesh to shreds; who is 't?
    ANN. (*Sings*) *Che morte più dolce che
morire per amore?* [44]
    SOR. Thus will I pull thy hair, and thus
    I'll drag

[41] Commonly used in sense of lust.
[42] Jumbled mess.   [43] Harlot.
[44] "What death more sweet than to die for
love?"

Thy lust be-lepered body through the dust—
    (*Hales her up and down*)
Yet tell his name.

Ann. (*Sings*) *Morendo in grazia dee
morire senza dolore.*[45]

 Sor. Dost thou triumph? The treasure of
  the earth
Shall not redeem thee. Were there kneeling
  kings
Did beg thy life, or angels did come down
To plead in tears, yet should not all prevail
Against my rage. Dost thou not tremble yet?

 Ann. At what? To die? No, be a gallant
  hangman;
I dare thee to the worst. Strike, and strike
  home.
I leave revenge behind, and thou shalt feel 't.

 Sor. Yet tell me ere thou diest, and tell
  me truly,
Knows thy old father this?

 Ann. No, by my life.

 Sor. Wilt thou confess, and I will spare
thy life?

 Ann. My life! I will not buy my life so
dear.

 Sor. I will not slack my vengeance.
       (*Draws his sword*)

     (*Enter* Vasques)

 Vas. What d' you mean, sir?

 Sor. Forbear, Vasques; such a damned
  whore
Deserves no pity.

 Vas. Now the gods forefend!
And would you be her executioner, and kill
her in your rage too? O 'twere most unman-
like; she is your wife, what faults have been
done by her before she married you, were
not against you. Alas! poor lady, what hath
she committed, which any lady in Italy in
the like case would not? Sir, you must be
ruled by your reason, and not by your fury;
that were inhuman and beastly.

 Sor. She shall not live.

 Vas. Come, she must. You would have her
confess the authors of her present misfortunes, I warrant'ee; 'tis an unconscionable demand, and she should lose the estimation
that I, for my part, hold of her worth, if she
had done it. Why, sir, you ought not, of all

 [45] "To die in grace is to die without grief."

men living, to know it. Good sir, be reconciled. Alas, good gentlewoman!

 Ann. Pish, do not beg for me, I prize my
  life
As nothing; if the man will needs be mad,
Why let him take it.

 Sor. Vasques, hear'st thou this?

 Vas. Yes, and commend her for it; in this
she shews the nobleness of a gallant spirit,
and beshrew my heart, but it becomes her
rarely.—(*Aside to* Sor.)—Sir, in any case
smother your revenge; leave the scenting out
your wrongs to me; be ruled, as you respect
your honor, or you mar all.—(*Aloud*)—Sir,
if ever my service were of any credit with
you, be not so violent in your distractions.
You are married now; what a triumph might
the report of this give to other neglected
suitors! 'Tis as manlike to bear extremities,
as godlike to forgive.

 Sor. O Vasques, Vasques, in this piece
  of flesh,
This faithless face of hers, had I laid up
The treasure of my heart.—Hadst thou been
  virtuous,
Fair, wicked woman, not the matchless joys
Of life itself had made me wish to live
With any saint but thee. Deceitful creature,
How hast thou mocked my hopes, and in
  the shame
Of thy lewd womb even buried me alive!
I did too dearly love thee.

 Vas. (*Aside*) This is well; follow this temper with some passion. Be brief and moving,
'tis for the purpose.

 Sor. Be witness to my words thy soul and
  thoughts,
And tell me, didst not think that in my heart
I did too superstitiously adore thee?

 Ann. I must confess, I know you loved
me well.

 Sor. And would'st thou use me thus! O
  Annabella,
Be thou assured, whoe'er the villain was
That thus hath tempted thee to this disgrace,
Well he might lust, but never loved like
  me.
He doted on the picture that hung out
Upon thy cheeks, to please his humorous
  eye;
Not on the part I loved, which was thy heart,
And, as I thought, thy virtues.

 Ann. O, my lord!

These words wound deeper than your sword
    could do.

Vas. Let me not ever take comfort, but I
begin to weep myself, so much I pity him;
why, madam, I knew, when his rage was
over-past, what it would come to.

Sor. Forgive me, Annabella. Though thy
    youth
Hath tempted thee above thy strength to
    folly,
Yet will I not forget what I should be,
And what I am,—a husband; in that name
Is hid divinity. If I do find
That thou wilt yet be true, here I remit
All former faults, and take thee to my bosom.

Vas. By my troth, and that's a point of
noble charity.

Ann. Sir, on my knees—

Sor. Rise up, you shall not kneel.
Get you to your chamber, see you make no
    shew
Of alteration; I'll be with you straight.
My reason tells me now that "'tis as common
To err in frailty as to be a woman."
Go to your chamber.   (Exit Ann.)

Vas. So! This was somewhat to the matter.
What do you think of your heaven of happiness now, sir?

Sor. I carry hell about me; all my blood
Is fired in swift revenge.

Vas. That may be; but know you how,
or on whom? Alas! to marry a great woman,
being made great in the stock to your hand,
is a usual sport in these days; but to know
what ferret it was that hunted your coney-
burrow,—there's the cunning.

Sor. I'll make her tell herself, or—

Vas. Or what?—You must not do so; let
me yet persuade your sufferance a little while.
Go to her, use her mildly; win her, if it be
possible, to a voluntary, to a weeping tune.
For the rest, if all hit, I will not miss my
mark. Pray, sir, go in; the next news I tell
you shall be wonders.

Sor. Delay in vengeance gives a heavier
blow.   (Exit)

Vas. Ah, sirrah, here's work for the nonce!
I had a suspicion of a bad matter in my head
a pretty while ago; but after my madam's
scurvy looks here at home, her waspish perverseness, and loud fault-finding, then I remembered the proverb, that "where hens
crow, and cocks hold their peace, there are
sorry houses." 'Sfoot! if the lower parts of a
she-tailor's cunning can cover such a swelling
in the stomach, I'll never blame a false stitch
in a shoe whilst I live again. Up, and up so
quick? And so quickly too? 'Twere a fine
policy to learn by whom this must be known;
and I have thought on 't—

(*Enter* Putana, *in tears*)

Here's the way, or none.—What, crying, old
mistress! Alas, alas, I cannot blame 'ee; we
have a lord, Heaven help us, is so mad as the
devil himself, the more shame for him.

Put. O Vasques, that ever I was born to
see this day! Doth he use thee so too, sometimes, Vasques?

Vas. Me? Why he makes a dog of me;
but if some were of my mind, I know what
we would do. As sure as I am an honest man,
he will go near to kill my lady with unkindness. Say she be with child, is that such a
matter for a young woman of her years to
be blamed for?

Put. Alas, good heart, it is against her will
full sore.

Vas. I durst be sworn, all his madness is
for that she will not confess whose 'tis, which
he will know; and when he doth know it, I
am so well acquainted with his humor, that
he will forget all straight. Well, I could wish
she would in plain terms tell all, for that's
the way, indeed.

Put. Do you think so?

Vas. Foh, I know't; provided that he did
not win her to't by force. He was once in
a mind that you could tell and meant to have
wrung it out of you; but I somewhat pacified
him from that; yet sure you know a great
deal.

Put. Heaven forgive us all! I know a
little, Vasques.

Vas. Why should you not? Who else
should? Upon my conscience she loves you
dearly; and you would not betray her to any
affliction for the world.

Put. Nor for all the world, by my faith
and troth, Vasques.

Vas. 'Twere pity of your life if you should;
but in this you should both relieve her present
discomforts, pacify my lord, and gain yourself everlasting love and preferment.

Put. Dost think so, Vasques?

VAS. Nay, I know't; sure it was some near and entire friend.

PUT. 'Twas a dear friend indeed; but—

VAS. But what? Fear not to name him; my life between you and danger. 'Faith, I think it was no base fellow.

PUT. Thou wilt stand between me and harm?

VAS. 'Uds pity, what else? You shall be rewarded too; trust me.

PUT. 'Twas even no worse than her own brother.

VAS. Her brother Giovanni, I warrant 'ee!

PUT. Even he, Vasques; as brave a gentleman as ever kissed fair lady. O, they love most perpetually.

VAS. A brave gentleman indeed! Why therein I commend her choice—(Aside) Better and better—You are sure 'twas he?

PUT. Sure; and you shall see he will not be long from her too.

VAS. He were to blame if he would; but may I believe thee?

PUT. Believe me! Why, dost think I am a Turk or a Jew? No, Vasques, I have known their dealings too long, to belie them now.

VAS. (Calling) Where are you? There, within, sirs!

(Enter BANDITTI)

PUT. How now, what are these?

VAS. You shall know presently.—Come, sirs, take me this old damnable hag, gag her instantly, and put out her eyes, quickly, quickly!

PUT. Vasques! Vasques!

VAS. Gag her, I say; 'sfoot, do 'ee suffer her to prate? What do 'ee fumble about? Let me come to her. I'll help your old gums, you toad-bellied bitch! Sirs, carry her closely unto the coal-house and put out her eyes instantly; if she roars, slit her nose. Do 'ee hear, be speedy and sure. (Exeunt BAN. with PUT.) Why this is excellent, and above expectation!

Her own brother! O horrible! To what a height of liberty in damnation hath the devil trained our age! Her brother, well! There's yet but a beginning; I must to my lord and tutor him better in his points of vengeance. Now I see how a smooth tale goes beyond a smooth tail.—But soft, what thing comes next? (Enter GIOVANNI) Giovanni! As I could wish; my belief is strengthened, 'tis as firm as winter and summer.

GIO. Where's my sister?

VAS. Troubled with a new sickness, my lord; she's somewhat ill.

GIO. Took too much of the flesh, I believe.

VAS. Troth, sir, and you I think have even hit it; but my virtuous lady—

GIO. Where's she?

VAS. In her chamber. Please you visit her; she is alone. (GIO. gives him money) Your liberality hath doubly made me your servant, and ever shall, ever—   (Exit GIO.)

(Re-enter SORANZO)

Sir, I am made a man; I have plied my cue with cunning and success. I beseech you let us be private.

SOR. My lady's brother's come; now he'll know all.

VAS. Let him know't; I have made some of them fast enough. How have you dealt with my lady?

SOR. Gently, as thou hast counselled. O my soul
Runs circular in sorrow for revenge.
But, Vasques, thou shalt know—

VAS. Nay, I will know no more, for now comes your turn to know; I would not talk so openly with you—(Aside) Let my young master take time enough, and go at pleasure; he is sold to death, and the devil shall not ransom him.—Sir, I beseech you, your privacy.

SOR. No conquest can gain glory of my fear.   (Exeunt)

Act V

SCENE I. *The Street before* SORANZO'S *House.*

(ANNABELLA *appears at a window above*)

ANN. Pleasures, farewell, and all ye thrift-
less minutes
Wherein false joys have spun a weary life!
To these my fortunes now I take my leave.
Thou, precious Time, that swiftly rid'st in
post
Over the world, to finish up the race
Of my last fate, here stay thy restless course,
And bear to ages that are yet unborn
A wretched, woeful woman's tragedy!
My conscience now stands up against my
lust,
With depositions charactered in guilt,

(*Enter* FRIAR, *below*)

And tells me I am lost. Now I confess;
Beauty that clothes the outside of the face,
Is cursed if it be not clothed with grace.
Here like a turtle,[46] mewed up in a cage,
Unmated, I converse with air and walls
And descant on my vile unhappiness.
O Giovanni, that hast had the spoil
Of thine own virtues, and my modest fame;
Would thou hadst been less subject to those
stars
That luckless reigned at my nativity!
O would the scourge, due to my black of-
fence,
Might pass from thee, that I alone might
feel
The torment of an uncontrolled flame!
FRIAR. (*Aside*) What's this I hear?
ANN. That man, that blessed friar,
Who joined in ceremonial knot my hand
To him whose wife I now am, told me oft,
I trod the path to death, and shewed me how.
But they who sleep in lethargies of lust,
Hug their confusion, making Heaven un-
just;
And so did I.

[46] Turtle-dove.

FRIAR. (*Aside*) Here's music to the soul!
ANN. Forgive me, my good Genius, and
this once
Be helpful to my ends. Let some good man
Pass this way, to whose trust I may commit
This paper, double lined with tears and
blood;
Which being granted, here I sadly vow
Repentance and a leaving of that life
I long have died in.
FRIAR. Lady, Heaven hath heard you,
And hath by providence ordained that I
Should be his minister for your behoof.
ANN. Ha, what are you?
FRIAR. Your brother's friend, the Friar;
Glad in my soul that I have lived to hear
This free confession 'twixt your peace and
you.
What would you, or to whom? Fear not to
speak.
ANN. Is Heaven so bountiful?—then I
have found
More favor than I hoped. Here, holy man—
(*Throws down a letter*)
Commend me to my brother, give him that,
That letter; bid him read it and repent.
Tell him that I, imprisoned in my chamber,
Barred of all company, even of my guard-
ian,—
Which gives me cause of much suspect,—
have time
To blush at what hath past; bid him be wise
And not believe the friendship of my lord.
I fear much more than I can speak. Good
father,
The place is dangerous, and spies are busy;
I must break off.—You'll do't?
FRIAR. Be sure I will
And fly with speed.—My blessing ever rest
With thee, my daughter; live, to die more
blest! (*Exit*)
ANN. Thanks to the heavens, who have
prolonged my breath
To this good use! Now I can welcome death.
(*Exit*)

Scene II. *A Room in* Soranzo's *House.*

(*Enter* Soranzo *and* Vasques)

Vas. Am I to be believed now? First,
marry a strumpet that cast herself away upon
you but to laugh at your horns, to feast on
your disgrace, riot in your vexations, cuckold
you in your bride-bed, waste your estate
upon panders and bawds!—

Sor. No more, I say, no more!

Vas. A cuckold is a goodly tame beast, my
lord.

Sor. I am resolved; urge not another word.
My thoughts are great, and all as resolute
As thunder. In mean time, I'll cause our lady
To deck herself in all her bridal robes,
Kiss her, and fold her gently in my arms.
Begone—yet, hear you, are the banditti ready
To wait in ambush?

Vas. Good sir, trouble not yourself about
other business than your own resolution; remember that time lost cannot be recalled.

Sor. With all the cunning words thou
canst, invite
The states [47] of Parma to my birth-day's feast.
Haste to my brother-rival and his father,
Entreat them gently, bid them not to fail;
Be speedy, and return.

Vas. Let not your pity betray you, till my
coming back; think upon incest and cuck-
oldry.

Sor. Revenge is all the ambition I aspire,
To that I'll climb or fall; my blood's on
fire.

(*Exeunt*)

Scene III. *A Room in* Florio's *House.*

(*Enter* Giovanni)

Gio. Busy opinion is an idle fool,
That, as a school-rod keeps a child in awe,
Frights th' unexperienced temper of the
mind.
So did it me, who, ere my precious sister
Was married, thought all taste of love would
die
In such a contract; but I find no change
Of pleasure in this formal law of sports.
She is still one to me, and every kiss
As sweet and as delicious as the first
I reaped, when yet the privilege of youth
Entitled her a virgin. O the glory
Of two united hearts like hers and mine!
Let poring book-men dream of other worlds;
My world, and all of happiness is here,
And I'd not change it for the best to come.—
A life of pleasure is Elysium.

(*Enter* Friar)

Father, you enter on the jubilee
Of my retired delights; now I can tell you,
The hell you oft have prompted is nought
else
But slavish and fond superstitious fear;
And I could prove it too—

Friar. Thy blindness slays thee.
Look there, 'tis writ to thee.

(*Gives him the letter*)

Gio. From whom?

Friar. Unrip the seals and see.
The blood's yet seething hot that will anon
Be frozen harder than congealed coral.
Why d'ye change color, son?

Gio. 'Fore heaven, you make
Some petty devil factor [48] 'twixt my love
And your religion-masked sorceries.
Where had you this?

Friar. Thy conscience, youth, is seared;
Else thou would'st stoop to warning.

Gio. 'Tis her hand,
I know't; and 'tis all written in her blood.
She writes I know not what. Death? I'll not
fear
An armed thunderbolt aimed at my heart.
She writes, we are discovered—pox on dreams
Of low faint-hearted cowardice!—discovered?
The devil we are! Which way is't possible?
Are we grown traitors to our own delights?
Confusion take such dotage! 'Tis but forged;
This is your peevish chattering, weak old
man!—

[47] The nobles.   [48] Agent.

(Enter Vasques*)*

Now, sir, what news bring you?

Vas. My lord, according to his yearly custom, keeping this day a feast in honor of his birth-day, by me invites you thither. Your worthy father, with the pope's reverend nuncio and other magnificoes of Parma, have promised their presence; will't please you to be of the number?

Gio. Yes, tell him I dare come.

Vas. Dare come?

Gio. So I said; and tell him more, I will come.

Vas. These words are strange to me.

Gio. Say, I will come.

Vas. You will not miss?

Gio. Yet more! I'll come, sir. Are you answered?

Vas. So I'll say.—My service to you.
(Exit)

Friar. You will not go, I trust.

Gio. Not go? For what?

Friar. O, do not go; this feast, I'll gage my life,
Is but a plot to train you to your ruin;
Be ruled, you shall not go.

Gio. Not go! Stood death
Threatening his armies of confounding plagues,
With hosts of dangers hot as blazing stars,
I would be there. Not go! yes, and resolve
To strike as deep in slaughter as they all;
For I will go.

Friar. Go where thou wilt. I see
The wildness of thy fate draws to an end,
To a bad fearful end. I must not stay
To know thy fall; back to Bononia I
With speed will haste and shun this coming blow.
Parma, farewell; would I had never known thee,
Or aught of thine! Well, young man, since no prayer
Can make thee safe, I leave thee to despair.
(Exit)

Gio. Despair, or tortures of a thousand hells,
All's one to me; I have set up my rest.[49]
Now, now, work serious thoughts on baneful plots.
Be all a man, my soul; let not the curse
Of old prescription rend from me the gall
Of courage, which enrolls a glorious death.
If I must totter like a well-grown oak,
Some under-shrubs shall in my weighty fall
Be crushed to splits; with me they all shall perish! *(Exit)*

Scene IV. *A Hall in* Soranzo's *House.*

(Enter Soranzo, Vasques *with masks, and* Banditti*)*

Sor. You will not fail or shrink in the attempt?

Vas. I will undertake for their parts.—Be sure, my masters, to be bloody enough, and as unmerciful as if you were preying upon a rich booty on the very mountains of Liguria. For your pardons, trust to my lord; but for reward, you shall trust none but your own pockets.

Banditti. We'll make a murder.

Sor. Here's gold, here's more; want nothing. What you do
Is noble, and an act of brave revenge.
I'll make you rich, banditti, and all free.

Omnes. Liberty! Liberty!

Vas. Hold, take every man a vizard. When you are withdrawn, keep as much silence as you can possibly. You know the watch-word, till which be spoken, move not; but when you hear that, rush in like a stormy flood. I need not instruct you in your own profession.

Omnes. No, no, no.

Vas. In, then; your ends are profit and preferment.—Away! *(Exeunt* Ban.*)*

Sor. The guests will all come, Vasques?

Vas. Yes, sir. And now let me a little edge your resolution. You see nothing is unready to this great work, but a great mind in you. Call to your remembrance your disgraces, your loss of honor, Hippolita's blood, and arm your courage in your own wrongs. So

[49] Made my resolution.

shall you best right those wrongs in vengeance, which you may truly call your own.

Sor. 'Tis well; the less I speak, the more
    I burn,
And blood shall quench that flame.

Vas. Now you begin to turn Italian. This
beside:—When my young incest-monger
comes, he will be sharp set on his old bit.
Give him time enough, let him have your
chamber and bed at liberty; let my hot hare
have law ere he be hunted to his death, that,
if it be possible, he may post to hell in the
very act of his damnation.

Sor. It shall be so; and see, as we would
    wish,
He comes himself first—

(Enter GIOVANNI*)*

Welcome, my much-loved brother.
Now I perceive you honor me; you are wel-
    come.
But where's my father?

Gio. With the other states,
Attending on the nuncio of the pope,
To wait upon him hither. How's my sister?

Sor. Like a good housewife, scarcely ready
    yet.
You were best walk to her chamber.

Gio. If you will.

Sor. I must expect my honorable friends;
Good brother, get her forth.

Gio. You are busy, sir.   *(Exit)*

Vas. Even as the great devil himself
would have it! Let him go and glut himself
in his own destruction— *(Flourish)*—Hark,
the nuncio is at hand; good sir, be ready to
receive him.

(Enter CARDINAL, FLORIO, DONADO, RICH-
    ARDETTO, *and* ATTENDANTS*)*

Sor. Most reverend lord, this grace hath
    made me proud,
That you vouchsafe my house; I ever rest
Your humble servant for this noble favor.

Car. You are our friend, my lord; his Hol-
    iness
Shall understand how zealously you honor
Saint Peter's vicar in his substitute.
Our special love to you.

Sor. Signiors, to you
My welcome, and my ever best of thanks
For this so memorable courtesy.
Pleaseth your grace, walk near?

Car. My lord, we come
To celebrate your feast with civil mirth,
As ancient custom teacheth; we will go.

Sor. Attend his grace there. Signiors, keep
your way.   *(Exeunt)*

SCENE V. ANNABELLA's *Bed Chamber in the Same.*

*(*ANNABELLA, *richly dressed, lying on a
bed, and* GIOVANNI*)*

Gio. What, changed so soon! Hath your
    new sprightly lord
Found out a trick in night-games more than
    we
Could know, in our simplicity? Ha! Is 't so?
Or does the fit come on you to prove
    treacherous
To your past vows and oaths?

Ann. Why should you jest
At my calamity, without all sense
Of the approaching dangers you are in?

Gio. What dangers half so great as thy
    revolt?
Thou art a faithless sister, else thou know'st
Malice or any treachery beside

Would stoop to my bent brows.[60] Why, I
    hold fate
Clasped in my fist, and could command the
    course
Of time's eternal motion, hadst thou been
One thought more steady than an ebbing sea.
And what? You'll now be honest, that's re-
    solved?

Ann. Brother, dear brother, know what I
    have been,
And know that now there's but a dining-time
'Twixt us and our confusion; let's not waste
These precious hours in vain and useless
    speech.
Alas! These gay attires were not put on
But to some end. This sudden solemn feast
Was not ordained to riot in expense;

    [60] Would dwindle at my frown.

I, that have now been chambered here alone,
Barred of my guardian or of any else,
Am not for nothing at an instant freed
To fresh access. Be not deceived, my brother;
This banquet is an harbinger of death
To you and me; resolve yourself it is,
And be prepared to welcome it.

Gio. Well, then,
The schoolmen teach that all this globe of earth
Shall be consumed to ashes in a minute.

Ann. So I have read too.

Gio. But 'twere somewhat strange
To see the waters burn; could I believe
This might be true, I could believe as well
There might be hell or heaven.

Ann. That's most certain.

Gio. A dream, a dream! Else in this other world
We should know one another.

Ann. So we shall.

Gio. Have you heard so?

Ann. For certain.

Gio. But d'you think
That I shall see you there?—You look on me?
May we kiss one another, prate, or laugh,
Or do as we do here?

Ann. I know not that.
But—brother, for the present, what d'ye mean
To free yourself from danger? Some way think
How to escape; I'm sure the guests are come.

Gio. Look up, look here; what see you in my face?

Ann. Distraction and a troubled conscience.

Gio. Death, and a swift repining wrath.
—Yet look;
What see you in mine eyes?

Ann. Me thinks you weep.

Gio. I do indeed; these are the funeral tears
Shed on your grave; these furrowed up my cheeks
When first I loved and knew not how to woo.
Fair Annabella, should I here repeat
The story of my life, we might lose time.
Be record all the spirits of the air,
And all things else that are, that day and night,
Early and late, the tribute which my heart
Hath paid to Annabella's sacred love

Hath been these tears, which are her mourners now!
Never till now did nature do her best
To shew a matchless beauty to the world,
Which in an instant, ere it scarce was seen,
The jealous destinies required again.
Pray, Annabella, pray! Since we must part,
Go thou, white in thy soul, to fill a throne
Of innocence and sanctity in heaven.
Pray, pray, my sister!

Ann. Then I see your drift—
Ye blessed angels guard me!

Gio. So say I!
Kiss me! If ever aftertimes should hear
Of our fast-knit affections, though perhaps
The laws of conscience and of civil use
May justly blame us, yet when they but know
Our loves, that love will wipe away that rigor
Which would in other incests be abhorred.
Give me your hand. How sweetly life doth run
In these well-colored veins! How constantly
These palms do promise health! But I could chide
With nature for this cunning flattery—
Kiss me again—forgive me.

Ann. With my heart.

Gio. Farewell!

Ann. Will you be gone?

Gio. Be dark, bright sun,
And make this mid-day night, that thy gilt rays
May not behold a deed, will turn their splendor
More sooty than the poets feign their Styx!—
One other kiss, my sister.

Ann. What means this?

Gio. To save thy fame, and kill thee in a kiss. (Stabs her)
Thus die, and die by me, and by my hand!
Revenge is mine; honor doth love command.

Ann. Oh brother, by your hand!

Gio. When thou art dead
I'll give my reasons for 't; for to dispute
With thy (even in thy death) most lovely beauty,
Would make me stagger to perform this act
Which I most glory in.

Ann. Forgive him, Heaven—and me my sins! Farewell,

Brother unkind, unkind,—mercy, great
    Heaven, oh—oh!   (*Dies*)
    Gio. She's dead, alas, good soul! The hap-
    less fruit
That in her womb received its life from me,
Hath had from me a cradle and a grave.
I must not dally.—This sad marriage-bed
In all her best, bore her alive and dead.
Soranzo, thou hast missed thy aim in this!
I have prevented now thy reaching plots,

And killed a love for whose each drop of
    blood
I would have pawned my heart.—Fair Anna-
    bella,
How over-glorious art thou in thy wounds,
Triumphing over infamy and hate!—
Shrink not, courageous hand, stand up, my
    heart,
And boldly act my last and greater part!
        (*Exit with the body*)

SCENE VI. *A Banqueting Room in the Same.*

(*A Banquet.—Enter the* CARDINAL, FLORIO,
DONADO, SORANZO, RICHARDETTO, VASQUES,
and Attendants; they take their places)

    VAS. (*Apart to* SOR.) Remember, sir, what
you have to do; and be wise and resolute.
    SOR. (*Aside to* VAS.) Enough: my heart is
    fixed.—Pleaseth your grace
To taste these coarse confections; though the
    use
Of such set entertainments more consists
In custom than in cause, yet, reverend sir,
I am still made your servant by your presence.
    CAR. And we your friend.
    SOR. But where's my brother Giovanni?

(*Enter* GIOVANNI, *with a heart upon his
dagger*)

    GIO. Here, here, Soranzo! Trimmed in
    reeking blood
That triumphs over death! Proud in the spoil
Of love and vengeance! Fate, or all the pow-
    ers
That guide the motions of immortal souls,
Could not prevent me.
    CAR. What means this?
    FLO. Son Giovanni!
    SOR. (*Aside*) Shall I be forestalled?
    GIO. Be not amazed. If your misgiving
    hearts
Shrink at an idle sight, what bloodless fear
Of coward passion would have seized your
    senses,
Had you beheld the rape of life and beauty
Which I have acted?—My sister, oh my sister!
    FLO. Ha! What of her?
    GIO. The glory of my deed

Darkened the mid-day sun, made noon as
    night.
You came to feast, my lords, with dainty fare;
I came to feast too, but I digged for food
In a much richer mine than gold or stone
Of any value balanced; 'tis a heart,
A heart, my lords, in which is mine en-
    tombed.
Look well upon 't; do you know it?
    VAS. What strange riddle's this?
    GIO. 'Tis Annabella's heart, 'tis; why d'you
    startle?
I vow 'tis hers;—this dagger's point ploughed
    up
Her fruitful womb, and left to me the fame
Of a most glorious executioner.
    FLO. Why, madman, art thyself?
    GIO. Yes, father, and, that times to come
    may know
How, as my fate, I honored my revenge,
List, father, to your ears I will yield up
How much I have deserved to be your son.
    FLO. What is 't thou say'st?
    GIO. Nine moons have had their changes
Since I first thoroughly viewed and truly
    loved
Your daughter and my sister.
    FLO. How! Alas, my lords,
He is a frantic madman!
    GIO. Father, no.
For nine months space, in secret, I enjoyed
Sweet Annabella's sheets; nine months I lived
A happy monarch of her heart and her.—
Soranzo, thou know'st this. Thy paler cheek
Bears the confounding print of thy disgrace,
For her too fruitful womb too soon bewrayed
The happy passage of our stolen delights,
And made her mother to a child unborn.

CAR. Incestuous villain!

FLO. Oh, his rage belies him.

GIO. It does not, 'tis the oracle of truth;
I vow it is so.

SOR. I shall burst with fury.—
Bring the strumpet forth!

VAS. I shall, sir.   (*Exit*)

GIO. Do, sir.—Have you all no faith
To credit yet my triumphs? Here I swear
By all that you call sacred, by the love
I bore my Annabella whilst she lived,
These hands have from her bosom ripped this
   heart.

(*Re-enter* VASQUES)

Is 't true or no, sir?

VAS. 'Tis most strangely true.

FLO. Cursed man!—have I lived to—
                          (*Dies*)

CAR. Hold up Florio!
Monster of children! See what thou hast
   done—
Broke thy old father's heart! Is none of you
Dares venture on him?

GIO. Let 'em! O my father,
How well his death becomes him in his griefs!
Why this was done with courage. Now sur-
   vives
None of our house but I, gilt in the blood
Of a fair sister and a hapless father.

SOR. Inhuman scorn of men, hast thou a
   thought
T' outlive thy murders?   (*Draws*)

GIO. Yes, I tell thee, yes,
For in my fists I bear the twists of life.
Soranzo, see this heart, which was thy wife's;
Thus I exchange it royally for thine.
                          (*Stabs him*)
And thus and thus! Now brave revenge is
   mine.   (SORANZO *falls*)

VAS. I cannot hold any longer. You, sir,
are you grown insolent in your butcheries?
Have at you.

GIO. Come, I am armed to meet thee.
                          (*They fight*)

VAS. No! will it not be yet? If this will not,
another shall. Not yet? I shall fit you anon—
VENGEANCE! [51]

(*The* BANDITTI *rush in*)

[51] The watchword or cue agreed upon in
Scene IV.

GIO. Welcome! come more of you; what-
e'er you be,
I dare your worst—
                          (*They surround and wound him*)
Oh I can stand no longer! Feeble arms,
Have you so soon lost strength?   (*Falls*)

VAS. Now, you are welcome, sir!—(*Aside
to* BAND.) Away, my masters, all is done;
shift for yourselves, your reward is your own;
shift for yourselves.

BAND. Away, away!   (*Exeunt* BANDITTI)

VAS. How d'ee my lord? See you this?
(*Pointing to* GIO.) How is 't?

SOR. Dead; but in death well pleased, that
   I have lived
To see my wrongs revenged on that black
   devil.—
O Vasques, to thy bosom let me give
My last of breath; let not that lecher live—
Oh!—   (*Dies*)

VAS. The reward of peace and rest be with
you, my ever dearest lord and master!

GIO. Whose hand gave me this wound?

VAS. Mine, sir; I was your first man. Have
you enough?

GIO. I thank thee, thou hast done for me
But what I would have else done on myself.
Art sure thy lord is dead?

VAS. Oh impudent slave!
As sure as I am sure to see thee die!

CAR. Think on thy life and end, and call
for mercy.

GIO. Mercy? why, I have found it in this
justice.

CAR. Strive yet to cry to Heaven.

GIO. Oh I bleed fast!
Death, thou'rt a guest long looked for; I em-
   brace
Thee and thy wounds. Oh, my last minute
   comes!
Where'er I go, let me enjoy this grace,
Freely to view my Annabella's face.   (*Dies*)

DON. Strange miracle of justice!

CAR. Raise up the city, we shall be murdered all!

VAS. You need not fear, you shall not; this
strange task being ended, I have paid the
duty to the son, which I have vowed to the
father.

CAR. Speak, wretched villain, what incar-
nate fiend
Hath led thee on to this?

VAS. Honesty, and pity of my master's

wrongs. For know, my lord, I am by birth a Spaniard, brought forth my country in my youth by lord Soranzo's father, whom, whilst he lived, I served faithfully; since whose death I have been to this man as I was to him. What I have done was duty, and I repent nothing but that the loss of my life had not ransomed his.

CAR. Say, fellow, know'st thou any yet unnamed

Of council in this incest?

VAS. Yes, an old woman, sometime [52] guardian to this murdered lady.

CAR. And what's become of her?

VAS. Within this room she is; whose eyes after her confession I caused to be put out, but kept alive to confirm what from Giovanni's own mouth you have heard. Now, my lord, what I have done you may judge of, and let your own wisdom be a judge in your own reason.

CAR. Peace! First, this woman, chief in these effects,

My sentence is, that forthwith she be ta'en Out of the city, for example's sake, There to be burnt to ashes.

DON. 'Tis most just.

CAR. Be it your charge, Donado, see it done.

DON. I shall.

VAS. What for me? If death, 'tis welcome.

I have been honest to the son, as I was to the father.

CAR. Fellow, for thee, since what thou didst was done

Not for thyself, being no Italian,
We banish thee for ever, to depart
Within three days. In this we do dispense
With grounds of reason, not of thine offence.

VAS. 'Tis well; this conquest is mine, and I rejoice that a Spaniard outwent an Italian in revenge. (Exit)

CAR. Take up these slaughtered bodies, see them buried;

And all the gold and jewels, or whatsoever,
Confiscate by the canons of the church,
We seize upon to the Pope's proper use.

RICH. (Discovers himself) Your grace's pardon; thus long I lived disguised,

To see the effect of pride and lust at once
Brought both to shameful ends.

CAR. What! Richardetto, whom we thought for dead?

DON. Sir, was it you—

RICH. Your friend.

CAR. We shall have time
To talk at large of all; but never yet
Incest and murder have so strangely met.
Of one so young, so rich in nature's store,
Who could not say, 'TIS PITY SHE'S A WHORE? (Exeunt)

[52] Formerly.

SIR ROBERT HOWARD
JOHN DRYDEN

The Indian Queen

~~~~~~~~~~~~~~~~~~~~~~

PRINCIPAL EVENTS IN HOWARD'S LIFE

1626, He was born in this year, the sixth son of Thomas Howard, first earl of Berkshire.

1644, Knighted at the second battle of Newbury for his signal courage on the Royalist side.

?, Imprisoned during the Commonwealth.

1660, Published *Poems*; the volume included a comedy, *The Blind Lady*, which was never acted.

1661-98, Member of Parliament.

1662, April, The Surprisal, a comedy, was acted at the Theatre Royal.

1662, c. Oct., The Committee, or the Faithful Irishman, a comedy, was produced at the Theatre Royal. A political satire, it was long popular because of the character of Teague, a comic Irishman.

1664, Jan., The Indian Queen, produced at the Theatre Royal.

1664, The Vestal Virgin, a tragedy, produced at the Theatre Royal.

1665, Published the last in *Foure New Plays*, with a preface attacking Dryden's view that rhymed couplets were better suited to heroic tragedy than blank verse, to which Dryden replied in his *Essay of Dramatic Poesie*, 1668.

1668, Published *The Duel of the Stags*, a rhymed satire.

1668, Feb., The Great Favourite, or the Duke of Lerma was produced at the Theatre Royal; published in the same year with a reply to Dryden, who thereupon made a vigorous and sarcastic answer in *A Defence of an Essay of Dramatic Poesie*, prefixed to the second edition (1668) of *The Indian Emperor*.

1692, Published *Five New Plays*, containing his last productions.

1698, Sept. 3, Died; buried in Westminster Abbey.

PRINCIPAL EVENTS IN DRYDEN'S LIFE

1631, 9 Aug., Dryden was born at Aldwinkle, Northamptonshire, of a Puritan family.

c. 1644, Entered Westminster School in London.

1650, Entered Trinity College, Cambridge, on a Westminster scholarship.

1654, Took his B.A. at Cambridge.

1659, Published a poem on the death of Cromwell.

1660, Published *Astraea Redux* on the return of Charles II.

1663, Feb., The Wild Gallant acted at the Theatre Royal.

1663, 1 Dec., Married Lady Elizabeth Howard, sister of Sir Robert Howard.

1664, Jan., Dryden and Howard's *Indian Queen* acted at the Theatre Royal in a spectacular production.

1664, June, The Rival Ladies acted at the Theatre Royal.

1665, April (?), The Indian Emperor acted at the Theatre Royal.

1666, Annus Mirabilis, celebrating great events of the year, published.

1667, Aug., Sir Martin Mar-all acted at the Lincoln's Inn Fields Theatre.

1667, Nov., Dryden and Davenant's adaptation of Shakespeare's *Tempest* acted at Lincoln's Inn Fields Theatre.

1667-78, Dryden was under contract to write three plays a year for the King's Company in return for 1¼ shares of the profits of the company. He actually averaged only one play a year for them.

1668, Published *An Essay of Dramatic Poesie.*

1668, June, An Evening's Love acted at the Theatre Royal.

1670, Dryden was appointed Poet Laureate and Historiographer Royal.

1670, Dec. (?), The Conquest of Granada, Part I, acted at the Theatre Royal.

1671, Jan., The Conquest of Granada, Part II, acted at the Theatre Royal.

1672, May (?), Marriage à la Mode acted at the Lincoln's Inn Fields Theatre.

1673, June (?), Amboyna acted at the Lincoln's Inn Fields Theatre.

1675, Nov., Aurung-Zebe acted at the Drury Lane Theatre.

1677, Dec., All for Love acted at the Drury Lane Theatre.

1679, April (?), Troilus and Cressida, an adaptation of Shakespeare's play, acted at the Dorset Garden Theatre and published later in the same year with an important critical preface.

1680, March, The Spanish Friar acted at the Dorset Garden Theatre.

1681, Absolom and Achitophel, a distinguished satire on contemporary political affairs, published.

1682, MacFlecknoe, a distinguished literary satire, published.

1685, Shortly after the accession of James II, Dryden became a Catholic.

1685, June, Albion and Albianus, an opera, acted at Dorset Garden Theatre.

1687, The Hind and the Panther, Dryden's defense of Roman Catholicism, published.

1688, On the accession of William and Mary, Dryden lost all his appointments and political preferments.

1690, Amphitryon, one of many adaptations of Plautus' comedy, acted at the Drury Lane Theatre.

1693, Dryden's translations of Juvenal and Persius published.

1694, Love Triumphant acted at the Drury Lane Theatre.

1700, Fables Ancient and Modern, popular translations from Homer, Ovid, Chaucer, and Boccaccio, published.

1700, 1 May, Dryden died. He was buried in Westminster Abbey with great honor.

A number of Dryden's plays and poems have been omitted from this list.

INTRODUCTION

This play is representative of a type both popular and admired in the Restoration theatre but which seems utter dramatic folly to modern audiences. It is worth examining not because of its dramatic excellence, but as an example of one odd variety of dramatic appeal which has had an important place in the history of the English theatre.

The Indian Queen is an heroic tragedy. One of its authors, John Dryden, the most prominent dramatist, dramatic critic, and poet of his time, discussed the form and its essentials in an essay, *Of Heroique Playes,* which he published with his play *The Conquest of Granada* in 1672, eight years after *The Indian Queen* had been performed. He noted that Love and Valor ought to be the subject of such plays, that the characters should have noble traits exalted beyond those of ordinary mortals, that the plot should be full and elaborate and need not be tied to true or probable actions; in short, that heroic plays ought to be analogous to heroic poems like the *Odyssey*. Though this is not a dramatic formula which has much appeal in the twentieth century, it was closely followed in *The Indian Queen,* and the play was a notable success in its time.

Clearly the valor of Montezuma is enlarged to superhuman proportions, for the routed army and the victorious army automatically reverse their roles as soon as he changes sides. The honor of both Montezuma and Acacis is made so fantastically sensitive and so much more powerful than all normal instincts and desires that the spectator can scarcely follow the honorable surrenders, honorable escapes, honorable duels, and honorable suicides or threatened suicides of these magnanimous heroes. Orazia's love and honor and the lust and cruelty of Zempoalla and Traxalla are similarly magnified beyond any resemblance to the normal. To the audience at the Theatre Royal this made them admirable; to the modern audience it makes them ridiculous.

These exaggerated characters are manipulated through a constantly twisting plot of victory, defeat, betrayal, murder, suicide, and revolt, a plot which constantly alters their respective positions but pays scant regard to probability, for in probability neither authors nor audience were much interested. Intricacy of action to provide for repeated displays of exalted nobility was the aim of Dryden and Howard, and they willingly sacrificed qualities which seem more important to us.

The dialogue of *The Indian Queen,* like the plot and the characters, is intended to be impressive, not natural. Most of it is written in couplets, which are excellent vehicles for noble or aphoristic statements, but which give no illusion of real speech. Again the authors were content with their choice, for no form of verse or prose could have made the action or the characters of *The Indian Queen* seem normal or credible, and the couplets tend to emphasize the remoteness from ordinary life and to make heroic sentiments more memorable—if the audience can accept them at all, as the Restoration audience could.

The Indian Queen's exemplification of the Restoration ideals of heroic tragedy is part of the reason for its contemporary success. A further reason was the spectacular production which the play was given at the Theatre Royal in January, 1664. Scenery and costumes were the most magnificent the Restoration theatre had seen, as the diarist John Evelyn noted, and he thought that probably no commercial theatre any place had staged such a beautiful spectacle before. The stage directions at the opening of Acts III and V give a faint suggestion of how elaborate this spectacle was. Such a production was appropriate to the heroic character of the play and to the fabulous contemporary reputation of the riches of Mexico and Peru.

❦

THE INDIAN QUEEN

Dramatis personae

In the order of first appearance

INDIAN BOY
INDIAN GIRL, QUEVIRA } Prologue
THE INCA, The proud and haughty emperor of Peru, at war with Mexico.
ORAZIA, His fair and lovely daughter.
MONTEZUMA, The valorous hero. A hand-

some young man who as the Inca's general has triumphantly defeated the Mexican army; in love with Orazia.
FIRST PERUVIAN } Courtiers attendant on
SECOND PERUVIAN } the Inca.
ACACIS, A gentle and noble youth, fantasti-

cally honorable. The son of the usurping Queen of Mexico and a prince, captured in the war and in love with Orazia.

ZEMPOALLA, The usurping Queen of Mexico, vengeful, cruel, lustful, and without pity.

TRAXALLA, Her general and confidant, crafty, ambitious, and unscrupulous.

ISMERON, A soothsayer of Mexico.

GOD OF DREAMS

JAILER

AMEXIA, The lawful Queen of Mexico, deposed by Zempoalla.

GARUCCA, Her faithful subject, supposed father of Montezuma.

Guards, prisoners, messengers, priests, officers and soldiers, attendants, ladies, Peruvians, and Mexicans.

SCENE: *Mexico*

Prologue

(*As the music plays a soft air, the curtain rises slowly and discovers an* INDIAN BOY *and* GIRL *sleeping under two plantain-trees; and, when the curtain is almost up, the music turns into a tune expressing an alarm, at which the* BOY *wakes and speaks*)

BOY. Wake, wake, Quevira! Our soft rest must cease,
And fly together with our country's peace!
No more must we sleep under the plantain shade,
Which neither heat could pierce, nor cold invade;
Where bounteous nature never feels decay,
And opening buds drive falling fruits away.
    QUEVIRA. Why should men quarrel here, where all possess
As much as they can hope for by success?—
None can have most, where nature is so kind

As to exceed man's use, though not his mind.
    BOY. By ancient prophecies we have been told
Our world shall be subdued by one more old;
And, see, that world already's hither come.
    QUEVIRA. If these be they, we welcome then our doom!
Their looks are such that mercy flows from thence,
More gentle than our native innocence.
    BOY. Why should we then fear these are enemies,
That rather seem to us like deities?
    QUEVIRA. By their protection let us beg to live;
They came not here to conquer, but forgive.—
If so, your goodness may your power express,
And we shall judge both best by our success.

Act I

SCENE I.

(*Enter* INCA, *the* PRINCESS ORAZIA, MONTEZUMA, *the prisoner* ACACIS, *and other Prisoners, with* PERUVIANS)

INCA. Thrice have the Mexicans before us fled,
Their armies broke, their prince in triumph led;
Both to thy valor, brave young man, we owe;
Ask thy reward, but such as it may show

It is a king thou hast obliged, whose mind
Is large, and, like his fortune, unconfined.
    MONTEZUMA. Young and a stranger to your court I came,
There, by your favor, raised to what I am;
I conquer but in right of your great fate,

And so your arms, not mine, are fortunate.
    INCA. I am impatient till this debt be paid
Which still increases on me while delayed;
A bounteous monarch to himself is kind.
Ask such a gift as may forever bind
Thy service to my empire and to me.
    MONTEZUMA. (*Aside*) What can this gift
    he bids me ask him be!
Perhaps he has perceived our mutual fires
    (*Gazing at* ORAZIA)
And now, with ours, would crown his own
    desires;
'Tis so, he sees my service is above
All other payments but his daughter's love.
    INCA. So quick to merit, and to take so
    slow?
I first prevent [1] small wishes, and bestow
This prince (*turning to* ACACIS) his sword
    and fortunes, to thy hand;
He's thine unasked; now make thy free de-
    mand.
    MONTEZUMA. Here, prince, receive this
    sword, as only due
        (*Gives* ACACIS *his sword*)
To that excess of courage shown in you.—
(*To* INCA) When you, without demand, a
    prince bestow,
Less than a prince to ask of you were low.
    INCA. Then ask a kingdom; say where
    thou wilt reign.
    MONTEZUMA. I beg not empires, those my
    sword can gain;
But for my past and future service, too,
What I have done, and what I mean to do—
For this of Mexico which I have won,
And kingdoms I will conquer yet unknown—
I only ask from fair Orazia's eyes
To reap the fruits of all my victories.
    FIRST PERUVIAN. Our Inca's color mounts
into his face.
    SECOND PERUVIAN. His looks speak death.
    INCA. Young man of unknown race,
Ask once again; so well thy merits plead,
Thou shalt not die for that which thou hast
    said;
The price of what thou ask'st, thou dost not
    know;
That gift's too high.
    MONTEZUMA. And all besides too low.
    INCA. Once more I bid thee ask.
    MONTEZUMA. Once more I make
The same demand.
   [1] Anticipate.

    INCA. The Inca bids thee take
Thy choice, what towns, what kingdoms thou
    wouldst have.
    MONTEZUMA. Thou giv'st me only what
    before I gave.
Give me thy daughter.
    INCA. Thou deserv'st to die.
O thou great author of our progeny,
Thou glorious sun, dost thou not blush to
    shine,
While such base blood attempts to mix with
    thine!
    MONTEZUMA. That sun thou speak'st of
    did not hide his face
When he beheld me conquering for his race.
    INCA. My fortunes gave thee thy success
    in fight!
Convey thy boasted valor from my sight;
I can o'ercome without thy feeble aid.
    (*Exeunt* INCA, ORAZIA, *and* PERUVIANS)
    MONTEZUMA. And is it thus my services
    are paid?
Not all his guards—
    (*Starts after* INCA, ACACIS *holds him*)
    ACACIS. Hold, sir.
    MONTEZUMA. Unhand me.
    ACACIS. No, I must your rage prevent
From doing what your reason would repent;
Like the vast seas, your mind no limits
    knows,
Like them, lies open to each wind that blows.
    MONTEZUMA. Can a revenge that is so just
be ill?
    ACACIS. It is Orazia's father you would kill.
    MONTEZUMA. Orazia! How that name has
charmed my sword!
    ACACIS. Compose these wild distempers
    in your breast;
Anger, like madness, is appeased by rest.
    MONTEZUMA. Bid children sleep, my spir-
    its boil too high;
But, since Orazia's father must not die,
A nobler vengeance shall my actions guide:
I'll bear the conquest to the conquered side,
Until this Inca for my friendship sues,
And proffers what his pride does now refuse.
    ACACIS. Your honor is obliged to keep your
trust.
    MONTEZUMA. He broke that bond in ceas-
ing to be just.
    ACACIS. Subjects to kings should more
obedience pay.

MONTEZUMA. Subjects are bound, not strangers, to obey.

ACACIS. Can you so little your Orazia prize,
To give the conquest to her enemies?
Can you so easily forego her sight?
I, that hold liberty more dear than light,
Yet to my freedom should my chains prefer,
And think it were well lost to stay with her.

MONTEZUMA. (*Aside*) How unsuccessfully I still o'ercome!
I brought a rival, not a captive, home.
Yet I may be deceived—but 'tis too late
To clear those doubts; my stay brings certain fate.—
Come, prince, you shall to Mexico return,
Where your sad armies do your absence mourn;
And in one battle I will gain you more
Than I have made you lose in three before.

ACACIS. No, Montezuma, though you change your side,
I, as a prisoner, am by honor tied.

MONTEZUMA. You are my prisoner, and I set you free.

ACACIS. 'Twere baseness to accept such liberty.

MONTEZUMA. From him that conquered you it should be sought.

ACACIS. No, but from him for whom my conqueror fought.

MONTEZUMA. Still you are mine, his gift has made you so.

ACACIS. He gave me to his general, not his foe.

MONTEZUMA. How poorly have you pleaded honor's laws!
Yet shun the greatest in your country's cause.

ACACIS. What succor can the captive give the free?

MONTEZUMA. A needless captive is an enemy.
In painted honor you would seem to shine;
But 'twould be clouded, were your wrongs like mine.

ACACIS. When choler such unbridled power can have,
Thy virtue seems but thy revenge's slave;
If such injustice should my honor stain,
My aid would prove my nation's loss, not gain.

MONTEZUMA. Be cozened by thy guilty honesty
To make thyself thy country's enemy.

ACACIS. I do not mean in the next fight to stain
My sword in blood of any Mexican,
But will be present in the fatal strife
To guard Orazia's and the Inca's life.

MONTEZUMA. Orazia's life, fond man! First guard thy own;
Her safety she must owe to me alone.

ACACIS. Your sword, that does such wonders, cannot be
In an ill cause secure of victory.

MONTEZUMA. Hark, hark!
(*Noise of trampling*)

ACACIS. What noise is this invades my ear?
Fly, Montezuma, fly! The guards are near;
To favor your retreat I'll freely pay
That life which you so frankly gave this day.

MONTEZUMA. I must retire; but those that follow me
Pursue their deaths, and not their victory.
(*Exit* MONTEZUMA)

ACACIS. Our quarrels kinder than our friendships prove;
You for my country fight, I for your love.

(*Enter* INCA *and Guards*)

INCA. I was to blame to leave this madman free;
Perhaps he may revolt to the enemy,
Or stay and raise some fatal mutiny.

ACACIS. Stop your pursuits, for they must pass through me.

INCA. Where is the slave?

ACACIS. Gone.

INCA. Whither?

ACACIS. O'er the plain;
Where he may soon the camp, or city, gain.

INCA. Curse on my dull neglect!
And yet I do less cause of wonder find
That he is gone than that thou stayest behind.

ACACIS. My treatment, since you took me, was so free,
It wanted but the name of liberty.
I with less shame can still your captive live
Than take that freedom which you did not give.

INCA. Thou brave young man, that hast thy years outdone
And, losing liberty, hast honor won,
I must myself thy honor's rival make,
And give that freedom which thou would'st not take.
Go, and be safe—
 ACACIS. But that you may be so—
Your dangers must be past before I go.

Fierce Montezuma will for fight prepare,
And bend on you the fury of the war,
Which, by my presence, I will turn away,
If fortune gives my Mexicans the day.
 INCA. Come, then, we are alike to honor just,
Thou to be trusted thus, and I to trust.
          (*Exeunt*)

SCENE II. *Mexico.*

(*Enter* ZEMPOALLA, TRAXALLA, *and Attendants*)

ZEMPOALLA. O my Acacis!
Does not my grief, Traxalla, seem too rude,
Thus to press out before my gratitude
Has paid my debts to you?—yet it does move
My rage and grief to see those powers above
Punish such men as, if they be divine,
They know will most adore, and least repine.
 TRAXALLA. Those that can only mourn when they are crossed
May lose themselves with grieving for the lost.
Rather to your retreated troops appear,
And let them see a woman void of fear;
The shame of that may call their spirits home.
Were the prince safe, we were not overcome,
Though we retired. O his too youthful heat,
That thrust him where the dangers are so great!
Heaven wanted power his person to protect
From that which he had courage to neglect;
But since he's lost, let us draw forth, and pay
His funeral rites in blood, that we are they
May in our fates perform his obsequies,
And make death triumph when Acacis dies.
 ZEMPOALLA. That courage thou hast shown in fight seems less
Than this, amidst despair to have excess;
Let thy great deeds force fate to change her mind;
He that courts fortune boldly makes her kind.
 TRAXALLA. If e'er Traxalla so successful proves,
May he then say he hopes as well as loves;
And that aspiring passion boldly own
Which gave my prince his fate, and you his throne?

I did not feel remorse to see his blood
Flow from the spring of life into a flood;
Nor did it look like treason, since to me
You were a sovereign much more great than he.
 ZEMPOALLA. He was my brother, yet I scorned to pay
Nature's mean debts, but threw those bonds away;
When his own issue did my hopes remove,
Not only from his empire, but his love,
You, that in all my wrongs then bore a part,
Now need not doubt a place within my heart.
I could not offer you my crown and bed
Till fame and envy with long time were dead;
But fortune now does happily present
Occasions fit to second my intent.
Your valor may regain the public love,
And make the people's choice their queen's approve.   (*Shout*)
Hark, hark! What noise is this that strikes my ear?
 TRAXALLA. 'Tis not a sound that should beget a fear;
Such shouts as these have I heard often fly
From conquering armies, crowned with victory.
 ZEMPOALLA. Great god of vengeance, here I firmly vow,
Make but my Mexicans successful now,
And with a thousand feasts thy flames I'll feed;
And them I take shall on thy altars bleed;
Princes themselves shall fall, and make thy shrine,
Dyed with their blood, in glorious blushes shine.

(*Enter* MESSENGER)

TRAXALLA. How now!
What news is this that makes thy haste a
    flight?
    MESSENGER. Such as brings victory with-
    out a fight.
The prince Acacis lives—
    ZEMPOALLA. Oh, I am blest!—
    MESSENGER. Reserve some joy till I have
    told the rest.
He's safe, and only wants his liberty.
But that great man that carries victory
Where'er he goes; that mighty man, by whom
In three set battles we were overcome;
Ill used (it seems) by his ungrateful king,
Does to our camp his fate and valor bring.
The troops gaze on him as if some bright star
Shot to their aids, call him the god of war;
Whilst he, as if all conquest did of right
Belong to him, bids them prepare to fight;

Which if they should delay one hour, he
    swears
He'll leave them to their dangers, or their
    fears
And shame, which is the ignoble coward's
    choice.
At this the army seemed to have one voice,
United in a shout, and called upon
The god-like stranger, "Lead us, lead us
    on."
Make haste, great sir, lest you should come
    too late
To share with them in victory, or fate.
    ZEMPOALLA. My general, go; the gods be
    on our side;
Let valor act, but let discretion guide.
                            (*Exit* TRAXALLA)
Great god of vengeance,
I see thou dost begin to hear me now;
Make me thy offering if I break my vow.
                            (*Exeunt*)

Act II

SCENE I.

(*Enter* INCA *and* ORAZIA, *as pursued in
    battle*)

ORAZIA. O fly, sir, fly! Like torrents your
    swift foes
Come rolling on—
    INCA. The gods can but destroy.
The noblest way to fly is that death shows;
I'll court her now, since victory's grown coy.
    ORAZIA. Death's winged to your pursuit,
    and yet you wait
To meet her—
    INCA. Poor Orazia, time and fate
Must once o'ertake me, though I now should
    fly.
    ORAZIA. Do not meet death; but when it
comes, then die.

(*Enter three* SOLDIERS)

THIRD SOLDIER. Stand, sir, and yield
yourself, and that fair prey.
    INCA. You speak to one unpractised to
obey.

(*Enter* MONTEZUMA)

MONTEZUMA. Hold, villains, hold, or your
    rude lives shall be
Lost in the midst of your own victory.
These have I hunted for;—nay, do not stare;
Be gone, and in the common plunder share.
                            (*Exeunt* SOLDIERS)
How different is my fate from theirs whose
    fame
From conquest grows! From conquest grows
    my shame.
    INCA. Why dost thou pause? thou canst
    not give me back,
With fruitless grief, what I enjoyed before.
No more than seas, repenting of a wrack,
Can with a calm our buried wealth restore.
    MONTEZUMA. 'Twere vain to own repent-
    ance, since I know
Thy scorn, which did my passions once de-
    spise,
Once more would make my swelling anger
    flow,
Which now ebbs lower than your miseries.
The gods, that in my fortunes were unkind,
Gave me not sceptres, nor such gilded things;

But whilst I wanted crowns, enlarged my
    mind
To despise sceptres and dispose of kings.
    INCA. Thou art but grown a rebel by suc-
    cess,
And I, that scorned Orazia should be tied
To thee, my slave, must now esteem thee
    less;
Rebellion is a greater guilt than pride.
    MONTEZUMA. Princes see others' faults,
    but not their own.
'Twas you that broke that bond and set me
    free;
Yet I attempted not to climb your throne
And raise myself, but level you to me.
    ORAZIA. O Montezuma, could thy love
    engage
Thy soul so little, or make banks so low
About thy heart, that thy revenge and rage,
Like sudden floods, so soon should overflow?
Ye gods, how much was I mistaken here!
I thought you gentle as the gall-less dove;
But you as humorsome as winds appear,
And subject to more passions than your love.
    MONTEZUMA. How have I been betrayed
    by guilty rage,
Which, like a flame, rose to so vast a height,
That nothing could resist, nor yet assuage,
Till it wrapt all things in one cruel fate.
But I'll redeem myself, and act such things
That you shall blush Orazia was denied;
And yet make conquest, though with wearied
    wings,
Take a new flight to your now fainting side.
    INCA. Vain man, what foolish thoughts
    fill thy swelled mind!
It is too late our ruin to recall;
Those that have once great buildings un-
    dermined,
Will prove too weak to prop them in their
    fall.

(*Enter* TRAXALLA, *with the former*
SOLDIERS)

FIRST SOLDIER. See, mighty sir, where the
    bold stranger stands,
Who snatched these glorious prisoners from
    our hands.
    TRAXALLA. 'Tis the great Inca; seize him
    as my prey,
To crown the triumphs of this glorious day.

    MONTEZUMA. Stay your bold hands from
    reaching at what's mine,
If any title springs from victory;
You safer may attempt to rob a shrine
And hope forgiveness from the deity.

(*Enters* ACACIS)

    TRAXALLA. O my dear prince, my joys to
    see you live
Are more than all that victory can give.
    ACACIS. (*To the* INCA) How are my best
    endeavors crossed by fate!
Else you had ne'er been lost, or found so late.
Hurried by the wild fury of the fight,
Far from your presence, and Orazia's sight,
I could not all that care and duty show
Which, as your captive, mighty prince, I owe.
    INCA. You often have preserved our lives
    this day,
And one small debt with many bounties pay.
But human actions hang on springs that be
Too small, or too remote, for us to see.
My glories freely I to yours resign,
And am your prisoner now, that once were
    mine.
    MONTEZUMA. (*To* TRAXALLA) These
    prisoners, sir, are mine by right of war;
And I'll maintain that right, if any dare.
    TRAXALLA. Yes, I would snatch them from
    thy weak defence,
But that due reverence which I owe my
    prince
Permits me not to quarrel in his sight;
To him I shall refer his general's right.
    MONTEZUMA. I knew too well what justice
    I should find
From an armed plaintiff, and a judge so kind.
    ACACIS. Unkindly urged, that I should
    use thee so;
Thy virtue is my rival, not my foe;
The prisoners fortune gave thee shall be
    thine.
    TRAXALLA. Would you so great a prize to
him resign?
    ACACIS. Should he, who boldly for his prey
    designed
To dive the deepest under swelling tides,
Have the less title if he chance to find
The richest jewel that the ocean hides?
They are his due—
But in his virtue I repose that trust
That he will be as kind as I am just.

Dispute not my commands, but go with haste,
Rally our men; they may pursue too fast,
And the disorders of the inviting prey
May turn again the fortune of the day.
                              (*Exit* Traxalla)
Montezuma. How gentle all this prince's actions be!
Virtue is calm in him, but rough in me.
Acacis. Can Montezuma place me in his breast?
Montezuma. My heart's not large enough for such a guest.
Acacis. See, Montezuma, see, Orazia weeps.   (Orazia *weeps*)
Montezuma. Acacis! Is he deaf, or, waking, sleeps?
He does not hear me, sees me not, nor moves;

How firm his eyes are on Orazia fixed!
Gods, that take care of men, let not our loves
Become divided by their being mixed.
    Acacis. Weep not, fair princess, nor believe you are
A prisoner, subject to the chance of war.
Why should you waste the stock of those fair eyes,
That from mankind can take their liberties?
And you, great sir, think not a generous mind
To virtuous princes dares appear unkind
Because those princes are unfortunate,
Since over all men hangs a doubtful fate.
One gains by what another is bereft;
The frugal deities have only left
A common bank [2] of happiness below,
Maintained, like nature, by an ebb and flow.
                              (*Exeunt*)

Scene II.

(Zempoalla *appears seated upon a throne, frowning upon her Attendants; then comes down and speaks*)

Zempoalla. No more, you that above your prince's dare proclaim
With your rebellious breath a stranger's name.
First Peruvian. Dread empress—
Zempoalla. Slave, perhaps you grieve to see
Your young prince glorious, 'cause he sprang from me;
Had he been one of base Amexia's brood,
Your tongues, though silent now, had then been loud.

(*Enter* Traxalla)

Traxalla, welcome; welcomer to me
Than what thou bring'st, a crown and victory.
    Traxalla. All I have done is nothing; fluttering fame
Now tells no news but of the stranger's name
And his great deeds; 'tis he, they cry, by whom
Not men, but war itself, is overcome;
Who, bold with his success, dares think to have
A prince to wear his chains and be his slave.

Zempoalla. What prince?
    Traxalla. The great Peruvian Inca, that of late
In three set battles was so fortunate,
Till this strange man had power to turn the tide
And carry conquest unto any side.
    Zempoalla. Would you permit a private man to have
The great Peruvian Inca for his slave?
Shame to all princes! Was it not just now
I made a sacred and a solemn vow
To offer up (if blest with victory)
The prisoners that were took? And they shall die.
    Traxalla. I soon had snatched from this proud stranger's hand
That too great object for his bold demand,
Had not the prince, your son, to whom I owe
A kind obedience, judged it should be so.
    Zempoalla. I'll hear no more; go quickly, take my guards,
And from that man force those usurped rewards;
That prince, upon whose ruins I must rise,
Shall be the gods', but more *my* sacrifice.
They, with my slaves, in triumph shall be tied,

² An elevation under the sea; e.g., the banks of Newfoundland.

While my devotion justifies my pride;
Those deities in whom I place my trust
Shall see, when they are kind, that I am just.

(*Exit*)

TRAXALLA. How gladly I obey!
There's something shoots from my enlivened frame,
Like a new soul, but yet without a name,

Nor can I tell what the bold guest will prove;
It must be envy, or it must be love.
Let it be either, 'tis the greatest bliss
For man to grant himself, all he dares wish;
For he that to himself himself denies
Proves meanly wretched, to be counted wise.

(*Exit* TRAXALLA)

SCENE III.

(*Enter* MONTEZUMA *and* ACACIS)

ACACIS. You wrong me, my best friend, not to believe
Your kindness gives me joy; and when I grieve,
Unwillingly my sorrows I obey;
Showers sometimes fall upon a shining day.
MONTEZUMA. Let me, then, share your griefs, that in your fate
Would have took part.
ACACIS. Why should you ask me that?
Those must be mine, though I have such excess;
Divided griefs increase, and not grow less.
MONTEZUMA. It does not lessen fate, nor satisfy
The grave, 'tis true, when friends together die,
And yet they are unwilling to divide.
ACACIS. To such a friend nothing can be denied.
You, when you hear my story, will forgive
My grief, and rather wonder that I live.
Unhappy in my title to a throne,
Since blood made way for my succession,
Blood of an uncle, too, a prince so free
From being cruel, it taught cruelty.
His queen Amexia then was big with child,
Nor was he gentler than his queen was mild;
Th' impatient people longed for what would come
From such a father, bred in such a womb;
When false Traxalla, weary to obey,
Took with his life their joys and hopes away.
Amexia, by the assistance of the night,
When this dark deed was acted took her flight,
Only with true Garucca for her aid;
Since when, for all the searches that were made,

The queen was never heard of more. Yet still
This traitor lives, and prospers by the ill;
Nor does my mother seem to reign alone,
But with this monster shares the guilt and throne.
Horror chokes up my words; now you'll believe
'Tis just I should do nothing else but grieve.
MONTEZUMA. Excellent prince!
How great a proof of virtue have you shown,
To be concerned for griefs, though not your own!
ACACIS. Pray, say no more.

(*Enter a* MESSENGER *hastily*)

MONTEZUMA. How now, whither so fast?
MESSENGER. O sir, I come too slow with all my haste!
The fair Orazia—
MONTEZUMA. Ha, what dost thou say?
MESSENGER. Orazia with the Inca's forced away
Out of your tent; Traxalla, at the head
Of the rude soldiers, forced the door and led
Those glorious captives, who on thrones once shined,
To grace the triumph that is now designed.

(*Exit*)

MONTEZUMA. Orazia forced away!—What tempests roll
About my thoughts, and toss my troubled soul!
Can there be gods to see, and suffer this?
Or does mankind make his own fate or bliss,
While every good and bad happens by chance,
Not from their orders, but from ignorance?—
But I will pull a ruin on them all,
And turn their triumph to a funeral.

ACACIS. Be temperate, friend.

MONTEZUMA. You may as well advise
That I should have less love, as grow more
    wise.

ACACIS. Yet stay—I did not think to have
    revealed
A secret which my heart has still concealed;
But, in this cause since I must share with
    you,
'Tis fit you know—I love Orazia, too!
Delay not then, nor waste the time in words;
Orazia's cause calls only for our swords.

MONTEZUMA. That ties my hand, and
    turns from thee that rage

Another way, thy blood should else assuage;
The storm on our proud foes shall higher
    rise,
And, changing, gather blackness as it flies;
So, when winds turn, the wandering waves
    obey,
And all the tempest rolls another way.

ACACIS. Draw then a rival's sword, as I
    draw mine,
And, like friends suddenly to part, let's
    join
In this one act, to seek one destiny;
Rivals with honor may together die.

(Exeunt)

Act III

SCENE I.

(ZEMPOALLA appears, borne by her Slaves in
triumph, followed by TRAXALLA leading
INCA and ORAZIA bound. The Indians, as to
celebrate the victory, advance in a warlike
dance; in the midst of which triumph, ACACIS
and MONTEZUMA fall upon them. ZEMPO-
ALLA descends from her triumphant throne,
and ACACIS and MONTEZUMA are brought in
            before her)

ZEMPOALLA. Shame of my blood and
    traitor to thy own,
Born to dishonor, not command, a throne!
Hast thou with envious eyes my triumph
    seen?
Or couldst not see thy mother in the queen?
Couldst thou a stranger above me prefer?

ACACIS. It was my honor made my duty
    err;
I could not see his prisoners forced away
To whom I owed my life, and you, the day.

ZEMPOALLA. Is that young man the war-
rior so renowned?

MONTEZUMA. Yes, he that made thy men
    thrice quit their ground.
Do, smile at Montezuma's chains; but know
His valor gave thee power to use him so.

TRAXALLA. Grant that it did, what can
    his merits be
That sought his vengeance, not our victory?
What has thy brutish fury gained us more
Than only healed the wounds it gave before?

Die then, for whilst thou liv'st, wars cannot
    cease;
Thou mayst bring victory, but never peace.
Like a black storm thou roll'st about us all,
Even to thyself unquiet, till thy fall.

(Draws to kill him)

ACACIS. Unthankful villain, hold!

TRAXALLA. You must not give
Him succor, sir.

ACACIS. Why, then, I must not live.
Posterity shall ne'er report they had
Such thankless fathers, or a prince so bad.

ZEMPOALLA. You're both too bold to will
    or to deny:
On me alone depends his destiny.
Tell me, audacious stranger, whence could
    rise
The confidence of this rash enterprise?

MONTEZUMA. First tell me how you dared
    to force from me
The fairest spoils of my own victory?

ZEMPOALLA. Kill him—(Aside) hold,
    must he die?—why, let him die.—
Whence should proceed this strange diversity
In my resolves?
Does he command in chains? What would
    he do,
Proud slave, if he were free, and I were so?
But is he bound, ye gods, or am I free?
'Tis love, 'tis love, that thus disorders me.
How pride and love tear my divided soul!
For each too narrow, yet both claim it whole.

Love, as the younger, must be forced away.—
(*To* TRAXALLA) Hence with the captives,
general, and convey
To several prisons that—young man, and
this—
Peruvian woman.

TRAXALLA. (*Aside*) How concerned she
is! I must know more.

MONTEZUMA. (*To* ORAZIA) Fair princess,
why should I
Involve that sweetness in my destiny?
I could out-brave my death, were I alone
To suffer, but my fate must pull yours on.
My breast is armed against all sense of fear;
But where your image lies, 'tis tender there.

INCA. Forbear thy saucy love, she cannot
be
So low but still she is too high for thee.

ZEMPOALLA. Be gone, and do as I command: away!

MONTEZUMA. I ne'er was truly wretched
till this day.

ORAZIA. Think half your sorrows on
Orazia fall,
And be not so unkind to suffer all;
Patience in cowards is tame, hopeless fear,
But in brave minds, a scorn of what they
bear.   (*Exeunt* INCA, MONTEZUMA,
ORAZIA, *and* TRAXALLA)

ZEMPOALLA. What grief is this which in
your face appears?

ACACIS. The badge of sorrow which my
soul still wears.

ZEMPOALLA. Though thy late actions did
my anger move,
It cannot rob thee of a mother's love.
Why shouldst thou grieve?
Grief seldom joined with blooming youth is
seen.
Can sorrow be where knowledge scarce has
been?
Fortune does well for heedless youth provide,
But wisdom does unlucky age misguide;
Cares are the train of present power and
state,
But hope lives best that on himself does wait.
O happiest fortune if well understood,
The certain prospect of a future good!

ACACIS. What joy can empire bring me,
when I know
That all my greatness to your crimes I owe?

ZEMPOALLA. Yours be the joy, be mine the
punishment.

ACACIS. In vain, alas, that wish to heaven
is sent
For me, if fair Orazia must not live.

ZEMPOALLA. Why should you ask me
what I cannot give?
She must be sacrificed. Can I bestow
What to the gods, by former vows, I owe?

ACACIS. O plead not vows; I wish you had
not shown
You slighted all things sacred for a throne.

ZEMPOALLA. I love thee so, that though
fear follows still,
And horror urges, all that have been ill,
I could for thee
Act o'er my crimes again, and not repent,
Even when I bore the shame and punish-
ment.

ACACIS. Could you so many ill acts undertake,
And not perform one good one for my sake?

ZEMPOALLA. Prudence permits not pity
should be shown
To those that raised the war to shake my
throne.

ACACIS. As you are wise, permit me to be
just;
What prudence will not venture, honor must;
We owe our conquest to the stranger's sword,
'Tis just his prisoners be to him restored.
I love Orazia, but a nobler way
Than for my love my honor to betray.

ZEMPOALLA. Honor is but an itch in
youthful blood
Of doing acts extravagantly good;
We call that virtue which is only heat
That reigns in youth, till age finds out the
cheat.

ACACIS. Great actions first did her affections move,
And I, by greater, would regain her love.

ZEMPOALLA. Urge not a suit which I must
still deny;
Orazia and her father both shall die.
Begone, I'll hear no more.

ACACIS. You stop your ears—
But though a mother will not, heaven will
hear.
Like you I vow, when to the powers divine
You pay her guiltless blood, I'll offer mine.
                                        (*Exit*)

ZEMPOALLA. She dies, this happy rival
that enjoys
The stranger's love and all my hopes destroys;

Had she triùmphed, what could she more
   have done
Than robbed the mother and enslaved the
   son?
Nor will I, at the name of cruel, stay.
Let dull successive monarchs mildly sway;
Their conquering fathers did the laws for-
   sake,
And broke the old ere they the new could
   make.
I must pursue my love; yet love, enjoyed,
Will, with esteem that caused it first, grow
   less;
But thirst and hunger fear not to be cloyed,
And when they be, are cured by their excess.

(*Enter* TRAXALLA)

TRAXALLA. (*Aside*) Now I shall see what
   thoughts her heart conceals;
For that which wisdom covers, love reveals.—
Madam, the prisoners are disposed.
ZEMPOALLA. They are?
And how fares our young blustering man of
   war?
Does he support his chains with patience yet?
   TRAXALLA. He and the princess, madam—
ZEMPOALLA. Are they met?
   TRAXALLA. No; but from whence is all
this passion grown?
   ZEMPOALLA. 'Twas a mistake.
   TRAXALLA. I find this rash unknown
Is dangerous; and, if not timely slain,
May plunge your empire in new wars again.
   ZEMPOALLA. Thank ye; I shall consider.
   TRAXALLA. Is that all?
The army dote on him, already call
You cruel; and, for aught I know, they may
By force unchain and crown him in a day.
   ZEMPOALLA. You say I have already had
   their curse
For his bad usage; should I use him worse?
   TRAXALLA. Yet once you feared his repu-
   tation might
Obscure the prince's in the people's sight.
   ZEMPOALLA. Time will inform us best
   what course to steer,
But let us not our sacred vows defer:
The Inca and his daughter both shall die.
   TRAXALLA. He suffers justly for the war;
   but why

Should she share his sad fate? A poor pre-
   tence,
That birth should make a crime of innocence.
   ZEMPOALLA. Yet we destroy the poisonous
   viper's young,
Not for themselves but those from whom
   they sprung.
   TRAXALLA. O no, they die not for their
   parents' sake,
But for the poisonous seed which they par-
   take.
Once more behold her, and then let her die
If in that face or person you can see
But any place to fix a cruelty.
The heavens have clouds, and spots are in
   the moon,
But faultless beauty shines in her alone.
   ZEMPOALLA. Beauty has wrought compas-
sion in your mind!
   TRAXALLA. And you to valor are become
   as kind.
To former services there's something due,
Yet be advised—
   ZEMPOALLA. Yes, by myself, not you.
   TRAXALLA. Princes are sacred.
   ZEMPOALLA. True, whilst they are free;
But power once lost, farewell their sanctity.
'Tis power to which the gods their worship
   owe,
Which, uncontrolled, makes all things just
   below.
Thou dost the plea of saucy rebels use;
They will be judge of what their prince must
   choose.
Hard fate of monarchs, not allowed to know
When safe, but as their subjects tell them so!
Then princes but like public pageants move,
And seem to sway because they sit above.
                   (*Exit*)
   TRAXALLA. She loves him; in one moment
   this new guest
Has drove me out from this false woman's
   breast;
They that would fetter love with constancy
Make bonds to chain themselves, but leave
   him free.
With what impatience I her falsehood bear!
Yet do myself that which I blame in her.
But interest in my own cause makes me see
That act unjust in her, but just in me.
                   (*Exit*)

Scene II.

(Ismeron *asleep in a cave. Enter*
Zempoalla)

Zempoalla. Ho, Ismeron, Ismeron!
He stirs not; ha, in such a dismal cell
Can gentle sleep with his soft blessings dwell?
Must I feel tortures in a human breast,
While beasts and monsters can enjoy their
  rest?
What quiet they possess in sleep's calm bliss!
The lions cease to roar, the snakes to hiss,
While I am kept awake
Only to entertain my miseries.
Or if a slumber steal upon my eyes,
Some horrid dream my laboring soul be-
  numbs,
And brings fate to me sooner than it comes.
Fears most oppress when sleep has seized
  upon
The outward parts and left the soul alone.
What envied blessings these cursed things
  enjoy!
Next to possess, 'tis pleasure to destroy.
Ismeron! Ho, Ismeron, Ismeron!   (*Stamps*)
    Ismeron. Who's that, that with so loud
      and fierce a call
Disturbs my rest?
    Zempoalla. She that has none at all,
Nor ever must, unless thy powerful art
Can charm the passions of a troubled heart.
    Ismeron. How can you have a discon-
      tented mind,
To whom the gods have lately been so kind?
    Zempoalla. Their envious kindness how
      can I enjoy,
When they give blessings and the use de-
  stroy?
    Ismeron. Dread empress, tell the cause of
      all your grief;
If art can help, be sure of quick relief.
    Zempoalla. I dreamed before the altar
      that I led
A mighty lion in a twisted thread;
I shook to hold him in so slight a tie,
Yet had not power to seek a remedy,
When, in the midst of all my fears, a dove
With hovering wings descended from above,
Flew to the lion, and embraces spread
With wings like clasping arms about his
  head,

Making that murmuring noise that cooing
  doves
Use in the soft expression of their loves;
While I, fixed by my wonder, gazed to see
So mild a creature with so fierce agree.
At last the gentle dove turned from his head,
And, pecking, tried to break the slender
  thread,
Which instantly she severed and released
From that small bond the fierce and mighty
  beast,
Who presently turned all his rage on me
And with his freedom brought my destiny.
    Ismeron. Dread empress, this strange
      vision you relate
Is big with wonder, and too full of fate,
Without the god's assistance, to expound.
In those low regions where sad night hangs
  round
The drowsy vaults, and where moist vapors
  steep
The god's dull brows, that sways the realm of
  sleep;
There all the informing elements repair,
Swift messengers of water, fire, and air,
To give account of actions, whence they came
And how they govern every mortal frame;
How, from their various mixture or their
  strife,
Are known the calms and tempests of our life.
Thence souls, when sleep their bodies over-
  come,
Have some imperfect knowledge of their
  doom.
From those dark caves those powers shall
  straight appear;
Be not afraid, whatever shapes they wear.
    Zempoalla. There's nothing thou canst
      raise can make me start;
A living form can only shake my heart.

(Ismeron *raises his arms and intones*)

Ismeron. *You twice ten hundred deities,*
To whom we daily sacrifice;
You powers that dwell with fate below,
And see what men are doomed to do,
Where elements in discord dwell;
Thou god of sleep, arise and tell

Great Zempoalla what strange fate
Must on her dismal vision wait.

ZEMPOALLA. How slow these spirits are!
  Call, make them rise,
Or they shall fast from flame and sacrifice.
  ISMERON. Great empress,
Let not your rage offend what we adore,
And vainly threaten when we must implore.
Sit, and silently attend—
While my powerful charms I end.

  By the croaking of the toad
  In their caves that makes abode,
  Earthy, dun, that pants for breath
  With her swelled sides full of death;
  By the crested adders' pride
  That along the cliffs do glide;
  By the visage fierce and black;
  By the death's-head on thy back;
  By the twisted serpents placed
  For a girdle round thy waist;
  By the hearts of gold that deck
  Thy breast, thy shoulders, and thy neck:
  From thy sleepy mansion rise,
  And open thy unwilling eyes,
  While bubbling springs their music keep,
  That used to lull thee in thy sleep.

(GOD OF DREAMS *rises*)

GOD. Seek not to know what must not be
  revealed;
Joys only flow where fate is most concealed.
Too busy man would find his sorrows more,
If future fortunes he should know before;
For, by that knowledge of his destiny,
He would not live at all, but always die.
Inquire not, then, who shall from bonds be
  freed,
Who 'tis shall wear a crown, and who shall
  bleed.
All must submit to their appointed doom;
Fate and misfortune will too quickly come.
Let me no more with powerful charms be
  prest;
I am forbid by fate to tell the rest.
(*The* GOD *descends*)

ZEMPOALLA. Stay, cozener, thou that
  hat'st clear truth like light,
And usest words dark as thy own dull night.
You tyrant gods, do you refuse to free
The soul you gave from its perplexity?
Why should we in your mercies still believe,

When you can never pity, though we grieve?
For you have bound yourselves by harsh de-
  crees,
And those, not you, are now the deities.
        (*Sits down despondently*)
  ISMERON. She droops under the weight of
    rage and care.
You spirits that inhabit in the air,
With all your powerful charms of music try
To bring her soul back to its harmony.

(SONG *from above, as if sung by aerial*
        spirits)

Poor mortals that are clogged with earth
    below,
    Sink under love and care,
    While we that dwell in air,
  Such heavy passions never know.
    Why then should mortals be
    Unwilling to be free
    From blood, that sullen cloud,
    Which shining souls does shroud?
    Then they'll show bright,
    And like us light,
  When leaving bodies with their care,
    They slide to us and air.

ZEMPOALLA. Death on these trifles! Can-
  not your art find
Some means to ease the passions of the
  mind?
Or, if you cannot give a lover rest,
Can you force love into a scornful breast?
  ISMERON. 'Tis reason only can make pas-
    sions less;
Art gives not new, but may the old, increase;
Nor can it alter love in any breast
That is with other flames before possessed.
  ZEMPOALLA. If this be all your slighted art
    can do,
I'll be a fate both to your gods and you;
I'll kindle other flames, since I must burn,
And all their temples into ashes turn.
  ISMERON. Great queen—
  ZEMPOALLA. If you would have this sen-
    tence stayed,
Summon their godheads quickly to your aid,
And presently compose a charm that may
Love's flames into the stranger's breast con-
  vey,
The captive stranger, he whose sword and
  eyes,

Where'er they strike, meet ready victories;
Make him but burn for me, in flames like
    mine,
Victims shall bleed, and feasted altars shine.
If not—

Down go your temples, and your gods shall
    see
They have small use of their divinity.
                        (*Exeunt*)

Act IV

Scene I.

(*The scene opens and discovers* Montezuma
sleeping in prison. Enter Traxalla *leading
in* Orazia)

Traxalla. Now take your choice, and bid
    him live or die;
To both show pity or show cruelty.
'Tis you that must condemn, I'll only act;
Your sentence is more cruel than my fact.
    Orazia. You are most cruel to disturb a
    mind
Which to approaching fate was so resigned.
    Traxalla. Reward my passions, and you'll
    quickly prove
There's none dare sacrifice what I dare
    love.—
(*To* Montezuma) Next to thee, stranger;
    wake, and now resign
The bold pretences of thy love to mine,
Or in this fatal minute thou shalt find—
    Montezuma. Death, fool; in that, thou
    mayst be just and kind.
'Twas I that loved Orazia, yet did raise
The storm in which she sinks. Why dost thou
    gaze,
Or stay thy hand from giving that just stroke
Which, rather than prevent, I would pro-
    voke?
When I am dead, Orazia may forgive;
She never must, if I dare wish to live.
    Orazia. Hold, hold—O Montezuma, can
    you be
So careless of yourself, but more of me?
Though you have brought me to this misery,
I blush to say I cannot see you die.
    Montezuma. Can my approaching fate
    such pity move?
The gods and you at once forgive and love.
    Traxalla. Fond fool, thus to mis-spend
    that little breath
I lent thee to prevent, not hasten, death!
Let her thank you she was unfortunate,

And you thank her for pulling on your fate;
Prove to each other your own destinies.
                        (*Draws*)

(*Enter* Zempoalla *hastily, and sets a dagger to* Orazia's *breast*)

    Zempoalla. Hold, hold, Traxalla, or
    Orazia dies.—
Oh, is't Orazia's name that makes you stay?
'Tis her great power, not mine, that you obey!
Inhuman wretch, dar'st thou the murderer be
Of him that is not yet condemned by me?
    Traxalla. The wretch that gave you all
    the power you have
May venture sure to execute a slave,
And quench a flame your fondness would
    have burn,
Which may this city into ashes turn,
The nation in your guilty passion lost;
To me ungrateful, to your country most.
(*Threatening* Montezuma) But this shall
    be their offering, I their priest.
    Zempoalla. The wounds thou giv'st I'll
    copy on her breast.
Strike, and I'll open here a spring of blood
Shall add new rivers to the crimson flood.
How his pale looks are fixed on her!—'tis so.
Oh, does amazement on your spirit grow?
What, is your public love Orazia's grown?
Couldst thou see mine, and yet not hide thy
    own?
Suppose I should strike first, would it not
    breed
Grief in your public heart to see her bleed?
    Traxalla. (*Aside*) She mocks my pas-
    sions; in her sparkling eyes
Death and a close dissembled fury lies.
I dare not trust her thus.—If she must die,
The way to her loved life through mine shall
    lie.

(*He pushes* ZEMPOALLA *aside and steps*
before ORAZIA; ZEMPOALLA *runs*
to stand before MONTEZUMA)

ZEMPOALLA. And he that does this stranger's fate design
Must to his heart a passage force through mine.
   TRAXALLA. Can fair Orazia yet no pity have?
'Tis just she should her own preserver save.
   ZEMPOALLA. Can Montezuma so ungrateful prove
To her that gave him life and offers love?
   ORAZIA. Can Montezuma live, and live to be
Just to another and unjust to me?
You need not be ungrateful; can she give
A life to you, if you refuse to live?—
Forgive me, Passion; I had rather see
You dead than kind to anything but me.
   MONTEZUMA. O my Orazia!
To what new joys and knowledge am I brought!
Are death's hard lessons by a woman taught?
How to despise my fate I always knew,
But ne'er durst think, at once, of death and you;
Yet since you teach this generous jealousy,
I dare not wish your life, if I must die.
How much your love my courage does exceed!
Courage alone would shrink to see you bleed!
   ZEMPOALLA. Ungrateful stranger! Thou shalt please thy eyes,
And gaze upon Orazia while she dies!—
I'll keep my vow!—It is some joy to see
That my revenge will prove my piety.
   TRAXALLA. Then both shall die!—We have too long withstood,
By private passions urged, the public good.
   ZEMPOALLA. (*Aside*) Sure he dissembles; and perhaps may prove
My ruin with his new, ambitious love.
Were but this stranger kind, I'd cross his art,
And give my empire where I gave my heart.—
Yet, thou ungrateful man,
Let thy approaching ruin make thee wise.
   MONTEZUMA. Thee, and thy love, and mischief, I despise!
   ZEMPOALLA. (*Aside*) What shall I do?
Some way must yet be tried;—
What reasons can she use whom passions guide!

   TRAXALLA. (*Aside*) Some black designs are hatching now.—False eyes
Are quick to see another's treacheries.
   ZEMPOALLA. Rash stranger, thus to pull down thy own fate!
   MONTEZUMA. You, and that life you offer me, I hate.

(*Enter* JAILER)

ZEMPOALLA. Here, jailer, take—What title must he have?
Slave, slave!—Am I then captive to a slave?—
Why art thou thus unwilling to be free?
   MONTEZUMA. Death will release me from these chains and thee.
   ZEMPOALLA. Here, jailer, take this monster from my sight,
And keep him where it may be always night.
Let none come near him; if thou dost, expect
To pay thy life, the price of the neglect.
   MONTEZUMA. I scorn thy pity and thy cruelty,
And should despise a blessing sent from thee.
   ZEMPOALLA. Oh, horror to my soul! Take him away!—
My rage, like dammed-up streams swelled by some stay,
Shall from this opposition get new force,
And leave the bound of its old easy course.—
     (*Exeunt* MONTEZUMA *and* Jailer)
Come, my Traxalla, let us both forgive,
And in these wretches' fate begin to live.
The altars shall be crowned with funeral boughs,
Peace-offerings paid,—but with unquiet vows.
     (*Exeunt* ZEMPOALLA *and* TRAXALLA)
   ORAZIA. How are things ordered, that the wicked should
Appear more kind and gentle than the good?
Her passion seems to make her kinder prove,
And I seem cruel through excess of love.
She loves, and would prevent his death; but I,
That love him better, fear he should not die.
My jealousy, immortal as my love,
Would rob my grave below, and me above,
Of rest.—Ye gods, if I repine, forgive!
You neither let me die in peace, nor live.

(*Enter* ACACIS, JAILER, *and* INDIANS)

JAILER. They are just gone, sir.
   ACACIS. 'Tis well. Be faithful to my just design,

And all thy prince's fortune shall be thine.
(*Exit* ACACIS)
INDIAN. This shall to the empress.
(*Exit* INDIAN)
ORAZIA. What can this mean!
'Twas Prince Acacis, if I durst believe
My sight; but sorrow may like joy deceive.
Each object different from itself appears
That comes not to the eyes, but through their
tears.

(*Enter* ACACIS, *bringing in* MONTEZUMA)

Ha!—
ACACIS. Here, sir, wear this again.—
(*Gives* MONTEZUMA *a sword*)
Now follow me.
MONTEZUMA. So, very good.—
I dare not think, for I may guess amiss.
None can deceive me while I trust to this.
(*Exeunt*)

SCENE II.

(*Enter* ORAZIA, *conducted by two Indians with their swords drawn,* MONTEZUMA, *followed by* ACACIS *whispering to another* INDIAN)

ACACIS. Think what a weight upon thy faith I lay.
INDIAN. I ne'er did more unwillingly obey.
ACACIS. First, Montezuma, take thy liberty.
Thou gav'st me freedom, here I set thee free.
We're equal now. Madam, the danger's great
Of close pursuit; to favor your retreat,
Permit we two a little while remain
Behind, while you go softly o'er the plain.
ORAZIA. Why should I go before?—What's your intent?
Where is my father?—Whither am I sent?
ACACIS. Your doubts shall soon be cleared.
Conduct her on.
(*Exit* ORAZIA *and Indian guards*)
So, Montezuma, we are now alone.
That which my honor owed thee I have paid;
As honor was, so love must be obeyed.
I set Orazia, as thy captive, free;
But, as my mistress, ask her back from thee.
MONTEZUMA. Thou hast performed what honor bid thee do,
But friendship bars what honor prompts me to.—
Friends should not fight.
ACACIS. If friendship we profess,
Let us secure each other's happiness.
One needs must die, and he shall happy prove
In her remembrance, t'other in her love.
My guards wait near; and, if I fail, they must
Give up Orazia or betray their trust.

MONTEZUMA. Suppose thou conquer'st, wouldst thou wander o'er
The south-sea sands or the rough northern shore
That parts thy spacious kingdom from Peru,
And, leaving empire, hopeless love pursue?
ACACIS. By which of all my actions could you guess,
Though more your merit, that my love was less?
What prize can empire with Orazia bear?
Or, where love fills the breast, what room for fear?
MONTEZUMA. Let fair Orazia then the sentence give,
Else he may die whom she desires to live.
ACACIS. Your greater merits bribe her to your side;
My weaker title must by arms be tried.
MONTEZUMA. Oh, tyrant love, how cruel are thy laws!
I forfeit friendship or betray thy cause.
That person whom I would defend from all
The world, that person by my hand must fall.
ACACIS. Our lives we to each other's friendships owe,
But love calls back what friendship did bestow;
Love has its cruelties, but friendship none,
And we now fight in quarrels not our own.
(*They fight.* ACACIS *is wounded.*)

(*Enter* ORAZIA)

ORAZIA. What noise is this?—
Hold, hold! What cause could be so great to move
This furious hatred?—

MONTEZUMA. 'Twas our furious love.—

ACACIS. Love, which I hid till I had set you free
And bought your pardon with my liberty;
That done, I thought I less unjustly might
With Montezuma for Orazia fight.
He has prevailed, and I must now confess
His fortune greater, not my passion less;
Yet cannot yield you, till his sword remove
A dying rival that holds fast his love.

ORAZIA. Whoever falls, 'tis my protector still,
And then the crime's as great to die as kill.—
Acacis, do not hopeless love pursue,
But live, and this soft malady subdue.

ACACIS. You bid me live, and yet command me die!
I am not worth your care.—Fly, madam, fly,
(While I fall here unpitied) o'er this plain;
Free from pursuit, the faithless mountains gain!
And these I charge,
As they would have me think their friendship true,
Leave me alone, to serve and follow you.
Make haste, fair princess, to avoid that fate
Which does for your unhappy father wait.

ORAZIA. Is he then left to die, and shall he see
Himself forsaken, ere his death, by me?

MONTEZUMA. What would you do?

ORAZIA. To prison I'll return,
And there in fetters with my father mourn.

MONTEZUMA. That saves not his, but throws your life away.

ORAZIA. Duty shall give what nature once must pay.

ACACIS. Life is the gift which heaven and parents give,
And duty best preserves it, if you live.

ORAZIA. I should but further from my fountain fly,
And like an unfed stream run on and die.
Urge me no more, and do not grieve to see
Your honor rivalled by my piety.

(*She goes softly off, and often looks back*)

MONTEZUMA. If honor would not, shame would lead the way;
I'll back with her.

ACACIS. Stay, Montezuma, stay!—
Thy rival cannot let thee go alone;
My love will bear me, though my blood is gone.

(*As they are going off, enter* ZEMPOALLA, TRAXALLA, *the Indian that went to tell her, and the rest, and seize them*)

ZEMPOALLA. Seize them!—

ACACIS. Oh, Montezuma, thou art lost!

MONTEZUMA. No more, proud heart, thy useless courage boast!—
Courage, thou curse of the unfortunate,
That canst encounter, not resist, ill fate!—

ZEMPOALLA. Acacis bleeds!—
What barbarous hand has wounded thus my son?

MONTEZUMA. 'Twas I; by my unhappy sword 'twas done.—
Thou bleedst, poor prince, and I am left to grieve
My rival's fall.

TRAXALLA. He bleeds, but yet may live.

ACACIS. Friendship and love my failing strength renew;
I dare not die when I should live for you;
My death were now my crime, as it would be
My guilt to live when I have set you free.
Thus I must still remain unfortunate,
Your life and death are equally my fate.

(ORAZIA *comes back*)

ORAZIA. A noise again!—Alas, what do I see!
Love, thou didst once give place to piety—
Now, piety, let love triùmph awhile;—
Here, bind my hands. Come, Montezuma, smile
At fortune; since thou sufferest for my sake,
Orazia will her captive's chains partake.

MONTEZUMA. Now, fate, thy worst.

ZEMPOALLA. Lead to the temple straight;
A priest and altar for these lovers wait.
They shall be joined, they shall.

TRAXALLA. And I will prove
Those joys in vengeance which I want in love.

ACACIS. I'll quench your thirst with blood, and will destroy
Myself, and with myself, your cruel joy.
Now, Montezuma, since Orazia dies,
I'll fall before thee, the first sacrifice;
My title in her death shall exceed thine,
As much as, in her life, thy hopes did mine,
And when with our mixed blood the altar's dyed,
Then our new title let the gods decide.

(*Exeunt*)

Act V

Scene I.

(The Scene opens, and discovers the Temple of the Sun, all of gold, and four Priests in habits of white and red feathers, attending by a bloody altar, as ready for sacrifice. Then enter the Guards, ZEMPOALLA, and TRAXALLA; INCA, ORAZIA, and MONTEZUMA, bound. As soon as they are placed, the Priest sings)

SONG

You to whom victory we owe,
  Whose glories rise
    By sacrifice,
  And from our fates below;
Never did your altars shine
Feasted with blood so near divine;
  Princes to whom we bow,
    As they to you.—
Thus you can ravish from a throne,
And by their loss of power declare your own.

ZEMPOALLA. Now to inflict those punishments that are
Due to the authors of invasive war,
Who, to deceive the oppressed world, like you
Invent false quarrels to conceal the true.
  INCA. My quarrel was the same that all the gods
Must have to thee, if there be any odds
Betwixt those titles that are bad or good,
To crowns descended, or usurped by blood.—
Swell not with this success; 'twas not to thee,
But to this man, the gods gave victory.
  MONTEZUMA. Since I must perish by my own success,
Think my misfortunes more, my crimes the less;
And so, forgiving, make me pleased to die,
Thus punished for this guilty victory.
  INCA. Death can make virtue easy; I forgive.
That word would prove too hard, were I to live;
The honor of a prince would then deny,
But in the grave all our distinctions die.

MONTEZUMA. Forgive me one thing yet; to say, I love,
Let it no more your scorn and anger move,
Since, dying in one flame, my ashes must
Embrace and mingle with Orazia's dust.
  INCA. Name thy bold love no more, lest that last breath
Which should forgive, I stifle with my death.
  ORAZIA. Oh, my dear father! Oh, why may not I,
Since you gave life to me, for you now die?
  MONTEZUMA. 'Tis I that wrought this mischief, ought to fall
A just and willing sacrifice for all.
Now, Zempoalla, be both just and kind,
And, in my fate, let me thy mercy find.
Be grateful, then, and grant me that esteem,
That as alive, so dead, I may redeem.
  ORAZIA. O do not for her cruel mercy move;
None should ask pity but from those they love.   *(Weeps)*
  INCA. Fond girl, to let thy disobedient eyes
Show a concern for him whom I despise!
  ORAZIA. How love and nature may divide a breast
At once by both their powers severely pressed!
Yet, sir, since love seems less, you may forgive;
I would not have you die, nor have him live;
Yet if he dies, alas! what shall I do?
I cannot die with him, and live with you.
  MONTEZUMA. How vainly we pursue this generous strife,
Parting in death more cruel than in life!—
Weep not, we both shall have one destiny;
As in one flame we lived, in one we'll die.
  TRAXALLA. Why do we waste in vain these precious hours?
Each minute of his life may hazard ours.
The nation does not live whilst he enjoys
His life; it is his safety that destroys.
He shall fall first, and teach the rest to die.
  ZEMPOALLA. Hold!—
Who is it that commands—ha! you, or I?—
Your zeal grows saucy!—Sure, you may allow

Your empress freedom first to pay her vow.

TRAXALLA. She may allow—a justice to be
    done

By him that raised his empress to her throne.

ZEMPOALLA. You are too bold—

TRAXALLA. And you, too passionate.

ZEMPOALLA. Take heed, with his, you
urge not your own fate.—

For all this pity is now due to me.

MONTEZUMA. I hate thy offered mercy
more than thee.

TRAXALLA. Why will not then the fair
    Orazia give

Life to herself, and let Traxalla live?

MONTEZUMA. Orazia will not live and let
    me die;

She taugh me first this cruel jealousy.

ORAZIA. I joy that you have learned it!—

That flame not like immortal love appears,

Where death can cool its warmth or kill its
fears.

ZEMPOALLA. (Aside) What shall I do?
    Am I so quite forlorn,

No help from my own pride, nor from his
scorn!

My rival's death may more effectual prove;

He that is robbed of hope may cease to
love.—

(To the Guards) Here, lead these offerings
    to their deaths.

TRAXALLA. Let none

Obey but he that will pull on his own!

ZEMPOALLA. Tempt me not thus; false
and ungrateful, too!

TRAXALLA. Just as ungrateful and as false
as you!

ZEMPOALLA. 'Tis thy false love that fears
her destiny.

TRAXALLA. And your false love that fears
to have him die.

ZEMPOALLA. Seize the bold traitor!
        (The Guards stand motionless)

TRAXALLA. (Tauntingly) What a slighted
    frown

Troubles your brow! feared nor obeyed by
none!

Come, prepare for sacrifice.

(Enter ACACIS weakly)

ACACIS. Hold, hold! Such sacrifices can-
    not be

Devotions, but a solemn cruelty.

How can the gods delight in human blood?

Think them not cruel, if you think them
    good.

In vain we ask that mercy which they want,

And hope that pity which they hate to grant.

ZEMPOALLA. Retire, Acacis.—

Preserve thyself, for 'tis in vain to waste

Thy breath for them. The fatal vow is past.

ACACIS. To break that vow is juster than
    commit

A greater crime by your preserving it.

ZEMPOALLA. The gods themselves their
    own will best express

To like the vow, by giving the success.

ACACIS. If all things by success are under-
    stood,

Men that make war grow wicked to be good;

But did you vow, those that were overcome

And he that conquered, both should share
    one doom?

There's no excuse; for one of these must be

Not your devotion, but your cruelty.

TRAXALLA. To that rash stranger, sir, we
    nothing owe;

What he had raised, he strove to overthrow;

That duty lost which should our actions
    guide,

Courage proves guilt, when merit swells to
    pride.

ACACIS. Darest thou, who didst thy
    prince's life betray,

Once name that duty thou hast thrown away?

Like thy injustice to this stranger shown,

To tax him with a guilt that is thy own?—

(To the Guards) Can you, brave soldiers,
    suffer him to die

That gave you life in giving victory?

Look but upon this stranger, see those hands

That brought you freedom, fettered up in
    bands.

Not one looks up,—

Lest sudden pity should your hearts surprise,

And steal into their bosoms through their
    eyes.

ZEMPOALLA. Why thus, in vain, are thy
    weak spirits pressed?

Restore thyself to thy more needful rest.

ACACIS. And leave Orazia!—

ZEMPOALLA. Go, you must resign,

For she must be the gods'—not yours nor
    mine.

ACACIS. You are my mother, and my
    tongue is tied

So much by duty that I dare not chide.—
Divine Orazia!
Can you have so much mercy to forgive?
I do not ask it with design to live,
But in my death to have my torments cease.
Death is not death when it can bring no
    peace.
    ORAZIA. I both forgive and pity.—
    ACACIS. O say no more, lest words less
        kind destroy
What these have raised in me of peace and
    joy.
You said you did both pity and forgive;
You would do neither, should Acacis live.
By death alone the certain way appears
Thus to hope mercy and deserve your tears.
                    (Stabs himself)
    ZEMPOALLA. O my Acacis!
What cruel cause could urge this fatal
    deed?—   (Weeps)
He faints!—Help, help! Some help, or he
    will bleed
His life and mine away!—
Some water there!—(The Guards look at
    TRAXALLA and do not move) Not one
    stirs from his place!
I'll use my tears to sprinkle on his face.
            (She kneels beside ACACIS)
    ACACIS. Orazia—
    ZEMPOALLA. Fond child! Why dost thou
        call upon her name?
I am thy mother.
    ACACIS. No, you are my shame.
That blood is shed that you had title in,
And with your title may it end your sin!
Unhappy prince, you may forgive me now,
Thus bleeding for my mother's cruel vow.
    INCA. Be not concerned for me;
Death's easier than the changes I have seen.
I would not live to trust the world again.
    MONTEZUMA. Into my eyes sorrow begins
        to creep;
When hands are tied, it is no shame to weep.
    ACACIS. Dear Montezuma,
I may be still your friend, though I must die
Your rival in her love. Eternity
Has room enough for both; there's no desire
Where to enjoy is only to admire.
There we'll meet friends, when this short
    storm is past.
    MONTEZUMA. Why must I tamely wait to
perish last?

    ACACIS. Orazia weeps, and my parched
        soul appears
Refreshed by that kind shower of pitying
    tears.
Forgive those faults my passion did commit;
'Tis punished with the life that nourished it.
I had no power in this extremity
To save your life, and less to see you die.
My eyes would ever on this object stay,
But sinking nature takes the props away.
Kind death,
To end with pleasures all my miseries,
Shuts up your image in my closing eyes.
                    (Dies)

(Enter a MESSENGER)

    MESSENGER. To arms, to arms!
    TRAXALLA. From whence this sudden
fear?
    MESSENGER. Stand to your guard, my
        lord, the danger's near;
From every quarter crowds of people meet
And, leaving houses empty, fill the street.
                    (Exit MESSENGER)
    TRAXALLA. Fond queen, thy fruitless tears
        a while defer;
Rise, we must join again. (ZEMPOALLA still
    kneels)—Not speak, nor stir!
I hear the people's voice like winds that roar
When they pursue the flying waves to shore.

(Enter SECOND MESSENGER)

    SECOND MESSENGER. Prepare to fight, my
        lord; the banished queen,
With old Garucca, in the streets are seen.
    TRAXALLA. We must go meet them or it
        be too late;
Yet, madam, rise! Have you no sense of fate?

(Enter THIRD MESSENGER)

    THIRD MESSENGER. King Montezuma
        their loud shouts proclaim,
The city rings with their new sovereign's
    name;
The banished queen declares he is her son,
And to his succor all the people run.
                    (ZEMPOALLA rises)
    ZEMPOALLA. Can this be true? O love! O
        fate! Have I
Thus doted on my mortal enemy?

TRAXALLA. (*Hand on sword he approaches* MONTEZUMA) To my new prince I thus my homage pay;
Your reign is short, young king—
ZEMPOALLA. Traxalla, stay!
'Tis to my hand that he must owe his fate;
I will revenge at once my love and hate.
    (*She sets a dagger to* MONTEZUMA's *breast*)
TRAXALLA. Strike, strike, the conquering enemy is near.
My guards are passed while you detain me here.
ZEMPOALLA. Die, then, ungrateful, die!
Amexia's son
Shall never triumph on Acacis' throne.
Thy death must my unhappy flames remove:
Now where is thy defence—against my love?
    (*She cuts the cords and gives him the dagger*)
TRAXALLA. Am I betrayed?
    (*He draws and thrusts at* MONTEZUMA, *who parries the thrust and kills him*)
MONTEZUMA. So may all rebels die:
This end has treason joined with cruelty.
ZEMPOALLA. Live thou whom I must love and yet must hate;
She gave thee life who knows it brings her fate.
MONTEZUMA. Life is a trifle which I would not take,
But for Orazia's and her father's sake.
Now, Inca, hate me if thou canst; for he
Whom thou hast scorned will die, or rescue thee.
(*As he goes to attack the guard with* TRAXALLA's *sword, enter* AMEXIA, GARUCCA, *Indians, driving some of the other party before them*)
GARUCCA. He lives, ye gods, he lives!
Great queen, see here
Your coming joys and your departing fear.
AMEXIA. Wonder and joy so fast together flow,
Their haste to pass has made their passage slow;
Like struggling waters in a vessel pent,
Whose crowding drops choke up the narrow vent.
My son!—   (*She embraces him*)
MONTEZUMA. I am amazed! It cannot be
That fate has such a joy in store for me.

AMEXIA. Can I not gain belief that this is true?
MONTEZUMA. It is my fortune I suspect, not you.
GARUCCA. First ask him if he old Garucca know.
MONTEZUMA. (*Kneeling*) My honored father! Let me fall thus low.
GARUCCA. Forbear, great prince; 'tis I must pay to you
That adoration as my sovereign's due;
For, from my humble race you did not spring;
You are the issue of our murdered king,
Sent by that traitor (*pointing to* TRAXALLA) to his blest abode,
Whom, to be made a king, he made a god.
The story is too full of fate to tell,
Or what strange fortune our lost queen befell.
AMEXIA. That sad relation longer time will crave;
I lived obscure, he bred you in a cave,
But kept the mighty secret from your ear,
Lest heat of blood to some strange course should steer
Your youth.
MONTEZUMA. I owe him all that now I am.
He taught me first the noble thirst of fame,
Showed me the baseness of unmanly fear,
Till the unlicked whelp I plucked from the rough bear,
And made the ounce and tiger give me way
While from their hungry jaws I snatched the prey.
'Twas he that charged my young arms first with toils,
And dressed me glorious in my savage spoils.
GARUCCA. You spent in shady forest all the day,
And joyed, returning, to show me the prey,
To tell the story, to describe the place,
With all the pleasures of the boasted chase,
Till fit for arms, I reaved[3] you from your sport,
To train your youth in the Peruvian court.
I left you there, and ever since have been
The sad attendant of my exiled queen.
ZEMPOALLA. My fatal dream comes to my memory;
That lion, whom I held in bonds, was he;
Amexia was the dove that broke his chains.

[3] Tore.

What now but Zempoalla's death remains?

MONTEZUMA. Pardon, fair princess, if I
  must delay
My love a while, my gratitude to pay.
Live, Zempoalla—free from dangers live,
For present merits I past crimes forgive.
Oh, might she hope Orazia's pardon, too!

ORAZIA. I would have none condemned
  for loving you;
In me her merit much her fault o'erpowers;
She sought my life, but she preserved me
  yours.

AMEXIA. Taught by my own, I pity her
  estate,
And wish her penitence, but not her fate.

INCA. I would not be the last to bid her
  live;
Kings best revenge their wrongs when they
  forgive.

ZEMPOALLA. I cannot yet forget what I
  have been.
Would you give life to her that was a queen?
Must you then give, and must I take? There's
  yet
One way, that's by refusing to be great.
You bid me live—bid me be wretched, too.
Think, think what pride, unthroned, must
  undergo.
(*Pointing to the body of* ACACIS) Look on
  this youth, Amexia, look, and then
Suppose him yours, and bid me live again;
A greater sweetness on these lips there grows
Than breath shut out from a new-folded
  rose;
What lovely charms on these cold cheeks ap-
  pear!
Could any one hate death, and see it here?
But thou are gone—

MONTEZUMA. O that you would believe
Acacis lives in me, and cease to grieve.

ZEMPOALLA. Yes, I will cease to grieve,
  and cease to be.
His soul stays watching in his wound for me;
All that could render life desired is gone,
Orazia has my life, and you, my throne,
And death, Acacis—yet I need not die,
You leave me mistress of my destiny.
In spite of dreams, how am I pleased to see
Heaven's truth or falsehood should depend
  on me!
But I will help the gods;
The greatest proof of courage we can give
Is then to die when we have power to live.
(*Draws a concealed dagger and kills herself*)

MONTEZUMA. How fatally that instrument
  of death
Was hid—

AMEXIA. She has expired her latest breath.

MONTEZUMA. (*Pointing to* ACACIS) But
there lies one to whom all grief is due.

ORAZIA. None e'er was so unhappy and so
true.

MONTEZUMA. Your pardon, royal sir.

INCA. You have my love.
               (*Gives him* ORAZIA)

AMEXIA. The gods, my son, your happy
choice approve.

MONTEZUMA. Come, my Orazia, then,
  and pay with me
             (*Leads her to* ACACIS)
Some tears to poor Acacis' memory.
So strange a fate for me the gods ordain,
Our clearest sunshine should be mixed with
  rain;
How equally our joys and sorrows move!
Death's fatal triumphs, joined with those of
  love.
Love crowns the dead, and death crowns him
  that lives,
Each gains the conquest which the other
  gives.   (*Exeunt omnes*)

Epilogue

Spoken by MONTEZUMA

You see what shifts we are enforced to try,
To help our wit with some variety;
Shows may be found that never yet were
  seen,
'Tis hard to find such wit as ne'er has been.

You have seen all that this old world can do;
We therefore try the fortune of the new,
And hope it is below your aim to hit
At untaught nature with your practised wit.
Our naked Indians, then, when wits appear,

Would as soon choose to have the Spaniards
    here.
'Tis true, you have marks enough, the plot,
    the show,
The poet's scenes, nay, more, the painter's
    too; [1]

[1] A reference to the sensationally elaborate
scenery prepared for the production.

If all this fail, considering the cost,
'Tis a true voyage to the Indies lost.
But if you smile on all, then these designs,
Like the imperfect treasure of our mines,
Will pass for current wheresoe'er they go,
When to your bounteous hands their stamps
    they owe.

JOHN DRYDEN *

All for Love

or

The World Well Lost

INTRODUCTION

Dryden was well aware when he wrote this play that the famous story of Antony and Cleopatra had been a popular one with dramatists, and he knew and admired Shakespeare's *Antony and Cleopatra*. When he published his tragedy in 1678, he wrote a preface commenting on his purpose and methods. Particularly notable for students of the development of English drama are his comments in the preface on the moral, the characters, the structure, and the verse form of the play.

All writers of serious plays have given thought to the moral implications of the actions they set on the stage, but English tragedies from the Restoration to the middle of the nineteenth century tend to make their moralizing more insistent and more obvious than their predecessors had done. In his preface Dryden exemplifies this tendency when he accounts for the popularity of the Antony and Cleopatra story among dramatists by saying,

I doubt not but the same motive has prevailed with all of us in this attempt; I mean the excellency of the moral: for the chief persons represented were famous patterns of unlawful love, and their end accordingly was unfortunate.

* See pp. 395-96 for biographical details.

That word "accordingly" nicely reveals the moral certitude which characterizes the comparatively feeble tragedies of the next two hundred years, but which is not typical of Renaissance or twentieth-century tragedy.

Dryden also sets forth one of the basic principles which guided the creation of the character of Antony.

All reasonable men have long since concluded that the hero of the poem ought not to be a character of perfect virtue, for then he could not without injustice be made unhappy; nor yet altogether wicked, because he could not then be pitied. I have therefore steered the middle course.

The attempt to steer a middle course with Antony, though undoubtedly sound in theory, has led Dryden into the most frequently noted weakness of his play: Antony's vacillation between Cleopatra and empire, between Cleopatra and Octavia, makes him appear not a great man with pitiable weaknesses, but an indecisive weakling who could never have attained Antony's world significance. Dryden's application of Aristotle's theory has resulted in an Antony who is turned aside from his stated course, at one time or another, by every major figure in the cast.

Dryden's most notable deviation from the

methods of his admired predecessor, Shakespeare, are pointed out in his statement,

The fabric of the play is regular enough, as to the inferior parts of it; and the unities of time, place, and action, more exactly observed than, perhaps, the English theatre requires. Particularly, the action is so much one, that it is the only one of the kind without episode, or under-plot; every scene in the tragedy conducing to the main design, and every act concluding with a turn of it.

This unity of place and near-unity of time have robbed the play of the great scope which Shakespeare gave *Antony and Cleopatra,* the feeling that Antony was truly a world figure, vital in events which affected the fate of millions of subjects and the history of the world. Yet with the disappearance of the flexible Elizabethan stage after the Restoration, it was scarcely possible to bring into the theatre world actions like those set out by Marlowe and Shakespeare at the Theatre or the Globe. Dryden's *All for Love* is an excellent example of the drawing in of the scope of dramatic action necessitated by the adoption of the proscenium arch theatre.

Finally Dryden's comments on his verse are noteworthy, for they show a deliberate deviation from the Restoration norm exhibited in his other principles. Though he had been one of the most influential dramatists in popularizing heroic couplets in Restoration plays, he here turns to blank verse under the admitted influence of Shakespeare. He says,

In my style, I have professed to imitate the divine Shakespeare; which that I might perform more freely, I have disencumbered myself from rhyme. Not that I condemn my former way, but that this is more proper to my present purpose. . . . I hope, I may affirm, and without vanity, that, by imitating him, I have excelled myself throughout the play.

To just what extent the high rank of this play among Restoration tragedies is due to Dryden's blank verse it would be difficult to say, but it is clear that he has attained a flexibility of dialogue and an emotional force which he did not achieve in his couplet tragedies.

❦

ALL FOR LOVE

Dramatis personae

In order of first appearance

SERAPION ⎱ Priests of Isis.
MYRIS ⎰

ALEXAS, An eunuch, Cleopatra's shrewd and scheming but cowardly advisor.

VENTIDIUS, A veteran general of Mark Antony's army, brave, upright, uncorruptible, blunt in speech, devoted to Antony.

MARK ANTONY, Friend of Julius Caesar, conqueror of Brutus and Cassius. With Augustus, the ruler of the Roman Empire. For several years the lover of Cleopatra.

FIRST GENTLEMAN ⎱ Members of Antony's
SECOND GENTLEMAN ⎰ train.

CLEOPATRA, Queen of Egypt, the former mistress of Caesar and for ten years mistress of Antony; possessed of great beauty, charm, and fire.

IRAS ⎱ Her attendants and companions.
CHARMION ⎰

DOLABELLA, A bosom friend of Antony, younger than he, handsome and accomplished.

OCTAVIA, Caesar's sister and Antony's wife, a handsome Roman matron of upright virtue and pride, but lacking in tact and tenderness.

AGRIPPINA ⎱ Young daughters of Antony
ANTONIA ⎰ and Octavia.

Guards, attendants, lictors, commanders.

SCENE: *Alexandria*

Prologue

What flocks of critics hover here to-day,
As vultures wait on armies for their prey,
All gaping for the carcass of a play!
With croaking notes they bode some dire
     event,
And follow dying poets by the scent.
Ours gives himself for gone; y' have watched
     your time!
He fights this day unarmed,—without his
     rhyme;—
And brings a tale which often has been told,
As sad as Dido's; and almost as old.
His hero, whom you wits his bully call,
Bates of his mettle, and scarce rants at all:
He's somewhat lewd; but a well-meaning
     mind;
Weeps much; fights little; but is wond'rous
     kind.
In short, a pattern, and companion fit,
For all the keeping Tonies of the pit.
I could name more: a wife, and mistress too;
Both (to be plain) too good for most of you:
The wife well-natured, and the mistress true.
     Now, poets, if your fame has been his care,
Allow him all the candor you can spare.
A brave man scorns to quarrel once a day,
Like Hectors in at every petty fray.
Let those find fault whose wit's so very small,
They've need to show that they can think
     at all.
Errors like straws upon the surface flow;
He who would search for pearls must dive
     below.
Fops may have leave to level all they can,
As pigmies would be glad to lop a man.
Half-wits are fleas; so little and so light,
We scarce could know they live, but that
     they bite.
But, as the rich, when tired with daily feasts,
For change, become their next poor tenant's
     guests,
Drink hearty draughts of ale from plain
     brown bowls,
And snatch the homely rasher from the coals:
So you, retiring from much better cheer,
For once, may venture to do penance here.
And since that plenteous autumn now is
     past,
Whose grapes and peaches have indulged
     your taste,
Take in good part, from our poor poet's board,
Such rivelled fruits as winter can afford.

Act I

The Temple of Isis

(*Enter* SERAPION, MYRIS, *Priests of Isis*)

SERAP. Portents and prodigies are grown
     so frequent
That they have lost their name. Our fruitful
     Nile
Flowed ere the wonted season, with a torrent
So unexpected and so wondrous fierce,
That the wild deluge overtook the haste
Ev'n of the hinds that watched it; men and
     beasts
Were borne above the tops of trees that grew
On the utmost margin of the water-mark.
Then with so swift an ebb the flood drove
     backward,
It slipt from underneath the scaly herd.
Here monstrous phocæ panted on the shore;
Forsaken dolphins there with their broad
     tails
Lay lashing the departing waves; hard by
     'em,
Sea horses flound'ring in the slimy mud
Tossed up their heads, and dashed the ooze
     about 'em.

(*Enter* ALEXAS *behind them*)

MYR. Avert these omens, Heav'n!
SERAP. Last night, between the hours of
     twelve and one,
In a lone aisle o' th' temple while I walked,
A whirlwind rose that with a violent blast

Shook all the dome. The doors around me
    clapt;
The iron wicket, that defends the vault
Where the long race of Ptolemies is laid,
Burst open and disclosed the mighty dead.
From out each monument, in order placed,
An armed ghost starts up: the boy-king last
Reared his inglorious head. A peal of groans
Then followed, and a lamentable voice
Cried, "Egypt is no more!" My blood ran
    back,
My shaking knees against each other
    knocked;
On the cold pavement down I fell entranced,
And so unfinished left the horrid scene.
                (ALEXAS *comes forward*)
    ALEX. And dreamed you this? or did in-
    vent the story,
To frighten our Egyptian boys withal,
And train 'em up betimes in fear of priest-
    hood?
    SERAP. My lord, I saw you not,
Nor meant my words should reach your ears;
    but what
I uttered was most true.
    ALEX. A foolish dream,
Bred from the fumes of indigested feasts
And holy luxury.
    SERAP. I know my duty:
This goes no farther.
    ALEX. 'Tis not fit it should;
Nor would the times now bear it, were it
    true.
All southern, from yon hills, the Roman
    camp
Hangs o'er us black and threat'ning, like a
    storm
Just breaking on our heads.
    SERAP. Our faint Egyptians pray for
    Antony,
But in their servile hearts they own Octavius.
    MYR. Why then does Antony dream out
    his hours,
And tempts not fortune for a noble day,
Which might redeem what Actium lost?
    ALEX. He thinks 'tis past recovery.
    SERAP. Yet the foe
Seems not to press the siege.
    ALEX. Oh, there's the wonder.
Mæcenas and Agrippa, who can most
With Cæsar, are his foes. His wife Octavia,
Driv'n from his house, solicits her revenge;
And Dolabella, who was once his friend,

Upon some private grudge now seeks his
    ruin.
Yet still war seems on either side to sleep.
    SERAP. 'Tis strange that Antony for some
    days past
Has not beheld the face of Cleopatra,
But here in Isis' temple lives retired,
And makes his heart a prey to black despair.
    ALEX. 'Tis true; and we much fear he
    hopes by absence
To cure his mind of love.
    SERAP. If he be vanquished
Or make his peace, Egypt is doomed to be
A Roman province, and our plenteous har-
    vests
Must then redeem the scarceness of their soil.
While Antony stood firm, our Alexandria
Rivalled proud Rome (dominion's other
    seat),
And Fortune striding, like a vast Colossus,
Could fix an equal foot of empire here.
    ALEX. Had I my wish, these tyrants of all
    nature
Who lord it o'er mankind, should perish—
    perish,
Each by the other's sword; but since our will
Is lamely followed by our pow'r, we must
Depend on one, with him to rise or fall.
    SERAP. How stands the queen affected?
    ALEX. Oh, she dotes,
She dotes, Serapion, on this vanquished man,
And winds herself about his mighty ruins;
Whom would she yet forsake, yet yield him
    up,
This hunted prey, to his pursuers' hands,
She might preserve us all. But 'tis in vain—
This changes my designs, this blasts my
    counsels,
And makes me use all means to keep him
    here,
Whom I could wish divided from her arms
Far as the earth's deep center. Well, you
    know
The state of things; no more of your ill omens
And black prognostics; labor to confirm
The people's hearts.

    (*Enter* VENTIDIUS, *talking aside with a*
        GENTLEMAN *of* ANTONY'S)

    SERAP. These Romans will o'erhear us.
But who's that stranger? By his warlike port,
His fierce demeanor, and erected look,

He's of no vulgar note.

ALEX. Oh, 'tis Ventidius,
Our emp'ror's great lieutenant in the East,
Who first showed Rome that Parthia could
    be conquered.
When Antony returned from Syria last,
He left this man to guard the Roman fron-
    tiers.

SERAP. You seem to know him well.

ALEX. Too well. I saw him in Cilicia first,
When Cleopatra there met Antony.
A mortal foe he was to us, and Egypt.
But let me witness to the worth I hate,
A braver Roman never drew a sword;
Firm to his prince, but as a friend, not slave.
He ne'er was of his pleasures, but presides
O'er all his cooler hours and morning coun-
    sels.
In short the plainness, fierceness, rugged vir-
    tue
Of an old true-stamped Roman lives in him.
His coming bodes I know not what of ill
To our affairs. Withdraw, to mark him better,
And I'll acquaint you why I sought you here,
And what's our present work.

(*They withdraw to a corner of the stage, and*
    VENTIDIUS, *with the other, comes for-*
    ward to the front)

VENT. Not see him, say you?
I say, I must, and will.

GENT. He has commanded,
On pain of death, none should approach his
    presence.

VENT. I bring him news will raise his
    drooping spirits,
Give him new life.

GENT. He sees not Cleopatra.

VENT. Would he had never seen her!

GENT. He eats not, drinks not, sleeps not,
    has no use
Of anything, but thought; or, if he talks,
'Tis to himself, and then 'tis perfect raving.
Then he defies the world and bids it pass;
Sometimes he gnaws his lip, and curses loud
The boy Octavius; then he draws his mouth
Into a scornful smile and cries, "Take all,
The world's not worth my care."

VENT. Just, just his nature.
Virtue's his path; but sometimes 'tis too nar-
    row
For his vast soul, and then he starts out wide
And bounds into a vice that bears him far
From his first course, and plunges him in ills:

But when his danger makes him find his
    fault,
Quick to observe and full of sharp remorse,
He censures eagerly his own misdeeds,
Judging himself with malice to himself
And not forgiving what as man he did,
Because his other parts are more than man.
He must not thus be lost.

(ALEXAS *and the* PRIESTS *come forward*)

ALEX. (*To* SERAPION) You have your full
    instructions, now advance;
Proclaim your orders loudly.

SERAP. Romans, Egyptians, hear the
    queen's command.
Thus Cleopatra bids: "Let labor cease,
To pomp and triumphs give this happy day,
That gave the world a lord: 'tis Antony's."
Live, Antony! And Cleopatra live!
Be this the general voice sent up to heav'n,
And every public place repeat this echo.

VENT. (*Aside*) Fine pageantry!

SERAP. Set out before your doors
The images of all your sleeping fathers,
With laurels crowned; with laurels wreathe
    your posts,
And strow with flow'rs the pavement; let the
    priests
Do present sacrifice; pour out the wine,
And call the gods to join with you in glad-
    ness.

VENT. Curse on the tongue that bids this
    general joy!
Can they be friends of Antony, who revel
When Antony's in danger? Hide, for shame,
You Romans, your great grandsires' images,
For fear their souls should animate their
    marbles,
To blush at their degenerate progeny.

ALEX. A love which knows no bounds to
    Antony,
Would mark the day with honors, when all
    heaven
Labored for him, when each propitious star
Stood wakeful in his orb to watch that hour,
And shed his better influence. Her own
    birthday
Our queen neglected, like a vulgar fate
That passed obscurely by.

VENT. Would it had slept,
Divided far from his, till some remote
And future age had called it out to ruin
Some other prince, not him.

ALEX. Your emperor,

Though grown unkind, would be more
    gentle than
T' upbraid my queen for loving him too well.
    VENT. Does the mute sacrifice upbraid the
    priest?
He knows him not his executioner.
Oh, she has decked his ruin with her love,
Led him in golden bands to gaudy slaughter,
And made perdition pleasing; she has left
    him
The blank of what he was.
I tell thee, eunuch, she has quite unmanned
    him.
Can any Roman see and know him now,
Thus altered from the lord of half mankind,
Unbent, unsinewed, made a woman's toy,
Shrunk from the vast extent of all his honors,
And cramped within a corner of the world?
O Antony!
Thou bravest soldier, and thou best of
    friends!
Bounteous as nature; next to nature's God!
Couldst thou but make new worlds, so
    wouldst thou give 'em,
As bounty were thy being! Rough in battle,
As the first Romans when they went to war,
Yet, after victory, more pitiful
Than all their praying virgins left at home!
    ALEX. Would you could add to those more
    shining virtues,
His truth to her who loves him.
    VENT. Would I could not!
But wherefore waste I precious hours with
    thee?
Thou art her darling mischief, her chief
    engine,
Antony's other fate. Go, tell thy queen
Ventidius is arrived, to end her charms.
Let your Egyptian timbrels play alone,
Nor mix effeminate sounds with Roman
    trumpets.
You dare not fight for Antony; go pray,
And keep your cowards' holiday in temples.
                    (*Exeunt* ALEXAS, SERAPION)

(*Enter a* SECOND GENTLEMAN *of*
M. ANTONY)

2 GENT. The emperor approaches, and
    commands,
On pain of death, that none presume to stay.
1 GENT. I dare not disobey him.
                    (*Going out with the other*)

VENT. Well, I dare.
But I'll observe him first unseen, and find
Which way his humor drives; the rest I'll
    venture.   (*Withdraws*)

(*Enter* ANTONY, *walking restlessly about
before he speaks*)

ANT. They tell me 'tis my birthday, and
    I'll keep it
With double pomp of sadness.
'Tis what the day deserves which gave me
    breath.
Why was I raised the meteor of the world,
Hung in the skies, and blazing as I travelled,
Till all my fires were spent, and then cast
    downward
To be trod out by Cæsar?
    VENT. (*Aside*) On my soul,
'Tis mournful, wond'rous mournful!
    ANT. Count thy gains.
Now, Antony, wouldst thou be born for this?
Glutton of fortune, thy devouring youth
Has starved thy wanting age.
                    (*Throws himself down*)
    VENT. (*Aside*) How sorrow shakes him!
So, now the tempest tears him up by th'
    roots,
And on the ground extends the noble ruin.
    ANT. Lie there, thou shadow of an em-
    peror;
The place thou pressest on thy mother earth
Is all thy empire now. Now it contains thee;
Some few days hence, and then 'twill be too
    large,
When thou'rt contracted in thy narrow urn,
Shrunk to a few cold ashes; then Octavia
(For Cleopatra will not live to see it),
Octavia then will have thee all her own,
And bear thee in her widowed hand to
    Cæsar.
Cæsar will weep, the crocodile will weep,
To see his rival of the universe
Lie still and peaceful there. I'll think no
    more on't.
(*Calls*) Give me some music; look that it be
    sad:
I'll soothe my melancholy, till I swell
And burst myself with sighing.—
                    (*Soft music*)
'Tis somewhat to my humor. Stay, I fancy
I'm now turned wild, a commoner of nature,
Of all forsaken and forsaking all;

Live in a shady forest's sylvan scene;
Stretched at my length beneath some blasted
    oak
I lean my head upon the mossy bark
And look just of a piece as I grew from it.
My uncombed locks, matted like mistletoe,
Hang o'er my hoary face; a murm'ring brook
Runs at my foot.
    VENT. (*Aside*) Methinks I fancy
Myself there too.
    ANT. The herd come jumping by me,
And, fearless, quench their thirst, while I
    look on,
And take me for their fellow-citizen.
More of this image, more; it lulls my
    thoughts. (*Soft music again*)
    VENT. I must disturb him; I can hold no
    longer. (*Stands before him*)
    ANT. (*Starting up*) Art thou Ventidius?
    VENT. Are you Antony?
I'm liker what I was, than you to him
I left you last.
    ANT. I'm angry.
    VENT. So am I.
    ANT. I would be private: leave me.
    VENT. Sir, I love you,
And therefore will not leave you.
    ANT. Will not leave me!
Where have you learnt that answer? Who
    am I?
    VENT. My emperor; the man I love next
    heaven;
If I said more, I think 'twere scarce a sin;
Y'are all that's good and god-like.
    ANT. All that's wretched.
You will not leave me then?
    VENT. 'Twas too presuming
To say I would not, but I dare not leave you;
And 'tis unkind in you to chide me hence
So soon, when I so far have come to see you.
    ANT. Now thou hast seen me, art thou
    satisfied?
For, if a friend, thou hast beheld enough;
And, if a foe, too much.
    VENT. (*Weeping*) Look, emperor, this is
    no common dew.
I have not wept this forty year, but now
My mother comes afresh into my eyes;
I cannot help her softness.
    ANT. By heav'n, he weeps, poor good old
    man, he weeps!
The big round drops course one another
    down

The furrows of his cheeks. Stop 'em, Ven-
    tidius,
Or I shall blush to death; they set my shame,
That caused 'em, full before me.
    VENT. I'll do my best.
    ANT. Sure there's contagion in the tears
    of friends:
See, I have caught it too. Believe me, 'tis not
For my own griefs, but thine.—Nay, father.
    VENT. Emperor.
    ANT. Emperor! Why, that's the style of
    victory;
The conqu'ring soldier, red with unfelt
    wounds,
Salutes his general so, but never more
Shall that sound reach my ears.
    VENT. I warrant you.
    ANT. Actium, Actium! Oh!——
    VENT. It sits too near you.
    ANT. Here, here it lies; a lump of lead by
    day,
And, in my short, distracted, nightly slum-
    bers,
The hag that rides my dreams.——
    VENT. Out with it; give it vent.
    ANT. Urge not my shame.
I lost a battle.
    VENT. So has Julius done.
    ANT. Thou favor'st me, and speak'st not
    half thou think'st;
For Julius fought it out, and lost it fairly.
But Antony——
    VENT. Nay, stop not.
    ANT. Antony,
(Well, thou wilt have it) like a coward, fled,
Fled while his soldiers fought; fled first, Ven-
    tidius.
Thou long'st to curse me, and I give thee
    leave.
I know thou cam'st prepared to rail.
    VENT. I did.
    ANT. I'll help thee.—I have been a man,
Ventidius—
    VENT. Yes, and a brave one; but——
    ANT. I know thy meaning.
But I have lost my reason, have disgraced
The name of soldier, with inglorious ease.
In the full vintage of my flowing honors,
Sat still, and saw it pressed by other hands.
Fortune came smiling to my youth and
    wooed it,
And purple greatness met my ripened years.
When first I came to empire, I was borne

On tides of people crowding to my triumphs,
The wish of nations; and the willing world
Received me as its pledge of future peace.
I was so great, so happy, so beloved,
Fate could not ruin me; till I took pains,
And worked against my fortune, chid her
  from me,
And turned her loose; yet still she came
  again.
My careless days and my luxurious nights
At length have wearied her, and now she's
  gone,
Gone, gone, divorced for ever. Help me, sol-
  dier,
To curse this madman, this industrious fool,
Who labored to be wretched; pr'ythee, curse
  me.
  VENT. No.
  ANT. Why?
  VENT. You are too sensible already
Of what y' have done, too conscious of your
  failings;
And, like a scorpion, whipped by others first
To fury, sting yourself in mad revenge.
I would bring balm, and pour it in your
  wounds,
Cure your distempered mind, and heal your
  fortunes.
  ANT. I know thou would'st.
  VENT. I will.
  ANT. Ha, ha, ha, ha!
  VENT. You laugh.
  ANT. I do, to see officious love
Give cordials to the dead.
  VENT. You would be lost, then?
  ANT. I am.
  VENT. I say you are not. Try your for-
tune.
  ANT. I have, to th' utmost. Dost thou
  think me desperate
Without just cause? No, when I found all
  lost
Beyond repair, I hid me from the world,
And learned to scorn it here; which now I do
So heartily, I think it is not worth
The cost of keeping.
  VENT. Cæsar thinks not so;
He'll thank you for the gift he could not
  take.
You would be killed like Tully, would you?
  Do,
Hold out your throat to Cæsar, and die
  tamely.

  ANT. No, I can kill myself; and so resolve.
  VENT. I can die with you too, when time
  shall serve;
But fortune calls upon us now to live,
To fight, to conquer.
  ANT. Sure thou dream'st, Ventidius.
  VENT. No, 'tis you dream; you sleep away
  your hours
In desperate sloth, miscalled philosophy.
Up, up, for honor's sake! Twelve legions
  wait you
And long to call you chief; by painful jour-
  neys
I led 'em, patient both of heat and hunger,
Down from the Parthian marches to the
  Nile.
'Twill do you good to see their sunburned
  faces,
Their scarred cheeks, and chopped hands;
  there's virtue in 'em.
They'll sell those mangled limbs at dearer
  rates
Than yon trim bands can buy.
  ANT. Where left you them?
  VENT. I said in Lower Syria.
  ANT. Bring 'em hither;
There may be life in these.
  VENT. They will not come.
  ANT. Why didst thou mock my hopes
  with promised aids,
To double my despair? They're mutinous.
  VENT. Most firm and loyal.
  ANT. Yet they will not march
To succor me. O trifler!
  VENT. They petition
You would make haste to head 'em.
  ANT. I'm besieged.
  VENT. There's but one way shut up. How
came I hither?
  ANT. I will not stir.
  VENT. They would perhaps desire
A better reason.
  ANT. I have never used
My soldiers to demand a reason of
My actions. Why did they refuse to march?
  VENT. They said they would not fight for
Cleopatra.
  ANT. What was't they said?
  VENT. They said they would not fight for
  Cleopatra.
Why should they fight indeed, to make her
  conquer

And make you more a slave? to gain you
kingdoms
Which, for a kiss, at your next midnight feast
You'll sell to her? Then she new-names her
jewels,
And calls this diamond such or such a tax;
Each pendant in her ear shall be a province.
    ANT. Ventidius, I allow your tongue free
license
On all my other faults, but, on your life,
No word of Cleopatra; she deserves
More worlds than I can lose.
    VENT. Behold, you Pow'rs,
To whom you have intrusted humankind;
See Europe, Africa, Asia, put in balance,
And all weighed down by one light, worth-
less woman!
I think the gods are Antonies and give,
Like prodigals, this nether world away
To none but wasteful hands.
    ANT. You grow presumptuous.
    VENT. I take the privilege of plain love to
speak.
    ANT. Plain love! plain arrogance, plain in-
solence!
Thy men are cowards; thou, an envious trai-
tor,
Who, under seeming honesty, hast vented
The burden of thy rank, o'erflowing gall.
Oh, that thou wert my equal, great in arms
As the first Cæsar was, that I might kill thee
Without a stain to honor!
    VENT. You may kill me;
You have done more already—called me
traitor.
    ANT. Art thou not one?
    VENT. For showing you yourself,
Which none else durst have done? but had I
been
That name which I disdain to speak again,
I needed not have sought your abject for-
tunes,
Come to partake your fate, to die with you.
What hindered me t' have led my conqu'ring
eagles
To fill Octavius's bands? I could have been
A traitor then, a glorious, happy traitor,
And not have been so called.
    ANT. Forgive me, soldier;
I've been too passionate.
    VENT. You thought me false;
Thought my old age betrayed you. Kill me,
sir;

Pray, kill me; yet you need not, your un-
kindness
Has left your sword no work.
    ANT. I did not think so;
I said it in my rage. Pr'ythee, forgive me.
Why didst thou tempt my anger, by dis-
covery
Of what I would not hear?
    VENT. No prince but you
Could merit that sincerity I used,
Nor durst another man have ventured it;
But you, ere love misled your wand'ring eyes,
Were sure the chief and best of human race,
Framed in the very pride and boast of na-
ture;
So perfect, that the gods who formed you
wondered
At their own skill, and cried, "A lucky hit
Has mended our design." Their envy hin-
dered,
Else you had been immortal and a pattern,
When heav'n would work for ostentation
sake,
To copy out again.
    ANT. But Cleopatra—
Go on; for I can bear it now.
    VENT. No more.
    ANT. Thou dar'st not trust my passion, but
thou may'st;
Thou only lov'st, the rest have flattered me.
    VENT. Heav'n's blessing on your heart for
that kind word!
May I believe you love me? Speak again.
    ANT. Indeed I do. Speak this, and this,
and this.
                      (Hugging him)
Thy praises were unjust; but I'll deserve 'em,
And yet mend all. Do with me what thou
wilt;
Lead me to victory, thou know'st the way.
    VENT. And, will you leave this——
    ANT. Pr'ythee, do not curse her,
And I will leave her; though heav'n knows I
love
Beyond life, conquest, empire, all but honor;
But I will leave her.
    VENT. That's my royal master;
And shall we fight?
    ANT. I warrant thee, old soldier,
Thou shalt behold me once again in iron,
And at the head of our old troops, that beat
The Parthians, cry aloud, "Come, follow
me!"

VENT. Oh, now I hear my emperor! in
  that word
Octavius fell. Gods, let me see that day,
And, if I have ten years behind, take all;
I'll thank you for th' exchange.
  ANT. O Cleopatra!
  VENT. Again?
  ANT. I've done; in that last sigh she went.
Cæsar shall know what 'tis to force a lover
From all he holds most dear.
  VENT. Methinks you breathe
Another soul; your looks are more divine,
You speak a hero, and you move a god.
  ANT. Oh, thou hast fired me; my soul's up
  in arms
And mans each part about me. Once again,
That noble eagerness of fight has seized me,
That eagerness with which I darted upward

To Cassius's camp. In vain the steepy hill
Opposed my way; in vain a war of spears
Sung round my head and planted all my
  shield;
I won the trenches, while my foremost men
Lagged on the plain below.
  VENT. Ye gods, ye gods,
For such another hour!
  ANT. Come on, my soldier!
Our hearts and arms are still the same. I long
Once more to meet our foes, that thou and I,
Like Time and Death, marching before our
  troops,
May taste fate to 'em, mow 'em out a passage,
And, ent'ring where the foremost squadrons
  yield,
Begin the noble harvest of the field.
                                  (*Exeunt*)

Act II

A Courtyard of the Palace

(*Enter* CLEOPATRA, IRAS, *and* ALEXAS)

  CLEO. What shall I do, or whither shall I
  turn?
Ventidius has o'ercome, and he will go.
  ALEX. He goes to fight for you.
  CLEO. Then he would see me, ere he went
  to fight.
Flatter me not; if once he goes, he's lost,
And all my hopes destroyed.
  ALEX. Does this weak passion
Become a mighty queen?
  CLEO. I am no queen!
Is this to be a queen, to be besieged
By yon insulting Roman, and to wait
Each hour the victor's chain? These ills are
  small,
For Antony is lost, and I can mourn
For nothing else but him. Now come, Oc-
  tavius,
I have no more to lose; prepare thy bands.
I'm fit to be a captive—Antony
Has taught my mind the fortune of a slave.
  IRAS. Call reason to assist you.
  CLEO. I have none,
And none would have; my love's a noble
  madness
Which shows the cause deserved it. Moderate
  sorrow

Fits vulgar love, and for a vulgar man,
But I have loved with such transcendent pas-
  sion
I soared at first quite out of reason's view,
And now am lost above it. No, I'm proud
'Tis thus; would Antony could see me now!
Think you he would not sigh? Though he
  must leave me,
Sure he would sigh; for he is noble-natured,
And bears a tender heart. I know him well.
Ah, no, I know him not; I knew him once,
But now 'tis past.
  IRAS. Let it be past with you;
Forget him, madam.
  CLEO. Never, never, Iras.
He once was mine; and once, though now
  'tis gone,
Leaves a faint image of possession still.
  ALEX. Think him unconstant, cruel, and
ungrateful.
  CLEO. I cannot; if I could, those thoughts
  were vain.
Faithless, ungrateful, cruel, though he be,
I still must love him.

(*Enter* CHARMION)

Now, what news, my Charmion?
Will he be kind? and will he not forsake me?

Am I to live, or die?—nay, do I live?
Or am I dead? for when he gave his answer,
Fate took the word, and then I lived or died.
    CHAR. I found him, madam——
    CLEO. A long speech preparing?
If thou bring'st comfort, haste, and give it
    me,
For never was more need.
    IRAS. I know he loves you.
    CLEO. Had he been kind, her eyes had
    told me so
Before her tongue could speak it; now she
    studies
To soften what he said. But give me death,
Just as he sent it, Charmion, undisguised,
And in the words he spoke.
    CHAR. I found him, then,
Incompassed round, I think, with iron stat-
    ues,
So mute, so motionless his soldiers stood,
While awfully he cast his eyes about,
And ev'ry leader's hopes or fears surveyed;
Methought he looked resolved, and yet not
    pleased.
When he beheld me struggling in the crowd,
He blushed, and bade make way.
    ALEX. There's comfort yet.
    CHAR. Ventidius fixed his eyes upon my
    passage
Severely, as he meant to frown me back,
And sullenly gave place; I told my message,
Just as you gave it, broken and disordered;
I numbered in it all your sighs and tears,
And while I moved your pitiful request,
That you but only begged a last farewell,
He fetched an inward groan, and ev'ry time
I named you, sighed, as if his heart were
    breaking,
But shunned my eyes and guiltily looked
    down.
He seemed not now that awful Antony
Who shook an armed assembly with his nod,
But, making show as he would rub his eyes,
Disguised and blotted out a falling tear.
    CLEO. Did he then weep? And was I worth
    a tear?
If what thou hast to say be not as pleasing,
Tell me no more, but let me die contented.
    CHAR. He bid me say, he knew himself so
    well
He could deny you nothing, if he saw you;
And therefore——

    CLEO. Thou wouldst say, he would not
see me?
    CHAR. And therefore begged you not to
    use a power
Which he could ill resist; yet he should ever
Respect you as he ought.
    CLEO. Is that a word
For Antony to use to Cleopatra?
O that faint word, *respect!* how I disdain it!
Disdain myself, for loving after it!
He should have kept that word for cold
    Octavia.
Respect is for a wife. Am I that thing,
That dull, insipid lump, without desires
And without pow'r to give 'em?
    ALEX. You misjudge;
You see through love, and that deludes your
    sight,
As what is straight seems crooked through
    the water.
But I, who bear my reason undisturbed,
Can see this Antony, this dreaded man,
A fearful slave who fain would run away
And shuns his master's eyes. If you pursue
    him,
My life on't, he still drags a chain along
That needs must clog his flight.
    CLEO. Could I believe thee!—
    ALEX. By ev'ry circumstance I know he
    loves.
True, he's hard pressed by int'rest and by
    honor;
Yet he but doubts, and parleys, and casts out
Many a long look for succor.
    CLEO. He sends word,
He fears to see my face.
    ALEX. And would you more?
He shows his weakness who declines the
    combat,
And you must urge your fortune. Could he
    speak
More plainly? To my ears, the message
    sounds—
"Come to my rescue, Cleopatra, come;
Come, free me from Ventidius, from my
    tyrant.
See me, and give me a pretence to leave
    him!"—
I hear his trumpets. This way he must pass.
Please you, retire a while; I'll work him first,
That he may bend more easy.
    CLEO. You shall rule me;

But all, I fear, in vain.
> (*Exit with* CHARMION *and* IRAS)

ALEX. I fear so too,
Though I concealed my thoughts to make
   her bold;
But 'tis our utmost means, and fate befriend
   it!   (*Withdraws*)

(*Enter* LICTORS *with fasces, one bearing the
eagle; then enter* ANTONY *with* VENTIDIUS,
followed by other Commanders)

ANT. Octavius is the minion of blind
   chance,
But holds from virtue nothing.
VENT. Has he courage?
ANT. But just enough to season him from
   coward.
Oh, 'tis the coldest youth upon a charge,
The most deliberate fighter! if he ventures
(As in Illyria once they say he did,
To storm a town), 'tis when he cannot
   choose,
When all the world have fixed their eyes
   upon him;
And then he lives on that for seven years
   after.
But at a close revenge he never fails.
VENT. I heard you challenged him.
ANT. I did, Ventidius.
What think'st thou was his answer? 'Twas
   so tame!
He said he had more ways than one to die;
I had not.
VENT. Poor!
ANT. He has more ways than one,
But he would choose 'em all before that one.
VENT. He first would choose an ague, or a
fever.
ANT. No, it must be an ague, not a fever;
He has not warmth enough to die by that.
VENT. Or old age and a bed.
ANT. Aye, there's his choice;
He would live, like a lamp, to the last wink,
And crawl upon the utmost verge of life.
O Hercules! Why should a man like this,
Who dares not trust his fate for one great
   action,
Be all the care of heav'n? Why should he
   lord it
O'er fourscore thousand men, of whom each
   one
Is braver than himself?

VENT. You conquered for him!
Philippi knows it—there you shared with him
That empire which your sword made all your
   own.
ANT. Fool that I was, upon my eagle's
   wings
I bore this wren till I was tired with soaring,
And now he mounts above me.
Good heav'ns, is this—is this the man who
   braves me?
Who bids my age make way, drives me be-
   fore him
To the world's ridge, and sweeps me off like
   rubbish?
VENT. Sir, we lose time; the troops are
   mounted all.
ANT. Then give the word to march.
I long to leave this prison of a town,
To join thy legions, and in open field
Once more to show my face. Lead, my de-
   liverer.

(*Enter* ALEXAS)

ALEX. Great emperor,
In mighty arms renowned above mankind,
But in soft pity to th' oppressed, a god,
This message sends the mournful Cleopatra
To her departing lord.
VENT. (*Aside*) Smooth sycophant!
ALEX. A thousand wishes and ten thou-
   sand prayers,
Millions of blessings wait you to the wars;
Millions of sighs and tears she sends you too,
And would have sent
As many dear embraces to your arms,
As many parting kisses to your lips;
But those, she fears, have wearied you al-
   ready.
VENT. (*Aside*) False crocodile!
ALEX. And yet she begs not now, you
   would not leave her;
That were a wish too mighty for her hopes,
Too presuming
For her low fortune and your ebbing love;
That were a wish for her more prosp'rous
   days,
Her blooming beauty, and your growing
   kindness.
ANT. (*Aside*) Well, I must man it out!—
What would the queen?
ALEX. (*Turning to Commanders*) First,
   to these noble warriors who attend

Your daring courage in the chase of fame
(Too daring, and too dang'rous for her
    quiet),
She humbly recommends all she holds dear,
All her own cares and fears—the care of you.
    VENT. (*Scornfully*) Yes, witness Actium.
    ANT. Let him speak, Ventidius.
    ALEX. You, when his matchless valor bears
    him forward
With ardor too heroic on his foes,
Fall down, as she would do, before his feet,
Lie in his way, and stop the paths of death.
Tell him, this god is not invulnerable;
That absent Cleopatra bleeds in him;
And, that you may remember her petition,
She begs you wear these trifles, as a pawn
Which, at your wished return, she will re-
    deem
With all the wealth of Egypt.
        (*Gives jewels to the Commanders*)
This to the great Ventidius she presents,
Whom she can never count her enemy
Because he loves her lord.
    VENT. Tell her, I'll none on't;
I'm not ashamed of honest poverty.
Not all the diamonds of the East can bribe
Ventidius from his faith. I hope to see
These and the rest of all her sparkling store
Where they shall more deservingly be placed.
    ANT. And who must wear 'em then?
    VENT. The wronged Octavia.
    ANT. You might have spared that word.
    VENT. And he that bribe.
    ANT. But have I no remembrance?
    ALEX. Yes, a dear one;
Your slave the queen——
    ANT. My mistress.
    ALEX. Then your mistress.
Your mistress would, she says, have sent her
    soul,
But that you had long since; she humbly begs
This ruby bracelet, set with bleeding hearts
(The emblems of her own), may bind your
    arm.   (*Presenting a bracelet*)
    VENT. Now, my best lord, in honor's name
I ask you,
For manhood's sake, and for your own dear
    safety,
Touch not these poisoned gifts,
Infected by the sender; touch 'em not!
Myriads of bluest plagues lie underneath 'em,
And more than aconite has dipped the silk.

    ANT. Nay, now you grow too cynical,
    Ventidius;
A lady's favors may be worn with honor.
What, to refuse her bracelet! On my soul,
When I lie pensive in my tent alone,
'Twill pass the wakeful hours of winter
    nights
To tell these pretty beads upon my arm,
To count for every one a soft embrace,
A melting kiss at such and such a time,
And now and then the fury of her love,
When——And what harm's in this?
    ALEX. None, none, my lord,
But what's to her, that now 'tis past for ever.
    ANT. (*Going to tie it*) We soldiers are so
awkward—help me tie it.
    ALEX. In faith, my lord, we courtiers too
    are awkward
In these affairs; so are all men indeed;
Even I, who am not one. But shall I speak?
    ANT. Yes, freely.
    ALEX. Then, my lord, fair hands alone
Are fit to tie it; she, who sent it, can.
    VENT. Hell, death! this eunuch pander
    ruins you.
You will not see her?
        (ALEXAS *whispers to an Attendant,*
        who goes out)
    ANT. But to take my leave.
    VENT. Then I have washed an Æthiope.
    Y'are undone;
Y'are in the toils; y'are taken; y'are destroyed!
Her eyes do Cæsar's work.
    ANT. You fear too soon.
I'm constant to myself, I know my strength;
And yet she shall not think me barbarous
    neither,
Born in the depths of Afric. I'm a Roman,
Bred to the rules of soft humanity.
A guest, and kindly used, should bid farewell.
    VENT. You do not know
How weak you are to her, how much an in-
    fant.
You are not proof against a smile, or glance;
A sigh will quite disarm you.
    ANT. See, she comes!
Now you shall find your error. Gods, I thank
    you;
I formed the danger greater than it was,
And now 'tis near, 'tis lessened.
    VENT. Mark the end yet.

(*Enter* CLEOPATRA, CHARMION, *and* IRAS)

Ant. Well, madam, we are met.
Cleo. Is this a meeting?
Then we must part?
Ant. We must.
Cleo. Who says we must?
Ant. Our own hard fates.
Cleo. We make those fates ourselves.
Ant. Yes, we have made 'em; we have
   loved each other
Into our mutual ruin.
Cleo. The gods have seen my joys with
   envious eyes;
I have no friends in heav'n and all the world
(As 'twere the bus'ness of mankind to part
   us)
Is armed against my love. Ev'n you yourself
Join with the rest; you, you are armed against
   me.
Ant. I will be justified in all I do
To late posterity, and therefore hear me.
If I mix a lie
With any truth, reproach me freely with it;
Else, favor me with silence.
Cleo. You command me,
And I am dumb.
Vent. (Aside) I like this well; he shows
authority.
Ant. That I derive my ruin
From you alone——
Cleo. O heav'ns! I ruin you!
Ant. You promised me your silence, and
   you break it
Ere I have scarce begun.
Cleo. Well, I obey you.
Ant. When I beheld you first, it was in
   Egypt,
Ere Cæsar saw your eyes; you gave me love,
And were too young to know it. That I settled
Your father in his throne, was for your sake;
I left th' acknowledgment for time to ripen.
Cæsar stepped in and with a greedy hand
Plucked the green fruit, ere the first blush of
   red,
Yet cleaving to the bough. He was my lord
And was, beside, too great for me to rival,
But I deserved you first, though he enjoyed
   you.
When, after, I beheld you in Cilicia,
An enemy to Rome, I pardoned you.
Cleo. I cleared myself——
Ant. Again you break your promise.
I loved you still, and took your weak excuses,
Took you into my bosom, stained by Cæsar,

And not half mine. I went to Egypt with you
And hid me from the bus'ness of the world,
Shut out inquiring nations from my sight,
To give whole years to you.
Vent. (Aside) Yes, to your shame be't
spoken.
Ant. How I loved,
Witness, ye days and nights, and all your
   hours
That danced away with down upon your feet,
As all your bus'ness were to count my pas-
   sion!
One day passed by, and nothing saw but love;
Another came, and still 'twas only love;
The suns were wearied out with looking on,
And I untired with loving.
I saw you ev'ry day, and all the day;
And ev'ry day was still but as the first,
So eager was I still to see you more.
Vent. (Aside) 'Tis all too true.
Ant. Fulvia, my wife, grew jealous,
As she indeed had reason; raised a war
In Italy, to call me back.
Vent. (Aside) But yet
You went not.
Ant. While within your arms I lay,
The world fell mould'ring from my hands
   each hour,
And left me scarce a grasp (I thank your love
   for't).
Vent. (Aside) Well pushed: that last
was home.
Cleo. Yet may I speak?
Ant. If I have urged a falsehood, yes;
else, not.
Your silence says I have not. Fulvia died
(Pardon, you gods, with my unkindness
   died).
To set the world at peace, I took Octavia,
This Cæsar's sister; in her pride of youth
And flow'r of beauty did I wed that lady,
Whom blushing I must praise, because I left
   her.
You called; my love obeyed the fatal sum-
   mons.
This raised the Roman arms; the cause was
   yours.
I would have fought by land, where I was
   stronger;
You hindered it, yet when I fought at sea
Forsook me fighting, and (O stain to honor!
O lasting shame!) I knew not that I fled,
But fled to follow you.

VENT. (*Aside*) What haste she made to hoist her purple sails!
And, to appear magnificent in flight,
Drew half our strength away.

ANT. All this you caused.
And would you multiply more ruins on me?
This honest man, my best, my only friend,
Has gathered up the shipwreck of my fortunes.
Twelve legions I have left, my last recruits.
And you have watched the news, and bring your eyes
To seize them too. If you have aught to answer,
Now speak, you have free leave.

ALEX. (*Aside*) She stands confounded;
Despair is in her eyes.

VENT. (*Aside*) Now lay a sigh i' th' way
to stop his passage;
Prepare a tear, and bid it for his legions;
'Tis like they shall be sold.

CLEO. How shall I plead my cause, when you, my judge,
Already have condemned me? Shall I bring
The love you bore me for my advocate?
That now is turned against me, that destroys me;
For love, once past, is at the best forgotten,
But oft'ner sours to hate. 'Twill please my lord
To ruin me, and therefore I'll be guilty.
But could I once have thought it would have pleased you,
That you would pry with narrow searching eyes
Into my faults, severe to my destruction,
And watching all advantages with care,
That serve to make me wretched? Speak, my lord,
For I end here. Though I deserve this usage,
Was it like you to give it?

ANT. Oh, you wrong me
To think I sought this parting, or desired
To accuse you more than what will clear myself,
And justify this breach.

CLEO. Thus low I thank you.
And, since my innocence will not offend,
I shall not blush to own it.

VENT. (*Aside*) After this,
I think she'll blush at nothing.

CLEO. You seemed grieved
(And therein you are kind) that Cæsar first
Enjoyed my love, though you deserved it better;
I grieve for that, my lord, much more than you,
For had I first been yours, it would have saved
My second choice; I never had been his,
And ne'er had been but yours. But Cæsar first,
You say, possessed my love. Not so, my lord.
He first possessed my person; you, my love.
Cæsar loved me, but I loved Antony.
If I endured him after, 'twas because
I judged it due to the first name of men;
And, half constrained, I gave, as to a tyrant,
What he would take by force.

VENT. (*Breaks out at last*) O siren! siren!
Yet grant that all the love she boasts were true,
Has she not ruined you? I still urge that,
The fatal consequence.

CLEO. The consequence indeed,
For I dare challenge him, my greatest foe,
To say it was designed. 'Tis true, I loved you,
And kept you far from an uneasy wife
(Such Fulvia was).
Yes, but he'll say you left Octavia for me;—
And can you blame me to receive that love
Which quitted such desert, for worthless me?
How often have I wished some other Cæsar,
Great as the first and as the second young,
Would court my love, to be refused for you!

VENT. Words, words! But Actium, sir, remember Actium.

CLEO. Ev'n there, I dare his malice. True,
I counselled
To fight at sea; but I betrayed you not.
I fled, but not to the enemy. 'Twas fear;
Would I had been a man, not to have feared!
For none would then have envied me your friendship
Who envy me your love.

ANT. We're both unhappy;
If nothing else, yet our ill fortune parts us.
Speak; would you have me perish by my stay?

CLEO. If as a friend you ask my judgment, go;
If as a lover, stay. If you must perish——
'Tis a hard word—but stay.

VENT. See now th' effects of her so boasted love!
She strives to drag you down to ruin with her;
But, could she 'scape without you, oh, how soon

Would she let go her hold, and haste to shore,
And never look behind!

CLEO. Then judge my love by this.
(*Giving* ANTONY *a writing*)
Could I have borne
A life or death, a happiness or woe,
From yours divided, this had giv'n me means.

ANT. By Hercules, the writing of Octavius!
I know it well: 'tis that proscribing hand,
Young as it was, that led the way to mine,
And left me but the second place in murder.—
See, see, Ventidius! here he offers Egypt,
And joins all Syria to it, as a present,
So, in requital, she forsake my fortunes
And join her arms with his.

CLEO. And yet you leave me!
You leave me, Antony; and yet I love you,
Indeed I do. I have refused a kingdom;
That's a trifle,
For I could part with life, with anything,
But only you. Oh, let me die but with you!
Is that a hard request?

ANT. Next living with you,
'Tis all that heav'n can give.

ALEX. (*Aside*) He melts; we conquer.

CLEO. No, you shall go; your int'rest calls
you hence.
Yes, your dear interest pulls too strong for
these
Weak arms to hold you here.—
(*Takes his hand*)
Go, leave me, soldier
(For you're no more a lover); leave me dying.
Push me all pale and panting from your
bosom,
And when your march begins, let one run
after,
Breathless almost for joy, and cry, "She's
dead."
The soldiers shout; you then, perhaps, may
sigh
And muster all your Roman gravity.
Ventidius chides; and straight your brow
clears up,
As I had never been.

ANT. Gods, 'tis too much;
Too much for man to bear!

CLEO. What is't for me then,
A weak, forsaken woman, and a lover?—
(*She throws herself on* ANTONY)
Here let me breathe my last; envy me not
This minute in your arms; I'll die apace,
As fast as e'er I can, and end your trouble.

ANT. Die! rather let me perish; loosened
nature
Leap from its hinges! Sink the props of
heav'n,
And fall the skies to crush the nether world!
My eyes, my soul, my all!—
(*Embraces her*)

VENT. And what's this toy,
In balance with your fortune, honor, fame?

ANT. What is't, Ventidius?—it outweighs
'em all.
Why, we have more than conquered Cæsar
now;
My queen's not only innocent, but loves me.
This, this is she who drags me down to ruin!
"But, could she 'scape without me, with what
haste
Would she let slip her hold, and make to
shore,
And never look behind!"
Down on thy knees, blasphemer as thou art,
And ask forgiveness of wronged innocence.

VENT. I'll rather die than take it. Will you
go?

ANT. Go! whither? Go from all that's excellent?
Faith, honor, virtue, all good things forbid
That I should go from her who sets my love
Above the price of kingdoms! Give, you gods,
Give to your boy, your Cæsar,
This rattle of a globe to play withal,
This gewgaw world, and put him cheaply off.
I'll not be pleased with less than Cleopatra.

CLEO. She's wholly yours. My heart's so
full of joy
That I shall do some wild extravagance
Of love in public; and the foolish world,
Which knows not tenderness, will think me
mad.

VENT. O women! women! women! all the
gods
Have not such pow'r of doing good to man
As you of doing harm. (*Exit*)

ANT. Our men are armed.
Unbar the gate that looks to Cæsar's camp;
I would revenge the treachery he meant me,
And long security makes conquest easy.
I'm eager to return before I go,
For all the pleasures I have known beat thick
On my remembrance. How I long for night!

That both the sweets of mutual love may try,
And once triumph o'er Cæsar ere we die.
(*Exeunt*)

Act III

A Great Hall in CLEOPATRA's Palace

(*At one door enter* CLEOPATRA, CHARMION, IRAS, *and* ALEXAS, *a train of Egyptians; at the other* ANTONY *and Romans. The entrance on both sides is prepared by music, the trumpets first sounding on* ANTONY'S *part, then answered by timbrels, etc., on* CLEOPATRA'S. CHARMION *and* IRAS *hold a laurel wreath betwixt them. A dance of Egyptians. After the ceremony,* CLEOPATRA *crowns* ANTONY.)

ANT. I thought how those white arms
    would fold me in,
And strain me close, and melt me into love;
So pleased with that sweet image, I sprung
    forwards,
And added all my strength to every blow.
    CLEO. Come to me, come, my soldier, to
    my arms!
You've been too long away from my embraces.
But when I have you fast and all my own,
With broken murmurs and with amorous
    sighs
I'll say you were unkind, and punish you,
And mark you red with many an eager kiss.
    ANT. My brighter Venus!
    CLEO. O my greater Mars!
    ANT. Thou join'st us well, my love!
Suppose me come from the Phlegræan plains,
Where gasping giants lay, cleft by my sword,
And mountain-tops pared off each other blow,
To bury those I slew. Receive me, goddess!
Let Cæsar spread his subtle nets, like Vulcan;
In thy embraces I would be beheld
By heav'n and earth at once,
And make their envy what they meant their
    sport.
Let those who took us blush; I would love on
With awful state, regardless of their frowns,
As their superior god.
There's no satiety of love in thee.
Enjoyed, thou still art new; perpetual spring
Is in thy arms; the ripened fruit but falls,
And blossoms rise to fill its empty place,
And I grow rich by giving.

(*Enter* VENTIDIUS, *and stands apart*)

ALEX. Oh, now the danger's past, your
    general comes!
He joins not in your joys, nor minds your
    triumphs;
But with contracted brows looks frowning on,
As envying your success.
    ANT. Now, on my soul, he loves me, truly
    loves me.
He never flattered me in any vice,
But awes me with his virtue; ev'n this minute,
Methinks, he has a right of chiding me.
Lead to the temple. I'll avoid his presence;
It checks too strong upon me.
    (*Exeunt the rest. As* ANTONY *is going,*
      VENTIDIUS *pulls him by the robe.*)
    VENT. Emperor!
    ANT. (*Looking back*) 'Tis the old argument;
I pr'ythee, spare me.
    VENT. But this one hearing, emperor.
    ANT. Let go
My robe, or by my father Hercules—
    VENT. By Hercules his father, that's yet
    greater,
I bring you somewhat you would wish to
    know.
    ANT. Thou see'st we are observed; attend
    me here,
And I'll return.   (*Exit*)
    VENT. I'm waning in his favor, yet I love
    him;
I love this man, who runs to meet his ruin;
And sure the gods, like me, are fond of him.
His virtues lie so mingled with his crimes
As would confound their choice to punish
    one
And not reward the other.

(*Enter* ANTONY)

ANT. We can conquer,
You see, without your aid.
We have dislodged their troops;
They look on us at distance, and, like curs
'Scaped from the lion's paws, they bay far off,
And lick their wounds, and faintly threaten
    war.

Five thousand Romans, with their faces up-
     ward,
Lie breathless on the plain.
     VENT. 'Tis well; and he
Who lost 'em could have spared ten thousand
     more.
Yet if by this advantage you could gain
An easier peace, while Cæsar doubts the
     chance
Of arms!——
     ANT. Oh, think not on't, Ventidius!
The boy pursues my ruin, he'll no peace;
His malice is considerate in advantage.
Oh, he's the coolest murderer! so staunch,
He kills, and keeps his temper.
     VENT. Have you no friend
In all his army who has power to move him?
Mæcenas or Agrippa might do much.
     ANT. They're both too deep in Cæsar's
     interests.
We'll work it out by dint of sword, or perish.
     VENT. Fain I would find some other.
     ANT. Thank thy love.
Some four or five such victories as this
Will save thy farther pains.
     VENT. Expect no more; Cæsar is on his
     guard.
I know, sir, you have conquered against odds,
But still you draw supplies from one poor
     town,
And of Egyptians; he has all the world,
And at his back nations come pouring in
To fill the gaps you make. Pray, think again.
     ANT. Why dost thou drive me from my-
     self, to search
For foreign aids?—to hunt my memory,
And range all o'er a waste and barren place
To find a friend? The wretched have no
     friends.——
Yet I had one, the bravest youth of Rome,
Whom Cæsar loves beyond the love of
     women;
He could resolve his mind as fire does wax,
From that hard rugged image melt him down
And mold him in what softer form he
     pleased.
     VENT. Him would I see, that man of all
     the world;
Just such a one we want.
     ANT. He loved me too,
I was his soul; he lived not but in me.
We were so closed within each other's breasts,

The rivets were not found that joined us
     first.
That does not reach us yet: we were so mixed
As meeting streams, both to ourselves were
     lost;
We were one mass; we could not give or take,
But from the same; for he was I, I he.
     VENT. (Aside) He moves as I would wish
     him.
     ANT. After this,
I need not tell his name—'twas Dolabella.
     VENT. He's now in Cæsar's camp.
     ANT. No matter where,
Since he's no longer mine. He took unkindly
That I forbade him Cleopatra's sight
Because I feared he loved her; he confessed
He had a warmth which, for my sake, he
     stifled;
For 'twere impossible that two, so one,
Should not have loved the same. When he
     departed,
He took no leave, and that confirmed my
     thoughts.
     VENT. It argues that he loved you more
     than her,
Else he had stayed; but he perceived you
     jealous,
And would not grieve his friend. I know he
     loves you.
     ANT. I should have seen him, then, ere
     now.
     VENT. Perhaps
He has thus long been lab'ring for your peace.
     ANT. Would he were here!
     VENT. Would you believe he loved you?
I read your answer in your eyes, you would.
Not to conceal it longer, he has sent
A messenger from Cæsar's camp, with letters.
     ANT. Let him appear.
     VENT. I'll bring him instantly.
          (Exit VENTIDIUS, and re-enters imme-
               diately with DOLABELLA)
     ANT. 'Tis he himself! himself, by holy
          friendship!   (Runs to embrace him)
Art thou returned at last, my better half?
Come, give me all myself!
Let me not live,
If the young bridegroom, longing for his
     night,
Was ever half so fond.
     DOLA. I must be silent, for my soul is busy
About a nobler work: she's new come home,
Like a long-absent man, and wanders o'er

Each room, a stranger to her own, to look
If all be safe.

ANT. Thou hast what's left of me;
For I am now so sunk from what I was,
Thou find'st me at my lowest water-mark.
The rivers that ran in and raised my fortunes
Are all dried up, or take another course.
What I have left is from my native spring;
I've still a heart that swells in scorn of fate,
And lifts me to my banks.

DOLA. Still you are lord of all the world to
me.

ANT. Why, then I yet am so; for thou art
all.
If I had any joy when thou wert absent,
I grudged it to myself; methought I robbed
Thee of thy part. But, O my Dolabella!
Thou hast beheld me other than I am.
Hast thou not seen my morning chambers
filled
With sceptered slaves, who waited to salute
me?
With eastern monarchs, who forgot the sun
To worship my uprising? Menial kings
Ran coursing up and down my palace-yard,
Stood silent in my presence, watched my
eyes,
And at my least command all started out,
Like racers to the goal.

DOLA. Slaves to your fortune.

ANT. Fortune is Cæsar's now; and what
am I?

VENT. What you have made yourself; I
will not flatter.

ANT. Is this friendly done?

DOLA. Yes, when his end is so, I must
join with him;
Indeed I must, and yet you must not chide.
Why am I else your friend?

ANT. Take heed, young man,
How thou upbraid'st my love; the queen has
eyes,
And thou too hast a soul. Canst thou remember
When, swelled with hatred, thou beheld'st
her first,
As accessary to thy brother's death?

DOLA. Spare my remembrance; 'twas a
guilty day,
And still the blush hangs here.

ANT. To clear herself
For sending him no aid, she came from
Egypt.

Her galley down the silver Cydnos rowed,
The tackling silk, the streamers waved with
gold;
The gentle winds were lodged in purple sails;
Her nymphs like Nereids round her couch
were placed,
Where she, another sea-born Venus lay.

DOLA. No more; I would not hear it.

ANT. Oh, you must!
She lay, and leaned her cheek upon her hand,
And cast a look so languishingly sweet,
As if, secure of all beholders' hearts,
Neglecting, she could take 'em. Boys, like
Cupids,
Stood fanning with their painted wings the
winds
That played about her face; but if she smiled,
A darting glory seemed to blaze abroad,
That men's desiring eyes were never wearied,
But hung upon the object. To soft flutes
The silver oars kept time; and while they
played,
The hearing gave new pleasure to the sight,
And both to thought. 'Twas heaven, or some-
what more;
For she so charmed all hearts that gazing
crowds
Stood panting on the shore, and wanted
breath
To give their welcome voice.
Then, Dolabella, where was then thy soul?
Was not thy fury quite disarmed with won-
der?
Didst thou not shrink behind me from those
eyes,
And whisper in my ear, "Oh, tell her not
That I accused her with my brother's death?"

DOLA. And should my weakness be a plea
for yours?
Mine was an age when love might be excused,
When kindly warmth, and when my spring-
ing youth
Made it a debt to nature. Yours——

VENT. Speak boldly.
Yours, he would say, in your declining age,
When no more heat was left but what you
forced,
When all the sap was needful for the trunk;
When it went down, then you constrained
the course,
And robbed from nature to supply desire;
In you (I would not use so harsh a word)

But 'tis plain dotage.

ANT. Ha!

DOLA. 'Twas urged too home.[1]
But yet the loss was private that I made;
'Twas but myself I lost: I lost no legions;
I had no world to lose, no people's love.

ANT. This from a friend?

DOLA. Yes, Antony, a true one;
A friend so tender that each word I speak
Stabs my own heart before it reach your ear.
Oh, judge me not less kind, because I chide!
To Cæsar I excuse you.

ANT. O ye gods!
Have I then lived to be excused to Cæsar?

DOLA. As to your equal.

ANT. Well, he's but my equal;
                    (Grasping his sword)
While I wear this, he never shall be more.

DOLA. I bring conditions from him.

ANT. Are they noble?
Methinks thou shouldst not bring 'em else;
      yet he
Is full of deep dissembling, knows no honor
Divided from his int'rest. Fate mistook him,
For nature meant him for an usurer.
He's fit indeed to buy, not conquer kingdoms.

VENT. Then, granting this,
What pow'r was theirs who wrought so hard
      a temper
To honorable terms?

ANT. It was my Dolabella, or some god.

DOLA. Nor I, nor yet Mæcenas, nor
      Agrippa.
They were your enemies, and I, a friend,
Too weak alone; yet 'twas a Roman's deed.

ANT. 'Twas like a Roman done. Show me
      that man,
Who has preserved my life, my love, my
      honor;
Let me but see his face.

VENT. That task is mine,
And, Heav'n, thou know'st how pleasing.
                    (Exit VENTIDIUS)

DOLA. You'll remember
To whom you stand obliged?

ANT. When I forget it,
Be thou unkind, and that's my greatest curse.
My queen shall thank him too.

DOLA. I fear she will not.

ANT. But she shall do't. The queen, my
      Dolabella!

[1] Too near the mark.

Has thou not still some grudgings of thy
      fever?

DOLA. I would not see her lost.

ANT. When I forsake her,
Leave me, my better stars! for she has truth
Beyond her beauty. Cæsar tempted her,
At no less price than kingdoms, to betray me;
But she resisted all; and yet thou chid'st me
For loving her too well. Could I do so?

DOLA. Yes; there's my reason.

(Re-enter VENTIDIUS, with OCTAVIA, leading ANTONY's two little DAUGHTERS)

ANT. (Starting back) Where?—Octavia
there!

VENT. What, is she poison to you?—a dis-
ease?
Look on her, view her well, and those she
      brings:
Are they all strangers to your eyes? Has
      nature
No secret call, no whisper they are yours?

DOLA. For shame, my lord, if not for love,
      receive 'em
With kinder eyes. If you confess a man,
Meet 'em, embrace 'em, bid 'em welcome to
      you.
Your arms should open ev'n without your
      knowledge
To clasp 'em in; your feet should turn to
      wings
To bear you to 'em; and your eyes dart out
And aim a kiss, ere you could reach the lips.

ANT. I stood amazed, to think how they
came hither.

VENT. I sent for 'em; I brought 'em in unknown
To Cleopatra's guards.

DOLA. Yet are you cold?

OCTAV. Thus long I have attended for my
      welcome,
Which, as a stranger, sure I might expect.
Who am I?

ANT. Cæsar's sister.

OCTAV. That's unkind.
Had I been nothing more than Cæsar's sister,
Know, I had still remained in Cæsar's camp;
But your Octavia, your much injured wife,
Though banished from your bed, driv'n from
      your house,
In spite of Cæsar's sister, still is yours.

'Tis true, I have a heart disdains your cold-
    ness
And prompts me not to seek what you should
    offer;
But a wife's virtue still surmounts that pride.
I come to claim you as my own; to show
My duty first; to ask, nay beg, your kindness.
Your hand, my lord; 'tis mine, and I will have
    it.   (*Taking his hand*)
    VENT. Do, take it; thou deserv'st it.
    DOLA. On my soul,
And so she does; she's neither too submissive,
Nor yet too haughty; but so just a mean
Shows, as it ought, a wife and Roman too.
    ANT. I fear, Octavia, you have begged my
life.
    OCTAV. Begged it, my lord?
    ANT. Yes, begged it, my ambassadress,
Poorly and basely begged it of your brother.
    OCTAV. Poorly and basely I could never
    beg;
Nor could my brother grant.
    ANT. Shall I, who, to my kneeling slave,
    could say,
"Rise up, and be a king," shall I fall down
And cry, "Forgive me, Cæsar"? Shall I set
A man, my equal, in the place of Jove,
As he could give me being? No; that word,
"Forgive," would choke me up,
And die upon my tongue.
    DOLA. You shall not need it.
    ANT. I will not need it. Come, you've all
betrayed me,—
My friend too!—to receive some vile condi-
tions,
My wife has bought me, with her prayers and
tears;
And now I must become her branded slave.
In every peevish mood, she will upbraid
The life she gave; if I but look awry,
She cries, "I'll tell my brother."
    OCTAV. My hard fortune
Subjects me still to your unkind mistakes;
But the conditions I have brought are such
You need not blush to take. I love your honor,
Because 'tis mine; it never shall be said,
Octavia's husband was her brother's slave.
Sir, you are free, free, ev'n from her you
    loathe;
For though my brother bargains for your love,
Makes me the price and cement of your
    peace,
I have a soul like yours; I cannot take

Your love as alms, nor beg what I deserve.
I'll tell my brother we are reconciled;
He shall draw back his troops, and you shall
    march
To rule the East; I may be dropped at Athens,
No matter where. I never will complain,
But only keep the barren name of wife,
And rid you of the trouble.
    VENT. (*Aside to* DOLA.) Was ever such a
    strife of sullen honor!
Both scorn to be obliged.
    DOLA. (*Aside to* VENT.) Oh, she has
    touched him in the tender'st part;
See how he reddens with despite and shame,
To be outdone in generosity!
    VENT. (*Aside to* DOLA.) See how he
    winks! how he dries up a tear
That fain would fall!
    ANT. Octavia, I have heard you, and must
    praise
The greatness of your soul
But cannot yield to what you have proposed;
For I can ne'er be conquered but by love,
And you do all for duty. You would free me,
And would be dropped at Athens; was't not
    so?
    OCTAV. It was, my lord.
    ANT. Then I must be obliged
To one who loves me not, who, to herself,
May call me thankless and ungrateful man.—
I'll not endure it; no.
    VENT. (*Aside*) I am glad it pinches there.
    OCTAV. Would you triumph o'er poor
    Octavia's virtue?
That pride was all I had to bear me up,
That you might think you owed me for your
    life
And owed it to my duty, not my love.
I have been injured, and my haughty soul
Could brook but ill the man who slights my
    bed.
    ANT. Therefore you love me not.
    OCTAV. Therefore, my lord,
I should not love you.
    ANT. Therefore you would leave me?
    OCTAV. And therefore I should leave you
—if I could.
    DOLA. Her soul's too great, after such in-
    juries,
To say she loves; and yet she lets you see it.
Her modesty and silence plead her cause.
    ANT. O Dolabella, which way shall I turn?
I find a secret yielding in my soul;

But Cleopatra, who would die with me,
Must she be left? Pity pleads for Octavia;
But does it not plead more for Cleopatra?
 Vent. Justice and pity both plead for
  Octavia;
For Cleopatra, neither.
One would be ruined with you, but she first
Had ruined you: the other, you have ruined,
And yet she would preserve you.
In everything their merits are unequal.
 Ant. O my distracted soul!
 Octav. Sweet heaven compose it!—
Come, come, my lord, if I can pardon you,
Methinks you should accept it. (*Drawing
 the* Children *to her*) Look on these;
Are they not yours? Or stand they thus
 neglected,
As they are mine? Go to him, children, go;
Kneel to him, take him by the hand, speak to
 him;
For you may speak, and he may own you too,
Without a blush; and so he cannot all
His children. Go, I say, and pull him to me,
And pull him to yourselves, from that bad
 woman.
You, Agrippina, hang upon his arms;
And you, Antonia, clasp about his waist.
If he will shake you off, if he will dash you
Against the pavement, you must bear it, chil-
 dren;
For you are mine, and I was born to suffer.
  (*The* Children *run to* Antony *and
  embrace him*)
 Vent. Was ever sight so moving?—Em-
peror!
 Dola. Friend!
 Octav. Husband!
 Both Child. Father!
 Ant. I am vanquished; take me,
Octavia; take me, children; share me all.
     (*Embracing them*)
I've been a thriftless debtor to your loves,
And run out much, in riot, from your stock;
But all shall be amended.
 Octav. O blest hour!
 Dola. O happy change!
 Vent. My joy stops at my tongue;
But it has found two channels here for one,
And bubbles out above.
 Ant. (*To* Octav.) This is thy triumph;
 lead me where thou wilt,
Ev'n to thy brother's camp.
 Octav. All there are yours.

(*Enter* Alexas *hastily*)

 Alex. The queen, my mistress, sir, and
yours——
 Ant. 'Tis past.—
Octavia, you shall stay this night; tomorrow,
Cæsar and we are one.
  (*Exit leading* Octavia; Dolabella
  and the Children *follow*)
 Vent. There's news for you; run, my
 officious eunuch,
Be sure to be the first; haste forward;
Haste, my dear eunuch, haste! (*Exit*)
 Alex. This downright fighting fool, this
 thick-skulled hero,
This blunt, unthinking instrument of death,
With plain dull virtue has outgone my wit.
Pleasure forsook my earliest infancy;
The luxury of others robbed my cradle,
And ravished thence the promise of a man.
Cast out from nature, disinherited
Of what her meanest children claim by kind,
Yet greatness kept me from contempt; that's
 gone.
Had Cleopatra followed my advice,
Then he had been betrayed who now for-
 sakes.
She dies for love; but she has known its joys.
Gods, is this just, that I, who know no joys,
Must die, because she loves?

(*Enter* Cleopatra, Charmion, Iras,
  Attendants)

O madam, I have seen what blasts my eyes!
Octavia's here!
 Cleo. Peace with that raven's note.
I know it too; and now am in
The pangs of death.
 Alex. You are no more a queen;
Egypt is lost.
 Cleo. What tell'st thou me of Egypt?
My life, my soul is lost! Octavia has him!—
O fatal name to Cleopatra's love!
My kisses, my embraces now are hers;
While I—— But thou hast seen my rival;
 speak,
Does she deserve this blessing? Is she fair?
Bright as a goddess? And is all perfection
Confined to her? It is. Poor I was made
Of that coarse matter which, when she was
 finished,
The gods threw by for rubbish.

ALEX. She's indeed a very miracle.

CLEO. Death to my hopes, a miracle!

ALEX. (*Bowing*) A miracle;
I mean of goodness; for in beauty, madam,
You make all wonders cease.

CLEO. I was too rash:
Take this in part of recompense. (*Giving a
ring*) But, oh!
I fear thou flatter'st me.

CHAR. She comes! she's here!

IRAS. Fly, madam, Cæsar's sister!

CLEO. Were she the sister of the thund'rer
Jove,
And bore her brother's lightning in her eyes,
Thus would I face my rival.

(*Enter* OCTAVIA *with* VENTIDIUS. OCTAVIA
and CLEOPATRA *approach each other. Their
Attendants come up on either side*)

OCTAV. I need not ask if you are Cleopatra;
Your haughty carriage——

CLEO. Shows I am a queen;
Nor need I ask you, who you are.

OCTAV. A Roman;
A name that makes and can unmake a queen.

CLEO. Your lord, the man who serves me,
is a Roman.

OCTAV. He was a Roman, till he lost that
name
To be a slave in Egypt; but I come
To free him thence.

CLEO. Peace, peace, my lover's Juno.
When he grew weary of that household clog,
He chose my easier bonds.

OCTAV. I wonder not
Your bonds are easy; you have long been
practised
In that lascivious art. He's not the first
For whom you spread your snares: let Cæsar
witness.

CLEO. I loved not Cæsar; 'twas but grati-
tude
I paid his love. The worst your malice can,
Is but to say the greatest of mankind
Has been my slave. The next, but far above
him
In my esteem, is he whom law calls yours,
But whom his love made mine.

OCTAV. (*Coming up close to her*) I would
view nearer

That face which has so long usurped my
right,
To find th' inevitable charms that catch
Mankind so sure, that ruined my dear lord.

CLEO. Oh, you do well to search; for had
you known
But half these charms, you had not lost his
heart.

OCTAV. Far be their knowledge from a
Roman lady,
Far from a modest wife! Shame of our sex,
Dost thou not blush to own those black en-
dearments
That make sin pleasing?

CLEO. You may blush, who want 'em.
If bounteous nature, if indulgent heav'n
Have giv'n me charms to please the bravest
man,
Should I not thank 'em? Should I be
ashamed,
And not be proud? I am, that he has loved
me;
And when I love not him, heav'n change this
face
For one like that.

OCTAV. Thou lov'st him not so well.

CLEO. I love him better, and deserve him
more.

OCTAV. You do not, cannot; you have been
his ruin.
Who made him cheap at Rome, but Cleo-
patra?
Who made him scorned abroad, but Cleo-
patra?
At Actium, who betrayed him? Cleopatra.
Who made his children orphans, and poor me
A wretched widow? Only Cleopatra.

CLEO. Yet she who loves him best is Cleo-
patra.
If you have suffered, I have suffered more.
You bear the specious title of a wife
To gild your cause and draw the pitying
world
To favor it; the world contemns poor me,
For I have lost my honor, lost my fame,
And stained the glory of my royal house,
And all to bear the branded name of mistress.
There wants but life, and that too I would
lose
For him I love.

OCTAV. Be't so, then; take thy wish.
(*Exit with* VENTIDIUS *and Attendants*)

CLEO. And 'tis my wish,

Now he is lost for whom alone I lived.
My sight grows dim, and every object dances
And swims before me, in the maze of death.
My spirits, while they were opposed, kept up;
They could not sink beneath a rival's scorn.
But now she's gone, they faint.
   ALEX. Mine have had leisure
To recollect their strength, and furnish
   counsel
To ruin her who else must ruin you.
   CLEO. Vain promiser!

Lead me, my Charmion; nay, your hand too,
   Iras.
My grief has weight enough to sink you both.
Conduct me to some solitary chamber,
And draw the curtains round;
Then leave me to myself, to take alone
My fill of grief.

There I till death will his unkindness weep,
As harmless infants moan themselves asleep.
                            (*Exeunt*)

Act IV

The Same

(*Enter* ANTONY *and* DOLABELLA, *talking
earnestly*)

   DOLA. Why would you shift it from your-
   self on me?
Can you not tell her you must part?
   ANT. I cannot.
I could pull out an eye and bid it go,
And t'other should not weep. O Dolabella,
How many deaths are in this word "depart!"
I dare not trust my tongue to tell her so:
One look of hers would thaw me into tears,
And I should melt till I were lost again.
   DOLA. Then let Ventidius; he's rough by
nature.
   ANT. Oh, he'll speak too harshly;
He'll kill her with the news. Thou, only
   thou.
   DOLA. Nature has cast me in so soft a
   mold,
That but to hear a story feigned for pleasure
Of some sad lover's death, moistens my eyes
And robs me of my manhood. I should speak
So faintly, with such fear to grieve her heart,
She'd not believe it earnest.
   ANT. Therefore—therefore
Thou only, thou art fit. Think thyself me;
And when thou speak'st (but let it first be
   long),
Take off the edge from every sharper sound,
And let our parting be as gently made
As other loves begin. Wilt thou do this?
   DOLA. What you have said so sinks into
   my soul
That if I must speak, I shall speak just so.

   ANT. I leave you then to your sad task.
   Farewell.
I sent her word to meet you.
        (*Goes to the door, and comes back*)
I forgot;
Let her be told, I'll make her peace with
   mine.
Her crown and dignity shall be preserved,
If I have pow'r with Cæsar.——Oh, be sure
To think on that.
   DOLA. Fear not, I will remember.
      (ANTONY *goes again to the door, and
      comes back*)
   ANT. And tell her, too, how much I was
   constrained;
I did not this, but with extremest force.
Desire her not to hate my memory,
For I still cherish hers——insist on that.
   DOLA. Trust me, I'll not forget it.
   ANT. Then that's all.
         (*Goes out, and returns again*)
Wilt thou forgive my fondness this once
   more?
Tell her, though we shall never meet again,
If I should hear she took another love,
The news would break my heart.—Now I
   must go;
For every time I have returned I feel
My soul more tender, and my next command
Would be to bid her stay, and ruin both.
                         (*Exit*)
   DOLA. Men are but children of a larger
   growth;
Our appetites as apt to change as theirs,
And full as craving too, and full as vain;

And yet the soul, shut up in her dark room,
Viewing so clear abroad, at home sees nothing;
But, like a mole in earth, busy and blind,
Works all her folly up, and casts it outward
To the world's open view. Thus I discovered,
And blamed the love of ruined Antony;
Yet wish that I were he, to be so ruined.

(*Enter* VENTIDIUS *above*)

VENT. (*Aside*) Alone? and talking to himself? concerned too?
Perhaps my guess is right; he loved her once,
And may pursue it still.
  DOLA. O friendship! friendship!
Ill canst thou answer this; and reason, worse.
Unfaithful in th' attempt; hopeless to win;
And if I win, undone—mere madness all.
And yet the occasion's fair. What injury
To him, to wear the robe which he throws by?
  VENT. (*Aside*) None, none at all. This happens as I wish,
To ruin her yet more with Antony.

(*Enter* CLEOPATRA, *talking with* ALEXAS;
  CHARMION, IRAS, *on the other side*)

  DOLA. She comes! What charms have sorrow on that face!
Sorrow seems pleased to dwell with so much sweetness;
Yet, now and then, a melancholy smile
Breaks lose, like lightning in a winter's night,
And shows a moment's day.
  VENT. (*Aside*) If she should love him too!
  her eunuch there!
That porcpisce [2] bodes ill weather. Draw, draw nearer,
Sweet devil, that I may hear.
  (DOLABELLA *goes over to* CHARMION
    and IRAS *and talks with them*)
  ALEX. Believe me; try
To make him jealous. Jealousy is like
A polished glass held to the lips when life's in doubt;
If there be breath, 'twill catch the damp and show it.
  CLEO. I grant you, jealousy's a proof of love,
But 'tis a weak and unavailing med'cine;
It puts out the disease and makes it show,

[2] Porpoise.

But has no pow'r to cure.
  ALEX. 'Tis your last remedy, and strongest too.
And then this Dolabella—who so fit
To practise on? He's handsome, valiant, young,
And looks as he were laid for nature's bait
To catch weak women's eyes.
He stands already more than half suspected
Of loving you; the least kind word or glance
You give this youth will kindle him with love.
Then, like a burning vessel set adrift,
You'll send him down amain before the wind
To fire the heart of jealous Antony.
  CLEO. Can I do this? Ah, no; my love's so true,
That I can neither hide it where it is,
Nor show it where it is not. Nature meant me
A wife, a silly, harmless, household dove,
Fond without art, and kind without deceit;
But Fortune, that has made a mistress of me,
Has thrust me out to the wide world, unfurnished
Of falsehood to be happy.
  ALEX. Force yourself.
Th' event will be, your lover will return
Doubly desirous to possess the good
Which once he feared to lose.
  CLEO. I must attempt it;
But oh, with what regret!
    (*Exit* ALEXAS. *She comes up to* DOLA-
      BELLA)
  VENT. (*Aside*) So, now the scene draws near; they're in my reach.
  CLEO. (*To* DOLA.) Discoursing with my women! Might not I
Share in your entertainment?
  CHAR. You have been
The subject of it, madam.
  CLEO. How! and how?
  IRAS. Such praises of your beauty!
  CLEO. Mere poetry.
Your Roman wits, your Gallus and Tibullus,
Have taught you this from Cytheris and Delia.
  DOLA. Those Roman wits have never been in Egypt;
Cytheris and Delia else had been unsung.
I, who have seen——had I been born a poet,
Should choose a nobler name.
  CLEO. You flatter me.

But 'tis your nation's vice; all of your country
Are flatterers, and all false. Your friend's like
    you.
I'm sure he sent you not to speak these words.
    Dola. No, madam; yet he sent me——
    Cleo. Well, he sent you——
    Dola. Of a less pleasing errand.
    Cleo. How less pleasing?
Less to yourself, or me?
    Dola. Madam, to both;
For you must mourn, and I must grieve to
    cause it.
    Cleo. You, Charmion, and your fellow
    stand at distance.—(Charmion and
    Iras move away and talk)
(Aside)—Hold up, my spirits.——Well, now
    your mournful matter;
For I'm prepared, perhaps can guess it too.
    Dola. I wish you would; for 'tis a thank-
    less office,
To tell ill news; and I, of all your sex,
Most fear displeasing you.
    Cleo. Of all your sex,
I soonest could forgive you, if you should.
    Vent. (Aside) Most delicate advances!
    Woman! Woman!
Dear, damned, inconstant sex!
    Cleo. In the first place,
I am to be forsaken; is't not so?
    Dola. I wish I could not answer to that
question.
    Cleo. Then pass it o'er, because it troubles
    you;
I should have been more grieved another
    time.
Next, I'm to lose my kingdom.——Farewell,
    Egypt!
Yet, is there any more?
    Dola. Madam, I fear
Your too deep sense of grief has turned your
    reason.
    Cleo. No, no, I'm not run mad; I can bear
    fortune;
And love may be expelled by other love,
As poisons are by poisons.
    Dola. You o'erjoy me, madam,
To find your griefs so moderately borne.
You've heard the worst; all are not false like
    him.
    Cleo. No; heav'n forbid they should.
    Dola. Some men are constant.
    Cleo. And constancy deserves reward,
that's certain.

    Dola. Deserves it not; but give it leave to
hope.
    Vent. (Aside) I'll swear, thou hast my
    leave. I have enough.
But how to manage this! Well, I'll consider.
                   (Exit)
    Dola. I came prepared
To tell you heavy news; news, which I
    thought
Would fright the blood from your pale cheeks
    to hear;
But you have met it with a cheerfulness
That makes my task more easy; and my
    tongue,
Which on another's message was employed,
Would gladly speak its own.
    Cleo. Hold, Dolabella.
First tell me, were you chosen by my lord?
Or sought you this employment?
    Dola. He picked me out; and, as his
    bosom friend,
He charged me with his words.
    Cleo. The message then
I know was tender, and each accent smooth,
To mollify that rugged word "depart."
    Dola. Oh, you mistake; he chose the
    harshest words;
With fiery eyes, and with contracted brows,
He coined his face in the severest stamp,
And fury shook his fabric, like an earth-
    quake;
He heaved for vent, and burst like bellowing
    Ætna,
In sounds scarce human—"Hence, away for-
    ever;
Let her begone, the blot of my renown,
And bane of all my hopes!
    (All the time of this speech, Cleopatra
      seems more and more concerned,
      till she sinks quite down)
Let her be driv'n as far as men can think
From man's commerce! She'll poison to the
    center."
    Cleo. Oh, I can bear no more!
    Dola. Help, help—(Charmion and Iras
    rush to Cleopatra) O wretch! O
    cursed, cursed wretch!
What have I done!
    Char. Help, chafe her temples, Iras.
    Iras. Bend, bend her forward quickly.
    Char. Heav'n be praised,
She comes again.
    Cleo. Oh, let him not approach me.

Why have you brought me back to this
    loathed being,
Th' abode of falsehood, violated vows,
And injured love? For pity, let me go;
For, if there be a place of long repose,
I'm sure I want it. My disdainful lord
Can never break that quiet, nor awake
The sleeping soul with hollowing in my
    tomb
Such words as fright her hence.—Unkind,
    unkind!
    Dola. (*Kneeling*) Believe me, 'tis against
    myself I speak;
That sure deserves belief. I injured him:
My friend ne'er spoke those words. Oh, had
    you seen
How often he came back, and every time
With something more obliging and more
    kind,
To add to what he said; what dear farewells;
How almost vanquished by his love he
    parted,
And leaned to what unwillingly he left!
I, traitor as I was, for love of you
(But what can you not do, who made me
    false!)
I forged that lie; for whose forgiveness kneels
This self-accused, self-punished criminal.
    Cleo. With how much ease believe we
    what we wish!
Rise, Dolabella; if you have been guilty,
I have contributed, and too much love
Has made me guilty too.
Th' advance of kindness which I made was
    feigned,
To call back fleeting love by jealousy;
But 'twould not last. Oh, rather let me lose,
Than so ignobly trifle with his heart.
    Dola. I find your breast fenced round
    from human reach,
Transparent as a rock of solid crystal,
Seen through, but never pierced. My friend,
    my friend!
What endless treasure hast thou thrown
    away,
And scattered, like an infant, in the ocean,
Vain sums of wealth, which none can gather
    thence!
    Cleo. Could you not beg
An hour's admittance to his private ear?
Like one who wanders through long barren
    wilds
And yet foreknows no hospitable inn

Is near to succor hunger, eats his fill,
Before his painful march:
So would I feed a while my famished eyes
Before we part; for I have far to go,
If death be far, and never must return.

(*Enter at the rear* Ventidius *with* Octavia.
They are at first unobserved by Cleopatra
    and Dolabella.)

    Vent. (*To* Octavia) From hence you
    may discover—oh, sweet, sweet!
Would you indeed? the pretty hand in
    earnest?
    Dola. (*To* Cleopatra) I will, for this re-
    ward.—(*Takes her hand*) Draw it not
    back,
'Tis all I e'er will beg. (*Starts as he sees*
    Ventidius *and* Octavia)
    Vent. (*To* Octavia) They turn upon us.
    Octav. What quick eyes has guilt!
    Vent. Seem not to have observed 'em, and
    go on.
(Ventidius *and* Octavia *come forward*)
    Dola. Saw you the emperor, Ventidius?
    Vent. No.
I sought him, but I heard that he was private,
None with him but Hipparchus, his freed-
    man.
    Dola. Know you his bus'ness?
    Vent. Giving him instructions,
And letters to his brother Cæsar.
    Dola. Well,
He must be found.
    (*Exeunt* Dolabella *and* Cleopatra)
    Octav. Most glorious impudence!
    Vent. She looked, methought,
As she would say, "Take your old man, Oc-
    tavia;
Thank you, I'm better here."
Well, but what use
Make we of this discovery?
    Octav. Let it die.
    Vent. I pity Dolabella; but she's danger-
    ous:
Her eyes have pow'r beyond Thessalian
    charms
To draw the moon from heav'n; for elo-
    quence,
The sea-green Sirens taught her voice their
    flatt'ry;
And, while she speaks, night steals upon the
    day,

Unmarked of those that hear. Then she's so
    charming,
Age buds at sight of her, and swells to youth:
The holy priests gaze on her when she smiles,
And with heaved hands, forgetting gravity,
They bless her wanton eyes. Even I, who hate
    her,
With a malignant joy behold such beauty,
And, while I curse, desire it. Antony
Must needs have some remains of passion
    still,
Which may ferment into a worse relapse,
If now not fully cured. I know, this minute,
With Cæsar he's endeavoring her peace.
  OCTAV. You have prevailed. (*Aside*) But
    for a farther purpose
I'll prove how he will relish this discovery.
What, make a strumpet's peace! it swells my
    heart:
It must not, sha' not be.
  VENT. His guards appear.
Let me begin, and you shall second me.

(*Enter* ANTONY)

  ANT. Octavia, I was looking you, my love:
What, are your letters ready? I have giv'n
My last instructions.
  OCTAV. Mine, my lord, are written.
  ANT. Ventidius! (*Drawing him aside*)
  VENT. My lord?
  ANT. A word in private.
When saw you Dolabella?
  VENT. Now, my lord,
He parted hence; and Cleopatra with him.
  ANT. Speak softly.—'Twas by my com-
    mand he went,
To bear my last farewell.
  VENT. (*Aloud*) It looked indeed
Like your farewell.
  ANT. More softly.—My farewell?
What secret meaning have you in those
    words
Of "my farewell"? He did it by my order.
  VENT. (*Aloud*) Then he obeyed your
    order. I suppose
You bid him do it with all gentleness,
All kindness, and all——love.
  ANT. How she mourned,
The poor forsaken creature!
  VENT. She took it as she ought; she bore
    your parting
As she did Cæsar's, as she would another's,

Were a new love to come.
  ANT. (*Aloud*) Thou dost belie her;
Most basely, and maliciously belie her.
  VENT. I thought not to displease you; I
have done.
  OCTAV. (*Coming up*) You seemed dis-
turbed, my lord.
  ANT. A very trifle.
Retire, my love.
  VENT. It was indeed a trifle.
He sent——
  ANT. (*Angrily*) No more. Look how thou
disobey'st me;
Thy life shall answer it.
  OCTAV. Then 'tis no trifle.
  VENT. (*To* OCTAV.) 'Tis less, a very noth-
ing: you too saw it,
As well as I, and therefore 'tis no secret.
  ANT. She saw it!
  VENT. Yes; she saw young Dolabella——
  ANT. Young Dolabella!
  VENT. Young, I think him young,
And handsome too; and so do others think
him.
But what of that? He went by your com-
mand,
Indeed 'tis probable with some kind message,
For she received it graciously; she smiled;
And then he grew familiar with her hand,
Squeezed it, and worried it with ravenous
kisses;
She blushed, and sighed, and smiled, and
blushed again;
At last she took occasion to talk softly,
And brought her cheek up close, and leaned
on his;
At which, he whispered kisses back on hers;
And then she cried aloud that constancy
Should be rewarded.
  OCTAV. This I saw and heard.
  ANT. What woman was it whom you
heard and saw
So playful with my friend? Not Cleopatra?
  VENT. Ev'n she, my lord.
  ANT. My Cleopatra?
  VENT. Your Cleopatra;
Dolabella's Cleopatra; every man's Cleopatra.
  ANT. Thou li'st.
  VENT. I do not lie, my lord.
Is this so strange? Should mistresses be left
And not provide against a time of change?
You know she's not much used to lonely
    nights.

Ant. I'll think no more on't.
I know 'tis false, and see the plot betwixt you.
You needed not have gone this way, Octavia.
What harms it you that Cleopatra's just?
She's mine no more. I see, and I forgive.
Urge it no farther, love.
Octav. Are you concerned,
That she's found false?
Ant. I should be, were it so;
For, though 'tis past, I would not that the world
Should tax my former choice, that I loved one
Of so light note; but I forgive you both.
Vent. What has my age deserved, that you should think
I would abuse your ears with perjury?
If heav'n be true, she's false.
Ant. Though heav'n and earth
Should witness it, I'll not believe her tainted.
Vent. I'll bring you, then, a witness
From hell, to prove her so. (Sees Alexas just entering and starting back)—Nay, go not back,
For stay you must and shall.
Alex. What means my lord?
Vent. To make you do what most you hate—speak truth.
You are of Cleopatra's private counsel,
Of her bed-counsel, her lascivious hours;
Are conscious of each nightly change she makes,
And watch her, as Chaldeans do the moon,
Can tell what signs she passes through, what day.
Alex. My noble lord!
Vent. My most illustrious pander,
No fine set speech, no cadence, no turned periods,
But a plain homespun truth is what I ask.
I did, myself, o'erhear your queen make love
To Dolabella. Speak! for I will know
By your confession what more passed betwixt 'em;
How near the bus'ness draws to your employment;
And when the happy hour.
Ant. Speak truth, Alexas; whether it offend
Or please Ventidius, care not. Justify
Thy injured queen from malice; dare his worst.
Octav. (Aside) See how he gives him courage! how he fears

To find her false! and shuts his eyes to truth,
Willing to be misled!
Alex. As far as love may plead for woman's frailty,
Urged by desert and greatness of the lover,
So far, divine Octavia, may my queen
Stand ev'n excused to you for loving him
Who is your lord; so far, from brave Ventidius,
May her past actions hope a fair report.
Ant. 'Tis well and truly spoken. Mark, Ventidius.
Alex. To you, most noble emperor, her strong passion
Stands not excused, but wholly justified.
Her beauty's charms alone, without her crown,
From Ind and Meroe drew the distant vows
Of sighing kings; and at her feet were laid
The sceptres of the earth, exposed on heaps,
To choose where she would reign.
She thought a Roman only could deserve her,
And, of all Romans, only Antony;
And, to be less than wife to you, disdained
Their lawful passion.
Ant. 'Tis but truth.
Alex. And yet, though love and your unmatched desert
Have drawn her from the due regard of honor,
At last heav'n opened her unwilling eyes
To see the wrongs she offered fair Octavia,
Whose holy bed she lawlessly usurped.
The sad effects of this improsperous war
Confirmed those pious thoughts.
Vent. (Aside) Oh, wheel you there?
Observe him now; the man begins to mend,
And talk substantial reason.—Fear not, eunuch,
The emperor has giv'n thee leave to speak.
Alex. Else had I never dared t'offend his ears
With what the last necessity has urged
On my forsaken mistress; yet I must not
Presume to say her heart is wholly altered.
Ant. No, dare not for thy life, I charge thee dare not
Pronounce that fatal word!
Octav. (Aside) Must I bear this? Good heav'n, afford me patience.
Vent. On, sweet eunuch, my dear half-man, proceed.
Alex. Yet Dolabella

Has loved her long. He, next my god-like
    lord,
Deserves her best; and should she meet his
    passion,
Rejected as she is by him she loved——
    ANT. Hence from my sight! for I can bear
    no more.
Let furies drag thee quick to hell; let all
The longer damned have rest! Each torturing
    hand
Do thou employ till Cleopatra comes,
Then join thou too, and help to torture her!
    (*Exit* ALEXAS, *thrust out by* ANTONY)
    OCTAV. 'Tis not well,
Indeed, my lord, 'tis much unkind to me
To show this passion, this extreme concern-
    ment,
For an abandoned, faithless prostitute.
    ANT. Octavia, leave me. I am much dis-
    ordered.
Leave me, I say.
    OCTAV. My lord!
    ANT. I bid you leave me.
    VENT. Obey him, madam. (*Aside to her*)
    Best withdraw a while,
And see how this will work.
    OCTAV. Wherein have I offended you, my
    lord,
That I am bid to leave you? Am I false,
Or infamous? Am I a Cleopatra?
Were I she,
Base as she is, you would not bid me leave
    you,
But hang upon my neck, take slight excuses,
And fawn upon my falsehood.
    ANT. 'Tis too much,
Too much, Octavia. I am pressed with sor-
    rows
Too heavy to be borne, and you add more.
I would retire and recollect what's left
Of man within, to aid me.
    OCTAV. You would mourn,
In private, for your love who has betrayed
    you.
You did but half return to me; your kindness
Lingered behind with her. I hear, my lord,
You make conditions for her
And would include her treaty. Wond'rous
    proofs
Of love to me!
    ANT. Are you my friend, Ventidius?
Or are you turned a Dolabella too,
And let this Fury loose?

    VENT. Oh, be advised,
Sweet madam, and retire.
    OCTAV. Yes, I will go, but never to return.
You shall no more be haunted with this Fury.
My lord, my lord, love will not always last,
When urged with long unkindness and dis-
    dain.
Take her again whom you prefer to me;
She stays but to be called. Poor cozened man!
Let a feigned parting give her back your
    heart,
Which a feigned love first got. For injured
    me,
Though my just sense of wrongs forbid my
    stay,
My duty shall be yours.
To the dear pledges of our former love
My tenderness and care shall be transferred,
And they shall cheer, by turns, my widowed
    nights.
So, take my last farewell, for I despair
To have you whole, and scorn to take you
    half.   (*Exit*)
    VENT. (*Aside*) I combat heav'n, which
    blasts my best designs;
My last attempt must be to win her back,
But oh! I fear in vain.   (*Exit*)
    ANT. Why was I framed with this plain,
    honest heart
Which knows not to disguise its griefs and
    weakness,
But bears its workings outward to the world?
I should have kept the mighty anguish in,
And forced a smile at Cleopatra's falsehood:
Octavia had believed it, and had stayed.
But I am made a shallow-forded stream,
Seen to the bottom, all my clearness scorned,
And all my faults exposed!—See where he
    comes,

(*Enter* DOLABELLA)

Who has profaned the sacred name of friend
And worn it into vileness!
With how secure a brow and specious form
He gilds the secret villain! Sure that face
Was meant for honesty, but heav'n mis-
    matched it,
And furnished treason out with nature's
    pomp,
To make its work more easy.
    DOLA. O my friend!

ANT. Well, Dolabella, you performed my message?

DOLA. I did, unwillingly.

ANT. Unwillingly?
Was it so hard for you to bear our parting?
You should have wished it.

DOLA. Why?

ANT. Because you love me.
And she received my message with as true,
With as unfeigned a sorrow as you brought it?

DOLA. She loves you, even to madness.

ANT. Oh, I know it.
You, Dolabella, do not better know
How much she loves me. And should I
Forsake this beauty, this all-perfect creature?

DOLA. I could not, were she mine.

ANT. And yet you first
Persuaded me! How come you altered since?

DOLA. I said at first I was not fit to go—
I could not hear her sighs and see her tears
But pity must prevail. And so, perhaps,
It may again with you, for I have promised,
That she should take her last farewell. And see,
She comes to claim my word.

(*Enter* CLEOPATRA)

ANT. False Dolabella!

DOLA. What's false, my lord?

ANT. Why, Dolabella's false,
And Cleopatra's false, both false and faith-
less.
Draw near, you well-joined wickedness, you serpents,
Whom I have in my kindly bosom warmed
Till I am stung to death.

DOLA. My lord, have I
Deserved to be thus used?

CLEO. Can heav'n prepare
A newer torment? Can it find a curse
Beyond our separation?

ANT. Yes, if fate
Be just, much greater! Heav'n should be ingenious
In punishing such crimes. The rolling stone
And gnawing vulture were slight pains, in-
vented
When Jove was young and no examples known
Of mighty ills; but you have ripened sin

To such a monstrous growth, 'twill pose the gods
To find an equal torture. Two, two such!—
Oh, there's no further name, two such!—to me,
To me, who locked my soul within your breasts,
Had no desires, no joys, no life, but you.
When half the globe was mine, I gave it you
In dowry with my heart; I had no use,
No fruit of all, but you; a friend and mistress
Was what the world could give. O Cleopatra!
O Dolabella! how could you betray
This tender heart, which with an infant fondness
Lay lulled betwixt your bosoms, and there slept,
Secure of injured faith?

DOLA. If she has wronged you,
Heav'n, hell, and you revenge it.

ANT. If she wronged me!
Thou wouldst evade thy part of guilt. But swear
Thou lov'st not her.

DOLA. Not so as I love you.

ANT. Not so? Swear, swear, I say, thou dost not love her.

DOLA. No more than friendship will allow.

ANT. No more?
Friendship allows thee nothing. Thou art perjured—
And yet thou didst not swear thou lov'dst her not,
But not so much, no more. O trifling hypo-
crite,
Who dar'st not own to her thou dost not love,
Nor own to me thou dost! Ventidius heard it;
Octavia saw it.

CLEO. They are enemies.

ANT. Alexas is not so. He, he confessed it;
He, who, next hell, best knew it, he avowed it.
(*To* DOLA.) Why do I seek a proof beyond yourself?
You, whom I sent to bear my last farewell,
Returned to plead her stay.

DOLA. What shall I answer?
If to have loved be guilt, then I have sinned;
But if to have repented of that love
Can wash away my crime, I have repented.
Yet if I have offended past forgiveness,
Let not her suffer: she is innocent.

CLEO. Ah, what will not a woman do, who
    loves!
What means will she refuse, to keep that
    heart
Where all her joys are placed? 'Twas I en-
    couraged,
'Twas I blew up the fire that scorched his
    soul,
To make you jealous, and by that regain you.
But all in vain; I could not counterfeit.
In spite of all the dams my love broke o'er
And drowned my heart again. Fate took th'
    occasion,
And thus one minute's feigning has de-
    stroyed
My whole life's truth.
    ANT. Thin cobweb arts of falsehood,
Seen, and broke through at first.
    DOLA. Forgive your mistress.
    CLEO. Forgive your friend.
    ANT. You have convinced yourselves,
You plead each other's cause. What witness
    have you
That you but meant to raise my jealousy?
    CLEO. Ourselves, and heav'n.
    ANT. Guilt witnesses for guilt. Hence, love
        and friendship!
You have no longer place in human breasts,
These two have driv'n you out. Avoid my
    sight!
I would not kill the man whom I have loved,
And cannot hurt the woman, but avoid me—
I do not know how long I can be tame.
For if I stay one minute more to think
How I am wronged, my justice and revenge
Will cry so loud within me that my pity
Will not be heard for either.
    DOLA. Heav'n has but
Our sorrow for our sins, and then delights
To pardon erring man. Sweet mercy seems
Its darling attribute, which limits justice
As if there were degrees in infinite,
And infinite would rather want perfection
Than punish to extent.
    ANT. I can forgive
A foe, but not a mistress and a friend.
Treason is there in its most horrid shape
Where trust is greatest, and the soul resigned
Is stabbed by its own guards. I'll hear no
    more.
Hence from my sight for ever!
    CLEO. How? for ever!
I cannot go one moment from your sight,

And must I go for ever?
My joys, my only joys, are centered here.
What place have I to go to? My own king-
    dom?
That I have lost for you. Or to the Romans?
They hate me for your sake. Or must I
    wander
The wide world o'er, a helpless, banished
    woman,
Banished for love of you, banished from you?
Ay, there's the banishment! Oh, hear me!
    hear me,
With strictest justice, for I beg no favor;
And if I have offended you, then kill me,
But do not banish me.
    ANT. I must not hear you.
I have a fool within me takes your part,
But honor stops my ears.
    CLEO. For pity hear me!
Would you cast off a slave who followed you?
Who crouched beneath your spurn?—He has
    no pity!
See if he gives one tear to my departure,
One look, one kind farewell! O iron heart!
Let all the gods look down and judge betwixt
    us,
If he did ever love!
    ANT. No more.——Alexas!
    DOLA. A perjured villain!
    ANT. (To CLEO.) Your Alexas, yours!
    CLEO. Oh, 'twas his plot, his ruinous
        design,
T'engage you in my love by jealousy.
Hear him; confront him with me; let him
    speak.
    ANT. I have, I have.
    CLEO. And if he clear me not——
    ANT. Your creature! one who hangs upon
        your smiles!
Watches your eye, to say or to unsay
Whate'er you please! I am not to be moved.
    CLEO. Then must we part? Farewell, my
        cruel lord!
Th' appearance is against me, and I go,
Unjustified, for ever from your sight.
How I have loved, you know; how yet I love,
My only comfort is, I know myself.
I love you more, ev'n now you are unkind,
Than when you loved me most; so well, so
    truly,
I'll never strive against it, but die pleased,
To think you once were mine.

Ant. (*Aside*) Good heav'n, they weep at
    parting!
Must I weep too? That calls 'em innocent.
I must not weep; and yet I must, to think
That I must not forgive.——
Live, but live wretched; 'tis but just you
    should,
Who made me so. Live from each other's
    sight;
Let me not hear you meet. Set all the earth
And all the seas betwixt your sundered loves;
View nothing common but the sun and skies.
Now, all take several ways;
And each your own sad fate, with mine,
    deplore
That you were false, and I could trust no
    more.

(*Exeunt severally*)

Act V

The Same

(*Enter* Cleopatra, Charmion, *and* Iras)

Char. Be juster, heav'n; such virtue
    punished thus
Will make us think that chance rules all
    above,
And shuffles with a random hand the lots
Which man is forced to draw.
    Cleo. I could tear out these eyes that
    gained his heart
And had not pow'r to keep it. Oh, the curse
Of doting on, ev'n when I find it dotage!
Bear witness, gods, you heard him bid me go;
You, whom he mocked with imprecating
    vows
Of promised faith!——I'll die! I will not bear
    it.
    (*She pulls out her dagger, and they
        hold her*)
You may hold me——
But I can keep my breath; I can die inward
And choke this love.

(*Enter* Alexas)

Iras. Help, O Alexas, help!
The queen grows desperate; her soul strug-
    gles in her
With all the agonies of love and rage
And strives to force its passage.
    Cleo. Let me go.
Art thou there, traitor!—Oh,
Oh, for a little breath to vent my rage!
Give, give me way, and let me loose upon
    him.
    Alex. Yes, I deserve it, for my ill-timed
    truth.

Was it for me to prop
The ruins of a falling majesty?
To place myself beneath the mighty flaw,
Thus to be crushed and pounded into atoms
By its o'erwhelming weight? 'Tis too pre-
    suming
For subjects to preserve that wilful pow'r
Which courts its own destruction.
    Cleo. I would reason
More calmly with you. Did not you o'errule,
And force my plain, direct, and open love
Into these crooked paths of jealousy?
Now, what's th' event? Octavia is removed,
But Cleopatra's banished. Thou, thou,
    villain,
Hast pushed my boat to open sea, to prove,
At my sad cost, if thou canst steer it back.
It cannot be; I'm lost too far; I'm ruined!
Hence, thou impostor, traitor, monster,
    devil!—
I can no more. Thou and my griefs have sunk
Me down so low that I want voice to curse
    thee.
    Alex. Suppose some shipwrecked seaman
    near the shore,
Dropping and faint with climbing up the
    cliff,
If, from above, some charitable hand
Pull him to safety, hazarding himself
To draw the other's weight, would he look
    back
And curse him for his pains? The case is
    yours;
But one step more, and you have gained the
    height.
    Cleo. Sunk, never more to rise.

ALEX. Octavia's gone, and Dolabella banished.
Believe me, madam, Antony is yours.
His heart was never lost, but started off
To jealousy, love's last retreat and covert,
Where it lies hid in shades, watchful in silence,
And list'ning for the sound that calls it back.
Some other, any man ('tis so advanced),
May perfect this unfinished work, which I
(Unhappy only to myself) have left
So easy to his hand.
    CLEO. Look well thou do't; else——
    ALEX. Else, what your silence threatens.—
Antony
Is mounted up the Pharos, from whose turret
He stands surveying our Egyptian galleys,
Engaged with Cæsar's fleet. Now death or conquest!
If the first happen, fate acquits my promise;
If we o'ercome, the conqueror is yours.
                (*A distant shout within*)
    CHAR. Have comfort, madam. Did you mark that shout?
                (*Second shout nearer*)
    IRAS. Hark! they redouble it.
    ALEX. 'Tis from the port.
The loudness shows it near. Good news, kind heavens!
    CLEO. Osiris make it so!

(*Enter* SERAPION)

    SERAP. Where, where's the queen?
    ALEX. How frightfully the holy coward stares!
As if not yet recovered of th' assault,
When all his gods and, what's more dear to him,
His offerings, were at stake.
    SERAP. O horror, horror!
Egypt has been; our latest hour is come.
The queen of nations from her ancient seat
Is sunk for ever in the dark abyss.
Time has unrolled her glories to the last
And now closed up the volume.
    CLEO. Be more plain.
Say whence thou com'st (though fate is in thy face,
Which from thy haggard eyes looks wildly out
And threatens ere thou speak'st).
    SERAP. I came from Pharos,
From viewing (spare me, and imagine it)
Our land's last hope, your navy——
    CLEO. Vanquished?
    SERAP. No.
They fought not.
    CLEO. Then they fled?
    SERAP. Nor that. I saw,
With Antony, your well-appointed fleet
Row out; and thrice he waved his hand on high,
And thrice with cheerful cries they shouted back.
'Twas then false Fortune, like a fawning strumpet
About to leave the bankrupt prodigal,
With a dissembled smile would kiss at parting
And flatter to the last. The well-timed oars
Now dipped from every bank, now smoothly run
To meet the foe; and soon indeed they met,
But not as foes. In few, we saw their caps
On either side thrown up; th' Egyptian galleys
(Received like friends) passed through, and fell behind
The Roman rear; and now, they all come forward
And ride within the port.
    CLEO. Enough, Serapion.
I've heard my doom.—This needed not, you gods.
When I lost Antony, your work was done;
'Tis but superfluous malice.—Where's my lord?
How bears he this last blow?
    SERAP. His fury cannot be expressed by words.
Thrice he attempted headlong to have fall'n
Full on his foes and aimed at Cæsar's galley.
Withheld, he raves on you; cries, he's betrayed.
Should he now find you—
    ALEX. Shun him; seek your safety
Till you can clear your innocence.
    CLEO. I'll stay.
    ALEX. You must not. Haste you to your monument,
While I make speed to Cæsar.
    CLEO. Cæsar! No,
I have no business with him.
    ALEX. I can work him

To spare your life, and let this madman
   perish.
CLEO. Base fawning wretch! wouldst
   thou betray him too?
Hence from my sight! I will not hear a
   traitor;
'Twas thy design brought all this ruin on us.
Serapion, thou art honest; counsel me.
But haste, each moment's precious.
   SERAP. Retire; you must not yet see An-
   tony.
He who began this mischief,
'Tis just he tempt the danger; let him clear
   you,
And, since he offered you his servile tongue
To gain a poor precarious life from Cæsar,
Let him expose that fawning eloquence,
And speak to Antony.
   ALEX. O heavens! I dare not;
I meet my certain death.
   CLEO. Slave, thou deserv'st it.—
Not that I fear my lord, will I avoid him;
I know him noble. When he banished me
And thought me false, he scorned to take my
   life;
But I'll be justified, and then die with him.
   ALEX. Oh, pity me, and let me follow you!
   CLEO. To death, if thou stir hence. Speak
   if thou canst
Now, for thy life, which basely thou wouldst
   save,
While mine I prize at—this! Come, good
   Serapion.
   (*Exeunt* CLEOPATRA, SERAPION, CHAR-
   MION, IRAS)
   ALEX. Oh, that I less could fear to lose
   this being,
Which, like a snowball in my coward hand,
The more 'tis grasped, the faster melts away.
Poor reason! what a wretched aid art thou!
For still, in spite of thee,
These two long lovers, soul and body, dread
Their final separation. Let me think:
What can I say to save myself from death?
No matter what becomes of Cleopatra.
   ANT. (*Within*) Which way? where?
   VENT. (*Within*) This leads to th' monu-
ment.
   ALEX. Ah me! I hear him, yet I'm un-
   prepared.
My gift of lying's gone,
And this court-devil, which I so oft have
   raised,

Forsakes me at my need. I dare not stay,
Yet cannot far go hence.   (*Exit*)

   (*Enter* ANTONY *and* VENTIDIUS)

   ANT. O happy Cæsar! thou hast men to
   lead.
Think not 'tis thou hast conquered Antony,
But Rome has conquered Egypt. I'm be-
   trayed.
   VENT. Curse on this treach'rous train!
Their soil and heav'n infect 'em all with
   baseness,
And their young souls come tainted to the
   world
With the first breath they draw.
   ANT. Th' original villain sure no god
   created;
He was a bastard of the sun, by Nile,
Aped into man, with all his mother's mud
Crusted about his soul.
   VENT. The nation is
One universal traitor, and their queen
The very spirit and extract of 'em all.
   ANT. Is there yet left
A possibility of aid from valor?
Is there one god unsworn to my destruction?
The least unmortgaged hope? For if there be,
Methinks I cannot fall beneath the fate
Of such a boy as Cæsar.
The world's one half is yet in Antony,
And from each limb of it that's hewed away,
The soul comes back to me.
   VENT. There yet remain
Three legions in the town; the last assault
Lopped off the rest. If death be your design
(As I must wish it now), these are sufficient
To make a heap about us of dead foes,
An honest pile for burial.
   ANT. They're enough.
We'll not divide our stars, but side by side
Fight emulous, and with malicious eyes
Survey each other's acts. So every death
Thou giv'st, I'll take on me as a just debt,
And pay thee back a soul.
   VENT. Now you shall see I love you. Not
   a word
Of chiding more. By my few hours of life,
I am so pleased with this brave Roman fate
That I would not be Cæsar, to outlive you.
When we put off this flesh and mount
   together,
I shall be shown to all th' ethereal crowd,—

"Lo, this is he who died with Antony!"
ANT. Who knows but we may pierce
through all their troops
And reach my veterans yet? 'Tis worth the
tempting,
T' o'erleap this gulf of fate
And leave our wond'ring destinies behind.

(*Enter* ALEXAS, *trembling*)

VENT. See, see, that villain!
See Cleopatra stamped upon that face,
With all her cunning, all her arts of false-
hood!
How she looks out through those dissembling
eyes!
How he has set his count'nance for deceit,
And promises a lie, before he speaks!
Let me despatch him first.   (*Drawing*)
ALEX. Oh, spare me, spare me!
ANT. Hold; he's not worth your killing.—
On thy life
(Which thou may'st keep, because I scorn to
take it),
No syllable to justify thy queen;
Save thy base tongue its office.
ALEX. Sir, she's gone,
Where she shall never be molested more
By love, or you.
ANT. Fled to her Dolabella!
Die, traitor! I revoke my promise! die!
                    (*Going to kill him*)
ALEX. Oh, hold! she is not fled.
ANT. She is! My eyes
Are open to her falsehood; my whole life
Has been a golden dream of love and friend-
ship.
But, now I wake, I'm like a merchant, roused
From soft repose to see his vessel sinking
And all his wealth cast o'er. Ingrateful
woman!
Who followed me but as the swallow sum-
mer,
Hatching her young ones in my kindly
beams,
Singing her flatt'ries to my morning wake;
But, now my winter comes, she spreads her
wings
And seeks the spring of Cæsar.
ALEX. Think not so.
Her fortunes have in all things mixed with
yours.
Had she betrayed her naval force to Rome,

How easily might she have gone to Cæsar,
Secure by such a bribe!
VENT. She sent it first,
To be more welcome after.
ANT. 'Tis too plain;
Else would she have appeared to clear herself.
ALEX. Too fatally she has. She could not
bear
To be accused by you, but shut herself
Within her monument; looked down and
sighed;
While, from her unchanged face, the silent
tears
Dropped, as they had not leave, but stole
their parting.
Some undistinguished words she inly mur-
mured;
At last, she raised her eyes, and with such
looks
As dying Lucrece cast——
ANT. My heart forebodes——
VENT. All for the best; go on.
ALEX. She snatched her poniard,
And, ere we could prevent the fatal blow,
Plunged it within her breast. Then turned
to me:
"Go, bear my lord," said she, "my last fare-
well,
And ask him if he yet suspect my faith."
More she was saying, but death rushed be-
twixt.
She half pronounced your name with her last
breath,
And buried half within her.
VENT. Heav'n be praised!
ANT. Then art thou innocent, my poor
dear love,
And art thou dead?
Oh, those two words! their sound should be
divided.
Hadst thou been false, and died; or hadst
thou lived,
And hadst been true.—But innocence and
death!
This shows not well above. Then what am I,
The murderer of this truth, this innocence!
Thoughts cannot form themselves in words
so horrid
As can express my guilt!
VENT. Is't come to this? The gods have
been too gracious,
And thus you thank 'em for't!
ANT. (*To* ALEX.) Why stay'st thou here?

Is it for thee to spy upon my soul,
And see its inward mourning? Get thee
    hence!
Thou are not worthy to behold what now
Becomes a Roman emperor to perform.
    ALEX. (*Aside*) He loves her still:
His grief betrays it. Good! The joy to find
She's yet alive completes the reconcilement.
I've saved myself and her. But, oh! the
    Romans!
Fate comes too fast upon my wit,
Hunts me too hard, and meets me at each
    double.   (*Exit*)
    VENT. Would she had died a little sooner,
    though,
Before Octavia went; you might have treated.
Now 'twill look tame, and would not be
    received.
Come, rouse yourself, and let's die warm
    together.
    ANT. I will not fight; there's no more work
    for war.
The bus'ness of my angry hours is done.
    VENT. Cæsar is at your gates.
    ANT. Why, let him enter;
He's welcome now.
    VENT. What lethargy has crept into your
    soul?
    ANT. 'Tis but a scorn of life and just desire
To free myself from bondage.
    VENT. Do it bravely.
    ANT. I will, but not by fighting. O Ven-
    tidius!
What should I fight for now? My queen is
    dead.
I was but great for her; my pow'r, my empire,
Were but my merchandise to buy her love,
And conquered kings, my factors. Now she's
    dead,
Let Cæsar take the world—
An empty circle, since the jewel's gone
Which made it worth my strife. My being's
    nauseous,
For all the bribes of life are gone away.
    VENT. Would you be taken?
    ANT. Yes, I would be taken,
But as a Roman ought—dead, my Ventidius.
For I'll convey my soul from Cæsar's reach,
And lay down life myself. 'Tis time the world
Should have a lord and know whom to obey.
We two have kept its homage in suspense
And bent the globe, on whose each side we
    trod,

Till it was dinted inwards. Let him walk
Alone upon't; I'm weary of my part.
My torch is out, and the world stands before
    me
Like a black desert at th' approach of night.
I'll lay me down, and stray no farther on.
    VENT. I could be grieved,
But that I'll not outlive you. Choose your
    death;
For I have seen him in such various shapes,
I care not which I take. I'm only troubled,
The life I bear is worn to such a rag,
'Tis scarce worth giving. I could wish, indeed,
We threw it from us with a better grace,
That, like two lions taken in the toils,
We might at least thrust out our paws and
    wound
The hunters that inclose us.
    ANT. I have thought on't.
Ventidius, you must live.
    VENT. I must not, sir.
    ANT. Wilt thou not live, to speak some
    good of me?
To stand by my fair fame, and guard th'
    approaches
From the ill tongues of men?
    VENT. Who shall guard mine,
For living after you?
    ANT. Say I command it.
    VENT. If we die well, our deaths will speak
    themselves
And need no living witness.
    ANT. Thou hast loved me,
And fain I would reward thee. I must die.
Kill me, and take the merit of my death
To make thee friends with Cæsar.
    VENT. Thank your kindness.
You said I loved you, and in recompense
You bid me turn a traitor. Did I think
You would have used me thus?—that I should
    die
With a hard thought of you?
    ANT. Forgive me, Roman.
Since I have heard of Cleopatra's death,
My reason bears no rule upon my tongue,
But let's my thoughts break all at random
    out.
I've thought better; do not deny me twice.
    VENT. By heav'n, I will not.
Let it not be t' outlive you.
    ANT. Kill me first,
And then die thou; for 'tis but just thou serve
Thy friend before thyself.

Vent. Give me your hand.
We soon shall meet again. Now, farewell,
    emperor!—   (*Embrace*)
Methinks that word's too cold to be my last.
Since death sweeps all distinctions, farewell,
    friend!
That's all.——
I will not make a bus'ness of a trifle,
And yet I cannot look on you and kill you;
Pray turn your face.
    Ant. I do: strike home, be sure.
    Vent. Home as my sword will reach.
                  (*Kills himself*)
    Ant. Oh, thou mistak'st!
That wound was none of thine; give it me
    back;
Thou robb'st me of my death!
    Vent. I do indeed;
But think 'tis the first time I e'er deceived
    you,
If that may plead my pardon.—And you,
    gods,
Forgive me, if you will; for I die perjured
Rather than kill my friend.   (*Dies*)
    Ant. Farewell! Ever my leader, ev'n in
    death!
My queen and thou have got the start of me,
And I'm the lag of honor.—Gone so soon?
Is Death no more? He used him carelessly,
With a familiar kindness; ere he knocked,
Ran to the door and took him in his arms,
As who should say, "Y'are welcome at all
    hours,
A friend need give no warning." Books had
    spoiled him,
For all the learned are cowards by profession.
'Tis not worth
My farther thought; for death, for aught I
    know,
Is but to think no more. Here's to be satisfied.
               (*Falls on his sword*)
I've missed my heart. O unperforming hand!
Thou never couldst have erred in a worse
    time.
My fortune jades me to the last, and death,
Like a great man, takes state and makes me
    wait
For my admittance.——
             (*Trampling within*)
Some, perhaps, from Cæsar.
If he should find me living, and suspect
That I played booty with my life! I'll mend

My work ere they can reach me.
        (*Rises upon his knees*)

(*Enter* Cleopatra, Charmion, Iras)

    Cleo. Where is my lord! where is he?
    Char. There he lies,
And dead Ventidius by him.
    Cleo. My fears were prophets; I am come
    too late.
Oh, that accursed Alexas!   (*Runs to him*)
    Ant. Art thou living?
Or am I dead before I knew, and thou
The first kind ghost that meets me?
    Cleo. Help me seat him.
Send quickly, send for help!
          (*They place him in a chair*)
    Ant. I am answered.
We live both. Sit thee down, my Cleopatra.
I'll make the most I can of life, to stay
A moment more with thee.
    Cleo. How is it with you?
    Ant. 'Tis as with a man
Removing in a hurry; all packed up,
But one dear jewel that his haste forgot,
And he, for that, returns upon the spur.
So I come back, for thee.
    Cleo. Too long, you heav'ns, you have
    been cruel to me;
Now show your mended faith and give me
    back
His fleeting life!
    Ant. It will not be, my love.
I keep my soul by force.
Say but thou art not false.
    Cleo. 'Tis now too late
To say I'm true: I'll prove it, and die with
    you.
Unknown to me, Alexas feigned my death;
Which, when I knew, I hasted to prevent
This fatal consequence. My fleet betrayed
Both you and me.
    Ant. And Dolabella——
    Cleo. Scarce
Esteemed before he loved; but hated now.
    Ant. Enough: my life's not long enough
    for more.
Thou say'st thou wilt come after. I believe
    thee;
For I can now believe whate'er thou sayst
That we may part more kindly.
    Cleo. I will come.
Doubt not, my life, I'll come, and quickly too.

Cæsar shall triumph o'er no part of thee.

ANT. But grieve not, while thou stay'st,
My last disastrous times.
Think we have had a clear and glorious day,
And heav'n did kindly to delay the storm,
Just till our close of ev'ning. Ten years' love,
And not a moment lost, but all improved
To th' utmost joys!—What ages have we
    lived!
And now to die each other's; and, so dying,
While hand in hand we walk in groves
    below,
Whole troops of lovers' ghosts shall flock
    about us,
And all the train be ours.

CLEO. Your words are like the notes of
    dying swans,
Too sweet to last. Were there so many hours
For your unkindness, and not one for love?

ANT. No, not a minute.—This one kiss—
    more worth
Than all I leave to Cæsar.   (Dies)

CLEO. Oh, tell me so again,
And take ten thousand kisses for that word.
My lord, my lord! speak, if you yet have
    being;
Sigh to me, if you cannot speak; or cast
One look! Do anything that shows you live.

IRAS. He's gone too far to hear you;
And this you see, a lump of senseless clay,
The leavings of a soul.

CHAR. Remember, madam,
He charged you not to grieve.

CLEO. And I'll obey him.
I have not loved a Roman not to know
What should become his wife; his wife, my
    Charmion,
For 'tis to that high title I aspire,
And now I'll not die less! Let dull Octavia
Survive, to mourn him dead. My nobler fate
Shall knit our spousals with a tie too strong
For Roman laws to break.

IRAS. Will you then die?

CLEO. Why shouldst thou make that question?

IRAS. Cæsar is merciful.

CLEO. Let him be so
To those that want his mercy; my poor lord
Made no such cov'nant with him, to spare me
When he was dead. Yield me to Cæsar's
    pride?
What! to be led in triumph through the
    streets,

A spectacle to base plebian eyes,
While some dejected friend of Antony's,
Close in a corner, shakes his head and mut-
    ters
A secret curse on her who ruined him?
I'll none of that.

CHAR. Whatever you resolve,
I'll follow, ev'n to death.

IRAS. I only feared
For you, but more should fear to live without
    you.

CLEO. Why, now 'tis as it should be.
    Quick, my friends,
Dispatch; ere this, the town's in Cæsar's
    hands.
My lord looks down concerned and fears my
    stay,
Lest I should be surprised;
Keep him not waiting for his love too long.
You, Charmion, bring my crown and richest
    jewels;
With 'em, the wreath of victory I made
(Vain augury!) for him who now lies dead.
You, Iras, bring the cure of all our ills.

IRAS. The aspics, madam?

CLEO. Must I bid you twice?
            (Exeunt CHARMION and IRAS)
'Tis sweet to die when they would force life
    on me,
To rush into the dark abode of Death
And seize him first; if he be like my love,
He is not frightful, sure.
We're now alone, in secrecy and silence;
And is not this like lovers? I may kiss
These pale, cold lips; Octavia does not see
    me.
And, oh! 'tis better far to have him thus
Than see him in her arms.—(Enter CHAR-
    MION and IRAS) Oh, welcome, wel-
    come!

CHAR. What must be done?

CLEO. Short ceremony, friends,
But yet it must be decent. First, this laurel
Shall crown my hero's head: he fell not
    basely,
Nor left his shield behind him.—Only thou
Couldst triumph o'er thyself, and thou alone
Wert worthy so to triumph.

CHAR. To what end
These ensigns of your pomp and royalty?

CLEO. Dull that thou art! why, 'tis to
    meet my love,
As when I saw him first on Cydnos' bank,

All sparkling, like a goddess. So adorned,
I'll find him once again; my second spousals
Shall match my first in glory. Haste, haste, both,
And dress the bride of Antony.
    (*They put her crown and jewels on her*)
    CHAR. 'Tis done.
    CLEO. Now seat me by my lord. I claim
this place;
For I must conquer Cæsar too, like him,
And win my share o' th' world.—Hail, you dear relics
Of my immortal love!
Oh, let no impious hand remove you hence;
But rest for ever here! Let Egypt give
His death that peace which it denied his life.—
Reach me the casket.
    IRAS. Underneath the fruit
The aspic lies.
    CLEO. (*Putting aside the leaves*) Welcome, thou kind deceiver!
Thou best of thieves, who with an easy key
Dost open life and, unperceived by us,
Ev'n steal us from ourselves; discharging so
Death's dreadful office better than himself,
Touching our limbs so gently into slumber
That Death stands by, deceived by his own image,
And thinks himself but Sleep.
    SERAP. (*Within*) The queen, where is she?
The town is yielded, Cæsar's at the gates.
    CLEO. He comes too late t' invade the rights of death.
Haste, bare my arm, and rouse the serpent's fury.
    (*Holds out her arm, and draws it back*)
Coward flesh,
Wouldst thou conspire with Cæsar to betray me,
As thou wert none of mine? I'll force thee to't,
And not be sent by him,
But bring, myself, my soul to Antony.
    (*Turns aside, and then shows her arm bloody*)
Take hence; the work is done.
    SERAP. (*Within*) Break ope the door
And guard the traitor well.
    CHAR. The next is ours.

    IRAS. Now, Charmion, to be worthy
Of our great queen and mistress.
        (*They apply the aspics*)
    CLEO. Already, death, I feel thee in my veins.
I go with such a will to find my lord
That we shall quickly meet.
A heavy numbness creeps through every limb,
And now 'tis at my head; my eyelids fall,
And my dear love is vanished in a mist.
Where shall I find him, where? Oh, turn me to him,
And lay me on his breast!—Cæsar, thy worst;
Now part us, if thou canst.   (*Dies*)
(IRAS *sinks down at her feet, and dies;* CHARMION *stands behind her chair, as dressing her head*)

(*Enter* SERAPION, *two* PRIESTS, ALEXAS *bound, Egyptians*)

    2 PRIESTS. Behold, Serapion,
What havoc death has made!
    SERAP. 'Twas what I feared.—
Charmion, is this well done?
    CHAR. Yes, 'tis well done, and like a queen, the last
Of her great race. I follow her.
        (*Sinks down and dies*)
    ALEX. 'Tis true,
She has done well. Much better thus to die,
Than live to make a holiday in Rome.
    SERAP. See, see how the lovers sit in state together,
As they were giving laws to half mankind!
Th' impression of a smile, left in her face,
Shows she died pleased with him for whom she lived,
And went to charm him in another world.
Cæsar's just ent'ring: grief has now no leisure.
Secure that villain, as our pledge of safety,
To grace th' imperial triumph.—Sleep, blessed pair,
Secure from human chance, long ages out,
While all the storms of fate fly o'er your tomb;

And fame to late posterity shall tell
No lovers lived so great, or died so well.

Epilogue

Poets, like disputants when reasons fail,
Have one sure refuge left—and that's to rail.
Fop, coxcomb, fool, are thundered through
    the pit;
And this is all their equipage of wit.
We wonder how the devil this diff'rence
    grows
Betwixt our fools in verse, and yours in prose:
For, 'faith, the quarrel rightly understood,
'Tis civil war with their own flesh and blood.
The threadbare author hates the gaudy coat,
And swears at the gilt coach, but swears afoot.
For 'tis observed of every scribbling man,
He grows a fop as fast as e'er he can;
Prunes up, and asks his oracle, the glass,
If pink or purple best become his face.
For our poor wretch, he neither rails nor
    prays;
Nor likes your wit just as you like his plays;
He has not yet so much of Mr. Bayes.

He does his best; and if he cannot please,
Would quietly sue out his writ of ease.
Yet, if he might his own grand jury call,
By the fair sex he begs to stand or fall.
Let Cæsar's pow'r the men's ambition move,
But grace you him who lost the world for
    love!
Yet if some antiquated lady say,
The last age is not copied in his play,
Heav'n help the man who for that face must
    drudge,
Which only has the wrinkles of a judge.
Let not the young and beauteous join with
    those;
For should you raise such numerous hosts of
    foes,
Young wits and sparks he to his aid must
    call;
'Tis more than one man's work to please you
    all.

WILLIAM CONGREVE

Love for Love

~~~~~~~~~~~~~~~~

PRINCIPAL EVENTS IN CONGREVE'S LIFE

1670, 10 Feb., William, son of William Congreve, an army officer, was baptized at Bardsey, near Leeds. The Congreve family had lived in the county of Staffordshire for more than three hundred years.

c. 1674, William Congreve, Sr., was made commander of the English garrison at Youghal, in Ireland, and took his family with him.

c. 1681, Young Congreve was entered at Kilkenny School, where Jonathan Swift was for a time one of his school fellows.

1685, April, He entered Trinity College, Dublin.

c. 1688, The family returned to England after William Congreve, Sr., inherited his father's estate. The young William Congreve apparently lived with his family in the country for about two years.

1691, March, Congreve was entered in the Middle Temple and began to enjoy the fashionable life of London.

1692, His novel *Incognita* was published.

1693, Jan., Congreve's first play, *The Old Bachelor,* written two or three years before and revised with the help of John Dryden, was acted with sensational success at the Drury Lane Theatre. The success of the play made Congreve one of the most admired literary figures in London.

1693, Dryden's translation of Juvenal and Persius, in which Congreve had assisted, was published.

1693, Nov., Congreve's second comedy, *The Double Dealer,* was acted at Drury Lane. Many spectators objected to the keenness of the satire, and it was not so popular as *The Old Bachelor* had been.

1694, The Double Dealer was published with highly commendatory verses by John Dryden.

1695, 30 April, His *Love for Love* was acted as the opening play by the new company at the new Duke's Theatre in Lincoln's Inn Fields. The play was a great success.

1695, May, Congreve was made one of three Commissioners for Hackney Coaches; the office was a sinecure.

1696, Congreve's *Essay on Humour in Comedy,* written the previous year as a letter to John Dennis, published in Dennis's *Letters upon Several Occasions.*

1697, Feb., Congreve's only tragedy, *The Mourning Bride,* was acted at the Duke's Theatre in Lincoln's Inn Fields. It became the most fashionable tragedy of its time and was regularly performed in repertory for more than one hundred years.

1698, Congreve published a pamphlet in reply to Jeremy Collier's *A Short View of the Immorality and Profaneness of the English Stage.*

1700, March, The Way of the World was acted at the Duke's Theatre in Lincoln's Inn Fields. Though it was the wittiest play of its time, it was not very successful in its first run.

1701, Congreve's short masque, *The Judgment of Paris*, published. It had been written for musicians in a musical competition.

1704, March, An adaptation of Molière's *Monsieur Pourceaugnac* called *Squire Trelooby,* by Congreve, Vanbrugh, and Walsh, was acted.

1705, April, Congreve joined Vanbrugh in the joint management of the new theatre in the Haymarket.

1705, Dec., Congreve made Commissioner of Wine Licenses, another sinecure.

1710, A collected edition of Congreve's plays and poems published in three volumes.

1714, Dec., Congreve made one of the Searchers of Customs and later Secretary of Jamaica.

1720, Pope dedicated his *Iliad* to Congreve.

1729, 19 Jan., Congreve died. A week later he was buried in Westminster Abbey with great ceremony.

INTRODUCTION

The Restoration audience for which Congreve and his contemporary playwrights wrote was a very restricted one: the middle classes and the lower classes generally stayed away from the theatres, and the plays were written primarily for the courtiers and the gentry and their parasites, male and female. The subject matter and the appeal for such an audience were naturally limited, and as a consequence the drama displays much less variety than the Elizabethan. The principal subject matter of the comedies is love and seduction, and the most popular appeal is wit and satire. Given these restrictions, the Restoration comedy of manners is a brilliant achievement. The principal comic dramatists of the time, Sir George Etheredge, William Wycherley, William Congreve, Sir John Vanbrugh, and George Farquhar, are among the most distinguished writers of this form of comedy in English; Congreve is the most accomplished of them all.

Love for Love exhibits the same basic attitudes as most other Restoration comedies of manners—preoccupation with the game of courtship and seduction, amusement at eccentricities and variations from the polished norm of select society, delight in intrigue, and very little interest in moral values. Congreve lavishes most of his skill on dialogue and character, but he has a very special purpose in mind. The dialogue is intended to be the most scintillating type of conversation, graceful, witty, allusive, spirited, and personal. It is not designed primarily to convey ideas, much of it does not

pretend to advance the plot, and neither dramatist nor audience had any notion that it was a transcript of life. Many persons in the Restoration audience would have liked to talk as these characters did, and perhaps a few of them could on occasion, but none believed that any group ever continued to talk for three hours as wittily and as subtly as the characters in Mr. Congreve's play.

The dramatist's interest in character is also of a limited and peculiar type. He was not trying for detailed and profound analysis like Shakespeare's, nor flashes of insight like Webster's, nor the castigation of vices like Jonson's. Congreve wanted to set forth those foibles and petty vices, those mental quirks and peccadillos, which make people amusing to watch—amusing, that is, so long as one does not have too much sympathy or is not himself forced to live with them. His satire is directed against such minor traits, and his characters are built up out of them. The superstition of Foresight, the salacious garrulity of Tattle, the hoyden amorousness of Miss Prue, were more interesting to Congreve and the audience at Lincoln's Inn Fields than more fundamental qualities. Superficially these interests sound somewhat like Jonson's, but Congreve had none of Jonson's moral earnestness, none of his deep concern with the social functions of the drama.

In *Love for Love* Congreve has masterfully fused his dual interests in dialogue and character. Not only are the more conspicuous peccadillos of certain characters, like Tattle and Mrs. Frail, frequently the subject of witty sallies in the dialogue, but the speakers themselves often exhibit their own foibles unconsciously through their own wit. Tattle does so when he says, "Why there, as I hope to be saved, I believe a woman only obliges a man to secrecy that she may have the pleasure of telling herself." Cunningly devised lines like these, which enable a sophisticated audience to laugh first at the witty observation itself, second at the revelation of the speaker's idea of pleasure, and finally at the spectacle of a self-conscious character unconsciously exposing himself, are a hall-mark of Congreve's genius at comic dialogue.

Such an interest in affectations and follies and in clever, sophisticated dialogue is characteristic of the Restoration comedy of manners. No English dramatist has ever handled the type more brilliantly than William Congreve.

LOVE FOR LOVE

Dramatis personae

In order of first appearance

VALENTINE, A handsome, witty, extravagant man-about-town, son of Sir Sampson Legend. He has spent his fortune in gay living and in the pursuit of Angelica.

JEREMY, His servant, sophisticated and urbane, with a knack for fine phrases and witty turns, knowing and cynical but loyal to his master.

SCANDAL, A friend of Valentine's, like him a man-about-town; disillusioned and cynical, a misogynist, with a clever, biting tongue and a jaundiced view of human nature.

TRAPLAND, A loan broker to whom Valentine is deeply in debt.

MR. SNAP, An officer brought by Trapland to arrest Valentine for Sir Sampson.

TATTLE, A silly young man whose chief ambition is to dress the dandy and act the gay seducer; he pretends to more confidences than he has received, reveals them in the guise of secrecy, and boasts of his feigned conquests while affecting modesty and discretion.

MRS.[1] FRAIL, Lively, quick-tongued, light-minded, devoted to the pleasures of society and determined, for the convenience of it, to get a husband.

FORESIGHT, Angelica's uncle, a foolish old fellow, peevish and positive, superstitious, devoted to Astrology, Palmistry, Physiognomy, Omens, Dreams, etc.

NURSE, A privileged old Foresight retainer, simple-minded and easily fussed, free and vulgar in her speech.

ANGELICA, The beautiful, witty, intelligent niece of Foresight, whose considerable fortune in her own right both makes her a desirable catch and gives her independence of importunity.

SIR SAMPSON LEGEND, Father of Valentine and Ben, choleric, opinionated, and stubborn, too dazzled by his own good opinion of himself to see when he is being made a fool of.

MRS. FORESIGHT, Old Foresight's second wife, young, pretty, fond of gaiety and society, sophisticated and seducible.

MISS PRUE, Foresight's daughter by his first wife, who has just come up from the country. She is a young hoyden full of naiveté and gusto who romps through the artifices of London society life with untamed heartiness.

BEN LEGEND, Sir Sampson's younger son and brother to Valentine. His years at sea have kept from him the polish of sophistication and made him bluff, hearty, and simple; he is good-natured and direct.

JENNY, Angelica's maid.

BUCKRAM, Sir Sampson's lawyer.

Steward, officers (i.e., policemen), sailors, musicians, and servants.

[1] The term "Mrs." was used for both married and unmarried women in the time.

SCENE: London

Prologue

Spoken at the Opening of the New House,
By Mr. Betterton

The husbandman in vain renews his toil,
To cultivate each year a hungry soil;
And fondly hopes for rich and generous
    fruit,
When what should feed the tree, devours
    the root:
Th' unladen boughs, he sees, bode certain
    dearth,
Unless transplanted to more kindly earth.
So, the poor husbands of the stage, who
    found
Their labors lost upon ungrateful ground,
This last and only remedy have proved;
And hope new fruit from ancient stocks
    removed.
Well may they hope, when you so kindly
    aid,
Well plant a soil which you so rich have
    made.
As Nature gave the world to man's first
    age,
So from your bounty, we receive this stage;
The freedom man was born to, you've⌉
    restored, |
And to our world, such plenty you afford, }
It seems like *Eden*, fruitful of its own |
    accord.   ⌋
But since in *Paradise* frail flesh gave way,
And when but two were made, both went
    astray,
Forebear your wonder, and the fault for-⌉
    give,   }
If in our larger family we grieve |
One falling *Adam*, and one tempted *Eve*. ⌋

We who remain, would gratefully repay ⌉
What our endeavors can, and bring, this |
    day,   }
The first-fruit offering, of a virgin play. ⌋
We hope there's something that may ⌉
    please each taste, |
And tho' of homely fare we make the }
    feast, |
Yet you will find variety at least. ⌋
There's humor, which for cheerful friends
    we got,
And for the thinking party there's a plot.
We've something too, to gratify ill nature,
(If there be any here) and that is Satire.
Tho' Satire scarce dares grin, 'tis grown so
    mild
Or only shews its teeth, as if it smiled.
As asses thistles, poets mumble wit,
And dare not bite, for fear of being bit.
They hold their pens, as swords are held by
    fools,
And are afraid to use their own edge-tools.
Since the *Plain-Dealer's* scenes of manly
    rage,
Not one has dared to lash this crying age.
This time, the poet owns the bold essay,
Yet hopes there's no ill-manners in his play:
And he declares by me, he has designed
Affront to none, but frankly speaks his mind.
And should th'ensuing scenes not chance ⌉
    to hit, |
He offers but this one excuse, 'twas writ }
Before your late encouragement of wit. ⌋

Act I

VALENTINE'S *Lodging.*

(VALENTINE *in negligent costume reading
at a table on which a number of books are
piled.* JEREMY *waiting*)

VAL. Jeremy.

JERE. Sir.

VAL. Here, take away; I'll walk a turn,
and digest what I have read——

JERE. (*Aside*) You'll grow devilish fat
upon this paper diet. (*He takes away the*

books. VALENTINE *strides up and down.*)

VAL. And d'ye hear, go you to break-fast——There's a page doubled down in Epictetus, that is a feast for an emperor.

JERE. Was Epictetus a real cook, or did he only write receipts?

VAL. Read, read, sirrah, and refine your appetite; learn to live upon instruction; feast your mind, and mortify your flesh; read, and take your nourishment in at your eyes; shut up your mouth, and chew the cud of understanding. So Epictetus advises.

JERE. O Lord! I have heard much of him, when I waited upon a gentleman at Cambridge. Pray what was that Epictetus?

VAL. A very rich man,—not worth a groat.

JERE. Humph, and so he has made a very fine feast, where there is nothing to be eaten.

VAL. Yes.

JERE. Sir, you're a gentleman, and prob-ably understand this fine feeding: but if you please, I had rather be at board-wages. Does your Epictetus, or your Seneca here, or any of these poor rich rogues, teach you how to pay your debts without money? Will they shut up the mouths of your creditors? Will Plato be bail for you? Or Diogenes, because he understands confinement, and lived in a tub, go to prison for you? 'Slife, sir, what do you mean, to mew your self up here with three or four musty books, in commendation of starving and poverty?

VAL. Why, sirrah, I have no money, you know it; and therefore resolve to rail at all that have. And in that I but follow the ex-amples of the wisest and wittiest men in all ages—these poets and philosophers whom you naturally hate, for just such another rea-son: because they abound in sense, and you are a fool.

JERE. Ay, sir, I am a fool, I know it. And yet, heav'n help me, I'm poor enough to be a wit. But I was always a fool, when I told you what your expenses would bring you to; your coaches and your liveries; your treats and your balls; your being in love with a lady, that did not care a farthing for you in your prosperity; and keeping company with wits, that cared for nothing but your pros-perity; and now when you are poor, hate you as much as they do one another.

VAL. Well, and now I am poor, I have an opportunity to be reveng'd on them all. I'll pursue Angelica with more love than ever, and appear more notoriously her admirer in this restraint, than when I openly rivaled the rich fops that made court to her; so shall my poverty be a mortification to her pride and, perhaps, make her compassionate the love which has principally reduced me to this low-ness of fortune. And for the wits, I'm sure I am in a condition to be even with them.

JERE. Nay, your condition is pretty even with theirs, that's the truth on't.

VAL. I'll take some of their trade out of their hands.

JERE. Now heav'n of mercy continue the tax upon paper; you don't mean to write!

VAL. Yes, I do; I'll write a play.

JERE. Hem! (*Distantly*) Sir, if you please to give me a small certificate of three lines ——only to certify those whom it may con-cern; that the bearer hereof, Jeremy Fetch by name, has for the space of seven years truly and faithfully served Valentine Legend, Esq.; and that he is not now turned away for any misdemeanor, but does voluntarily dismiss his master from any future authority over him—

VAL. No, sirrah, you shall live with me still.

JERE. Sir, it's impossible—I may die with you, starve with you, or be damned with your works; but to live, even three days, the life of a play, I no more expect it, than to be canonized for a Muse after my decease.

VAL. You are witty, you rogue! I shall want your help—I'll have you learn to make couplets, to tag the ends of acts. D'ye hear, get the maids to Crambo[2] in an eve-ning, and learn the knack of rhyming. You may arrive at the height of a song sent by an unknown hand, or a chocolate-house lam-poon.

JERE. But sir, is this the way to recover your father's favor? Why, Sir Sampson will be irreconcilable. If your younger brother should come from sea, he'd never look upon you again. You're undone, sir; you're ruined; you won't have a friend left in the world, if you turn poet.——Ah, pox confound that Will's coffee-house,[3] it has ruined more young

[2] A game in which one player gives a word to which each of the others has to find a rhyme.

[3] A favorite gathering-place for authors and wits after the Restoration. Its popularity con-tinued into the 18th century.

men than the Royal Oak Lottery—nothing thrives that belongs to't. The man of the house would have been an Alderman by this time with half the trade, if he had set up in the City. For my part, I never sit at the door, that I don't get double the stomach that I do at a horse race—the air upon Banstead-Downs is nothing to it for a whetter. Yet I never see it, but the Spirit of Famine appears to me: sometimes like a decayed porter, worn out with pimping, and carrying *billet doux* and songs, not like other porters for hire, but for the jest's sake; now like a thin chairman, melted down to half his proportion with carrying a poet upon tick to visit some great fortune, and his fare to be paid him like the wages of sin, either at the day of marriage, or the day of death.

VAL. Very well, sir; can you proceed?

JERE. Sometimes like a bilked bookseller, with a meagre terrified countenance, that looks as if he had written for himself, or were resolved to turn author, and bring the rest of his brethren into the same condition. And lastly, in the form of a worn-out punk,[4] with verses in her hand which her vanity had preferred to settlements, without a whole tatter to her tail, but as ragged as one of the Muses; or as if she were carrying her linen to the paper-mill, to be converted into folio books of warning to all young maids, not to prefer poetry to good sense, or lying in the arms of a needy wit, before the embraces of a wealthy fool.

(*Enter* SCANDAL)

SCAN. What, Jeremy holding forth?

VAL. The rogue has (with all the wit he could muster up) been declaiming against wit.

SCAN. Ay? Why then I'm afraid Jeremy has wit: for whatever it is, it's always contriving its own ruin.

JERE. Why, so I have been telling my master, sir. Mr. Scandal, for Heaven's sake, sir, try if you can dissuade him from turning poet.

SCAN. Poet! He shall turn soldier first, and rather depend upon the outside of his head than the lining. Why, what the devil, has not your poverty made you enemies

[4] Prostitute.

enough? Must you needs show your wit to get more?

JERE. Ay, more indeed; for who cares for any body that has more wit than himself?

SCAN. Jeremy speaks like an oracle. Don't you see how worthless great men, and dull rich rogues, avoid a witty man of small fortune? Why, he looks like a writ of enquiry into their titles and estates, and seems commissioned by Heaven to seize the better half.

VAL. Therefore I would rail in my writings, and be revenged.

SCAN. Rail? At whom? the whole world? Impotent and vain! Who would die a martyr to sense in a country where the religion is folly? You may stand at bay for a while; but when the full cry is against you, you shan't have fair play for your life. If you can't be fairly run down by the hounds, you will be treacherously shot by the huntsmen.—No, turn pimp, flatterer, quack, lawyer, parson; be chaplain to an atheist, or stallion to an old woman—any thing but poet. A modern poet is worse, more servile, timorous, and fawning, than any I have named, without you could retrieve the ancient honors of the name, recall the stage of Athens, and be allowed the force of open honest satire.

VAL. You are as inveterate against our poets as if your character had been lately exposed upon the stage.——Nay, I am not violently bent upon the trade.——(*A knock at the door*) Jeremy, see who's there. (JEREMY *goes out*) But tell me what you would have me do?——What does the world say of me and my forced confinement?

SCAN. The world behaves itself as it uses to do on such occasions: some pity you, and condemn your father; others excuse him, and blame you; only the ladies are merciful, and wish you well, since love and pleasurable expense have been your greatest faults.

(*Re-enter* JEREMY)

VAL. How now?

JERE. Nothing new, sir. I have dispatched some half a dozen duns with as much dexterity as a hungry judge does causes at dinner time.

VAL. What answer have you given 'em?

SCAN. Patience, I suppose, the old receipt.

JERE. No, faith, sir; I have put 'em off so long with patience and forbearance and other fair words, that I was forced now to tell 'em in plain downright English——

VAL. What?

JERE. That they should be paid.

VAL. When?

JERE. Tomorrow.

VAL. And how the devil do you mean to keep your word?

JERE. Keep it? Not at all; it has been so very much stretched, that I reckon it will break of course by tomorrow, and nobody be surprised at the matter. (*Knocking*)—Again! Sir, if you don't like my negotiation, will you be pleased to answer these yourself.

VAL. See who they are.   (*Exit* JEREMY)

VAL. By this, Scandal, you may see what it is to be great! Secretaries of State, Presidents of the Council, and generals of an army lead just such a life as I do, have just such crowds of visitants in a morning, all soliciting of past promises, which are but a civiller sort of duns, that lay claim to voluntary debts.

SCAN. And you, like a true great man, having engaged their attendance, and promised more than ever you intended to perform, are more perplexed to find evasions than you would be to invent the honest means of keeping your word and gratifying your creditors.

VAL. Scandal, learn to spare your friends, and do not provoke your enemies; this liberty of your tongue, will one day bring a confinement on your body, my friend.

(*Enter* JEREMY)

JERE. O, sir, there's Trapland the scrivener, with two suspicious fellows like lawful pads, that would knock a man down with pocket-tipstaves. And there's your father's steward, and the nurse with one of your children from Twitnam.

VAL. Pox on her, could she find no other time to fling my sins in my face? Here, give her this (*Gives money*), and bid her trouble me no more. (*To* SCANDAL) A thoughtless, two-handed whore, she knows my condition well enough, and might have overlaid the child a fortnight ago, if she had had any forecast in her.

SCAN. What, is it bouncing Margery, with my godson?

JERE. Yes, sir.

SCAN. My blessing to the boy, with this token (*Gives money*) of my love. And, d'ye hear, bid Margery put more flocks in her bed, shift twice a week, and not work so hard, that she may not smell so vigorously.——I shall take the air shortly.

VAL. Scandal, don't spoil my boy's milk! ——(*To* JEREMY) Bid Trapland come in. (*Exit* JEREMY) If I can give that Cerberus a sop, I shall be at rest for one day.

(JEREMY *ushers in* TRAPLAND)

VAL. O Mr. Trapland! my old friend! Welcome. Jeremy, a chair quickly: a bottle of sack and a toast—fly—a chair first.

TRAP. A good morning to you, Mr. Valentine, and to you, Mr. Scandal.

SCAN. The morning's a very good morning, if you don't spoil it.

VAL. Come sit you down, you know his way.

TRAP. (*Sits*) There is a debt, Mr. Valentine, of £1500 of pretty long standing——

VAL. I cannot talk about business with a thirsty palate.——Sirrah, the sack. (JEREMY *brings the glasses and wine*)

TRAP. And I desire to know what course you have taken for the payment?

VAL. Faith and troth, I am heartily glad to see you,——my service to you, (JEREMY *fills the glasses*)—fill, fill, to honest Mr. Trapland——fuller.

TRAP. Hold, sweetheart.——This is not to our business.——My service to you, Mr. Scandal—(*Drinks*)—I have forborn as long—

VAL. T'other glass, and then we'll talk. Fill, Jeremy.

TRAP. No more, in truth.—I have forborn, I say—

VAL. (*To* JEREMY) Sirrah, fill when I bid you.——And how does your handsome daughter?——Come, a good husband to her.

(*Drinks*)

TRAP. Thank you——I have been out of this money——

VAL. Drink first. Scandal, why do you not drink?   (*They drink*)

TRAP. And in short, I can be put off no longer.

VAL. I was much obliged to you for your supply: it did me signal service in my necessity. But you delight in doing good.—Scandal, drink to me, my friend Trapland's health. An honester man lives not, nor one more ready to serve his friend in distress, tho' I say it to his face. Come, fill each man his glass.

SCAN. What, I know Trapland has been a whoremaster, and loves a wench still. You never knew a whoremaster that was not an honest fellow.

TRAP. Fie, Mr. Scandal, you never knew—

SCAN. What don't I know?——I know the buxom black widow in the Poultry—£800 a year jointure, and £20,000 in money. Ahah, old Trap!

VAL. Say you so, i'faith! Come, we'll remember the widow: I know whereabouts you are; come, to the widow—(*Fills the glasses*)

TRAP. No more, indeed.

VAL. What, the widow's health! give it him—off with it. (*They drink*) A lovely girl, i'faith, black sparkling eyes, soft pouting ruby-lips? better sealing there, than a bond for a million, hah!

TRAP. No, no, there's no such thing, we'd better mind our business—(*Suddenly succumbs to the wine and their raillery*) you're a wag.

VAL. No faith, we'll mind the widow's business, fill again. Pretty round heaving breasts, a Barbary shape, and a jut with her bum would stir an anchorite. And the prettiest foot! Oh, if a man could but fasten his eyes to her feet, as they steal in and out, and play at Bo-peep under her petticoats! ah, Mr. Trapland?

TRAP. Verily, give me a glass,—you're a wag,——and here's to the widow. (*Drinks*)

SCAN. He begins to chuckle; ply him close, or he'll relapse into a dun.

(*Enter* SNAP)

SNAP. By your leave, gentlemen.——Mr. Trapland, if we must do our office, tell us. We have half a dozen gentlemen to arrest in Pall-Mall and Covent-Garden; and if we don't make haste, the chairmen will be abroad and block up the chocolate-houses, and then our labor's lost.

TRAP. Udso, that's true. Mr. Valentine,

I love mirth, but business must be done. Are you ready to——

JERE. (*Coming from the door*) Sir, your father's steward says he comes to make proposals concerning your debts.

VAL. Bid him come in.—Mr. Trapland, send away your officer; you shall have an answer presently.

TRAP. Mr. Snap, stay within call.

(*Exit* SNAP)

(*Enter* STEWARD. *He and* VALENTINE *go to one side and talk quietly*)

SCAN. Here's a dog now, a traitor in his wine. (*To* TRAPLAND) Sirrah, refund the sack. Jeremy, fetch him some warm water, or I'll rip up his stomach and go the shortest way to his conscience.

TRAP. Mr. Scandal, you are uncivil; I did not value your sack; but you cannot expect it again, when I have drunk it.

SCAN. And how do you expect to have your money again, when a gentleman has spent it?

VAL. (*Coming forward, to* STEWARD) You need say no more, I understand the conditions; they are very hard, but my necessity is very pressing: I agree to 'em. Take Mr. Trapland with you, and let him draw the writing.—Mr. Trapland, you know this man; he shall satisfy you.

TRAP. Sincerely, I am loth to be thus pressing, but my necessity—

VAL. No apology, good Mr. Scrivener, you shall be paid.

TRAP. I hope you forgive me, my business requires—

(JEREMY *ushers out* STEWARD *and* TRAPLAND, *the latter bowing and scraping*)

SCAN. He begs pardon like a hangman at an execution.

VAL. But I have got a reprieve.

SCAN. I am surprised; what, does your father relent?

VAL. No; he has sent me the hardest conditions in the world. You have heard of a booby brother of mine, that was sent to sea three years ago? This brother, my father hears, is landed; whereupon he very affectionately sends me word, if I will make a deed of conveyance of my right to his estate after his death to my younger brother, he will immediately furnish me with four thousand pound to pay my debts, and make my fortune. This was once proposed before, and I refused it; but the present impatience of my creditors for their money, and my own impatience of confinement, and absence from Angelica, force me to consent.

SCAN. A very desperate demonstration of your love to Angelica, and I think she has never given you any assurance of hers.

VAL. You know her temper; she never gave me any great reason either for hope or despair.

SCAN. Women of her airy temper, as they seldom think before they act, so they rarely give us any light to guess at what they mean. But you have little reason to believe that a woman of this age, who has had an indifference for you in your prosperity, will fall in love with your ill fortune; besides, Angelica has a great fortune of her own; and great fortunes either expect another great fortune, or a fool.

(*To them* JEREMY)

JERE. More misfortunes, sir.

VAL. What, another dun?

JERE. No, sir, but Mr. Tattle is come to wait upon you.

VAL. Well, I can't help it, you must bring him up; he knows I don't go abroad.

(*Exit* JEREMY)

SCAN. Pox on him, I'll be gone.

VAL. No, prithee stay. Tattle and you should never be asunder; you are light and shadow, and show one another; he is perfectly thy reverse both in humor and understanding; and as you set up for defamation, he is a mender of reputations.

SCAN. A mender of reputations! Ay, just as he is a keeper of secrets, another virtue that he sets up for in the same manner. For the rogue will speak aloud in the posture of a whisper, and deny a woman's name while he gives you the marks of her person. He will forswear receiving a letter from her, and at the same time show you her hand in the superscription. And yet perhaps he has counterfeited the hand too, and sworn to a truth; but he hopes not to be believed, and refuses the reputation of a lady's favor, as a Doctor says no to a bishopric, only that it may be granted him.—In short, he is a public professor of secrecy, and makes proclamation that he holds private intelligence.——He's here.

(*To them* TATTLE)

TATT. Valentine, good morrow; Scandal, I am yours,——that is, when you speak well of me.

SCAN. That is, when I am yours; for while I am my own, or any body's else, that will never happen.

TATT. How inhuman!

VAL. Why, Tattle, you need not be much concerned at anything that he says; for to converse with Scandal is to play at Losing Loadum;[5] you must lose a good name to him, before you can win it for your self.

TATT. But how barbarous that is, and how unfortunate for him, that the world shall think the better of any person for his calumniation! I thank Heaven, it has always been a part of my character to handle the reputations of others very tenderly indeed.

SCAN. Ay, such rotten reputations as you have to deal with are to be handled tenderly indeed.

TATT. Nay, but why rotten? Why should you say rotten, when you know not the persons of whom you speak? How cruel that is!

SCAN. Not know 'em? Why, thou never hadst to do with anybody that did not stink to all the town.

TATT. Ha, ha, ha! nay, now you make a jest of it indeed. For there is nothing more known, than that nobody knows any thing of that nature of me. As I hope to be saved, Valentine, I never exposed a woman, since I knew what woman was.

VAL. And yet you have conversed with several.

TATT. To be free with you, I have—I don't care if I own that. Nay more (I'm going to say a bold word now) I never could meddle with a woman that had to do with anybody else.

SCAN. How!

VAL. Nay, faith, I'm apt to believe him. Except her husband, Tattle.

TATT. Oh, that——

SCAN. What think you of that noble commoner, Mrs. Drab?

[5] A game of cards in which the loser won the game.

TATT. Pooh, I know Madam Drab has made her brags in three or four places, that I said this and that, and writ to her, and did I know not what. But, upon my reputation, she did me wrong. Well, well, that was malice. But I know the bottom of it. She was bribed to that by one we all know— a man, too. Only to bring me into disgrace with a certain woman of quality.

SCAN. Whom we all know.

TATT. No matter for that. Yes, yes, everybody knows——no doubt on't, everybody knows my secrets. But I soon satisfied the lady of my innocence; for I told her—— Madam, says I, there are some persons who make it their business to tell stories, and say this and that of one and t'other, and every thing in the world; and, says I, if your grace—

SCAN. Grace!

TATT. O Lord, what have I said? My unlucky tongue!

VAL. Ha, ha, ha!

SCAN. Why, Tattle, thou hast more impudence than one can in reason expect: I shall have an esteem for thee. Well, and ha, ha, ha! Well, go on, and what did you say to her grace?

VAL. I confess this is something extraordinary.

TATT. Not a word, as I hope to be saved; an errant *lapsus linguæ*. Come, let's talk of something else.

VAL. Well, but how did you acquit yourself?

TATT. Pooh, pooh, nothing at all, I only rallied with you. A woman of ordinary rank was a little jealous of me, and I told her something or other, faith, I know not what. ——Come, let's talk of something else.

(*Hums a song*)

SCAN. Hang him, let him alone, he has a mind we should inquire.

TATT. Valentine, I supped last night with your mistress and her uncle, old Foresight. I think your father lies at Foresight's.

VAL. Yes.

TATT. Upon my soul, Angelica's a fine woman. And so is Mrs. Foresight, and her sister, Mrs. Frail.

SCAN. Yes, Mrs. Frail is a very fine woman; we all know her.

TATT. Oh, that is not fair.

SCAN. What?

TATT. To tell.

SCAN. To tell what? Why, what do you know of Mrs. Frail?

TATT. Who, I? Upon honor I don't know whether she be man or woman, but by the smoothness of her chin, and roundness of her hips.

SCAN. No!

TATT. No.

SCAN. She says otherwise.

TATT. Impossible!

SCAN. Yes, faith. Ask Valentine else.

TATT. Why then, as I hope to be saved, I believe a woman only obliges a man to secrecy that she may have the pleasure of telling herself.

SCAN. No doubt on't. Well, but has she done you wrong, or no? You have had her? Ha?

TATT. Tho' I have more honor than to tell first, I have more manners than to contradict what a lady has declared.

SCAN. Well, you own it?

TATT. I am strangely surprised! Yes, yes, I can't deny't, if she taxes me with it.

SCAN. She'll be here by and by, she sees Valentine every morning.

TATT. How!

VAL. She does me the favor——I mean of a visit sometimes. I did not think she had granted more to any body.

SCAN. Nor I, faith. But Tattle does not use to belie a lady; it is contrary to his character. How one may be deceived in a woman, Valentine?

TATT. Nay, what do you mean, gentlemen?

SCAN. I'm resolved I'll ask her.

TATT. O barbarous! Why did you not tell me——

SCAN. No, you told us.

TATT. And bid me ask Valentine?

VAL. What did I say? I hope you won't bring me to confess an answer, when you never asked me the question?

TATT. But, gentlemen, this is the most inhuman proceeding——

VAL. Nay, if you have known Scandal thus long, and cannot avoid such a palpable decoy as this was, the ladies have a fine time whose reputations are in your keeping.

(To them JEREMY*)*

JERE. Sir, Mrs. Frail has sent to know if you are stirring.

VAL. Show her up when she comes.

(Exit JEREMY*)*

TATT. *(In alarm)* I'll be gone.

VAL. You'll meet her.

TATT. Is there not a back way?

VAL. If there were, you have more discretion than to give Scandal such an advantage; why, your running away will prove all that he can tell her.

TATT. Scandal, you will not be so ungenerous——O, I shall lose my reputation of secrecy for ever!——I shall never be received but upon public days, and my visits will never be admitted beyond a drawing-room. I shall never see a bed-chamber again, never be locked in a closet, nor run behind a screen, or under a table; never be distinguished among the waiting-women by the name of trusty Mr. Tattle more. You will not be so cruel!

VAL. Scandal, have pity on him; he'll yield to any conditions.

TATT. Any, any terms.

SCAN. Come, then, sacrifice half a dozen women of good reputation to me presently. Come, where are you familiar? And see that they are women of quality too, the first quality—

TATT. 'Tis very hard. Won't a baronet's lady pass?

SCAN. No, nothing under a right honorable.

TATT. O inhuman! You don't expect their names.

SCAN. No, their titles shall serve.

TATT. Alas, that's the same thing. Pray spare me their titles; I'll describe their persons.

SCAN. Well, begin then.—But take notice, if you are so ill a painter, that I cannot know the person by your picture of her, you must be condemned, like other bad painters, to write the name at the bottom.

TATT. Well, first then——

(Enter MRS. FRAIL*)*

TATT. O unfortunate! she's come already;

will you have patience 'till another time—I'll double the number.

SCAN. Well, on that condition. Take heed you don't fail me.

MRS. FRAIL. I shall get a fine reputation, by coming to see fellows in a morning. Scandal, you devil, are you here too? Oh, Mr. Tattle, everything is safe with you, we know.

SCAN. *(Railing)* Tattle!

TATT. *(Aside to him, finger on lip)* Mum.—O madam, you do me too much honor.

VAL. Well, Lady Galloper, how does Angelica?

MRS. FRAIL. Angelica? Manners!

VAL. What, you will allow an absent lover——

MRS. FRAIL. No, I'll allow a lover present with his mistress to be particular. But otherwise I think his passion ought to give place to his manners.

VAL. But what if he has more passion than manners?

MRS. FRAIL. Then let him marry and reform.

VAL. Marriage indeed may qualify the fury of his passion, but it very rarely mends a man's manners.

MRS. FRAIL. You are the most mistaken in the world; there is no creature perfectly civil but a husband. For in a little time he grows only rude to his wife, and that is the highest good breeding, for it begets his civility to other people.—Well, I'll tell you news; but I suppose you hear your brother Benjamin is landed. And my brother Foresight's daughter is come out of the country——I assure you, there's a match talked of by the old people. Well, if he be but as great a sea-beast, as she is a land-monster, we shall have a most amphibious breed. The progeny will be all otters: he has been bred at sea, and she has never been out of the country.

VAL. Pox take 'em, their conjunction bodes me no good, I'm sure.

MRS. FRAIL. Now you talk of conjunction, my brother Foresight has cast both their nativities, and prognosticates an admiral and an eminent justice of the peace to be the issue-male of their two bodies. 'Tis the most superstitious old fool! He would have persuaded me that this was an unlucky day, and would not let me come abroad. But I invented a dream, and sent him to Artimedorus for interpretation, and so stole out to see you. Well, and what will you give me now? Come, I must have something.

VAL. Step into the next room, and I'll give you something.

SCAN. Ay, we'll all give you something.

MRS. FRAIL. Well, what will you all give me?

VAL. Mine's a secret.

MRS. FRAIL. I thought you would give me something that would be a trouble to you to keep.

VAL. And Scandal shall give you a good name.

MRS. FRAIL. That's more than he has for himself. And what will you give me, Mr. Tattle?

TATT. I? My soul, madam.

MRS. FRAIL. Pooh, no I thank you, I have enough to do to take care of my own. Well, but I'll come and see you one of these mornings. I hear you have a great many pictures.

TATT. I have a pretty good collection at your service, some originals.

SCAN. Hang him, he has nothing but the Seasons and the Twelve Cæsars, paltry copies; and the Five Senses, as ill represented as they are in himself; and he himself is the only original you will see there.

MRS. FRAIL. Ay, but I hear he has a closet of beauties.

SCAN. Yes, all that have done him favors, if you will believe him.

MRS. FRAIL. Ay, let me see those, Mr. Tattle.

TATT. Oh, madam, those are sacred to love and contemplation. No man but the painter and myself was ever blest with the sight.

MRS. FRAIL. Well, but a woman——

TATT. Nor woman, 'till she consented to have her picture there too——for then she's obliged to keep the secret.

SCAN. No, no; come to me if you'd see pictures.

MRS. FRAIL. You?

SCAN. Yes, faith, I can show you your own picture, and most of your acquaintance to the life, and as like as at Kneller's.[6]

MRS. FRAIL. O lying creature—Valentine, does not he lie?——I can't believe a word he says.

VAL. No, indeed, he speaks truth now. For as Tattle has pictures of all that have granted him favors, he has the pictures of all that have refused him, if satires, descriptions, characters, and lampoons are pictures.

SCAN. Yes, mine are most in black and white. And yet there are some set out in their true colors, both men and women. I can show you pride, folly, affectation, wantonness, inconstancy, covetousness, dissimulation, malice and ignorance, all in one piece. Then I can show you lying, foppery, vanity, cowardice, bragging, lechery, impotence and ugliness in another piece; and yet one of these is a celebrated beauty, and t'other a professed beau. I have paintings too, some pleasant enough.

MRS. FRAIL. Come, let's hear 'em.

SCAN. Why, I have a beau in a bagnio,[7] cupping for a complexion, and sweating for a shape.

MRS. FRAIL. So.

SCAN. Then I have a lady burning brandy in a cellar with a hackney coachman.

MRS. FRAIL. O devil! Well, but that story is not true.

SCAN. I have some hieroglyphics too. I have a lawyer with a hundred hands, two heads, and but one face; a divine with two faces, and one head; and I have a soldier with his brains in his belly, and his heart where his head should be.

MRS. FRAIL. And no head?

SCAN. No head.

MRS. FRAIL. Pooh, this is all invention. Have you ne'er a poet?

SCAN. Yes, I have a poet weighing words, and selling praise for praise, and a critic picking his pocket. I have another large piece too, representing a school, where there are huge proportioned critics, with long wigs, laced coats, Steinkirk cravats, and terrible faces, with cat-calls in their hands, and hornbooks about their necks. I have many more of this kind, very well painted, as you shall see.

[6] Sir Godfrey Kneller was a popular and prolific portrait painter.   [7] Bath-house.

Mrs. Frail. Well, I'll come, if it be but to disprove you.

(*Enter* Jeremy)

Jere. Sir, here's the steward again from your father.

Val. I'll come to him.——Will you give me leave? I'll wait on you again presently.

Mrs. Frail. No, I'll be gone. Come, who squires me to the Exchange? I must call my sister Foresight there.

Scan. I will: I have a mind to your sister.

Mrs. Frail. Civil!

Tatt. I will; because I have a *tendre* for your ladyship.

Mrs. Frail. That's somewhat the better reason, to my opinion.

Scan. Well, if Tattle entertains you, I have the better opportunity to engage your sister.

Val. Tell Angelica, I am about making hard conditions to come abroad and be at liberty to see her.

Scan. I'll give an account of you and your proceedings. If indiscretion be a sign of love, you are the most a lover of any body that I know: you fancy that parting with your estate will help you to your mistress. In my mind he is a thoughtless adventurer,

Who hopes to purchase wealth, by selling land;
Or win a mistress, with a losing hand.
(*Exeunt*)

Act II

A Room in Foresight's *House*

(*Enter* Foresight *and* Servant)

Fore. Hey day! What, are all the women of my family abroad? Is not my wife come home? Nor my sister, nor my daughter?

Serv. No, sir.

Fore. Mercy on us, what can be the meaning of it? Sure the moon is in all her fortitudes. Is my niece Angelica at home?

Serv. Yes, sir.

Fore. I believe you lie, sir.

Serv. Sir?

Fore. I say you lie, sir. It is impossible that anything should be as I would have it; for I was born, sir, when the crab was ascending, and all my affairs go backward.

Serv. I can't tell, indeed, sir.

Fore. No, I know you can't, sir. But I can tell, and foretell, sir.

(*Enter* Nurse)

Fore. Nurse, where's your young mistress?

Nurse. Wee'st heart, I know not, they're none of 'em come home yet. Poor child, I warrant she's fond o' seeing the town. Marry, pray heaven they ha' given her any dinner. (*Suddenly doubles up in laughter*) Good lack-a-day, ha, ha, ha, O strange! I'll vow and swear now, ha, ha, ha, marry, and did you ever see the like!

Fore. Why, how now, what's the matter?

Nurse. Pray heaven send your worship good luck, marry and amen with all my heart, for you have put on one stocking with the wrong side outward.

Fore. Ha, how? Faith and troth, I'm glad of it! and so I have! That may be good luck in troth, in troth it may, very good luck. Nay, I have had some omens: I got out of bed backwards too this morning, without premeditation; pretty good that too; but then I stumbled coming down stairs, and met a weasel; bad omens those. Some bad, some good, our lives are checquered: mirth and sorrow, want and plenty, night and day, make up our time. But in troth I am pleased at my stocking; very well pleased at my stocking. Oh, here's my niece! (*To* Servant) Sirrah, go tell Sir Sampson Legend I'll wait on him if he's at leisure. 'Tis now three o'clock, a very good hour for business, Mercury governs this hour. (*Exit* Servant)

(*Enter* Angelica)

Ang. Is it not a good hour for pleasure too,

uncle? Pray lend me your coach, mine's out of order.

FORE. What, would you be gadding too? Sure all females are mad today. It is of evil portent, and bodes mischief to the master of a family. I remember an old prophecy written by Messahalah the Arabian, and thus translated by a reverend Buckinghamshire bard.

When housewives all the house forsake,
And leave good man to brew and bake,
Withouten guile, then be it said,
That house doth stand upon its head;
And when the head is set in grond,
Ne marl, if it be fruitful fond.

Fruitful, the head fruitful, that bodes horns; the fruit of the head is horns. Dear niece, stay at home——for by the head of the house is meant the husband; the prophecy needs no explanation.

ANG. Well, but I can neither make you a cuckold, uncle, by going abroad, nor secure you from being one, by staying at home.

FORE. Yes, yes; while there's one woman left, the prophecy is not in full force.

ANG. But my inclinations are in force; I have a mind to go abroad; and if you won't lend me your coach, I'll take a hackney, or a chair, and leave you to erect a scheme, and find who's in conjunction with your wife. Why don't you keep her at home, if you're jealous of her when she's abroad? You know my aunt is a little retrograde (as you call it) in her nature. Uncle, I'm afraid you are not lord of the ascendant, ha, ha, ha!

FORE. Well, Jill-flirt, you are very pert, and always ridiculing that celestial science.

ANG. Nay, uncle, don't be angry. If you are, I'll reap up all your false prophecies, ridiculous dreams, and idle divinations. I'll swear you are a nuisance to the neighborhood. What a bustle did you keep against the last invisible eclipse, laying in provision as 'twere for a siege? What a world of fire and candle, matches and tinderboxes did you purchase! One would have thought we were ever after to live under ground, or at least making a voyage to Greenland, to inhabit there all the dark season.

FORE. Why, you malapert slut——

ANG. Will you lend me your coach? or I'll go on——nay, I'll declare how you prophesied popery was coming, only because the butler had mislaid some of the apostle spoons and thought they were lost. Away went religion and spoon-meat together. Indeed, uncle, I'll indite you for a wizard.

FORE. How, hussy! was there ever such a provoking minx?

NURSE. O merciful father, how she talks!

ANG. Yes, I can make oath of your unlawful midnight practices; you and the old nurse there——

NURSE. Marry, heaven defend! I at midnight practices—O Lord, what's here to do? I in unlawful doings with my master's worship! Why, did you ever hear the like now? Sir, did ever I do anything of your midnight concerns——but warm your bed, and tuck you up, and set the candle and your tobacco-box, and your urinal by you, and now and then rub the soles of your feet? O Lord, I!

ANG. Yes, I saw you together, thro' the keyhole of the closet, one night, like Saul and the Witch of Endor, turning the sieve and shears, and pricking your thumbs, to write poor innocent servants' names in blood, about a little nutmeg grater, which she had forgot in the caudle-cup. Nay, I know something worse, if I would speak of it——

FORE. (*Dancing about in a rage*) I defy you, hussy! But I'll remember this, I'll be revenged on you, cockatrice; I'll hamper you. You have your fortune in your own hands, but I'll find a way to make your lover, your prodigal spendthrift gallant, Valentine, pay for all, I will.

ANG. Will you? I care not, but all shall out then. Look to't, nurse; I can bring witness that you have a great unnatural teat under your left arm, and he another; and that you suckle a young devil in the shape of a tabby-cat, by turns, I can.

NURSE. A teat, a teat, I an unnatural teat! O the false, slanderous thing! Feel, feel here, if I have anything but like another Christian. (*Crying*)

FORE. I will have patience, since it is the will of the stars I should be thus tormented. This is the effect of the malicious conjunctions and oppositions in the third house of my nativity; there the curse of kindred was foretold. But I will have my doors locked up

——I'll punish you, not a man shall enter my house.

ANG. Do, uncle, lock 'em up quickly before my aunt come home. You'll have a letter for alimony tomorrow morning. But let me be gone first, and then let no mankind come near the house, but converse with spirits and the celestial signs, the bull, and the ram, and the goat. Bless me! There are a great many horned beasts among the twelve signs, uncle. But cuckolds go to heaven.

FORE. But there's but one virgin among the twelve signs, spitfire, but one virgin.

ANG. Nor there had not been that one, if she had had to do with any thing but astrologers, uncle. That makes my aunt go abroad.

FORE. How? How? Is that the reason? Come, you know something; tell me, and I'll forgive you; do, good niece. Come, you shall have my coach and horses, faith and troth you shall. Does my wife complain? Come, I know women tell one another. She is young and sanguine, has a wanton hazel eye, and was born under Gemini, which may incline her to society; she has a mole upon her lip, with a moist palm, and an open liberality on the mount of Venus.

ANG. Ha, ha, ha!

FORE. Do you laugh? Well, gentlewoman, I'll——but come, be a good girl, don't perplex your poor uncle, tell me——won't you speak? Odd, I'll——

(*Enter* SERVANT)

SERV. Sir Sampson is coming down to wait upon you—

ANG. Good bye, uncle. (*To* SERVANT) Call me a chair. (*Exit* SERVANT) I'll find out my aunt, and tell her she must not come home. (*Exit* ANGELICA)

FORE. I'm so perplexed and vexed, I am not fit to receive him; I shall scarce recover myself before the hour be past. Go, nurse, tell Sir Sampson I'm ready to wait on him.

NURSE. Yes, sir. (*Exit* NURSE)

FORE. Well—why, if I was born to be a cuckold, there's no more to be said—he's here already.

(*Enter* SIR SAMPSON LEGEND *with a paper*)

SIR SAMP. Nor no more to be done, old boy; that's plain.—Here 'tis, I have it in my hand, old Ptolemy; I'll make the ungracious prodigal know who begat him; I will, old Nostrodamus. What, I warrant my son thought nothing belonged to a father, but forgiveness and affection; no authority, no correction, no arbitrary power; nothing to be done, but for him to offend and me to pardon. I warrant you, if he danced till doomsday, he thought I was to pay the piper. Well, but here it is under black and white, signatum, sigillatum, and deliberatum; that as soon as my son Benjamin is arrived, he is to make over to him his right of inheritance. Where's my daughter that is to be?——Hah! old Merlin! body o'me, I'm so glad I'm revenged on this undutiful rogue.

FORE. Odso, let me see; let me see the paper. Ay, faith and troth, here 'tis, if it will but hold. I wish things were done, and the conveyance made. When was this signed, what hour? Odso, you should have consulted me for the time. Well, but we'll make haste——

SIR SAMP. Haste, ay, ay; haste enough. My son Ben will be in town tonight. I have ordered my lawyer to draw up writings of settlement and jointure. All shall be done tonight. No matter for the time; prithee, brother Foresight, leave superstition. Pox o'th' time; there's no time but the time present, there's no more to be said of what's past, and all that is to come will happen. If the sun shine by day, and the stars by night, why, we shall know one another's faces without the help of a candle, and that's all the stars are good for.

FORE. How, how? Sir Sampson, that all? Give me leave to contradict you, and tell you, you are ignorant.

SIR SAMP. I tell you I am wise; and *sapiens dominabitur astris;* there's Latin for you to prove it, and an argument to confound your Ephemeris. Ignorant! I tell you, I have travelled old Fircu, and know the globe. I have seen the Antipodes, where the sun rises at midnight, and sets at noon-day.

FORE. But I tell you, I have travelled, and travelled in the celestial spheres, known the signs and the planets, and their houses. Can judge of motions direct and retrograde, of sextiles, quadrates, trines and oppositions, fiery trigons and aquatical trigons. Know whether life shall be long or short, happy or unhappy, whether diseases are curable or incurable. If journeys shall be prosperous, undertakings successful; or goods stolen recovered, I know——

SIR SAMP. I know the length of the Emperor of China's foot; have kissed the Great Mogul's slipper, and rid a hunting upon an elephant with the Cham of Tartary. Body o'me, I have made a cuckold of a king, and the present majesty of Bantam is the issue of these loins.

FORE. I know when travellers lie or speak truth, when they don't know it themselves.

SIR SAMP. I have known an astrologer made a cuckold in the twinkling of a star; and seen a conjurer, that could not keep the devil out of his wife's circle.

FORE. (Aside) What, does he twit me with my wife too? I must be better informed of this.——Do you mean my wife, Sir Sampson? Tho' you made a cuckold of the king of Bantam, yet by the body of the sun——

SIR SAMP. By the horns of the moon, you would say, brother Capricorn.

FORE. Capricorn in your teeth, thou modern Mandevil; Ferdinand Mendez Pinto was but a type of thee, thou liar of the first magnitude. Take back your paper of inheritance; send your son to sea again. I'll wed my daughter to an Egyptian mummy, e'er she shall incorporate with a contemner of sciences, and a defamer of virtue.

SIR SAMP. (Aside) Body o'me, I have gone too far; I must not provoke honest Albumazar.——An Egyptian mummy is an illustrious creature, my trusty hieroglyphic; and may have significations of futurity about him; odsbud, I would my son were an Egyptian mummy for thy sake. What, thou art not angry for a jest, my good Haly? I reverence the sun, moon and stars with all my heart. What, I'll make thee a present of a mummy: now I think on't, body o'me, I have a shoulder of an Egyptian king, that I purloined from one of the pyramids, powdered with hieroglyphics; thou shalt have it brought home to thy house, and make an entertainment for all the Philomaths, and students in physic and astrology in and about London.

FORE. But what do you know of my wife, Sir Sampson?

SIR SAMP. Thy wife is a constellation of virtues; she's the moon, and thou art the man in the moon. Nay, she is more illustrious than the moon; for she has her chastity without her inconstancy. S'bud, I was but in jest.

(Enter JEREMY unnoticed by FORESIGHT)

SIR SAMP. How now, who sent for you? Ha! What would you have? (JEREMY speaks to him)

FORE. Nay, if you were but in jest—— who's that fellow? I don't like his physiognomy.

SIR SAMP. My son, sir; what son, sir? My son Benjamin, hoh?

JERE. No, sir, Mr. Valentine, my master, —'tis the first time he has been abroad since his confinement, and he comes to pay his duty to you.

SIR SAMP. Well, sir.

(Enter VALENTINE)

JERE. He is here, sir.

VAL. Your blessing, sir.

SIR SAMP. You've had it already, sir. I think I sent it you today in a bill of four thousand pound. A great deal of money, brother Foresight.

FORE. Ay, indeed, Sir Sampson, a great deal of money for a young man. I wonder what he can do with it!

SIR SAMP. Body o'me, so do I. Hark ye, Valentine, if there be too much, refund the superfluity; do'st hear, boy?

VAL. Superfluity, sir, it will scarce pay my debts. I hope you will have more indulgence than to oblige me to those hard conditions, which my necessity signed to.

SIR SAMP. Sir, how, I beseech you? What were you pleased to intimate, concerning indulgence?

VAL. Why, sir, that you would not go to the extremity of the conditions, but release me at least from some part.

SIR SAMP. Oh, sir, I understand you— that's all, ha?

VAL. Yes, sir, all that I presume to ask. But what you, out of fatherly fondness, will be pleased to add, shall be doubly welcome.

SIR SAMP. No doubt of it, sweet sir, but your filial piety and my fatherly fondness would fit like two tallies. Here's a rogue, brother Foresight, makes a bargain under hand and seal in the morning, and would be released from it in the afternoon! Here's a rogue, dog, here's conscience and honesty; this is your wit now, this is the morality of your wits! You are a wit, and have been a beau, and may be a——why, sirrah, is it not here under hand and seal? Can you deny it?

VAL. Sir, I don't deny it.

SIR SAMP. Sirrah, you'll be hanged; I shall live to see you go up Holborn-Hill.[8] Has he not a rogue's face? Speak, brother, you understand physiognomy. A hanging look to me——of all my boys the most unlike me; he has a damned Tyburn-face, without the benefit o'the clergy.

FORE. Hum—truly I don't care to discourage a young man,——he has a violent death in his face; but I hope no danger of hanging.

VAL. Sir, is this usage for your son? For that old weather-headed fool, I know how to laugh at him; but you, sir——

SIR SAMP. You, sir; and you, sir!—Why, who are you, sir?

VAL. Your son, sir.

SIR SAMP. That's more than I know, sir, and I believe not.

VAL. Faith, I hope not.

SIR SAMP. What, would you have your mother a whore! Did you ever hear the like! Did you ever hear the like! Body o'me——

VAL. I would have an excuse for your barbarity and unnatural usage.

SIR SAMP. Excuse! Impudence! Why, sirrah, mayn't I do what I please? Are not you my slave? Did I not beget you? And might not I have chosen whether I would have begot you or no? 'Oons, who are you? Whence came you? What brought you into the world? How came you here, sir? Here, to stand here, upon those two legs, and look erect with that audacious face, hah? Answer me that! Did you come a volunteer into the world? Or did I, with the lawful authority of a parent, press you to the service?

VAL. I know no more why I came, than you do why you called me. But here I am, and if you don't mean to provide for me, I desire you would leave me as you found me.

SIR SAMP. With all my heart. Come, un-

case, strip, and go naked out of the world, as you came into't.

VAL. My clothes are soon put off. But you must also divest me of reason, thought, passions, inclinations, affections, appetites, senses, and the huge train of attendants that you begot along with me.

SIR SAMP. Body o'me, what a many-headed monster have I propagated!

VAL. I am of myself, a plain, easy, simple creature, and to be kept at small expense; but the retinue that you gave me are craving and invincible; they are so many devils that you have raised, and will have employment.

SIR SAMP. 'Oons, what had I to do to get children,——can't a private man be born without all these followers? Why, nothing under an emperor should be born with appetites. Why, at this rate a fellow that has but a groat in his pocket, may have a stomach capable of a ten shilling ordinary.

JERE. Nay, that's as clear as the sun; I'll make oath of it before any justice in Middlesex.

SIR SAMP. Here's a cormorant, too. 'S'heart, this fellow was not born with you? I did not beget him, did I?

JERE. By the provision that's made for me, you might have begot me too. Nay, and to tell your worship another truth, I believe you did, for I find I was born with those same whoreson appetites, too, that my master speaks of.

SIR SAMP. Why, look you there now. I'll maintain it, that by the rule of right reason, this fellow ought to have been born without a palate. 'S'heart, what should he do with a distinguishing taste? I warrant now he'd rather eat a pheasant, than a piece of poor John;[9] and smell, now, why I warrant he can smell, and loves perfumes above a stink.—— Why, there's it; and music, don't you love music, scoundrel?

JERE. Yes, I have a reasonable good ear, sir, as to jigs and country dances, and the like. I don't much matter your solos or sonatas; they give me the spleen.

SIR SAMP. The spleen, ha, ha, ha! a pox confound you!—Solos or sonatas? 'Oons, whose son are you? How were you engendered, muckworm?

---

[8] On his way to Tyburn to be hanged.

[9] An inferior kind of dried fish.

JERE. I am by my father, the son of a chairman; my mother sold oysters in winter, and cucumbers in summer; and I came upstairs into the world, for I was born in a cellar.

FORE. By your looks, you should go upstairs out of the world too, friend.

SIR SAMP. And if this rogue were anatomized now, and dissected, he has his vessels of digestion and concoction, and so forth, large enough for the inside of a cardinal, this son of a cucumber. These things are unaccountable and unreasonable. Body o'me, why was not I a bear, that my cubs might have lived upon sucking their paws? Nature has been provident only to bears and spiders; the one has its nutriment in his own hands, and t'other spins his habitation out of his own entrails.

VAL. Fortune was provident enough to supply all the necessities of my nature, if I had my right of inheritance.

SIR SAMP. Again! 'Oons, han't you four thousand pound?—if I had it again, I would not give thee a groat. What, would'st thou have me turn pelican, and feed thee out of my own vitals? 'S'heart, live by your wits. You were always fond of the wits, now let's see if you have wit enough to keep your self. Your brother will be in town tonight, or tomorrow morning, and then look you perform covenants, and so (*bowing angrily*) your friend and servant. Come, brother Foresight.

(*Exeunt* SIR SAMPSON *and* FORESIGHT)

JERE. I told you what your visit would come to.

VAL. 'Tis as much as I expected. I did not come to see him; I came to Angelica, but since she was gone abroad, it was easily turned another way; and at least looked well on my side.—What's here? Mrs. Foresight and Mrs. Frail; they are earnest. I'll avoid 'em. Come this way, and go and inquire when Angelica will return.

(*Exeunt* VALENTINE *and* JEREMY)

(*Enter* MRS. FORESIGHT *and* MRS. FRAIL)

MRS. FRAIL. What have you to do to watch me? 'S'life, I'll do what I please.

MRS. FORE. You will?

MRS. FRAIL. Yes, marry will I. A great piece of business to go to Covent-Garden Square in a hackney-coach and take a turn with one's friend.

MRS. FORE. Nay, two or three turns, I'll take my oath.

MRS. FRAIL. Well, what if I took twenty? ——I warrant if you had been there, it had been only innocent recreation. Lord, where's the comfort of this life, if we can't have the happiness of conversing where we like?

MRS. FORE. But can't you converse at home?——I own it, I think there's no happiness like conversing with an agreeable man; I don't quarrel at that, nor I don't think but your conversation was very innocent; but the place is public, and to be seen with a man in a hackney-coach is scandalous. What if anybody else should have seen you alight, as I did? How can anybody be happy, while they're in perpetual fear of being seen and censured? Besides it would not only reflect upon you, Sister, but me.

MRS. FRAIL. Pooh, here's a clutter. Why should it reflect upon you? I don't doubt but you have thought yourself happy in a hackney-coach before now. If I had gone to Knightsbridge, or to Chelsea, or to Spring-Garden, or Barn-Elms with a man alone—— something might have been said.

MRS. FORE. Why, was I ever in any of those places? What do you mean, sister?

MRS. FRAIL. Was I? What do you mean?

MRS. FORE. You have been at a worse place.

MRS. FRAIL. I at a worse place, and with a man!

MRS. FORE. I suppose you would not go alone to the World's-End.[10]

MRS. FRAIL. The World's-End! What, do you mean to banter me?

MRS. FORE. Poor innocent! You don't know that there's a place called the World's-End? I'll swear you can keep your countenance purely; you'd make an admirable player.

MRS. FRAIL. I'll swear you have a great deal of confidence, and in my mind too much for the stage.

MRS. FORE. Very well, that will appear who has most; you never were at the World's-End?

MRS. FRAIL. No.

[10] A somewhat disreputable tavern in Knightsbridge.

MRS. FORE. You deny it positively to my face.

MRS. FRAIL. Your face, what's your face?

MRS. FORE. No matter for that, it's as good a face as yours.

MRS. FRAIL. Not by a dozen years wearing. But I do deny it positively to your face then.

MRS. FORE. I'll allow you now to find fault with my face; for I'll swear your impudence has put me out of countenance. But look you here now,—where did you lose this gold bodkin?——Oh, sister, sister!

MRS. FRAIL. My bodkin!

MRS. FORE. Nay, 'tis yours, look at it.

MRS. FRAIL. Well, if you go to that, where did you find this bodkin?——Oh, sister, sister! Sister every way.

MRS. FORE. (*Aside*) O Devil on't, that I could not discover her, without betraying myself.

MRS. FRAIL. I have heard gentlemen say, sister, that one should take great care, when one makes a thrust in fencing, not to lie open one's self.

MRS. FORE. It's very true, sister. Well, since all's out, and as you say, since we are both wounded, let us do what is often done in duels, take care of one another, and grow better friends than before.

MRS. FRAIL. With all my heart. Ours are but slight flesh wounds, and if we keep 'em from air, not at all dangerous. Well, give me your hand in token of sisterly secrecy and affection.

MRS. FORE. Here 'tis, with all my heart.

MRS. FRAIL. Well, as an earnest of friendship and confidence, I'll acquaint you with a design that I have. To tell truth, and speak openly one to another, I'm afraid the world have observed us more than we have observed one another. You have a rich husband, and are provided for. I am at a loss, and have no great stock either of fortune or reputation, and therefore must look sharply about me. Sir Sampson has a son that is expected to-night; and by the account I have heard of his education, can be no conjurer. The estate you know is to be made over to him. Now if I could wheedle him, sister, ha? You understand me?

MRS. FORE. I do; and will help you to the utmost of my power. And I can tell you one thing that falls out luckily enough; my awkward daughter-in-law,[11] who you know is designed to be his wife, is grown fond of Mr. Tattle. Now if we can improve that, and make her have an aversion for the booby, it may go a great way towards his liking you. Here they come together; and let us contrive some way or other to leave 'em together.

(*Enter* TATTLE *and* MISS PRUE)

MISS. Mother, mother, mother, look you here!

MRS. FORE. Fie, fie, Miss, how you bawl! Besides, I have told you, you must not call me mother.

MISS. What must I call you then? Are you not my father's wife?

MRS. FORE. Madam; you must say madam. —By my soul, I shall fancy myself old indeed, to have this great girl call me mother.—Well, but Miss, what are you so over-joyed at?

MISS. Look you here, madam then, what Mr. Tattle has given me. Look you here, cousin, here's a snuff-box; nay, there's snuff in't. Here, will you have any? Oh good! How sweet it is! Mr. Tattle is all over sweet, his peruke is sweet, and his gloves are sweet, and his handkerchief is sweet, pure sweet, sweeter than roses. Smell him, mother, madam, I mean. He gave me this ring for a kiss.

TATT. O fie, Miss, you must not kiss and tell.

MISS. Yes; I may tell my mother. And he says he'll give me something to make me smell so. Oh, pray lend me your handkerchief. Smell, cousin; he says he'll give me something that will make my smocks smell this way. Is not it pure? It's better than lavender, mun. I'm resolved I won't let nurse put any more lavender among my smocks— ha, cousin?

MRS. FRAIL. Fie, Miss; amongst your linen, you must say. You must never say smock.

MISS. Why, it is not bawdy, is it, cousin?

TATT. Oh, madam; you are too severe upon Miss; you must not find fault with her pretty simplicity, it becomes her strangely. Pretty Miss, don't let 'em persuade you out of your innocency.

MRS. FORE. Oh, demn you, toad! I wish

[11] Step-daughter.

you don't persuade her out of her innocency.

TATT. Who, I, madam? Oh Lord, how can your ladyship have such a thought? Sure, you don't know me?

MRS. FRAIL. Ah, devil, sly devil. He's as close, sister, as a confessor. He thinks we don't observe him.

MRS. FORE. A cunning cur, how soon he could find out a fresh harmless creature; and left us, sister, presently.

TATT. Upon reputation——

MRS. FORE. They're all so, sister, these men—they love to have the spoiling of a young thing; they are as fond of it, as of being first in the fashion, or of seeing a new play the first day. I warrant it would break Mr. Tattle's heart, to think that any body else should be beforehand with him.

TATT. Oh Lord, I swear I would not for the world——

MRS. FRAIL. O hang you! who'll believe you? You'd be hanged before you'd confess. We know you—she's very pretty!—Lord, what pure red and white!—she looks so wholesome; ne'er stir, I don't know, but I fancy, if I were a man—

MISS. How you love to jeer one, cousin.

MRS. FORE. Hark'ee, sister, by my soul the girl is spoiled already. D'ee think she'll ever endure a great lubberly tarpaulin? Gad, I warrant you she won't let him come near her, after Mr. Tattle.

MRS. FRAIL. O'my soul, I'm afraid not—eh!—filthy creature, that smells all of pitch and tar! Devil take you, you confounded toad——why did you see her before she was married?

MRS. FORE. Nay, why did we let him? My husband will hang us. He'll think we brought 'em acquainted.

MRS. FRAIL. Come, faith, let us be gone. If my brother Foresight should find us with them, he'd think so, sure enough.

MRS. FORE. So he would. But then, leaving 'em together is as bad. And he's such a sly devil, he'll never miss an opportunity.

MRS. FRAIL. I don't care; I won't be seen in't.

MRS. FORE. Well, if you should, Mr. Tattle, you'll have a world to answer for; remember I wash my hands of it, I'm thoroughly innocent.

(*Exeunt* MRS. FORESIGHT *and* MRS. FRAIL)

MISS. What makes 'em go away, Mr. Tattle? What do they mean——do you know?

TATT. Yes, my dear, I think I can guess. But hang me if I know the reason of it.

MISS. Come, must not we go too?

TATT. No, no, they don't mean that.

MISS. No! What then? What shall you and I do together?

TATT. I must make love to you, pretty Miss; will you let me make love to you?

MISS. Yes, if you please.

TATT. (*Aside*) Frank, egad, at least. What a pox does Mrs. Foresight mean by this civility? Is it to make a fool of me? Or does she leave us together out of good morality, and do as she would be done by——Gad, I'll understand it so.

MISS. Well; and how will you make love to me? Come, I long to have you begin. Must I make love too? You must tell me how.

TATT. You must let me speak, Miss, you must not speak first; I must ask you questions, and you must answer.

MISS. What, is it like the catechism? Come, then, ask me.

TATT. D'ye think you can love me?

MISS. Yes.

TATT. Pooh, pox, you must not say yes already; I shan't care a farthing for you then in a twinkling.

MISS. What must I say then?

TATT. Why you must say no, or you believe not, or you can't tell——

MISS. Why, must I tell a lie then?

TATT. Yes, if you'd be well bred. All well-bred persons lie. Besides, you are a woman, you must never speak what you think. Your words must contradict your thoughts, but your actions may contradict your words. So, when I ask you if you can love me, you must say no, but you must love me too. If I tell you you are handsome, you must deny it, and say I flatter you——but you must think yourself more charming than I speak you. And like me, for the beauty which I say you have, as much as if I had it myself. If I ask you to kiss me, you must be angry, but you must not refuse me. If I ask you for more, you must be more angry, but more complying; and as soon as ever I make you say you'll cry out, you must be sure to hold your tongue.

Miss. O Lord, I swear this is pure. I like it better than our old-fashioned country way of speaking one's mind. And must not you lie too?

Tatt. Hum——yes—but you must believe I speak truth.

Miss. O Gemini! Well, I always had a great mind to tell lies, but they frighted me, and said it was a sin.

Tatt. Well, my pretty creature; will you make me happy by giving me a kiss?

Miss. No, indeed; I'm angry at you.
(Runs and kisses him)

Tatt. Hold, hold, that's pretty well, but you should not have given it me, but have suffered me to have taken it.

Miss. Well, we'll do it again.

Tatt. With all my heart. Now then, my little angel.   *(Kisses her)*

Miss. Pish.

Tatt. That's right,——again, my charmer.
(Kisses again)

Miss. O fie, nay, now I can't abide you.

Tatt. Admirable! That was as well as if you had been born and bred in Covent-Garden. And won't you show me, pretty Miss, where your bed-chamber is?

Miss. No, indeed won't I: but I'll run there, and hide myself from you behind the curtains.

Tatt. I'll follow you.

Miss. Ah, but I'll hold the door with both hands, and be angry; and you shall push me down before you come in.

Tatt. No, I'll come in first, and push you down afterwards.

Miss. Will you? Then I'll be more angry, and more complying.

Tatt. Then I'll make you cry out.

Miss. Oh, but you shan't, for I'll hold my tongue.

Tatt. Oh, my dear apt scholar.

Miss. Well, now I'll run and make more haste than you.   *(Exit)*

Tatt. You shall not fly so fast as I'll pursue. *(He runs after her)*

Act III

Outside Miss Prue's *Bedroom*.

(Enter Nurse)

Nurse. Miss, Miss, Miss Prue! Mercy on me, marry and amen. Why, what's become of the child? Why Miss, Miss Foresight! *(She tries to open the door)* Sure she has locked herself up in her chamber, and gone to sleep, or to prayers. Miss, Miss! I hear her. Come to your father, child. Open the door—open the door, Miss. I hear you cry "hush!" O Lord, who's there? *(Peeps through the keyhole)* What's here to do?——O the Father! a man with her! Why, Miss, I say; God's my life, here's fine doings towards. O Lord, we're all undone! O you young harlotry! *(Knocks)* Od's my life, won't you open the door? I'll come in the back way.
(Exit Nurse)

(Enter Tattle, Miss Prue)

Miss. O Lord, she's coming, and she'll tell my father; what shall I do now?

Tatt. Pox take her! if she had stayed two minutes longer, I should have wished for her coming.

Miss. O dear, what shall I say? Tell me, Mr. Tattle, tell me a lie.

Tatt. There's no occasion for a lie; I could never tell a lie to no purpose. But since we have done nothing, we must say nothing, I think. I hear her——I'll leave you together, and come off as you can.
(Thrusts her in, and shuts the door)

(Enter Valentine, Scandal, Angelica)

Ang. You can't accuse me of inconstancy; I never told you that I loved you.

Val. But I can accuse you of uncertainty, for not telling me whether you did or not.

Ang. You mistake indifference for uncertainty; I never had concern enough to ask myself the question.

Scan. Nor good nature enough to answer

him that did ask you; I'll say that for you, madam.

Ang. What, are you setting up for good nature?

Scan. Only for the affectation of it, as the women do for ill nature.

Ang. Persuade your friend that it is all affectation.

Scan. I shall receive no benefit from the opinion, for I know no effectual difference between continued affectation and reality.

Tatt. (*Coming up and speaking aside to* Scandal) Scandal, are you in private discourse, anything of secrecy?

Scan. Yes, but I dare trust you; we were talking of Angelica's love to Valentine; you won't speak of it.

Tatt. No, no, not a syllable. I know that's a secret, for it's whispered everywhere.

Scan. Ha, ha, ha!

Ang. What is, Mr. Tattle? I heard you say something was whispered everywhere.

Scan. Your love of Valentine.

Ang. How!

Tatt. No, madam, his love for your ladyship. Gad take me, I beg your pardon, for I never heard a word of your ladyship's passion till this instant.

Ang. My passion! And who told you of my passion, pray sir?

Scan. Why, is the devil in you? Did not I tell it you for a secret?

Tatt. Gadso; but I thought she might have been trusted with her own affairs.

Scan. Is that your discretion? Trust a woman with herself?

Tatt. You say true; I beg your pardon. I'll bring all off. It was impossible, madam, for me to imagine that a person of your ladyship's wit and gallantry could have so long received the passionate addresses of the accomplished Valentine, and yet remain insensible; therefore you will pardon me, if from a just weight of his merit with your ladyship's good judgment, I formed the balance of a reciprocal affection.

Val. O the devil, what damned costive poet has given thee this lesson of fustian to get by rote?

Ang. I dare swear you wrong him. It is his own. And Mr. Tattle only judges of the success of others from the effects of his own

merit. For certainly Mr. Tattle was never denied anything in his life.

Tatt. O Lord! Yes indeed, madam, several times.

Ang. I swear I don't think 'tis possible.

Tatt. Yes, I vow and swear I have. Lord, madam, I'm the most unfortunate man in the world, and the most cruelly used by the ladies.

Ang. Nay, now you're ungrateful.

Tatt. No, I hope not——'tis as much ingratitude to own some favors, as to conceal others.

Val. There, now it's out.

Ang. I don't understand you now. I thought you had never asked anything but what a lady might modestly grant, and you confess.

Scan. So faith, your business is done here; now you may go brag somewhere else.

Tatt. Brag! O heavens! Why, did I name any body?

Ang. No; I suppose that is not in your power; but you would if you could, no doubt on't.

Tatt. Not in my power, madam! What does your ladyship mean, that I have no woman's reputation in my power?

Scan. (*Aside to* Tattle) 'Oons, why you won't own it, will you?

Tatt. Faith, madam, you're in the right; no more I have, as I hope to be saved; I never had it in my power to say any thing to a lady's prejudice in my life. For as I was telling you, madam, I have been the most unsuccessful creature living in things of that nature; and never had the good fortune to be trusted once with a lady's secret, not once.

Ang. No.

Val. Not once, I dare answer for him.

Scan. And I'll answer for him; for I'm sure if he had, he would have told me. I find, madam, you don't know Mr. Tattle.

Tatt. No indeed, madam, you don't know me at all, I find. For sure my intimate friends would have known——

Ang. Then it seems you would have told, if you had been trusted.

Tatt. O pox, Scandal, that was too far put.—Never have told particulars, madam. Perhaps I might have talked as of a third person, or have introduced an amour of my own, in conversation, by way of novel; but never have explained particulars.

ANG. But whence comes the reputation of Mr. Tattle's secrecy, if he was never trusted?

SCAN. Why thence it arises—the thing is proverbially spoken, but may be applied to him——as if we should say in general terms, he only is secret who never was trusted: a satirical proverb upon our sex. There's another upon yours: as, she is chaste, who was never asked the question. That's all.

VAL. A couple of very civil proverbs, truly! 'Tis hard to tell whether the lady or Mr. Tattle be the more obliged to you, for you found her virtue upon the backwardness of the men, and his secrecy upon the mistrust of the women.

TATT. Gad, it's very true, madam, I think we are obliged to acquit ourselves. And for my part——but your ladyship is to speak first—

ANG. Am I? Well, I freely confess I have resisted a great deal of temptation.

TATT. And I, Gad, I have given some temptation that has not been resisted.

VAL. Good.

ANG. I cite Valentine here, to declare to the court how fruitless he has found his endeavors, and to confess all his solicitations and my denials.

VAL. I am ready to plead not guilty for you, and guilty for myself.

SCAN. So, why this is fair, here's demonstration with a witness.

TATT. Well, my witnesses are not present. But I confess I have had favors from persons——But as the favors are numberless, so the persons are nameless.

SCAN. Pooh, this proves nothing.

TATT. No? I can show letters, lockets, pictures, and rings; and if there be occasion for witnesses, I can summon the maids at the chocolate-houses, all the porters at Pall-Mall and Covent-Garden, the door-keepers at the play-house, the drawers at Locket's, Pontack's, the Rummer, Spring-Garden; my own landlady and valet de chambre; all who shall make oath that I receive more letters than the secretary's office, and that I have more vizor-masks to enquire for me than ever went to see the hermaphrodite, or the naked prince. And it is notorious that in a country church, once, an enquiry being made who I was, it was answered, I was the famous Tattle, who had ruined so many women.

VAL. It was there, I suppose, you got the nickname of the Great Turk.

TAT. True; I was called Turk-Tattle all over the parish. The next Sunday all the old women kept their daughters at home, and the parson had not half his congregation. He would have brought me into the spiritual court, but I was revenged upon him, for he had a handsome daughter whom I initiated into the science. But I repented it afterwards, for it was talked of in town, and a lady of quality that shall be nameless, in a raging fit of jealousy, came down in her coach and six horses, and exposed herself upon my account. Gad, I was sorry for it with all my heart. You know whom I mean —you know where we raffled——

SCAN. Mum, Tattle.

VAL. 'Sdeath, are not you ashamed?

ANG. O barbarous! I never heard so insolent a piece of vanity. Fie, Mr. Tattle, I'll swear I could not have believed it. Is this your secrecy?

TATT. Gad so, the heat of my story carried me beyond my discretion, as the heat of the lady's passion hurried her beyond her reputation. But I hope you don't know whom I mean, for there was a great many ladies raffled. Pox on't, now could I bite off my tongue.

SCAN. No, don't; for then you'll tell us no more. Come, I'll recommend a song to you upon the hint of my two proverbs, and I see one in the next room that will sing it.

(Goes to the door and beckons in SINGER)

TATT. For Heaven's sake, if you do guess, say nothing; Gad, I'm very unfortunate.

SCAN. Pray sing the first song in the last new play.

SONG

I.

A nymph and a swain to Apollo once prayed,
The swain had been jilted, the nymph been
*   betrayed:*
Their intent was to try if his oracle knew
E'er a nymph that was chaste, or a swain
*   that was true.*

II.

*Apollo was mute, and had like t'have been
    posed,
But sagely at length he this secret disclosed:
He alone won't betray in whom none will
    confide;
And the nymph may be chaste that has never
    been tried.* (*Exit* SINGER)

(*Enter* SIR SAMPSON, MRS. FRAIL, MISS
    PRUE, *and Servant*)

SIR SAMP. Is Ben come? Odso, my son
Ben come? Odd, I'm glad on't. Where is
he? I long to see him. Now, Mrs. Frail, you
shall see my son Ben——Body o'me, he's
the hopes of my family. I han't seen him
these three years. I warrant he's grown.
Call him in, bid him make haste. (*Exit
Servant*) I'm ready to cry for joy.

MRS. FRAIL. Now, Miss, you shall see
your husband.

MISS. (*Aside to* MRS. FRAIL) Pish, he
shall be none of my husband.

MRS. FRAIL. (*Aside to* PRUE) Hush.
Well he shan't——leave that to me. I'll
beckon Mr. Tattle to us.

ANG. Won't you stay and see your
brother?

VAL. We are the twin-stars, and cannot
shine in one sphere; when he rises I must
set. Besides, if I should stay, I don't know
but my father in good nature may press me
to the immediate signing the deed of conveyance of my estate, and I'll defer it as
long as I can. Well, you'll come to a resolution.

ANG. I can't. Resolution must come to me,
or I shall never have one.

SCAN. Come, Valentine, I'll go with you;
I've something in my head to communicate
to you.

(*Exeunt* VALENTINE *and* SCANDAL)

SIR SAMP. What, is my son Valentine
gone? What, is he sneaked off, and would
not see his brother? There's an unnatural
whelp! There's an ill-natured dog! What,
were you here too, madam, and could not
keep him! Could neither love, nor duty,
nor natural affection oblige him? Odsbud,
madam, have no more to say to him; he is
not worth your consideration. The rogue has

not a dram of generous love about him—
all interest, all interest. He's an undone
scoundrel, and courts your estate; body o'me,
he does not care a doit for your person.

ANG. I'm pretty even with him, Sir Sampson; for if ever I could have liked anything
in him, it should have been his estate too.
But since that's gone, the bait's off, and
the naked hook appears.

SIR SAMP. Odsbud, well spoken; and you
are a wiser woman than I thought you were,
for most young women now a-days are to
be tempted with a naked hook.

ANG. If I marry, Sir Sampson, I'm for a
good estate with any man, and for any man
with a good estate. Therefore if I were
obliged to make a choice, I declare I'd rather
have you than your son.

SIR SAMP. Faith and troth, you're a wise
woman, and I'm glad to hear you say so;
I was afraid you were in love with the repro-
bate. Odd, I was sorry for you with all my
heart. Hang him, mongrel! Cast him off—
you shall see the rogue show himself, and
make love to some desponding Cadua of
fourscore for sustenance. Odd, I love to see
a young spendthrift forced to cling to an
old woman for support, like ivy round a
dead oak, faith I do; I love to see 'em hug
and cotton together, like down upon a
thistle.

(*Enter* BEN. LEGEND *and* SERVANT)

BEN. Where's Father?

SERV. There, sir; his back's towards you.

SIR SAMP. My son Ben! Bless thee, my
dear boy; body o'me, thou art heartily welcome.

BEN. Thank you, Father, and I'm glad to
see you.

SIR SAMP. Odsbud, and I'm glad to see
thee. Kiss me, boy, kiss me again and again,
dear Ben. (*Kisses him*)

BEN. So, so, enough, Father. Mess, I'd
rather kiss these gentlewomen.

SIR SAMP. And so thou shalt. Mrs. Angelica, my son Ben.

BEN. Forsooth if you please. (*Salutes her*)
Nay, mistress, I'm not for dropping anchor
here. About ship, i'faith. (*Kisses* MRS.
FRAIL) Nay, and you too, my little cock-
boat——so. (*Kisses* MISS)

Tatt. Sir, you're welcome ashore.

Ben. Thank you, thank you, friend.

Sir. Samp. Thou hast been many a weary league, Ben, since I saw thee.

Ben. Ey, ey, been! Been far enough, an that be all. Well, father, and how do all at home? How does brother Dick, and brother Val?

Sir Samp. Dick, body o'me, Dick has been dead these two years; I writ you word when you were at Leghorn.

Ben. Mess, that's true. Marry, I had forgot. Dick's dead, as you say. Well, and how? I have a many questions to ask you. Well, you ben't married again, father, be you?

Sir Samp. No, I intend you shall marry, Ben; I would not marry for thy sake.

Ben. Nay, what does that signify? An you marry again——why then, I'll go to sea again, so there's one for t'other, an that be all. Pray don't let me be your hindrance; e'en marry, a God's name, an the wind sit that way. As for my part, mayhap I have no mind to marry.

Mrs. Frail. That would be pity, such a handsome young gentleman.

Ben. Handsome! He, he, he! Nay, forsooth, an you be for joking, I'll joke with you, for I love my jest, an the ship were sinking, as we say at sea. But I'll tell you why I don't much stand towards matrimony. I love to roam about from port to port, and from land to land; I could never abide to be port-bound, as we call it. Now a man that is married has, as it were, d'ye see, his feet in the bilboes, and mayhap mayn't get 'em out again when he would.

Sir Samp. Ben's a wag.

Ben. A man that is married, d'ye see, is no more like another man, than a galley-slave is like one of us free sailors; he is chained to an oar all his life, and mayhap forced to tug a leaky vessel into the bargain.

Sir Samp. A very wag, Ben's a very wag; only a little rough, he wants a little polishing.

Mrs. Frail. Not at all; I like his humor mightily, it's plain and honest. I should like such a humor in a husband extremely.

Ben. Say you so, forsooth? Marry, and I should like such a handsome gentlewoman for a bedfellow hugely. How say you, mistress, would you like going to sea? Mess, you're a tight vessel, and well rigged, an you were but as well manned.

Mrs. Frail. I should not doubt that, if you were master of me.

Ben. But I'll tell you one thing, an you come to sea in a high wind, or that lady (pointing to Angelica)——you mayn't carry so much sail o'your head——top and top gallant, by the mess.

Mrs. Frail. No, why so?

Ben. Why, an you do, you may run the risk to be over-set, and then you'll carry your keels above water, he, he, he!

Ang. I swear, Mr. Benjamin is the veriest wag in nature; an absolute sea-wit.

Sir Samp. Nay, Ben has parts, but as I told you before, they want a little polishing. You must not take anything ill, madam.

Ben. No, I hope the gentlewoman is not angry; I mean all in good part. For if I give a jest, I'll take a jest, and so, forsooth, you may be as free with me.

Ang. I thank you, sir, I am not at all offended. But methinks, Sir Sampson, you should leave him alone with his mistress. Mr. Tattle, we must not hinder lovers.

Tatt. (Aside to Miss) Well, Miss, I have your promise.

Sir Samp. Body o'me, madam, you say true. (Taking Prue's hand) Look you, Ben; this is your mistress. Come, Miss, you must not be shame-faced; we'll leave you together.

Miss. (Pulling away) I can't abide to be left alone; mayn't my cousin stay with me?

Sir Samp. No, no. Come, let's away.

Ben. (Backing off) Look you, father, mayhap the young woman mayn't take a liking to me.

Sir Samp. I warrant thee, boy; come, come, we'll be gone; I'll venture that.

(Exeunt Angelica, Mrs. Frail, Sir Sampson, and Tattle)

Ben. Come, mistress, will you please to sit down? For an you stand a stern a that'n, we shall never grapple together. Come, I'll haul a chair; there, an you please to sit, I'll sit by you.

Miss. You need not sit so near me. If you have anything to say, I can hear you farther off; I an't deaf.

Ben. Why, that's true, as you say, nor I an't dumb, I can hear as far as another. I'll heave off to please you. (Sits farther off)

An we were a league asunder, I'd undertake to hold discourse with you, an 'twere not a main high wind indeed, and full in my teeth. Look you, forsooth, I am, as it were, bound for the land of matrimony; 'tis a voyage, d'ye see, that was none of my seeking. I was commanded by father, and if you like of it, mayhap I may steer into your harbor. How say you, mistress? The short of the thing is, that if you like me, and I like you, we may chance to swing in a hammock together.

Miss. I don't know what to say to you, nor I don't care to speak with you at all.

Ben. No, I'm sorry for that. But pray, why are you so scornful?

Miss. As long as one must not speak one's mind, one had better not speak at all, I think, and truly I won't tell a lie for the matter.

Ben. Nay, you say true in that, it's but a folly to lie. For to speak one thing, and to think just the contrary way, is, as it were, to look one way, and to row another. Now, for my part, d'ye see, I'm for carrying things above board, I'm not for keeping any thing under hatches,—so that if you ben't as willing as I, say so, a God's name, there's no harm done. Mayhap you may be shamefaced; some maidens, tho'f they love a man well enough, yet they don't care to tell'n so to's face. If that's the case, why silence gives consent.

Miss. But I'm sure it is not so, for I'll speak sooner than you should believe that; and I'll speak truth, tho' one should always tell a lie to a man; and I don't care, let my father do what he will! I'm too big to be whipt, so I'll tell you plainly, I don't like you, nor love you at all, nor ever will, what's more. So, there's your answer for you; and don't trouble me no more, you ugly thing.

Ben. Look you, young woman, you may learn to give good words, however. I spoke you fair, d'ye see, and civil. As for your love or your liking, I don't value it of a rope's end. And mayhap I like you as little as you do me. What I said was in obedience to father; Gad, I fear a whipping no more than you do. But I tell you one thing, if you should give such language at sea, you'd have a cat o' nine tails laid cross your shoulders. Flesh! Who are you? You heard t'other

handsome young woman speak civilly to me, of her own accord. Whatever you think of yourself, Gad, I don't think you are any more to compare to her than a can of small-beer to a bowl of punch.

Miss. Well, and there's a handsome gentleman, and a fine gentleman, and a sweet gentleman, that was here, that loves me, and I love him. And if he sees you speak to me any more, he'll thrash your jacket for you, he will, you great sea-calf.

Ben. What, do you mean that fair-weather spark that was here just now? Will he thrash my jacket? Let'n——let'n. But an he comes near me, mayhap I may giv'n a salt eel for's supper, for all that. What does father mean to leave me alone as soon as I come home, with such a dirty dowdy? Sea-calf? I an't calf enough to lick your chalked face, you cheese-curd you. Marry thee! Oons, I'll marry a Lapland witch as soon, and live upon selling contrary winds and wrecked vessels.

Miss. I won't be called names, nor I won't be abused thus, so I won't. If I were a man——(Cries)——you durst not talk at this rate. No, you durst not, you stinking tar-barrel.

(Enter Mrs. Foresight and Mrs. Frail)

Mrs. Fore. They have quarreled just as we could wish.

Ben. Tar-barrel? Let your sweetheart there call me so, if he'll take your part, your Tom Essence, and I'll say something to him! Gad, I'll lace his musk-doublet for him, I'll make him stink; he shall smell more like a weasel than a civet-cat, afore I ha' done with 'en.

Mrs. Fore. Bless me, what's the matter, Miss? What, does she cry? Mr. Benjamin, what have you done to her?

Ben. Let her cry: the more she cries, the less she'll——she has been gathering foul weather in her mouth, and now it rains out at her eyes.

Mrs. Fore. Come, Miss, come along with me, and tell me, poor child.

Mrs. Frail. Lord, what shall we do? There's my brother Foresight and Sir Sampson coming. Sister, do you take Miss down into the parlor, and I'll carry Mr. Benjamin into my chamber, for they must not know that they are fallen out. Come, sir, will you venture yourself with me?

(*Looking kindly on him*)

BEN. Venture, Mess, and that I will, though 'twere to sea in a storm.

(*Exeunt* MRS. FORESIGHT *with* MISS, *and* MRS. FRAIL *with* BEN)

(*Enter* SIR SAMPSON *and* FORESIGHT)

SIR SAMP. I left 'em together here; what, are they gone? Ben's a brisk boy. He has got her into a corner. Father's own son! Faith, he'll touzle her, and mouzle her. The rogue's sharp set, coming from sea. If he should not stay for saying grace, old Foresight, but fall to without the help of a parson, ha? Odd, if he should I could not be angry with him; 'twould be but like me, a chip of the old block. Ha! thou'rt melancholic, old prognostication; as melancholic as if thou hadst spilt the salt, or pared thy nails on a Sunday. Come, cheer up, look about thee: look up old star-gazer. (*Aside*) Now is he poring upon the ground for a crooked pin, or an old horse-nail with the head towards him.

FORE. Sir Sampson, we'll have the wedding tomorrow morning.

SIR SAMP. With all my heart.

FORE. At ten o'clock, punctually at ten.

SIR SAMP. To a minute, to a second; thou shall set thy watch, and the bridegroom shall observe its motions. They shall be married to a minute, go to bed to a minute; and when the alarm strikes, they shall keep time like the figures of St. Dunstan's clock, and *consummatum est* shall ring all over the parish.

(*Enter* SCANDAL)

SCAN. Sir Sampson, sad news.

FORE. Bless us!

SIR SAMP. Why, what's the matter?

SCAN. Can't you guess at what ought to afflict you and him, and all of us, more than anything else?

SIR SAMP. Body o'me, I don't know any universal grievance, but a new tax, or the loss of the Canary fleet. Unless Popery should be landed in the West, or the French fleet were at anchor at Blackwall.

SCAN. No. Undoubtedly, Mr. Foresight knew all this, and might have prevented it.

FORE. 'Tis no earthquake!

SCAN. No, not yet; nor whirlwind. But we don't know what it may come to. But it has had a consequence already that touches us all.

SIR SAMP. Why, body o'me, out with't.

SCAN. Something has appeared to your son Valentine. He's gone to bed upon't, and very ill. He speaks little, yet he says he has a world to say. Asks for his father and the wise Foresight; talks of Raymond Lully, and the ghost of Lilly. He has secrets to impart I suppose to you two. I can get nothing out of him but sighs. He desires he may see you in the morning, but would not be disturbed to-night, because he has some business to do in a dream.

SIR SAMP. Hoity toity! What have I to do with his dreams or his divination? Body o'me, this is a trick to defer signing the conveyance. I warrant the devil will tell him in a dream that he must not part with his estate. But I'll bring him a parson to tell him that the devil's a liar——or if that won't do, I'll bring a lawyer that shall out-lie the devil. And so I'll try whether my black-guard or his shall get the better of the day.

(*Exit* SIR SAMPSON)

SCAN. Alas, Mr. Foresight, I'm afraid all is not right. You are a wise man, and a conscientious man, a searcher into obscurity and futurity, and if you commit an error, it is with a great deal of consideration, and discretion, and caution——

FORE. Ah, good Mr. Scandal——

SCAN. Nay, nay, 'tis manifest; I do not flatter you. But Sir Sampson is hasty, very hasty. I'm afraid he is not scrupulous enough, Mr. Foresight. He has been wicked, and Heaven grant he may mean well in his affair with you. But my mind gives me, these things cannot be wholly insignificant. You are wise, and should not be overreached, methinks you should not——

FORE. Alas, Mr. Scandal,—*humanum est errare.*

SCAN. You say true, man will err; mere man will err—but you are something more. There have been wise men; but they were such as you, men who consulted the stars, and were observers of omens——Solomon was wise, but how?—by his judgment in astrology. So says Pineda in his third book and eighth chapter.

FORE. You are learned, Mr. Scandal!

SCAN. A trifler—but a lover of art. And the wise men of the East owed their instruction to a star, which is rightly observed by Gregory the Great in favor of astrology. And Albertus Magnus makes it the most valuable science, because, says he, it teaches us to consider the causation of causes, in the causes of things.

FORE. I protest I honor you, Mr. Scandal. I did not think you had been read in these matters. Few young men are inclined——

SCAN. I thank my stars that have inclined me. But I fear this marriage and making over this estate, this transferring of a rightful inheritance, will bring judgments upon us. I prophesy it, and I would not have the fate of Cassandra, not to be believed. Valentine is disturbed; what can be the cause of that? And Sir Sampson is hurried on by an unusual violence. I fear he does not act wholly from himself; methinks he does not look as he used to do.

FORE. He was always of an impetuous nature. But as to his marriage, I have consulted the stars, and all appearances are prosperous——

SCAN. Come, come, Mr. Foresight, let not the prospect of worldly lucre carry you beyond your judgment, nor against your conscience. You are not satisfied that you act justly.

FORE. How!

SCAN. You are not satisfied, I say. I am loth to discourage you, but it is palpable that you are not satisfied.

FORE. How does it appear, Mr. Scandal? I think I am very well satisfied.

SCAN. Either you suffer yourself to deceive yourself, or you do not know yourself.

FORE. Pray explain yourself.

SCAN. Do you sleep well o'nights?

FORE. Very well.

SCAN. Are you certain? You do not look so.

FORE. I am in health, I think.

SCAN. So was Valentine this morning, and looked just so.

FORE. How! Am I altered any way? I don't perceive it.

SCAN. That may be, but your beard is longer than it was two hours ago.

FORE. Indeed! bless me!

(*Enter* MRS. FORESIGHT)

MRS. FORE. Husband, will you go to bed? It's ten o'clock. Mr. Scandal, your servant.

SCAN. (*Aside*) Pox on her! She has interrupted my design——but I must work her into the project.——You keep early hours, madam.

MRS. FORE. Mr. Foresight is punctual; we sit up after him.

FORE. My dear, pray lend me your glass, your little looking-glass.

SCAN. Pray lend it him, madam. I'll tell you the reason. (*She gives him the glass. While he anxiously examines his face in it,* SCANDAL *and she whisper.*) My passion for you is grown so violent that I am no longer master of myself. I was interrupted in the morning, when you had charity enough to give me your attention, and I had hopes of finding another opportunity of explaining myself to you, but was disappointed all this day; and the uneasiness that has attended me ever since, brings me now hither at this unseasonable hour.

MRS. FORE. Was there ever such impudence, to make love to me before my husband's face? I'll swear I'll tell him.

SCAN. Do, I'll die a martyr, rather than disclaim my passion. But come a little farther this way, and I'll tell you what project I had to get him out of the way, that I might have an opportunity of waiting upon you.

(*They whisper aside*)

FORE. (*Looking in the glass*) I do not see any revolution here. Methinks I look with a serene and benign aspect——pale, a little pale——but the roses of these cheeks have been gather'd many years. Ha! I do not like that sudden flushing. Gone already!—hem, hem, hem! Faintish. My heart is pretty good; yet it beats; and my pulses, ha!——I have none——mercy on me——hum. Yes, here they are——gallop, gallop, gallop, gallop, gallop, gallop, hey! Whither will they hurry me? Now they're gone again—and now I'm faint again; and pale again, and hem! and my—hem!—breath, hem!—grows short; hem! hem! he, he, hem!

SCAN. (*To* MRS. FORESIGHT) It takes, pursue it in the name of love and pleasure.

MRS. FORE. How do you do, Mr. Foresight?

FORE. Hum, not so well as I thought I was. Lend me your hand.

SCAN. Look you there now. Your lady says your sleep has been unquiet of late.

FORE. Very likely.

MRS. FORE. O mighty restless, but I was afraid to tell him so. He has been subject to talking and starting.

SCAN. And did not use to be so?

MRS. FORE. Never, never, 'till within these three nights; I cannot say that he has once broken my rest since we have been married.

FORE. (*Feebly*) I will go to bed.

SCAN. Do so, Mr. Foresight, and say your prayers. He looks better than he did.

MRS. FORE. (*Calling*) Nurse, nurse!

FORE. Do you think so, Mr. Scandal?

SCAN. Yes, yes, I hope this will be gone by morning, taking it in time.

FORE. I hope so.

(*Enter* NURSE)

MRS. FORE. Nurse, your master is not well; put him to bed.

SCAN. I hope you will be able to see Valentine in the morning. You had best take a little diacodion and cowslip-water, and lie upon your back; maybe you may dream.

FORE. I thank you, Mr. Scandal, I will. Nurse, let me have a watch-light, and lay the Crumbs of Comfort by me.

NURSE. Yes, sir.

FORE. And——hem, hem! I am very faint.

SCAN. No, no, you look much better.

FORE. Do I? (*To* NURSE) And d'ye hear ——bring me, let me see——within a quarter of twelve—hem—he, hem!—just upon the turning of the tide, bring me the urinal. And I hope neither the lord of my ascendant, nor the moon will be combust; and then I may do well.

SCAN. I hope so. Leave that to me; I will erect a scheme; and I hope I shall find both Sol and Venus in the sixth house.

FORE. I thank you, Mr. Scandal; indeed that would be a great comfort to me. Hem, hem! good night.

(*Exit* FORESIGHT *supported by* NURSE)

SCAN. Good night, good Mr. Foresight. And I hope Mars and Venus will be in conjunction——while your wife and I are together.

MRS. FORE. Well; and what use do you hope to make of this project? You don't think that you are ever like to succeed in your design upon me?

SCAN. Yes, faith I do; I have a better opinion both of you and myself than to despair.

MRS. FORE. Did you ever hear such a toad? Hark'ee, devil, do you think any woman honest?

SCAN. Yes, several, very honest; they'll cheat a little at cards, sometimes, but that's nothing.

MRS. FORE. Pshaw! but virtuous I mean.

SCAN. Yes, faith, I believe some women are virtuous too; but 'tis as I believe some men are valiant, thro' fear. For why should a man court danger, or a woman shun pleasure?

MRS. FORE. O monstrous! What are conscience and honor?

SCAN. Why, honor is a public enemy, and conscience a domestic thief; and he that would secure his pleasure must pay a tribute to one, and go halves with t'other. As for honor, that you have secured, for you have purchased a perpetual opportunity for pleasure.

MRS. FORE. An opportunity for pleasure!

SCAN. Ay, your husband; a husband is an opportunity for pleasure; so you have taken care of honor, and 'tis the least I can do to take care of conscience.

MRS. FORE. And so you think we are free for one another?

SCAN. Yes, faith, I think so; I love to speak my mind.

MRS. FORE. Why, then, I'll speak my mind. Now as to this affair between you and me. Here you make love to me; why, I'll confess it does not displease me. Your person is well enough, and your understanding is not amiss.

SCAN. I have no great opinion of myself, but I think I'm neither deformed, nor a fool.

MRS. FORE. But you have a villainous character; you are a libertine in speech, as well as practice.

SCAN. Come. I know what you would say: you think it more dangerous to be seen in conversation with me than to allow some other men the last favor. You mistake, the liberty I take in talking is purely affected for the service of your sex. He that first cries out stop thief, is often he that has stolen the treasure. I am a juggler that act by confederacy; and if you please, we'll put a trick upon the world.

MRS. FORE. Ay; but you are such a universal juggler, that I'm afraid you have a great many confederates.

SCAN. Faith, I'm sound.

MRS. FORE. O, fie——I'll swear you're impudent.

SCAN. I'll swear you're handsome.

MRS. FORE. Pish, you'd tell me so, tho' you did not think so.

SCAN. And you'd think so, tho' I should not tell you so. And now I think we know one another pretty well.

MRS. FORE. O Lord, who's here?

(*They talk aside*)

(*Enter* MRS. FRAIL *and* BEN)

BEN. Mess, I love to speak my mind. Father has nothing to do with me. Nay, I can't say that neither; he has something to do with me. But what does that signify? If so be, that I ben't minded to be steer'd by him, 'tis as tho'f he should strive against wind and tide.

MRS. FRAIL. Ay, but my dear, we must keep it secret, 'till the estate be settled; for you know, marrying without an estate is like sailing in a ship without ballast.

BEN. He, he, he! Why, that's true; just so, for all the world it is indeed, as like as two cable ropes.

MRS. FRAIL. And tho' I have a good portion, you know one would not venture all in one bottom.

BEN. Why, that's true again; for mayhap one bottom may spring a leak. You have hit it indeed; mess, you've nicked the channel.

MRS. FRAIL. Well, but if you should forsake me after all, you'd break my heart.

BEN. Break your heart? I'd rather the *Marygold* should break her cable in a storm, as well as I love her. Flesh, you don't think I'm false-hearted, like a land-man. A sailor will be honest, tho'f mayhap he has never a penny of money in his pocket. Mayhap I may not have so fair a face as a citizen or a courtier, but for all that, I've as good blood in my veins, and a heart as sound as a biscuit.

MRS. FRAIL. And will you love me always?

BEN. Nay, an I love once, I'll stick like pitch; I'll tell you what. Come, I'll sing you a song of a sailor.

MRS. FRAIL. Hold, there's my sister, I'll call her to hear it.

MRS. FORE. (*To* SCANDAL) Well, I won't go to bed to my husband tonight, because I'll retire to my own chamber, and think of what you have said.

SCAN. Well; you'll give me leave to wait upon you to your chamber door, and leave you my last instructions?

MRS. FORE. Hold, here's my sister coming towards us.

MRS. FRAIL. If it won't interrupt you, I'll entertain you with a song.

BEN. The song was made upon one of our ships-crew's wife; our boat-swain made the song; mayhap you may know her, sir. Before she was married, she was called Buxom Joan of Deptford.

SCAN. I have heard of her. (BEN *sings*)

BALLAD

I.

A soldier and a sailor,
A tinker, and a tailor,
Had once a doubtful strife, sir,
To make a maid a wife, sir,
  Whose name was Buxom Joan.
For now the time was ended,
When she no more intended,
To lick her lips at men, sir,
And gnaw the sheets in vain, sir,
  And lie o' nights alone.

II.

The soldier swore like thunder,
He loved her more than plunder;
And showed her many a scar, sir,
That he had brought from far, sir,

With fighting for her sake.
The tailor thought to please her,
With off'ring her his measure.
The tinker too with mettle,
Said he could mend her kettle,
And stop up every leak.

III.

But while these three were prating,
The sailor slyly waiting,
Thought if it came about, sir,
That they should all fall out, sir:
He then might play his part.
And just e'en as he meant, sir,
To loggerheads they went, sir,
And then he let fly at her,
A shot 'twixt wind and water,
That won this fair maid's heart.

BEN. If some of our crew that came to see me are not gone, you shall see that we sailors can dance sometimes, as well as other folks. (*Whistles*) I warrant that brings 'em, an they be within hearing.

(*Enter Seamen*)

Oh, here they be. And fiddles along with 'em; come, my lads, let's have a round, and I'll make one.

(*They dance*)

BEN. We're merry folks, we sailors, we han't much to care for. Thus we live at sea; eat biscuit, and drink flip; put on a clean shirt once a quarter; come home, and lie with our landladies once a year, get rid of a little money; and then put off with the next fair wind. How d'ye like us?

MRS. FRAIL. Oh, you are the happiest, merriest men alive!

MRS. FORE. We're beholden to Mr. Benjamin for this entertainment.——I believe it's late.

BEN. Why, forsooth, an you think so, you had best go to bed. For my part, I mean to toss a can, and remember my sweetheart, a-fore I turn in; mayhap I may dream of her.

MRS. FORE. Mr. Scandal, you had best go to bed and dream too.

SCAN. Why faith, I have a good lively imagination, and can dream as much to the purpose as another, if I set about it. But dreaming is the poor retreat of a lazy, hopeless, and imperfect lover; 'tis the last glimpse of love to worn-out sinners, and the faint dawning of a bliss to wishing girls and growing boys.

There's nought but willing, waking Love, that can
Make blest the ripen'd maid and finish'd man.

(*Exeunt*)

Act IV

VALENTINE'S *Lodging.*

(*Enter* SCANDAL *and* JEREMY)

SCAN. Well, is your master ready? Does he look madly, and talk madly?

JERE. Yes sir; you need make no great doubt of that. He that was so near turning poet yesterday morning, can't be much to seek in playing the madman today.

SCAN. Would he have Angelica acquainted with the reason of his design?

JERE. No, sir, not yet. He has a mind to try whether his playing the madman won't make her play the fool, and fall in love with him; or at least own that she has loved him all this while, and concealed it.

SCAN. I saw her take coach just now with her maid, and think I heard her bid the coachman drive hither.

JERE. Like enough, sir, for I told her maid this morning, my master was run stark mad only for love of her mistress. I hear a coach stop; if it should be she, sir, I believe he would not see her till he hears how she takes it.

SCAN. Well, I'll try her.——'Tis she, here she comes.

(*Enter* ANGELICA *with* JENNY)

ANG. Mr. Scandal, I suppose you don't think it a novelty to see a woman visit a man at his own lodgings in a morning?

SCAN. Not upon a kind occasion, madam. But when a lady comes tyrannically to insult a ruined lover, and make manifest the cruel triumphs of her beauty, the barbarity of it something surprises me.

ANG. I don't like raillery from a serious face. (*To* JEREMY) Pray tell me what is the matter?

JERE. No strange matter, madam; my master's mad, that's all. I suppose your ladyship has thought him so a great while.

ANG. How d'ye mean, mad?

JERE. Why, faith, madam, he's mad for want of his wits, just as he was poor for want of money; his head is e'en as light as his pockets; and any body that has a mind to a bad bargain, can't do better than to beg him for his estate.

ANG. If you speak truth, your endeavoring at wit is very unseasonable——

SCAN. (*Aside*) She's concerned, and loves him.

ANG. Mr. Scandal, you can't think me guilty of so much inhumanity, as not to be concerned for a man I must own myself obliged to? Pray tell me truth.

SCAN. Faith, madam, I wish telling a lie would mend the matter. But this is no new effect of an unsuccessful passion.

ANG. (*Aside*) I know not what to think. Yet I should be vext to have a trick put upon me.——May I not see him?

SCAN. I'm afraid the physician is not willing you should see him yet. Jeremy, go in and enquire.

(*Exit* JEREMY)

ANG. (*Aside*) Ha! I saw him wink and smile. I fancy 'tis a trick! I'll try.——I would disguise to all the world a failing, which I must own to you——I fear my happiness depends upon the recovery of Valentine. Therefore I conjure you, as you are his friend, and as you have compassion upon one fearful of affliction, to tell me what I am to hope for.— I cannot speak.—But you may tell me, tell me, for you know what I wou'd ask?

SCAN. (*Aside*) So, this is pretty plain.—— Be not too much concerned, madam; I hope his condition is not desperate. An acknowledgement of love from you, perhaps, may work a cure, as the fear of your aversion occasioned his distemper.

ANG. (*Aside*) Say you so; nay then I'm convinced. And if I don't play trick for trick, may I never taste the pleasure of revenge. ——Acknowledgement of love! I find you have mistaken my compassion, and think me guilty of a weakness I am a stranger to. But I have too much sincerity to deceive you, and too much charity to suffer him to be deluded with vain hopes. Good nature and humanity oblige me to be concerned for him; but to love is neither in my power nor inclination, and if he can't be cured without I suck the poison from his wounds, I'm afraid he won't recover his senses 'till I lose mine.

SCAN. (*Aside*) Hey, brave woman, i' faith! ——Won't you see him then, if he desire it?

ANG. What signify a madman's desires? Besides, 'twould make me uneasy. If I don't see him, perhaps my concern for him may lessen.—If I forget him, 'tis no more than he has done by himself; and now the surprise is over, methinks I am not half so sorry as I was.

SCAN. So, faith, good nature works apace; you were confessing just now an obligation to his love.

ANG. But I have consider'd that passions are unreasonable and involuntary. If he loves, he can't help it; and if I don't love, I can't help it; no more than he can help his being a man, or I my being a woman; or no more than I can help my want of inclination to stay longer here. Come, Jenny.

(*Exeunt* ANGELICA *and* JENNY)

SCAN. Humh! An admirable composition, faith, this same womankind.

(*Enter* JEREMY)

JERE. What, is she gone, sir?

SCAN. Gone! Why she was never here, nor any where else; nor I don't know her if I see her, nor you neither.

JERE. Good lack! What's the matter now? Are any more of us to be mad? Why, sir, my master longs to see her, and is almost mad in good earnest, with the joyful news of her being here.

SCAN. We are all under a mistake. Ask no questions, for I can't resolve you; but I'll inform your master. In the mean time, if our project succeed no better with his father than it does with his mistress, he may descend from his exaltation of madness into the road of common sense, and be content only to be made a fool with other reasonable people. I hear Sir Sampson. You know your cue; I'll to your master.

(*Enter* SIR SAMPSON LEGEND, *with* BUCKRAM)

SIR SAMP. D'ye see, Mr. Buckram, here's the paper signed with his own hand.

BUCK. Good, sir. And the conveyance is ready drawn in this box, if he be ready to sign and seal.

SIR SAMP. Ready, body o'me! he must be ready. His sham-sickness shan't excuse him. O, here's his scoundrel. Sirrah, where's your master?

JERE. Ah, sir, he's quite gone.

SIR SAMP. Gone! What, he is not dead?

JERE. No, sir, not dead.

SIR SAMP. What, is he gone out of town, run away, ha? has he trick'd me? Speak, varlet.

JERE. No, no, sir, he's safe enough, sir, an he were but as sound, poor gentleman. He is indeed here, sir, and not here, sir.

SIR SAMP. Hey day, rascal, do you banter me? Sirrah, d'ye banter me? Speak, sirrah, where is he? for I will find him.

JERE. Would you could, sir, for he has lost himself. Indeed, sir, I have a' most broke my heart about him—I can't refrain tears when I think of him, sir. I'm as melancholy for him as a passing-bell, sir, or a horse in a pound.

SIR SAMP. A pox confound your similitudes, sir. Speak to be understood, and tell me in plain terms what the matter is with him, or I'll crack your fool's skull.

JERE. Ah, you've hit it, sir; that's the matter with him, sir; his skull's cracked, poor gentleman; he's stark mad, sir.

SIR SAMP. Mad!

BUCK. What, is he *non compos?*

JERE. Quite *non compos,* sir.

BUCK. Why, then, all's obliterated, Sir Sampson, if he be *non compos mentis;* his act and deed will be of no effect, it is not good in law.

SIR SAMP. Oons, I won't believe it; let me

see him, sir. Mad, I'll make him find his senses.

JERE. Mr. Scandal is with him, sir; I'll knock at the door.

(*The scene opens to show* VALENTINE *upon a couch, disorderly dressed, with* SCANDAL *beside him*)

SIR SAMP. How now, what's here to do?

VAL. (*Starting*) Ha! Who's that?

SCAN. For heav'ns sake, softly, sir, and gently; don't provoke him.

VAL. Answer me; who is that, and that? (*Rises and roams about*)

SIR SAMP. Gads bobs, does he not know me? Is he mischievous? I'll speak gently. Val, Val, dost thou not know me, boy? Not know thy own father, Val? I am thy own father, and this is honest Brief Buckram, the lawyer.

VAL. It may be so——I did not know you ——the world is full. There are people that we do know, and people that we do not know; and yet the sun shines upon all alike. There are fathers that have many children, and there are children that have many fathers. 'Tis strange! But I am Truth, and come to give the world the lie.

SIR SAMP. Body o'me, I know not what to say to him.

VAL. Why does that lawyer wear black? Does he carry his conscience withoutside? (*Clutches* BUCKRAM) Lawyer, what art thou? Dost thou know me?

BUCK. O Lord, what must I say? Yes, sir.

VAL. Thou liest, for I am Truth. 'Tis hard I cannot get a livelihood amongst you. I have been sworn out of Westminster Hall the first day of every term—let me see—no matter how long. But I'll tell you one thing; it's a question that would puzzle an arithmetician, if you should ask him whether the Bible saves more souls in Westminster Abbey, or damns more in Westminster Hall. For my part, I am Truth, and can't tell; I have very few acquaintance.

SIR SAMP. Body o'me, he talks sensibly in his madness. Has he no intervals?

JERE. Very short, sir.

BUCK. Sir, I can do you no service while he's in this condition. Here's your paper, sir ——he may do me a mischief if I stay. The conveyance is ready, sir, if he recovers his senses. (*Exit* BUCKRAM *hastily*)

SIR SAMP. Hold, hold, don't you go yet.

SCAN. You'd better let him go, sir, and send for him if there be occasion; for I fancy his presence provokes him more.

VAL. Is the lawyer gone? 'Tis well, then we may drink about without going together by the ears—heigh ho! What a 'clock is't? My father here! Your blessing, sir.

SIR SAMP. He recovers——bless thee, Val. How dost thou do, boy?

VAL. Thank you, sir, pretty well. I have been a little out of order. Won't you please to sit, sir?

SIR SAMP. Ay, boy. Come, thou shalt sit down by me.

VAL. Sir, 'tis my duty to wait.

SIR SAMP. No, no, come, come, sit thee down, honest Val. How do'st thou do? Let me feel thy pulse. Oh, pretty well now, Val. Body o'me, I was sorry to see thee indisposed; but I'm glad thou art better, honest Val.

VAL. I thank you, sir.

SCAN. (*Aside*) Miracle! the monster grows loving.

SIR SAMP. Let me feel thy hand again, Val. It does not shake; I believe thou canst write, Val. Ha, boy? thou canst write thy name, Val? (*Whispers to* JEREMY) Jeremy, step and overtake Mr. Buckram, bid him make haste back with the conveyance—quick, quick. (*Exit* JEREMY)

SCAN. (*Aside*) That ever I should suspect such a heathen of any remorse!

SIR SAMP. Dost thou know this paper, Val? I know thou'rt honest, and wilt perform articles.

(*Shows him the paper, but holds it out of his reach*)

VAL. Pray let me see it, sir. You hold it so far off that I can't tell whether I know it or no.

SIR SAMP. See it, boy? Ay, ay, why thou dost see it—'tis thy own hand, Vally. Why, let me see, I can read it as plain as can be. Look you here. (*Reads*) *The condition of this obligation*——Look you, as plain as can be, so it begins——and then at the bottom—— *As witness my hand,* VALENTINE LEGEND, in great letters. Why, 'tis as plain as the nose in one's face. What, are my eyes better than thine? I believe I can read it farther off yet;

let me see. (*Stretches his arm as far as he can*)

VAL. Will you please let me hold it, sir?

SIR SAMP. Let thee hold it, say'st thou? Ay, with all my heart. What matter is it who holds it? What need anybody hold it? I'll put it up in my pocket, Val, and then nobody need hold it. (*Puts the paper in his pocket*) There, Val: it's safe enough, boy. But thou shalt have it as soon as thou hast set thy hand to another paper, little Val.

(*Enter* JEREMY *with* BUCKRAM)

VAL. What, is my bad genius here again! Oh no, 'tis the lawyer with an itching palm; and he's come to be scratched. (*Darts at* BUCKRAM) My nails are not long enough. Let me have a pair of red-hot tongs quickly, quickly, and you shall see me act St. Dunstan, and lead the devil by the nose.

BUCK. O Lord, let me be gone; I'll not venture myself with a madman.

(*Exit* BUCKRAM)

VAL. Ha, ha, ha! You need not run so fast, honesty will not overtake you. Ha, ha, ha, the rogue found me out to be *in forma pauperis* presently.

SIR SAMP. Oons! What a vexation is here! I know not what to do, or say, nor which way to go.

VAL. Who's that, that's out of his way? I am Truth, and can set him right. Harkee, friend, the straight road is the worst way you can go. He that follows his nose always, will very often be led into a stink. *Probatum est.* But what are you for? Religion or politics? There's a couple of topics for you, no more like one another than oil and vinegar; and yet those two beaten together by a state-cook, make sauce for the whole nation.

SIR SAMP. What the devil had I to do, ever to beget sons? Why did I ever marry?

VAL. Because thou wert a monster, old boy! The two greatest monsters in the world are a man and a woman. What's thy opinion?

SIR SAMP. Why, my opinion is, that those two monsters join'd together, make yet a greater, that's a man and his wife.

VAL. Aha! Old True-penny, say'st thou so? Thou hast nicked it. But it's wonderful strange, Jeremy.

JERE. What is, sir?

VAL. That gray hairs should cover a green head—and I make a fool of my father. (*Looks out the door*) What's here! *Erra Pater*, or a bearded sibyl? If Prophecy comes, Truth must give place.

(*Exeunt* VALENTINE *with* JEREMY)

(*Enter* FORESIGHT, MRS. FORESIGHT, MRS. FRAIL)

FORE. What says he? What, did he prophesy? Ha, Sir Sampson, bless us! How are we?

SIR SAMP. Are we? A pox o'your prognostication. Why, we are fools as we used to be. Oons, that you could not foresee that the moon would predominate, and my son be mad. Where's your oppositions, your trines, and your quadrates? What did your Cardan and your Ptolemy tell you? Your Messahalah and your Longomontanus, your harmony of chiromancy with astrology. Ah! pox on't, that I that know the world, and men and manners, that don't believe a syllable in the sky and stars, and sun and almanacs, and trash, should be directed by a dreamer, an omen-hunter, and defer business in expectation of a lucky hour, when, body o'me, there never was a lucky hour after the first opportunity.

(*Exit* SIR SAMPSON)

FORE. Ah, Sir Sampson, heav'n help your head. This is none of your lucky hour; *Nemo omnibus horis sapit.* What, is he gone, and in contempt of science? Ill stars and unconvertible ignorance attend him.

SCAN. You must excuse his passion, Mr. Foresight, for he has been heartily vexed. His son is *non compos mentis,* and thereby incapable of making any conveyance in law; so that all his measures are disappointed.

FORE. Ha! say you so?

MRS. FRAIL. (*Aside to* MRS. FORESIGHT) What, has my sea-lover lost his anchor of hope then?

MRS. FORE. Oh sister, what will you do with him?

MRS. FRAIL. Do with him? Send him to sea again in the next foul weather. He's used to an inconstant element, and won't be surprised to see the tide turned.

FORE. (*Considers*) Wherein was I mistaken, not to foresee this?

SCAN. (*Aside to* MRS. FORESIGHT) Madam, you and I can tell him something

else that he did not foresee, and more particularly relating to his own fortune.

MRS. FORE. What do you mean? I don't understand you.

SCAN. Hush, softly! The pleasures of last night, my dear, too considerable to be forgot so soon.

MRS. FORE. Last night! And what would your impudence infer from last night? Last night was like the night before, I think.

SCAN. 'S death, do you make no difference between me and your husband?

MRS. FORE. Not much. He's superstitious, and you are mad, in my opinion.

SCAN. You make me mad. You are not serious. Pray recollect yourself.

MRS. FORE. Oh yes, now I remember, you were very impertinent and impudent, and would have come to bed to me.

SCAN. And did not?

MRS. FORE. Did not! With what face can you ask the question?

SCAN. This I have heard of before, but never believed. I have been told she had that admirable quality of forgetting to a man's face in the morning that she had lain with him all night, and denying that she had done favors with more impudence than she could grant 'em. Madam, I'm your humble servant, and honor you.—You look pretty well, Mr. Foresight. How did you rest last night?

FORE. Truly, Mr. Scandal, I was so taken up with broken dreams and distracted visions that I remember little.

SCAN. 'Twas a very forgetting night. But would you not talk with Valentine? Perhaps you may understand him; I'm apt to believe there is something mysterious in his discourses, and sometimes rather think him inspired than mad.

FORE. You speak with singular good judgment, Mr. Scandal, truly. I am inclining to your Turkish opinion in this matter, and do reverence a man whom the vulgar think mad. Let us go to him.

(*Exeunt* FORESIGHT *and* SCANDAL)

MRS. FRAIL. Sister, do you stay with them. I'll find out my lover, and give him his discharge, and come to you. O'my conscience, here he comes. (*Exit* MRS. FORESIGHT)

(*Enter* BEN)

BEN. All mad, I think. Flesh, I believe all the calentures of the sea are come ashore, for my part.

MRS. FRAIL. Mr. Benjamin in choler!

BEN. No, I'm pleased well enough, now I have found you. Mess, I have had such a hurricane upon your account yonder.

MRS. FRAIL. My account! pray, what's the matter?

BEN. Why, father came and found me squabbling with yon chitty-faced thing, as he would have me marry, so he asked what was the matter. He asked in a surly sort of a way —it seems brother Val is gone mad, and so that put'n into a passion; but what did I know that? what's that to me?—so he asked in a surly sort of manner, and gad, I answered 'en as surlily. What tho'f he be my father, I an't bound prentice to 'en; so faith, I told'n in plain terms, if I were minded to marry, I'd marry to please myself, not him. And for the young woman that he provided for me, I thought it more fitting for her to learn her sampler and make dirt-pies, than to look after a husband. For my part, I was none of her man; I had another voyage to make, let him take it as he will.

MRS. FRAIL. So then, you intend to go to sea again?

BEN. Nay, nay, my mind run upon you, but I would not tell him so much. So he said he'd make my heart ache; and if so be that he could get a woman to his mind, he'd marry himself. Gad, says I, an you play the fool and marry at these years, there's more danger of your head's aching than my heart. He was woundy angry when I gav'n that wipe. He hadn't a word to say, and so I left'n, and the green girl together; mayhap the bee may bite, and he'll marry her himself, with all my heart.

MRS. FRAIL. And were you this undutiful and graceless wretch to your father?

BEN. Then why was he graceless first? If I am undutiful and graceless, why did he beget me so? I did not get myself.

MRS. FRAIL. O impiety! How have I been mistaken! What an inhuman merciless creature have I set my heart upon? O, I am happy to have discovered the shelves and quicksands that lurk beneath that faithless smiling face.

BEN. Hey toss! What's the matter now? Why, you ben't angry, be you?

MRS. FRAIL. O, see me no more,——for thou wert born amongst rocks, suckled by whales, cradled in a tempest, and whistled to by winds; and thou art come forth with fins and scales, and three rows of teeth, a most outrageous fish of prey.

BEN. O Lord, O Lord, she's mad, poor young woman. Love has turn'd her senses, her brain is quite overset. Well-a-day, how shall I do to set her to rights?

MRS. FRAIL. No, no, I am not mad, monster, I am wise enough to find you out. Hadst thou the impudence to aspire at being a husband with that stubborn and disobedient temper? You that know not how to submit to a father, presume to have a sufficient stock of duty to undergo a wife? I should have been finely fobbed indeed, very finely fobbed.

BEN. Harkee forsooth; if so be that you are in your right senses, d'ye see, for ought as I perceive I'm like to be finely fobbed,——if I have got anger here upon your account, and you are tacked about already. What d'ye mean, after all your fair speeches, and stroking my cheeks, and kissing and hugging, what, would you sheer off so? Would you, and leave me aground?

MRS. FRAIL. No, I'll leave you adrift, and go which way you will.

BEN. What, are you false-hearted then?

MRS. FRAIL. Only the wind's changed.

BEN. More shame for you——the wind's chang'd? It's an ill wind blows nobody good. Mayhap I have a good riddance on you, if these be your tricks. What did you mean all this while, to make a fool of me?

MRS. FRAIL. Any fool, but a husband.

BEN. Husband! Gad, I would not be your husband if you would have me, now I know your mind, tho'f you had your weight in gold and jewels, and tho'f I loved you never so well.

MRS. FRAIL. Why, can'st thou love, Porpoise?

BEN. No matter what I can do; don't call names. I don't love you so well as to bear that, whatever I did. I'm glad you show yourself, mistress.—Let them marry you, as don't know you. Gad, I know you too well, by sad experience; I believe he that marries you will go to sea in a hen-peck'd frigate—I believe that, young woman——and mayhap may come to an anchor at Cuckold's-Point; so there's a dash for you, take it as you will. Mayhap you may holla after me when I won't come to.   (*Exit* BEN)

MRS. FRAIL. Ha, ha, ha! No doubt on't, —(*Sings*) *My true Love is gone to Sea*——

(*Enter* MRS. FORESIGHT)

MRS. FRAIL. O sister, had you come a minute sooner, you would have seen the resolution of a lover! Honest Tar and I are parted, and with the same indifference that we met. O' my life, I am half vex'd at the insensibility of a brute that I despised.

MRS. FORE. What then, he bore it most heroically?

MRS. FRAIL. Most tyrannically; for you see he has got the start of me, and I, the poor forsaken maid, am left complaining on the shore. But I'll tell you a hint that he has given me. Sir Sampson is enraged, and talks desperately of committing matrimony himself. If he has a mind to throw himself away, he can't do it more effectually than upon me, if we could bring it about.

MRS. FORE. Oh, hang him, old fox, he's too cunning, besides he hates both you and me. But I have a project in my head for you, and I have gone a good way towards it. I have almost made a bargain with Jeremy, Valentine's man, to sell his master to us.

MRS. FRAIL. Sell him! How?

MRS. FORE. Valentine raves upon Angelica, and took me for her, and Jeremy says will take any body for her that he imposes on him. Now I have promised him mountains, if in one of his mad fits he will bring you to him in her stead, and get you married together, and put to bed together; and after consummation, girl, there's no revoking. And if he should recover his senses, he'll be glad at least to make you a good settlement. Here they come, stand aside a little, and tell me how you like the design.

(*They withdraw to a corner*)

(*Enter* VALENTINE, FORESIGHT, SCANDAL, *and* JEREMY)

SCAN. (*To* JEREMY) And have you given your master a hint of their plot upon him?

JERE. Yes, sir; he says he'll favor it, and mistake her for Angelica.

SCAN. It may make us sport.

FORE. Mercy on us!

VAL. Hush——interrupt me not——I'll whisper prediction to thee, and thou shalt prophesy. I am Truth, and can teach thy tongue a new trick. I have told thee what's past, now I'll tell you what's to come. Dost thou know what will happen tomorrow?—— Answer me not, for I will tell thee. Tomorrow, knaves will thrive through craft, and fools through fortune, and honesty will go as it did, frost-nipt in a summer suit. Ask me questions concerning tomorrow.

SCAN. Ask him, Mr. Foresight.

FORE. Pray, what will be done at court?

VAL. Scandal will tell you. I am Truth, I never come there.

FORE. In the city?

VAL. Oh, prayers will be said in empty churches, at the usual hours. Yet you will see such zealous faces behind counters, as if religion were to be sold in every shop. Oh, things will go methodically in the city, the clocks will strike twelve at noon, and the horned herd buzz in the Exchange at two. Wives and husbands will drive distinct trades, and care and pleasure separately occupy the family. Coffee-houses will be full of smoke and stratagem. And the cropt prentice, that sweeps his master's shop in the morning, may ten to one dirty his sheets before night. But there are two things that you will see very strange: which are wanton wives, with their legs at liberty, and tame cuckolds, with chains about their necks. But hold, I must examine you before I go further. You look suspiciously. Are you a husband?

FORE. I am married.

VAL. Poor creature! Is your wife of Covent Garden parish?

FORE. No; St. Martin's-in-the-Fields.

VAL. Alas, poor man; his eyes are sunk, and his hands shrivelled; his legs dwindled, and his back bowed. Pray, pray, for a metamorphosis. Change thy shape, and shake off age; get thee Medea's kettle, and be boiled anew; come forth with laboring callous hands, a chine of steel, and Atlas shoulders. Let Taliacotius trim the calves of twenty chairmen, and make thee pedestals to stand erect upon, and look matrimony in the face. Ha, ha, ha! That a man should have a stomach to a wedding supper, when the pigeons ought rather to be laid to his feet, ha, ha, ha!

Fore. His frenzy is very high now, Mr. Scandal.

Scan. I believe it is a spring tide.

Fore. Very likely, truly. You understand these matters. Mr. Scandal, I shall be very glad to confer with you about these things which he has uttered. His sayings are very mysterious and hieroglyphical.

Val. Oh, why would Angelica be absent from my eyes so long?

Jere. She's here, sir.

Mrs. Fore. (*To* Mrs. Frail) Now, sister.

Mrs. Frail. (*Aside*) O Lord, what must I say? (*She approaches* Valentine)

Scan. Humor him, madam, by all means.

Val. Where is she? Oh, I see her——she comes, like riches, health, and liberty at once, to a despairing, starving, and abandoned wretch. Oh, welcome, welcome!

Mrs. Frail. How d'ye, sir? Can I serve you?

Val. Harkee——I have a secret to tell you. Endymion and the moon shall meet us upon Mount Latmos, and we'll be married in the dead of night. But say not a word. Hymen shall put his torch into a dark lanthorn, that it may be secret; and Juno shall give her peacock poppy-water, that he may fold his ogling tail, and Argus's hundred eyes be shut. Ha? Nobody shall know but Jeremy.

Mrs. Frail. No, no! We'll keep it secret; it shall be done presently.

Val. The sooner the better. Jeremy, come hither——closer——that none may over-hear us. Jeremy, I can tell you news: Angelica is turned nun, and I am turning friar, and yet we'll marry one another in spite of the pope. Get me a cowl and beads, that I may play my part, for she'll meet me two hours hence in black and white, and a long veil to cover the project, and we won't see one another's faces till we have done something to be ashamed of; and then we'll blush once for all.

(*Enter* Tattle *and* Angelica)

Jere. I'll take care, and——

Val. Whisper. (*They whisper aside*)

Ang. Nay, Mr. Tattle, if you make love to me, you spoil my design, for I intend to make you my confidant.

Tatt. But, madam, to throw away your person, such a person! and such a fortune, on a madman!

Ang. I never loved him 'till he was mad; but don't tell anybody so.

Scan. (*Aside*) How's this! Tattle making love to Angelica!

Tatt. Tell, madam! Alas, you don't know me. I have much ado to tell your ladyship how long I have been in love with you; but encouraged by the impossibility of Valentine's making any more addresses to you, I have ventured to declare the very inmost passion of my heart. Oh, madam, look upon us both. There you see the ruins of a poor decayed creature——here, a complete and lively figure, with youth and health, and all his five senses in perfection, madam, and to all this, the most passionate lover——

Ang. O, fie for shame! Hold your tongue. A passionate lover, and five senses in perfection! When you are as mad as Valentine, I'll believe you love me, and the maddest shall take me.

Val. It is enough. Ha! Who's here?

Mrs. Frail. (*To* Jeremy) O Lord, her coming will spoil all.

Jere. No, no, madam, he won't know her; if he should, I can persuade him.

Val. Scandal, who are these? Foreigners? If they are, I'll tell you what I think. (*Whispers to* Scandal) Get away all the company but Angelica, that I may discover my design to her.

Scan. (*Whispering*) I will. I have discovered something of Tattle, that is of a piece with Mrs. Frail: he courts Angelica! If we could contrive to couple 'em together, hark'ee——(*They talk aside*)

Mrs. Fore. He won't know you, cousin, he knows nobody.

Fore. But he knows more than anybody. Oh, niece, he knows things past and to come, and all the profound secrets of time.

Tatt. Look you, Mr. Foresight, it is not my way to make many words of matters, and so I shan't say much; but in short, d'ye see, I will hold you a hundred pounds now, that I know more secrets than he.

Fore. How! I cannot read that knowledge in your face, Mr. Tattle. Pray, what do you know?

Tatt. Why, d'ye think I'll tell you, sir!

Read it in my face? No, sir, 'tis written in my heart; and safer there, sir, than letters writ in juice of lemon, for no fire can fetch it out. I am no blab, sir.

VAL. (*Aside to* SCANDAL) Acquaint Jeremy with it; he may easily bring it about. (*To the others*) They are welcome, and I'll tell 'em so myself. What, do you look strange upon me? Then I must be plain. (*Coming up to them*) I am Truth, and hate an old acquaintance with a new face.

(SCANDAL *goes aside with* JEREMY)

TATT. Do you know me, Valentine?

VAL. You? Who are you? No, I hope not.

TATT. I am Jack Tattle, your friend.

VAL. My friend? What to do? I am no married man, and thou canst not lie with my wife; I am very poor, and thou canst not borrow money of me; then what employment have I for a friend?

TATT. Hah! A good open speaker, and not to be trusted with a secret.

ANG. Do you know me, Valentine?

VAL. Oh, very well.

ANG. Who am I?

VAL. You're a woman. One to whom Heav'n gave beauty, when it grafted roses on a briar. You are the reflection of heav'n in a pond, and he that leaps at you is sunk. You are all white, a sheet of lovely spotless paper, when you first are born; but you are to be scrawled and blotted by every goose's quill. I know you; for I loved a woman, and loved her so long, that I found out a strange thing: I found out what a woman was good for.

TATT. Ay, prithee, what's that?

VAL. Why, to keep a secret.

TATT. O Lord!

VAL. O exceeding good to keep a secret. For though she should tell, yet she is not to be believed.

TATT. Hah! good again, faith.

VAL. I would have music. Sing me the song that I like.

SONG

I.

I tell thee, Charmion, could I time retrieve,
And could again begin to love and live,
To you I should my earliest off'ring give;

I know, my eyes would lead my heart to
you,
And I should all my vows and oaths re-
new,
But to be plain, I never would be true.

II.

For by our weak and weary truth, I find,
Love hates to center in a point assign'd;
But runs with joy the circle of the mind.
Then never let us chain what should be
free,
But for relief of either sex agree,
Since women love to change, and so do
we.

No more, for I am melancholy.

(*Walks musing*)

JERE. (*To* SCANDAL) I'll do't, sir.

SCAN. Mr. Foresight, we had best leave him. He may grow outrageous, and do mischief.

FORE. I will be directed by you.

JERE. (*Aside to* MRS. FRAIL) You'll meet, madam? I'll take care everything shall be ready.

MRS. FRAIL. Thou shalt do what thou wilt, in short, I will deny thee nothing.

TATT. (*To* ANGELICA) Madam, shall I wait upon you?

ANG. No, I'll stay with him; Mr. Scandal will protect me. Aunt, Mr. Tattle desires you would give him leave to wait on you.

TATT. (*Aside*) Pox on't, there's no coming off, now she has said that. (*Aloud*) Madam, will you do me the honor?

MRS. FORE. Mr. Tattle might have used less ceremony.

(*Exeunt* FORESIGHT, MRS. FRAIL, MRS. FORESIGHT, *and* TATTLE)

SCAN. Jeremy, follow Tattle.

ANG. Mr. Scandal, I only stay 'till my maid comes, and because I had a mind to be rid of Mr. Tattle.

SCAN. Madam, I am very glad that I overheard a better reason, which you gave to Mr. Tattle; for his impertinence forced you to acknowledge a kindness for Valentine, which you denied to all his sufferings and my solicitations. So I'll leave him to make use of the discovery, and your ladyship to the free confession of your inclinations.

ANG. Oh Heav'ns! You won't leave me alone with a madman?

SCAN. No, madam, I only leave a madman to his remedy.   (*Exit* SCANDAL)

VAL. Madam, you need not be very much afraid, for I fancy I begin to come to myself.

ANG. (*Aside*) Ay, but if I don't fit you, I'll be hang'd.

VAL. You see what disguises love makes us put on. Gods have been in counterfeited shapes for the same reason; and the divine part of me, my mind, has worn this masque of madness, and this motley livery, only as the slave of love and menial creature of your beauty.

ANG. Mercy on me, how he talks! Poor Valentine.

VAL. Nay, faith, now let us understand one another, hypocrisy apart. The comedy draws toward an end, and let us think of leaving acting, and be ourselves; and since you have loved me, you must own, I have at length deserved you should confess it.

ANG. (*Sighs*) I would I had loved you—— for Heav'n knows I pity you; and could I have foreseen the bad effects, I would have striven. But that's too late.   (*Sighs*)

VAL. What sad effects? What's too late? My seeming madness has deceived my father, and procured me time to think of means to reconcile me to him, and preserve the right of my inheritance to his estate; which otherwise, by articles, I must this morning have resign'd. And this I had inform'd you of today, but you were gone before I knew you had been here.

ANG. How! I thought your love of me had caused this transport in your soul, which, it seems, you only counterfeited for mercenary ends, and sordid interest.

VAL. Nay, now you do me wrong; for if any interest was considered it was yours, since I thought I wanted more than love to make me worthy of you.

ANG. Then you thought me mercenary. But how am I deluded by this interval of sense, to reason with a madman!

VAL. Oh, 'tis barbarous to misunderstand me longer.

(*Enter* JEREMY)

ANG. Oh here's a reasonable creature——

sure he will not have the impudence to persevere. Come, Jeremy, acknowledge your trick, and confess your master's madness counterfeit.

JERE. Counterfeit, madam! I'll maintain him to be as absolutely and substantially mad, as any freeholder in Bethlehem. Nay, he's as mad as any projector, fanatic, chemist, lover, or poet in Europe.

VAL. Sirrah, you lie! I am not mad.

ANG. Ha, ha, ha! you see he denies it.

JERE. O Lord, madam, did you ever know any madman mad enough to own it?

VAL. Sot, can't you apprehend?

ANG. Why he talked very sensibly just now.

JERE. Yes, madam; he has intervals. But you see he begins to look wild again now.

VAL. Why, you thick-skulled rascal, I tell you the farce is done, and I will be mad no longer.   (*Beats him*)

ANG. Ha, ha, ha! Is he mad, or no, Jeremy?

JERE. Partly I think—for he does not know his own mind two hours. I'm sure I left him just now in the humor to be mad, and I think I have not found him very quiet at this present. (*Knock at the door*) Who's there?

VAL. Go see, you sot. (*Exit* JEREMY) I'm very glad that I can move your mirth, though not your compassion.

ANG. I did not think you had apprehension enough to be exceptious. But madmen show themselves most, by over-pretending to a sound understanding, as drunken men do by over-acting sobriety. I was half inclining to believe you, 'till I accidentally touched upon your tender part, but now you have restored me to my former opinion and compassion.

(*Enter* JEREMY)

JERE. Sir, your father has sent to know if you are any better yet. Will you please to be mad, sir, or how?

VAL. Stupidity! You know the penalty of all I'm worth must pay for the confession of my senses. I'm mad, and will be mad to everybody but this lady.

JERE. So! Just the very backside of truth. But lying is a figure in speech that interlards the greatest part of my conversation. Madam, your ladyship's woman. (*Exit* JEREMY)

(*Enter* JENNY)

ANG. Well, have you been there?—— Come hither.

JENNY. Yes, madam. (*Aside to* ANGELICA) Sir Sampson will wait upon you presently.

VAL. You are not leaving me in this uncertainty?

ANG. Would anything but a madman complain of uncertainty? Uncertainty and expectation are the joys of life. Security is an insipid thing, and the overtaking and possessing of a wish, discovers the folly of the chase. Never let us know one another better; for the pleasure of a masquerade is done when we come to show our faces. But I'll tell you two things before I leave you: I am not the fool you take me for, and you are mad, and don't know it.

(*Exeunt* ANGELICA *and* JENNY)

VAL. From a riddle, you can expect nothing but a riddle. There's my instruction, and the moral of my lesson.

(*Enter* JEREMY)

JERE. What, is the lady gone again, sir? I hope you understood one another before she went.

VAL. Understood! She is harder to be understood than a piece of Egyptian antiquity or an Irish manuscript; you may pore 'till you spoil your eyes, and not improve your knowledge.

JERE. I have heard 'em say, sir, they read hard Hebrew books backwards. Maybe you begin to read at the wrong end.

VAL. They say so of a witch's prayer, and dreams and Dutch almanacs are to be understood by contraries. But there's regularity and method in that; she is a medal without a reverse or inscription, for indifference has both sides alike. Yet while she does not seem to hate me, I will pursue her, and know her if it be possible, in spite of the opinion of my satirical friend, Scandal, who says,

That women are like tricks by slight of hand,
Which, to admire, we should not understand.

Act V

A Room in FORESIGHT'S House.

(*Enter* ANGELICA *and* JENNY)

ANG. Where is Sir Sampson? Did you not tell me he would be here before me?

JENNY. He's at the great glass in the dining room, madam, setting his cravat and wig.

ANG. How! I'm glad on't! If he has a mind I should like him, it's a sign he likes me; and that's more than half my design.

JENNY. I hear him, madam.

ANG. Leave me, and d'ye hear, if Valentine should come, or send, I am not to be spoken with. (*Exit* JENNY)

(*Enter* SIR SAMPSON)

SIR SAMP. I have not been honored with the commands of a fair lady a great while —odd, madam, you have revived me—not since I was five and thirty.

ANG. Why, you have no great reason to complain, Sir Sampson, that is not long ago.

SIR SAMP. Zooks, but it is, madam, a very great while, to a man that admires a fine woman as much as I do.

ANG. You're an absolute courtier, Sir Sampson.

SIR SAMP. Not at all, madam. Odsbud, you wrong me; I am not so old neither, to be a bare courtier, only a man of words. Odd, I have warm blood about me yet, and can serve a lady any way. Come, come, let me tell you, you women think a man old too soon, faith and troth you do. Come, don't despise fifty; odd, fifty, in a hale constitution, is no such contemptible age.

ANG. Fifty a contemptible age! Not at all, a very fashionable age, I think. I assure you, I know very considerable beaux that set a good face upon fifty. Fifty! I have seen fifty in a side-box by candlelight out-blossom five and twenty.

SIR SAMP. Outsides, outsides; a pize take 'em, mere outsides! Hang your side-box beaux! No, I'm none of those, none of your forced trees, that pretend to blossom in the fall, and bud when they should bring forth fruit. I am of a long lived race, and inherit vigor; none of my ancestors married 'till fifty, yet they begot sons and daughters 'till fourscore. I am of your patriarchs, I; a branch of one of your antediluvian families, fellows that the flood could not wash away. Well, madam, what are your commands? Has any young rogue affronted you, and shall I cut his throat? or——

ANG. No, Sir Sampson, I have no quarrel upon my hands—I have more occasion for your conduct than your courage at this time. To tell you the truth, I'm weary of living single, and want a husband.

SIR SAMP. Odsbud, and 'tis pity you should—(Aside) Odd, would she would like me, then I should hamper my young rogues! Odd, would she would; faith and troth she's devilish handsome. (Aloud) Madam, you deserve a good husband, and 'twere pity you should be thrown away upon any of these young idle rogues about the town. Odd, there's ne'er a young fellow worth hanging—that is a very young fellow. Pize on 'em, they never think beforehand of any thing; and if they commit matrimony, 'tis as they commit murder, out of a frolic, and are ready to hang themselves, or to be hanged by the law, the next morning. Odso, have a care, madam.

ANG. Therefore I ask your advice, Sir Sampson: I have fortune enough to make any man easy that I can like. If there were such a thing as a young agreeable man, with a reasonable stock of good nature and sense ——for I would neither have an absolute wit, nor a fool.

SIR SAMP. Odd, you are hard to please, madam; to find a young fellow that is neither a wit in his own eye, nor a fool in the eye of the world, is a very hard task. But, faith and troth, you speak very discreetly; for I hate both a wit and a fool.

ANG. She that marries a fool, Sir Sampson, forfeits the reputation of her honesty

or understanding; and she that marries a very witty man is a slave to the severity and insolent conduct of her husband. I should like a man of wit for a lover, because I would have such an one in my power; but I would no more be his wife, than his enemy. For his malice is not a more terrible consequence of his aversion, than his jealousy is of his love.

SIR SAMP. None of old Foresight's Sibyls ever uttered such a truth. Odsbud, you have won my heart. I hate a wit; I had a son that was spoiled among 'em; a good hopeful lad, 'till he learned to be a wit——and might have risen in the state——but, a pox on't, his wit run him out of his money, and now his poverty has run him out of his wits.

ANG. Sir Sampson, as your friend, I must tell you, you are very much abused in that matter; he's no more mad than you are.

SIR SAMP. How, madam! Would I could prove it.

ANG. I can tell you how that may be done. But it is a thing that would make me appear to be too much concerned in your affairs.

SIR SAMP. (Aside) Odsbud, I believe she likes me!——Ah, madam, all my affairs are scarce worthy to be laid at your feet; and I wish, madam, they were in a better posture, that I might make a more becoming offer to a lady of your incomparable beauty and merit. If I had Peru in one hand, and Mexico in t'other, and the Eastern Empire under my feet, it would make me only a more glorious victim to be offered at the shrine of your beauty.

ANG. Bless me, Sir Sampson, what's the matter?

SIR SAMP. Odd, madam, I love you. And if you would take my advice in a husband——

ANG. Hold, hold, Sir Sampson. I asked your advice for a husband, and you are giving me your consent. I was indeed thinking to propose something like it in jest, to satisfy you about Valentine; for if a match were seemingly carried on between you and me, it would oblige him to throw off his disguise of madness, in apprehension of losing me: for you know he has long pretended a passion for me.

SIR SAMP. Gadzooks, a most ingenious contrivance—if we were to go through with it. But why must the match only be seemingly carried on? Odd, let it be a real contract.

Ang. O fie, Sir Sampson, what would the world say?

Sir Samp. Say! They would say you were a wise woman, and I a happy man. Odd, madam, I'll love you as long as I live, and leave you a good jointure when I die.

Ang. Ay, but that is not in your power, Sir Sampson; for when Valentine confesses himself in his senses, he must make over his inheritance to his younger brother.

Sir Samp. Odd, you're cunning, a wary baggage! Faith and troth, I like you the better! But, I warrant you, I have a proviso in the obligation in favor of myself. Body o'me, I have a trick to turn the settlement upon the issue male of our two bodies begotten. Odsbud, let us find children, and I'll find an estate!

Ang. Will you? Well, do you find the estate, and leave the t'other to me.

Sir Samp. O rogue! But I'll trust you. And will you consent? Is it a match then?

Ang. Let me consult my lawyer concerning this obligation, and if I find what you propose practicable, I'll give you my answer.

Sir Samp. With all my heart. Come in with me, and I'll lend you the bond. You shall consult your lawyer, and I'll consult a parson. Odzooks, I'm a young man—odzooks, I'm a young man, and I'll make it appear—odd, you're devilish handsome. Faith and troth, you're very handsome, and I'm very young, and very lusty. Odsbud, hussy, you know how to choose, and so do I. Odd, I think we are very well met. Give me your hand, odd, let me kiss it; 'tis as warm and as soft—as what?——odd, as t'other hand—give me t'other hand, and I'll mumble 'em, and kiss 'em 'till they melt in my mouth.

Ang. Hold, Sir Sampson——you're profuse of your vigor before your time; you'll spend your estate before you come to it.

Sir Samp. No, no, only give you a rent-roll of my possessions. Ah! Baggage——I warrant you for little Sampson. Odd, Sampson's a very good name for an able fellow; your Sampsons were strong dogs from the beginning.

Ang. Have a care, and don't over-act your part. If you remember, Sampson, the strongest of the name, pulled an old house over his head at last.

Sir Samp. Say you so, hussy? Come, let's go then; odd, I long to be pulling too, come away. Odso, here's somebody coming.

(Exeunt Angelica and Sir Sampson)

(Enter by another door Tattle and Jeremy)

Tatt. Is not that she, gone out just now?

Jere. Ay, sir, she's just going to the place of appointment. Ah, sir, if you are not very faithful and close in this business, you'll certainly be the death of a person that has a most extraordinary passion for your honor's service.

Tatt. Ay, who's that?

Jere. Even my unworthy self, sir. Sir, I have had an appetite to be fed with your commands a great while; and now, sir, my former master, having much troubled the fountain of his understanding, it is a very plausible occasion for me to quench my thirst at the spring of your bounty. I thought I could not recommend myself better to you, sir, than by the delivery of a great beauty and fortune into your arms, whom I have heard you sigh for.

Tatt. I'll make thy fortune; say no more. Thou art a pretty fellow, and canst carry a message to a lady in a pretty soft kind of phrase, and with a good persuading accent.

Jere. Sir, I have the seeds of rhetoric and oratory in my head——I have been at Cambridge.

Tatt. Ay! 'tis well enough for a servant to be bred at an university, but the education is a little too pedantic for a gentleman. I hope you are secret in your nature, private, close, ha?

Jere. O sir, for that, sir, 'tis my chief talent; I'm as secret as the head of Nilus.

Tatt. Ay? Who's he, though? A privy counsellor?

Jere. (Aside) O Ignorance!—A cunning Egyptian, sir, that with his arms would overrun the country, yet no body could ever find out his headquarters.

Tatt. Close dog! A good whoremaster, I warrant him. The time draws nigh, Jeremy. Angelica will be veiled like a nun, and I must be hooded like a friar; ha, Jeremy?

JERE. Ay, sir, hooded like a hawk, to seize at first sight upon the quarry. It is the whim of my master's madness to be so dressed; and she is so in love with him, she'll comply with anything to please him. Poor lady, I'm sure she'll have reason to pray for me when she finds what a happy exchange she has made, between a madman and so accomplished a gentleman.

TATT. Ay, faith, so she will, Jeremy. You're a good friend to her, poor creature. I swear I do it hardly so much in consideration of myself, as compassion to her.

JERE. 'Tis an act of charity, sir, to save a fine woman with thirty thousand pound from throwing herself away.

TATT. So 'tis, faith! I might have saved several others in my time; but, gad, I could never find in my heart to marry anybody before.

JERE. Well, sir, I'll go and tell her my master's coming, and meet you in half a quarter of an hour, with your disguise, at your own lodgings. You must talk a little madly, she won't distinguish the tone of your voice.

TATT. No, no, let me alone for a counterfeit; I'll be ready for you.   (*Exit* JEREMY)

(*Enter* MISS PRUE)

MISS. O Mr. Tattle, are you here! I'm glad I have found you; I have been looking up and down for you like anything, 'till I'm as tired as anything in the world.

TATT. (*Aside*) Oh, pox, how shall I get rid of this foolish girl?

MISS. O, I have pure news, I can tell you, pure news. I must not marry the seaman now—my father says so. Why won't you be my husband? You say you love me, and you won't be my husband. And I know you may be my husband now if you please.

TATT. O fie, Miss. Who told you so, child?

MISS. Why, my father—I told him that you loved me.

TATT. O fie, Miss, why did you do so? And who told you so, child?

MISS. Who? Why you did; did not you?

TATT. Oh, pox, that was yesterday, Miss, that was a great while ago, child. I have been asleep since; slept a whole night, and did not so much as dream of the matter.

MISS. Pshaw. Oh, but I dreamt that it was so, though.

TATT. Ay, but your father will tell you that dreams come by contraries, child. O fie! what, we must not love one another now. Pshaw, that would be a foolish thing indeed. Fie, fie, you're a woman now, and must think of a new man every morning, and forget him every night. No, no, to marry is to be a child again, and play with the same rattle always. O fie, marrying is a paw thing!

MISS. Well, but don't you love me as well as you did last night then?

TATT. No, no, child, you would not have me.

MISS. No? Yes but I would though.

TATT. Pshaw, but I tell you, you would not. You forget you're a woman, and don't know your own mind.

MISS. But here's my father, and he knows my mind.

(*Enter* FORESIGHT)

FORE. Oh, Mr. Tattle, your servant (*bows hastily*), you are a close man, but methinks your love to my daughter was a secret I might have been trusted with. Or had you a mind to try if I could discover it by my art? Hum, ha! I think there is something in your physiognomy that has a resemblance of her; and the girl is like me.

TATT. And so you would infer, that you and I are alike——(*Aside*) what does the old prig mean? I'll banter him, and laugh at him, and leave him.—I fancy you have a wrong notion of faces.

FORE. How? What? A wrong notion! How so?

TATT. In the way of art: I have some taking features, not obvious to vulgar eyes, that are indications of a sudden turn of good fortune in the lottery of wives, and promise a great beauty and great fortune reserved alone for me, by a private intrigue of destiny, kept secret from the piercing eye of perspicuity, from all astrologers and the stars themselves.

FORE. How! I will make it appear that what you say is impossible.

TATT. Sir, I beg your pardon, I'm in haste——

FORE. For what?

TATT. To be married, sir, married.

Fore. Ay, but pray take me along with you, sir——

Tatt. No, sir; 'tis to be done privately. I never make confidents.

Fore. Well, but my consent, I mean. You won't marry my daughter without my consent?

Tatt. Who, I, sir? I'm an absolute stranger to you and your daughter, sir.

Fore. Hey day! What time of the moon is this?

Tatt. Very true, sir, and desire to continue so. I have no more love for your daughter than I have likeness of you; and I have a secret in my heart, which you would be glad to know, and shan't know; and yet you shall know it too, and be sorry for't afterwards. I'd have you to know, sir, that I am as knowing as the stars, and as secret as the night. And I'm going to be married just now, yet did not know of it half an hour ago; and the lady stays for me, and does not know of it yet. There's a mystery for you——I know you love to untie difficulties. Or if you can't solve this, stay here a quarter of an hour, and I'll come and explain it to you.   (Exit Tattle)

Miss. O father, why will you let him go? Won't you make him to be my husband?

Fore. Mercy on us, what do these lunacies portend? Alas! he's mad, child, stark wild.

Miss. What, and must not I have e'er a husband, then? What, must I go to bed to nurse again, and be a child as long as she's an old woman? Indeed but I won't. For now my mind is set upon a man, I will have a man some way or other. Oh! methinks I'm sick when I think of a man; and if I can't have one, I would go to sleep all my life. For when I'm awake it makes me wish and long, and I don't know for what. And I'd rather be always asleep, than sick with thinking.

Fore. O fearful! I think the girl's influenced too. Hussy, you shall have a rod.

Miss. A fiddle of a rod, I'll have a husband; and if you won't get me one, I'll get one for myself. I'll marry our Robin the butler, he says he loves me, and he's a handsome man, and shall be my husband. I warrant he'll be my husband, and thank me too, for he told me so.

(Enter Scandal, Mrs. Foresight,
and Nurse)

Fore. Did he so? I'll dispatch him for't presently. Rogue! Oh, nurse, come hither.

Nurse. What is your worship's pleasure?

Fore. Here, take your young mistress, and lock her up presently, 'till farther orders from me. (To Miss Prue) Not a word, hussy ——do what I bid you, no reply, away. (To Nurse) And bid Robin make ready to give an account of his plate and linen, d'ye hear. (To Miss Prue) Be gone when I bid you.
(Exit Miss Prue)

Mrs. Fore. What's the matter, husband?

Fore. 'Tis not convenient to tell you now. Mr. Scandal, Heaven keep us all in our senses. I fear there is a contagious frenzy abroad. How does Valentine?

Scan. Oh, I hope he will do well again. I have a message from him to your niece Angelica.

Fore. I think she has not returned since she went abroad with Sir Sampson. Nurse, why are you not gone?   (Exit Nurse)

(Enter Ben)

Mrs. Fore. Here's Mr. Benjamin, he can tell us if his father be come home.

Ben. Who, father? Ay, he's come home with a vengeance.

Mrs. Fore. Why, what's the matter?

Ben. Matter! Why, he's mad.

Fore. Mercy on us, I was afraid of this.

Ben. And there's the handsome young woman, she, as they say, brother Val went mad for, she's mad too, I think.

Fore. O my poor niece, my poor niece, is she gone too? Well, I shall run mad next.

Mrs. Fore. Well, but how mad? how d'ye mean?

Ben. Nay, I'll give you leave to guess. I'll undertake to make a voyage to Antegoa—— no, hold, I mayn't say so neither——but I'll sail as far as Leghorn, and back again, before you shall guess at the matter, and do nothing else. Mess, you may take in all the points of the compass, and not hit right.

Mrs. Fore. Your experiment will take up a little too much time.

Ben. Why then, I'll tell you. There's a new wedding upon the stocks, and they two are a—going to be married to rights.

Scan. Who?

BEN. Why, father, and——the young woman, I can't hit of her name.

SCAN. Angelica?

BEN. Ay, the same.

MRS. FORE. Sir Sampson and Angelica! Impossible!

BEN. That may be, but I'm sure it is as I tell you.

SCAN. 'Sdeath, it's a jest. I can't believe it.

BEN. Look you, friend, it's nothing to me, whether you believe it or no. What I say is true; d'ye see, they are married, or just going to be married, I know not which.

FORE. Well, but they are not mad, that is, not lunatic?

BEN. I don't know what you call madness. But she's mad for a husband, and he's horn mad, I think, or they'd ne'er make a match together. Here they come.

(*Enter* SIR SAMPSON, ANGELICA, BUCKRAM)

SIR SAMP. Where is this old soothsayer, this uncle of mine elect? Aha, old Foresight, Uncle Foresight, wish me joy, Uncle Foresight, double joy, both as uncle and astrologer; here's a conjunction that was not foretold in all your Ephemeris. The brightest star in the blue firmament——is *shot from above, in a jelly of Love*, and so forth; and I'm lord of the ascendant. Odd, you're an old fellow, Foresight; uncle, I mean, a very old fellow, Uncle Foresight; and yet you shall live to dance at my wedding; faith and troth you shall. Odd, we'll have the music of the spheres for thee, old Lilly, that we will, and thou shalt lead up a dance *in via lactea*.

FORE. I'm thunder-struck! You are not married to my niece?

SIR SAMP. Not absolutely married, uncle; but very near it, within a kiss of the matter, as you see.   (*Kisses* ANGELICA)

ANG. 'Tis very true indeed, uncle. I hope you'll be my father, and give me.

SIR SAMP. That he shall, or I'll burn his globes. Body o'me, he shall be thy father, I'll make him thy father, and thou shalt make me a father, and I'll make thee a mother, and we'll beget sons and daughters enough to put the weekly bills [12] out of countenance.

SCAN. Death and Hell! Where's Valentine?   (*Exit* SCANDAL)

[12] Reports of deaths.

MRS. FORE. This is so surprising——

SIR SAMP. How! What does my aunt say? Surprising, aunt? Not at all, for a young couple to make a match in winter, not at all! It's a plot to undermine cold weather, and destroy that usurper of a bed called a warming-pan.

MRS. FORE. I'm glad to hear you have so much fire in you, Sir Sampson.

BEN. Mess, I fear his fire's little better than tinder; mayhap it will only serve to light up a match for somebody else. The young woman's a handsome young woman, I can't deny it. But father, if I might be your pilot in this case, you should not marry her. It's just the same thing, as if so be you should sail so far as the Straits without provision.

SIR SAMP. Who gave you authority to speak, sirrah? To your element, fish, be mute, fish, and to sea; rule your helm, sirrah, don't direct me.

BEN. Well, well, take you care of your own helm, or you mayn't keep your new vessel steady.

SIR SAMP. Why, you impudent tarpaulin! Sirrah, do you bring your forecastle jests upon your father? But I shall be even with you; I won't give you a groat. Mr. Buckram, is the conveyance so worded that nothing can possibly descend to this scoundrel? I would not so much as have him there have the prospect of an estate, though there were no way to come to it but by the North-East passage.

BUCK. Sir, it is drawn according to your directions; there is not the least cranny of the law unstopt.

BEN. Lawyer, I believe there's many a cranny and leak unstopt in your conscience. If so be that one had a pump to your bosom, I believe we should discover a foul hold. They say a witch will sail in a sieve, but I believe the devil would not venture aboard o'your conscience. And that's for you.

SIR SAMP. Hold your tongue, sirrah. How now, who's here?

(*Enter* TATTLE *and* MRS. FRAIL)

MRS. FRAIL. O, sister, the most unlucky accident!

MRS. FORE. What's the matter?

TATT. O, the two most unfortunate poor creatures in the world we are!

FORE. Bless us! How so?

MRS. FRAIL. Ah, Mr. Tattle and I, poor Mr. Tattle and I are——I can't speak it out.

TATT. Nor I——but poor Mrs. Frail and I are——

MRS. FRAIL. Married.

MRS. FORE. Married! How?

TATT. Suddenly——before we knew where we were—that villian Jeremy, by the help of disguises, tricked us into one another.

FORE. Why, you told me just now you went hence in haste to be married.

ANG. But I believe Mr. Tattle meant the favor to me, I thank him.

TATT. I did, as I hope to be saved, madam; my intentions were good. But this is the most cruel thing, to marry one does not know how, nor why, nor wherefore. The devil take me if ever I was so much concerned at anything in my life.

ANG. 'Tis very unhappy if you don't care for one another.

TATT. The least in the world—that is for my part; I speak for myself. Gad, I never had the least thought of serious kindness. I never liked anybody less in my life. Poor woman! Gad, I'm sorry for her too, for I have no reason to hate her neither, but I believe I shall lead her a damned sort of a life.

MRS. FORE. (To MRS. FRAIL) He's better than no husband at all—though he's a coxcomb.

MRS. FRAIL. (To her) Ay, ay, it's well it's no worse. (Aloud) Nay, for my part I always despised Mr. Tattle of all things; nothing but his being my husband could have made me like him less.

TATT. Look you there, I thought as much! Pox on't, I wish we could keep it secret! Why, I don't believe any of this company would speak of it.

MRS. FRAIL. But, my dear, that's impossible; the parson and that rogue Jeremy will publish it.

TATT. Ay, my dear, so they will, as you say.

ANG. O, you'll agree very well in a little time; custom will make it easy to you.

TATT. Easy! Pox on't, I don't believe I shall sleep tonight.

SIR SAMP. Sleep, quotha! No! Why you would not sleep o' your wedding-night? I'm an older fellow than you, and don't mean to sleep.

BEN. Why, there's another match now, as tho'f a couple of privateers were looking for a prize, and should fall foul of one another. I'm sorry for the young man with all my heart. Look you, friend, if I may advise you, when she's going——for that you must expect, I have experience of her——when she's going, let her go. For no matrimony is tough enough to hold her, and if she can't drag her anchor along with her, she'll break her cable, I can tell you that.——Who's here? The madman?

(Enter VALENTINE, SCANDAL, and JEREMY)

VAL. No, here's the fool; and if occasion be, I'll give it under my hand.

SIR SAMP. How now?

VAL. Sir, I'm come to acknowledge my errors, and ask your pardon.

SIR SAMP. What, have you found your senses at last then? In good time, sir.

VAL. You were abused, sir; I never was distracted.

FORE. How! Not mad! Mr. Scandal——

SCAN. No really, sir; I'm his witness, it was all counterfeit.

VAL. I thought I had reasons——but it was a poor contrivance; the effect has shown it such.

SIR SAMP. Contrivance! What, to cheat me? to cheat your father! Sirrah, could you hope to prosper?

VAL. Indeed, I thought, sir, when the father endeavored to undo the son, it was a reasonable return of nature.

SIR SAMP. Very good, sir. Mr. Buckram, are you ready? Come, sir, will you sign and seal?

VAL. If you please, sir. But first I would ask this lady one question.

SIR SAMP. Sir, you must ask me leave first. That lady? No, sir; you shall ask that lady no questions till you have asked her blessing, sir. That lady is to be my wife.

VAL. I have heard as much, sir; but I would have it from her own mouth.

SIR SAMP. That's as much as to say I lie, sir, and you don't believe what I say.

VAL. Pardon me, sir. But I reflect that I

very lately counterfeited madness; I don't know but the frolic may go round.

SIR SAMP. Come, chuck, satisfy him, answer him. Come, come, Mr. Buckram, the pen and ink.

BUCK. Here it is, sir, with the deed; all is ready. (VALENTINE *goes to* ANGELICA)

ANG. 'Tis true, you have a great while pretended love to me; nay, what if you were sincere? Still you must pardon me, if I think my own inclinations have a better right to dispose of my person than yours.

SIR SAMP. Are you answered now, sir?

VAL. Yes, sir.

SIR SAMP. Where's your plot, sir? And your contrivance now, sir? Will you sign, sir? Come, will you sign and seal?

VAL. With all my heart, sir.

SCAN. 'Sdeath, you are not mad indeed, to ruin yourself?

VAL. I have been disappointed of my only hope; and he that loses hope may part with any thing. I never valued fortune but as it was subservient to my pleasure; and my only pleasure was to please this lady. I have made many vain attempts, and find at last that nothing but my ruin can effect it; which, for that reason, I will sign to——give me the paper.

ANG. (*Aside*) Generous Valentine!

BUCK. Here is the deed, sir.

VAL. But where is the bond by which I am obliged to sign this?

BUCK. Sir Sampson, you have it.

ANG. No, I have it; and I'll use it as I would everything that is an enemy to Valentine. (*Tears the paper*)

SIR SAMP. How now!

VAL. Ha!

ANG. (*To* VALENTINE) Had I the world to give you, it could not make me worthy of so generous and faithful a passion. Here's my hand; my heart was always yours, and struggled very hard to make this utmost trial of your virtue.

VAL. Between pleasure and amazement, I am lost, but on my knees I take the blessing.

SIR SAMP. Oons, what is the meaning of this?

BEN. Mess, here's the wind changed again. Father, you and I may make a voyage together now.

ANG. Well, Sir Sampson, since I have played you a trick, I'll advise you how you may avoid such another. Learn to be a good father, or you'll never get a second wife. I always loved your son, and hated your unforgiving nature. I was resolved to try him to the utmost; I have tried you too, and know you both. You have not more faults than he has virtues; and 'tis hardly more pleasure to me that I can make him and myself happy than that I can punish you.

VAL. If my happiness could receive addition, this kind surprise would make it double.

SIR SAMP. Oons, you're a crocodile.

FORE. Really, Sir Sampson, this is a sudden eclipse.

SIR SAMP. You're an illiterate old fool, and I'm another.

TATT. If the gentleman is in disorder for want of a wife, I can spare him mine. (*He suddenly notices* JEREMY) Oh, are you there, sir? I'm indebted to you for my happiness.

JERE. Sir, I ask you ten thousand pardons, 'twas an errant mistake. You see, sir, my master was never mad, nor anything like it. Then how could it be otherwise?

VAL. Tattle, I thank you; you would have interposed between me and Heav'n, but providence laid purgatory in your way. You have but justice.

SCAN. I hear the fiddles that Sir Sampson provided for his own wedding; methinks 'tis pity they should not be employed when the match is so much mended. Valentine, though it be morning, we may have a dance.

VAL. Anything, my friend, everything that looks like joy and transport.

SCAN. Call 'em, Jeremy. (*Exit* JEREMY)

ANG. I have done disassembling now, Valentine; and if that coldness which I have always worn before you should turn to an extreme fondness, you must not suspect it.

VAL. I'll prevent that suspicion. For I intend to dote to that immoderate degree, that your fondness shall never distinguish itself enough to be taken notice of. If ever you seem to love too much, it must be only when I can't love enough.

ANG. Have a care of promises; you know you are apt to run more in debt than you are able to pay.

VAL. Therefore I yield my body as your prisoner, and make your best on't.

(*Re-enter* JEREMY)

JERE. The music stays for you.

(*They dance*)

SCAN. Well, madam, you have done exemplary justice in punishing an inhuman father and rewarding a faithful lover. But there is a third good work, which I, in particular, must thank you for; I was an infidel to your sex, and you have converted me. For now I am convinced that all women are not like Fortune, blind in bestowing favors, either on those who do not merit, or who do not want 'em.

ANG. 'Tis an unreasonable accusation that you lay upon our sex. You tax us with injustice, only to cover your own want of merit. You would all have the reward of love; but few have the constancy to stay 'till it becomes your due. Men are generally hypocrites and infidels: they pretend to worship, but have neither zeal nor faith. How few, like Valentine, would persevere even to martyrdom, and sacrifice their interest to their constancy! In admiring me, you misplace the novelty.

The miracle today is, that we find
A lover true, not that a woman's kind.

Epilogue

Spoken at the Opening of the New House,[13]

By MRS. BRACEGIRDLE[14]

Sure Providence at first designed this place
To be the player's refuge in distress;
For still in every storm, they all run hither,
As to a shed, that shields 'em from the
weather.
But thinking of this change which last befell us,
It's like what I have heard our poets tell us:
For when behind our scenes their suits are
pleading,
To help their love, sometimes they show their
reading;
And wanting ready cash to pay for hearts,
They top their learning on us, and their parts.
Once of philosophers they told us stories,
Whom, as I think, they called—Py—Pythagories,
I'm sure 'tis some such *Latin* name they give
'em,
And we, who know no better, must believe
'em.
Now to these men (say they) such souls
were given,
That after death, ne'er went to Hell, nor
Heaven,
But lived, I know not how, in beasts; and
then
When many years were past, in men again.
Methinks, we *Players* resemble such a soul,
That, does from bodies, we from houses stroll.

[13] The Duke's Theatre in Lincoln's Inn Fields.
It was a remodeled tennis court.

[14] The actress for whom Congreve wrote the
part of Angelica.

Thus *Aristotle's* soul, of old that was,
May now be damned to animate an ass;
Or in this very house, for ought we know,
Is doing painful penance in some *Beau*:
And thus our audience, which did once
resort
To shining theatres to see our sport,
Now find us tossed into a tennis-court.
These walls but t'other day were filled with
noise
Of roaring gamesters, and your *Damne Boys;*
Then bounding balls and rackets they encompast,
And now they're filled with jests, and flights,
and bombast!
I vow, I don't much like this transmigration,
Strolling from place to place, by circulation;
Grant Heaven, we don't return to our first
station.
I know not what these think, but for my
part,
I can't reflect without an aching heart,
How we should end in our original, a cart.
But we can't fear, since you're so good to
save us,
That you have only set us up, to leave us.
Thus from the past, we hope for future grace,
I beg it——
And some here know I have a begging face.
Then pray continue this your kind behavior,
For a clear stage won't do, without your favor.

WILLIAM CONGREVE *

The Way of the World

~~~~~~

INTRODUCTION

The Way of the World is generally thought to be Congreve's comic masterpiece, and it has more than once been called the most brilliant comedy of manners in the English language. It presents serious difficulties to most readers, however, for Congreve has not kept Mirabell's intrigues very clear, and readers usually concentrate more on plot developments than do audiences in the theatre. Perhaps the best way to obviate this difficulty is to outline the intrigues first, so that the reader will waste only a minimum of energy in trying to follow them.

Mirabell has been for some time in love with Millamant, the niece of Lady Wishfort. Millamant's fortune has been left to her with the proviso that half of it, £6,000, is to be forfeited to Lady Wishfort if Millimant marries without her aunt's consent. Before the play opens, Mirabell has pretended to be in love with Lady Wishfort in order to secure her favor, but Mrs. Marwood has revealed his scheme to her, and now she hates him. Mirabell lays a new plot to force her consent. He plans for his serving man Waitwell to pose as his uncle, Sir Rowland, and court Lady Wishfort. He is confident that Lady Wishfort will accept the pretended Sir Rowland because of her vanity and her eagerness to spite Mirabell of his inheritance from his uncle. Before Waitwell begins his imposture, Mirabell arranges Waitwell's marriage with Lady Wishfort's maid, Foible, and promises to set the couple up on a farm if the plot succeeds. He plans that when Lady Wishfort discovers her entanglement with a serving man,

* See p. 462 for biographical details.

he will agree to extricate her at the price of her consent to his marriage to Millamant; this he will accomplish by revealing Waitwell's previous marriage to Foible.

Unfortunately Mrs. Marwood discovers this plot too. She is the mistress of Mr. Fainall, the husband of Lady Wishfort's daughter. Marwood and Fainall form a counter-plot to gain the money of both Millamant and Mrs. Fainall and to be revenged on Mirabell, of whom they are both jealous because he has had both Mrs. Fainall and Mrs. Marwood for his mistresses. Their scheme is first to expose the phony Sir Rowland and enrage Lady Wishfort still further against Mirabell and then to reveal the former affair of Mrs. Fainall to Lady Wishfort and threaten to make the scandal public. They are sure that Lady Wishfort will be terrified of the scandal for her daughter and agree as the price of silence to make both her daughter's fortune and Millamant's over to Fainall. Their machinations are successful, and Lady Wishfort is blackmailed into accepting the demands of Fainall. In her despair she agrees to give her consent for Millamant to marry Mirabell if he can rescue her. First Mirabell has two maids reveal the intimacy of Mrs. Marwood and Mr. Fainall, but though this disillusions Lady Wishfort about her supposed friend Marwood, Fainall does not relent. Then Mirabell reveals a witnessed document whereby Mrs. Fainall, before her marriage to Fainall, made over her entire estate in trust to Mirabell. Thus Fainall loses both his wife's money because of the deed and Millamant's money because Lady Wishfort has consented to her match with Mirabell. Fainall and Marwood leave, futilely swearing revenge, and all prepare for the wedding of Mirabell and Millamant.

These intrigues of the play are of only minor significance. Each scene can be enjoyed for itself, for each has its own pace, its own wit, its own charm. Here is manner, wit, and elegance refined to the last distillation, an elegance of which the elaborate and colorful costumes are only the most external manifestation. The handicapped reader of the comedy must visualize the magnificent embroidered waistcoats, the satin coats, the elaborately curled wigs, and the costly lace at the wrists, for dialogue and costume are equally representative of manners. The elaborate formality of the dialogue receives its proper setting from the costumes, and the gaucherie of a character like Petulant is fully apparent only in its proper setting. Mincing's affectation of elegance, the mincing gesture accompanying the mincing talk, serve as a foil to the superb ease and assurance of her mistress, Millamant. Both are posing and affected, but the maid is clumsily so, while the mistress achieves her effects with the ease and precision of a ballerina. This is the comedy of manners at its peak. The ideas and the emotional effects are negligible, the polish of the dialogue and the exquisite calculation of the pose of the mannered characters are the subjects of Congreve's primary concern.

∾

THE WAY OF THE WORLD

Dramatis personae

In order of first appearance

MIRABELL, A witty and dashing man-about-town. He loves Millamant and is constantly scheming to win her hand without forfeiting her fortune.

FAINALL, A callous adventurer, husband of Mrs. Fainall and lover of Mrs. Marwood.

BETTY, A pert waitress at a chocolate-house.

SERVANT, In the employ of Mirabell.

MESSENGER

WITWOUD, A silly admirer of Mrs. Millamant who strives to be witty. Boon companion of Petulant.

COACHMAN

PETULANT, A silly, quarrelsome fellow who pretends to be pursued by ladies.

MRS. FAINALL, Daughter of Lady Wishfort, wife of Fainall, formerly mistress of Mirabell and still in love with him.

MRS. MARWOOD, Mistress of Mr. Fainall, in love with Mirabell, pretended friend of Mrs. Fainall.

MRS. MILLAMANT, The belle of the town. She is the niece of Lady Wishfort, and half her fortune is contingent on Lady Wishfort's approval of her marriage.

Though she is witty and sophisticated, with a keen eye for folly and the cool arrogance of the acknowledged beauty, she is also possessed of moral sense and capable of sincere emotion.

MINCING, Her affected maid.

WAITWELL, A competent servant of Mirabell.

FOIBLE, Lady Wishfort's clever and scheming maid.

LADY WISHFORT, Mother of Mrs. Fainall and aunt of Millamant and Sir Wilfull. A vain and foolish woman of 55, easily persuaded that men admire and desire her.

PEG, A stupid and awkward maid in Lady Wishfort's house.

SIR WILFULL WITWOUD, Witwoud's elder half-brother and nephew of Lady Wishfort. He has just come to London from his Shropshire estate and dresses and acts like a farmer, to the disgust or amusement of the ladies and gentlemen of London society.

Singer, dancers, servants, etc.

SCENE: *London*

Prologue

Spoken by Mr. Betterton

Of those few fools who with ill stars are
    cursed,
Sure scribbling fools called poets, fare the
    worst:
For they're a sort of fools which Fortune
    makes,
And after she has made 'em fools, forsakes.
With Nature's oafs 'tis quite a different case,
For Fortune favors all her idiot-race.
In her own nest the cuckoo-eggs we find,
O'er which she broods to hatch the change-
    ling-kind.
No portion for her own she has to spare,
So much she dotes on her adopted care.

Poets are bubbles, by the town drawn in,
Suffered at first some trifling stakes to win;
But what unequal hazards do they run!
Each time they write they venture all
    they've won:
The squire that's buttered [1] still, is sure to
    be undone.
This author heretofore has found your favor;
But pleads no merit from his past behavior.
To build on that might prove a vain pre-
    sumption,
Should grants, to poets made, admit resump-
    tion:
And in Parnassus he must lose his seat,
If that be found a forfeited estate.

He owns with toil he wrought the follow-
    ing scenes;
But, if they're naught, ne'er spare him for
    his pains:
Damn him the more; have no commiseration
For dullness on mature deliberation.
He swears he'll not resent one hissed-off
    scene,
Nor, like those peevish wits, his play
    maintain,
Who, to assert their sense, your taste
    arraign.
Some plot we think he has, and some new
    thought;
Some humor too, no farce—but that's a fault.
Satire, he thinks, you ought not to expect;
For so reformed a town who dares correct?
To please, this time, has been his sole pre-
    tence,
He'll not instruct, lest it should give offence.
Should he by chance a knave or fool expose,
That hurts none here; sure, here are none of
    those.
In short, our play shall (with your leave to
    show it)
Give you one instance of a passive poet,
Who to your judgments yields all resigna-
    tion;
So save or damn, after your own discretion.

Act I

Scene I. *A Room in a Chocolate-House.*

(Mirabell *and* Fainall *at a card table;*
Betty *waiting*)

Mirabell. You are a fortunate man, Mr.
Fainall!

Fainall. Have we done?

Mirabell. What you please. I'll play on
to entertain you.

Fainall. No, I'll give you your revenge

[1] Fulsomely praised.

another time, when you are not so indifferent; you are thinking of something else now,
and play too negligently. The coldness of a
losing gamester lessens the pleasure of the
winner. (*He leaves the table;* Mirabell
pushes back his chair) I'd no more play with
a man that slighted his ill fortune than I'd
make love to a woman who undervalued the
loss of her reputation.

Mirabell. You have a taste extremely

delicate, and are for refining on your pleasures.

FAINALL. Prithee, why so reserved? Something has put you out of humor.

MIRABELL. Not at all. I happen to be grave to-day, and you are gay; that's all.

FAINALL. Confess, Millamant and you quarrelled last night after I left you; my fair cousin has some humors that would tempt the patience of a stoic. What, some coxcomb came in, and was well received by her, while you were by?

MIRABELL. Witwoud and Petulant; and what was worse, her aunt, your wife's mother, my evil genius; or to sum up all in her own name, my old Lady Wishfort came in.

FAINALL. Oh, there it is then! She has a lasting passion for you, and with reason.— What, then my wife was there?

MIRABELL. Yes, and Mrs. Marwood, and three or four more, whom I never saw before. Seeing me, they all put on their grave faces, whispered one another; then complained aloud of the vapors,[1a] and after fell into a profound silence.

FAINALL. They had a mind to be rid of you.

MIRABELL. (*Rises and strides about as he talks*) For which reason I resolved not to stir. At last the good old lady broke through her painful taciturnity with an invective against long visits. I would not have understood her, but Millamant joining in the argument, I rose, and with a constrained smile, told her I thought nothing was so easy as to know when a visit began to be troublesome. She reddened, and I withdrew without expecting her reply.

FAINALL. You were to blame to resent what she spoke only in compliance with her aunt.

MIRABELL. She is more mistress of herself than to be under the necessity of such a resignation.

FAINALL. What! Though half her fortune depends upon her marrying with my lady's approbation?

MIRABELL. I was then in such a humor, that I should have been better pleased if she had been less discreet.

FAINALL. Now I remember, I wonder not

they were weary of you; last night was one of their cabal nights. They have 'em three times a week, and meet by turns at one another's apartments, where they come together like the coroner's inquest, to sit upon the murdered reputations of the week. You and I are excluded, and it was once proposed that all the male sex should be excepted; but somebody moved that, to avoid scandal, there might be one man of the community, upon which motion Witwoud and Petulant were enrolled members.

MIRABELL. And who may have been the foundress of this sect? My Lady Wishfort, I warrant, who publishes her detestation of mankind, and, full of the vigor of fifty-five, declares for a friend and ratafia;[2] and let posterity shift for itself, she'll breed no more.

FAINALL. The discovery of your sham addresses to her, to conceal your love to her niece, has provoked this separation; had you dissembled better, things might have continued in the state of nature.

MIRABELL. I did as much as man could, with any reasonable conscience; I proceeded to the very last act of flattery with her, and was guilty of a song in her commendation. Nay, I got a friend to put her into a lampoon and compliment her with the imputation of an affair with a young fellow, which I carried so far that I told her the malicious town took notice that she was grown fat of a sudden; and when she lay in of a dropsy, persuaded her she was reported to be in labor. The devil's in't, if an old woman is to be flattered further, unless a man should endeavor downright personally to debauch her; and that my virtue forbade me. But for the discovery of this amour I am indebted to your friend, or your wife's friend, Mrs. Marwood.

FAINALL. What should provoke her to be your enemy unless she has made you advances which you have slighted? Women do not easily forgive omissions of that nature.

MIRABELL. She was always civil to me till of late. I confess I am not one of those coxcombs who are apt to interpret a woman's good manners to her prejudice, and think that she who does not refuse 'em everything, can refuse 'em nothing.

[1a] Depression, low spirits, boredom.

[2] A liqueur flavored with the kernels of peach, cherry, apricot, or almond.

FAINALL. You are a gallant man, Mirabell; and though you may have cruelty enough not to satisfy a lady's longing, you have too much generosity not to be tender of her honor. Yet you speak with an indifference which seems to be affected and confesses you are conscious of a negligence.

MIRABELL. You pursue the argument with a distrust that seems to be unaffected and confesses you are conscious of a concern for which the lady is more indebted to you than is your wife.

FAINALL. Fie, fie, friend! If you grow censorious I must leave you.—I'll look upon the gamesters in the next room.

MIRABELL. Who are they?

FAINALL. (At the door) Petulant and Witwoud.—(To BETTY) Bring me some chocolate. (Exit FAINALL)

MIRABELL. Betty, what says your clock?

BETTY. Turned of the last canonical hour,[2a] sir. (Exit BETTY)

MIRABELL. How pertinently the jade answers me!—(Looking on his watch)—Ha, almost one o'clock!—Oh, y'are come!

(Enter a SERVANT)

Well, is the grand affair over? You have been something tedious.

SERVANT. Sir, there's such coupling at Pancras[3] that they stand behind one another, as 'twere in a country dance. Ours was the last couple to lead up, and no hopes appearing of dispatch—besides, the parson growing hoarse, we were afraid his lungs would have failed before it came to our turn; so we drove round to Duke's-place,[4] and there they were riveted in a trice.

MIRABELL. So, so! You are sure they are married?

SERVANT. Married and bedded, sir; I am witness.

MIRABELL. Have you the certificate?

SERVANT. Here it is, sir.

MIRABELL. Has the tailor brought Waitwell's clothes home, and the new liveries?

SERVANT. Yes, sir.

MIRABELL. That's well. Do you go home again, d'ye hear, and adjourn the consummation till further orders. Bid Waitwell shake his ears, and Dame Partlet[5] rustle up her feathers and meet me at one o'clock by Rosamond's Pond,[6] that I may see her before she returns to her lady; and as you tender your ears be secret. (Exit SERVANT)

(Enter FAINALL, followed by BETTY, who goes to the window)

FAINALL. Joy of your success, Mirabell; you look pleased.

MIRABELL. Aye; I have been engaged in a matter of some sort of mirth, which is not yet ripe for discovery. I am glad this is not a cabal night. I wonder, Fainall, that you, who are married and of consequence should be discreet, will suffer your wife to be of such a party.

FAINALL. Faith, I am not jealous. Besides, most who are engaged are women and relations; and for the men, they are of a kind too contemptible to give scandal.

MIRABELL. I am of another opinion. The greater the coxcomb, always the more the scandal; for a woman who is not a fool can have but one reason for associating with a man who is one.

FAINALL. Are you jealous as often as you see Witwoud entertained by Millamant?

MIRABELL. Of her understanding I am, if not of her person.

FAINALL. You do her wrong; for, to give her her due, she has wit.

MIRABELL. She has beauty enough to make any man think so; and complaisance enough not to contradict him who shall tell her so.

FAINALL. For a passionate lover, methinks you are a man somewhat too discerning in the failings of your mistress.

MIRABELL. And for a discerning man, somewhat too passionate a lover; for I like her with all her faults—nay, like her for her faults. Her follies are so natural, or so artful, that they become her; and those affectations which in another woman would be odious

[2a] Hour of legal marriage.

[3] St. Pancras Church, where marriages could be performed at any time without a license.

[4] Site of St. James's Church, well known for the irregular and hurried marriages performed there.

[5] I.e., the hen.

[6] In St. James's Park, which was much frequented by lovers. See Act II.

serve but to make her more agreeable. I'll tell thee, Fainall, she once used me with that insolence, that in revenge I took her to pieces, sifted her, and separated her failings; I studied 'em, and got 'em by rote. The catalogue was so large that I was not without hopes one day or other to hate her heartily: to which end I so used myself to think of 'em, that at length, contrary to my design and expectation, they gave me every hour less and less disturbance, till in a few days it became habitual to me to remember 'em without being displeased. They are now grown as familiar to me as my own frailties, and, in all probability, in a little time longer I shall like 'em as well.

FAINALL. Marry her, marry her! Be half as well acquainted with her charms as you are with her defects, and my life on't, you are your own man again.

MIRABELL. Say you so?

FAINALL. Aye, aye, I have experience: I have a wife, and so forth.

(*Enter* MESSENGER)

MESSENGER. Is one Squire Witwoud here?

BETTY. Yes, what's your business?

MESSENGER. I have a letter for him from his brother Sir Wilfull, which I am charged to deliver into his own hands.

BETTY. He's in the next room, friend—that way. (*Exit* MESSENGER)

MIRABELL. What, is the chief of that noble family in town—Sir Wilfull Witwoud?

FAINALL. He is expected to-day. Do you know him?

MIRABELL. I have seen him; he promises to be an extraordinary person. I think you have the honor to be related to him.

FAINALL. Yes; he is half-brother to this Witwoud by a former wife, who was sister to my Lady Wishfort, my wife's mother. If you marry Millamant, you must call cousins too.

MIRABELL. I had rather be his relation than his acquaintance.

FAINALL. He comes to town in order to equip himself for travel.

MIRABELL. For travel! Why, the man that I mean is above forty.

FAINALL. No matter for that; 'tis for the honor of England that all Europe should know we have blockheads of all ages.

MIRABELL. I wonder there is not an act of parliament to save the credit of the nation, and prohibit the exportation of fools.

FAINALL. By no means; 'tis better as 'tis. 'Tis better to trade with a little loss, than to be quite eaten up with being overstocked.

MIRABELL. Pray, are the follies of this knight-errant and those of the squire his brother anything related?

FAINALL. Not at all; Witwoud grows by the knight, like a medlar [7] grafted on a crab. One will melt in your mouth, and t'other set your teeth on edge; one is all pulp, and the other all core.

MIRABELL. So one will be rotten before he be ripe, and the other will be rotten without ever being ripe at all.

FAINALL. Sir Wilfull is an odd mixture of bashfulness and obstinacy.—But when he's drunk, he's as loving as the monster in *The Tempest*, and much after the same manner. To give t'other his due, he has something of good nature, and does not always want wit.

MIRABELL. Not always; but as often as his memory fails him, and his commonplace [8] of comparisons. He is a fool with a good memory and some few scraps of other folks' wit. He is one whose conversation can never be approved; yet it is now and then to be endured. He has indeed one good quality—he is not exceptious; for he so passionately affects the reputation of understanding raillery that he will construe an affront into a jest, and call downright rudeness and ill language, satire and fire.

FAINALL. If you have a mind to finish his picture, you have an opportunity to do it at full length.—Behold the original!

(*Enter* WITWOUD)

WITWOUD. Afford me your compassion, my dears! Pity me, Fainall! Mirabell, pity me!

MIRABELL. I do, from my soul.

FAINALL. Why, what's the matter?

WITWOUD. No letters for me, Betty?

BETTY. Did not a messenger bring you one but now, sir?

[7] A fruit resembling a crabapple which is eaten only when it is decayed.

[8] A commonplace book was a collection of quotations.

WITWOUD. Aye, but no other?

BETTY. No, sir.

WITWOUD. That's hard, that's very hard. —A messenger, a mule, a beast of burden! He has brought me a letter from the fool my brother, as heavy as a panegyric in a funeral sermon, or a copy of commendatory verses from one poet to another. And what's worse, 'tis as sure a forerunner of the author as an epistle dedicatory.

MIRABELL. A fool,—and your brother, Witwoud!

WITWOUD. Aye, aye, my half-brother. My half-brother he is, no nearer, upon honor.

MIRABELL. Then 'tis possible he may be but half a fool.

WITWOUD. Good, good, Mirabell, le drôle! Good, good; hang him, don't let's talk of him. —Fainall, how does your lady? Gad, I say anything in the world to get this fellow out of my head. I beg pardon that I should ask a man of pleasure and the town, a question at once so foreign and domestic. But I talk like an old maid at a marriage; I don't know what I say. But she's the best woman in the world.

FAINALL. 'Tis well you don't know what you say, or else your commendation would go near to make me either vain or jealous.

WITWOUD. No man in town lives well with a wife but Fainall.—Your judgment, Mirabell?

MIRABELL. You had better step and ask his wife if you would be credibly informed.

WITWOUD. Mirabell?

MIRABELL. Aye.

WITWOUD. My dear, I ask ten thousand pardons—gad, I have forgot what I was going to say to you!

MIRABELL. I thank you heartily, heartily.

WITWOUD. No, but prithee, excuse me— my memory is such a memory.

MIRABELL. Have a care of such apologies, Witwoud; for I never knew a fool but he affected to complain either of the spleen or his memory.

FAINALL. What have you done with Petulant?

WITWOUD. He's reckoning his money—my money it was. I have no luck to-day.

FAINALL. You may allow him to win of you at play, for you are sure to be too hard for him at repartee. Since you monopolize the wit that is between you, the fortune must be his, of course.

MIRABELL. I don't find that Petulant confesses the superiority of wit to be your talent, Witwoud.

WITWOUD. Come, come, you are malicious now, and would breed debates.—Petulant's my friend, and a very honest fellow, and a very pretty fellow, and has a smattering— faith and troth, a pretty deal of an odd sort of a small wit. Nay, I'll do him justice. I'm his friend, I won't wrong him.—And if he had any judgment in the world, he would not be altogether contemptible. Come, come, don't detract from the merits of my friend.

FAINALL. You don't take your friend to be over-nicely bred?

WITWOUD. No, no, hang him, the rogue has no manners at all, that I must own—no more breeding than a bumbaily,[9] that I grant you—'tis pity, faith; the fellow has fire and life.

MIRABELL. What, courage?

WITWOUD. Hum, faith I don't know as to that; I can't say as to that. Yes, faith, in a controversy, he'll contradict anybody.

MIRABELL. Though 'twere a man whom he feared, or a woman whom he loved?

WITWOUD. Well, well, he does not always think before he speaks—we have all our failings. You're too hard upon him—you are, faith. Let me excuse him. I can defend most of his faults, except one or two. One he has, that's the truth on't; if he were my brother, I could not acquit him—that, indeed, I could wish were otherwise.

MIRABELL. Aye, marry, what's that, Witwoud?

WITWOUD. O pardon me!—Expose the infirmities of my friend?—No, my dear, excuse me there.

FAINALL. What! I warrant he's unsincere, or 'tis some such trifle.

WITWOUD. No, no, what if he be? 'Tis no matter for that; his wit will excuse that. A wit should no more be sincere than a woman constant; one argues a decay of parts, as t'other of beauty.

MIRABELL. Maybe you think him too positive?

WITWOUD. No, no, his being positive is

---

[9] Bailiff who made seizures.

an incentive to argument, and keeps up conversation.

FAINALL. Too illiterate?

WITWOUD. That? That's his happiness: his want of learning gives him the more opportunities to show his natural parts.

MIRABELL. He wants words?

WITWOUD. Aye, but I like him for that, now; for his want of words gives me the pleasure very often to explain his meaning.

FAINALL. He's impudent?

WITWOUD. No, that's not it.

MIRABELL. Vain?

WITWOUD. No.

MIRABELL. What! He speaks unseasonable truths sometimes, because he has not wit enough to invent an evasion?

WITWOUD. Truths! ha! ha! ha! No, no; since you will have it—I mean, he never speaks truth at all—that's all. He will lie like a chambermaid, or a woman of quality's porter. Now, that is a fault.

(*Enter* COACHMAN)

COACHMAN. Is Master Petulant here, mistress?

BETTY. Yes.

COACHMAN. Three gentlewomen in a coach would speak with him.

FAINALL. O brave Petulant!—three!

BETTY. I'll tell him.

COACHMAN. You must bring two dishes of chocolate and a glass of cinnamon-water.[10]

(*Exit* COACHMAN. *Exit* BETTY *to the other room; she returns immediately*)

WITWOUD. That should be for two fasting strumpets, and a bawd troubled with wind. Now you may know what the three are.

MIRABELL. You are very free with your friend's acquaintance.

WITWOUD. Aye, aye, friendship without freedom is as dull as love without enjoyment, or wine without toasting. But to tell you a secret, these are trulls whom he allows coach-hire, and something more, by the week, to call on him once a day at public places.

MIRABELL. How!

WITWOUD. You shall see he won't go to 'em, because there's no more company here to take notice of him.—Why, this is nothing to what he used to do; before he found out this way, I have known him call for himself.

[10] Cinnamon cordial.

FAINALL. Call for himself! What dost thou mean?

WITWOUD. Mean! Why, he would slip you out of this chocolate-house just when you had been talking to him; as soon as your back was turned—whip, he was gone!—then trip to his lodging, clap on a hood and scarf and a mask, slap into a hackney-coach, and drive hither to the door again in a trice, where he would send in for himself, that is, I mean—call for himself, wait for himself; nay, and what's more, not finding himself, sometimes leave a letter for himself.

MIRABELL. I confess this is something extraordinary.—I believe he waits for himself now, he is so long a-coming.—Oh! I ask his pardon.

(*Enter* PETULANT)

BETTY. Sir, the coach stays.

PETULANT. (*With over-acted irritation*) Well, well; I come.—'Sbud, a man had as good be a professed midwife as a professed whoremaster, at this rate! To be knocked up and raised at all hours, and in all places! Pox on 'em, I won't come!—D'ye hear, tell 'em I won't come—let 'em snivel and cry their hearts out.

FAINALL. You are very cruel, Petulant.

PETULANT. All's one, let it pass. I have a humor to be cruel.

MIRABELL. I hope they are not persons of condition that you use at this rate.

PETULANT. Condition! Condition's a dried fig if I am not in humor!—By this hand, if they were your—a—a—your what-d'ye-call-'ems themselves, they must wait or rub off, if I want appetite.

MIRABELL. What-d'ye-call-'ems! What are they, Witwoud?

WITWOUD. Empresses, my dear; by your what-d'ye-call-'ems he means sultana queens.

PETULANT. Aye, Roxolanas.

MIRABELL. Cry you mercy.

FAINALL. Witwoud says they are—

PETULANT. What does he say th' are?

WITWOUD. I? Fine ladies, I say.

PETULANT. Pass on, Witwoud.—Hark'ee, by this light, his relations—two co-heiresses, his cousins, and an old aunt who loves caterwauling better than a conventicle.[11]

[11] A clandestine, non-conformist religious meeting.

WITWOUD. Ha, ha, ha! I had a mind to see how the rogue would come off.—Ha, ha, ha! Gad, I can't be angry with him if he had said they were my mother and my sisters.

MIRABELL. No?

WITWOUD. No; the rogue's wit and readiness of invention charm me. Dear Petulant!

BETTY. (*Looking out the window*) They are gone, sir, in great anger.

PETULANT. Enough; let 'em trundle. Anger helps complexion—saves paint.

FAINALL. This continence is all dissembled; this is in order to have something to brag of the next time he makes court to Millamant and swear he has abandoned the whole sex for her sake.

MIRABELL. Have you not left off your impudent pretensions there yet? I shall cut your throat some time or other, Petulant, about that business.

PETULANT. Aye, aye, let that pass—there are other throats to be cut.

MIRABELL. Meaning mine, sir?

PETULANT. Not I—I mean nobody—I know nothing. But there are uncles and nephews in the world—and they may be rivals—what then? All's one for that.

MIRABELL. How! Hark'ee, Petulant, come hither—explain, or I shall call your interpreter.

PETULANT. Explain? I know nothing. Why, you have an uncle, have you not, lately come to town, and lodges by my Lady Wishfort's?

MIRABELL. True.

PETULANT. Why, that's enough—you and he are not friends; and if he should marry and have a child you may be disinherited, ha?

MIRABELL. Where hast thou stumbled upon all this truth?

PETULANT. All's one for that; why, then, say I know something.

MIRABELL. Come, thou art an honest fellow, Petulant, and shalt make love to my mistress; thou sha't, faith. What hast thou heard of my uncle?

PETULANT. I? Nothing, I. If throats are to be cut, let swords clash! snug's the word; I shrug and am silent.

MIRABELL. Oh, raillery, raillery! Come, I know thou art in the women's secrets.— What, you're a cabalist; I know you stayed at Millamant's last night after I went. Was there any mention made of my uncle or me? Tell me. If thou hadst but good nature equal to thy wit, Petulant, Tony Witwoud, who is now thy competitor in fame, would show as dim by thee as a dead whiting's eye by a pearl of orient; he would no more be seen by thee than Mercury is by the sun. Come, I'm sure thou wo't tell me.

PETULANT. If I do, will you grant me common sense then, for the future?

MIRABELL. Faith, I'll do what I can for thee, and I'll pray that Heaven may grant it thee in the meantime.

PETULANT. Well, hark'ee.

(MIRABELL and PETULANT *talk apart*)

FAINALL. (*To* WITWOUD) Petulant and you both will find Mirabell as warm a rival as a lover.

WITWOUD. Pshaw! pshaw! that she laughs at Petulant is plain. And for my part, but that it is almost a fashion to admire her, I should—hark'ee—to tell you a secret, but let it go no further—between friends, I shall never break my heart for her.

FAINALL. How!

WITWOUD. She's handsome; but she's a sort of an uncertain woman.

FAINALL. I thought you had died for her.

WITWOUD. Umh—no—

FAINALL. She has wit.

WITWOUD. 'Tis what she will hardly allow anybody else. Now, demme! I should hate that, if she were as handsome as Cleopatra. Mirabell is not so sure of her as he thinks for.

FAINALL. Why do you think so?

WITWOUD. We stayed pretty late there last night, and heard something of an uncle to Mirabell, who is lately come to town—and is between him and the best part of his [12] estate. Mirabell and he are at some distance, as my Lady Wishfort has been told; and you know she hates Mirabell worse than a Quaker hates a parrot, or than a fishmonger hates a hard frost. Whether this uncle has seen Mrs. Millamant or not, I cannot say, but there were items of such a treaty being in embryo; and if it should come to life, poor Mirabell would be in some sort unfortunately fobbed,[13] i'faith.

---

[12] A false rumor which Mirabell himself has planted.   [13] Cheated.

FAINALL. 'Tis impossible Millamant should hearken to it.

WITWOUD. Faith, my dear, I can't tell; she's a woman, and a kind of humorist.

MIRABELL. (*To* PETULANT) And this is the sum of what you could collect last night?

PETULANT. The quintessence. Maybe Witwoud knows more, he stayed longer. Besides, they never mind him; they say anything before him.

MIRABELL. I thought you had been the greatest favorite.

PETULANT. Aye, *tête-à-tête,* but not in public, because I make remarks.

MIRABELL. Do you?

PETULANT. Aye, aye; pox, I'm malicious, man! Now, he's soft, you know; they are not in awe of him—the fellow's well-bred; he's what you call a—what-d'ye-call-'em, a fine gentleman.—But he's silly withal.

MIRABELL. I thank you. I know as much as my curiosity requires.—Fainall, are you for the Mall?

FAINALL. Aye, I'll take a turn before dinner.

WITWOUD. Aye, we'll all walk in the Park; the ladies talked of being there.

MIRABELL. I thought you were obliged to watch for your brother Sir Wilfull's arrival.

WITWOUD. No, no; he comes to his aunt's, my Lady Wishfort. Pox on him! I shall be troubled with him, too; what shall I do with the fool?

PETULANT. Beg him for his estate, that I may beg you afterwards, and so have but one trouble with you both.

WITWOUD. Oh, rare Petulant! Thou art as quick as fire in a frosty morning. Thou shalt to the Mall with us, and we'll be very severe.

PETULANT. Enough! I'm in a humor to be severe.

MIRABELL. Are you? Pray then, walk by yourselves: let not us be accessory to your putting the ladies out of countenance with your senseless ribaldry, which you roar out aloud as often as they pass by you; and when you have made a handsome woman blush, then you think you have been severe.

PETULANT. What, what? Then let 'em either show their innocence by not understanding what they hear, or else show their discretion by not hearing what they would not be thought to understand.

MIRABELL. But hast not thou then sense enough to know that thou oughtest to be most ashamed thyself when thou hast put another out of countenance?

PETULANT. Not I, by this hand!—I always take blushing either for a sign of guilt or ill breeding.

MIRABELL. I confess you ought to think so. You are in the right, that you may plead the error of your judgment in defence of your practice.

Where modesty's ill manners, 'tis but fit
That impudence and malice pass for wit.

(*Exeunt*)

Act II

SCENE I. *St. James's Park.*

(*Enter* MRS. FAINALL *and* MRS. MARWOOD)

MRS. FAINALL. Aye, aye, dear Marwood, if we will be happy, we must find the means in ourselves and among ourselves. Men are ever in extremes—either doting or averse. While they are lovers, if they have fire and sense, their jealousies are insupportable; and when they cease to love—(we ought to think at least) they loathe; they look upon us with horror and distaste; they meet us like the ghosts of what we were, and as from such, fly from us.

MRS. MARWOOD. True, 'tis an unhappy circumstance of life, that love should ever die before us and that the man so often should outlive the lover. But say what you will, 'tis better to be left than never to have been loved. To pass our youth in dull indifference, to refuse the sweets of life because they once must leave us, is as preposterous as to wish to have been born old because we one day must be old. For my part, my youth may wear and waste, but it shall never rust in my possession.

MRS. FAINALL. Then it seems you dissemble an aversion to mankind only in compliance to my mother's humor?

Mrs. Marwood. Certainly. To be free: I have no taste of those insipid dry discourses with which our sex of force must entertain themselves apart from men. We may affect endearments to each other, profess eternal friendships, and seem to dote like lovers; but 'tis not in our natures long to persevere. Love will resume his empire in our breasts and every heart, or soon or late, receive and readmit him as its lawful tyrant.

Mrs. Fainall. Bless me, how have I been deceived! Why, you profess a libertine.

Mrs. Marwood. You see my friendship by my freedom. Come, be as sincere; acknowledge that your sentiments agree with mine.

Mrs. Fainall. Never!

Mrs. Marwood. You hate mankind?

Mrs. Fainall. Heartily, inveterately.

Mrs. Marwood. Your husband?

Mrs. Fainall. Most transcendently; aye, though I say it, meritoriously.

Mrs. Marwood. Give me your hand upon it.

Mrs. Fainall. There.

Mrs. Marwood. I join with you; what I have said has been to try you.

Mrs. Fainall. Is it possible? Dost thou hate those vipers, men?

Mrs. Marwood. I have done hating 'em, and am now come to despise 'em; the next thing I have to do, is eternally to forget 'em.

Mrs. Fainall. There spoke the spirit of an Amazon, a Penthesilea!

Mrs. Marwood. And yet I am thinking sometimes to carry my aversion further.

Mrs. Fainall. How?

Mrs. Marwood. Faith, by marrying; if I could but find one that loved me very well and would be thoroughly sensible of ill usage, I think I should do myself the violence of undergoing the ceremony.

Mrs. Fainall. You would not make him a cuckold?

Mrs. Marwood. No; but I'd make him believe I did, and that's as bad.

Mrs. Fainall. Why had not you as good do it?

Mrs. Marwood. Oh, if he should ever discover it, he would then know the worst and be out of his pain; but I would have him

ever to continue upon the rack of fear and jealousy.

Mrs. Fainall. Ingenious mischief! Would thou wert married to Mirabell.

Mrs. Marwood. Would I were!

Mrs. Fainall. You change color.

Mrs. Marwood. Because I hate him.

Mrs. Fainall. So do I, but I can hear him named. But what reason have you to hate him in particular?

Mrs. Marwood. I never loved him; he is, and always was, insufferably proud.

Mrs. Fainall. By the reason you give for your aversion, one would think it dissembled; for you have laid a fault to his charge, of which his enemies must acquit him.

Mrs. Marwood. Oh, then it seems you are one of his favorable enemies! Methinks you look a little pale—and now you flush again.

Mrs. Fainall. Do I? I think I am a little sick o' the sudden.

Mrs. Marwood. What ails you?

Mrs. Fainall. My husband. Don't you see him? He turned short upon me unawares, and has almost overcome me.

(*Enter* Fainall *and* Mirabell)

Mrs. Marwood. Ha, ha, ha! He comes opportunely for you.

Mrs. Fainall. For you, for he has brought Mirabell with him.

Fainall. (*To* Mrs. Fainall) My dear!

Mrs. Fainall. My soul!

Fainall. You don't look well to-day, child.

Mrs. Fainall. D'ye think so?

Mirabell. He is the only man that does, madam.

Mrs. Fainall. The only man that would tell me so, at least, and the only man from whom I could hear it without mortification.

Fainall. Oh, my dear, I am satisfied of your tenderness; I know you cannot resent anything from me, especially what is an effect of my concern.

Mrs. Fainall. Mr. Mirabell, my mother interrupted you in a pleasant relation last night; I would fain hear it out.

Mirabell. The persons concerned in that affair have yet a tolerable reputation. I am afraid Mr. Fainall will be censorious.

Mrs. Fainall. He has a humor more prevailing than his curiosity, and will willingly dispense with the hearing of one scandalous story, to avoid giving an occasion to make another by being seen to walk with his wife. This way, Mr. Mirabell, and I dare promise you will oblige us both.

(*Exeunt* Mrs. FAINALL *and* MIRABELL)

FAINALL. Excellent creature! Well, sure if I should live to be rid of my wife, I should be a miserable man.

MRS. MARWOOD. Aye?

FAINALL. For having only that one hope, the accomplishment of it, of consequence, must put an end to all my hopes; and what a wretch is he who must survive his hopes! Nothing remains when that day comes but to sit down and weep like Alexander when he wanted other worlds to conquer.

MRS. MARWOOD. Will you not follow 'em?

FAINALL. Faith, I think not.

MRS. MARWOOD. Pray, let us; I have a reason.

FAINALL. You are not jealous?

MRS. MARWOOD. Of whom?

FAINALL. Of Mirabell.

MRS. MARWOOD. If I am, is it inconsistent with my love to you that I am tender of your honor?

FAINALL. You would intimate, then, as if there were a fellow-feeling between my wife and him.

MRS. MARWOOD. I think she does not hate him to that degree she would be thought.

FAINALL. But he, I fear, is too insensible.

MRS. MARWOOD. It may be you are deceived.

FAINALL. It may be so. I do not now begin to apprehend it.

MRS. MARWOOD. What?

FAINALL. That I have been deceived, madam, and you are false.

MRS. MARWOOD. That I am false! What mean you?

FAINALL. To let you know I see through all your little arts.—Come, you both love him, and both have equally dissembled your aversion. Your mutual jealousies of one another have made you clash till you have both struck fire. I have seen the warm confession reddening on your cheeks and sparkling from your eyes.

MRS. MARWOOD. You do me wrong.

FAINALL. I do not. 'Twas for my ease to oversee and wilfully neglect the gross advances made him by my wife, that by permitting her to be engaged, I might continue unsuspected in my pleasures and take you oftener to my arms in full security. But could you think, because the nodding husband would not wake, that e'er the watchful lover slept?

MRS. MARWOOD. And wherewithal can you reproach me?

FAINALL. With infidelity, with loving another—with love of Mirabell.

MRS. MARWOOD. 'Tis false! I challenge you to show an instance that can confirm your groundless accusation. I hate him!

FAINALL. And wherefore do you hate him? He is insensible, and your resentment follows his neglect. An instance!—the injuries you have done him are a proof—your interposing in his love. What cause had you to make discoveries of his pretended passion?—to undeceive the credulous aunt, and be the officious obstacle of his match with Millamant?

MRS. MARWOOD. My obligations to my lady urged me. I had professed a friendship to her, and could not see her easy nature so abused by that dissembler.

FAINALL. What, was it conscience, then? Professed a friendship! Oh, the pious friendships of the female sex!

MRS. MARWOOD. More tender, more sincere, and more enduring than all the vain and empty vows of men, whether professing love to us or mutual faith to one another.

FAINALL. Ha, ha, ha! You are my wife's friend, too.

MRS. MARWOOD. Shame and ingratitude! Do you reproach me? You, you upbraid me? Have I been false to her, through strict fidelity to you, and sacrificed my friendship to keep my love inviolate? And have you the baseness to charge me with the guilt, unmindful of the merit? To you it should be meritorious that I have been vicious, and do you reflect that guilt upon me which should lie buried in your bosom?

FAINALL. You misinterpret my reproof. I meant but to remind you of the slight account you once could make of strictest ties when set in competition with your love to me.

MRS. MARWOOD. 'Tis false; you urged it with deliberate malice! 'Twas spoken in scorn, and I never will forgive it.

FAINALL. Your guilt, not your resentment, begets your rage. If yet you loved, you could forgive a jealousy; but you are stung to find you are discovered.

MRS. MARWOOD. It shall be all discovered. —You too shall be discovered; be sure you shall. I can but be exposed.—If I do it myself I shall prevent your baseness.

FAINALL. Why, what will you do?

MRS. MARWOOD. Disclose it to your wife; own what has passed between us.

FAINALL. Frenzy!

MRS. MARWOOD. By all my wrongs I'll do't!—I'll publish to the world the injuries you have done me, both in my fame and fortune! With both I trusted you,—you, bankrupt in honor, as indigent of wealth.

FAINALL. Your fame I have preserved. Your fortune has been bestowed as the prodigality of your love would have it, in pleasures which we both have shared. Yet, had not you been false, I had ere this repaid it—'tis true. Had you permitted Mirabell with Millamant to have stolen their marriage, my lady had been incensed beyond all means of reconcilement; Millamant had forfeited the moiety of her fortune, which then would have descended to my wife—and wherefore did I marry but to make lawful prize of a rich widow's wealth, and squander it on love and you?

MRS. MARWOOD. Deceit and frivolous pretence!

FAINALL. Death, am I not married? What's pretence? Am I not imprisoned, fettered? Have I not a wife?—nay, a wife that was a widow, a young widow, a handsome widow; and would be again a widow, but that I have a heart of proof, and something of a constitution to bustle through the ways of wedlock and this world! Will you yet be reconciled to truth and me?

MRS. MARWOOD. Impossible. Truth and you are inconsistent—I hate you, and shall forever.

FAINALL. For loving you?

MRS. MARWOOD. I loathe the name of love after such usage; and next to the guilt with which you would asperse me, I scorn you most. Farewell!

FAINALL. Nay, we must not part thus.

MRS. MARWOOD. Let me go.

FAINALL. Come, I'm sorry.

MRS. MARWOOD. I care not—let me go— break my hands, do! I'd leave 'em to get loose.

FAINALL. I would not hurt you for the world. Have I no other hold to keep you here?

MRS. MARWOOD. Well, I have deserved it all.

FAINALL. You know I love you.

MRS. MARWOOD. Poor dissembling!—Oh, that—well, it is not yet—

FAINALL. What? What is it not? What is it not yet? It is not yet too late—

MRS. MARWOOD. No, it is not yet too late —I have that comfort.

FAINALL. It is, to love another.

MRS. MARWOOD. But not to loathe, detest, abhor mankind, myself, and the whole treacherous world.

FAINALL. Nay, this is extravagance!— Come, I ask your pardon—no tears—I was to blame, I could not love you and be easy in my doubts. Pray, forbear—I believe you; I'm convinced I've done you wrong, and any way, every way will make amends. I'll hate my wife yet more, damn her! I'll part with her, rob her of all she's worth, and we'll retire somewhere—anywhere—to another world. I'll marry thee—be pacified.—'Sdeath, they come! Hide your face, your tears.—You have a mask; wear it a moment. This way, this way —be persuaded. (*Exeunt*)

(*Enter* MIRABELL *and* MRS. FAINALL)

MRS. FAINALL. They are here yet.

MIRABELL. They are turning into the other walk.

MRS. FAINALL. While I only hated my husband, I could bear to see him; but since I have despised him, he's too offensive.

MIRABELL. Oh, you should hate with prudence.

MRS. FAINALL. Yes, for I have loved with indiscretion.

MIRABELL. You should have just so much disgust for your husband as may be sufficient to make you relish your lover.

MRS. FAINALL. You have been the cause that I have loved without bounds, and would you set limits to that aversion of which you have been the occasion? Why did you make me marry this man?

MIRABELL. Why do we daily commit disagreeable and dangerous actions? To save that idol, reputation. If the familiarities of our loves had produced that consequence of which you were apprehensive, where could you have fixed a father's name with credit but on a husband? I knew Fainall to be a man lavish of his morals, an interested and professing friend, a false and a designing lover, yet one whose wit and outward fair behavior have gained a reputation with the town enough to make that woman stand excused who has suffered herself to be won by his addresses. A better man ought not to have been sacrificed to the occasion, a worse had not answered to the purpose. When you are weary of him, you know your remedy.

MRS. FAINALL. I ought to stand in some degree of credit with you, Mirabell.

MIRABELL. In justice to you, I have made you privy to my whole design, and put it in your power to ruin or advance my fortune.

MRS. FAINALL. Whom have you instructed to represent your pretended uncle?

MIRABELL. Waitwell, my servant.

MRS. FAINALL. He is an humble servant [14] to Foible, my mother's woman, and may win her to your interest.

MIRABELL. Care is taken for that—she is won and worn by this time. They were married this morning.

MRS. FAINALL. Who?

MIRABELL. Waitwell and Foible. I would not tempt any servant to betray me by trusting him too far. If your mother, in hopes to ruin me, should consent to marry my pretended uncle, he might, like Mosca in *The Fox*,[15] stand upon terms; so I made him sure beforehand.

MRS. FAINALL. So if my poor mother is caught in a contract,[16] you will discover the imposture betimes, and release her by producing a certificate of her gallant's former marriage.

MIRABELL. Yes, upon condition that she consent to my marriage with her niece, and surrender the moiety of her fortune in her possession.

MRS. FAINALL. She talked last night of endeavoring at a match between Millamant and your uncle.

[14] That is, suitor.

[15] Volpone's servant in Ben Jonson's *Volpone, or the Fox*.   [16] Of marriage.

MIRABELL. That was by Foible's direction and my instruction, that she might seem to carry it more privately.

MRS. FAINALL. Well, I have an opinion of your success; for I believe my lady will do anything to get a husband; and when she has this which you have provided for her, I suppose she will submit to anything to get rid of him.

MIRABELL. Yes, I think the good lady would marry anything that resembled a man, though 'twere no more than what a butler could pinch out of a napkin.

MRS. FAINALL. Female fraility! We must all come to it if we live to be old and feel the craving of a false appetite when the true is decayed.

MIRABELL. An old woman's appetite is depraved like that of a girl—'tis the green sickness of a second childhood, and, like the faint offer of a latter spring, serves but to usher in the fall and withers in an affected bloom.

MRS. FAINALL. Here's your mistress.

(*Enter* MRS. MILLAMANT, WITWOUD, *and* MINCING)

MIRABELL. Here she comes, i'faith, full sail, with her fan spread and her streamers out, and a shoal of fools for tenders. Ha, no, I cry her mercy!

MRS. FAINALL. I see but one poor empty sculler, and he tows her woman after him.

MIRABELL. (*To* MRS. MILLAMANT) You seem to be unattended, madam. You used to have the *beau monde* throng after you, and a flock of gay fine perukes hovering round you.

WITWOUD. Like moths about a candle.— I had like to have lost my comparison for want of breath.

MRS. MILLAMANT. Oh, I have denied myself airs to-day. I have walked as fast through the crowd—

WITWOUD. As a favorite just disgraced, and with as few followers.

MRS. MILLAMANT. Dear Mr. Witwoud, truce with your similitudes; for I'm as sick of 'em—

WITWOUD. As a physician of a good air. —I cannot help it, madam, though 'tis against myself.

Mrs. Millamant. Yet again! Mincing, stand between me and his wit.

Witwoud. Do, Mrs. Mincing, like a screen before a grate fire.—I confess I do blaze to-day; I am too bright.

Mrs. Fainall. But, dear Millamant, why were you so long?

Mrs. Millamant. Long! Lord, have I not made violent haste? I have asked every living thing I met for you; I have inquired after you as after a new fashion.

Witwoud. Madam, truce with your similitudes.—No, you met her husband, and did not ask him for her.

Mrs. Millamant. By your leave, Witwoud, that were like inquiring after an old fashion, to ask a husband for his wife.

Witwoud. Hum, a hit! a hit! A palpable hit! I confess it.

Mrs. Fainall. You were dressed before I came abroad.

Mrs. Millamant. Aye, that's true.—Oh, but then I had—Mincing, what had I? Why was I so long?

Mincing. O mem, your la'ship stayed to peruse a pecquet [17] of letters.

Mrs. Millamant. Oh, aye, letters—I had letters—I am persecuted with letters—I hate letters.—Nobody knows how to write letters—and yet one has 'em, one does not know why. They serve one to pin up one's hair.

Witwoud. Is that the way? Pray, madam, do you pin up your hair with all your letters? I find I must keep copies.

Mrs. Millamant. Only with those in verse, Mr. Witwoud; I never pin up my hair with prose. I think I tried once, Mincing.

Mincing. O mem, I shall never forget it.

Mrs. Millamant. Aye, poor Mincing tift and tift [18] all the morning.

Mincing. Till I had the cremp in my fingers, I'll vow, mem; and all to no purpose. But when your la'ship pins it up with poetry, it sits so pleasant the next day as anything, and is so pure and so crips.

Witwoud. Indeed, so "crips"?

Mincing. You're such a critic, Mr. Witwoud.

Mrs. Millamant. Mirabell, did you take exceptions last night? Oh, aye, and went away—now I think on't I'm angry—No,

now I think on't I'm pleased—for I believe I gave you some pain.

Mirabell. Does that please you?

Mrs. Millamant. Infinitely; I love to give pain.

Mirabell. You would affect a cruelty which is not in your nature; your true vanity is in the power of pleasing.

Mrs. Millamant. Oh, I ask your pardon for that—one's cruelty is one's power; and when one parts with one's cruelty, one parts with one's power; and when one has parted with that, I fancy one's old and ugly.

Mirabell. Aye, aye, suffer your cruelty to ruin the object of your power, to destroy your lover—and then how vain, how lost a thing you'll be! Nay, 'tis true: you are no longer handsome when you've lost your lover; your beauty dies upon the instant, for beauty is the lover's gift. 'Tis he bestows your charms—your glass is all a cheat. The ugly and the old, whom the looking-glass mortifies, yet after commendation can be flattered by it and discover beauties in it; for that reflects our praises, rather than your face.

Mrs. Millamant. Oh, the vanity of these men! Fainall, d'ye hear him? If they did not commend us, we were not handsome! Now you must know they could not commend one, if one was not handsome. Beauty the lover's gift!—Lord, what is a lover, that it can give? Why, one makes lovers as fast as one pleases, and they live as long as one pleases, and they die as soon as one pleases: and then, if one pleases, one makes more.

Witwoud. Very pretty. Why, you make no more of making of lovers, madam, than of making so many card-matches.

Mrs. Millamant. One no more owes one's beauty to a lover, than one's wit to an echo. They can but reflect what we look and say—vain empty things if we are silent or unseen, and want a being.

Mirabell. Yet to those two vain empty things you owe the two greatest pleasures of your life.

Mrs. Millamant. How so?

Mirabell. To your lover you owe the pleasure of hearing yourselves praised, and to an echo the pleasure of hearing yourselves talk.

Witwoud. But I know a lady that loves talking so incessantly, she won't give an echo

---

[17] Mincing's affected pronunciation of packet.
[18] Arranged.

fair play; she has that everlasting rotation of tongue, that an echo must wait till she dies before it can catch her last words.

Mrs. Millamant. Oh, fiction!—Fainall, let us leave these men.

Mirabell. (*Aside to* Mrs. Fainall) Draw off Witwoud.

Mrs. Fainall. (*Aside*) Immediately.—I have a word or two for Mr. Witwoud.

(*Exeunt* Witwoud *and* Mrs. Fainall)

Mirabell. (*To* Mrs. Millamant) I would beg a little private audience too.—You had the tyranny to deny me last night, though you knew I came to impart a secret to you that concerned my love.

Mrs. Millamant. You saw I was engaged.

Mirabell. Unkind! You had the leisure to entertain a herd of fools—things who visit you from their excessive idleness, bestowing on your easiness that time which is the encumbrance of their lives. How can you find delight in such society? It is impossible they should admire you; they are not capable—or if they were, it should be to you as a mortification, for sure, to please a fool is some degree of folly.

Mrs. Millamant. I please myself. Besides, sometimes to converse with fools is for my health.

Mirabell. Your health! Is there a worse disease than the conversation of fools?

Mrs. Millamant. Yes, the vapors; fools are physic for it, next to asafœtida.

Mirabell. You are not in a course of fools?

Mrs. Millamant. Mirabell, if you persist in this offensive freedom, you'll displease me.—I think I must resolve, after all, not to have you; we shan't agree.

Mirabell. Not in our physic, it may be.

Mrs. Millamant. And yet our distemper, in all likelihood, will be the same; for we shall be sick of one another. I shan't endure to be reprimanded nor instructed; 'tis so dull to act always by advice, and so tedious to be told of one's faults—I can't bear it. Well, I won't have you, Mirabell,—I'm resolved—I think—you may go.—Ha, ha, ha! What would you give, that you could help loving me?

Mirabell. I would give something that you did not know I could not help it.

Mrs. Millamant. Come, don't look grave, then. Well, what do you say to me?

Mirabell. I say that a man may as soon make a friend by his wit, or a fortune by his honesty, as win a woman by plain dealing and sincerity.

Mrs. Millamant. Sententious Mirabell! Prithee, don't look with that violent and inflexible wise face, like Solomon at the dividing of the child in an old tapestry hanging.

Mirabell. You are merry, madam, but I would persuade you for a moment to be serious.

Mrs. Millamant. What, with that face? No, if you keep your countenance, 'tis impossible I should hold mine. Well, after all, there is something very moving in a lovesick face. Ha, ha, ha!—Well, I won't laugh; don't be peevish—Heigho! now I'll be melancholy —as melancholy as a watch-light.[19] Well, Mirabell, if ever you will win me, woo me now.—Nay, if you are so tedious, fare you well; I see they are walking away.

Mirabell. Can you not find in the variety of your disposition one moment—

Mrs. Millamant. To hear you tell me Foible's married, and your plot like to speed? No.

Mirabell. (*Astonished*) But how came you to know it?

Mrs. Millamant. Without the help of the devil, you can't imagine—unless she should tell me herself. Which of the two it may have been I will leave you to consider; and when you have done thinking of that, think of me. (*Exit* Mrs. Millamant)

Mirabell. I have something more!— Gone!—Think of you? To think of a whirlwind, though 'twere in a whirlwind, were a case of more steady contemplation—a very tranquillity of mind and mansion. A fellow that lives in a windmill has not a more whimsical dwelling than the heart of a man that is lodged in a woman. There is no point of the compass to which they cannot turn, and by which they are not turned; and by one as well as another. For motion, not method, is their occupation. To know this, and yet continue to be in love, is to be made wise from the dictates of reason, and yet

[19] A small candle in a sick room.

persevere to play the fool by the force of instinct.—(*He sees* WAITWELL *and* FOIBLE *approaching*) Oh, here come my pair of turtles! [20]—What, billing so sweetly! Is not Valentine's Day over with you yet?

(*Enter* WAITWELL *and* FOIBLE)

Sirrah Waitwell; why, sure you think you were married for your own recreation, and not for my conveniency.

WAITWELL. Your pardon, sir. With submission, we have indeed been solacing in lawful delights; but still with an eye to business, sir. I have instructed her as well as I could. If she can take your directions as readily as my instructions, sir, your affairs are in a prosperous way.

MIRABELL. Give you joy, Mrs. Foible.

FOIBLE. Oh, 'las, sir, I'm so ashamed!— I'm afraid my lady has been in a thousand inquietudes for me. But I protest, sir, I made as much haste as I could.

WAITWELL. That she did indeed, sir. It was my fault that she did not make more.

MIRABELL. That I believe.

FOIBLE. But I told my lady as you instructed me, sir, that I had a prospect of seeing Sir Rowland, your uncle; and that I would put her ladyship's picture in my pocket to show him, which I'll be sure to say has made him so enamored of her beauty that he burns with impatience to lie at her ladyship's feet and worship the original.

MIRABELL. Excellent Foible! Matrimony has made you eloquent in love.

WAITWELL. I think she has profited, sir; I think so.

FOIBLE. You have seen Madam Millamant, sir?

MIRABELL. Yes.

FOIBLE. I told her, sir, because I did not know that you might find an opportunity; she had so much company last night.

MIRABELL. Your diligence will merit more—in the meantime— (*Gives her money*)

FOIBLE. O dear sir, your humble servant!

WAITWELL. (*Putting forth his hand*) Spouse.

MIRABELL. Stand off, sir, not a penny!— Go on and prosper, Foible—the lease shall be made good and the farm stocked if we succeed.

FOIBLE. I don't question your generosity, sir, and you need not doubt of success. If you have no more commands, sir, I'll be gone; I'm sure my lady is at her toilet, and can't dress till I come.—Oh, dear, I'm sure that was Mrs. Marwood that went by in a mask! If she has seen me with you, I'm sure she'll tell my lady. I'll make haste home and prevent her. Your servant, sir.—B'w'y,[21] Waitwell.   (*Exit* FOIBLE)

WAITWELL. Sir Rowland, if you please.— The jade's so pert upon her preferment she forgets herself.

MIRABELL. Come, sir, will you endeavor to forget yourself, and transform into Sir Rowland?

WAITWELL. Why, sir, it will be impossible I should remember myself.—Married, knighted, and attended all in one day! 'Tis enough to make any man forget himself. The difficulty will be how to recover my acquaintance and familiarity with my former self, and fall from my transformation to a reformation into Waitwell. Nay, I shan't be quite the same Waitwell neither; for now, I remember me, I'm married and can't be my own man again.

Aye, there's the grief; that's the sad change of life,

To lose my title, and yet keep my wife.
                (*Exeunt*)

Act III

SCENE I. A Room in LADY WISHFORT's House.

(LADY WISHFORT *at her toilet,* PEG *waiting*)

LADY WISHFORT. Merciful! No news of Foible yet?

PEG. No, madam.

LADY WISHFORT. I have no more patience.—If I have not fretted myself till I am pale again, there's no veracity in me!

---

[20] Turtle-doves.

[21] Shortened form of "God be with you."

Fetch me the red—the red, do you hear, sweetheart?—An arrant ash-color, as I am a person! Look you how this wench stirs! Why dost thou not fetch me a little red? Didst thou not hear me, Mopus? [22]

PEG. The red ratafia, does your ladyship mean, or the cherry-brandy?

LADY WISHFORT. Ratafia, fool! No, fool. Not the ratafia, fool—grant me patience!—I mean the Spanish paper,[23] idiot—complexion, darling. Paint, paint, paint!—dost thou understand that, changeling, dangling thy hands like bobbins before thee? Why dost thou not stir, puppet? Thou wooden thing upon wires!

PEG. Lord, madam, your ladyship is so impatient!—I cannot come at the paint, madam; Mrs. Foible has locked it up and carried the key with her.

LADY WISHFORT. A pox take you both!—Fetch me the cherry-brandy then. (*Exit* PEG) I'm as pale and as faint, I look like Mrs. Qualmsick, the curate's wife, that's always breeding.—Wench! Come, come, wench, what art thou doing? Sipping? Tasting?—Save thee, dost thou not know the bottle?

(*Enter* PEG *with a bottle and china cup*)

PEG. Madam, I was looking for a cup.

LADY WISHFORT. A cup, save thee! and what a cup hast thou brought!—Dost thou take me for a fairy, to drink out of an acorn? Why didst thou not bring thy thimble? Hast thou ne'er a brass thimble clinking in thy pocket with a bit of nutmeg?—I warrant thee. Come, fill, fill!—So—again.—(*One knocks*) —See who that is.—Set down the bottle first. —Here, here, under the table.—What, wouldst thou go with the bottle in thy hand, like a tapster? As I'm a person, this wench has lived in an inn upon the road before she came to me, like Maritornes the Asturian in *Don Quixote!*—No Foible yet?

PEG. No, madam, Mrs. Marwood.

LADY WISHFORT. Oh, Marwood; let her come in.—Come in, good Marwood.

(*Enter* MRS. MARWOOD)

MRS. MARWOOD. I'm surprised to find your ladyship in dishabille at this time of day.

[22] Stupid person.   [23] Rouge.

LADY WISHFORT. Foible's a lost thing—has been abroad since morning, and never heard of since.

MRS. MARWOOD. I saw her but now as I came masked through the park, in conference with Mirabell.

LADY WISHFORT. With Mirabell!—You call my blood into my face, with mentioning that traitor. She durst not have the confidence! I sent her to negotiate an affair in which, if I'm detected, I'm undone. If that wheedling villain has wrought upon Foible to detect me, I'm ruined. Oh, my dear friend, I'm a wretch of wretches if I'm detected.

MRS. MARWOOD. O madam, you cannot suspect Mrs. Foible's integrity.

LADY WISHFORT. Oh, he carries poison in his tongue that would corrupt integrity itself! If she has given him an opportunity, she has as good as put her integrity into his hands. Ah, dear Marwood, what's integrity to an opportunity?—Hark! I hear her! (*To* PEG) Go, you thing, and send her in. (*Exit* PEG) —Dear friend, retire into my closet, that I may examine her with more freedom.—You'll pardon me, dear friend; I can make bold with you.—There are books over the chimney—Quarles and Prynne, and *The Short View of the Stage*, with Bunyan's works, to entertain you.[24]

(*Exit* MRS. MARWOOD, *leaving the door slightly ajar*)

(*Enter* FOIBLE *at another door*)

LADY WISHFORT. O Foible, where hast thou been? What hast thou been doing?

FOIBLE. Madam, I have seen the party.

LADY WISHFORT. But what hast thou done?

FOIBLE. Nay, 'tis your ladyship has done, and are to do; I have only promised. But a man so enamored—so transported!—Well, if worshiping of pictures be a sin—poor Sir Rowland, I say—

LADY WISHFORT. The miniature has been counted like—but hast thou not betrayed me, Foible? Hast thou not detected me to that faithless Mirabell?—What hadst thou to do with him in the Park? Answer me; has he got nothing out of thee?

[24] All the books are pious, and two are anti-theatrical.

FOIBLE. (*Aside*) So the devil has been beforehand with me. What shall I say?—(*Aloud*)—Alas, madam, could I help it if I met that confident thing? Was I in fault? If you had heard how he used me, and all upon your ladyship's account, I'm sure you would not suspect my fidelity. Nay, if that had been the worst, I could have borne; but he had a fling at your ladyship too. And then I could not hold, but i'faith I gave him his own.

LADY WISHFORT. Me? What did the filthy fellow say?

FOIBLE. Oh, madam! 'tis a shame to say what he said—with his taunts and his fleers, tossing up his nose. Humh! (says he) what, you are a hatching some plot (says he), you are so early abroad, or catering (says he), ferreting for some disbanded officer, I warrant.—Half-pay is but thin subsistence (says he)—well, what pension does your lady propose? Let me see (says he); what, she must come down pretty deep now, she's superannuated (says he) and—

LADY WISHFORT. Odds my life, I'll have him—I'll have him murdered! I'll have him poisoned! Where does he eat?—I'll marry a drawer[25] to have him poisoned in his wine. I'll send for Robin from Locket's[26] immediately.

FOIBLE. Poison him! Poisoning's too good for him. Starve him, madam, starve him; marry Sir Rowland, and get him disinherited. Oh, you would bless yourself to hear what he said!

LADY WISHFORT. A villain! Superannuated!

FOIBLE. Humh (says he), I hear you are laying designs against me too (says he), and Mrs. Millamant is to marry my uncle (he does not suspect a word of your ladyship); but (says he) I'll fit you for that. I warrant you (says he) I'll hamper you for that (says he)—you and your old frippery too (says he); I'll handle you—

LADY WISHFORT. Audacious villain! Handle me, would he durst!—Frippery? Old frippery! Was there ever such a foul-mouthed fellow? I'll be married to-morrow; I'll be contracted to-night.

FOIBLE. The sooner the better, madam.

LADY WISHFORT. Will Sir Rowland be here, sayest thou? When, Foible?

FOIBLE. Incontinently, madam. No new sheriff's wife expects the return of her husband after knighthood with that impatience in which Sir Rowland burns for the dear hour of kissing your ladyship's hand after dinner.

LADY WISHFORT. Frippery! Superannuated frippery! I'll frippery the villain; I'll reduce him to frippery and rags! a tatterdemalion! I hope to see him hung with tatters, like a Long-lane penthouse[27] or a gibbet thief. A slander-mouthed railer! I warrant the spendthrift prodigal's in debt as much as the million lottery, or the whole court upon a birthday. I'll spoil his credit with his tailor. Yes, he shall have my niece with her fortune, he shall.

FOIBLE. He! I hope to see him lodge in Ludgate[28] first, and angle into Blackfriars for brass farthings with an old mitten.

LADY WISHFORT. Aye, dear Foible; thank thee for that, dear Foible. He has put me out of all patience. I shall never recompose my features to receive Sir Rowland with any economy of face. This wretch has fretted me that I am absolutely decayed. Look, Foible.

FOIBLE. Your ladyship has frowned a little too rashly, indeed, madam. There are some cracks discernible in the white varnish.

LADY WISHFORT. Let me see the glass.—Cracks, sayest thou?—why, I am arrantly flayed—I look like an old peeled wall. Thou must repair me, Foible, before Sir Rowland comes, or I shall never keep up to my picture.

FOIBLE. I warrant you, madam, a little art once made your picture like you, and now a little of the same art must make you like your picture. Your picture must sit for you, madam.

LADY WISHFORT. But art thou sure Sir Rowland will not fail to come? Or will he not fail when he does come? Will he be importunate, Foible, and push? For if he should not be importunate, I shall never break decorums —I shall die with confusion if I am forced to advance.—Oh, no, I can never advance!—I

[27] A shed or shop with an overhanging roof. Long Lane was occupied by old-clothes dealers.

[28] A prison in which debtors were confined, from the windows of which they let down baskets (in this case, an old mitten) to beg money from the passers-by.

[25] A tavern waiter.   [26] A London tavern.

shall swoon if he should expect advances. No, I hope Sir Rowland is better bred than to put a lady to the necessity of breaking her forms. I won't be too coy, neither.—I won't give him despair—but a little disdain is not amiss; a little scorn is alluring.

FOIBLE. A little scorn becomes your ladyship.

LADY WISHFORT. Yes, but tenderness becomes me best—a sort of dyingness—you see that picture has a sort of a—ha, Foible? a swimmingness in the eye—yes, I'll look so.— My niece affects it, but she wants features. Is Sir Rowland handsome? Let my toilet[29] be removed—I'll dress above. I'll receive Sir Rowland here.—Is he handsome? Don't answer me. I won't know; I'll be surprised. I'll be taken by surprise.

FOIBLE. By storm, madam. Sir Rowland's a brisk man.

LADY WISHFORT. Is he? Oh, then he'll importune, if he's a brisk man. I shall save decorums if Sir Rowland importunes. I have a mortal terror at the apprehension of offending against decorums. Oh, I'm glad he's a brisk man!—Let my things be removed, good Foible.

(Exit LADY WISHFORT. MRS. MARWOOD peers out and then steps back)

(Enter MRS. FAINALL)

MRS. FAINALL. Oh, Foible, I have been in a fright lest I should come too late! That devil Marwood saw you in the Park with Mirabell, and I'm afraid will discover it to my lady.

FOIBLE. Discover what, madam?

MRS. FAINALL. Nay, nay, put not on that strange face! I am privy to the whole design and know that Waitwell, to whom thou wert this morning married, is to personate Mirabell's uncle, and as such, winning my lady, to involve her in those difficulties from which Mirabell only must release her, by his making his conditions to have my cousin and her fortune left to her own disposal.

FOIBLE. Oh, dear madam, I beg your pardon. It was not my confidence in your ladyship that was deficient, but I thought the former good correspondence between your ladyship and Mr. Mirabell might have hindered his communicating this secret.

[29] Toilet case or service.

MRS. FAINALL. Dear Foible, forget that.

FOIBLE. O dear madam, Mr. Mirabell is such a sweet, winning gentleman—but your ladyship is the pattern of generosity.—Sweet lady, to be so good! Mr. Mirabell cannot choose but be grateful. I find your ladyship has his heart still. Now, madam, I can safely tell your ladyship our success: Mrs. Marwood had told my lady, but I warrant I managed myself. I turned it all for the better. I told my lady that Mr. Mirabell railed at her; I laid horrid things to his charge, I'll vow; and my lady is so incensed that she'll be contracted to Sir Rowland to-night, she says. I warrant I worked her up, that he may have her for asking for, as they say of a Welsh maidenhead.

MRS. FAINALL. O rare Foible!

FOIBLE. Madam, I beg your ladyship to acquaint Mr. Mirabell of his success. I would be seen as little as possible to speak to him: besides, I believe Madam Marwood watches me.—She has a month's mind[30]; but I know Mr. Mirabell can't abide her.—(Enter Footman) John, remove my lady's toilet.—Madam, your servant: my lady is so impatient I fear she'll come for me if I stay.

MRS. FAINALL. I'll go with you up the back stairs lest I should meet her. (Exeunt)

(Enter MRS. MARWOOD)

MRS. MARWOOD. Indeed, Mrs. Engine, is it thus with you? Are you become a go-between of this importance?—Yes, I shall watch you. Why, this wench is the passe-partout, a very master-key to everybody's strong-box. My friend Fainall, have you carried it so swimmingly? I thought there was something in it, but it seems it's over with you. Your loathing is not from a want of appetite, then, but from a surfeit. Else you could never be so cool to fall from a principal to be an assistant,—to procure for him! A pattern of generosity, that, I confess. Well, Mr. Fainall, you have met with your match.—O man, man! Woman, woman! The devil's an ass; if I were a painter, I would draw him like an idiot, a driveller with a bib and bells. Man should have his head and horns,[31] and woman the rest of him. Poor simple fiend!—"Madam Marwood has a month's mind, but he can't abide her."—'Twere better for him you had

[30] Strong desire.   [31] The symbol of a cuckold.

not been his confessor in that affair, without you could have kept his counsel closer. I shall not prove another pattern of generosity; he has not obliged me to that with those excesses of himself! And now I'll have none of him.—Here comes the good lady, panting ripe, with a heart full of hope, and a head full of care, like any chemist[32] upon the day of projection.

(Enter LADY WISHFORT)

LADY WISHFORT. Oh, dear Marwood, what shall I say for this rude forgetfulness?—but my dear friend is all goodness.

MRS. MARWOOD. No apologies, dear madam; I have been very well entertained.

LADY WISHFORT. As I'm a person, I am in a very chaos to think I should so forget myself: but I have such an olio[33] of affairs, really I know not what to do.—(Calls) Foible!—I expect my nephew, Sir Wilfull, every moment, too.—(Calls again) Why, Foible!—He means to travel for improvement.

MRS. MARWOOD. Methinks Sir Wilfull should rather think of marrying than travelling, at his years. I hear he is turned of forty.

LADY WISHFORT. Oh, he's in less danger of being spoiled by his travels—I am against my nephew's marrying too young. It will be time enough when he comes back and has acquired discretion to choose for himself.

MRS. MARWOOD. Methinks Mrs. Millamant and he would make a very fit match. He may travel afterwards.—'Tis a thing very usual with young gentlemen.

LADY WISHFORT. I promise you I have thought on't—and since 'tis your judgment, I'll think on't again. I assure you I will. I value your judgment extremely. On my word, I'll propose it.

(Enter FOIBLE)

LADY WISHFORT. Come, come, Foible—I had forgot my nephew will be here before dinner. I must make haste.

FOIBLE. Mr. Witwoud and Mr. Petulant are come to dine with your ladyship.

LADY WISHFORT. Oh, dear, I can't appear till I'm dressed! Dear Marwood, shall I be

free with you again, and beg you to entertain 'em? I'll make all imaginable haste. Dear friend, excuse me.

(Exeunt LADY WISHFORT and FOIBLE)

(Enter MRS. MILLAMANT and MINCING)

MRS. MILLAMANT. Sure never anything was so unbred as that odious man!—Marwood, your servant.

MRS. MARWOOD. You have a color; what's the matter?

MRS. MILLAMANT. That horrid fellow, Petulant, has provoked me into a flame: I have broken my fan.—Mincing, lend me yours. Is not all the powder out of my hair?

MRS. MARWOOD. No. What has he done?

MRS. MILLAMANT. Nay, he has done nothing; he has only talked—nay, he has said nothing neither, but he has contradicted everything that has been said. For my part, I thought Witwoud and he would have quarrelled.

MINCING. I vow, mem, I thought once they would have fit.

MRS. MILLAMANT. Well, 'tis a lamentable thing, I swear, that one has not the liberty of choosing one's acquaintance as one does one's clothes.

MRS. MARWOOD. If we had that liberty, we should be as weary of one set of acquaintance, though never so good, as we are of one suit, though never so fine. A fool and a doily stuff[34] would now and then find days of grace, and be worn for variety.

MRS. MILLAMANT. I could consent to wear 'em if they would wear alike; but fools never wear out—they are such drap du Berri[35] things—Without one could give 'em to one's chambermaid after a day or two!

MRS. MARWOOD. 'Twere better so indeed. Or what think you of the playhouse? A fine, gay, glossy fool should be given there, like a new masking habit, after the masquerade is over and we have done with the disguise. For a fool's visit is always a disguise, and never admitted by a woman of wit but to blind her affair with a lover of sense. If you would but appear barefaced now, and own Mirabell, you might as easily put off Petulant and Witwoud as your hood and scarf. And

[32] Like any alchemist about to undertake the last step in producing gold.   [33] Hodgepodge.

[34] A kind of woollen material.
[35] French woollen cloth.

indeed, 'tis time, for the town has found it; the secret is grown too big for the pretence. 'Tis like Mrs. Primly's great belly; she may lace it down before, but it burnishes on her hips. Indeed, Millamant, you can no more conceal it than my Lady Strammel can her face—that goodly face, which, in defiance of her Rhenish-wine tea,[36] will not be comprehended in a mask.

MRS. MILLAMANT. I'll take my death, Marwood, you are more censorious than a decayed beauty or a discarded toast.—Mincing, tell the men they may come up. My aunt is not dressing here.—Their folly is less provoking than your malice. (*Exit* MINCING) —The town has found it! What has it found? That Mirabell loves me is no more a secret than it is a secret that you discovered it to my aunt, or than the reason why you discovered it is a secret.

MRS. MARWOOD. You are nettled.

MRS. MILLAMANT. You're mistaken. Ridiculous!

MRS. MARWOOD. Indeed, my dear, you'll tear another fan if you don't mitigate those violent airs.

MRS. MILLAMANT. Oh, silly! ha, ha, ha! I could laugh immoderately.—Poor Mirabell! His constancy to me has quite destroyed his complaisance for all the world beside. I swear, I never enjoined it him to be so coy. If I had the vanity to think he would obey me, I would command him to show more gallantry —'tis hardly well-bred to be so particular on one hand, and so insensible on the other. But I despair to prevail, and so let him follow his own way. Ha, ha, ha! Pardon me, dear creature, I must laugh—ha, ha, ha!—though I grant you 'tis a little barbarous—ha, ha, ha!

MRS. MARWOOD. What pity 'tis, so much fine raillery and delivered with so significant gesture, should be so unhappily directed to miscarry.

MRS. MILLAMANT. Ha! Dear creature, I ask your pardon. I swear, I did not mind you.

MRS. MARWOOD. Mr. Mirabell and you both may think it a thing impossible, when I shall tell him by telling you—

MRS. MILLAMANT. Oh dear, what? for it is the same thing if I hear it—ha, ha, ha!

MRS. MARWOOD. That I detest him, hate him, madam.

[36] White Rhine wine, used for reducing.

MRS. MILLAMANT. O, Madam! why, so do I—and yet the creature loves me—ha, ha, ha! How can one forbear laughing to think of it. —I am a sibyl if I am not amazed to think what he can see in me. I'll take my death, I think you are handsomer—and within a year or two as young; if you could but stay for me, I should overtake you—but that cannot be.—Well, that thought makes me melancholic.—Now I'll be sad.

MRS. MARWOOD. Your merry note may be changed sooner than you think.

MRS. MILLAMANT. D'ye say so? Then I'm resolved I'll have a song to keep up my spirits.

(*Enter* MINCING)

MINCING. The gentlemen stay but to comb,[37] madam, and will wait on you.

MRS. MILLAMANT. Desire Mrs.——that is in the next room to sing the song I would have learned yesterday.—You shall hear it, madam—not that there's any great matter in it, but 'tis agreeable to my humor.

SONG

I.

Love's but the frailty of the mind,
When 'tis not with ambition joined;
A sickly flame, which, if not fed, expires,
And feeding, wastes in self-consuming fires.

II.

'Tis not to wound a wanton boy
Or amorous youth, that gives the joy;
But 'tis the glory to have pierced a swain,
For whom inferior beauties sighed in vain.

III.

Then I alone the conquest prize,
When I insult a rival's eyes:
If there's delight in love, 'tis when I see
That heart, which others bleed for, bleed for
* me.*

(*Enter* PETULANT *and* WITWOUD)

MRS. MILLAMANT. Is your animosity composed, gentlemen?

WITWOUD. Raillery, raillery, madam; we have no animosity—we hit off a little wit now

[37] *I.e.*, to comb their wigs.

and then, but no animosity. The falling out of wits is like the falling out of lovers. We agree in the main, like treble and bass. Ha, Petulant?

PETULANT. Aye, in the main—but when I have a humor to contradict—

WITWOUD. Aye, when he has a humor to contradict, then I contradict, too. What! I know my cue. Then we contradict one another like two battledores; for contradictions beget one another like Jews.

PETULANT. If he says black's black—if I have a humor to say 'tis blue—let that pass —all's one for that. If I have a humor to prove it, it must be granted.

WITWOUD. Not positively must—but it may—it may.

PETULANT. Yes, it positively must, upon proof positive.

WITWOUD. Aye, upon proof positive it must; but upon proof presumptive it only may.—That's a logical distinction now, madam.

MRS. MARWOOD. I perceive your debates are of importance and very learnedly handled.

PETULANT. Importance is one thing, and learning's another. But a debate's a debate; that I assert.

WITWOUD. Petulant's an enemy to learning; he relies altogether on his parts.

PETULANT. No, I'm no enemy to learning. It hurts not me.

MRS. MARWOOD. That's a sign indeed it's no enemy to you.

PETULANT. No, no, it's no enemy to anybody but them that have it.

MRS. MILLAMANT. Well, an illiterate man's my aversion. I wonder at the impudence of any illiterate man to offer to make love.

WITWOUD. That I confess I wonder at, too.

MRS. MILLAMANT. Ah! to marry an ignorant that can hardly read or write!

PETULANT. Why should a man be any further from being married, though he can't read, than he is from being hanged? The ordinary's[38] paid for setting the psalm,[39] and the parish priest for reading the ceremony. And for the rest which is to follow in both

cases, a man may do it without book—so all's one for that.

MRS. MILLAMANT. D'ye hear the creature? —Lord, here's company, I'll be gone.

(*Exeunt* Mrs. MILLAMANT *and* MINCING)

(*Enter* SIR WILFULL WITWOUD *in a country riding habit, and* SERVANT *to* LADY WISHFORT)

WITWOUD. In the name of Bartlemew and his fair,[40] what have we here?

MRS. MARWOOD. 'Tis your brother, I fancy. Don't you know him?

WITWOUD. Not I.—Yes, I think it is he— I've almost forgot him; I have not seen him since the Revolution.[41]

SERVANT. (*To* SIR WILFULL) Sir, my lady's dressing. Here's company; if you please to walk in, in the meantime.

SIR WILFULL. Dressing! What, it's but morning here I warrant, with you in London; we should count it towards afternoon in our parts, down in Shropshire.—Why, then belike, my aunt han't dined yet,—ha, friend?

SERVANT. Your aunt, sir?

SIR WILFULL. My aunt, sir! Yes, my aunt, sir, and your lady, sir; your lady is my aunt, sir.—Why, what! Dost thou not know me, friend? Why, then send somebody hither that does. How long hast thou lived with thy lady, fellow,—ha?

SERVANT. A week, sir—longer than anybody in the house, except my lady's woman.

SIR WILFULL. Why, then belike thou dost not know thy lady, if thou seest her,—ha, friend?

SERVANT. Why, truly, sir, I cannot safely swear to her face in a morning, before she is dressed. 'Tis like I may give a shrewd guess at her by this time.

SIR WILFULL. Well, prithee try what thou canst do; if thou canst not guess, inquire her out, dost hear, fellow? And tell her, her nephew, Sir Wilfull Witwoud, is in the house.

SERVANT. I shall, sir.

SIR WILFULL. Hold ye; hear me, friend; a word with you in your ear. Prithee, who are these gallants?

[38] Chaplain to the condemned criminals.
[39] Selecting the psalm.
[40] The annual Bartholomew Fair in Smithfield, famous for its side shows.   [41] Of 1688.

Servant. Really, sir, I can't tell; there come so many here, 'tis hard to know 'em all.
(*Exit* Servant)

Sir Wilfull. Oons, this fellow knows less than a starling; I don't think a' knows his own name.

Mrs. Marwood. Mr. Witwoud, your brother is not behindhand in forgetfulness—I fancy he has forgot you too.

Witwoud. I hope so—the devil take him that remembers first, I say.

Sir Wilfull. Save you, gentlemen and lady!

Mrs. Marwood. For shame, Mr. Witwoud; why don't you speak to him?—(*To* Sir Wilfull) And you, sir.

Witwoud. Petulant, speak.

Petulant. (*To* Sir Wilfull) And you, sir.

Sir Wilfull. No offense, I hope.
            (*Salutes* Mrs. Marwood)

Mrs. Marwood. No, sure, sir.

Witwoud. (*Aside*) This is a vile dog, I see that already. No offence! Ha, ha, ha!—To him; to him, Petulant, smoke him.[42]

Petulant. (*Surveying him round*) It seems as if you had come a journey, sir;—hem, hem.

Sir Wilfull. Very likely, sir, that it may seem so.

Petulant. No offence, I hope, sir.

Witwoud. (*Aside*) Smoke the boots, the boots, Petulant, the boots! Ha, ha, ha!

Sir Wilfull. May be not, sir; thereafter, as 'tis meant, sir.

Petulant. Sir, I presume upon the information of your boots.

Sir Wilfull. Why, 'tis like you may, sir; if you are not satisfied with the information of my boots, sir, if you will step to the stable, you may inquire further of my horse, sir.

Petulant. Your horse, sir? Your horse is an ass, sir!

Sir Wilfull. Do you speak by way of offence, sir?

Mrs. Marwood. The gentleman's merry, that's all, sir.—(*Aside*) 'Slife, we shall have a quarrel betwixt an horse and an ass before they find one another out.—(*Aloud*) You must not take anything amiss from your friends, sir. You are among your friends here,

though it may be you don't know it.—If I am not mistaken, you are Sir Wilfull Witwoud.

Sir Wilfull. Right, lady; I am Sir Wilfull Witwoud—so I write myself. No offence to anybody, I hope—and nephew to the Lady Wishfort of this mansion.

Mrs. Marwood. Don't you know this gentleman, sir?

Sir Wilfull. Hum! What, sure 'tis not —yea, by'r Lady, but 'tis—'sheart, I know not whether 'tis or no—yea, but 'tis, by the Rekin,[43] Brother Anthony! What, Tony, i'faith!—what, dost thou not know me? By'r Lady, nor I thee, thou art so be-cravated, and so be-periwigged!—'Sheart, why dost not speak? Art thou overjoyed?

Witwoud. Odso, brother, is it you? Your servant, brother.

Sir Wilfull. Your servant!—why yours, sir. Your servant again—'sheart, and your friend and servant to that—and a (*puff*)—and a—flap-dragon for your service, sir! and a hare's foot and a hare's scut for your service, sir, an you be so cold and so courtly.

Witwoud. No offence, I hope, brother.

Sir Wilfull. 'Sheart, sir, but there is, and much offence!—A pox, is this your Inns o' Court breeding, not to know your friends and your relations, your elders, and your betters?

Witwoud. Why, brother Wilfull of Salop,[44] you may be as short as a Shrewsbury-cake, if you please. But I tell you 'tis not modish to know relations in town. You think you're in the country, where great lubberly brothers slabber and kiss one another when they meet, like a call of sergeants[45]—'tis not the fashion here; 'tis not indeed, dear brother.

Sir Wilfull. The fashion's a fool; and you're a fop, dear brother. 'Sheart, I've suspected this—by'r Lady, I conjectured you were a fop since you began to change the style of your letters, and write on a scrap of paper gilt round the edges, no bigger than a *subpœna*. I might expect this when you left off "Honored Brother," and "hoping you are in good health," and so forth—to begin with

---

[42] Ridicule him.

[43] The Wrekin, a small mountain in Shropshire.   [44] Shropshire.

[45] When a sergeant-at-law is called to the bar.

a "Rat me, knight, I'm so sick of a last night's debauch—'ods heart," and then tell a familiar tale of a cock and a bull, and a whore and a bottle, and so conclude.—You could write news before you were out of your time,[46] when you lived with honest Pumple Nose, the attorney of Furnival's Inn—you could entreat to be remembered then to your friends round the Rekin. We could have gazettes, then, and Dawks's Letter,[47] and the Weekly Bill,[48] till of late days.

PETULANT. 'Slife, Witwoud, were you ever an attorney's clerk? Of the family of the Furnivals? Ha, ha, ha!

WITWOUD. Aye, aye, but that was but for a while—not long, not long. Pshaw! I was not in my own power then; an orphan, and this fellow was my guardian. Aye, aye, I was glad to consent to that man to come to London. He had the disposal of me then. If I had not agreed to that, I might have been bound 'prentice to a felt-maker in Shrewsbury; this fellow would have bound me to a maker of felts.

SIR WILFULL. 'Sheart, and better than to be bound to a maker of fops—where, I suppose, you have served your time, and now you may set up for yourself.

MRS. MARWOOD. You intend to travel, sir, as I'm informed.

SIR WILFULL. Belike I may, madam. I may chance to sail upon the salt seas, if my mind hold.

PETULANT. And the wind serve.

SIR WILFULL. Serve or not serve, I shan't ask license of you, sir; nor the weathercock your companion. I direct my discourse to the lady, sir.—'Tis like my aunt may have told you, madam—yes, I have settled my concerns, I may say now, and am minded to see foreign parts—if an' how that the peace holds, whereby that is, taxes abate.

MRS. MARWOOD. I thought you had designed for France at all adventures.

SIR WILFULL. I can't tell that; 'tis like I may, and 'tis like I may not. I am somewhat dainty in making a resolution because when I make it I keep it. I don't stand shill I, shall

I, then; if I say't, I'll do't. But I have thoughts to tarry a small matter in town to learn somewhat of your lingo first, before I cross the seas. I'd gladly have a spice of your French, as they say, whereby to hold discourse in foreign countries.

MRS. MARWOOD. Here's an academy in town for that use.

SIR WILFULL. There is? 'Tis like there may.

MRS. MARWOOD. No doubt you will return very much improved.

WITWOUD. Yes, refined, like a Dutch skipper from a whale-fishing.

(Enter LADY WISHFORT and FAINALL)

LADY WISHFORT. Nephew, you are welcome.

SIR WILFULL. Aunt, your servant.

FAINALL. Sir Wilfull, your most faithful servant.

SIR WILFULL. Cousin Fainall, give me your hand.

LADY WISHFORT. Cousin Witwoud, your servant; Mr. Petulant, your servant; nephew, you are welcome again. Will you drink anything after your journey, nephew, before you eat? Dinner's almost ready.

SIR WILFULL. I'm very well, I thank you, aunt—however, I thank you for your courteous offer. 'Sheart, I was afraid you would have been in the fashion, too, and have remembered to have forgot your relations. Here's your cousin Tony; belike, I mayn't call him brother for fear of offence.

LADY WISHFORT. Oh, he's a rallier, nephew—my cousin's a wit. And your great wits always rally their best friends to choose.[49] When you have been abroad, nephew, you'll understand raillery better.

(FAINALL and MRS. MARWOOD talk apart)

SIR WILFULL. Why then, let him hold his tongue in the meantime, and rail when that day comes.

(Enter MINCING)

MINCING. Mem, I am come to acquaint your la'ship that dinner is impatient.

SIR WILFULL. Impatient! Why, then, belike it won't stay till I pull off my boots.—

---

[46] Had served your apprenticeship.

[47] A news sheet intended for country consumption.

[48] The bills of mortality for London, then issued weekly.

[49] As they please.

Sweetheart, can you help me to a pair of slippers?—My man's with his horses, I warrant.

LADY WISHFORT. Fie, fie, nephew! You would not pull off your boots here!—Go down into the hall—dinner shall stay for you.
(*Exit* SIR WILFULL)
My nephew's a little unbred; you'll pardon him, madam.—Gentlemen, will you walk? Marwood?

MRS. MARWOOD. I'll follow you, madam —before Sir Wilfull is ready.
(*Exeunt all but* MRS. MARWOOD *and* FAINALL)

FAINALL. Why then, Foible's a bawd, an arrant, rank, match-making bawd. And I, it seems, am a husband, a rank husband; and my wife a very errant, rank wife—all in the way of the world. 'Sdeath, to be an anticipated cuckold, a cuckold in embryo! Sure, I was born with budding antlers, like a young satyr or a citizen's child. 'Sdeath! To be outwitted, to be out-jilted—out-matrimony'd!— If I had kept my speed like a stag, 'twere somewhat—but to crawl after, with my horns like a snail, and be outstripped by my wife— 'tis scurvy wedlock.

MRS. MARWOOD. Then shake it off. You have often wished for an opportunity to part, and now you have it. But first prevent their plot—the half of Millamant's fortune is too considerable to be parted with to a foe, to Mirabell.

FAINALL. Damn him! That had been mine, had you not made that fond discovery. —That had been forfeited, had they been married. My wife had added lustre to my horns by that increase of fortune; I could have worn 'em tipped with gold, though my forehead had been furnished like a deputy-lieutenant's hall.

MRS. MARWOOD. They may prove a cap of maintenance to you still, if you can away with your wife. And she's no worse than when you had her—I dare swear she had given up her game before she was married.

FAINALL. Hum! that may be. She might throw up her cards, but I'll be hanged if she did not put pam [50] in her pocket.

MRS. MARWOOD. You married her to keep you; and if you can contrive to have her

[50] The jack of clubs, the highest trump in the fashionable card game, loo.

keep you better than you expected, why should you not keep her longer than you intended?

FAINALL. The means, the means?

MRS. MARWOOD. Discover to my lady your wife's conduct; threaten to part with her! My lady loves her, and will come to any composition to save her reputation. Take the opportunity of breaking it just upon the discovery of this imposture. My lady will be enraged beyond bounds, and sacrifice niece, and fortune, and all, at that conjuncture. And let me alone to keep her warm; if she should flag in her part, I will not fail to prompt her.

FAINALL. Faith, this has an appearance.

MRS. MARWOOD. I'm sorry I hinted to my lady to endeavor a match between Millamant and Sir Wilfull; that may be an obstacle.

FAINALL. Oh, for that matter, leave me to manage him. I'll disable him for that; he will drink like a Dane. After dinner I'll set his hand in.

MRS. MARWOOD. Well, how do you stand affected towards your lady?

FAINALL. Why, faith, I'm thinking of it. —Let me see—I am married already, so that's over. My wife has played the jade with me —well, that's over, too. I never loved her, or if I had, why, that would have been over, too, by this time.—Jealous of her I cannot be, for I am certain, so there's an end of jealousy; weary of her I am, and shall be— no, there's no end of that—no, no, that were too much to hope. Thus far concerning my repose; now for my reputation. As to my own, I married not for it, so that's out of the question; and as to my part in my wife's —why, she had parted with hers before; so bringing none to me, she can take none from me. 'Tis against all rule of play that I should lose to one who has not wherewithal to stake.

MRS. MARWOOD. Besides, you forgot marriage is honorable.

FAINALL. Hum, faith, and that's well thought on. Marriage is honorable, as you say; and if so, wherefore should cuckoldom be a discredit, being derived from so honorable a root?

MRS. MARWOOD. Nay, I know not; if the root be honorable, why not the branches?

FAINALL. So, so; why, this point's clear. —Well, how do we proceed?

MRS. MARWOOD. I will contrive a letter which shall be delivered to my lady at the time when that rascal who is to act Sir Rowland is with her. It shall come as from an unknown hand—for the less I appear to know of the truth, the better I can play the incendiary. Besides, I would not have Foible provoked if I could help it—because you know she knows some passages—nay, I expect all will come out. But let the mine be sprung first, and then I care not if I am discovered.

FAINALL. If the worst come to the worst, I'll turn my wife to grass. I have already a deed of settlement of the best part of her estate, which I wheedled out of her, and that you shall partake at least.

MRS. MARWOOD. I hope you are convinced that I hate Mirabell. Now you'll be no more jealous?

FAINALL. Jealous! No, by this kiss. Let husbands be jealous, but let the lover still believe; or, if he doubt, let it be only to endear his pleasure, and prepare the joy that follows when he proves his mistress true. But let husbands' doubts convert to endless jealousy; or, if they have belief, let it corrupt to superstition and blind credulity. I am single, and will herd no more with 'em. True, I wear the badge, but I'll disown the order. And since I take my leave of 'em, I care not if I leave 'em a common motto to their common crest:

All husbands must or pain or shame endure;
The wise too jealous are, fools too secure.

(*Exeunt*)

Act IV

SCENE I. *The Same Place.*

(*Enter* LADY WISHFORT *and* FOIBLE)

LADY WISHFORT. Is Sir Rowland coming, sayest thou, Foible? And are things in order?

FOIBLE. Yes, madam, I have put wax lights in the sconces, and placed the footmen in a row in the hall, in their best liveries, with the coachman and postilion to fill up the equipage.

LADY WISHFORT. Have you pulvilled [51] the coachman and postilion, that they may not stink of the stable when Sir Rowland comes by?

FOIBLE. Yes, madam.

LADY WISHFORT. And are the dancers and the music ready, that he may be entertained in all points with correspondence to his passion?

FOIBLE. All is ready, madam.

LADY WISHFORT. And—well—how do I look, Foible?

FOIBLE. Most killing well, madam.

LADY WISHFORT. Well, and how shall I receive him? In what figure shall I give his heart the first impression? There is a great deal in the first impression. Shall I sit?—

[51] Perfumed.

no, I won't sit—I'll walk—aye, I'll walk from the door upon his entrance, and then turn full upon him—no, that will be too sudden. I'll lie,—aye, I'll lie down—I'll receive him in my little dressing-room; there's a couch— yes, yes, I'll give the first impression on a couch.—I won't lie neither, but loll and lean upon one elbow with one foot a little dangling off, jogging in a thoughtful way —yes—and then as soon as he appears, start, aye, start and be surprised, and rise to meet him in a pretty disorder—yes.—Oh, nothing is more alluring than a levee from a couch, in some confusion; it shows the foot to advantage, and furnishes with blushes, and recomposing airs beyond comparison. Hark! There's a coach.

FOIBLE. 'Tis he, madam.

LADY WISHFORT. Oh, dear, has my nephew made his addresses to Millamant? I ordered him.

FOIBLE. Sir Wilfull is set in drinking, madam, in the parlor.

LADY WISHFORT. Odds my life, I'll send him to her. Call her down, Foible; bring her hither. I'll send him as I go.—When they are together, then come to me, Foible, that

I may not be too long alone with Sir Rowland. (*Exit* LADY WISHFORT)

(*Enter* MRS. MILLAMANT *and* MRS. FAINALL)

FOIBLE. Madam, I stayed here to tell your ladyship that Mr. Mirabell has waited this half-hour for an opportunity to talk with you—though my lady's orders were to leave you and Sir Wilfull together. Shall I tell Mr. Mirabell that you are at leisure?

MRS. MILLAMANT. No. What would the dear man have? I am thoughtful, and would amuse myself—bid him come another time.
(*Reciting, and walking about*)

There never yet was woman made
Nor shall, but to be cursed.

That's hard!

MRS. FAINALL. You are very fond of Sir John Suckling to-day, Millamant, and the poets.

MRS. MILLAMANT. He? Aye, and filthy verses—so I am.

FOIBLE. Sir Wilfull is coming, madam. Shall I send Mr. Mirabell away?

MRS. MILLAMANT. Aye, if you please, Foible, send him away, or send him hither—just as you will, dear Foible. I think I'll see him—shall I? Aye, let the wretch come.
(*Exit* FOIBLE)
MRS. MILLAMANT. (*Reciting*)

Thyrsis, a youth of the inspired train.

Dear Fainall, entertain Sir Wilfull—thou hast philosophy to undergo a fool. Thou art married and hast patience—I would confer with my own thoughts.

MRS. FAINALL. I am obliged to you that you would make me your proxy in this affair, but I have business of my own.

(*Enter* SIR WILFULL)

O Sir Wilfull, you are come at the critical instant. There's your mistress up to the ears in love and contemplation; pursue your point now or never.

SIR WILFULL. Yes; my aunt will have it so—I would gladly have been encouraged with a bottle or two, because I'm somewhat wary at first before I am acquainted.—(MILLAMANT *walks about repeating verses to herself*)—But I hope, after a time, I shall break my mind—that is, upon further acquaintance.—So for the present, cousin, I'll take my leave. If so be you'll be so kind to make my excuse, I'll return to my company—

MRS. FAINALL. Oh, fie, Sir Wilfull! What! You must not be daunted.

SIR WILFULL. Daunted! No, that's not it; it is not so much for that—for if so be that I set on't, I'll do't. But only for the present, 'tis sufficient till further acquaintance, that's all—your servant.
(*Bows and edges toward the door*)
MRS. FAINALL. Nay, I'll swear you shall never lose so favorable an opportunity if I can help it. I'll leave you together, and lock the door. (*Exit*)

SIR WILFULL. Nay, nay, cousin—I have forgot my gloves!—What d'ye do?—'Sheart, a' has locked the door indeed, I think. Nay, Cousin Fainall, open the door! Pshaw, what a vixen trick is this?—Nay, now a' has seen me too.—Cousin, I made bold to pass through as it were—I think this door's enchanted!

MRS. MILLAMANT. (*Reciting*)

I prithee spare me, gentle boy,
Press me no more for that slight toy.

SIR WILFULL. Anan? Cousin, your servant. (*Bows*)
MRS. MILLAMANT.

—That foolish trifle of a heart.—

Sir Wilfull!

SIR WILFULL. Yes—your servant. (*Bows again*) No offence, I hope, cousin.

MRS. MILLAMANT. (*Reciting*)

I swear it will do its part,
Though thou dost thine, employ'st thy power and art.

Natural, easy Suckling!

SIR WILFULL. Anan? Suckling! No such suckling neither, cousin, nor stripling; I thank heaven, I'm no minor.

MRS. MILLAMANT. Ah, rustic, ruder than Gothic!

SIR WILFULL. Well, well, I shall understand your lingo one of these days, cousin; in the meanwhile I must answer in plain English.

MRS. MILLAMANT. Have you any business with me, Sir Wilfull?

SIR WILFULL. Not at present, cousin.—Yes, I made bold to see, to come and know if that how you were disposed to fetch a walk this evening; if so be that I might not be troublesome, I would have sought a walk with you.

MRS. MILLAMANT. A walk! What then?

SIR WILFULL. Nay, nothing—only for the walk's sake, that's all.

MRS. MILLAMANT. I nauseate walking; 'tis a country diversion. I loathe the country, and everything that relates to it.

SIR WILFULL. Indeed! Ha! Look ye, look ye—you do? Nay, 'tis like you may—here are choice of pastimes here in town, as plays and the like; that must be confessed, indeed.

MRS. MILLAMANT. Ah, l'étourdi! [52] I hate the town too.

SIR WILFULL. Dear heart, that's much—ha! that you should hate 'em both! Ha! 'Tis like you may; there are some can't relish the town, and others can't away with the country—'tis like you may be one of those, cousin.

MRS. MILLAMANT. Ha, ha, ha! Yes, 'tis like I may.—You have nothing further to say to me?

SIR WILFULL. Not at present, cousin.—'Tis like when I have an opportunity to be more private, I may break my mind in some measure—I conjecture you partly guess—however, that's as time shall try—but spare to speak and spare to speed, as they say.

MRS. MILLAMANT. If it is of no great importance, Sir Wilfull, you will oblige me to leave me; I have just now a little business—

SIR WILFULL. Enough, enough, cousin; yes, yes, all a case.—When you're disposed, when you're disposed. Now's as well as another time, and another time as well as now. All's one for that—Yes, yes, if your concerns call you, there's no haste; it will keep cold, as they say. Cousin, your servant. (Bows)—I think this door's locked.

MRS. MILLAMANT. You may go this way, sir.

SIR WILFULL. Your servant; then with your leave I'll return to my company.

(Exit)

MRS. MILLAMANT. Aye, aye; ha, ha, ha!

Like Phœbus sung the no less amorous boy.[52a]

(Enter MIRABELL)

MIRABELL. "Like Daphne she, as lovely and as coy." Do you lock yourself up from me, to make my search more curious, or is this pretty artifice contrived to signify that here the chase must end, and my pursuits be crowned? For you can fly no further.

MRS. MILLAMANT. Vanity! No—I'll fly, and be followed to the last moment. Though I am upon the very verge of matrimony, I expect you should solicit me as much as if I were wavering at the grate of a monastery, with one foot over the threshold. I'll be solicited to the very last—nay, and afterwards.

MIRABELL. What, after the last?

MRS. MILLAMANT. Oh, I should think I was poor and had nothing to bestow, if I were reduced to an inglorious ease and freed from the agreeable fatigues of solicitation.

MIRABELL. But do not you know that when favors are conferred upon instant and tedious solicitation, that they diminish in their value, and that both the giver loses the grace, and the receiver lessens his pleasure?

MRS. MILLAMANT. It may be in things of common application; but never, sure, in love. Oh, I hate a lover that can dare to think he draws a moment's air, independent of the bounty of his mistress. There is not so impudent a thing in nature as the saucy look of an assured man, confident of success. The pedantic arrogance of a very husband has not so pragmatical an air. Ah! I'll never marry unless I am first made sure of my will and pleasure.

MIRABELL. Would you have 'em both before marriage? Or will you be contented with the first now, and stay for the other till after grace?

MRS. MILLAMANT. Ah! don't be impertinent.—My dear liberty, shall I leave thee? My faithful solitude, my darling contemplation, must I bid you then adieu? Ay-h adieu—my morning thoughts, agreeable wakings, indolent slumbers, all ye *douceurs,* ye *sommeils du matin, adieu.*—I can't do't, 'tis more than impossible.—Positively, Mirabell, I'll lie abed in a morning as long as I please.

MIRABELL. Then I'll get up in a morning as early as I please.

MRS. MILLAMANT. Ah? Idle creature, get up when you will—and d'ye hear, I won't be called names after I'm married; positively, I won't be called names.

MIRABELL. Names!

MRS. MILLAMANT. Aye, as wife, spouse, my dear, joy, jewel, love, sweetheart, and the rest of that nauseous cant, in which men and their wives are so fulsomely familiar—I shall never bear that. Good Mirabell, don't let us be familiar or fond, nor kiss before folks, like my Lady Fadler and Sir Francis; nor go to Hyde Park together the first Sunday in a new chariot, to provoke eyes and whispers, and then never to be seen there together again, as if we were proud of one another the first week, and ashamed of one another ever after. Let us never visit together, nor go to a play together; but let us be very strange and well-bred. Let us be as strange as if we had been married a great while, and as well-bred as if we were not married at all.

MIRABELL. Have you any more conditions to offer? Hitherto your demands are pretty reasonable.

MRS. MILLAMANT. Trifles—as liberty to pay and receive visits to and from whom I please; to write and receive letters, without interrogatories or wry faces on your part; to wear what I please, and choose conversation with regard only to my own taste; to have no obligation upon me to converse with wits that I don't like, because they are your acquaintance: or to be intimate with fools, because they may be your relations.—Come to dinner when I please; dine in my dressing-room when I'm out of humor, without giving a reason. To have my closet inviolate; to be sole empress of my tea-table, which you must never presume to approach without first asking leave. And lastly, wherever I am, you shall always knock at the door before you come in. These articles subscribed, if I continue to endure you a little longer, I may by degrees dwindle into a wife.

MIRABELL. Your bill of fare is something advanced in this latter account.—Well, have I liberty to offer conditions—that when you are dwindled into a wife, I may not be beyond measure enlarged into a husband?

MRS. MILLAMANT. You have free leave. Propose your utmost; speak and spare not.

MIRABELL. I thank you.—*Imprimis* then, I covenant that your acquaintance be general; that you admit no sworn confidante or intimate of your own sex—no she-friend to screen her affairs under your countenance, and tempt you to make trial of a mutual secrecy. No decoy-duck to wheedle you a fop—scrambling to the play in a mask—then bring you home in a pretended fright, when you think you shall be found out—and rail at me for missing the play and disappointing the frolic which you had, to pick me up and prove my constancy.

MRS. MILLAMANT. Detestable *imprimis!* I go to the play in a mask!

MIRABELL. *Item,* I article, that you continue to like your own face, as long as I shall; and while it passes current with me, that you endeavor not to new-coin it. To which end, together with all vizards for the day, I prohibit all masks for the night, made of oiled-skins and I know not what—hogs' bones, hares' gall, pig-water, and the marrow of a roasted cat. In short, I forbid all commerce with the gentlewoman in what-d'ye-call-it Court. *Item,* I shut my doors against all bawds with baskets, and pennyworths of muslin, china, fans, atlases, etc.—*Item,* when you shall be breeding—

MRS. MILLAMANT. Ah! Name it not.

MIRABELL. Which may be presumed, with a blessing on our endeavors—

MRS. MILLAMANT. Odious endeavors!

MIRABELL. I denounce against all strait lacing, squeezing for a shape, till you mold my boy's head like a sugar-loaf, and instead of a man-child, make me father to a crooked billet. Lastly, to the dominion of the tea-table I submit—but with proviso, that you exceed not in your province, but restrain yourself to native and simple tea-table drinks, as tea, chocolate, and coffee; as likewise to genuine and authorized tea-table talk—such as mending of fashions, spoiling reputations, railing at absent friends, and so forth—but that on no account you encroach upon the men's prerogative, and presume to drink healths, or toast fellows; for prevention of which I banish all foreign forces, all auxiliaries to the tea-table, as orange-brandy, all aniseed, cinnamon, citron, and Barbadoes waters, together with ratafia, and the most noble spirit of clary, but for cowslip wine, poppy water, and all dormitives, those I allow.—These provisos admitted, in other things I may prove a tractable and complying husband.

MRS. MILLAMANT. O horrid provisos! Filthy strong-waters! I toast fellows! Odious men! I hate your odious provisos.

MIRABELL. Then we're agreed. Shall I kiss your hand upon the contract? And here comes one to be a witness to the sealing of the deed.

(*Enter* MRS. FAINALL)

MRS. MILLAMANT. Fainall, what shall I do? Shall I have him? I think I must have him.

MRS. FAINALL. Aye, aye, take him, take him; what should you do?

MRS. MILLAMANT. Well then—I'll take my death, I'm in a horrid fright.—Fainall, I shall never say it—well—I think—I'll endure you.

MRS. FAINALL. Fie! fie! Have him, have him, and tell him so in plain terms; for I am sure you have a mind to him.

MRS. MILLAMANT. Are you? I think I have—and the horrid man looks as if he thought so too. Well, you ridiculous thing you, I'll have you—I won't be kissed, nor I won't be thanked—here, kiss my hand though.—So, hold your tongue now; don't say a word.

MRS. FAINALL. Mirabell, there's a necessity for your obedience; you have neither time to talk nor stay. My mother is coming, and in my conscience if she should see you, would fall into fits, and maybe not recover time enough to return to Sir Rowland, who, as Foible tells me, is in a fair way to succeed. Therefore spare your ecstasies for another occasion, and slip down the backstairs, where Foible waits to consult you.

MRS. MILLAMANT. Aye, go, go. In the meantime I suppose you have said something to please me.

MIRABELL. I am all obedience.

(*Exit* MIRABELL)

MRS. FAINALL. Yonder Sir Wilfull's drunk, and so noisy that my mother has been forced to leave Sir Rowland to appease him; but he answers her only with singing and drinking. What they may have done by this time I know not, but Petulant and he were upon quarreling as I came by.

MRS. MILLAMANT. Well, if Mirabell should not make a good husband, I am a lost thing, for I find I love him violently.

MRS. FAINALL. So it seems, when you mind not what's said to you.—If you doubt him, you had best take up with Sir Wilfull.

MRS. MILLAMANT. How can you name that superannuated lubber?—Foh!

(*Enter* WITWOUD *from drinking*)

MRS. FAINALL. So! Is the fray made up, that you have left 'em?

WITWOUD. Left 'em? I could stay no longer. I have laughed like ten christ'nings—I am tipsy with laughing. If I had stayed any longer I should have burst—I must have been let out and pieced in the sides like an unfixed camlet.—Yes, yes, the fray is composed; my lady came in like a *noli prosequi,*[53] and stopped their proceedings.

MRS. MILLAMANT. What was the dispute?

WITWOUD. That's the jest; there was no dispute. They could neither of 'em speak for rage, and so fell a sputtering at one another like two roasting apples.

(*Enter* PETULANT, *drunk*)

Now, Petulant, all's over, all's well. Gad, my head begins to whim it about.—Why dost thou not speak? Thou art both as drunk and mute as a fish.

PETULANT. Look you, Mrs. Millamant—if you can love me, dear nymph, say it—and that's the conclusion. Pass on, or pass off—that's all.

WITWOUD. Thou hast uttered volumes, folios, in less than *decimo sexto,* my dear Lacedemonian. Sirrah Petulant, thou art an epitomizer of words.

[53] Legal term: unwilling to prosecute.

PETULANT. Witwoud—you are an annihilator of sense.

WITWOUD. Thou art a retailer of phrases, and dost deal in remnants of remnants, like a maker of pincushions—thou art in truth (metaphorically speaking) a speaker of shorthand.

PETULANT. Thou art (without a figure) just one-half of an ass, and Baldwin[54] yonder, thy half-brother, is the rest.—A Gemini[55] of asses split would make just four of you.

WITWOUD. Thou dost bite, my dear mustard seed; kiss me for that.

PETULANT. Stand off!—I'll kiss no more males—I have kissed your twin yonder in a humor of reconciliation, till he (*hiccup*) rises upon my stomach like a radish.

MRS. MILLAMANT. Eh! Filthy creature! —What was the quarrel?

PETULANT. There was no quarrel—there might have been a quarrel.

WITWOUD. If there had been words enow between 'em to have expressed provocation, they had gone together by the ears like a pair of castanets.

PETULANT. You were the quarrel.

MRS. MILLIMANT. Me!

PETULANT. If I have a humor to quarrel, I can make less matters conclude premises. —If you are not handsome, what then, if I have a humor to prove it? If I shall have my reward, say so; if not, fight for your face the next time yourself. I'll go sleep.

WITWOUD. Do; wrap thyself up like a wood-louse, and dream revenge—and hear me; if thou canst learn to write by tomorrow morning, pen me a challenge.—I'll carry it for thee.

PETULANT. Carry your mistress's monkey a spider!—Go, flea dogs, and read romances! —I'll go to bed to my maid.

(*Exit* PETULANT)

MRS. FAINALL. He's horridly drunk. How came you all in this pickle?

WITWOUD. A plot, a plot, to get rid of the knight—your husband's advice, but he sneaked off.

(*Enter* LADY WISHFORT, *and then* SIR WILFULL, *drunk*)

[54] The ass in *Reynard the Fox.*
[55] Twins.

LADY WISHFORT. Out upon't, out upon't! At years of discretion, and comport yourself at this rantipole rate!

SIR WILFULL. No offence, aunt.

LADY WISHFORT. Offence! As I'm a person, I'm ashamed of you. Fob! How you stink of wine! D'ye think my niece will ever endure such a borachio! you're an absolute borachio.[55a]

SIR WILFULL. Borachio?

LADY WISHFORT. At a time when you should commence an amour and put your best foot foremost—

SIR WILFULL. 'Sheart, an you grutch me your liquor, make a bill—give me more drink, and take my purse—(*Sings*)

> Prithee fill me the glass,
>   Till it laugh in my face,
> With ale that is potent and mellow;
>   He that whines for a lass,
>   Is an ignorant ass,
> For a bumper has not its fellow.

But if you would have me marry my cousin —say the word, and I'll do't. Wilfull will do't; that's the word. Wilfull will do't; that's my crest—My motto I have forgot.

LADY WISHFORT. (*To* MRS. MILLAMANT) My nephew's a little overtaken, cousin, but 'tis with drinking your health.— O' my word, you are obliged to him.

SIR WILFULL. *In vino veritas,* aunt.—If I drunk your health to-day, cousin—I am a Borachio. But if you have a mind to be married, say the word, and send for the piper; Wilfull will do't. If not, dust it away, and let's have t'other round.—Tony!—Odds heart, where's Tony?—Tony's an honest fellow; but he spits after a bumper, and that's a fault.—

(*Sings*)

> We'll drink, and we'll never ha' done, boys,
>   Put the glass then around with the sun, boys,
> Let Apollo's example invite us;
>   For he's drunk every night,
>   And that makes him so bright,
> That he's able next morning to light us.

The sun's a good pimple, an honest soaker; he has a cellar at your Antipodes. If I travel,

[55a] Winebag; hence, drunkard.

aunt, I touch at your Antipodes.—Your Antipodes are a good, rascally sort of topsy-turvy fellows; if I had a bumper, I'd stand upon my head and drink a health to 'em.—A match or no match, cousin with the hard name?—Aunt, Wilfull will do't. If she has her maidenhead, let her look to't; if she has not, let her keep her own counsel in the meantime, and cry out at the nine months' end.

MRS. MILLAMANT. Your pardon, madam, I can stay no longer—Sir Wilfull grows very powerful. Eh! How he smells! I shall be overcome, if I stay. Come, cousin.

(*Exeunt* MRS. MILLAMANT *and* MRS. FAINALL)

LADY WISHFORT. Smells! He would poison a tallow-chandler and his family! Beastly creature, I know not what to do with him!—Travel, quotha! Aye, travel, travel—get thee gone, get thee gone; get thee but far enough, to the Saracens, or the Tartars, or the Turks!—for thou art not fit to live in a Christian commonwealth, thou beastly pagan!

SIR WILFULL. Turks? No; no Turks, aunt. Your Turks are infidels, and believe not in the grape. Your Mahometan, your Mussulman, is a dry stinkard—no offence, aunt. My map says that your Turk is not so honest a man as your Christian. I cannot find by the map that your Mufti is orthodox —whereby it is a plain case that orthodox is a hard word, aunt, and (*hiccups*)—Greek for claret.— (*Sings*)

To drink is a Christian diversion,
Unknown to the Turk or the Persian:
Let Mahometan fools
Live by heathenish rules,
And be damned over tea-cups and coffee.
But let British lads sing,
Crown a health to the king,
And a fig for your sultan and sophy!

Ah, Tony!

(*Enter* FOIBLE, *and whispers to* LADY WISHFORT)

LADY WISHFORT. (*Aside to* FOIBLE) Sir Rowland impatient? Good lack! What shall I do with this beastly tumbril?—(*Aloud*) Go lie down and sleep, you sot!—or, as I'm a person, I'll have you bastinadoed with broomsticks.—Call up the wenches.

(*Exit* FOIBLE)

SIR WILFULL. Ahey! Wenches; where are the wenches?

LADY WISHFORT. Dear Cousin Witwoud, get him away, and you will bind me to you inviolably. I have an affair of moment that invades me with some precipitation—you will oblige me to all futurity.

WITWOUD. Come, knight.—Pox on him. I don't know what to say to him.—Will you go to a cock-match?

SIR WILFULL. With a wench, Tony? Is she a shakebag, sirrah? Let me bite your cheek for that.

WITWOUD. Horrible! he has a breath like a bagpipe—Aye, aye; come, will you march, my Salopian?

SIR WILFULL. Lead on, little Tony—I'll follow thee, my Anthony, my Tantony. Sirrah, thou shalt be my Tantony, and I'll be thy pig.[56] (*Sings*)

And a fig for your sultan and sophy.

(*Exeunt* SIR WILFULL *and* WITWOUD)

LADY WISHFORT. This will never do. It will never make a match—at least before he has been abroad.

(*Enter* WAITWELL, *disguised as* SIR ROWLAND)

LADY WISHFORT. Dear Sir Rowland, I am confounded with confusion at the retrospection of my own rudeness!—I have more pardons to ask than the pope distributes in the year of jubilee. But I hope, where there is likely to be so near an alliance, we may unbend the severity of decorums and dispense with a little ceremony.

WAITWELL. My impatience, madam, is the effect of my transport; and till I have the possession of your adorable person, I am tantalized on the rack; and do but hang, madam, on the tenter of expectation.

LADY WISHFORT. You have excess of gallantry, Sir Rowland, and press things to a conclusion with a most prevailing vehe-

[56] The pig is associated with St. Anthony in legend.

mence.—But a day or two for decency of marriage—

WAITWELL. For decency of funeral, madam! The delay will break my heart—or, if that should fail, I shall be poisoned. My nephew will get an inkling of my designs, and poison me; and I would willingly starve him before I die—I would gladly go out of the world with that satisfaction.—That would be some comfort to me, if I could but live so long as to be revenged on that unnatural viper!

LADY WISHFORT. Is he so unnatural, say you? Truly, I would contribute much, both to the saving of your life and the accomplishment of your revenge—not that I respect myself, though he has been a perfidious wretch to me.

WAITWELL. Perfidious to you!

LADY WISHFORT. O Sir Rowland, the hours that he has died away at my feet, the tears that he has shed, the oaths that he has sworn, the palpitations that he has felt, the trances and the tremblings, the ardors and the ecstasies, the kneelings and the risings, the heart-heavings and the hand-grippings, the pangs and the pathetic regards of his protesting eyes! Oh, no memory can register!

WAITWELL. What, my rival! Is the rebel my rival?—a' dies!

LADY WISHFORT. No, don't kill him at once, Sir Rowland; starve him gradually, inch by inch.

WAITWELL. I'll do't. In three weeks he shall be barefoot; in a month out at knees with begging an alms.—He shall starve upward and upward, till he has nothing living but his head, and then go out in a stink like a candle's end upon a save-all.[57]

LADY WISHFORT. Well, Sir Rowland, you have the way—you are no novice in the labyrinth of love; you have the clue. But as I am a person, Sir Rowland, you must not attribute my yielding to any sinister appetite, or indigestion of widowhood; nor impute my complacency to any lethargy of continence. I hope you do not think me prone to any iteration of nuptials—

WAITWELL. Far be it from me—

LADY WISHFORT. If you do, I protest I must recede—or think that I have made a

prostitution of decorums; but in the vehemence of compassion, and to save the life of a person of so much importance—

WAITWELL. I esteem it so—

LADY WISHFORT. Or else you wrong my condescension.

WAITWELL. I do not, I do not—

LADY WISHFORT. Indeed you do.

WAITWELL. I do not, fair shrine of virtue!

LADY WISHFORT. If you think the least scruple of carnality was an ingredient,—

WAITWELL. Dear madam, no. You are all camphor and frankincense, all chastity and odor.

LADY WISHFORT. Or that—

(Enter FOIBLE)

FOIBLE. Madam, the dancers are ready; and there's one with a letter, who must deliver it into your own hands.

LADY WISHFORT. Sir Rowland, will you give me leave? Think favorably, judge candidly, and conclude you have found a person who would suffer racks in honor's cause, dear Sir Rowland, and will wait on you incessantly.   (Exit LADY WISHFORT)

WAITWELL. Fie, fie!—What a slavery have I undergone! Spouse, hast thou any cordial? I want spirits.

FOIBLE. What a washy rogue art thou, to pant thus for a quarter of an hour's lying and swearing to a fine lady.

WAITWELL. Oh, she is the antidote to desire! Spouse, thou wilt fare the worse for't— I shall have no appetite to iteration of nuptials this eight-and-forty hours.—By this hand, I'd rather be a chairman[57a] in the dog-days than act Sir Rowland till this time tomorrow!

(Enter LADY WISHFORT, with a letter)

LADY WISHFORT. Call in the dancers.— Sir Rowland, we'll sit, if you please, and see the entertainment. (A dance) Now, with your permission, Sir Rowland, I will peruse my letter.—I would open it in your presence, because I would not make you uneasy. If it should make you uneasy, I would burn it. Speak, if it does—but you may see by the superscription it is like a woman's hand.

FOIBLE. (Aside to WAITWELL) By

---

[57] A device for burning candle ends.

[57a] A sedan chair carrier.

heaven! Mrs. Marwood's, I know it.—My heart aches—get it from her.

WAITWELL. A woman's hand? No, madam, that's no woman's hand; I see that already. That's somebody whose throat must be cut.

LADY WISHFORT. Nay, Sir Rowland, since you give me a proof of your passion by your jealousy, I promise you I'll make a return by a frank communication.—You shall see it—we'll open it together—look you here.—(Reads)—"Madam, though unknown to you"—Look you there, 'tis from nobody that I know—"I have that honor for your character, that I think myself obliged to let you know you are abused. He who pretends to be Sir Rowland, is a cheat and a rascal."—Oh, heavens! What's this?

FOIBLE. (Aside) Unfortunate, all's ruined!

WAITWELL. How, how! Let me see, let me see!—(Reads) "A rascal, and disguised and suborned for that imposture,"—O villainy! O villainy!—"by the contrivance of—"

LADY WISHFORT. I shall faint!—I shall die, I shall die!—Oh!

FOIBLE. (Aside to WAITWELL) Say 'tis your nephew's hand—quickly, his plot,—swear it, swear it!

WAITWELL. Here's a villain! Madam, don't you perceive it? Don't you see it?

LADY WISHFORT. Too well, too well! I have seen too much.

WAITWELL. I told you at first I knew the hand.—A woman's hand! The rascal writes a sort of a large hand—your Roman hand.—I saw there was a throat to be cut presently. If he were my son, as he is my nephew, I'd pistol him!

FOIBLE. O treachery!—But are you sure, Sir Rowland, it is his writing?

WAITWELL. Sure? Am I here? Do I live? Do I love this pearl of India? I have twenty letters in my pocket from him in the same character.

LADY WISHFORT. How!

FOIBLE. Oh, what luck it is, Sir Rowland, that you were present at this juncture! This was the business that brought Mr. Mirabell disguised to Madam Millamant this after-noon. I thought something was contriving when he stole by me and would have hid his face.

LADY WISHFORT. How, how!—I heard the villain was in the house, indeed; and now I remember, my niece went away abruptly when Sir Wilfull was to have made his addresses.

FOIBLE. Then, then, madam, Mr. Mirabell waited for her in her chamber; but I would not tell your ladyship to discompose you when you were to receive Sir Rowland.

WAITWELL. Enough; his date is short.

FOIBLE. No, good Sir Rowland, don't incur the law.

WAITWELL. Law! I care not for law. I can but die and 'tis in a good cause.—My lady shall be satisfied of my truth and innocence, though it cost me my life.

LADY WISHFORT. No, dear Sir Rowland, don't fight. If you should be killed, I must never show my face; or hanged—oh, consider my reputation, Sir Rowland!—No, you shan't fight.—I'll go in and examine my niece; I'll make her confess. I conjure you, Sir Rowland, by all your love, not to fight.

WAITWELL. I am charmed, madam; I obey. But some proof you must let me give you; I'll go for a black box which contains the writings of my whole estate, and deliver that into your hands.

LADY WISHFORT. Aye, dear Sir Rowland, that will be some comfort. Bring the black box.

WAITWELL. And may I presume to bring a contract to be signed this night? May I hope so far?

LADY WISHFORT. Bring what you will, but come alive, pray, come alive! Oh, this is a happy discovery!

WAITWELL. Dead or alive I'll come—and married we will be in spite of treachery; aye, and get an heir that shall defeat the last remaining glimpse of hope in my abandoned nephew. Come, my buxom widow:
Ere long you shall substantial proofs receive,
That I'm an errant knight—

FOIBLE. (Aside) Or arrant knave.

(Exeunt)

Act V

Scene I. *Same Place.*

(LADY WISHFORT *and* FOIBLE)

LADY WISHFORT. Out of my house! Out of my house, thou viper, thou serpent, that I have fostered! Thou bosom traitress, that I raised from nothing!—Begone, begone, begone, go! go!—That I took from washing of old gauze and weaving of dead hair, with a bleak blue nose over a chafing-dish of starved embers, and dining behind a traverse rag, in a shop no bigger than a bird-cage!—Go, go! Starve again! Do, do!

FOIBLE. Dear madam, I'll beg pardon on my knees.

LADY WISHFORT. Away! out, out!—Go, set up for yourself again!—Do, drive a trade, do, with your three-pennyworth of small ware, flaunting upon a packthread under a brandy-seller's bulk, or against a dead wall by a ballad-monger! Go, hang out an old Frisoneer gorget, with a yard of yellow colbertine again, do! An old gnawed mask, two rows of pins, and a child's fiddle; a glass necklace with the beads broken, and a quilted nightcap with one ear! Go, go, drive a trade!—These were your commodities, you treacherous trull! This was the merchandise you dealt in when I took you into my house, placed you next myself, and made you governante of my whole family! You have forgot this, have you, now you have feathered your nest?

FOIBLE. No, no, dear madam. Do but hear me; have but a moment's patience. I'll confess all. Mr. Mirabell seduced me. I am not the first that he has wheedled with his dissembling tongue; your ladyship's own wisdom has been deluded by him—then how should I, a poor ignorant, defend myself? O madam, if you knew but what he promised me, and how he assured me your ladyship should come to no damage!—Or else the wealth of the Indies should not have bribed me to conspire against so good, so sweet, so kind a lady as you have been to me.

LADY WISHFORT. No damage! What, to betray me, and marry me to a cast serving-man! To make me a receptacle, an hospital for a decayed pimp! No damage! O thou frontless impudence, more than a big-bellied actress!

FOIBLE. Pray, do but hear me, madam! He could not marry your ladyship, madam. —No, indeed; his marriage was to have been void in law, for he was married to me first, to secure your ladyship. He could not have bedded your ladyship; for if he had consummated with your ladyship, he must have run the risk of the law, and been put upon his clergy.—Yes, indeed, I inquired of the law in that case before I would meddle or make.

LADY WISHFORT. What, then I have been your property, have I? I have been convenient to you, it seems!—While you were catering for Mirabell, I have been broker for you! What, have you made a passive bawd of me?—This exceeds all precedent! I am brought to fine uses, to become a botcher of second-hand marriages between Abigails and Andrews. I'll couple you! Yes, I'll baste you together, you and your Philander.[58] I'll Duke's-place [59] you, as I'm a person! Your turtle [60] is in custody already; you shall coo in the same cage if there be a constable or warrant in the parish. (*Exit* LADY WISHFORT)

FOIBLE. Oh, that ever I was born! Oh, that I was ever married!—A bride!—aye, I shall be a Bridewell-bride.—Oh!

(*Enter* MRS. FAINALL)

MRS. FAINALL. Poor Foible, what's the matter?

FOIBLE. O madam, my lady's gone for a constable! I shall be had to a justice and put to Bridewell to beat hemp. Poor Waitwell's gone to prison already.

MRS. FAINALL. Have a good heart, Foible; Mirabell's gone to give security for him. This is all Marwood's and my husband's doing.

FOIBLE. Yes, yes; I know it, madam. She was in my lady's closet, and overheard all

[58] Lover.
[59] Where irregular marriages were performed.
[60] Turtle-dove.

that you said to me before dinner. She sent the letter to my lady, and that missing effect, Mr. Fainall laid this plot to arrest Waitwell when he pretended to go for the papers, and in the meantime Mrs. Marwood declared all to my lady.

MRS. FAINALL. Was there no mention made of me in the letter? My mother does not suspect my being in the confederacy? I fancy Marwood has not told her, though she has told my husband.

FOIBLE. Yes, madam, but my lady did not see that part; we stifled the letter before she read so far—Has that mischievous devil told Mr. Fainall of your ladyship, then?

MRS. FAINALL. Aye, all's out, my affair with Mirabell—everything discovered. This is the last day of our living together, that's my comfort.

FOIBLE. Indeed, madam; and so 'tis a comfort if you knew all—he has been even with your ladyship, which I could have told you long enough since, but I love to keep peace and quietness by my goodwill. I had rather bring friends together than set 'em at distance. But Mrs. Marwood and he are nearer related than ever their parents thought for.

MRS. FAINALL. Sayest thou so, Foible? Canst thou prove this?

FOIBLE. I can take my oath of it, madam; so can Mrs. Mincing. We have had many a fair word from Madam Marwood, to conceal something that passed in our chamber one evening when you were at Hyde Park, and we were thought to have gone a-walking, but we went up unawares—though we were sworn to secrecy, too; Madam Marwood took a book and swore us upon it, but it was but a book of poems. So long as it was not a Bible oath, we may break it with a safe conscience.

MRS. FAINALL. This discovery is the most opportune thing I could wish.—(*Sees* MINCING *at the door*) Now, Mincing!

(*Enter* MINCING)

MINCING. My lady would speak with Mrs. Foible, mem. Mr. Mirabell is with her; he has set your spouse at liberty, Mrs. Foible, and would have you hide yourself in my lady's closet till my old lady's anger is abated. Oh, my old lady is in a perilous passion at something Mr. Fainall has said; he swears, and my old lady cries. There's a fearful hurricane, I vow. He says, mem, how that he'll have my lady's fortune made over to him, or he'll be divorced.

MRS. FAINALL. Does your lady or Mirabell know that?

MINCING. Yes, mem; they have sent me to see if Sir Wilfull be sober, and to bring him to them. My lady is resolved to have him, I think, rather than lose such a vast sum as six thousand pounds.—Oh, come, Mrs. Foible, I hear my old lady.

MRS. FAINALL. Foible, you must tell Mincing that she must prepare to vouch when I call her.

FOIBLE. Yes, yes, madam.

MINCING. Oh, yes! mem, I'll vouch anything for your ladyship's service, be what it will. (*Exeunt* MINCING *and* FOIBLE)

(*Enter* LADY WISHFORT *and* MRS. MARWOOD)

LADY WISHFORT. Oh, my dear friend, how can I enumerate the benefits that I have received from your goodness! To you I owe the timely discovery of the false vows of Mirabell; to you I owe the detection of the impostor Sir Rowland.—And now you are become an intercessor with my son-in-law, to save the honor of my house and compound for the frailties of my daughter. Well, friend, you are enough to reconcile me to the bad world, or else I would retire to deserts and solitudes, and feed harmless sheep by droves and purling streams. Dear Marwood, let us leave the world, and retire by ourselves and be shepherdesses.

MRS. MARWOOD. Let us first dispatch the affair in hand, madam. We shall have leisure to think of retirement afterwards. Here is one who is concerned in the treaty.

LADY WISHFORT. Oh, daughter, daughter! Is it possible thou shouldst be my child, bone of my bone, and flesh of my flesh, and, as I may say, another me, and yet transgress the most minute particle of severe virtue? Is it possible you should lean aside to iniquity, who have been cast in the direct mold of virtue? I have not only been a mold but a pattern for you and a model for you, after you were brought into the world.

MRS. FAINALL. I don't understand your ladyship.

LADY WISHFORT. Not understand? Why, have you not been naught? Have you not been sophisticated? Not understand! Here I am ruined to compound for your caprices and your cuckoldoms. I must pawn my plate and my jewels, and ruin my niece, and all little enough—

MRS. FAINALL. I am wronged and abused, and so are you. 'Tis a false accusation—as false as hell, as false as your friend there, aye, or your friend's friend, my false husband!

MRS. MARWOOD. My friend, Mrs. Fainall! Your husband my friend? What do you mean?

MRS. FAINALL. I know what I mean, madam, and so do you; and so shall the world at a time convenient.

MRS. MARWOOD. I am sorry to see you so passionate, madam. More temper[61] would look more like innocence. But I have done. I am sorry my zeal to serve your ladyship and family should admit of misconstruction, or make me liable to affronts. You will pardon me, madam, if I meddle no more with an affair in which I am not personally concerned.

LADY WISHFORT. O dear friend, I am so ashamed that you should meet with such returns!—(To MRS. FAINALL) You ought to ask pardon on your knees, ungrateful creature; she deserves more from you than all your life can accomplish.—(To MRS. MARWOOD) Oh, don't leave me destitute in this perplexity! No, stick to me, my good genius.

MRS. FAINALL. I tell you, madam, you are abused.—Stick to you! Aye, like a leech, to suck your best blood—she'll drop off when she's full. Madam, you shan't pawn a bodkin, nor part with a brass counter, in composition for me. I defy 'em all. Let 'em prove their aspersions; I know my own innocence, and dare stand a trial. (Exit MRS. FAINALL)

LADY WISHFORT. Why, if she should be innocent, if she should be wronged after all —ha! I don't know what to think—and I promise you her education has been unexceptionable—I may say it; for I chiefly made it my own care to initiate her very infancy in the rudiments of virtue, and to impress upon her tender years a young odium and aversion to the very sight of men. Aye, friend, she would ha' shrieked if she had but seen a man, till she was in her teens. As I am a person, 'tis true—she was never suffered to play with a male child, though but in coats; nay, her very babies[62] were of the feminine gender. Oh, she never looked a man in the face but her own father, or the chaplain, and him we made a shift to put upon her for a woman, by the help of his long garments and his sleek face, till she was going in her fifteen.

MRS. MARWOOD. 'Twas much she should be deceived so long.

LADY WISHFORT. I warrant you, or she would never have borne to have been catechized by him; and have heard his long lectures against singing and dancing, and such debaucheries; and going to filthy plays, and profane music-meetings, where the lewd trebles squeak nothing but bawdy, and the basses roar blasphemy. Oh, she would have swooned at the sight or name of an obscene play-book!—and can I think, after all this, that my daughter can be naught? What, a whore? And thought it excommunication to set her foot within the door of a playhouse! O dear friend, I can't believe it. No, no! As she says, let him prove it—let him prove it.

MRS. MARWOOD. Prove it, madam? What, and have your name prostituted in a public court—yours and your daughter's reputation worried at the bar by a pack of bawling lawyers? To be ushered in with an "O yez" of scandal, and have your case opened by an old fumbling lecher in a quoif like a man-midwife; to bring your daughter's infamy to light; to be a theme for legal punsters and quibblers by the statute; and become a jest against a rule of court, where there is no precedent for a jest in any record—not even in Domesday Book; to discompose the gravity of the bench, and provoke naughty interrogatories in more naughty law Latin; while the good judge, tickled with the proceeding, simpers under a grey beard, and fidgets off and on his cushion as if he had swallowed cantharides, or sat upon cow-itch.—

LADY WISHFORT. Oh, 'tis very hard!

MRS. MARWOOD. And then to have my young revellers of the Temple take notes, like 'prentices at a conventicle, and after,

[61] Temperance.

[62] Dolls.

talk it all over again in commons, or before drawers [63] in an eating-house.

LADY WISHFORT. Worse and worse!

MRS. MARWOOD. Nay, this is nothing; if it would end here, 'twere well. But it must, after this, be consigned by the shorthand writers to the public press; and from thence be transferred to the hands, nay into the throats and lungs of hawkers, with voices more licentious than the loud flounder-man's, or the woman that cries grey peas. And this you must hear till you are stunned—nay, you must hear nothing else for some days.

LADY WISHFORT. Oh, 'tis insupportable! No, no, dear friend, make it up, make it up; aye, aye, I'll compound. I'll give up all, myself and my all, my niece and her all—anything, everything for composition.

MRS. MARWOOD. Nay, madam, I advise nothing; I only lay before you, as a friend, the inconveniences which perhaps you have overseen. Here comes Mr. Fainall. If he will be satisfied to huddle up all in silence, I shall be glad. You must think I would rather congratulate than condole with you.

LADY WISHFORT. Aye, aye, I do not doubt it, dear Marwood; no, no, I do not doubt it.

(*Enter* FAINALL)

FAINALL. Well, madam, I have suffered myself to be overcome by the importunity of this lady, your friend; and am content you shall enjoy your own proper estate during life, on condition you oblige yourself never to marry, under such penalty as I think convenient.

LADY WISHFORT. Never to marry!

FAINALL. No more Sir Rowlands; the next imposture may not be so timely detected.

MRS. MARWOOD. That condition, I dare answer, my lady will consent to without difficulty; she has already but too much experienced the perfidiousness of men.—Besides, madam, when we retire to our pastoral solitude we shall bid adieu to all other thoughts.

LADY WISHFORT. Aye, that's true; but in case of necessity, as of health, or some such emergency—

FAINALL. Oh, if you are prescribed marriage, you shall be considered; I only will reserve to myself the power to choose for

[63] Waiters in a tavern.

you. If your physic be wholesome, it matters not who is your apothecary. Next, my wife shall settle on me the remainder of her fortune not made over already, and for her maintenance depend entirely on my discretion.

LADY WISHFORT. This is most inhumanly savage, exceeding the barbarity of a Muscovite husband.

FAINALL. I learned it from his Czarish majesty's retinue, in a winter evening's conference over brandy and pepper, amongst other secrets of matrimony and policy as they are at present practised in the northern hemisphere. But this must be agreed unto, and that positively. Lastly, I will be endowed, in right of my wife, with that six thousand pounds which is the moiety of Mrs. Millamant's fortune in your possession, and which she has forfeited (as will appear by the last will and testament of your deceased husband, Sir Jonathan Wishfort) by her disobedience in contracting herself against your consent or knowledge and by refusing the offered match with Sir Wilfull Witwoud, which you, like a careful aunt, had provided for her.

LADY WISHFORT. My nephew was *non compos* and could not make his addresses.

FAINALL. I come to make demands—I'll hear no objections.

LADY WISHFORT. You will grant me time to consider?

FAINALL. Yes, while the instrument is drawing, to which you must set your hand till more sufficient deeds can be perfected—which I will take care shall be done with all possible speed. In the meanwhile I will go for the said instrument, and till my return you may balance this matter in your own discretion. (*Exit* FAINALL)

LADY WISHFORT. This insolence is beyond all precedent, all parallel. Must I be subject to this merciless villain?

MRS. MARWOOD. 'Tis severe indeed, madam, that you should smart for your daughter's wantonness.

LADY WISHFORT. 'Twas against my consent that she married this barbarian, but she would have him, though her year was not out.—Ah, her first husband, my son Languish, would not have carried it thus! Well, that was my choice, this is hers; she is matched now with a witness.—I shall be mad!

—Dear friend, is there no comfort for me? Must I live to be confiscated at this rebel-rate?—Here come two more of my Egyptian plagues too.

(*Enter* MRS. MILLAMANT *and* SIR WILFULL WITWOUD)

SIR WILFULL. Aunt, your servant.

LADY WISHFORT. Out, caterpillar! Call not me aunt! I know thee not!

SIR WILFULL. I confess I have been a little in disguise, as they say.—'Sheart! and I'm sorry for't. What would you have? I hope I have committed no offence, aunt—and if I did I am willing to make satisfaction; and what can a man say fairer? If I have broke anything, I'll pay for't, and it cost a pound. And so let that content for what's past, and make no more words. For what's to come, to pleasure you I'm willing to marry our cousin; so pray let's all be friends. She and I are agreed upon the matter before a witness.

LADY WISHFORT. How's this, dear niece? Have I any comfort? Can this be true?

MRS. MILLAMANT. I am content to be a sacrifice to your repose, madam, and to convince you that I had no hand in the plot, as you were misinformed. I have laid my commands on Mirabell to come in person and be a witness that I give my hand to this flower of knighthood; and for the contract that passed between Mirabell and me, I have obliged him to make a resignation of it in your ladyship's presence. He is without, and waits your leave for admittance.

LADY WISHFORT. Well, I'll swear I am something revived at this testimony of your obedience, but I cannot admit that traitor—I fear I cannot fortify myself to support his appearance. He is as terrible to me as a gorgon; if I see him I fear I shall turn to stone, and petrify incessantly.

MRS. MILLAMANT. If you disoblige him, he may resent your refusal and insist upon the contract still. Then 'tis the last time he will be offensive to you.

LADY WISHFORT. Are you sure it will be the last time?—If I were sure of that—shall I never see him again?

MRS. MILLAMANT. Sir Wilfull, you and he are to travel together, are you not?

SIR WILFULL. 'Sheart, the gentleman's a civil gentleman, aunt; let him come in. Why, we are sworn brothers and fellow-travellers.—We are to be Pylades and Orestes, he and I. He is to be my interpreter in foreign parts. He has been overseas once already, and with proviso that I marry my cousin, will cross 'em once again only to bear me company.—'Sheart, I'll call him in. An I set on't once, he shall come in; and see who'll hinder him.

(*Exit* SIR WILFULL)

MRS. MARWOOD. (*Aside*) This is precious fooling, if it would pass; but I'll know the bottom of it.

LADY WISHFORT. O dear Marwood, you are not going?

MRS. MARWOOD. Not far, madam; I'll return immediately.   (*Exit* MRS. MARWOOD)

(*Re-enter* SIR WILFULL *and* MIRABELL)

SIR WILFULL. Look up, man, I'll stand by you. 'Sbud an she do frown, she can't kill you; besides—harkee, she dare not frown desperately, because her face is none of her own. 'Sheart, an she should, her forehead would wrinkle like the coat of a cream-cheese; but mum for that, fellow-traveller.

MIRABELL. If a deep sense of the many injuries I have offered to so good a lady, with a sincere remorse and a hearty contrition, can but obtain the least glance of compassion, I am too happy. Ah, madam, there was a time! —but let it be forgotten—I confess I have deservedly forfeited the high place I once held, of sighing at your feet. Nay, kill me not, by turning from me in disdain. I come not to plead for favor—nay, not for pardon; I am a suppliant only for your pity. I am going where I never shall behold you more—

SIR WILFULL. How, fellow-traveller! You shall go by yourself then.

MIRABELL. Let me be pitied first, and afterwards forgotten.—I ask no more.

SIR WILFULL. By'r Lady, a very reasonable request, and will cost you nothing, aunt! Come, come, forgive and forget, aunt. Why, you must, an you are a Christian.

MIRABELL. Consider, madam, in reality you could not receive much prejudice. It was an innocent device; though I confess it had a face of guiltiness, it was at most an artifice which love contrived—and errors which love produces have ever been accounted venial. At least think it is punishment enough that I have lost what in my heart I hold most dear, that to your cruel indignation I have offered up this beauty, and with her my peace and quiet—nay, all my hopes of future comfort.

SIR WILFULL. An he does not move me, would I may never be o' the quorum! An it were not as good a deed as to drink, to give her to him again, I would I might never take shipping!—Aunt, if you don't forgive quickly, I shall melt, I can tell you that. My contract went no farther than a little mouth glue, and that's hardly dry—one doleful sigh more from my fellow-traveller, and 'tis dissolved.

LADY WISHFORT. Well, nephew, upon your account—Ah, he has a false insinuating tongue!—Well sir, I will stifle my just resentment at my nephew's request. I will endeavor what I can to forget, but on proviso that you resign the contract with my niece immediately.

MIRABELL. It is in writing, and with papers of concern; but I have sent my servant for it, and will deliver it to you with all acknowledgements for your transcendent goodness.

LADY WISHFORT. (*Aside*) Oh, he has witchcraft in his eyes and tongue!—When I did not see him, I could have bribed a villain to his assassination; but his appearance rakes the embers which have so long lain smothered in my breast.

(*Enter* FAINALL *and* MRS. MARWOOD)

FAINALL. Your date of deliberation, madam, is expired. Here is the instrument; are you prepared to sign?

LADY WISHFORT. If I were prepared, I am not impowered. My niece exerts a lawful claim, having matched herself by my direction to Sir Wilfull.

FAINALL. That sham is too gross to pass on me—though 'tis imposed on you, madam.

MRS. MILLAMANT. Sir, I have given my consent.

MIRABELL. And, sir, I have resigned my pretensions.

SIR WILFULL. And, sir, I assert my right and will maintain it in defiance of you, sir, and of your instrument. 'Sheart, an you talk of an instrument, sir, I have an old fox by my thigh shall hack your instrument of ram vel-

lum to shreds, sir! It shall not be sufficient for a mittimus or a tailor's measure. Therefore withdraw your instrument, sir, or by'r Lady, I shall draw mine.

LADY WISHFORT. Hold, nephew, hold!

MRS. MILLAMANT. Good Sir Wilfull, respite your valor!

FAINALL. Indeed! Are you provided of a guard, with your single beef-eater [64] there? But I'm prepared for you, and insist upon my first proposal. You shall submit your own estate to my management, and absolutely make over my wife's to my sole use, as pursuant to the purport and tenor of this other covenant.—(*To* MRS. MILLAMANT) I suppose, madam, your consent is not requisite in this case; nor, Mr. Mirabell, your resignation; nor, Sir Wilfull, your right.—You may draw your fox if you please, sir, and make a bear-garden flourish somewhere else, for here it will not avail. This, my Lady Wishfort, must be subscribed, or your darling daughter's turned adrift, like a leaky hulk, to sink or swim, as she and the current of this lewd town can agree.

LADY WISHFORT. Is there no means, no remedy to stop my ruin? Ungrateful wretch! Dost thou not owe thy being, thy subsistence, to my daughter's fortune?

FAINALL. I'll answer you when I have the rest of it in my possession.

MIRABELL. But that you would not accept of a remedy from my hands—I own I have not deserved you should owe any obligation to me; or else perhaps I could advise—

LADY WISHFORT. Oh, what?—what? To save me and my child from ruin, from want, I'll forgive all that's past; nay, I'll consent to anything to come, to be delivered from this tyranny.

MIRABELL. Aye, madam, but that is too late; my reward is intercepted. You have disposed of her who only could have made me a compensation for all my services. But be it as it may, I am resolved I'll serve you! You shall not be wronged in this savage manner.

LADY WISHFORT. How! Dear Mr. Mirabell, can you be so generous at last? But it is not possible. Harkee, I'll break my nephew's match; you shall have my niece yet, and all

[64] Guards at the Tower of London who wore medieval uniforms.

her fortune, if you can but save me from this imminent danger.

MIRABELL. Will you? I'll take you at your word. I ask no more. I must have leave for two criminals to appear.

LADY WISHFORT. Aye, aye;—anybody, anybody!

MIRABELL. Foible is one, and a penitent.

(*Enter* MRS. FAINALL, FOIBLE, *and* MINCING)

MRS. MARWOOD. (*To* FAINALL) Oh my shame! These corrupt things are brought hither to expose me.

(MIRABELL *and* LADY WISHFORT *go to* MRS. FAINALL *and* FOIBLE)

FAINALL. If it must all come out, why let 'em know it; 'tis but the way of the world. That shall not urge me to relinquish or abate one tittle of my terms; no, I will insist the more.

FOIBLE. Yes, indeed, madam, I'll take my Bible oath of it.

MINCING. And so will I, mem.

LADY WISHFORT. O Marwood, Marwood, art thou false? My friend deceive me? Hast thou been a wicked accomplice with that profligate man?

MRS. MARWOOD. Have you so much ingratitude and injustice to give credit against your friend to the aspersions of two such mercenary trulls?

MINCING. Mercenary, mem? I scorn your words. 'Tis true we found you and Mr. Fainall in the blue garret; by the same token, you swore us to secrecy upon Messalina's poems. Mercenary? No, if we would have been mercenary, we should have held our tongues; you would have bribed us sufficiently.

FAINALL. Go, you are an insignificant thing!—Well, what are you the better for this? Is this Mr. Mirabell's expedient? I'll be put off no longer.—You, thing that was a wife, shall smart for this! I will not leave thee wherewithal to hide thy shame; your body shall be naked as your reputation.

MRS. FAINALL. I despise you and defy your malice!—You have aspersed me wrongfully—I have proved your falsehood! Go, you and your treacherous—I will not name it, but starve together. Perish!

FAINALL. Not while you are worth a groat,

indeed, my dear. Madam, I'll be fooled no longer.

LADY WISHFORT. Ah, Mr. Mirabell, this is small comfort, the detection of this affair.

MIRABELL. Oh, in good time. Your leave for the other offender and penitent to appear, madam.

(*Enter* WAITWELL *with a box of writings*)

LADY WISHFORT. O Sir Rowland!—Well, rascal!

WAITWELL. What your ladyship pleases. I have brought the black box at last, madam.

MIRABELL. Give it me. Madam, you remember your promise?

LADY WISHFORT. Aye, dear sir.

MIRABELL. Where are the gentlemen?

WAITWELL. At hand, sir, rubbing their eyes—just risen from sleep.

FAINALL. 'Sdeath, what's this to me? I'll not wait your private concerns.

(*Enter* PETULANT *and* WITWOUD)

PETULANT. How now! What's the matter? Whose hand's out?

WITWOUD. Heyday! What, are you all got together like players at the end of the last act?

MIRABELL. You may remember, gentlemen, I once requested your hands as witnesses to a certain parchment.

WITWOUD. Aye, I do; my hand I remember—Petulant set his mark.

MIRABELL. You wrong him. His name is fairly written, as shall appear.—(*Undoing the box*) You do not remember, gentlemen, anything of what that parchment contained?

WITWOUD. No.

PETULANT. Not I; I writ, I read nothing.

MIRABELL. Very well, now you shall know.—Madam, your promise.

LADY WISHFORT. Aye, aye, sir, upon my honor.

MIRABELL. Mr. Fainall, it is now time that you should know that your lady, while she was at her own disposal, and before you had by your insinuations wheedled her out of a pretended settlement of the greatest part of her fortune—

FAINALL. Sir! Pretended!

MIRABELL. Yes, sir. I say that this lady while a widow, having, it seems, received some cautions respecting your inconstancy and tyranny of temper, which from her own partial opinion and fondness of you she could never have suspected—she did, I say, by the wholesome advice of friends and of sages learned in the laws of this land, deliver this same as her act and deed to me in trust, and to the uses within mentioned. You may read if you please—(*Holding out the parchment*) though perhaps what is written on the back may serve your occasions.

FAINALL. Very likely, sir. What's here?—Damnation! (*Reads*) "A deed of conveyance of the whole estate real of Arabella Languish, widow, in trust to Edward Mirabell."—Confusion!

MIRABELL. Even so, sir; 'tis the way of the world, sir,—of the widows of the world. I suppose this deed may bear an elder date than what you have obtained from your lady?

FAINALL. Perfidious fiend! Then thus I'll be revenged.

(*Offers to run at* MRS. FAINALL)

SIR WILFULL. Hold, sir! Now you may make your bear-garden flourish somewhere else, sir.

FAINALL. Mirabell, you shall hear of this, sir, be sure you shall.—Let me pass, oaf!

(*Exit* FAINALL)

MRS. FAINALL. Madam, you seem to stifle your resentment; you had better give it vent.

MRS. MARWOOD. Yes, it shall have vent—and to your confusion, or I'll perish in the attempt.   (*Exit* MRS. MARWOOD)

LADY WISHFORT. O daughter, daughter! 'Tis plain thou hast inherited thy mother's prudence.

MRS. FAINALL. Thank Mr. Mirabell, a cautious friend, to whose advice all is owing.

LADY WISHFORT. Well, Mr. Mirabell, you have kept your promise—and I must perform mine.—First, I pardon, for your sake, Sir Rowland there, and Foible. The next thing is to break the matter to my nephew—and how to do that—

MIRABELL. For that, madam, give yourself no trouble; let me have your consent. Sir Wilfull is my friend. He has had compassion upon lovers, and generously engaged a volunteer in this action for our service, and now designs to prosecute his travels.

SIR WILFULL. 'Sheart, aunt, I have no mind to marry. My cousin's a fine lady, and

the gentleman loves her, and she loves him, and they deserve one another. My resolution is to see foreign parts—I have set on't—and when I'm set on't I must do't. And if these two gentlemen would travel too, I think they may be spared.

PETULANT. For my part, I say little—I think things are best off or on.

WITWOUD. 'Ygad, I understand nothing of the matter; I'm in a maze yet, like a dog in a dancing-school.

LADY WISHFORT. Well, sir, take her, and with her all the joy I can give you.

MRS. MILLAMANT. Why does not the man take me? Would you have me give myself to you over again?

MIRABELL. Aye, and over and over again; (*Kisses her hand*) I would have you as often as possibly I can. Well, Heaven grant I love you not too well; that's all my fear.

SIR WILFULL. 'Sheart, you'll have time enough to toy after you're married; or if you will toy now, let us have a dance in the meantime, that we who are not lovers may have some other employment besides looking on.

MIRABELL. With all my heart, dear Sir Wilfull. What shall we do for music?

FOIBLE. Oh, sir, some that were provided for Sir Rowland's entertainment are yet within call.   (*A dance*)

LADY WISHFORT. As I am a person, I can hold out no longer. I have wasted my spirits so to-day already, that I am ready to sink under the fatigue, and I cannot but have some fears upon me yet, that my son Fainall will pursue some desperate course.

MIRABELL. Madam, disquiet not yourself on that account; to my knowledge his circumstances are such he must of force comply. For my part, I will contribute all that in me lies to a reunion; in the meantime, madam—(*To* MRS. FAINALL) let me before these witnesses restore to you this deed of trust. It may be a means, well-managed, to make you live easily together.

From hence let those be warned who mean
   to wed,
Lest mutual falsehood stain the bridal bed;
For each deceiver to his cost may find
That marriage-frauds too oft are paid in kind.

(*Exeunt omnes*)

Epilogue

Spoken by Mrs. BRACEGIRDLE [65]

After our epilogue this crowd dismisses,
I'm thinking how this play'll be pulled to
    pieces.
But pray consider, ere you doom its fall,
How hard a thing 'twould be to please you
    all.
There are some critics so with spleen dis-
    eased,
They scarcely come inclining to be
    pleased:
And sure he must have more than mortal
    skill,
Who pleases anyone against his will.
Then, all bad poets we are sure of foes,
And how their number's swelled, the town
    well knows:
In shoals I've marked 'em judging in the ⎤
    pit; |
Though they're on no pretense for judg- ⎬
    ment fit, |
But that they have been damned for want |
    of wit.   ⎦
Since when, they by their own offences
    taught,
Set up for spies on plays and finding
    fault.

[65] She played Millamant in the original performance.

Others there are whose malice we'd pre- ⎤
    vent; |
Such who watch plays with scurrilous in- ⎬
    tent |
To mark out who by characters are meant. ⎦
And though no perfect likeness they can
    trace,
Yet each pretends to know the copied face.
These with false glosses feed their own ill
    nature,
And turn to libel what was meant a satire.
May such malicious fops this fortune find,
To think themselves alone the fools de-
    signed!
If any are so arrogantly vain,   ⎤
To think they singly can support a scene, ⎬
And furnish fool enough to entertain.   ⎦
For well the learn'd and the judicious   ⎤
    know |
That satire scorns to stoop so meanly low ⎬
As any one abstracted fop to show.   ⎦
For, as when painters form a matchless face,
They from each fair one catch some different
    grace,
And shining features in one portrait blend,
To which no single beauty must pretend;
So poets oft do in one piece expose
Whole *belles-assemblées* of coquettes and
    beaux.

GEORGE LILLO

The London Merchant

~~~~~~

PRINCIPAL EVENTS IN LILLO'S LIFE

1693, 4 Feb., Born in London, the son of a Dutch jeweller and an English mother.

c. 1713-1739, He is said to have been an active London jeweller, though very little is known of his life.

1730, 10 Nov., Silvia, or the Country Burial, a ballad opera, opened at Lincoln's Inn Fields theatre.

1731, 22 June, The London Merchant, or The History of George Barnwell acted with great success at Drury Lane theatre.

1734, Probably in this year Lillo wrote a masque called *Brittania and Batavia* to celebrate the marriage of Princess Anne and William of Orange. It was published in 1740 but never acted.

1735, 13 Jan., The Christian Hero, a blank verse tragedy, acted at Drury Lane theatre.

1736, 27 May, Fatal Curiosity, a tragedy, acted at the Haymarket theatre.

1738, 1 Aug., Marina, adapted from Shakespeare's *Pericles, Prince of Tyre*, acted at Covent Garden theatre.

1739, 3 Sept., George Lillo died. He was buried in St. Leonard's Shoreditch, London.

1740, 23 Feb., Elmerick, or Justice Triumphant, an adaptation by Lillo of an Elizabethan domestic tragedy of the same name, acted at Drury Lane theatre.

INTRODUCTION

Though they were never usual, several tragedies about ordinary middle-class English men and women appeared in late Elizabethan and early Jacobean times, but such plays had been rare from 1615 until Lillo wrote this tragedy in 1731. Comedies about middle-class Londoners were common enough, but English tragedies in these years generally concerned characters of high social rank and significance; they were written in verse and were usually set in foreign countries or in the distant past.

Lillo turned to tragic characters who were within the daily knowledge of most of the members of his audience, to recognizable London scenes, and to events which, if not quite so common, were still familiar enough to all Londoners who read contemporary accounts of crimes and who flocked to the public executions. The attempt to make the audience feel that the poor murderer, George Barnwell, was one of *them* and that the events of the play were real London occurrences is illustrated by the distribution of the ballad-account of the real-life George Barnwell just before the performance of the play and by the title, *The Merchant, or The True History of George Barnwell*, which Lillo first chose for his play, before altering it to its present form.

555

These attempts at realism are obscured for most modern readers by Lillo's pompous dialogue, sometimes so inappropriate as to be ludicrous, by his juvenile moralizing, and by the persistent sentimentality which was the curse of the eighteenth-century English theatre. There is no doubt, however, that the play succeeded in pleasing its audience. It was frequently acted before Lillo's death, the Queen asked for a copy of the play to read, and Lillo is said to have made several thousand pounds from his tragedy. The play had a great influence on continental drama, and more than a hundred years after Lillo's death it was commonly revived in English theatres during Christmas and Easter holidays as a lesson for apprentices; Sir Henry Irving played George Barnwell a number of times in provincial theatres.

When Lillo's tragedy was written, the London theatre was no longer primarily the resort of the upper classes, as it had been in the Restoration; there were not only several times as many theatres as in the reign of Charles II, but they were larger. The middle classes were becoming a more and more important element in the average audience, and as a consequence middle-class interests bulk much larger in the plays. *The London Merchant* demonstrates this development in its elimination of noble and high society characters and its magnification of the virtue and significance of London business men, notably in Thorowgood's speeches in the first scene. Though these lines are per-

haps the most obvious illustration of the new orientation of the drama, the entire action of the play, the moral tone which pervades it, and the particular virtues and vices which are selected for emphasis are eloquent of an admiration for the London business man and his ideals which does not characterize earlier drama.

The London Merchant is what some modern theatre people would call a "tear-jerker," but whereas this designation is now used as a term of contempt, in Lillo's time the weeping audience was accepted as an important and significant achievement by the dramatist, an indication that the play was not only theatrically effective but that it had accomplished one of the prime functions of great drama on the minds and characters of the auditory. The playwright is not concerned with the psychological steps in Barnwell's downfall, or with more than a superficial understanding of the characters; he is not really concerned with the power of love or lust, as Ford was, for he scrupulously plays down the seduction scenes, and he expects the audience to take Millwood's attraction for granted without any demonstration; he *is* concerned with teaching a very simple and obvious lesson about the importance of honesty and purity for young men, and he is especially concerned that the pitiful, pitiful fate of poor Barnwell should be held before the audience as constantly and affectingly as possible.

                                                       ~

THE LONDON MERCHANT

Dramatis personae

In order of first appearance

TRUEMAN, The model employee, docile, industrious, virtuous, and devoted to all the interests of his employer Thorowgood.

THOROWGOOD, Lillo's ideal business man; rich, proud of his business and his class, generous to his employees. The virtues that he prizes are industry, honesty, probity, and moral rectitude.

MARIA, Thorowgood's daughter, pretty, modest, and dutiful, admired and sought after by the young nobles but secretly pining for Barnwell.

MILLWOOD, A scheming, heartless, avaricious harlot, experienced in fleecing men in order to support her extravagance.

Lucy, Her maid, cynical, not overly scrupulous, but with promptings of decency.

Barnwell, Thorowgood's second clerk, young and handsome, trusted with affairs of some consequence; by nature honest, grateful, and loyal, but untried and susceptible.

Blunt, Millwood's servant, the masculine counterpart of Lucy.

Barnwell's Uncle, A wealthy and virtuous old man.

Servants, officer and attendants, jailer.

Place: *London and an adjacent village*

Time: *Shortly before 1588*

Dedication

Sir John Eyles, Bar. Member of Parliament for, and Alderman of, the City of *London,* and Sub-Governor of the *South-Sea* Company

Sir,

If tragic poetry be, as Mr. Dryden has some where said, the most excellent and most useful kind of writing, the more extensively useful the moral of any tragedy is, the more excellent that piece must be of its kind.

I hope I shall not be thought to insinuate that this, to which I have presumed to prefix your name, is such; that depends on its fitness to answer the end of tragedy, the exciting of the passions in order to the correcting such of them as are criminal, either in their nature, or through their excess. Whether the following scenes do this in any tolerable degree, is, with the deference that becomes one who would not be thought vain, submitted to your candid and impartial judgment.

What I would infer is this, I think, evident truth: that tragedy is so far from losing its dignity by being accommodated to the circumstances of the generality of mankind that it is more truly august in proportion to the extent of its influence, and the numbers that are properly affected by it. As it is more truly great to be the instrument of good to many, who stand in need of our assistance, than to a very small part of that number.

If princes, &c., were alone liable to misfortunes arising from vice or weakness in themselves or others there would be good reason for confining the characters in tragedy to those of superior rank; but, since the con-

trary is evident, nothing can be more reasonable than to proportion the remedy to the disease.

I am far from denying that tragedies founded on any instructive and extraordinary events in history or a well-invented fable where the persons introduced are of the highest rank are without their use, even to the bulk of the audience. The strong contrast between a *Tamerlane* and a *Bajazet,* may have its weight with an unsteady people and contribute to the fixing of them in the interest of a prince of the character of the former, when, thro' their own levity or the arts of designing men, they are rendered factious and uneasy though they have the highest reason to be satisfied. The sentiments and example of a *Cato* may inspire his spectators with a just sense of the value of liberty when they see that honest patriot prefer death to an obligation from a tyrant who would sacrifice the constitution of his country and the liberties of mankind to his ambition or revenge. I have attempted, indeed, to enlarge the province of the graver kind of poetry, and should be glad to see it carried on by some abler hand. Plays founded on moral tales in private life may be of admirable use by carrying conviction to the mind with such irresistible force as to engage all the faculties and powers of the soul in the cause of virtue by stifling vice in its first principles. They who imagine this to be too much to be attributed to tragedy must be strangers to the energy of that noble species of poetry. Shakespeare, who has given such amazing proofs of his genius in that as well as in comedy, in his *Hamlet,* has the following lines:

Had he the motive and the cause for passion
That I have, he would drown the stage with
  tears
And cleave the general ear with horrid
  speech;
Make mad the guilty, and appall the free,
Confound the ignorant, and amaze indeed
The very faculty of eyes and ears.

And farther, in the same speech,

I've heard that guilty creatures at a play,
Have, by the very cunning of the scene,
Been so struck to the soul that presently
They have proclaim'd their malefactions.

Prodigious! yet strictly just. But I shan't take up your valuable time with my remarks; only give me leave just to observe that he seems so firmly persuaded of the power of a well wrote piece to produce the effect here ascribed to it, as to make Hamlet venture his soul on the event, and rather trust that, than a messenger from the other world, tho' it assumed, as he expresses it, his noble father's form, and assured him that it was his spirit. I'll have, says Hamlet, grounds more relative.

  . . . The Play's the thing
Wherein I'll catch the conscience of the king.

Such plays are the best answers to them who deny the lawfulness of the stage.

Considering the novelty of this attempt, I thought it would be expected from me to say something in its excuse; and I was unwilling to lose the opportunity of saying something of the usefulness of tragedy in general, and what may be reasonably expected from the farther improvement of this excellent kind of poetry.

Sir, I hope you will not think I have said too much of an art, a mean specimen of which I am ambitious enough to recommend to your favor and protection. A mind conscious of superior worth as much despises flattery as it is above it. Had I found in myself an inclination to so contemptible a vice, I should not have chose Sir John Eyles for my patron. And indeed the best writ panegyric, tho' strictly true, must place you in a light, much inferior to that in which you have long been fixed by the love and esteem of your fellow citizens, whose choice of you for one of their representatives in Parliament, has sufficiently declared their sense of your merit. Nor hath the knowledge of your worth been confined to the City. The proprietors in the South-Sea Company, in which are included numbers of persons as considerable for their rank, fortune, and understanding as any in the kingdom, gave the greatest proof of their confidence in your capacity and probity when they chose you Sub-Governor of their company, at a time when their affairs were in the utmost confusion, and their properties in the greatest danger. Nor is the court insensible of your importance. I shall not therefore attempt your character, nor pretend to add any thing to a reputation so well established.

Whatever others may think of a dedication, wherein there is so much said of other things and so little of the person to whom it is addressed, I have reason to believe that you will the more easily pardon it on that very account.

I am, sir,
Your most obedient
humble servant,
GEORGE LILLO

Prologue

Spoken by BARNWELL

The tragic muse, sublime, delights to show
Princes distressed, and scenes of royal woe;
In awful pomp, majestic, to relate
The fall of nations or some hero's fate,
That sceptered chiefs may by example know
The strange vicissitude of things below;
What danger on security attend;
How pride and cruelty in ruin end;

Hence Providence supreme to know; and own
Humanity adds glory to a throne.
　In ev'ry former age, and foreign tongue,
With native grandeur thus the goddess sung.
Upon our stage indeed with wished success
You've sometimes seen her in a humbler dress,
Great only in distress. When she complains
In Southerne's, Rowe's, or Otway's moving strains [1]
The brilliant drops that fall from each bright eye,
The absent pomp with brighter gems supply.
Forgive us then, if we attempt to show
In artless strains a tale of private woe.
A London prentice ruined is our theme,
Drawn from the famed old song that bears his name.
We hope your taste is not so high to scorn
A moral tale esteemed e'er you were born,
Which for a century of rolling years
Has filled a thousand-thousand eyes with tears.
If thoughtless youth to warn and shame the age
From vice destructive well becomes the stage,
If this example innocence secure,
Prevents our guilt, or by reflection cure,
If Millwood's dreadful guilt, and sad despair,
Commend the virtue of the good and fair,
Though art be wanting, and our numbers fail,
Indulge th' attempt in justice to the tale.

Act I

Scene I. *A Room in* Thorowgood's *House.*

(*Enter* Thorowgood *and* Trueman)

TRUEMAN. Sir, the packet from Genoa is arrived.　　　　　　　　(*Gives letters*)

THOROWGOOD. (*Hastily glancing over first letter*) Heaven be praised, the storm that threatened our royal mistress, pure religion, liberty, and laws is for a time diverted; the haughty and revengeful Spaniard, disappointed of the loan on which he depended from Genoa, must now attend the slow return of wealth from his new world to supply his empty coffers, e'er he can execute his purposed invasion of our happy island; [2] by which means time is gained to make such preparations on our part as may, Heaven concurring, prevent his malice or turn the meditated mischief on himself.

TRUEMAN. He must be insensible indeed who is not affected when the safety of his country is concerned.—(*Hesitantly*) Sir, may I know by what means,—if I am too bold—

THOROWGOOD. Your curiosity is laudable; and I gratify it with the greater pleasure because from thence you may learn how honest merchants, as such, may sometimes contribute to the safety of their country as they do at all times to its happiness; that if hereafter you should be tempted to any action that has the appearance of vice or meanness in it, upon reflecting on the dignity of our profession, you may with honest scorn reject whatever is unworthy of it.

TRUEMAN. Should Barnwell or I, who have the benefit of your example, by our ill conduct bring any imputation on that honorable name, we must be left without excuse.

THOROWGOOD. You compliment, young man.—　　(TRUEMAN *bows respectfully*) Nay, I'm not offended. As the name of merchant never degrades the gentleman, so by no means does it exclude him; only take heed not to purchase the character of complaisant at the expense of your sincerity.—But to answer your question,—the bank of Genoa had agreed, at excessive interest and on good security, to advance the King of Spain a sum of money sufficient to equip his vast armada, of which our peerless Elizabeth (more than in name the mother of her people), being well informed, sent Walsingham, her wise and faithful secretary, to consult the merchants of this loyal city, who all agreed to direct their

[1] Southerne, Rowe, and Otway all wrote tragedies more domestic than heroic.
[2] These allusions date the action some time before the sailing of the Spanish Armada, 1588.

several agents to influence, if possible, the Genoese to break their contract with the Spanish court. 'Tis done, the state and bank of Genoa, having maturely weighed and rightly judged of their true interest, prefer the friendship of the merchants of London to that of a monarch who proudly styles himself King of both Indies.

TRUEMAN. Happy success of prudent councils. What an expense of blood and treasure is here saved!—Excellent queen! O how unlike to former princes, who made the danger of foreign enemies a pretense to oppress their subjects, by taxes great and grievous to be borne.

THOROWGOOD. Not so our gracious queen, whose richest exchequer is her people's love as their happiness her greatest glory.

TRUEMAN. On these terms to defend us, is to make our protection a benefit worthy her who confers it, and well worth our acceptance. Sir, have you any commands for me at this time?

THOROWGOOD. Only to look carefully over the files to see whether there are any tradesmen's bills unpaid; and if there are, to send and discharge 'em. We must not let artificers lose their time, so useful to the public and their families, in unnecessary attendance.

(*Exit* TRUEMAN)

(*Enter* MARIA)

THOROWGOOD. Well, Maria, have you given orders for the entertainment? I would have it in some measure worthy the guests. Let there be plenty, and of the best, that the courtiers, though they should deny us citizens politeness, may at least commend our hospitality.

MARIA. Sir, I have endeavored not to wrong your well-known generosity by an ill-timed parsimony.

THOROWGOOD. Nay, 'twas a needless caution; I have no cause to doubt your prudence.

MARIA. Sir! I find myself unfit for conversation at present. I should but increase the number of the company, without adding to their satisfaction.

THOROWGOOD. Nay, my child, this melancholy must not be indulged.

MARIA. Company will but increase it. I wish you would dispense with my absence; [3] solitude best suits my present temper.

THOROWGOOD. You are not insensible that it is chiefly on your account these noble lords do me the honor so frequently to grace my board; should you be absent, the disappointment may make them repent their condescension and think their labor lost.

MARIA. He that shall think his time or honor lost in visiting you, can set no real value on your daughter's company, whose only merit is that she is yours. The man of quality, who chooses to converse with a gentleman and merchant of your worth and character, may confer honor by so doing, but he loses none.

THOROWGOOD. Come, come, Maria, I need not tell you that a young gentleman may prefer your conversation to mine, yet intend me no disrespect at all; for though he may lose no honor in my company, 'tis very natural for him to expect more pleasure in yours. I remember the time when the company of the greatest and wisest man in the kingdom would have been insipid and tiresome to me, if it had deprived me of an opportunity of enjoying your mother's.

MARIA. Yours no doubt was as agreeable to her; for generous minds know no pleasure in society but where 'tis mutual.

THOROWGOOD. Thou know'st I have no heir, no child, but thee; the fruits of many years' successful industry must all be thine. Now it would give me pleasure great as my love, to see on whom you would bestow it. I am daily solicited by men of the greatest rank and merit for leave to address you, but I have hitherto declined it, in hopes that by observation I should learn which way your inclination tends; for as I know love to be essential to happiness in the marriage state, I had rather my approbation should confirm your choice than direct it.

MARIA. What can I say? How shall I answer as I ought this tenderness, so uncommon even in the best of parents; but you are without example; yet had you been less indulgent, I had been most wretched. That I look on the crowd of courtiers that visit here with equal esteem but equal indifference you have observed, and I must needs confess; yet had you asserted your authority, and insisted

[3] Lillo must mean "presence."

on a parent's right to be obeyed, I had submitted, and to my duty sacrificed my peace.

THOROWGOOD. From your perfect obedience in every other instance, I feared as much; and therefore would leave you without a bias in an affair wherein your happiness is so immediately concerned.

MARIA. Whether from a want of that just ambition that would become your daughter or from some other cause I know not; but I find high birth and titles don't recommend the man who owns them, to my affections.

THOROWGOOD. I would not that they should, unless his merit recommends him more. A noble birth and fortune, though they make not a bad man good, yet they are a real advantage to a worthy one, and place his virtues in the fairest light.

MARIA. I cannot answer for my inclinations, but they shall ever be submitted to your wisdom and authority; and as you will not compel me to marry where I cannot love, so love shall never make me act contrary to my duty. Sir, have I your permission to retire?

THOROWGOOD. I'll see you to your chamber. (*Exeunt*)

SCENE II. *A Room in* MILLWOOD'S *House.*

(MILLWOOD *before a mirror, attended by* LUCY)

MILLWOOD. How do I look to-day, Lucy?

LUCY. O, killingly, madam!—A little more red, and you'll be irresistible!—But why this more than ordinary care of your dress and complexion? What new conquest are you aiming at?

MILLWOOD. A conquest would be new indeed!

LUCY. Not to you, who make 'em every day,—but to me.—Well! 'tis what I'm never to expect,—unfortunate as I am.—But your wit and beauty—

MILLWOOD. First made me a wretch, and still continue me so.—Men, however generous or sincere to one another, are all selfish hypocrites in their affairs with us. We are no otherwise esteemed or regarded by them, but as we contribute to their satisfaction.

LUCY. You are certainly, madam, on the wrong side in this argument. Is not the expense all theirs? And I am sure it is our own fault if we haven't our share of the pleasure.

MILLWOOD. We are but slaves to men.

LUCY. Nay, 'tis they that are slaves most certainly; for we lay them under contribution.

MILLWOOD. Slaves have no property; no, not even in themselves.—All is the victor's.

LUCY. You are strangely arbitrary in your principles, madam.

MILLWOOD. I would have my conquests complete, like those of the Spaniards in the New World, who first plundered the natives of all the wealth they had, and then condemned the wretches to the mines for life to work for more.

LUCY. Well, I shall never approve of your scheme of government. I should think it much more politic, as well as just, to find my subjects an easier employment.

MILLWOOD. It's a general maxim among the knowing part of mankind that a woman without virtue, like a man without honor or honesty, is capable of any action, though never so vile; and yet what pains will they not take, what arts not use, to seduce us from our innocence and make us contemptible and wicked even in their own opinions? Then is it not just, the villains, to their cost, should find us so?—But guilt makes them suspicious, and keeps them on their guard; therefore we can take advantage only of the young and innocent part of the sex, who, having never injured women, apprehend no injury from them.

LUCY. Ay, they must be young indeed.

MILLWOOD. Such a one, I think, I have found.—As I've passed through the City, I have often observed him receiving and paying considerable sums of money; from thence I conclude he is employed in affairs of consequence.

LUCY. Is he handsome?

MILLWOOD. Ay, ay, the stripling is well made.

LUCY. About—

MILLWOOD. Eighteen—

LUCY. Innocent, handsome, and about

eighteen.—You'll be vastly happy.—Why, if you manage well, you may keep him to your self these two or three years.

MILLWOOD. If I manage well, I shall have done with him much sooner; having long had a design on him, and meeting him yesterday, I made a full stop and gazing wishfully on his face, asked him his name. He blushed, and bowing very low, answered, George Barnwell. I begged his pardon for the freedom I had taken, and told him that he was the person I had long wished to see, and to whom I had an affair of importance to communicate at a proper time and place. He named a tavern; I talked of honor and reputation, and invited him to my house. He swallowed the bait, promised to come, and this is the time I expect him. (*Knocking at the door*) Somebody knocks,—d'ye hear? I am at home to nobody to-day, but him.—   (*Exit* LUCY)

MILLWOOD. Less affairs must give way to those of more consequence; and I am strangely mistaken if this does not prove of great importance to me and him, too, before I have done with him.—Now, after what manner shall I receive him? Let me consider—What manner of person am I to receive?—He is young, innocent, and bashful; therefore I must take care not to shock him at first.—But then, if I have any skill in physiognomy, he is amorous, and, with a little assistance, will soon get the better of his modesty.—I'll trust to nature, who does wonders in these matters.—If to seem what one is not, in order to be the better liked for what one really is; if to speak one thing, and mean the direct contrary, be art in a woman, I know nothing of nature.

(*Enter to her* BARNWELL, *bowing very low, and* LUCY *at a distance*)

MILLWOOD. Sir, the surprise and joy!—
BARNWELL. Madam.—
MILLWOOD. This is such a favor,—
                              (*Advancing*)
BARNWELL. Pardon me, madam,—
MILLWOOD. So unhoped for,—
(*Still advances.* BARNWELL *salutes her, and retires in confusion*)
MILLWOOD. To see you here—Excuse the confusion—
BARNWELL. I fear I am too bold.—

MILLWOOD. Alas, sir! All my apprehensions proceed from my fears of your thinking me so.—Please, sir, to sit.—I am as much at a loss how to receive this honor as I ought, as I am surprised at your goodness in conferring it.

BARNWELL. I thought you had expected me.—I promised to come.

MILLWOOD. That is the more surprising; few men are such religious observers of their word.

BARNWELL. All who are honest are.

MILLWOOD. To one another.—But we silly women are seldom thought of consequence enough to gain a place in your remembrance. (*Laying her hand on his, as by accident*)

BARNWELL. (*Aside*) Her disorder is so great, she don't perceive she has laid her hand on mine.—Heaven! how she trembles!—What can this mean!

MILLWOOD. The interest I have in all that relates to you (the reason of which you shall know hereafter) excites my curiosity; and, were I sure you would pardon my presumption, I should desire to know your real sentiments on a very particular affair.

BARNWELL. Madam, you may command my poor thoughts on any subject;—I have none that I would conceal.

MILLWOOD. You'll think me bold.

BARNWELL. No, indeed.

MILLWOOD. What then are your thoughts of love?

BARNWELL. If you mean the love of women, I have not thought of it at all.—My youth and circumstances make such thoughts improper in me yet. But if you mean the general love we owe to mankind, I think no one has more of it in his temper than myself.—I don't know that person in the world whose happiness I don't wish, and wouldn't promote, were it in my power.—In an especial manner I love my uncle, and my master, but above all my friend.

MILLWOOD. You have a friend then whom you love?

BARNWELL. As he does me, sincerely.

MILLWOOD. He is, no doubt, often blessed with your company and conversation.—

BARNWELL. We live in one house together, and both serve the same worthy merchant.

MILLWOOD. Happy, happy youth!—Who e'er thou art, I envy thee, and so must all who see and know this youth.—What I have lost, by being formed a woman!—I hate my sex, myself.—Had I been a man, I might, perhaps, have been as happy in your friendship as he who now enjoys it:—But as it is,—Oh!—

BARNWELL. (*Aside*) I never observed women before, or this is sure the most beautiful of her sex.—You seem disordered, madam! May I know the cause?

MILLWOOD. Do not ask me.—I can never speak it, whatever is the cause;—I wish for things impossible;—I would be a servant, bound to the same master as you are, to live in one house with you.

BARNWELL. (*Aside*) How strange, and yet how kind, her words and actions are!—And the effect they have on me is as strange.—I feel desires I never knew before;—I must be gone, while I have power to go.—Madam, I humbly take my leave.—

MILLWOOD. You will not sure leave me so soon!

BARNWELL. Indeed I must.

MILLWOOD. You cannot be so cruel!—I have prepared a poor supper, at which I promised myself your company.

BARNWELL. I am sorry I must refuse the honor that you designed me;—but my duty to my master calls me hence.—I never yet neglected his service. He is so gentle and so good a master that should I wrong him, though he might forgive me, I never should forgive myself.

MILLWOOD. Am I refused, by the first man, the second favor I ever stooped to ask? —Go then, thou proud, hard-hearted youth. —But know, you are the only man that could be found, who would let me sue twice for greater favors.

BARNWELL. (*Aside*) What shall I do!— How shall I go or stay!

MILLWOOD. Yet do not, do not, leave me. I wish my sex's pride would meet your scorn; but when I look upon you, when I behold those eyes,—oh! spare my tongue, and let my blushes speak. This flood of tears to that will force their way, and declare—what woman's modesty should hide.

BARNWELL. Oh, heavens! she loves me, worthless as I am; her looks, her words, her flowing tears confess it. And can I leave her then? Oh, never, never! Madam, dry up those tears. You shall command me always; I will stay here for ever, if you'd have me.

LUCY. (*Aside*) So! she has wheedled him out of his virtue of obedience already and will strip him of all the rest one after another till she has left him as few as her ladyship or myself.

MILLWOOD. Now you are kind, indeed; but I mean not to detain you always: I would have you shake off all slavish obedience to your master;—but you may serve him still.

LUCY. (*Aside*) Serve him still!—Aye, or he'll have no opportunity of fingering his cash, and then he'll not serve your end, I'll be sworn.

(*Enter to them* BLUNT)

BLUNT. Madam, supper's on the table.

MILLWOOD. Come, sir, you'll excuse all defects. My thoughts were too much employed on my guest to observe the entertainment.

(*Exeunt* MILLWOOD *and* BARNWELL)

BLUNT. What! is all this preparation, this elegant supper, variety of wines and music, for the entertainment of that young fellow!

LUCY. So it seems.

BLUNT. What, is our mistress turned fool at last! She's in love with him, I suppose.

LUCY. I suppose not, but she designs to make him in love with her if she can.

BLUNT. What will she get by that? He seems under age, and can't be supposed to have much money.

LUCY. But his master has; and that's the same thing, as she'll manage it.

BLUNT. I don't like this fooling with a handsome young fellow; while she's endeavoring to ensnare him, she may be caught herself.

LUCY. Nay, were she like me, that would certainly be the consequence;—for, I confess, there is something in youth and innocence that moves me mightily.

BLUNT. Yes, so does the smoothness and plumpness of a partridge move a mighty desire in the hawk to be the destruction of it.

LUCY. Why, birds are their prey, as men are ours; though, as you observed, we are sometimes caught ourselves. But that, I dare say, will never be the case with our mistress.

BLUNT. I wish it may prove so; for you

know we all depend upon her. Should she trifle away her time with a young fellow that there's nothing to be got by, we must all starve.

LUCY. There's no danger of that, for I am sure she has no view in this affair but interest.

BLUNT. Well, and what hopes are there of success in that?

LUCY. The most promising that can be.— 'Tis true, the youth has his scruples; but she'll soon teach him to answer them, by stifling his conscience.—O, the lad is in a hopeful way, depend upon't.   (*Exeunt*)

SCENE III. *Another Room in* MILLWOOD's *House.*

(*Discovered* BARNWELL *and* MILLWOOD *at an entertainment*)

BARNWELL. What can I answer! All that I know is, that you are fair and I am miserable.

MILLWOOD. We are both so, and yet the fault is in ourselves.

BARNWELL. To ease our present anguish, by plunging into guilt, is to buy a moment's pleasure with an age of pain.

MILLWOOD. I should have thought the joys of love as lasting as they are great. If ours prove otherwise, 'tis your inconstancy must make them so.

BARNWELL. The law of Heaven will not be reversed; and that requires us to govern our passions.

MILLWOOD. To give us sense of beauty and desires, and yet forbid us to taste and be happy, is cruelty to nature. Have we passions only to torment us!

BARNWELL. To hear you talk, tho' in the cause of vice, to gaze upon your beauty, press your hand, and see your snow-white bosom heave and fall, enflames my wishes; my pulse beats high, my senses all are in a hurry, and I am on the rack of wild desire; yet for a moment's guilty pleasure, shall I lose my innocence, my peace of mind, and hopes of solid happiness?

MILLWOOD. Chimeras all,—
Come on with me and prove,
No joy's like woman, kind, nor heaven like love.

BARNWELL. I would not, yet I must on.
Reluctant thus, the merchant quits his ease
And trusts to rocks and sands and stormy seas;
In hopes some unknown golden coast to find,
Commits himself, tho' doubtful, to the wind,
Longs much for joys to come, yet mourns those left behind.   (*Exeunt*)

Act II

SCENE I. *A Room in* THOROWGOOD's *House.*

(*Enter* BARNWELL)

BARNWELL. How strange are all things round me! Like some thief who treads forbidden ground, fearful I enter each apartment of this well-known house. To guilty love, as if that was too little, already have I added breach of trust. A thief! Can I know myself that wretched thing, and look my honest friend and injured master in the face? Though hypocrisy may a while conceal my guilt, at length it will be known, and public shame and ruin must ensue. In the meantime, what must be my life? Ever to speak a language foreign to my heart; hourly to add to the number of my crimes in order to conceal 'em. Sure, such was the condition of the grand apostate,[4] when first he lost his purity; like me disconsolate he wandered, and while yet in heaven, bore all his future hell about him.

(*Enter* TRUEMAN)

[4] Lucifer.

TRUEMAN. Barnwell! O how I rejoice to see you safe! So will our master and his gentle daughter, who during your absence often inquired after you.

BARNWELL. (*Aside*) Would he were gone; his officious love will pry into the secrets of my soul.

TRUEMAN. Unless you knew the pain the whole family has felt on your account, you can't conceive how much you are beloved. But why thus cold and silent? When my heart is full of joy for your return, why do you turn away? Why thus avoid me? What have I done? How am I altered since you saw me last? Or rather what have you done, and why are you thus changed, for I am still the same?

BARNWELL. (*Aside*) What have I done indeed?

TRUEMAN. Not speak nor look upon me!

BARNWELL. (*Aside*) By my face he will discover all I would conceal; methinks already I begin to hate him.

TRUEMAN. I cannot bear this usage from a friend, one whom till now I ever found so loving, whom yet I love, though this unkindness strikes at the root of friendship, and might destroy it in any breast but mine.

BARNWELL. I am not well. (*Turning to him*) Sleep has been a stranger to these eyes since you beheld them last.

TRUEMAN. Heavy they look indeed, and swollen with tears; now they o'erflow; rightly did my sympathizing heart forebode last night when thou wast absent something fatal to our peace.

BARNWELL. Your friendship engages you too far. My troubles, whate'er they are, are mine alone; you have no interest in them, nor ought your concern for me give you a moment's pain.

TRUEMAN. You speak as if you knew of friendship nothing but the name. Before I saw your grief I felt it. Since we parted last I have slept no more than you, but, pensive in my chamber, sat alone and spent the tedious night in wishes for your safety and return; e'en now, though ignorant of the cause, your sorrow wounds me to the heart.

BARNWELL. 'Twill not be always thus. Friendship and all engagements cease, as circumstances and occasions vary; and since you once may hate me, perhaps it might be better for us both that now you loved me less.

TRUEMAN. Sure I but dream! Without a cause would Barnwell use me thus? Ungenerous and ungrateful youth, farewell.—I shall endeavor to follow your advice.—(*Starts to leave, then pauses and speaks aside*) Yet stay, perhaps I am too rash and angry when the cause demands compassion. Some unforeseen calamity may have befallen him, too great to bear.

BARNWELL. (*Aside*) What part am I reduced to act; 'tis vile and base to move his temper thus, the best of friends and men.

TRUEMAN. (*Turns back*) I am to blame, prithee forgive me, Barnwell. Try to compose your ruffled mind, and let me know the cause that thus transports you from yourself; my friendly counsel may restore your peace.

BARNWELL. All that is possible for man to do for man, your generous friendship may effect; but here even that's in vain.

TRUEMAN. Something dreadful is laboring in your breast. O give it vent and let me share your grief! 'Twill ease your pain should it admit no cure and make it lighter by the part I bear.

BARNWELL. Vain supposition! My woes increase by being observed; should the cause be known they would exceed all bounds.

TRUEMAN. So well I know thy honest heart, guilt cannot harbor there.

BARNWELL. (*Aside*) O torture insupportable!

TRUEMAN. Then why am I excluded? Have I a thought I would conceal from you?

BARNWELL. If still you urge me on this hated subject, I'll never enter more beneath this roof, nor see your face again.

TRUEMAN. 'Tis strange. But I have done; say but you hate me not.

BARNWELL. Hate you!—I am not that monster yet.

TRUEMAN. Shall our friendship still continue?

BARNWELL. It's a blessing I never was worthy of, yet now must stand on terms; and but upon conditions can confirm it.

TRUEMAN. What are they?

BARNWELL. Never hereafter, though you should wonder at my conduct, desire to know more than I am willing to reveal.

TRUEMAN. 'Tis hard, but upon any conditions I must be your friend.

BARNWELL. Then, as much as one lost to himself can be another's, I am yours.

(*They embrace*)

TRUEMAN. Be ever so, and may heaven restore your peace.

BARNWELL. Will yesterday return? We have heard the glorious sun, that till then incessant rolled, once stopped his rapid course and once went black. The dead have risen; and parched rocks poured forth a liquid stream to quench the people's thirst. The sea divided and formed walls of water while a whole nation passed in safety through its sandy bosom. Hungry lions have refused their prey; and men unhurt have walked amidst consuming flames; but never yet did time once past, return.

TRUEMAN. Though the continued chain of time has never once been broke, nor ever will, but uninterrupted must keep on its course till lost in eternity it ends there where it first begun; yet as heaven can repair whatever evils time can bring upon us, he who trusts heaven ought never to despair. But business requires our attendance, business, the youth's best preservative from ill, as idleness is his worst of snares. Will you go with me?

BARNWELL. I'll take a little time to reflect on what has past, and follow you.

(*Exit* TRUEMAN)

BARNWELL. I might have trusted Trueman to have applied to my uncle to have repaired the wrong I have done my master; but what of Millwood? Must I expose her too? Ungenerous and base! Then heaven requires it not. But heaven requires that I forsake her. What! Never see her more! Does heaven require that! I hope I may see her, and heaven not be offended. Presumptuous hope! Dearly already have I proved my frailty; should I once more tempt heaven, I may be left to fall never to rise again. Yet shall I leave her, forever leave her, and not let her know the cause? She who loves me with such a boundless passion? Can cruelty be duty? I judge of what she then must feel, by what I now endure. The love of life and fear of shame, opposed by inclination strong as death or shame, like wind and tide in raging conflict met, when neither can prevail, keep me in doubt. How then can I determine?

(*Enter* THOROWGOOD)

THOROWGOOD. Without a cause assigned, or notice given, to absent yourself last night was a fault, young man, and I came to chide you for it, but hope I am prevented. That modest blush, the confusion so visible in your face, speak grief and shame. When we have offended heaven, it requires no more; and shall man, who needs himself to be forgiven, be harder to appease? If my pardon or love be of moment to your peace, look up, secure of both.

BARNWELL. (*Aside*) This goodness has o'ercome me.—O sir! You know not the nature and extent of my offence; and I should abuse your mistaken bounty to receive 'em. Though I had rather die than speak my shame; though racks could not have forced the guilty secret from my breast, your kindness has.

THOROWGOOD. Enough, enough! Whate'er it be, this concern shows you're convinced, and I am satisfied. How painful is the sense of guilt to an ingenuous mind!—some youthful folly, which it were prudent not to enquire into. When we consider the frail condition of humanity, it may raise our pity, not our wonder, that youth should go astray; when reason, weak at the best when opposed to inclination, scarce formed, and wholly unassisted by experience, faintly contends, or willingly becomes the slave of sense. The state of youth is much to be deplored, and the more so because they see it not; they being then to danger most exposed, when they are least prepared for their defence.

BARNWELL. It will be known, and you recall your pardon and abhor me.

THOROWGOOD. I never will; so heaven confirm to me the pardon of my offences. Yet be upon your guard in this gay, thoughtless season of your life; now, when the sense of pleasure's quick, and passion high, the voluptuous appetites, raging and fierce, demand the strongest curb; take heed of a relapse. When vice becomes habitual, the very power of leaving it is lost.

BARNWELL. Hear me, then, on my knees confess.

THOROWGOOD. I will not hear a syllable more upon this subject; it were not mercy, but cruelty, to hear what must give you such torment to reveal.

BARNWELL. This generosity amazes and distracts me.

THOROWGOOD. This remorse makes thee dearer to me than if thou hadst never offended; whatever is your fault, of this I'm certain, 'twas harder for you to offend than me to pardon. (*Exit* THOROWGOOD)

BARNWELL. Villain, villain, villain! basely to wrong so excellent a man. Should I again return to folly?—detested thought!—But what of Millwood then? Why, I renounce her; I give her up; the struggle's over, and virtue has prevailed. Reason may convince, but gratitude compels. This unlooked for generosity has saved me from destruction. (*Going*)

(*Enter a* FOOTMAN)

FOOTMAN. Sir, two ladies, from your uncle in the country, desire to see you.

BARNWELL. (*Aside*) Who should they be? Tell them I'll wait upon 'em. (*Exit* Footman)

BARNWELL. Methinks I dread to see 'em. Guilt, what a coward hast thou made me? Now everything alarms me. (*Exit*)

SCENE II. *Another Room in* THOROWGOOD's *House.*

(MILLWOOD *and* LUCY *seated. Enter a* FOOTMAN)

FOOTMAN. Ladies, he'll wait upon you immediately.

MILLWOOD. 'Tis very well. I thank you. (*Exit* FOOTMAN)

(*Enter* BARNWELL)

BARNWELL. Confusion! Millwood!

MILLWOOD. That angry look tells me that here I'm an unwelcome guest; I feared as much—the unhappy are so everywhere.

BARNWELL. Will nothing but my utter ruin content you?

MILLWOOD. Unkind and cruel! Lost myself, your happiness is now my only care.

BARNWELL. How did you gain admission?

MILLWOOD. Saying we were desired by your uncle to visit and deliver a message to you, we were received by the family without suspicion, and with much respect directed here.

BARNWELL. Why did you come at all?

MILLWOOD. I never shall trouble you more; I'm come to take my leave forever. Such is the malice of my fate, I go hopeless, despairing ever to return. This hour is all I have left me. One short hour is all I have to bestow on love and you, for whom I thought the longest life too short.

BARNWELL. Then we are met to part forever?

MILLWOOD. It must be so; yet think not that time or absence ever shall put a period to my grief or make me love you less; though I must leave you, yet condemn me not.

BARNWELL. Condemn you? No, I approve your resolution, and rejoice to hear it; 'tis just, 'tis necessary. I have well weighed, and found it so.

LUCY. (*Aside*) I'm afraid the young man has more sense than she thought he had.

BARNWELL. Before you came I had determined never to see you more.

MILLWOOD. (*Aside*) Confusion!

LUCY. (*Aside*) Ay, we are all out; this is a turn so unexpected, that I shall make nothing of my part; they must e'en play the scene betwixt themselves. (*She withdraws*)

MILLWOOD. 'Twas some relief to think, though absent, you would love me still; but to find, though fortune had been kind, that you, more cruel and inconstant, had resolved to cast me off! This, as I never could expect, I have not learnt to bear.

BARNWELL. I am sorry to hear you blame in me a resolution that so well becomes us both.

MILLWOOD. I have reason for what I do, but you have none.

BARNWELL. Can we want a reason for parting, who have so many to wish we never had met?

MILLWOOD. Look on me, Barnwell; am I deformed or old, that satiety so soon succeeds enjoyment? Nay, look again; am I not she whom yesterday you thought the fairest and the kindest of her sex, whose hand, trembling with ecstasy, you pressed and molded thus, while on my eyes you gazed with such delight, as if desire increased by being fed?

BARNWELL. No more! Let me repent my former follies, if possible, without remembering what they were.

MILLWOOD. Why?

BARNWELL. Such is my frailty that 'tis dangerous.

MILLWOOD. Where is the danger, since we are to part?

BARNWELL. The thought of that already is too painful.

MILLWOOD. If it be painful to part, then I may hope at least you do not hate me?

BARNWELL. No,—no,—I never said I did! —O my heart!

MILLWOOD. Perhaps you pity me?

BARNWELL. I do, I do, indeed, I do.

MILLWOOD. You'll think upon me?

BARNWELL. Doubt it not while I can think at all.

MILLWOOD. You may judge an embrace at parting too great a favor, though it would be the last? (*He draws back*) A look shall then suffice,—farewell forever.

(*Exeunt* MILLWOOD *and* LUCY)

BARNWELL. If to resolve to suffer be to conquer, I have conquered. Painful victory!

(*Re-enter* MILLWOOD *and* LUCY)

MILLWOOD. One thing I had forgot. I never must return to my own house again. This I thought proper to let you know, lest your mind should change, and you should seek in vain to find me there. Forgive me this second intrusion; I only came to give you this caution, and that, perhaps, was needless.

BARNWELL. I hope it was, yet it is kind, and I must thank you for it.

MILLWOOD. (*To* LUCY) My friend, your arm.—Now I am gone forever. (*Going*)

BARNWELL. One thing more—sure, there's no danger in my knowing where you go? If you think otherwise—

MILLWOOD. Alas! (*Weeping*)

LUCY. (*Aside*) We are right I find, that's my cue.—Ah, dear sir, she's going she knows not whither; but go she must.

BARNWELL. Humanity obliges me to wish you well; why will you thus expose yourself to needless troubles?

LUCY. Nay, there's no help for it. She must quit the town immediately, and the kingdom as soon as possible; it was no small matter, you may be sure, that could make her resolve to leave you.

MILLWOOD. No more, my friend, since he for whose dear sake alone I suffer, and am content to suffer, is kind and pities me. Where'er I wander through wilds and deserts, benighted and forlorn, that thought shall give me comfort.

BARNWELL. For my sake! O tell me how; which way am I so cursed as to bring such ruin on thee?

MILLWOOD. No matter, I am contented with my lot.

BARNWELL. Leave me not in this incertainty.

MILLWOOD. I have said too much.

BARNWELL. How, how am I the cause of your undoing?

MILLWOOD. 'Twill but increase your troubles.

BARNWELL. My troubles can't be greater than they are.

LUCY. Well, well, sir, if she won't satisfy you, I will.

BARNWELL. I am bound to you beyond expression.

MILLWOOD. Remember, sir, that I desired you not to hear it.

BARNWELL. Begin, and ease my racking expectation.

LUCY. Why you must know, my lady here was an only child; but her parents dying while she was young, left her and her fortune (no inconsiderable one, I assure you) to the care of a gentleman who has a good estate of his own.

MILLWOOD. Ay, ay, the barbarous man is rich enough;—but what are riches when compared to love?

LUCY. For a while he performed the office of a faithful guardian, settled her in a house, hired her servants—but you have seen in what manner she lived, so I need say no more of that.

MILLWOOD. How I shall live hereafter, heaven knows.

LUCY. All things went on as one could wish, till, some time ago, his wife dying, he fell violently in love with his charge, and would fain have married her. Now the man is neither old nor ugly, but a good, personable sort of a man, but I don't know how it was, she could never endure him. In short, her ill usage so provok'd him, that he brought in an account of his executorship, wherein he makes her debtor to him—

MILLWOOD. A trifle in itself, but more than enough to ruin me, whom, by this unjust account, he had stripped of all before.

LUCY. Now she having neither money nor friend, except me, who am as unfortunate as herself, he compelled her to pass his account, and give bond for the sum he demanded; but still provided handsomely for her and continued his courtship, till, being informed by his spies (truly I suspect some in her own family) that you were entertained at her house, and stayed with her all night, he came this morning raving and storming like a madman, talks no more of marriage (so there's no hopes of making up matters that way) but vows her ruin, unless she'll allow him the same favor that he supposes she granted you.

BARNWELL. Must she be ruined, or find her refuge in another's arms?

MILLWOOD. He gave me but an hour to resolve in. That's happily spent with you—and now I go.—

BARNWELL. To be exposed to all the rigors of the various seasons; the summer's parching heat, and winter's cold; unhoused to wander friendless through the unhospitable world, in misery and want; attended with fear and danger, and pursued by malice and revenge, wouldst thou endure all this for me, and can I do nothing, nothing to prevent it?

LUCY. 'Tis really a pity, there can be no way found out.

BARNWELL. O where are all my resolutions now? Like early vapors, or the morning dew, chased by the sun's warm beams they're vanished and lost, as though they had never been.

LUCY. Now I advised her, sir, to comply with the gentleman, that would not only put an end to her troubles, but make her fortune at once.

BARNWELL. Tormenting fiend, away!—I had rather perish, nay, see her perish, than have her saved by him; I will myself prevent her ruin, though with my own. A moment's patience, I'll return immediately.— (Exit)

LUCY. 'Twas well you came, or, by what I can perceive, you had lost him.

MILLWOOD. That, I must confess, was a danger I did not foresee; I was only afraid he should have come without money. You know a house of entertainment like mine is not kept with nothing.

LUCY. That's very true; but then you should be reasonable in your demands; 'tis pity to discourage a young man.

(Enter BARNWELL)

BARNWELL. (Aside) What am I about to do! Now you, who boast your reason all sufficient, suppose yourselves in my condition, and determine for me, whether it's right to let her suffer for my faults, or, by this small addition to my guilt, prevent the ill effects of what is past.

LUCY. (Aside) These young sinners think everything in the ways of wickedness so strange,—but I could tell him that this is nothing but what's very common; for one vice as naturally begets another, as a father a son. But he'll find out that himself, if he lives long enough.

BARNWELL. Here take this, and with it purchase your deliverance; return to your house, and live in peace and safety.

MILLWOOD. So I may hope to see you there again.

BARNWELL. Answer me not,—but fly,—lest, in the agonies of my remorse, I take again what is not mine to give, and abandon thee to want and misery.

MILLWOOD. Say but you'll come.—

BARNWELL. You are my fate, my heaven, or my hell. Only leave me now, dispose of me hereafter as you please.

(Exeunt MILLWOOD and LUCY)

BARNWELL. What have I done? Were my resolutions founded on reason, and sincerely made? Why then has heaven suffered me to fall? I sought not the occasion; and, if my heart deceives me not, compassion and generosity were my motives. Is virtue inconsistent with itself, or are vice and virtue only empty names? Or do they depend on accidents beyond our power to produce, or to prevent, wherein we have no part, and yet must be determined by the event?—But why should I attempt to reason? All is confusion, horror, and remorse;—I find I am lost, cast down from all my late erected hopes and plunged again in guilt, yet scarce know how or why—

Such undistinguished horrors make my brain,
Like hell, the seat of darkness, and of pain.
(*Exit*)

Act III

Scene I. *A Room in* Thorowgood's *House.*

(*Enter* Thorowgood *and* Trueman)

Thorowgood. Methinks I would not have you only learn the method of merchandize and practise it hereafter merely as a means of getting wealth. 'Twill be well worth your pains to study it as a science. See how it is founded in reason and the nature of things. How it has promoted humanity, as it has opened and yet keeps up an intercourse between nations far remote from one another in situation, customs, and religion; promoting arts, industry, peace and plenty, by mutual benefits diffusing mutual love from pole to pole.

Trueman. Something of this I have considered, and hope, by your assistance, to extend my thoughts much farther. I have observed those countries where trade is promoted and encouraged do not make discoveries to destroy, but to improve mankind by love and friendship, to tame the fierce, and polish the most savage, to teach them the advantages of honest traffic by taking from them with their own consent their useless superfluities, and giving them in return what, from their ignorance in manual arts, their situation, or some other accident they stand in need of.

Thorowgood. 'Tis justly observed. The populous east, luxuriant, abounds with glittering gems, bright pearls, aromatic spices, and health-restoring drugs. The late found western world glows with unnumbered veins of gold and silver ore. On every climate, and on every country, heaven has bestowed some good peculiar to itself. It is the industrious merchant's business to collect the various blessings of each soil and climate, and, with the product of the whole, to enrich his native country.

Well! I have examined your accounts. They are not only just, as I have always found

them, but regularly kept, and fairly entered. I commend your diligence. Method in business is the surest guide. He who neglects it frequently stumbles, and always wanders perplexed, uncertain, and in danger. Are Barnwell's accounts ready for my inspection? He does not use to be the last on these occasions.

Trueman. Upon receiving your orders he retired, I thought in some confusion. If you please, I'll go and hasten him. I hope he hasn't been guilty of any neglect.

Thorowgood. I'm now going to the Exchange; let him know, at my return, I expect to find him ready.   (*Exeunt*)

(*Enter* Maria *with a book; she sits and reads*)

Maria. How forcible is truth! The weakest mind, inspired with love of that, fixed and collected in itself, with indifference beholds the united force of earth and hell opposing. Such souls are raised above the sense of pain, or so supported that they regard it not. The martyr cheaply purchases his heaven. Small are his sufferings, great is his reward; not so the wretch who combats love with duty, when the mind, weakened and dissolved by the soft passion, feeble and hopeless opposes its own desire. What is an hour, a day, a year of pain, to a whole life of tortures, such as these?

(*Enter* Trueman)

Trueman. O, Barnwell! O, my friend, how art thou fallen!

Maria. Ha! Barnwell! What of him? Speak, say what of Barnwell?

Trueman. 'Tis not to be concealed. I've news to tell of him that will afflict your generous father, yourself, and all who knew him.

MARIA. Defend us, Heaven!

TRUEMAN. I cannot speak it.—See there.
(Gives a letter)

MARIA. *(Reads)*

Trueman,

I know my absence will surprise my honored master, and yourself; and the more, when you shall understand that the reason of my withdrawing, is my having embezzled part of the cash with which I was entrusted. After this, 'tis needless to inform you that I intend never to return again. Though this might have been known by examining my accounts; yet, to prevent that unnecessary trouble, and to cut all fruitless expectations of my return, I have left this from the lost
GEORGE BARNWELL.

TRUEMAN. Lost indeed! Yet how he should be guilty of what he there charges himself withal, raises my wonder equal to my grief. Never had youth a higher sense of virtue. Justly he thought, and as he thought he practised; never was life more regular than his; an understanding uncommon at his years; an open, generous, manliness of temper; his manners easy, unaffected and engaging.

MARIA. This and much more you might have said with truth.—He was the delight of every eye, and joy of every heart that knew him.

TRUEMAN. Since such he was, and was my friend, can I support his loss? See, the fairest and happiest maid this wealthy city boasts, kindly condescends to weep for thy unhappy fate, poor, ruined Barnwell!

MARIA. Trueman, do you think a soul so delicate as his, so sensible of shame, can e'er submit to live a slave to vice?

TRUEMAN. Never, never! So well I know him, I'm sure this act of his, so contrary to his nature, must have been caused by some unavoidable necessity.

MARIA. Is there no means yet to preserve him?

TRUEMAN. O! that there were!—But few men recover reputation lost, a merchant never. Nor would he, I fear, though I should find him, ever be brought to look his injured master in the face.

MARIA. I fear as much,—and therefore would never have my father know it.

TRUEMAN. That's impossible.

MARIA. What's the sum?

TRUEMAN. 'Tis considerable.—I've marked it here, to show it, with the letter, to your father, at his return.

MARIA. If I should supply the money, could you so dispose of that, and the account, as to conceal this unhappy mismanagement from my father?

TRUEMAN. Nothing more easy.—But can you intend it? Will you save a helpless wretch from ruin? Oh! 'twere an act worthy such exalted virtue as Maria's.—Sure, heaven in mercy to my friend inspired the generous thought!

MARIA. Doubt not but I would purchase so great a happiness at a much dearer price. —But how shall he be found?

TRUEMAN. Trust to my diligence for that. —In the meantime, I'll conceal his absence from your father, or find such excuses for it, that the real cause shall never be suspected.

MARIA. In attempting to save from shame one whom we hope may yet return to virtue, to heaven and you, the judges of this action, I appeal, whether I have done anything misbecoming my sex and character.

TRUEMAN. Earth must approve the deed, and heaven, I doubt not, will reward it.

MARIA. If heaven succeed it, I am well rewarded. A virgin's fame is sullied by suspicion's slightest breath; and therefore as this must be a secret from my father and the world for Barnwell's sake, for mine, let it be so to him.

SCENE II. A *Room in* MILLWOOD'S *House.*

(Enter LUCY *and* BLUNT*)*

LUCY. Well! What do you think of Millwood's conduct now?

BLUNT. I own it is surprising. I don't know which to admire most, her feigned, or his real passion, though I have sometimes been afraid that her avarice would discover her.—But his youth and want of experience make it the easier to impose on him.

Lucy. No, it is his love. To do him justice, notwithstanding his youth, he don't want understanding; but you men are much easier imposed on in these affairs than your vanity will allow you to believe. Let me see the wisest of you all as much in love with me as Barnwell is with Millwood, and I'll engage to make as great a fool of him.

Blunt. And all circumstances considered, to make as much money of him, too.

Lucy. I can't answer for that. Her artifice in making him rob his master at first, and the various stratagems by which she has obliged him to continue in that course, astonish even me, who know her so well.

Blunt. But then you are to consider that the money was his master's.

Lucy. There was the difficulty of it. Had it been his own, it had been nothing. Were the world his, she might have it for a smile. But these golden days are done; he's ruined, and Millwood's hopes of farther profits there are at an end.

Blunt. That's no more than we all expected.

Lucy. Being called by his master to make up his accounts, he was forced to quit his house and service, and wisely flies to Millwood for relief and entertainment.

Blunt. I have not heard of this before! How did she receive him?

Lucy. As you would expect. She wondered what he meant, was astonished at his impudence, and, with an air of modesty peculiar to herself, swore so heartily that she never saw him before that she put me out of countenance.

Blunt. That's much indeed! But how did Barnwell behave?

Lucy. He grieved, and at length, enraged at this barbarous treatment, was preparing to be gone; and, making toward the door, showed a bag of money, which he had stolen from his master,—the last he's ever like to have from thence.

Blunt. But then Millwood?

Lucy. Aye, she, with her usual address, returned to her old arts of lying, swearing, and dissembling. Hung on his neck, and wept, and swore 'twas meant in jest, till the easy fool, melted into tears, threw the money into her lap, and swore he had rather die than think her false.

Blunt. Strange infatuation!

Lucy. But what followed was stranger still. As doubts and fears followed by reconcilement ever increase love where the passion is sincere, so in him it caused so wild a transport of excessive fondness, such joy, such grief, such pleasure, and such anguish, that nature in him seemed sinking with the weight, and the charmed soul disposed to quit his breast for hers.—Just then, when every passion with lawless anarchy prevailed, and reason was in the raging tempest lost, the cruel, artful Millwood prevailed upon the wretched youth to promise what I tremble but to think on.

Blunt. I am amazed! What can it be?

Lucy. You will be more so to hear it is to attempt the life of his nearest relation and best benefactor.

Blunt. His uncle, whom we have often heard him speak of as a gentleman of a large estate and fair character in the country where he lives?

Lucy. The same. She was no sooner possessed of the last dear purchase of his ruin, but her avarice, insatiate as the grave, demands this horrid sacrifice, Barnwell's near relation; and unsuspected virtue must give too easy means to seize the good man's treasure, whose blood must seal the dreadful secret, and prevent the terrors of her guilty fears.

Blunt. Is it possible she could persuade him to do an act like that! He is, by nature, honest, grateful, compassionate, and generous. And though his love and her artful persuasions have wrought him to practise what he most abhors, yet we all can witness for him with what reluctance he has still complied! So many tears he shed o'er each offence, as might, if possible, sanctify theft and make a merit of a crime.

Lucy. 'Tis true, at the naming the murder of his uncle, he started into rage; and, breaking from her arms, where she till then had held him with well dissembled love and false endearments, called her cruel monster, devil; and told her she was born for his destruction. She thought it not for her purpose to meet his rage with rage, but affected a most passionate fit of grief, railed at her fate, and cursed her wayward stars, that still her wants should force her to press him to act such deeds as she must needs abhor as well as he; but told him necessity had no law and love no bounds; that therefore he never truly loved, but meant in her necessity to forsake her. Then kneeled and swore, that since by his refusal he had given her cause to doubt his love, she never would see him more, unless, to prove it true, he robbed his uncle to supply her wants and murdered him to keep it from discovery.

BLUNT. I am astonished! What said he?

LUCY. Speechless he stood; but in his face you might have read that various passions tore his very soul. Oft he in anguish threw his eyes towards heaven, and then as often bent their beams on her; then wept and groaned and beat his breast; at length, with horror not to be expressed, he cried, "Thou cursed fair! have I not given dreadful proofs of love? What drew me from my youthful innocence to stain my then unspotted soul but love? What caused me to rob my gentle master but cursed love? What makes me now a fugitive from his service, loathed by myself, and scorned by all the world, but love? What fills my eyes with tears, my soul with torture, never felt on this side death before? Why love, love, love! And why, above all, do I resolve (for, tearing his hair, he cried, I do resolve!) to kill my uncle?"

BLUNT. Was she not moved? It makes me weep to hear the sad relation.

LUCY. Yes, with joy that she had gained her point. She gave him no time to cool, but urged him to attempt it instantly. He's now gone; if he performs it and escapes, there's more money for her; if not, he'll ne'er return, and then she's fairly rid of him.

BLUNT. 'Tis time the world was rid of such a monster.—

LUCY. If we don't do our endeavors to prevent this murder, we are as bad as she.

BLUNT. I'm afraid it is too late.

LUCY. Perhaps not. Her barbarity to Barnwell makes me hate her. We've run too great a length with her already. I did not think her or myself so wicked, as I find upon reflection we are.

BLUNT. 'Tis true, we have all been too much so. But there is something so horrid in murder that all other crimes seem nothing when compared to that. I would not be involved in the guilt of that for all the world.

LUCY. Nor I, heaven knows; therefore let us clear ourselves by doing all that is in our power to prevent it. I have just thought of a way that, to me, seems probable. Will you join with me to detect this cursed design?

BLUNT. With all my heart. How else shall I clear myself? He who knows of a murder intended to be committed and does not discover it in the eye of the law and reason is a murderer.

LUCY. Let us lose no time; I'll acquaint you with the particulars as we go.

(*Exeunt*)

SCENE III. *A Country Walk near a Wood.*

(*Enter* BARNWELL)

BARNWELL. A dismal gloom obscures the face of day; either the sun has slipped behind a cloud, or journeys down the west of heaven with more than common speed to avoid the sight of what I'm doomed to act. Since I set forth on this accursed design, where'er I tread, methinks, the solid earth trembles beneath my feet. Yonder limpid stream, whose hoary fall has made a natural cascade, as I passed by, in doleful accents seemed to murmur, "Murder." The earth, the air, the water, seem concerned; but that's not strange, the world is punished, and nature feels the shock when Providence permits a good man's fall! Just heaven! Then what should I be! For him that was my father's only brother, and since his death has been to me a father, who took me up an infant and an orphan, reared me with tenderest care, and still indulged me with most paternal fondness; yet here I stand avowed his destined murderer!—I stiffen with horror at my own impiety; 'tis yet unperformed. What if I quit my bloody purpose and fly the place! (*Going, then stops*)—But whither, O whither, shall I fly! My master's once friendly doors are ever shut against me; and without money Millwood will never see me more, and life is not to be endured with-

out her! She's got such firm possession of my heart, and governs there with such despotic sway! Aye, there's the cause of all my sin and sorrow. 'Tis more than love; 'tis the fever of the soul and madness of desire. In vain does nature, reason, conscience, all oppose it; the impetuous passion bears down all before it, and drives me on to lust, to theft, and murder.—Oh conscience! feeble guide to virtue, who only shows us when we go astray, but wants the power to stop us in our course. —Ha! in yonder shady walk I see my uncle. He's alone. Now for my disguise. (*Plucks out a visor*) This is his hour of private meditation. Thus daily he prepares his soul for heaven, whilst I—but what have I to do with heaven!—Ha! No struggles, Conscience!— Hence! Hence remorse, and ev'ry thought that's good;
The storm that lust began must end in blood.
(*Puts on the visor, and draws a pistol*)

(*Enter* UNCLE)

UNCLE. If I was superstitious, I should fear some danger lurked unseen, or death were nigh. A heavy melancholy clouds my spirits; my imagination is filled with gashly forms of dreary graves, and bodies changed by death, when the pale lengthened visage attracts each weeping eye, and fills the musing soul at once with grief and horror, pity and aversion. I will indulge the thought. The wise man prepares himself for death by making it familiar to his mind. When strong reflections hold the mirror near, and the living in the dead behold their future selves, how does each inordinate passion and desire cease or sicken at the view! The mind scarce moves; the blood, curdling and chilled, creeps slowly through the veins, fixed, still, and motionless, like the solemn object of our thoughts. We are almost at present what we must be hereafter, till curiosity awakes the soul, and sets it on inquiry.—

(GEORGE BARNWELL *steals towards him*)

UNCLE. O death, thou strange mysterious power, seen every day, yet never understood but by the incommunicative dead, what art thou? The extensive mind of man, that with a thought circles the earth's vast globe, sinks to the center, or ascends above the stars; that worlds exotic finds, or thinks it finds, thy thick clouds attempts to pass in vain; lost and bewildered in the horrid gloom, defeated she returns more doubtful than before; of nothing certain, but of labor lost.
(*During this speech,* BARNWELL *sometimes presents the pistol, and draws it back again; at last he drops it,—at which his uncle starts, and draws his sword*)
BARNWELL. Oh, 'tis impossible!
UNCLE. A man so near me, armed and masked!
BARNWELL. Nay, then there's no retreat. (*Plucks a poinard from his bosom, and stabs him*)
UNCLE. Oh! I am slain! All gracious heaven, regard the prayer of thy dying servant! Bless with thy choicest blessings my dearest nephew, forgive my murderer, and take my fleeting soul to endless mercy.
(BARNWELL *throws off his mask, runs to him, and, kneeling by him, raises and chafes him*)
BARNWELL. Expiring saint! Oh, murdered, martyred uncle! Lift up your dying eyes, and view your nephew in your murderer. O do not look so tenderly upon me! Let indignation lighten from your eyes, and blast me ere you die. By heaven, he weeps in pity of my woes. Tears, tears, for blood! The murdered, in the agonies of death, weeps for his murderer! O, speak your pious purpose, pronounce my pardon then, and take me with you!—He would, but cannot. O why, with such fond affection do you press my murdering hand!—What! will you kiss me! (*Kisses him.*—UNCLE *groans and dies*) He's gone forever, and oh! I follow.—(*Swoons away upon his uncle's dead body*) Do I still live to press the suffering bosom of the earth? Do I still breathe, and taint with my infectious breath the wholesome air? Let Heaven, from its high throne, in justice or in mercy, now look down on that dear murdered saint, and me the murderer. And, if his vengeance spares, let pity strike and end my wretched being.—Murder the worst of crimes, and parricide the worst of murders, and this the worst of parricides! Cain, who stands on record from the birth of time, and must to its last final period, as accursed, slew a

brother favored above him. Detested Nero, by another's hand, dispatched a mother, that he feared and hated. But I, with my own hand, have murdered a brother, mother, father, and a friend; most loving and beloved. This execrable act of mine's without a parallel.—O may it ever stand alone!—the last of murders, as it is the worst.—

The rich man thus, in torment and despair, Preferred his vain, but charitable prayer. The fool, his own soul lost, would fain be wise For others' good; but heaven his suit denies. By laws and means well known we stand or fall, And one eternal rule remains for all.

Act IV

SCENE I. THOROWGOOD'S *House.*

(*Enter* MARIA)

MARIA. How falsely do they judge who censure or applaud, as we're afflicted or rewarded here! I know I am unhappy, yet cannot charge myself with any crime more than the common frailties of our kind that should provoke just heaven to mark me out for sufferings so uncommon and severe. Falsely to accuse ourselves, heaven must abhor; then it is just and right that innocence should suffer, for heaven must be just in all its ways. Perhaps by that they are kept from moral evils, much worse than penal, or more improved in virtue; or may not the lesser ills that they sustain, be the means of greater good to others? Might all the joyless days and sleepless nights that I have passed, but purchase peace for thee—

Thou dear, dear cause of all my grief and pain, Small were the loss, and infinite the gain: Tho' to the grave in secret love I pine, So life, and fame, and happiness were thine.

(*Enter* TRUEMAN)

MARIA. What news of Barnwell?

TRUEMAN. None.—I have sought him with the greatest diligence, but all in vain.

MARIA. Doth my father yet suspect the cause of his absenting himself?

TRUEMAN. All appeared so just and fair to him, it is not possible he ever should; but his absence will no longer be concealed. Your father's wise; and though he seems to hearken to the friendly excuses I would make for Barnwell, yet, I am afraid, he regards 'em only as such, without suffering them to influence his judgment.

MARIA. How does the unhappy youth defeat all our designs to serve him! Yet I can never repent what we have done. Should he return, 'twill make his reconciliation with my father easier, and preserve him from future reproach from a malicious, unforgiving world.

(*Enter* THOROWGOOD *and* LUCY)

THOROWGOOD. This woman here has given me a sad, (and bating some circumstances) too probable account of Barnwell's defection.

LUCY. I am sorry, sir, that my frank confession of my former unhappy course of life should cause you to suspect my truth on this occasion.

THOROWGOOD. It is not that; your confession has in it all the appearance of truth. (*To them*) Among many other particulars, she informs me that Barnwell had been influenced to break his trust, and wrong me, at several times, of considerable sums of money; now, as I know this to be false, I would fain doubt the whole of her relation, too dreadful to be willingly believed.

MARIA. Sir, your pardon; I find myself on a sudden so indisposed, that I must retire. —(*Aside*) Providence opposes all attempts to save him.—Poor ruined Barnwell!—Wretched lost Maria!— (*Exit* MARIA)

THOROWGOOD. How am I distressed on every side! Pity for that unhappy youth, fear for the life of a much valued friend—and then my child—the only joy and hope of my declining life. Her melancholy increases hourly and gives me painful apprehensions of her loss.—O Trueman! this person informs me, that your friend, at the instigation of an impious woman, is gone to rob and murder his venerable uncle.

TRUEMAN. O execrable deed! I am blasted with the horror of the thought.

LUCY. This delay may ruin all.

THOROWGOOD. What to do or think I know not; that he ever wronged me, I know is false; the rest may be so too, there's all my hope.

TRUEMAN. Trust not to that, rather suppose all true than lose a moment's time; even now the horrid deed may be a-doing—dreadful imagination! or it may be done, and we are vainly debating on the means to prevent what is already past.

THOROWGOOD. (Aside) This earnestness convinces me that he knows more than he has yet discovered. What ho! Without there! Who waits?

(Enter a Servant)

THOROWGOOD. Order the groom to saddle the swiftest horse, and prepare himself to set out with speed. An affair of life and death demands his diligence.   (Exit Servant)

THOROWGOOD. (To LUCY) For you, whose behavior on this occasion I have no time to commend as it deserves, I must engage your farther assistance.—Return and observe this Millwood till I come. I have your directions, and will follow you as soon as possible.

(Exit LUCY)

THOROWGOOD. Trueman, you, I am sure, would not be idle on this occasion.

(Exit THOROWGOOD)

TRUEMAN. He only who is a friend can judge of my distress.   (Exit)

SCENE II. MILLWOOD's *House.*

(Enter MILLWOOD)

MILLWOOD. I wish I knew the event of his design; the attempt without success would ruin him. Well! what have I to apprehend from that? I fear too much. The mischief being only intended, his friends, in pity of his youth, turn all their rage on me. I should have thought of that before. Suppose the deed done; then, and then only, I shall be secure; or what if he returns without attempting it at all?

(Enter BARNWELL, *bloody*)

MILLWOOD. But he is here, and I have done him wrong; his bloody hands show he has done the deed, but show he wants the prudence to conceal it.

BARNWELL. Where shall I hide me? Whither shall I fly to avoid the swift unerring hand of justice?

MILLWOOD. Dismiss those fears; though thousands have pursued you to the door, yet being entered here, you are safe as innocence; I have such a cavern, by art so cunningly contrived, that the piercing eyes of jealousy and revenge may search in vain, nor find the entrance to the safe retreat. There will I hide you if any danger's near.

BARNWELL. O hide me from myself if it be possible, for while I bear my conscience in my bosom, tho' I were hid where man's eye never saw, nor light e'er dawned, 'twere all in vain. For that inmate, that impartial judge, will try, convict, and sentence me for murder; and execute me with never-ending torments. Behold these hands all crimsoned o'er with my dear uncle's blood! Here's a sight to make a statue start with horror or turn a living man into a statue.

MILLWOOD. Ridiculous! Then it seems you are afraid of your own shadow; or what's less than a shadow, your conscience.

BARNWELL. Though to man unknown I did the accursed act, what can we hide from heaven's omniscient eye?

MILLWOOD. No more of this stuff; what advantage have you made of his death, or what advantage may yet be made of it? Did you secure the keys of his treasure? Those no doubt were about him? What gold, what jewels, or what else of value have you brought me?

BARNWELL. Think you I added sacrilege to murder? Oh! had you seen him as his life flowed from him in a crimson flood, and heard him praying for me by the double name of nephew and of murderer; alas, alas! he knew not then that his nephew was his murderer; how would you have wished as I did, tho' you had a thousand years of life to come, to have given them all to have lengthened his one hour. But being dead, I fled the sight of what my hands had done, nor could I, to have gained the empire of the world, have violated by theft his sacred corpse.

MILLWOOD. Whining preposterous canting villain! To murder your uncle, rob him of life, nature's first, last, dear prerogative, after which there's no injury—then fear to take what he no longer wanted! and bring to me your penury and guilt. Do you think I'll hazard my reputation, nay my life, to entertain you?

BARNWELL. Oh!—Millwood!—This from thee?—But I have done, if you hate me, if you wish me dead; then are you happy,—for oh! 'tis sure my grief will quickly end me.

MILLWOOD. (Aside) In his madness he will discover all, and involve me in his ruin; we are on a precipice from whence there's no retreat for both.—Then to preserve myself— (Pauses) There is no other way;—'tis dreadful, but reflection comes too late when danger's pressing, and there's no room for choice. It must be done. (Stamps)

(Enter a Servant)

MILLWOOD. Fetch me an officer and seize this villain; he has confessed himself a murderer. Should I let him escape, I justly might be thought as bad as he. (Exit Servant)

BARNWELL. O Millwood! Sure thou dost not, cannot mean it. Stop the messenger, upon my knees I beg you, call him back. 'Tis fit I die indeed, but not by you. I will this instant deliver myself into the hands of justice; indeed I will, for death is all I wish. But thy ingratitude so tears my wounded soul, 'tis worse ten thousand times than death with torture!

MILLWOOD. Call it what you will, I am willing to live; and live secure; which nothing but your death can warrant.

BARNWELL. If there be a pitch of wickedness that seats the author beyond the reach of vengeance, you must be secure. But what remains for me but a dismal dungeon, hard-galling fetters, an awful trial, and ignominious death, justly to fall unpitied and abhorred?—After death to be suspended between heaven and earth, a dreadful spectacle, the warning and horror of a gaping crowd. This I could bear, nay wish not to avoid, had it but come from any hand but thine.—

(Enter BLUNT, Officer and Attendants)

MILLWOOD. Heaven defend me! Conceal a murderer! Here, sir, take this youth into your custody; I accuse him of murder and will appear to make good my charge.
(They seize him)

BARNWELL. To whom, of what, or how shall I complain? I'll not accuse her; the hand of heaven is in it, and this, the punishment of lust and parricide! Yet heaven, that justly cuts me off, still suffers her to live, perhaps to punish others. Tremendous mercy! So friends are cursed with immortality to be the executioners of heaven—

Be warned, ye youths, who see my sad despair,
Avoid lewd women, false as they are fair;
By reason guided, honest joys pursue;
The fair, to honor, and to virtue true,
Just to herself, will ne'er be false to you.
By my example learn to shun my fate,
(How wretched is the man who's wise too late!)
Ere innocence, and fame, and life be lost,
Here purchase wisdom cheaply, at my cost.
(Exeunt BARNWELL, manacled, Officer, and Attendants)

MILLWOOD. Where's Lucy? Why is she absent at such a time?

BLUNT. Would I had been so too, thou devil!

MILLWOOD. Insolent! This to me?

BLUNT. The worst that we know of the devil is, that he first seduces to sin, and then betrays to punishment. (Exit BLUNT)

MILLWOOD. They disapprove of my conduct, and mean to take this opportunity to set up for themselves. My ruin is resolved; I see my danger, but scorn both it and them. I was not born to fall by such weak instruments.

(*Enter* THOROWGOOD)

THOROWGOOD. Where is the scandal of her own sex, and curse of ours?

MILLWOOD. What means this insolence? Who do you seek?

THOROWGOOD. Millwood.

MILLWOOD. Well, you have found her then. I am Millwood.

THOROWGOOD. Then you are the most impious wretch that e'er the sun beheld.

MILLWOOD. From your appearance I should have expected wisdom and moderation, but your manners belie your aspect. What is your business here? I know you not.

THOROWGOOD. Hereafter you may know me better; I am Barnwell's master.

MILLWOOD. Then you are master to a villain, which, I think, is not much to your credit.

THOROWGOOD. Had he been as much above thy arts as my credit is superior to thy malice, I need not blush to own him.

MILLWOOD. My arts? I don't understand you, sir! If he has done amiss, what's that to me? Was he my servant, or yours? You should have taught him better.

THOROWGOOD. Why should I wonder to find such uncommon impudence in one arrived to such a height of wickedness! When innocence is banished, modesty soon follows. Know, sorceress, I'm not ignorant of any of your arts by which you first deceived the unwary youth. I know how, step by step, you've led him on, reluctant and unwilling, from crime to crime to this last horrid act which you contrived and by your cursed wiles even forced him to commit, and then betrayed him.

MILLWOOD. (*Aside*) Ha! Lucy has got the advantage of me, and accused me first; unless I can turn the accusation, and fix it upon her and Blunt, I am lost.

THOROWGOOD. Had I known your cruel design sooner, it had been prevented. To see you punished as the law directs, is all that now remains. Poor satisfaction, for he, innocent as he is compared to you, must suffer too. But heaven, who knows our frame, and graciously distinguishes between frailty and presumption, will make a difference, though man cannot, who sees not the heart, but only judges by the outward action.

MILLWOOD. I find, sir, we are both unhappy in our servants. I was surprised at such ill treatment from a gentleman of your appearance, without cause, and therefore too hastily returned it, for which I ask your pardon. I now perceive you have been so far imposed on, as to think me engaged in a former correspondence with your servant, and, some way or other, accessory to his undoing.

THOROWGOOD. I charge you as the cause, the sole cause of all his guilt, and all his suffering, of all he now endures, and must endure, till a violent and shameful death shall put a dreadful period to his life and miseries together.

MILLWOOD. 'Tis very strange; but who's secure from scandal and detraction? So far from contributing to his ruin, I never spoke to him till since that fatal accident, which I lament as much as you. 'Tis true, I have a servant, on whose account he has of late frequented my house; if she has abused my good opinion of her, am I to blame? Hasn't Barnwell done the same by you?

THOROWGOOD. I hear you; pray go on.

MILLWOOD. I have been informed he had a violent passion for her, and she for him; but I always thought it innocent; I know her poor and given to expensive pleasures. Now who can tell but she may have influenced the amorous youth to commit this murder, to supply her extravagancies? It must be so. I now recollect a thousand circumstances that confirm it. I'll have her and a man servant that I suspect as an accomplice, secured immediately. I hope, sir, you will lay aside your ill-grounded suspicions of me, and join to punish the real contrivers of this bloody deed.

(*Offers to go*)

THOROWGOOD. Madam, you pass not this way. I see your design, but shall protect them from your malice.

MILLWOOD. I hope you will not use your influence and the credit of your name to screen such guilty wretches. Consider, sir, the wickedness of persuading a thoughtless youth to such a crime.

THOROWGOOD. I do, and of betraying him when it was done.

MILLWOOD. That which you call betraying him, may convince you of my innocence. She who loves him, though she contrived the murder, would never have delivered him into the hands of justice, as I, struck with the horror of his crimes, have done.

THOROWGOOD. (*Aside*) How should an unexperienced youth escape her snares? The powerful magic of her wit and form might betray the wisest to simple dotage and fire the blood that age had froze long since. Even I, that with just prejudice came prepared, had, by her artful story, been deceived, but that my strong conviction of her guilt makes even a doubt impossible.—Those whom subtly you would accuse, you know are your accusers; and what proves unanswerably their innocence and your guilt—they accused you before the deed was done, and did all that was in their power to have prevented it.

MILLWOOD. Sir, you are very hard to be convinced; but I have such a proof, which, when produced, will silence all objections.

(*Exit*)

(*Enter* LUCY, TRUEMAN, BLUNT, *Officers, &c.*)

LUCY. Gentlemen, pray place yourselves, some on one side of that door, and some on the other; watch her entrance, and act as your prudence shall direct you.—This way—(*to* THOROWGOOD) and note her behavior; I have observed her, she's driven to the last extremity, and is forming some desperate resolution.—I guess at her design.—

(*Enter* MILLWOOD *with a pistol;* TRUEMAN *secures her*)

TRUEMAN. Here thy power of doing mischief ends, deceitful, cruel, bloody woman!

MILLWOOD. Fool, hypocrite, villain!—Man! thou can'st not call me that.

TRUEMAN. To call thee woman were to wrong the sex, thou devil!

MILLWOOD. That imaginary being is an emblem of thy cursed sex collected. A mirror, wherein each particular man may see his own likeness and that of all mankind!

TRUEMAN. Think not, by aggravating the fault of others, to extenuate thy own, of which the abuse of such uncommon perfections of mind and body is not the least.

MILLWOOD. If such I had, well may I curse your barbarous sex, who robbed me of 'em ere I knew their worth, then left me, too

late, to count their value by their loss! Another and another spoiler came, and all my gain was poverty and reproach. My soul disdained, and yet disdains, dependence and contempt. Riches, no matter by what means obtained, I saw, secured the worst of men from both; I found it therefore necessary to be rich; and, to that end, I summoned all my arts. You call 'em wicked; be it so, they were such as my conversation with your sex had furnished me withal.

THOROWGOOD. Sure none but the worst of men conversed with thee.

MILLWOOD. Men of all degrees and all professions I have known, yet found no difference, but in their several capacities; all were alike wicked to the utmost of their power. In pride, contention, avarice, cruelty, and revenge, the reverend priesthood were my unerring guides. From suburb-magistrates,[5] who live by ruined reputations, as the unhospitable natives of Cornwall do by shipwrecks, I learned that to charge my innocent neighbors with my crimes was to merit their protection; for to screen the guilty, is the less scandalous, when many are suspected, and detraction, like darkness and death, blackens all objects and levels all distinction. Such are your venal magistrates, who favor none but such as, by their office, they are sworn to punish. With them, not to be guilty is the worst of crimes; and large fees privately paid is every needful virtue.

THOROWGOOD. Your practice has sufficiently discovered your contempt of laws, both human and divine; no wonder then that you should hate the officers of both.

MILLWOOD. I hate you all, I know you, and expect no mercy; nay, I ask for none; I have done nothing that I am sorry for; I followed my inclinations, and that the best of you does every day. All actions are alike natural and indifferent to man and beast, who devour, or are devoured, as they meet with others weaker or stronger than themselves.

THOROWGOOD. What pity it is, a mind so comprehensive, daring and inquisitive, should be a stranger to religion's sweet, but powerful charms.

MILLWOOD. I am not fool enough to be an

[5] The notoriously corrupt magistrates in the disreputable suburban districts of London.

atheist, though I have known enough of men's hypocrisy to make a thousand simple women so. Whatever religion is in itself, as practised by mankind, it has caused the evils you say it was designed to cure. War, plague, and famine have not destroyed so many of the human race, as this pretended piety has done, and with such barbarous cruelty, as if the only way to honor heaven were to turn the present world into hell.

THOROWGOOD. Truth is truth, though from an enemy and spoke in malice. You bloody, blind, and superstitious bigots, how will you answer this?

MILLWOOD. What are your laws, of which you make your boast, but the fool's wisdom and the coward's valor; the instrument and screen of all your villainies, by which you punish in others what you act yourselves, or would have acted, had you been in their circumstances? The judge who condemns the poor man for being a thief had been a thief himself had he been poor. Thus you go on deceiving and being deceived, harassing, plaguing, and destroying one another; but women are your universal prey.

Women, by whom you are, the source of joy,
With cruel arts you labor to destroy.
A thousand ways our ruin you pursue,
Yet blame in us those arts, first taught by you.
O may, from hence, each violated maid,
By flattering, faithless, barb'rous man betrayed;
When robbed of innocence and virgin fame
From your destruction raise a nobler name;
To right their sex's wrongs devote their mind,
And future Millwoods prove to plague mankind.

Act V

SCENE I. *A Room in a Prison.*

(*Enter* THOROWGOOD, BLUNT *and* LUCY)

THOROWGOOD. I have recommended to Barnwell a reverend divine whose judgment and integrity I am well acquainted with; nor has Millwood been neglected, but she, unhappy woman, still obstinate, refuses his assistance.

LUCY. This pious charity to the afflicted well becomes your character; yet pardon me, sir, if I wonder you were not at their trial.

THOROWGOOD. I knew it was impossible to save him, and I and my family bear so great a part in his distress, that to have been present would have aggravated our sorrows without relieving his.

BLUNT. It was mournful, indeed. Barnwell's youth and modest deportment as he passed drew tears from every eye. When placed at the bar and arraigned before the reverend judges, with many tears and interrupting sobs he confessed and aggravated his offences, without accusing, or once reflecting on, Millwood, the shameless author of his ruin, who, dauntless and unconcerned, stood by his side, viewing with visible pride and contempt the vast assembly, who all with sympathizing sorrow wept for the wretched youth. Millwood, when called upon to answer, loudly insisted upon her innocence, and made an artful and a bold defence; but finding all in vain, the impartial jury and the learned bench concurring to find her guilty, how did she curse herself, poor Barnwell, us, her judges, all mankind; but what could that avail? She was condemned, and is this day to suffer with him.

THOROWGOOD. The time draws on; I am going to visit Barnwell, as you are Millwood.

LUCY. We have not wronged her, yet I dread this interview. She's proud, impatient, wrathful, and unforgiving. To be the branded instruments of vengeance, to suffer in her shame, and sympathize with her in all she suffers, is the tribute we must pay for our former ill-spent lives and long confederacy with her in wickedness.

THOROWGOOD. Happy for you it ended when it did. What you have done against Millwood, I know, proceeded from a just abhorrence of her crimes, free from interest, malice, or revenge. Proselytes to virtue should be encouraged. Pursue your proposed reformation, and know me hereafter for your friend.

LUCY. This is a blessing as unhoped for as unmerited, but heaven, that snatched us from impending ruin, sure intends you as its instrument to secure us from apostasy.

THOROWGOOD. With gratitude to impute your deliverance to heaven is just. Many, less virtuously disposed than Barnwell was, have never fallen in the manner he has done,—may not such owe their safety rather to Providence than to themselves? With pity and compassion let us judge him. Great were his faults, but strong was the temptation. Let his ruin learn us diffidence, humanity and circumspection; for we, who wonder at his fate, perhaps had we like him, been tried,—like him, we had fallen, too.

SCENE II. *A Dungeon with a Table and Lamp.*

(BARNWELL *is reading by the table.*
Enter THOROWGOOD)

THOROWGOOD. See there the bitter fruits of passion's detested reign and sensual appetite indulged. Severe reflections, penitence, and tears!

BARNWELL. (*Rising*) My honored, injured master, whose goodness has covered me a thousand times with shame, forgive this last unwilling disrespect,—indeed I saw you not.

THOROWGOOD. 'Tis well. I hope you were better employed in viewing of yourself; your journey's long, your time for preparation almost spent. I sent a reverend divine to teach you to improve it and should be glad to hear of his success.

BARNWELL. The word of truth, which he recommended for my constant companion in this my sad retirement, has at length removed the doubts I labored under. From thence I've learned the infinite extent of heavenly mercy; that my offences, though great, are not unpardonable; and that 'tis not my interest only, but my duty, to believe and to rejoice in that hope. So shall heaven receive the glory, and future penitents the profit of my example.

THOROWGOOD. Go on. How happy am I who live to see this!

BARNWELL. 'Tis wonderful that words should charm despair, speak peace and pardon to a murderer's conscience; but truth and mercy flow in every sentence, attended with force and energy divine. How shall I describe my present state of mind? I hope in doubt, and trembling I rejoice. I feel my grief increase, even as my fears give way. Joy and gratitude now supply more tears than the horror and anguish of despair before.

THOROWGOOD. These are the genuine signs of true repentance, the only preparatory, certain way to everlasting peace. O the joy it gives to see a soul formed and prepared for heaven! For this the faithful minister devotes himself to meditation, abstinence, and prayer, shunning the vain delights of sensual joys, and daily dies that others may live forever. For this he turns the sacred volumes o'er, and spends his life in painful search of truth. The love of riches and the lust of power, he looks on with just contempt and detestation; who only counts for wealth the souls he wins, and whose highest ambition is to serve mankind. If the reward of all his pains be to preserve one soul from wandering or turn one from the error of his ways, how does he then rejoice and own his little labors over-paid!

BARNWELL. What do I owe for all your generous kindness! But though I cannot, heaven can, and will, reward you.

THOROWGOOD. To see thee thus is joy too great for words. Farewell! Heaven strengthen thee! Farewell!

BARNWELL. Oh, sir, there's something I could say, if my sad swelling heart would give me leave.

THOROWGOOD. Give it vent a while and try.

BARNWELL. I had a friend ('tis true I am unworthy) yet methinks your generous example might persuade—could I not see him once before I go from whence there's no return?

THOROWGOOD. He's coming, and as much thy friend as ever; but I'll not anticipate his sorrow. (*Aside*) Too soon he'll see the sad effect of his contagious ruin. This torrent of domestic misery bears too hard upon me; I must retire to indulge a weakness I find impossible to overcome.—Much loved—and much lamented youth,—farewell! Heaven strengthen thee! Eternally farewell!

BARNWELL. The best of masters and of men, farewell—While I live, let me not want your prayers!

THOROWGOOD. Thou shalt not;—thy peace being made with Heaven, death's already vanquished; bear a little longer the pains that attend this transitory life, and cease from pain forever. (*Exit*)

BARNWELL. I find a power within that bears my soul above the fears of death, and, spite of conscious shame and guilt, gives me a taste of pleasure more than mortal.

(*Enter* TRUEMAN *and* KEEPER)

KEEPER. Sir, there's the prisoner. (*Exit*)

BARNWELL. Trueman!—my friend, whom I so wished to see, yet now he's here I dare not look upon him. (*Weeps*)

TRUEMAN. O Barnwell! Barnwell!

BARNWELL. Mercy! Mercy! Gracious Heaven! for death, but not for this, was I prepared!

TRUEMAN. What have I suffered since I saw you last!—What pain has absence given me! But oh! to see thee thus!

BARNWELL. I know it is dreadful! I feel the anguish of thy generous soul,—but I was born to murder all who love me.

(*Both weep*)

TRUEMAN. I came not to reproach you;—I thought to bring you comfort,—but I'm deceived, for I have none to give;—I came to share thy sorrow, but cannot bear my own.

BARNWELL. My sense of guilt, indeed, you cannot know; 'tis what the good and innocent like you can ne'er conceive; but other griefs at present I have none but what I feel for you. In your sorrow I read you love me still, but yet methinks 'tis strange, when I consider what I am.

TRUEMAN. No more of that. I can re-member nothing but thy virtue, thy honest, tender friendship, our former happy state and present misery. O had you trusted me when first the fair seducer tempted you, all might have been prevented!

BARNWELL. Alas, thou know'st not what a wretch I've been! Breach of friendship was my first and least offence. So far was I lost to goodness,—so devoted to the author of my ruin,—that had she insisted on my murdering thee,—I think I should have done it.

TRUEMAN. Prithee, aggravate thy faults no more.

BARNWELL. I think I should! Thus good and generous as you are, I should have murdered you!

TRUEMAN. We have not yet embraced, and may be interrupted. Come to my arms.

BARNWELL. Never, never will I taste such joys on earth; never will I so soothe my just remorse. Are those honest arms and faithful bosom fit to embrace and to support a murderer? These iron fetters only shall clasp and flinty pavement bear me. (*Throwing himself on the ground*) Even these too good for such a bloody monster!

TRUEMAN. Shall fortune sever those whom friendship joined! Thy miseries cannot lay thee so low, but love will find thee. (*Lies down by him*) Upon this rugged couch then let us lie, for well it suits our most deplorable condition. Here will we offer to stern calamity, this earth the altar, and ourselves the sacrifice. Our mutual groans shall echo to each other through the dreary vault. Our sighs shall number the moments as they pass, and mingling tears communicate such anguish as words were never made to express.

BARNWELL. Then be it so. Since you propose an intercourse of woe, pour all your griefs into my breast,—and in exchange take mine. (*Embracing*) Where's now the anguish that you promised? You've taken mine, and make me no return.—Sure peace and comfort dwell within these arms, and sorrow can't approach me while I'm here! This, too, is the work of Heaven, who, having before spoke peace and pardon to me, now sends thee to confirm it. O take, take some of the joy that overflows my breast!

TRUEMAN. I do, I do. Almighty Power,

how have you made us capable to bear, at once, the extremes of pleasure and pain?

(*Enter* KEEPER)

KEEPER. Sir.

TRUEMAN. I come.   (Exit KEEPER)

BARNWELL. Must you leave me? Death would soon have parted us forever.

TRUEMAN. O, my Barnwell, there's yet another task behind. –Again your heart must bleed for others' woes.

BARNWELL. To meet and part with you, I thought was all I had to do on earth! What is there more for me to do or suffer?

TRUEMAN. I dread to tell thee, yet it must be known.—Maria—

BARNWELL. Our master's fair and virtuous daughter!

TRUEMAN. The same.

BARNWELL. No misfortune, I hope, has reached that lovely maid! Preserve her, Heaven, from every ill, to show mankind that goodness is your care.

TRUEMAN. Thy, thy misfortunes, my unhappy friend, have reached her. Whatever you and I have felt, and more, if more be possible, she feels for you.

BARNWELL. (*Aside*) I know he doth abhor a lie, and would not trifle with his dying friend.—This is, indeed, the bitterness of death!

TRUEMAN. You must remember, for we all observed it, for some time past, a heavy melancholy weighed her down. Disconsolate she seemed, and pined and languished from a cause unknown; till hearing of your dreadful fate, the long stifled flame blazed out. She wept, she wrung her hands, and tore her hair, and in the transport of her grief discovered her own lost state, whilst she lamented yours.

BARNWELL. Will all the pain I feel restore thy ease, lovely unhappy maid? (*Weeping*) Why didn't you let me die and never know it?

TRUEMAN. It was impossible; she makes no secret of her passion for you, and is determined to see you ere you die. She waits for me to introduce her.   (*Exit*)

BARNWELL. Vain busy thoughts be still! What avails it to think on what I might have been. I now am what I've made myself.

(*Enter* TRUEMAN *and* MARIA)

TRUEMAN. Madam, reluctant I lead you to this dismal scene. This is the seat of misery and guilt. Here awful justice reserves her public victims. This is the entrance to shameful death.

MARIA. To this sad place, then, no improper guest, the abandoned, lost Maria brings despair; and see! the subject and the cause of all this world of woe! Silent and motionless he stands, as if his soul had quitted her abode, and the lifeless form alone was left behind; yet that so perfect, that beauty and death, ever at enmity, now seem united there.

BARNWELL. I groan, but murmur not. Just Heaven, I am your own; do with me what you please.

MARIA. Why are your streaming eyes still fixed below as though thou'dst give the greedy earth thy sorrows, and rob me of my due? Were happiness within your power, you should bestow it where you pleased; but in your misery I must and will partake.

BARNWELL. Oh! say not so, but fly, abhor, and leave me to my fate. Consider what you are! How vast your fortune, and how bright your fame! Have pity on your youth, your beauty, and unequalled virtue, for which so many noble peers have sighed in vain. Bless with your charms some honorable lord. Adorn with your beauty, and, by your example, improve the English court, that justly claims such merit; so shall I quickly be to you as though I had never been.

MARIA. When I forget you, I must be so, indeed. Reason, choice, virtue, all forbid it. Let women like Millwood, if there be more such women, smile in prosperity and in adversity forsake. Be it the pride of virtue to repair or to partake the ruin such have made.

TRUEMAN. Lovely, ill-fated maid! Was there ever such generous distress before? How must this pierce his grateful heart and aggravate his woes!

BARNWELL. Ere I knew guilt or shame, when fortune smiled, and when my youthful hopes were at the highest; if then to have raised my thoughts to you had been presumption in me, never to have been pardoned, think how much beneath yourself you condescend to regard me now.

MARIA. Let her blush, who, professing love, invades the freedom of your sex's choice and meanly sues in hopes of a return. Your inevitable fate hath rendered hope impossible as vain. Then why should I fear to avow a passion so just and so disinterested?

TRUEMAN. If any should take occasion from Millwood's crimes to libel the best and fairest part of the creation, here let them see their error. The most distant hopes of such a tender passion from so bright a maid might add to the happiness of the most happy and make the greatest proud. Yet here 'tis lavished in vain. Though by the rich present the generous donor is undone, he on whom it is bestowed receives no benefit.

BARNWELL. So the aromatic spices of the East, which all the living covet and esteem, are with unavailing kindness wasted on the dead.

MARIA. Yes, fruitless is my love, and unavailing all my sighs and tears. Can they save thee from approaching death, from such a death? O terrible idea! What is her misery and distress, who sees the first last object of her love, for whom alone she'd live, for whom she'd die a thousand, thousand deaths if it were possible, expiring in her arms? Yet she is happy, when compared to me. Were millions of worlds mine, I'd gladly give them in exchange for her condition. The most consummate woe is light to mine. The last of curses to other miserable maids, is all I ask; and that's denied me.

TRUEMAN. Time and reflection cure all ills.

MARIA. All but this; his dreadful catastrophe virtue herself abhors. To give a holiday to suburb slaves; and, passing, entertain the savage herd who, elbowing each other for a sight, pursue and press upon him like his fate. A mind with piety and resolution armed may smile on death. But public ignominy! everlasting shame! shame the death of souls! to die a thousand times and yet survive even death itself, in never-dying infamy,—is this to be endured? Can I, who live in him, and must each hour of my devoted life feel all these woes renewed, can I endure this!—

TRUEMAN. Grief has impaired her spirits; she pants, as in the agonies of death.

BARNWELL. Preserve her, Heaven, and restore her peace,—nor let her death be added to my crime.—(*Bell tolls*) I am summoned to my fate.

(*Enter* KEEPER)

KEEPER. The officers attend you, sir. Mrs. Millwood is already summoned.

BARNWELL. Tell 'em I'm ready. And now, my friend, farewell. (*Embracing*) Support and comfort the best you can this mourning fair. No more. Forget not to pray for me. (*Turning to* MARIA) Would you, bright excellence, permit me the honor of a chaste embrace, the last happiness this world could give were mine. (*She inclines towards him; they embrace*) Exalted goodness! O turn your eyes from earth and me to heaven, where virtue like yours is ever heard. Pray for the peace of my departing soul.—Early my race of wickedness began, and soon has reached the summit, ere nature has finished her work, and stamped me man. Just at the time that others begin to stray, my course is finished! Though short my span of life, and few my days, yet count my crimes for years, and I have lived whole ages. Justice and mercy are in heaven the same. Its utmost severity is mercy to the whole, thereby to cure man's folly and presumption, which else would render even infinite mercy vain and ineffectual. Thus justice in compassion to mankind cuts off a wretch like me,—by one such example to secure thousands from future ruin. (*Turning to audience*)

If any youth, like you, in future times,
Shall mourn my fate, though he abhor my
   crimes;
Or tender maid, like you, my tale shall hear,
And to my sorrows give a pitying tear:
To each such melting eye, and throbbing
   heart,
Would gracious heaven this benefit impart,
Never to know my guilt, nor feel my pain; ⎤
Then must you own, you ought not to ⎟
   complain; ⎬
Since you nor weep, nor shall I die, in ⎟
   vain. ⎦
        (*Exeunt* KEEPER *and* BARNWELL)

(*Enter* TRUEMAN, BLUNT, *and* LUCY)

Lucy. Heart-breaking sight! O wretched, wretched Millwood!

Trueman. You came from her then—how is she disposed to meet her Fate?

Blunt. Who can describe unalterable woe?

Lucy. She goes to death encompassed with horror, loathing life, and yet afraid to die; no tongue can tell her anguish and despair.

Trueman. Heaven be better to her than her fears; may she prove a warning to others, a monument of mercy in herself.

Lucy. O sorrow insupportable! Break, break, my heart!

Trueman. In vain

With bleeding hearts and weeping eyes we show
A human gen'rous sense of others' woe;
Unless we mark what drew their ruin on,
And by avoiding that, prevent our own.[6]

Epilogue

Spoken by Maria

Since Fate has robbed me of the hopeless youth,
For whom my heart had hoarded up its truth;
By all the laws of love and honor, now,
I'm free again to choose,—and one of you.

But soft! With caution first I'll round me peep;
Maids, in my case, should look before they leap:
Here's choice enough, of various sorts, and hue,
The cit, the wit, the rake cocked up in cue,[7]
The fair spruce mercer, and the tawny[8] Jew.

Suppose I search the sober gallery. No,
There's none but prentices,—and cuckolds all a row;
And these, I doubt, are those that make 'em so.[9]

(*Points to the boxes*)

'Tis very well, enjoy the jest. But you,
Fine powdered sparks, nay, I'm told 'tis true,
Your happy spouses—can make cuckolds too.
'Twixt you and them, the diff'rence this perhaps,
The cit's ashamed whene'er his duck he traps;
But you, when madam's tripping, let her fall,
Cock up your hats, and take no shame at all.

What if some savored poet I could meet?
Whose love would lay his laurels at my feet?
No,—painted passion real love abhors,—
His flame would prove the suit of creditors.

Not to detain you then with longer pause,
In short; my heart to this conclusion draws,
I yield it to the hand, that's loudest in applause.

---

[6] This is the last scene of the play as originally produced. Certain later editions contain a scene at the place of execution.

[7] With hat tipped over the queue of his wig.

[8] Yellow, the color of the head dress which Jews had been compelled to wear.

[9] The boxes were generally occupied by courtiers.

RICHARD CUMBERLAND

The West Indian

~~~~~~~~~~~~~~~

PRINCIPAL EVENTS IN CUMBERLAND'S LIFE

1732, 19 Feb., Born in the Master's Lodge of Trinity College, Cambridge. The Master, the famous classical scholar Richard Bentley, was his grandfather.

1744, Entered Westminster school, London.

1745, Entered Trinity College, Cambridge.

1751, Made a Fellow of Trinity College.

1751, Made private secretary to the Earl of Halifax, First Lord of Trade and Plantations in the cabinet.

1759, Married his cousin, Elizabeth Ridge.

1761, Accompanied Halifax to Ireland as Ulster Secretary.

1762, Made Clerk of Reports at the Board of Trade.

1765, 6 Dec., The Summer's Tale, a musical comedy, acted at Covent Garden Theatre.

1769, 2 Dec., The Brothers, a comedy, acted at Covent Garden Theatre.

1771, 19 Jan., The West Indian acted at Drury Lane Theatre with great success.

1771, 4 Dec., Timon of Athens, an alteration of Shakespeare's play, acted at Drury Lane.

1772, 20 Jan., The Fashionable Lovers acted at Drury Lane.

1774, 9 Feb., The Note of Hand, or A Trip to Newmarket acted at Drury Lane.

1775-1782, Secretary to the Board of Trade and Plantations.

1780, Sent to Spain to negotiate peace treaty.

1783, 28 Jan., The Mysterious Husband acted at Covent Garden.

1789, 26 Jan., The Impostors acted at Drury Lane.

1794, 8 May, The Jew acted at Drury Lane.

1795, 28 Feb., The Wheel of Fortune acted at Drury Lane.

1811, 7 May, Died in London and was buried in Westminster Abbey.

In addition to writing about fifty-four plays, Cumberland turned out essays, poems, art books, stories, two novels, and memoirs and edited a critical journal.

INTRODUCTION

Cumberland's *West Indian* is one of the least offensive, as it was one of the most popular, sentimental comedies of the eighteenth century. This regrettable form of comedy became the most popular type on the stage from about the first decade of the eighteenth century until past the end—a type of play whose chief comic attributes were the happy ending and the triumph of virtue, but whose most admired and most carefully developed traits were the presentation of virtue in distress with many, many tears, the iteration and reiteration of elementary moral maxims about benevolence and virtue and pity, and the arrangement of spectacles of repentance and forgiveness as crises of tearful ecstasy.

The sentimentality of Cumberland's comedy is apparent enough in the distressed Louisa Dudley, the penitently reformed rake Belcour, redeemed by his soft heart and easy generosity, the villainous Fulmers and Lady Rusport, soundly punished by means of the lucky chances which always work for the virtuous. It is apparent in the barely relevant preaching of Louisa Dudley on virtue (V, 2) and of Captain Dudley on morality (II, 1). This latter speech very aptly expresses a central tenet of the sentimentalists. In commenting on a novelist, Captain Dudley says;

I hold him to be a moralist in the noblest sense; he plays indeed with the fancy, and sometimes perhaps too wantonly, but while he thus designedly masks his main attack, he comes at once upon the heart, refines, amends it, softens it, beats down each selfish barrier from about it, and opens every sluice of pity and benevolence.

The writers of sentimental comedy all tried to open "every sluice of pity and benevolence," and this sluicing is generally more disgusting than affecting for modern theatregoers.

Yet these excessively sentimental elements do not make *The West Indian* quite the mawkish moral tract which so many eighteenth-century sentimental comedies are. The sentimentality of the play is more pervasively but less offensively seen in the underlying assumptions that a good heart will redeem irresponsible impetuosity like Belcour's or fatuous incompetence like Major O'Flaherty's; that the virtuous poor need only hold to the path of rectitude to come into a fortune, as the Dudleys do.

Cumberland's comedy has, moreover, virtues which helped to keep it a favorite in the theatre for two generations. Belcour's impetuosity is made both amusing and attractive, even though it is so improbably rewarded. Charlotte Rusport has an effective coquettishness adroitly woven into her part which makes her more amusing though less exemplary than most of the sentimental heroines. Major O'Flaherty is a most effective stage Irishman, who furnished an excellent model for Sheridan's famous Sir Lucius O'Trigger of *The Rivals*, presented at the same theatre three years later. Several scenes, like Mrs. Fulmer's ensnaring of Belcour, or Major O'Flaherty's scene with Lady Rusport, or the cross-purposes scenes with Charlotte, Belcour, and Louisa, are very nicely written to point up the comic values without the overwriting so common in plays of the time. The interweaving of the threads of the plotting is seldom so violently abrupt or unconvincing as in most eighteenth-century comedies, and sometimes, as in the arrangements for the Dudley-Belcour duel and its adjustment, it is very neatly handled. The contemporary popularity of the play is more understandable now than that of many others of the time. One contemporary said, "Its success exceeded that of any comedy within the memory of the oldest man living."

The West Indian is by no means one of the great English comedies, but considering the time and the comic type from which it derives, it exhibits its essential characteristics with less crudeness, obviousness, and mawkishness than one could expect.

THE WEST INDIAN

Dramatis personae

In order of first appearance

STUKELY, Mr. Stockwell's trusted chief clerk.
STOCKWELL, An honest and successful business man and Member of Parliament, kindly and sentimental.
SAILOR

BELCOUR, The West Indian, a rich young planter of Jamaica, handsome, highly impetuous, and generous.
LADY RUSPORT, A selfish, vain, and stupid woman, the puritan widow of the recently

deceased Sir Stephen Rusport, Lord Mayor of London, and heiress of her father's large fortune.

CHARLOTTE RUSPORT, Daughter of Sir Stephen and therefore step-daughter to Lady Rusport, within a few months of coming of age and the inheritance of £40,000 from her father's estate. A girl of independent mind and pleasing person, in love with Charles Dudley.

CHARLES DUDLEY, Nephew of Lady Rusport and rightful heir to the estate of Sir Oliver Roundhead, his grandfather. He is an ensign in the army, a proper and sincere young man, acutely aware of his poverty.

MAJOR DENNIS O'FLAHERTY, A retired Irish officer, ebullient, friendly, and generous.

MR. FULMER, A petty criminal, posing as a bookseller.

MRS. MARTHA FULMER, His common-law wife and accomplice.

CAPTAIN DUDLEY, A very poor retired army officer, brother-in-law to Lady Rusport. He is kindly and honest but depressed by his poverty.

LOUISA DUDLEY, His daughter, beautiful and modest.

LUCY, Lady Rusport's maid.

VARLAND, Sir Oliver Roundhead's solicitor.

Clerks in Stockwell's counting house, English and West Indian servants, housekeeper, constable, sailors.

SCENE: *London*

Prologue

Critics, hark forward! noble game and new;
A fine West Indian started full in view:
Hot as the soil, the clime, which gave him birth,
You'll run him on a burning scent to earth;
Yet don't devour him in his hiding place;
Bag him, he'll serve you for another chase;
For sure that country has no feeble claim,
Which swells your commerce, and supports your fame.
And in this humble sketch, we hope you'll find,
Some emanations of a noble mind;
Some little touches, which, tho' void of art,
May find perhaps their way into the heart.
Another hero your excuse implores,
Sent by your sister kingdom to your shores;
Doomed by Religion's too severe command,
To fight for bread against his native land:
A brave, unthinking, animated rogue,
With here and there a touch upon the brogue;
Laugh, but despise him not, for on his lip
His errors lie; his heart can never trip.
Others there are—but may we not prevail
To let the gentry tell their own plain tale?
Shall they come in? They'll please you, if they can;

If not, condemn the bard—but spare the Man.
For speak, think, act, or write in angry times,
A wish to please is made the worst of crimes;
Dire slander now with black envenomed dart,
Stands ever armed to stab you to the heart.
  Rouse, Britons, rouse, for honor of your isle,
Your old good humor; and be seen to smile.
You say we write not like our fathers—true,
Nor were our fathers half so strict as you,
Damned not each error of the poet's pen,
But judging man, remembered they were men.
Awed into silence by the times' abuse,
Sleeps many a wise, and many a witty muse;
We that for mere experiment come out,
Are but the light armed rangers on the scout:
High on Parnassus' lofty summit stands
The immortal camp; there lie the chosen bands!
But give fair quarter to us puny elves,
The giants then will sally forth themselves;
With wit's sharp weapons vindicate the age,
And drive even *Arthur's* magic from the Stage.

Act I

Scene I. *A Merchant's Counting House.*

(*In an inner room, set off by glass doors, several clerks are to be seen busy at their desks. At a writing table in the front room, STOCKWELL is reading a letter; STUKELY comes quietly out of the back room and observes him some time before he speaks*)

STUKELY. He seems disordered; something in that letter, and I'm afraid of an unpleasant sort. He has many ventures of great account at sea: a ship richly freighted for Barcelona; another for Lisbon; and others expected from Cadiz of still greater value. Besides these, I know he has many deep concerns in foreign bottoms, and underwritings to a vast amount. I'll accost him. Sir! Mr. Stockwell!

STOCK. (*Starts*) Stukely!—Well, have you shipped the cloths?

STUKELY. I have, sir. Here's the bill of lading, and copy of the invoice; the assortments are all compared. Mr. Traffick will give you the policy upon 'Change.

STOCK. 'Tis very well. Lay these papers by, and no more of business for a while. Shut the door, Stukely. (*STUKELY closes the door to the inner room and comes forward. There is a moment's silence*) I have had long proof of your friendship and fidelity to me; a matter of most intimate concern lies on my mind, and 'twill be a sensible relief to unbosom myself to you. I have just now been informed of the arrival of the young West Indian I have so long been expecting; you know who I mean.

STUKELY. Yes, sir; Mr. Belcour, the young gentleman who inherited old Belcour's great estates in Jamaica.

STOCK. Hush, not so loud; come a little nearer this way.—This Belcour is now in London; part of his baggage is already arrived, and I expect him every minute. Is it to be wondered at if his coming throws me into some agitation, when I tell you, Stukely, he is my son?

STUKELY. Your son!

STOCK. Yes, sir, my only son. Early in life

I accompanied his grandfather to Jamaica as his clerk; he had an only daughter, somewhat older than myself, the mother of this gentleman. It was my chance (call it good or ill) to engage her affections, and, as the inferiority of my condition made it hopeless to expect her father's consent, her fondness provided an expedient, and we were privately married; the issue of that concealed engagement is, as I have told you, this Belcour.

STUKELY. That event, surely, discovered your connexion.

STOCK. You shall hear. Not many days after our marriage old Belcour set out for England; and, during his abode here, my wife was with great secrecy delivered of this son. Fruitful in expedients to disguise her situation without parting from her infant, she contrived to have it laid and received at her door as a foundling. After some time her father returned, having left me here; in one of those favorable moments that decide the fortunes of prosperous men, this child was introduced; from that instant, he treated him as his own, gave him his name, and brought him up in his family.

STUKELY. And did you never reveal this secret, either to old Belcour or your son?

STOCK. Never.

STUKELY. Therein you surprise me. A merchant of your eminence, and a member of the British parliament, might surely aspire without offence to the daughter of a planter. In this case too, natural affection would prompt to a discovery.

STOCK. Your remark is obvious; nor could I have persisted in this painful silence, but in obedience to the dying injunctions of a beloved wife. The letter you found me reading conveyed those injunctions to me; it was dictated in her last illness, and almost in the article of death (you'll spare me the recital of it). She there conjures me, in terms as solemn as they are affecting, never to reveal the secret of our marriage, or withdraw my son, while her father survived.

STUKELY. But on what motives did your unhappy lady found these injunctions?

STOCK. Principally, I believe, from apprehension on my account, lest old Belcour, on whom at her decease I wholly depended, should withdraw his protection; in part from consideration of his repose, as well knowing the discovery would deeply affect his spirit, which was haughty, vehement, and unforgiving; and lastly, in regard to the interest of her infant, whom he had warmly adopted, and for whom, in case of a discovery, every thing was to be dreaded from his resentment. And, indeed, though the alteration in my condition might have justified me in discovering myself, yet I always thought my son safer in trusting to the caprice than to the justice of his grandfather. My judgment has not suffered by the event; old Belcour is dead, and has bequeathed his whole estate to him we are speaking of.

STUKELY. Now then you are no longer bound to secrecy.

STOCK. True. But before I publicly reveal myself, I could wish to make some experiment of my son's disposition. This can only be done by letting his spirit take its course without restraint; by these means, I think I shall discover much more of his real character under the title of his merchant than I should under that of his father.

(A SAILOR *enters, ushering in several* black SERVANTS, *carrying portmanteaus, trunks, etc.*)

SAILOR. Save your honor! Is your name Stockwell, pray?

STOCK. It is.

SAILOR. Part of my master Belcour's baggage an't please you; there's another cargo not far a-stern of us; and the cock-swain has got charge of the dumb creatures.

STOCK. Pr'ythee, friend, what dumb creatures do you speak of? Has Mr. Belcour brought over a collection of wild beasts?

SAILOR. No, Lord love him; no, not he. Let me see; there's two green monkeys, a pair of grey parrots, a Jamaica sow and pigs, and a Mangrove dog; that's all.

STOCK. Is that all?

SAILOR. Yes, your honor; yes, that's all. Bless his heart, a'might have brought over the whole island if he would; a didn't leave a dry eye in it.

STOCK. Indeed! Stukely, show 'em where to bestow their baggage. (*To* SAILOR) Follow that gentleman.

SAILOR. Come, bear a hand, my lads, bear a hand. (*Exit with* STUKELY *and* SERVANTS)

STOCK. If the principle tallies with his purveyors, he must be a singular spectacle in this place. He has a friend, however, in this sea-faring fellow; 'tis no bad prognostic of a man's heart when his ship-mates give him a good word. (*Exit*)

SCENE II. *The Drawing Room in* STOCKWELL's *House, Furnished with Substantial Elegance.*

(A SERVANT *in handsome livery is arranging the draperies, pulling forward chairs, adjusting the fire-screen, etc., when the* HOUSEKEEPER, *a dignified and now somewhat indignant matron, enters*)

HOUSEK. Why, what a fuss does our good master put himself in about this West Indian! See what a bill of fare I've been forced to draw out. Seven and nine I'll assure you, and only a family dinner as he calls it. Why if my Lord Mayor was expected, there couldn't be a greater to-do about him.

SERV. I wish to my heart you had but seen the loads of trunks, boxes, and portmanteaus he has sent hither. An ambassador's baggage, with all the smuggled goods of his family, does not exceed it.

HOUSEK. A fine pickle he'll put the house into. Had he been master's own son, and a Christian Englishman, there could not be more rout than there is about this Creolian, as they call 'em.

SERV. No matter for that; he's very rich, and that's sufficient. They say he has rum and sugar enough belonging to him to make all the water in the Thames into punch. But I see my master's coming. (*Exeunt*)

(STOCKWELL *enters with a letter in his hand, followed by a* SERVANT)

STOCK. Where is Mr. Belcour? Who brought this note from him?

SERV. A waiter from the London Tavern, sir; he says the young gentleman is just dressed and will be with you directly.

STOCK. Show him in when he arrives.

SERV. I shall, sir. (*Aside*) I'll have a peep at him first, however; I've a great mind to see this outlandish spark. The sailor fellow says he'll make rare doings amongst us.

STOCK. (*Looks up from his letter*) You need not wait; leave me. (*Exit* SERVANT) Let me see (*reads*).

"SIR,

I write to you under the hands of the hairdresser; as soon as I have made myself decent and slipped on some fresh clothes, I will have the honor of paying you my devoirs.

Yours,

BELCOUR."

He writes at his ease, for he's unconscious to whom his letter is addressed; but what a palpitation does it throw my heart into—a father's heart! 'Tis an affecting interview! When my eyes meet a son whom yet they never saw, where shall I find constancy to support it? Should he resemble his mother, I am overthrown. All the letters I have had from him (for I industriously drew him into a correspondence with me) bespeak him of quick and ready understanding. All the reports I ever received give me favorable impressions of his character, wild, perhaps, as the manner of his country is, but, I trust, not frantic or unprincipled.

(SERVANT *enters*)

SERV. Sir, the foreign gentleman is come.

(*Another* SERVANT)

SERV. Mr. Belcour.

(BELCOUR *enters*)

STOCK. Mr. Belcour, I'm rejoiced to see you; you're welcome to England.
(*Exeunt* SERVANTS)

BEL. I thank you heartily, good Mr. Stock-well. You and I have long conversed at a distance; now we are met, and the pleasure this meeting gives me amply compensates for the perils I have run through in accomplishing it.

STOCK. What perils, Mr. Belcour? I could not have thought you would have made a bad passage at this time o'year.

BEL. Nor did we. Courier like, we came posting to your shores upon the pinions of the swiftest gales that ever blew. 'Tis upon English ground all my difficulties have arisen; 'tis the passage from the river-side I complain of.

STOCK. Ay, indeed! What obstructions can you have met between this and the river-side?

BEL. Innumerable! Your town's as full of defiles as the Island of Corsica; and I believe they are as obstinately defended. So much hurry, bustle, and confusion on your quays; so many sugar-casks, porter-butts, and common council-men in your streets, that, unless a man marched with artillery in his front, 'tis more than the labor of a Hercules can effect to make any tolerable way through your town.

STOCK. I am sorry you have been so incommoded.

BEL. Why, faith, 'twas all my own fault. Accustomed to a land of slaves, and out of patience with the whole tribe of custom-house extortioners, boatmen, tide-waiters, and water-bailiffs that beset me on all sides, worse than a swarm of mosquitos, I proceeded a little too roughly to brush them away with my rattan; the sturdy rogues took this in dudgeon, and beginning to rebel, the mob chose different sides, and a furious scuffle ensued, in the course of which my person and apparel suffered so much that I was obliged to step into the first tavern to refit, before I could make my approaches in any decent trim.

STOCK. (*Aside*) All without is as I wish; dear Nature add the rest, and I am happy.— Well, Mr. Belcour, 'tis a rough sample you have had of my countrymen's spirit, but I trust you'll not think the worse of them for it.

BEL. Not at all, not at all; I like 'em the better. Was I only a visitor, I might, perhaps, wish them a little more tractable; but as a fellow subject and a sharer in their freedom,

I applaud their spirit, though I feel the effects of it in every bone of my skin.

STOCK. (*Aside*) That's well; I like that well. How gladly I could fall upon his neck, and own myself his father!

BEL. Well, Mr. Stockwell, for the first time in my life here am I in England; at the fountain-head of pleasure, in the land of beauty, of arts, and elegancies. My happy stars have given me a good estate, and the conspiring winds have blown me hither to spend it.

STOCK. To use it, not to waste it, I should hope; to treat it, Mr. Belcour, not as a vassal, over whom you have a wanton and a despotic power, but as a subject, which you are bound to govern with a temperate and restrained authority.

BEL. True, sir, most truly said; mine's a commission, not a right. I am the offspring of distress, and every child of sorrow is my brother; while I have hands to hold, therefore, I will hold them open to mankind. But, sir, my passions are my masters; they take me where they will, and oftentimes they leave to reason and to virtue nothing but my wishes and my sighs.

STOCK. Come, come, the man who can accuse corrects himself.

BEL. Ah! that's an office I am weary of. I wish a friend would take it up. I would to Heaven you had leisure for the employ; but, did you drive a trade to the four corners of the world, you would not find the task so toilsome as to keep me free from faults.

STOCK. Well, I am not discouraged. This candor tells me I should not have the fault of self-conceit to combat; that, at least, is not amongst the number.

BEL. No; if I knew that man on earth who thought more humbly of me than I do of myself, I would take up his opinion and forego my own.

STOCK. And, was I to choose a pupil, it should be one of your complexion. So if you'll come along with me, we'll agree upon your admission and enter on a course of lectures directly.

BEL. With all my heart.   (*Exeunt*)

SCENE III. *An Elegant Sitting Room in* LADY RUSPORT'S *House.*

L. RUS. Miss Rusport, I desire to hear no more of Captain Dudley and his destitute family. Not a shilling of mine shall ever cross the hands of any of them. Because my sister chose to marry a beggar, am I bound to support him and his posterity?

CHAR. I think you are.

L. RUS. You think I am; and pray where do you find the law that tells you so?

CHAR. I am not proficient enough to quote chapter and verse, but I take charity to be a main clause in the great statute of Christianity.

L. RUS. I say charity, indeed! And pray, Miss, are you sure that it is charity, pure charity, which moves you to plead for Captain Dudley? Amongst all your pity, do you find no spice of a certain anti-spiritual passion, called love? Don't mistake yourself; you are no saint, child, believe me; and I am apt to think the distresses of old Dudley, and of his daughter into the bargain, would never break your heart if there was not a certain young fellow of two and twenty in the case; who, by the happy recommendation of a good person and the brilliant appointments of an ensigncy, will, if I am not mistaken, cozen you out of a fortune of twice twenty thousand pounds, as soon as ever you are of age to bestow it upon him.

CHAR. A nephew of your ladyship's can never want any other recommendation with me; and, if my partiality for Charles Dudley is acquitted by the rest of the world, I hope Lady Rusport will not condemn me for it.

L. RUS. I condemn you! I thank Heaven, Miss Rusport, I am no ways responsible for your conduct; nor is it any concern of mine how you dispose of yourself. You are not my daughter; and, when I married your father, poor Sir Stephen Rusport, I found you a forward spoiled miss of fourteen, far above being instructed by me.

CHAR. Perhaps your ladyship calls this instruction.

L. RUS. You're strangely pert, but 'tis no

wonder. Your mother, I'm told, was a fine lady; and according to the modern style of education you was brought up. It was not so in my young days; there was then some decorum in the world, some subordination, as the great Locke expresses it. Oh! 'twas an edifying sight, to see the regular deportment observed in our family: no giggling, no gossiping was going on there. My good father, Sir Oliver Roundhead, never was seen to laugh himself, nor ever allowed it in his children.

CHAR. (Drily) Ay; those were happy times, indeed.

L. Rus. But in this forward age we have coquettes in the egg-shell and philosophers in the cradle, girls of fifteen that lead the fashion in new caps and new opinions, that have their sentiments and their sensations, and the idle fops encourage 'em in it. O' my conscience, I wonder what it is the men can see in such babies.

CHAR. True, madam; but all men do not overlook the maturer beauties of your ladyship's age. Witness your admirer Major Dennis O'Flaherty; there's an example of some discernment. I declare to you, when your ladyship is by, the Major takes no more notice of me than if I was part of the furniture of your chamber.

L. Rus. (Bridling) The Major, child, has travelled through various kingdoms and climates, and has more enlarged notions of female merit than falls to the lot of an English home-bred lover; in most other countries, no woman on your side forty would ever be named in a polite circle.

CHAR. Right, Madam; I've been told that in Vienna they have coquettes upon crutches, and Venuses in their grand climacteric; a lover there celebrates the wrinkles, not the dimples, in his mistress's face. The Major, I think, has served in the imperial army.

L. Rus. Are you piqued, my young madam? Had my sister Louisa yielded to the addresses of one of Major O'Flaherty's person and appearance, she would have had some excuse. But to run away, as she did, at the age of sixteen too, with a man of old Dudley's sort——

CHAR. Was, in my opinion, the most venial trespass that ever girl of sixteen committed. Of a noble family, an engaging person, strict honor, and sound understanding, what accomplishment was there wanting in Captain Dudley, but that which the prodigality of his ancestors had deprived him of?

L. Rus. They left him as much as he deserves; hasn't the old man captain's half pay? And is not the son an ensign?

CHAR. An ensign! Alas, poor Charles! Would to Heaven he knew what my heart feels and suffers for his sake.

(SERVANT enters)

SERV. Ensign Dudley to wait upon your ladyship.

L. Rus. Who! Dudley! What can have brought him to town?

CHAR. Dear madam, 'tis Charles Dudley, 'tis your nephew.

L. Rus. Nephew! I renounce him as my nephew! Sir Oliver renounced him as his grandson: wasn't he son of the eldest daughter and only male descendant of Sir Oliver, and didn't he cut him off with a shilling? Didn't the poor dear good man leave his whole fortune to me, except a small annuity to my maiden sister, who spoiled her constitution with nursing him? And, depend upon it, not a penny of that fortune shall ever be disposed of otherwise than according to the will of the donor.

(CHARLES DUDLEY enters)

So, young man, whence come you? What brings you to town?

CHARLES. If there is any offence in my coming to town, your ladyship is in some degree responsible for it, for part of my errand was to pay my duty here.

L. Rus. I hope you have some better excuse than all this.

CHARLES. 'Tis true, madam, I have other motives; but, if I consider my trouble repaid by the pleasure I now enjoy, I should hope my aunt would not think my company the less welcome for the value I set upon her's.

L. Rus. Coxcomb! And where is your father, child; and your sister? Are they in town too?

CHARLES. They are.

L. Rus. Ridiculous! I don't know what people do in London who have no money to spend in it.

Char. Dear madam, speak more kindly to your nephew; how can you oppress a youth of his sensibility?

L. Rus. Miss Rusport, I insist upon your retiring to your apartment; when I want your advice I'll send to you. (*Exit* Charlotte) So you have put on a red coat too, as well as your father; 'tis plain what value you set upon the good advice Sir Oliver used to give you. How often has he cautioned you against the army?

Charles. Had it pleased my grandfather to enable me to have obeyed his caution, I would have done it; but you well know how destitute I am, and 'tis not to be wondered at if I prefer the service of my king to that of any other master.

L. Rus. Well, well, take your own course; 'tis no concern of mine. You never consulted me.

Charles. I frequently wrote to your ladyship, but could obtain no answer; and since my grandfather's death, this is the first opportunity I have had of waiting upon you.

L. Rus. I must desire you not to mention the death of that dear good man in my hearing——my spirits cannot support it.

Charles. I shall obey you. Permit me to say that, as that event has richly supplied you with the materials of bounty, the distresses of my family can furnish you with objects of it.

L. Rus. The distresses of your family, child, are quite out of the question at present. Had Sir Oliver been pleased to consider them, I should have been well content; but he has absolutely taken no notice of you in his will, and that to me must and shall be a law. Tell your father and your sister I totally disapprove of their coming up to town.

Charles. Must I tell my father that before your ladyship knows the motive that brought him hither? Allured by the offer of exchanging for a commission on full pay, the veteran, after thirty years service, prepares to encounter the fatal heats of Senegambia, but wants a small supply to equip him for the expedition.

(Servant *enters, followed immediately by* Major O'Flaherty)

Serv. Major O'Flaherty to wait on your ladyship.

O'Fla. Spare your speeches, young man; don't you think her ladyship can take my word for that? I hope, madam, 'tis evidence enough of my being present when I've the honor of telling you so myself.

L. Rus. Major O'Flaherty, I am rejoiced to see you. Nephew Dudley, you perceive I'm engaged.

Charles. I shall not intrude upon your ladyship's more agreeable engagements. I presume I have my answer.

L. Rus. Your answer, child! What answer can you possibly expect, or how can your romantic father suppose that I am to abet him in all his idle and extravagant undertakings? Come, Major, let me show you the way into my dressing-room; and let us leave this young adventurer to his meditation. (*Exit*)

O'Fla. I follow you, my lady. (*Moves toward the door and bows to* Charles, *who is lost in unhappy thought and does not observe him*) Young gentleman, your obedient!—Upon my conscience, as fine a young fellow as I would wish to clap my eyes on. He might have answered my salute, however—well, let it pass. Fortune, perhaps, frowns upon the poor lad. She's a damned slippery lady, and very apt to jilt us poor fellows that wear cockades in our hats. Fare-thee-well, honey, whoever thou art. (*Exit*)

Charles. (*Sighs*) So much for the virtues of a puritan! Out upon it, her heart is flint. Yet that woman, that aunt of mine, without one worthy particle in her composition, would, I dare be sworn, as soon set her foot in a pest-house as in a play-house. (*Going*)

(Miss Rusport *enters to him*)

Char. Stop, stay a little, Charles, whither are you going in such haste?

Charles. Madam; Miss Rusport. What are your commands?

Char. Why so reserved? We had used to answer to no other names than those of Charles and Charlotte.

CHARLES. What ails you? You've been weeping.

CHAR. No, no; or if I have—your eyes are full too. But I have a thousand things to say to you. Before you go, tell me, I conjure you, where you are to be found. Here, give me your direction; write it upon the back of this visiting-ticket—Have you a pencil?

CHARLES. I have. But why should you desire to find us out? 'Tis a poor little incon-venient place; my sister has no apartment fit to receive you in.

(SERVANT enters)

SERV. Madam, my lady desires your company directly.

CHAR. I am coming—well, have you wrote it? Give it me. O Charles! either you do not, or you will not understand me.

(Exeunt severally)

Act II

SCENE I. A Small, Sparsely Furnished Room in FULMER's House.

(Enter FULMER and MRS. FULMER)

MRS. FUL. Why, how you sit, musing and moping, sighing and desponding! I'm ashamed of you, Mr. Fulmer. Is this the country you described to me, a second Eldorado, rivers of gold and rocks of diamonds? You found me in a pretty snug retired way of life at Boulogne, out of the noise and bustle of the world, and wholly at my ease. You, indeed, was upon the wing, with a fiery persecution at your back, but, like a true son of Loyola, you had then a thousand ingenious devices to repair your fortune, and this, your native country was to be the scene of your performances. Fool that I was, to be inveigled into it by you! But, thank Heaven, our partnership is revocable; I am not your wedded wife, praised be my stars! For what have we got, whom have we gulled but ourselves? Which of all your trains has taken fire? Even this poor expedient of your bookseller's shop seems abandoned, for if a chance customer drops in, who is there, pray, to help him to what he wants?

FUL. Patty, you know it is not upon slight grounds that I despair. There had used to be a livelihood to be picked up in this country, both for the honest and dishonest. I have tried each walk, and am likely to starve at last. There is not a point to which the wit and faculty of man can turn, that I have not set mine to, but in vain; I am beat through every quarter of the compass.

MRS. FUL. Ah! common efforts all. Strike me a masterstroke, Mr. Fulmer, if you wish to make any figure in this country.

FUL. But where, how, and what? I have blustered for prerogative; I have bellowed for freedom; I have offered to serve my country; I have engaged to betray it. A masterstroke, truly! Why, I have talked treason, writ treason, and if a man can't live by that he can live by nothing. Here I set up as a bookseller, why men left off reading; and if I was to turn butcher, I believe o'my conscience they'd leave off eating.

(CAPTAIN DUDLEY crosses the stage)

MRS. FUL. Why there now's your lodger, old Captain Dudley, as he calls himself. There's no flint without fire; something might be struck out of him, if you'd the wit to find the way.

FUL. Hang him, an old dry skinned curmudgeon. You may as well think to get truth out of a courtier, or candor out of a critic. I can make nothing of him; besides, he's poor, and therefore not for our purpose.

MRS. FUL. The more fool he! Would any man be poor that had such a prodigy in his possession?

FUL. His daughter, you mean; she is, indeed, uncommonly beautiful.

MRS. FUL. Beautiful! Why she need only be seen to have the first men in the kingdom at her feet. Egad, I wish I had the leasing of her beauty; what would some of our young Nabobs give——?

FUL. Hush! here comes the Captain; good girl, leave us to ourselves, and let me try what I can make of him.

MRS. FUL. Captain, truly! i'faith I'd have

a regiment, had I such a daughter, before I was three months older.　　　(*Exit*)

(Captain Dudley *enters to him*)

Ful. Captain Dudley, good morning to you.

Dud. Mr. Fulmer, I have borrowed a book from your shop; 'tis the sixth volume of my deceased friend Tristram. He is a flattering writer to us poor soldiers, and the divine story of Le Fevre, which makes part of this book, in my opinion of it does honor not to its author only but to human nature.

Ful. He's an author I keep in the way of trade, but one I never relished. He is much too loose and profligate for my taste.

Dud. That's being too severe. I hold him to be a moralist in the noblest sense; he plays indeed with the fancy, and sometimes perhaps too wantonly, but while he thus designedly masks his main attack, he comes at once upon the heart, refines, amends it, softens it, beats down each selfish barrier from about it, and opens every sluice of pity and benevolence.

Ful. We of the Catholic persuasion are not much bound to him.——Well, sir, I shall not oppose your opinion; a favorite author is like a favorite mistress, and there you know, Captain, no man likes to have his taste arraigned.

Dud. Upon my word, sir, I don't know what a man likes in that case; 'tis an experiment I never made.

Ful. Sir!—Are you serious?

Dud. 'Tis of little consequence whether you think so.

Ful. (*Aside*) What a formal old prig it is! —I apprehend you, sir; you speak with caution. You are married?

Dud. I have been.

Ful. And this young lady, which accompanies you—

Dud. Passes for my daughter.

Ful. (*Aside*) Passes for his daughter! humph—She is exceedingly beautiful, finely accomplished, of a most enchanting shape and air.

Dud. You are much too partial; she has the greatest defect a woman can have.

Ful. How so, pray?

Dud. She has no fortune.

Ful. Rather say that you have none; and that's a sore defect in one of your years, Captain Dudley. You've served, no doubt?

Dud. (*Aside*) Familiar coxcomb! But I'll humor him.

Ful. (*Aside*) A close old fox! But I'll unkennel him.

Dud. Above thirty years I've been in the service, Mr. Fulmer.

Ful. I guessed as much; I laid it at no less. Why 'tis a wearisome time, 'tis an apprenticeship to a profession fit only for a patriarch. But preferment must be closely followed. You never could have been so far behind hand in the chase unless you had palpably mistaken your way. You'll pardon me, but I begin to perceive you have lived in the world, not with it.

Dud. It may be so; and you, perhaps, can give me better council. I'm now soliciting a favor, an exchange to a company on full pay, nothing more, and yet I meet a thousand bars to that; tho', without boasting, I should think the certificate of services which I sent in might have purchased that indulgence to me.

Ful. Who thinks or cares about 'em? Certificate of services, indeed! Send in a certificate of your fair daughter; carry her in your hand with you.

Dud. What! Who! My daughter! Carry my daughter! Well, and what then?

Ful. Why, then your fortune's made, that's all.

Dud. I understand you. And this you call knowledge of the world? Despicable knowledge! But, sirrah, I will have you know— (*threatening him*).

Ful. Help! Who's within? Would you strike me, sir? would you lift up your hand against a man in his own house?

Dud. In a church, if he dare insult the poverty of a man of honor.

Ful. Have a care what you do! Remember there is such a thing in law as an assault and battery; ay, and such trifling forms as warrants and indictments.

Dud. Go, sir; you are too mean for my resentment. 'Tis that, and not the law, protects you. Hence!

Ful. (*Aside*) An old, absurd, incorrigible blockhead! I'll be revenged of him.　　(*Exit*)

(*Young* Dudley *enters*)

Charles. What is the matter, sir? Sure I heard an outcry as I entered the house.

Dud. Not unlikely; our landlord and his wife are forever wrangling.—Did you find your aunt Dudley at home?

Charles. I did.

Dud. And what was your reception?

Charles. Cold as our poverty and her pride could make it.

Dud. You told her the pressing occasion I had for a small supply to equip me for this exchange; has she granted me the relief I asked?

Charles. Alas, sir, she has peremptorily refused it.

Dud. That's hard; that's hard, indeed! My petition was for a small sum; she has refused it, you say. Well, be it so; I must not complain. Did you see the broker about the insurance on my life?

Charles. There again I am the messenger of ill news; I can raise no money, so fatal is the climate. Alas! that ever my father should be sent to perish in such a place!

(Miss Dudley *enters hastily*)

Dud. Louisa, what's the matter? You seem frighted.

Lou. I am, indeed. Coming from Miss Rusport's, I met a young gentleman in the streets who has beset me in the strangest manner.

Charles. Insufferable! Was he rude to you?

Lou. I cannot say he was absolutely rude to me, but he was very importunate to speak to me, and once or twice attempted to lift up my hat. He followed me to the corner of the street, and there I gave him the slip.

Dud. You must walk no more in the streets, child, without me, or your brother.

Lou. O Charles! Miss Rusport desires to see you directly. Lady Rusport is gone out, and she has something particular to say to you.

Charles. Have you any commands for me, sir?

Dud. None, my dear; by all means wait upon Miss Rusport. Come, Louisa, I shall desire you to go up to your chamber, and compose yourself. (*Exeunt*)

(Belcour *peeps round another door, surveys the empty room, and enters*)

Bel. Not a soul, as I'm alive. Why, what an odd sort of a house is this! Confound the little jilt, she has fairly given me the slip. A plague upon this London, I shall have no luck in it. Such a crowd, and such a hurry, and such a number of shops, and one so like the other, that whether the wench turned into this house or the next, or whether she went up stairs or down stairs (for there's a world above, and a world below, it seems), I declare, I know no more than if I was in the Blue Mountains. In the name of all the devils at once, why did she run away? If every handsome girl I meet in this town is to lead me such a wild-goose chase, I had better have stayed in the torrid zone. I shall be wasted to the size of a sugar-cane. What shall I do? Give the chase up? Hang it, that's cowardly. Shall I, a true born son of Phœbus, suffer this little nimble-footed Daphne to escape me? ——"Forbid it honor, and forbid it love." Hush! hush! here she comes! Oh! the devil! What tawdry thing have we got here?

(Mrs. Fulmer *enters to him*)

Mrs. Ful. Your humble servant, sir.

Bel. Your humble servant, madam.

Mrs. Ful. A fine summer's day, sir.

Bel. Yes, ma'am, and so cool that if the calendar didn't call it July, I should swear it was January.

Mrs. Ful. Sir!

Bel. Madam!

Mrs. Ful. Do you wish to speak to Mr. Fulmer, sir?

Bel. Mr. Fulmer, madam? I haven't the honor of knowing such a person.

Mrs. Ful. No, I'll be sworn, have you not. Thou art much too pretty a fellow, and too much of a gentleman, to be an author thyself, or to have anything to say to those that are so. 'Tis the Captain, I suppose, you are waiting for.

Bel. I rather suspect it is the Captain's wife.

Mrs. Ful. The Captain has no wife, sir.

BEL. No wife! I'm heartily sorry for it, for then she's his mistress, and that I take to be the more desperate case of the two. Pray, madam, wasn't there a lady just now turned into your house? 'Twas with her I wished to speak.

MRS. FUL. What sort of a lady, pray?

BEL. One of the loveliest sort my eyes ever beheld; young, tall, fresh, fair—in short, a goddess.

MRS. FUL. Nay, but dear, dear sir, now I'm sure you flatter, for 'twas me you followed into the shop-door this minute.

BEL. You! No, no, take my word for it, it was not you, madam.

MRS. FUL. But what is it you laugh at?

BEL. Upon my soul, I ask your pardon. But it was not you, believe me; be assured it wasn't.

MRS. FUL. Well, sir, I shall not contend for the honor of being noticed by you; I hope you think you wouldn't have been the first man that noticed me in the streets. However, this I'm positive of, that no living woman but myself has entered these doors this morning.

BEL. Why then I'm mistaken in the house, that's all, for 'tis not humanly possible I can be so far out in the lady. (*Going*)

MRS. FUL. (*Aside*) Coxcomb! But hold— a thought occurs. As sure as can be he has seen Miss Dudley.—A word with you, young gentleman; come back.

BEL. (*Turning back*) Well, what's your pleasure?

MRS. FUL. You seem greatly captivated with this young lady; are you apt to fall in love thus at first sight?

BEL. Oh, yes, 'tis the only way I can ever fall in love. Any man may tumble into a pit by surprise, none but a fool would walk into one by choice.

MRS. FUL. You are a hasty lover it seems; have you spirit to be a generous one? They that will please the eye mustn't spare the purse.

BEL. Try me; put me to the proof; bring me to an interview with the dear girl that has thus captivated me, and see whether I have spirit to be grateful.

MRS. FUL. But how, pray, am I to know the girl you have set your heart on?

BEL. By an undescribable grace that accompanies every look and action that falls

from her. There can be but one such woman in the world, and nobody can mistake that one.

MRS. FUL. Well, if I should stumble upon this angel in my walks, where am I to find you? What's your name?

BEL. Upon my soul, I can't tell you my name.

MRS. FUL. Not tell me! Why so?

BEL. Because I don't know what it is myself; as yet I have no name.

MRS. FUL. No name!

BEL. None; a friend, indeed, lent me his, but he forbad me to use it on any unworthy occasion.

MRS. FUL. But where is your place of abode?

BEL. I have none; I never slept a night in England in my life.

MRS. FUL. Hey-day!

(FULMER *enters, muttering*)

FUL. A fine case, truly, in a free country; a pretty pass things are come to, if a man is to be assaulted in his own house.

MRS. FUL. Who has assaulted you, my dear?

FUL. Who! why this Captain Drawcansir, this old Dudley, my lodger; but I'll unlodge him; I'll unharbor him, I warrant.

MRS. FUL. Hush! hush! Hold your tongue man, pocket the affront, and be quiet; I've a scheme on foot will pay you a hundred beatings. Why you surprise me, Mr. Fulmer; Captain Dudley assault you! Impossible.

FUL. Nay, I can't call it an absolute assault, but he threatened me.

MRS. FUL. Oh, was that all? I thought how it would turn out—A likely thing, truly, for a person of his obliging compassionate turn. No, no, poor Captain Dudley, he has sorrows and distresses enough of his own to employ his spirits, without setting them against other people. Make it up as fast as you can. (*Aside to* FULMER) Watch this gentleman out, follow him wherever he goes, and bring me word who and what he is. Be sure you don't lose sight of him; I've other business in hand. (*Exit*)

BEL. Pray, sir, what sorrows and distresses have befallen this old gentleman you speak of?

Ful. Poverty, disappointment, and all the distresses attendant thereupon. Sorrow enough of all conscience. I soon found how it was with him by his way of living, low enough of all reason; but what I overheard this morning put it out of all doubt.

Bel. What did you overhear this morning?

Ful. Why, it seems he wants to join his regiment, and has been beating the town over to raise a little money for that purpose upon his pay; but the climate, I find, where he is going is so unhealthy that nobody can be found to lend him any.

Bel. Why then your town is a damned good-for-nothing town, and I wish I had never come into it.

Ful. That's what I say, sir; the hard-heartedness of some folks is unaccountable. There's an old Lady Rusport, a near relation of this gentleman's; she lives hard by here, opposite to Stockwell's, the great merchant. He sent to her a-begging, but to no purpose; though she is as rich as a Jew, she would not furnish him with a farthing.

Bel. Is the Captain at home?

Ful. He is up stairs, sir.

Bel. Will you take the trouble to desire him to step hither? I want to speak to him.

Ful. I'll send him to you directly. (*Aside*) I don't know what to make of this young man; but, if I live, I will find him out, or know the reason why.   (*Exit*)

Bel. I've lost the girl it seems; that's clear. She was the first object of my pursuit; but the case of this poor officer touches me, and, after all, there may be as much true delight in rescuing a fellow creature from distress as there would be in plunging one into it—— But let me see; it's a point that must be managed with some delicacy—Apropos! there's pen and ink—I've struck upon a method that will do. (*Writes*) Ay, ay, this is the very thing; 'twas devilish lucky I happened to have these bills about me. There, there, fare you well, I'm glad to be rid of you; you stood a chance of being worse applied, I can tell you. (*Encloses and seals the paper*)

(FULMER *brings in* DUDLEY)

Ful. That's the gentleman, sir. (*Aside*) I shall make bold, however, to lend an ear.

(FULMER *leaves, but can be seen listening at the door*)

Dud. Have you any commands for me, sir?

Bel. Your name is Dudley, sir——?

Dud. It is.

Bel. You command a company, I think, Captain Dudley?

Dud. I did. I am now upon half-pay.

Bel. You've served some time?

Dud. A pretty many years; long enough to see some people of more merit, and better interest than myself, made general officers.

Bel. Their merit I may have some doubt of; their interest I can readily give credit to. There is little promotion to be looked for in your profession, I believe, without friends, Captain?

Dud. I believe so too. Have you any other business with me, may I ask?

Bel. Your patience for a moment. I was informed you was about to join your regiment in distant quarters abroad.

Dud. I have been soliciting an exchange to a company on full-pay, quartered at James's-Fort, in Senegambia; but I'm afraid I must drop the undertaking.

Bel. Why so, pray?

Dud. Why so, sir? 'Tis a home-question for a perfect stranger to put; there is something very particular in all this.

Bel. If it is not impertinent, sir, allow me to ask you what reason you have for despairing of success.

Dud. Why really, sir, mine is an obvious reason for a soldier to have—Want of money; simply that.

Bel. May I beg to know the sum you have occasion for?

Dud. Truly, sir, I cannot exactly tell you on a sudden, nor is it, I suppose, of any great consequence to you to be informed, but I should guess in the gross that two hundred pounds would serve.

Bel. And do you find a difficulty in raising that sum upon your pay? 'Tis done every day.

Dud. The nature of the climate makes it difficult: I can get no one to insure my life.

Bel. Oh! that's a circumstance may make for you, as well as against. In short, Captain Dudley, it so happens that I can command the sum of two hundred pounds. Seek no farther; I'll accommodate you with it upon easy terms.

Dud. Sir! do I understand you rightly?—I beg your pardon, but am I to believe that you are in earnest?

Bel. What is your surprise? Is it an uncommon thing for a gentleman to speak truth? Or is it incredible that one fellow creature should assist another?

Dud. I ask your pardon—May I beg to know to whom? Do you propose this in the way of business?

Bel. Entirely: I have no other business on earth.

Dud. Indeed! You are not a broker, I'm persuaded.

Bel. I am not.

Dud. Nor an army agent, I think?

Bel. I hope you will not think the worse of me for being neither. In short, sir, if you will peruse this paper, it will explain to you who I am, and upon what terms I act; while you read it, I will step home and fetch the money, and we will conclude the bargain without loss of time. In the meanwhile, good day to you. (*Exit hastily*)

Dud. Humph! there's something very odd in all this—let me see what we've got here—This paper is to tell me who he is, and what are his terms. In the name of wonder, why has he sealed it! Hey-dey! What's here? Two bank notes, of a hundred each! I can't comprehend what this means. Hold, here's a writing; perhaps that will show me. "Accept this trifle; pursue your fortune, and prosper." Am I in a dream? Is this a reality? (*He starts to run after* Belcour *and collides at the door with* Major O'Flaherty)

(*Enter* Major O'Flaherty)

O'Fla. Save you, my dear! Is it you now that are Captain Dudley, I would ask?——Whuh! What's the hurry the man's in? If 'tis the lad that run out of the shop you would overtake, you might as well stay where you are; by my soul he's as nimble as a Croat, you are a full hour's march in his rear. Ay, faith, you may as well turn back, and give over the pursuit. Well, Captain Dudley, if that's your name, there's a letter for you. Read, man; read it; and I'll have a word with you after you have done.

Dud. More miracles on foot! So, so, from Lady Rusport.

O'Fla. You're right; it's from her ladyship.

Dud. Well, sir, I have cast my eye over it; 'tis short and peremptory. Are you acquainted with the contents?

O'Fla. Not at all, my dear, not at all.

Dud. Have you any message from Lady Rusport?

O'Fla. Not a syllable, honey; only, when you've digested the letter, I've a little bit of a message to deliver you from myself.

Dud. And may I beg to know who yourself is?

O'Fla. Dennis O'Flaherty, at your service; a poor major of grenadiers, nothing better.

Dud. So much for your name and title, sir; now be so good to favor me with your message.

O'Fla. Why then, Captain, I must tell you I have promised Lady Rusport you shall do whatever it is she bids you to do in that letter there.

Dud. Ay, indeed. Have you undertaken so much, Major, without knowing either what she commands, or what I can perform?

O'Fla. That's your concern, my dear, not mine; I must keep my word, you know.

Dud. Or else, I suppose, you and I must measure swords.

O'Fla. Upon my soul you've hit it.

Dud. That would hardly answer to either of us; you and I have, probably, had enough of fighting in our time before now.

O'Fla. Faith and troth, Master Dudley, you may say that; 'tis thirty years, come the time, that I have followed the trade, and in a pretty many countries.—Let me see—In the war before last I served in the Irish brigade, d'ye see; there, after bringing off the French monarch, I left his service, with a British bullet in my body and this ribband in my buttonhole. Last war I followed the fortunes of the German eagle, in the corps of grenadiers; there I had my belly full of fighting and a plentiful scarcity of every thing else. After six and twenty engagements, great and small, I went off, with this gash on my skull, and a kiss of the Empress Queen's sweet hand (Heaven bless it!) for my pains. Since the peace, my dear, I took a little turn with the Confederates there in Poland—but such another set of madcaps!—by the lord Harry, I never knew what it was they were scuffling about.

Dud. Well, Major, I won't add another action to the list, you shall keep your promise with Lady Rusport. She requires me to leave London; I shall go in a few days, and you may take what credit you please from my compliance.

O'Fla. Give me your hand, my dear boy! This will make her my own; when that's the case, we shall be brothers, you know, and we'll share her fortune between us.

Dud. Not so, Major; the man who marries Lady Rusport will have a fair title to her whole fortune without division. But I hope your expectations of prevailing are founded upon good reasons.

O'Fla. Upon the best grounds in the world. First, I think she will comply, because she is a woman; secondly, I am persuaded she won't hold out long, because she's a widow; and thirdly, I make sure of her, because I've married five wives (*en militaire*, Captain) and never failed yet; and, for what I know, they're all alive and merry at this very hour.

Dud. Well, sir, go on and prosper. If you can inspire Lady Rusport with half your charity, I shall think you deserve all her fortune; at present, I must beg your excuse. Good morning to you.   (*Exit*)

O'Fla. A good sensible man, and very much of a soldier. I did not care if I was better acquainted with him, but 'tis an awkward kind of country for that; the English, I observe, are close friends but distant acquaintance. I suspect the old lady has not been overgenerous to poor Dudley; I shall give her a little touch about that. Upon my soul, I know but one excuse a person can have for giving nothing, and that is, like myself, having nothing to give.   (*Exit*)

Scene II. Lady Rusport's *House. A Dressing-Room.*

(*Enter* Miss Rusport *and* Lucy)

Char. Well, Lucy, you've dislodged the old lady at last, but methought you was a tedious time about it.

Lucy. A tedious time, indeed. I think they who have least to spare contrive to throw the most away; I thought I should never have got her out of the house.

Char. Why, she's as deliberate in canvassing every article of her dress as an ambassador would be in settling the preliminaries of a treaty.

Lucy. There was a new hood and handkerchief, that had come express from Holborn Hill on the occasion, that took as much time in adjusting——

Char. As they did in making, and she was as vain of them as an old maid of a young lover.

Lucy. Or a young lover of himself. Then, madam, this being a visit of great ceremony to a person of distinction, at the west end of the town, the old state chariot was dragged forth on the occasion, with strict charges to dress out the box with the leopard-skin hammer-cloth.

Char. Yes, and to hang the false tails on the miserable stumps of the old crawling cattle. Well, well, pray Heaven the crazy affair don't break down again with her! at least till she gets to her journey's end.——But where's Charles Dudley? Run down, dear girl, and be ready to let him in; I think he's as long in coming as she was in going.

Lucy. Why, indeed, madam, you seem the more alert of the two, I must say.   (*Exit*)

Char. Now the deuce take the girl for putting that notion into my head. I'm sadly afraid Dudley does not like me; so much encouragement as I have given him to declare himself, I never could get a word from him on the subject! This may be very honorable, but upon my life it's very provoking. By the way, I wonder how I look today. Oh! shockingly! hideously pale! like a witch! This is the old lady's glass, and she has left some of her wrinkles on it. How frightfully have I put on my cap! all awry! and my hair dressed so unbecomingly! Altogether, I'm a most complete fright.

(Charles Dudley *comes in unobserved*)

Charles. That I deny.
Char. Ah!

CHARLES. Quarrelling with your glass, cousin? Make it up, make it up and be friends. It cannot compliment you more than by reflecting you as you are.

CHAR. Well, I vow, my dear Charles, that is delightfully said, and deserves my very best curtsy. Your flattery, like a rich jewel, has a value not only from its superior lustre, but from its extraordinary scarceness. I verily think this is the only civil speech you ever directed to my person in your life.

CHARLES. And I ought to ask pardon of your good sense for having done it now.

CHAR. Nay, now you relapse again. Don't you know, if you keep well with a woman on the great score of beauty, she'll never quarrel with you on the trifling article of good sense? But any thing serves to fill up a dull yawning hour with an insipid cousin; you have brighter moments and warmer spirits for the dear girl of your heart.

CHARLES. Oh! fie upon you, fie upon you.

CHAR. You blush, and the reason is apparent. You are a novice at hypocrisy, but no practice can make a visit of ceremony pass for a visit of choice. Love is ever before its time; friendship is apt to lag a little after it. Pray, Charles, did you make any extraordinary haste hither?

CHARLES. By your question, I see you acquit me of the impertinence of being in love.

CHAR. But why impertinence? Why the impertinence of being in love? You have one language for me, Charles, and another for the woman of your affection.

CHARLES. You are mistaken; the woman of my affection shall never hear any other language from me than what I use to you.

CHAR. I am afraid then you'll never make yourself understood by her.

CHARLES. It is not fit I should. There is no need of love to make me miserable; 'tis wretchedness enough to be a beggar.

CHAR. A beggar, do you call yourself! O Charles, Charles, rich in every merit and accomplishment, whom may you not aspire to? And why think you so unworthily of our sex, as to conclude there is not one to be found with sense to discern your virtue, and generosity to reward it?

CHARLES. You distress me; I must beg to hear no more.

CHAR. Well, I can be silent.——(*Aside*) Thus does he always serve me, whenever I am about to disclose myself to him.

CHARLES. Why do you not banish me and my misfortunes forever from your thoughts?

CHAR. Ay, wherefore do I not, since you never allowed me a place in yours? But go, sir, I have no right to stay you; go where your heart directs you, go to the happy, the distinguished fair one.

CHARLES. Now, by all that's good, you do me wrong. There is no such fair one for me to go to, nor have I an acquaintance among the sex, yourself excepted, which answers to that description.

CHAR. Indeed!

CHARLES. In very truth. There, then let us drop the subject. May you be happy, though I never can!

CHAR. O Charles! give me your hand; if I have offended you, I ask your pardon. You have been long acquainted with my temper, and know how to bear with its infirmities.

CHARLES. Thus, my dear Charlotte, let us seal our reconciliation. (*Kissing her hand*) Bear with thy infirmities! By Heaven, I know not any one failing in thy whole composition, except that of too great a partiality for an undeserving man.

CHAR. And you are now taking the very course to augment that failing.—A thought strikes me: I have a commission that you must absolutely execute for me. I have immediate occasion for the sum of two hundred pounds; you know my fortune is shut up till I am of age; take this paltry box (it contains my ear-rings, and some other baubles I have no use for), carry it to our opposite neighbor, Mr. Stockwell (I don't know where else to apply), leave it as a deposit in his hands, and beg him to accommodate me with the sum.

CHARLES. Dear Charlotte, what are you about to do? How can you possibly want two hundred pounds?

CHAR. How can I possibly do without it, you mean? Doesn't every lady want two hundred pounds? Perhaps I have lost it at play; perhaps I mean to win as much to it; perhaps I want it for two hundred different uses.

CHARLES. Pooh! pooh! all this is nothing; don't I know you never play?

CHAR. You mistake. I have a spirit to set not only this trifle, but my whole fortune, upon a stake; therefore make no wry faces, but do as I bid you. You will find Mr. Stockwell a very honorable gentleman.

(LUCY *enters in haste*)

LUCY. Dear madam, as I live, here comes the old lady in a hackney-coach.

CHAR. The old chariot has given her a second tumble. Away with you, you know your way out without meeting her. Take the box, and do as I desire you.

CHARLES. I must not dispute your orders. Farewell!

(*Exeunt* CHARLES *and* CHARLOTTE)

(LADY RUSPORT *enters, leaning on* MAJOR O'FLAHERTY'S *arm*)

O'FLA. Rest yourself upon my arm, never spare it. 'Tis strong enough, it has stood harder service than you can put it to.

LUCY. Mercy upon me, what is the matter? I am frightened out of my wits—has your ladyship had an accident?

L. RUS. O Lucy, the most untoward one in nature. I know not how I shall repair it.

O'FLA. Never go about to repair it, my lady. Ev'n build a new one; 'twas but a crazy piece of business at best.

LUCY. Bless me, is the old chariot broke down with you again?

L. RUS. Broke, child? I don't know what might have been broke, if, by great good fortune, this obliging gentleman had not been at hand to assist me.

LUCY. Dear madam, let me run and fetch you a cup of the cordial drops.

L. RUS. Do, Lucy. (*Exit* LUCY) Alas! sir, ever since I lost my husband, my poor nerves have been shook to pieces. There hangs his beloved picture; that precious relic and a plentiful jointure is all that remains to console me for the best of men.

O'FLA. Let me see. I'faith a comely personage; by his fur cloak I suppose he was in the Russian service, and by the gold chain round his neck, I should guess he had been honored with the order of St. Catharine.

L. RUS. No, no; he meddled with no St. Catharines. That's the habit he wore in his mayoralty; Sir Stephen was Lord Mayor of London. But he is gone, and has left me a poor, weak, solitary widow behind him.

O'FLA. By all means, then, take a strong, able, hearty man to repair his loss. If such a plain fellow as one Dennis O'Flaherty can please you, I think I may venture to say, without any disparagement to the gentleman in the fur-gown there——

L. RUS. What are you going to say? Don't shock my ears with any comparisons, I desire.

O'FLA. Not I, by my soul; I don't believe there's any comparison in the case.

(*Enter* LUCY *with a goblet*)

L. RUS. Oh, are you come? Give me the drops; I'm all in a flutter.

O'FLA. Hark'e, sweetheart, what are those same drops? Have you any more left in the bottle? I didn't care if I took a little sip of them myself.

LUCY. Oh, sir, they are called the cordial restorative elixir, or the nervous golden drops; they are only for ladies' cases.

O'FLA. Yes, yes, my dear, there are gentlemen as well as ladies that stand in need of those same golden drops; they'd suit my case to a tittle.

(*Exit* LUCY *with an impudent curtsy*)

L. RUS. Well, Major, did you give old Dudley my letter, and will the silly man do as I bid him and be gone?

O'FLA. You are obeyed; he's on his march.

L. RUS. That's well; you have managed this matter to perfection. I didn't think he would have been so easily prevailed upon.

O'FLA. At the first word; no difficulty in life. 'Twas the very thing he was determined to do, before I came; I never met a more obliging gentleman.

L. RUS. Well, 'tis no matter, so I am but rid of him and his distresses. Would you believe it, Major O'Flaherty, it was but this morning he sent a begging to me for money to fit him out upon some wild-goose expedition to the coast of Africa, I know not where.

O'FLA. Well, you sent him what he wanted?

L. RUS. I sent him what he deserved, a flat refusal.

O'FLA. You refused him!

L. RUS. Most undoubtedly.

O'FLA. You sent him nothing!

L. RUS. Not a shilling.

O'FLA. Good morning to you—Your servant—(*Going*)

L. RUS. Hey-day! What ails the man? Where are you going?

O'FLA. Out of your house, before the roof falls on my head—to poor Dudley, to share the little modicum that thirty years hard service has left me; I wish it was more for his sake.

L. RUS. Very well, sir, take your course. I shan't attempt to stop you; I shall survive it; it will not break my heart if I never see you more.

O'FLA. Break your heart! No, o'my conscience will it not.—You preach, and you pray, and you turn up your eyes, and all the while you're as hard-hearted as an hyena—A hyena, truly! By my soul, there isn't in the whole creation so savage an animal as a human creature without pity. (*Exit*)

L. RUS. A hyena, truly! Where did the fellow blunder upon that word? Now the deuce take him for using it, and the Macaronies for inventing it. (*Exit*)

Act III

SCENE I. *A Room in* STOCKWELL'S *House.*

(*Enter* STOCKWELL *and* BELCOUR)

STOCK. Gratify me so far, however, Mr. Belcour, as to see Miss Rusport. Carry her the sum she wants, and return the poor girl her box of diamonds, which Dudley left in my hands. You know what to say on the occasion better than I do; that part of your commission I leave to your own discretion, and you may season it with what gallantry you think fit.

BEL. You could not have pitched upon a greater bungler at gallantry than myself, if you had rummaged every company in the city, and the whole court of aldermen into the bargain. Part of your errand, however, I will do; but whether it shall be with an ill grace or a good one depends upon the caprice of a moment, the humor of the lady, the mode of our meeting, and a thousand undefinable small circumstances that nevertheless determine us upon all the great occasions of life.

STOCK. I persuade myself you will find Miss Rusport an ingenious, worthy, animated girl.

BEL. Why I like her the better, as a woman; but name her not to me as a wife! No, if I ever marry, it must be a staid, sober, considerate damsel, with blood in her veins as cold as a turtle's; quick of scent as a vulture when danger's in the wind; wary and sharp-sighted as a hawk when treachery is on foot. With such a companion at my elbow, for ever whispering in my ear—"Have a care of this man, he's a cheat; don't go near that woman, she's a jilt; over head there's a scaffold, under foot there's a well." Oh! sir, such a woman might lead me up and down this great city without difficulty or danger. But with a girl of Miss Rusport's complexion, heaven and earth, sir, we should be duped, undone, and distracted in a fortnight.

STOCK. Ha! ha! ha! Why you are become wond'rous circumspect of a sudden, pupil; and if you can find such a prudent damsel as you describe, you have my consent—only beware how you choose. Discretion is not the reigning quality amongst the fine ladies of the present time, and I think in Miss Rusport's particular I have given you no bad counsel.

BEL. Well, well, if you'll fetch me the jewels, I believe I can undertake to carry them to her, but as for the money, I'll have nothing to do with that. Dudley would be your fittest ambassador on that occasion, and, if I mistake not, the most agreeable to the lady.

STOCK. Why, indeed, from what I know of the matter, it may not improbably be destined to find its way into his pockets. (*Exit*)

BEL. Then, depend upon it, these are not the only trinkets she means to dedicate to Captain Dudley. As for me, Stockwell indeed wants me to marry, but till I can get this bewitching girl, this incognita, out of my head, I can never think of any other woman.

(SERVANT *enters, and delivers a letter*)

Heyday! Where can I have picked up a correspondent already! 'Tis a most execrable manuscript—Let me see—Martha Fulmer—Who is Martha Fulmer? Pshaw! I won't be at the trouble of deciphering her damned pothooks. Hold, hold, hold; what have we got here!

"DEAR SIR,

I've discovered the lady you was so much smitten with, and can procure you an interview with her; if you can be as generous to a pretty girl as you was to a paltry old captain —how did she find that out!—you need not despair. Come to me immediately; the lady is now in my house, and expects you.

Yours,
MARTHA FULMER."

O thou dear, lovely, and enchanting paper, which I was about to tear into a thousand scraps, devoutly I entreat thy pardon. I have slighted thy contents, which are delicious; slandered thy characters, which are divine; and all the atonement I can make is implicitly to obey thy mandates.

(STOCKWELL *returns*)

STOCK. Mr. Belcour, here are the jewels. This letter encloses bills for the money, and if you will deliver it to Miss Rusport, you'll have no farther trouble on that score.

BEL. Ah, sir! the letter which I've been reading disqualifies me for delivering the letter which you have been writing. I have other game on foot; the loveliest girl my eyes ever feasted upon is started in view, and the world cannot now divert me from pursuing her.

STOCK. Hey-day! What has turned you thus on a sudden?

BEL. A woman: one that can turn, and overturn me and my tottering resolutions every way she will. Oh, sir, if this is folly in me, you must rail at Nature; you must chide the sun, that was vertical at my birth and would not wink upon my nakedness, but swaddled me in the broadest, hottest glare of his meridian beams.

STOCK. Mere rhapsody; mere childish rhapsody; the libertine's familiar plea——Nature made us, 'tis true, but we are the responsible creators of our own faults and follies.

BEL. Sir!

STOCK. Slave of every face you meet, some hussy has inveigled you, some handsome profligate (the town is full of them); and, when once fairly bankrupt in constitution, as well as fortune, nature no longer serves as your excuse for being vicious, necessity, perhaps, will stand your friend, and you'll reform.

BEL. You are severe.

STOCK. It fits me to be so—it well becomes a father——I would say a friend—(*Aside*) How strangely I forget myself—How difficult it is to counterfeit indifference, and put a mask upon the heart—I've struck him hard; he reddens.

BEL. How could you tempt me so? Had you not inadvertently dropped the name of father, I fear our friendship, short as it has been, would scarce have held me. But even your mistake I reverence—Give me your hand—'tis over.

STOCK. Generous young man——let me embrace you——How shall I hide my tears? I have been to blame; because I bore you the affection of a father, I rashly took up the authority of one. I ask your pardon. Pursue your course; I have no right to stop it.——What would you have me do with these things?

BEL. This, if I might advise: carry the money to Miss Rusport immediately; never let generosity wait for its materials; that part of the business presses. Give me the jewels; I'll find an opportunity of delivering them into her hands, and your visit may pave the way for my reception.

STOCK. Be it so. Good morning to you. (*Exit* BELCOUR) Farewell advice! Away goes he upon the wing for pleasure. What various passions he awakens in me! He pains, yet pleases me; affrights, offends, yet grows upon my heart. His very failings set him off —forever trespassing, forever atoning. I almost think he would not be so perfect, were he free from fault. I must dissemble longer, and yet how painful the experiment!—Even now he's gone upon some wild adventure, and who can tell what mischief may befall him. O Nature, what it is to be a father! Just such a thoughtless headlong thing was I when I beguiled his mother into love.

(*Exit*)

Scene II. Fulmer's *House*.

(*Enter* Fulmer *and his* Wife)

Ful. I tell you, Patty, you are a fool to think of bringing him and Miss Dudley together. 'Twill ruin every thing and blow your whole scheme up to the moon at once.

Mrs. Ful. Why, sure, Mr. Fulmer, I may be allowed to rear a chicken of my own hatching, as they say. Who first sprung the thought but I, pray? Who first contrived the plot? Who proposed the letter, but I, I?

Ful. And who dogged the gentleman home? Who found out his name, fortune, connection? That he was a West Indian, fresh landed, and full of cash; a gull to our heart's content; a hot-brained headlong spark, that would run into our trap like a wheat-ear under a turf?

Mrs. Ful. Hark! he's come. Disappear, march, and leave the field open to my machinations. (*Exit* Fulmer)

(Belcour *enters to her*)

Bel. O, thou dear minister to my happiness, let me embrace thee! Why, thou art my polar star, my propitious constellation, by which I navigate my impatient bark into the port of pleasure and delight.

Mrs. Ful. Oh, you men are sly creatures! Do you remember now, you cruel, what you said to me this morning?

Bel. All a jest, a frolic! Never think on't, bury it for ever in oblivion. Thou! why thou art all over nectar and ambrosia, powder of pearl and odor of roses; thou hast the youth of Hebe, the beauty of Venus, and the pen of Sappho. But in the name of all that's lovely, where's the lady? I expected to find her with you.

Mrs. Ful. No doubt you did, and these raptures were designed for her; but where have you loitered? The lady's gone, you are too late; girls of her sort are not to be kept waiting like negro slaves in your sugar plantations.

Bel. Gone! whither is she gone? Tell me that I may follow her.

Mrs. Ful. Hold, hold, not so fast, young gentleman, this is a case of some delicacy. Should Captain Dudley know that I introduced you to his daughter, he is a man of such scrupulous honor——

Bel. What do you tell me! Is she daughter to the old gentleman I met here this morning?

Mrs. Ful. The same; him you was so generous to.

Bel. There's an end of the matter then at once; it shall never be said of me, that I took advantage of the father's necessities to trepan the daughter. (*Going*)

Mrs. Ful. (*Aside*) So, so, I've made a wrong cast, he's one of your conscientious sinners I find; but I won't lose him thus—— Ha! ha! ha!

Bel. What is it you laugh at?

Mrs. Ful. Your absolute inexperience. Have you lived so very little time in this country, as not to know that between young people of equal ages, the term of sister often is a cover for that of mistress? This young lady is, in that sense of the word, sister to young Dudley, and consequently daughter to my old lodger.

Bel. Indeed! Are you serious?

Mrs. Ful. Can you doubt it! I must have been pretty well assured of that before I invited you hither.

Bel. That's true; she cannot be a woman of honor, and Dudley is an unconscionable young rogue to think of keeping one fine girl in pay, by raising contributions on another. He shall therefore give her up; she is a dear, bewitching, mischievous, little devil, and he shall positively give her up.

Mrs. Ful. Ay, now the freak has taken

you again; I say give her up. There's one way, indeed, and certain of success.

BEL. What's that?

MRS. FUL. Out-bid him, never dream of out-blust'ring him; buy out his lease of possession, and leave her to manage his ejectment.

BEL. Is she so venal? Never fear me then; when beauty is the purchase, I shan't think much of the price.

MRS. FUL. All things, then, will be made easy enough. Let me see; some little genteel present to begin with. What have you got about you? Ay, search; I can bestow it to advantage, there's no time to be lost.

BEL. Hang it, confound it; a plague upon't, say I! I haven't a guinea left in my pocket; I parted from my whole stock here this morning, and have forgot to supply myself since.

MRS. FUL. Mighty well, let it pass then, there's an end. Think no more of the lady, that's all.

BEL. Distraction! Think no more of her? Let me only step home and provide myself, I'll be back with you in an instant.

MRS. FUL. Pooh, pooh! that's a wretched shift. Have you nothing of value about you? Money's a coarse slovenly vehicle, fit only to bribe electors in a borough; there are more graceful ways of purchasing a lady's favors—rings, trinkets, jewels!

BEL. Jewels! Gadso, I protest I had forgot. I have a case of jewels; but they won't do, I must not part from them. No, no, they are appropriated; they are none of my own. (*He takes* MISS RUSPORT's *jewels from his pocket*)

MRS. FUL. Let me see, let me see! (*She takes them*) Ay, now, this were something like. Pretty creatures, how they sparkle! these would ensure success.

BEL. Indeed!

MRS. FUL. These would make her your own for ever.

BEL. Then the deuce take 'em for belonging to another person; I could find in my heart to give 'em the girl, and swear I've lost them.

MRS. FUL. Ay, do, say they were stolen out of your pocket.

BEL. No, hang it, that's dishonorable. Here, give me the paltry things, I'll write you an order on my merchant for double their value.

MRS. FUL. (*Holds the jewels behind her*) An order! No; order for me no orders upon merchants, with their value received, and three days grace; their noting, protesting, and endorsing, and all their counting house formalities; I'll have nothing to do with them. Leave your diamonds with me, and give your order for the value of them to the owner. The money would be as good as the trinkets, I warrant you.

BEL. Hey! how! I never thought of that. But a breach of trust, 'tis impossible. I never can consent; therefore give me the jewels back again.

MRS. FUL. (*Returns jewels*) Take 'em; I am now to tell you the lady is in this house?

BEL. In this house?

MRS. FUL. Yes, sir, in this very house; but what of that? You have got what you like better, your toys, your trinkets; go, go: Oh! you're a man of a notable spirit, are you not?

BEL. Provoking creature! Bring me to the sight of the dear girl, and dispose of me as you think fit.

MRS. FUL. And of the diamonds too?

BEL. Damn 'em, I would there was not such a bauble in nature! But come, come, dispatch; if I had the throne of Delhi I should give it to her.

MRS. FUL. Swear to me then that you will keep within bounds, remember she passes for the sister of young Dudley. Oh! if you come to your flights, and your rhapsodies, she'll be off in an instant.

BEL. Never fear me.

MRS. FUL. You must expect to hear her talk of her father, as she calls him, and her brother, and your bounty to her family.

BEL. Ay, ay, never mind what she talks of, only bring her.

MRS. FUL. You'll be prepared upon that head?

BEL. I shall be prepared, never fear; away with you.

MRS. FUL. But hold, I had forgot: not a word of the diamonds; leave that matter to my management.

BEL. Hell and vexation! Get out of the room, or I shall run distracted. (*Exit* MRS. FULMER) Of a certain, Belcour, thou art born to be the fool of woman. Sure no man sins with so much repentance, or repents with so little amendment, as I do. I cannot give away another person's property, honor forbids me; and I positively cannot give up the girl; love, passion, constitution, every thing protests against that. How shall I decide? I cannot bring myself to break a trust, and I am not at present in the humor to balk my inclinations. Is there no middle way? Let me consider—There is, there is! My good genius has presented me with one, apt, obvious, honorable. The girl shall not go without her baubles, I'll not go without the girl, Miss Rusport shan't lose her diamonds, I'll save Dudley from destruction, and every party shall be a gainer by the project.

(*Enter* Mrs. Fulmer *introducing* Miss Dudley)

Mrs. Ful. Miss Dudley, this is the worthy gentleman you wish to see; this is Mr. Belcour.

Lou. (*Aside*) As I live, the very man that beset me in the streets!

Bel. (*Aside*) An angel, by this light! Oh, I am gone past all retrieving!

Lou. Mrs. Fulmer, sir, informs me you are the gentleman from whom my father has received such civilities.

Bel. Oh! never name 'em.

Lou. Pardon me, Mr. Belcour, they must be both named and remembered; and if my father was here——

Bel. I am much better pleased with his representative.

Lou. That title is my brother's, sir; I have no claim to it.

Bel. I believe it.

Lou. But as neither he nor my father were fortunate enough to be at home, I could not resist the opportunity—

Bel. Nor I neither, by my soul, madam. Let us improve it, therefore. I am in love with you to distraction; I was charmed at the first glance; I attempted to accost you; you fled; I followed, but was defeated of an interview. At length I have obtained one,

and seize the opportunity of casting my person and my fortune at your feet.

Lou. You astonish me! Are you in your senses, or do you make a jest of my misfortunes? Do you ground pretences on your generosity, or do you make a practice of this folly with every woman you meet?

Bel. Upon my life, no. As you are the handsomest woman I ever met, so you are the first to whom I ever made the like professions. As for my generosity, madam, I must refer you on that score to this good lady, who I believe has something to offer in my behalf.

Lou. Don't build upon that, sir; I must have better proofs of your generosity than the mere divestment of a little superfluous dross, before I can credit the sincerity of professions so abruptly delivered.

(*Exit hastily*)

Bel. Oh! ye gods and goddesses, how her anger animates her beauty!   (*Going out*)

Mrs. Ful. Stay, sir, if you stir a step after her, I renounce your interest for ever. Why you'll ruin every thing.

Bel. Well, I must have her, cost what it will. I see she understands her own value tho'; a little superfluous dross, truly! She must have better proofs of my generosity.

Mrs. Ful. 'Tis exactly as I told you. Your money she calls dross; she's too proud to stain her fingers with your coin. Bait your hook well with jewels; try that experiment, and she's your own.

Bel. Take 'em, let 'em go, lay 'em at her feet. I must get out of the scrape as I can; my propensity is irresistible. There! (*Gives her the jewels*) You have 'em; they are yours; they are hers. But remember they are a trust; I commit them to her keeping till I can buy 'em off with something she shall think more valuable. Now tell me when shall I meet her?

Mrs. Ful. How can I tell that? Don't you see what an alarm you have put her into? Oh! you're a rare one! But go your ways for this while; leave her to my management, and come to me at seven this evening, but remember not to bring empty pockets with you——Ha! ha! ha!   (*Exeunt severally*)

Scene III. Lady Rusport's *House.*

(Miss Rusport *enters, followed by a Servant*)

CHAR. Desire Mr. Stockwell to walk in.
(*Exit Servant*)

(STOCKWELL *enters*)

STOCK. Madam, your most obedient servant. I am honored with your commands, by Captain Dudley, and have brought the the money with me as you directed. I understand the sum you have occasion for is two hundred pounds.

CHAR. It is, sir. I am quite confounded at your taking this trouble upon yourself, Mr. Stockwell.

STOCK. There is a bank note, madam, to the amount. Your jewels are in safe hands, and will be delivered to you directly. If I had been happy in being better known to you, I should have hoped you would not have thought it necessary to place a deposit in my hands for so trifling a sum as you have now required me to supply you with.

CHAR. The baubles I sent you may very well be spared, and as they are the only security in my present situation I can give you, I could wish you would retain them in your hands. When I am of age (which, if I live a few months, I shall be) I will replace your favor with thanks.

STOCK. It is obvious, Miss Rusport, that your charms will suffer no impeachment by the absence of those superficial ornaments, but they should be seen in the suite of a woman of fashion, not as creditors to whom you are indebted for your appearance, but as subservient attendants which help to make up your equipage.

CHAR. Mr. Stockwell is determined not to wrong the confidence I reposed in his politeness.

STOCK. I have only to request, madam, that you will allow Mr. Belcour, a young gentleman in whose happiness I particularly interest myself, to have the honor of delivering you the box of jewels.

CHAR. Most gladly; any friend of yours cannot fail of being welcome here.

STOCK. I flatter myself you will not find him totally undeserving your good opinion. An education not of the strictest kind, and strong animal spirits are apt sometimes to betray him into youthful irregularities; but an high principle of honor and an uncommon benevolence, in the eye of candor, will, I hope, atone for any faults by which these good qualities are not impaired.

CHAR. I dare say Mr. Belcour's behavior wants no apology. We've no right to be over strict in canvassing the morals of a common acquaintance.

STOCK. I wish it may be my happiness to see Mr. Belcour in the list, not of your common, but particular acquaintance, of your friends, Miss Rusport—I dare not be more explicit.

CHAR. Nor need you, Mr. Stockwell. I shall be studious to deserve his friendship; and, though I have long since unalterably placed my affections on another, I trust I have not left myself insensible to the merits of Mr. Belcour, and hope that neither you nor he will, for that reason, think me less worthy your good opinion and regards.

STOCK. Miss Rusport, I sincerely wish you happy. I have no doubt you have placed your affection on a deserving man, and I have no right to combat your choice.   (*Exit*)

CHAR. How honorable is that behavior! Now, if Charles were here, I should be happy. The old lady is so fond of her new Irish acquaintance that I have the whole house at my disposal.   (*Exit* CHARLOTTE)

(BELCOUR *enters, preceded by a* SERVANT)

SERV. I ask your honor's pardon; I thought my young lady was here. Who shall I inform her would speak to her?

BEL. Belcour is my name, sir; and pray beg your lady to put herself in no hurry on my account, for I'd sooner see the devil than see her face. (*Exit* SERVANT) In the name of all that's mischievous, why did Stockwell drive me hither in such haste? A pretty figure, truly, I shall make, an ambassador without credentials. Blockhead that I was to charge myself with her diamonds; officious, meddling puppy! Now they are irretrievably gone. That suspicious jade Fulmer wouldn't part even with a sight of them, tho' I would have ransomed 'em at twice their value. Now must I trust to my poor wits to bring me off —a lamentable dependance. Fortune be my helper! Here comes the girl—If she is noble minded, as she is said to be, she will forgive me; if not, 'tis a lost cause, for I have not thought of one word in my excuse.

(CHARLOTTE enters)

CHAR. Mr. Belcour, I'm proud to see you. Your friend, Mr. Stockwell, prepared me to expect this honor, and I am happy in the opportunity of being known to you.

BEL. (Aside) A fine girl, by my soul! Now what a cursed hang-dog do I look like!

CHAR. You are newly arrived in this country, sir?

BEL. Just landed, madam; just set a-shore, with a large cargo of Muscavado sugars, rum-puncheons, mahogany-slabs, wet sweet meats, and green paroquets.

CHAR. May I ask you how you like London, sir?

BEL. To admiration: I think the town and the town's-folk are exactly suited; 'tis a great, rich, overgrown, noisy, tumultuous place: the whole morning is a bustle to get money, and the whole afternoon is a hurry to spend it.

CHAR. Are these all the observations you have made?

BEL. No, madam; I have observed the women are very captivating, and the men very soon caught.

CHAR. Ay, indeed! Whence do you draw that conclusion?

BEL. From infallible guides; the first remark I collect from what I now see, the second from what I now feel.

CHAR. Oh, the deuce take you! But to waive this subject, I believe, sir, this was a visit of business, not compliment, was it not?

BEL. Ay. (Aside) Now comes on my execution.

CHAR. You have some foolish trinkets of mine, Mr. Belcour, haven't you?

BEL. No, in truth; they are gone in search of a trinket, still more foolish than themselves.

CHAR. Some diamonds I mean, sir; Mr. Stockwell informed me you was charged with 'em.

BEL. Oh, yes, madam; but I have the most treacherous memory in life—Here they are! Pray put them up; they're all right; you need not examine 'em. (Gives a box)

CHAR. (Opens the box) Hey-day! Right, sir! Why these are not my diamonds; these are quite different, and, as it should seem, of much greater value.

BEL. Upon my life I'm glad on't, for then I hope you value 'em more than your own.

CHAR. As a purchaser I should, but not as an owner; you mistake, these belong to somebody else.

BEL. 'Tis yours, I'm afraid, that belong to somebody else.

CHAR. What is it you mean? I must insist upon your taking 'em back again.

BEL. Pray, madam, don't do that; I shall infallibly lose them. I have the worst luck with diamonds of any man living.

CHAR. That you might well say, was you to give me these in the place of mine. But pray, sir, what is the reason of all this? Why have you changed the jewels? And where have you disposed of mine?

BEL. Miss Rusport, I cannot invent a lie for my life; and, if it was to save it, I couldn't tell one. I am an idle, dissipated, unthinking fellow, not worth your notice: in short, I am a West Indian, and you must try me according to the charter of my colony, not by a jury of English spinsters. The truth is, I've given away your jewels; caught with a pair of sparkling eyes, whose lustre blinded theirs, I served your property as I should my own and lavished it away. Let me not totally despair of your forgiveness. I frequently do wrong, but never with impunity; if your displeasure is added to my own, my punishment will be too severe. When I parted from the jewels, I had not the honor of knowing their owner.

CHAR. Mr. Belcour, your sincerity charms me; I enter at once into your character, and I make all the allowances for it you can desire. I take your jewels for the present, because I know there is no other way of reconciling you to yourself; but, if I give way to your spirit in one point, you must yield to mine in another. Remember I will not keep more than the value of my own jewels. There is no need to be pillaged by more than one woman at a time, sir.

BEL. Now, may every blessing that can crown your virtues and reward your beauty be showered upon you; may you meet admiration without envy, love without jealousy, and old age without malady; may the man of your heart be ever constant, and you never meet a less penitent, or less grateful offender, than myself!

(SERVANT *enters and delivers a letter*)

CHAR. Does your letter require such haste?

SERV. I was bade to give it into your own hands, madam.

CHAR. From Charles Dudley, I see—(*to* BELCOUR) have I your permission? Good Heaven, what do I read! Mr. Belcour, you are concern'd in this——"Dear Charlotte, in the midst of our distress, Providence has cast a benefactor in our way, after the most unexpected manner. A young West Indian, rich and with a warmth of heart peculiar to his climate, has rescued my father from his troubles, satisfied his wants, and enabled him to accomplish his exchange. When I relate to you the manner in which this was done, you will be charmed; I can only now add, that it was by chance we found out that his name is Belcour, and that he is a friend of Mr. Stockwell's. I lose not a moment's time in making you acquainted with this fortunate event, for reasons which delicacy obliges me to suppress; but perhaps if you have not received the money on your jewels, you will not think it necessary now to do it. I have the honor to be,

Dear Madam,

most faithfully, yours,

CHARLES DUDLEY."

Is this your doing, Sir? Never was generosity so worthily exerted.

BEL. Or so greatly overpaid.

CHAR. After what you have now done for this noble but indigent family, let me not scruple to unfold the whole situation of my heart to you. Know then, sir (and don't think the worse of me for the frankness of my declaration), that such is my attachment to the son of that worthy officer whom you relieved, that the moment I am of age and in possession of my fortune, I should hold myself the happiest of women to share it with young Dudley.

BEL. Say you so, madam! Then let me perish if I don't love and reverence you above all womankind; and if such is your generous resolution, never wait till you're of age. Life is too short, pleasure too fugitive; the soul grows narrower every hour. I'll equip you for your escape. I'll convey you to the man of your heart, and away with you then to the first hospitable parson that will take you in.

CHAR. O blessed be the torrid zone for ever, whose rapid vegetation quickens nature into such benignity! These latitudes are made for politics and philosophy; friendship has no root in this soil. But had I spirit to accept your offer, which is not improbable, wouldn't it be a mortifying thing for a fond girl to find herself mistaken and sent back to her home like a vagrant? And such, for what I know, might be my case.

BEL. Then he ought to be proscribed the society of mankind for ever——(*Aside*) Ay, ay, 'tis the sham sister that makes him thus indifferent; 'twill be a meritorious office to take that girl out of the way.

(SERVANT *enters*)

SERV. Miss Dudley to wait on you, madam.

BEL. (*Astonished*) Who?

SERV. Miss Dudley.

CHAR. What's the matter, Mr. Belcour? Are you frighted at the name of a pretty girl? 'Tis the sister of him we were speaking of—pray admit her.

BEL. The sister! (*Aside*) So, so; he has imposed on her too—this is an extraordinary visit, truly. Upon my soul, the assurance of some folks is not to be accounted for.

(*He starts toward the door*)

CHAR. I insist upon your not running away; you'll be charmed with Louisa Dudley.

BEL. Oh, yes, I am charmed with her.

CHAR. You've seen her then, have you?

BEL. Yes, yes, I've seen her.

CHAR. Well, isn't she a delightful girl?

BEL. Very delightful.

CHAR. Why, you answer as if you was in a court of justice. O' my conscience! I believe you are caught; I've a notion she has trick'd you out of your heart.

BEL. I believe she has, and you out of your jewels; for, to tell you the truth, she's the very person I gave 'em to.

CHAR. You gave her my jewels! Louisa Dudley my jewels? Admirable! Inimitable! Oh, the sly little jade! But hush, here she comes; I don't know how I shall keep my countenance. (LOUISA *enters*) My dear, I'm rejoiced to see you; how d'ye do? (*Roguishly*) I beg leave to introduce Mr. Belcour, a very worthy friend of mine; I believe, Louisa, you have seen him before.

LOU. I have met the gentleman.

CHAR. You have met the gentleman. Well, sir, and you have met the lady; in short, you have met each other. Why then don't you speak to each other? How you both stand! Tongue-tied, and fix'd as statues ——Ha! ha! ha! Why you'll fall asleep by-and-by.

LOU. Fie upon you, fie upon you; is this fair?

BEL. (*Aside*) Upon my soul, I never looked so like a fool in my life; the assurance of that girl puts me quite down.

CHAR. Sir—Mr. Belcour—Was it your pleasure to advance any thing? Not a syllable. Come, Louisa, women's wit, they say, is never at a loss—Nor you neither? Speechless both. Why you was merry enough before this lady came in.

LOU. I am sorry I have been any interruption to your happiness, sir.

BEL. Madam!

CHAR. Madam! Is that all you can say? But come, my dear girl, I won't tease you. Apropos! I must show you what a present this dumb gentleman has made me. Are not these handsome diamonds?

LOU. Yes, indeed, they seem very fine; but I am no judge of these things.

CHAR. Oh, you wicked little hypocrite, you are no judge of these things, Louisa; you have no diamonds, not you.

LOU. You know I haven't, Miss Rusport. You know those things are infinitely above my reach.

CHAR. Ha! ha! ha!

BEL. (*Aside*) She does tell a lie with an admirable countenance, that's true enough.

LOU. What ails you, Charlotte? What impertinence have I been guilty of that you should find it necessary to humble me at such a rate? If you are happy, long may you be so; but, surely, it can be no addition to it to make me miserable.

CHAR. So serious! there must be some mystery in this—Mr. Belcour, will you leave us together? You see I treat you with all the familiarity of an old acquaintance already.

BEL. Oh, by all means, pray command me. Miss Rusport, I'm your most obedient! By your condescension in accepting these poor trifles, I am under eternal obligations to you. —To you, Miss Dudley, I shall not offer a word on the subject. You despise finery. You have a soul above it; I adore your spirit. I was rather unprepared for meeting you here, but I shall hope for an opportunity of making myself better known to you.   (*Exit*)

CHAR. Louisa Dudley, you surprise me; I never saw you act thus before. Can't you bear a little innocent raillery before the man of your heart?

LOU. The man of my heart, madam? Be assured I never was so visionary to aspire to any man whom Miss Rusport honors with her choice.

CHAR. My choice, my dear! Why we are playing at cross purposes. How enter'd it into your head that Mr. Belcour was the man of my choice?

LOU. Why, didn't he present you with those diamonds?

CHAR. Well, perhaps he did—and pray, Louisa, have you no diamonds?

LOU. I, diamonds, truly! Who should give me diamonds?

CHAR. Who, but this very gentleman. Apropos! here comes your brother——

(CHARLES *enters*)

I insist upon referring our dispute to him. Your sister and I, Charles, have a quarrel. Belcour, the hero of your letter, has just left us. Somehow or other, Louisa's bright eyes have caught him, and the poor fellow's fallen desperately in love with her—(don't interrupt me, hussy)—Well, that's excusable enough, you'll say; but the jet[1] of the story is that this hair-brained spark, who does nothing like other people, has given her the very identical jewels which you pledged for me to Mr. Stockwell. And will you believe that this little demure slut made up a face and squeezed out three or four hypocritical tears, because I rallied her about it.

CHARLES. I'm all astonishment! Louisa, tell me without reserve, has Mr. Belcour given you any diamonds?

LOU. None, upon my honor.

CHARLES. Has he made any professions to you?

LOU. He has, but altogether in a style so whimsical and capricious that the best which can be said of them is to tell you that they seemed more the result of good spirits than good manners.

CHAR. Ay, ay, now the murder's out; he's in love with her, and she has no very great dislike to him, trust to my observation, Charles, for that. As to the diamonds, there's some mistake about them, and you must clear it up. Three minutes conversation with him will put every thing in a right train. Go, go, Charles, 'tis a brother's business; about it instantly. Ten to one you'll find him over the way at Mr. Stockwell's.

CHARLES. I confess I'm impatient to have the case cleared up; I'll take your advice, and find him out. Good bye to you.

CHAR. Your servant; my life upon it you'll find Belcour a man of honor. Come, Louisa, let us adjourn to my dressing-room; I've a little private business to transact with you before the old lady comes up to tea and interrupts us.

Act IV

SCENE I. FULMER's *House.*

(*Enter* FULMER *and* MRS. FULMER)

FUL. Patty, wasn't Mr. Belcour with you?

MRS. FUL. He was; and is now shut up in my chamber, in high expectation of an interview with Miss Dudley; she's at present with her brother, and 'twas with some difficulty I persuaded my hot-headed spark to wait till he has left her.

FUL. Well, child, and what then?

MRS. FUL. Why then, Mr. Fulmer, I think it will be time for you and me to steal a march, and be gone.

FUL. So this is all the fruit of your ingenious project, a shameful overthrow, or a sudden flight.

MRS. FUL. Why, my project was a mere impromptu, and can at worst but quicken our departure a few days; you know we had fairly outlived our credit here, and a trip to Boulogne is no ways unseasonable. Nay, never droop, man—Hark! hark! here's enough to bear charges. (*Showing a purse*)

FUL. Let me see, let me see! This weighs

¹ Gist.

well; this is of the right sort: why your West Indian bled freely.

MRS. FUL. But that's not all: look here! Here are the sparklers. (*Showing the jewels*) Now what d'ye think of my performances? Heh! a foolish scheme, isn't it—a silly woman?

FUL. Thou art a Judith, a Joan of Arc, and I'll march under thy banners, girl, to the world's end. Come, let's begone; I've little to regret; my creditors may share the old books amongst them; they'll have occasion for philosophy to support their loss; they'll find enough upon my shelves. The world is my library; I read mankind! Now, Patty, lead the way.

MRS. FUL. Adieu, Belcour!   (*Exeunt*)

(*Enter* CHARLES DUDLEY *and* LOUISA)

CHARLES. Well, Louisa, I confess the force of what you say. I accept Miss Rusport's bounty; and, when you see my generous Charlotte, tell her——but have a care, there is a selfishness even in gratitude, when it is too profuse; to be overthankful for any one favor, is in effect to lay out for another; the best return I could make my benefactress would be never to see her more.

Lou. I understand you.

CHARLES. We that are poor, Louisa, should be cautious; for this reason, I would guard you against Belcour; at least till I can unravel the mystery of Miss Rusport's diamonds. I was disappointed of finding him at Mr. Stockwell's, and am now going in search of him again. He may intend honorably; but, I confess to you, I am staggered. Think no more of him, therefore, for the present. Of this be sure, while I have life, and you have honor, I will protect you, or perish in your defence.

(Exit)

Lou. Think of him no more! Well, I'll obey; but if a wandering uninvited thought should creep by chance into my bosom, must I not give the harmless wretch a shelter? Oh! yes! The great artificer of the human heart knows every thread he wove into its fabric, nor puts his work to harder uses than it was made to bear. My wishes then, my guiltless ones, I mean, are free. How fast they spring within me at that sentence! Down, down, ye busy creatures! Whither would you carry me? Ah! there is one amongst you, a forward, new intruder, that, in the likeness of an offending, generous man, grows into favor with my heart. Fie, fie upon it! Belcour pursues, insults me; yet, such is the fatality of my condition, that what should rouse resentment, only calls up love.

(BELCOUR enters to her)

BEL. Alone, by all that's happy!

Lou. Ah!

BEL. Oh! shriek not, start not, stir not, loveliest creature! but let me kneel, and gaze upon your beauties. *(He kneels)*

Lou. Sir! Mr. Belcour, rise! What is it you do?

BEL. See, I obey you. Mould me as you will, behold your ready servant! New to your country, ignorant of your manners, habits, and desires, I put myself into your hands for instruction; make me only such as you can like yourself, and I shall be happy.

Lou. I must not hear this, Mr. Belcour. Go! Should he that parted from me but this minute now return, I tremble for the consequence.

BEL. Fear nothing; let him come. I love you, madam; he'll find it hard to make me unsay that.

Lou. You terrify me; your impetuous temper frightens me; you know my situation; it is not generous to pursue me thus.

BEL. True; I do know your situation, your real one, Miss Dudley, and am resolved to snatch you from it. 'Twill be a meritorious act; the old Captain shall rejoice; Miss Rusport shall be made happy; and even he, even your beloved brother, with whose resentment you threaten me, shall in the end applaud and thank me. Come, thou'rt a dear enchanting girl, and I'm determin'd not to live a minute longer without thee.

(He reaches for her)

Lou. *(Starting back)* Hold, are you mad? I see you are a bold assuming man, and know not where to stop.

BEL. Who that beholds such beauty can? By Heaven, you put my blood into a flame. Provoking girl! Is it within the stretch of my fortune to content you? What is it you can further ask that I am not ready to grant?

Lou. Yes, with the same facility that you bestowed upon me Miss Rusport's diamonds. For shame! for shame! Was that a manly story?

BEL. So! so! These devilish diamonds meet me every where! Let me perish if I meant you any harm! Oh! I could tear my tongue out for saying a word about the matter.

Lou. Go to her then, and contradict it; till that is done, my reputation is at stake.

BEL. *(Aside)* Her reputation! Now she has got upon that, she'll go on for ever.— What is there I will not do for your sake? I will go to Miss Rusport.

Lou. Do so; restore her own jewels to her, which I suppose you kept back for the purpose of presenting others to her of a greater value; but for the future, Mr. Belcour, when you would do a gallant action to that lady, don't let it be at my expense.

BEL. *(Aside)* I see where she points: she is willing enough to give up Miss Rusport's diamonds, now she finds she shall be a gainer by the exchange. Be it so! 'tis what I wished. —Well, madam, I will return Miss Rusport her own jewels, and you shall have others of tenfold their value.

Lou. No, sir, you err most widely; it is my good opinion, not my vanity, which you must bribe.

BEL. (*Aside*) Why, what the devil would she have now?—Miss Dudley, it is my wish to obey and please you, but I have some apprehension that we mistake each other.

Lou. I think we do: tell me, then, in few words, what it is you aim at.

BEL. In few words, then, and in plain honesty, I must tell you, so entirely am I captivated with you, that had you been such as it would have become me to have called my wife, I had been happy in knowing you by that name; as it is, you are welcome to partake my fortune, give me in return your person, give me pleasure, give me love——free, disencumbered, antimatrimonial love.

Lou. (*Horrified*) Stand off, and let me never see you more.

BEL. Hold, hold, thou dear, tormenting, tantalizing girl! Upon my knees I swear you shall not stir till you've consented to my bliss. (*He kneels and clasps her about the knees*)

Lou. Unhand me, sir! O Charles! protect me, rescue me, redress me. (*Exit*)

(CHARLES DUDLEY enters)

CHARLES. How's this! Rise, villain, and defend yourself.

BEL. Villain!

CHARLES. The man who wrongs that lady is a villain—Draw!

BEL. Never fear me, young gentleman; brand me for a coward if I baulk you.

CHARLES. Yet hold! Let me not be too hasty. Your name, I think, is Belcour.

BEL. Well, sir.

CHARLES. How is it, Mr. Belcour, you have done this mean, unmanly wrong, beneath the mask of generosity to give this fatal stab to our domestic peace? You might have had my thanks, my blessing; take my defiance now. 'Tis Dudley speaks to you, the brother, the protector of that injured lady.

BEL. The brother? Give yourself a truer title.

CHARLES. What is't you mean?

BEL. Come, come, I know both her and you. I found you, sir (but how or why I know not) in the good graces of Miss Rusport—yes, color at the name! I gave you no disturbance there, never broke in upon you in that rich and plenteous quarter; but, when I could have blasted all your projects with a word, spared you, in foolish pity spared you, nor roused her from the fond credulity in which your artifice had lulled her.

CHARLES. No, sir, nor boasted to her of the splendid present you had made my poor Louisa, the diamonds, Mr. Belcour. How was that? What can you plead to that arraignment?

BEL. You question me too late; the name of Belcour and of villain never met before. Had you enquired of me before you uttered that rash word, you might have saved yourself or me a mortal error. Now, sir, I neither give nor take an explanation. So, come on!

(*They draw swords and fight*)

(Enter LOUISA, *followed by* O'FLAHERTY)

Lou. Hold, hold, for Heaven's sake hold! Charles! Mr. Belcour! Help! Sir, sir, make haste, they'll murder one another.

O'FLA. Hell and confusion! What's all this uproar for? Can't you leave off cutting one another's throats, and mind what the poor girl says to you? (*He steps between them*) You've done a notable thing, haven't you both, to put her into such a flurry? I think, o' my conscience, she's the most frighted of the three.

CHARLES. Dear Louisa, recollect yourself. Why did you interfere? 'Tis in your cause.

BEL. Now could I kill him for caressing her.

O'FLA. O sir, your most obedient! You are the gentleman I had the honor of meeting here before. You was then running off at full speed like a Calmuck, now you are tilting and driving like a Bedlamite with this lad here, that seems as mad as yourself. 'Tis pity but your country had a little more employment for you both.

BEL. Mr. Dudley, when you've recovered the lady, you know where I am to be found. (*Exit*)

O'FLA. Well then, can't you stay where you are, and that will save the trouble of looking after you? Yon volatile fellow thinks to give a man the meeting by getting out of his way. By my soul 'tis a round-about method that of his. But I think he called you Dudley. Hark'e, young man, are you son of my friend the old captain?

CHARLES. I am. Help me to convey this lady to her chamber, and I shall be more at leisure to answer your questions.

O'FLA. Ay, will I. Come along, pretty one. If you've had wrong done you, young man, you need look no further for a second. Dennis O'Flaherty's your man for that. But never draw your sword before a woman, Dudley; damn it, never while you live draw your sword before a woman. (*Exeunt*)

SCENE II. LADY RUSPORT's *House*.

(*Enter* LADY RUSPORT *and* SERVANT)

SERV. An elderly gentleman, who says his name is Varland, desires leave to wait on your ladyship.

L. RUS. Show him in; the very man I wish to see. Varland, he was Sir Oliver's solicitor, and privy to all his affairs; he brings some good tidings, some fresh mortgage, or another bond come to light. They start up every day.

(VARLAND *enters*)

Mr. Varland, I'm glad to see you. You're heartily welcome, honest Mr. Varland; you and I haven't met since our late irreparable loss. How have you passed your time this age?

VAR. Truly, my lady, ill enough. I thought I must have followed good Sir Oliver.

L. RUS. Alack-a-day, poor man! Well, Mr. Varland, you find me here overwhelmed with trouble and fatigue, torn to pieces with a multiplicity of affairs, a great fortune poured upon me unsought for and unexpected. 'Twas my good father's will and pleasure it should be so, and I must submit.

VAR. Your ladyship inherits under a will made in the year forty-five, immediately after Captain Dudley's marriage with your sister.

L. RUS. I do so, Mr. Varland, I do so.

VAR. I well remember it. I engrossed every syllable. But I am surprised to find that your ladyship set so little store by this vast accession.

L. RUS. Why you know, Mr. Varland, I am a moderate woman; I had enough before. A small matter satisfies me; and Sir Stephen Rusport (Heaven be his portion!) took care I shouldn't want that.

VAR. Very true; very true, he did so. And I am overjoyed at finding your ladyship in

this disposition, for, truth to say, I was not without apprehension the news I have to communicate would have been of some prejudice to your ladyship's tranquillity.

L. RUS. News, sir! What news have you for me?

VAR. Nay, nothing to alarm you. A trifle, in your present way of thinking. I have a will of Sir Oliver's you have never seen.

L. RUS. A will! Impossible! How came you by it, pray?

VAR. I drew it up, at his command, in his last illness. It will save you a world of trouble. It gives his whole estate from you to his grandson, Charles Dudley.

L. RUS. To Dudley? His estate to Charles Dudley? I can't support it! I shall faint! You've killed me, you vile man! I never shall survive it!

VAR. Look'e there now! I protest, I thought you would have rejoiced at being clear of the incumbrance.

L. RUS. 'Tis false! 'Tis all a forgery, concerted between you and Dudley! Why else did I never hear of it before?

VAR. Have patience, my lady, and I'll tell you. By Sir Oliver's direction, I was to deliver this will into no hands but his grandson Dudley's. The young gentleman happened to be then in Scotland; I was dispatched thither in search of him. The hurry and fatigue of my journey brought on a fever by the way, which confined me in extreme danger for several days. Upon my recovery I pursued my journey, found young Dudley had left Scotland in the interim, and am now directed hither; where as soon I can find him, doubtless, I shall discharge my conscience and fulfil my commission.

L. RUS. Dudley then, as yet, knows nothing of this will?

VAR. Nothing. That secret rests with me.

L. RUS. (*Aside*) A thought occurs. By this fellow's talking of his conscience, I should guess it was upon sale.—Come, Mr. Varland, if 'tis as you say, I must submit. I was somewhat flurried at first, and forgot myself. I ask your pardon. This is no place to talk of business. Step with me into my room; we will there compare the will, and resolve accordingly——(*Aside*) Oh! would your fever had you, and I had your paper. (*Exeunt*)

(*Enter* MISS RUSPORT, CHARLES, *and* O'FLAHERTY)

CHAR. So, so! My lady and her lawyer have retired to close confabulation. Now, Major, if you are the generous man I take you for, grant me one favor.

O'FLA. Faith will I, and not think much of my generosity neither; for, though it may not be in my power to do the favor you ask, look you, it can never be in my heart to refuse it.

CHARLES. (*Aside*) Could this man's tongue do justice to his thoughts, how eloquent would he be!

CHAR. Plant yourself then in that room. Keep guard, for a few moments, upon the enemy's motions, in the chamber beyond, and, if they should attempt a sally, stop their march a moment, till your friend here can make good his retreat down the back-stairs.

O'FLA. A word to the wise! I'm an old campaigner. Make the best use of your time, and trust me for tying the old cat up to the picket.

CHAR. Hush! hush! not so loud.

CHARLES. 'Tis the office of a sentinel, Major, you have undertaken, rather than that of a field-officer.

O'FLA. 'Tis the office of a friend, my dear boy, and therefore no disgrace to a general. (*Exit*)

CHAR. Well, Charles, will you commit yourself to me for a few minutes?

CHARLES. Most readily; and let me, before one goes by, tender you the only payment I can ever make for your abundant generosity.

CHAR. Hold, hold! So vile a thing as money must not come between us. What shall I say! O Charles! O Dudley! What difficulties have you thrown upon me! Familiarly as we have lived, I shrink not at what I'm doing; and, anxiously as I have sought this opportunity, my fears almost persuade me to abandon it.

CHARLES. You alarm me!

CHAR. Your looks and actions have been so distant, and at this moment are so deterring, that, was it not for the hope that delicacy, and not disgust, inspires this conduct in you, I should sink with shame and apprehension. But times presses and I must speak; and plainly too. Was you now in possession of your grandfather's estate, as justly you ought to be, and, was you inclined to seek a companion for life, should you, or should you not, in that case, honor your unworthy Charlotte with your choice?

CHARLES. My unworthy Charlotte! So judge me Heaven, there is not a circumstance on earth so valuable as your happiness, so dear to me as your person! But to bring poverty, disgrace, reproach from friends, ridicule from all the world, upon a generous benefactress; thievishly to steal into an open, unreserved, ingenuous heart——O Charlotte! Dear, unhappy girl, it is not to be done.

CHAR. Nay, now you rate too highly the poor advantages fortune alone has given me over you. How otherwise could we bring our merits to any balance? Come, my dear Charles, I have enough. Make that enough still more by sharing it with me. Sole heiress of my father's fortune, a short time will put it in my disposal. In the mean while you will be sent to join your regiment. Let us prevent a separation, by setting out this very night for that happy country where marriage still is free. Carry me this moment to Belcour's lodgings.

CHARLES. Belcour's? (*Aside*) The name is ominous; there's murder in it: bloody inexorable honor!

CHAR. D'ye pause? Put me into his hands, while you provide the means for our escape. He is the most generous, the most honorable of men.

CHARLES. Honorable! most honorable!

CHAR. Can you doubt it? Do you demur? Have you forgot your letter? Why, Belcour 'twas that prompted me to this proposal, that promised to supply the means, that nobly offered his unasked assistance——

(O'FLAHERTY *enters hastily*)

O'FLA. Run, run, for holy St. Anthony's sake! To horse and away! The conference is broke up, and the old lady advances upon a full Piedmontese trot, within pistol-shot of your encampment.

CHAR. Here, here, down the back-stairs! O Charles, remember me!

CHARLES. Farewell! Now, now I feel myself a coward.   (*Exit*)

CHAR. What does he mean?

O'FLA. Ask no questions, but be gone. (*Exit* CHARLOTTE) She has cooled the lad's courage, and wonders he feels like a coward. There's a damned deal of mischief brewing between this hyena and her lawyer. Egad I'll step behind this screen and listen: a good soldier must sometimes fight in ambush as well as open field. (*Hides behind a screen*)

(*Enter* LADY RUSPORT *and* VARLAND *with the will*)

L. RUS. Sure I heard somebody. Hark! No, only the servants going down the back-stairs. Well, Mr. Varland, I think then we are agreed. You'll take my money, and your conscience no longer stands in your way.

VAR. Your father was my benefactor. His will ought to be sacred; but, if I commit it to the flames, how will he be the wiser? Dudley, 'tis true, has done me no harm; but five thousand pounds will do me much good. So, in short, madam, I take your offer. I will confer with my clerk, who witnessed the will, and to-morrow morning put it into your hands, upon condition you put five thousand good pounds into mine.

L. RUS. 'Tis a bargain. I'll be ready for you. Farewell.   (*Exit*)

VAR. Let me consider—Five thousand pounds prompt payment for destroying this scrap of paper, not worth five farthings. 'Tis a fortune easily earned. Yes, and 'tis another man's fortune easily thrown away. 'Tis a good round sum to be paid down at once for a bribe, but 'tis a damned rogue's trick in me to take it.

O'FLA. (*Aside*) So, so! this fellow speaks truth to himself, tho' he lies to other people—but hush!

VAR. 'Tis breaking the trust of my benefactor—that's a foul crime. But he's dead, and can never reproach me with it. And 'tis robbing young Dudley of his lawful patrimony. That's a hard case; but he's alive, and knows nothing of the matter.

O'FLA. (*Aside*) These lawyers are so used to bring off the rogueries of others that they are never without an excuse for their own.

VAR. Were I assured now that Dudley would give me half the money for producing this will that Lady Rusport does for concealing it, I would deal with him, and be an honest man at half price. I wish every gentleman of my profession could lay his hand on his heart and say the same thing.

O'FLA. (*Coming forth*) A bargain, old gentleman! Nay, never start, nor stare. You wasn't afraid of your own conscience, never be afraid of me.

VAR. Of you, sir. Who are you, pray?

O'FLA. I'll tell you who I am. You seem to wish to be honest, but want the heart to set about it. Now I am the very man in the world to make you so, for, if you do not give me up that paper this very instant, by the soul of me, fellow, I will not leave one whole bone in your skin that shan't be broken.

VAR. What right have you, pray, to take this paper from me?

O'FLA. What right have you, pray, to keep it from young Dudley? I don't know what it contains, but I am apt to think it will be safer in my hands than in yours. Therefore give it me without more words, and save yourself a beating. Do now, you had best.

VAR. Well, sir, I may as well make a grace of necessity. (*Gives* O'FLAHERTY *the will*) There! I have acquitted my conscience at the expense of five thousand pounds.

O'FLA. Five thousand pounds! Mercy upon me! When there are such temptations in the law, can we wonder if some of the corps are a disgrace to it?

VAR. Well, you have got the paper. If you are an honest man, give it to Charles Dudley.

O'FLA. An honest man! Look at me, friend, I am a soldier, this is not the livery of a knave. I am an Irishman, honey; mine is not the country of dishonor. Now, sirrah, be gone. If you enter these doors, or give Lady Rusport the least item of what has passed, I will cut off both your ears and rob the pillory of its due.

VAR. I wish I was once fairly out of his sight.   (*Exeunt*)

Scene III. *A Room in* Stockwell's *House.*

Stock. I must disclose myself to Belcour. This noble instance of his generosity, which old Dudley has been relating, allies me to him at once. Concealment becomes too painful; I shall be proud to own him for my son ——But see, he's here.

(Belcour *enters, and throws himself upon a sofa*)

Bel. O my curst tropical constitution! Would to Heaven I had been dropt upon the snows of Lapland, and never felt the blessed influence of the sun, so I had never burnt with these inflammatory passions!

Stock. So, so, you seem disordered, Mr. Belcour.

Bel. Disordered, sir! Why did I ever quit the soil in which I grew? What evil planet drew me from that warm sunny region, where naked nature walks without disguise, into this cold contriving artificial country?

Stock. Come, sir, you've met a rascal. What o'that? General conclusions are illiberal.

Bel. No, sir, I've met reflection by the way. I've come from folly, noise, and fury, and met a silent monitor—Well, well, a villain! 'Twas not to be pardoned—Pray never mind me, sir.

Stock. (*Aside*) Alas! my heart bleeds for him.

Bel. And yet, I might have heard him. Now, plague upon that blundering Irishman for coming in as he did. The hurry of the deed might palliate the event, deliberate execution has less to plead—Mr. Stockwell, I am bad company to you.

Stock. Oh, sir; make no excuse. I think you have not found me forward to pry into the secrets of your pleasures and pursuits, 'tis not my disposition. But there are times, when want of curiosity would be want of friendship.

Bel. Ah, sir, mine is a case wherein you and I shall never think alike. The punctilious rules by which I am bound are not to be found in your ledgers, nor will pass current in the compting house of a trader.

Stock. 'Tis very well, sir. If you think I can render you any service, it may be worth your trial to confide in me; if not, your secret is safer in your own bosom.

Bel. That sentiment demands my confidence; pray, sit down by me. You must know, I have an affair of honor on my hands with young Dudley, and, tho' I put up with no man's insult, yet I wish to take away no man's life.

Stock. I know the young man, and am apprised of your generosity to his father. What can have bred a quarrel between you?

Bel. A foolish passion on my side, and a haughty provocation on his. There is a girl, Mr. Stockwell, whom I have unfortunately seen, of most uncommon beauty. She has withall an air of so much natural modesty that had I not had good assurance of her being an attainable wanton, I declare I should as soon have thought of attempting the chastity of Diana.

(Servant *enters*)

Stock. Hey-day, do you interrupt us?

Serv. Sir, there's an Irish gentleman will take no denial. He says he must see Mr. Belcour directly upon business of the last consequence.

Bel. Admit him. 'Tis the Irish officer that parted us, and brings me young Dudley's challenge. I should have made a long story of it, and he'll tell you in three words.

(O'Flaherty *enters*)

O'Fla. Save you, my dear; and you, sir! I have a little bit of a word in private for you.

Bel. Pray deliver your commands; this gentleman is my intimate friend.

O'Fla. Why then, Ensign Dudley will be glad to measure swords with you, yonder, at the London Tavern, in Bishopsgate Street, at nine o'clock—you know the place.

Bel. I do, and shall observe the appointment.

O'Fla. Will you be of the party, sir? We shall want a fourth hand.

Stock. Savage as the custom is, I close with your proposal, and tho' I am not fully informed of the occasion of your quarrel, I shall rely on Mr. Belcour's honor for the justice of it, and willingly stake my life in his defence.

O'FLA. Sir, you're a gentleman of honor, and I shall be glad of being better known to you——But hark'e, Belcour, I had like to have forgot part of my errand. There is the money you gave old Dudley. You may tell it over, faith; 'tis a receipt in full. Now the lad can put you to death with a safe conscience, and when he has done that job for you, let it be a warning how you attempt the sister of a man of honor.

BEL. The sister?

O'FLA. Ay, the sister; 'tis English, is it not? Or Irish, 'tis all one. You understand me, his sister, or Louisa Dudley, that's her name I think, call her which you will. By St. Patrick, 'tis a foolish piece of a business, Belcour, to go about to take away a poor girl's virtue from her, when there are so many to be met in this town, who would have disposed of theirs to your hands. (*Exit*)

STOCK. Why I am thunderstruck! What is it you have done, and what is the shocking business in which I have engaged? If I understood him right, 'tis the sister of young Dudley you've been attempting. You talked to me of a profest wanton; the girl he speaks of has beauty enough indeed to inflame your desires, but she has honor, innocence and simplicity to awe the most licentious passion. If you have done that, Mr. Belcour, I renounce you, I abandon you, I forswear all fellowship or friendship with you for ever.

BEL. Have patience for a moment. We do indeed speak of the same person, but she is not innocent, she is not young Dudley's sister.

STOCK. Astonishing! Who told you this?

BEL. The woman where she lodges, the person who put me on the pursuit and contrived our meetings.

STOCK. What woman? What person?

BEL. Fulmer her name is. I warrant you I did not proceed without good grounds.

STOCK. Fulmer, Fulmer! (*Calls*) Who waits? (*A Servant enters*) Send Mr. Stukely hither directly. I begin to see my way into this dark transaction. Mr. Belcour, Mr. Belcour, you are no match for the cunning and contrivances of this intriguing town.

(STUKELY *enters*) Pr'ythee, Stukely, what is the name of the woman and her husband who were stopt upon suspicion of selling stolen diamonds at our next-door neighbor's, the jeweller?

STUKELY. Fulmer.

STOCK. So!

BEL. Can you procure me a sight of those diamonds?

STUKELY. (*Taking the case of jewels from his pocket*) They are now in my hand. I was desired to show them to Mr. Stockwell.

STOCK. Give 'em to me. What do I see? As I live, the very diamonds Miss Rusport sent hither, and which I intrusted to you to return.

BEL. Yes, but I betrayed that trust, and gave 'em Mrs. Fulmer to present to Miss Dudley.

STOCK. With a view no doubt to bribe her to compliance?

BEL. I own it.

STOCK. For shame, for shame! And 'twas this woman's intelligence you relied upon for Miss Dudley's character?

BEL. I thought she knew her. By Heaven, I would have died sooner than have insulted a woman of virtue or a man of honor.

STOCK. I think you would, but mark the danger of licentious courses. You are betrayed, robbed, abused, and, but for this providential discovery, in a fair way of being sent out of the world with all your follies on your head—Dear Stukely, go to my neighbor, tell him I have an owner for the jewels, and beg him to carry the people under custody to the London Tavern, and wait for me there.

(*Exit* STUKELY)

I fear the law does not provide a punishment to reach the villainy of these people. But how in the name of wonder could you take anything on the word of such an informer?

BEL. Because I had not lived long enough in your country to know how few informers' words are to be taken. Persuaded, however, as I was of Miss Dudley's guilt, I must own to you I was staggered with the appearance of such innocence, especially when I saw her admitted into Miss Rusport's company.

STOCK. Good Heaven! Did you meet her at Miss Rusport's, and could you doubt her being a woman of reputation?

BEL. By you perhaps such a mistake could not have been made, but in a perfect stranger, I hope it is venial. I did not know what artifices young Dudley might have used to conceal her character. I did not know what disgrace attended the detection of it.

STOCK. I see it was a trap laid for you, which you have narrowly escaped. You addressed a woman of honor with all the loose incense of a profane admirer, and you have drawn upon you the resentment of a man of honor who thinks himself bound to protect her. Well, sir, you must atone for this mistake.

BEL. To the lady the most penitent submission I can make is justly due, but in the execution of an act of justice it never shall be said my soul was swayed by the least particle of fear. I have received a challenge from her brother. Now, tho' I would give my fortune, almost my life itself, to purchase her happiness, yet I cannot abate her one scruple of my honor. I have been branded with the name of villain.

STOCK. Ay, sir, you mistook her character, and he mistook yours; error begets error.

BEL. Villain, Mr. Stockwell, is a harsh word.

STOCK. It is a harsh word, and should be unsaid.

BEL. Come, come, it shall be unsaid.

STOCK. Or else what follows? Why the sword is drawn, and to heal the wrongs you have done to the reputation of the sister, you make an honorable amends by murdering the brother.

BEL. Murdering!

STOCK. 'Tis thus religion writes and speaks the word. In the vocabulary of modern honor there is no such term—But come, I don't despair of satisfying the one without alarming the other; that done, I have a discovery to unfold that you will then I hope be fitted to receive.

Act V

SCENE I. *The London Tavern.*

(*Enter* O'FLAHERTY, STOCKWELL, CHARLES, *and* BELCOUR)

O'FLA. Gentlemen, well met! You understand each other's minds, and as I see you have brought nothing but your swords, you may set to without any further ceremony.

STOCK. You will not find us backward in any worthy cause; but before we proceed any further, I would ask this young gentleman, whether he has any explanation to require of Mr. Belcour.

CHARLES. Of Mr. Belcour none; his actions speak for themselves. But to you, sir, I would fain propose one question.

STOCK. Name it.

CHARLES. How is it, Mr. Stockwell, that I meet a man of your character on this ground?

STOCK. I will answer you directly, and my answer shall not displease you. I come hither in defence of the reputation of Miss Dudley, to redress the injuries of an innocent young lady.

O'FLA. By my soul the man knows he's to fight, only he mistakes which side he's to be of.

STOCK. You are about to draw your sword to refute a charge against your sister's honor. You would do well, if there were no better means within reach, but the proofs of her innocence are lodged in our bosoms, and if we fall, you destroy the evidence that most effectually can clear her fame.

CHARLES. How's that, sir?

STOCK. This gentleman could best explain it to you, but you have given him an undeserved name that seals his lips against you. I am not under the same inhibition, and if your anger can keep cool for a few minutes, I desire I may call in two witnesses who will solve all difficulties at once. Here, waiter! Bring those people in that are without.

O'FLA. Out upon it! What need is there for so much talking about the matter? Can't you settle your differences first, and dispute about 'em afterwards?

(FULMER *and* MRS. FULMER *brought in
by a Constable*)

CHARLES. Fulmer and his wife in custody?

STOCK. Yes, sir, these are your honest landlord and landlady, now in custody for defrauding this gentleman of certain diamonds intended to have been presented to your sister. Be so good, Mrs. Fulmer, to inform the company why you so grossly scandalized the reputation of an innocent lady by persuading Mr. Belcour that Miss Dudley was not the sister but the mistress of this gentleman.

MRS. FUL. Sir, I don't know what right you have to question me, and I shall not answer till I see occasion.

STOCK. Had you been as silent heretofore, madam, it would have saved you some trouble, but we don't want your confession. This letter, which you wrote to Mr. Belcour, will explain your design; and these diamonds, which of right belong to Miss Rusport, will confirm your guilt. The law, Mrs. Fulmer, will make you speak, tho' I can't. Constable, take charge of your prisoners.

FUL. Hold a moment. Mr. Stockwell, you are a gentleman that knows the world, and a member of parliament; we shall not attempt to impose upon you. We know we are open to the law, and we know the utmost it can do against us. Mr. Belcour has been ill used to be sure, and so has Miss Dudley; and, for my own part, I always condemned the plot as a very foolish plot, but it was a child of Mrs. Fulmer's brain, and she would not be put out of conceit with it.

MRS. FUL. You are a very foolish man, Mr. Fulmer, so pr'ythee hold your tongue.

FUL. Therefore, as I was saying, if you send her to Bridewell, it won't be amiss; and if you give her a little wholesome discipline, she may be the better for that too. But for me, Mr. Stockwell, who am a man of letters, I must beseech you, sir, not to bring any disgrace upon my profession.

STOCK. 'Tis you, Mr. Fulmer, not I, that disgrace your profession. Therefore begone, nor expect that I will betray the interests of mankind so far as to show favor to such incendiaries. Take 'em away; I blush to think such wretches should have the power to set two honest men at variance.

(*Exeunt* FULMER, *etc.*)

CHARLES. Mr. Belcour, we have mistaken each other; let us exchange forgiveness. I am convinced you intended no affront to my sister, and ask your pardon for the expression I was betrayed into.

BEL. 'Tis enough, sir; the error began on my side, and, was Miss Dudley here, I would be the first to atone.

STOCK. Let us all adjourn to my house and conclude the evening like friends. You will find a little entertainment ready for you, and, if I am not mistaken, Miss Dudley and her father will make part of our company. Come, Major, do you consent?

O'FLA. Most readily, Mr. Stockwell. A quarrel well made up is better than a victory hardly earned. Give me your hand, Belcour. O' my conscience, you are too honest for the country you live in. And now, my dear lad, since peace is concluded on all sides, I have a discovery to make to you which you must find out for yourself, for deuce take me if I rightly comprehend it, only that your aunt Rusport is in a conspiracy against you, and a vile rogue of a lawyer, whose name I forget, at the bottom of it.

CHARLES. What conspiracy? Dear Major, recollect yourself.

O'FLA. By my soul, I've no faculty at recollecting myself. But I've a paper somewhere about me that will tell you more of the matter than I can. When I get to the merchant's, I will endeavor to find it.

CHARLES. Well, it must be in your own way, but I confess you have thoroughly roused my curiosity.   (*Exeunt*)

Scene II. Stockwell's *House.*

(*Enter* Captain Dudley, Louisa, *and* Stukeley)

Dud. And are those wretches, Fulmer and his wife, in safe custody?

Stukely. They are in good hands. I accompanied them to the Tavern, where your son was to be, and then went in search of you. You may be sure Mr. Stockwell will enforce the law against them as far as it will go.

Dud. What mischief might their cursed machinations have produced, but for this timely discovery!

Lou. Still I am terrified. I tremble with apprehension lest Mr. Belcour's impetuosity and Charles's spirit should not wait for an explanation, but drive them both to extremes before the mistake can be unravelled.

Stukely. Mr. Stockwell is with them, madam, and you have nothing to fear. You cannot suppose he would ask you hither for any other purpose but to celebrate their reconciliation and to receive Mr. Belcour's atonement.

Dud. No, no, Louisa. Mr. Stockwell's honor and discretion guard us against all danger or offence. He well knows we will endure no imputation on the honor of our family, and he certainly has invited us to receive satisfaction on that score in an amicable way.

Lou. Would to Heaven they were returned!

Stukely. You may expect them every minute. And see madam, agreeable to your wish, they are here. (*Exit*)

(*Enter* Charles, *and afterwards* Stockwell *and* O'Flaherty)

Lou. O Charles! O brother, how could you serve me so? How could you tell me you was going to Lady Rusport's and then set out with a design of fighting Mr. Belcour? But where is he? Where is your antagonist?

Stock. Captain, I am proud to see you, and you, Miss Dudley, do me particular honor. We have been adjusting, sir, a very extraordinary and dangerous mistake, which I take for granted my friend Stukely has explained to you.

Dud. He has. I have too good an opinion of Mr. Belcour to believe he could be guilty of a designed affront to an innocent girl, and I am much too well acquainted with your character to suppose you could abet him in such design. I have no doubt, therefore, all things will be set to rights in very few words when we have the pleasure of seeing Mr. Belcour.

Stock. He has only stept into the compting-house and will wait upon you directly. You will not be over strict, madam, in weighing Mr. Belcour's conduct to the minutest scruple. His manners, passions and opinions are not as yet assimilated to this climate; he comes amongst you a new character, an inhabitant of a new world, and both hospitality as well as pity recommend him to our indulgence.

(*Enter* Belcour. *Bows to* Miss Dudley)

Bel. I am happy and ashamed to see you. No man in his senses would offend you; I forfeited mine and erred against the light of the sun when I overlooked your virtues, but your beauty was predominant, and hid them from my sight. I now perceive I was the dupe of a most improbable report, and humbly entreat your pardon.

Lou. Think no more of it; 'twas a mistake.

Bel. My life has been composed of little else; 'twas founded in mystery, and has continued in error. I was once given to hope, Mr. Stockwell, that you was to have delivered me from these difficulties, but either I do not deserve your confidence, or I was deceived in my expectations.

Stock. When this lady has confirmed your pardon, I shall hold you deserving of my confidence.

Lou. That was granted the moment it was asked.

Bel. To prove my title to his confidence, honor me so far with yours as to allow me a few minutes conversation in private with you.   (*She turns to her father*)

Dud. By all means, Louisa. Come, Mr. Stockwell, let us go into another room.

Charles. And now, Major O'Flaherty, I claim your promise of a sight of the paper that is to unravel this conspiracy of my aunt Rusport's. I think I have waited with great patience.

O'Fla. I have been endeavoring to call to mind what it was I overheard. I've got the paper, and will give you the best account I can of the whole transaction.

(*Exeunt all but* Belcour *and* Louisa)

Bel. Miss Dudley, I have solicited this audience to repeat to you my penitence and confusion. How shall I atone? What reparation can I make to you and virtue?

Lou. To me there's nothing due, nor anything demanded of you but your more favorable opinion for the future, if you should chance to think of me. Upon the part of virtue I'm not empowered to speak, but if, hereafter, as you range thro' life, you should surprise her in the person of some wretched female, poor as myself and not so well protected, enforce not your advantage, complete not your licentious triumph, but raise her, rescue her from shame and sorrow, and reconcile her to herself again.

Bel. I will, I will! By bearing your idea ever present in my thoughts, virtue shall keep an advocate within me. But tell me, loveliest, when you pardon the offence, can you, all perfect as you are, approve of the offender? As I now cease to view you in that false light I lately did, can you, and in the fulness of your bounty will you, cease also to reflect upon the libertine addresses I have paid you, and look upon me as your reformed, your rational admirer?

Lou. Are sudden reformations apt to last? And how can I be sure the first fair face you meet will not ensnare affections so unsteady, and that I shall not lose you lightly as I gained you?

Bel. Because tho' you conquered me by surprise, I have no inclination to rebel; because since the first moment that I saw you, every instant has improved you in my eyes; because by principle as well as passion I am unalterably yours; in short, there are ten thousand causes for my love to you. Would

to Heaven I could plant one in your soft bosom that might move you to return it!

Lou. Nay, Mr. Belcour——

Bel. I know I am not worthy your regard. I know I'm tainted with a thousand faults, sick of a thousand follies, but there's a healing virtue in your eyes that makes recovery certain. I cannot be a villain in your arms.

Lou. That you can never be. Whomever you shall honor with your choice, my life upon't, that woman will be happy. It is not from suspicion that I hesitate; it is from honor. 'Tis the severity of my condition; it is the world that never will interpret fairly in our case.

Bel. Oh, what am I, and who in this wide world concerns himself for such a nameless, such a friendless thing as I am? I see, Miss Dudley, I've not yet obtained your pardon.

Lou. Nay, that you are in full possession of.

Bel. Oh, seal it with your hand then, loveliest of women, confirm it with your heart. Make me honorably happy, and crown your penitent not with your pardon only, but your love.

Lou. My love!——

Bel. By Heaven, my soul is conquered with your virtues more than my eyes are ravished with your beauty. Oh, may this soft, this sensitive alarm be happy, be auspicious! Doubt not, deliberate not, delay not! If happiness be the end of life, why do we slip a moment?

(*Enter* O'Flaherty, *and afterwards* Captain Dudley *and* Charles, *with* Stockwell *reading the will*)

O'Fla. Joy, joy, joy! Sing, dance, leap, laugh for joy! Ha' done making love and fall down on your knees to every saint in the calendar, for they're all on your side, and honest St. Patrick at the head of them.

Charles. O Louisa, such an event! By the luckiest chance in life we have discovered a will of my grandfather's made in his last illness, by which he cuts off my aunt Rusport with a small annuity, and leaves me heir to his whole estate, with a fortune of fifteen thousand pounds to yourself.

Lou. What is it you tell me? (*To her*

father) O sir, instruct me to support this unexpected turn of fortune.

Dud. Name not fortune! 'Tis the work of providence, 'tis the justice of Heaven that would not suffer innocence to be oppressed, nor your base aunt to prosper in her cruelty and cunning.

(*A* Servant *whispers to* Belcour, *and he goes out*)

O'Fla. You shall pardon me, Captain Dudley, but you must not overlook St. Patrick neither, for by my soul if he had not put it into my head to slip behind the screen when your righteous aunt and the lawyer were plotting together, I don't see how you would ever have come at the paper there that Master Stockwell is reading.

Dud. True my good friend, you are the father of this discovery, but how did you contrive to get this will from the lawyer?

O'Fla. By force, my dear, the only way of getting anything from a lawyer's clutches.

Stock. Well, Major, when he brings his action of assault and battery against you, the least Dudley can do is to defend you with the weapons you have put into his hands.

Charles. That I am bound to do, and after the happiness I shall have in sheltering a father's age from the vicissitudes of life, my next delight will be in offering you an asylum in the bosom of your country.

O'Fla. And upon my soul, my dear, 'tis high time I was there, for 'tis now thirty long years since I set foot in my native country, and by the power of St. Patrick I swear I think it's worth all the rest of the world put together.

Dud. Ay, Major, much about that time have I been beating the round of service, and 'twere well for us both to give over; we have stood many a tough gale and abundance of hard blows, but Charles shall lay us up in a little private, but safe, harbor, where we'll rest from our labors, and peacefully wind up the remainder of our days.

O'Fla. Agreed, and you may take it as a proof of my esteem, young man, that Major O'Flaherty accepts a favor at your hands, for by Heaven I'd sooner starve, than say I thank you to the man I despise. But I believe you are an honest lad, and I'm glad you've trounced the old cat, for on my conscience I believe I must otherwise have married her myself to have let you in for a share of her fortune.

Stock. Hey-day, what's become of Belcour?

Lou. One of your servants called him out just now, and seemingly on some earnest occasion.

Stock. I hope, Miss Dudley, he has atoned to you as a gentleman ought.

Lou. Mr. Belcour, sir, will always do what a gentleman ought, and in my case I fear only you will think he has done too much.

Stock. (*Aside*) What has he done; and what can be too much? Pray Heaven, it may be as I wish!

Dud. Let us hear it, child.

Lou. With confusion for my own unworthiness, I confess to you he has offered me——

Stock. Himself.

Lou. 'Tis true.

Stock. (*Aside*) Then I am happy. All my doubts, my cares are over, and I may own him for my son.——Why these are joyful tidings. Come, my good friend, assist me in disposing your lovely daughter to accept this returning prodigal. He is no unprincipled, no hardened libertine; his love for you and virtue is the same.

Dud. 'Twere vile ingratitude in me to doubt his merit—What says my child?

O'Fla. Begging your pardon now, 'tis a frivolous sort of a question, that of yours; for you may see plainly enough by the young lady's looks that she says a great deal, though she speaks never a word.

Charles. Well, sister, I believe the Major has fairly interpreted the state of your heart.

Lou. I own it. And what must that heart be, which love, honor and beneficence like Mr. Belcour's can make no impression on?

Stock. I thank you. What happiness has this hour brought to pass.

O'Fla. Why don't we all sit down to supper then and make a night on't.

Stock. Hold, here comes Belcour.

(*Enter* Belcour *introducing* Miss Rusport)

Bel. Mr. Dudley, here is a fair refugee who properly comes under your protection; she is equipt for Scotland, but your good fortune, which I have related to her, seems inclined to save you both the journey.—— Nay, madam, never go back; you are amongst friends.

CHARLES. Charlotte!

CHAR. The same; that fond officious girl that haunts you everywhere, that persecuting spirit——

CHARLES. Say rather, that protecting angel; such you have been to me.

CHAR. O Charles, you have an honest but proud heart.

CHARLES. Nay, chide me not, dear Charlotte.

BEL. Seal up her lips then. She is an adorable girl, her arms are open to you, and love and happiness are ready to receive you.

CHARLES. Thus then I claim my dear, my destined wife.   (*Embracing her*)

(LADY RUSPORT *enters*)

L. RUS. Hey-day! Mighty fine! Wife, truly! Mighty well! Kissing, embracing—did ever anything equal this? Why, you shameless hussy!—But I won't condescend to waste a word upon you.——You, sir, you, Mr. Stockwell, you fine, sanctified, fair-dealing man of conscience, is this the principle you trade upon? Is this your neighborly system, to keep a house of reception for run-away daughters and young beggarly fortune-hunters?

O'FLA. Be advised now, and don't put yourself in such a passion; we were all very happy till you came.

L. RUS. Stand away, sir; haven't I a reason to be in a passion?

O'FLA. Indeed, honey, and you have, if you knew all.

L. RUS. Come, madam, I have found out your haunts. Dispose yourself to return home with me. Young man, let me never see you within my doors again. Mr. Stockwell, I shall report your behavior, depend on it.

STOCK. Hold, madam, I cannot consent to lose Miss Rusport's company this evening, and I am persuaded you won't insist upon it; 'tis an unmotherly action to interrupt your daughter's happiness in this manner, believe me it is.

L. RUS. Her happiness, truly; upon my word! And I suppose it's an unmotherly

action to interrupt her ruin; for what but ruin must it be to marry a beggar? (*To* CAPTAIN DUDLEY) I think my sister had a proof of that, sir, when she made choice of you.

DUD. Don't be too lavish of your spirits, Lady Rusport.

O'FLA. By my soul, you'll have occasion for a sip of the cordial Elixir by and bye.

STOCK. It don't appear to me, madam, that Mr. Dudley can be called a beggar.

L. RUS. But it appears to me, Mr. Stockwell. I am apt to think a pair of colors cannot furnish settlement quite sufficient for the heiress of Sir Stephen Rusport.

CHAR. But a good estate in aid of a commission may do something.

L. RUS. A good estate, truly! Where should he get a good estate, pray?

STOCK. Why, suppose now a worthy old gentleman on his death-bed should have taken it in mind to leave him one——

L. RUS. Hah! what's that you say?

O'FLA. O ho! you begin to smell a plot, do you?

STOCK. Suppose there should be a paper in the world that runs thus——(*reading from the will*) "I do hereby give and bequeath all my estates, real and personal, to Charles Dudley, son of my late daughter Louisa, &c. &c. &c."

L. RUS. Why I am thunder-struck! By what contrivance, what villainy did you get possession of that paper?

STOCK. There was no villainy, madam, in getting possession of it; the crime was in concealing it, none in bringing it to light.

L. RUS. Oh, that cursed lawyer, Varland!

O'FLA. You may say that, faith, he is a cursed lawyer, and a cursed piece of work I had to get the paper from him. Your ladyship now was to have paid him five thousand pounds for it, I forced him to give it me of his own accord for nothing at all, at all.

L. RUS. Is it you that have done this? Am I foiled by your blundering contrivances, after all?

O'FLA. 'Twas a blunder, faith, but as natural a one as if I'd made it o' purpose.

CHARLES. Come, let us not oppress the fallen. Do right even now, and you shall have no cause to complain.

L. RUS. Am I become an object of your pity then? Insufferable! Confusion light amongst you! Marry and be wretched; let me never see you more. (*Exit*)

CHAR. She is outrageous; I suffer for her, and blush to see her thus exposed.

CHARLES. Come, Charlotte, don't let this angry woman disturb our happiness. We will save her in spite of herself; your father's memory shall not be stained by the discredit of his second choice.

CHAR. I trust implicitly to your discretion and am in all things yours.

BEL. Now, lovely but obdurate, does not this example soften?

LOU. What can you ask for more? Accept my hand, accept my willing heart.

BEL. O bliss unutterable! Brother, father, friend, and you the author of this general joy——

O'FLA. Blessing of St. Patrick upon us all! 'tis a night of wonderful and surprising ups and downs. I wish we were all fairly set down to supper, and there was an end on't.

STOCK. Hold for a moment! I have yet one word to interpose.—Intitled by my friendship to a voice in your disposal, I have approved your match; there yet remains a father's consent to be obtained.

BEL. Have I a father?

STOCK. You have a father; did not I tell you I had a discovery to make? Compose yourself: you have a father, who observes, who knows, who loves you.

BEL. Keep me no longer in suspense; my heart is softened for the affecting discovery, and nature fits me to receive his blessing.

STOCK. I am your father.

BEL. My father? Do I live?

STOCK. I am your father.

BEL. It is too much, my happiness o'erpowers me; to gain a friend and find a father is too much; I blush to think how little I deserve you. (*They embrace*)

DUD. See, children, how many new relations spring from this night's unforeseen events, to endear us to each other.

O'FLA. O' my conscience, I think we shall be all related by and bye.

STOCK. How happily has this evening concluded, and yet how threatening was its approach! Let us repair to the supper room, where I will unfold to you every circumstance of my mysterious story. Yes, Belcour, I have watched you with a patient, but enquiring eye, and I have discovered thro' the veil of some irregularities, a heart beaming with benevolence, an animated nature, fallible indeed, but not incorrigible; and your election of this excellent young lady makes me glory in acknowledging you to be my son.

BEL. I thank you, and in my turn glory in the father I have gained. Sensibly imprest with gratitude for such extraordinary dispensations, I beseech you, amiable Louisa, for the time to come, whenever you perceive me deviating into error or offence, bring only to my mind the Providence of this night, and I will turn to reason and obey.

Epilogue

Written by D. G. Esq.

Spoken by MRS. ABINGTON *as* CHARLOTTE RUSPORT

N.B. The lines in italics are to be spoken in a catechise tone.

Confess, good folks, has not Miss Rusport shown,
Strange whims for SEVENTEEN HUNDRED SEVENTY-ONE?
What, pawn her jewels!——there's a precious plan!
To extricate from want a brave *old* man;
And fall in love with poverty and honor;

A girl of fortune, fashion!——Fie upon her.
But do not think we females of the stage,
So dead to the refinements of the age,
That we agree with our old fashioned poet:
I am point blank against him, and I'll show it:
And that my tongue may more politely run,
Make me a lady——Lady Blabington.
Now, with a rank and title to be free,
I'll make a catechism—and you shall see,
What is the *veritable Beaume de Vie:*

As I change place, I stand for that, or this,
My Lady questions first——then answers
    Miss.

               (*She speaks as my* LADY)
"Come, tell me, Child, what were our modes
    and dress,
In those strange times of that old fright
    Queen Bess?"——
And now for Miss————
    (*She changes place and speaks for* MISS)
When Bess was England's queen,
Ladies were dismal beings, seldom seen;
They rose betimes, and breakfasted as soon
On beef and beer, then studied Greek till
    noon;
Unpainted cheeks with blush of health
    did glow,
Beruffed and fardingaled from top to toe,
Nor necks, nor ankles would they ever
    show.
Learnt Greek!—(*laughs*)—Our outside head
    takes half a day;
Have we much time to dress the *inside*, pray?
No heads dressed *à la Greque*; the ancients
    quote,
There may be learning in a *papillote:*
Cards are our classics; and I, Lady B,
In learning will not yield to any she,
Of the late founded female university.
But now for Lady Blab————
               (*Speaks as my* LADY)
"Tell me, Miss Nancy,
What sports and what employments did they
    fancy?"
               (*Speaks as* MISS)
The vulgar creatures seldom left their
    houses,
But taught their children, worked, and
    loved their spouses;

The use of cards at Christmas only knew,
They played for little, and their games
    were few,
One-and-thirty, Put, All fours, and
    Lantera-Loo;
They bore a race of mortals stout and bony,
And never heard the name of Macaroni.——
               (*Speaks as my* LADY)
"Oh brava, brava! that's my pretty dear——
Now let a modern, modish fair appear;
No more of these old dowdy maids and
    wives,
Tell how superior beings pass their
    lives."————
               (*Speaks as* MISS)
Till noon they sleep, from noon till night
    they dress,
From night till morn they game it more or
    less,
Next night the same sweet course of joy
    run o'er,
Then the night after as the night before,
And the night after that, encore, encore!
    ————
               (*She comes forward*)
Thus with our cards we shuffle off all sorrow,
To-morrow, and to-morrow, and to-morrow!
We deal apace, from youth unto our prime,
To the last moment of our tabby-time;
And all our yesterdays, from rout and drum,
Have lighted fools with empty pockets home.
Thus do our lives with rapture roll away,
Not with the nonsense of our author's play;
This is true life—true spirit—give it praise;
Don't snarl and sigh for good Queen Bess's
    days:
For all you look so sour, and bend the brow,
You all rejoice with me, you're living now.

OLIVER GOLDSMITH

She Stoops to Conquer

PRINCIPAL EVENTS IN GOLDSMITH'S LIFE

1703?, Born in Ireland.

1749, Granted A.B. from Trinity College, Dublin.

1752-53, Studied medicine at Edinburgh University.

1753-56, Studied medicine at the University of Leyden and travelled in France, Switzerland, and Italy.

1756-58, Practiced medicine in London and wrote magazine reviews.

1757-62, Contributed to a large number of magazines.

1759, Published *An Enquiry into the Present State of Polite Learning in Europe.*

1759, Published *The Bee*, a periodical miscellany.

1760-61, *Citizen of the World* essays published in the *Public Ledger.*

1761-74, Translated, compiled, or revised a large number of histories, anthologies, and miscellaneous collections.

1764, Became a member of Dr. Johnson's famous club.

1766, Published *The Vicar of Wakefield.*

1768, 29 Jan., The Good Natured Man was performed at Covent Garden theatre.

1770, The Deserted Village published.

1773, Jan., Published in *The Westminster Magazine* "A Comparison Between Laughing and Sentimental Comedy."

1773, 15 March, She Stoops to Conquer was performed at Covent Garden.

1774, 4 April, Goldsmith died in London.

INTRODUCTION

Oliver Goldsmith deplored the sentimental or genteel comedy of his time. Shortly before *She Stoops to Conquer* was produced, he had written an essay for *The Westminster Magazine* entitled "A Comparison Between Laughing and Sentimental Comedy" in which he stated his opinion of popular comedy and his fear that laughter was disappearing from the stage:

Yet notwithstanding this weight of authority, and the universal practice of former ages, a new species of dramatic composition has been introduced under the name of *sentimental comedy,* in which the virtues of private life are exhibited, rather than the vices exposed; and the distresses rather than the faults of mankind make our interest in the piece. . . . In these plays almost all the characters are good, and exceedingly generous; they are lavish enough of their *tin* money on the stage; and though they want humor, have abundance of sentiment and feeling. If they happen to have faults or foibles, the spectator is taught not only to pardon, but to applaud, them, in consideration of the goodness of their hearts; so that folly, instead of being ridiculed, is commended, and the comedy aims at touching our passions, without the power of being truly pathetic. . . .

Humor, at present, seems to be departing from the stage; and it will soon happen that our comic players will have nothing left for it but a fine coat and a song. It depends upon the audience whether they will actually drive those poor merry creatures from the stage, or sit at a play as gloomy as at the tabernacle. It is not easy to recover an art when once lost; and it would be but a just punishment that when, by our being too fastidious, we have banished humor from the stage, we should ourselves be deprived of the art of laughing.

This same scorn for sentimental comedy and the plea for laughter in the theatre appear in the dedication of She Stoops to Conquer and in the prologue which the great actor, David Garrick, wrote for it. Goldsmith's play was an attempt to persuade the audience to enjoy the "laughing comedy" of former times.

The comedy of former times which Goldsmith admired was not, however, the satiric comedy of the Restoration, but Elizabethan comedy, especially plays like As You Like It and Twelfth Night. He made no attempt to imitate these comedies in detail, but their healthy vigor and good-natured ridicule are very similar to the spirit of She Stoops to Conquer. The amazement and indignation of the dignified Mr. Hardcastle at being taken for an innkeeper are elaborated for the entertainment of the audience, yet he is kept a sympathetic figure, neither castigated nor sentimentalized. Tony Lumpkin is a more remarkable comic figure. His ignorance and boorishness are made perfectly clear, yet he is by no means a butt; he is sympathetically treated, always entertaining, and sometimes the wittiest character in the play. He is an independent comic creation, devised to make an audience laugh.

The love affairs of the play are equally reminiscent of Elizabethan romantic comedy. Kate Hardcastle's dangling of Marlow is much in the spirit of Rosalind's treatment of Orlando; there is never much doubt that she will marry him in the end, but he is teased at length for the amusement of Kate and of the audience. The less entertaining affair of Constance Neville and George Hastings is never allowed to become too serious.

"The Mistakes of a Night" upon which the action is based are essentially of the nature of farce, but Goldsmith has kept his characters too independent and interesting in themselves to be dominated wholly by the plot, as in the usual farce. Characters and action combine in light-hearted, good-natured entertainment. Dr. Johnson's comment on the play aptly characterized its intent and its achievement: "I know of no comedy for many years that has answered so much the general end of comedy,—making an audience merry."

❧

SHE STOOPS TO CONQUER

Dramatis personae

In order of first appearance

MRS. HARDCASTLE, The second wife of Mr. Hardcastle, a vain, ignorant, rather mean woman. She dotes on her oafish son by her former husband, the wealthy Mr. Lumpkin.

MR. HARDCASTLE, A country gentleman, contemptuous of modern fashions and London society, pleased with old-fashioned things and hearty country ways.

TONY LUMPKIN, Mrs. Hardcastle's son by a former marriage. An ignorant, vulgar, boisterous young man, but good natured.

KATE HARDCASTLE, Mr. Hardcastle's only daughter by a former marriage, and his pride and joy. A merry and mischievous girl, devoted to her father.

CONSTANCE NEVILLE, A beautiful young

lady, niece to Mrs. Hardcastle, in love with George Hastings.

FIRST FELLOW
SECOND FELLOW   Village ne'er-do-wells,
THIRD FELLOW   Tony Lumpkin's ale-
FOURTH FELLOW   house companions.

LANDLORD, Proprietor of The Three Pigeons, the village alehouse.

CHARLES MARLOW, A gay young man, but bashful in polite society, the son and heir of Sir Charles Marlow.

GEORGE HASTINGS, His friend and companion, in love with Constance Neville.

DIGGORY, A stableman on Mr. Hardcastle's estate.

ROGER, A plowman on Mr. Hardcastle's estate.

FIRST SERVANT   Country fellows, servants
SECOND SERVANT   in   Mr.   Hardcastle's
THIRD SERVANT   household.

PIMPLE, Miss Hardcastle's maid.

JEREMY, Charles Marlow's man.

SIR CHARLES MARLOW, An old and trusted friend of Mr. Hardcastle, father of Charles Marlow.

To Samuel Johnson, LL.D.

DEAR SIR,

By inscribing this slight performance to you, I do not mean so much to compliment you as myself. It may do me some honor to inform the public, that I have lived many years in intimacy with you. It may serve the interests of mankind also to inform them, that the greatest wit may be found in a character, without impairing the most unaffected piety.

I have, particularly, reason to thank you for your partiality to this performance. The undertaking a comedy, not merely sentimental, was very dangerous; and Mr. Colman, who saw this piece in its various stages, always thought it so. However, I ventured to trust it to the public; and, though it was necessarily delayed till late in the season, I have every reason to be grateful.

I am, dear sir,
Your most sincere friend
And admirer,
OLIVER GOLDSMITH.

Prologue

BY DAVID GARRICK, ESQ.

(*Enter* MR. WOODWARD, *dressed in black, and holding a handkerchief to his eyes*)

Excuse me, sirs, I pray—I can't yet speak—
I'm crying now—and have been all the week!
'Tis not alone this mourning suit, good masters;
I've that within—for which there are no plasters!
Pray would you know the reason why I'm crying?
The Comic Muse, long sick, is now a-dying!
And if she goes, my tears will never stop;
For, as a player, I can't squeeze out one drop;
I am undone, that's all—shall lose my bread—
I'd rather, but that's nothing—lose my head.

When the sweet maid is laid upon the bier,
Shuter[1] and I shall be chief mourners here.
To her a mawkish drab of spurious breed,
Who deals in sentimentals, will succeed.
Poor Ned and I are dead to all intents;
We can as soon speak Greek as sentiments!
Both nervous grown, to keep our spirits up,
We now and then take down a hearty cup.
What shall we do? If Comedy forsake us,
They'll turn us out, and no one else will take us.
But why can't I be moral?—Let me try:
(*striking a pose*)
My heart thus pressing—fix'd my face and eye—

[1] Edward Shuter, who played Hardcastle.

With a sententious look, that nothing means,
(Faces are blocks in sentimental scenes,)
Thus I begin—*All is not gold that glitters,*
Pleasure seems sweet, but proves a glass of
bitters.
When Ignorance enters, Folly is at hand;
Learning is better far than house and land.
Let not your virtue trip; who trips may stum-
ble,
And virtue is not virtue, if she tumble.
   I give it up—morals won't do for me;
To make you laugh, I must play tragedy.
One hope remains,—hearing the maid was ill,
A Doctor comes this night to show his skill.
To cheer her heart, and give your muscles
   motion,

He, in Five Draughts prepared, presents a
   potion:
A kind of magic charm; for, be assured,
If you will swallow it, the maid is cured:
But desperate the Doctor, and her case is,
If you reject the dose, and make wry faces.
This truth he boasts, will boast it while he
   lives,
No poisonous drugs are mixed in what he
   gives.
Should he succeed, you'll give him his de-
   gree;
If not, within he will receive no fee!
The college, you, must his pretensions
   back,
Pronounce him Regular, or dub him Quack.

Act I

Scene I. *A Chamber in an Old-Fashioned House.*

(*Enter* Mrs. Hardcastle *and*
Mr. Hardcastle)

Mrs. Hardcastle. I vow, Mr. Hard-
castle, you're very particular. Is there a creature in the whole country but ourselves that
does not take a trip to town now and then, to
rub off the rust a little? There's the two Miss
Hoggs, and our neighbor Mrs. Grigsby, go to
take a month's polishing every winter.

Hardcastle. Ay, and bring back vanity
and affectation to last them the whole year.
I wonder why London cannot keep its own
fools at home. In my time, the follies of the
town crept slowly among us, but now they
travel faster than a stagecoach. Its fopperies
come down not only as inside passengers, but
in the very basket.

Mrs. Hardcastle. Ay, your times were
fine times indeed; you have been telling us of
them for many a long year. Here we live in
an old rumbling mansion, that looks for all
the world like an inn, but that we never see
company. Our best visitors are old Mrs. Odd-
fish, the curate's wife, and little Cripplegate,
the lame dancing-master; and all our entertainment your old stories of Prince Eugene
and the Duke of Marlborough. I hate such
old-fashioned trumpery.

Hardcastle. And I love it. I love everything that's old: old friends, old times, old
manners, old books, old wine; and, I believe,
Dorothy, (*taking her hand*) you'll own I
have been pretty fond of an old wife.

Mrs. Hardcastle. Lord, Mr. Hardcastle,
you're forever at your Dorothys and your old
wifes. You may be a Darby, but I'll be no
Joan, I promise you. I'm not so old as you'd
make me by more than one good year. Add
twenty to twenty and make money of that.

Hardcastle. Let me see; twenty added to
twenty—makes just fifty and seven!

Mrs. Hardcastle. It's false, Mr. Hardcastle; I was but twenty when I was brought
to bed of Tony, that I had by Mr. Lumpkin,
my first husband; and he's not come to years
of discretion yet.

Hardcastle. Nor ever will, I dare answer
for him. Ay, you have taught *him* finely!

Mrs. Hardcastle. No matter. Tony
Lumpkin has a good fortune. My son is not
to live by his learning. I don't think a boy
wants much learning to spend fifteen hundred a year.

Hardcastle. Learning, quotha! a mere
composition of tricks and mischief!

Mrs. Hardcastle. Humor, my dear;
nothing but humor. Come, Mr. Hardcastle,
you must allow the boy a little humor.

Hardcastle. I'd sooner allow him a horse-pond! If burning the footmen's shoes, fright-ing the maids, and worrying the kittens, be humor, he has it. It was but yesterday he fas-tened my wig to the back of my chair, and when I went to make a bow, I popped my bald head in Mrs. Frizzle's face.

MRS. HARDCASTLE. And I am to blame? The poor boy was always too sickly to do any good. A school would be his death. When he comes to be a little stronger, who knows what a year or two's Latin may do for him?

HARDCASTLE. Latin for him! A cat and fid-dle! No, no; the alehouse and the stable are the only schools he'll ever go to.

MRS. HARDCASTLE. Well, we must not snub the poor boy now, for I believe we shan't have him long among us. Anybody that looks in his face may see he's consump-tive.

HARDCASTLE. Ay, if growing too fat be one of the symptoms.

MRS. HARDCASTLE. He coughs sometimes.

HARDCASTLE. Yes, when his liquor goes the wrong way.

MRS. HARDCASTLE. I'm actually afraid of his lungs.

HARDCASTLE. And truly, so am I; for he sometimes whoops like a speaking-trumpet—(TONY *hallooing behind the scenes*)—Oh, there he goes—a very consumptive figure, truly!

(*Enter* TONY, *crossing the stage*)

MRS. HARDCASTLE. Tony, where are you going, my charmer? Won't you give papa and I a little of your company, lovey?

TONY. I'm in haste, mother; I cannot stay.

MRS. HARDCASTLE. You shan't venture out this raw evening, my dear; you look most shockingly.

TONY. I can't stay, I tell you. *The Three Pigeons* expects me down every moment. There's some fun going forward.

HARDCASTLE. Ay, the alehouse, the old place; I thought so.

MRS. HARDCASTLE. A low, paltry set of fellows.

TONY. Not so low, neither. There's Dick Muggins, the exciseman; Jack Slang, the horse-doctor; little Aminadab, that grinds the music-box; and Tom Twist, that spins the pewter platter.

MRS. HARDCASTLE. Pray, my dear, disap-point them for one night at least.

TONY. As for disappointing them, I should not so much mind; but I can't abide to dis-appoint myself.

MRS. HARDCASTLE. (*Detaining him*) You shan't go.

TONY. I will, I tell you.

MRS. HARDCASTLE. I say you shan't.

TONY. We'll see which is the strongest, you or I.   (*Exit, hauling her out*)

HARDCASTLE. Ay, there goes a pair that only spoil each other. But is not the whole age in a combination to drive sense and discretion out of doors? There's my pretty darling, Kate; the fashions of the times have almost infected her too. By living a year or two in town, she is as fond of gauze and French frippery as the best of them.

(*Enter* MISS HARDCASTLE)

Blessings on my pretty innocence! Dressed out as usual, my Kate. Goodness! what a quantity of superfluous silk hast thou got about thee, girl! I could never teach the fools of this age that the indigent world could be clothed out of the trimmings of the vain.

MISS HARDCASTLE. You know our agree-ment, sir. You allow me the morning to re-ceive and pay visits, and to dress in my own manner; and in the evening I put on my housewife's dress to please you.

HARDCASTLE. Well, remember, I insist on the terms of our agreement; and, by the bye, I believe I shall have occasion to try your obedience this very evening.

MISS HARDCASTLE. I protest, sir, I don't comprehend your meaning.

HARDCASTLE. Then, to be plain with you, Kate, I expect the young gentleman I have chosen to be your husband from town this very day. I have his father's letter, in which he informs me his son is set out, and that he intends to follow himself shortly after.

MISS HARDCASTLE. Indeed! I wish I had known something of this before. Bless me, how shall I behave? It's a thousand to one I shan't like him; our meeting will be so for-mal, and so like a thing of business, that I shall find no room for friendship or esteem.

HARDCASTLE. Depend upon it, child, I'll never control your choice; but Mr. Marlow, whom I have pitched upon, is the son of my old friend, Sir Charles Marlow, of whom you have heard me talk so often. The young gentleman has been bred a scholar, and is designed for an employment in the service of his country. I am told he's a man of excellent understanding.

Miss Hardcastle. Is he?

Hardcastle. Very generous.

Miss Hardcastle. I believe I shall like him.

Hardcastle. Young and brave.

Miss Hardcastle. I'm sure I shall like him.

Hardcastle. And very handsome.

Miss Hardcastle. My dear papa, say no more; (kissing his hand) he's mine, I'll have him!

Hardcastle. And, to crown all, Kate, he's one of the most bashful and reserved young fellows in all the world.

Miss Hardcastle. Eh! you have frozen me to death again. That word reserved has undone all the rest of his accomplishments. A reserved lover, it is said, always makes a suspicious husband.

Hardcastle. On the contrary, modesty seldom resides in a breast that is not enriched with nobler virtues. It was the very feature in his character that first struck me.

Miss Hardcastle. He must have more striking features to catch me, I promise you. However, if he be so young, so handsome, and so everything as you mention, I believe he'll do still; I think I'll have him.

Hardcastle. Ay, Kate, but there is still an obstacle. It's more than an even wager he may not have you.

Miss Hardcastle. My dear papa, why will you mortify one so? Well, if he refuses, instead of breaking my heart at his indifference, I'll only break my glass for its flattery, set my cap to some newer fashion, and look out for some less difficult admirer.

Hardcastle. Bravely resolved! In the mean time, I'll go prepare the servants for his reception; as we seldom see company, they want as much training as a company of recruits the first day's muster. (Exit)

Miss Hardcastle. Lud, this news of papa's puts me all in a flutter. Young, handsome; these he put last, but I put them foremost. Sensible, good-natured; I like all

that. But then, reserved and sheepish; that's much against him. Yet, can't he be cured of his timidity by being taught to be proud of his wife? Yes; and can't I—but I vow I'm disposing of the husband, before I have secured the lover.

(Enter Miss Neville)

Miss Hardcastle. I'm glad you're come, Neville, my dear. Tell me, Constance, how do I look this evening? Is there anything whimsical about me? Is it one of my well-looking days, child? Am I in face to-day?

Miss Neville. Perfectly, my dear. Yet, now I look again—bless me!—surely no accident has happened among the canary birds or the gold-fishes? Has your brother or the cat been meddling? Or has the last novel been too moving?

Miss Hardcastle. No; nothing of all this. I have been threatened—I can scarce get it out—I have been threatened with a lover.

Miss Neville. And his name—

Miss Hardcastle. Is Marlow.

Miss Neville. Indeed!

Miss Hardcastle. The son of Sir Charles Marlow.

Miss Neville. As I live, the most intimate friend of Mr. Hastings, my admirer. They are never asunder. I believe you must have seen him when we lived in town.

Miss Hardcastle. Never.

Miss Neville. He's a very singular character, I assure you. Among women of reputation and virtue, he is the modestest man alive; but his acquaintance give him a very different character among creatures of another stamp. You understand me.

Miss Hardcastle. An odd character, indeed! I shall never be able to manage him. What shall I do? Pshaw, think no more of him, but trust to occurrences for success. But how goes on your own affair, my dear? Has my mother been courting you for my brother Tony, as usual?

Miss Neville. I have just come from one of our agreeable tête-à-têtes. She has been saying a hundred tender things, and setting off her pretty monster as the very pink of perfection.

Miss Hardcastle. And her partiality is such that she actually thinks him so. A fortune like yours is no small temptation. Besides, as she has the sole management of it, I'm not surprised to see her unwilling to let it go out of the family.

MISS NEVILLE. A fortune like mine, which chiefly consists in jewels, is no such mighty temptation. But at any rate, if my dear Hastings be but constant, I make no doubt to be too hard for her at last. However, I let her suppose that I am in love with her son; and she never once dreams that my affections are fixed upon another.

MISS HARDCASTLE. My good brother holds out stoutly. I could almost love him for hating you so.

MISS NEVILLE. It is a good-natured creature at bottom, and I'm sure would wish to see me married to anybody but himself. But my aunt's bell rings for our afternoon's walk round the improvements. *Allons.* Courage is necessary, as our affairs are critical.

MISS HARDCASTLE. Would it were bedtime, and all were well. (*Exeunt*)

SCENE II. *An Alehouse Room.*

(*Several shabby* FELLOWS *with punch and tobacco;* TONY *at the head of the table, a little higher than the rest; a mallet in his hand*)

OMNES. Hurrea, hurrea, hurrea, bravo!

FIRST FELLOW. Now, gentlemen, silence for a song. The Squire is going to knock himself down for a song.

OMNES. Ay, a song, a song!

TONY. Then I'll sing you, gentlemen, a song I made upon this alehouse, *The Three Pigeons.*

SONG

Let schoolmasters puzzle their brain,
    With grammar, and nonsense, and learning;
Good liquor, I stoutly maintain,
    Gives genus a better discerning.
Let them brag of their heathenish gods,
    Their Lethes, their Styxes, and Stygians,
Their quis, and their quæs, and their quods,
    They're all but a parcel of pigeons.
        Toroddle, toroddle, toroll!

When Methodist preachers come down,
    A-preaching that drinking is sinful,
I'll wager the rascals a crown,
    They always preach best with a skinful.
But when you come down with your pence,
    For a slice of their scurvy religion,
I'll leave it to all men of sense,
    That you, my good friend, are the pigeon.
        Toroddle, toroddle, toroll!

Then come, put the jorum about,
    And let us be merry and clever,

Our hearts and our liquors are stout,
    Here's the Three Jolly Pigeons for ever.
Let some cry up woodcock or hare,
    Your bustards, your ducks, and your widgeons;
But of all the birds in the air,
    Here's a health to the Three Jolly Pigeons.
        Toroddle, toroddle, toroll!

OMNES. Bravo, bravo!

FIRST FELLOW. The Squire has got some spunk in him.

SECOND FELLOW. I loves to hear him sing, bekeays he never gives us nothing that's low.

THIRD FELLOW. Oh, damn anything that's low, I cannot bear it!

FOURTH FELLOW. The genteel thing is the genteel thing any time; if so be that a gentleman bees in a concatenation accordingly.

THIRD FELLOW. I like the maxum of it, Master Muggins. What though I am obligated to dance a bear, a man may be a gentleman for all that. May this be my poison, if my bear ever dances but to the very genteelest of tunes: *Water Parted,* or the minuet in *Ariadne.*

SECOND FELLOW. What a pity it is the Squire is not come to his own. It would be well for all the publicans within ten miles round of him.

TONY. Ecod, and so it would, Master Slang. I'd then show what it was to keep choice of company.

SECOND FELLOW. Oh, he takes after his own father for that. To be sure, old Squire Lumpkin was the finest gentleman I ever set my eyes on. For winding the straight horn, or beating a thicket for a hare, or a wench, he never had his fellow. It was a saying in the place, that he kept the best horses, dogs, and girls in the whole county.

TONY. Ecod, and when I'm of age I'll be no bastard, I promise you. I have been thinking of Bet Bouncer and the miller's gray mare to begin with. But come, my boys, drink about and be merry, for you pay no reckoning. Well, Stingo, what's the matter?

(Enter LANDLORD*)*

LANDLORD. There be two gentlemen in a post-chaise at the door. They have lost their way upo' the forest; and they are talking something about Mr. Hardcastle.

TONY. As sure as can be, one of them must be the gentleman that's coming down to court my sister. Do they seem to be Londoners?

LANDLORD. I believe they may. They look woundily like Frenchmen.

TONY. Then desire them to step this way, and I'll set them right in a twinkling. *(Exit* LANDLORD*)* Gentlemen, as they mayn't be good enough company for you, step down for a moment, and I'll be with you in the squeezing of a lemon.   *(Exeunt mob)*

TONY. Father-in-law has been calling me whelp and hound this half year. Now, if I pleased, I could be so revenged upon the old grumbletonian. But then I'm afraid,— afraid of what? I shall soon be worth fifteen hundred a year, and let him frighten me out of *that* if he can.

(Enter LANDLORD, *conducting* MARLOW *and* HASTINGS*)*

MARLOW. What a tedious, uncomfortable day have we had of it! We were told it was but forty miles across the country, and we have come above threescore!

HASTINGS. And all, Marlow, from that unaccountable reserve of yours, that would not let us inquire more frequently on the way.

MARLOW. I own, Hastings, I am unwilling to lay myself under an obligation to every one I meet, and often stand the chance of an unmannerly answer.

HASTINGS. At present, however, we are not likely to receive any answer.

TONY. No offence, gentlemen. But I'm told you have been inquiring for one Mr. Hardcastle, in these parts. Do you know what part of the country you are in?

HASTINGS. Not in the least, sir, but should thank you for information.

TONY. Nor the way you came?

HASTINGS. No, sir; but if you can inform us—

TONY. Why, gentlemen, if you know neither the road you are going, nor where you are, nor the road you came, the first thing I have to inform you is, that—you have lost your way.

MARLOW. We wanted no ghost to tell us that.

TONY. Pray, gentlemen, may I be so bold as to ask the place from whence you came?

MARLOW. That's not necessary towards directing us where we are to go.

TONY. No offence; but question for question is all fair, you know.—Pray, gentlemen, is not this same Hardcastle a cross-grained, old-fashioned, whimsical fellow, with an ugly face, a daughter, and a pretty son?

HASTINGS. We have not seen the gentleman, but he has the family you mention.

TONY. The daughter, a tall, trapesing, trolloping, talkative maypole; the son, a pretty, well-bred, agreeable youth, that everybody is fond of?

MARLOW. Our information differs in this. The daughter is said to be well-bred, and beautiful; the son an awkward booby, reared up and spoiled at his mother's apron-string.

TONY. He-he-hem!—Then, gentlemen, all I have to tell you is, that you won't reach Mr. Hardcastle's house this night, I believe.

HASTINGS. Unfortunate!

TONY. It's a damned long, dark, boggy, dirty, dangerous way. Stingo, tell the gentlemen the way to Mr. Hardcastle's; *(winking upon the* LANDLORD*)* Mr. Hardcastle's of Quagmire Marsh, you understand me.

LANDLORD. Master Hardcastle's! Lack-a-daisy, my masters, you're come a deadly deal wrong! When you came to the bottom of the hill, you should have crossed down Squash-lane.

MARLOW. Cross down Squash-lane!

LANDLORD. Then you were to keep straight forward, till you came to four roads.

MARLOW. Come to where four roads meet!

TONY. Ay; but you must be sure to take only one of them.

MARLOW. Oh sir, you're facetious.

TONY. Then, keeping to the right, you are to go sideways till you come upon Crackskull Common. There you must look sharp for the track of the wheel, and go forward till you come to farmer Murrain's barn. Coming to the farmer's barn, you are to turn to the right, and then to the left, and then to the right about again, till you find out the old mill—

MARLOW. Zounds, man! we could as soon find out the longitude!

HASTINGS. What's to be done, Marlow?

MARLOW. This house promises but a poor reception; though perhaps the landlord can accommodate us.

LANDLORD. Alack, master, we have but one spare bed in the whole house.

TONY. And to my knowledge, that's taken up by three lodgers already. (*After a pause in which the rest seem disconcerted*) I have hit it. Don't you think, Stingo, our landlady could accommodate the gentlemen by the fireside, with—three chairs and a bolster?

HASTINGS. I hate sleeping by the fireside.

MARLOW. And I detest your three chairs and a bolster.

TONY. You do, do you?—then, let me see —what if you go on a mile further, to the Buck's Head; the old Buck's Head on the hill, one of the best inns in the whole county?

HASTINGS. O ho! so we have escaped an adventure for this night, however.

LANDLORD. (*Apart to* TONY) Sure, you ben't sending them to your father's as an inn, be you?

TONY. Mum, you fool you. Let *them* find that out. (*To them*) You have only to keep on straight forward, till you come to a large old house by the road side. You'll see a pair of large horns over the door. That's the sign. Drive up the yard, and call stoutly about you.

HASTINGS. Sir, we are obliged to you. The servants can't miss the way?

TONY. No, no; but I tell you, though, the landlord is rich, and going to leave off business; so he wants to be thought a gentleman, saving your presence, he! he! he! He'll be for giving you his company; and, ecod, if you mind him, he'll persuade you that his mother was an alderman and his aunt a justice of peace.

LANDLORD. A troublesome old blade, to be sure; but a keeps as good wines and beds as any in the whole country.

MARLOW. Well, if he supplies us with these, we shall want no further connection. We are to turn to the right, did you say?

TONY. No, no; straight forward. I'll just step myself, and show you a piece of the way. (*To the* LANDLORD) Mum!

LANDLORD. Ah, bless your heart, for a sweet, pleasant—damn'd mischievous son of a whore. (*Exeunt*)

Act II

The Parlor of an Old-Fashioned House

(*Enter* HARDCASTLE, *followed by three or four awkward* SERVANTS)

HARDCASTLE. Well, I hope you are perfect in the table exercise I have been teaching you these three days. You all know your posts and your places, and can show that you have been used to good company, without ever stirring from home.

OMNES. Ay, ay.

HARDCASTLE. When company comes, you are not to pop out and stare, and then run in again, like frighted rabbits in a warren.

OMNES. No, no.

HARDCASTLE. You, Diggory, whom I have taken from the barn, are to make a show at the side-table; and you, Roger, whom I have advanced from the plough, are to place yourself behind my chair. But you're not to stand so, with your hands in your pockets. Take your hands from your pockets, Roger; and from your head, you blockhead, you. See how Diggory carries his hands. They're a little too stiff, indeed, but that's no great matter.

DIGGORY. Ay, mind how I hold them. I

learned to hold my hands this way, when I was upon drill for the militia. And so being upon drill—

HARDCASTLE. You must not be so talkative, Diggory. You must be all attention to the guests. You must hear us talk, and not think of talking; you must see us drink, and not think of drinking; you must see us eat, and not think of eating.

DIGGORY. By the laws, your worship, that's parfectly unpossible. Whenever Diggory sees yeating going forward, ecod, he's always wishing for a mouthful himself.

HARDCASTLE. Blockhead! Is not a bellyful in the kitchen as good as a bellyful in the parlor? Stay your stomach with that reflection.

DIGGORY. Ecod, I thank your worship, I'll make a shift to stay my stomach with a slice of cold beef in the pantry.

HARDCASTLE. Diggory, you are too talkative.—Then, if I happen to say a good thing, or tell a good story at table, you must not all burst out a-laughing, as if you made part of the company.

DIGGORY. Then, ecod, your worship must not tell the story of Ould Grouse in the gunroom. I can't help laughing at that—he! he! he!—for the soul of me. We have laughed at that these twenty years—ha! ha! ha!

HARDCASTLE. Ha! ha! ha! The story is a good one. Well, honest Diggory, you may laugh at that; but still remember to be attentive. Suppose one of the company should call for a glass of wine, how will you behave? A glass of wine, sir, if you please. (*To* DIGGORY)—Eh, why don't you move?

DIGGORY. Ecod, your worship, I never have courage till I see the eatables and drinkables brought upo' the table, and then I'm as bauld as a lion.

HARDCASTLE. What, will nobody move?

FIRST SERVANT. I'm not to leave this pleace.

SECOND SERVANT. I'm sure it's no pleace of mine.

THIRD SERVANT. Nor mine, for sartain.

DIGGORY. Wauns, and I'm sure it canna be mine.

HARDCASTLE. You numskulls! and so while, like your betters, you are quarrelling for places, the guests must be starved. Oh you dunces! I find I must begin all over

again—But don't I hear a coach drive into the yard? To your posts, you blockheads! I'll go in the meantime, and give my old friend's son a hearty reception at the gate.

(*Exit* HARDCASTLE)

DIGGORY. By the elevens, my pleace is quite gone out my head!

ROGER. I know that my pleace is to be everywhere!

FIRST SERVANT. Where the devil is mine?

SECOND SERVANT. My pleace is to be nowhere at all; and so I'ze go about my business!

(*Exeunt* SERVANTS, *running about as if frighted, different ways*)

(*Enter* SERVANT *with candles, showing in* MARLOW *and* HASTINGS)

SERVANT. Welcome, gentlemen, very welcome! This way.

HASTINGS. After the disappointments of the day, welcome once more, Charles, to the comforts of a clean room and a good fire. Upon my word, a very well-looking house; antique but creditable.

MARLOW. The usual fate of a large mansion. Having first ruined the master by good house-keeping, it at last comes to levy contributions as an inn.

HASTINGS. As you say, we passengers are to be taxed to pay all these fineries. I have often seen a good side-board, or a marble chimney-piece, though not actually put in the bill, inflame a reckoning confoundedly.

MARLOW. Travellers, George, must pay in all places. The only difference is that in good inns you pay dearly for luxuries; in bad inns you are fleeced and starved.

HASTINGS. You have lived pretty much among them. In truth, I have been often surprised that you, who have seen so much of the world, with your natural good sense, and your many opportunities, could never yet acquire a requisite share of assurance.

(*They seat themselves near the fire*)

MARLOW. The Englishman's malady. But tell me, George, where could I have learned that assurance you talk of? My life has been chiefly spent in a college or an inn, in seclusion from that lovely part of the creation that chiefly teach men confidence. I don't know that I was ever familiarly acquainted with a single modest woman, except my mother. But among females of another class, you know—

HASTINGS. Ay, among them you are impudent enough, of all conscience.

MARLOW. They are of *us*, you know.

HASTINGS. But in the company of women of reputation I never saw such an idiot, such a trembler; you look for all the world as if you wanted an opportunity of stealing out of the room.

MARLOW. Why, man, that's because I *do* want to steal out of the room. Faith, I have often formed a resolution to break the ice, and rattle away at any rate. But I don't know how, a single glance from a pair of fine eyes has totally overset my resolution. An impudent fellow may counterfeit modesty, but I'll be hanged if a modest man can ever counterfeit impudence.

HASTINGS. If you could but say half the fine things to them that I have heard you lavish upon the bar-maid of an inn, or even a college bed-maker—

MARLOW. Why, George, I can't say fine things to them. They freeze, they petrify me. They may talk of a comet, or a burning mountain, or some such bagatelle; but to me a modest woman, dressed out in all her finery, is the most tremendous object of the whole creation.

HASTINGS. Ha! ha! ha! At this rate, man, how can you ever expect to marry?

MARLOW. Never; unless, as among kings and princes, my bride were to be courted by proxy. If, indeed, like an Eastern bridegroom, one were to be introduced to a wife he never saw before, it might be endured. But to go through all the terrors of a formal courtship, together with the episode of aunts, grandmothers, and cousins, and at last to blurt out the broad staring question of "Madam, will you marry me?" No, no, that's a strain much above me, I assure you.

HASTINGS. I pity you. But how do you intend behaving to the lady you are come down to visit at the request of your father?

MARLOW. As I behave to all other ladies. Bow very low; answer yes or no to all her demands. But for the rest, I don't think I shall venture to look in her face till I see my father's again.

HASTINGS. I'm surprised that one who is so warm a friend can be so cool a lover.

MARLOW. To be explicit, my dear Hastings, my chief inducement down was to be instrumental in forwarding your happiness, not my own. Miss Neville loves you, the family don't know you; as my friend, you are sure of a reception, and let honor do the rest.

HASTINGS. My dear Marlow! But I'll suppress the emotion. Were I a wretch, meanly seeking to carry off a fortune, you should be the last man in the world I would apply to for assistance. But Miss Neville's person is all I ask, and that is mine, both from her deceased father's consent and her own inclination.

MARLOW. Happy man! you have talents and art to captivate any woman. I'm doomed to adore the sex, and yet to converse with the only part of it I despise. This stammer in my address, and this awkward unprepossessing visage of mine, can never permit me to soar above the reach of a milliner's 'prentice, or one of the Duchesses of Drury Lane. Pshaw! this fellow here to interrupt us.

(Enter HARDCASTLE*)*

HARDCASTLE. Gentlemen, once more you are heartily welcome. Which is Mr. Marlow? Sir, you are heartily welcome. It's not my way, you see, to receive my friends with my back to the fire. I like to give them a hearty reception, in the old style, at my gate. I like to see their horses and trunks taken care of.

MARLOW. *(Aside)* He has got our names from the servants already. *(To him)* We approve your caution and hospitality, sir. *(To* HASTINGS*)* I have been thinking, George, of changing our travelling dresses in the morning. I am grown confoundedly ashamed of mine.

HARDCASTLE. I beg, Mr. Marlow, you'll use no ceremony in this house.

HASTINGS. I fancy, Charles, you're right; the first blow is half the battle. I intend opening the campaign with the white and gold.

HARDCASTLE. Mr. Marlow—Mr. Hastings —gentlemen, pray be under no restraint in this house. This is Liberty Hall, gentlemen. You may do just as you please here.

MARLOW. Yet, George, if we open the

campaign too fiercely at first, we may want ammunition before it is over. I think to reserve the embroidery to secure a retreat.

HARDCASTLE. Your talking of a retreat, Mr. Marlow, puts me in mind of the Duke of Marlborough, when we went to besiege Denain. He first summoned the garrison—

MARLOW. Don't you think the *ventre d'or* waistcoat will do with the plain brown?

HARDCASTLE. He first summoned the garrison, which might consist of about five thousand men—

HASTINGS. I think not: brown and yellow mix but very poorly.

HARDCASTLE. I say, gentlemen, as I was telling you, he summoned the garrison, which might consist of about five thousand men—

MARLOW. The girls like finery.

HARDCASTLE. Which might consist of about five thousand men, well appointed with stores, ammunition, and other implements of war. "Now," says the Duke of Marlborough to George Brooks, that stood next to him—you must have heard of George Brooks—"I'll pawn my dukedom," says he, "but I take that garrison without spilling a drop of blood." So—

MARLOW. What, my good friend, if you gave us a glass of punch in the meantime; it would help us to carry on the siege with vigor.

HARDCASTLE. Punch, sir! (*Aside*) This is the most unaccountable kind of modesty I ever met with!

MARLOW. Yes, sir, punch! A glass of warm punch, after our journey, will be comfortable. This is Liberty Hall, you know.

HARDCASTLE. Here's cup, sir.

MARLOW. (*Aside*) So this fellow, in his Liberty Hall, will only let us have just what he pleases.

HARDCASTLE. (*Taking the cup*) I hope you'll find it to your mind. I have prepared it with my own hands, and I believe you'll own the ingredients are tolerable. Will you be so good as to pledge me, sir? Here, Mr. Marlow, here is to our better acquaintance.
(*Drinks*)

MARLOW. (*Aside*) A very impudent fellow this! But he's a character, and I'll humor him a little.—Sir, my service to you.
(*Drinks*)

HASTINGS. (*Aside*) I see this fellow wants to give us his company, and forgets that he's an innkeeper before he has learned to be a gentleman.

MARLOW. From the excellence of your cup, my old friend, I suppose you have a good deal of business in this part of the country. Warm work, now and then, at elections, I suppose.

HARDCASTLE. No, sir, I have long given that work over. Since our betters have hit upon the expedient of electing each other, there is no business "for us that sell ale."

HASTINGS. So, then, you have no turn for politics, I find.

HARDCASTLE. Not in the least. There was a time, indeed, I fretted myself about the mistakes of government, like other people; but, finding myself every day grow more angry, and the government growing no better, I left it to amend itself. Since that, I no more trouble my head about Hyder Ally, or Ally Cawn, than about Ally Croaker. Sir, my service to you.

HASTINGS. So that with eating above stairs, and drinking below, with receiving your friends within, and amusing them without, you lead a good, pleasant, bustling life of it.

HARDCASTLE. I do stir about a great deal, that's certain. Half the differences of the parish are adjusted in this very parlor.

MARLOW. (*After drinking*) And you have an argument in your cup, old gentleman, better than any in Westminster Hall.

HARDCASTLE. Ay, young gentleman, that, and a little philosophy.

MARLOW. (*Aside*) Well, this is the first time I ever heard of an innkeeper's philosophy.

HASTINGS. So, then, like an experienced general, you attack them on every quarter. If you find their reason manageable, you attack it with your philosophy; if you find they have no reason, you attack them with this. Here's your health, my philosopher.
(*Drinks*)

HARDCASTLE. Good, very good, thank you; ha! ha! ha! Your generalship puts me in mind of Prince Eugene, when he fought the Turks at the battle of Belgrade. You shall hear—

MARLOW. Instead of the battle of Belgrade, I believe it's almost time to talk about supper. What has your philosophy got in the house for supper?

HARDCASTLE. For supper, sir! (*Aside*) Was ever such a request to a man in his own house!

MARLOW. Yes, sir, supper, sir; I begin to feel an appetite. I shall make devilish work to-night in the larder, I promise you.

HARDCASTLE. (*Aside*) Such a brazen dog sure never my eyes beheld. (*To him*) Why, really, sir, as for supper, I can't well tell. My Dorothy and the cook-maid settle these things between them. I leave these kind of things entirely to them.

MARLOW. You do, do you?

HARDCASTLE. Entirely. By the bye, I believe they are in actual consultation upon what's for supper this moment in the kitchen.

MARLOW. Then I beg they'll admit *me* as one of their privy-council. It's a way I have got. When I travel I always choose to regulate my own supper. Let the cook be called. No offence, I hope, sir.

HARDCASTLE. Oh, no, sir, none in the least; yet I don't know how. Our Bridget, the cook-maid, is not very communicative upon these occasions. Should we send for her, she might scold us all out of the house.

HASTINGS. Let's see your list of the larder, then. I ask it as a favor. I always match my appetite to my bill of fare.

MARLOW. (*To* HARDCASTLE, *who looks at them with surprise*) Sir, he's very right, and it's my way, too.

HARDCASTLE. Sir, you have a right to command here. Here, Roger, bring us the bill of fare for to-night's supper; I believe it's drawn out. (*Exit* ROGER) Your manner, Mr. Hastings, puts me in mind of my uncle, Colonel Wallop. It was a saying of his, that no man was sure of his supper till he had eaten it.

HASTINGS. (*Aside*) All upon the high ropes! His uncle a colonel! We shall soon hear of his mother being a justice of peace. (*Re-enter* ROGER) But let's hear the bill of fare.

MARLOW. (*Perusing*) What's here? For the first course; for the second course; for the dessert. The devil, sir, do you think we have brought down the whole Joiners' Company, or the Corporation of Bedford, to eat up such a supper? Two or three little things, clean and comfortable, will do.

HASTINGS. But let's hear it.

MARLOW. (*Reading*) For the first course, at the top, a pig, and prune sauce.

HASTINGS. Damn your pig, I say!

MARLOW. And damn your prune sauce, say I!

HARDCASTLE. And yet, gentlemen, to men that are hungry, pig with prune sauce is very good eating.

MARLOW. At the bottom, a calf's tongue and brains.

HASTINGS. Let your brains be knocked out, my good sir; I don't like them.

MARLOW. Or you may clap them on a plate by themselves. I do.

HARDCASTLE. (*Aside*) Their impudence confounds me. (*To them*) Gentlemen, you are my guests; make what alterations you please. Is there anything else you wish to retrench, or alter, gentlemen?

MARLOW. Item: a pork pie, a boiled rabbit and sausages, a Florentine, a shaking pudding, and a dish of tiff—taff—taffety cream!

HASTINGS. Confound your made dishes! I shall be as much at a loss in this house as at a green and yellow dinner at the French Ambassador's table. I'm for plain eating.

HARDCASTLE. I'm sorry, gentlemen, that I have nothing you like; but if there be anything you have a particular fancy to—

MARLOW. Why, really, sir, your bill of fare is so exquisite, that any one part of it is full as good as another. Send us what you please. So much for supper. And now to see that our beds are aired, and properly taken care of.

HARDCASTLE. I entreat you'll leave all that to me. You shall not stir a step.

MARLOW. Leave that to you! I protest, sir, you must excuse me; I always look to these things myself.

HARDCASTLE. I must insist, sir, you'll make yourself easy on that head.

MARLOW. You see I am resolved on it. (*Aside*) A very troublesome fellow this, as ever I met with.

HARDCASTLE. Well, sir, I'm resolved at least to attend you. (*Aside*) This may be modern modesty, but I never saw anything look so like old-fashioned impudence.

(*Exeunt* MARLOW *and* HARDCASTLE)

HASTINGS. So I find this fellow's civilities begin to grow troublesome. But who can be angry at those assiduities which are meant to please him? Ha! what do I see? Miss Neville, by all that's happy!

(*Enter* MISS NEVILLE)

MISS NEVILLE. My dear Hastings! To what unexpected good fortune, to what accident, am I to ascribe this happy meeting?

HASTINGS. Rather let me ask the same question, as I could never have hoped to meet my dearest Constance at an inn.

MISS NEVILLE. An inn! sure you mistake! My aunt, my guardian, lives here. What could induce you to think this house an inn?

HASTINGS. My friend, Mr. Marlow, with whom I came down, and I, have been sent here as to an inn, I assure you. A young fellow, whom we accidentally met at a house hard by, directed us hither.

MISS NEVILLE. Certainly it must be one of my hopeful cousin's tricks, of whom you have heard me talk so often. Ha! ha! ha!

HASTINGS. He whom your aunt intends for you? He of whom I have such just apprehensions?

MISS NEVILLE. You have nothing to fear from him, I assure you. You'd adore him if you knew how heartily he despises me. My aunt knows it too, and has undertaken to court me for him, and actually begins to think she has made a conquest.

HASTINGS. Thou dear dissembler! You must know, my Constance, I have just seized this happy opportunity of my friend's visit here to get admittance into the family. The horses that carried us down are now fatigued with their journey, but they'll soon be refreshed; and then, if my dearest girl will trust in her faithful Hastings, we shall soon be landed in France, where even among slaves the laws of marriage are respected.

MISS NEVILLE. I have often told you that, though ready to obey you, I yet should leave my little fortune behind with reluctance. The greatest part of it was left me by my uncle, the India director, and chiefly consists in jewels. I have been for some time persuading my aunt to let me wear them. I fancy I'm very near succeeding. The instant they are put into my possession, you shall find me ready to make them and myself yours.

HASTINGS. Perish the baubles! Your person is all I desire. In the meantime, my friend Marlow must not be let into his mistake. I know the strange reserve of his temper is such that, if abruptly informed of it, he would instantly quit the house before our plan was ripe for execution.

MISS NEVILLE. But how shall we keep him in the deception? Miss Hardcastle is just returned from walking; what if we still continue to deceive him?—This, this way—

(*They confer*)

(*Enter* MARLOW)

MARLOW. The assiduities of these good people tease me beyond bearing. My host seems to think it ill manners to leave me alone, and so he claps not only himself but his old-fashioned wife on my back. They talk of coming to sup with us too; and then, I suppose, we are to run the gauntlet through all the rest of the family.—What have we got here?

HASTINGS. My dear Charles! Let me congratulate you! The most fortunate accident! Who do you think is just alighted?

MARLOW. Cannot guess.

HASTINGS. Our mistresses, boy, Miss Hardcastle and Miss Neville. Give me leave to introduce Miss Constance Neville to your acquaintance. Happening to dine in the neighborhood, they called on their return to take fresh horses here. Miss Hardcastle has just stepped into the next room, and will be back in an instant. Wasn't it lucky? eh!

MARLOW. (*Aside*) I have just been mortified enough of all conscience, and here comes something to complete my embarrassment.

HASTINGS. Well, but wasn't it the most fortunate thing in the world?

MARLOW. Oh, yes. Very fortunate—a most joyful encounter—But our dresses, George, you know, are in disorder—What if we should postpone the happiness till to-morrow?—to-morrow at her own house—It will be every bit as convenient—and rather more respectful—To-morrow let it be.

(Offering to go)

HASTINGS. By no means, sir. Your ceremony will displease her. The disorder of your dress will show the ardor of your impatience. Besides, she knows you are in the house, and will permit you to see her.

MARLOW. Oh, the devil! how shall I support it? Hem! hem! Hastings, you must not go. You are to assist me, you know. I shall be confoundedly ridiculous. Yet, hang it, I'll take courage! Hem!

HASTINGS. Pshaw, man! it's but the first plunge, and all's over! She's but a woman, you know.

MARLOW. And of all women, she that I dread most to encounter!

(Enter MISS HARDCASTLE, *as returned from walking, fashionably dressed and wearing a bonnet which obscures her face)*

HASTINGS. *(Introducing them)* Miss Hardcastle, Mr. Marlow; I'm proud of bringing two persons of such merit together, that only want to know, to esteem each other.

MISS HARDCASTLE. *(Aside)* Now for meeting my modest gentleman with a demure face, and quite in his own manner. *(After a pause, in which he appears very uneasy and disconcerted)* I'm glad of your safe arrival, sir. I'm told you had some accidents by the way.

MARLOW. Only a few, madam. Yes, we had some. Yes, madam, a good many accidents, but should be sorry—madam—or rather glad of any accidents—that are so agreeably concluded. Hem!

HASTINGS. *(To him)* You never spoke better in our whole life. Keep it up, and I'll insure you the victory.

MISS HARDCASTLE. I'm afraid you flatter, sir. You that have seen so much of the finest company, can find little entertainment in an obscure corner of the country.

MARLOW. *(Gathering courage)* I have lived, indeed, in the world, madam; but I have kept very little company. I have been but an observer upon life, madam, while others were enjoying it.

MISS NEVILLE. But that, I am told, is the way to enjoy it at last.

HASTINGS. *(To him)* Cicero never spoke better. Once more, and you are confirmed in assurance for ever.

MARLOW. *(To him)* Hem! stand by me then, and when I'm down, throw in a word or two to set me up again.

MISS HARDCASTLE. An observer, like you, upon life, were, I fear, disagreeably employed, since you must have had much more to censure than to approve.

MARLOW. Pardon me, madam. I was always willing to be amused. The folly of most people is rather an object of mirth than uneasiness.

HASTINGS. *(To him)* Bravo, bravo! Never spoke so well in your whole life.—Well, Miss Hardcastle, I see that you and Mr. Marlow are going to be very good company. I believe our being here will but embarrass the interview.

MARLOW. Not in the least, Mr. Hastings. We like your company of all things. *(To him)* Zounds, George, sure you won't go? How can you leave us?

HASTINGS. Our presence will but spoil conversation, so we'll retire to the next room. *(To him)* You don't consider, man, that we are to manage a little *tête-à-tête* of our own.

(Exeunt HASTINGS *with* MISS NEVILLE*)*

MISS HARDCASTLE. *(After a pause)* But you have not been wholly an observer, I presume, sir. The ladies, I should hope, have employed some part of your addresses.

MARLOW. *(Relapsing into timidity)* Pardon me, madam, I—I—I—as yet have studied—only—to—deserve them.

MISS HARDCASTLE. And that, some say, is the very worst way to obtain them.

MARLOW. Perhaps so, madam. But I love to converse only with the more grave and sensible part of the sex.—But I'm afraid I grow tiresome.

MISS HARDCASTLE. Not at all, sir; there is nothing I like so much as grave conversation myself; I could hear it for ever. Indeed I have often been surprised how a man of sentiment could ever admire those light, airy pleasures, where nothing reaches the heart.

MARLOW. It's—a disease—of the mind, madam. In the variety of tastes there must be some who, wanting a relish—for—um—a —um—

Miss Hardcastle. I understand you, sir. There must be some who, wanting a relish for refined pleasures, pretend to despise what they are incapable of tasting.

Marlow. My meaning, madam, but infinitely better expressed. And I can't help observing—a—

Miss Hardcastle. (*Aside*) Who could ever suppose this fellow impudent upon some occasions! (*To him*) You were going to observe, sir,—

Marlow. I was observing, madam—I protest, madam, I forget what I was going to observe.

Miss Hardcastle. (*Aside*) I vow and so do I. (*To him*) You were observing, sir, that in this age of hypocrisy,—something about hypocrisy, sir.

Marlow. Yes, madam. In this age of hypocrisy there are few who, upon strict inquiry, do not—a—a—

Miss Hardcastle. I understand you perfectly, sir.

Marlow. (*Aside*) Egad! and that's more than I do myself!

Miss Hardcastle. You mean that in this hypocritical age there are few who do not condemn in public what they practice in private; and think they pay every debt to virtue when they praise it.

Marlow. True, madam; those who have most virtue in their mouths have least of it in their bosoms. But I'm sure I tire you, madam.

Miss Hardcastle. Not in the least, sir; there's something so agreeable and spirited in your manner, such life and force,—pray, sir, go on.

Marlow. Yes, madam, I was saying—that there are some occasions—when a total want of courage, madam, destroys all the—and puts us—upon—a—a—a—

Miss Hardcastle. I agree with you entirely; a want of courage upon some occasions, assumes the appearance of ignorance, and betrays us when we most want to excel. I beg you'll proceed.

Marlow. Yes, madam. Morally speaking, madam—But I see Miss Neville expecting us in the next room. I would not intrude for the world.

Miss Hardcastle. I protest, sir, I never was more agreeably entertained in all my life. Pray go on.

Marlow. Yes, madam, I was—But she beckons us to join her. Madam, shall I do myself the honor to attend you?

Miss Hardcastle. Well, then, I'll follow.

Marlow. (*Aside*) This pretty smooth dialogue has done for me.   (*Exit*)

Miss Hardcastle. Ha! ha! ha! Was there ever such a sober, sentimental interview? I'm certain he scarce looked in my face the whole time. Yet the fellow, but for his unaccountable bashfulness, is pretty well, too. He has good sense, but then so buried in his fears, that it fatigues one more than ignorance. If I could teach him a little confidence, it would be doing somebody that I know of a piece of service. But who is that somebody? That, faith, is a question I can scarce answer.   (*Exit*)

(*Enter* Tony *and* Miss Neville, *followed by* Mrs. Hardcastle *and* Hastings)

Tony. What do you follow me for, cousin Con? I wonder you're not ashamed to be so very engaging.

Miss Neville. I hope, cousin, one may speak to one's own relations, and not be to blame.

Tony. Ay, but I know what sort of a relation you want to make me, though; but it won't do. I tell you, cousin Con, it won't do; so I beg you'll keep your distance. I want no nearer relationship.

(*She follows, coquetting him to the back scene*)

Mrs. Hardcastle. Well, I vow, Mr. Hastings, you are very entertaining. There's nothing in the world I love to talk of so much as London, and the fashions, though I was never there myself.

Hastings. Never there! You amaze me! From your air and manner, I concluded you had been bred all your life either at Ranelagh, St. James's, or Tower Wharf.[2]

Mrs. Hardcastle. Oh, sir, you're only pleased to say so. We country persons can have no manner at all. I'm in love with the town, and that serves to raise me above some

[2] Hastings deliberately mixes fashionable and disreputable places.

of our neighboring rustics; but who can have a manner, that has never seen the Pantheon, the Grotto Gardens, the Borough, and such places, where the nobility chiefly resort? All I can do is to enjoy London at second-hand. I take care to know every *tête-à-tête* from the *Scandalous Magazine,* and have all the fashions, as they come out, in a letter from the two Miss Rickets of Crooked-lane. Pray, how do you like this head, Mr. Hastings?

HASTINGS. Extremely elegant and *dégagée,* upon my word, madam. Your *friseur* is a Frenchman, I suppose?

MRS. HARDCASTLE. I protest, I dressed it myself from a print in the *Ladies' Memorandum-book* for the last year.

HASTINGS. Indeed! Such a head in a side-box, at the play-house, would draw as many gazers as my Lady Mayoress at a city ball.

MRS. HARDCASTLE. I vow, since inoculation[3] began, there is no such thing to be seen as a plain woman; so one must dress a little particular, or one may escape in the crowd.

HASTINGS. But that can never be your case, madam, in any dress. (*Bowing*)

MRS. HARDCASTLE. Yet what signifies my dressing, when I have such a piece of antiquity by my side as Mr. Hardcastle? All I can say will never argue down a single button from his clothes. I have often wanted him to throw off his great flaxen wig, and where he was bald to plaster it over, like my Lord Pately, with powder.

HASTINGS. You are right, madam; for, as among the ladies there are none ugly, so among the men there are none old.

MRS. HARDCASTLE. But what do you think his answer was? Why, with his usual Gothic vivacity, he said I only wanted him to throw off his wig to convert it into a *tête* for my own wearing.

HASTINGS. Intolerable! At your age you may wear what you please, and it must become you.

MRS. HARDCASTLE. Pray, Mr. Hastings, what do you take to be the most fashionable age about town?

HASTINGS. Some time ago forty was all the mode; but I'm told the ladies intend to bring up fifty for the ensuing winter.

[3] Against smallpox.

MRS. HARDCASTLE. Seriously? Then I shall be too young for the fashion.

HASTINGS. No lady begins now to put on jewels till she's past forty. For instance, Miss there, in a polite circle, would be considered as a child, as a mere maker of samplers.

MRS. HARDCASTLE. And yet, Mistress Niece thinks herself as much a woman, and is as fond of jewels, as the oldest of us all.

HASTINGS. Your niece, is she? And that young gentleman,—a brother of yours, I should presume?

MRS. HARDCASTLE. My son, sir. They are contracted to each other. Observe their little sports. They fall in and out ten times a day, as if they were man and wife already. (*To them*) Well, Tony, child, what soft things are you saying to your cousin Constance this evening?

TONY. I have been saying no soft things; but that it's very hard to be followed about so. Ecod! I've not a place in the house now that's left to myself, but the stable.

MRS. HARDCASTLE. Never mind him, Con, my dear. He's in another story behind your back.

MISS NEVILLE. There's something generous in my cousin's manner. He falls out before faces, to be forgiven in private.

TONY. That's a damned confounded—crack.

MRS. HARDCASTLE. Ah, he's a sly one! Don't you think they're like each other about the mouth, Mr. Hastings? The Blenkinsop mouth to a T. They're of a size, too. Back to back, my pretties, that Mr. Hastings may see you. Come, Tony.

TONY. You had as good not make me, I tell you.

(*While measuring,* TONY *deliberately bumps her head*)

MISS NEVILLE. Oh, lud! He has almost cracked my head.

MRS. HARDCASTLE. Oh, the monster! For shame, Tony. You a man, and behave so!

TONY. If I'm a man, let me have my fortin. Ecod, I'll not be made a fool of no longer.

MRS. HARDCASTLE. Is this, ungrateful boy, all that I'm to get for the pains I have taken in your education? I that have rocked you in your cradle, and fed that pretty mouth with a spoon! Did not I work that waistcoat to make you genteel? Did not I prescribe for you every day, and weep while the receipt was operating?

TONY. Ecod! you had reason to weep, for you have been dosing me ever since I was born. I have gone through every receipt in *The Complete Huswife* ten times over; and you have thoughts of coursing me through *Quincy* next spring. But, Ecod! I tell you, I'll not be made a fool of no longer.

MRS. HARDCASTLE. Wasn't it all for your good, viper? Wasn't it all for your good?

TONY. I wish you'd let me and my good alone, then. Snubbing this way when I'm in spirits! If I'm to have any good, let it come of itself; not to keep dinging it, dinging it into one so.

MRS. HARDCASTLE. That's false; I never see you when you're in spirits. No, Tony, you then go to the alehouse or kennel. I'm never to be delighted with your agreeable wild notes, unfeeling monster!

TONY. Ecod! mamma, your own notes are the wildest of the two.

MRS. HARDCASTLE. Was ever the like? But I see he wants to break my heart; I see he does.

HASTINGS. Dear madam, permit me to lecture the young gentleman a little. I'm certain I can persuade him to his duty.

MRS. HARDCASTLE. Well, I must retire. Come, Constance, my love. You see, Mr. Hastings, the wretchedness of my situation. Was ever poor woman so plagued with a dear, sweet, pretty, provoking, undutiful boy?

(*Exeunt* MRS. HARDCASTLE *and* MISS NEVILLE)

TONY. (*Singing*)
There was a young man riding by,
And fain would have his will.
Rang do didlo dee.

—Don't mind her. Let her cry. It's the comfort of her heart. I have seen her and sister cry over a book for an hour together; and they said they liked the book the better the more it made them cry.

HASTINGS. Then you're no friend to the ladies, I find, my pretty young gentleman?

TONY. That's as I find 'um.

HASTINGS. Not to her of your mother's choosing, I dare answer? And she appears to me a pretty, well-tempered girl.

TONY. That's because you don't know her

as well as I. Ecod! I know every inch about her; and there's not a more bitter, cantankerous toad in all Christendom.

HASTINGS. (*Aside*) Pretty encouragement, this, for a lover.

TONY. I have seen her since the height of that. She has as many tricks as a hare in a thicket, or a colt the first day's breaking.

HASTINGS. To me she appears sensible and silent.

TONY. Ay, before company. But when she's with her playmates, she's as loud as a hog in a gate.

HASTINGS. But there is a meek modesty about her that charms me.

TONY. Yes, but curb her never so little, she kicks up, and you're flung in a ditch.

HASTINGS. Well, but you must allow her a little beauty.—Yes, you must allow her some beauty.

TONY. Bandbox! She's all a made-up thing, mun. Ah! could you but see Bet Bouncer of these parts, you might then talk of beauty. Ecod! she has two eyes as black as sloes, and cheeks as broad and red as a pulpit cushion. She'd make two of she.

HASTINGS. Well, what say you to a friend that would take this bitter bargain off your hands?

TONY. Anon!

HASTINGS. Would you thank him that would take Miss Neville, and leave you to happiness and your dear Betsy?

TONY. Ay; but where is there such a friend, for who would take *her*?

HASTINGS. I am he. If you but assist me, I'll engage to whip her off to France, and you shall never hear more of her.

TONY. Assist you! Ecod I will, to the last drop of my blood. I'll clap a pair of horses to your chaise that shall trundle you off in a twinkling, and may be get you a part of her fortin besides, in jewels, that you little dream of.

HASTINGS. My dear Squire, this looks like a lad of spirit.

TONY. Come along then, and you shall see more of my spirit before you have done with me. (*Singing*)

We are the boys
That fears no noise
Where the thundering cannons roar.
(*Exeunt*)

Act III

The Parlor of MR. HARDCASTLE'S House

(*Enter* HARDCASTLE *solus*)

HARDCASTLE. What could my old friend Sir Charles mean by recommending his son as the modestest young man in town? To me he appears the most impudent piece of brass that ever spoke with a tongue. He has taken possession of the easy chair by the fire-side already. He took off his boots in the parlor, and desired me to see them taken care of. I'm desirous to know how his impudence affects my daughter. She will certainly be shocked at it.

(*Enter* MISS HARDCASTLE, *plainly dressed*)

HARDCASTLE. Well, my Kate, I see you have changed your dress, as I bid you; and yet, I believe, there was no great occasion.

MISS HARDCASTLE. I find such a pleasure, sir, in obeying your commands, that I take care to observe them without ever debating their propriety.

HARDCASTLE. And yet, Kate, I sometimes give you some cause, particularly when I recommended my *modest* gentleman to you as a lover to-day.

MISS HARDCASTLE. You taught me to expect something extraordinary, and I find the original exceeds the description.

HARDCASTLE. I was never so surprised in my life! He has quite confounded all my faculties.

MISS HARDCASTLE. I never saw anything like it; and a man of the world, too!

HARDCASTLE. Ay, he learned it all abroad; what a fool was I, to think a young man could learn modesty by travelling. He might as soon learn wit at a masquerade.

MISS HARDCASTLE. It seems all natural to him.

HARDCASTLE. A good deal assisted by bad company and a French dancing-master.

MISS HARDCASTLE. Sure, you mistake, papa. A French dancing-master could never have taught him that timid look—that awkward address—that bashful manner.

HARDCASTLE. Whose look, whose manner, child?

MISS HARDCASTLE. Mr. Marlow's: his *mauvaise honte,* his timidity, struck me at the first sight.

HARDCASTLE. Then your first sight deceived you; for I think him one of the most brazen first sights that ever astonished my senses.

MISS HARDCASTLE. Sure, sir, you rally! I never saw any one so modest.

HARDCASTLE. And can you be serious! I never saw such a bouncing, swaggering puppy since I was born. Bully Dawson was but a fool to him.

MISS HARDCASTLE. Surprising! He met me with a respectful bow, a stammering voice, and a look fixed on the ground.

HARDCASTLE. He met me with a loud voice, a lordly air, and a familiarity that made my blood freeze again.

MISS HARDCASTLE. He treated me with diffidence and respect; censured the manners of the age; admired the prudence of girls that never laughed; tired me with apologies for being tiresome; then left the room with a bow, and "Madam, I would not for the world detain you."

HARDCASTLE. He spoke to me as if he knew me all his life before; asked twenty questions, and never waited for an answer; interrupted my best remarks with some silly pun; and when I was in my best story of the Duke of Marlborough and Prince Eugene, he asked if I had not a good hand at making punch. Yes, Kate, he asked your father if he was a maker of punch!

MISS HARDCASTLE. One of us must certainly be mistaken.

HARDCASTLE. If he be what he has shown himself, I'm determined he shall never have my consent.

MISS HARDCASTLE. And if he be the sullen thing I take him, he shall never have mine.

HARDCASTLE. In one thing then we are agreed—to reject him.

MISS HARDCASTLE. (*Hesitating*) Yes—but upon conditions. For if you should find him less impudent, and I more presuming; if you find him more respectful, and I more importunate—I don't know—the fellow is well enough for a man—Certainly we don't meet many such at a horse-race in the country.

HARDCASTLE. If we should find him so— but that's impossible. The first appearance has done my business. I'm seldom deceived in that.

MISS HARDCASTLE. And yet there may be many good qualities under that first appearance.

HARDCASTLE. Ay, when a girl finds a fellow's outside to her taste, she then sets about guessing the rest of his furniture. With her a smooth face stands for good sense, and a genteel figure for every virtue.

MISS HARDCASTLE. I hope, sir, a conversation begun with a compliment to my good sense, won't end with a sneer at my understanding!

HARDCASTLE. Pardon me, Kate. But if young Mr. Brazen can find the art of reconciling contradictions, he may please us both, perhaps.

MISS HARDCASTLE. And as one of us must be mistaken, what if we go to make farther discoveries?

HARDCASTLE. Agreed. But depend on't, I'm in the right.

MISS HARDCASTLE. And, depend on't, I'm not much in the wrong.　　　(*Exeunt*)

(*Enter* TONY, *running in with a jewel casket*)

TONY. Ecod! I have got them. Here they are. My cousin Con's necklaces, bobs and all. My mother shan't cheat the poor souls out of their fortin neither. Oh! my genus, is that you?

(*Enter* HASTINGS)

HASTINGS. My dear friend, how have you managed with your mother? I hope you have amused her with pretending love for your cousin, and that you are willing to be reconciled at last? Our horses will be refreshed in a short time, and we shall soon be ready to set off.

TONY. And here's something to bear your charges by the way (*giving the casket*);— your sweetheart's jewels. Keep them; and hang those, I say, that would rob you of one of them!

HASTINGS. But how have you procured them from your mother?

TONY. Ask me no questions, and I'll tell you no fibs. I procured them by the rule of thumb. If I had not a key to every drawer in my mother's bureau, how could I go to the alehouse so often as I do? An honest man may rob himself of his own at any time.

HASTINGS. Thousands do it every day. But, to be plain with you, Miss Neville is endeavoring to procure them from her aunt this very instant. If she succeeds, it will be the most delicate way, at least, of obtaining them.

TONY. Well, keep them, till you know how it will be. But I know how it will be well enough; she'd as soon part with the only sound tooth in her head.

HASTINGS. But I dread the effects of her resentment when she finds she has lost them.

TONY. Never you mind her resentment; leave *me* to manage that. I don't value her resentment the bounce of a cracker. Zounds! here they are! Morrice! Prance! [4]

(*Exit* HASTINGS)

(*Enter* MRS. HARDCASTLE *and* MISS NEVILLE)

MRS. HARDCASTLE. Indeed, Constance, you amaze me. Such a girl as you want jewels? It will be time enough for jewels, my dear, twenty years hence, when your beauty begins to want repairs.

MISS NEVILLE. But what will repair beauty at forty, will certainly improve it at twenty, madam.

MRS. HARDCASTLE. Yours, my dear, can admit of none. That natural blush is beyond a thousand ornaments. Besides, child, jewels are quite out at present. Don't you see half the ladies of our acquaintance, my Lady Kill-day-light, and Mrs. Crump, and the rest of them, carry their jewels to town, and bring nothing but paste and marcasites back?

MISS NEVILLE. But who knows, madam, but somebody that shall be nameless would like me best with all my little finery about me?

MRS. HARDCASTLE. Consult your glass, my dear, and then see if, with such a pair of eyes, you want any better sparklers. What

[4] *I.e.*, dance away, as if at a country morris dance.

do you think, Tony, my dear? Does your cousin Con want any jewels, in your eyes, to set off her beauty?

Tony. That's as hereafter may be.

Miss Neville. My dear aunt, if you knew how it would oblige me.

Mrs. Hardcastle. A parcel of old-fashioned rose and table-cut things. They would make you look like the court of King Solomon at a puppet-show. Besides, I believe I can't readily come at them. They may be missing, for aught I know to the contrary.

Tony. (Apart to Mrs. Hardcastle) Then why don't you tell her so at once, as she's so longing for them? Tell her they're lost. It's the only way to quiet her. Say they're lost, and call me to bear witness.

Mrs. Hardcastle. (Apart to Tony) You know, my dear, I'm only keeping them for you. So if I say they're gone, you'll bear me witness, will you? He! he! he!

Tony. Never fear me. Ecod! I'll say I saw them taken out with my own eyes.

Miss Neville. I desire them but for a day, madam, just to be permitted to show them as relics, and then they may be locked up again.

Mrs. Hardcastle. To be plain with you, my dear Constance, if I could find them you should have them. They're missing, I assure you. Lost, for aught I know; but we must have patience, wherever they are.

Miss Neville. I'll not believe it; this is but a shallow pretence to deny me. I know they are too valuable to be so slightly kept, and as you are to answer for the loss—

Mrs. Hardcastle. Don't be alarmed, Constance. If they be lost, I must restore an equivalent. But my son knows they are missing, and not to be found.

Tony. That I can bear witness to. They are missing, and not to be found; I'll take my oath on't.

Mrs. Hardcastle. You must learn resignation, my dear; for though we lose our fortune, yet we should not lose our patience. See me, how calm I am.

Miss Neville. Ay, people are generally calm at the misfortunes of others.

Mrs. Hardcastle. Now, I wonder a girl of your good sense should waste a thought upon such trumpery. We shall soon find them; and in the mean time you shall make use of my garnets till your jewels be found.

Miss Neville. I detest garnets!

Mrs. Hardcastle. The most becoming things in the world to set off a clear complexion. You have often seen how well they look upon me. You *shall* have them. (Exit)

Miss Neville. I dislike them of all things. —You shan't stir. Was ever anything so provoking,—to mislay my own jewels, and force me to wear her trumpery?

Tony. Don't be a fool. If she gives you the garnets take what you can get. The jewels are your own already. I have stolen them out of her bureau, and she does not know it. Fly to your spark; he'll tell you more of the matter. Leave me to manage *her*.

Miss Neville. My dear cousin!

Tony. Vanish. She's here, and has missed them already. (Exit Miss Neville) Zounds! how she fidgets and spits about like a Catherine wheel.

(Enter Mrs. Hardcastle)

Mrs. Hardcastle. Confusion! thieves! robbers! We are cheated, plundered, broke open, undone!

Tony. What's the matter, what's the matter, mamma? I hope nothing has happened to any of the good family?

Mrs. Hardcastle. We are robbed. My bureau has been broke open, the jewels taken out, and I'm undone!

Tony. Oh! is that all! Ha! ha! ha! By the laws, I never saw it better acted in my life. Ecod, I thought you was ruined in earnest, ha, ha, ha!

Mrs. Hardcastle. Why, boy, I *am* ruined in earnest. My bureau has been broke open, and all taken away.

Tony. Stick to that; ha, ha, ha! stick to that. I'll bear witness, you know! call me to bear witness.

Mrs. Hardcastle. I tell you, Tony, by all that's precious, the jewels are gone, and I shall be ruined forever.

Tony. Sure I know they are gone, and I am to say so.

Mrs. Hardcastle. My dearest Tony, but hear me. They're gone, I say.

Tony. By the laws, mamma, you make me for to laugh, ha! ha! I know who took them well enough, ha! ha! ha!

MRS. HARDCASTLE. Was there ever such a blockhead, that can't tell the difference between jest and earnest? I can tell you I'm not in jest, booby.

TONY. That's right, that's right! You must be in a bitter passion, and then nobody will suspect either of us. I'll bear witness that they are gone.

MRS. HARDCASTLE. Was there ever such a cross-grained brute, that won't hear me? Can you bear witness that you're no better than a fool? Was ever poor woman so beset with fools on one hand, and thieves on the other?

TONY. I can bear witness to that.

MRS. HARDCASTLE. Bear witness again, you blockhead, you, and I'll turn you out of the room directly. My poor niece, what will become of *her*? Do you laugh, you unfeeling brute, as if you enjoyed my distress?

TONY. I can bear witness to that.

MRS. HARDCASTLE. Do you insult me, monster. I'll teach you to vex your mother, I will!

TONY. I can bear witness to that.

(*He runs off; she follows him*)

(*Enter* MISS HARDCASTLE *and* MAID)

MISS HARDCASTLE. What an unaccountable creature is that brother of mine, to send them to the house as an inn; ha! ha! I don't wonder at his impudence.

MAID. But what is more, madam, the young gentleman, as you passed by in your present dress, asked me if you were the bar-maid. He mistook you for the bar-maid, madam!

MISS HARDCASTLE. Did he? Then, as I live, I'm resolved to keep up the delusion. Tell me, Pimple, how do you like my present dress? Don't you think I look something like Cherry in the *Beaux' Stratagem*?

MAID. It's the dress, madam, that every lady wears in the country, but when she visits or receives company.

MISS HARDCASTLE. And are you sure he does not remember my face or person?

MAID. Certain of it.

MISS HARDCASTLE. I vow I thought so; for though we spoke for some time together, yet his fears were such that he never once looked up during the interview. Indeed, if he had, my bonnet would have kept him from seeing me.

MAID. But what do you hope from keeping him in his mistake?

MISS HARDCASTLE. In the first place, I shall be *seen*, and that is no small advantage to a girl who brings her face to market. Then I shall perhaps make an acquaintance, and that's no small victory gained over one who never addresses any but the wildest of her sex. But my chief aim is to take my gentleman off his guard, and, like an invisible champion of romance, examine the giant's force before I offer to combat.

MAID. But are you sure you can act your part and disguise your voice so that he may mistake that, as he has already mistaken your person?

MISS HARDCASTLE. Never fear me. I think I have got the true bar cant—(*Imitating a bar-maid*) Did your honor call?—Attend the Lion there.—Pipes and tobacco for the Angel. —The Lamb has been outrageous this half hour!

MAID. (*Giggling*) It will do, madam.— But he's here. (*Exit* MAID)

(*Enter* MARLOW)

MARLOW. What a bawling in every part of the house; I have scarce a moment's repose. If I go to the best room, there I find my host and his story; if I fly to the gallery, there we have my hostess with her curtsey down to the ground. I have at last got a moment to myself, and now for recollection. (*Walks and muses*)

MISS HARDCASTLE. Did you call, sir? Did your honor call?

MARLOW. (*Musing*) As for Miss Hardcastle, she's too grave and sentimental for me.

MISS HARDCASTLE. Did your honor call?
(*She still places herself before him, he turning away*)

MARLOW. No, child. (*Musing*) Besides, from the glimpse I had of her, I think she squints.

MISS HARDCASTLE. I'm sure, sir, I heard the bell ring.

MARLOW. No, no. (*Musing*) I have pleased my father, however, by coming down, and I'll to-morrow please myself by returning.

(*Taking out his tablets and perusing*)

Miss Hardcastle. Perhaps the other gentleman called, sir?

Marlow. I tell you no.

Miss Hardcastle. I should be glad to know, sir. We have such a parcel of servants.

Marlow. No, no, I tell you. (*Looks full in her face*) Yes, child, I think I did call. I wanted—I wanted—I vow, child, you are vastly handsome.

Miss Hardcastle. Oh, la, sir, you'll make one ashamed.

Marlow. Never saw a more sprightly, malicious eye. Yes, yes, my dear, I did call. Have you got any of your—a—what d'ye call it, in the house?

Miss Hardcastle. No, sir, we have been out of that these ten days.

Marlow. One may call in this house, I find, to very little purpose. Suppose I should call for a taste, just by way of trial, of the nectar of your lips; perhaps I might be disappointed in that too.

Miss Hardcastle. Nectar? nectar? That's a liquor there's no call for in these parts. French, I suppose. We keep no French wines here, sir.

Marlow. Of true English growth, I assure you.

Miss Hardcastle. Then it's odd I should not know it. We brew all sorts of wines in this house, and I have lived here these eighteen years.

Marlow. Eighteen years! Why, one would think, child, you kept the bar before you were born. How old are you?

Miss Hardcastle. Oh, sir, I must not tell my age. They say women and music should never be dated.

Marlow. To guess at this distance, you can't be much above forty. (*Approaching*) Yet nearer, I don't think so much. (*Approaching*) By coming close to some women, they look younger still; but when we come very close indeed—   (*Attempting to kiss her*)

Miss Hardcastle. Pray, sir, keep your distance. One would think you wanted to know one's age as they do horses, by mark of mouth.

Marlow. I protest, child, you use me extremely ill. If you keep me at this distance, how is it possible you and I can be ever acquainted?

Miss Hardcastle. And who wants to be acquainted with you? I want no such acquaintance, not I. I'm sure you did not treat Miss Hardcastle, that was here a while ago, in this obstropalous manner. I'll warrant me, before her you looked dashed, and kept bowing to the ground, and talked, for all the world, as if you was before a justice of peace.

Marlow. (*Aside*) Egad, she has hit it, sure enough! (*To her*) In awe of her, child? Ha! ha! ha! A mere awkward, squinting thing! No, no. I find you don't know me. I laughed and rallied her a little; but I was unwilling to be too severe. No, I could not be too severe, curse me!

Miss Hardcastle. Oh, then, sir, you are a favorite, I find, among the ladies!

Marlow. Yes, my dear, a great favorite. And yet, hang me, I don't see what they find in me to follow. At the Ladies' Club in town I'm called their agreeable Rattle. Rattle, child, is not my real name, but one I'm known by. My name is Solomons; Mr. Solomons, my dear, at your service.

(*Offering to kiss her*)

Miss Hardcastle. Hold, sir, you are introducing me to your club, not to yourself. And you're so great a favorite there, you say?

Marlow. Yes, my dear. There's Mrs. Mantrap, Lady Betty Blackleg, the Countess of Sligo, Mrs. Langhorns, old Miss Biddy Buckskin, and your humble servant, keep up the spirit of the place.

Miss Hardcastle. Then it's a very merry place, I suppose?

Marlow. Yes, as merry as cards, suppers, wine, and old women can make us.

Miss Hardcastle. And their agreeable Rattle, ha! ha! ha!

Marlow. (*Aside*) Egad! I don't quite like this chit. She looks knowing, methinks.— You laugh, child?

Miss Hardcastle. I can't but laugh to think what time they all have for minding their work, or their family.

Marlow. (*Aside*) All's well; she don't laugh at me. (*To her*) Do *you* ever work, child?

Miss Hardcastle. Ay, sure. There's not a screen or a quilt in the whole house but what can bear witness to that.

Marlow. Odso! then you must show me your embroidery. I embroider and draw patterns myself a little. If you want a judge of your work, you must apply to me.

(Seizing her hand)

(Enter HARDCASTLE, *who stands in surprise)*

MISS HARDCASTLE. Ay, but the colors don't look well by candle-light. You shall see it all in the morning. *(Struggling)*

MARLOW. And why not now, my angel? Such beauty fires beyond the power of resistance.—Pshaw! the father here! My old luck; I never nicked seven that I did not throw ames ace three times following.

(Exit MARLOW)

HARDCASTLE. So, madam! So I find *this* is your *modest* lover. This is your humble admirer, that kept his eyes fixed on the ground, and only adored at humble distance. Kate, Kate, art thou not ashamed to deceive your father so?

MISS HARDCASTLE. Never trust me, dear papa, but he's still the modest man I first took him for; you'll be convinced of it as well as I.

HARDCASTLE. By the hand of my body, I believe his impudence is infectious! Didn't I see him seize your hand? Didn't I see him haul you about like a milk-maid? And now you talk of his respect and his modesty, forsooth!

MISS HARDCASTLE. But if I shortly convince you of his modesty, that he has only the faults that will pass off with time, and the virtues that will improve with age, I hope you'll forgive him.

HARDCASTLE. The girl would actually make one run mad! I tell you I'll not be convinced. I am convinced. He has scarcely been three hours in the house, and he has already encroached on all my prerogatives. You may like his impudence and call it modesty, but my son-in-law, madam, must have very different qualifications.

MISS HARDCASTLE. Sir, I ask but this night to convince you.

HARDCASTLE. You shall not have half the time, for I have thoughts of turning him out this very hour.

MISS HARDCASTLE. Give me that hour, then, and I hope to satisfy you.

HARDCASTLE. Well, an hour let it be then. But I'll have no trifling with your father. All fair and open; do you mind me?

MISS HARDCASTLE. I hope, sir, you have ever found that I considered your commands as my pride; for your kindness is such that my duty as yet has been inclination. *(Exeunt)*

Act IV

The Parlor of MR. HARDCASTLE's House

(Enter HASTINGS *and* MISS NEVILLE)

HASTINGS. You surprise me! Sir Charles Marlow expected here this night? Where have you had your information?

MISS NEVILLE. You may depend upon it. I just saw his letter to Mr. Hardcastle, in which he tells him he intends setting out a few hours after his son.

HASTINGS. Then, my Constance, all must be completed before he arrives. He knows me; and should he find me here, would discover my name, and perhaps my designs, to the rest of the family.

MISS NEVILLE. The jewels, I hope, are safe?

HASTINGS. Yes, yes. I have sent them to Marlow, who keeps the keys of our baggage. In the mean time, I'll go to prepare matters for our elopement. I have had the Squire's promise of a fresh pair of horses; and, if I should not see him again, will write him further directions. *(Exit)*

MISS NEVILLE. Well, success attend you! In the mean time, I'll go amuse my aunt with the old pretence of a violent passion for my cousin. *(Exit)*

(Enter MARLOW, *followed by a* SERVANT)

MARLOW. I wonder what Hastings could mean by sending me so valuable a thing as a casket to keep for him, when he knows the only place I have is the seat of a post-coach at an inn-door. Have you deposited the casket with the landlady, as I ordered you? Have you put it into her own hands?

SERVANT. Yes, your honor.

MARLOW. She said she'd keep it safe, did she?

SERVANT. Yes; she said she'd keep it safe enough. She asked me how I came by it; and she said she had a great mind to make me give an account of myself. (*Exit* SERVANT)

MARLOW. Ha! ha! ha! They're safe, however. What an unaccountable set of beings have we got amongst! This little bar-maid, though, runs in my head most strangely, and drives out the absurdities of all the rest of the family. She's mine, she must be mine, or I'm greatly mistaken!

(*Enter* HASTINGS)

HASTINGS. (*Aside*) Bless me! I quite forgot to tell her that I intended to prepare at the bottom of the garden. Marlow here, and in spirits too!

MARLOW. Give me joy, George! Crown me, shadow me with laurels! Well, George, after all, we modest fellows don't want for success among the women.

HASTINGS. Some women, you mean. But what success has your honor's modesty been crowned with now, that it grows so insolent upon us?

MARLOW. Didn't you see the tempting, brisk, lovely little thing, that runs about the house with a bunch of keys to its girdle?

HASTINGS. Well, and what then?

MARLOW. She's mine, you rogue, you. Such fire, such motion, such eyes, such lips— but, egad! she would not let me kiss them though.

HASTINGS. But are you sure, so very sure of her?

MARLOW. Why, man, she talked of showing me her work above stairs, and I am to improve the pattern.

HASTINGS. But how can *you*, Charles, go about to rob a woman of her honor?

MARLOW. Pshaw! pshaw! We all know the honor of the bar-maid of an inn. I don't intend to *rob* her, take my word for it; there's nothing in this house I shan't honestly *pay* for.

HASTINGS. I believe the girl has virtue.

MARLOW. And if she has, I should be the last man in the world that would attempt to corrupt it.

HASTINGS. You have taken care, I hope, of the casket I sent you to lock up? It's in safety?

MARLOW. Yes, yes; it's safe enough. I have taken care of it. But how could you think the seat of a post-coach at an inn-door a place of safety? Ah! numskull! I have taken better precautions for you than you did for yourself—I have—

HASTINGS. What?

MARLOW. I have sent it to the landlady to keep for you.

HASTINGS. To the landlady!

MARLOW. The landlady.

HASTINGS. You did?

MARLOW. I did. She's to be answerable for its forthcoming, you know.

HASTINGS. Yes, she'll bring it forth with a witness.

MARLOW. Wasn't I right? I believe you'll allow that I acted prudently upon this occasion.

HASTINGS. (*Aside*) He must not see my uneasiness.

MARLOW. You seem a little disconcerted, though, methinks. Sure nothing has happened?

HASTINGS. No, nothing. Never was in better spirits in all my life. And so you left it with the landlady, who, no doubt, very readily undertook the charge.

MARLOW. Rather too readily; for she not only kept the casket, but, through her great precaution, was going to keep the messenger too. Ha! ha! ha!

HASTINGS. He! he! he! They're safe, however.

MARLOW. As a guinea in a miser's purse.

HASTINGS. (*Aside*) So now all hopes of fortune are at an end, and we must set off without it. (*To him*) Well, Charles, I'll leave you to your meditations on the pretty bar-maid, and he! he! he! may you be as successful for yourself as you have been for me!
(*Exit*)

MARLOW. Thank ye, George; I ask no more.—Ha! ha! ha!

(*Enter* HARDCASTLE)

HARDCASTLE. (*Aside*) I no longer know my own house. It's turned all topsy-turvy. His servants have got drunk already. I'll bear it no longer; and yet, from my respect for his father, I'll be calm. (*To him*) Mr. Marlow, your servant. I'm your very humble servant.
(*Bowing low*)

MARLOW. Sir, your humble servant. (*Aside*) What's to be the wonder now?

HARDCASTLE. I believe, sir, you must be sensible, sir, that no man alive ought to be more welcome than your father's son, sir. I hope you think so?

MARLOW. I do from my soul, sir. I don't want much entreaty. I generally make my father's son welcome wherever he goes.

HARDCASTLE. I believe you do, from my soul, sir. But though I say nothing to your own conduct, that of your servants is insufferable. Their manner of drinking is setting a very bad example in this house, I assure you.

MARLOW. I protest, my very good sir, that is no fault of mine. If they don't drink as they ought, *they* are to blame. I ordered them not to spare the cellar; I did, I assure you. (*Calling*) Here, let one of my servants come up. (*To him*) My positive directions were, that as I did not drink myself, they should make up for my deficiencies below.

HARDCASTLE. Then they had your orders for what they do? I'm satisfied!

MARLOW. They had, I assure you. You shall hear from one of themselves.

(*Enter* SERVANT, *drunk*)

MARLOW. You, Jeremy! Come forward, sirrah! What were my orders? Were you not told to drink freely, and call for what you thought fit, for the good of the house?

HARDCASTLE. (*Aside*) I begin to lose my patience.

JEREMY. Please your honor, liberty and Fleet-street forever! Though I'm but a servant, I'm as good as another man. I'll drink for no man before supper, sir, damme! Good liquor will sit upon a good supper, but a good supper will not sit upon—hiccup—upon my conscience, sir. (*Exit*)

MARLOW. You see, my old friend, the fellow is as drunk as he can possibly be. I don't know what you'd have more, unless you'd have the poor devil soused in a beer barrel.

HARDCASTLE. Zounds! He'll drive me distracted if I contain myself any longer. Mr. Marlow, sir! I have submitted to your insolence for more than four hours, and I see no likelihood of its coming to an end. I'm now resolved to be master here, sir, and I desire that you and your drunken pack may leave my house directly.

MARLOW. Leave your house!—Sure, you jest, my good friend? What? when I am doing what I can to please you!

HARDCASTLE. I tell you, sir, you don't please me; so I desire you'll leave my house.

MARLOW. Sure you cannot be serious? At this time of night, and such a night? You only mean to banter me.

HARDCASTLE. I tell you, sir, I'm serious! and now that my passions are roused, I say this house is mine, sir; this house is mine, and I command you to leave it directly.

MARLOW. Ha! ha! ha! A puddle in a storm. I shan't stir a step, I assure you. (*In a serious tone*) This your house, fellow! It's my house. This is my house. Mine, while I choose to stay. What right have you to bid me leave this house, sir? I never met with such impudence, curse me; never in my whole life before.

HARDCASTLE. Nor I, confound me if ever I did! To come to my house, to call for what he likes, to turn me out of my own chair, to insult the family, to order his servants to get drunk, and then to tell me, "This house is mine, sir!" By all that's impudent, it makes me laugh. Ha! ha! ha! Pray, sir, (*bantering*) as you take the house, what think you of taking the rest of the furniture? There's a pair of silver candlesticks, and there's a fire-screen, and here's a pair of brazen-nosed bellows; perhaps you may take a fancy to them?

MARLOW. (*Angrily*) Bring me your bill, sir; bring me your bill, and let's make no more words about it.

HARDCASTLE. There are a set of prints, too. What think you of *The Rake's Progress* for your own apartment?

MARLOW. Bring me your bill, I say, and I'll leave you and your infernal house directly.

HARDCASTLE. Then there's a mahogany table that you may see your face in.

MARLOW. My bill, I say.

HARDCASTLE. I had forgot the great chair for your own particular slumbers, after a hearty meal.

MARLOW. Zounds! bring me my bill, I say, and let's hear no more on't.

HARDCASTLE. Young man, young man, from your father's letter to me, I was taught to expect a well-bred, modest man as a visitor here, but now I find him no better than a coxcomb and a bully; but he will be down here presently, and shall hear more of it.

(Exit)

MARLOW. How's this! Sure I have not mistaken the house? Everything looks like an inn; the servants cry "coming"; the attendance is awkward; the bar-maid, too, to attend us. But she's here, and will further inform me. Whither so fast, child? A word with you.

(Enter MISS HARDCASTLE*)*

MISS HARDCASTLE. Let it be short, then. I'm in a hurry. *(Aside)* I believe he begins to find out his mistake. But it's too soon quite to undeceive him.

MARLOW. Pray, child, answer me one question. What are you, and what may your business in this house be?

MISS HARDCASTLE. A relation of the family, sir.

MARLOW. What! a poor relation?

MISS HARDCASTLE. Yes, sir, a poor relation, appointed to keep the keys, and to see that the guests want nothing in my power to give them.

MARLOW. That is, you act as the bar-maid of this inn.

MISS HARDCASTLE. Inn! O law—what brought that into your head? One of the best families in the county keep an inn!—Ha! ha! ha! Old Mr. Hardcastle's house an inn!

MARLOW. Mr. Hardcastle's house! Is this house Mr. Hardcastle's house, child?

MISS HARDCASTLE. Ay, sure. Whose else should it be?

MARLOW. So then all's out, and I have been damnably imposed on. Oh, confound my stupid head, I shall be laughed at over the whole town! I shall be stuck up in caricatura in all the print-shops. The *Dullissimo-Macaroni*. To mistake this house of all others for an inn, and my father's old friend for an inn-keeper! What a swaggering puppy must he take me for! What a silly puppy do I find myself! There again, may I be hanged, my dear, but I mistook you for the bar-maid.

MISS HARDCASTLE. Dear me! dear me! I'm sure there's nothing in my *behavior* to put me upon a level with one of that stamp.

MARLOW. Nothing, my dear, nothing. But I was in for a list of blunders, and could not help making you a subscriber. My stupidity saw everything the wrong way. I mistook your assiduity for assurance, and your simplicity for allurement. But it's over—this house I no more show *my* face in.

MISS HARDCASTLE. I hope, sir, I have done nothing to disoblige you. I'm sure I should be sorry to affront any gentleman who has been so polite, and said so many civil things to me. I'm sure I should be sorry *(pretending to cry)* if he left the family upon my account. I'm sure I should be sorry people said anything amiss, since I have no fortune but my character.

MARLOW. *(Aside)* By Heaven! She weeps! This is the first mark of tenderness I ever had from a modest woman, and it touches me. *(To her)* Excuse me, my lovely girl; you are the only part of the family I leave with reluctance. But, to be plain with you, the difference of our birth, fortune, and education, make an honorable connection impossible; and I can never harbor a thought of seducing simplicity that trusted in my honor, or bringing ruin upon one whose only fault was being too lovely.

MISS HARDCASTLE. *(Aside)* Generous man! I now begin to admire him. *(To him)* But I am sure my family is as good as Miss Hardcastle's; and though I'm poor, that's no great misfortune to a contented mind; and, until this moment, I never thought that it was bad to want a fortune.

MARLOW. And why now, my pretty simplicity?

MISS HARDCASTLE. Because it puts me at a distance from one, that, if I had a thousand pound, I would give it all to.

MARLOW. *(Aside)* This simplicity bewitches me so, that if I stay I'm undone. I must make one bold effort and leave her. *(To her)* Your partiality in my favor, my dear, touches me most sensibly; and were I to live for myself alone, I could easily fix my choice. But I owe too much to the opinion of the world, too much to the authority of a father; so that—I can scarcely speak it—it affects me! Farewell.

(Exit)

MISS HARDCASTLE. I never knew half his merit till now. He shall not go if I have power or art to detain him. I'll still preserve the character in which I *stooped to conquer,* but will undeceive my papa, who, perhaps, may laugh him out of his resolution.   (*Exit*)

(*Enter* TONY *and* MISS NEVILLE)

TONY. Ay, you may steal for yourselves the next time. I have done my duty. She has got the jewels again, that's a sure thing; but she believes it was all a mistake of the servants.

MISS NEVILLE. But, my dear cousin, sure you won't forsake us in this distress? If she in the least suspects that I am going off, I shall certainly be locked up, or sent to my aunt Pedigree's, which is ten times worse.

TONY. To be sure, aunts of all kinds are damned bad things. But what can I do? I have got you a pair of horses that will fly like Whistle Jacket; and I'm sure you can't say but I have courted you nicely before her face. Here she comes; we must court a bit or two more, for fear she should suspect us.

(*They retire and seem to fondle*)

(*Enter* MRS. HARDCASTLE)

MRS. HARDCASTLE. Well, I was greatly fluttered, to be sure. But my son tells me it was all a mistake of the servants. I shan't be easy, however, till they are fairly married, and then let her keep her own fortune. But what do I see? Fondling together, as I'm alive. I never saw Tony so sprightly before. Ah! have I caught you, my pretty doves? What, billing, exchanging stolen glances, and broken murmurs? Ah!

TONY. As for murmurs, mother, we grumble a little now and then, to be sure. But there's no love lost between us.

MRS. HARDCASTLE. A mere sprinkling, Tony, upon the flame, only to make it burn brighter.

MISS NEVILLE. Cousin Tony promises to give us more of his company at home. Indeed, he shan't leave us any more. It won't leave us, Cousin Tony, will it?

TONY. Oh, it's a pretty creature! No, I'd sooner leave my horse in a pound than leave you when you smile upon one so. Your laugh makes you so becoming.

MISS NEVILLE. Agreeable cousin! Who can help admiring that natural humor, that pleasant, broad, red, thoughtless (*patting his cheek*),—Ah! it's a bold face!

MRS. HARDCASTLE. Pretty innocence!

TONY. I'm sure I always loved cousin Con's hazel eyes, and her pretty long fingers that she twists this way and that over the haspicholls,[5] like a parcel of bobbins.

MRS. HARDCASTLE. Ah! he would charm the bird from the tree. I was never so happy before. My boy takes after his father, poor Mr. Lumpkin, exactly. The jewels, my dear Con, shall be yours incontinently. You shall have them. Isn't he a sweet boy, my dear? You shall be married to-morrow, and we'll put off the rest of his education, like Dr. Drowsy's sermons, to a fitter opportunity.

(*Enter* DIGGORY)

DIGGORY. Where's the Squire? I have got a letter for your worship.

TONY. Give it to my mamma. She reads all my letters first.

DIGGORY. I had orders to deliver it into your own hands.

TONY. Who does it come from?

DIGGORY. Your worship mun ask that o' the letter itself.   (*Exit* DIGGORY)

TONY. I could wish to know, though.

(*Turning the letter and gazing on it*)

MISS NEVILLE. (*Aside*) Undone! undone! A letter to him from Hastings. I know the hand. If my aunt sees it, we are ruined forever. I'll keep her employed a little if I can. (*To* MRS. HARDCASTLE) But I have not told you, madam, of my cousin's smart answer just now to Mr. Marlow. We so laughed—you must know, madam—this way a little, for he must not hear us.   (*They confer*)

TONY. (*Still gazing*) A damned cramp piece of penmanship as ever I saw in my life. I can read your print-hand very well; but here there are such handles and shanks and dashes that one can scarce tell the head from the tail. *To Anthony Lumpkin, Esquire.* It's very odd, I can read the outside of my letters, where my own name is, well enough. But when I come to open it, it's all—buzz. That's

[5] Harpsichord.

hard, very hard; for the inside of the letter is always the cream of the correspondence.

MRS. HARDCASTLE. Ha! ha! ha! Very well, very well! And so my son was too hard for the philosopher?

MISS NEVILLE. Yes, madam; but you must hear the rest, madam. A little more this way, or he may hear us. You'll hear how he puzzled him again.

MRS. HARDCASTLE. He seems strangely puzzled now himself, methinks.

TONY. (*Still gazing*) A damned up-and-down hand, as if it was disguised in liquor. (*Reading*) Dear Sir,—Ay, that's that. Then there's an *M*, and a *T*, and an *S*, but whether the next be an *izzard* or an *R*, confound me, I cannot tell!

MRS. HARDCASTLE. What's that, my dear; can I give you any assistance?

MISS NEVILLE. Pray, aunt, let me read it. Nobody reads a cramp hand better than I. (*Twitching the letter from her*) Do you know who it is from?

TONY. Can't tell, except from Dick Ginger, the feeder.

MISS NEVILLE. Ay, so it is. (*Pretending to read*) DEAR SQUIRE, Hoping that you're in health, as I am at this present. The gentlemen of the Shake-bag club has cut the gentlemen of the Goose-green quite out of feather. The odds—um—odd battle—um—long fighting—um—here, here, it's all about cocks, and fighting; it's of no consequence; here, put it up, put it up.

(*Thrusting the crumpled letter upon him*)

TONY. But I tell you, miss, it's of all the consequence in the world! I would not lose the rest of it for a guinea. Here, mother, do you make it out? Of no consequence!

(*Giving* MRS. HARDCASTLE *the letter*)

MRS. HARDCASTLE. How's this? (*Reads*): *Dear Squire, I'm now waiting for Miss Neville with a postchaise and pair, at the bottom of the garden, but I find my horses yet unable to perform the journey. I expect you'll assist us with a pair of fresh horses, as you promised. Dispatch is necessary, as the hag*—ay, the hag—*your mother, will otherwise suspect us. Yours, Hastings.* Grant me patience. I shall run distracted! My rage chokes me!

MISS NEVILLE. I hope, madam, you'll suspend your resentment for a few moments and not impute to me any impertinence or sinister design that belongs to another.

MRS. HARDCASTLE. (*Curtseying very low*) Fine spoken, madam; you are most miraculously polite and engaging, and quite the very pink of courtesy and circumspection, madam. (*Changing her tone*) And you, you great ill-fashioned oaf, with scarce sense enough to keep your mouth shut,—were you too joined against me? But I'll defeat all your plots in a moment. As for you, madam, since you have got a pair of fresh horses ready, it would be cruel to disappoint them. So, if you please, instead of running away with your spark, prepare, this very moment, to run off with *me*. Your old Aunt Pedigree will keep you secure, I'll warrant me. You, too, sir, may mount your horse, and guard us upon the way. (*Calling*) Here, Thomas, Roger, Diggory! I'll show you that I wish you better than you do yourselves. (*Exit*)

MISS NEVILLE. So, now I'm completely ruined.

TONY. Ay, that's a sure thing.

MISS NEVILLE. What better could be expected from being connected with such a stupid fool,—and after all the nods and signs I made him!

TONY. By the laws, miss, it was your own cleverness and not my stupidity, that did your business. You were so nice and so busy with your Shake-bags and Goose-greens that I thought you could never be making believe.

(*Enter* HASTINGS)

HASTINGS. So, sir, I find by my servant that you have shown my letter, and betrayed us. Was this well done, young gentleman?

TONY. Here's another. Ask miss, there, who betrayed you. Ecod! it was her doing, not mine.

(*Enter* MARLOW)

MARLOW. So, I have been finely used here among you. Rendered contemptible, driven into ill-manners, despised, insulted, laughed at.

TONY. Here's another. We shall have old Bedlam broke loose presently.

MISS NEVILLE. And there, sir, is the gentleman to whom we all owe every obligation.

MARLOW. What can I say to him? A mere boy, an idiot, whose ignorance and age are a protection.

HASTINGS. A poor, contemptible booby, that would but disgrace correction.

MISS NEVILLE. Yet with cunning and malice enough to make himself merry with all our embarrassments.

HASTINGS. An insensible cub.

MARLOW. Replete with tricks and mischief.

TONY. Baw! damme, but I'll fight you both, one after the other,—with baskets.[6]

MARLOW. As for him, he's below resentment. But your conduct, Mr. Hastings, requires an explanation. You knew of my mistakes, yet would not undeceive me.

HASTINGS. Tortured as I am with my own disappointments, is this a time for explanations? It is not friendly, Mr. Marlow.

MARLOW. But, sir—

MISS NEVILLE. Mr. Marlow, we never kept on your mistake, till it was too late to undeceive you. Be pacified.

(Enter SERVANT)

SERVANT. My mistress desires you'll get ready immediately, madam. The horses are putting to. Your hat and things are in the next room. We are to go thirty miles before morning.   *(Exit SERVANT)*

MISS NEVILLE. Well, well, I'll come presently.

MARLOW. *(To HASTINGS)* Was it well done, sir, to assist in rendering me ridiculous? To hang me out for the scorn of all my acquaintance? Depend upon it, sir, I shall expect an explanation.

HASTINGS. Was it well done, sir, if you're upon that subject, to deliver what I entrusted to yourself to the care of another, sir?

MISS NEVILLE. Mr. Hastings! Mr. Marlow! Why will you increase my distress by this groundless dispute? I implore, I entreat you—

(Enter SERVANT)

[6] Basket-hilt swords.

SERVANT. Your cloak, madam. My mistress is impatient.

MISS NEVILLE. I come. *(Exit SERVANT)* Pray, be pacified. If I leave you thus, I shall die with apprehension!

(Enter SERVANT)

SERVANT. Your fan, muff, and gloves, madam. The horses are waiting.
                                  (Exit SERVANT)

MISS NEVILLE. Oh, Mr. Marlow! if you knew what a scene of constraint and ill-nature lies before me, I am sure it would convert your resentment into pity.

MARLOW. I'm so distracted with a variety of passions that I don't know what I do. Forgive me, madam. George, forgive me. You know my hasty temper, and should not exasperate it.

HASTINGS. The torture of my situation is my only excuse.

MISS NEVILLE. Well, my dear Hastings, if you have that esteem for me that I think, that I am sure you have, your constancy for three years will but increase the happiness of our future connection. If—

MRS. HARDCASTLE. *(Within)* Miss Neville! Constance! why, Constance, I say!

MISS NEVILLE. I'm coming! Well, constancy. Remember, constancy is the word.
                                          (Exit)

HASTINGS. My heart! How can I support this! To be so near happiness, and such happiness!

MARLOW. *(To TONY)* You see now, young gentleman, the effects of your folly. What might be amusement to you is here disappointment, and even distress.

TONY. *(From a reverie)* Ecod, I have hit it. It's here! Your hands. Yours, and yours, my poor Sulky.—*(Calling)* My boots there, ho!—Meet me, two hours hence, at the bottom of the garden; and if you don't find Tony Lumpkin a more good-natured fellow than you thought for, I'll give you leave to take my best horse, and Bet Bouncer into the bargain! Come along. My boots, ho!   *(Exeunt)*

Act V

Scene I. *The Same Room.*

(*Enter* Hastings *and* Servant)

Hastings. You saw the old lady and Miss Neville drive off, you say?

Servant. Yes, your honor. They went off in a postcoach, and the young Squire went on horseback. They're thirty miles off by this time.

Hastings. Then all my hopes are over.

Servant. Yes, sir. Old Sir Charles is arrived. He and the old gentleman of the house have been laughing at Mr. Marlow's mistake this half hour. They are coming this way.

(*Exit*)

Hastings. Then I must not be seen. So now to my fruitless appointment at the bottom of the garden. This is about the time.

(*Exit*)

(*Enter* Sir Charles Marlow *and* Hardcastle)

Hardcastle. Ha! ha! ha! The peremptory tone in which he sent forth his sublime commands!

Sir Charles. And the reserve with which I suppose he treated all your advances.

Hardcastle. And yet he might have seen something in me above a common innkeeper, too.

Sir Charles. Yes, Dick, but he mistook you for an uncommon innkeeper; ha! ha! ha!

Hardcastle. Well, I'm in too good spirits to think of anything but joy. Yes, my dear friend, this union of our families will make our personal friendships hereditary; and though my daughter's fortune is but small—

Sir Charles. Why, Dick, will you talk of fortune to *me?* My son is possessed of more than a competence already, and can want nothing but a good and virtuous girl to share his happiness and increase it. If they like each other, as you say they do—

Hardcastle. *If,* man! I tell you they *do* like each other. My daughter as good as told me so.

Sir Charles. But girls are apt to flatter themselves, you know.

Hardcastle. I saw him grasp her hand in the warmest manner, myself; and here he comes to put you out of your *ifs,* I warrant him.

(*Enter* Marlow)

Marlow. I come, sir, once more, to ask pardon for my strange conduct. I can scarce reflect on my insolence without confusion.

Hardcastle. Tut, boy, a trifle. You take it too gravely. An hour or two's laughing with my daughter will set all to rights again. She'll never like you the worse for it.

Marlow. Sir, I shall be always proud of her approbation.

Hardcastle. Approbation is but a cold word, Mr. Marlow; if I am not deceived, you have something more than approbation thereabouts. You take me?

Marlow. Really, sir, I have not that happiness.

Hardcastle. Come, boy, I'm an old fellow, and know what's what as well as you that are younger. I know what has passed between you; but mum.

Marlow. Sure, sir, nothing has passed between us but the most profound respect on my side, and the most distant reserve on hers. You don't think, sir, that my impudence has been passed upon all the rest of the family?

Hardcastle. Impudence! No, I don't say that—not quite impudence—though girls like to be played with, and rumpled a little, too, sometimes. But she has told no tales, I assure you.

Marlow. I never gave her the slightest cause.

Hardcastle. Well, well, I like modesty in its place well enough; but this is overacting, young gentleman. You *may* be open. Your father and I will like you the better for it.

Marlow. May I die, sir, if I ever—

Hardcastle. I tell you she don't dislike you; and as I am sure you like her—

Marlow. Dear sir,—I protest, sir—

HARDCASTLE. I see no reason why you should not be joined as fast as the parson can tie you.

MARLOW. But hear me, sir—

HARDCASTLE. Your father approves the match; I admire it; every moment's delay will be doing mischief; so—

MARLOW. But why won't you hear me? By all that's just and true, I never gave Miss Hardcastle the slightest mark of my attachment, or even the most distant hint to suspect me of affection. We had but one interview, and that was formal, modest, and uninteresting.

HARDCASTLE. (*Aside*) This fellow's formal, modest impudence is beyond bearing.

SIR CHARLES. And you never grasped her hand, or made any protestations?

MARLOW. As heaven is my witness, I came down in obedience to your commands. I saw the lady without emotion, and parted without reluctance. I hope you'll exact no further proofs of my duty, nor prevent me from leaving a house in which I suffer so many mortifications. (*Exit*)

SIR CHARLES. I'm astonished at the air of sincerity with which he parted.

HARDCASTLE. And I'm astonished at the deliberate intrepidity of his assurance.

SIR CHARLES. I dare pledge my life and honor upon his truth.

HARDCASTLE. Here comes my daughter, and I would stake my happiness upon her veracity.

(*Enter* MISS HARDCASTLE)

HARDCASTLE. Kate, come hither, child. Answer us sincerely, and without reserve; has Mr. Marlow made you any professions of love and affection?

MISS HARDCASTLE. The question is very abrupt, sir. But since you require unreserved sincerity, I think he has.

HARDCASTLE. (*To* SIR CHARLES) You see.

SIR CHARLES. And pray, madam, have you and my son had more than one interview?

MISS HARDCASTLE. Yes, sir, several.

HARDCASTLE. (*To* SIR CHARLES) You see.

SIR CHARLES. But did he profess any attachment?

MISS HARDCASTLE. A lasting one.

SIR CHARLES. Did he talk of love?

MISS HARDCASTLE. Much, sir.

SIR CHARLES. Amazing! And all this formally?

MISS HARDCASTLE. Formally.

HARDCASTLE. Now, my friend, I hope you are satisfied.

SIR CHARLES. And how did he behave, madam?

MISS HARDCASTLE. As most professed admirers do; said some civil things of my face; talked much of his want of merit, and the greatness of mine; mentioned his heart, gave a short tragedy speech, and ended with pretended rapture.

SIR CHARLES. Now I'm perfectly convinced, indeed. I know his conversation among women to be modest and submissive. This forward, canting, ranting manner by no means describes him, and, I am confident, he never sate for the picture.

MISS HARDCASTLE. Then what, sir, if I should convince you to your face of my sincerity? If you and my papa, in about half an hour, will place yourselves behind that screen, you shall hear him declare his passion to me in person.

SIR CHARLES. Agreed. And if I find him what you describe, all my happiness in him must have an end. (*Exit*)

MISS HARDCASTLE. And if you don't find him what I describe—I fear my happiness must never have a beginning. (*Exeunt*)

SCENE II. *The Back of the Garden.*

(*Enter* HASTINGS)

HASTINGS. What an idiot am I to wait here for a fellow who probably takes a delight in mortifying me. He never intended to be punctual, and I'll wait no longer. What do I see? It is he, and perhaps with news of my Constance.

(*Enter* TONY, *booted and spattered*)

HASTINGS. My honest Squire! I now find you a man of your word. This looks like friendship.

TONY. Ay, I'm your friend, and the best friend you have in the world, if you knew but all. This riding by night, by the bye, is cursedly tiresome. It has shook me worse than the basket of a stage-coach.

HASTINGS. But how? Where did you leave your fellow-travellers? Are they in safety? Are they housed?

TONY. Five and twenty miles in two hours and a half is no such bad driving. The poor beasts have smoked for it; rabbit me, but I'd rather ride forty miles after a fox, than ten with such *varment.*

HASTINGS. Well, but where have you left the ladies? I die with impatience.

TONY. Left them! Why, where should I leave them but where I found them?

HASTINGS. This is a riddle.

TONY. Riddle me this, then. What's that goes round the house, and round the house, and never touches the house?

HASTINGS. I'm still astray.

TONY. Why, that's it, man. I have led them astray. By jingo, there's not a pond nor slough within five miles of the place but they can tell the taste of.

HASTINGS. Ha! ha! ha! I understand; you took them in a round, while they supposed themselves going forward. And so you have at last brought them home again.

TONY. You shall hear. I first took them down Feather-bed lane, where we stuck fast in the mud. I then rattled them crack over the stones of Up-and-down Hill. I then introduced them to the gibbet on Heavy-tree Heath; and from that, with a circumbendibus, I fairly lodged them in the horse-pond at the bottom of the garden.

HASTINGS. But no accident, I hope?

TONY. No, no; only mother is confoundedly frightened. She thinks herself forty miles off. She's sick of the journey; and the cattle can scarce crawl. So, if your own horses be ready, you may whip off with Cousin, and I'll be bound that no soul here can budge a foot to follow you.

HASTINGS. My dear friend, how can I be grateful?

TONY. Ay, now it's "dear friend," "noble Squire." Just now, it was all "idiot," "cub,"

and "run me through the guts." Damn *your* way of fighting, I say. After we take a knock in this part of the country, we kiss and be friends. But if you had run me through the guts, then I should be dead, and you might go kiss the hangman.

HASTINGS. The rebuke is just. But I must hasten to relieve Miss Neville; if you keep the old lady employed, I promise to take care of the young one.

TONY. Never fear me. Here she comes. Vanish! (*Exit* HASTINGS) She's got from the pond, and draggled up to the waist like a mermaid.

(*Enter* MRS. HARDCASTLE)

MRS. HARDCASTLE. Oh, Tony, I'm killed! Shook! Battered to death! I shall never survive it. That last jolt, that laid us against the quickset hedge, has done my business.

TONY. Alack, mamma, it was all your own fault. You would be for running away by night, without knowing one inch of the way.

MRS. HARDCASTLE. I wish we were at home again. I never met so many accidents in so short a journey. Drenched in the mud, overturned in a ditch, stuck fast in a slough, jolted to a jelly, and at last to lose our way! Whereabouts do you think we are, Tony?

TONY. By my guess, we should be upon Crack-skull Common, about forty miles from home.

MRS. HARDCASTLE. O lud! O lud! The most notorious spot in all the country. We only want a robbery to make a complete night on't.

TONY. Don't be afraid, mamma; don't be afraid. Two of the five that kept here are hanged, and the other three may not find us. Don't be afraid. Is that a man that's galloping behind us? No, it's only a tree. Don't be afraid.

MRS. HARDCASTLE. The fright will certainly kill me.

TONY. Do you see anything like a black hat moving behind the thicket?

MRS. HARDCASTLE. Oh, death!

TONY. No, it's only a cow. Don't be afraid, mamma, don't be afraid.

MRS. HARDCASTLE. As I'm alive, Tony, I see a man coming towards us. Ah, I am sure on't! If he perceives us, we are undone.

Tony. (*Aside*) Father-in-law, by all that's unlucky, come to take one of his night walks. (*To her*) Ah, it's a highwayman, with pistols as long as my arm. A damned ill-looking fellow!

Mrs. Hardcastle. Good Heaven defend us! He approaches.

Tony. Do you hide yourself in that thicket, and leave me to manage him. If there be any danger, I'll cough and cry hem. When I cough, be sure to keep close.

(Mrs. Hardcastle *hides behind a tree in the back scene*)

(*Enter* Hardcastle)

Hardcastle. I'm mistaken, or I heard voices of people in want of help. Oh, Tony, is that you? I did not expect you so soon back. Are your mother and her charge in safety?

Tony. Very safe, sir, at my Aunt Pedigree's. Hem.

Mrs. Hardcastle. (*From behind*) Ah, death! I find there's danger.

Hardcastle. Forty miles in three hours; sure that's too much, my youngster.

Tony. Stout horses and willing minds make short journeys, as they say. Hem.

Mrs. Hardcastle. (*From behind*) Sure, he'll do the dear boy no harm.

Hardcastle. But I heard a voice here; I should be glad to know from whence it came.

Tony. It was I, sir, talking to myself, sir. I was saying that forty miles in four hours was very good going. Hem. As to be sure it was. Hem. I have got a sort of cold by being out in the air. We'll go in, if you please. Hem.

Hardcastle. But if you talked to yourself, you did not answer yourself. I'm certain I heard two voices, and resolved (*raising his voice*) to find the other out.

Mrs. Hardcastle. (*From behind*) Oh! he's coming to find me out. Oh!

Tony. What need you go, sir, if I tell you? Hem. I'll lay down my life for the truth—hem—I'll tell you all, sir. (*Detaining him*)

Hardcastle. I tell you I will not be detained. I insist on seeing. It's in vain to expect I'll believe you.

Mrs. Hardcastle. (*Running forward from behind*) O lud! He'll murder my poor boy, my darling! Here, good gentleman, whet your rage upon me. Take my money, my life, but spare that young gentleman; spare my child, if you have any mercy.

Hardcastle. My wife, as I'm a Christian! From whence can she come, or what does she mean?

Mrs. Hardcastle. (*Kneeling*) Take compassion on us, good Mr. Highwayman. Take our money, our watches, all we have, but spare our lives. We will never bring you to justice; indeed we won't, good Mr. Highwayman.

Hardcastle. I believe the woman's out of her senses. What, Dorothy, don't you know *me*?

Mrs. Hardcastle. Mr. Hardcastle, as I'm alive! My fears blinded me. But who, my dear, could have expected to meet you here, in this frightful place, so far from home? What has brought you to follow us?

Hardcastle. Sure, Dorothy, you have not lost your wits? So far from home, when you are within forty yards of your own door! (*To him*) This is one of your old tricks, you graceless rogue, you! (*To her*) Don't you know the gate, and the mulberry tree; and don't you remember the horse-pond, my dear?

Mrs. Hardcastle. Yes, I shall remember the horse-pond as long as I live; I have caught my death in it. (*To* Tony) And is it to you, you graceless varlet, I owe all this? I'll teach you to abuse your mother, I will.

Tony. Ecod, mother, all the parish says you have spoiled me, so you may take the fruits on't.

Mrs. Hardcastle. I'll spoil you, I will.
(*Follows him off the stage*)

Hardcastle. There's morality, however, in his reply. (*Exit*)

(*Enter* Hastings *and* Miss Neville)

Hastings. My dear Constance, why will you deliberate thus? If we delay a moment, all is lost forever. Pluck up a little resolution, and we shall soon be out of the reach of her malignity.

Miss Neville. I find it impossible. My spirits are so sunk with the agitations I have suffered, that I am unable to face any new danger. Two or three years' patience will at last crown us with happiness.

HASTINGS. Such a tedious delay is worse than inconstancy. Let us fly, my charmer! Let us date our happiness from this very moment. Perish fortune. Love and content will increase what we possess beyond a monarch's revenue. Let me prevail!

MISS NEVILLE. No, Mr. Hastings, no. Prudence once more comes to my relief, and I will obey its dictates. In the moment of passion, fortune may be despised, but it ever produces a lasting repentance. I'm resolved to apply to Mr. Hardcastle's compassion and justice for redress.

HASTINGS. But though he had the will he has not the power to relieve you.

MISS NEVILLE. But he has influence, and upon that I am resolved to rely.

HASTINGS. I have no hopes. But, since you persist, I must reluctantly obey you.

(*Exeunt*)

SCENE III. *The House.*

(*Enter* SIR CHARLES *and* MISS HARD-CASTLE)

SIR CHARLES. What a situation am I in! If what you say appears, I shall then find a guilty son. If what he says be true, I shall then lose one that, of all others, I most wished for—a daughter.

MISS HARDCASTLE. I am proud of your approbation; and to show I merit it, if you place yourselves as I directed, you shall hear his explicit declaration. But he comes.

SIR CHARLES. I'll to your father, and keep him to the appointment.

(*Exit* SIR CHARLES)

(*Enter* MARLOW)

MARLOW. Though prepared for setting out, I come once more to take leave; nor did I, till this moment, know the pain I feel in the separation.

MISS HARDCASTLE. (*In her own natural manner*) I believe these sufferings cannot be very great, sir, which you can so easily remove. A day or two longer, perhaps, might lessen your uneasiness, by showing the little value of what you now think proper to regret.

MARLOW. (*Aside*) This girl every moment improves upon me. (*To her*) It must not be, madam; I have already trifled too long with my heart. My very pride begins to submit to my passion. The disparity of education and fortune, the anger of a parent, and the contempt of my equals begin to lose their weight; and nothing can restore me to myself but this painful effort of resolution.

MISS HARDCASTLE. Then go, sir; I'll urge nothing more to detain you. Though my family be as good as hers you came down to visit, and my education, I hope, not inferior, what are these advantages without equal affluence? I must remain contented with the slight approbation of imputed merit; I must have only the mockery of your addresses, while all your serious aims are fixed on fortune.

(*Enter* HARDCASTLE *and* SIR CHARLES *from behind*)

SIR CHARLES. Here, behind this screen.

HARDCASTLE. Ay, ay; make no noise. I'll engage my Kate covers him with confusion at last.

MARLOW. By heavens, madam, fortune was ever my smallest consideration. Your beauty at first caught my eye; for who could see that without emotion? But every moment that I converse with you, steals in some new grace, heightens the picture, and gives it stronger expression. What at first seemed rustic plainness, now appears refined simplicity. What seemed forward assurance, now strikes me as the result of courageous innocence and conscious virtue.

SIR CHARLES. What can it mean? He amazes me!

HARDCASTLE. I told you how it would be. Hush!

MARLOW. I am now determined to stay, madam, and I have too good an opinion of my father's discernment, when he sees you, to doubt his approbation.

MISS HARDCASTLE. No, Mr. Marlow, I

will not, cannot detain you. Do you think
I could suffer a connection in which there
is the smallest room for repentance? Do you
think I would take the mean advantage of
a transient passion to load you with confusion? Do you think I could ever relish that
happiness which was acquired by lessening
yours?

MARLOW. By all that's good, I can have
no happiness but what's in your power to
grant me! Nor shall I ever feel repentance
but in not having seen your merits before.
I will stay, even contrary to your wishes; and
though you should persist to shun me, I
will make my respectful assiduities atone for
the levity of my past conduct.

MISS HARDCASTLE. Sir, I must entreat
you'll desist. As our acquaintance began, so
let it end, in indifference. I might have given
an hour or two to levity; but seriously, Mr.
Marlow, do you think I could ever submit
to a connection where I must appear mercenary, and you imprudent? Do you think
I could ever catch at the confident addresses
of a secure admirer?

MARLOW. (*Kneeling*) Does this look like
security? Does this look like confidence? No,
madam, every moment that shows me your
merit, only serves to increase my diffidence
and confusion. Here let me continue—

SIR CHARLES. I can hold it no longer.
Charles, Charles, how hast thou deceived
me! Is this your indifference, your uninteresting conversation?

HARDCASTLE. Your cold contempt! Your
formal interview! What have you to say
now?

MARLOW. That I'm all amazement! What
can it mean?

HARDCASTLE. It means that you can say
and unsay things at pleasure; that you can
address a lady in private, and deny it in
public; that you have one story for us, and
another for my daughter.

MARLOW. Daughter!—this lady your
daughter?

HARDCASTLE. Yes, sir, my only daughter
—my Kate; whose else should she be?

MARLOW. Oh, the devil!

MISS HARDCASTLE. Yes, sir, that very
identical tall, squinting lady you were
pleased to take me for (*curtseying*); she that
you addressed as the mild, modest, senti-

mental man of gravity, and the bold, forward, agreeable Rattle of the Ladies' Club.
Ha! ha! ha!

MARLOW. Zounds, there's no bearing this;
it's worse than death!

MISS HARDCASTLE. In which of your
characters, sir, will you give us leave to address you? As the faltering gentleman, with
looks on the ground, that speaks just to be
heard, and hates hypocrisy; or the loud, confident creature, that keeps it up with Mrs.
Mantrap, and old Miss Biddy Buckskin, till
three in the morning? Ha! ha! ha!

MARLOW. Oh, curse on my noisy head!
I never attempted to be impudent yet that
I was not taken down. I must be gone.

HARDCASTLE. By the hand of my body,
but you shall not. I see it was all a mistake,
and I am rejoiced to find it. You shall not,
sir, I tell you. I know she'll forgive you.
Won't you forgive him, Kate? We'll all forgive you. Take courage, man.

(*They retire, she tormenting him, to
the back scene*)

(*Enter* MRS. HARDCASTLE *and* TONY)

MRS. HARDCASTLE. So, so, they're gone
off. Let them go, I care not.

HARDCASTLE. Who gone?

MRS. HARDCASTLE. My dutiful niece and
her gentleman, Mr. Hastings, from town.
He who came down with our modest visitor
here.

SIR CHARLES. Who, my honest George
Hastings! As worthy a fellow as lives, and
the girl could not have made a more prudent
choice.

HARDCASTLE. Then, by the hand of my
body, I'm proud of the connection.

MRS. HARDCASTLE. Well, if he has taken
away the lady, he has not taken her fortune;
that remains in this family to console us for
her loss.

HARDCASTLE. Sure, Dorothy, you would
not be so mercenary?

MRS. HARDCASTLE. Ay, that's my affair,
not yours.

HARDCASTLE. But you know if your son,
when of age, refuses to marry his cousin,
her whole fortune is then at her own disposal.

MRS. HARDCASTLE. Ay, but he's not of

age, and she has not thought proper to wait for his refusal.

(*Enter* HASTINGS *and* MISS NEVILLE)

MRS. HARDCASTLE. (*Aside*) What, returned so soon? I begin not to like it.

HASTINGS. (*To* HARDCASTLE) For my late attempt to fly off with your niece, let my present confusion be my punishment. We are now come back, to appeal from your justice to your humanity. By her father's consent I first paid her my addresses, and our passions were first founded in duty.

MISS NEVILLE. Since his death, I have been obliged to stoop to dissimulation to avoid oppression. In an hour of levity, I was ready even to give up my fortune to secure my choice. But I am now recovered from the delusion, and hope from your tenderness what is denied me from a nearer connection.

MRS. HARDCASTLE. Pshaw! pshaw; this is all but the whining end of a modern novel.

HARDCASTLE. Be it what it will, I'm glad they're come back to reclaim their due. Come hither, Tony, boy. Do you refuse this lady's hand, whom I now offer you?

TONY. What signifies my refusing? You know I can't refuse her till I'm of age, father.

HARDCASTLE. While I thought concealing your age, boy, was likely to conduce to your improvement, I concurred with your mother's desire to keep it secret. But since I find she turns it to a wrong use, I must now declare you have been of age this three months.

TONY. Of age! Am I of age, father?

HARDCASTLE. Above three months.

TONY. Then you'll see the first use I'll make of my liberty. (*Taking* MISS NEVILLE's *hand*) Witness all men, by these presents, that I, Anthony Lumpkin, Esquire, of BLANK place, refuse you, Constantia Neville, spinster, of no place at all, for my true and lawful wife. So Constance Neville may marry whom she pleases, and Tony Lumpkin is his own man again!

SIR CHARLES. Oh, brave Squire!

HASTINGS. My worthy friend!

MRS. HARDCASTLE. My undutiful offspring.

MARLOW. Joy, my dear George, I give you joy sincerely! And could I prevail upon my little tyrant here to be less arbitrary, I should be the happiest man alive, if you would return me the favor.

HASTINGS. (*To* MISS HARDCASTLE) Come, madam, you are now driven to the very last scene of all your contrivances. I know you like him, I'm sure he loves you, and you must and shall have him.

HARDCASTLE. (*Joining their hands*) And I say so, too. And, Mr. Marlow, if she makes as good a wife as she has a daughter, I don't believe you'll ever repent your bargain. So now to supper. To-morrow we shall gather all the poor of the parish about us, and the Mistakes of the Night shall be crowned with a merry morning. So, boy, take her; and as you have been mistaken in the mistress, my wish is, that you may never be mistaken in the wife.

(*Exeunt Omnes*)

Epilogue

By DR. GOLDSMITH

Spoken by MRS. BULKLEY in the Character of MISS HARDCASTLE

WELL, having stooped to conquer with success,
And gained a husband without aid from dress,
Still, as a bar-maid, I could wish it too,
As I have conquered him to conquer you:
And let me say, for all your resolution,

That pretty bar-maids have done execution.
Our life is all a play, composed to please;
"We have our exits and our entrances."
The first act shows the simple country maid,
Harmless and young, of everything afraid;
Blushes when hired, and with unmeaning action,

"I hopes as how to give you satisfaction."
Her second act displays a livelier scene,—
Th' unblushing bar-maid of a country inn,
Who whisks about the house, at market
    caters,
Talks loud, coquets the guests, and scolds
    the waiters.
Next the scene shifts to town, and there she
    soars,
The chop-house toast of ogling connoisseurs.
On Squires and Cits she there displays her
    arts,
And on the gridiron broils her lovers' hearts;
And, as she smiles, her triumphs to com-
    plete,
E'en common-councilmen forget to eat.

The fourth act shows her wedded to the
    Squire,
And Madam now begins to hold it higher;
Pretends to taste, at Operas cries *caro!*
And quits her *Nancy Dawson* for *Che Faro:*
Doats upon dancing, and in all her pride,
Swims round the room, the Heinel of Cheap-
    side;
Ogles and leers, with artificial skill,
Till, having lost in age the power to kill,
She sits all night at cards, and ogles at
    spadille.
Such, through our lives, th' eventful history!
The fifth and last act still remains for me:
The bar-maid now for your protection prays,
Turns female barrister, and pleads for Bayes.

Epilogue

To be Spoken in the Character of TONY LUMPKIN

WELL, now all's ended, and my comrades
    gone,
Pray what becomes of *mother's nonly son?*
A hopeful blade!—in town I'll fix my sta-
    tion,
And try to make a bluster in the nation.
As for my cousin Neville, I renounce her,
Off, in a crack, I'll carry big Bet Bouncer.
  Why should not I in the great world
    appear?
I soon shall have a thousand pounds a year;
No matter what a man may here inherit,
In London—gad, they've some regard to
    spirit.
I see the horses prancing up the streets,

And big Bet Bouncer bobs to all she meets;
Then hoiks to jigs and pastimes every
    night—
Not to the plays—they say it a'n't polite:
To Sadler's Wells, perhaps, or operas go,
And once, by chance, to the roratorio.
Thus, here and there, forever up and down,
We'll set the fashions, too, to half the town;
And then at auctions—money ne'er regard—
Buy pictures, like the great, ten pounds a
    yard:
Zounds! we shall make these London gentry
    say,
We know what's damned genteel as well as
    they!

RICHARD BRINSLEY SHERIDAN

The School for Scandal

PRINCIPAL EVENTS IN SHERIDAN'S LIFE

1751, 30 Oct., Born in Dublin, son of an actor and theatre-manager.

1758, Left Ireland with his parents.

1762, Entered Harrow School.

1770, Assisted his father in an Academy of Oratory at Bath.

1772, March, Eloped with Elizabeth Linley, a young singer, to get her away from the unwelcome attentions of a Major Mathews.

1772, May & July, Fought two duels with Major Mathews, in one of which he was wounded.

1775, 17 Jan., Sheridan's play, *The Rivals,* was produced at Covent Garden theatre.

1775, 21 Nov., His comic opera, *The Duenna,* was acted with sensational success at Covent Garden theatre. The music was written by Sheridan's wife and father-in-law.

1775, 2 May, St. Patrick's Day, or the Scheming Lieutenant, a short farce, was acted at Covent Garden. Sheridan wrote it for Lawrence Clinch, who had made a great success of the role of Sir Lucius O'Trigger in *The Rivals.*

1776, June, Sheridan and two friends bought David Garrick's share in the Drury Lane theatre. Sheridan became manager of the company.

1776, Nov., Dec., Sheridan put on his own revisions of Congreve's *The Old Bachelor,* *Love for Love,* and *The Way of the World* at Drury Lane.

1777, 5 May, The School for Scandal produced at Drury Lane with great success.

1778, Sept., Sheridan's father took over the management of Drury Lane from him.

1778, 15 Nov., His musical entertainment, *The Camp,* produced at Drury Lane.

1779, 30 Oct., Sheridan's burlesque, *The Critic,* produced at Drury Lane.

1780, Entered Parliament as a member for Stafford.

1782, He was made an under-secretary for foreign affairs in the ministry of Lord Rockingham.

1787, 7 Feb., His speech against Warren Hastings was said to be one of the greatest ever delivered in the House of Commons.

1799, 24 May, Sheridan's tragedy, *Pizzaro,* adapted from Kotzebue, was performed with great success at Drury Lane.

1806, Sheridan became Treasurer of the Navy in Pitt's new ministry.

1809, 24 Feb., Drury Lane theatre burned to the ground, a great financial loss to Sheridan.

1812, His defeat in the election at Stafford ended his Parliamentary career.

1816, 7 July, Sheridan died; he was buried in the Poets' Corner in Westminster Abbey.

INTRODUCTION

Sheridan, like his contemporary Oliver Goldsmith, deplored the sentimental comedy which dominated the London theatres of his time. He refused to believe that the function of comedy was to preach sermons on the obvious and to dissolve the audience in sympathetic tears, though the audiences of his time had shown again and again that this was exactly what they did like. The plays Sheridan admired were the comedies of the Restoration and especially those of William Congreve. When he became manager of the great Drury Lane theatre, less than a year before *The School for Scandal* was produced, one of his first acts was to prepare versions of Congreve's *The Old Bachelor, Love for Love,* and *The Way of the World* for immediate performance. These plays, even though expurgated, were thought "exceedingly gross and unrefined" and were not very successful. Clearly the wit, satire, and amorality of Restoration comedies had to be diluted for this eighteenth-century London audience, and Sheridan's greatest success, *The School for Scandal,* is the most splendid example of the compromise.

Like Restoration comedies, *The School for Scandal* portrays characters drawn from the best London society and satirizes certain high society types; its scenes are set in London drawing rooms; it deals with the trials of a man who has married a wife too young for him; its plot consists in part of love intrigues; and it depends for much of its appeal on witty dialogue. Nevertheless, *The School for Scandal* is not written to the Restoration formula. The bickerings of Sir Peter and Lady Teazle do not end as in Restoration comedies, the plot interest is much greater, and the satire of Joseph Surface's moralizing would have been wholly lost on a Restoration audience, which would have assumed from the beginning that any man who spouted morality as he did was necessarily a hypocrite. Indeed, certain aspects of the comedy, though much more palatable to modern taste, are not very far from the sentimentality of the usual eighteenth-century comedy, like *The West Indian.* The apportioning of rewards and punishments in the fifth act is in the style of Cumberland, especially the triumph of Charles Surface, who has, in fact, earned his great reward by a fine display of tender regard toward his uncle's portrait. These characteristics fall far short of the sentimentality and cheap moralizing of Steele's *Conscious Lovers* or Kelly's *False Delicacy,* but they do indicate that the play was by no means a revival of pure Restoration comedy of manners. *The School for Scandal* is, in fact, a compromise between Sheridan's Restoration comedy ideal and the sure-fire appeal of eighteenth-century sentimentalism.

For more than a century and a half, *The School for Scandal* has been a favorite on the English and American stage. Its amusing and not very bitter satire of scandal-mongering, its witty dialogue, its sharp if somewhat superficial character portrayal, its clever construction culminating in the brilliant screen scene, and its wealth of effective acting roles have made it a perennial success. After the original performance, a London newspaper writer observed of it and of the birth of Sheridan's son: "Yesterday morning Mrs. Sheridan was delivered of a son. The mother and child are likely to do well. In the evening of the same day, Mr. Sheridan's muse was delivered of a bantling which is likely to live forever." More than a century after the first performance, the leading English actor of his time said, "Sheridan brought the comedy of manners to its highest perfection in *The School for Scandal.* It remains to this day the most popular comedy in the English language."

THE SCHOOL FOR SCANDAL

Dramatis personae

In order of first appearance

LADY SNEERWELL, A well-to-do widow, unscrupulous and malicious, who moves in the best social circles. The scandalmongers of the play frequently gather in her fashionable town house.

MR. SNAKE, Her friend and confidant, secretly her social agent. He is a fawning and obsequious young man.

SERVANT, A liveried footman in Lady Sneerwell's town house, who announces her callers.

JOSEPH SURFACE, A serious and discreet young man, much admired in London high society because of his piously reiterated moral sentiments. He is a protégé of Sir Peter Teazle, who favors his suit to Maria. Elder brother of Charles Surface.

MARIA, An attractive young lady, rather shy and self-effacing. She is the ward of Sir Peter Teazle and lives in his household; in love with Charles Surface, but courted by Joseph Surface, Sir Peter's favorite.

MRS. CANDOUR, A member of Lady Sneerwell's scandal-mongering circle. She is famed for her ability to spread scandal while insisting that she thinks only the best of everyone.

MR. CRABTREE, A silly old gentleman, one of the most active of the scandal circle.

SIR BENJAMIN BACKBITE, Crabtree's nephew, an affected young rattlebrain. He is the constant companion of Mr. Crabtree, who dotes on him.

SIR PETER TEAZLE, A substantial, serious-minded gentleman of property, guardian of Maria, and formerly "a kind of guardian" to Joseph and Charles Surface. He deplores the extravagance, frivolity, and heartlessness of London society, to which his recently-married young wife is devoted.

MR. ROWLEY, Formerly steward to the father of Joseph and Charles Surface, now retired. He is devoted to the family.

LADY TEAZLE, The frivolous young wife of Sir Peter. She is pretty and quick-witted and still rather dazzled by London society, to the distress of her sedate husband.

SIR OLIVER SURFACE, A wealthy merchant, uncle of Joseph and Charles, just returned to England after an absence of fifteen years in India.

MOSES, A Jewish moneylender, accustomed to lending money to reckless young-men-about-town at exorbitant rates.

TRIP, Charles Surface's elegant liveried servant who apes the ways of society gentlemen.

CHARLES SURFACE, A wildly extravagant and dissipated, but honest and charming young man, the younger brother of Joseph Surface. He is disapproved of in high society because of his frank contempt for social hypocrisy. Formerly he was protected and befriended by Sir Peter, whom he has alienated by his extravagance. He is in love with Maria.

SIR HARRY BUMPER, A wild young man, friend and drinking companion of Charles Surface.

MR. CARELESS, Another friend and drinking companion.

FIRST GENTLEMAN } Other drinking companions.
SECOND GENTLEMAN }

WILLIAM, Servant to Joseph Surface.

MAID to Lady Sneerwell.

SCENE: *London*

Prologue

Written by MR. GARRICK

A School for Scandal! tell me, I beseech you,
Needs there a school this modish art to teach
　　you?
No need of lessons now, the knowing think;
We might as well be taught to eat and drink.
Caused by a dearth of scandal, should the
　　vapors
Distress our fair ones—let them read the pa-
　　pers;
Their powerful mixtures such disorders hit;
Crave what you will—there's *quantum suf-
ficit.*
"Lord!" cries my Lady Wormwood (who
　　loves tattle,
And puts much salt and pepper in her prat-
tle),
Just risen at noon, all night at cards when
　　threshing
Strong tea and scandal—"Bless me, how re-
freshing!
Give me the papers, Lisp—how bold and free!
　　　　　　　　　　　　　　(Sips)
*Last night Lord L. (Sips) was caught with
　　Lady D.*
For aching heads what charming sal volatile!
　　　　　　　　　　　　　　(Sips)
If Mrs. B. will still continue flirting,
We hope she'll DRAW, *or we'll* UNDRAW *the
　　curtain.*
Fine satire, poz[1]—in public all abuse it,
But, by ourselves *(Sips)*, our praise we can't
　　refuse it.

Now, Lisp, read you—there, at that dash and
　　star."
"Yes, ma'am—*A certain Lord had best be-
ware,*
*Who lives not twenty miles from Grosvenor
　　Square;*
For should he Lady W. find willing,
Wormwood is bitter"——"Oh! that's me! the
　　villain!
Throw it behind the fire, and never more
Let that vile paper come within my door."
Thus at our friends we laugh, who feel the
　　dart;
To reach our feelings, we ourselves must
　　smart.
Is our young bard so young, to think that he
Can stop the full spring-tide of calumny?
Knows he the world so little, and its trade?
Alas! the devil's sooner raised than laid.
So strong, so swift, the monster there's no
　　gagging:
Cut Scandal's head off, still the tongue is
　　wagging.
Proud of your smiles once lavishly bestow'd,
Again our young Don Quixote takes the road;
To show his gratitude he draws his pen,
And seeks his hydra, Scandal, in his den.
For your applause all perils he would
　　through—
He'll fight—that's write—a cavalliero true,
Till every drop of blood—that's ink—is spilt
　　for you.

Act I

SCENE I. LADY SNEERWELL's *Dressing-room.*

*(*LADY SNEERWELL *discovered at her toilet;*
SNAKE *drinking chocolate)*

LADY SNEER. The paragraphs, you say,
Mr. Snake, were all inserted?

SNAKE. They were, madam; and, as I

[1] Positively.

copied them myself in a feigned hand, there
can be no suspicion whence they came.

LADY SNEER. Did you circulate the report
of Lady Brittle's intrigue with Captain Boast-
all?

SNAKE. That's in as fine a train as your
ladyship could wish. In the common course

of things, I think it must reach Mrs. Clack-itt's ears within four-and-twenty hours; and then, you know, the business is as good as done.

LADY SNEER. Why, truly, Mrs. Clackitt has a very pretty talent, and a great deal of industry.

SNAKE. True, madam, and has been toler-ably successful in her day. To my knowledge, she has been the cause of six matches being broken off, and three sons being disinherited; of four forced elopements, and as many close confinements; nine separate maintenances, and two divorces. Nay, I have more than once traced her causing a *tête-à-tête* in the "Town and Country Magazine," when the parties, perhaps, had never seen each other's face before in the course of their lives.

LADY SNEER. She certainly has talents, but her manner is gross.

SNAKE. 'Tis very true. She generally de-signs well, has a free tongue and a bold in-vention; but her coloring is too dark, and her outlines often extravagant. She wants that delicacy of tint, and mellowness of sneer, which distinguish your ladyship's scandal.

LADY SNEER. You are partial, Snake.

SNAKE. Not in the least; everybody allows that Lady Sneerwell can do more with a word or look than many can with the most labored detail, even when they happen to have a lit-tle truth on their side to support it.

LADY SNEER. Yes, my dear Snake; and I am no hypocrite to deny the satisfaction I reap from the success of my efforts. Wounded myself, in the early part of my life, by the envenomed tongue of slander, I confess I have since known no pleasure equal to the reducing others to the level of my own in-jured reputation.

SNAKE. Nothing can be more natural. But, Lady Sneerwell, there is one affair in which you have lately employed me, wherein, I confess, I am at a loss to guess your motives.

LADY SNEER. I conceive you mean with respect to my neighbor, Sir Peter Teazle, and his family?

SNAKE. I do. Here are two young men, to whom Sir Peter has acted as a kind of guard-ian since their father's death; the eldest pos-sessing the most amiable character, and universally well spoken of—the youngest, the most dissipated and extravagant young fellow in the kingdom, without friends or character: the former an avowed admirer of your lady-ship, and apparently your favorite; the latter attached to Maria, Sir Peter's ward, and con-fessedly beloved by her. Now, on the face of these circumstances, it is utterly unaccount-able to me, why you, the widow of a city knight, with a good jointure, should not close with the passion of a man of such character and expectations as Mr. Surface; and more so why you should be so uncommonly earnest to destroy the mutual attachment subsisting between his brother Charles and Maria.

LADY SNEER. Then, at once to unravel this mystery, I must inform you that love has no share whatever in the intercourse between Mr. Surface and me.

SNAKE. No!

LADY SNEER. His real attachment is to Maria or her fortune; but, finding in his brother a favored rival, he has been obliged to mask his pretensions, and profit by my assistance.

SNAKE. Yet still I am more puzzled why you should interest yourself in his success.

LADY SNEER. Heavens! how dull you are! Cannot you surmise the weakness which I hitherto, through shame, have concealed even from you? Must I confess that Charles —that libertine, that extravagant, that bank-rupt in fortune and reputation—that he it is for whom I am thus anxious and malicious, and to gain whom I would sacrifice every-thing?

SNAKE. Now, indeed, your conduct ap-pears consistent; but how came you and Mr. Surface so confidential?

LADY SNEER. For our mutual interest. I have found him out a long time since. I know him to be artful, selfish, and malicious—in short, a sentimental knave; while with Sir Peter, and indeed with all his acquaintance, he passes for a youthful miracle of prudence, good sense, and benevolence.

SNAKE. Yes; yet Sir Peter vows he has not his equal in England; and, above all, he praises him as a man of sentiment.

LADY SNEER. True; and with the assist-ance of his sentiment and hypocrisy he has brought Sir Peter entirely into his interest with regard to Maria; while poor Charles has no friend in the house—though, I fear, he has a powerful one in Maria's heart, against whom we must direct our schemes.

(*Enter* SERVANT)

SER. Mr. Surface.

LADY SNEER. Show him up.—(*Exit* SERVANT) He generally calls about this time. I don't wonder at people giving him to me for a lover.

(*Enter* JOSEPH SURFACE)

JOS. SURFACE. My dear Lady Sneerwell, how do you do to-day? Mr. Snake, (*bowing*) your most obedient.

LADY SNEER. Snake has just been rallying me on our mutual attachment; but I have informed him of our real views. You know how useful he has been to us; and, believe me, the confidence is not ill-placed.

JOS. SURF. Madam, it is impossible for me to suspect a man of Mr. Snake's sensibility and discernment.

LADY SNEER. Well, well, no compliments now; but tell me when you saw your mistress, Maria—or, what is more material to me, your brother.

JOS. SURF. I have not seen either since I left you; but I can inform you that they never meet. Some of your stories have taken a good effect on Maria.

LADY SNEER. Ah, my dear Snake! the merit of this belongs to you. But do your brother's distresses increase?

JOS. SURF. Every hour. I am told he has had another execution in the house yesterday. In short, his dissipation and extravagance exceed anything I have ever heard of.

LADY SNEER. Poor Charles!

JOS. SURF. True, madam; notwithstanding his vices, one can't help feeling for him. (*Shaking his head sadly*) Poor Charles! I'm sure I wish it were in my power to be of any essential service to him; for the man who does not share in the distresses of a brother, even though merited by his own misconduct, deserves——

LADY SNEER. O Lud! you are going to be moral, and forget that you are among friends.

JOS. SURF. Egad, that's true! I'll keep that sentiment till I see Sir Peter. However, it is certainly a charity to rescue Maria from such a libertine, who, if he is to be reclaimed, can be so only by a person of your ladyship's superior accomplishments and understanding.

SNAKE. (*Looking out the window*) I believe, Lady Sneerwell, here's company coming; I'll go and copy the letter I mentioned to you. Mr Surface, (*bowing*) your most obedient.

JOS. SURF. Sir, (*bowing*) your very devoted.—(*Exit* SNAKE) Lady Sneerwell, I am very sorry you have put any farther confidence in that fellow.

LADY SNEER. Why so?

JOS. SURF. I have lately detected him in frequent conference with old Rowley, who was formerly my father's steward, and has never, you know, been a friend of mine.

LADY SNEER. And do you think he would betray us?

JOS. SURF. Nothing more likely: take my word for't, Lady Sneerwell, that fellow hasn't virtue enough to be faithful even to his own villainy. Ah, Maria!

(*Enter* MARIA *flushed and panting*)

LADY SNEER. Maria, my dear, how do you do? What's the matter?

MAR. Oh! there's that disagreeable lover of mine, Sir Benjamin Backbite, has just called at my guardian's, with his odious uncle, Crabtree; so I slipped out, and ran hither to avoid them.

LADY SNEER. Is that all?

JOS. SURF. If my brother Charles had been of the party, madam, perhaps you would not have been so much alarmed.

LADY SNEER. Nay, now you are severe; for I dare swear the truth of the matter is, Maria heard you were here. But, my dear, what has Sir Benjamin done, that you should avoid him so?

MAR. Oh, he has done nothing—but 'tis for what he has said: his conversation is a perpetual libel on all his acquaintance.

JOS. SURF. Ay, and the worst of it is, there is no advantage in not knowing him; for he'll abuse a stranger just as soon as his best friend: and his uncle's as bad.

LADY SNEER. Nay, but we should make allowance; Sir Benjamin is a wit and a poet.

MAR. For my part, I own, madam, wit

loses its respect with me, when I see it in company with malice. What do you think, Mr. Surface?

Jos. Surf. Certainly, madam; to smile at the jest which plants a thorn in another's breast is to become a principal in the mischief.

Lady Sneer. Psha! there's no possibility of being witty without a little ill-nature: the malice of a good thing is the barb that makes it stick. What's your opinion, Mr. Surface?

Jos. Surf. To be sure, madam; that conversation, where the spirit of raillery is suppressed, will ever appear tedious and insipid.

Mar. Well, I'll not debate how far scandal may be allowable; but in a man, I am sure, it is always contemptible. We have pride, envy, rivalship, and a thousand motives to depreciate each other; but the male slanderer must have the cowardice of a woman before he can traduce one.

(*Re-enter* Servant)

Ser. Madam, Mrs. Candour is below, and, if your ladyship's at leisure, will leave her carriage.

Lady Sneer. Beg her to walk in.—(*Exit* Servant) Now, Maria, here is a character to your taste; for, though Mrs. Candour is a little talkative, everybody knows her to be the best-natured and best sort of woman.

Mar. Yes, with a very gross affectation of good nature and benevolence, she does more mischief than the direct malice of old Crabtree.

Jos. Surf. I'faith that's true, Lady Sneerwell: whenever I hear the current running against the characters of my friends, I never think them in such danger as when Candour undertakes their defence.

Lady Sneer. Hush!—here she is!

(*Enter* Mrs. Candour)

Mrs. Can. My dear Lady Sneerwell, how have you been this century?—Mr. Surface, what news do you hear?—though indeed it is no matter, for I think one hears nothing else but scandal.

Jos. Surf. Just so, indeed, ma'am.

Mrs. Can. Oh, Maria! child,—what, is the whole affair off between you and Charles? His extravagance, I presume—the town talks of nothing else.

Mar. (*Offended*) I am very sorry, ma'am, the town has so little to do.

Mrs. Can. True, true, child: but there's no stopping people's tongues. I own I was hurt to hear it, as I indeed was to learn, from the same quarter, that your guardian, Sir Peter, and Lady Teazle have not agreed lately as well as could be wished.

Mar. 'Tis strangely impertinent for people to busy themselves so.

Mrs. Can. Very true, child; but what's to be done? People will talk—there's no preventing it. Why, it was but yesterday I was told that Miss Gadabout had eloped with Sir Filagree Flirt. But, Lord! there's no minding what one hears; though, to be sure, I had this from very good authority.

Mar. Such reports are highly scandalous.

Mrs. Can. So they are, child—shameful, shameful! But the world is so censorious, no character escapes. Lord, now who would have suspected your friend, Miss Prim, of an indiscretion? Yet such is the ill-nature of people, that they say her uncle stopped her last week, just as she was stepping into the York mail with her dancing-master.

Mar. I'll answer for't there are no grounds for that report.

Mrs. Can. Ah, no foundation in the world, I dare swear: no more, probably, than the story circulated last month, of Mrs. Festino's affair with Colonel Cassino—though, to be sure, that matter was never rightly cleared up.

Jos. Surf. The license of invention some people take is monstrous indeed.

Mar. 'Tis so; but, in my opinion, those who report such things are equally culpable.

Mrs. Can. To be sure they are; talebearers are as bad as the tale-makers—'tis an old observation, and a very true one: but what's to be done, as I said before? how will you prevent people from talking? To-day, Mrs. Clackitt assured me, Mr. and Mrs. Honeymoon were at last become mere man and wife, like the rest of their acquaintance. She likewise hinted that a certain widow, in the next street, had got rid of her dropsy and recovered her shape in a most surprising manner. And at the same time Miss Tattle, who was by, affirmed, that Lord Buffalo had discovered his lady at a house of no extraordinary fame; and that Sir Harry Bouquet and Tom Saunter were to measure swords on a similar provocation. But, Lord, do you think I would report these things! No, no! Tale-bearers, as I said before, are just as bad as the tale-makers.

Jos. SURF. Ah! Mrs. Candour, if everybody had your forbearance and good nature!

MRS. CAN. I confess, Mr. Surface, I cannot bear to hear people attacked behind their backs; and when ugly circumstances come out against our acquaintance I own I always love to think the best. By-the-by, I hope 'tis not true that your brother is absolutely ruined?

Jos. SURF. I am afraid his circumstances are very bad indeed, ma'am.

MRS. CAN. Ah!—I heard so—but you must tell him to keep up his spirits; everybody almost is in the same way: Lord Spindle, Sir Thomas Splint, Captain Quinze, and Mr. Nickit—all up, I hear, within this week; so, if Charles is undone, he'll find half his acquaintance ruined too, and that, you know, is a consolation.

Jos. SURF. Doubtless, ma'am—a very great one.

(Re-enter SERVANT)

SER. Mr. Crabtree and Sir Benjamin Backbite.   *(Exit)*

LADY SNEER. So, Maria, you see your lover pursues you; positively you shan't escape.

(Enter CRABTREE and SIR BENJAMIN BACKBITE)

CRAB. Lady Sneerwell, I kiss your hand. Mrs. Candour, I don't believe you are acquainted with my nephew, Sir Benjamin Backbite? Egad, ma'am, he has a pretty wit, and is a pretty poet too. Isn't he, Lady Sneerwell?

SIR BEN. *(Simpering)* Oh, fie, uncle!

CRAB. Nay, egad it's true: I back him at a rebus or a charade against the best rhymer in the kingdom. Has your ladyship heard the epigram he wrote last week on Lady Frizzle's feather catching fire?—Do, Benjamin, repeat it, or the charade you made last night extempore at Mrs. Drowzie's conver-

sazione. Come now; your first is the name of a fish, your second a great naval commander, and——

SIR BEN. Uncle, now—pr'ythee——

CRAB. I'faith, ma'am, 'twould surprise you to hear how ready he is at all these sort of things.

LADY SNEER. I wonder, Sir Benjamin, you never publish anything.

SIR BEN. To say truth, ma'am, 'tis very vulgar to print; and, as my little productions are mostly satires and lampoons on particular people, I find they circulate more by giving copies in confidence to the friends of the parties. However, I have some elegies, which, when favored with this lady's smiles (*bowing to MARIA*), I mean to give the public.

CRAB. (*To MARIA*) 'Fore heaven, ma'am, they'll immortalize you—you will be handed down to posterity, like Petrarch's Laura, or Waller's Sacharissa.

SIR BEN. (*To MARIA*) Yes, madam, I think you will like them, when you shall see them on a beautiful quarto page, where a neat rivulet of text shall meander through a meadow of margin. 'Fore Gad, they will be the most elegant things of their kind!

CRAB. But, ladies, that's true—have you heard the news?

MRS. CAN. What, sir, do you mean the report of—

CRAB. No, ma'am, that's not it.—Miss Nicely is going to be married to her own footman.

MRS. CAN. Impossible!

CRAB. Ask Sir Benjamin.

SIR BEN. 'Tis very true, ma'am: everything is fixed, and the wedding liveries bespoke.

CRAB. Yes—and they do say there were pressing reasons for it.

LADY SNEER. Why, I have heard something of this before.

MRS. CAN. It can't be—and I wonder any one should believe such a story of so prudent a lady as Miss Nicely.

SIR BEN. O Lud! ma'am, that's the very reason 'twas believed at once. She has always been so cautious and so reserved, that everybody was sure there was some reason for it at bottom.

MRS. CAN. Why, to be sure, a tale of scandal is as fatal to the credit of a prudent lady of her stamp as a fever is generally to those of the strongest constitutions. But there is a sort of puny sickly reputation, that is always ailing, yet will outlive the robuster characters of a hundred prudes.

SIR BEN. True, madam, there are valetudinarians in reputation as well as constitution, who, being conscious of their weak part, avoid the least breath of air, and supply their want of stamina by care and circumspection.

MRS. CAN. Well, but this may be all a mistake. You know, Sir Benjamin, very trifling circumstances often give rise to the most injurious tales.

CRAB. That they do, I'll be sworn, ma'am. Did you ever hear how Miss Piper came to lose her lover and her character last summer at Tunbridge?—Sir Benjamin, you remember it?

SIR BEN. Oh, to be sure!—the most whimsical circumstance.

LADY SNEER. How was it, pray?

CRAB. Why, one evening, at Mrs. Ponto's assembly, the conversation happened to turn on the breeding Nova Scotia sheep in this country. Says a young lady in company, I have known instances of it; for Miss Letitia Piper, a first cousin of mine, had a Nova Scotia sheep that produced her twins. "What!" cries the Lady Dowager Dundizzy (who you know is as deaf as a post), "has Miss Piper had twins?" This mistake, as you may imagine, threw the whole company into a fit of laughter. However, 'twas the next morning everywhere reported, and in a few days believed by the whole town, that Miss Letitia Piper had actually been brought to bed of a fine boy and girl: and in less than a week there were some people who could name the father, and the farm-house where the babies were put to nurse.

LADY SNEER. Strange, indeed!

CRAB. Matter of fact, I assure you. O Lud! Mr. Surface, pray is it true that your uncle, Sir Oliver, is coming home?

JOS. SURF. Not that I know of, indeed, sir.

CRAB. He has been in the East Indies a long time. You can scarcely remember him, I believe? Sad comfort, whenever he returns, to hear how your brother has gone on!

JOS. SURF. Charles has been imprudent, sir, to be sure; but I hope no busy people have

already prejudiced Sir Oliver against him. He may reform.

SIR BEN. To be sure he may; for my part I never believed him to be so utterly void of principle as people say; and though he has lost all his friends, I am told nobody is better spoken of by the Jews.

CRAB. That's true, egad, nephew. If the old Jewry was a ward, I believe Charles would be an alderman: no man more popular there, 'fore Gad! I hear he pays as many annuities as the Irish tontine;[2] and that, whenever he is sick, they have prayers for the recovery of his health in all the synagogues.

SIR BEN. Yet no man lives in greater splendor. They tell me, when he entertains his friends he will sit down to dinner with a dozen of his own securities; have a score of tradesmen in the antechamber, and an officer behind every guest's chair.

JOS. SURF. This may be entertainment to you, gentlemen, but you pay very little regard to the feelings of a brother.

MAR. (Aside) Their malice is intolerable! —(Aloud) Lady Sneerwell, I must wish you a good morning: I'm not very well. (Exit)

MRS. CAN. O dear! she changes color very much.

LADY SNEER. Do, Mrs. Candour, follow her; she may want your assistance.

MRS. CAN. That I will, with all my soul, ma'am.—(With a leer) Poor dear girl, who knows what her situation may be! (Exit)

LADY SNEER. 'Twas nothing but that she could not bear to hear Charles reflected on, notwithstanding their difference.

SIR BEN. The young lady's penchant is obvious.

CRAB. But, Benjamin, you must not give up the pursuit for that: follow her, and put her into good humor. Repeat her some of your own verses. Come, I'll assist you.

SIR BEN. Mr. Surface, I did not mean to hurt you; but depend on't your brother is utterly undone.

CRAB. O Lud, ay! undone as ever man was —can't raise a guinea.

SIR BEN. And everything sold, I'm told, that was movable.

CRAB. I have seen one that was at his

[2] A species of Irish government loan by which subscribers bought annuities from the government.

house. Not a thing left but some empty bottles that were overlooked, and the family pictures, which I believe are framed in the wainscots.

SIR BEN. And I'm very sorry also to hear some bad stories against him.   (*Going*)

CRAB. Oh, he has done many mean things, that's certain.

SIR BEN. But, however, as he's your brother——   (*Going*)

CRAB. We'll tell you all, another opportunity.

(*Exeunt* CRABTREE *and* SIR BENJAMIN)

LADY SNEER. Ha, ha! 'tis very hard for them to leave a subject they have not quite run down.

JOS. SURF. And I believe the abuse was no more acceptable to your ladyship than to Maria.

LADY SNEER. I doubt her affections are further engaged than we imagine. But the family are to be here this evening, so you may as well dine where you are, and we shall have an opportunity of observing further; in the meantime, I'll go and plot mischief, and you shall study sentiment.   (*Exeunt*)

SCENE II. *A Room in* SIR PETER TEAZLE's *House.*

(*Enter* SIR PETER TEAZLE)

SIR PET. When an old bachelor marries a young wife, what is he to expect? 'Tis now six months since Lady Teazle made me the happiest of men—and I have been the most miserable dog ever since! We tift a little going to church, and fairly quarrelled before the bells had done ringing. I was more than once nearly choked with gall during the honeymoon, and had lost all comfort in life before my friends had done wishing me joy. Yet I chose with caution—a girl bred wholly in the country, who never knew luxury beyond one silk gown, nor dissipation above the annual gala of a race ball. Yet she now plays her part in all the extravagant fopperies of fashion and the town, with as ready a grace as if she never had seen a bush or a grass-plot out of Grosvenor Square! I am sneered at by all my acquaintance, and paragraphed in the newspapers. She dissipates my fortune, and contradicts all my humors; yet the worst of it is, I doubt I love her, or I should never bear all this. However, I'll never be weak enough to own it.

(*Enter* ROWLEY)

Row. Oh! Sir Peter, your servant: how is it with you, sir?

SIR PET. Very bad, Master Rowley, very bad. I meet with nothing but crosses and vexations.

Row. What can have happened since yesterday?

SIR PET. A good question to a married man!

Row. Nay, I'm sure, Sir Peter, your lady can't be the cause of your uneasiness.

SIR PET. Why, has anybody told you she was dead?

Row. Come, come, Sir Peter, you love her, notwithstanding your tempers don't exactly agree.

SIR PET. But the fault is entirely hers, Master Rowley. I am, myself, the sweetest-tempered man alive, and hate a teasing temper; and so I tell her a hundred times a day.

Row. Indeed!

SIR PET. Ay; and what is very extraordinary, in all our disputes she is always in the wrong! But Lady Sneerwell, and the set she meets at her house, encourage the perverseness of her disposition. Then, to complete my vexation, Maria, my ward, whom I ought to have the power of a father over, is determined to turn rebel too, and absolutely refuses the man whom I have long resolved on for her husband; meaning, I suppose, to bestow herself on his profligate brother.

Row. You know, Sir Peter, I have always taken the liberty to differ with you on the subject of these two young gentlemen. I only wish you may not be deceived in your opinion of the elder. For Charles, my life on't! he will retrieve his errors yet. Their worthy father, once my honored master, was, at his years, nearly as wild a spark; yet, when he died, he did not leave a more benevolent heart to lament his loss.

Sɪʀ Pᴇᴛ. You are wrong, Master Rowley. On their father's death, you know, I acted as a kind of guardian to them both, till their uncle Sir Oliver's liberality gave them an early independence: of course, no person could have more opportunities of judging of their hearts, and I was never mistaken in my life. Joseph is indeed a model for the young men of the age. He is a man of sentiment, and acts up to the sentiments he professes; but, for the other, take my word for't, if he had any grain of virtue by descent, he has dissipated it with the rest of his inheritance. Ah! my old friend, Sir Oliver, will be deeply mortified when he finds how part of his bounty has been misapplied.

Row. I am sorry to find you so violent against the young man, because this may be the most critical period of his fortune. I came hither with news that will surprise you.

Sɪʀ Pᴇᴛ. What! let me hear.

Row. Sir Oliver is arrived, and at this moment in town.

Sɪʀ Pᴇᴛ. How! you astonish me! I thought you did not expect him this month.

Row. I did not: but his passage has been remarkably quick.

Sɪʀ Pᴇᴛ. Egad, I shall rejoice to see my old friend. 'Tis sixteen years since we met. We have had many a day together: but does he still enjoin us not to inform his nephews of his arrival?

Row. Most strictly. He means, before it is known, to make some trial of their dispositions.

Sɪʀ Pᴇᴛ. Ah! There needs no art to discover their merits—however, he shall have his way; (*apprehensively*) but, pray, does he know I am married?

Row. Yes, and will soon wish you joy.

Sɪʀ Pᴇᴛ. What, as we drink health to a friend in consumption! Ah, Oliver will laugh at me. We used to rail at matrimony together, but he has been steady to his text. Well, he must be soon at my house, though—I'll instantly give orders for his reception. But, Master Rowley, don't drop a word that Lady Teazle and I ever disagree.

Row. By no means.

Sɪʀ Pᴇᴛ. For I should never be able to stand Noll's jokes; so I'll have him think, Lord forgive me! that we are a very happy couple.

Row. I understand you:—but then you must be very careful not to differ while he is in the house with you.

Sɪʀ Pᴇᴛ. Egad, and so we must—and that's impossible. Ah! Master Rowley, when an old bachelor marries a young wife, he deserves—no—the crime carries its punishment along with it. (*Exeunt*)

Act II

Scᴇɴᴇ I. *A Room in* Sɪʀ Pᴇᴛᴇʀ Tᴇᴀᴢʟᴇ's *House.*

(*Enter* Sɪʀ Pᴇᴛᴇʀ *and* Lᴀᴅʏ Tᴇᴀᴢʟᴇ *quarrelling violently*)

Sɪʀ Pᴇᴛ. Lady Teazle, Lady Teazle, I'll not bear it!

Lᴀᴅʏ Tᴇᴀᴢ. Sir Peter, Sir Peter, you may bear it or not, as you please; but I ought to have my own way in everything, and what's more, I will too. What though I was educated in the country, I know very well that women of fashion in London are accountable to nobody after they are married.

Sɪʀ Pᴇᴛ. Very well, ma'am, very well; so a husband is to have no influence, no authority?

Lᴀᴅʏ Tᴇᴀᴢ. Authority! No, to be sure:—if you wanted authority over me, you should have adopted me, and not married me: I am sure you were old enough.

Sɪʀ Pᴇᴛ. Old enough!—ay, there it is! Well, well, Lady Teazle, though my life may be made unhappy by your temper, I'll not be ruined by your extravagance!

Lᴀᴅʏ Tᴇᴀᴢ. My extravagance! I'm sure I'm not more extravagant than a woman of fashion ought to be.

Sɪʀ Pᴇᴛ. No, no, madam, you shall throw away no more sums on such unmeaning luxury. 'Slife! to spend as much to furnish your dressing-room with flowers in winter as would suffice to turn the Pantheon into a green-house, and give a *fête champêtre* at Christmas.

LADY TEAZ. And am I to blame, Sir Peter, because flowers are dear in cold weather? You should find fault with the climate, and not with me. For my part, I'm sure I wish it was spring all the year round, and that roses grew under our feet!

SIR PET. Oons! madam—if you had been born to this, I shouldn't wonder at your talking thus; but you forget what your situation was when I married you.

LADY TEAZ. No, no, I don't; 'twas a very disagreeable one, or I should never have married you.

SIR PET. Yes, yes, madam, you were then in somewhat a humbler style—the daughter of a plain country squire. Recollect, Lady Teazle, when I saw you first sitting at your tambour, in a pretty figured linen gown, with a bunch of keys at your side, your hair combed smooth over a roll, and your apartment hung round with fruits in worsted, of your own working.

LADY TEAZ. Oh, yes! I remember it very well, and a curious life I led. My daily occupation to inspect the dairy, superintend the poultry, make extracts from the family receipt-book, and comb my aunt Deborah's lap-dog.

SIR PET. Yes, yes, ma'am, 'twas so indeed.

LADY TEAZ. And then, you know, my evening amusements! To draw patterns for ruffles, which I had not the materials to make up; to play Pope Joan with the Curate; to read a sermon to my aunt; or to be stuck down to an old spinet to strum my father to sleep after a fox-chase.

SIR PET. I am glad you have so good a memory. Yes, madam, these were the recreations I took you from; but now you must have your coach—*vis-à-vis*—and three powdered footmen before your chair; and, in the summer, a pair of white cats[3] to draw you to Kensington Gardens. No recollection, I suppose, when you were content to ride double, behind the butler, on a docked coach-horse?

LADY TEAZ. No—I swear I never did that; I deny the butler and the coach-horse.

SIR PET. This, madam, was your situation; and what have I done for you? I have made

[3] Ponies.

you a woman of fashion, of fortune, of rank—in short, I have made you my wife.

LADY TEAZ. Well, then, and there is but one thing more you can make me to add to the obligation, that is——

SIR PET. My widow, I suppose?

LADY TEAZ. Hem! hem!

SIR PET. I thank you, madam—but don't flatter yourself; for, though your ill-conduct may disturb my peace of mind, it shall never break my heart, I promise you: however, I am equally obliged to you for the hint.

LADY TEAZ. Then why will you endeavor to make yourself so disagreeable to me, and thwart me in every little elegant expense?

SIR PET. 'Slife, madam, I say, had you any of these little elegant expenses when you married me?

LADY TEAZ. Lud, Sir Peter! would you have me be out of the fashion?

SIR PET. The fashion, indeed! what had you to do with the fashion before you married me?

LADY TEAZ. For my part, I should think you would like to have your wife thought a woman of taste.

SIR PET. Ay—there again—taste! Zounds! madam, you had no taste when you married me!

LADY TEAZ. That's very true, indeed, Sir Peter! and, after having married you, I should never pretend to taste again, I allow. But now, Sir Peter, since we have finished our daily jangle, I presume I may go to my engagement at Lady Sneerwell's?

SIR PET. Ay, there's another precious circumstance—a charming set of acquaintance you have made there!

LADY TEAZ. Nay, Sir Peter, they are all people of rank and fortune, and remarkably tenacious of reputation.

SIR PET. Yes, egad, they are tenacious of reputation with a vengeance; for they don't choose anybody should have a character but themselves! Such a crew! Ah! many a wretch has rid on a hurdle who has done less mischief than these utterers of forged tales, coiners of scandal, and clippers of reputation.

LADY TEAZ. What, would you restrain the freedom of speech?

SIR PET. Ah! they have made you just as bad as any one of the society.

LADY TEAZ. Why, I believe I do bear a

part with a tolerable grace. But I vow I bear no malice against the people I abuse: when I say an ill-natured thing, 'tis out of pure good humor; and I take it for granted they deal exactly in the same manner with me. But, Sir Peter, you know you promised to come to Lady Sneerwell's too.

Sir Pet. Well, well, I'll call in just to look after my own character.

Lady Teaz. Then, indeed, you must make haste after me or you'll be too late. So goodbye to ye. (*Exit*)

Sir Pet. So—I have gained much by my intended expostulation! Yet with what a charming air she contradicts everything I say, and how pleasantly she shows her contempt for my authority! Well, though I can't make her love me, there is great satisfaction in quarrelling with her; and I think she never appears to such advantage as when she is doing everything in her power to plague me.

(*Exit*)

Scene II. *A Room in* Lady Sneerwell's *House.*

(Lady Sneerwell, Mrs. Candour, Crabtree, Sir Benjamin Backbite, *and* Joseph Surface, *discovered*)

Lady Sneer. Nay, positively, we will hear it.

Jos. Surf. Yes, yes, the epigram, by all means.

Sir Ben. O plague on't, uncle! 'tis mere nonsense.

Crab. No, no; 'fore Gad, very clever for an extempore!

Sir Ben. But, ladies, you should be acquainted with the circumstance. You must know, that one day last week, as Lady Betty Curricle was taking the dust in Hyde Park, in a sort of duodecimo phaeton, she desired me to write some verses on her ponies; upon which, I took out my pocket-book, and in one moment produced the following:—

Sure never were seen two such beautiful ponies;
Other horses are clowns, but these macaronies:
To give them this title I am sure can't be wrong.
Their legs are so slim, and their tails are so long.

Crab. There, ladies, done in the smack of a whip, and on horseback too.

Jos. Surf. A very Phœbus, mounted—indeed, Sir Benjamin!

Sir Ben. Oh dear, sir!—trifles—trifles.—

(*Enter* Lady Teazle *and* Maria)

Mrs. Can. I must have a copy.

Lady Sneer. Lady Teazle, I hope we shall see Sir Peter?

Lady Teaz. I believe he'll wait on your ladyship presently.

Lady Sneer. Maria, my love, you look grave. Come, you shall sit down to piquet with Mr. Surface.

Mar. I take very little pleasure in cards—however, I'll do as your ladyship pleases.

Lady Teaz. (*Aside*) I am surprised Mr. Surface should sit down with her; I thought he would have embraced this opportunity of speaking to me before Sir Peter came.

Mrs. Can. Now, I'll die; but you are so scandalous, I'll forswear your society.

Lady Teaz. What's the matter, Mrs. Candour?

Mrs. Can. They'll not allow our friend Miss Vermillion to be handsome.

Lady Sneer. Oh, surely she is a pretty woman.

Crab. I am very glad you think so, ma'am.

Mrs. Can. She has a charming fresh color.

Lady Teaz. Yes, when it is fresh put on.

Mrs. Can. Oh, fie! I'll swear her color is natural: I have seen it come and go!

Lady Teaz. I dare swear you have, ma'am: it goes off at night, and comes again in the morning.

Sir Ben. True, ma'am, it not only comes and goes; but, what's more, egad, her maid can fetch and carry it!

Mrs. Can. Ha! ha! ha! how I hate to hear you talk so! But surely, now, her sister is, or was, very handsome.

CRAB. Who? Mrs. Evergreen? O Lord! she's six-and-fifty if she's an hour!

MRS. CAN. Now positively you wrong her; fifty-two or fifty-three is the utmost—and I don't think she looks more.

SIR BEN. Ah! there's no judging by her looks, unless one could see her face.

LADY SNEER. Well, well, if Mrs. Evergreen does take some pains to repair the ravages of time, you must allow she effects it with great ingenuity; and surely that's better than the careless manner in which the widow Ochre caulks her wrinkles.

SIR BEN. Nay, now, Lady Sneerwell, you are severe upon the widow. Come, come, 'tis not that she paints so ill—but, when she has finished her face, she joins it on so badly to her neck, that she looks like a mended statue, in which the connoisseur may see at once that the head's modern, though the trunk's antique!

CRAB. Ha! ha! ha! Well said, nephew!

MRS. CAN. Ha! ha! ha! Well, you make me laugh; but I vow I hate you for it. What do you think of Miss Simper?

SIR BEN. Why, she has very pretty teeth.

LADY TEAZ. Yes; and on that account, when she is neither speaking nor laughing (which very seldom happens), she never absolutely shuts her mouth, but leaves it always on a jar, as it were—thus. (Grins foolishly)

MRS. CAN. How can you be so ill-natured?

LADY TEAZ. Nay, I allow even that's better than the pains Mrs. Prim takes to conceal her losses in front. She draws her mouth till it positively resembles the aperture of a poor's-box, and all her words appear to slide out edge-wise, as it were—thus: How do you do, madam? Yes, madam.

LADY SNEER. Very well, Lady Teazle; I see you can be a little severe.

LADY TEAZ. In defence of a friend it is but justice. But here comes Sir Peter to spoil our pleasantry.

(Enter SIR PETER TEAZLE)

SIR PET. (Bowing) Ladies, your most obedient—(Aside) Mercy on me, here is the whole set! a character dead at every word, I suppose.

MRS. CAN. I am rejoiced you are come, Sir Peter. They have been so censorious—and Lady Teazle as bad as any one.

SIR PET. That must be very distressing to you, Mrs. Candour, I dare swear.

MRS. CAN. Oh, they will allow good qualities to nobody; not even good nature to our friend Mrs. Pursy.

LADY TEAZ. What, the fat dowager who was at Mrs. Quadrille's last night?

MRS. CAN. Nay, her bulk is her misfortune; and, when she takes so much pains to get rid of it, you ought not to reflect on her.

LADY SNEER. That's very true, indeed.

LADY TEAZ. Yes, I know she almost lives on acids and small whey; laces herself by pulleys; and often, in the hottest noon in summer, you may see her on a little squat pony, with her hair plaited up behind like a drummer's and puffing round the Ring on a full trot.

MRS. CAN. I thank you, Lady Teazle, for defending her.

SIR PET. Yes, a good defence, truly.

MRS. CAN. Truly, Lady Teazle is as censorious as Miss Sallow.

CRAB. Yes, and she is a curious being to pretend to be censorious—an awkward gawky, without any one good point under heaven.

MRS. CAN. Positively you shall not be so very severe. Miss Sallow is a near relation of mine by marriage, and, as for her person, great allowance is to be made; for, let me tell you, a woman labors under many disadvantages who tries to pass for a girl of six-and-thirty.

LADY SNEER. Though, surely, she is handsome still—and for the weakness in her eyes, considering how much she reads by candlelight, it is not to be wondered at.

MRS. CAN. True; and then as to her manner, upon my word I think it is particularly graceful, considering she never had the least education; for you know her mother was a Welsh milliner, and her father a sugar-baker at Bristol.

SIR BEN. Ah! you are both of you too good-natured!

SIR PET. (Aside) Yes, damned good-natured! This their own relation! mercy on me!

MRS. CAN. For my part, I own I cannot bear to hear a friend ill-spoken of.

SIR PET. No, to be sure.

SIR BEN. Oh! you are of a moral turn. Mrs. Candour and I can sit for an hour and hear Lady Stucco talk sentiment.

LADY TEAZ. Nay, I vow Lady Stucco is very well with the dessert after dinner; for she's just like the French fruit one cracks for mottoes—made up of paint and proverb.

MRS. CAN. Well, I will never join in ridiculing a friend; and so I constantly tell my cousin Ogle, and you all know what pretensions she has to be critical on beauty.

CRAB. Oh, to be sure! she has herself the oddest countenance that ever was seen; 'tis a collection of features from all the different countries of the globe.

SIR BEN. So she has, indeed—an Irish front——

CRAB. Caledonian locks——

SIR BEN. Dutch nose——

CRAB. Austrian lips——

SIR BEN. Complexion of a Spaniard——

CRAB. And teeth à la Chinoise——

SIR BEN. In short, her face resembles a table d'hôte at Spa—where no two guests are of a nation——

CRAB. Or a congress at the close of a general war—wherein all the members, even to her eyes, appear to have a different interest, and her nose and her chin are the only parties likely to join issue.

MRS. CAN. Ha! ha! ha!

SIR PET. (Aside) Mercy on my life!—a person they dine with twice a week!

LADY SNEER. Go—go—you are a couple of provoking toads.

MRS. CAN. Nay, but I vow you shall not carry the laugh off so—for give me leave to say, that Mrs. Ogle——

SIR PET. Madam, madam, I beg your pardon—there's no stopping these good gentlemen's tongues. But when I tell you, Mrs. Candour, that the lady they are abusing is a particular friend of mine, I hope you'll not take her part.

LADY SNEER. Ha! ha! ha! well said, Sir Peter! but you are a cruel creature—too phlegmatic yourself for a jest, and too peevish to allow wit in others.

SIR PET. Ah, madam, true wit is more nearly allied to good nature than your ladyship is aware of.

LADY TEAZ. True, Sir Peter: I believe they are so near akin that they can never be united.

SIR BEN. Or rather, madam, I suppose them man and wife, because one seldom sees them together.

LADY TEAZ. But Sir Peter is such an enemy to scandal, I believe he would have it put down by parliament.

SIR PET. 'Fore heaven, madam, if they were to consider the sporting with reputation of as much importance as poaching on manors, and pass an act for the preservation of fame, I believe many would thank them for the bill.

LADY SNEER. O Lud! Sir Peter; would you deprive us of our privileges?

SIR PET. Ay, madam; and then no person should be permitted to kill characters and run down reputations, but qualified old maids and disappointed widows.

LADY SNEER. Go, you monster!

MRS. CAN. But, surely, you would not be quite so severe on those who only report what they hear?

SIR PET. Yes, madam, I would have law merchant for them too; and in all cases of slander currency, whenever the drawer of the lie was not to be found, the injured parties should have a right to come on any of the indorsers.

CRAB. Well, for my part, I believe there never was a scandalous tale without some foundation.

LADY SNEER. Come, ladies, shall we sit down to cards in the next room?

(Enter SERVANT, who whispers to SIR PETER)

SIR PET. I'll be with them directly. (Exit SERVANT)—(Aside) I'll get away unperceived.

LADY SNEER. Sir Peter, you are not going to leave us?

SIR PET. You ladyship must excuse me; I'm called away by particular business. But I leave my character behind me. (Exit)

SIR BEN. Well—certainly, Lady Teazle, that lord of yours is a strange being: I could tell you some stories of him would make you laugh heartily if he were not your husband.

LADY TEAZ. Oh, pray don't mind that; come, do let's hear them.

(*Exeunt all but* JOSEPH SURFACE *and* MARIA)

JOS. SURF. Maria, I see you have no satisfaction in this society.

MAR. How is it possible I should? If to raise malicious smiles at the infirmities or misfortunes of those who have never injured us be the province of wit or humor, Heaven grant me a double portion of dullness!

JOS. SURF. Yet they appear more ill-natured than they are; they have no malice at heart.

MAR. Then is their conduct still more contemptible; for, in my opinion, nothing could excuse the intemperance of their tongues but a natural and uncontrollable bitterness of mind.

JOS. SURF. Undoubtedly, madam; and it has always been a sentiment of mine, that to propagate a malicious truth wantonly is more despicable than to falsify from revenge. But can you, Maria, feel thus for others, and be unkind to me alone? Is hope to be denied the tenderest passion?

MAR. Why will you distress me by renewing this subject?

JOS. SURF. Ah, Maria! you would not treat me thus, and oppose your guardian, Sir Peter's will, but that I see that profligate Charles is still a favored rival.

MAR. Ungenerously urged! But, whatever my sentiments are for that unfortunate young man, be assured I shall not feel more bound to give him up, because his distresses have lost him the regard even of a brother.

JOS. SURF. Nay, but, Maria, do not leave me with a frown: by all that's honest, I swear—— (*Kneels*)

(*Re-enter* LADY TEAZLE *behind*)

(*Aside*) Gad's life, here's Lady Teazle.—(*Aloud to* MARIA) You must not—no, you shall not—for, though I have the greatest regard for Lady Teazle——

MAR. Lady Teazle!

JOS. SURF. Yet were Sir Peter to suspect——

LADY TEAZ. (*Coming forward angrily*) What is this, pray? Do you take her for me? —Child, you are wanted in the next room.— (*Exit* MARIA) What is all this, pray?

JOS. SURF. Oh, the most unlucky circumstance in nature! Maria has somehow suspected the tender concern I have for your happiness, and threatened to acquaint Sir Peter with her suspicions, and I was just endeavoring to reason with her when you came in.

LADY TEAZ. Indeed! but you seemed to adopt a very tender mode of reasoning—do you usually argue on your knees?

JOS. SURF. Oh, she's a child, and I thought a little bombast——but, Lady Teazle, when are you to give me your judgment on my library, as you promised?

LADY TEAZ. No, no; I begin to think it would be imprudent, and you know I admit you as a lover no farther than fashion requires.

JOS. SURF. True—a mere Platonic cicisbeo.[4] What every wife is entitled to.

LADY TEAZ. Certainly, one must not be out of the fashion. However, I have so many of my country prejudices left, that, though Sir Peter's ill humor may vex me ever so, it never shall provoke me to——

JOS. SURF. The only revenge in your power. Well, I applaud your moderation.

LADY TEAZ. Go—you are an insinuating wretch! But we shall be missed—let us join the company.

JOS. SURF. But we had best not return together.

LADY TEAZ. Well, don't stay; for Maria shan't come to hear any more of your reasoning, I promise you. (*Exit*)

JOS. SURF. A curious dilemma, truly, my politics have run me into! I wanted, at first, only to ingratiate myself with Lady Teazle, that she might not be my enemy with Maria; and I have, I don't know how, become her serious lover. Sincerely I begin to wish I had never made such a point of gaining so very good a character, for it has led me into so many cursed rogueries that I doubt I shall be exposed at last. (*Exit*)

4 Gallant.

SCENE III. *A Room in* SIR PETER TEAZLE's *House.*

(*Enter* SIR OLIVER SURFACE *and* ROWLEY)

SIR OLIV. Ha! ha! ha! so my old friend is married, hey?—a young wife out of the country. Ha! ha! ha! that he should have stood bluff to old bachelor so long, and sink into a husband at last!

ROW. But you must not rally him on the subject, Sir Oliver; 'tis a tender point, I assure you, though he has been married only seven months.

SIR OLIV. Then he has been just half a year on the stool of repentance!—Poor Peter! But you say he has entirely given up Charles—never sees him, hey?

ROW. His prejudice against him is astonishing, and I am sure greatly increased by a jealousy of him with Lady Teazle, which he has industriously been led into by a scandalous society in the neighborhood, who have contributed not a little to Charles's ill name. Whereas the truth is, I believe, if the lady is partial to either of them, his brother is the favorite.

SIR OLIV. Ay, I know there are a set of malicious, prating, prudent gossips, both male and female, who murder characters to kill time, and will rob a young fellow of his good name before he has years to know the value of it. But I am not to be prejudiced against my nephew by such, I promise you! No, no; if Charles has done nothing false or mean, I shall compound for his extravagance.

ROW. Then, my life on't, you will reclaim him. Ah, sir, it gives me new life to find that your heart is not turned against him, and that the son of my good old master has one friend, however, left.

SIR OLIV. What! shall I forget, Master Rowley, when I was at his years myself? Egad, my brother and I were neither of us very prudent youths; and yet, I believe, you have not seen many better men than your old master was?

ROW. Sir, 'tis this reflection gives me assurance that Charles may yet be a credit to his family. But here comes Sir Peter.

SIR OLIV. Egad, so he does! Mercy on me, he's greatly altered, and seems to have a settled married look! One may read husband in his face at this distance!

(*Enter* SIR PETER TEAZLE)

SIR PET. Ha! Sir Oliver—my old friend! Welcome to England a thousand times!

SIR OLIV. Thank you, thank you, Sir Peter! and i'faith I am glad to find you well, believe me!

SIR PET. Oh! 'tis a long time since we met—fifteen years, I doubt, Sir Oliver, and many a cross accident in the time.

SIR OLIV. Ay, I have had my share. But, what! I find you are married, hey, my old boy? Well, well, it can't be helped; and so—I wish you joy with all my heart!

SIR PET. Thank you, thank you, Sir Oliver.—Yes, I have entered into—the happy state; but we'll not talk of that now.

SIR OLIV. True, true, Sir Peter; old friends should not begin on grievances at first meeting. No, no, no.

ROW. (*Aside to* SIR OLIVER) Take care, pray, sir.

SIR OLIV. Well, so one of my nephews is a wild rogue, hey?

SIR PET. Wild! Ah! my old friend, I grieve for your disappointment there; he's a lost young man, indeed. However, his brother will make you amends; Joseph is, indeed, what a youth should be—everybody in the world speaks well of him.

SIR OLIV. I am sorry to hear it; he has too good a character to be an honest fellow. Everybody speaks well of him! Psha! then he has bowed as low to knaves and fools as to the honest dignity of genius and virtue.

SIR PET. What, Sir Oliver! do you blame him for not making enemies?

SIR OLIV. Yes, if he has merit enough to deserve them.

SIR PET. Well, well—you'll be convinced when you know him. 'Tis edification to hear him converse; he professes the noblest sentiments.

SIR OLIV. Oh, plague of his sentiments! If he salutes me with a scrap of morality in his mouth, I shall be sick directly. But, however, don't mistake me, Sir Peter; I don't mean to defend Charles's errors: but, before I form my judgment of either of them, I intend to make a trial of their hearts; and my friend Rowley and I have planned something for the purpose.

Row. And Sir Peter shall own for once he has been mistaken.

Sir Pet. Oh, my life on Joseph's honor!

Sir Oliv. Well—come, give us a bottle of good wine, and we'll drink the lads' health, and tell you our scheme.

Sir Pet. *Allons,* then!

Sir Oliv. And don't, Sir Peter, be so severe against your old friend's son. Odds my life! I am not sorry that he has run out of the course a little: for my part, I hate to see prudence clinging to the green suckers of youth; 'tis like ivy round a sapling, and spoils the growth of the tree. (*Exeunt*)

Act III

Scene I. *A Room in* Sir Peter Teazle's *House.*

(*Enter* Sir Peter Teazle, Sir Oliver Surface, *and* Rowley)

Sir Pet. Well, then, we will see this fellow first, and have our wine afterwards. But how is this, Master Rowley? I don't see the jet of your scheme.

Row. Why, sir, this Mr. Stanley, whom I was speaking of, is nearly related to them by their mother. He was once a merchant in Dublin, but has been ruined by a series of undeserved misfortunes. He has applied, by letter, since his confinement, both to Mr. Surface and Charles: from the former he has received nothing but evasive promises of future service, while Charles has done all that his extravagance has left him power to do; and he is, at this time, endeavoring to raise a sum of money, part of which, in the midst of his own distresses, I know he intends for the service of poor Stanley.

Sir Oliv. Ah, he is my brother's son.

Sir Pet. Well, but how is Sir Oliver personally to——

Row. Why, sir, I will inform Charles and his brother that Stanley has obtained permission to apply personally to his friends; and, as they have neither of them ever seen him, let Sir Oliver assume his character, and he will have a fair opportunity of judging, at least, of the benevolence of their dispositions: and believe me, sir, you will find in the youngest brother one who, in the midst of folly and dissipation, has still, as our immortal bard expresses it,—

"a heart to pity, and a hand Open as day, for melting charity."

Sir Pet. Psha! What signifies his having an open hand or purse either, when he has nothing left to give? Well, well, make the trial, if you please. But where is the fellow whom you brought for Sir Oliver to examine, relative to Charles's affairs?

Row. Below, waiting his commands, and no one can give him better intelligence.— This, Sir Oliver, is a friendly Jew, who, to do him justice, has done everything in his power to bring your nephew to a proper sense of his extravagance.

Sir Pet. Pray let us have him in.

Row. (*Calls offstage to a servant*) Desire Mr. Moses to walk upstairs.

Sir Pet. But, pray, why should you suppose he will speak the truth?

Row. Oh, I have convinced him that he has no chance of recovering certain sums advanced to Charles but through the bounty of Sir Oliver, who he knows is arrived; so that you may depend on his fidelity to his own interests. I have also another evidence in my power, one Snake, whom I have detected in a matter little short of forgery, and shall shortly produce to remove some of your prejudices, Sir Peter, relative to Charles and Lady Teazle.

Sir Pet. I have heard too much on that subject.

Row. Here comes the honest Israelite.

(*Enter* Moses)

—This is Sir Oliver.

(MOSES *bows to* SIR OLIVER)

SIR OLIV. Sir, I understand you have lately had great dealings with my nephew Charles.

MOS. Yes, Sir Oliver, I have done all I could for him; but he was ruined before he came to me for assistance.

SIR OLIV. That was unlucky, truly; for you have had no opportunity of showing your talents.

MOS. None at all; I hadn't the pleasure of knowing his distresses till he was some thousands worse than nothing.

SIR OLIV. Unfortunate, indeed! But I suppose you have done all in your power for him, honest Moses?

MOS. Yes, he knows that. This very evening I was to have brought him a gentleman from the city, who does not know him, and will, I believe, advance him some money.

SIR PET. What, one Charles has never had money from before?

MOS. Yes, Mr. Premium, of Crutched Friars, formerly a broker.

SIR PET. Egad, Sir Oliver, a thought strikes me!—Charles, you say, does not know Mr. Premium?

MOS. Not at all.

SIR PET. Now then, Sir Oliver, you may have a better opportunity of satisfying yourself than by an old romancing tale of a poor relation: go with my friend Moses, and represent Premium, and then, I'll answer for it, you'll see your nephew in all his glory.

SIR OLIV. Egad, I like this idea better than the other, and I may visit Joseph afterwards as old Stanley.

SIR PET. True—so you may.

ROW. Well, this is taking Charles rather at a disadvantage, to be sure. However, Moses, you understand Sir Peter, and will be faithful.

MOS. You may depend upon me.—(*Looks at his watch*) This is near the time I was to have gone.

SIR OLIV. I'll accompany you as soon as you please, Moses—— But hold! I have forgot one thing—how the plague shall I be able to pass for a Jew?

MOS. There's no need—the principal is Christian.

SIR OLIV. Is he? I'm very sorry to hear it.

But, then again, an't I rather too smartly dressed to look like a money-lender?

SIR PET. Not at all; 'twould not be out of character, if you went in your carriage—would it, Moses?

MOS. Not in the least.

SIR OLIV. Well, but how must I talk? there's certainly some cant of usury and mode of treating that I ought to know.

SIR PET. Oh, there's not much to learn. The great point, as I take it, is to be exorbitant enough in your demands. Hey, Moses?

MOS. Yes, that's a very great point.

SIR OLIV. I'll answer for't I'll not be wanting in that. I'll ask him eight or ten per cent. on the loan, at least.

MOS. If you ask him no more than that, you'll be discovered immediately.

SIR OLIV. Hey! what, the plague! how much then?

MOS. That depends upon the circumstances. If he appears not very anxious for the supply, you should require only forty or fifty per cent.; but if you find him in great distress, and want the moneys very bad, you may ask double.

SIR PET. A good honest trade you're learning, Sir Oliver!

SIR OLIV. Truly I think so—and not unprofitable.

MOS. Then, you know, you haven't the moneys yourself, but are forced to borrow them for him of a friend.

SIR OLIV. Oh! I borrow it of a friend, do I?

MOS. And your friend is an unconscionable dog: but you can't help that.

SIR OLIV. My friend an unconscionable dog, is he?

MOS. Yes, and he himself has not the moneys by him, but is forced to sell stocks at a great loss.

SIR OLIV. He is forced to sell stocks at a great loss, is he? Well, that's very kind of him.

SIR PET. I'faith, Sir Oliver—Mr. Premium, I mean—you'll soon be master of the trade. But, Moses! would not you have him run out a little against the annuity bill? That would be in character, I should think.

MOS. Very much.

ROW. And lament that a young man now must be at years of discretion before he is suffered to ruin himself?

Mos. Ay, great pity!

Sir Pet. And abuse the public for allowing merit to an act whose only object is to snatch misfortune and imprudence from the rapacious grip of usury, and give the minor a chance of inheriting his estate without being undone by coming into possession.

Sir Oliv. So, so—Moses shall give me further instructions as we go together.

Sir Pet. You will not have much time, for your nephew lives hard by.

Sir Oliv. Oh, never fear! my tutor appears so able, that though Charles lived in the next street, it must be my own fault if I am not a complete rogue before I turn the corner.

(*Exit with* Moses)

Sir Pet. So, now, I think Sir Oliver will be convinced: you are partial, Rowley, and would have prepared Charles for the other plot.

Row. No, upon my word, Sir Peter.

Sir Peter. Well, go bring me this Snake, and I'll hear what he has to say presently. I see Maria, and want to speak with her.— (*Exit* Rowley) I should be glad to be convinced my suspicions of Lady Teazle and Charles were unjust. I have never yet opened my mind on this subject to my friend Joseph —I am determined I will do it—he will give me his opinion sincerely.

(*Enter* Maria)

So, child, has Mr. Surface returned with you?

Mar. No, sir; he was engaged.

Sir Pet. Well, Maria, do you not reflect, the more you converse with that amiable young man, what return his partiality for you deserves?

Mar. Indeed, Sir Peter, your frequent importunity on this subject distresses me extremely—you compel me to declare, that I know no man who has ever paid me a particular attention whom I would not prefer to Mr. Surface.

Sir Pet. So—here's perverseness! No, no, Maria, 'tis Charles only whom you would prefer. 'Tis evident his vices and follies have won your heart.

Mar. This is unkind, sir. You know I have obeyed you in neither seeing nor corresponding with him: I have heard enough to convince me that he is unworthy my regard. Yet

I cannot think it culpable, if, while my understanding severely condemns his vices, my heart suggests pity for his distresses.

Sir Pet. Well, well, pity him as much as you please; but give your heart and hand to a worthier object.

Mar. Never to his brother!

Sir Pet. Go, perverse and obstinate! But take care, madam; you have never yet known what the authority of a guardian is: don't compel me to inform you of it.

Mar. I can only say, you shall not have just reason. 'Tis true, by my father's will, I am for a short period bound to regard you as his substitute; but must cease to think you so, when you would compel me to be miserable.

(*Exit*)

Sir Pet. Was ever man so crossed as I am, everything conspiring to fret me! I had not been involved in matrimony a fortnight, before her father, a hale and hearty man, died, on purpose, I believe, for the pleasure of plaguing me with the care of his daughter.— (Lady Teazle *is heard singing offstage*) But here comes my helpmate! She appears in great good humor. How happy I should be if I could tease her into loving me, though but a little!

(*Enter* Lady Teazle)

Lady Teaz. Lud! Sir Peter, I hope you haven't been quarrelling with Maria? It is not using me well to be ill humored when I am not by.

Sir Pet. Ah, Lady Teazle, you might have the power to make me good humored at all times.

Lady Teaz. I am sure I wish I had; for I want you to be in a charming sweet temper at this moment. (*Sweetly*) Do be good humored now, and let me have two hundred pounds, will you?

Sir Pet. Two hundred pounds! What, an't I to be in a good humor without paying for it! But speak to me thus, and i'faith there's nothing I could refuse you. You shall have it; but seal me a bond for the repayment.

Lady Teaz. Oh, no—there—my note of hand will do as well. (*Offering her hand*)

Sir Pet. And you shall no longer reproach me with not giving you an independent settlement. I mean shortly to surprise you; (*put-*

ting his arm about her) but shall we always live thus, hey?

LADY TEAZ. If you please, I'm sure I don't care how soon we leave off quarrelling, provided you'll own you were tired first.

SIR PET. Well—then let our future contest be, who shall be most obliging.

LADY TEAZ. I assure you, Sir Peter, good nature becomes you. You look now as you did before we were married, when you used to walk with me under the elms, and tell me stories of what a gallant you were in your youth, and chuck me under the chin, you would; and ask me if I thought I could love an old fellow, who would deny me nothing—didn't you?

SIR PET. Yes, yes, and you were as kind and attentive——

LADY TEAZ. Ay, so I was, and would always take your part, when my acquaintance used to abuse you, and turn you into ridicule.

SIR PET. Indeed!

LADY TEAZ. Ay, and when my cousin Sophy has called you a stiff, peevish old bachelor, and laughed at me for thinking of marrying one who might be my father, I have always defended you, and said, I didn't think you so ugly by any means, and that you'd make a very good sort of a husband.

SIR PET. And you prophesied right; and we shall now be the happiest couple——

LADY TEAZ. And never differ again?

SIR PET. No, never—though at the same time, indeed, my dear Lady Teazle, you must watch your temper very seriously; for in all our little quarrels, my dear, if you recollect, my love, you always began first.

LADY TEAZ. I beg your pardon, my dear Sir Peter: indeed, you always gave the provocation.

SIR PET. Now, see, my angel! take care—contradicting isn't the way to keep friends.

LADY TEAZ. Then, don't you begin it, my love!

SIR PET. There, now! you—you are going on. You don't perceive, my life, that you are just doing the very thing which you know always makes me angry.

LADY TEAZ. Nay, you know if you will be angry without any reason, my dear——

SIR PET. There! now you want to quarrel again.

LADY TEAZ. No, I'm sure I don't: but, if you will be so peevish——

SIR PET. There now! who begins first?

LADY TEAZ. Why, you, to be sure. I said nothing—but there's no bearing your temper.

SIR PET. No, no, madam: the fault's in your own temper.

LADY TEAZ. Ay, you are just what my cousin Sophy said you would be.

SIR PET. Your cousin Sophy is a forward, impertinent gipsy.

LADY TEAZ. You are a great bear, I am sure, to abuse my relations.

SIR PET. Now may all the plagues of marriage be doubled on me, if ever I try to be friends with you any more!

LADY TEAZ. So much the better.

SIR PET. No, no, madam: 'tis evident you never cared a pin for me, and I was a madman to marry you—a pert, rural coquette, that had refused half the honest squires in the neighborhood!

LADY TEAZ. And I am sure I was a fool to marry you—an old dangling bachelor, who was single at fifty, only because he never could meet with any one who would have him.

SIR PET. Ay, ay, madam; but you were pleased enough to listen to me: you never had such an offer before.

LADY TEAZ. No? Didn't I refuse Sir Tivy Terrier, who everybody said would have been a better match? for his estate is just as good as yours, and he has broke his neck since we have been married.

SIR PET. I have done with you, madam! You are an unfeeling, ungrateful—but there's an end of everything. I believe you capable of everything that is bad. Yes, madam, I now believe the reports relative to you and Charles, madam. Yes, madam, you and Charles are, not without grounds——

LADY TEAZ. Take care, Sir Peter! You had better not insinuate any such thing! I'll not be suspected without cause, I promise you.

SIR PET. (*Furious*) Very well, madam! very well! a separate maintenance as soon as you please. Yes, madam, or a divorce! I'll make an example of myself for the benefit of all old bachelors. Let us separate, madam.

LADY TEAZ. Agreed! agreed! And now, my dear Sir Peter, we are of a mind once more, we may be the happiest couple, and never differ again, you know: ha! ha! ha! Well, you are going to be in a passion, I see, and I shall only interrupt you—so, bye! bye!

(Exit laughing at him)

SIR PET. Plagues and tortures! can't I make her angry either! Oh, I am the most miserable fellow! But I'll not bear her presuming to keep her temper: no! she may break my heart, but she shan't keep her temper. *(Exit)*

SCENE II. *A Room in* CHARLES SURFACE'S *House.*

(Enter TRIP, *in a footman's livery,* MOSES, *and* SIR OLIVER SURFACE)

TRIP. Here, Master Moses! if you'll stay a moment; I'll try whether—what's the gentleman's name?

SIR OLIV. *(Aside to* MOSES) Mr. Moses, what is my name?

MOS. Mr. Premium.

TRIP. Premium—very well.

(Exit, taking snuff)

SIR OLIV. To judge by the servants, one wouldn't believe the master was ruined. But what!—sure, this was my brother's house?

MOS. Yes, sir; Mr. Charles bought it of Mr. Joseph, with the furniture, pictures, &c., just as the old gentleman left it. Sir Peter thought it a piece of extravagance in him.

SIR OLIV. In my mind, the other's economy in selling it to him was more reprehensible by half.

(Re-enter TRIP)

TRIP. My master says you must wait, gentlemen: he has company, and can't speak with you yet.

SIR OLIV. If he knew who it was wanted to see him, perhaps he would not send such a message?

TRIP. Yes, yes, sir; he knows you are here —I did not forget little Premium: no, no, no.

SIR OLIV. Very well; and I pray, sir, what may be your name?

TRIP. Trip, sir; my name is Trip, at your service.

SIR OLIV. Well, then, Mr. Trip, you have a pleasant sort of place here, I guess?

TRIP. Why, yes—here are three or four of us pass our time agreeably enough; but then our wages are sometimes a little in arrear—and not very great either—but fifty pounds a year, and find our own bags and bouquets.

SIR OLIV. *(Aside)* Bags and bouquets! halters and bastinadoes!

TRIP. And *à propos*, Moses, have you been able to get me that little bill discounted?

SIR OLIV. *(Aside)* Wants to raise money, too!—mercy on me! Has his distresses too, I warrant, like a lord, and affects creditors and duns.

MOS. 'Twas not to be done, indeed, Mr. Trip.

TRIP. Good lack, you surprise me! My friend Brush has indorsed it, and I thought when he put his name at the back of a bill 'twas the same as cash.

MOS. No, 'twouldn't do.

TRIP. A small sum—but twenty pounds. Hark'ee, Moses, do you think you couldn't get it me by way of annuity?

SIR OLIV. *(Aside)* An annuity! ha! ha! A footman raise money by way of annuity! Well done, luxury, egad!

MOS. Well, but you must insure your place.

TRIP. Oh, with all my heart! I'll insure my place, and my life too, if you please.

SIR OLIV. *(Aside)* It's more than I would your neck.

MOS. But is there nothing you could deposit?

TRIP. Why, nothing capital of my master's wardrobe has dropped lately; but I could give you a mortgage on some of his winter clothes, with equity of redemption before November—or you shall have the reversion of the French velvet, or a post-obit on the blue and silver;—these, I should think, Moses, with a few pair of point ruffles, as a collateral security—hey, my little fellow?

MOS. Well, well. *(Bell rings)*

TRIP. Egad, I heard the bell! I believe,

gentlemen, I can now introduce you. Don't forget the annuity, little Moses! This way, gentlemen, I'll insure my place, you know.

Sir Oliv. (*Aside*) If the man be a shadow of the master, this is the temple of dissipation indeed! (*Exeunt*)

Scene III. *Another Room in the Same.*

(Charles Surface, Sir Harry Bumper, Careless, *and* Gentlemen, *sit about a table, drinking*)

Chas. Surf. 'Fore heaven, 'tis true!—there's the great degeneracy of the age. Many of our acquaintance have taste, spirit, and politeness; but plague on't they won't drink.

Care. It is so, indeed, Charles! they give in to all the substantial luxuries of the table, and abstain from nothing but wine and wit. Oh, certainly society suffers by it intolerably! for now, instead of the social spirit of raillery that used to mantle over a glass of bright Burgundy, their conversation is become just like the Spa-water they drink, which has all the pertness and flatulency of champagne, without its spirit or flavor.

1 Gent. But what are they to do who love play better than wine?

Care. True! there's Sir Harry diets himself for gaming, and is now under a hazard regimen.

Chas. Surf. Then he'll have the worst of it. What! you wouldn't train a horse for the course by keeping him from corn? For my part, egad, I'm never so successful as when I am a little merry: let me throw on a bottle of champagne, and I never lose—at least I never feel my losses, which is exactly the same thing.

2 Gent. Ay, that I believe.

Chas. Surf. And, then, what man can pretend to be a believer in love, who is an abjurer of wine? 'Tis the test by which the lover knows his own heart. Fill a dozen bumpers to a dozen beauties, and she that floats at the top is the maid that has bewitched you.

Care. Now then, Charles, be honest, and give us your real favorite.

Chas. Surf. Why, I have withheld her only in compassion to you. If I toast her, you must give a round of her peers, which is impossible—on earth.

Care. Oh, then we'll find some canonized vestals or heathen goddesses that will do, I warrant!

Chas. Surf. Here then, bumpers, you rogues! (*They fill their glasses*) Bumpers! Maria! Maria—

Sir Har. Maria who?

Chas. Surf. Oh, damn the surname!—'tis too formal to be registered in Love's calendar—but now, Sir Harry, beware, we must have beauty superlative.

Care. Nay, never study, Sir Harry: we'll stand to the toast, though your mistress should want an eye, and you know you have a song will excuse you.

Sir Har. Egad, so I have! and I'll give him the song instead of the lady. (*Sings*)

> Here's to the maiden of bashful fifteen;
> Here's to the widow of fifty;
> Here's to the flaunting extravagant quean,
> And here's to the housewife that's
> thrifty.

Chorus. Let the toast pass,—
Drink to the lass,
I'll warrant she'll prove an excuse for a glass.

> Here's to the charmer whose dimples we
> prize;
> Now to the maid who has none, sir;
> Here's to the girl with a pair of blue eyes,
> And here's to the nymph with but one,
> sir.

Chorus. Let the toast pass,—
Drink to the lass,
I'll warrant she'll prove an excuse for a glass.

> Here's to the maid with a bosom of snow:
> Now to her that's as brown as a berry:
> Here's to the wife with a face full of woe,
> And now to the damsel that's merry.

CHORUS.   *Let the toast pass,—*
       Drink to the lass,
I'll warrant she'll prove an excuse for a glass.

   For let 'em be clumsy, or let 'em be slim,
     Young or ancient, I care not a feather;
   So fill a pint bumper quite up to the brim,
   So fill up your glasses, nay, fill to the brim,
   And let us e'en toast them together.

CHORUS.   *Let the toast pass,—*
       Drink to the lass,
I'll warrant she'll prove an excuse for a glass.

ALL. Bravo! Bravo!

(*Enter* TRIP, *and whispers to* CHARLES
         SURFACE)

CHAS. SURF. Gentlemen, you must excuse me a little.—Careless, take the chair, will you?

CARE. Nay, pr'ythee, Charles, what now? This is one of your peerless beauties, I suppose, dropped in by chance?

CHAS. SURF. No, faith! To tell you the truth, 'tis a Jew and a broker, who are come by appointment.

CARE. Oh, damn it! let's have the Jew in.

1 GENT. Ay, and the broker too, by all means.

2 GENT. Yes, yes, the Jew and the broker.

CHAS. SURF. Egad, with all my heart!— Trip, bid the gentlemen walk in.—(*Exit* TRIP) Though there's one of them a stranger, I can tell you.

CARE. Charles, let us give them some generous Burgundy, and perhaps they'll grow conscientious.

CHAS. SURF. Oh, hang 'em, no! wine does but draw forth a man's natural qualities; and to make them drink would only be to whet their knavery.

(*Re-enter* TRIP, *with* SIR OLIVER SURFACE
         and MOSES)

CHAS. SURF. So, honest Moses; walk in, pray, Mr. Premium—that's the gentleman's name, isn't it, Moses?

MOS. Yes, sir.

CHAS. SURF. Set chairs, Trip.—Sit down, Mr. Premium.—Glasses, Trip.—(TRIP *places*

chairs and glasses, and exit*) Sit down, Moses.—Come, Mr. Premium, I'll give you a sentiment; here's *Success to usury!*—Moses, fill the gentleman a bumper.

MOS. Success to usury!   (*Drinks*)

CARE. Right, Moses—usury is prudence and industry, and deserves to succeed.

SIR OLIV. Then here's—All the success it deserves!   (*Drinks*)

CARE. No, no, that won't do! Mr. Premium, you have demurred at the toast, and must drink it in a pint bumper.

1 GENT. A pint bumper, at least.

MOS. Oh, pray, sir, consider—Mr. Premium's a gentleman.

CARE. And therefore loves good wine.

2 GENT. Give Moses a quart glass—this is mutiny, and a high contempt for the chair.

CARE. Here, now for't! I'll see justice done, to the last drop of my bottle.

SIR OLIV. Nay, pray, gentlemen—I did not expect this usage.

CHAS. SURF. No, hang it, you shan't; Mr. Premium's a stranger.

SIR OLIV. (*Aside*) Odd! I wish I was well out of their company.

CARE. Plague on 'em then! if they won't drink, we'll not sit down with them. Come, Harry, the dice are in the next room.— Charles, you'll join us when you have finished your business with the gentlemen?

CHAS. SURF. I will! I will!—(*Exeunt* SIR HARRY BUMPER *and* GENTLEMEN; CARELESS *following*) Careless.

CARE. (*Returning*) Well!

CHAS. SURF. Perhaps I may want you.

CARE. Oh, you know I am always ready: word, note, or bond, 'tis all the same to me.   (*Exit*)

MOS. Sir, this is Mr. Premium, a gentleman of the strictest honor and secrecy; and always performs what he undertakes. Mr. Premium, this is——

CHAS. SURF. Psha! have done. Sir, my friend Moses is a very honest fellow, but a little slow at expression: he'll be an hour giving us our titles. Mr. Premium, the plain state of the matter is this: I am an extravagant young fellow who wants to borrow money; you I take to be a prudent old fellow, who has got money to lend. I am blockhead enough to give fifty per cent. sooner than not have it! and you, I presume, are rogue enough to take a hundred if you can get it. Now, sir, you see we are acquainted at once, and may proceed to business without further ceremony.

SIR OLIV. Exceeding frank, upon my word. I see, sir, you are not a man of many compliments.

CHAS. SURF. Oh, no, sir! plain dealing in business I always think best.

SIR OLIV. Sir, I like you the better for it. However, you are mistaken in one thing; I have no money to lend, but I believe I could procure some of a friend; but then he's an unconscionable dog. Isn't he, Moses? And must sell stock to accommodate you. Mustn't he, Moses?

MOS. Yes, indeed! You know I always speak the truth, and scorn to tell a lie!

CHAS. SURF. Right. People that speak truth generally do. But these are trifles, Mr. Premium. What! I know money isn't to be bought without paying for't!

SIR OLIV. Well, but what security could you give? You have no land, I suppose?

CHAS. SURF. Not a mole-hill, nor a twig, but what's in the bough-pots out of the window!

SIR OLIV. Nor any stock, I presume?

CHAS. SURF. Nothing but live stock—and that's only a few pointers and ponies. But pray, Mr. Premium, are you acquainted at all with any of my connections?

SIR OLIV. Why, to say the truth, I am.

CHAS. SURF. Then you must know that I have a devilish rich uncle in the East Indies, Sir Oliver Surface, from whom I have the greatest expectations?

SIR OLIV. That you have a wealthy uncle, I have heard; but how your expectations will turn out is more, I believe, than you can tell.

CHAS. SURF. Oh, no!—there can be no doubt. They tell me I'm a prodigious favorite, and that he talks of leaving me everything.

SIR OLIV. Indeed! this is the first I've heard of it.

CHAS. SURF. Yes, yes, 'tis just so. Moses knows 'tis true; don't you, Moses?

MOS. Oh, yes! I'll swear to't.

SIR OLIV. (*Aside*) Egad, they'll persuade me presently I'm at Bengal.

CHAS. SURF. Now I propose, Mr. Pre-

mium, if it's agreeable to you, a post-obit on Sir Oliver's life: though at the same time the old fellow has been so liberal to me, that I give you my word, I should be very sorry to hear that anything had happened to him.

SIR OLIV. Not more than I should, I assure you. But the bond you mention happens to be just the worst security you could offer me—for I might live to a hundred and never see the principal.

CHAS. SURF. Oh, yes, you would! the moment Sir Oliver dies, you know, you would come on me for the money.

SIR OLIV. Then I believe I should be the most unwelcome dun you ever had in your life.

CHAS. SURF. What! I suppose you're afraid that Sir Oliver is too good a life?

SIR OLIV. No, indeed I am not; though I have heard he is as hale and healthy as any man of his years in Christendom.

CHAS. SURF. There again, now, you are misinformed. No, no, the climate has hurt him considerably, poor uncle Oliver. Yes, yes, he breaks apace, I'm told—and is so much altered lately that his nearest relations would not know him.

SIR OLIV. No! Ha! ha! ha! so much altered lately that his nearest relations would not know him! Ha! ha! ha! egad—ha! ha! ha!

CHAS. SURF. Ha! ha!—you're glad to hear that, little Premium?

SIR OLIV. No, no, I'm not.

CHAS. SURF. Yes, yes, you are—ha! ha! ha! —you know that mends your chance.

SIR OLIV. But I'm told Sir Oliver is coming over; nay, some say he has actually arrived.

CHAS. SURF. Psha! sure I must know better than you whether he's come or not. No, no, rely on't he's at this moment at Calcutta. Isn't he, Moses?

MOS. Oh, yes, certainly.

SIR OLIV. Very true, as you say, you must know better than I, though I have it from pretty good authority. Haven't I, Moses?

MOS. Yes, most undoubted!

SIR OLIV. But, sir, as I understand you want a few hundreds immediately, is there nothing you could dispose of?

CHAS. SURF. How do you mean?

SIR OLIV. For instance, now, I have heard

that your father left behind him a great quantity of massy old plate.

CHAS. SURF. O Lud, that's gone long ago. Moses can tell you how better than I can.

SIR OLIV. (*Aside*) Good lack! all the family race-cups and corporation-bowls!—(*Aloud*) Then it was also supposed that his library was one of the most valuable and compact.

CHAS. SURF. Yes, yes, so it was—vastly too much so for a private gentleman. For my part, I was always of a communicative disposition, so I thought it a shame to keep so much knowledge to myself.

SIR OLIV. (*Aside*) Mercy upon me! learning that had run in the family like an heirloom!—(*Aloud*) Pray, what has become of the books?

CHAS. SURF. You must inquire of the auctioneer, Master Premium, for I don't believe even Moses can direct you.

MOS. I know nothing of books.

SIR OLIV. So, so, nothing of the family property left, I suppose?

CHAS. SURF. Not much, indeed; unless you have a mind to the family pictures. I have got a room full of ancestors above: and if you have a taste for old paintings, egad, you shall have 'em a bargain!

SIR OLIV. Hey! what the devil! sure, you wouldn't sell your forefathers, would you?

CHAS. SURF. Every man of them, to the best bidder.

SIR OLIV. What! your great-uncles and aunts?

CHAS. SURF. Ay, and my great-grandfathers and grandmothers too.

SIR OLIV. (*Aside*) Now I give him up!—(*Aloud*) What the plague, have you no bowels for your own kindred? Odd's life! do you take me for Shylock in the play, that

you would raise money of me on your own flesh and blood?

CHAS. SURF. Nay, my little broker, don't be angry: what need you care, if you have your money's worth?

SIR OLIV. Well, I'll be the purchaser: I think I can dispose of the family canvas.—(*Aside*) Oh, I'll never forgive him this! never!

(*Re-enter* CARELESS)

CARE. Come, Charles, what keeps you?

CHAS. SURF. I can't come yet. I'faith, we are going to have a sale above stairs, here's little Premium will buy all my ancestors!

CARE. Oh, burn your ancestors!

CHAS. SURF. No, he may do that afterwards, if he pleases. Stay, Careless, we want you: egad, you shall be auctioneer—so come along with us.

CARE. Oh, have with you, if that's the case. I can handle a hammer as well as a dice box; Going! going!

SIR OLIV. (*Aside*) Oh, the profligates!

CHAS. SURF. Come, Moses, you shall be appraiser, if we want one. Gad's life, little Premium, you don't seem to like the business?

SIR OLIV. Oh, yes, I do, vastly! Ha! ha! ha! yes, yes, I think it a rare joke to sell one's family by auction—ha! ha!—(*Aside*) Oh, the prodigal!

CHAS. SURF. To be sure! when a man wants money, where the plague should he get assistance, if he can't make free with his own relations?

(*Exeunt all except* SIR OLIVER)

SIR OLIV. I'll never forgive him; never! never! (*Exit*)

Act IV

SCENE I. *A Picture Gallery in* CHARLES SURFACE'S *House.*

(*Enter* CHARLES SURFACE, SIR OLIVER SURFACE, MOSES, *and* CARELESS)

CHAS. SURF. Walk in, gentlemen, pray walk in.—Here they are, the family of the Surfaces, up to the Conquest.

SIR OLIV. And, in my opinion, a goodly collection.

CHAS. SURF. Ay, ay, these are done in the true spirit of portrait-painting; no *volontière grace* or expression. Not like the works of your modern Raphaels, who give you the strongest resemblance, yet contrive to make your portrait independent of you; so that you may sink the original and not hurt the picture. No, no; the merit of these is the inveterate likeness—all stiff and awkward as the originals, and like nothing in human nature besides.

SIR OLIV. Ah! we shall never see such figures of men again.

CHAS. SURF. I hope not. Well, you see, Master Premium, what a domestic character I am; here I sit of an evening surrounded by my family. But come, get to your pulpit, Mr. Auctioneer; here's an old gouty chair of my grandfather's will answer the purpose.

CARE. Ay, ay, this will do. But, Charles, I haven't a hammer; and what's an auctioneer without his hammer?

CHAS. SURF. Egad, that's true. (*Looking about and picking up a roll of parchment, which he examines*) What parchment have we here? Oh, our genealogy in full. Here, Careless, you shall have no common bit of mahogany, here's the family tree for you, you rogue! This shall be your hammer, and now you may knock down my ancestors with their own pedigree.

SIR OLIV. (*Aside*) What an unnatural rogue!—an *ex post facto* parricide!

CARE. Yes, yes, here's a list of your generation indeed;—faith, Charles, this is the most convenient thing you could have found for the business, for 'twill not only serve as a hammer, but a catalogue into the bargain. Come, begin—A-going, a-going, a-going!

CHAS. SURF. Bravo, Careless! Well, here's my great uncle, Sir Richard Ravelin, a marvellous good general in his day, I assure you. He served in all the Duke of Marlborough's wars, and got that cut over his eye at the battle of Malplaquet. What say you, Mr. Premium? look at him—there's a hero! not cut out of his feathers, as your modern clipped captains are, but enveloped in wig and regimentals, as a general should be. What do you bid?

SIR OLIV. (*Aside to* MOSES) Bid him speak.

MOS. Mr. Premium would have you speak.

CHAS. SURF. Why, then, he shall have him for ten pounds, and I'm sure that's not dear for a staff-officer.

SIR OLIV. (*Aside*) Heaven deliver me! his famous uncle Richard for ten pounds!—(*Aloud*) Very well, sir, I take him at that.

CHAS. SURF. Careless, knock down my uncle Richard.—Here, now, is a maiden sister of his, my great-aunt Deborah, done by Kneller, in his best manner, and esteemed a very formidable likeness. There she is, you see, a shepherdess feeding her flock. You shall have her for five pounds ten—the sheep are worth the money.

SIR OLIV. (*Aside*) Ah! poor Deborah! a woman who set such a value on herself!—(*Aloud*) Five pounds ten—she's mine.

CHAS. SURF. Knock down my aunt Deborah! Here, now, are two that were a sort of cousins of theirs.—You see, Moses, these pictures were done some time ago, when beaux wore wigs, and the ladies their own hair.

SIR OLIV. Yes, truly, head-dresses appear to have been a little lower in those days.

CHAS. SURF. Well, take that couple for the same.

MOS. 'Tis a good bargain.

CHAS. SURF. Careless!—This, now, is a grandfather of my mother's, a learned judge, well known on the western circuit.—What do you rate him at, Moses?

MOS. Four guineas.

CHAS. SURF. Four guineas! Gad's life, you don't bid me the price of his wig.—Mr. Premium, you have more respect for the woolsack; do let us knock his lordship down at fifteen.

SIR OLIV. By all means.

CARE. Gone.

CHAS. SURF. And there are two brothers of his, William and Walter Blunt, Esquires, both members of Parliament, and noted speakers; and, what's very extraordinary, I believe, this is the first time they were ever bought or sold.

SIR OLIV. That is very extraordinary, indeed! I'll take them at your own price, for the honor of Parliament.

CARE. Well said, little Premium! I'll knock them down at forty.

CHAS. SURF. Here's a jolly fellow—I don't know what relation, but he was mayor of Norwich: take him at eight pounds.

SIR OLIV. No, no; six will do for the mayor.

CHAS. SURF. Come, make it guineas, and

I'll throw you the two aldermen there into the bargain.

SIR OLIV. They're mine.

CHAS. SURF. Careless, knock down the mayor and aldermen. But, plague on't! we shall be all day retailing in this manner; do let us deal wholesale: what say you, little Premium? Give me three hundred pounds for the rest of the family in the lump.

CARE. Ay, ay, that will be the best way.

SIR OLIV. Well, well, anything to accommodate you; they are mine. But there is one portrait which you have always passed over.

CARE. What, that ill-looking little fellow over the settee?

SIR OLIV. Yes, sir, I mean that; though I don't think him so ill-looking a little fellow, by any means.

CHAS. SURF. What, that? Oh; that's my uncle Oliver! 'Twas done before he went to India.

CARE. Your uncle Oliver! Gad, then you'll never be friends, Charles. That, now, to me, is as stern a looking rogue as ever I saw; an unforgiving eye, and a damned disinheriting countenance! an inveterate knave, depend on't. Don't you think so, little Premium?

SIR OLIV. Upon my soul, sir, I do not; I think it is as honest a looking face as any in the room, dead or alive. But I suppose uncle Oliver goes with the rest of the lumber?

CHAS. SURF. No, hang it! I'll not part with poor Noll. The old fellow has been very good to me, and, egad, I'll keep his picture while I've a room to put it in.

SIR OLIV. (Aside) The rogue's my nephew after all!—(Aloud) But, sir, I have somehow taken a fancy to that picture.

CHAS. SURF. I'm sorry for't, for you certainly will not have it. Oons, haven't you got enough of them?

SIR OLIV. (Aside) I forgive him everything!—(Aloud) But, sir, when I take a whim in my head, I don't value money. I'll give you as much for that as for all the rest.

CHAS. SURF. Don't tease me, master broker; I tell you I'll not part with it, and there's an end of it.

SIR OLIV. (He sits down to write, saying aside) How like his father the dog is.—(Aloud) Well, well, I have done.—(Aside) I did not perceive it before, but I think I never saw such a striking resemblance.—

(Aloud) Here is a draught for your sum.

CHAS. SURF. Why, 'tis for eight hundred pounds!

SIR OLIV. You will not let Sir Oliver go?

CHAS. SURF. Zounds! no! I tell you, once more.

SIR OLIV. Then never mind the difference, we'll balance that another time. But give me your hand on the bargain; you are an honest fellow, Charles—I beg pardon, sir, for being so free.—Come, Moses.

CHAS. SURF. Egad, this is a whimsical old fellow!—But hark'ee, Premium, you'll prepare lodgings for these gentlemen.

SIR OLIV. Yes, yes, I'll send for them in a day or two.

CHAS. SURF. But hold; do now send a genteel conveyance for them, for, I assure you, they were most of them used to ride in their own carriages.

SIR OLIV. I will, I will—for all but Oliver.

CHAS. SURF. Ay, all but the little nabob.

SIR OLIV. You're fixed on that?

CHAS. SURF. Peremptorily.

SIR OLIV. (Aside) A dear extravagant rogue!—(Aloud) Good day!—Come, Moses. —(Aside) Let me hear now who dares call him profligate! (Exit with MOSES)

CARE. Why, this is the oddest genius of the sort I ever met with!

CHAS. SURF. Egad, he's the prince of brokers, I think. I wonder how the devil Moses got acquainted with so honest a fellow.—(Looks out the door) Ha! here's Rowley.—Do, Careless, say I'll join the company in a few moments.

CARE. I will—but don't let that old blockhead persuade you to squander any of that money on old musty debts, or any such nonsense; for tradesmen, Charles, are the most exorbitant fellows.

CHAS. SURF. Very true, and paying them is only encouraging them.

CARE. Nothing else.

CHAS. SURF. Ay, ay, never fear.—(Exit CARELESS) So! this was an odd old fellow, indeed. Let me see, two-thirds of these five hundred and thirty odd pounds are mine by right. 'Fore Heaven! I find one's ancestors are more valuable relations than I took them for!—(Bows ceremoniously to the pictures) Ladies and gentlemen, your most obedient and very grateful servant.

(*Enter* ROWLEY)

Ha! old Rowley! egad, you are just come in time to take leave of your old acquaintance.

Row. Yes, I heard they were a-going. But I wonder you can have such spirits under so many distresses.

CHAS. SURF. Why, there's the point! my distresses are so many, that I can't afford to part with my spirits; but I shall be rich and splenetic, all in good time. However, I suppose you are surprised that I am not more sorrowful at parting with so many near relations; to be sure, 'tis very affecting; but you see they never move a muscle, so why should I?

Row. There's no making you serious a moment.

CHAS. SURF. Yes, faith, I am so now. (*Giving him the draught*) Here, my honest Rowley, here, get me this changed directly, and take a hundred pounds of it immediately to old Stanley.

Row. A hundred pounds! Consider only——

CHAS. SURF. Gad's life, don't talk about it! poor Stanley's wants are pressing, and, if you don't make haste, we shall have some one call that has a better right to the money.

Row. Ah! there's the point! I never will cease dunning you with the old proverb——

CHAS. SURF. *Be just before you're generous.*—Why, so I would if I could; but Justice is an old hobbling beldame, and I can't get her to keep pace with Generosity, for the soul of me.

Row. Yet, Charles, believe me, one hour's reflection——

CHAS. SURF. Ay, ay, it's very true; but, hark'ee, Rowley, while I have, by Heaven I'll give; so, damn your economy! And now for hazard. (*Exeunt*)

SCENE II. *Another Room in* CHARLES SURFACE'S *House.*

(*Enter* SIR OLIVER SURFACE *and* MOSES)

Mos. Well, sir, I think, as Sir Peter said, you have seen Mr. Charles in high glory; 'tis great pity he's so extravagant.

SIR OLIV. True, but he would not sell my picture.

Mos. And loves wine and women so much.

SIR OLIV. But he would not sell my picture.

Mos. And games so deep.

SIR OLIV. But he would not sell my picture. Oh, here's Rowley.

(*Enter* ROWLEY)

Row. So, Sir Oliver, I find you have made a purchase——

SIR OLIV. Yes, yes, our young rake has parted with his ancestors like old tapestry.

Row. And here has he commissioned me to re-deliver you part of the purchase-money —I mean, though, in your necessitous character of old Stanley.

Mos. Ah! there is the pity of all: he is so damned charitable.

Row. And I left a hosier and two tailors in the hall, who, I'm sure, won't be paid, and this hundred would satisfy them.

SIR OLIV. Well, well, I'll pay his debts, and his benevolence too. But now I am no more a broker, and you shall introduce me to the elder brother as old Stanley.

Row. Not yet awhile; Sir Peter, I know, means to call there about this time.

(*Enter* TRIP)

TRIP. Oh, gentlemen, I beg pardon for not showing you out; this way—Moses, a word. (*Exit with* MOSES)

SIR OLIV. There's a fellow for you! Would you believe it, that puppy intercepted the Jew on our coming, and wanted to raise money before he got to his master!

Row. Indeed.

SIR OLIV. Yes, they are now planning an annuity business. Ah, Master Rowley, in my days servants were content with the follies of their masters, when they were worn a little threadbare; but now they have their vices, like their birthday clothes, with the gloss on. (*Exeunt*)

SCENE III. *A Library in* JOSEPH SURFACE'S *House.*

(*Enter* JOSEPH SURFACE *and* SERVANT)

JOS. SURF. No letter from Lady Teazle?

SER. No, sir.

JOS. SURF. (*Aside*) I am surprised she has not sent, if she is prevented from coming. Sir Peter certainly does not suspect me. Yet I wish I may not lose the heiress through the scrape I have drawn myself into with the wife; however, Charles's imprudence and bad character are great points in my favor.

(*Knocking off stage*)

SER. Sir, I believe that must be Lady Teazle.

JOS. SURF. Hold! See whether it is or not, before you go to the door: I have a particular message for you if it should be my brother.

SER. (*Looking out the window*) 'Tis her ladyship, sir; she always leaves the chair at the milliner's in the next street.

JOS. SURF. Stay, stay: draw that screen before the window—that will do;—my opposite neighbor is a maiden lady of so curious a temper.—(SERVANT *draws the screen, and exit*) I have a difficult hand to play in this affair. Lady Teazle has lately suspected my views on Maria; but she must by no means be let into that secret,—at least, till I have her more in my power.

(*Enter* LADY TEAZLE)

LADY TEAZ. What sentiment in soliloquy now? Have you been very impatient? O Lud! don't pretend to look grave. I vow I couldn't come before.

JOS. SURF. O madam, punctuality is a species of constancy very unfashionable in a lady of quality.

(*Places chairs, and sits after* LADY TEAZLE *is seated*)

LADY TEAZ. Upon my word, you ought to pity me. Do you know Sir Peter is grown so ill-natured to me of late, and so jealous of Charles too—that's the best of the story, isn't it?

JOS. SURF. (*Aside*) I am glad my scandalous friends keep that up.

LADY TEAZ. I am sure I wish he would let Maria marry him, and then perhaps he would be convinced; don't you, Mr. Surface?

JOS. SURF. (*Aside*) Indeed I do not.—(*Aloud*) Oh, certainly I do! for then my dear Lady Teazle would also be convinced how wrong her suspicions were of my having any design on the silly girl.

LADY TEAZ. Well, well, I'm inclined to believe you. But isn't it provoking, to have the most ill-natured things said at one? And there's my friend Lady Sneerwell has circulated I don't know how many scandalous tales of me, and all without any foundation, too; that's what vexes me.

JOS. SURF. Ay, madam, to be sure, that is the provoking circumstance—(*Slyly*) without foundation. Yes, yes, there's the mortification, indeed; for, when a scandalous story is believed against one, there certainly is no comfort like the consciousness of having deserved it.

LADY TEAZ. No, to be sure, then I'd forgive their malice; but to attack me, who am really so innocent, and who never say an ill-natured thing of anybody—that is, of any friend; and then Sir Peter, too, to have him so peevish, and so suspicious, when I know the integrity of my own heart—indeed 'tis monstrous!

JOS. SURF. But, my dear Lady Teazle, 'tis your own fault if you suffer it. When a husband entertains a groundless suspicion of his wife, and withdraws his confidence from her, the original compact is broken, and she owes it to the honor of her sex to endeavor to outwit him.

LADY TEAZ. Indeed! So that, if he suspects me without cause, it follows, that the best way of curing his jealousy is to give him reason for't?

JOS. SURF. Undoubtedly—for your husband should never be deceived in you: and in that case it becomes you to be frail in compliment to his discernment.

LADY TEAZ. To be sure, what you say is very reasonable, and when the consciousness of my innocence——

JOS. SURF. Ah, my dear madam, there is the great mistake; 'tis this very conscious innocence that is of the greatest prejudice to you. What is it makes you negligent of forms, and careless of the world's opinion? why, the consciousness of your own innocence. What makes you thoughtless in your conduct, and apt to run into a thousand little imprudences? why, the consciousness of your own innocence. What makes you impatient of Sir Peter's temper, and outrageous at his suspicions? why, the consciousness of your innocence.

LADY TEAZ. 'Tis very true!

Jos. SURF. Now, my dear Lady Teazle, if you would but once make a trifling *faux pas,* you can't conceive how cautious you would grow, and how ready to humor and agree with your husband.

LADY TEAZ. Do you think so?

Jos. SURF. Oh, I'm sure on't; and then you would find all scandal would cease at once, for—in short, your character at present is like a person in a plethora, absolutely dying from too much health.

LADY TEAZ. So, so; then I perceive your prescription is, that I must sin in my own defence, and part with my virtue to preserve my reputation?

Jos. SURF. Exactly so, upon my credit, ma'am.

LADY TEAZ. Well, certainly this is the oddest doctrine, and the newest receipt for avoiding calumny?

Jos. SURF. An infallible one, believe me. Prudence, like experience, must be paid for.

LADY TEAZ. Why, if my understanding were once convinced——

Jos. SURF. Oh, certainly, madam, your understanding should be convinced. Yes, yes—Heaven forbid I should persuade you to do anything you thought wrong. No, no, I have too much honor to desire it.

LADY TEAZ. Don't you think we may as well leave honor out of the argument?
(*Rises*)

Jos. SURF. Ah, the ill effects of your country education, I see, still remain with you.

LADY TEAZ. I doubt they do, indeed; and I will fairly own to you, that if I could be persuaded to do wrong, it would be by Sir Peter's ill-usage sooner than your honorable logic, after all.

Jos. SURF. Then, by this hand, which he is unworthy of—— (*Taking her hand*)

(*Re-enter* SERVANT)

(*Jumping away from* LADY TEAZLE) 'Sdeath, you blockhead—what do you want?

SER. I beg your pardon, sir, but I thought you would not choose Sir Peter to come up without announcing him.

Jos. SURF. Sir Peter!—Oons—the devil!

LADY TEAZ. Sir Peter! O Lud! I'm ruined! I'm ruined!

SER. Sir, 'twasn't I let him in.

LADY TEAZ. Oh! I'm quite undone! What will become of me? Now, Mr. Logic—Oh! mercy, sir, he's on the stairs—I'll get behind here—and if ever I'm so imprudent again——
(*Goes behind the screen*)

Jos. SURF. Give me that book.
(*Sits down.* SERVANT *pretends to adjust his chair*)

(*Enter* SIR PETER TEAZLE)

SIR PET. Ay, ever improving himself. (JOSEPH *pretends to be absorbed in his book*) Mr. Surface, Mr. Surface——
(*Pats* JOSEPH *on the shoulder*)

Jos. SURF. Oh, my dear Sir Peter, I beg your pardon. (*Gaping, throws away the book*) I have been dozing over a stupid book. Well, I am much obliged to you for this call. You haven't been here, I believe, since I fitted up this room. Books, you know, are the only things I am a coxcomb in.

SIR PET. 'Tis very neat indeed. Well, well, that's proper; and you can make even your screen a source of knowledge—hung, I perceive, with maps.

Jos. SURF. Oh, yes, I find great use in that screen.

SIR PET. I dare say you must, certainly, when you want to find anything in a hurry.

Jos. SURF. (*Aside*) Ay, or to hide anything in a hurry either.

SIR PET. Well, I have a little private business——

Jos. SURF. (*To* SERVANT) You need not stay.

SER. No, sir. (*Exit*)

Jos. SURF. Here's a chair, Sir Peter—I beg——

SIR PET. Well, now we are alone, there is a subject, my dear friend, on which I wish to unburden my mind to you—a point of the greatest moment to my peace; in short, my good friend, Lady Teazle's conduct of late has made me very unhappy.

Jos. Surf. Indeed! I am very sorry to hear it.

Sir Pet. Yes, 'tis but too plain she has not the least regard for me; but, what's worse, I have pretty good authority to suppose she has formed an attachment to another.

Jos. Surf. Indeed! you astonish me!

Sir Pet. Yes! and, between ourselves, I think I've discovered the person.

Jos. Surf. How! you alarm me exceedingly.

Sir Pet. Ay, my dear friend, I knew you would sympathize with me!

Jos. Surf. Yes, believe me, Sir Peter, such a discovery would hurt me just as much as it would you.

Sir Pet. I am convinced of it. Ah! it is a happiness to have a friend whom we can trust even with one's family secrets. But have you no guess who I mean?

Jos. Surf. I haven't the most distant idea. It can't be Sir Benjamin Backbite!

Sir Pet. Oh, no! what say you to Charles?

Jos. Surf. My brother! impossible!

Sir Pet. Oh, my dear friend, the goodness of your own heart misleads you. You judge of others by yourself.

Jos. Surf. Certainly, Sir Peter, the heart that is conscious of its own integrity is ever slow to credit another's treachery.

Sir Pet. True; but your brother has no sentiment—you never hear him talk so.

Jos. Surf. Yet I can't but think Lady Teazle herself has too much principle.

Sir Pet. Ay; but what is principle against the flattery of a handsome, lively young fellow?

Jos. Surf. That's very true.

Sir Pet. And then, you know, the difference of our ages makes it very improbable that she should have any great affection for me; and if she were to be frail, and I were to make it public, why the town would only laugh at me, the foolish old bachelor, who had married a girl.

Jos. Surf. That's true, to be sure—they would laugh.

Sir Pet. Laugh! ay, and make ballads, and paragraphs, and the devil knows what of me.

Jos. Surf. No, you must never make it public.

Sir Pet. But then again—that the nephew of my old friend, Sir Oliver, should be the person to attempt such a wrong, hurts me more nearly.

Jos. Surf. Ay, there's the point. When ingratitude barbs the dart of injury, the wound has double danger in it.

Sir Pet. Ay—I, that was, in a manner, left his guardian; in whose house he had been so often entertained; who never in my life denied him—my advice!

Jos. Surf. Oh, 'tis not to be credited! There may be a man capable of such baseness, to be sure; but, for my part, till you can give me positive proofs, I cannot but doubt it. However, if it should be proved on him, he is no longer a brother of mine—I disclaim kindred with him: for the man who can break the laws of hospitality, and tempt the wife of his friend, deserves to be branded as the pest of society.

Sir Pet. What a difference there is between you! What noble sentiments!

Jos. Surf. Yet I cannot suspect Lady Teazle's honor.

Sir Pet. I am sure I wish to think well of her, and to remove all ground of quarrel between us. She has lately reproached me more than once with having made no settlement on her; and, in our last quarrel, she almost hinted that she should not break heart if I was dead. Now, as we seem to differ in our ideas of expense, I have resolved she shall have her own way, and be her own mistress in that respect for the future; and, if I were to die, she will find I have not been inattentive to her interest while living. (*Taking papers from his pocket*) Here, my friend, are the drafts of two deeds, which I wish to have your opinion on. By one, she will enjoy eight hundred a year independent while I live; and, by the other, the bulk of my fortune at my death.

Jos. Surf. This conduct, Sir Peter, is indeed truly generous.—(*Aside*) I wish it may not corrupt my pupil.

Sir Pet. Yes, I am determined she shall have no cause to complain, though I would not have her acquainted with the latter instance of my affection yet awhile.

Jos. Surf. (*Aside*) Nor I, if I could help it.

Sir Pet. And now, my dear friend, if you please, we will talk over the situation of your hopes with Maria.

Jos. Surf. (*Softly*) Oh, no, Sir Peter; another time, if you please.

Sir Pet. I am sensibly chagrined at the little progress you seem to make in her affections.

Jos. Surf. (*Softly*) I beg you will not mention it. What are my disappointments when your happiness is in debate!—(*Aside*) 'Sdeath, I shall be ruined every way!

Sir Pet. And though you are averse to my acquainting Lady Teazle with your passion, I'm sure she's not your enemy in the affair.

Jos. Surf. Pray, Sir Peter, now oblige me. I am really too much affected by the subject we have been speaking of to bestow a thought on my own concerns. The man who is entrusted with his friend's distresses can never——

(*Re-enter* Servant)

Well, sir?

Ser. Your brother, sir, is speaking to a gentleman in the street, and says he knows you are within.

Jos. Surf. 'Sdeath, blockhead, I'm not within—I'm out for the day.

Sir Pet. Stay—hold—a thought has struck me:—you shall be at home.

Jos. Surf. Well, well, let him up. (*Exit* Servant)—(*Aside*) He'll interrupt Sir Peter, however.

Sir Pet. Now, my good friend, oblige me, I entreat you. Before Charles comes, let me conceal myself somewhere, then do you tax him on the point we have been talking, and his answer may satisfy me at once.

Jos. Surf. Oh, fie, Sir Peter! would you have me join in so mean a trick?—to trepan my brother too?

Sir Pet. Nay, you tell me you are sure he is innocent; if so, you do him the greatest service by giving him an opportunity to clear himself, and you will set my heart at rest. Come, you shall not refuse me. (*Going up to the screen*) Here, behind the screen will be —(*As he starts around the screen he sees a corner of* Lady Teazle's *skirt and starts back*) Hey! what the devil! there seems to be one listener here already—I'll swear I saw a petticoat!

Jos. Surf. Ha! ha! ha! Well, this is ridiculous enough. I'll tell you, Sir Peter, though I hold a man of intrigue to be a most despicable character, yet you know, it does not follow that one is to be an absolute Joseph either! Hark'ee, 'tis a little French milliner, a silly rogue that plagues me; and having some character to lose, on your coming, sir, she ran behind the screen.

Sir Pet. Ah, a rogue—— But, egad, she has overheard all I have been saying of my wife.

Jos. Surf. Oh, 'twill never go any farther, you may depend upon it!

Sir Pet. No! then, faith, let her hear it out.—Here's a closet will do as well.

Jos. Surf. Well, go in there.

Sir Pet. (*Shaking his finger at* Joseph) Sly rogue! sly rogue!   (*Goes into the closet*)

Jos. Surf. A narrow escape, indeed! and a curious situation I'm in, to part man and wife in this manner.

Lady Teaz. (*Peeping*) Couldn't I steal off?

Jos. Surf. Keep close, my angel!

Sir Pet. (*Peeping*) Joseph, tax him home.

Jos. Surf. Back, my dear friend!

Lady Teaz. (*Peeping*) Couldn't you lock Sir Peter in?

Jos. Surf. Be still, my life!

Sir Pet. (*Peeping*) You're sure the little milliner won't blab?

Jos. Surf. In, in, my dear Sir Peter!— 'Fore Gad, I wish I had a key to the door.

(*Enter* Charles Surface)

Chas. Surf. Holla! brother, what has been the matter? Your fellow would not let me up at first. What! have you had a Jew or a wench with you?

Jos. Surf. (*With dignity*) Neither, brother, I assure you.

Chas. Surf. But what has made Sir Peter steal off? I thought he had been with you.

Jos. Surf. He was, brother; but, hearing you were coming, he did not choose to stay.

Chas. Surf. What! was the old gentleman afraid I wanted to borrow money of him!

Jos. Surf. No, sir: but I am sorry to find, Charles, you have lately given that worthy man grounds for great uneasiness.

Chas. Surf. Yes, they tell me I do that to

a great many worthy men. But how so, pray?

Jos. Surf. To be plain with you, brother, he thinks you are endeavoring to gain Lady Teazle's affections from him.

Chas. Surf. Who, I? O Lud! not I, upon my word.—Ha! ha! ha! ha! so the old fellow has found out that he has got a young wife, has he?—or, what is worse, Lady Teazle has found out she has an old husband?

Jos. Surf. This is no subject to jest on, brother. He who can laugh——

Chas. Surf. True, true, as you were going to say—then, seriously, I never had the least idea of what you charge me with, upon my honor.

Jos. Surf. (Raising his voice) Well, it will give Sir Peter great satisfaction to hear this.

Chas. Surf. To be sure, I once thought the lady seemed to have taken a fancy to me; but, upon my soul, I never gave her the least encouragement. Besides, you know my attachment to Maria.

Jos. Surf. But sure, brother, even if Lady Teazle had betrayed the fondest partiality for you——

Chas. Surf. Why, look'ee, Joseph, I hope I shall never deliberately do a dishonorable action; but if a pretty woman was purposely to throw herself in my way—and that pretty woman married to a man old enough to be her father——

Jos. Surf. Well!

Chas. Surf. Why, I believe I should be obliged to borrow a little of your morality, that's all. But, brother, do you know now that you surprise me exceedingly, by naming me with Lady Teazle; for i'faith, I always understood you were her favorite.

Jos. Surf. Oh, for shame, Charles! This retort is foolish.

Chas. Surf. Nay, I swear I have seen you exchange such significant glances——

Jos. Surf. Nay, nay, sir, this is no jest.

Chas. Surf. Egad, I'm serious! Don't you remember one day, when I called here——

Jos. Surf. Nay, pr'ythee, Charles——

Chas. Surf. And found you together——

Jos. Surf. Zounds, sir, I insist——

Chas. Surf. And another time, when your servant——

Jos. Surf. Brother, brother, a word with you!—(Aside) Gad, I must stop him.

Chas. Surf. Informed, I say, that——

Jos. Surf. Hush! I beg your pardon, but Sir Peter has overheard all we have been saying. I knew you would clear yourself, or I should not have consented.

Chas. Surf. How, Sir Peter! Where is he?

Jos. Surf. Softly, there!

                    (Points to the closet)

Chas. Surf. (Starting toward the closet) Oh, 'fore Heaven, I'll have him out. Sir Peter, come forth!

Jos. Surf. No, no——

Chas. Surf. I say, Sir Peter, come into court.—(Opens the closet door and pulls out Sir Peter) What! my old guardian!—What! —turn inquisitor, and take evidence, incog.? Oh, fie! Oh, fie!

Sir Pet. Give me your hand, Charles—I believe I have suspected you wrongfully; but you mustn't be angry with Joseph—'twas my plan!

Chas. Surf. Indeed!

Sir Pet. But I acquit you. I promise you I don't think near so ill of you as I did. What I have heard has given me great satisfaction.

Chas. Surf. Egad, then, 'twas lucky you didn't hear any more. Wasn't it, Joseph?

Sir Pet. Ah! you would have retorted on him.

Chas. Surf. Ah, ay, that was a joke.

Sir Pet. Yes, yes, I know his honor too well.

Chas. Surf. But you might as well have suspected him as me in this matter, for all that. Mightn't he, Joseph?

Sir Pet. Well, well, I believe you.

Jos. Surf. (Aside) Would they were both out of the room!

Sir Pet. And in future, perhaps, we may not be such strangers.

(Re-enter Servant and whispers to Joseph Surface)

Ser. Lady Sneerwell is below, and says she will come up.

Jos. Surf. Gentlemen, I beg pardon—I must wait on you downstairs; here's a person come on particular business.

Chas. Surf. Well, you can see him in another room. Sir Peter and I have not met a long time, and I have something to say to him.

Jos. Surf. (*Aside*) They must not be left together.—(*Aloud*) I'll send Lady Sneerwell away, and return directly.—(*Aside to* Sir Peter) Sir Peter, not a word of the French milliner.

Sir Pet. (*Aside to* Joseph Surface) I! not for the world!—(*Exit* Joseph Surface) Ah, Charles, if you associated more with your brother, one might indeed hope for your reformation. He is a man of sentiment. Well, there is nothing in the world so noble as a man of sentiment.

Chas. Surf. Psha! he is too moral by half; and so apprehensive of his good name, as he calls it, that I suppose he would as soon let a priest into his house as a wench.

Sir Pet. No, no,—come, come,—you wrong him. No, no, Joseph is no rake, but he is no such saint either, in that respect.—(*Aside*) I have a great mind to tell him—we should have such a laugh at Joseph.

Chas. Surf. Oh, hang him! he's a very anchorite, a young hermit!

Sir Pet. Hark'ee—you must not abuse him: he may chance to hear of it again, I promise you.

Chas. Surf. Why, you won't tell him?

Sir Pet. No—but—this way.—(*Aside*) Egad, I'll tell him. (*Aloud*) Hark'ee, have you a mind to have a good laugh at Joseph?

Chas. Surf. I should like it of all things.

Sir Pet. Then, i'faith, we will! I'll be quit with him for discovering me. (*Whispering*) He had a girl with him when I called.

Chas. Surf. What! Joseph? you jest.

Sir Pet. Hush!—a little French milliner—and the best of the jest is—she's in the room now.

Chas. Surf. The devil she is!

Sir Pet. Hush! I tell you.
(*Points to the screen*)

Chas. Surf. Behind the screen! Odds life, let's unveil her!

Sir Pet. No, no, he's coming:—you shan't, indeed!

Chas. Surf. Oh, egad, we'll have a peep at the little milliner!

Sir Pet. Not for the world!—Joseph will never forgive me.

Chas. Surf. I'll stand by you——

Sir Pet. Odds, here he is!
(Charles Surface *throws down the screen*)

(*Re-enter* Joseph Surface)

Chas. Surf. Lady Teazle, by all that's wonderful!

Sir Pet. Lady Teazle, by all that's damnable!

Chas. Surf. Sir Peter, this is one of the smartest French milliners I ever saw. (*Looking from one to another with glee*) Egad, you seem all to have been diverting yourselves here at hide and seek, and I don't see who is out of the secret. Shall I beg your ladyship to inform me? Not a word!—Brother, will you be pleased to explain this matter? What! is Morality dumb too?—Sir Peter, though I found you in the dark, perhaps you are not so now! All mute! Well—though I can make nothing of the affair, I suppose you perfectly understand one another; so I'll leave you to yourselves.—(*Going*) Brother, "I'm sorry to find you have given that worthy man grounds for so much uneasiness."—Sir Peter! "There's nothing in the world so noble as a man of sentiment!" (*Exit*)

Jos. Surf. Sir Peter—notwithstanding—I confess—that appearances are against me—if you will afford me your patience—I make no doubt—but I shall explain everything to your satisfaction.

Sir Pet. If you please, sir.

Jos. Surf. The fact is, sir, that Lady Teazle, knowing my pretensions to your ward Maria—I say, sir, Lady Teazle, being apprehensive of the jealousy of your temper—and knowing my friendship to the family—she, sir, I say—called here—in order that—I might explain these pretensions—but on your coming—being apprehensive—as I said—of your jealousy—she withdrew—and this, you may depend on it, is the whole truth of the matter.

Sir Pet. A very clear account, upon my word; and I dare swear the lady will vouch for every article of it.

Lady Teaz. For not one word of it, Sir Peter!

Sir Pet. How! don't you think it worth while to agree in the lie?

Lady Teaz. There is not one syllable of truth in what that gentleman has told you.

Sir Pet. I believe you, upon my soul, ma'am!

Jos. Surf. (*Aside to* Lady Teazle) 'Sdeath, madam, will you betray me?

LADY TEAZ. Good Mr. Hypocrite, by your leave, I'll speak for myself.

SIR PET. Ay, let her alone, sir; you'll find she'll make out a better story than you, without prompting.

LADY TEAZ. Hear me, Sir Peter!—I came here on no matter relating to your ward, and even ignorant of this gentleman's pretensions to her. But I came, seduced by his insidious arguments, at least to listen to his pretended passion, if not to sacrifice your honor to his baseness.

SIR PET. Now, I believe, the truth is coming, indeed!

JOS. SURF. The woman's mad!

LADY TEAZ. No, sir; she has recovered her senses, and your own arts have furnished her with the means.—Sir Peter, I do not expect you to credit me—but the tenderness you expressed for me, when I am sure you could not think I was a witness to it, has penetrated so to my heart, that had I left the place without the shame of this discovery, my future life should have spoken the sincerity of my gratitude. As for that smooth-tongued hypocrite, who would have seduced the wife of his too credulous friend, while he affected honorable addresses to his ward—I behold him now in a light so truly despicable, that I shall never again respect myself for having listened to him. (*She marches out*)

JOS. SURF. Notwithstanding all this, Sir Peter, Heaven knows——

SIR PET. That you are a villain! and so I leave you to your conscience. (*Going*)

JOS. SURF. (*Following* SIR PETER) You are too rash, Sir Peter; you shall hear me. The man who shuts out conviction by refusing to——

(*Exit* SIR PETER *followed by* JOSEPH, *still protesting*)

Act V

SCENE I. *The Library in* JOSEPH SURFACE's *House.*

(*Enter* JOSEPH SURFACE *and* SERVANT)

JOS. SURF. Mr. Stanley! and why should you think I would see him? You must know he comes to ask something.

SER. Sir, I should not have let him in, but that Mr. Rowley came to the door with him.

JOS. SURF. Psha! blockhead! to suppose that I should now be in a temper to receive visits from poor relations!—Well, why don't you show the fellow up?

SER. I will, sir.—Why, sir, it was not my fault that Sir Peter discovered my lady——

JOS. SURF. Go, fool!—(*Exit* SERVANT) Sure Fortune never played a man of my policy such a trick before! My character with Sir Peter, my hopes with Maria, destroyed in a moment! I'm in a rare humor to listen to other people's distresses! I shan't be able to bestow even a benevolent sentiment on Stanley.—So! here he comes, and Rowley with him. I must try to recover myself, and put a little charity into my face, however.

(*Exit*)

(*Enter* SIR OLIVER SURFACE *and* ROWLEY)

SIR OLIV. What! does he avoid us? That was he, was it not?

ROW. It was, sir. But I doubt you are come a little too abruptly. His nerves are so weak, that the sight of a poor relation may be too much for him. I should have gone first to break it to him.

SIR OLIV. Oh, plague of his nerves! Yet this is he whom Sir Peter extols as a man of the most benevolent way of thinking!

ROW. As to his way of thinking, I cannot pretend to decide; for, to do him justice, he appears to have as much speculative benevolence as any private gentleman in the kingdom, though he is seldom so sensual as to indulge himself in the exercise of it.

SIR OLIV. Yet he has a string of charitable sentiments at his fingers' ends.

ROW. Or, rather, at his tongue's end, Sir Oliver; for I believe there is no sentiment he has such faith in as that *Charity begins at home.*

SIR OLIV. And his, I presume, is of that domestic sort which never stirs abroad at all.

ROW. I doubt you'll find it so;—but he's coming. I mustn't seem to interrupt you; and you know, immediately as you leave him, I come in to announce your arrival in your real character.

Sir Oliv. True; and afterwards you'll meet me at Sir Peter's.

Row. Without losing a moment. (*Exit*)

Sir Oliv. I don't like the complaisance of his features.

(*Re-enter* Joseph Surface)

Jos. Surf. Sir, I beg you ten thousand pardons for keeping you a moment waiting.—Mr. Stanley, I presume.

Sir Oliv. At your service.

Jos. Surf. Sir, I beg you will do me the honor to sit down—I entreat you, sir.

Sir Oliv. Dear sir—there's no occasion.—(*Aside*) Too civil by half!

Jos. Surf. I have not the pleasure of knowing you, Mr. Stanley; but I am extremely happy to see you look so well. You were nearly related to my mother, I think, Mr. Stanley?

Sir Oliv. I was, sir; so nearly that my present poverty, I fear, may do discredit to her wealthy children, else I should not have presumed to trouble you.

Jos. Surf. Dear sir, there needs no apology: he that is in distress, though a stranger, has a right to claim kindred with the wealthy. I am sure I wish I was one of that class, and had it in my power to offer you even a small relief.

Sir Oliv. If your uncle, Sir Oliver, were here, I should have a friend.

Jos. Surf. I wish he was, sir, with all my heart; you should not want an advocate with him, believe me, sir.

Sir Oliv. I should not need one—my distresses would recommend me. But I imagined his bounty would enable you to become the agent of his charity.

Jos. Surf. My dear sir, you were strangely misinformed. Sir Oliver is a worthy man, a very worthy man; but avarice, Mr. Stanley, is the vice of age. I will tell you, my good sir, in confidence, what he has done for me has been a mere nothing; though people, I know, have thought otherwise, and, for my part, I never chose to contradict the report.

Sir Oliv. What! has he never transmitted you bullion—rupees—pagodas?

Jos. Surf. Oh, dear sir, nothing of the kind! No, no; a few presents now and then—china, shawls, congou tea, avadavats, and Indian crackers—little more, believe me.

Sir Oliv. (*Aside*) Here's gratitude for twelve thousand pounds!—Avadavats and Indian crackers!

Jos. Surf. Then, my dear sir, you have heard, I doubt not, of the extravagance of my brother; there are very few would credit what I have done for that unfortunate young man.

Sir Oliv. (*Aside*) Not I, for one!

Jos. Surf. The sums I have lent him! Indeed I have been exceedingly to blame; it was an amiable weakness; however, I don't pretend to defend it—and now I feel it doubly culpable, since it has deprived me of the pleasure of serving you, Mr. Stanley, as my heart dictates.

Sir Oliv. (*Aside*) Dissembler!—(*Aloud*) Then, sir, you can't assist me?

Jos. Surf. At present, it grieves me to say, I cannot; but, whenever I have the ability, you may depend upon hearing from me.

Sir Oliv. I am extremely sorry——

Jos. Surf. Not more than I, believe me. To pity, without the power to relieve, is still more painful than to ask and be denied.

Sir Oliv. Kind sir, your most obedient humble servant.

Jos. Surf. You leave me deeply affected, Mr. Stanley.—(*Calling to* Servant) William, be ready to open the door.

Sir Oliv. O, dear sir, no ceremony.

Jos. Surf. (*Bowing*) Your very obedient.

Sir Oliv. (*Bowing*) Your most obsequious.

Jos. Surf. You may depend upon hearing from me, whenever I can be of service.

Sir Oliv. Sweet sir, you are too good.

Jos. Surf. In the meantime I wish you health and spirits.

Sir Oliv. Your ever grateful and perpetual humble servant.

Jos. Surf. Sir, yours as sincerely.

Sir Oliv. (*Aside*) Charles!—you are my heir. (*Exit*)

Jos. Surf. This is one bad effect of a good character; it invites application from the unfortunate, and there needs no small degree of address to gain the reputation of benevolence without incurring the expense. The

silver ore of pure charity is an expensive article in the catalogue of man's good qualities;
whereas the sentimental French plate I use
instead of it makes just as good a show, and
pays no tax.

(*Re-enter* ROWLEY)

Row. Mr. Surface, your servant: I was
apprehensive of interrupting you, though my
business demands immediate attention, as
this note will inform you.

Jos. Surf. Always happy to see Mr. Rowley.—(*Reads the letter*) Sir Oliver Surface!—
My uncle arrived!

Row. He is, indeed: we have just parted
—quite well, after a speedy voyage, and impatient to embrace his worthy nephew.

Jos. Surf. I am astonished!—(*Calling to*
SERVANT) William! stop Mr. Stanley, if he's
not gone.

Row. Oh! he's out of reach, I believe.

Jos. Surf. Why did you not let me know
this when you came in together?

Row. I thought you had particular business. But I must be gone to inform your
brother, and appoint him here to meet your
uncle. He will be with you in a quarter of an
hour.

Jos. Surf. So he says. Well, I am strangely overjoyed at his coming.—(*Aside*) Never,
to be sure, was anything so damned unlucky!

Row. You will be delighted to see how
well he looks.

Jos. Surf. Oh! I'm overjoyed to hear it.—
(*Aside*)—Just at this time!

Row. I'll tell him how impatiently you expect him.

Jos. Surf. Do, do; pray give my best duty
and affection. Indeed, I cannot express the
sensations I feel at the thought of seeing him.
—(*Exit* ROWLEY) Certainly his coming just
at this time is the cruellest piece of ill fortune.   (*Exit*)

SCENE II. *A Room in* SIR PETER TEAZLE'S *House.*

(*Enter* MRS. CANDOUR *and* MAID)

MAID. Indeed, ma'am, my lady will see
nobody at present.

MRS. CAN. Did you tell her it was her
friend Mrs. Candour?

MAID. Yes, ma'am; but she begs you will
excuse her.

MRS. CAN. Do go again; I shall be glad to
see her, if it be only for a moment, for I am
sure she must be in great distress.—(*Exit*
MAID) Dear heart, how provoking! I'm not
mistress of half the circumstances! We shall
have the whole affair in the newspapers, with
the names of the parties at length, before I
have dropped the story at a dozen houses.

(*Enter* SIR BENJAMIN BACKBITE)

Oh, dear Sir Benjamin! you have heard, I
suppose——

SIR BEN. Of Lady Teazle and Mr. Surface——

MRS. CAN. And Sir Peter's discovery——

SIR BEN. Oh, the strangest piece of business, to be sure!

MRS. CAN. Well, I never was so surprised

in my life. I am so sorry for all parties, indeed.

SIR BEN. Now, I don't pity Sir Peter at all:
he was so extravagantly partial to Mr. Surface.

MRS. CAN. Mr. Surface! Why, 'twas with
Charles Lady Teazle was detected.

SIR BEN. No, no, I tell you: Mr. Surface
is the gallant.

MRS. CAN. No such thing! Charles is the
man. 'Twas Mr. Surface brought Sir Peter
on purpose to discover them.

SIR BEN. I tell you I had it from one——

MRS. CAN. And I have it from one——

SIR BEN. Who had it from one, who had
it——

MRS. CAN. From one immediately——But
here comes Lady Sneerwell; perhaps she
knows the whole affair.

(*Enter* LADY SNEERWELL)

LADY SNEER. So, my dear Mrs. Candour,
here's a sad affair of our friend Lady Teazle!

MRS. CAN. Ay, my dear friend, who would
have thought——

LADY SNEER. Well, there is no trusting to

appearances; though indeed, she was always too lively for me.

MRS. CAN. To be sure, her manners were a little too free; but then she was so young!

LADY SNEER. And had, indeed, some good qualities.

MRS. CAN. So she had, indeed. But have you heard the particulars?

LADY SNEER. No; but everybody says that Mr. Surface——

SIR BEN. Ay, there; I told you Mr. Surface was the man.

MRS. CAN. No, no: indeed the assignation was with Charles.

LADY SNEER. With Charles! You alarm me, Mrs. Candour.

MRS. CAN. Yes, yes: he was the lover. Mr. Surface, to do him justice, was only the in- former.

SIR BEN. Well, I'll not dispute with you, Mrs. Candour; but, be it which it may, I hope that Sir Peter's wound will not——

MRS. CAN. Sir Peter's wound! Oh, mercy! I didn't hear a word of their fighting.

LADY SNEER. Nor I, a syllable.

SIR BEN. No! what, no mention of the duel?

MRS. CAN. Not a word.

SIR BEN. Oh, yes: they fought before they left the room.

LADY SNEER. Pray let us hear.

MRS. CAN. Ay, do oblige us with the duel.

SIR BEN. "Sir," says Sir Peter, immediately after the discovery, "you are a most ungrateful fellow."

MRS. CAN. Ay, to Charles——

SIR BEN. No, no—to Mr. Surface—"a most ungrateful fellow; and old as I am, sir," says he, "I insist on immediate satisfaction."

MRS. CAN. Ay, that must have been to Charles; for 'tis very unlikely Mr. Surface should fight in his own house.

SIR BEN. 'Gad's life, ma'am, not at all— "giving me immediate satisfaction."—On this, ma'am, Lady Teazle, seeing Sir Peter in such danger, ran out of the room in strong hysterics, and Charles after her, calling out for hartshorn and water; then, madam, they began to fight with swords——

(Enter CRABTREE)

CRAB. With pistols, nephew—pistols! I have it from undoubted authority.

MRS. CAN. Oh, Mr. Crabtree, then it is all true!

CRAB. Too true, indeed, madam, and Sir Peter is dangerously wounded——

SIR BEN. By a thrust in second quite through his left side——

CRAB. By a bullet lodged in the thorax.

MRS. CAN. Mercy on me! Poor Sir Peter!

CRAB. Yes, madam; though Charles would have avoided the matter, if he could.

MRS. CAN. I knew Charles was the person.

SIR BEN. My uncle, I see, knows nothing of the matter.

CRAB. But Sir Peter taxed him with the basest ingratitude——

SIR BEN. That I told you, you know——

CRAB. Do, nephew, let me speak!—and insisted on immediate——

SIR BEN. Just as I said——

CRAB. Odds life, nephew, allow others to know something too! A pair of pistols lay on the bureau (for Mr. Surface, it seems, had come home the night before late from Salt-hill, where he had been to see the Montem with a friend, who has a son at Eton), so, unluckily, the pistols were left charged.

SIR BEN. I heard nothing of this.

CRAB. Sir Peter forced Charles to take one, and they fired, it seems, pretty nearly together. Charles's shot took effect, as I tell you, and Sir Peter's missed; but, what is very extraordinary, the ball struck against a little bronze Shakespeare that stood over the fire-place, grazed out of the window at a right angle, and wounded the postman, who was just coming to the door with a double letter from Northamptonshire.

SIR BEN. My uncle's account is more circumstantial, I confess; but I believe mine is the true one for all that.

LADY SNEER. (Aside) I am more interested in this affair than they imagine, and must have better information. (Exit)

SIR BEN. Ah! Lady Sneerwell's alarm is very easily accounted for.

CRAB. Yes, yes, they certainly do say—but that's neither here nor there.

MRS. CAN. But, pray, where is Sir Peter at present?

CRAB. Oh! they brought him home, and

he is now in the house, though the servants are ordered to deny him.

MRS. CAN. I believe so, and Lady Teazle, I suppose, attending him.

CRAB. Yes, yes; and I saw one of the faculty enter just before me.

SIR BEN. Hey! who comes here?

CRAB. Oh, this is he: the physician, depend on't.

MRS. CAN. Oh, certainly! it must be the physician; and now we shall know.

(*Enter* SIR OLIVER SURFACE)

CRAB. Well, doctor, what hopes?

MRS. CAN. Ay, doctor, how's your patient?

SIR BEN. Now, doctor, isn't it a wound with a small-sword?

CRAB. A bullet lodged in the thorax, for a hundred!

SIR OLIV. Doctor! A wound with a small-sword! and a bullet in the thorax?—Oons! are you mad, good people?

SIR BEN. Perhaps, sir, you are not a doctor?

SIR OLIV. Truly, I am to thank you for my degree, if I am.

CRAB. Only a friend of Sir Peter's, then, I presume. But, sir, you must have heard of his accident?

SIR OLIV. Not a word!

CRAB. Not of his being dangerously wounded?

SIR OLIV. The devil he is!

SIR BEN. Run through the body——

CRAB. Shot in the breast——

SIR BEN. By one Mr. Surface——

CRAB. Ay, the younger.

SIR OLIV. Hey! what the plague! you seem to differ strangely in your accounts: however, you agree that Sir Peter is dangerously wounded.

SIR BEN. Oh, yes, we agree in that.

CRAB. Yes, yes, I believe there can be no doubt in that.

SIR OLIV. Then, upon my word, for a person in that situation, he is the most imprudent man alive; for here he comes, walking as if nothing at all was the matter.

(*Enter* SIR PETER TEAZLE)

Odds heart, Sir Peter! you are come in good time, I promise you; for we had just given you over!

SIR BEN. (*Aside to* CRABTREE) Egad, uncle, this is the most sudden recovery!

SIR OLIV. Why, man! what do you do out of bed with a small-sword through your body, and a bullet lodged in your thorax?

SIR PET. A small-sword and a bullet?

SIR OLIV. Ay; these gentlemen would have killed you without law or physic, and wanted to dub me a doctor, to make me an accomplice.

SIR PET. Why, what is all this?

SIR BEN. We rejoice, Sir Peter, that the story of the duel is not true, and are sincerely sorry for your other misfortune.

SIR PET. (*Aside*) So, so; all over the town already.

CRAB. Though, Sir Peter, you were certainly vastly to blame to marry at your years.

SIR PET. Sir, what business is that of yours?

MRS. CAN. Though, indeed, as Sir Peter made so good a husband, he's very much to be pitied.

SIR PET. Plague on your pity, ma'am! I desire none of it.

SIR BEN. However, Sir Peter, you must not mind the laughing and jests you will meet with on the occasion.

SIR PET. Sir, sir! I desire to be master in my own house.

CRAB. 'Tis no uncommon case, that's one comfort.

SIR PET. I insist on being left to myself: without ceremony, I insist on your leaving my house directly!

MRS. CAN. Well, well, we are going; and depend on't, we'll make the best report of it we can. (*Exit*)

SIR PET. Leave my house!

CRAB. And tell how hardly you've been treated. (*Exit*)

SIR PET. Leave my house!

SIR BEN. And how patiently you bear it. (*Exit*)

SIR PET. Fiends! vipers! furies! Oh! that their own venom would choke them!

SIR OLIV. They are very provoking indeed, Sir Peter.

(*Enter* ROWLEY)

Row. I heard high words: what has ruffled you, sir?

Sir Pet. Psha! what signifies asking? Do I ever pass a day without my vexations?

Row. Well, I'm not inquisitive.

Sir Oliv. Well, Sir Peter, I have seen both my nephews in the manner we proposed.

Sir Pet. A precious couple they are!

Row. Yes, and Sir Oliver is convinced that your judgment was right, Sir Peter.

Sir Oliv. (*With a wink at* Rowley) Yes, I find Joseph is indeed the man, after all.

Row. Ay, as Sir Peter says, he is a man of sentiment.

Sir Oliv. And acts up to the sentiments he professes.

Row. It certainly is edification to hear him talk.

Sir Oliv. Oh, he's a model for the young men of the age! But how's this, Sir Peter? You don't join us in your friend Joseph's praise, as I expected.

Sir Pet. Sir Oliver, we live in a damned wicked world, and the fewer we praise the better.

Row. What! do you say so, Sir Peter, who were never mistaken in your life? (*Laughing at* Sir Peter)

Sir Pet. Psha! plague on you both! I see by your sneering you have heard the whole affair. I shall go mad among you!

Row. Then, to fret you no longer, Sir Peter, we are indeed acquainted with it all. I met Lady Teazle coming from Mr. Surface's so humbled, that she deigned to request me to be her advocate with you.

Sir Pet. And does Sir Oliver know all this?

Sir Oliv. Every circumstance.

Sir Pet. What, of the closet and the screen, hey?

Sir Oliv. Yes, yes, and the little French milliner. Oh, I have been vastly diverted with the story! ha! ha! ha!

Sir Pet. 'Twas very pleasant.

Sir Oliv. I never laughed more in my life, I assure you: ha! ha! ha!

Sir Pet. (*Ironically*) Oh, vastly diverting! ha! ha! ha!

Row. To be sure, Joseph with his sentiments! ha! ha! ha!

Sir Pet. Yes, his sentiments! ha! ha! ha! Hypocritical villain!

Sir Oliv. Ay, and that rogue Charles to pull Sir Peter out of the closet: ha! ha! ha!

Sir Pet. Ha! ha! 'twas devilish entertaining, to be sure!

Sir Oliv. Ha! ha! ha! Egad, Sir Peter, I should like to have seen your face when the screen was thrown down: ha! ha!

Sir Pet. Yes, my face when the screen was thrown down: ha! ha! ha! Oh, I must never show my head again!

Sir Oliv. But come, come, it isn't fair to laugh at you neither, my old friend; though, upon my soul, I can't help it.

Sir Pet. Oh, pray don't restrain your mirth on my account: it does not hurt me at all! I laugh at the whole affair myself. Yes, yes, I think being a standing jest for all one's acquaintance a very happy situation. Oh, yes, and then of a morning to read the paragraphs about Mr. S——, Lady ——, and Sir P——, will be so entertaining!

Row. Without affectation, Sir Peter, you may despise the ridicule of fools. But I see Lady Teazle going towards the next room; I am sure you must desire a reconciliation as earnestly as she does.

Sir Oliv. Perhaps my being here prevents her coming to you. Well, I'll leave honest Rowley to mediate between you; but he must bring you all presently to Mr. Surface's, where I am now returning, if not to reclaim a libertine, at least to expose hypocrisy.

Sir Pet. Ah, I'll be present at your discovering yourself there with all my heart; though 'tis a vile unlucky place for discoveries.

Row. We'll follow.

(*Exit* Sir Oliver Surface)

Sir Pet. She is not coming here, you see, Rowley.

Row. No, (*Pointing*) but she has left the door of that room open, you perceive. See, she is in tears.

Sir Pet. Certainly a little mortification appears very becoming in a wife. Don't you think it will do her good to let her pine a little?

Row. Oh, this is ungenerous in you!

Sir Pet. Well, I know not what to think.

You remember the letter I found of hers evidently intended for Charles!

Row. A mere forgery, Sir Peter! laid in your way on purpose. This is one of the points which I intend Snake shall give you conviction of.

Sir Pet. I wish I were once satisfied of that. She looks this way. What a remarkably elegant turn of the head she has. Rowley, I'll go to her.

Row. Certainly.

Sir Pet. Though, when it is known that we are reconciled, people will laugh at me ten times more.

Row. Let them laugh, and retort their malice only by showing them you are happy in spite of it.

Sir Pet. I'faith, so I will! and, if I'm not mistaken, we may yet be the happiest couple in the country.

Row. Nay, Sir Peter, he who once lays aside suspicion——

Sir Pet. Hold, Master Rowley! if you have any regard for me, never let me hear you utter anything like a sentiment: I have had enough of them to serve me the rest of my life. (*Exeunt*)

Scene III. *The Library in* Joseph Surface's *House.*

(*Enter* Joseph Surface *and* Lady Sneerwell)

Lady Sneer. Impossible! Will not Sir Peter immediately be reconciled to Charles, and of course no longer oppose his union with Maria? The thought is distraction to me.

Jos. Surf. Can passion furnish a remedy?

Lady Sneer. No, nor cunning either. Oh, I was a fool, an idiot, to league with such a blunderer!

Jos. Surf. Surely, Lady Sneerwell, I am the greatest sufferer; yet you see I bear the accident with calmness.

Lady Sneer. Because the disappointment doesn't reach your heart; your interest only attached you to Maria. Had you felt for her what I have for that ungrateful libertine, neither your temper nor hypocrisy could prevent your showing the sharpness of your vexation.

Jos. Surf. But why should your reproaches fall on me for this disappointment?

Lady Sneer. Are you not the cause of it? Had you not a sufficient field for your roguery in imposing upon Sir Peter, and supplanting your brother, but you must endeavor to seduce his wife? I hate such an avarice of crimes; 'tis an unfair monopoly, and never prospers.

Jos. Surf. Well, I admit I have been to blame. I confess I deviated from the direct road of wrong, but I don't think we're so totally defeated either.

Lady Sneer. No!

Jos. Surf. You tell me you have made a trial of Snake since we met, and that you still believe him faithful to us?

Lady Sneer. I do believe so.

Jos. Surf. And that he has undertaken, should it be necessary, to swear and prove, that Charles is at this time contracted by vows and honor to your ladyship, which some of his former letters to you will serve to support?

Lady Sneer. This, indeed, might have assisted.

Jos. Surf. Come, come; it is not too late yet.—(*Knocking at the door*) But hark! this is probably my uncle, Sir Oliver: retire to that room; we'll consult further when he's gone.

Lady Sneer. Well, but if he should find you out too.

Jos. Surf. Oh, I have no fear of that. Sir Peter will hold his tongue for his own credit's sake—and you may depend on it I shall soon discover Sir Oliver's weak side!

Lady Sneer. I have no diffidence of your abilities! only be constant to one roguery at a time.

Jos. Surf. I will, I will!—(*Exit* Lady Sneerwell) So! 'tis confounded hard, after such bad fortune, to be baited by one's confederate in evil. Well, at all events, my character is so much better than Charles's, that I certainly (*looking out the door*)—hey!—what —this is not Sir Oliver, but old Stanley again. Plague on't that he should return to tease me just now! I shall have Sir Oliver come and find him here—and—

(Enter Sir Oliver Surface*)*

Gad's life, Mr. Stanley, why have you come back to plague me at this time? You must not stay now, upon my word.

Sir Oliv. Sir, I hear your uncle Oliver is expected here, and though he has been so penurious to you, I'll try what he'll do for me.

Jos. Surf. Sir, 'tis impossible for you to stay now, so I must beg——Come any other time, and I promise you, you shall be assisted.

Sir Oliv. No: Sir Oliver and I must be acquainted.

Jos. Surf. Zounds, sir! then I insist on your quitting the room directly.

Sir Oliv. Nay, sir——

Jos. Surf. Sir, I insist on't!—*(Calling)* Here, William! show this gentleman out. Since you compel me, sir, not one moment— *(pushing* Sir Oliver *toward the door)* this is such insolence.

(Enter Charles Surface*)*

Chas. Surf. Heyday! what's the matter now? What the devil have you got hold of my little broker here? Zounds, brother, don't hurt little Premium. What's the matter, my little fellow?

Jos. Surf. So! he has been with you, too, has he?

Chas. Surf. To be sure he has. Why, he's as honest a little——But sure, Joseph, you have not been borrowing money too, have you?

Jos. Surf. Borrowing! no! But, brother, you know we expect Sir Oliver here every——

Chas. Surf. O Gad, that's true! Noll mustn't find the little broker here, to be sure.

Jos Surf. Yet, Mr. Stanley insists——

Chas. Surf. Stanley! why his name's Premium.

Jos. Surf. No, sir, Stanley.

Chas. Surf. No, no, Premium.

Jos. Surf. Well, no matter which—but——

Chas. Surf. Ay, ay, Stanley or Premium, 'tis the same thing, as you say; for I suppose he goes by half a hundred names, besides A. B. at the coffee-house. *(Knocking)*

Jos. Surf. 'Sdeath! here's Sir Oliver at the door. Now I beg, Mr. Stanley——

Chas. Surf. Ay, ay, and I beg, Mr. Premium——

Sir Oliv. Gentlemen——

Jos. Surf. Sir, by heaven you shall go!

Chas. Surf. *(both seize* Sir Oliver*)* Ay, out with him, certainly.

Sir Oliv. This violence——

Jos. Surf. Sir, 'tis your own fault.

Chas. Surf. Out with him, to be sure. *(They hustle him to the door)*

(Enter Sir Peter *and* Lady Teazle, Maria, *and* Rowley*)*

Sir Pet. My old friend, Sir Oliver—hey! What in the name of wonder!—here are dutiful nephews—assault their uncle at his first visit!

Lady Teaz. Indeed, Sir Oliver, 'twas well we came in to rescue you.

Row. Truly it was; for I perceive, Sir Oliver, the character of old Stanley was no protection to you.

Sir Oliv. Nor of Premium either: the necessities of the former could not extort a shilling from that benevolent gentleman; and with the other I stood a chance of faring worse than my ancestors, and being knocked down without being bid for.

Jos. Surf. Charles!

Chas. Surf. Joseph!

Jos. Surf. 'Tis now complete!

Chas. Surf. Very.

Sir Oliv. Sir Peter, my friend, and Rowley too—look on that elder nephew of mine. You know what he has already received from my bounty; and you also know how gladly I would have regarded half my fortune as held in trust for him? Judge, then, my disappointment in discovering him to be destitute of truth, charity, and gratitude!

Sir Pet. Sir Oliver, I should be more surprised at this declaration, if I had not myself found him to be mean, treacherous, and hypocritical.

Lady Teaz. And if the gentleman pleads not guilty to these, pray let him call me to his character.

Sir Pet. Then, I believe, we need add no more: if he knows himself, he will consider it as the most perfect punishment that he is known to the world.

CHAS. SURF. (*Aside*) If they talk this way to Honesty, what will they say to me, by-and-by?

(SIR PETER, LADY TEAZLE, *and* MARIA *retire to a corner and talk together*)

SIR OLIV. As for that prodigal, his brother, there——

CHAS. SURF. (*Aside*) Ay, now comes my turn: the damned family pictures will ruin me!

JOS. SURF. Sir Oliver—uncle, will you honor me with a hearing?

CHAS. SURF. (*Aside*) Now, if Joseph would make one of his long speeches, I might recollect myself a little.

SIR OLIV. (*To* JOSEPH) I suppose you would undertake to justify yourself?

JOS. SURF. I trust I could.

SIR OLIV. (*To* CHARLES SURFACE) Well, sir!—and you could justify yourself too, I suppose?

CHAS. SURF. Not that I know of, Sir Oliver.

SIR OLIV. What!—Little Premium has been let too much into the secret, I suppose?

CHAS. SURF. True, sir; (*grinning at* SIR OLIVER) but they were family secrets, and should not be mentioned again, you know.

ROW. Come, Sir Oliver, I know you cannot speak of Charles's follies with anger.

SIR OLIVER. Odd's heart, no more I can; nor with gravity either. Sir Peter, do you know the rogue bargained with me for all his ancestors; sold me judges and generals by the foot, and maiden aunts as cheap as broken china.

CHAS. SURF. To be sure, Sir Oliver, I did make a little free with the family canvas, that's the truth on't. My ancestors may rise in judgment against me, there's no denying it; but believe me sincere when I tell you—and upon my soul I would not say so if I was not—that if I do not appear mortified at the exposure of my follies, it is because I feel at this moment the warmest satisfaction at seeing you, my liberal benefactor.

SIR OLIV. Charles, I believe you. Give me your hand again: the ill-looking little fellow over the settee has made your peace.

CHAS. SURF. Then, sir, my gratitude to the original is still increased.

LADY TEAZ. (*Walking over to* SIR OLIVER) Yet, I believe, Sir Oliver, here (*indicating* MARIA) is one whom Charles is still more anxious to be reconciled to.

SIR OLIV. Oh, I have heard of his attachment there; and, with the young lady's pardon, if I construe right—that blush——

SIR PET. Well, child, speak your sentiments.

MAR. (*Embarrassed*) Sir, I have little to say, but that I shall rejoice to hear that he is happy; for me, whatever claim I had to his attention, I willingly resign to one who has a better title.

CHAS. SURF. How, Maria!

SIR PET. Heyday! what's the mystery now? While he appeared an incorrigible rake, you would give your hand to no one else; and now that he is likely to reform I'll warrant you won't have him.

MAR. His own heart and Lady Sneerwell know the cause.

CHAS. SURF. Lady Sneerwell!

JOS. SURF. Brother, it is with great concern I am obliged to speak on this point, but my regard to justice compels me, and Lady Sneerwell's injuries can no longer be concealed. (*Walks over and opens the door*)

(*Enter* LADY SNEERWELL)

SIR PET. So! another French milliner! Egad, he has one in every room in the house, I suppose!

LADY SNEER. Ungrateful Charles! Well may you be surprised, and feel for the indelicate situation your perfidy has forced me into.

CHAS. SURF. Pray, uncle, is this another plot of yours? For, as I have life, I don't understand it.

JOS. SURF. I believe, sir, there is but the evidence of one person more necessary to make it extremely clear.

SIR PET. And that person, I imagine, is Mr. Snake.—Rowley, you were perfectly right to bring him with us, and pray let him appear.

ROW. Walk in, Mr. Snake.

(*Enter* SNAKE)

I thought his testimony might be wanted;

however, it happens unluckily, that he comes to confront Lady Sneerwell, not to support her.

LADY SNEER. (*Terrified*) A villain! Treacherous to me at last! Speak, fellows, have you too conspired against me?

SNAKE. I beg your ladyship ten thousand pardons: you paid me extremely liberally for the lie in question; but I unfortunately have been offered double to speak the truth.

LADY SNEER. The torments of shame and disappointment on you all!

(*She starts toward the door*)

LADY TEAZ. Hold, Lady Sneerwell—before you go, let me thank you for the trouble you and that gentleman have taken, in writing letters from me to Charles, and answering them yourself; and let me also request you to make my respects to the scandalous college, of which you are president, and inform them, that Lady Teazle, licentiate, begs leave to return the diploma they granted her, as she leaves off practice, and kills characters no longer.

LADY SNEER. You too, madam!—provoking —insolent! May your husband live these fifty years! (*Exit*)

SIR PET. Oons! what a fury!

LADY TEAZ. A malicious creature, indeed!

SIR PET. What! not for her last wish?

LADY TEAZ. Oh, no!

SIR OLIV. Well, sir, and what have you to say now?

JOS. SURF. Sir, I am so confounded, to find that Lady Sneerwell could be guilty of suborning Mr. Snake in this manner, to impose on us all, that I know not what to say: however, lest her revengeful spirit should prompt her to injure my brother, I had certainly better follow her directly. (*Exit*)

SIR PET. Moral to the last drop!

SIR OLIV. Ay, and marry her, Joseph, if you can. Oil and vinegar!—egad, you'll do very well together.

ROW. I believe we have no more occasion for Mr. Snake at present?

SNAKE. Before I go, I beg pardon once for all, for whatever uneasiness I have been the humble instrument of causing to the parties present.

SIR PET. Well, well, you have made atonement by a good deed at last.

SNAKE. But I must request of the company, that it shall never be known.

SIR PET. Hey! what the plague! are you ashamed of having done a right thing once in your life?

SNAKE. Ah, sir, consider—I live by the badness of my character; and, if it were once known that I had been betrayed into an honest action, I should lose every friend I have in the world.

SIR OLIV. Well, well—we'll not traduce you by saying anything in your praise, never fear. (*Exit* SNAKE)

SIR PET. There's a precious rogue!

LADY TEAZ. See, Sir Oliver, there needs no persuasion now to reconcile your nephew and Maria.

SIR OLIV. Ay, ay, that's as it should be, and, egad, we'll have the wedding to-morrow morning.

CHAS. SURF. Thank you, dear uncle.

SIR PET. What, you rogue! don't you ask the girl's consent first?

CHAS. SURF. Oh, I have done that a long time—a minute ago—and she has looked yes.

MAR. For shame, Charles!—I protest, Sir Peter, there has not been a word——

SIR OLIV. Well, then, the fewer the better: may your love for each other never know abatement.

SIR PET. And may you live as happily together as Lady Teazle and I intend to do!

CHAS. SURF. Rowley, my old friend, I am sure you congratulate me; and I suspect that I owe you much.

SIR OLIV. You do, indeed, Charles.

ROW. If my efforts to serve you had not succeeded you would have been in my debt for the attempt—but deserve to be happy— and you over-repay me.

SIR PET. Ay, honest Rowley always said you would reform.

CHAS. SURF. Why as to reforming, Sir Peter, I'll make no promises, and that I take to be a proof that I intend to set about it. (*Taking* MARIA *by the hand*) But here shall be my monitor—my gentle guide.—Ah! can I leave the virtuous path those eyes illumine?

Though thou, dear maid, shouldst wave thy
    beauty's sway,
Thou still must rule, because I will obey:

(*turning to the audience*) An humble fugitive from Folly view,
No sanctuary near but Love and you:

You can, indeed, each anxious fear remove,
For even Scandal dies, if you approve.

(*Exeunt omnes*)

Epilogue

By MR. COLMAN

Spoken by LADY TEAZLE

I, who was late so volatile and gay,
Like a trade-wind must now blow all one
way,
Bend all my cares, my studies, and my vows,
To one dull rusty weathercock—my spouse!
So wills our virtuous Bard—the motley Bayes
Of crying epilogues and laughing plays!
Old bachelors, who marry smart young wives,
Learn from our play to regulate your lives:
Each bring his dear to town, all faults upon
her—
London will prove the very source of honor.
Plunged fairly in, like a cold bath it serves,
When principles relax, to brace the nerves:
Such is my case; and yet I must deplore
That the gay dream of dissipation's o'er.
And say, ye fair! was ever lively wife,
Born with a genius for the highest life,
Like me untimely blasted in her bloom,
Like me condemn'd to such a dismal doom?
Save money—when I just knew how to waste
it!
Leave London—just as I began to taste it!
  Must I then watch the early crowing cock,
The melancholy ticking of a clock;
In a lone rustic hall for ever pounded,
With dogs, cats, rats, and squalling brats sur-
rounded?
With humble curate can I now retire,
(While good Sir Peter boozes with the
squire,)
And at backgammon mortify my soul,
That pants for loo, or flutters at a vole.

Seven's the main! Dear sound that must ex-
pire,
Lost at hot cockles round a Christmas fire;
The transient hour of fashion too soon spent,
Farewell the tranquil mind, farewell con-
tent!
Farewell the plumèd head, the cushion'd
tête,
That takes the cushion from its proper seat!
That spirit-stirring drum!—card drums I
mean,
Spadille—odd trick—pam—basto—king and
queen!
And you, ye knockers, that, with brazen
throat,
The welcome visitors' approach denote;
Farewell all quality of high renown,
Pride, pomp, and circumstance of glorious
town!
Farewell! your revels I partake no more,
And Lady Teazle's occupation's o'er!
All this I told our bard; he smiled, and said
'twas clear,
I ought to play deep tragedy next year.
Meanwhile he drew wise morals from his
play,
And in these solemn periods stalk'd away:—
"Bless'd were the fair like you; her faults
who stopp'd,
And closed her follies when the curtain
dropp'd!
No more in vice or error to engage,
Or play the fool at large on life's great stage."

DION BOUCICAULT

London Assurance

~~~~~~~~~~~~~~~~

PRINCIPAL EVENTS IN BOUCICAULT'S LIFE

1820, 26 Dec., Born in Dublin.

1839, Began acting career in the provinces under the name of Lee Moreton.

1841, 4 March, London Assurance was produced at Covent Garden.

1842, 7 Feb., The Irish Heiress was produced at Covent Garden.

1844, 18 Nov., Old Heads and Young Hearts was produced at the Theatre Royal, Haymarket.

1851, 29 March, The Queen of Spades was produced at Drury Lane.

1852, 14 June, First appearance as an actor under his own name in his own play, *The Vampire*, a melodrama, at the Princess Theatre.

1853-60, In the United States as an actor.

1857, The Poor of New York produced at Wallack's Theatre, New York; later revised as *The Streets of London*, and again as *The Poor of Liverpool*.

1859, 6 Dec., The Octaroon, or Life in Louisiana, produced at the Adelphi.

1860, 28 March, The Colleen Brawn, an adaptation of Gerald Griffin's novel, *The Collegians*, produced in New York; one of the most popular plays of its time, it was performed in almost every city of the United States and the United Kingdom.

1865, 4 Sept., Rip Van Winkle began a long run at the Adelphi.

1865, 23 March, Arrah-na-Pogue produced at the Princess Theatre. His portrayal of an Irish carman in this play and of Con in *The Shaughraun* gained him the reputation of being the best stage Irishman of his time.

1868, 12 Aug., After Dark produced at the Princess Theatre.

1873, 17 March, Daddy O'Dowd produced in New York.

1874, 14 Nov., The Shaughraun acted at Wallack's Theatre in New York.

1875, Returned to New York as permanent residence.

1886, Last appearance in London in *The Jilt*.

1890, 18 Sept., Died in New York.

INTRODUCTION

If the English drama of the late eighteenth century was inferior, that of the first half of the nineteenth was worse. The principal theatres of the time were so large that the audience in the remoter parts of the house could not hear the lines unless they were almost shouted and could never see facial expressions. In such theatres great spectacles could be presented to advantage, but tragedy or high comedy was almost impossible, since the methods of the actors had to be so broad and over-emphasized that nothing more than the most obvious effects was possible. The best writers of the time, consequently, did not write for the stage, the audiences became more and more vulgar, and the plays were as crude and obvious as the average modern movie.

In such a state of the theatre, no great dramatists can be expected, and none appeared. Dion Boucicault is better than most, and his long career as both player and playwright in England and America make him a central figure of the mid-nineteenth-century theatre. His plays contain no subtly conceived characters, no presentations of significant problems, no memorable lines, not even any scenes handled with masterly skill, but they are better than most of the pieces written for presentation in the early Victorian theatres.

London Assurance is good entertainment for an unthinking audience. There are no uncomfortable comments about contemporary society, no suggestions of any ideas which might be difficult for a twelve-year-old child, nothing risqué, no aspects of any character beyond the most superficial. One or two of the characters, like Sir Harcourt Courtly and Lady Gay Spanker, are not those one might meet any day on a London street, but they have no rare ingredients in their make-up; they simply display familiar dandyism or forthrightness in an exaggerated form.

The plot of the play concerns nothing of any significance, merely the usual sort of mild love affair between an eligible young woman and an eligible young man. Nobody says anything out of the ordinary except once or twice in the third act when Grace makes an inappropriate romantic speech. Yet *London Assurance* is not a bad play, merely an undistinguished play, prepared for an undiscriminating audience in a very large theatre. For such an audience and theatre it is well planned. The progress of the plot is kept clear and unambiguous, the characters are simple and direct, exhibiting the same familiar traits of character over and over in different situations—Sir Harcourt's vanity, Meddle's professional greed, Lady Gay's boisterous honesty and preoccupation with hunting. The measure of its effectiveness with the audience and theatre for which it was planned is seen in the success of the first production and in the fact that it continued to be performed with some frequency for half a century.

≈

LONDON ASSURANCE

Dramatis personae
In order of first appearance

COOL, Sir Harcourt Courtly's resourceful valet.

MARTIN, Servant to Sir Harcourt Courtly.

CHARLES COURTLY, An attractive and debonair young man, son to Sir Harcourt, supposed by him to be a retiring and serious student at Oxford but actually well-acquainted with the manners and pleasures of London.

DAZZLE, An accomplished and lively gentleman of fashion, who lives by his wits.

SIR HARCOURT COURTLY, An aging gallant, father of Charles. He fancies himself as a gay blade and a leader of London society.

MAXIMILIAN HARKAWAY, Called Max; a bluff, hearty country squire with a generous heart and a passion for hunting.

PERT, Lady's maid to Grace.

JAMES, Servant to Max Harkaway.

GRACE HARKAWAY, Niece of Max, a beautiful, spirited girl.

MARK MEDDLE, A ridiculous little attorney, ready to go to any lengths for fees.

LADY GAY SPANKER, Grace's cousin and friend, handsome, gay, boisterous; devoted to hunting.

ADOLPHUS (DOLLY) SPANKER, Her meek and devoted husband, a timid and irresolute example of the English gentleman.

SIMPSON, Servant to Max Harkaway.

MR. SOLOMON ISAACS, A London moneylender.

SERVANTS

Act I

SCENE I. *An ante-room in* SIR HARCOURT COURTLY'S *House in fashionable Belgrave Square.*

(*Enter* COOL)

COOL. Half-past nine, and Mr. Charles has not yet returned: I am in a fever of dread. If his father happen to rise earlier than usual on any morning, he is sure to ask first for Mr. Charles. Poor deluded old gentleman—he little thinks how he is deceived.

(*Enter* MARTIN, *lazily*)

Well, Martin, he has not come home yet?

MARTIN. No; and I have not had a wink of sleep all night—I cannot stand this any longer; I shall give warning. This is the fifth night Mr. Courtly has remained out, and I am obliged to stand at the hall window to watch for him.

COOL. You know if Sir Harcourt was aware that we connived at his son's irregularities, we should all be discharged.

MARTIN. I have used up all my common excuses on his duns.—"Call again," "Not at home," and "Send it down to you," won't serve any more; and Mr. Crust, the wine-merchant, swears he will be paid.

COOL. So they all say. Why, he has arrests out against him already. I've seen the fellows watching the door—(*loud knock and ring heard*)—there he is, just in time—quick, Martin, for I expect Sir William's bell every moment—(*bell rings*)—and there it is. (*Exit* MARTIN, *slowly*) Thank heaven, he will return to college to-morrow, and this heavy responsibility will be taken off my shoulders. A valet is as difficult a post to fill properly as that of prime minister.   (*Exit*)

YOUNG COURTLY. (*Without*) Hollo!

DAZZLE. (*Without*) Steady!

(*Enter* YOUNG COURTLY *and* DAZZLE *staggering*)

YOUNG COURTLY. Hollo-o-o!

DAZZLE. Hush! What are you about, howling like a Hottentot. Sit down there, and thank heaven you are in Belgrave Square, instead of Bow Street.

YOUNG COURTLY. D—d—damn Bow Street.

DAZZLE. Oh, with all my heart!—you have not seen as much of it as I have.

YOUNG COURTLY. I say—let me see—what was I going to say?—oh, look here—(*He pulls out a large assortment of knockers, bell-pulls, etc., from his pocket*) There! dam'me! I'll puzzle the two-penny postmen, —I'll deprive them of their right of disturbing the neighborhood. That black lion's head did belong to old Vampire, the money-lender; this bell-pull to Miss Stitch, the milliner.

DAZZLE. And this brass griffin—

YOUNG COURTLY. That! oh, let me see— I think—I twisted that off our own hall-door as I came in, while you were paying the cab.

DAZZLE. What shall I do with them?

YOUNG COURTLY. Pack 'em in a small hamper, and send 'em to the sitting magistrate with my father's compliments; in the mean time, come into my room, and I'll astonish you with some Burgundy.

(*Re-enter* COOL)

COOL. Mr. Charles—

YOUNG COURTLY. Out! out! not at home to any one.

COOL. And drunk—

YOUNG COURTLY. As a lord.

COOL. If Sir Harcourt knew this, he would go mad, he would discharge me.

YOUNG COURTLY. You flatter yourself; that would be no proof of his insanity.— (*To* DAZZLE) This is Cool, sir, Mr. Cool; he is the best liar in London—there is a pungency about his invention, and an originality in his equivocation, that is perfectly refreshing.

COOL. Why, Mr. Charles, where did you pick him up?

YOUNG COURTLY. You mistake, he picked *me* up. (*Bell rings*)

COOL. Here comes Sir Harcourt—pray do not let him see you in this state.

YOUNG COURTLY. State! What do you mean? I am in a beautiful state.

COOL. I should lose my character.

YOUNG COURTLY. That would be a fortunate epoch in your life, Cool.

COOL. Your father would discharge me.

YOUNG COURTLY. Cool, my dad is an old ass!

COOL. Retire to your own room, for heaven's sake, Mr. Charles.

YOUNG COURTLY. I'll do so for my own sake. (*To* DAZZLE) I say, old fellow, (*staggering*) just hold the door steady while I go in.

DAZZLE. This way. Now, then!—take care! (*Helps him out of the room*)

(*Enter by another door* SIR HARCOURT COURTLY *in an elegant dressing-gown, and Greek scull-cap and tassels, etc.*)

SIR HARCOURT. Cool, is breakfast ready?

COOL. Quite ready, Sir Harcourt.

SIR HARCOURT. Apropos. I omitted to mention that I expect Squire Harkaway to join us this morning, and you must prepare for my departure to Oak Hall immediately.

COOL. Leave town in the middle of the season, Sir Harcourt? So unprecedented a proceeding!

SIR HARCOURT. It is. I confess it, there is but one power could effect such a miracle, —that is divinity.

COOL. How!

SIR HARCOURT. In female form, of course. Cool, I am about to present society with a second Lady Courtly; young—blushing eighteen;—lovely! I have her portrait; rich! I have her banker's account;—an heiress, and a Venus!

COOL. Lady Courtly could be none other.

SIR HARCOURT. Ha! ha! Cool, your manners are above your station.—Apropos, I shall find no further use for my brocaded dressing-gown.

COOL. (*Bowing*) I thank you, Sir Harcourt.—Might I ask who the fortunate lady is?

SIR HARCOURT. Certainly; Miss Grace Harkaway, the niece of my old friend, Max.

COOL. Have you never seen the lady, sir?

SIR HARCOURT. Never—that is, yes— eight years ago. Having been, as you know, on the continent for the last seven years, I have not had the opportunity of paying my devoirs. Our connection and betrothal was a very extraordinary one. Her father's estates were contiguous to mine;—being a penurious, miserly, *ugly* old scoundrel, he made a market of my indiscretion, and supplied my extravagance with large sums of money on mortgages, his great desire being to unite the two properties. About seven years ago, he died—leaving Grace, a girl, to the guardianship of her uncle, with this will:—if, on attaining the age of nineteen, she would consent to marry me, I should receive those deeds, and all his property, as her dowry. If she refused to comply with this condition, they should revert to my heir-presumptive or apparent.—She consents.

COOL. Who would not?

SIR HARCOURT. I consent to receive her £15,000 a year.

COOL. (*Aside*) Who would not?

SIR HARCOURT. So prepare, Cool, prepare!—But where is my boy, where is Charles?

COOL. Why—oh, he is gone out, Sir Harcourt; yes, gone out to take a walk.

SIR HARCOURT. Poor child! A perfect child in heart—a sober, placid mind—the simplicity and verdure of boyhood, kept fresh and unsullied by any contact with society. Tell me, Cool, at what time was he in bed last night?

COOL. Half-past nine, Sir Harcourt.

SIR HARCOURT. Half-past nine! Beautiful! What an original idea! Reposing in cherub slumbers, while all around him teems with drinking and debauchery! Primitive sweetness of nature! No pilot-coated, bearskinned brawling!

COOL. Oh, Sir Harcourt!

SIR HARCOURT. No cigar-smoking—

COOL. Faints at the smell of one.

SIR HARCOURT. No brandy and water bibbing—

COOL. Doesn't know the taste of anything stronger than barley-water.

SIR HARCOURT. No night parading—

COOL. Never heard the clock strike twelve, except at noon.

SIR HARCOURT. In fact, he is my son, and became a gentleman by right of paternity. He inherited my manners.

(*Enter* MARTIN)

MARTIN. Mr. Harkaway!

(*Enter* MAX HARKAWAY)

MAX. Squire Harkaway, fellow, or Max Harkaway, another time. (MARTIN *bows, and exit*) Ah! Ha! Sir Harcourt, I'm devilish glad to see ye! Gi' me your fist. Dang it, but I'm glad to see ye! Let me see. Six—seven years, or more, since we have met. How quickly they have flown!

SIR HARCOURT. (*Throwing off his studied manner*) Max, Max! Give me your hand, old boy.—(*Aside*) Ah! he *is* glad to see me. There is no fawning pretence about that squeeze.—Cool, you may retire. (*Exit* COOL)

MAX. Why, you are looking quite rosy.

SIR HARCOURT. Ah! ah! Rosy! Am I too florid?

MAX. Not a bit; not a bit.

SIR HARCOURT. I thought so.—(*Aside*) Cool said I had put too much on.

MAX. How comes it, Courtly, that you manage to retain your youth? See, I'm as grey as on old badger, or a wild rabbit; while you are—are as black as a young rook. I say, whose head grew your hair, eh?

SIR HARCOURT. Permit me to remark that all the beauties of my person are of home manufacture. Why should you be surprised at my youth? I have scarcely thrown off the giddiness of a very boy—elasticity of limb—buoyancy of soul! Remark this position—(*Throws himself into an attitude*) I held that attitude for ten minutes at Lady Acid's last *réunion*, at the express desire of one of our first sculptors, while he was making a sketch of me for the Apollo.

MAX. (*Aside*) Making a butt of thee for their gibes.

SIR HARCOURT. Lady Sarah Sarcasm started up, and, pointing to my face, ejaculated, "Good gracious! Does not Sir Harcourt remind you of the countenance of Ajax, in the Pompeian portrait?"

MAX. Ajax!—humbug!

SIR HARCOURT. You are complimentary.

MAX. I'm a plain man, and always speak my mind. What's in a face or figure? Does a Grecian nose entail a good temper? Does a waspish waist indicate a good heart? Or do oily perfumed locks necessarily thatch a well-furnished brain?

SIR HARCOURT. It's an undeniable fact, —*plain* people always praise the beauties of the *mind*.

MAX. Excuse the insinuation; I had thought the first Lady Courtly had surfeited you with beauty.

SIR HARCOURT. No; she lived fourteen months with me, and then eloped with an intimate friend. Etiquette compelled me to challenge the seducer; so I received satisfaction—and a bullet in my shoulder at the same time. However, I had the consolation of knowing that he was the handsomest man of the age. She did not insult me by running away with a d—d ill-looking scoundrel.

MAX. That certainly was flattering.

SIR HARCOURT. I felt so, as I pocketed the ten thousand pounds damages.

MAX. That must have been a great balm to your sore honor.

SIR HARCOURT. It was—Max, my honor would have died without it; for on that year the wrong horse won the Derby—by some mistake. It was one of the luckiest chances—a thing that does not happen twice in a man's life—the opportunity of getting rid of his wife and his debts at the same time.

MAX. Tell the truth, Courtly! Did you not feel a little frayed in your delicacy?—your honor, now? Eh?

SIR HARCOURT. Not a whit. Why should I? I married *money*, and I received it,—virgin gold! My delicacy and honor had nothing to do with hers. The world pities the bereaved husband, when it should congratulate. No,—the affair made a sensation, and I was the object. Besides, it is vulgar to make a parade of one's feelings, however acute they may be: impenetrability of countenance is the sure sign of your highly-bred man of fashion.

MAX. So, a man must, therefore, lose his wife and his money with a smile,—in fact, every thing he possesses but his temper.

SIR HARCOURT. Exactly,—and greet ruin with *vive la bagatelle!* For example,—your modish beauty never discomposes the shape of her features with convulsive laughter. A smile rewards the *bon mot,* and also shows the whiteness of her teeth. She never weeps impromptu,—tears might destroy the economy of her cheek. Scenes are vulgar,—hysterics obsolete; she exhibits a calm, placid, impenetrable lake, whose surface is reflection, but of unfathomable depth,—a statue, whose life is hypothetical, and not a *prima facie* fact.

MAX. Well, give me the girl that will fly at your eyes in an argument, and stick to her point like a fox to his own tail.

SIR HARCOURT. But etiquette! Max,—remember etiquette!

MAX. Damn etiquette! I have seen a man who thought it sacrilege to eat fish with a knife, that would not scruple to rise up and rob his brother of his birthright in a gambling-house. Your thoroughbred, well-blooded heart will seldom kick over the traces of good feeling. That's my opinion, and I don't care who knows it.

SIR HARCOURT. Pardon me,—etiquette is the pulse of society, by regulating which the body politic is retained in health. I consider myself one of the faculty in the art.

MAX. Well, well; you are a living libel upon common sense, for you are old enough to know better.

SIR HARCOURT. Old enough! What do you mean? Old! I still retain all my little juvenile indiscretions, which your niece's beauties must teach me to discard. I have not sown my wild oats yet.

MAX. Time you did, at sixty-three.

SIR HARCOURT. Sixty-three! Good God!—forty, 'pon my life! Forty, next March.

MAX. Why, you are older than I am.

SIR HARCOURT. Oh, you are old enough to be my father!

MAX. Well, if I am, I am; that's etiquette, I suppose. Poor Grace! How often I have pitied her fate! That a young and beautiful creature should be driven into wretched splendor, or miserable poverty!

SIR HARCOURT. Wretched! Wherefore? Lady Courtly wretched! Impossible!

MAX. Will she not be compelled to marry you, whether she likes you or not?—a choice between you and poverty. (*Aside*) And hang me if it isn't a tie!—But why do you not introduce your son Charles to me? I have not seen him since he was a child. You would never permit him to accept any of my invitations to spend his vacation at Oak Hall,—of course, we shall have the pleasure of his company now.

SIR HARCOURT. He is not fit to enter society yet. He is a studious, sober boy.

MAX. Boy! Why, he's five-and-twenty.

SIR HARCOURT. Good gracious! Max,—you will permit me to know my own son's age,—he is not twenty.

MAX. I'm dumb.

SIR HARCOURT. You will excuse me while I indulge in the process of dressing.—Cool!

(*Enter* COOL)

Prepare my toilet. (*Exit* COOL) That is a ceremony, which, with me, supersedes all others. I consider it a duty which every gentleman owes to society—to render himself as agreeable an object as possible—and the least compliment a mortal can pay to nature, when she honors him by bestowing extra care in the manufacture of his person, is to display her taste to the best possible advantage; and so, *au revoir.* (*Exit*)

MAX. That's a good soul—he has his faults, and who has not? Forty years of age! Oh, monstrous!—But he does look uncommonly young for sixty, spite of his foreign locks and complexion.

(*Enter* DAZZLE)

DAZZLE. (*Aside, on seeing* HARKAWAY) Who's my friend, with the stick and gaiters, I wonder—one of the family—the governor maybe.

MAX. Who's this? Oh, Charles—is that you, my boy? How are you? (*Aside*) This is the *boy.*

DAZZLE. (*Aside*) He knows me—he is too respectable for a bailiff. (*Aloud*) How are you?

MAX. Your father has just left me.

DAZZLE. (*Aside*) The devil he has! He's been dead these ten years. Oh! I see, he thinks I'm young Courtly. (*Aloud*) The honor you would confer upon me, I must unwillingly disclaim,—I am not Mr. Courtly.

MAX. I beg pardon—a friend, I suppose.

DAZZLE. Oh, a most intimate friend—a friend of years—distantly related to the family—one of my ancestors married one of his. (*Aside*) Adam and Eve.

MAX. Are you on a visit here?

DAZZLE. Yes. Oh! yes. (*Aside*) Rather a short one, I'm afraid.

MAX. (*Aside*) This appears a dashing kind of fellow—as he is a friend of Sir Harcourt's, I'll invite him to the wedding. (*Aloud*) Sir, if you are not otherwise engaged, I shall feel honored by your company at my house, Oak Hall, Gloucestershire.

DAZZLE. Your name is—

MAX. Harkaway—Max Harkaway.

DAZZLE. Harkaway—let me see—I ought to be related to the Harkaways, somehow.

MAX. A wedding is about to come off—will you take a part on the occasion?

DAZZLE. With pleasure! Any part, but that of the husband.

MAX. Have you any previous engagement?

DAZZLE. I was thinking—eh! why, let me see. (*Aside*) Promised to meet my tailor and his account to-morrow; however, I'll postpone that. (*Aloud*) Have you good shooting?

MAX. Shooting! Why, there's no shooting at this time of the year.

DAZZLE. Oh! I'm in no hurry—I can wait till the season, of course. I was only speaking precautionally—you have good shooting?

MAX. The best in the country.

DAZZLE. Make yourself comfortable!—Say no more—I'm your man—wait till you see how I'll murder your preserves.

MAX. Do you hunt?

DAZZLE. Pardon me—but will you repeat that? (*Aside*) Delicious and expensive idea!

MAX. You ride?

DAZZLE. Anything! Everything! From a blood to a broomstick. Only catch me a flash of lightning, and let me get on the back of it, and dam'me if I wouldn't astonish the elements.

MAX. Ha! ha!

DAZZLE. I'd put a girdle round about the earth, in very considerably less than forty minutes.

MAX. Ah! ha! We'll show old Fiddlestrings how to spend the day. He imagines that Nature, at the earnest request of Fashion, made summer days long for him to saunter in the Park, and winter nights, that he might have good time to get cleared out at hazard or at whist. Give me the yelping of a pack of hounds before the shuffling of a pack of cards. What state can match the chase in full cry, each vying with his fellow which shall be most happy? A thousand deaths fly by unheeded in that one hour's life of ecstasy. Time is outrun, and Nature seems to grudge our bliss by making the day so short.

DAZZLE. No, for then rises up the idol of my great adoration.

MAX. Who's that?

DAZZLE. The bottle—that lends a lustre to the soul!—When the world puts on its nightcap and extinguishes the sun—then comes the bottle! Oh, mighty wine! Don't ask me to apostrophise. Wine and love are the only two indescribable things in nature; but I prefer the wine, because its consequences are not entailed, and are more easily got rid of.

MAX. How so?

DAZZLE. Love ends in matrimony, wine in soda water.

MAX. Well, I can promise you as fine a bottle as ever was cracked.

DAZZLE. Never mind the bottle, give me the wine. Say no more; but, when I arrive, just shake one of my hands, and put the key of the cellar into the other, and if I don't make myself intimately acquainted with its internal organization—well, I say nothing,—time will show.

MAX. I foresee some happy days.

DAZZLE. And I some glorious nights.

MAX. It mustn't be a flying visit.

DAZZLE. I despise the word—I'll stop a month with you.

MAX. Or a year or two.

DAZZLE. I'll live and die with you!

MAX. Ha! ha! Remember Max Harkaway, Oak Hall, Gloucestershire.

DAZZLE. I'll remember—fare ye well. (MAX *is going*) I say, holloa!—Tallyho-o-o-o!

MAX. Yoicks!—Tallyho-o-o-o! (*Exit*)

DAZZLE. There I am—quartered for a couple of years at the least. The old boy wants somebody to ride his horses, shoot his game, and keep a restraint on the morals of the parish: I'm eligible. What a lucky accident to meet young Courtly last night! Who could have thought it?—Yesterday, I could not make certain of a dinner, except at my own proper peril; to-day, I would flirt with a banquet.

(*Enter* YOUNG COURTLY)

YOUNG COURTLY. What infernal row was that? Why, (*seeing* DAZZLE) are you here still?

DAZZLE. Yes. Ain't you delighted? I'll ring, and send the servant for my luggage.

YOUNG COURTLY. The devil you will! Why, you don't mean to say you seriously intend to take up a permanent residence here?   (*He rings bell*)

DAZZLE. Now, that's a most inhospitable insinuation.

YOUNG COURTLY. Might I ask your name?

DAZZLE. With a deal of pleasure—Richard Dazzle, late of the Unattached Volunteers, vulgarly entitled the Dirty Buffs.

(*Enter* MARTIN)

YOUNG COURTLY. Then, Mr. Richard Dazzle, I have the honor of wishing you a very good morning. Martin, show this gentleman the door.

DAZZLE. If he does, I'll kick Martin out of it.—No offence. (*Exit* MARTIN) Now, sir, permit me to place a dioramic view of your conduct before you. After bringing you safely home this morning—after indulgently waiting, whenever you took a passing fancy to a knocker or bell-pull—after conducting a retreat that would have reflected honor on Napoleon—you would kick me into the street, like a mangy cur: and that's what you call gratitude. Now, to show you how superior I am to petty malice, I give you an unlimited invitation to my house—my country house—to remain as long as you please.

YOUNG COURTLY. Your house!

DAZZLE. Oak Hall, Gloucestershire,—fine old place—for further particulars see roadbook; that is, it *nominally* belongs to my old friend and relation, Max Harkaway; but I'm privileged. Capital old fellow—say, shall we be honored?

YOUNG COURTLY. Sir, permit me to hesitate a moment. (*Aside*) Let me see—I go back to college to-morrow, so I shall not be missing; tradesmen begin to dun—

(*Enter* COOL)

I hear thunder; here is shelter ready for me.

COOL. Oh, Mr. Charles, Mr. Solomon Isaacs is in the hall, and swears he will remain till he has arrested you!

YOUNG COURTLY. Does he!—sorry he is so obstinate—take him my compliments, and I will bet him five to one he will not.

DAZZLE. Double or quits, with my kind regards.

COOL. But, sir, he has discovered the house in Curzon Street; he says he is aware the furniture, at least, belongs to you, and he will put a man in immediately.

YOUNG COURTLY. That's awkward—what's to be done?

DAZZLE. Ask him whether he couldn't make it a woman.

YOUNG COURTLY. I must trust that to fate.

DAZZLE. I will give you my acceptance, if it will be of any use to you; it is of none to me.

YOUNG COURTLY. No, sir; but in reply to your most generous and kind invitation, if you be in earnest, I shall feel delighted to accept it.

DAZZLE. Certainly.

YOUNG COURTLY. Then off we go—through the stables—down the mews, and so slip through my friend's fingers.

DAZZLE. But, stay, you must do the polite; say farewell to him before you part. Damn it, don't cut him!

YOUNG COURTLY. You jest!

DAZZLE. Here, lend me a card. (COURTLY *gives him one*) Now, then, (*writes*) "Our respects to Mr. Isaacs—sorry to have been prevented from seeing him."—Ha! ha!

YOUNG COURTLY. Ha! ha!

DAZZLE. We'll send him up some game.

YOUNG COURTLY. (*To* COOL) Don't let my father see him.   (*Exeunt*)

COOL. What's this?—"Mr. Charles Courtly, P.P.C., returns thanks for obliging inquiries."   (*Exit*)

Act II

SCENE I. *The next day. The lawn before Oak Hall, a fine Elizabethan mansion; a drawing-room is seen through large French windows at the back. Statues, urns, and garden chairs about the stage.*

(*Enter* PERT *and* JAMES)

PERT. James, Miss Grace desires me to request that you will watch at the avenue, and let her know when the squire's carriage is seen on the London road.

JAMES. I will go to the lodge.   (*Exit*)

PERT. How I do long to see what kind of a man Sir Harcourt Courtly is! They say he is sixty; so he must be old, and consequently ugly. If I was Miss Grace, I would rather give up all my fortune and marry the man I liked, than go to church with a stuffed eel-skin. But taste is everything,—she doesn't seem to care whether he is sixty or sixteen; jokes at love; prepares for matrimony as she would for dinner; says it is a necessary evil, and what can't be cured must be endured. Now, I say this is against all nature; and she is either no woman, or a deeper one than I am, if she prefers an old man to a young one. Here she comes! looking as cheerfully as if she was going to marry Mr. Jenks! my Mr. Jenks! whom nobody won't lead to the halter till I have that honor.

(*Enter* GRACE *from the drawing-room*)

GRACE. Well, Pert? Any sign of the squire yet?

PERT. No, Miss Grace; but James has gone to watch the road.

GRACE. In my uncle's letter he mentions a Mr. Dazzle, whom he has invited; so you must prepare a room for him. He is some friend of my husband that is to be, and my uncle seems to have taken an extraordinary predilection for him. Apropos! I must not forget to have a bouquet for the dear old man when he arrives.

PERT. The dear old man! Do you mean Sir Harcourt?

GRACE. Law, no! My uncle, of course. (*Plucking flowers*) What do I care for Sir Harcourt Courtly?

PERT. Isn't it odd, Miss, you have never seen your intended, though it has been so long since you were betrothed?

GRACE. Not at all; marriage matters are conducted now-a-days in a most mercantile manner; consequently a previous acquaintance is by no means indispensable. Besides, my *prescribed* husband has been upon the continent for the benefit of his—property! They say a southern climate is a great restorer of consumptive estates.

PERT. Well, Miss, for my own part, I should like to have a good look at my bargain before I paid for it; 'specially when one's life is the price of the article. But why, ma'am, do you consent to marry in this blind-man's-buff sort of manner? What would you think if he were not quite so old?

GRACE. I should think he was a little younger.

PERT. I should like him all the better.

GRACE. That wouldn't I. A young husband might expect affection and nonsense, which 'twould be deceit in me to render; nor would he permit me to remain with my uncle.—Sir Harcourt takes me with the incumbrances on his estate, and I shall beg to be left among the rest of the livestock.

PERT. Ah, Miss, but some day you might chance to stumble over *the* man,—what could you do then?

GRACE. Do! Beg *the* man's pardon, and request *the* man to pick me up again.

PERT. Ah, you were never in love, Miss?

GRACE. I never was, nor will be, till I am tired of myself and common sense. Love is a pleasant scape-goat for a little epidemic madness. I must have been inoculated in my infancy, for the infection passes over poor me in contempt.

(*Enter* JAMES)

JAMES. Two gentlemen, Miss Grace, have just alighted.

GRACE. Very well, James. (*Exit* JAMES)
Love is pictured as a boy; in another century
they will be wiser, and paint him as a fool,
with cap and bells, without a thought above
the jingling of his own folly. Now, Pert, remember this as a maxim,—A woman is always
in love with one of two things.

PERT. What are they, Miss?

GRACE. A man, or herself—and I know
which is the most profitable.   (*Exit*)

PERT. I wonder what my Jenks would say,
if I was to ask him.—Law! Here comes Mr.
Meddle, his rival, contemporary solicitor, as
he calls him,—a nasty, prying, ugly wretch—
what brings him here? He comes puffed with
some news.   (*Retires*)

(*Enter* MEDDLE, *with a newspaper*)

MEDDLE. I have secured the only newspaper in the village—my character as an attorney-at-law depended on the monopoly of
its information.—I took it up by chance, when
this paragraph met my astonished view:
(*Reads*) "We understand that the contract of
marriage so long in abeyance on account of
the lady's minority, is about to be celebrated,
at Oak Hall, Gloucestershire, the well-known
and magnificent mansion of Maximilian
Harkaway, Esq., between Sir Harcourt
Courtly, Baronet, of fashionable celebrity,
and Miss Grace Harkaway, niece to the said
Mr. Harkaway. The preparations are proceeding on the good old English style." Is it possible! I seldom swear, except in a witness box,
but damme, had it been known in the village,
my reputation would have been lost; my voice
in the parlor of the Red Lion mute, and Jenks,
a fellow who calls himself a lawyer, without
more capability than a broomstick, and as
much impudence as a young barrister after
getting a verdict by mistake; why, he would
actually have taken the Reverend Mr. Spout
by the button, which is now my sole privilege.
Ah! Here is Mrs. Pert; couldn't have hit upon
a better person. I'll cross-examine her—Lady's
maid to Miss Grace, confidential purloiner of
second-hand silk—a *nisi prius* of her mistress
—Ah! sits on the woolsack in the pantry, and
dictates the laws of kitchen etiquette.—Ah!
Mrs. Pert, good morning; permit me to say,—
and my word as a legal character is not un-

duly considered—I venture to affirm, that you
look a—quite like the—a—

PERT. Law! Mr. Meddle.

MEDDLE. Exactly like the law.

PERT. Ha! Indeed. Complimentary, I confess; like the law: tedious, prosy, made up of
musty paper. You sha'n't have a long suit of
me. Good morning! (*Going*)

MEDDLE. Stay, Mrs. Pert; don't calumni-
ate my calling, or disseminate vulgar prejudices.

PERT. Vulgar! you talk of vulgarity to me!
You, whose sole employment is to sneak about
like a pig, snouting out the dust-hole of society and feeding upon the bad ends of vice!
You, who live upon the world's iniquity; you
miserable specimen of a bad six-and-eight-
pence!

MEDDLE. But, Mrs. Pert—

PERT. Don't but me, sir; I won't be butted
by any such low fellow.

MEDDLE. This is slander; an action will lie.

PERT. Let it lie; lying is your trade. I'll tell
you what, Mr. Meddle: if I had my will, I
would soon put a check on your prying
propensities. I'd treat you as the farmers do
the inquisitive hogs.

MEDDLE. How?

PERT. I would ring your nose.   (*Exit*)

MEDDLE. Not much information elicited
from that witness. Jenks is at the bottom of
this. I have very little hesitation in saying,
Jenks is a libellous rascal; I heard reports that
he was undermining my character here,
through Mrs. Pert. Now, I'm certain of it.
Assault is expensive; but I certainly will put
by a small weekly stipendium, until I can
afford to kick Jenks.

DAZZLE. (*Outside*) Come along; this
way!

MEDDLE. Ah! Whom have we here?
Visitors; I'll address them.

(*Enter* DAZZLE)

DAZZLE. Who's this, I wonder; one of the
family? I must know him. (*To* MEDDLE) Ah!
How are ye?

MEDDLE. Quite well. Just arrived?—ah!—
um!—Might I request the honor of knowing
whom I address?

DAZZLE. Richard Dazzle, Esquire; and
you—

MEDDLE. Mark Meddle, Attorney-at-law.

(*Enter* YOUNG COURTLY)

DAZZLE. What detained you?

YOUNG COURTLY. My dear fellow, I have just seen such a woman!

DAZZLE. (*Aside*) Hush! (*Aloud*) Permit me to introduce you to my very old friend, Meddle. He's a capital fellow; know him.

MEDDLE. I feel honored. Who is your friend?

DAZZLE. Oh, he? What, my friend? Oh! Augustus Hamilton.

YOUNG COURTLY. How d'ye do? (*Looking off*) There she is again!

MEDDLE. (*Looking off*) Why, that is Miss Grace.

DAZZLE. Of course, Grace.

YOUNG COURTLY. I'll go and introduce myself. (DAZZLE *stops him*)

DAZZLE. (*Aside*) What are you about? Would you insult my old friend, Puddle, by running away? (*Aloud*) I say, Puddle, just show my friend the lions, while I say how d'ye do to my young friend, Grace. (*Aside*) Cultivate his acquaintance.

(*Exit.*—YOUNG COURTLY *looks after him*)

MEDDLE. Mr. Hamilton, might I take the liberty?

YOUNG COURTLY. (*Looking off*) Confound the fellow!

MEDDLE. Sir, what did you remark?

YOUNG COURTLY. She's gone! Oh, are you here still, Mr. Thingomerry Puddle?

MEDDLE. Meddle, sir, Meddle, in the list of attorneys.

YOUNG COURTLY. Well, Muddle, or Puddle, or whoever you are, you are a bore.

MEDDLE. (*Aside*) How excessively odd! Mrs. Pert said I was a pig; now I'm a boar! I wonder what they'll make of me next.

YOUNG COURTLY. Mr. Thingamy, will you take a word of advice?

MEDDLE. Feel honored.

YOUNG COURTLY. Get out.

MEDDLE. Do you mean to—I don't understand.

YOUNG COURTLY. Delighted to quicken your apprehension. You are an ass, Puddle.

MEDDLE. Ha! ha! Another quadruped! Yes; beautiful—(*Aside*) I wish he'd call me

something libellous: but that would be too much to expect.—(*Aloud*) Anything else?

YOUNG COURTLY. Some miserable, pettifogging scoundrel!

MEDDLE. Good! ha! ha!

YOUNG COURTLY. What do you mean by laughing at me?

MEDDLE. Ha! ha! ha! excellent! delicious!

YOUNG COURTLY. Mr. —— are you ambitious of a kicking?

MEDDLE. Very, very—Go on—kick—go on.

YOUNG COURTLY. (*Looking off*) Here she comes! I'll speak to her.

MEDDLE. But, sir—sir—

YOUNG COURTLY. Oh, go to the devil!

(*He runs off*)

MEDDLE. There, there's a chance lost—gone! I have no hesitation in saying that, in another minute, I should have been kicked; literally kicked—a legal luxury. Costs, damages, and actions rose up like sky-rockets in my aspiring soul. With golden tails reaching to the infinity of my hopes, (*looking*)—they are coming this way, Mr. Hamilton in close conversation with Lady Courtly that is to be. Crim. Con.—Courtly versus Hamilton—damages problematical—Meddle, chief witness for plaintiff—guinea a day—professional man! I'll take down their conversation verbatim.

(*He retires behind a bush*)

(*Enter* GRACE, *followed by* YOUNG COURTLY)

GRACE. Perhaps you would follow your friend into the dining-room; refreshment after your long journey must be requisite.

YOUNG COURTLY. Pardon me, madam; but the lovely garden and the loveliness before me is better refreshment than I could procure in any dining-room.

GRACE. Ha! Your company and compliments arrive together.

YOUNG COURTLY. I trust that a passing remark will not spoil so welcome an introduction as this by offending you.

GRACE. I am not certain that anything you could say would offend me.

YOUNG COURTLY. I never meant—

GRACE. I thought not. In turn, pardon me, when I request you will commence your visit with this piece of information: I consider compliments impertinent, and sweetmeat language fulsome.

YOUNG COURTLY. I would condemn my tongue to a Pythagorean silence if I thought it could attempt to flatter.

GRACE. It strikes me, sir, that you are a stray bee from the hive of fashion; if so, reserve your honey for its proper cell. A truce to compliments.—You have just arrived *from town,* I apprehend.

YOUNG COURTLY. This moment I left mighty London, under the fever of a full season, groaning with the noisy pulse of wealth and the giddy whirling brain of fashion. Enchanting, busy London! How have I prevailed on myself to desert you! Next week the new ballet comes out,—the week after comes Ascot.—Oh!

GRACE. How agonizing must be the reflection.

YOUNG COURTLY. Torture! Can you inform me how you manage to avoid suicide here? If there was but an opera, even, within twenty miles! We couldn't get up a rustic ballet among the village girls? No?—ah!

GRACE. I am afraid you would find that difficult. How I contrive to support life I don't know—it is wonderful—but I have not precisely contemplated suicide yet, nor do I miss the opera.

YOUNG COURTLY. How can you manage to kill time?

GRACE. I can't. Men talk of killing time, while time quietly kills them. I have many employments—this week I devote to study and various amusements—next week to being married—the following week to repentance, perhaps.

YOUNG COURTLY. Married!

GRACE. You seem surprised; I believe it is of frequent occurrence in the metropolis.—Is it not?

YOUNG COURTLY. Might I ask to whom?

GRACE. A gentleman who has been strongly recommended to me for the situation of husband.

YOUNG COURTLY. What an extraordinary match! Would you not consider it advisable to see him, previous to incurring the consequences of such an act?

GRACE. You must be aware that fashion says otherwise. The gentleman swears eternal devotion to the lady's fortune, and the lady swears she will outvie him still. My lord's horses, and my lady's diamonds, shine through a few seasons, until a seat in Parliament, or the continent, stares them in the face; then, when thrown upon each other for resources of comfort, they begin to quarrel about the original conditions of the sale.

YOUNG COURTLY. Sale! No! That would be degrading civilization into Turkish barbarity.

GRACE. Worse, sir, a great deal worse; for there at least they do not attempt concealment of the barter; but here, every London ballroom is a marriage mart—young ladies are trotted out, while the mother, father, or chaperone plays auctioneer, and knocks them down to the highest bidder,—young men are ticketed up with their fortunes on their backs, —and Love, turned into a dapper shopman, descants on the excellent qualities of the material.

YOUNG COURTLY. Oh, that such a custom could have ever emanated from the healthy soil of an English heart!

GRACE. No. It never did—like most of our literary dandyisms and dandy literature, it was borrowed from the French.

YOUNG COURTLY. You seem to laugh at love.

GRACE. Love! Why, the very word is a breathing satire upon man's reason—a mania, indigenous to humanity—nature's jester, who plays off tricks upon the world, and trips up common sense. When I'm in love, I'll write an almanac, for very lack of wit—prognosticate the sighing season—when to beware of tears—about this time, expect matrimony to be prevalent! Ha! ha! Why should I lay out my life in love's bonds upon the bare security of a man's word?

(Enter JAMES)

JAMES. The Squire, madam, has just arrived, and another gentleman with him.

GRACE. *(Aside)* My intended, I suppose.
(Exit JAMES)

YOUNG COURTLY. I perceive you are one of the railers against what is termed the follies of high life.

GRACE. No, not particularly; I deprecate all folly. By what prerogative can the West-end mint issue absurdity, which, if coined in the east, would be voted vulgar?

YOUNG COURTLY. By a sovereign right—because it has Fashion's head upon its side, and that stamps it current.

GRACE. Poor Fashion, for how many sins hast thou to answer! The gambler pawns his birth-right for fashion—the *roué* steals his friend's wife for fashion—each abandons himself to the storm of impulse, calling it the breeze of fashion.

YOUNG COURTLY. Is this idol of the world so radically vicious?

GRACE. No; the root is well enough, as the body was, until it had outgrown its native soil; but now, like a mighty giant lying over Europe, it pillows its head in Italy, its heart in France, leaving the heels alone its sole support for England.

YOUNG COURTLY. Pardon me, madam, you wrong yourself to rail against your own inheritance—the kingdom to which loveliness and wit attest your title.

GRACE. A mighty realm, forsooth,—with milliners for ministers, a cabinet of coxcombs, envy for my homage, ruin for my revenue—my right of rule depending on the shape of a bonnet or the sit of a pelisse, with the next grand noodle as my heir-apparent. Mr. Hamilton, when I am crowned, I shall feel happy to abdicate in your favor.

(Curtseys and exit)

YOUNG COURTLY. What did she mean by that? Hang me if I can understand her—she is evidently not used to society. Ha!—takes every word I say for infallible truth—requires the solution of a compliment, as if it were a problem in Euclid. She said she was about to marry, but I rather imagine she was in jest. 'Pon my life, I feel very queer at the contemplation of such an idea—I'll follow her. (MEDDLE *comes out from behind the bush*) Oh! Perhaps this booby can inform me something about her. (MEDDLE *makes signs at him*) What the devil is he at!

MEDDLE. It won't do—no—ah! um—it's not to be done.

YOUNG COURTLY. What do you mean?

MEDDLE. (*Points after* GRACE) Counsel retained—cause to come off!

YOUNG COURTLY. Cause to come off!

MEDDLE. Miss Grace is about to be married.

YOUNG COURTLY. Is it possible?

MEDDLE. Certainly. If *I* have the drawing out of the deeds—

YOUNG COURTLY. To whom?

MEDDLE. Ha! hem! Oh, yes! I dare say—Information being scarce in the market, I hope to make mine valuable.

YOUNG COURTLY. Married! Married!

MEDDLE. Now I shall have another chance.

YOUNG COURTLY. I'll run and ascertain the truth of this from Dazzle. *(Exit)*

MEDDLE. It's of no use. He either dare not kick me, or he can't afford it—in either case, he is beneath my notice. Ah, who comes here?—can it be Sir Harcourt Courtly himself? It can be no other.

(Enter COOL*)*

Sir, I have the honor to bid you welcome to Oak Hall and the village of Oldborough.

COOL. (*Aside*) Excessively polite. (*Aloud*) —Sir, thank you.

MEDDLE. The township contains two thousand inhabitants.

COOL. Does it! I am delighted to hear it.

MEDDLE. (*Aside*) I can charge him for that—ahem—six and eightpence is not much —but it is a beginning. (*Aloud*) If you will permit me, I can inform you of the different commodities for which it is famous.

COOL. Much obliged—but here comes Sir Harcourt Courtly, my master, and Mr. Harkaway—any other time I shall feel delighted.

MEDDLE. Oh! (*Aside*) Mistook the man for the master. *(He retires up)*

(Enter MAX *and* SIR HARCOURT*)*

MAX. Here we are at last. Now give ye welcome to Oak Hall, Sir Harcourt, heartily!

SIR HARCOURT. (*Languidly*) Cool, assist me.

*(COOL *takes off his furred cloak and gloves; gives him white gloves and a white handkerchief*)*

MAX. Why, you require unpacking as carefully as my best bin of port. Well, now you are decanted, tell me, what did you think of my park as we came along?

SIR HARCOURT. That it would never come to an end. You said it was only a stone's throw from your infernal lodge to the house; why, it's ten miles at least.

MAX. I'll do it in ten minutes any day.

SIR HARCOURT. Yes, in a steam carriage. Cool, perfume my handkerchief.

MAX. Don't do it. Don't! Perfume in the country! Why, it's high treason in the very face of Nature; 'tis introducing the robbed to the robber. Here are the sweets from which your fulsome essences are pilfered, and libelled with their names,—don't insult them, too.

SIR HARCOURT. (To MEDDLE) Oh! Cull me a bouquet, my man!

MAX. (Turning) Ah, Meddle! How are you? This is Lawyer Meddle.

SIR HARCOURT. Oh! I took him for one of your people.

MEDDLE. Ah! naturally—um—Sir Harcourt Courtly, I have the honor to congratulate—happy occasion approaches. Ahem! I have no hesitation in saying this very happy occasion approaches.

SIR HARCOURT. Cool, is the conversation addressed towards me?

COOL. I believe so, Sir Harcourt.

MEDDLE. Oh, certainly! I was complimenting you.

SIR HARCOURT. Sir, you are very good; the honor is undeserved; but I am only in the habit of receiving compliments from the fair sex. Men's admiration is so damnably insipid.

MEDDLE. I had hoped to make a unit on that occasion.

SIR HARCOURT. Yes, and you hoped to put an infernal number of ciphers after your unit on that and any other occasion.

MEDDLE. Ha! ha! Very good. Why, I did hope to have the honor of drawing out the deeds; for, whatever Jenks may say to the contrary, I have no hesitation in saying—

SIR HARCOURT. (Putting him aside) (To MAX) If the future Lady Courtly be visible at so unfashionable an hour as this, I shall beg to be introduced.

MAX. Visible! Ever since six this morning, I'll warrant ye. Two to one she is at dinner.

SIR HARCOURT. Dinner! Is it possible? Lady Courtly dine at half-past one P.M.!

MEDDLE. I rather prefer that hour to peck a little my—

SIR HARCOURT. Dear me! Who was addressing you?

MEDDLE. Oh! I beg pardon.

MAX. (Calling) Here, James!

(Enter JAMES*)*

Tell Miss Grace to come here directly. (Exit JAMES) Now prepare, Courtly, for, though I say it, she is—with the exception of my bay mare, Kitty—the handsomest thing in the country. Considering she is a biped, she is a wonder! Full of blood, sound wind and limb, plenty of bone, sweet coat, in fine condition, with a thorough-bred step, as dainty as a pet greyhound.

SIR HARCOURT. Damme, don't compare her to a horse!

MAX. Well, I wouldn't, but she's almost as fine a creature,—close similarities.

MEDDLE. Oh, very fine creature! Close similarity, amounting to identity.

SIR HARCOURT. Good gracious, sir! What can a lawyer know about women!

MEDDLE. Everything. The consistorial court is fine study of the character, and I have no hesitation in saying that I have examined more women than Jenks, or—

SIR HARCOURT. Oh, damn Jenks!

MEDDLE. Sir, thank you. Damn him again, sir, damn him again!

(Enter GRACE*)*

GRACE. My dear uncle!

MAX. Ah, Grace, you little jade, come here.

SIR HARCOURT. (Eyeing her through his glass) Oh, dear! she is a rural Venus. I'm astonished and delighted.

MAX. Won't you kiss your old uncle?

(He kisses her)

SIR HARCOURT. (Draws an agonizing face) Oh!—ah—um!—N'importe!—my privilege in embryo—hem! It's very tantalizing, though.

MAX. You are not glad to see me, you are not. (Kissing her)

SIR HARCOURT. Oh; no, no! (Aside) That is too much. I shall do something horrible presently, if this goes on. (Aloud) I should be sorry to curtail any little ebullition of affection; but—ahem! May I be permitted?

MAX. Of course you may. There Grace, is Sir Harcourt, your husband that will be. Go to him, girl.

Sir Harcourt. Permit me to do homage to the charms, the presence of which have placed me in sight of Paradise.

(Sir Harcourt *and* Grace *retire*)

(*Enter* Dazzle)

Dazzle. Ah, old fellow, how are you?

Max. I'm glad to see you! Are you comfortably quartered, yet, eh?

Dazzle. Splendidly quartered! What a place you've got here! Here, Hamilton.

(*Enter* Young Courtly)

Permit me to introduce my friend, Augustus Hamilton. (*Aside*) Capital fellow! drinks like a sieve, and rides like a thunder-storm.

Max. Sir, I'm devilish glad to see you. Here, Sir Harcourt, permit me to introduce to you—

Young Courtly. The devil!

Dazzle. (*Aside*) What's the matter?

Young Courtly. (*Aside*) Why, that is my governor, by Jupiter!

Dazzle. (*Aside*) What, old Whiskers? You don't say that!

Young Courtly. (*Aside*) It is; what's to be done now?

Max. Mr. Hamilton, Sir Harcourt Courtly —Sir Harcourt Courtly, Mr. Hamilton.

Sir Harcourt. Hamilton! Good gracious! God bless me!—why, Charles, is it possible?— why, Max, that's my son!

Young Courtly. (*Aside*) What shall I do!

Max. Your son!

Grace. Your son, Sir Harcourt! Have you a son as old as that gentleman!

Sir Harcourt. No—that is—a—yes,—not by twenty years—a—Charles, why don't you answer me, sir?

Young Courtly. (*Aside to* Dazzle) What shall I say?

Dazzle. (*Aside*) Deny your identity.

Young Courtly. (*Aside*) Capital! (*Aloud*) What's the matter, sir?

Sir Harcourt. How came you down here, sir?

Young Courtly. By one of Newman's— best fours—in twelve hours and a quarter.

Sir Harcourt. Isn't your name Charles Courtly?

Young Courtly. Not to my knowledge.

Sir Harcourt. Do you mean to say that you are usually called Augustus Hamilton?

Young Courtly. Lamentable fact—and quite correct.

Sir Harcourt. Cool, is that my son?

Cool. No, sir—it is not Mr. Charles—but is very like him.

Max. I cannot understand all this.

Grace. (*Aside*) I think I can.

Dazzle. (*Aside to* Young Courtly) Give him a touch of the indignant.

Young Courtly. Allow me to say, Sir What-d'ye-call-'em Hartly—

Sir Harcourt. Hartly, sir! Courtly, sir! Courtly!

Young Courtly. Well, Hartly, or Court-heart, or whatever your name may be, I say your conduct is—a—a—, and were it not for the presence of this lady, I should feel inclined—to—to—

Sir Harcourt. No, no, that can't be my son,—he never would address me in that way.

Max. What is all this?

Sir Harcourt. Sir, your likeness to my son Charles is so astonishing, that it, for a moment—the equilibrium of my etiquette— 'pon my life, I—permit me to request your pardon.

Meddle. (*To* Sir Harcourt) Sir Harcourt, don't apologize, don't—bring an action. I'm witness.

Sir Harcourt. Some one take this man away.

(*Enter* James)

James. Luncheon is on the table, sir.

(*Exit*)

Sir Harcourt. Miss Harkaway, I never swore before a lady in my life—except when I promised to love and cherish the late Lady Courtly, which I took care to preface with an apology,—I was compelled to the ceremony, and consequently not answerable for the language—but to that gentleman's identity I would have pledged—my hair.

Grace. (*Aside*) If that security were called for, I suspect the answer would be— no effects.

(*Exeunt* Sir Harcourt *and* Grace)

Meddle. (*To* Max) I have something very particular to communicate.

Max. Can't listen at present. (*Exit*)

MEDDLE. (*To* DAZZLE *and* YOUNG COURTLY) I can afford you information, which I—

DAZZLE. Oh, don't bother!

YOUNG COURTLY. Go to the devil!

(*Exeunt*)

MEDDLE. Now, I have no hesitation in saying that is the height of ingratitude.—Oh—Mr. Cool—can you oblige me?

(*Presents his account*)

COOL. Why, what is all this?

MEDDLE. Small account *versus* you—to giving information concerning the last census of the population of Oldborough and vicinity, six and eightpence.

COOL. Oh, you mean to make me pay for this, do you?

MEDDLE. Unconditionally.

COOL. Well, I have no objection—the charge is fair—but remember, I am a servant on board wages,—will you throw in a little advice gratis—if I give you the money?

MEDDLE. Ahem!—I will.

COOL. A fellow has insulted me. I want to abuse him—what terms are actionable?

MEDDLE. You may call him anything you please, providing there are no witnesses.

COOL. Oh, may I? (*Looks round*)—then you rascally, pettifogging scoundrel!

MEDDLE. Hallo!

COOL. You mean—dirty—disgrace to your profession.

MEDDLE. Libel—slander—

COOL. Aye, but where are your witnesses?

MEDDLE. Give me the costs—six and eight pence.

COOL. I deny that you gave me information at all.

MEDDLE. You do!

COOL. Yes, where are your witnesses?

(*Exit*)

MEDDLE. Ah—damme!   (*Exit*)

Act III

SCENE I. *Two days later. A morning-room in Oak Hall, French windows opening to the lawn.*

(MAX *and* SIR HARCOURT *seated on one side,* DAZZLE *on the other;* GRACE *and* YOUNG COURTLY *are playing chess at back. All dressed for dinner*)

MAX. (*Aside to* SIR HARCOURT) What can I do?

SIR HARCOURT. Get rid of them civilly.

MAX. What, turn them out, after I particularly invited them to stay a month or two?

SIR HARCOURT. Why, they are disreputable characters; as for that young fellow, in whom my Lady Courtly appears so particularly absorbed,—I am bewildered—I have written to town for my Charles, my boy—it certainly is the most extraordinary likeness—

DAZZLE. (*Calls across the room*) Sir Harcourt, I have an idea—

SIR HARCOURT. Sir, I am delighted to hear it.—(*Aside to* MAX) That fellow is a swindler.

MAX. I met him at your house.

SIR HARCOURT. Never saw him before in all my life.

DAZZLE. (*Crossing to* SIR HARCOURT) I will bet you five to one that I can beat you three out of four games at billiards, with one hand.

SIR HARCOURT. No, sir.

DAZZLE. I don't mind giving you ten points in fifty.

SIR HARCOURT. Sir, I never gamble.

DAZZLE. You don't! Well, I'll teach you—easiest thing in life—you have every requisite—good temper.

SIR HARCOURT. I have not, sir.

DAZZLE. A long-headed, knowing old buck.

SIR HARCOURT. Sir!

(*They go up conversing with* MAX)

GRACE. Really, Mr. Hamilton, you improve.—A young man pays us a visit, as you half intimate, to escape inconvenient friends—that is complimentary to us, his hosts.

YOUNG COURTLY. Nay, that is too severe.

GRACE. After an acquaintanceship of two days, you sit down to teach me chess, and domestic economy at the same time.—Might I ask where you graduated in that science—

where you learned all that store of matrimonial advice which you have obliged me with?

YOUNG COURTLY. I imbibed it, madam, from the moment I beheld you, and having studied my subject *con amore*, took my degrees from your eyes.

GRACE. Oh, I see you are a Master of Arts already.

YOUNG COURTLY. Unfortunately, no—I shall remain a bachelor—till you can assist me to that honor. (*Aside to* DAZZLE *as he sees* SIR HARCOURT *approaching*) Keep the old boy away.

DAZZLE. (*Aside*) How do you get on?

YOUNG COURTLY. (*Aside*) Splendidly!

SIR HARCOURT. Is the conversation strictly confidential?—or might I join?

DAZZLE. (*Taking his arm*) Oh, not in the least, my dear sir—we were remarking that rifle shooting was an excellent diversion during the summer months.

SIR HARCOURT. (*Drawing himself up*) Sir, I was addressing—

DAZZLE. And I was saying what a pity it was I couldn't find any one reasonable enough to back his opinion with long odds—come out on the lawn, and pitch up your hat, and I will hold you ten to one I put a bullet into it every time, at forty paces.

SIR HARCOURT. No, sir—I consider you—

MAX. Here, all of you—look, here is Lady Gay Spanker coming across the lawn at a hand gallop!

SIR HARCOURT. (*Running to the window*) Bless me, the horse is running away!

MAX. Look how she takes that fence! There's a seat!

SIR HARCOURT. Lady Gay Spanker—who may she be?

GRACE. Gay Spanker, Sir Harcourt? My cousin and dearest friend—you *must* like her.

SIR HARCOURT. It will be my devoir, since it is your wish—though it will be a hard task in your presence.

GRACE. I am sure she will like you.

SIR HARCOURT. Ha! ha! I flatter myself.

YOUNG COURTLY. Who, and what is she?

GRACE. Glee, glee made a living thing— Nature in some frolic mood shut up a merry devil in her eye, and, spiting Art, stole joy's brightest harmony to thrill her laugh, which peals out sorrow's knell. Her cry rings loudest in the field—the very echo loves it best, and,

as each hill attempts to ape her voice, earth seems to laugh that it made a thing so glad.

MAX. Ay, the merriest minx I ever kissed.

(LADY GAY *laughs without*)

LADY GAY. (*Without*) Max!

MAX. Come in, you mischievous puss.

(*Enter* JAMES)

JAMES. Mr. Adolphus and Lady Gay Spanker. (*Exit*)

(*Enter* LADY GAY, *fully equipped in riding habit, etc.*)

LADY GAY. Ha! ha! Well, Governor, how are ye? I have been down five times, climbing up your stairs in my long clothes. How are you, Grace, dear? (*Kisses her*) There, don't fidget, Max. And there—(*kisses him*)—there's one for you.

SIR HARCOURT. Ahem!

LADY GAY. Oh, gracious, I didn't see you had visitors.

MAX. Permit me to introduce—Sir Harcourt Courtly, Lady Gay Spanker. Mr. Dazzle, Mr. Hamilton—Lady Gay Spanker.

SIR HARCOURT. (*Aside*) A devilish fine woman!

DAZZLE. (*Aside to* SIR HARCOURT) She's a devilish fine woman.

LADY GAY. You mustn't think anything of the liberties I take with my old papa here— bless him!

SIR HARCOURT. Oh, no! (*Aside*) I only thought I should like to be in his place.

LADY GAY. I am so glad you have come, Sir Harcourt. Now we shall be able to make a decent figure at the heels of a hunt.

SIR HARCOURT. Does your ladyship hunt?

LADY GAY. Ha! I say, Governor, does my ladyship hunt? I rather flatter myself that I do hunt! Why, Sir Harcourt, one might as well live without laughing as without hunting. Man was fashioned expressly to fit a horse. Are not hedges and ditches created for leaps? Of course! And I look upon foxes to be one of the most blessed dispensations of a benign Providence.

SIR HARCOURT. Yes, it is all very well in the abstract: I tried it once.

LADY GAY. Once! Only once?

SIR HARCOURT. Once, only once. And then the animal ran away with me.

LADY GAY. Why, you would not have him walk!

SIR HARCOURT. Finding my society disagreeable, he instituted a series of kicks, with a view to removing the annoyance; but aided by the united stays of the mane and tail, I frustrated his intentions. His next resource, however, was more effectual, for he succeeded in rubbing me off against a tree.

MAX *and* LADY GAY. Ha! ha! ha!

DAZZLE. How absurd you must have looked with your legs and arms in the air, like a shipwrecked tea-table.

SIR HARCOURT. Sir, I never looked absurd in my life. Ah, it may be very amusing in relation, I dare say, but very unpleasant in effect.

LADY GAY. I pity you, Sir Harcourt; it was criminal in your parents to neglect your education so shamefully.

SIR HARCOURT. Possibly; but be assured I shall never break my neck awkwardly from a horse, when it might be accomplished with less trouble from a bedroom window.

YOUNG COURTLY. (*Aside*) My dad will be caught by this she-Bucephalus tamer.

MAX. Ah! Sir Harcourt, had you been here a month ago, you would have witnessed the most glorious run that ever swept over merry England's green cheek—a steeple-chase, sir, which I intended to win, but my horse broke down the day before. I had a chance, notwithstanding, and but for Gay here, I should have won. How I regretted my absence from it! How did my filly behave herself, Gay?

LADY GAY. Gloriously, Max! gloriously! There were sixty horses in the field, all mettle to the bone: the start was a picture—away we went in a cloud—pell-mell—helter-skelter— the fools first, as usual, using themselves up —we soon passed them—first your Kitty, then my Blueskin, and Craven's colt last. Then came the tug—Kitty skimmed the walls— Blueskin flew o'er the fences—the Colt neck and neck, and half a mile to run—at last the Colt baulked a leap and went wild. Kitty and and I had it all to ourselves—she was three lengths ahead as we breasted the last wall, six feet, if an inch, and a ditch on the other side. Now, for the first time, I gave Blueskin his head—ha! ha!—Away he flew like a thunderbolt—over went the filly—I over the same spot, leaving Kitty in the ditch—walked the

steeple, eight miles in thirty minutes, and scarcely turned a hair.

ALL. Bravo! Bravo!

LADY GAY. Do you hunt?

DAZZLE. Hunt! I belong to a hunting family. I was born on horseback and cradled in a kennel! Aye, and I hope I may die with a whoo-whoop!

MAX. (*To* SIR HARCOURT) You must leave your town habits in the smoke of London; here we rise with the lark.

SIR HARCOURT. Haven't the remotest conception when that period is.

GRACE. The man that misses sunrise loses the sweetest part of his existence.

SIR HARCOURT. Oh, pardon me; I have seen sunrise frequently after a ball, or from the window of my travelling carriage, and I always considered it disagreeable.

GRACE. I love to watch the first tear that glistens in the opening eye of morning, the silent song the flowers breathe, the thrilly choir of the woodland minstrels, to which the modest brook trickles applause;—these, swelling out the sweetest chord of sweet creation's matins, seem to pour some soft and merry tale into the daylight's ear, as if the waking world had dreamed a happy thing, and now smiled o'er the telling of it.

SIR HARCOURT. The effect of a rustic education! Who could ever discover music in a damp foggy morning, except those confounded waits, who never play in tune, and a miserable wretch who makes a point of crying coffee under my window just as I am persuading myself to sleep; in fact, I never heard any music worth listening to, except in Italy.

LADY GAY. No? Then you never heard a well-trained English pack, full cry.

SIR HARCOURT. Full cry!

LADY GAY. Aye! there is harmony, if you will. Give me the trumpet-neigh; the spotted pack just catching scent! What a chorus is their yelp! The view-hallo, blent with a peal of free and fearless mirth! That's our old English music—match it where you can.

SIR HARCOURT. (*Aside*) I must see about Lady Gay Spanker.

DAZZLE. (*Aside to* SIR HARCOURT) Ah, would you—

LADY GAY. Time then appears as young as love, and plumes as swift a wing. Away we go! The earth flies back to aid our course!

Horse, man, hound, earth, heaven!—all—all—one piece of glowing ecstasy! Then I love the world, myself, and every living thing,—a jocund soul cries out for very glee, as it could wish that all creation had but one mouth that I might kiss it!

SIR HARCOURT. (*Aside*) I wish I was the mouth!

MAX. Why, we will regenerate you, baronet! But Gay, where is your husband?—Where is Adolphus!

LADY GAY. Bless me, where is my Dolly?

SIR HARCOURT. You are married, then?

LADY GAY. I have a husband somewhere, though I can't find him just now. Dolly, dear! (*Aside to* MAX) Governor, at home I always whistle when I want him.

(*Enter* SPANKER)

SPANKER. Here I am,—did you call me, Gay?

SIR HARCOURT. (*Eyeing him*) Is that your husband?

LADY GAY. (*Aside*) Yes, bless his stupid face, that's my Dolly.

MAX. Permit me to introduce you to Sir Harcourt Courtly.

SPANKER. How d'ye do? I—ah!—um!

(*Appears frightened*)

LADY GAY. (*Prompting him*) Delighted to have the honor of making the acquaintance of a gentleman so highly celebrated in the world of fashion.

SPANKER. Oh, yes, delighted, I'm sure—quite—very, so delighted—delighted!

(*Gets quite confused, draws on his glove, and tears it*)

LADY GAY. Where have you been, Dolly?

SPANKER. Oh, ah, I was just outside.

MAX. Why did you not come in?

SPANKER. I'm sure I didn't—I don't exactly know, but I thought as—perhaps—I can't remember.

DAZZLE. Shall we have the pleasure of your company to dinner?

SPANKER. I always dine—usually—that is, unless Gay remains.

LADY GAY. Stay dinner, of course; we came on purpose to stop three or four days with you.

GRACE. Will you excuse my absence, Gay?

MAX. What! what! Where are you going? What takes you away?

GRACE. We must postpone the dinner till Gay is dressed.

MAX. Oh, never mind,—stay where you are.

GRACE. No, I must go.

MAX. I say you sha'n't! I will be king in my own house.

GRACE. Do, my dear uncle;—you shall be king, and I'll be your prime minister,—that is, I will rule, and you shall have the honor of taking the consequences. (*Exit*)

LADY GAY. Well said, Grace; have your own way; it is the only thing we women ought to be allowed.

MAX. Come, Gay, dress for dinner.

SIR HARCOURT. Permit me, Lady Gay Spanker.

LADY GAY. With pleasure,—what do you want?

SIR HARCOURT. To escort you.

LADY GAY. Oh, never mind, I can escort myself, thank you, and Dolly too;—come, dear! (*Exit*)

SIR HARCOURT. Au revoir!

SPANKER. Ah, thank you!

(*Exit awkwardly*)

SIR HARCOURT. What an ill-assorted pair!

MAX. Not a bit! She married him for freedom, and she has it; he married her for protection, and he has it.

SIR HARCOURT. How he ever summoned courage to propose to her, I can't guess.

MAX. Bless you, he never did. She proposed to him! She says he would, if he could; but as he couldn't, she did for him.

(*Exeunt* MAX *and* SIR HARCOURT, *laughing*)

(*Enter* COOL *with a letter*)

COOL. Mr. Charles, I have been watching to find you alone. Sir Harcourt has written to town for you.

YOUNG COURTLY. The devil he has!

COOL. He expects you down to-morrow evening.

DAZZLE. Oh! he'll be punctual. (*Turning to* YOUNG COURTLY) A thought strikes me.

YOUNG COURTLY. Pooh! Confound your thoughts! I can think of nothing but the idea of leaving Grace, at the very moment when I had established the most—

DAZZLE. What if I can prevent her marriage with your Governor?

YOUNG COURTLY. Impossible!

DAZZLE. He's pluming himself for the conquest of Lady Gay Spanker. It will not be difficult to make him believe she accedes to his suit. And if she would but join in the plan—

YOUNG COURTLY. I see it all. And do you think she would?

DAZZLE. I mistake my game if she would not.

COOL. Here comes Sir Harcourt!

DAZZLE. I'll begin with him. Retire, and watch how I'll open the campaign for you.
(*Exeunt* YOUNG COURTLY *and* COOL)

(*Enter* SIR HARCOURT)

SIR HARCOURT. Here is that cursed fellow again.

DAZZLE. Ah, my dear old friend!

SIR HARCOURT. Mr. Dazzle.

DAZZLE. I have a secret of importance to disclose to you. Are you a man of honor? Hush! don't speak; you are. It is with the greatest pain I am compelled to request you, as a gentleman, that you will shun studiously the society of Lady Gay Spanker!

SIR HARCOURT. Good gracious! Wherefore, and by what right, do you make such a demand?

DAZZLE. Why, I am distantly related to the Spankers.

SIR HARCOURT. Why, damme, sir, if you don't appear to be related to every family in Great Britain!

DAZZLE. A good many of the nobility claim me as a connection. But, to return—she is much struck with your address; evidently, she laid herself out for display.

SIR HARCOURT. Ha! You surprise me!

DAZZLE. To entangle you.

SIR HARCOURT. Ha! ha! Why, it did appear like it.

DAZZLE. You will spare her for my sake; give her no encouragement; if disgrace come upon my relatives, the Spankers, I should never hold up my head again.

SIR HARCOURT. (*Aside*) I shall achieve an easy conquest, and a glorious. Ha! ha! I never remarked it before; but this is a gentleman.

DAZZLE. May I rely on your generosity?

SIR HARCOURT. Faithfully. (*Shakes his hand*) Sir, I honor and esteem you; but, might I ask, how came you to meet our friend, Max Harkaway, in my house in Belgrave Square?

(*Re-enter* YOUNG COURTLY. *Sits on sofa at back*)

DAZZLE. Certainly. I had an acceptance of your son's for one hundred pounds.

SIR HARCOURT. (*Astonished*) Of my son's? Impossible!

DAZZLE. Ah, sir, fact! He paid a debt for a poor, unfortunate man— fifteen children —half-a-dozen wives—the devil knows what all.

SIR HARCOURT. Simple boy!

DAZZLE. Innocent youth, I have no doubt; when you have the hundred convenient, I shall feel delighted.

SIR HARCOURT. Oh! Follow me to my room, and if you have the document, it will be happiness to me to pay it. Poor Charles! Good heart!

DAZZLE. Oh, a splendid heart! I dare say. (*Exit* SIR HARCOURT) Come here; write me the bill.

YOUNG COURTLY. What for?

DAZZLE. What for? Why, to release the unfortunate man and his family, to be sure, from jail.

YOUNG COURTLY. Who is he?

DAZZLE. Yourself.

YOUNG COURTLY. But I haven't fifteen children!

DAZZLE. Will you take your oath of that?

YOUNG COURTLY. Nor four wives.

DAZZLE. More shame for you, with all that family. Come, don't be obstinate; write and date it back.

YOUNG COURTLY. Ay, but where is the stamp?

DAZZLE. Here they are, of all patterns. (*Pulls out a pocketbook*) I keep them ready drawn in case of necessity, all but the date and acceptance. Now, if you are in an autographic humor, you can try how your signature will look across half a dozen of them;— there—write—exactly—you know the place—

across—good—and thank your lucky stars that you have found a friend at last, that gives you money and advice.

(*Takes paper and exit*)

YOUNG COURTLY. Things are approaching to a climax; I must appear *in propria persona*—and immediately—but I must first ascertain what are the real sentiments of this riddle of a woman. Does she love me? I flatter myself.—By Jove, here she comes—I shall never have such an opportunity again!

(*Enter* GRACE)

GRACE. I wish I had never seen Mr. Hamilton. Why does every object appear robbed of the charm it once presented to me? Why do I shudder at the contemplation of this marriage, which, till now, was to me a subject of indifference? Am I in love? In love!—if I am, my past life has been the work of raising up a pedestal to place my own folly on—I—the infidel—the railer!

YOUNG COURTLY. Meditating upon matrimony, madam?

GRACE. (*Aside*) He little thinks he was the subject of my meditations! (*Aloud*) No.

YOUNG COURTLY. (*Aside*) I must unmask my battery now.

GRACE. (*Aside*) How foolish I am—he will perceive that I tremble—I must appear at ease.

YOUNG COURTLY. Eh! ah! um!

GRACE. Ah! (*They sink into silence again. Aside*) How very awkward!

YOUNG COURTLY. (*Aside*) It is a very difficult subject to begin. (*Aloud*) Madam—ahem—there was—is—I mean—I was about to remark—a—(*Aside*) Hang me if it is not a very slippery subject. I must brush up my faculties; attack her in her own way. (*Aloud*) Sing! oh, muse.—(*Aside*) Why, I have made love before to a hundred women!

GRACE. (*Aside*) I wish I had something to do, for I have nothing to say.

YOUNG COURTLY. Madam—there is—a subject so fraught with fate to my future life, that you must pardon my lack of delicacy, should a too hasty expression mar the fervent courtesy of its intent. To you, I feel aware, I must appear in the light of a comparative stranger.

GRACE. (*Aside*) I know what's coming.

YOUNG COURTLY. Of you— I know perhaps too much for my own peace.

GRACE. (*Aside*) He *is* in love.

YOUNG COURTLY. I forget all that befell before I saw your beauteous self: I seem born into another world—my nature changed—the beams of that bright face falling on my soul, have, from its chaos, warmed into life the flowrets of affection, whose maiden odors now float toward the sun, pouring forth on their pure tongue a mite of adoration, midst the voices of a universe. (*Aside*) That's something in her own style.

GRACE. Mr. Hamilton!

YOUNG COURTLY. You cannot feel surprised—

GRACE. I am more than surprised. (*Aside*) I am delighted.

YOUNG COURTLY. Do not speak so coldly.

GRACE. You have offended me.

YOUNG COURTLY. No, madam; no woman, whatever her state, can be offended by the adoration even of the meanest; it is myself whom I have offended and deceived—but still I ask your pardon.

GRACE. (*Aside*) Oh! he thinks I'm refusing him. (*Aloud*) I am not exactly offended, but—

YOUNG COURTLY. Consider my position—a few days—and an insurmountable barrier would have placed you beyond my wildest hopes—you would have been my mother.

GRACE. I should have been your mother! (*Aside*) I thought so.

YOUNG COURTLY. No—that is, I meant Sir Harcourt Courtly's bride.

GRACE. (*With great emphasis*) Never!

YOUNG COURTLY. How! never! may I then hope?—you turn away—you would not lacerate me by a refusal?

GRACE. (*Aside*) How stupid he is!

YOUNG COURTLY. Still silent! I thank you, Miss Grace—I ought to have expected this—fool that I have been—one course alone remains—farewell!

GRACE. (*Aside*) Now he's going.

YOUNG COURTLY. Farewell forever! (*Sits*) Will you not speak one word? I shall leave this house immediately—I shall not see you again.

GRACE. Unhand me, sir, I insist.

YOUNG COURTLY. (*Aside*) Oh! what an ass I've been! (*Rushes up to her, and seizes her hand*) Release this hand? Never! never! (*Kissing it*) Never will I quit this hand! it shall be my companion in misery—in solitude —when you are far away.

GRACE. Oh! should any one come! (*Drops her handkerchief; he stoops to pick it up*) For heaven's sake, do not kneel.

YOUNG COURTLY. (*Kneels*) Forever thus prostrate, before my soul's saint, I will lead a pious life of eternal adoration.

GRACE. Should we be discovered thus— pray, Mr. Hamilton—pray—pray.

YOUNG COURTLY. Pray! I am praying; what more can I do?

GRACE. Your conduct is shameful.

YOUNG COURTLY. It is.   (*Rises*)

GRACE. And if I do not scream, it is not for your sake—that—but it might alarm the family.

YOUNG COURTLY. It might—it would. Say, am I wholly indifferent to you? I entreat one word—I implore you—do not withdraw your hand—(*She snatches it away— he puts his round her waist*)—you smile.

GRACE. Leave me, dear Mr. Hamilton!

YOUNG COURTLY. Dear! Then I am dear to you; that word once more; say—say you love me!

GRACE. Is this fair?

(*He catches her in his arms, and kisses her*)

(*Enter* LADY GAY SPANKER *dressed for dinner*)

LADY GAY. Ha! oh!

GRACE. Gay! Destruction!   (*Exit*)

YOUNG COURTLY. Fizgig! The devil!

LADY GAY. Don't mind me—pray, don't let me be any interruption!

YOUNG COURTLY. I was just—

LADY GAY. Yes, I see you were.

YOUNG COURTLY. Oh! madam, how could you mar my bliss, in the very ecstasy of its fulfilment?

LADY GAY. I always like to be in at the death. Never drop your ears; bless you, she is only a little fresh—give her her head, and she will outrun herself.

YOUNG COURTLY. Possibly; but what am I to do?

LADY GAY. Keep your seat.

YOUNG COURTLY. But in a few days she will take a leap that must throw me—she marries Sir Harcourt Courtly.

LADY GAY. Why, that is awkward, certainly; but you can challenge him, and shoot him.

YOUNG COURTLY. Unfortunately, that is out of the question.

LADY GAY. How so?

YOUNG COURTLY. You will not betray a secret, if I inform you?

LADY GAY. All right—what is it?

YOUNG COURTLY. I am his son.

LADY GAY. What—his son? But does he not know you?

YOUNG COURTLY. No. I met him here, by chance, and faced it out. I never saw him before in my life.

LADY GAY. Beautiful!—I see it all—you're in love with your mother, that should be— your wife, that will be.

YOUNG COURTLY. Now, I think I could distance the old gentleman, if you will but lend us your assistance.

LADY GAY. I will, in anything.

YOUNG COURTLY. You must know, then, that my father, Sir Harcourt, has fallen desperately in love with you.

LADY GAY. With me!— (*Utters a scream of delight*)—That is delicious!

YOUNG COURTLY. Now, if you only could—

LADY GAY. Could!—I will. Ha! ha! I see my cue. I'll cross his scent—I'll draw him after me. Ho! ho! won't I make love to him? Ha!

YOUNG COURTLY. The only objection might be Mr. Spanker, who might—

LADY GAY. No, he mightn't,—he's no objection. Bless him, he's an inestimable little character—you don't know him as well as I do, I dare say—ha! ha! (*Dinner-bell rings*) Here they come to dinner. I'll commence my operations on your Governor immediately. Ha! ha! how I shall enjoy it!

YOUNG COURTLY. Be guarded!

(*Enter* MAX HARKAWAY, SIR HARCOURT, DAZZLE, GRACE, *and* SPANKER)

MAX. Now, gentlemen—Sir Harcourt, do you lead Grace.

LADY GAY. I believe Sir Harcourt is engaged to me. (*Takes his arm*)

MAX. Well, please yourselves.

(*They file out*, MAX *first*, YOUNG COURTLY *and* GRACE, SIR HARCOURT *coquetting with* LADY GAY, *leaving* DAZZLE, *who offers his arm to* SPANKER)

Act IV

SCENE I. *After dinner. A handsome drawing-room in Oak Hall, chandeliers, tables with books, drawings, etc.*

(GRACE *and* LADY GAY *discovered. Servant handing coffee*)

GRACE. If there be one habit more abominable than another, it is that of the gentlemen sitting over their wine; it is a selfish, unfeeling fashion, and a gross insult to our sex.

LADY GAY. We are turned out just when the fun begins. How happy the poor wretches look at the contemplation of being rid of us.

GRACE. The conventional signal for the ladies to withdraw is anxiously and deliberately waited for.

LADY GAY. Then I begin to wish I were a man.

GRACE. The instant the door is closed upon us, there rises a roar!

LADY GAY. In celebration of their short-lived liberty, my love; rejoicing over their emancipation.

GRACE. I think it very insulting, whatever it may be.

LADY GAY. Ah! my dear, philosophers say that man is the creature of an hour—it is the dinner hour, I suppose.

(*Loud noise. Cries of* "A song, a song.")

GRACE. I am afraid they are getting too pleasant to be agreeable.

LADY GAY. I hope the squire will restrict himself; after his third bottle, he becomes rather voluminous. (*Cries of* "Silence") Some one is going to sing. (*Jumps up*) Let us hear! (SPANKER *is heard to sing*)

GRACE. Oh, no, Gay, for heaven's sake!

LADY GAY. Oho! ha! ha! why, that is my Dolly. (*At the conclusion of the verse*) Well, I never heard my Dolly sing before! Happy wretches, how I envy them!

(*Enter* JAMES, *with a note*)

JAMES. Mr. Hamilton has just left the house for London.

GRACE. Impossible!—that is, without see-ing—that is—

LADY GAY. Ha! ha!

GRACE. He never—speak, sir!

JAMES. He left, Miss Grace, in a desperate hurry, and this note, I believe, for you.

(*Presenting a note on a salver*)

GRACE. For me!

(*She is about to snatch it, but restraining herself, takes it coolly. Exit* JAMES.)

(*Reads*) "Your manner during dinner has left me no alternative but instant departure; my absence will release you from the oppression which my society must necessarily inflict on your sensitive mind. It may tend also to smother, though it can never extinguish, that indomitable passion, of which I am the passive victim. Dare I supplicate pardon and oblivion for the past? It is the last request of the self-deceived, but still loving

AUGUSTUS HAMILTON."

(*Puts her hand to her forehead and appears giddy*)

LADY GAY. Hallo, Grace! what's the matter?

GRACE. (*Recovering herself*) Nothing—the heat of the room.

LADY GAY. Oh! what excuse does he make? Particular unforeseen business, I suppose?

GRACE. Why, yes—a mere formula—a—a—you may put it in the fire.

(*She puts it in her bosom*)

LADY GAY. (*Aside*) It is near enough to the fire where it is.

GRACE. I'm glad he's gone.

LADY GAY. So am I.

GRACE. He was a disagreeable, ignorant person.

LADY GAY. Yes; and so vulgar.

GRACE. No, he was not at all vulgar.

LADY GAY. I mean in appearance.

GRACE. Oh! how can you say so; he was very *distingué*.

LADY GAY. Well, I might have been mistaken, but I took him for a forward, intrusive—

GRACE. Good gracious, Gay! He was very retiring—even shy.

LADY GAY. (*Aside*) It's all right. *She* is in love,—blows hot and cold, in the same breath.

GRACE. How can you be a competent judge? Why, you have not known him more than a few hours,—while I—I—

LADY GAY. Have known him two days and a quarter! I yield—I confess, I never was, or will be, so intimate with him as you appeared to be! Ha! ha!

(*Loud noise of argument. The folding-doors are thrown open*)

(*Enter the whole party of gentlemen apparently engaged in warm discussion. They assemble in knots, while the servants hand coffee, etc.,* MAX, SIR HARCOURT, DAZZLE, *and* SPANKER, *together*)

DAZZLE. But, my dear sir, consider the position of the two countries under such a constitution.

SIR HARCOURT. The two countries! What have they to do with the subject?

MAX. Everything. Look at their two legislative bodies.

SPANKER. Ay, look at their two legislative bodies.

SIR HARCOURT. Why, it would inevitably establish universal anarchy and confusion.

GRACE. I think they are pretty well established already.

SPANKER. Well, suppose it did, what has anarchy and confusion to do with the subject?

LADY GAY. Do look at my Dolly; he is arguing—talking politics—'pon my life he is. (*Calling*) Mr. Spanker, my dear!

SPANKER. Excuse me, love, I am discussing a point of importance.

LADY GAY. Oh, that is delicious; he must discuss that to me.—(*She goes up and leads him down; he appears to have shaken off his gaucherie; she shakes her head*) Dolly! Dolly!

SPANKER. Pardon me, Lady Gay Spanker, I conceive your mutilation of my sponsorial appellation derogatory to my *amour propre*.

LADY GAY. Your what? Ho! ho!

SPANKER. And I particularly request that, for the future, I may not be treated with that cavalier spirit which does not become your sex, nor your station, your ladyship.

LADY GAY. You have been indulging till you have lost the little wit nature dribbled into your unfortunate little head—your brains want the whipper-in—you are not yourself.

SPANKER. Madam, I am doubly myself, and permit me to inform you, that unless you voluntarily pay obedience to my commands, I shall enforce them.

LADY GAY. Your commands!

SPANKER. Yes, madam; I mean to put a full stop to your hunting.

LADY GAY. You do! ah! (*Aside*) I can scarcely speak from delight. (*Aloud*) Who put such an idea into your head, for I am sure it is not an original emanation of your genius?

SPANKER. Sir Harcourt Courtly, my friend; and now, mark me! I request, for your own sake, that I may not be compelled to assert my a—my authority, as your husband. I shall say no more than this—if you persist in this absurd rebellion—

LADY GAY. Well?

SPANKER. Contemplate a separation.

(*He looks at her haughtily, and retires*)

LADY GAY. Now I'm happy! My own little darling, inestimable Dolly, has tumbled into a spirit, somehow. Sir Harcourt, too! Ha! ha! he's trying to make him ill-treat me, so that his own suit may thrive.

SIR HARCOURT. (*Advances*) Lady Gay!

LADY GAY. Now for it.

SIR HARCOURT. What hours of misery were those I passed, when, by your secession, the room suffered a total eclipse.

LADY GAY. Ah! you flatter.

SIR HARCOURT. No, pardon me, that were impossible. No, believe me, I tried to join in the boisterous mirth, but my thoughts would desert to the drawing-room. Ah! how I envied the careless levity and cool indifference with which Mr. Spanker enjoyed your absence.   (*They talk aside*)

DAZZLE. (*Who is lounging in a chair*) Max, that Madeira is worth its weight in gold; I hope you have more of it.

MAX. A pipe, I think.

DAZZLE. I consider a magnum of that nectar, and a meerschaum of kanaster, to consummate the ultimatum of all mundane bliss. To drown myself in liquid ecstasy, and then blow a cloud on which the enfranchised soul could soar above Olympus.—Oh!

(*Enter* JAMES)

JAMES. Mr Charles Courtly!   (*Exit*)

SIR HARCOURT. Ah, now, Max, you must see a living apology for my conduct.

(*Enter* YOUNG COURTLY, *dressed very plainly*)

Well, Charles, how are you? Don't be afraid. There, Max, what do you say now?

MAX. Well, this is the most extraordinary likeness.

GRACE. (*Aside*) Yes—considering it is the original. I am not so easily deceived!

MAX. Sir, I am delighted to see you.

YOUNG COURTLY. Thank you, sir.

DAZZLE. Will you be kind enough to introduce me, Sir Harcourt?

SIR HARCOURT. This is Mr. Dazzle, Charles.

YOUNG COURTLY. Which?
(*Looking from* MR. SPANKER *to* DAZZLE)

SIR HARCOURT. (*To* LADY GAY) Is not that refreshing? Miss Harkaway—Charles, this is your mother, or rather will be.

YOUNG COURTLY. Madam, I shall love, honor, and obey you punctually.
(*Takes out a book, sighs, and goes up reading*)

(*Enter* JAMES)

SIR HARCOURT. You perceive. Quite unused to society—perfectly ignorant of every conventional rule of life.

JAMES. The Doctor and the young ladies have arrived.   (*Exit*)

MAX. The young ladies—now we must to the ball—I make it a rule always to commence the festivities with a good old country dance—a rattling Sir Roger de Coverly; come, Sir Harcourt.

SIR HARCOURT. Does this antiquity require a war-whoop in it?

MAX. Nothing but a nimble foot and a light heart.

SIR HARCOURT. Very antediluvian indispensables! Lady Gay Spanker, will you honor me by becoming my preceptor?

LADY GAY. Why, I am engaged—but (*aloud*) on such a plea as Sir Harcourt's, I must waive all obstacles.

MAX. Now, Grace, girl—give your hand to Mr. Courtly.

GRACE. Pray, excuse me, uncle—I have a headache.

SIR HARCOURT. (*Aside*) Jealousy! by the gods!—Jealous of my devotions at another's fane! (*Aloud*) Charles, my boy! Amuse Miss Grace during our absence.
(*Exit with* LADY GAY)

MAX. But don't you dance, Mr. Courtly!

YOUNG COURTLY. Dance, sir!—I never dance—I can procure exercise in a much more rational manner—and music disturbs my meditations.

MAX. Well, do the gallant.   (*Exit*)

YOUNG COURTLY. I never studied that Art —but I have a Prize Essay on a Hydrostatic subject, which would delight her—for it enchanted the Reverend Doctor Pump, of Corpus Christi.

GRACE. (*Aside*) What on earth could have induced him to disfigure himself in that frightful way!—I rather suspect some plot to entrap me into a confession.

YOUNG COURTLY. (*Aside*) Dare I confess this trick to her? No! Not until I have proved her affection indisputably.—Let me see—I must concoct. (*He takes a chair, and, forgetting his assumed character, is about to take his natural free manner.—*GRACE *looks surprised.—He turns abashed*) Madam, I have been desired to amuse you.

GRACE. Thank you.

YOUNG COURTLY. "The labor we delight in, physics pain." I will draw you a moral, ahem! Subject, the effects of inebriety!— which, according to Ben Jonson—means perplexion of the intellects, caused by imbibing spirituous liquors.—About an hour **before** my arrival, I passed an appalling evidence of the effects of this state—a carriage was overthrown—horses killed—gentleman in a helpless state, with his neck broken—all occasioned by the intoxication of the post-boy.

GRACE. That is very amusing.

YOUNG COURTLY. I found it edifying—nutritious food for reflection—the expiring man desired his best compliments to you.

GRACE. To me—

YOUNG COURTLY. Yes.

GRACE. His name was—

YOUNG COURTLY. Mr. Augustus Hamilton.

GRACE. Augustus! Oh! (*Affects to faint*)

YOUNG COURTLY. (*Aside*) Huzza!

GRACE. But where, sir, did this happen?

YOUNG COURTLY. About four miles down the road.

GRACE. He must be conveyed here.

(*Enter* SERVANT)

SERVANT. Mr. Meddle, madam.

(*Enter* MEDDLE)

MEDDLE. On very particular business.

GRACE. The very person. My dear sir!

MEDDLE. My dear madam!

GRACE. You must execute a very particular commission for me immediately. Mr. Hamilton has met with a frightful accident on the London road, and is in a dying state.

MEDDLE. Well! I have no hesitation in saying, he takes it uncommonly easy—he looks as if he was used to it.

GRACE. You mistake: that is not Mr. Hamilton, but Mr. Courtly, who will explain everything, and conduct you to the spot.

YOUNG COURTLY. (*Aside*) Oh! I must put a stop to all this, or I shall be found out.—(*Aloud*) Madam, that were useless; for I omitted to mention a small fact which occurred before I left Mr. Hamilton—he died.

GRACE. Dear me! Oh, then we needn't trouble you, Mr. Meddle. Hark! I hear they are commencing a waltz—if you will ask me —perhaps your society and conversation may tend to dispel the dreadful sensation you have aroused.

YOUNG COURTLY. (*Aside*) Hears of my death—screams out—and then asks me to

waltz! I am bewildered! Can she suspect me? I wonder which she likes best—me or my double? Confound this disguise—I must retain it—I have gone too far with my dad to pull up now.—At your service, madam.

GRACE. (*Aside*) I will pay him well for this trick!   (*Exeunt*)

MEDDLE. Well, if that is not Mr. Hamilton, scratch me out with a big blade, for I am a blot—a mistake upon the rolls. There is an error in the pleadings somewhere, and I will discover it.—I would swear to his identity before the most discriminating jury. By the bye, this accident will form a capital excuse for my presence here. I just stepped in to see how matters worked, and—stay—here comes the bridegroom elect—and, oh! in his very arms, Lady Gay Spanker! (*Looks round*) Where are my witnesses? Oh, that some one else were here! However, I can retire and get some information, eh—Spanker *versus* Courtly—damages—witness.

(*Gets into an arm-chair, which he turns round*)

(*Enter* SIR HARCOURT, *supporting* LADY GAY)

SIR HARCOURT. This cool room will recover you.

LADY GAY. Excuse my trusting to you for support.

SIR HARCOURT. I am transported! Allow me thus ever to support this lovely burden, and I shall conceive that Paradise is regained.   (*They sit*)

LADY GAY. Oh! Sir Harcourt, I feel very faint.

SIR HARCOURT. The waltz made you giddy.

LADY GAY. And I have left my salts in the other room.

SIR HARCOURT. I always carry a flacon, for the express accommodation of the fair sex.   (*Producing a smelling-bottle*)

LADY GAY. Thank you—ah! (*She sighs*)

SIR HARCOURT. What a sigh was there!

LADY GAY. The vapor of consuming grief.

SIR HARCOURT. Grief? Is it possible, have you a grief? Are you unhappy? Dear me!

LADY GAY. Am I not married?

SIR HARCOURT. What a horrible state of existence!

LADY GAY. I am never contradicted, so there are none of those enlivening, interesting little differences which so pleasingly diversify the monotony of conjugal life, like spots of verdure—no quarrels, like oases in the desert of matrimony—no rows.

SIR HARCOURT. How vulgar! What a brute!

LADY GAY. I never have anything but my own way; and he won't permit me to spend more than I like.

SIR HARCOURT. Mean-spirited wretch!

LADY GAY. How can I help being miserable?

SIR HARCOURT. Miserable! I wonder you are not in a lunatic asylum, wth such unheard-of barbarism!

LADY GAY. But worse than all that!

SIR HARCOURT. Can it be out-Heroded?

LADY GAY. Yes, I could forgive that—I do—it is my duty. But only imagine—picture to yourself, my dear Sir Harcourt, though I, the third daughter of an Earl, married him out of pity for his destitute and helpless situation as a bachelor with ten thousand a year—conceive, if you can—he actually permits me, with the most placid indifference, to flirt with any old fool I may meet.

SIR HARCOURT. Good gracious! Miserable idiot!

LADY GAY. I fear there is an incompatibility of temper which renders a separation inevitable.

SIR HARCOURT. Indispensable, my dear madam! Ah! had I been the happy possessor of such a realm of bliss—what a beatific eternity unfolds itself to my extending imagination! Had another man but looked at you, I should have annihilated him at once; and if he had the temerity to speak, his life alone could have expiated his crime.

LADY GAY. Oh, an existence of such a nature is too bright for the eye of thought—too sweet to bear reflection.

SIR HARCOURT. My devotion, eternal, deep—

LADY GAY. Oh, Sir Harcourt!

SIR HARCOURT. (More fervently) Your every thought should be a separate study,—each wish forestalled by the quick apprehension of a kindred soul.

LADY GAY. Alas! how can I avoid my fate?

SIR HARCOURT. If a life—a heart—were offered to your astonished view by one who is considered the index of fashion—the vane of the *beau monde,*—if you saw him at your feet, begging, beseeching your acceptance of all, and more than this, what would your answer—

LADY GAY. Ah! I know of none so devoted!

SIR HARCOURT. You do! (*Throwing himself upon his knees*) Behold Sir Harcourt Courtly!

(MEDDLE *jumps up in the chair and peers round at them, but they are not aware of him*)

LADY GAY. (*Aside*) Ha! ha! Yoicks! Puss has broken cover.

SIR HARCOURT. Speak, adored, dearest Lady Gay!—speak—will you fly from the tyranny, the wretched misery of such a monster's roof, and accept the soul which lives but in your presence!

LADY GAY. Do not press me. Oh, spare a weak, yielding woman,—be contented to know that you are, alas! too dear to me. But the world—the world would say—

SIR HARCOURT. Let us be a precedent, to open a more extended and liberal view of matrimonial advantages to society.

LADY GAY. How irresistible is your argument! Oh! pause!

SIR HARCOURT. I have ascertained for a fact, every tradesman of mine lives with his wife, and thus you see it has become a vulgar and plebeian custom.

LADY GAY. Leave me; I feel I cannot withstand your powers of persuasion. Swear that you will never forsake me.

SIR HARCOURT. Dictate the oath. May I grow wrinkled,—may two inches be added to the circumference of my waist,—may I lose the fall in my back,—may I be old and ugly the instant I forego one tithe of adoration!

LADY GAY. I must believe you.

SIR HARCOURT. Shall we leave this detestable spot—this horrible vicinity?

LADY GAY. The sooner the better; to-morrow evening let it be. Now let me return; my absence will be remarked. (*He kisses her hand*) Do I appear confused? Has my agitation rendered me unfit to enter the room?

SIR HARCOURT. More angelic by a lovely tinge of heightened color.

LADY GAY. To-morrow, in this room, which opens on the lawn.

SIR HARCOURT. At eleven o'clock.

LADY GAY. Have your carriage in waiting, and four horses. Remember please, be particular to have four; don't let the affair come off shabbily. Adieu, dear Sir Harcourt!

(*Exit*)

SIR HARCOURT. Veni, vidi, vici! Hannibal, Cæsar, Napoleon, Alexander never completed so fair a conquest in so short a time. She dropped fascinated. This is an unprecedented example of the irresistible force of personal appearance combined with polished address. Poor creature! how she loves me! I pity so prostrating a passion, and ought to return it. I will; it is a duty I owe to society and fashion. (*Exit*)

MEDDLE. (*Turns the chair round*) "There is a tide in the affairs of men, which, taken at the flood, leads on to fortune." This is my tide—I am the only witness. "Virtue is sure to find its own reward." But I've no time to contemplate what I shall be—something huge. Let me see—Spanker *versus* Courtly—Crim. Con.—Damages placed at £150,000, at least, for juries always decimate your hopes.

(*Enter* MR. SPANKER, *looking about*)

SPANKER. I cannot find Gay anywhere.

MEDDLE. The plaintiff himself—I must commence the action.—Mr. Spanker, as I have information of deep, vital importance to impart, will you take a seat? (*They sit solemnly.* MEDDLE *takes out a note-book and pencil*) Ahem! You have a wife?

(*Re-enter* LADY GAY, *behind*)

SPANKER. Yes, I believe I—

MEDDLE. Will you be kind enough, without any prevarication, to answer my questions?

SPANKER. You alarm—I—

MEDDLE. Compose yourself and reserve your feelings; take time to consider. You have a wife?

SPANKER. Yes—

MEDDLE. He has a wife—good—a *bona-fide* wife—bound morally and legally to be your wife, and nobody else's in effect, except on your written permission—

SPANKER. But what has this—

MEDDLE. Hush! allow me, my dear sir, to congratulate you. (*Shakes his hand*)

SPANKER. What for?

MEDDLE. Lady Gay Spanker is about to dishonor the bond of wedlock by eloping from you.

SPANKER. (*Starting*) What!

MEDDLE. Be patient—I thought you would be overjoyed. Will you place the affair in my hands, and I will venture to promise the largest damages on record.

SPANKER. Damn the damages! I want my wife. Oh, I'll go and ask her not to run away. She may run away with me—she may hunt—she may ride—anything she likes. Oh, sir, let us put a stop to this affair.

MEDDLE. Put a stop to it! Do not alarm me, sir. Sir, you will spoil the most exquisite brief that was ever penned. It must proceed—it shall proceed. It is illegal to prevent it, and I will bring an action against you for wilful intent to injure the profession.

SPANKER. Oh, what an ass I am! Oh, I have driven her to this. It was all that damned brandy punch on the top of Burgundy. What a fool I was!

MEDDLE. It was the happiest moment of your life.

SPANKER. So I thought at the time; but we live to grow wiser. Tell me, who is the vile seducer?

MEDDLE. Sir Harcourt Courtly.

SPANKER. Ha! he is my best friend.

MEDDLE. I should think he is. If you will accompany me—here is a verbatim copy of the whole transaction in shorthand—sworn to by me.

SPANKER. Only let me have Gay back again.

MEDDLE. Even that may be arranged—this way.

SPANKER. That ever I should live to see my wife run away. Oh, I will do anything—keep two packs of hounds—buy up every horse and ass in England—myself included—oh! (*Exit with* MEDDLE)

LADY GAY. Ha! ha! ha! Poor Dolly! I'm sorry I must continue to deceive him. If he would kindle up a little—so that fellow overheard all—well, so much the better.

(*Enter* YOUNG COURTLY)

YOUNG COURTLY. My dear madam, how fares the plot? Does my Governor nibble?

LADY GAY. Nibble! He is caught and in the basket. I have just left him with a hook in his gills, panting for very lack of element. But how goes on your encounter?

YOUNG COURTLY. Bravely. By a simple ruse, I have discovered that she loves me. I see but one chance against the best termination I could hope.

LADY GAY. What is that?

YOUNG COURTLY. My father has told me that I return to town again to-morrow afternoon.

LADY GAY. Well, I insist you stop and dine—keep out of the way.

YOUNG COURTLY. Oh, but what excuse can I offer for disobedience? What can I say when he sees me before dinner?

LADY GAY. Say—say Grace.

(*Enter* GRACE, *who gets behind the window curtains*)

YOUNG COURTLY. Ha! ha!

LADY GAY. I have arranged to elope with Sir Harcourt myself to-morrow night.

YOUNG COURTLY. The deuce you have!

LADY GAY. Now if you could persuade Grace to follow that example—his carriage will be waiting at the Park—be there a little before eleven—and it will just prevent our escape. Can you make her agree to that?

YOUNG COURTLY. Oh, without the slightest difficulty, if Mr. Augustus Hamilton supplicates.

LADY GAY. Success attend you. (*Going*)

YOUNG COURTLY. I will bend the haughty Grace.   (*Going*)

LADY GAY. Do.   (*Exeunt severally*)

GRACE. Will you?

Act V

SCENE I. *The next morning. A drawing-room in Oak Hall.*

(*Enter* COOL)

COOL. This is the most serious affair Sir Harcourt has ever been engaged in. I took the liberty of considering him a fool when he told me he was going to marry, but voluntarily to incur another man's incumbrance is very little short of madness. If he continues to conduct himself in this absurd manner, I shall be compelled to dismiss him.

(*Enter* SIR HARCOURT, *equipped for travelling*)

SIR HARCOURT. Cool!

COOL. Sir Harcourt.

SIR HARCOURT. Is my chariot in waiting?

COOL. For the last half hour at the park wicket. But, pardon the insinuation, sir; would it not be more advisable to hesitate a little for a short reflection before you undertake the heavy responsibility of a woman?

SIR HARCOURT. No, hesitation destroys the romance of a *faux pas*, and reduces it to the level of a mere mercantile calculation.

COOL. What is to be done with Mr. Charles?

SIR HARCOURT. Ay, much against my will, Lady Gay prevailed on me to permit him to remain. You, Cool, must return him to college. Pass through London, and deliver these papers: here is a small notice of the coming elopement for the *Morning Post*; this, by an eye-witness, for the *Herald*; this, with all the particulars, for the *Chronicle*; and the full and circumstantial account for the evening journals—after which, meet us at Boulogne.

COOL. Very good, Sir Harcourt. (*Going*)

SIR HARCOURT. Lose no time. Remember—Hotel Anglais, Boulogne-sur-Mer. And, Cool, bring a few copies with you, and don't forget to distribute some amongst very particular friends.

COOL. It shall be done.   (*Exit* COOL)

SIR HARCOURT. With what indifference does a man of the world view the approach of the most perilous catastrophe! My position, hazardous as it is, entails none of that nervous excitement which a neophyte in the school of fashion would feel. I am as cool and steady as possible. Habit, habit! Oh! how many roses will fade upon the cheek of beauty, when the defalcation of Sir Harcourt Courtly is whispered—then hinted—at last, confirmed and bruited. I think I see them. Then, on my return, they will not dare to eject me—I am their sovereign! Whoever attempts to think of treason, I'll banish him from the West End—I'll cut him—I'll put him out of fashion!

(*Enter* LADY GAY)

LADY GAY. Sir Harcourt!

SIR HARCOURT. At your feet.

LADY GAY. I had hoped you would have repented.

SIR HARCOURT. Repented!

LADY GAY. Have you not come to say it was a jest?—say you have!

SIR HARCOURT. Love is too sacred a subject to be trifled with. Come, let us fly! See, I have procured disguises—

LADY GAY. My courage begins to fail me. Let me return.

SIR HARCOURT. Impossible!

LADY GAY. Where do you intend to take me?

SIR HARCOURT. You shall be my guide. The carriage waits.

LADY GAY. You will never desert me?

SIR HARCOURT. Desert! Oh, heavens! Nay, do not hesitate—flight, now, alone is left to your desperate situation! Come, every moment is laden with danger.

(*They are going*)

LADY GAY. Oh! gracious!

SIR HARCOURT. Hush! what is it?

LADY GAY. I have forgotten—I must return.

SIR HARCOURT. Impossible!

LADY GAY. I must! I must! I have left Max—a pet staghound, in his basket—without whom, life would be unendurable—I could not exist!

SIR HARCOURT. No, no. Let him be sent after us in a hamper.

LADY GAY. In a hamper! Remorseless man! Go—you love me not. How would you like to be sent after me—in a hamper? Let me fetch him. Hark! I hear him squeal! Oh! Max—Max!

SIR HARCOURT. Hush! for heaven's sake. They'll imagine you're calling the Squire. I hear footsteps; where can I retire?

(*He hides behind the curtains*)

(*Enter* MEDDLE, SPANKER, DAZZLE, *and* MAX. LADY GAY *screams*)

MEDDLE. Spanker *versus* Courtly!—I subpœna every one of you as witnesses!—I have 'em ready—here they are—shilling a-piece.

(*Giving them round*)

LADY GAY. Where is Sir Harcourt?

MEDDLE. There!—bear witness!—calling on the vile delinquent for protection!

SPANKER. Oh! his protection!

LADY GAY. What? ha!

MEDDLE. I'll swear I overheard the whole elopement planned—before any jury!—where's the book?

SPANKER. Do you hear, you profligate?

LADY GAY. Ha! ha! ha! ha!

DAZZLE. But where is this wretched Lothario?

MEDDLE. Aye, where is the defendant?

SPANKER. Where lies the hoary villain?

LADY GAY. What villain?

SPANKER. That will not serve you!—I'll not be blinded that way!

MEDDLE. We won't be blinded any way!

MAX. I must seek Sir Harcourt, and demand an explanation!—Such a thing never occurred in Oak Hall before!—It must be cleared up!   (*Exit*)

MEDDLE. (*Aside to* SPANKER) Now, take my advice, remember your gender. Mind the notes I have given you.

SPANKER. (*Aside*) All right! Here they are.—Now, madam, I have procured the highest legal opinion on this point.

MEDDLE. Hear! hear!

SPANKER. And the question resolves itself into a—into—What's this? (*Looks at notes*)

MEDDLE. A nutshell!

SPANKER. Yes, we are in a nutshell. Will you, in every respect, subscribe to my requests—desires—commands—(*looks at notes*) —orders—imperative—indicative—injunctive —or otherwise?

LADY GAY. (*Aside*) 'Pon my life, he's actually going to assume the ribbons, and take the box-seat. I must put a stop to this. I will! It will all end in smoke. I know Sir Harcourt would rather run than fight!

DAZZLE. Oh! I smell powder!—command my services. My dear madam, can I be of any use?

SPANKER. Oh! a challenge!—I must consult my legal adviser.

MEDDLE. No!—impossible!

DAZZLE. Pooh! the easiest thing in life! —Leave it to me—what has an attorney to do with affairs of honor?—they are out of his element!

MEDDLE. Compromise the question!—pull his nose!—we have no objection to that!

DAZZLE. (*Turning to* LADY GAY) Well, we have no objection either—have we?

LADY GAY. No!—pull his nose—that will be something.

MEDDLE. And, moreover, it is not exactly actionable!

DAZZLE. Isn't it!—thank you—I'll note down that piece of information—it may be useful.

MEDDLE. How! cheated out of my legal knowledge.

LADY GAY. Mr. Spanker, I am determined!—I insist upon a challenge being sent to Sir Harcourt Courtly!—and—mark me— if you refuse to fight him—I will.

MEDDLE. Don't. Take my advice—you'll incapacit—

LADY GAY. Look you, Mr. Meddle, unless you wish me to horsewhip you, hold your tongue.

MEDDLE. What a she-tiger—I shall retire and collect my costs. (*Exit*)

LADY GAY. Mr. Spanker, oblige me by writing as I dictate.

SPANKER. He's gone—and now I am defenceless! Is this the fate of husbands?—A duel!—Is this the result of becoming master of my own family? (*He sits down to write*)

LADY GAY. "Sir, the situation in which you were discovered with my wife, admits neither of explanation nor apology."

SPANKER. Oh, yes! but it does—I don't believe you really intended to run quite away.

LADY GAY. You do not; but I know better, I say I did; and if it had not been for your unfortunate interruption, I do not know where I might have been by this time.—Go on.

SPANKER. "Nor apology." I'm writing my own death-warrant, committing suicide on compulsion.

LADY GAY. "The bearer will arrange all preliminary matters, for another day must

see this sacrilege expiated by your life, or that of

Yours very sincerely,
"DOLLY SPANKER"

(*She takes the note from him*) Now, Mr. Dazzle. (*Gives it over his head*)

DAZZLE. The document is as sacred as if it were a hundred-pound bill.

LADY GAY. We trust to your discretion.

SPANKER. His discretion! Oh, put your head in a tiger's mouth, and trust to his discretion!

DAZZLE. (*Sealing letter, etc., with* SPANKER'S *seal*) My dear Lady Gay, matters of this kind are indigenous to my nature, independently of their pervading fascination to all humanity; but this is more especially delightful, as you may perceive I shall be the intimate and bosom friend of both parties.

LADY GAY. Is it not the only alternative in such a case?

DAZZLE. It is a beautiful panacea in any, in every case. (*Going—returns*) By the way, where would you like this party of pleasure to come off? Open air shooting is pleasant enough, but if I might venture to advise, we could order half a dozen of that Madeira and a box of cigars into the billiard-room, so make a night of it; take up the irons every now and then, string for first shot, and blaze away at one another in an amicable and gentlemanlike way; so conclude the matter before the potency of the liquor could disturb the individuality of the object, or the smoke of the cigars render its outline dubious. Does such an arrangement coincide with your views?

LADY GAY. Perfectly.

DAZZLE. I trust shortly to be the harbinger of happy tidings. (*Exit*)

SPANKER. (*Coming forward*) Lady Gay Spanker, are you ambitious of becoming a widow?

LADY GAY. Why, Dolly, woman is at best but weak, and weeds become me.

SPANKER. Female! Am I to be immolated on the altar of your vanity?

LADY GAY. If you become pathetic, I shall laugh.

SPANKER. Farewell—base, heartless, unfeeling woman! (*Exit*)

LADY GAY. Ha! well, so I am. I am heartless, for he is a dear, good little fellow, and

I ought not to play upon his feelings; but 'pon my life he sounds so well up at concert pitch, that I feel disinclined to untune him. Poor Dolly, I didn't think he cared so much about me. I will put him out of pain.

(*Exit.* SIR HARCOURT *comes down*)

SIR HARCOURT. I have been a fool! a dupe of my own vanity. I shall be pointed at as a ridiculous old coxcomb—and so I am. The hour of conviction is *arrived.* Have I deceived myself?—Have I turned all my senses inwards—looking towards self—always self? —and has the world been ever laughing at me? Well, if they have, I will revert the joke; —they may say I am an old ass; but I will prove that I am neither too old to repent my folly, nor such an ass as to flinch from confessing it. A blow half met is but half felt.

(*Enter* DAZZLE)

DAZZLE. Sir Harcourt, may I be permitted the honor of a few minutes' conversation with you?

SIR HARCOURT. With pleasure.

DAZZLE. Have the kindness to throw your eye over that. (*Gives the letter*)

SIR HARCOURT. (*Reads*) "Situation—my wife—apology—expiate—my life." Why, this is intended for a challenge.

DAZZLE. Why, indeed, I am perfectly aware that it is not quite *en règle* in the couching, for with that I had nothing to do; but I trust that the irregularity of the composition will be confounded in the beauty of the subject.

SIR HARCOURT. Mr. Dazzle, are you in earnest?

DAZZLE. Sir Harcourt Courtly, upon my honor I am, and I hope that no previous engagement will interfere with an immediate reply *in propria persona.* We have fixed upon the billiard-room as the scene of action, which I have just seen properly illuminated in honor of the occasion; and, by-the-bye, if your implements are not handy, I can oblige you with a pair of the sweetest things you ever handled—hair-triggered—saw grip; heir-looms in my family. I regard them almost in the light of relations.

SIR HARCOURT. Sir, I shall avail myself of one of your relatives. (*Aside*) One of the hereditaments of my folly—I must accept it.

(*Aloud*) Sir, I shall be happy to meet Mr. Spanker at any time or place he may appoint.

DAZZLE. The sooner the better, sir. Allow me to offer you my arm. I see you understand these matters;—my friend Spanker is woefully ignorant—miserably uneducated.

(*Exeunt*)

(*Re-enter* MAX, *with* GRACE)

MAX. Give ye joy, girl, give ye joy. Sir Harcourt Courtly must consent to waive all title to your hand in favor of his son Charles.

GRACE. Oh, indeed! Is that the pith of your congratulation—humph! the exchange of an old fool for a young one? Pardon me if I am not able to distinguish the advantage.

MAX. Advantage!

GRACE. Moreover, by what right am I a transferable cipher in the family of Courtly? So, then, my fate is reduced to this, to sacrifice my fortune, or unite myself with a worm-eaten edition of the Classics!

MAX. Why, he certainly is not such a fellow as I could have chosen for my little Grace; but consider, to retain fifteen thousand a-year! Now, tell me honestly—but why should I say *honestly?* Speak, girl, would you rather not have the lad?

GRACE. Why do you ask me?

MAX. Why, look ye, I'm an old fellow, another hunting season or two and I shall be in at my own death—I can't leave you this house and land, because they are entailed, nor can I say I'm sorry for it, for it is a good law; but I have a little box with my Grace's name upon it, where, since your father's death and miserly will, I have yearly placed a certain sum to be yours, should you refuse to fulfil the conditions prescribed.

GRACE. My own dear uncle!

(*Clasping him round the neck*)

MAX. Pooh! pooh! what's to do now? Why, it was only a trifle—why, you little rogue, what are you crying about?

GRACE. Nothing, but—

MAX. But what? Come, out with it, will you have young Courtly?

(*Re-enter* LADY GAY)

LADY GAY. Oh! Max, Max!

MAX. Why, what's amiss with you?

LADY GAY. I'm a wicked woman!

MAX. What have you done?

LADY GAY. Everything—oh, I thought Sir Harcourt was a coward, but now I find a man may be a coxcomb without being a poltroon. Just to show my husband how inconvenient it is to hold the ribands sometimes, I made him send a challenge to the old fellow, and he, to my surprise, accepted it, and is going to blow my Dolly's brains out in the billiard-room.

MAX. The devil!

LADY GAY. Just when I imagined I had got my whip hand of him again, out comes my linch-pin—and over I go—oh!

MAX. I will soon put a stop to that—a duel under my roof! Murder in Oak Hall! I'll shoot them both! (*Exit*)

GRACE. Are you really in earnest?

LADY GAY. Do you think it looks like a joke? Oh! Dolly, if you allow yourself to be shot, I will never forgive you—never! Ah, he is a great fool, Grace; but I can't tell why, but I would sooner lose my bridle hand than he should be hurt on my account.

(*Enter* SIR HARCOURT COURTLY)

Tell me—tell me—have you shot him—is he dead—my dear Sir Harcourt—you horrid old brute—have you killed him? I shall never forgive myself. (*Exit*)

GRACE. Oh! Sir Harcourt, what has happened?

SIR HARCOURT. Don't be alarmed, I beg—your uncle interrupted us—discharged the weapons—locked the challenger up in the billiard-room to cool his rage.

GRACE. Thank heaven!

SIR HARCOURT. Miss Grace, to apologize for my conduct were useless, more especially as I am confident that no feelings of indignation or sorrow for my late acts are cherished by you; but still, reparation is in my power, and I not only waive all title, right, or claim to your person or your fortune, but freely admit your power to bestow them on a more worthy object.

GRACE. This generosity, Sir Harcourt, is most unexpected.

SIR HARCOURT. No, not generosity, but simply justice, justice!

GRACE. May I still beg a favor?

SIR HARCOURT. Claim anything that is mine to grant.

GRACE. You have been duped by Lady Gay Spanker, I have also been cheated and played upon by her and Mr. Hamilton—may I beg that the contract between us may, to all appearances, be still held good?

SIR HARCOURT. Certainly, although I confess I cannot see the point of your purpose.

(*Enter* MAX, *with* YOUNG COURTLY)

MAX. Now, Grace, I have brought the lad.

GRACE. Thank you, uncle, but the trouble was quite unnecessary—Sir Harcourt holds to his original contract.

MAX. The deuce he does!

GRACE. And I am willing—nay, eager, to become Lady Courtly.

YOUNG COURTLY. (*Aside*) The deuce you are!

MAX. But, Sir Harcourt—

SIR HARCOURT. One word, Max, for an instant. (*They retire*)

YOUNG COURTLY. (*Aside*) What can this mean? Can it be possible that I have been mistaken—that she is not in love with Augustus Hamilton?

GRACE. (*Aside*) Now we shall find how he intends to bend the haughty Grace.

YOUNG COURTLY. Madam—Miss, I mean, —are you really in earnest—are you in love with my father?

GRACE. No, indeed I am not.

YOUNG COURTLY. Are you in love with any one else?

GRACE. No, or I should not marry him.

YOUNG COURTLY. Then you actually accept him as your real husband?

GRACE. In the common acceptation of the word.

YOUNG COURTLY. (*Aside*) Hang me if I have not been a pretty fool! (*Aloud*) Why do you marry him, if you don't care about him?

GRACE. To save my fortune.

YOUNG COURTLY. (*Aside*) Mercenary, cold-hearted girl! (*Aloud*) But if there be any one you love in the least—marry him;— were you never in love?

GRACE. Never!

YOUNG COURTLY. (*Aside*) Oh! what an ass I've been! (*Aloud*) I heard Lady Gay mention something about a Mr. Hamilton.

GRACE. Ah, yes, a person who, after an acquaintanceship of two days, had the assurance to make love to me, and I—

YOUNG COURTLY. Yes,—you—Well?

GRACE. I pretended to receive his attentions.

YOUNG COURTLY. (Aside) It was the best pretence I ever saw.

GRACE. An absurd, vain, conceited coxcomb, who appeared to imagine that I was so struck with his fulsome speech, that he could turn me round his finger.

YOUNG COURTLY. (Aside) My very thoughts!

GRACE. But he was mistaken.

YOUNG COURTLY. (Aside) Confoundedly! (Aloud) Yet you seemed rather concerned about the news of his death?

GRACE. His accident! No, but—

YOUNG COURTLY. But what?

GRACE. (Aside) What can I say? (Aloud) Ah! but my maid Pert's brother is a post-boy, and I thought he might have sustained an injury, poor boy.

YOUNG COURTLY. (Aside) Damn the post-boy! (Aloud) Madam, if the retention of your fortune be the plea on which you are about to bestow your hand on one you do not love, and whose very actions speak his carelessness for that inestimable jewel he is incapable of appreciating—Know that I am devotedly, madly attached to you.

GRACE. You, sir? Impossible!

YOUNG COURTLY. Not at all,—but inevitable,—I have been so for a long time.

GRACE. Why, you never saw me until last night.

YOUNG COURTLY. I have seen you in imagination—you are the ideal I have worshipped.

GRACE. Since you press me into a confession,—which nothing but this could bring me to speak,—know, I did love poor Augustus Hamilton—

(Re-enter MAX and SIR HARCOURT)

but he—he is—no—more! Pray, spare me, sir.

YOUNG COURTLY. (Aside) She loves me! And, oh! what a situation I am in!—if I own I am the man, my Governor will overhear,

and ruin me—if I do not, she'll marry him.— What is to be done?

(Enter LADY GAY)

LADY GAY. Where have you put my Dolly? I have been racing all round the house—tell me, is he quite dead!

MAX. I'll have him brought in.   (Exit)

SIR HARCOURT. My dear madam, you must perceive this unfortunate occurrence was no fault of mine. I was compelled to act as I have done—I was willing to offer any apology, but that resource was excluded, as unacceptable.

LADY GAY. I know—I know—'twas I made him write that letter—there was no apology required—'twas I that apparently seduced you from the paths of propriety,—'twas all a joke, and here is the end of it.

(Enter MAX, MR. SPANKER, and DAZZLE)

Oh! if he had but lived to say, "I forgive you, Gay!"

SPANKER. So I do!

LADY GAY. (Seeing SPANKER) Ah! he is alive!

SPANKER. Of course I am!

LADY GAY. Ha! ha! ha! (Embraces him) I will never hunt again—unless you wish it. Sell your stable—

SPANKER. No, no—do what you like—say what you like, for the future! I find the head of a family has less ease and more responsibility than I, as a member, could have anticipated. I abdicate!

(Enter COOL)

SIR HARCOURT. Ah! Cool, here! (Aside) You may destroy those papers—I have altered my mind,—and I do not intend to elope at present. Where are they?

COOL. As you seemed particular, Sir Harcourt, I sent them off by mail to London.

SIR HARCOURT. Why, then, a full description of the whole affair will be published to-morrow.

COOL. Most irretrievably!

SIR HARCOURT. You must post to town immediately, and stop the press.

COOL. Beg pardon—they would see me

hanged first, Sir Harcourt; they don't frequently meet with such a profitable lie.

SERVANT. (*Without*) No, sir! no, sir!

(*Enter* SIMPSON)

SIMPSON. Sir, there is a gentleman, who
calls himself Mr. Solomon Isaacs, insists
upon following me up.   (*Exit*)

(*Enter* MR. SOLOMON ISAACS)

ISAACS. Mr. Courtly, you will excuse my
performance of a most disagreeable duty at
any time, but more especially in such a manner. I must beg the honor of your company
to town.

SIR HARCOURT. What!—how!—what for?

ISAACS. For debt, Sir Harcourt.

SIR HARCOURT. Arrested?—impossible!
Here must be some mistake.

ISAACS. Not the slightest, sir. Judgment
has been given in five cases, for the last three
months; but Mr. Courtly is an eel, rather
too nimble for my men.—We have been on
his track, and traced him down to this village, with Mr. Dazzle.

DAZZLE. Ah! Isaacs! How are you?

ISAACS. Thank you, sir.

(*Speaks aside to* SIR HARCOURT)

MAX. Do you know him?

DAZZLE. Oh, intimately—distantly related
to his family—same arms on our escutcheon
—empty purse falling though a hole in a
pocket: motto, "Requiescat in pace"—which
means, "Let virtue be its own reward."

SIR HARCOURT. (*To* ISAACS) Oh, I
thought there was a mistake! Know, to your
misfortune, that Mr. Hamilton was the person you dogged to Oak Hall, between whom
and my son a most remarkable likeness exists.

ISAACS. Ha! ha! Know, to your misfortune, Sir Harcourt, that Mr. Hamilton and
Mr. Courtly are one and the same person!

SIR HARCOURT. Charles!

YOUNG COURTLY. Concealment is in vain
—I am Augustus Hamilton.

SIR HARCOURT. Hang me, if I didn't
think it all along! Oh, you infernal, cozening
dog!

ISAACS. Now, then, Mr. Hamilton—

GRACE. Stay, sir—Mr. Charles Courtly is
under age—ask his father.

SIR HARCOURT. Ahem!—I won't—I won't
pay a shilling of the rascal's debts—not a
sixpence!

GRACE. Then, I will—you may retire.

(*Exit* ISAACS)

YOUNG COURTLY. I can now perceive the
generous point of your conduct towards me;
and, believe me, I appreciate, and will endeavor to deserve it.

MAX. Ha! ha! Come, Sir Harcourt, you
have been fairly beaten—you must forgive
him—say you will.

SIR HARCOURT. So, sir, it appears you
have been leading, covertly, an infernal town
life.

YOUNG COURTLY. (*Imitating* MASTER
CHARLES) Yes, please, father.

SIR HARCOURT. None of your humbug,
sir! (*Aside*) He is my own son—how could
I expect him to keep out of the fire? (*Aloud*)
And you, Mr. Cool!—have you been deceiving me?

COOL. Oh! Sir Harcourt, if your perception was played upon, how could I be expected to see?

SIR HARCOURT. Well, it would be useless
to withhold my hand. There, boy! (*He gives
his hand to* YOUNG COURTLY. GRACE *comes
down on the other side, and offers her hand;
he takes it*) What is all this? What do you
want?

YOUNG COURTLY. Your blessing, father.

GRACE. If you please, father.

SIR HARCOURT. Oho! the mystery is being solved. So, so, you young scoundrel, you
have been making love—under the rose.

LADY GAY. He learnt that from you, Sir
Harcourt.

SIR HARCOURT. Ahem! What would you
do now, if I were to withhold my consent?

GRACE. *Do* without it.

MAX. The will says, if Grace marries any
one but you,—her property reverts to your
heir-apparent—and there he stands.

LADY GAY. Make a virtue of necessity.

SPANKER. I married from inclination; and
see how happy I am. And if ever I have a
son—

LADY GAY. Hush! Dolly, dear!

SIR HARCOURT. Well! take her, boy! Although you are too young to marry.

(*They retire with* MAX)

LADY GAY. Am I forgiven, Sir Harcourt?

Sir Harcourt. Ahem! Why—a—(*Aside*) Have you really deceived me?

Lady Gay. Can you not see through this?

Sir Harcourt. And you still love me?

Lady Gay. As much as I ever did.

Sir Harcourt. (*Is about to kiss her hand, when* Spanker *interposes between*) A very handsome ring, indeed.

Spanker. Very.

(*Puts her arm in his, and they go up*)

Sir Harcourt. Poor little Spanker!

Max. (*Coming down, aside to* Sir Harcourt) One point I wish to have settled. Who is Mr. Dazzle?

Sir Harcourt. A relative of the Spankers, he told me.

Max. Oh, no,—a near connection of yours.

Sir Harcourt. Never saw him before I came down here, in all my life. (*To* Young Courtly) Charles, who is Mr. Dazzle?

Young Courtly. Dazzle, Dazzle,—will you excuse an impertinent question?—but who the deuce are you?

Dazzle. Certainly. I have not the remotest idea!

All. How, sir?

Dazzle. Simple question as you may think it, it would puzzle half the world to answer. One thing I can vouch—Nature made me a gentleman—that is, I live on the best that can be procured for credit. I never spend my own money when I can oblige a friend. I'm always thick on the winning horse. I'm an epidemic on the trade of a tailor. For further particulars, inquire of any sitting magistrate.

Sir Harcourt. And these are the deeds which attest your title to the name of gentleman? I perceive that you have caught the infection of the present age. Charles, permit me, as your father, and you, sir, as his friend, to correct you on one point. Barefaced assurance is the vulgar substitute for gentlemanly ease; and there are many who, by aping the *vices* of the great, imagine that they elevate themselves to the rank of those whose faults alone they copy. No, sir! The title of gentleman is the only one *out* of any monarch's gift, yet within the reach of every peasant. It should be engrossed by *Truth*—stamped with *Honor*—sealed with *good-feeling*—signed *Man*—and enrolled in every true young English heart.

OSCAR FINGAL O'FLAHERTIE WILLS WILDE

Lady Windermere's Fan

~~~~~~~~~~~~~~~~~~~~~~~~~~~~~~~~~~~~

PRINCIPAL EVENTS IN WILDE'S LIFE

1856, 15 Oct., Born in Dublin, the son of Sir William Wilde, a famous surgeon, and his wife Jane Francisca Elgee, an accomplished writer.

1871, Entered Trinity College, Dublin.

1874, Entered Magdalen College, Oxford.

1878, Won the Newdigate Prize with his poem "Ravenna."

1878, Took first-class honors in classics and in literature.

1881, His affectations in following the cult of aestheticism, which he had begun in Oxford with elaborate interior decoration and costumes and a languid manner, were ridiculed in Gilbert and Sullivan's *Patience.* His witty sayings were constantly quoted, and his espousal of Art for Art's sake had great influence.

1881, Published *Poems,* a selection of his verse.

1882, 2 Jan.—27 Dec., Lectured in the United States, very successfully. Covered the country, from cities like New York, Boston, and San Francisco to mining towns in Colorado and ranch towns in Texas.

1883, 21 Aug., Vera, or The Nihilists produced in New York.

1884, Married Constance Lloyd.

1888, May, Published *The Happy Prince and Other Tales,* a collection of fairy tales.

1891, Published *The Picture of Dorian Gray.*

1891, Published *Intentions,* a volume of essays.

1891, 26 Jan., The Duchess of Padua, modelled on the Elizabethan tragedies of blood, produced in New York.

1892, Nov., The House of Pomegranates, more fairy stories, published.

1892, Published *Collected Poems.*

1892, 20 Feb., Lady Windermere's Fan produced at St. James's Theatre, London, with great success.

1893, Feb., Salome published in Paris in French; English translation published in London in 1894.

1893, 19 April, A Woman of No Importance produced at the Theatre Royal, Haymarket.

1895, 3 Jan., An Ideal Husband produced at the Theatre Royal, Haymarket.

1895, 14 Feb., The Importance of Being Earnest produced at St. James's.

1896, 11 Feb., Salome produced in Paris by Sarah Bernhardt.

1895, May, Sentenced to two year's imprisonment for criminal immorality.

1897, May, Stripped of health, financial resources, and reputation, he went to live in France.

1900, 30 Nov., Died in poverty in Paris.

INTRODUCTION

Lady Windermere's Fan is far superior to *London Assurance* and even more superior to most of the plays of Boucicault's contemporaries. Intelligent audiences still listen to Wilde's plays with delight and still quote his lines, when most of his nineteenth-century predecessors are forgotten except for occasional academic revivals. The obvious superiority of Wilde's plays sometimes misleads theatregoers and readers into crediting his amusing pieces with more virtues than they really have. *Lady Windermere's Fan* is a characteristic example.

What is the real distinction of this play? The characters are no more notable than those of a hundred other nineteenth-century comedies and melodramas. Lady Windermere is young and innocent, rather self-righteous and stubborn, but none of these qualities is developed by the dramatist any more than the plot requires; after the performance the audience may remember Lady Windermere's awkward situation or her costume, but as a character she is no more memorable than Maria Thorowgood or Grace Harkaway. Lord Windermere is an upright and troubled husband, no more. Lord Darlington is a clever man-about-town attracted by his friend's wife. Mrs. Erlynne is a woman with a past, trying to make a social come-back, who suddenly discovers a maternal feeling for her long-neglected daughter. All these characters are placed in situations which make them examine their deepest convictions, but none does any more than go through the motions of self-analysis. If Wilde had any profound understanding of human nature, he revealed none of it in any of the characters he created in *Lady Windermere's Fan.*

The situations of the play and their evolution suggest no revealing commentary on contemporary society comparable to those the novelists of the time had been making for several years or to the ones soon to be made in the drama by Shaw and Galsworthy and Granville-Barker. The plot of the play is contrived and sentimental: Lady Windermere's proposed betrayal of her husband is a plot device flatly contradictory of the character previously built up; Mrs. Erlynne's sudden and melodramatic sacrifice of herself for the daughter she has ignored since her birth and whose husband she has been blackmailing is grossly improbable; her hastily announced engagement to Lord Horton is an equally improbable reward for her heroic conduct. So far as plot and characters are concerned, *Lady Windermere's Fan* is not much above the class of *The West Indian.*

The real distinction of the play is the brilliant wit of the dialogue; the characters and situation are primarily devices for the display of finely turned epigrams. Oscar Wilde was the greatest wit of late Victorian England, and his comedies are vehicles for his wit such as few of his predecessors had ever achieved. It is not what the characters *are* or what they *do* which is important, but what they *say*—and even more how they say it! Many of these epigrams ridicule the hypocrisy of Victorian England or its snug complacency about moral values and so suggest a social criticism which is not found in the plots. Though many of the epigrams carry penetrating social comments, many others are simply witty inversions with no particular significance, but superbly polished. Clearly Wilde's prime purpose was to elicit the laughter of a sophisticated and intelligent audience. No plays have been more successful in achieving this end than *Lady Windermere's Fan, A Woman of No Importance, An Ideal Husband,* and *The Importance of Being Earnest.*

LADY WINDERMERE'S FAN

Dramatis personae

In order of first appearance

PARKER, Butler in Lord Windermere's London house.

LADY WINDERMERE, The young, lovely, innocent wife of Lord Windermere.

LORD DARLINGTON, A sophisticated man-about-town.

THE DUCHESS OF BERWICK, A shallow, scandal-mongering leader of London society.

LADY AGATHA CARLISLE, Her pretty and simple daughter.

LORD WINDERMERE, The devoted and high-principled husband of Lady Windermere.

MR. DUMBY, A stupid, fashionable young man.

LADY PLUMDALE
MRS. COWPER-COWPER
LADY STUTFIELD
SIR JAMES ROYSTON

MR. GUY BERKELEY
LADY JEDBURGH
MR. RUFFORD
MISS GRAHAM
MR. AND MRS. ARTHUR BOWDEN
LORD AND LADY PAISLEY
⎱ Guests at Lady Windermere's birthday ball.

MR. HOPPER, The son of an Australian millionaire.

LORD AUGUSTUS LORTON (TUPPY), A silly, impressionable, middle-aged beau, brother of the Duchess of Berwick.

MR. CECIL GRAHAM, A young man-about-town.

MRS. ERLYNNE, Handsome, clever, and smart, a woman of dash and calculated charm, of dubious background.

ROSALIE, Lady Windermere's maid.

SCENES

ACT   I. *Morning-Room in* LORD WINDERMERE'S *House*
ACT II. *Drawing-Room in* LORD WINDERMERE'S *House*
ACT III. LORD DARLINGTON'S *Rooms*
ACT IV. *Same as* ACT I

TIME. *The Present* (i.e. 1892)

PLACE. *London*

The action of the play takes place within twenty-four hours, beginning on a Tuesday afternoon at five o'clock, and ending the next day at 1:30 P.M.

Act I

SCENE. *Morning-room of* LORD WINDERMERE'S *house in Carlton House Terrace. Doors* C. *and* R. *Bureau with books and papers* R. *Sofa with small tea-table* L. *Window opening on to terrace* L. *Table* R.

(LADY WINDERMERE *is at table* R. *arranging roses in a blue bowl*)

(*Enter* PARKER)

PARKER. Is your ladyship at home this afternoon?

LADY W. Yes—who has called?

PARKER. Lord Darlington, my lady.

LADY W. (*Hesitates for a moment*) Show him up—and I'm at home to any one who calls.

PARKER. Yes, my lady.   (*Exit* C.)

LADY W. It's best for me to see him before to-night. I'm glad he's come.

(*Enter* PARKER C.)

PARKER. Lord Darlington.

(*Enter* LORD D. C. *Exit* PARKER)

LORD D. How do you do, Lady Windermere?

LADY W. How do you do, Lord Darlington? No, I can't shake hands with you. My hands are all wet with these roses. Aren't they lovely? They came up from Selby this morning.

LORD D. They are quite perfect. (*Sees a fan lying on the table*) And what a wonderful fan! May I look at it?

LADY W. Do. Pretty, isn't it! It's got my name on it, and everything. I have only just seen it myself. It's my husband's birthday present to me. You know to-day is my birthday?

LORD D. No? Is it really?

LADY W. Yes; I'm of age to-day. Quite an important day in my life, isn't it? That is why I am giving this party to-night. Do sit down.
(*Still arranging flowers*)

LORD D. (*Sitting down*) I wish I had known it was your birthday, Lady Windermere. I would have covered the whole street in front of your house with flowers to walk on. They are made for you. (*A short pause*)

LADY W. Lord Darlington, you annoyed me last night at the Foreign Office. I am afraid you are going to annoy me again.

LORD D. I, Lady Windermere?

(*Enter* PARKER *and* Footman C. *with tray and tea-things*)

LADY W. Put it there, Parker. That will do. (*Wipes her hands with her pocket-hand-kerchief, goes to tea-table* L. *and sits down*) Won't you come over, Lord Darlington?
(*Exit* PARKER C.)

LORD D. (*Takes chair and goes across* L. C.) I am quite miserable, Lady Windermere. You must tell me what I did.
(*Sits down at table* L.)

LADY W. Well, you kept paying me elaborate compliments the whole evening.

LORD D. (*Smiling*) Ah, nowadays we are all of us so hard up, that the only pleasant things to pay *are* compliments. They're the only thing we *can* pay.

LADY W. (*Shaking her head*) No, I am talking very seriously. You mustn't laugh, I am quite serious. I don't like compliments, and I don't see why a man should think he is pleasing a woman enormously when he says to her a whole heap of things that he doesn't mean.

LORD D. Ah, but I did mean them.
(*Takes tea which she offers him*)

LADY W. (*Gravely*) I hope not. I should be sorry to have to quarrel with you, Lord Darlington. I like you very much, you know that. But I shouldn't like you at all if I thought you were what most other men are. Believe me, you are better than most other men, and I sometimes think you pretend to be worse.

LORD D. We all have our little vanities, Lady Windermere.

LADY W. Why do you make that your special one?

(Still seated at table L.*)*

LORD D. *(Still seated* L. C.*)* Oh, nowadays so many conceited people go about Society pretending to be good, that I think it shows rather a sweet and modest disposition to pretend to be bad. Besides, there is this to be said. If you pretend to be good, the world takes you very seriously. If you pretend to be bad, it doesn't. Such is the astounding stupidity of optimism.

LADY W. Don't you *want* the world to take you seriously, then, Lord Darlington?

LORD D. No, not the world. Who are the people the world takes seriously? All the dull people one can think of, from the bishops down to the bores. I should like *you* to take me very seriously, Lady Windermere, *you* more than any one else in life.

LADY W. Why—why me?

LORD D. *(After a slight hesitation)* Because I think we might be great friends. Let us be great friends. You may want a friend some day.

LADY W. Why do you say that?

LORD D. Oh!—we all want friends at times.

LADY W. I think we're very good friends already, Lord Darlington. We can always remain so as long as you don't—

LORD D. Don't what?

LADY W. Don't spoil it by saying extravagant, silly things to me. You think I am a Puritan, I suppose? Well, I have something of the Puritan in me. I was brought up like that. I am glad of it. My mother died when I was a mere child. I lived always with Lady Julia, my father's eldest sister, you know. She was stern to me, but she taught me, what the world is forgetting, the difference that there is between what is right and what is wrong. *She* allowed of no compromise. *I* allow of none.

LORD D. My dear Lady Windermere!

LADY W. *(Leaning back on the sofa)* You look on me as being behind the age.—Well, I am! I should be sorry to be on the same level as an age like this.

LORD D. Do you think the age very bad?

LADY W. Yes. Nowadays people seem to look on life as a speculation. It is not a spec-ulation. It is a sacrament. Its ideal is Love. Its purification is sacrifice.

LORD D. *(Smiling)* Oh, anything is better than being sacrificed!

LADY W. *(Leaning forward)* Don't say that.

LORD D. I do say it. I feel it—I know it.

(Enter PARKER C.*)*

PARKER. The men want to know if they are to put the carpets on the terrace for tonight, my lady?

LADY W. You don't think it will rain, Lord Darlington, do you?

LORD D. I won't hear of its raining on your birthday!

LADY W. Tell them to do it at once, Parker. *(Exit* PARKER C.*)*

LORD D. *(Still seated)* Do you think then —of course I am only putting an imaginary instance—do you think, that in the case of a young married couple, say about two years married, if the husband suddenly becomes the intimate friend of a woman of—well, more than doubtful character, is always calling upon her, lunching with her, and probably paying her bills—do you think that the wife should not console herself?

LADY W. *(Frowning)* Console herself?

LORD D. Yes, I think she should—I think she has the right.

LADY W. Because the husband is vile should the wife be vile also?

LORD D. Vileness is a terrible word, Lady Windermere.

LADY W. It is a terrible thing, Lord Darlington.

LORD D. Do you know I am afraid that good people do a great deal of harm in this world. Certainly the greatest harm they do is that they make badness of such extraordinary importance. It is absurd to divide people into good and bad. People are either charming or tedious. I take the side of the charming, and you, Lady Windermere, can't help belonging to them.

LADY W. Now, Lord Darlington. *(Rising and crossing* R.*, front of him)* Don't stir, I am merely going to finish my flowers.

(Goes to table R. C.*)*

LORD D. *(Rising and moving chair)* And I must say I think you are very hard on modern life, Lady Windermere. Of course there is much against it, I admit. Most women, for instance, nowadays, are rather mercenary.

LADY W. Don't talk about such people.

LORD D. Well, then, setting mercenary people aside, who, of course, are dreadful, do you think seriously that women who have committed what the world calls a fault should never be forgiven?

LADY W. (*Standing at table*) I think they should never be forgiven.

LORD D. And me? Do you think that there should be the same laws for men as there are for women?

LADY W. Certainly!

LORD D. I think life too complex a thing to be settled by these hard and fast rules.

LADY W. If we had "these hard and fast rules," we should find life much more simple.

LORD D. You allow of no exceptions?

LADY W. None!

LORD D. Ah, what a fascinating Puritan you are, Lady Windermere!

LADY W. The adjective was unnecessary, Lord Darlington.

LORD D. I couldn't help it. I can resist everything except temptation.

LADY W. You have the modern affectation of weakness.

LORD D. (*Looking at her*) It's only an affectation, Lady Windermere.

(*Enter* PARKER C.)

PARKER. The Duchess of Berwick and Lady Agatha Carlisle.   (*Exit* PARKER C.)

(*Enter the* DUCHESS OF B. *and* LADY A. C. C.)

DUCHESS OF B. (*Coming down* C. *and shaking hands*) Dear Margaret, I am so pleased to see you. You remember Agatha, don't you? (*Crossing* L. C.) How do you do, Lord Darlington? I won't let you know my daughter, you are far too wicked.

LORD D. Don't say that, Duchess. As a wicked man I am a complete failure. Why, there are lots of people who say I have never really done anything wrong in the whole course of my life. Of course they only say it behind my back.

DUCHESS OF B. Isn't he dreadful? Agatha,

this is Lord Darlington. Mind you don't believe a word he says. (LORD DARLINGTON *crosses* R. C.) No, no tea, thank you, dear. (*Crosses and sits on sofa*) We have just had tea at Lady Markby's. Such bad tea, too. It was quite undrinkable. I wasn't at all surprised. Her own son-in-law supplies it. Agatha is looking forward so much to your ball to-night, dear Margaret.

LADY W. (*Seated* L. C.) Oh, you mustn't think it is going to be a ball, Duchess. It is only a dance in honor of my birthday. A small and early.

LORD D. (*Standing* L. C.) Very small, very early, and very select, Duchess.

DUCHESS OF B. (*On sofa* L.) Of course it's going to be select. But we know *that*, dear Margaret, about *your* house. It is really one of the few houses in London where I can take Agatha, and where I feel perfectly secure about poor Berwick. I don't know what Society is coming to. The most dreadful people seem to go everywhere. They certainly come to my parties—the men get quite furious if one doesn't ask them. Really, some one should make a stand against it.

LADY W. *I* will, Duchess, I will have no one in my house about whom there is any scandal.

LORD D. (R. C.) Oh, don't say that, Lady Windermere. I should never be admitted! (*Sitting*)

DUCHESS OF B. Oh, men don't matter. With women it is different. We're good. Some of us are, at least. But we are positively getting elbowed into the corner. Our husbands would really forget our existence if we didn't nag at them from time to time, just to remind them that we have a perfect legal right to do so.

LORD D. It's a curious thing, Duchess, about the game of marriage—a game, by the way, that is going out of fashion—the wives hold all the honors, and invariably lose the odd trick.

DUCHESS OF B. The odd trick? Is that the husband, Lord Darlington?

LORD D. It would be rather a good name for the modern husband.

DUCHESS OF B. Dear Lord Darlington, how thoroughly depraved you are!

LADY W. Lord Darlington is trivial.

LORD D. Ah, don't say that, Lady Windermere.

LADY W. Why do you *talk* so trivially about life, then?

LORD D. Because I think that life is far too important a thing ever to talk seriously about it.   (*Moves up* C.)

DUCHESS OF B. What does he mean? Do, as a concession to my poor wits, Lord Darlington, just explain to me what you really mean?

LORD D. (*Coming down back of table*) I think I had better not, Duchess. Nowadays to be intelligible is to be found out. Goodbye! (*Shakes hands with* DUCHESS) And now (*goes up stage*), Lady Windermere, good-bye. I may come to-night, mayn't I? Do let me come.

LADY W. (*Standing up stage with* LORD D.) Yes, certainly. But you are not to say foolish, insincere things to people.

LORD D. (*Smiling*) Ah, you are beginning to reform me. It is a dangerous thing to reform any one, Lady Windermere.

(*Bows, and exit* C.)

DUCHESS OF B. (*Who has risen, goes* C.) What a charming, wicked creature! I like him so much. I'm quite delighted he's gone! How sweet you're looking! Where *do* you get your gowns? And now I must tell you how sorry I am for you, dear Margaret. (*Crosses to sofa and sits with* LADY W.) Agatha, darling!

LADY A. Yes, mamma.   (*Rises*)

DUCHESS OF B. Will you go and look over the photograph album that I see there?

LADY A. Yes, mamma. (*Goes to table* L.)

DUCHESS OF B. Dear girl! She is so fond of photographs of Switzerland. Such a pure taste, I think. But I really am so sorry for you, Margaret.

LADY W. (*Smiling*) Why, Duchess?

DUCHESS OF B. Oh, on account of that horrid woman. She dresses so well, too, which makes it much worse, sets such a dreadful example. Augustus—you know my disreputable brother—such a trial to us all—well, Augustus is completely infatuated about her. It is quite scandalous, for she is absolutely inadmissible into society. Many a woman has a past, but I am told that she has at least a dozen, and that they all fit.

LADY W. Whom are you talking about, Duchess?

DUCHESS OF B. About Mrs. Erlynne.

LADY W. Mrs. Erlynne? I never heard of her, Duchess. And what *has* she to do with me?

DUCHESS OF B. My poor child! Agatha, darling!

LADY A. Yes, mamma.

DUCHESS OF B. Will you go out on the terrace and look at the sunset?

LADY A. Yes, mamma.

(*Exit through window* L.)

DUCHESS OF B. Sweet girl! So devoted to sunsets! Shows such refinement of feeling, does it not? After all, there is nothing like nature, is there?

LADY W. But what is it, Duchess? Why do you talk to me about this person?

DUCHESS OF B. Don't you really know? I assure you we're all so distressed about it. Only last night at dear Lady Fansen's every one was saying how extraordinary it was that, of all men in London, Windermere should behave in such a way.

LADY W. My husband—what has *he* to do with any woman of that kind?

DUCHESS OF B. Ah, what indeed, dear? That is the point. He goes to see her continually, and stops for hours at a time, and while he is there she is not at home to any one. Not that many ladies call on her, dear, but she has a great many disreputable men friends—my own brother in particular, as I told you—and that is what makes it so dreadful about Windermere. We looked upon *him* as being such a model husband, but I am afraid there is no doubt about it. My dear nieces—you know the Saville girls, don't you?—such nice domestic creatures—plain, dreadfully plain, but so good—well, they're always at the window doing fancy work, and making ugly things for the poor, which I think so useful of them in these dreadful socialistic days, and this terrible woman has taken a house in Curzon Street, right opposite them—such a respectable street, too. I don't know what we're coming to! And they tell me that Windermere goes there four and five times a week—they *see* him. They can't help it—and although they never talk scandal, they—well, of course —they remark on it to every one. And the worst of it all is, that I have been told that this woman has got a great deal of money out of somebody, for it seems that she came to

London six months ago without anything at all to speak of, and now she has this charming house in Mayfair, drives her pony in the Park every afternoon, and all—well, all—since she has known poor dear Windermere.

LADY W. Oh, I can't believe it!

DUCHESS OF B. But it's quite true, my dear. The whole of London knows it. That is why I felt it was better to come and talk to you, and advise you to take Windermere away at once to Homburg or to Aix where he'll have something to amuse him, and where you can watch him all day long. I assure you, my dear, that on several occasions after I was first married I had to pretend to be very ill, and was obliged to drink the most unpleasant mineral waters, merely to get Berwick out of town. He was so extremely susceptible. Though I am bound to say he never gave away any large sums of money to anybody. He is far too high-principled for that.

LADY W. (*Interrupting*) Duchess, Duchess, it's impossible! (*Rising and crossing stage c.*) We are only married two years. Our child is but six months old.

(*Sits in chair* R. *of* L. *table*)

DUCHESS OF B. Ah, the dear, pretty baby! How is the little darling? Is it a boy or a girl? I hope a girl—Ah, no, I remember it's a boy! I'm so sorry. Boys are so wicked. My boy is excessively immoral. You wouldn't believe at what hours he comes home. And he's only left Oxford a few months—I really don't know what they teach them there.

LADY W. Are *all* men bad?

DUCHESS OF B. Oh, all of them, my dear, all of them, without any exception. And they never grow any better. Men become old, but they never become good.

LADY W. Windermere and I married for love.

DUCHESS OF B. Yes, we begin like that. It was only Berwick's brutal and incessant threats of suicide that made me accept him at all, and before the year was out he was running after all kinds of petticoats, every color, every shape, every material. In fact, before the honeymoon was over, I caught him winking at my maid, a most pretty, respectable girl. I dismissed her at once without a character.—No, I remember I passed her on to my sister; poor dear Sir George is so short-sighted, I thought it wouldn't matter. But it

did, though it was most unfortunate. (*Rises*) And now, my dear child, I must go, as we are dining out. And mind you don't take this little aberration of Windermere's too much to heart. Just take him abroad, and he'll come back to you all right.

LADY W. Come back to me? (C.)

DUCHESS OF B. (L. C.) Yes, dear, these wicked women get our husbands away from us, but they always come back, slightly damaged, of course. And don't make scenes, men hate them!

LADY W. It is very kind of you, Duchess, to come and tell me all this. But I can't believe that my husband is untrue to me.

DUCHESS OF B. Pretty child! I was like that once. Now I know that all men are monsters. (LADY W. *rings bell*) The only thing to do is to feed the wretches well. A good cook does wonders, and that I know you have. My dear Margaret, you are not going to cry?

LADY W. You needn't be afraid, Duchess, I never cry.

DUCHESS OF B. That's quite right, dear. Crying is the refuge of plain women, but the ruin of pretty ones. Agatha, darling.

LADY A. (*Entering* L.) Yes, mamma.

(*Stands back of table* L. C.)

DUCHESS OF B. Come and bid good-bye to Lady Windermere, and thank her for your charming visit. (*Coming down again*) And by the way, I must thank you for sending a card to Mr. Hopper—he's that rich young Australian people are taking such notice of just at present. His father made a great fortune by selling some kind of food in circular tins—most palatable, I believe,—I fancy it is the thing the servants always refuse to eat. But the son is quite interesting. I think he's attracted by dear Agatha's clever talk. Of course, we should be very sorry to lose her, but I think that a mother who doesn't part with a daughter every season has no real affection. We're coming to-night, dear.

(PARKER *opens* C. *doors*)

And remember my advice, take the poor fellow out of town at once, it is the only thing to do. Good-bye, once more; come, Agatha.

(*Exeunt* DUCHESS *and* LADY A. C.)

LADY W. How horrible! I understand now what Lord Darlington meant by the imaginary instance of the couple not two years married. Oh! it can't be true—she spoke of enormous sums of money paid to this woman. I know where Arthur keeps his bank-book— in one of the drawers of that desk. I might find out by that. I *will* find out. (*Opens drawer*) No, it is some hideous mistake. (*Rises and goes* C.) Some silly scandal! He loves *me*! He loves *me*! But why should I not look? I am his wife, I have a right to look! (*Returns to bureau, takes out book and examines it, page by page, smiles and gives a sigh of relief*) I knew it, there is not a word of truth in this stupid story. (*Puts book back in drawer. As she does so, starts and takes out another book*) A second book—private— locked! (*Tries to open it, but fails. Sees paper knife on bureau, and with it cuts cover from book. Begins to start at the first page*) Mrs. Erlynne—£600—Mrs. Erlynne—£700—Mrs. Erlynne—£400. Oh! it is true! it is true! How horrible! (*Throws book on floor*)

(*Enter* Lord W. C.)

Lord W. Well, dear, has the fan been sent home yet? (*Going* R. C. *sees book*) Margaret, you have cut open my bank book. You have no right to do such a thing!

Lady W. You think it wrong that you are found out, don't you?

Lord W. I think it wrong that a wife should spy on her husband.

Lady W. I did not spy on you. I never knew of this woman's existence till half an hour ago. Some one who pitied me was kind enough to tell me what every one in London knows already—your daily visits to Curzon Street, your mad infatuation, the monstrous sums of money you squander on this infamous woman! (*Crossing* L.)

Lord W. Margaret, don't talk like that of Mrs. Erlynne, you don't know how unjust it is!

Lady W. (*Turning to him*) You are very jealous of Mrs. Erlynne's honor. I wish you had been as jealous of mine.

Lord W. Your honor is untouched, Margaret. You don't think for a moment that— (*Puts book back into desk*)

Lady W. I think that you spend your money strangely. That is all. Oh, don't imagine I mind about the money. As far as I am concerned, you may squander everything we have. But what I *do* mind is that you who have loved me, you who have taught me to love you, should pass from the love that is given to the love that is bought. Oh, it's horrible! (*Sits on sofa*) And it is I who feel degraded. *You* don't feel anything. I feel stained, utterly stained. You can't realize how hideous the last six months seem to me now— every kiss you have given me is tainted in my memory.

Lord W. (*Crossing to her*) Don't say that, Margaret, I never loved any one in the whole world but you.

Lady W. (*Rises*) Who is this woman, then? Why do you take a house for her?

Lord W. I did not take a house for her.

Lady W. You gave her the money to do it, which is the same thing.

Lord W. Margaret, as far as I have known Mrs. Erlynne—

Lady W. Is there a Mr. Erlynne—or is he a myth?

Lord W. Her husband died many years ago. She is alone in the world.

Lady W. No relations? (*A pause*)

Lord W. None.

Lady W. Rather curious, isn't it? (L.)

Lord W. (L. C.) Margaret, I was saying to you—and I beg you to listen to me—that as far as I have known Mrs. Erlynne, she has conducted herself well. If years ago—

Lady W. Oh! (*Crossing* R. C.) I don't want details about her life.

Lord W. I am not going to give you any details about her life. I tell you simply this— Mrs. Erlynne was once honored, loved, respected. She was well born, she had a position —she lost everything—threw it away, if you like. That makes it all the more bitter. Misfortunes one can endure—they come from outside, they are accidents. But to suffer for one's own faults—ah! there is the sting of life. It was twenty years ago, too. She was little more than a girl then. She had been a wife for even less time than you have.

Lady W. I am not interested in her—and —you should not mention this woman and me in the same breath. It is an error of taste. (*Sitting* R. *at desk*)

Lord W. Margaret, you could save this woman. She wants to get back into society, and she wants you to help her. (*Crossing to her*)

Lady W. Me!

LORD W. Yes, you.

LADY W. How impertinent of her!

(*A pause*)

LORD W. Margaret, I came to ask you a great favor, and I still ask it of you, though you have discovered what I had intended you should never have known, that I have given Mrs. Erlynne a large sum of money. I want you to send her an invitation for our party to-night.   (*Standing* L. *of her*)

LADY W. You are mad.   (*Rises*)

LORD W. I entreat you. People may chatter about her, do chatter about her, of course, but they don't know anything definite against her. She has been to several houses—not to houses where you would go, I admit, but still to houses where women who are in what is called Society nowadays do go. That does not content her. She wants you to receive her once.

LADY W. As a triumph for her, I suppose.

LORD W. No; but because she knows that you are a good woman—and that if she comes here once she will have a chance of a happier, a surer life, than she has had. She will make no further effort to know you. Won't you help a woman who is trying to get back?

LADY W. No! If a woman really repents, she never wishes to return to the society that has made or seen her ruin.

LORD W. I beg of you.

LADY W. (*Crossing to door* R.) I am going to dress for dinner, and don't mention the subject again this evening. Arthur (*going to him* C.), you fancy because I have no father or mother that I am alone in the world and you can treat me as you choose. You are wrong, I have friends, many friends.

LORD W. (L. C.) Margaret, you are talking foolishly, recklessly. I won't argue with you, but I insist upon your asking Mrs. Erlynne to-night.

LADY W. (R. C.) I shall do nothing of the kind.   (*Crossing* L. C.)

LORD W. (C.) You refuse?

LADY W. Absolutely!

LORD W. Ah, Margaret, do this for my sake; it is her last chance.

LADY W. What has that to do with me?

LORD W. How hard good women are!

LADY W. How weak bad men are!

LORD W. Margaret, none of us men may be good enough for the women we marry—

that is quite true—but you don't imagine I would ever—oh, the suggestion is monstrous!

LADY W. Why should *you* be different from other men? I am told that there is hardly a husband in London who does not waste his life over *some* shameful passion.

LORD W. I am not one of them.

LADY W. I am not sure of that.

LORD W. You are sure in your heart. But don't make chasm after chasm between us. God knows the last few minutes have thrust us wide enough apart. Sit down and write the card.

LADY W. Nothing in the whole world would induce me.

LORD W. (*Crossing to the bureau*) Then I will.

(*Rings electric bell, sits down and writes card*)

LADY W. You are going to invite this woman?   (*Crossing to him*)

LORD W. Yes.   (*Pause*)

(*Enter* PARKER)

LORD W. Parker!

PARKER. Yes, my lord. (*Comes down* L. C.)

LORD W. Have this note sent to Mrs. Erlynne at No. 84A Curzon Street. (*Crossing to* L. C. *and giving note to* PARKER) There is no answer.   (*Exit* PARKER C.)

LADY W. Arthur, if that woman comes here, I shall insult her.

LORD W. Margaret, don't say that.

LADY W. I mean it.

LORD W. Child, if you did such a thing, there's not a woman in London who wouldn't pity you.

LADY W. There is not a *good* woman in London who would not applaud me. We have been too lax. We must make an example. I propose to begin to-night. (*Picking up fan*) Yes, you gave me this fan to-day; it was your birthday present. If that woman crosses my threshold, I shall strike her across the face with it.

LORD W. Margaret, you couldn't do such a thing.

LADY W. You don't know me! (*Moves* R.)

(*Enter* PARKER)

LADY W. Parker!

PARKER. Yes, my lady.

LADY W. I shall dine in my own room. I don't want dinner, in fact. See that everything is ready by half-past ten. And, Parker, be sure you pronounce the names of the guests very distinctly to-night. Sometimes you speak so fast that I miss them. I am particularly anxious to hear the names quite clearly, so as to make no mistake. You understand, Parker?

PARKER. Yes, my lady.

LADY W. That will do!

(*Exit* PARKER C.)

(*Speaking to* LORD W.) Arthur, if that woman comes here—I warn you—

LORD W. Margaret, you'll ruin us!

LADY W. Us! From this moment my life is separate from yours. But if you wish to avoid a public scandal, write at once to this woman, and tell her that I forbid her to come here!

LORD W. I will not!—I cannot—she must come!

LADY W. Then I shall do exactly as I have said. (*Goes* R.) You leave me no choice.

(*Exit* R.)

LORD W. (*Calling after her*) Margaret! Margaret! (*A pause*) My God! What shall I do! I dare not tell her who this woman really is. The shame would kill her.

(*Sinks down into a chair and buries his face in his hands*)

Act II

SCENE: *Drawing-room in* LORD WINDERMERE'S *house. Door* R. U. *opening into ballroom, where band is playing. Door* L. *through which guests are entering. Door* L. U. *opens on an illuminated terrace. Palms, flowers, and brilliant lights. Room crowded with guests.*

(LADY W. *is receiving them*)

DUCHESS OF B. (*Up* C.) So strange Lord Windermere isn't here. Mr. Hopper is very late, too. You have kept those five dances for him, Agatha! (*Comes down*)

LADY A. Yes, mamma.

DUCHESS OF B. (*Sitting on sofa*) Just let me see your card. I'm so glad Lady Windermere has revived cards.—They're a mother's only safeguard. You dear simple little thing! (*Scratches out two names*) No nice girl should ever waltz with such particularly younger sons! It looks so fast! The last two dances you must pass on the terrace with Mr. Hopper.

(*Enter* MR. DUMBY *and* LADY PLYMDALE *from the ballroom*)

LADY A. Yes, mamma.

DUCHESS OF B. (*Fanning herself*) The air is so pleasant there.

PARKER. Mrs. Cowper-Cowper. Lady Stutfield. Sir James Royston. Mr. Guy Berkeley.

(*These people enter as announced*)

DUMBY. Good-evening, Lady Stutfield. I suppose this will be the last ball of the season?

LADY S. I suppose so, Mr. Dumby. It's been a delightful season, hasn't it?

DUMBY. Quite delightful! Good-evening, Duchess. I suppose this will be the last ball of the season?

DUCHESS OF B. I suppose so, Mr. Dumby. It has been a very dull season, hasn't it?

DUMBY. Dreadfully dull! Dreadfully dull!

MRS. C.-C. Good-evening, Mr. Dumby. I suppose this will be the last ball of the season?

DUMBY. Oh, I think not. There'll probably be two more.

(*Wanders back to* LADY P.)

PARKER. Mr. Rufford. Lady Jedburgh and Miss Graham. Mr. Hopper.

(*These people enter as announced*)

HOPPER. How do you do, Lady Windermere? How do you do, Duchess?

(*Bows to* LADY A.)

DUCHESS OF B. Dear Mr. Hopper, how nice of you to come so early. We all know how you are run after in London.

HOPPER. Capital place, London! They are not nearly so exclusive in London as they are in Sydney.

DUCHESS OF B. Ah! we know your value, Mr. Hopper. We wish there were more like you. It would make life so much easier. Do you know, Mr. Hopper, dear Agatha and I are so much interested in Australia. It must be so pretty with all the dear little kangaroos flying about. Agatha has found it on the map. What a curious shape it is! Just like a large packing-case. However, it is a very young country, isn't it?

HOPPER. Wasn't it made at the same time as the others, Duchess?

DUCHESS OF B. How clever you are, Mr. Hopper. You have a cleverness quite of your own. Now I mustn't keep you.

HOPPER. But I should like to dance with Lady Agatha, Duchess.

DUCHESS OF B. Well, I *hope* she has a dance left. Have you got a dance left, Agatha?

LADY A. Yes, mamma.

DUCHESS OF B. The next one?

LADY A. Yes, mamma.

HOPPER. May I have the pleasure?

(LADY AGATHA *bows*)

DUCHESS OF B. Mind you take great care of my little chatter-box, Mr. Hopper.

(LADY A. *and* MR. H. *pass into ballroom*)

(*Enter* LORD W. c.)

LORD W. Margaret, I want to speak to you.

LADY W. In a moment.

(*The music stops*)

PARKER. Lord Augustus Lorton.

(*Enter* LORD A.)

LORD A. Good-evening, Lady Windermere.

DUCHESS OF B. Sir James, will you take me into the ballroom? Augustus has been dining with us to-night. I really have had quite enough of dear Augustus for the moment.

(SIR JAMES R. *gives the* DUCHESS *his arm and escorts her into the ballroom*)

PARKER. Mr. and Mrs. Arthur Bowden. Lord and Lady Paisley. Lord Darlington.

(*These people enter as announced*)

LORD A. (*Coming up to* LORD W.) Want to speak to you particularly, dear boy. I'm worn to a shadow. Know I don't look it. None of us men do look what we really are. Demmed good thing, too. What I want to know is this. Who is she? Where does she come from? Why hasn't she got any demmed relations? Demmed nuisance, relations! But they make one so demmed respectable.

LORD W. You are talking of Mrs. Erlynne, I suppose? I only met her six months ago. Till then I never knew of her existence.

LORD A. You have seen a good deal of her since then.

LORD W. (*Coldly*) Yes, I have seen a good deal of her since then. I have just seen her.

LORD A. Egad! the women are very down on her. I have been dining with Arabella this evening! By Jove! you should have heard what she said about Mrs. Erlynne. She didn't leave a rag on her. . . . (*Aside*) Berwick and I told her that didn't matter much, as the lady in question must have an extremely fine figure. You should have seen Arabella's expression! . . . But, look here, dear boy. I don't know what to do about Mrs. Erlynne. Egad! I might be married to her; she treats me with such demmed indifference. She's deuced clever, too! She explains everything. Egad! She explains you. She has got any amount of explanations for you—and all of them different.

LORD W. No explanations are necessary about my friendship with Mrs. Erlynne.

LORD A. Hem! Well, look here, dear old fellow. Do you think she will ever get into this demmed thing called Society? Would you introduce her to your wife? No use beating about the confounded bush. Would you do that?

LORD W. Mrs. Erlynne is coming here to-night.

LORD A. Your wife has sent her a card?

LORD W. Mrs. Erlynne has received a card.

LORD A. Then she's all right, dear boy. But why didn't you tell me that before? It would have saved me a heap of worry and demmed misunderstandings!

(LADY A. *and* MR. H. *cross and exit on terrace* L. U. E.)

PARKER. Mr. Cecil Graham!

(*Enter* MR. CECIL G.)

CECIL G. (*Bows to* LADY W., *passes over and shakes hands with* LORD W.) Good-evening, Arthur. Why don't you ask me how I am? I like people to ask me how I am. It shows a widespread interest in my health. Now to-night I am not at all well. Been dining with my people. Wonder why it is one's people are always so tedious? My father would talk morality after dinner. I told him he was old enough to know better. But my experience is that as soon as people are old enough to know better, they don't know anything at all. Hullo, Tuppy! Hear you're going to be married again; thought you were tired of that game.

LORD A. You're excessively trivial, my dear boy, excessively trivial!

CECIL G. By the way, Tuppy, which is it? Have you been twice married and once divorced, or twice divorced and once married? I say, you've been twice divorced and once married. It seems so much more probable.

LORD A. I have a very bad memory. I really don't remember which. (*Moves away* R.)

LADY P. Lord Windermere, I've something most particular to ask you.

LORD W. I am afraid—if you will excuse me—I must join my wife.

LADY P. Oh, you mustn't dream of such a thing. It's most dangerous nowadays for a husband to pay any attention to his wife in public. It always makes people think that he beats her when they're alone. The world has grown so suspicious of anything that looks like a happy married life. But I'll tell you what it is at supper.

(*Moves towards door of ballroom*)

LORD W. (C.) Margaret, I *must* speak to you.

LADY W. Will you hold my fan for me, Lord Darlington? Thanks.

(*Comes down to him*)

LORD W. (*Crossing to her*) Margaret, what you said before dinner was, of course, impossible?

LADY W. That woman is not coming here to-night!

LORD W. (R. C.) Mrs. Erlynne is coming here, and if you in any way annoy or wound her, you will bring shame and sorrow on us both. Remember that! Ah, Margaret! only trust me! A wife should trust her husband!

LADY W. (C.) London is full of women who trust their husbands. One can always recognize them. They look so thoroughly unhappy. I am not going to be one of them. (*Moves up*) Lord Darlington, will you give me back my fan, please? Thanks.... A useful thing, a fan, isn't it? . . . I want a friend to-night, Lord Darlington. I didn't know I would want one so soon.

LORD D. Lady Windermere! I knew the time would come some day; but why to-night!

LORD W. I *will* tell her. I must. It would be terrible if there were any scene. Margaret—

PARKER. Mrs. Erlynne.

(LORD W. *starts.* MRS. E. *enters, very beautifully dressed and very dignified.* LADY W. *clutches at her fan, then lets it drop on the floor. She bows coldly to* MRS. E., *who bows to her sweetly in turn, and sails into the room*)

LORD D. You have dropped your fan, Lady Windermere.

(*Picks it up and hands it to her*)

MRS. E. (C.) How do you do again, Lord Windermere? How charming your sweet wife looks! Quite a picture!

LORD W. (*In a low voice*) It was terribly rash of you to come!

MRS. E. (*Smiling*) The wisest thing I ever did in my life. And, by the way, you must pay me a good deal of attention this evening. I am afraid of the women. You must introduce me to some of them. The men I can always manage. How do you do, Lord Augustus? You have quite neglected me lately. I have not seen you since yesterday. I am afraid you're faithless. Every one told me so.

LORD A. (R.) Now really, Mrs. Erlynne, allow me to explain.

MRS. E. (R. C.) No, dear Lord Augustus, you can't explain anything. It is your chief charm.

LORD A. Ah! if you find charms in me, Mrs. Erlynne—(*They converse together.*

LORD W. *moves uneasily about the room watching* MRS. E.)

LORD D. (*To* LADY W.) How pale you are!

LADY W. Cowards are always pale.

LORD D. You look faint. Come out on the terrace.

LADY W. Yes. (*To* PARKER) Parker, send my cloak out.

MRS. E. (*Crossing to her*) Lady Windermere, how beautifully your terrace is illuminated. Reminds me of Prince Doria's at Rome. (LADY W. *bows coldly, and goes off with* LORD D.) Oh, how do you do, Mr. Graham? Isn't that your aunt, Lady Jedburgh? I should so much like to know her.

CECIL G. (*After a moment's hesitation and embarrassment*) Oh, certainly, if you wish it. Aunt Caroline, allow me to introduce Mrs. Erlynne.

MRS. E. So pleased to meet you, Lady Jedburgh. (*Sits beside her on the sofa*) Your nephew and I are great friends. I am so much interested in his political career. I think he's sure to be a wonderful success. He thinks like a Tory, and talks like a Radical, and that's so important nowadays. He's such a brilliant talker, too. But we all know from whom he inherits that. Lord Allendale was saying to me only yesterday in the Park, that Mr. Graham talks almost as well as his aunt.

LADY J. (R.) Most kind of you to say these charming things to me! (MRS. E. *smiles and continues conversation*)

DUMBY. (*To* CECIL G.) Did you introduce Mrs. Erlynne to Lady Jedburgh?

CECIL G. Had to, my dear fellow. Couldn't help it. That woman can make one do anything she wants. How, I don't know.

DUMBY. Hope to goodness she won't speak to me! (*Saunters towards* LADY P.)

MRS. E. (C. *to* LADY J.) On Thursday? With great pleasure. (*Rises and speaks to* LORD W. *laughing*) What a bore it is to have to be civil to these old dowagers. But they always insist on it.

LADY P. (*To* MR. D.) Who is that well-dressed woman talking to Windermere?

DUMBY. Haven't got the slightest idea. Looks like an *édition de luxe* of a wicked French novel, meant specially for the English market.

MRS. E. So that is poor Dumby with Lady Plymdale? I hear she is frightfully jealous of him. He doesn't seem anxious to speak to me to-night. I suppose he is afraid of her. Those straw-colored women have dreadful tempers. Do you know, I think I'll dance with you first, Windermere. (LORD W. *bites his lip and frowns*) It will make Lord Augustus so jealous! Lord Augustus! (LORD A. *comes down*) Lord Windermere insists on my dancing with him first, and, as it's his own house, I can't well refuse. You know I would much sooner dance with you.

LORD A. (*With a low bow*) I wish I could think so, Mrs. Erlynne.

MRS. E. You know it far too well. I can fancy a person dancing through life with you and finding it charming.

LORD A. (*Placing his hand on his white waistcoat*) Oh, thank you, thank you. You are the most adorable of all ladies!

MRS. E. What a nice speech! So simple and so sincere! Just the sort of speech I like. Well, you shall hold my bouquet. (*Goes towards ballroom on* LORD W.'s *arm*) Ah, Mr. Dumby, how are you? I am so sorry I have been out the last three times you have called. Come and lunch on Friday.

DUMBY. (*With perfect nonchalance*) Delighted.

(LADY P. *glares with indignation at* MR. D.

LORD A. *follows* MRS. E. *and* LORD W. *into the ballroom holding bouquet*)

LADY P. (*To* MR. D.) What an absolute brute you are! I never can believe a word you say! Why did you tell me you didn't know her? What do you mean by calling on her three times running? You are not to go to lunch there; of course you understand that?

DUMBY. My dear Laura, I wouldn't dream of going!

LADY P. You haven't told me her name yet. Who is she?

DUMBY. (*Coughs slightly and smooths his hair*) She's a Mrs. Erlynne.

LADY P. *That* woman!

DUMBY. Yes, that is what every one calls her.

LADY P. How very interesting! How intensely interesting! I really must have a good stare at her. (*Goes to door of ballroom and looks in*) I have heard the most shocking things about her. They say she is ruining poor Windermere. And Lady Windermere, who goes in for being so proper, invites her! How extremely amusing! It takes a thoroughly good woman to do a thoroughly stupid thing. You are to lunch there on Friday.

DUMBY. Why?

LADY P. Because I want you to take my husband with you. He has been so attentive lately, that he has become a perfect nuisance. Now, this woman is just the thing for him. He'll dance attendance upon her as long as she lets him, and won't bother me. I assure you, women of that kind are most useful. They form the basis of other people's marriages.

DUMBY. What a mystery you are!

LADY P. (Looking at him) I wish you were!

DUMBY. I am—to myself. I am the only person in the world I should like to know thoroughly; but I don't see any chance of it just at present.

(They pass into the ballroom, and LADY W. and LORD D. enter from the terrace)

LADY W. Yes. Her coming here is monstrous, unbearable. I know now what you meant to-day at tea-time. Why didn't you tell me right out? You should have!

LORD D. I couldn't! A man can't tell these things about another man! But if I had known he was going to make you ask her here to-night, I think I would have told you. That insult, at any rate, you would have been spared.

LADY W. I did not ask her. He insisted on her coming—against my entreaties—against my commands. Oh! the house is tainted for me! I feel that every woman here sneers at me as she dances by with my husband. What have I done to deserve this? I gave him all my life. He took it—used it—spoiled it! I am degraded in my own eyes; and I lack courage—I am a coward! (Sits down on sofa)

LORD D. If I know you at all, I know that you can't live with a man who treats you like this! What sort of life would you have with him? You would feel that he was lying to you every moment of the day. You would feel that the look in his eyes was false, his voice false, his touch false, his passion false. He would come to you when he was weary of others; you would have to comfort him. He would come to you when he was devoted to others; you would have to charm him. You would

have to be to him the mask of his real life, the cloak to hide his secret.

LADY W. You are right—you are terribly right. But where am I to turn? You said you would be my friend, Lord Darlington.—Tell me, what am I to do? Be my friend now.

LORD D. Between men and women there is no friendship possible. There is passion, enmity, worship, love, but no friendship. I love you—

LADY W. No, no! (Rises)

LORD D. Yes, I love you! You are more to me than anything in the whole world. What does your husband give you? Nothing. Whatever is in him he gives to this wretched woman, whom he has thrust into your society, into your home, to shame you before every one. I offer you my life—

LADY W. Lord Darlington!

LORD D. My life—my whole life. Take it, and do with it what you will. . . . I love you —love you as I have never loved any living thing. From the moment I met you I loved you, loved you blindly, adoringly, madly! You did not know it then—you know it now! Leave this house to-night. I won't tell you that the world matters nothing, or the world's voice, or the voice of Society. They matter a good deal. They matter far too much. But there are moments when one has to choose between living one's own life, fully, entirely, completely—or dragging out some false, shallow, degrading existence that the world in its hypocrisy demands. You have that moment now. Choose! Oh, my love, choose!

LADY W. (Moving slowly away from him, and looking at him with startled eyes) I have not the courage.

LORD D. (Following her) Yes; you have the courage. There may be six months of pain, of disgrace even, but when you no longer bear his name, when you bear mine, all will be well. Margaret, my love, my wife that shall be some day—yes, my wife! You know it! What are you now? This woman has the place that belongs by right to you. Oh! go—go out of this house, with head erect, with a smile upon your lips, with courage in your eyes. All London will know why you did it; and who will blame you? No one. If they do, what matter. Wrong? What is wrong? It's wrong for a man to abandon his wife for a shameless woman. It is wrong for a wife to remain with a man who so dishonors her. You said once you would make no compromise with things. Make none now. Be brave! Be yourself!

LADY W. I am afraid of being myself. Let me think! Let me wait! My husband may return to me. (*Sits down on sofa*)

LORD D. And you would take him back! You are not what I thought you were. You are just the same as every other woman. You would stand anything rather than face the censure of a world whose praise you would despise. In a week you will be driving with this woman in the Park. She will be your constant guest—your dearest friend. You would endure anything rather than break with one blow this monstrous tie. You are right. You have no courage; none.

LADY W. Ah, give me time to think. I cannot answer you now.

(*Passes her hand nervously over her brow*)

LORD D. It must be now or not at all.

LADY W. (*Rising from the sofa*) Then not at all!   (*A pause*)

LORD D. You break my heart!

LADY W. Mine is already broken.

(*A pause*)

LORD D. To-morrow I leave England. This is the last time I shall ever look on you. You will never see me again. For one moment our lives met—our souls touched. They must never meet or touch again. Good-bye, Margaret.   (*Exit*)

LADY W. How alone I am in life! How terribly alone!

(*The music stops. Enter the* DUCHESS OF B. *and* LORD P. *laughing and talking. Other guests come on from ballroom*)

DUCHESS OF B. Dear Margaret, I've just been having such a delightful chat with Mrs. Erlynne. I am so sorry for what I said to you this afternoon about her. Of course, she must be all right if *you* invite her. A most attractive woman, and has such sensible views on life. Told me she entirely disapproved of people marrying more than once, so I feel quite safe about poor Augustus. Can't imagine why people speak against her. It's those horrid nieces of mine—the Saville girls—they're always talking scandal. Still, I should go to Homburg, dear, I really should. She is just a little too attractive. But where is Agatha? Oh, there she is. (LADY A. *and* MR. H. *enter*

from the terrace L. U. E.) Mr. Hopper, I am very angry with you. You have taken Agatha out on the terrace, and she is so delicate.

HOPPER. (L. C.) Awfully sorry, Duchess. We went out for a moment and then got chatting together.

DUCHESS OF B. (C.) Ah, about dear Australia, I suppose?

HOPPER. Yes.

DUCHESS OF B. Agatha, darling!

(*Beckons her over*)

LADY A. Yes, mamma!

DUCHESS OF B. (*Aside*) Did Mr. Hopper definitely—

LADY A. Yes, mamma.

DUCHESS OF B. And what answer did you give him, dear child?

LADY A. Yes, mamma.

DUCHESS OF B. (*Affectionately*) My dear one! You always say the right thing. Mr. Hopper! James! Agatha has told me everything. How cleverly you have both kept your secret.

HOPPER. You don't mind my taking Agatha off to Australia, then, Duchess?

DUCHESS OF B. (*Indignantly*) To Australia? Oh, don't mention that dreadful vulgar place.

HOPPER. But she said she'd like to come with me.

DUCHESS OF B. (*Severely*) Did you say that, Agatha?

LADY A. Yes, mamma.

DUCHESS OF B. Agatha, you say the most silly things possible. I think on the whole that Grosvenor Square would be a more healthy place to reside in. There are lots of vulgar people live in Grosvenor Square, but at any rate there are no horrid kangaroos crawling about. But we'll talk about that to-morrow. James, you can take Agatha down. You'll come to lunch, of course, James. At half past one instead of two. The Duke will wish to say a few words to you, I am sure.

HOPPER. I should like to have a chat with the Duke, Duchess. He has not said a single word to me yet.

DUCHESS OF B. I think you'll find he will have a great deal to say to you to-morrow. (*Exit* LADY A. *with* MR. H.) And now good-night, Margaret. I'm afraid it's the old, old story, dear. Love—well, not love at first sight, but love at the end of the season, which is so much more satisfactory.

LADY W. Good-night, Duchess.

(*Exit the* DUCHESS OF B. *on* LORD P.'s *arm*)

LADY P. My dear Margaret, what a handsome woman your husband has been dancing with! I should be quite jealous if I were you! Is she a great friend of yours?

LADY W. No!

LADY P. Really? Good-night, dear.

(*Looks at* MR. D. *and exit*)

DUMBY. Awful manners young Hopper has!

CECIL G. Ah! Hopper is one of Nature's gentlemen, the worst type of gentlemen I know.

DUMBY. Sensible woman, Lady Windermere. Lots of wives would have objected to Mrs. Erlynne coming. But Lady Windermere has that uncommon thing called common sense.

CECIL G. And Windermere knows that nothing looks so like innocence as an indiscretion.

DUMBY. Yes; dear Windermere is becoming almost modern. Never thought he would.

(*Bows to* LADY W. *and exit*)

LADY J. Good-night, Lady Windermere. What a fascinating woman Mrs. Erlynne is! She is coming to lunch on Thursday, won't you come too? I expect the Bishop and dear Lady Merton.

LADY W. I am afraid I am engaged, Lady Jedburgh.

LADY J. So sorry. Come, dear.

(*Exeunt* LADY J. *and* MISS G.)

(*Enter* MRS. E. *and* LORD W.)

MRS. E. Charming ball it has been! Quite reminds me of old days. (*Sits on the sofa*) And I see that there are just as many fools in society as there used to be. So pleased to find that nothing has altered! Except Margaret. She's grown quite pretty. The last time I saw her—twenty years ago, she was a fright in flannel. Positive fright, I assure you. The dear Duchess! and that sweet Lady Agatha! Just the type of girl I like. Well, really, Windermere, if I am to be the Duchess's sister-in-law—

LORD W. (*Sitting* L. *of her*) But are you—?

(*Exit* MR. CECIL G. *with rest of guests.* LADY W. *watches with a look of scorn and pain* MRS. E. *and her husband. They are unconscious of her presence*)

MRS. E. Oh, yes! He's to call to-morrow at twelve o'clock. He wanted to propose to-night. In fact he did. He kept on proposing. Poor Augustus, you know how he repeats himself. Such a bad habit! But I told him I wouldn't give him an answer till to-morrow. Of course I am going to take him. And I dare say I'll make him an admirable wife, as wives go. And there is a great deal of good in Lord Augustus. Fortunately it is all on the surface. Just where good qualities should be. Of course you must help me in this matter.

LORD W. I am not called on to encourage Lord Augustus, I suppose?

MRS. E. Oh, no! I do the encouraging. But you will make me a handsome settlement, Windermere, won't you?

LORD W. (*Frowning*) Is that what you want to talk to me about to-night?

MRS. E. Yes.

LORD W. (*With a gesture of impatience*) I will not talk of it here.

MRS. E. (*Laughing*) Then we will talk of it on the terrace. Even business should have a picturesque background. Should it not, Windermere? With a proper background women can do anything.

LORD W. Won't to-morrow do as well?

MRS. E. No; you see, to-morrow I am going to accept him. And I think it would be a good thing if I was able to tell him that—well, what shall I say—£2000 a year left me by a third cousin—or a second husband—or some distant relative of that kind. It would be an additional attraction, wouldn't it? You have a delightful opportunity now of paying me a compliment, Windermere. But you are not very clever at paying compliments. I am afraid Margaret doesn't encourage you in that excellent habit. It's a great mistake on her part. When men give up saying what is charming, they give up thinking what is charming. But seriously, what do you say to £2000? £2500, I think. In modern life margin is everything. Windermere, don't you

think the world an intensely amusing place?
I do!

(*Exit on terrace with* LORD W. *Music
strikes up in ballroom*)

LADY W. To stay in this house any longer
is impossible. To-night a man who loves me
offered me his whole life. I refused it. It was
foolish of me. I will offer him mine now.
I will give him mine. I will go to him!
(*Puts on cloak and goes to door, then turns
back. Sits down at table and writes a letter,
puts it into an envelope, and leaves it on
table*) Arthur has never understood me.
When he reads this, he will. He may do as
he chooses now with his life. I have done
with mine as I think best, as I think right.
It is he who has broken the bond of marriage
—not I. I only break its bondage.   (*Exit*)

(PARKER *enters* L. *and crosses towards the
ballroom* R. *Enter* MRS. E.)

MRS. E. Is Lady Windermere in the ballroom?

PARKER. Her ladyship has just gone out.

MRS. E. Gone out? She's not on the terrace?

PARKER. No, madam. Her ladyship has
just gone out of the house.

MRS. E. (*Starts and looks at the servant
with a puzzled expression on her face*) Out
of the house?

PARKER. Yes, madam—her ladyship told
me she had left a letter for his lordship on
the table.

MRS. E. A letter for Lord Windermere?

PARKER. Yes, madam.

MRS. E. Thank you. (*Exit* PARKER. *The
music in the ballroom stops*) Gone out of
her house! A letter addressed to her husband!
(*Goes over to table and looks at letter. Takes
it up and lays it down again with a shudder
of fear*) No, no! It would be impossible!
Life doesn't repeat its tragedies like that!
Oh, why does this horrible fancy come across
me? Why do I remember now the one moment of my life I most wish to forget? Does
life repeat its tragedies? (*Tears letter open
and reads it, then sinks down into a chair
with a gesture of anguish*) Oh, how terrible!
the same words that twenty years ago I wrote
to her father! and how bitterly I have been

punished for it! No; my punishment, my
real punishment is to-night, is now!
(*Still seated* R.)

(*Enter* LORD W. L. U. E.)

LORD W. Have you said good-night to my
wife?   (*Comes* C.)

MRS. E. (*Crushing letter in her hand*)
Yes.

LORD W. Where is she?

MRS. E. She is very tired. She has gone
to bed. She said she had a headache.

LORD W. I must go to her. You'll excuse
me?

MRS. E. (*Rising hurriedly*) Oh, no! It's
nothing serious. She's only very tired, that
is all. Besides, there are people still in the
supper-room. She wants you to make her
apologies to them. She said she didn't wish
to be disturbed. (*Drops letter*) She asked
me to tell you.

LORD W. (*Picks up letter*) You have
dropped something.

MRS. E. Oh, yes, thank you, that is mine.
(*Puts out her hand to take it*)

LORD W. (*Still looking at letter*) But it's
my wife's handwriting, isn't it?

MRS. E. (*Takes the letter quickly*) Yes,
it's—an address. Will you ask them to call
my carriage, please?

LORD W. Certainly.   (*Goes* L. *and exit*)

MRS. E. Thanks. What can I do? What
can I do? I feel a passion awakening within
me that I never felt before. What can it
mean? The daughter must not be like the
mother—that would be terrible. How can I
save her? How can I save my child? A moment may ruin a life. Who knows that better
than I? Windermere must be got out of the
house; that is absolutely necessary. (*Goes* L.)
But how shall I do it? It must be done somehow. Ah!

(*Enter* LORD A. R. U. E. *carrying bouquet*)

LORD A. Dear lady, I am in such suspense!
May I not have an answer to my request?

MRS. E. Lord Augustus, listen to me.
You are to take Lord Windermere down to
your club at once, and keep him there as
long as possible. You understand?

LORD A. But you said you wished me to keep early hours!

MRS. E. (*Nervously*) Do what I tell you. Do what I tell you.

LORD A. And my reward?

MRS. E. Your reward? Your reward? Oh! ask me that to-morrow. But don't let Windermere out of your sight to-night. If you do I will never forgive you. I will never speak to you again. I'll have nothing to do with you. Remember you are to keep Windermere at your club, and don't let him come back to-night. (*Exit*)

LORD A. Well, really, I might be her husband already. Positively I might.

(*Follows her in a bewildered manner*)

Act III

SCENE. LORD DARLINGTON'S *rooms. A large sofa is in front of fireplace* R. *At the back of the stage a curtain is drawn across the window. Doors* L. *and* R. *Table* R. *with writing materials. Table* C. *with syphons, glasses, and Tantalus frame. Table* L. *with cigars and cigarette box. Lamps lit.*

LADY W. (*Standing by the fireplace*) Why doesn't he come? This waiting is horrible. He should be here. Why is he not here, to wake by passionate words some fire within me? I am cold—cold as a loveless thing. Arthur must have read my letter by this time. If he cared for me, he would have come after me, would have taken me back by force. But he doesn't care. He's entrammeled by this woman—fascinated by her—dominated by her. If a woman wants to hold a man, she has merely to appeal to what is worst in him. We make gods of men, and they leave us. Others make brutes of them, and they fawn and are faithful. How hideous life is! . . . Oh! it was mad of me to come here, horribly mad. And yet which is the worst, I wonder, to be at the mercy of a man who loves one, or the wife of a man who in one's own house dishonors one? What woman knows? What woman in the whole world? But will he love me always, this man to whom I am giving my life? What do I bring him? Lips that have lost the note of joy, eyes that are blighted by tears, chill hands and icy heart. I bring him nothing. I must go back—no; I can't go back, my letter has put me in their power—Arthur would not take me back! That fatal letter! No! Lord Darlington leaves England to-morrow. I will go with him—I have no choice. (*Sits down for a few moments. Then starts up and puts on her cloak*) No, no! I will go back, let Arthur do with me what he pleases. I can't wait here. It has been madness my coming. I must go at once. As for Lord Darlington—Oh! here he is! What shall I do? What can I say to him? Will he let me go away at all? I have heard that men are brutal, horrible. . . . Oh! (*Hides her face in her hands*)

(*Enter* MRS. E. L.)

MRS. E. Lady Windermere! (LADY W. *starts and looks up. Then recoils in contempt*) Thank Heaven I am in time. You must go back to your husband's house immediately.

LADY W. Must?

MRS. E. (*Authoritatively*) Yes, you must! There is not a second to be lost. Lord Darlington may return at any moment.

LADY W. Don't come near me!

MRS. E. Oh! you are on the brink of ruin; you are on the brink of a hideous precipice. You must leave this place at once, my carriage is waiting at the corner of the street. You must come with me and drive straight home. (LADY W. *throws off her cloak and flings it on the sofa*) What are you doing?

LADY W. Mrs. Erlynne—if you had not come here, I would have gone back. But now that I see you, I feel that nothing in the whole world would induce me to live under the same roof as Lord Windermere. You fill me with horror. There is something about you that stirs the wildest rage within me. And I know why you are here. My husband sent you to lure me back that I might serve as a blind to whatever relations exist between you and him.

Mrs. E. Oh! You don't think that—you can't.

Lady W. Go back to my husband, Mrs. Erlynne. He belongs to you and not to me. I suppose he is afraid of a scandal. Men are such cowards. They outrage every law of the world, and are afraid of the world's tongue. But he had better prepare himself. He shall have a scandal. He shall have the worst scandal there has been in London for years. He shall see his name in every vile paper, mine on every hideous placard.

Mrs. E. No—no—

Lady W. Yes! he shall. Had he come himself, I admit I would have gone back to the life of degradation you and he had prepared for me—I was going back—but to stay himself at home, and send you as his messenger—oh! it was infamous—infamous.

Mrs. E. (c.) Lady Windermere, you wrong me horribly—you wrong your husband horribly. He doesn't know you are here—he thinks you are safe in your own house. He thinks you are asleep in your own room. He never read the mad letter you wrote to him!

Lady W. (r.) Never read it!

Mrs. E. No—he knows nothing about it.

Lady W. How simple you think me! (Going to her) You are lying to me!

Mrs. E. (Restraining herself) I am not. I am telling you the truth.

Lady W. If my husband didn't read my letter, how is it that you are here? Who told you I had left the house you were shameless enough to enter? Who told you where I had gone to? My husband told you, and sent you to decoy me back.   (Crosses L.)

Mrs. E. (r. c.) Your husband has never seen the letter. I—saw it, I opened it. I—read it.

Lady W. (Turning to her) You opened a letter of mine to my husband? You wouldn't dare!

Mrs. E. Dare! Oh! to save you from the abyss into which you are falling, there is nothing in the world I would not dare, nothing in the whole world. Here is the letter. Your husband has never read it. He never

shall read it. (Going to fireplace) It should never have been written.

(Tears it and throws it into the fire)

Lady W. (With infinite contempt in her voice and look) How do I know that was my letter after all? You seem to think the commonest device can take me in!

Mrs. E. Oh! Why do you disbelieve everything I tell you! What object do you think I have in coming here, except to save you from utter ruin, to save you from the consequence of a hideous mistake? That letter that is burning now was your letter. I swear it to you!

Lady W. (Slowly) You took good care to burn it before I had examined it. I cannot trust you. You, whose whole life is a lie, how could you speak the truth about anything?   (Sits down)

Mrs. E. (Hurriedly) Think as you like about me—say what you choose against me, but go back, go back to the husband you love.

Lady W. (Sullenly) I do not love him!

Mrs. E. You do, and you know that he loves you.

Lady W. He does not understand what love is. He understands it as little as you do—but I see what you want. It would be a great advantage for you to get me back. Dear Heaven! what a life I would have then! Living at the mercy of a woman who has neither mercy nor pity in her, a woman whom it is an infamy to meet, a degradation to know, a vile woman, a woman who comes between husband and wife!

Mrs. E. (With a gesture of despair) Lady Windermere, Lady Windermere, don't say such terrible things. You don't know how terrible they are, how terrible and how unjust. Listen, you must listen! Only go back to your husband, and I promise you never to communicate with him again on any pretext—never to see him—never to have anything to do with his life or yours. The money that he gave me, he gave me not through love, but through hatred, not in worship, but in contempt. The hold I have over him—

Lady W. (Rising) Ah! you admit you have a hold!

Mrs. E. Yes, and I will tell you what it is. It is his love for you, Lady Windermere.

Lady W. You expect me to believe that?

Mrs. E. You must believe it! It is true.

It is his love for you that has made him submit to—oh! call it what you like, tyranny, threats, anything you choose. But it is his love for you. His desire to spare you—shame, yes, shame and disgrace.

LADY W. What do you mean? You are insolent! What have I to do with you?

MRS. E. (*Humbly*) Nothing. I know it —but I tell you that your husband loves you —that you may never meet with such love again in your whole life—that such love you will never meet—and that if you throw it away, the day may come when you will starve for love and it will not be given to you, beg for love and it will be denied you —Oh! Arthur loves you!

LADY W. Arthur? And you tell me there is nothing between you?

MRS. E. Lady Windermere, before Heaven your husband is guiltless of all offense towards you! And I—I tell you that had it ever occurred to me that such a monstrous suspicion would have entered your mind, I would have died rather than have crossed your life or his—oh! died, gladly died!

(*Moves away to sofa* R.)

LADY W. You talk as if you had a heart. Women like you have no hearts. Heart is not in you. You are bought and sold.

(*Sits* L. C.)

MRS. E. (*Starts, with a gesture of pain. Then restrains herself, and comes over to where* LADY W. *is sitting. As she speaks, she stretches out her hands towards her, but does not dare to touch her*) Believe what you choose about me, I am not worth a moment's sorrow. But don't spoil your beautiful young life on my account! You don't know what may be in store for you, unless you leave this house at once. You don't know what it is to fall into the pit, to be despised, mocked, abandoned, sneered at— to be an outcast! to find the door shut against one, to have to creep in by hideous byways, afraid every moment lest the mask should be stripped from one's face, and all the while to hear the laughter, the horrible laughter of the world, a thing more tragic than all the tears the world has ever shed. You don't know what it is. One pays for one's sin, and then one pays again, and all one's life one pays. You must never know that.—As for me, if suffering be an expiation, then at this moment I have expiated all my faults, whatever they have been; for to-night you have made a heart in one who had it not, made it and broken it.—But let that pass. I may have wrecked my own life, but I will not let you wreck yours. You—why, you are a mere girl, you would be lost. You haven't got the kind of brains that enables a woman to get back. You have neither the wit nor the courage. You couldn't stand dishonor. No! Go back, Lady Windermere, to the husband who loves you, whom you love. You have a child, Lady Windermere. Go back to that child who even now, in pain or in joy, may be calling to you. (LADY W. *rises*) God gave you that child. He will require from you that you make his life fine, that you watch over him. What answer will you make to God if his life is ruined through you? Back to your house, Lady Windermere —your husband loves you. He has never swerved for a moment from the love he bears you. But even if he had a thousand loves, you must stay with your child. If he was harsh to you, you must stay with your child. If he ill-treated you, you must stay with your child. If he abandoned you, your place is with your child.

(LADY W. *bursts into tears and buries her face in her hands*)

(*Rushing to her*) Lady Windermere!

LADY W. (*Holding out her hands to her, helplessly, as a child might do*) Take me home. Take me home.

MRS. E. (*Is about to embrace her. Then restrains herself. There is a look of wonderful joy in her face*) Come! Where is your cloak? (*Getting it from sofa*) Here. Put it on. Come at once!   (*They go to the door*)

LADY W. Stop! Don't you hear voices?

MRS. E. No, no! There is no one!

LADY W. Yes, there is! Listen! Oh! that is my husband's voice! He is coming in! Save me! Oh, it's some plot! You have sent for him!   (*Voices outside*)

MRS. E. Silence! I am here to save you if I can. But I fear it is too late! There! (*Points to the curtain across the window*) The first chance you have, slip out, if you ever get a chance!

LADY W. But you!

MRS. E. Oh! never mind me. I'll face them.

(LADY W. *hides herself behind the curtain*)

LORD A. (*Outside*) Nonsense, dear Windermere, you must not leave me!

MRS. E. Lord Augustus! Then it is I who am lost!

(*Hesitates for a moment, then looks round and sees door R., and exit through it*)

(*Enter* LORD D., MR. D., LORD W., LORD A. L., *and* CECIL G.)

DUMBY. What a nuisance their turning us out of the club at this hour! It's only two o'clock. (*Sinks into a chair*) The lively part of the evening is only just beginning.

(*Yawns and closes his eyes*)

LORD W. It is very good of you, Lord Darlington, allowing Augustus to force our company on you, but I'm afraid I can't stay long.

LORD D. Really! I am so sorry! You'll take a cigar, won't you?

LORD W. Thanks! (*Sits down*)

LORD A. (*To* LORD W.) My dear boy, you must not dream of going. I have a great deal to talk to you about, of demmed importance, too.

(*Sits down with him at L. table*)

CECIL G. Oh! we all know what that is! Tuppy can't talk about anything but Mrs. Erlynne!

LORD W. Well, that is no business of yours, is it, Cecil?

CECIL G. None! That is why it interests me. My own business always bores me to death. I prefer other people's.

LORD D. Have something to drink, you fellows. Cecil, you'll have a whiskey and soda?

CECIL G. Thanks. (*Goes to the table with* LORD D.) Mrs. Erlynne looked very handsome to-night, didn't she?

LORD D. I am not one of her admirers.

CECIL G. I usen't to be, but I am now. Why! she actually made me introduce her to poor dear Aunt Caroline. I believe she is going to lunch there.

LORD D. (*In surprise*) No?

CECIL G. She is, really.

LORD D. Excuse me, you fellows. I'm going away to-morrow. And I have to write a few letters.

(*Goes to writing table and sits down*)

DUMBY. Clever woman, Mrs. Erlynne.

CECIL G. Hallo, Dumby! I thought you were asleep.

DUMBY. I am, I usually am!

LORD A. A very clever woman. Knows perfectly well what a demmed fool I am—knows it as well as I do myself. (CECIL G. *comes towards him laughing*) Ah! you may laugh, my boy, but it is a great thing to come across a woman who thoroughly understands one.

DUMBY. It is an awfully dangerous thing. They always end by marrying one.

CECIL G. But I thought, Tuppy, you were never going to see her again. Yes! you told me so yesterday evening at the club. You said you'd heard—

(*Whispering to him*)

LORD A. Oh, she's explained that.

CECIL G. And the Wiesbaden affair?

LORD A. She's explained that, too.

DUMBY. And her income, Tuppy? Has she explained that?

LORD A. (*In a very serious voice*) She's going to explain that to-morrow.

(CECIL G. *goes back to* C. *table*)

DUMBY. Awfully commercial, women nowadays. Our grandmothers threw their caps over the mills, of course, but by Jove, their granddaughters only throw their caps over mills that can raise the wind for them.

LORD A. You want to make her out a wicked woman. She is not!

CECIL G. Oh! Wicked women bother one. Good women bore one. That is the only difference between them.

LORD D. (*Puffing a cigar*) Mrs. Erlynne has a future before her.

DUMBY. Mrs. Erlynne has a past before her.

LORD A. I prefer women with a past. They're always so demmed amusing to talk to.

CECIL G. Well, you'll have lots of topics of conversation with *her*, Tuppy.

(*Rising and going to him*)

LORD A. You're getting annoying, dear boy; you're getting demmed annoying.

CECIL G. (*Puts his hands on his shoulders*) Now, Tuppy, you've lost your figure and you've lost your character. Don't lose your temper; you have only got one.

LORD A. My dear boy, if I wasn't the most good-natured man in London—

CECIL G. We'd treat you with more respect, wouldn't we, Tuppy? (*Strolls away*)

DUMBY. The youth of the present day are quite monstrous. They have absolutely no respect for dyed hair.

(LORD A. *looks round angrily*)

CECIL G. Mrs. Erlynne has a very great respect for dear Tuppy.

DUMBY. Then Mrs. Erlynne sets an admirable example to the rest of her sex. It is perfectly brutal the way most women nowadays behave to men who are not their husbands.

LORD W. Dumby, you are ridiculous, and Cecil, you let your tongue run away with you. You must leave Mrs. Erlynne alone. You don't really know anything about her, and you're always talking scandal against her.

CECIL G. (*Coming towards him* L. C.) My dear Arthur, I never talk scandal. I only talk gossip.

LORD W. What is the difference between scandal and gossip?

CECIL G. Oh! gossip is charming! History is merely gossip. But scandal is gossip made tedious by morality. Now I never moralize. A man who moralizes is usually a hypocrite, and a woman who moralizes is invariably plain. There is nothing in the whole world so unbecoming to a woman as a Non-conformist conscience. And most women know it, I'm glad to say.

LORD A. Just my sentiments, dear boy, just my sentiments.

CECIL G. Sorry to hear it, Tuppy; whenever people agree with me, I always feel I must be wrong.

LORD A. My dear boy, when I was your age—

CECIL G. But you never were, Tuppy, and you never will be. (*Goes up* C.) I say, Darlington, let us have some cards. You'll play, Arthur, won't you?

LORD W. No, thanks, Cecil.

DUMBY. (*With a sigh*) Good heavens! how marriage ruins a man! It's as demoralizing as cigarettes, and far more expensive.

CECIL G. You'll play, of course, Tuppy?

LORD A. (*Pouring himself out a brandy and soda at table*) Can't, dear boy. Promised Mrs. Erlynne never to play or drink again.

CECIL G. Now, my dear Tuppy, don't be led astray into the paths of virtue. Reformed, you would be perfectly tedious. That is the worst of women. They always want one to be good. And if we are good, when they meet us, they don't love us at all. They like to find us quite irretrievably bad, and to leave us quite unattractively good.

LORD D. (*Rising from* R. *table, where he has been writing letters*) They always do find us bad!

DUMBY. I don't think we are bad. I think we are all good except Tuppy.

LORD D. No, we are all in the gutter, but some of us are looking at the stars.

(*Sits down at* C. *table*)

DUMBY. We are all in the gutter, but some of us are looking at the stars? Upon my word, you are very romantic, to-night, Darlington.

CECIL G. Too romantic! You must be in love. Who is the girl?

LORD D. The woman I love is not free, or thinks she isn't.

(*Glances instinctively at* LORD W. *while he speaks*)

CECIL G. A married woman, then! Well, there's nothing in the world like the devotion of a married woman. It's a thing no married man knows anything about.

LORD D. Oh! she doesn't love me. She is a good woman. She is the only good woman I have ever met in my life.

CECIL G. The only good woman you have ever met in your life?

LORD D. Yes!

CECIL G. (*Lighting a cigarette*) Well, you are a lucky fellow! Why, I have met hundreds of good women. I never seem to meet any but good women. The world is perfectly packed with good women. To know them is a middle-class education.

LORD D. This woman has purity and innocence. She has everything we men have lost.

CECIL G. My dear fellow, what on earth should we men do going about with purity and innocence? A carefully thought-out buttonhole is much more effective.

DUMBY. She doesn't really love you then?

LORD D. No, she does not!

DUMBY. I congratulate you, my dear fel-

low. In this world there are only two tragedies. One is not getting what one wants,
and the other is getting it. The last is much
the worst, the last is a real tragedy! But
I am interested to hear she does not love
you. How long could you love a woman
who didn't love you, Cecil?

CECIL G. A woman who didn't love me?
Oh, all my life!

DUMBY. So could I. But it's so difficult to
meet one.

LORD D. How can you be so conceited,
Dumby?

DUMBY. I didn't say it as a matter of
conceit. I said it as a matter of regret. I have
been wildly, madly adored. I am sorry I
have. It has been an immense nuisance. I
should like to be allowed a little time to
myself, now and then.

LORD A. (*Looking round*) Time to edu-
cate yourself, I suppose.

DUMBY. No, time to forget all I have
learned. That is much more important, dear
Tuppy.

(LORD A. *moves uneasily in his chair*)

LORD D. What cynics you fellows are!

CECIL G. What is a cynic?

(*Sitting on the back of the sofa*)

LORD D. A man who knows the price of
everything, and the value of nothing.

CECIL G. And a sentimentalist, my dear
Darlington, is a man who sees an absurd
value in everything, and doesn't know the
market price of any single thing.

LORD D. You always amuse me, Cecil.
You talk as if you were a man of experience.

CECIL G. I am.

(*Moves up to front of fireplace*)

LORD D. You are far too young!

CECIL G. That is a great error. Experience
is a question of instinct about life. I have
got it. Tuppy hasn't. Experience is the name
Tuppy gives to his mistakes. That is all.

(LORD A. *looks round indignantly*)

DUMBY. Experience is the name every
one gives to their mistakes.

CECIL G. (*Standing with his back to fireplace*) One shouldn't commit any.

(*Sees* LADY W.'*s fan on sofa*)

DUMBY. Life would be very dull without
them.

CECIL G. Of course you are quite faithful to this woman you are in love with,
Darlington, to this good woman?

LORD D. Cecil, if one really loves a
woman, all other women in the world become absolutely meaningless to one. Love
changes one—I am changed.

CECIL G. Dear me! How very interesting.
Tuppy, I want to talk to you.

(LORD A. *takes no notice*)

DUMBY. It's no use talking to Tuppy.
You might as well talk to a brick wall.

CECIL G. But I like talking to a brick
wall—it's the only thing in the world that
never contradicts me! Tuppy!

LORD A. Well, what is it? What is it?

(*Rising and going over to* CECIL G.)

CECIL G. Come over here. I want you
particularly. (*Aside*) Darlington has been
moralizing and talking about the purity of
love, and that sort of thing, and he has got
some woman in his rooms all the time.

LORD A. No, really! really!

CECIL G. (*In a low voice*) Yes, here is
her fan.   (*Points to the fan*)

LORD A. (*Chuckling*) By Jove! By Jove!

LORD W. (*Up by door*) I am really off
now, Lord Darlington. I am sorry you are
leaving England so soon. Pray call on us
when you come back! My wife and I will be
charmed to see you!

LORD D. (*Up stage with* LORD W.) I am
afraid I shall be away for many years. Good-
night!

CECIL G. Arthur!

LORD W. What?

CECIL G. I want to speak to you for a
moment. No, do come!

LORD W. (*Putting on his coat*) I can't—
I'm off!

CECIL G. It is something very particular.
It will interest you enormously.

LORD W. (*Smiling*) It is some of your
nonsense, Cecil.

CECIL G. It isn't. It isn't really!

LORD A. (*Going to him*) My dear fellow,
you mustn't go yet. I have a lot to talk to
you about. And Cecil has something to show
you.

LORD W. (*Walking over*) Well, what is
it?

CECIL G. Darlington has got a woman
here in his rooms. Here is her fan. Amusing,
isn't it?   (*A pause*)

Lord W. Good God!

    (*Seizes the fan—*Dumby *rises*)

Cecil G. What is the matter?

Lord W. Lord Darlington!

Lord D. (*Turning round*) Yes!

Lord W. What is my wife's fan doing here in your rooms? Hands off, Cecil. Don't touch me.

Lord D. Your wife's fan?

Lord W. Yes, here it is!

Lord D. (*Walking towards him*) I don't know!

Lord W. You must know. I demand an explanation. (*To* Cecil G.) Don't hold me, you fool.

Lord D. (*Aside*) She is here after all!

Lord W. Speak, sir! Why is my wife's fan here? Answer me, by God! I'll search your rooms, and if my wife's here, I'll—

    (*Moves*)

Lord D. You shall not search my rooms. You have no right to do so. I forbid you.

Lord W. You scoundrel! I'll not leave your room till I have searched every corner of it! What moves behind that curtain?

    (*Rushes towards the curtain* c.)

Mrs. E. (*Enters behind* r.) Lord Windermere!

Lord W. Mrs. Erlynne!

(*Every one starts and turns round.* Lady W. *slips out from behind the curtain and glides from the room* l.)

Mrs. E. I am afraid I took your wife's fan in mistake for my own, when I was leaving your house to-night. I am so sorry. (*Takes fan from him.* Lord W. *looks at her in contempt.* Lord D. *in mingled astonishment and anger.* Lord A. *turns away. The other men smile at each other*)

Act IV

Scene: *Same as in Act I.*

Lady W. (*Lying on sofa*) How can I tell him? I can't tell him. It would kill me. I wonder what happened after I escaped from that horrible room. Perhaps she told them the true reason of her being there, and the real meaning of that—fatal fan of mine. Oh, if he knows—how can I look him in the face again? He would never forgive me. (*Touches bell*) How securely one thinks one lives—out of reach of temptation, sin, folly. And then suddenly—Oh! Life is terrible. It rules us, we do not rule it.

(*Enter* Rosalie r.)

Rosalie. Did your ladyship ring for me?

Lady W. Yes. Have you found out at what time Lord Windermere came in last night?

Rosalie. His lordship did not come in till five o'clock.

Lady W. Five o'clock! He knocked at my door this morning, didn't he?

Rosalie. Yes, my lady—at half past nine. I told him your ladyship was not awake yet.

Lady W. Did he say anything?

Rosalie. Something about your ladyship's fan. I didn't quite catch what his lordship said. Has the fan been lost, my lady? I can't find it, and Parker says it was not left in any of the rooms. He has looked in all of them and on the terrace as well.

Lady W. It doesn't matter. Tell Parker not to trouble. That will do.

    (*Exit* Rosalie)

Lady W. (*Rising*) She is sure to tell him. I can fancy a person doing a wonderful act of self-sacrifice, doing it spontaneously, recklessly, nobly—and afterwards finding out that it costs too much. Why should she hesitate between her ruin and mine? . . . How strange! I would have publicly disgraced her in my own house. She accepts public disgrace in the house of another to save me. . . . There is a bitter irony in things, a bitter irony in the way we talk of good and bad women. . . . Oh, what a lesson! and what a pity that in life we only get our lessons when they are of no use to us! For even if she doesn't tell, I must. Oh! the shame of it, the shame of it. To tell it is to live through it all again. Actions are the first tragedy in life, words are the second. Words are perhaps the worst. Words are merciless. . . . Oh!

              (*Starts as* LORD W. *enters*)

LORD W. (*Kisses her*) Margaret—how pale you look!

LADY W. I slept very badly.

LORD W. (*Sitting on sofa with her*) I am so sorry. I came in dreadfully late, and I didn't like to wake you. You are crying, dear.

LADY W. Yes, I am crying, for I have something to tell you, Arthur.

LORD W. My dear child, you are not well. You've been doing too much. Let us go away to the country. You'll be all right at Selby. The season is almost over. There is no use staying on. Poor darling! We'll go away to-day, if you like. (*Rises*) We can easily catch the 4:30. I'll send a wire to Fannen.

    (*Crosses and sits down at table to write a telegram*)

LADY W. Yes; let us go away to-day. No; I can't go away to-day, Arthur. There is some one I must see before I leave town—some one who has been kind to me.

LORD W. (*Rising and leaning over sofa*) Kind to you?

LADY W. Far more than that. (*Rises and goes to him*) I will tell you, Arthur, but only love me, love me as you used to love me.

LORD W. Used to? You are not thinking of that wretched woman who came here last night? (*Coming round and sitting* R. *of her*) You don't still imagine—no, you couldn't.

LADY W. I don't. I know now I was wrong and foolish.

LORD W. It was very good of you to receive her last night—but you are never to see her again.

LADY W. Why do you say that?

              (*A pause*)

LORD W. (*Holding her hand*) Margaret, I thought Mrs. Erlynne was a woman more sinned against than sinning, as the phrase goes. I thought she wanted to be good, to get back into a place that she had lost by a moment's folly, to lead again a decent life. I believed what she told me—I was mistaken in her. She is bad—as bad as a woman can be.

LADY W. Arthur, Arthur, don't talk so bitterly about any woman. I don't think now that people can be divided into the good and the bad, as though they were two separate races or creations. What are called good women may have terrible things in them, mad moods of recklessness, assertion, jealousy, sin. Bad women, as they are termed, may have in them sorrow, repentance, pity, sacrifice. And I don't think Mrs. Erlynne a bad woman—I know she's not.

LORD W. My dear child, the woman's impossible. No matter what harm she tries to do us, you must never see her again. She is inadmissible anywhere.

LADY W. But I want to see her. I want her to come here.

LORD W. Never!

LADY W. She came here once as *your* guest. She must come now as *mine*. That is but fair.

LORD W. She should never have come here.

LADY W. (*Rising*) It is too late, Arthur, to say that now.   (*Moves away*)

LORD W. (*Rising*) Margaret, if you knew where Mrs. Erlynne went last night, after she left this house, you would not sit in the same room with her. It was absolutely shameless, the whole thing.

LADY W. Arthur, I can't bear it any longer. I must tell you. Last night—

    (*Enter* PARKER *with a tray on which lie* LADY W.'s *fan and a card*)

PARKER. Mrs. Erlynne has called to return your ladyship's fan which she took away by mistake last night. Mrs. Erlynne has written a message on the card.

LADY W. Oh, ask Mrs. Erlynne to be kind enough to come up. (*Reads card*) Say I shall be very glad to see her. (*Exit* PARKER) She wants to see me, Arthur.

LORD W. (*Takes card and looks at it*) Margaret, I *beg* you not to. Let me see her first, at any rate. She's a very dangerous woman. She is the most dangerous woman I know. You don't realize what you're doing.

LADY W. It is right that I should see her.

LORD W. My child, you may be on the brink of a great sorrow. Don't go to meet it. It is absolutely necessary that I should see her before you do.

LADY W. Why should it be necessary?

(*Enter* PARKER)

PARKER. Mrs. Erlynne.

(*Enter* MRS. E. *Exit* PARKER)

MRS. E. How do you do, Lady Windermere? (*To* LORD W.) How do you do? Do you know, Lady Windermere, I am so sorry about your fan. I can't imagine how I made such a silly mistake. Most stupid of me. And as I was driving in your direction, I thought I would take the opportunity of returning your property in person, with many apologies for my carelessness, and of bidding you good-bye.

LADY W. Good-bye? (*Moves towards sofa with* MRS. E. *and sits down beside her*) Are you going away, then, Mrs. Erlynne?

MRS. E. Yes; I am going to live abroad again. The English climate doesn't suit me. My—heart is affected here, and that I don't like. I prefer living in the south. London is too full of fogs and—and serious people, Lord Windermere. Whether the fogs produce the serious people or whether the serious people produce the fogs, I don't know, but the whole thing rather gets on my nerves, and so I'm leaving this afternoon by the Club Train.

LADY W. This afternoon? But I wanted so much to come and see you.

MRS. E. How kind of you! But I am afraid I have to go.

LADY W. Shall I never see you again, Mrs. Erlynne?

MRS. E. I am afraid not. Our lives lie too far apart. But there is a little thing I would like you to do for me. I want a photograph of you, Lady Windermere—would you give me one? You don't know how gratified I should be.

LADY W. Oh, with pleasure. There is one on that table. I'll show it to you.

(*Goes across to the table*)

LORD W. (*Coming up to* MRS. E. *and speaking in a low voice*) It is monstrous your intruding yourself here after your conduct last night.

MRS. E. (*With an amused smile*) My dear Windermere, manners before morals!

LADY W. (*Returning*) I'm afraid it is very flattering—I am not so pretty as that.

(*Showing photograph*)

MRS. E. You are much prettier. But haven't you got one of yourself with your little boy?

LADY W. I have. Would you prefer one of those?

MRS. E. Yes.

LADY W. I'll go and get it for you, if you'll excuse me for a moment. I have one upstairs.

MRS. E. So sorry, Lady Windermere, to give you so much trouble.

LADY W. (*Moves to door* R.) No trouble at all, Mrs. Erlynne.

MRS. E. Thanks so much. (*Exit* LADY W. R.) You seem rather out of temper this morning, Windermere. Why should you be? Margaret and I get on charmingly together.

LORD W. I can't bear to see you with her. Besides, you have not told me the truth, Mrs. Erlynne.

MRS. E. I have not told *her* the truth, you mean.

LORD W. (*Standing* C.) I sometimes wish you had. I should have been spared then the misery, the anxiety, the annoyance of the last six months. But rather than my wife should know—that the mother whom she was taught to consider as dead, the mother whom she has mourned as dead, is living—a divorced woman going about under an assumed name, a bad woman preying upon life, as I know you now to be—rather than that, I was ready to supply you with money to pay bill after bill, extravagance after extravagance, to risk what occurred yesterday, the first quarrel I have ever had with my wife. You don't understand what that means to me. How could you? But I tell you that the only bitter words that ever came from those sweet lips of hers were on your account, and I hate to see you near her. You sully the innocence that is in her. (*Moves* L. C.) And then I used to think that with all your faults you were frank and honest. You are not.

MRS. E. Why do you say that?

LORD W. You made me get you an invitation to my wife's ball.

MRS. E. For my daughter's ball—yes.

LORD W. You came, and within an hour of your leaving the house, you are found in a man's rooms—you are disgraced before every one. (*Goes up stage* C.)

Mrs. E. Yes.

Lord W. (*Turning round on her*) Therefore I have a right to look upon you as what you are—a worthless, vicious woman. I have the right to tell you never to enter this house, never to attempt to come near my wife—

Mrs. E. (*Coldly*) My daughter, you mean.

Lord W. You have no right to claim her as your daughter. You left her, abandoned her, when she was but a child in the cradle, abandoned her for your lover, who abandoned you in turn.

Mrs. E. (*Rising*) Do you count that to his credit, Lord Windermere—or to mine?

Lord W. To his, now that I know you.

Mrs. E. Take care—you had better be careful.

Lord W. Oh, I am not going to mince words for you. I know you thoroughly.

Mrs. E. (*Looking steadily at him*) I question that.

Lord W. I *do* know you. For twenty years of your life you lived without your child, without a thought of your child. One day you read in the papers that she had married a rich man. You saw your hideous chance. You knew that to spare her the ignominy of learning that a woman like you was her mother, I would endure anything. You began your blackmailing.

Mrs. E (*Shrugging her shoulders*) Don't use ugly words, Windermere. They are vulgar. I saw my chance, it is true, and took it.

Lord W. Yes, you took it—and spoiled it all last night by being found out.

Mrs. E. (*With a strange smile*) You are quite right, I spoiled it all last night.

Lord W. And as for your blunder in taking my wife's fan from here, and then leaving it about in Darlington's rooms, it is unpardonable. I can't bear the sight of it now. I shall never let my wife use it again. The thing is soiled for me. You should have kept it, and not brought it back.

Mrs. E. I think I *shall* keep it. (*Goes up*) It's extremely pretty. (*Takes up fan*) I shall ask Margaret to give it to me.

Lord W. I hope my wife will give it you.

Mrs. E. Oh, I'm sure she will have no objection.

Lord W. I wish that at the same time she would give you a miniature she kisses every night before she prays—It's the miniature of a young, innocent-looking girl with beautiful dark hair.

Mrs. E. Ah, yes, I remember. How long ago that seems! (*Goes to sofa and sits down*) It was done before I was married. Dark hair and an innocent expression were the fashion then, Windermere! (*A pause*)

Lord W. What do you mean by coming here this morning? What is your object?
(*Crossing* l. c. *and sitting*)

Mrs. E. (*With a note of irony in her voice*) To bid good-bye to my dear daughter, of course. (Lord W. *bites his underlip in anger.* Mrs. E. *looks at him, and her voice and manner become serious. In her accents as she talks there is a note of deep tragedy. For a moment she reveals herself*) Oh, don't imagine I am going to have a pathetic scene with her, weep on her neck and tell her who I am, and all that kind of thing. I have no ambition to play the part of a mother. Only once in my life have I known a mother's feelings. That was last night. They were terrible—they made me suffer—they made me suffer too much. For twenty years, as you say, I have lived childless—I want to live childless still. (*Hiding her feelings with a trivial laugh*) Besides, my dear Windermere, how on earth could I pose as a mother with a grown-up daughter? Margaret is twenty-one, and I have never admitted that I am more than twenty-nine, or thirty at the most. Twenty-nine when there are pink shades, thirty when there are not. So you see what difficulties it would involve. No, as far as I am concerned, let your wife cherish the memory of this dead, stainless mother. Why should I interfere with her illusions? I find it hard enough to keep my own. I lost one illusion last night. I thought I had no heart. I find I have, and a heart doesn't suit me, Windermere. Somehow it doesn't go with modern dress. It makes one look old. (*Takes up hand-mirror from table and looks into it*) And it spoils one's career at critical moments.

Lord W. You fill me with horror—with absolute horror.

Mrs. E. (*Rising*) I suppose, Windermere, you would like me to retire into a convent or become a hospital nurse or something of that kind, as people do in silly modern novels.

That is stupid of you, Arthur; in real life we don't do such things—not as long as we have any good looks left, at any rate. No—what consoles one nowadays is not repentance, but pleasure. Repentance is quite out of date. And, besides, if a woman really repents, she has to go to a bad dressmaker, otherwise no one believes in her. And nothing in the world would induce me to do that. No; I am going to pass entirely out of your two lives. My coming into them has been a mistake—I discovered that last night.

LORD W. A fatal mistake.

MRS. E. (*Smiling*) Almost fatal.

LORD W. I am sorry now I did not tell my wife the whole thing at once.

MRS. E. I regret my bad actions. You regret your good ones—that is the difference between us.

LORD W. I don't trust you. I *will* tell my wife. It's better for her to know, and from me. It will cause her infinite pain—it will humiliate her terribly, but it's right that she should know.

MRS. E. You propose to tell her?

LORD W. I am going to tell her.

MRS. E. (*Going up to him*) If you do, I will make my name so infamous that it will mar every moment of her life. It will ruin her and make her wretched. If you dare to tell her, there is no depth of degradation I will not sink to, no pit of shame I will not enter. You shall not tell her—I forbid you.

LORD W. Why?

MRS. E. (*After a pause*) If I said to you that I cared for her, perhaps loved her even—you would sneer at me, wouldn't you?

LORD W. I should feel it was not true. A mother's love means devotion, unselfishness, sacrifice. What could you know of such things?

MRS. E. You are right. What could I know of such things? Don't let us talk any more about *it*, as for telling my daughter who I am, that I do not allow. It is my secret, it is not yours. If I make up my mind to tell her, and I think I will, I shall tell her before I leave this house—if not, I shall never tell her.

LORD W. (*Angrily*) Then let me beg of you to leave our house at once. I will make your excuses to Margaret.

(*Enter* LADY W. R. *She goes over to* MRS. E. *with the photograph in her hand.* LORD W. *moves to back of sofa, and anxiously watches* MRS. E. *as the scene progresses*)

LADY W. I am so sorry, Mrs. Erlynne, to have kept you waiting. I couldn't find the photograph anywhere. At last I discovered it in my husband's dressing-room—he had stolen it.

MRS. E. (*Takes the photograph from her and looks at it*) I am not surprised—it is charming. (*Goes over to sofa with* LADY W. *and sits down beside her. Looks again at the photograph*) And so that is your little boy! What is he called?

LADY W. Gerard, after my dear father.

MRS. E. (*Laying the photograph down*) Really?

LADY W. Yes. If it had been a girl, I would have called it after my mother. My mother had the same name as myself, Margaret.

MRS. E. My name is Margaret, too.

LADY W. Indeed!

MRS. E. Yes. (*Pause*) You are devoted to your mother's memory, Lady Windermere, your husband tells me.

LADY W. We all have ideals in life. At least we all should have. Mine is my mother.

MRS. E. Ideals are dangerous things. Realities are better. They wound, but they are better.

LADY W. (*Shaking her head*) If I lost my ideals, I should lose everything.

MRS. E. Everything?

LADY W. Yes. (*Pause*)

MRS. E. Did your father often speak to you of your mother?

LADY W. No, it gave him too much pain. He told me how my mother had died a few months after I was born. His eyes filled with tears as he spoke. Then he begged me never to mention her name to him again. It made him suffer even to hear it. My father—my father really died of a broken heart. His was the most ruined life I know.

MRS. E. (*Rising*) I am afraid I must go now, Lady Windermere.

LADY W. (*Rising*) Oh, no, don't.

MRS. E. I think I had better. My carriage must have come back by this time. I sent it to Lady Jedburgh's with a note.

LADY W. Arthur, would you mind seeing if Mrs. Erlynne's carriage has come back?

MRS. E. Pray don't trouble Lord Windermere, Lady Windermere.

LADY W. Yes, Arthur, do go, please.

(LORD W. *hesitates for a moment, and looks at* MRS. E. *She remains quite impassive. He leaves the room*)

(*To* MRS. E.) Oh, what am I to say to you? You saved me last night!

(*Goes toward her*)

MRS. E. Hush—don't speak of it.

LADY W. I must speak of it. I can't let you think that I am going to accept this sacrifice. I am not. It is too great. I am going to tell my husband everything. It is my duty.

MRS. E. It is not your duty—at least you have duties to others besides him. You say you owe me something?

LADY W. I owe you everything.

MRS. E. Then pay your debt by silence. That is the only way in which it can be paid. Don't spoil the one good thing I have done in my life by telling it to any one. Promise me that what passed last night will remain a secret between us. You must not bring misery into your husband's life. Why spoil his love? You must not spoil it. Love is easily killed. Oh, how easily love is killed! Pledge me your word, Lady Windermere, that you will *never* tell him. I insist upon it.

LADY W. (*With bowed head*) It is your will, not mine.

MRS. E. Yes, it is my will. And never forget your child—I like to think of you as a mother. I like to think of yourself as one.

LADY W. (*Looking up*) I always will now. Only once in my life I have forgotten my own mother—that was last night. Oh, if I had remembered her, I should not have been so foolish, so wicked.

MRS. E. (*With a slight shudder*) Hush, last night is quite over.

(*Enter* LORD W.)

LORD W. Your carriage has not come back yet, Mrs. Erlynne.

MRS. E. It makes no matter. I'll take a hansom. There is nothing in the world so respectable as a good Shrewsbury and Talbot. And now, dear Lady Windermere, I am afraid it is really good-bye. (*Moves up* C.) Oh, I remember. You'll think me absurd, but do you know, I've taken a great fancy to this fan that I was silly enough to run away with last night from your ball. Now, I wonder would you give it to me? Lord Windermere says you may. I know it is his present.

LADY W. Oh, certainly, if it will give you any pleasure. But it has my name on it. It has "Margaret" on it.

MRS. E. But we have the same Christian name.

LADY W. Oh, I forgot. Of course, do have it. What a wonderful chance our names being the same!

MRS. E. Quite wonderful. Thanks—it will always remind me of you.

(*Shakes hands with her*)

(*Enter* PARKER)

PARKER. Lord Augustus Lorton. Mrs. Erlynne's carriage has come.

(*Enter* LORD A.)

LORD A. Good-morning, dear boy. Good-morning, Lady Windermere. (*Sees* MRS. E.) Mrs. Erlynne!

MRS. E. How do you do, Lord Augustus? Are you quite well this morning?

LORD A. (*Coldly*) Quite well, thank you, Mrs. Erlynne.

MRS. E. You don't look at all well, Lord Augustus. You stop up too late—it is so bad for you. You really should take more care of yourself. Good-bye, Lord Windermere. (*Goes towards door with a bow to* LORD A. *Suddenly smiles, and looks back at him*) Lord Augustus! Won't you see me to my carriage? You might carry the fan.

LORD W. Allow me!

MRS. E. No, I want Lord Augustus. I have a special message for the dear Duchess. Won't you carry the fan, Lord Augustus?

LORD A. If you really desire it, Mrs. Erlynne.

MRS. E. (*Laughing*) Of course I do. You'll carry it so gracefully. You would carry off anything gracefully, dear Lord Augustus.

(*When she reaches the door she looks back for a moment at* LADY W. *Their eyes meet. Then she turns, and exit* C., *followed by* LORD A.)

LADY W. You will never speak against Mrs. Erlynne again, Arthur, will you?

LORD W. (*Gravely*) She is better than one thought her.

LADY W. She is better than I am.

LORD W. (*Smiling as he strokes her hair*) Child, you and she belong to different worlds. Into your world evil has never entered.

LADY W. Don't say that, Arthur. There is the same world for all of us, and good and evil, sin and innocence, go through it hand in hand. To shut one's eyes to half of life that one may live securely is as though one blinded one's self that one might walk with more safety in a land of pit and precipice.

LORD W. (*Moves down with her*) Darling, why do you say that?

LADY W. (*Sits on sofa*) Because I, who had shut my eyes to life, came to the brink. And one who had separated us—

LORD W. We were never parted.

LADY W. We never must be again. Oh, Arthur, don't love me less, and I will trust you more. I will trust you absolutely. Let us go to Selby. In the Rose Garden at Selby, the roses are white and red.

(*Enter* LORD A.)

LORD A. Arthur, she has explained everything! (LADY W. *looks horribly frightened.* LORD W. *starts.* LORD A. *takes* LORD W. *by the arm, and brings him to front of stage*) My dear fellow, she has explained every demmed thing. We all wronged her immensely. It was entirely for my sake she went to Darlington's rooms—called first at the club. Fact is, wanted to put me out of suspense, and being told I had gone on, followed — naturally — frightened when she heard a lot of men coming in—retired to another room—I assure you, most gratifying to me, the whole thing. We all behaved brutally to her. She is just the woman for me. Suits me down to the ground. All the condition she makes is that we live out of England —a very good thing, too!—Demmed clubs, demmed climate, demmed cooks, demmed everything! Sick of it all.

LADY W. (*Frightened*) Has Mrs. Erlynne—?

LORD A. (*Advancing towards her with a bow*) Yes, Lady Windermere, Mrs. Erlynne has done me the honor of accepting my hand.

LORD W. Well, you are certainly marrying a very clever woman.

LADY W. (*Taking her husband's hand*) Ah! you're marrying a very good woman.

SIR ARTHUR WING PINERO

The Second Mrs. Tanqueray

PRINCIPAL EVENTS IN PINERO'S LIFE

1855, 24 May, Arthur Wing Pinero was born in London.

1865-74, Worked in his father's law office.

1874, At his father's death he joined the Wyndham's stock company at the Theatre Royal in Edinburgh.

1875, He joined the company of Henry Irving (later Sir Henry) and Ellen Terry at the Lyceum in London.

1877, 6 Oct., Pinero's first play, a one-act curtain-raiser called £200 *a Year* produced at the Globe Theatre in London.

1879, 20 Sept., Daisy's Escape, another one-act curtain-raiser, produced by Henry Irving at the Lyceum.

1880, 5 Nov., The Money Spinner, Pinero's first full-length play, was tried out at the Theatre Royal, Manchester. After revision, produced at St. James's, London, 8 January 1881.

1883, Pinero married the actress Myra Holme.

1882-84, He wrote a series of popular but undistinguished plays: *Girls and Boys, The Rector, The Rocket, Lords and Commons, Low-Water, The Iron Master,* and *In Chancery.*

1885, 21 March, The Magistrate was produced at the Court Theatre, where it established a record run.

1885-93, Pinero wrote a series of plays, most of them for the Court Theatre and generally known as the "Court Farces." Most of them were very popular—*The Magistrate, The School Mistress, Dandy Dick, Sweet Lavender, The Weaker Sex, The Cabinet Minister, The Amazons.*

1889, 24 April, The Profligate was produced at the Garrick theatre. It was a tragedy on the theme of the double standard, but a happy ending was substituted at the manager's insistence.

1893, 27 May, The Second Mrs. Tanqueray produced at St. James's Theatre. Because of the serious nature of the play, Pinero, in spite of his popularity, had great trouble in getting it produced. It was a great success with both critics and audience.

1895, 13 March, The Notorious Mrs. Ebbsmith produced at the Garrick.

1898, 20 Jan., Trelawny of the "Wells" produced at the Court.

1899, 8 April, The Gay Lord Quex produced at the Globe.

1901, 21 Sept., Iris performed at the Garrick with Dion Boucicault in the cast.

1906, 1 Feb., His House in Order began a long run at St. James's.

1908, 9 May, The Thunderbolt performed at St. James's.

1909, Pinero was knighted by King Edward VII.

1909, 2 Sept., Mid-Channel performed at

St. James's. It opened in New York five months later with Ethel Barrymore in the lead.

1915, 1 Sept., The Big Drum produced at St. James's.

1922, 1 March, The Enchanted Cottage

produced at the Duke of York's Theatre.

1932, 20 May, A Cold June, his last play, produced at the Duchess Theatre.

1934, 23 Nov., Pinero died in London. About half Pinero's plays have been omitted from this list.

INTRODUCTION

When Pinero wrote this play, the London audience was just beginning to be dissatisfied with the trivial, sentimental, and artificial fare which the English theatres had been providing for nearly two centuries. The serious social analyses of Ibsen had made their mark on the continent, and their virtues were being urged on the English by critics like William Archer and G. B. Shaw. In London J. T. Grein had established the Independent Theatre for the production of significant plays. These harbingers of the New Drama had already appeared when *The Second Mrs. Tanqueray* was produced and had attracted a few followers, but the vast majority of the London audience was still addicted to the old trivialities and was violently shocked by any honest presentation of the more serious aspects of contemporary life in the theatre.

Pinero had already made a reputation and a good income by the composition of amusing trivialities for the theatre when he decided to write *The Second Mrs. Tanqueray.* This play he did not expect to be popular; he intended it as a serious consideration of a significant subject for thoughtful audiences. Compared with the nineteenth-century plays which had preceded it, this is what *The Second Mrs. Tanqueray* is. But unfortunately for Pinero's reputation, his serious play was followed in a few years by the more penetrating and thoughtful plays of Shaw, Granville-Barker, and Galsworthy, and our tendency has been to compare his play with its successors instead of its predecessors.

The subject of the "fallen" woman was somewhat more absorbing to the Victorians than it is to us, and Pinero set out to present her sympathetically and to consider the

problem of her attempt to rehabilitate herself. His Paula was an effective piece of dramatic characterization, as is demonstrated by the number of important actresses eager to portray the role in the next twenty-five years. His conclusion that it was impossible for such a woman to live down her past seemed convincing, and it was a telling indictment of the "double standard of morality" about which many serious social critics of the nineties were agitated. Pinero has carefully excluded all theatrically attractive irrelevencies and conscientiously limited himself to the main issue of Aubrey and Paula's attempt to make a successful marriage and to live down her past. His play marks a notable advance in the serious social drama.

Yet in the light of succeeding plays, *The Second Mrs. Tanqueray* seems contrived and melodramatic. Paula's promiscuous past is attributed to the wickedness and cruelty of men, a scarcely adequate explanation; the opening expository scene, in which the host at an intimate farewell dinner party leaves his guests to catch up on his correspondence, seems almost as artificial as the old-fashioned explanatory soliloquy to the audience which Pinero eschewed; the wholly unprepared introduction of an unknown former lover of Paula's as Ellean's suitor smacks of the arrangements of farce. These criticisms of the play have been often made, and they cannot be wholly denied, yet they are not quite fair to Pinero. Though *The Second Mrs. Tanqueray* may not be one of the greatest of English plays, it is a serious and honest play by a gifted, if limited, man, and it helped to prepare the way for the dramatic renaissance of the twentieth century.

THE SECOND MRS. TANQUERAY

Dramatis personae

In order of first appearance

AUBREY TANQUERAY, A well-to-do widower of forty-two.

FRANK MISQUITH, Q.C., M.P., An old friend of Tanqueray.

GORDON JAYNE, M.D., Another old friend.

MORSE, Tanqueray's man servant.

CAYLEY DRUMMLE, A middle-aged bachelor, Tanqueray's closest friend.

PAULA RAY, A beautiful and vivacious woman.

ELLEAN TANQUERAY, Tanqueray's serious-minded nineteen-year-old daughter.

MRS. CORTELYON, A neighbor and old acquaintance of Tanqueray.

LADY ORREYED, An old friend of Paula.

SIR GEORGE ORREYED, BART., Her stupid husband.

CAPTAIN HUGH ARDALE, A young officer, recently decorated for conspicuous bravery in an Indian mutiny.

Servants.

SCENE: *London and Surrey.*

TIME: *The Present Day* (i.e. 1893)

The Scene of the First Act is laid at MR. TANQUERAY'S *rooms, No. 2 x, The Albany, in the month of November; the occurrences of the succeeding Acts take place at his house, "Highercoombe," near Willowmere, Surrey, during the early part of the following year.*

Act I

AUBREY TANQUERAY'S *chambers in the Albany—a richly and tastefully decorated room, elegantly and luxuriously furnished: on the right a large pair of doors opening into another room, on the left at the further end of the room a small door leading to a bed-chamber. A circular table is laid for a dinner for four persons, which has now reached the stage of dessert and coffee. Everything in the apartment suggests wealth and refinement. The fire is burning brightly.*

(AUBREY TANQUERAY, MISQUITH, *and* JAYNE *are seated at the dinner table.* AUBREY *is forty-two, handsome, winning in manner, his speech and bearing retaining some of the qualities of young manhood.* MISQUITH *is about forty-seven, genial and portly.* JAYNE *is a year or two* MISQUITH'S *senior; soft-speaking and precise—in appearance a type of the prosperous town physician.* MORSE, AUBREY'S *servant, places a little cabinet of cigars and the spirit-lamp on the table beside* AUBREY, *and goes out*)

MISQUITH. Aubrey, it is a pleasant yet dreadful fact to contemplate, but it's nearly fifteen years since I first dined with you. You lodged in Piccadilly in those days, over a hat-shop. Jayne, I met you at that dinner, and Cayley Drummle.

JAYNE. Yes, yes. What a pity it is that Cayley isn't here to-night.

AUBREY. Confound the old gossip! His empty chair has been staring us in the face all through dinner. I ought to have told Morse to take it away.

MISQUITH. Odd, his sending no excuse.

AUBREY. I'll walk round to his lodgings later on and ask after him.

MISQUITH. I'll go with you.

JAYNE. So will I.

AUBREY. (*Opening the cigar-cabinet*) Doctor, it's useless to tempt you, I know. Frank—(MISQUITH *and* AUBREY *smoke*) I particularly wished Cayley Drummle to be one of us to-night. You two fellows and Cayley are my closest, my best friends—

MISQUITH. My dear Aubrey!

JAYNE. I rejoice to hear you say so.

AUBREY. And I wanted to see the three of you round this table. You can't guess the reason.

MISQUITH. You desired to give us a most excellent dinner.

JAYNE. Obviously.

AUBREY. (*Hesitatingly*) Well—I—(*glancing at the clock*)—Cayley won't turn up now.

JAYNE. H'm, hardly.

AUBREY. Then you two shall hear it. Doctor, Frank, this is the last time we are to meet in these rooms.

JAYNE. The last time?

MISQUITH. You're going to leave the Albany?

AUBREY. Yes. You've heard me speak of a house I built in the country years ago, haven't you?

MISQUITH. In Surrey.

AUBREY. Well, when my wife died I cleared out of that house and let it. I think of trying the place again.

MISQUITH. But you'll go raving mad if ever you find yourself down there alone.

AUBREY. Ah, but I shan't be alone, and that's what I wanted to tell you. I'm going to be married.

JAYNE. Going to be married?

MISQUITH. Married?

AUBREY. Yes—to-morrow.

JAYNE. To-morrow?

MISQUITH. You take my breath away! My dear fellow, I—I—of course, I congratulate you.

JAYNE. And—and—so do I—heartily.

AUBREY. Thanks—thanks.

(*There is a moment or two of embarrassment*)

MISQUITH. Er—ah—this is an excellent cigar.

JAYNE. Ah—um—your coffee is remarkable.

AUBREY. Look here; I dare say you two old friends think this treatment very strange, very unkind. So I want you to understand me. You know a marriage often cools friendships. What's the usual course of things? A man's engagement is given out, he is congratulated, complimented upon his choice; the church is filled with troops of friends, and he goes away happily to a chorus of good wishes. He comes back, sets up house in town or country, and thinks to resume the old associations, the old companionships. My dear Frank, my dear good doctor, it's very seldom that it can be done. Generally, a worm has begun to eat its way into those hearty, unreserved, pre-nuptial friendships; a damnable constraint sets in and acts like a wasting disease; and so, believe me, in nine cases out of ten a man's marriage severs for him more close ties than it forms.

MISQUITH. Well, my dear Aubrey, I earnestly hope—

AUBREY. I know what you're going to say, Frank. I hope so, too. In the meantime let's face dangers. I've reminded you of the *usual* course of things, but my marriage isn't even the conventional sort of marriage likely to satisfy society. Now, Cayley's a bachelor, but you two men have wives. By the bye, my love to Mrs. Misquith and to Mrs. Jayne when you get home—don't forget that. Well, your wives may not—like—the lady I'm going to marry.

JAYNE. Aubrey, forgive me for suggesting that the lady you are going to marry may not like our wives—mine at least; I beg your pardon, Frank.

AUBREY. Quite so; then I must go the way my wife goes.

MISQUITH. Come, come, pray don't let us anticipate that either side will be called upon to make such a sacrifice.

AUBREY. Yes, yes, let us anticipate it. And let us make up our minds to have no slow bleeding to death of our friendship. We'll end a pleasant chapter here to-night, and after to-night start afresh. When my wife and I settle down at Willowmere it's possible that we shall all come together. But if this isn't to be, for Heaven's sake let us recognize that it is simply because it *can't* be, and not wear hypocritical faces and suffer and be wretched. Doctor, Frank—(*holding out his hands, one to* MISQUITH, *the other to* JAYNE) —good luck to all of us!

MISQUITH. But—but—do I understand we are to ask nothing? Not even the lady's name, Aubrey?

AUBREY. The lady, my dear Frank, belongs to the next chapter, and in that her name is Mrs. Aubrey Tanqueray.

JAYNE. (*Raising his coffee-cup*) Then, in an old-fashioned way, I propose a toast. Aubrey, Frank, I give you "The Next Chapter!"

(*They drink the toast, saying, "The Next Chapter!"*)

AUBREY. Doctor, find a comfortable chair; Frank, you too. As we're going to turn out by and by, let me scribble a couple of notes now while I think of them.

MISQUITH *and* JAYNE. Certainly—yes, yes.

AUBREY. It might slip my memory when I get back.

(AUBREY *sits at a writing-table at the other end of the room, and writes*)

JAYNE. (*To* MISQUITH *in a whisper*) Frank—(MISQUITH *quietly leaves his chair, and sits nearer to* JAYNE) What is all this? Simply a morbid crank of Aubrey's with regard to ante-nuptial acquaintances?

MISQUITH. H'm! Did you notice *one* expression he used?

JAYNE. Let me think—

MISQUITH. "My marriage is not even the conventional sort of marriage likely to satisfy society."

JAYNE. Bless me, yes! What does that suggest?

MISQUITH. That he has a particular rather than a general reason for anticipating estrangement from his friends, I'm afraid.

JAYNE. A horrible *mésalliance!* A dairymaid who has given him a glass of milk during a day's hunting, or a little anæmic shop-girl! Frank, I'm utterly wretched!

MISQUITH. My dear Jayne, speaking in absolute confidence, I have never been more profoundly depressed in my life.

(MORSE *enters*)

MORSE. (*Announcing*) Mr. Drummle. (CAYLEY DRUMMLE *enters briskly. He is a*

neat little man of about five-and-forty, in manner bright, airy, debonair, but with an undercurrent of seriousness. MORSE *retires*)

DRUMMLE. I'm in disgrace; nobody realizes that more thoroughly than I do. Where's my host?

AUBREY. (*Who has risen*) Cayley.

DRUMMLE. (*Shaking hands with him*) Don't speak to me till I have tendered my explanation. A harsh word from anybody would unman me.

(MISQUITH *and* JAYNE *shake hands with* DRUMMLE)

AUBREY. Have you dined?

DRUMMLE. No—unless you call a bit of fish, a cutlet, and a pancake dining.

AUBREY. Cayley, this is disgraceful.

JAYNE. Fish, a cutlet, and a pancake will require a great deal of explanation.

MISQUITH. Especially the pancake. My dear friend, your case looks miserably weak.

DRUMMLE. Hear me! hear me!

JAYNE. Now then!

MISQUITH. Come!

AUBREY. Well!

DRUMMLE. It so happens that to-night I was exceptionally early in dressing for dinner.

MISQUITH. For which dinner—the fish and cutlet?

DRUMMLE. For *this* dinner, of course— really, Frank! At a quarter to eight, in fact, I found myself trimming my nails, with ten minutes to spare. Just then enter my man with a note—would I hasten, as fast as cab could carry me, to old Lady Orreyed in Bruton Street?—"sad trouble." Now, recollect, please, I had ten minutes on my hands, old Lady Orreyed was a very dear friend of my mother's, and was in some distress.

AUBREY. Cayley, come to the fish and cutlet!

MISQUITH *and* JAYNE. Yes, yes, and the pancake!

DRUMMLE. Upon my word! Well, the scene in Bruton Street beggars description; the women servants looked scared, the men drunk; and there was poor old Lady Orreyed on the floor of her boudoir like Queen Bess among her pillows.

AUBREY. What's the matter?

DRUMMLE. (*To everybody*) You know

George Orreyed?

MISQUITH. Yes.

JAYNE. I've met him.

DRUMMLE. Well, he's a thing of the past.

AUBREY. Not dead!

DRUMMLE. Certainly, in the worst sense. He's married Mabel Hervey.

MISQUITH. What!

DRUMMLE. It's true—this morning. The poor mother showed me his letter—a dozen curt words, and some of those ill-spelt.

MISQUITH. (*Walking up to the fireplace*) I'm very sorry.

JAYNE. Pardon my ignorance—who *was* Mabel Hervey?

DRUMMLE. You don't—? Oh, of course not. Miss Hervey—Lady Orreyed, as she now is—was a lady who would have been, perhaps has been, described in the reports of the Police or the Divorce Court as an actress. Had she belonged to a lower stratum of our advanced civilization she would, in the event of judicial inquiry, have defined her calling with equal justification as that of a dressmaker. To do her justice, she is a type of a class which is immortal. Physically, by the strange caprice of creation, curiously beautiful; mentally, she lacks even the strength of deliberate viciousness. Paint her portrait, it would symbolize a creature perfectly patrician; lance a vein of her superbly-modelled arm, you would get the poorest *vin ordinaire!* Her affections, emotions, impulses, her very existence—a burlesque! Flaxen, five-and-twenty, and feebly frolicsome; anybody's in less gentle society I should say everybody's, property! That, doctor, was Miss Hervey who is the new Lady Orreyed. Dost thou like the picture?

MISQUITH. Very good, Cayley! Bravo!

AUBREY. (*Laying his hand on* DRUMMLE's *shoulder*) You'd scarcely believe it, Jayne, but none of us really know anything about this lady, our gay young friend here, I suspect, least of all.

DRUMMLE. Aubrey, I applaud your chivalry.

AUBREY. And perhaps you'll let me finish a couple of letters which Frank and Jayne have given me leave to write. (*Returning to the writing-table*) Ring for what you want, like a good fellow!

(AUBREY *resumes his writing*)

MISQUITH. (*To* DRUMMLE) Still, the fish and the cutlet remain unexplained.

DRUMMLE. Oh, the poor old woman was so weak that I insisted upon her taking some food, and felt there was nothing for it but to sit down opposite her. The fool! the blackguard!

MISQUITH. Poor Orreyed! Well, he's gone under for a time.

DRUMMLE. For a time! My dear Frank, I tell you he has absolutely ceased to be. (AUBREY, *who has been writing busily, turns his head towards the speakers and listens. His lips are set, and there is a frown upon his face*) For all practical purposes you may regard him as the late George Orreyed. To-morrow the very characteristics of his speech, as we remember them, will have become obsolete.

JAYNE. But surely, in the course of years, he and his wife will outlive—

DRUMMLE. No, no, doctor, don't try to upset one of my settled beliefs. You may dive into many waters, but there is *one* social Dead Sea—!

JAYNE. Perhaps you're right.

DRUMMLE. Right! Good God! I wish you could prove me otherwise! Why, for years I've been sitting, and watching and waiting.

MISQUITH. You're in form to-night, Cayley. May we ask where you've been in the habit of squandering your useful leisure?

DRUMMLE. Where? On the shore of that same sea.

MISQUITH. And, pray, what have you been waiting for?

DRUMMLE. For some of my best friends to come up. (AUBREY *utters a half-stifled exclamation of impatience; then he hurriedly gathers up his papers from the writing-table. The three men turn to him.*) Eh?

AUBREY. Oh, I—I'll finish my letters in the other room if you'll excuse me for five minutes. Tell Cayley the news.

(*He goes out*)

DRUMMLE. (*Hurrying to the door*) My dear fellow, my jabbering has disturbed you! I'll never talk again as long as I live!

MISQUITH. Close the door, Cayley.

(DRUMMLE *shuts the door*)

JAYNE. Cayley—

DRUMMLE. (*Advancing to the dinner table*) A smoke, a smoke, or I perish!

(Selects a cigar from the little cabinet)

JAYNE. Cayley, marriages are in the air.

DRUMMLE. Are they? Discover the bacillus, doctor, and destroy it.

JAYNE. I mean, among our friends.

DRUMMLE. Oh, Nugent Warrinder's engagement to Lady Alice Tring. I've heard of that. They're not to be married till the spring.

JAYNE. Another marriage that concerns us a little takes place to-morrow.

DRUMMLE. Whose marriage?

JAYNE. Aubrey's.

DRUMMLE. Aub—! *(Looking towards* MISQUITH) Is it a joke?

MISQUITH. No.

DRUMMLE. *(Looking from* MISQUITH *to* JAYNE) To whom?

MISQUITH. He doesn't tell us.

JAYNE. We three were asked here to-night to receive the announcement. Aubrey has some theory that marriage is likely to alienate a man from his friends, and it seems to me he has taken the precaution to wish us good-bye.

MISQUITH. No, no.

JAYNE. Practically, surely.

DRUMMLE. *(Thoughtfully)* Marriage in general, does he mean, or *this* marriage?

JAYNE. That's the point. Frank says—

MISQUITH. No, no, no; I feared it suggested—

JAYNE. Well, well, *(To* DRUMMLE) What do you think of it?

DRUMMLE. *(After a slight pause)* Is there a light there? *(Lighting his cigar)* He—wraps the lady—in mystery—you say?

MISQUITH. Most modestly.

DRUMMLE. Aubrey's—not—a very—young man.

JAYNE. Forty-three.

DRUMMLE. Ah! *L'âge critique!*

MISQUITH. A dangerous age—yes, yes.

DRUMMLE. When you two fellows go home, do you mind leaving me behind here?

MISQUITH. Not at all.

JAYNE. By all means.

DRUMMLE. All right. *(Anxiously)* Deuce take it, the man's second marriage mustn't be another mistake!

(With his head bent he walks up to the fireplace)

JAYNE. You knew him in his short married life, Cayley. Terribly unsatisfactory, wasn't it?

DRUMMLE. Well—*(Looking at the door)* I quite closed that door?

MISQUITH. Yes.

(Settles himself on the sofa; JAYNE *is seated in an arm-chair)*

DRUMMLE. *(Smoking with his back to the fire)* He married a Miss Herriott; that was in the year eighteen—confound dates—twenty years ago. She was a lovely creature—by Jove, she was; by religion a Roman Catholic. She was one of your cold sort, you know—all marble arms and black velvet. I remember her with painful distinctness as the only woman who ever made me nervous.

MISQUITH. Ha, ha!

DRUMMLE. He loved her—to distraction, as they say. Jupiter, how fervently that poor devil courted her! But I don't believe she allowed him even to squeeze her fingers. She *was* an iceberg! As for kissing, the mere contact would have given him chapped lips. However, he married her and took her away, the latter greatly to my relief.

JAYNE. Abroad, you mean?

DRUMMLE. Eh? Yes. I imagine he gratified her by renting a villa in Lapland, but I don't know. After a while they returned, and then I saw how woefully Aubrey had miscalculated results.

JAYNE. Miscalculated—?

DRUMMLE. He had reckoned, poor wretch, that in the early days of marriage she would thaw. But she didn't. I used to picture him closing his doors and making up the fire in the hope of seeing her features relax. Bless her, the thaw never set in! I believe she kept a thermometer in her stays and always registered ten degrees below zero. However, in time a child came—a daughter.

JAYNE. Didn't that—?

DRUMMLE. Not a bit of it; it made matters worse. Frightened at her failure to stir up in him some sympathetic religious belief, she determined upon strong measures with regard to the child. He opposed her for a miserable year or so, but she wore him down, and the insensible little brat was placed in a convent, first in France, then in Ireland. Not long afterwards the mother died, strangely enough, of fever, the only warmth,

I believe, that ever came to that woman's body.

MISQUITH. Don't, Cayley!

JAYNE. The child is living, we know.

DRUMMLE. Yes, if you choose to call it living. Miss Tanqueray—a young woman of nineteen now—is in the Loretto convent at Armagh. She professes to have found her true vocation in a religious life, and within a month or two will take final vows.

MISQUITH. He ought to have removed his daughter from the convent when the mother died.

DRUMMLE. Yes, yes, but absolutely at the end there was reconciliation between husband and wife, and she won his promise that the child should complete her conventual education. He reaped his reward. When he attempted to gain his girl's confidence and affection he was too late; he found he was dealing with the spirit of the mother. You remember his visit to Ireland last month?

JAYNE. Yes.

DRUMMLE. That was to wish his girl good-bye.

MISQUITH. Poor fellow!

DRUMMLE. He sent for me when he came back. I think he must have had a lingering hope that the girl would relent—would come to life, as it were—at the last moment, for, for an hour or so, in this room, he was terribly shaken. I'm sure he'd clung to that hope from the persistent way in which he kept breaking off in his talk to repeat one dismal word, as if he couldn't realize his position without dinning this damned word into his head.

JAYNE. What word was that?

DRUMMLE. Alone—alone.

(AUBREY *enters*)

AUBREY. A thousand apologies!

DRUMMLE. (*Gayly*) We are talking about you, my dear Aubrey.

(*During the telling of the story,* MISQUITH *has risen and gone to the fire, and* DRUMMLE *has thrown himself full-length on the sofa.* AUBREY *now joins* MISQUITH *and* JAYNE)

AUBREY. Well, Cayley, are you surprised?

DRUMMLE. Surp—! I haven't been surprised for twenty years.

AUBREY. And you're not angry with me?

DRUMMLE. Angry! (*Rising*) Because you considerately withhold the name of a lady with whom it is now the object of my life to become acquainted? My dear fellow, you pique my curiosity, you give zest to my existence! And as for a wedding, who on earth wants to attend that familiar and probably draughty function? Ugh! My cigar's out.

AUBREY. Let's talk about something else.

MISQUITH. (*Looking at his watch*) Not to-night, Aubrey.

AUBREY. My dear Frank!

MISQUITH. I go up to Scotland to-morrow, and there are some little matters—

JAYNE. I am off too.

AUBREY. No, no.

JAYNE. I must: I have to give a look to a case in Clifford Street on my way home.

AUBREY. (*Going to the door*) Well! (MISQUITH *and* JAYNE *exchange looks with* DRUMMLE. *Opening the door and calling*) Morse, hats and coats! I shall write to you all next week from Genoa or Florence. Now, doctor, Frank, remember, my love to Mrs. Misquith and to Mrs. Jayne!

(MORSE *enters with hats and coats*)

MISQUITH *and* JAYNE. Yes, yes—yes, yes.

AUBREY. And your young people!

(*As* MISQUITH *and* JAYNE *put on their coats there is the clatter of careless talk*)

JAYNE. Cayley, I meet you at dinner on Sunday.

DRUMMLE. At the Stratfields'. That's very pleasant.

MISQUITH. (*Putting on his coat with* AUBREY's *aid*) Ah-h!

AUBREY. What's wrong?

MISQUITH. A twinge. Why didn't I go to Aix in August?

JAYNE. (*Shaking hands with* DRUMMLE) Good-night, Cayley.

DRUMMLE. Good-night, my dear doctor!

MISQUITH. (*Shaking hands with* DRUMMLE) Cayley, are you in town for long?

DRUMMLE. Dear friend, I'm nowhere for long. Good-night.

MISQUITH. Good-night.

(AUBREY, JAYNE, *and* MISQUITH *go out,*

followed by Morse; *the hum of talk is continued outside*)

Aubrey. A cigar, Frank.

Misquith. No, thank you.

Aubrey. Going to walk, doctor?

Jayne. If Frank will.

Misquith. By all means.

Aubrey. It's a cold night.

(*The door is closed.* Drummle *remains standing with his coat on his arm and his hat in his hand*)

Drummle. (*To himself, thoughtfully*) Now then! What the devil!—

(Aubrey *returns*)

Aubrey. (*Eyeing* Drummle *a little awkwardly*) Well, Cayley?

Drummle. Well, Aubrey?

(Aubrey *walks up to the fire and stands looking into it*)

Aubrey. You're not going, old chap?

Drummle. (*Sitting*) No.

Aubrey. (*After a slight pause, with a forced laugh*) Hah, Cayley, I never thought I should feel—shy—with you.

Drummle. Why do you?

Aubrey. Never mind.

Drummle. Now, I can quite understand a man wishing to be married in the dark, as it were.

Aubrey. You can?

Drummle. In your place I should very likely adopt the same course.

Aubrey. You think so?

Drummle. And if I intended marrying a lady not prominently in society, as I presume you do—as I presume you do—

Aubrey. Well?

Drummle. As I presume you do, I'm not sure that I should tender her for preliminary dissection at afternoon tea-tables.

Aubrey. No?

Drummle. In fact, there is probably only one person—were I in your position to-night—with whom I should care to chat the matter over.

Aubrey. Who's that?

Drummle. Yourself, of course. (*Going to* Aubrey *and standing beside him*) Of course, yourself, old friend.

Aubrey. (*After a pause*) I must seem a brute to you, Cayley. But there are some acts which are hard to explain, hard to defend—

Drummle. To defend—

Aubrey. Some acts which one must trust to time to put right.

(Drummle *watches him for a moment, then takes up his hat and coat*)

Drummle. Well, I'll be moving.

Aubrey. Cayley! Confound you and your old friendship! Do you think I forget it? Put your coat down! Why did you stay behind here? Cayley, the lady I am going to marry is the lady—who is known as—Mrs. Jarman.

(*There is a pause*)

Drummle. (*In a low voice*) Mrs. Jarman! are you serious?

(*He walks to the fireplace, where he leans upon the mantelpiece uttering something like a groan*)

Aubrey. As you've got this out of me I give you leave to say all you care to say. Come, we'll be plain with each other. You know Mrs. Jarman?

Drummle. I first met her at—what does it matter?

Aubrey. Yes, yes, everything! Come!

Drummle. I met her at Homburg, two—three seasons ago.

Aubrey. Not as Mrs. Jarman?

Drummle. No.

Aubrey. She was then—?

Drummle. Mrs. Dartry.

Aubrey. Yes. She has also seen you in London, she says.

Drummle. Certainly.

Aubrey. In Alford Street. Go on.

Drummle. Please!

Aubrey. I insist.

Drummle. (*With a slight shrug of the shoulders*) Some time last year I was asked by a man to sup at his house, one night after the theater.

Aubrey. Mr. Selwyn Ethurst—a bachelor.

Drummle. Yes.

Aubrey. You were surprised therefore to find Mr. Ethurst aided in his cursed hospitality by a lady.

Drummle. I was unprepared.

Aubrey. The lady you had known as Mrs. Dartry? (Drummle *inclines his head silently*) There is something of a yachting cruise in the Mediterranean, too, is there not?

Drummle. I joined Peter Jarman's yacht

as Marseilles, in the Spring, a month before he died.

AUBREY. Mrs. Jarman was on board?

DRUMMLE. She was a kind hostess.

AUBREY. And an old acquaintance?

DRUMMLE. Yes.

AUBREY. You have told your story.

DRUMMLE. With your assistance.

AUBREY. I have put you to the pain of telling it to show you that this is not the case of a blind man entrapped by an artful woman. Let me add that Mrs. Jarman has no legal right to that name; that she is simply Miss Ray—Miss Paula Ray.

DRUMMLE. (After a pause) I should like to express my regret, Aubrey, for the way in which I spoke of George Orreyed's marriage.

AUBREY. You mean you compare Lady Orreyed with Miss Ray? (DRUMMLE is silent) Oh, of course! To you, Cayley, all women who have been roughly treated, and who dare to survive by borrowing a little of our philosophy, are alike. You see in the crowd of the ill-used only one pattern; you can't detect the shades of goodness, intelligence, even nobility there. Well, how should you? The crowd is dimly lighted! And, besides, yours is the way of the world.

DRUMMLE. My dear Aubrey, I live in the world.

AUBREY. The name we give our little parish of St. James's.

DRUMMLE. (Laying a hand on AUBREY's shoulder) And you are quite prepared, my friend, to forfeit the esteem of your little parish?

AURBEY. I avoid mortification by shifting from one parish to another. I give up Pall Mall for the Surrey hills; leave off varnishing my boots, and double the thickness of the soles.

DRUMMLE. And your skin—do you double the thickness of that also?

AUBREY. I know you think me a fool, Cayley—you needn't infer that I'm a coward into the bargain. No! I know what I'm doing, and I do it deliberately, defiantly. I'm alone: I injure no living soul by the step I'm going to take; and so you can't urge the one argument which might restrain me. Of course, I don't expect you to think compassionately,

fairly even, of the woman whom I—whom I am drawn to—

DRUMMLE. My dear Aubrey, I assure you I consider Mrs.—Miss Jarman—Mrs. Ray—Miss Ray—delightful. But I confess there is a form of chivalry which I gravely distrust, especially in a man of—our age.

AUBREY. Thanks. I've heard you say that from forty till fifty a man is at heart either a stoic or a satyr.

DRUMMLE. (Protestingly) Ah! now—

AUBREY. I am neither. I have a temperate, honorable affection for Mrs. Jarman. She has never met a man who has treated her well—I intend to treat her well. That's all. And in a few years, Cayley, if you've not quite forsaken me, I'll prove to you that it's possible to rear a life of happiness, of good repute, on a—miserable foundation.

DRUMMLE. (Offering his hand) Do prove it!

AUBREY. (Taking his hand) We have spoken too freely of—of Mrs. Jarman. I was excited—angry. Please forget it!

DRUMMLE. My dear Aubrey, when we next meet I shall remember nothing but my respect for the lady who bears your name.

(MORSE enters, closing the door behind him carefully)

AUBREY. What is it?

MORSE. (Hesitatingly) May I speak to you, sir? (In an undertone) Mrs. Jarman, sir.

AUBREY. (Softly to MORSE) Mrs. Jarman! Do you mean she is at the lodge in her carriage?

MORSE. No, sir—here. (AUBREY looks towards DRUMMLE, perplexed) There's a nice fire in your—in that room, sir.

(Glancing in the direction of the door leading to the bedroom)

AUBREY. (Between his teeth, angrily) Very well.

(MORSE retires)

DRUMMLE. (Looking at his watch) A quarter to eleven—horrible! (Taking up his hat and coat) Must get to bed—up late every night this week. (AUBREY assists DRUMMLE with his coat) Thank you. Well, good-night, Aubrey. I feel I've been dooced serious, quite out of keeping with myself; pray overlook it.

AUBREY. (*Kindly*) Ah, Cayley!

DRUMMLE. (*Putting on a neck-handkerchief*) And remember that, after all, I'm merely a spectator in life; nothing more than a man at a play, in fact; only, like the old-fashioned play goer, I love to see certain characters happy and comfortable at the finish. You understand?

AUBREY. I think I do.

DRUMMLE. Then, for as long as you can, old friend, will you—keep a stall for me?

AUBREY. Yes, Cayley.

DRUMMLE. (*Gayly*) Ah, ha! Good-night! (*Bustling to the door*) Don't bother! I'll let myself out! Good-night! God bless yer! (*He goes out;* AUBREY *follows him.* MORSE *enters by the other door, carrying some unopened letters, which after a little consideration he places on the mantelpiece against the clock.* AUBREY *returns*)

AUBREY. Yes?

MORSE. You hadn't seen your letters that came by the nine o'clock post, sir; I've put 'em where they'll catch your eye by and by.

AUBREY. Thank you.

MORSE. (*Hesitatingly*) Gunter's cook and waiter have gone, sir. Would you prefer me to go to bed?

AUBREY. (*Frowning*) Certainly not.

MORSE. Very well, sir.

             (*He goes out*)

AUBREY. (*Opening the upper door*) Paula! Paula!

(PAULA *enters and throws her arms round his neck. She is a young woman of about twenty-seven: beautiful, fresh, innocent-looking. She is in superb evening dress*)

PAULA. Dearest!

AUBREY. Why have you come here?

PAULA. Angry?

AUBREY. Yes—no. But it's eleven o'clock.

PAULA. (*Laughing*) I know.

AUBREY. What on earth will Morse think?

PAULA. Do you trouble yourself about what servants *think*?

AUBREY. Of course.

PAULA. Goose! They're only machines made to wait upon people—and to give evidence in the Divorce Court. (*Looking round*) Oh, indeed! A snug little dinner!

AUBREY. Three men.

PAULA. (*Suspiciously*) Men?

AUBREY. Men.

PAULA. (*Penitently*) Ah! (*Sitting at the table*) I'm so hungry.

AUBREY. Let me get you some game pie, or some—

PAULA. No, no, hungry for this. What beautiful fruit! I love fruit when it's expensive. (*He clears a space on the table, places a plate before her, and helps her to fruit*) I haven't dined, Aubrey dear.

AUBREY. My poor girl! Why?

PAULA. In the first place, I forgot to order any dinner, and my cook, who has always loathed me, thought he'd pay me out before he departed.

AUBREY. The beast!

PAULA. That's precisely what I—

AUBREY. No, Paula!

PAULA. What I told my maid to call him. What next will you think of me?

AUBREY. Forgive me. You must be starved.

PAULA. (*Eating fruit*) I didn't care. As there was nothing to eat, I sat in my best frock, with my toes on the dining-room fender, and dreamt, oh, such a lovely dinner party.

AUBREY. Dear lonely little woman!

PAULA. It was perfect. I saw you at the end of a very long table, opposite me, and we exchanged sly glances now and again over the flowers. We were host and hostess, Aubrey, and had been married about five years.

AUBREY. (*Kissing her hand*) Five years.

PAULA. And on each side of us was the nicest set imaginable—you know, dearest, the sort of men and women that can't be imitated.

AUBREY. Yes, yes. Eat some more fruit.

PAULA. But I haven't told you the best part of my dream.

AUBREY. Tell me.

PAULA. Well, although we had been married only such a few years, I seemed to know by the look on their faces that none of our guests had ever heard anything—anything—anything peculiar about the fascinating hostess.

AUBREY. That's just how it will be, Paula. The world moves so quickly. That's just how it will be.

PAULA. (*With a little grimace*) I wonder! (*Glancing at the fire*) Ugh! Do throw another log on.

AUBREY. (*Mending the fire*) There. But you mustn't be here long.

PAULA. Hospitable wretch! I've something important to tell you. No, stay where you are. (*Turning from him, her face averted*) Look here, that was my dream, Aubrey; but the fire went out while I was dozing, and I woke up with a regular fit of the shivers. And the result of it all was that I ran upstairs and scribbled you a letter.

AUBREY. Dear baby!

PAULA. Remain where you are. (*Taking a letter from her pocket*) This is it. I've given you an account of myself, furnished you with a list of my adventures since I—you know. (*Weighing the letter in her hand*) I wonder if it would go for a penny. Most of it you're acquainted with; I've told you a good deal, haven't I?

AUBREY. Oh, Paula!

PAULA. What I haven't told you I dare say you've heard from others. But in case they've omitted anything—the dears—it's all here.

AUBREY. In Heaven's name, why must you talk like this to-night?

PAULA. It may save discussion by and by, don't you think? (*Holding out the letter*) There you are.

AUBREY. No, dear, no.

PAULA. Take it. (*He takes the letter*) Read it through after I've gone, and then —read it again, and turn the matter over in your mind finally. And if, even at the very last moment, you feel you—oughtn't to go to church with me, send a messenger to Pont Street, any time before eleven to-morrow, telling me that you're afraid, and I—I'll take the blow.

AUBREY. Why, what—what do you think I am?

PAULA. That's it. It's because I know you're such a dear good fellow that I want to save you the chance of ever feeling sorry you married me. I really love you so much, Aubrey, that to save you that, I'd rather you treated me as—as the others have done.

AUBREY. (*Turning from her with a cry*) Oh!

PAULA. (*After a slight pause*) I suppose I've shocked you. I can't help it if I have. (*She sits with assumed languor and indifference. He turns to her, advances, and kneels by her*)

AUBREY. My dearest, you don't understand me. I—I can't bear to hear you always talking about—what's done with. I tell you I'll never remember it; Paula, can't you dismiss it? Try. Darling, if we promise each other to forget, to forget, we're bound to be happy. After all, it's a mechanical matter; the moment a wretched thought enters your head, you quickly think of something bright —it depends on one's will. Shall I burn this, dear? (*Referring to the letter he holds in his hand*) Let me, let me!

PAULA. (*With a shrug of the shoulders*) I don't suppose there's much that's new to you in it,—just as you like.

(*He goes to the fire and burns the letter*)

AUBREY. There's an end of it. (*Returning to her*) What's the matter?

PAULA. (*Rising coldly*) Oh, nothing! I'll go and put my cloak on.

AUBREY. (*Detaining her*) What *is* the matter?

PAULA. Well, I think you might have said, "You're very generous, Paula," or at least, "Thank you, dear," when I offered to set you free.

AUBREY. (*Catching her in his arms*) Ah!

PAULA. Ah! ah! Ha! ha! It's all very well, but you don't know what it cost me to make such an offer. I do so want to be married.

AUBREY. But you never imagined—?

PAULA. Perhaps not. And yet I *did* think of what I'd do at the end of our acquaintance if you had preferred to behave like the rest. (*Taking a flower from her bodice*)

AUBREY. Hush!

PAULA. Oh, I forgot!

AUBREY. What would you have done when we parted?

PAULA. Why, killed myself.

AUBREY. Paula, dear!

PAULA. It's true. (*Putting the flower in his buttonhole*) Do you know, I feel certain I should make away with myself if anything serious happened to me.

AUBREY. Anything serious! What, has

nothing ever been serious to you, Paula?

PAULA. Not lately; not since a long while ago. I made up my mind then to have done with taking things seriously. If I hadn't, I— However, we won't talk about that.

AUBREY. But now, now, life will be different to you, won't it—quite different? Eh, dear?

PAULA. Oh, yes, now. Only, Aubrey, mind you keep me always happy.

AUBREY. I will try to.

PAULA. I know I couldn't swallow a second big dose of misery. I know that if ever I felt wretched again—truly wretched—I should take a leaf out of Connie Tirlemont's book. You remember? They found her— (*With a look of horror*)

AUBREY. For God's sake, don't let your thoughts run on such things!

PAULA. (*Laughing*) Ha, ha, how scared you look! There, think of the time! Dearest, what will my coachman say? My cloak! (*She runs off, gayly, by the upper door. AUBREY looks after her for a moment, then he walks up to the fire and stands warming his feet at the bars. As he does so he raises his head and observes the letters upon the mantelpiece. He takes one down quickly*)

AUBREY. Ah! Ellean! (*Opening the letter and reading*) "My dear father,—A great change has come over me. I believe my mother in Heaven has spoken to me, and counseled me to turn to you in your loneliness. At any rate, your words have reached my heart, and I no longer feel fitted for this solemn life. I am ready to take my place by you. Dear father, will you receive me?— ELLEAN."

(PAULA *re-enters, dressed in a handsome cloak. He stares at her as if he hardly realized her presence*)

PAULA. What are you staring at? Don't you admire my cloak?

AUBREY. Yes.

PAULA. Couldn't you wait till I'd gone before reading your letters?

AUBREY. (*Putting the letter away*) I beg your pardon.

PAULA. Take me downstairs to the carriage. (*Slipping her arm through his*) How I tease you! To-morrow! I'm so happy! (*They go out*)

Act II

A morning-room in AUBREY TANQUERAY'S *house, "Highercoombe," near Willowmere, Surrey—a bright and prettily furnished apartment of irregular shape, with double doors opening into a small hall at the back, another door on the left, and a large recessed window through which is obtained a view of extensive grounds. Everything about the room is charming and graceful. The fire is burning in the grate, and a small table is tastefully laid for breakfast. It is a morning in early spring, and the sun is streaming in through the window.*

(AUBREY *and* PAULA *are seated at breakfast, and* AUBREY *is silently reading his letters. Two servants, a man and a woman, hand dishes and then retire. After a little while* AUBREY *puts his letters aside and looks across to the window*)

AUBREY. Sunshine! Spring!

PAULA. (*Glancing at the clock*) Exactly six minutes.

AUBREY. Six minutes?

PAULA. Six minutes, Aubrey dear, since you made your last remark.

AUBREY. I beg your pardon: I was reading my letters. Have you seen Ellean this morning?

PAULA. (*Coldly*) Your last observation but one was about Ellean.

AUBREY. Dearest, what shall I talk about?

PAULA. Ellean breakfasted two hours ago, Morgan tells me, and then went out walking with her dog.

AUBREY. She wraps up warmly, I hope; this sunshine is deceptive.

PAULA. I ran about the lawn last night, after dinner, in satin shoes. Were you anxious about me?

AUBREY. Certainly.

PAULA. (*Melting*) Really.

AUBREY. You make me wretchedly anxious; you delight in doing incautious things. You are incurable.

PAULA. Ah, what a beast I am! (*Going to him and kissing him, then glancing at the letters by his side*) A letter from Cayley?

AUBREY. He is staying very near here, with Mrs. —— Very near here.

PAULA. With the lady whose chimneys we have the honor of contemplating from our windows?

AUBREY. With Mrs. Cortelyon—Yes.

PAULA. Mrs. Cortelyon! The woman who might have set the example of calling on me when we first threw out roots in this deadly-lively soil! Deuce take Mrs. Cortelyon!

AUBREY. Hush! my dear girl!

PAULA. (*Returning to her seat*) Oh, I know she's an old acquaintance of yours—and of the first Mrs. Tanqueray. And she joins the rest of 'em in slapping the second Mrs. Tanqueray in the face. However, I have my revenge—she's six-and-forty, and I wish nothing worse to happen to any woman.

AUBREY. Well, she's going to town, Cayley says here, and his visit's at an end. He's coming over this morning to call on you. Shall we ask him to transfer himself to us? Do say yes.

PAULA. Yes.

AUBREY. (*Gladly*) Ah, ha! old Cayley.

PAULA. (*Coldly*) He'll amuse *you*.

AUBREY. And you too.

PAULA. Because you find a companion, shall I be boisterously hilarious?

AUBREY. Come, come! He talks London, and you know you like that.

PAULA. London! London or Heaven! which is farther from me!

AUBREY. Paula!

PAULA. Oh! Oh, I am so bored, Aubrey!

AUBREY. (*Gathering up his letters and going to her, leaning over her shoulder*) Baby, what can I do for you?

PAULA. I suppose, nothing. You have done all you can for me.

AUBREY. What do you mean?

PAULA. You have married me.

(*He walks away from her thoughtfully, to the writing table. As he places his letters on the table he sees an addressed letter, stamped for the post, lying on the blotting-book; he picks it up*)

AUBREY. (*In an altered tone*) You've been writing this morning before breakfast?

PAULA. (*Looking at him quickly, then away again*) Er—that letter.

AUBREY. (*With the letter in his hand*) To Lady Orreyed. Why?

PAULA. Why not? Mabel's an old friend of mine.

AUBREY. Are you—corresponding?

PAULA. I heard from her yesterday. They've just returned from the Riviera. She seems happy.

AUBREY. (*Sarcastically*) That's good news.

PAULA. Why are you always so cutting about Mabel? She's a kind-hearted girl. Everything's altered; she even thinks of letting her hair go back to brown. She's Lady Orreyed. She's married to George. What's the matter with her?

AUBREY. (*Turning away*) Oh!

PAULA. You drive me mad sometimes with the tone you take about things! Great goodness, if you come to that, George Orreyed's wife isn't a bit worse than yours! (*He faces her suddenly*) I suppose I needn't have made that observation.

AUBREY. No, there was scarcely a necessity.

(*He throws the letter on to the table, and takes up the newspaper*)

PAULA. I am very sorry.

AUBREY. All right, dear.

PAULA. (*Trifling with the letter*) I—I'd better tell you what I've written. I meant to do so, of course. I—I've asked the Orreyeds to come and stay with us. (*He looks at her, and lets the paper fall to the ground in a helpless way*) George was a great friend of Cayley's; I'm sure *he* would be delighted to meet them here.

AUBREY. (*Laughing mirthlessly*) Ha, ha, ha! They say Orreyed has taken to tippling at dinner. Heavens above!

PAULA. Oh! I've no patience with you! You'll kill me with this life! (*She selects some flowers from a vase on the table, cuts and arranges them, and fastens them in her bodice*) What is my existence, Sunday to Saturday? In the morning, a drive down to the village, with the groom, to give my orders to the tradespeople. At lunch, you and Ellean. In the afternoon, a novel, the newspapers; if fine, another drive—*if* fine! Tea —you and Ellean. Then two hours of dusk; then dinner—you and Ellean. Then a game of Bésique, you and I, while Ellean reads a religious book in a dull corner. Then a yawn from me, another from you, a sigh from Ellean; three figures suddenly rise— "Good-night, good-night, good-night!" (*Imitating a kiss*) "God bless you!" Ah!

AUBREY. Yes, yes, Paula—yes, dearest— that's what it is *now*. But by and by, if people begin to come round us—

PAULA. Hah! That's where we've made the mistake, my friend Aubrey! (*Pointing to the window*) Do you believe these people will *ever* come round us? Your former crony, Mrs. Cortelyon? Or the grim old vicar, or that wife of his whose huge nose is positively indecent? Or the Ullathornes, or the Gollans, or Lady William Petres? I know better! And when the young ones gradually take the place of the old, there will still remain the sacred tradition that the dreadful person who lives at the top of the hill is never, under any circumstances, to be called upon! And so we shall go on here, year in and year out, until the sap is run out of our lives, and we're stale and dry and withered from sheer, solitary respectability. Upon my word, I wonder we didn't see that we should have been far happier if we'd gone in for the devil-may-care, café-living sort of life in town! After all, *I* have a set, and you might have joined it. It's true, I did want, dearly, dearly, to be a married woman, but where's the pride in being a married woman among married women who are—married! If—(*Seeing that AUBREY's head has sunk into his hands*) Aubrey! My dear boy! You're not— crying?

(*He looks up, with a flushed face. ELLEAN enters, dressed very simply for walking. She is a low-voiced, grave girl of about nineteen, with a face somewhat re-* sembling a Madonna. Towards PAULA her manner is cold and distant*)

AUBREY. (*In an undertone*) Ellean!

ELLEAN. Good-morning, papa. Good-morning, Paula.

(*PAULA puts her arms round ELLEAN and kisses her. ELLEAN makes little response*)

PAULA. Good-morning. (*Brightly*) We've been breakfasting this side of the house, to get the sun.

(*She sits at the piano and rattles at a gay melody. Seeing that PAULA's back is turned to them, ELLEAN goes to AUBREY and kisses him; he returns the kiss almost furtively. As they separate, the servants re-enter, and proceed to carry out the breakfast table*)

AUBREY. (*To ELLEAN*) I guess where you've been: there's some gorse clinging to your frock.

ELLEAN. (*Removing a sprig of gorse from her skirt*) Rover and I walked nearly as far as Black Moor. The poor fellow has a thorn in his pad; I am going upstairs for my tweezers.

AUBREY. Ellean! (*She returns to him*) Paula is a little depressed—out of sorts. She complains that she has no companion.

ELLEAN. I am with Paula nearly all the day, papa.

AUBREY. Ah, but you're such a little mouse. Paula likes cheerful people about her.

ELLEAN. I'm afraid I am naturally rather silent; and it's so difficult to seem to be what one is not.

AUBREY. I don't wish that, Ellean.

ELLEAN. I will offer to go down to the village with Paula this morning—shall I?

AUBREY. (*Touching her hand gently*) Thank you—do.

ELLEAN. When I've looked after Rover, I'll come back to her.

(*She goes out; PAULA ceases playing, and turns on the music-stool, looking at AUBREY*)

PAULA. Well, have you and Ellean had your little confidence?

AUBREY. Confidence?

PAULA. Do you think I couldn't feel it, like a pain between my shoulders?

AUBREY. Ellean is coming back in a few

minutes to be with you. (*Bending over her*) Paula, Paula dear, is this how you keep your promise?

PAULA. Oh! (*Rising impatiently, and crossing swiftly to the settee, where she sits; moving restlessly*) I *can't* keep my promise; I *am* jealous; it won't be smothered. I see you looking at her, watching her; your voice drops when you speak to her. I know how fond you are of that girl, Aubrey.

AUBREY. What would you have? I've no other home for her. She is my daughter.

PAULA. She is your saint. Saint Ellean!

AUBREY. You have often told me how good and sweet you think her.

PAULA. Good!—Yes! Do you imagine *that* makes me less jealous? (*Going to him and clinging to his arm*) Aubrey, there are two sorts of affection—the love for a woman you respect, and the love for the woman you—love. She gets the first from you: I never can.

AUBREY. Hush, hush! you don't realize what you say.

PAULA. If Ellean cared for me only a little, it would be different. I shouldn't be jealous then. Why doesn't she care for me?

AUBREY. She—she—she will, in time.

PAULA. You can't say that without stuttering.

AUBREY. Her disposition seems a little unresponsive; she resembles her mother in many ways; I can see it every day.

PAULA. She's marble. It's a shame. There's not the slightest excuse; for all she knows, I'm as much a saint as she—only married. Dearest, help me to win her over!

AUBREY. Help you?

PAULA. You can. Teach her that it is her duty to love me; she hangs on to every word you speak. I'm sure, Aubrey, that the love of a nice woman who believed me to be like herself would do me a world of good. You'd get the benefit of it as well as I. It would soothe me; it would make me less horribly restless; it would take this—this—mischievous feeling from me. (*Coaxingly*) Aubrey!

AUBREY. Have patience; everything will come right.

PAULA. Yes, if you help me.

AUBREY. In the meantime you will tear up your letter to Lady Orreyed, won't you?

PAULA. (*Kissing his hand*) Of course I will—anything!

AUBREY. Ah, thank you, dearest! (*Laughing*) Why, good gracious!—ha, ha!—just imagine "Saint Ellean" and that woman side by side!

PAULA. (*Going back with a cry*) Ah!

AUBREY. What?

PAULA. (*Passionately*) It's Ellean you're considering, not me! It's all Ellean with you! Ellean! Ellean!

(ELLEAN *re-enters*)

ELLEAN. Did you call me, Paula? (*Clenching his hands,* AUBREY *turns away and goes out*) Is papa angry?

PAULA. I drive him distracted, sometimes. There, I confess it!

ELLEAN. Do you? Oh, why do you!

PAULA. Because I—because I'm jealous.

ELLEAN. Jealous?

PAULA. Yes—of you. (ELLEAN *is silent*) Well, what do you think of that?

ELLEAN. I knew it; I've seen it. It hurts me dreadfully. What do you wish me to do? Go away?

PAULA. Leave us! (*Beckoning her with a motion of the head*) Look here! (ELLEAN *goes to* PAULA *slowly and unresponsively*) You can cure me of my jealousy very easily. Why don't you—like me?

ELLEAN. What do you mean by—like you? I don't understand.

PAULA. Love me.

ELLEAN. Love is not a feeling that is under one's control. I shall alter as time goes on, perhaps. I didn't begin to love my father deeply till a few months ago, and then I obeyed my mother.

PAULA. Ah, yes, you dream things, don't you—see them in your sleep? You fancy your mother speaks to you?

ELLEAN. When you have lost your mother it is a comfort to believe that she is dead only to this life, that she still watches over her child. I do believe that of my mother.

PAULA. Well, and so you haven't been bidden to love *me*?

ELLEAN. (*After a pause, almost inaudibly*) No.

PAULA. Dreams are only a hash-up of one's day-thoughts, I suppose you know. Think intently of anything, and it's bound to come back to you at night. I don't culti-vate dreams myself.

ELLEAN. Ah, I knew you would only sneer!

PAULA. I'm not sneering; I'm speaking the truth. I say that if you cared for me in the daytime I should soon make friends with those nightmares of yours. Ellean, why don't you try to look on me as your second mother? Of course there are not many years between us, but I'm ever so much older than you—in experience. I shall have no children of my own, I know that; it would be a real comfort to me if you would make me feel we belonged to each other. Won't you? Perhaps you think I'm odd—not nice. Well, the fact is I've two sides to my nature, and I've let the one almost smother the other. A few years ago I went through some trouble, and since then I haven't shed a tear. I believe if you put your arms around me just once I should run upstairs and have a good cry. There, I've talked to you as I've never talked to a woman in my life. Ellean, you seem to fear me. Don't! Kiss me!

(*With a cry, almost of despair,* ELLEAN *turns from* PAULA *and sinks on to the settee, covering her face with her hands*)

PAULA. (*Indignantly*) Oh! Why is it! How dare you treat me like this? What do you mean by it? What do you mean?

(*A* Servant *enters*)

SERVANT. Mr. Drummle, ma'am.

(CAYLEY DRUMMLE, *in riding-dress, enters briskly. The* Servant *retires*)

PAULA. (*Recovering herself*) Well, Cay-ley!

DRUMMLE. (*Shaking hands with her cordially*) How are you? (*Shaking hands with* ELLEAN, *who rises*) I saw you in the distance an hour ago, in the gorse near Stapleton's.

ELLEAN. I didn't see you, Mr. Drummle.

DRUMMLE. My dear Ellean, it is my experience that no charming young lady of nineteen ever does see a man of forty-five. (*Laughing*) Ha, ha!

ELLEAN. (*Going to the door*) Paula, papa wishes me to drive down to the village with you this morning. Do you care to take me?

PAULA. (*Coldly*) Oh, by all means. Pray tell Watts to balance the cart for three.

(ELLEAN *goes out*)

DRUMMLE. How's Aubrey?

PAULA. Very well—when Ellean's about the house.

DRUMMLE. And you? I needn't ask.

PAULA. (*Walking away to the window*) Oh, a dog's life, my dear Cayley, mine.

DRUMMLE. Eh?

PAULA. Doesn't that define a happy marriage? I'm sleek, well-kept, well-fed, never without a bone to gnaw and fresh straw to lie upon. (*Gazing out of the window*) Oh, dear me!

DRUMMLE. H'm! Well, I heartily congratulate you on your kennel. The view from the terrace here is superb.

PAULA. Yes; I can see London.

DRUMMLE. London! Not quite so far, surely?

PAULA. I can. Also the Mediterranean, on a fine day. I wonder what Algiers looks like this morning from the sea! (*Impulsively*) Oh, Cayley, do you remember those jolly times on board Peter Jarman's yacht when we lay off—? (*Stopping suddenly, seeing* DRUMMLE *staring at her*) Good gracious! What are we talking about!

(AUBREY *enters*)

AUBREY. (*To* DRUMMLE) Dear old chap! Has Paula asked you?

PAULA. Not yet.

AUBREY. We want you to come to us, now that you're leaving Mrs. Cortelyon—at once, to-day. Stay a month, as long as you please—eh, Paula?

PAULA. As long as you can possibly endure it—do, Cayley.

DRUMMLE. (*Looking at* AUBREY) Delighted. (*To* PAULA) Charming of you to have me.

PAULA. My dear man, you're a blessing. I must telegraph to London for more fish! A strange appetite to cater for! Something to do, to do, to do!

(*She goes out in a mood of almost childish delight*)

DRUMMLE. (*Eyeing* AUBREY) Well?

AUBREY. (*With a wearied, anxious look*) Well, Cayley?

DRUMMLE. How are you getting on?

AUBREY. My position doesn't grow less difficult. I told you, when I met you last week, of this feverish, jealous attachment of Paula's for Ellean?

DRUMMLE. Yes. I hardly know why, but I came to the conclusion that you don't consider it an altogether fortunate attachment.

AUBREY. Ellean doesn't respond to it.

DRUMMLE. These are early days. Ellean will warm towards your wife by and by.

AUBREY. Ah, but there's the question, Cayley!

DRUMMLE. What question?

AUBREY. The question which positively distracts me. Ellean is so different from—most women; I don't believe a purer creature exists out of heaven. And I—I ask myself, am I doing right in exposing her to the influence of poor Paula's light, careless nature?

DRUMMLE. My dear Aubrey!

AUBREY. That shocks you! So it does me. I assure you I long to urge my girl to break down the reserve which keeps her apart from Paula, but somehow I can't do it—well, I don't do it. How can I make you understand? But when you come to us you'll understand quickly enough. Cayley, there's hardly a subject you can broach on which poor Paula hasn't some strange, out-of-the-way thought to give utterance to; some curious, warped notion. They are not mere worldly thoughts —unless, good God! they belong to the little hellish world which our blackguardism has created: no, her ideas have too little calculation in them to be called worldly. But it makes it more dreadful that such thoughts should be ready, spontaneous; that expressing them has become a perfectly natural process; that her words, acts even, have almost lost their proper significance for her, and seem beyond her control. Ah, and the pain of listening to it all from the woman one loves, the woman one hoped to make happy and contented, who is really and truly a good woman, as it were, maimed! Well, this is my burden, and I shouldn't speak to you of it but for my anxiety about Ellean. Ellean! What is to be her future? It is in my hands; what am I to do? Cayley, when I remember how Ellean comes to me, from another world I always think,—when I realize the charge that's laid on me, I find myself wishing, in a sort of terror, that my child were safe under the ground!

DRUMMLE. My dear Aubrey, aren't you making a mistake?

AUBREY. Very likely. What is it?

DRUMMLE. A mistake, not in regarding your Ellean as an angel, but in believing that, under any circumstances, it would be possible for her to go through life without getting her white robe—shall we say, a little dusty at the hem? Don't take me for a cynic. I am sure there are many women upon earth who are almost divinely innocent; but being on earth, they must send their robes to the laundry occasionally. Ah, and it's right that they should have to do so, for what can they learn from the checking of their little washing-bills but lessons of charity? Now I see but two courses open to you for the disposal of your angel.

AUBREY. Yes?

DRUMMLE. You must either restrict her to a paradise which is, like every earthly paradise, necessarily somewhat imperfect, or treat her as an ordinary flesh-and-blood young woman, and give her the advantages of that society to which she properly belongs.

AUBREY. Advantages?

DRUMMLE. My dear Aubrey, of all forms of innocence mere ignorance is the least admirable. Take my advice, let her walk and talk and suffer and be healed with the great crowd. Do it, and hope that she'll some day meet a good, honest fellow who'll make her life complete, happy, secure. Now you see what I'm driving at.

AUBREY. A sanguine programme, my dear Cayley! Oh, I'm not pooh-poohing it. Putting sentiment aside, of course I know that a fortunate marriage for Ellean would be the best —perhaps the only—solution of my difficulty. But you forget the danger of the course you suggest.

DRUMMLE. Danger?

AUBREY. If Ellean goes among men and women, how can she escape from learning, sooner or later, the history of—poor Paula's— old life?

DRUMMLE. H'm! You remember the episode of the Jeweler's Son in the Arabian Nights? Of course you don't. Well, if your daughter lives, she *can't* escape—what you're afraid of. (AUBREY *gives a half-stifled excla-*

mation of pain) And when she does hear the story, surely it would be better that she should have some knowledge of the world to help her to understand it.

AUBREY. To understand!

DRUMMLE. To understand, to—philosophize.

AUBREY. To philosophize?

DRUMMLE. Philosophy is toleration, and it is only one step from toleration to forgiveness.

AUBREY. You're right, Cayley; I believe you always are. Yes, yes. But, even if I had the courage to attempt to solve the problem of Ellean's future in this way, I—I'm helpless.

DRUMMLE. How?

AUBREY. What means have I now of placing my daughter in the world I've left?

DRUMMLE. Oh, some friend—some woman friend.

AUBREY. I have none; they're gone.

DRUMMLE. You're wrong there; I know one—

AUBREY. *(Listening)* That's Paula's cart. Let's discuss this again.

DRUMMLE. *(Going up to the window and looking out)* It isn't the dog-cart. *(Turning to AUBREY)* I hope you'll forgive me, old chap.

AUBREY. What for?

DRUMMLE. Whose wheels do you think have been cutting ruts in your immaculate drive?

(A SERVANT enters)

SERVANT. *(To AUBREY)* Mrs. Cortelyon, sir.

AUBREY. Mrs. Cortelyon! *(After a short pause)* Very well. *(The Servant withdraws)* What on earth is the meaning of this?

DRUMMLE. Ahem! While I've been our old friend's guest, Aubrey, we have very naturally talked a good deal about you and yours.

AUBREY. Indeed, have you?

DRUMMLE. Yes; and Alice Cortelyon has arrived at the conclusion that it would have been far kinder had she called on Mrs. Tanqueray long ago. She's going abroad for Easter before settling down in London for the season, and I believe she has come over this morning to ask for Ellean's companionship.

AUBREY. Oh, I see! *(Frowning)* Quite a friendly little conspiracy, my dear Cayley!

DRUMMLE. Conspiracy! Not at all, I assure you. *(Laughing)* Ha, ha!

(ELLEAN enters from the hall with MRS. CORTELYON, a handsome, good-humored, spirited woman of about forty-five)

ELLEAN. Papa—

MRS. CORTELYON. *(To AUBREY, shaking hands with him heartily)* Well, Aubrey, how are you? I've just been telling this great girl of yours that I knew her when she was a sad-faced, pale baby. How is Mrs. Tanqueray? I have been a bad neighbor, and I'm here to beg forgiveness. Is she indoors?

AUBREY. She's upstairs putting on a hat, I believe.

MRS. CORTELYON. *(Sitting comfortably)* Ah! *(She looks round; DRUMMLE and ELLEAN are talking together in the hall)* We used to be very frank with each other, Aubrey. I suppose the old footing is no longer possible, eh?

AUBREY. If so, I'm not entirely to blame, Mrs. Cortelyon.

MRS. CORTELYON. Mrs. Cortelyon? H'm! No, I admit it. But you must make some little allowance for me, *Mr. Tanqueray.* Your first wife and I, as girls, were like two cherries on one stalk, and then I was the confidential friend of your married life. That post, perhaps, wasn't altogether a sinecure. And now—well, when a woman gets to my age I suppose she's a stupid, prejudiced, conventional creature. However, I've got over it and—*(giving him her hand)*—I hope you'll be enormously happy and let me be a friend once more.

AUBREY. Thank you, Alice.

MRS. CORTELYON. That's right. I feel more cheerful than I've done for weeks. But I suppose it would serve me right if the second Mrs. Tanqueray showed me the door. Do you think she will?

AUBREY. *(Listening)* Here is my wife.

(MRS. CORTELYON rises, and PAULA enters, dressed for driving; she stops abruptly on seeing MRS. CORTELYON) Paula, dear, Mrs. Cortelyon has called to see you.

(PAULA starts, looks at MRS. CORTELYON irresolutely, then after a slight pause barely touches MRS. CORTELYON's extended hand)

PAULA. *(Whose manner now alternates*

between deliberate insolence and assumed sweetness) Mrs. ——? What name, Aubrey?

AUBREY. Mrs. Cortelyon.

PAULA. Cortelyon? Oh, yes, Cortelyon.

MRS. CORTELYON. (*Carefully guarding herself throughout against any expression of resentment*) Aubrey ought to have told you that Alice Cortelyon and he are very old friends.

PAULA. Oh, very likely he has mentioned the circumstance. I have quite a wretched memory.

MRS. CORTELYON. You know we are neighbors, Mrs. Tanqueray.

PAULA. Neighbors? Are we really? Won't you sit down? (*They both sit*) Neighbors! That's most interesting!

MRS. CORTELYON. Very near neighbors. You can see my roof from your windows.

PAULA. I fancy I *have* observed a roof. But you have been away from home; you have only just returned.

MRS. CORTELYON. I? What makes you think that?

PAULA. Why, because it is two months since we came to Highercoombe, and I don't remember your having called.

MRS. CORTELYON. Your memory is now terribly accurate. No, I've not been away from home, and it is to explain my neglect that I am here, rather unceremoniously, this morning.

PAULA. Oh, to explain—quite so. (*With mock solicitude*) Ah, you've been very ill; I ought to have seen that before.

MRS. CORTELYON. Ill!

PAULA. You look dreadfully pulled down. We poor women show illness so plainly in our faces, don't we?

AUBREY. (*Anxiously*) Paula dear, Mrs. Cortelyon is the picture of health.

MRS. CORTELYON. (*With some asperity*) I have never *felt* better in my life.

PAULA. (*Looking around innocently*) Have I said anything awkward? Aubrey, tell Mrs. Cortelyon how stupid and thoughtless I always am!

MRS. CORTELYON. (*To* DRUMMLE, *who is now standing close to her*) Really, Cayley—! (*He soothes her with a nod and smile and a motion of his finger to his lip*) Mrs. Tanqueray, I am afraid my explanation will not be quite so satisfactory as either of those

you have just helped me to. You may have heard—but, if you have heard, you have doubtless forgotten—that twenty years ago, when your husband first lived here, I was a constant visitor at Highercoombe.

PAULA. Twenty years ago—fancy! I was a naughty little child then.

MRS. CORTELYON. Possibly. Well, at that time, and till the end of her life, my affections were centered upon the lady of this house.

PAULA. Were they? That was very sweet of you.

(ELLEAN *approaches* MRS. CORTELYON, *listening intently to her*)

MRS. CORTELYON. I will say no more on that score, but I must add this: when, two months ago you came here, I realized, perhaps for the first time, that I was a middle-aged woman, and that it had become impossible for me to accept without some effort a breaking-in upon many tender associations. There, Mrs. Tanqueray, that is my confession. Will you try to understand it and pardon me?

PAULA. (*Watching* ELLEAN,—*sneeringly*) Ellean dear, you appear to be very interested in Mrs. Cortelyon's reminiscences; I don't think I can do better than make you my mouthpiece—there is such sympathy between us. What do you say—can we bring ourselves to forgive Mrs. Cortelyon for neglecting us for two weary months?

MRS. CORTELYON. (*To* ELLEAN, *pleasantly*) Well, Ellean? (*With a little cry of tenderness* ELLEAN *impulsively sits beside* MRS. CORTELYON *and takes her hand*) My dear child!

PAULA. (*In an undertone to* AUBREY) Ellean isn't so very slow in taking to Mrs. Cortelyon!

MRS. CORTELYON. (*To* PAULA *and* AUBREY) Come, this encourages me to broach my scheme. Mrs. Tanqueray, it strikes me that you two good people are just now excellent company for each other, while Ellean would perhaps be glad of a little peep into the world you are anxious to avoid. Now, I'm going to Paris to-morrow for a week or two before settling down in Chester Square, so—don't gasp, both of you!—if this girl is willing, and you have made no other arrangements for her, will you let her come with me to Paris, and afterwards remain with me in town during the season? (ELLEAN *utters an exclamation of surprise.* PAULA *is silent.*) What do you say?

AUBREY. Paula—Paula dear. (*Hesitatingly*) My dear Mrs. Cortelyon, this is wonderfully kind of you; I am really at a loss to—eh, Cayley?

DRUMMLE. (*Watching* PAULA *apprehensively*) Kind! Now I must say I don't think so! I begged Alice to take *me* to Paris, and she declined! I am thrown over for Ellean! Ha! ha!

MRS. CORTELYON. (*Laughing*) What nonsense you talk, Cayley!

(*The laughter dies out.* PAULA *remains quite still*)

AUBREY. Paula dear.

PAULA. (*Slowly collecting herself*) One moment. I—I don't quite—(*To* MRS. CORTELYON) You propose that Ellean leaves Highercoombe almost at once, and remains with you some months?

MRS. CORTELYON. It would be a mercy to me. You can afford to be generous to a desolate old widow. Come, Mrs. Tanqueray, won't you spare her?

PAULA. Won't *I* spare her. (*Suspiciously*) Have you mentioned your plan to Aubrey—before I came in?

MRS. CORTELYON. No; I had no opportunity.

PAULA. Nor to Ellean?

MRS. CORTELYON. Oh, no.

PAULA. (*Looking about her in suppressed excitement*) This hasn't been discussed at all, behind my back?

MRS. CORTELYON. My dear Mrs. Tanqueray!

PAULA. Ellean, let us hear your voice in the matter!

ELLEAN. I should like to go with Mrs. Cortelyon—

PAULA. Ah!

ELLEAN. That is, if—if—

PAULA. If—what?

ELLEAN. (*Looking towards* AUBREY, *appealingly*) Papa!

PAULA. (*In a hard voice*) Oh, of course—I forgot. (*To* AUBREY) My dear Aubrey, it rests with you, naturally, whether I am—to lose—Ellean.

AUBREY. Lose Ellean! (*Advancing to* PAULA) There is no question of losing El-

lean. You would see Ellean in town constantly when she returned from Paris; isn't that so, Mrs. Cortelyon?

MRS. CORTELYON. Certainly.

PAULA. (*Laughing softly*) Oh, I didn't know I should be allowed that privilege.

MRS. CORTELYON. Privilege, my dear Mrs. Tanqueray!

PAULA. Ha, ha! that makes all the difference, doesn't it?

AUBREY. (*With assumed gayety*) All the difference? I should think so! (*To* ELLEAN, *laying his hand upon her head tenderly*) And you are quite certain you wish to see what the world is like on the other side of Black Moor!

ELLEAN. If you are willing, papa, I am quite certain.

AUBREY. (*Looking at* PAULA *irresolutely, then speaking with an effort*) Then I—I am willing.

PAULA. (*Rising and striking the table lightly with her clenched hand*) That decides it! (*There is a general movement. Excitedly to* MRS. CORTELYON, *who advances towards her*) When do you want her?

MRS. CORTELYON. We go to town this afternoon at five o'clock, and sleep to-night at Bayliss's. There is barely time for her to make her preparations.

PAULA. I will undertake that she is ready.

MRS. CORTELYON. I've a great deal to scramble through at home too, as you may guess. Good-bye!

PAULA. (*Turning away*) Mrs. Cortelyon is going.

(PAULA *stands looking out of the window, with her back to those in the room*)

MRS. CORTELYON. (*To* DRUMMLE) Cayley—

DRUMMLE. (*To her*) Eh?

MRS. CORTELYON. I've gone through it, for the sake of Aubrey and his child, but I—I feel a hundred. Is that a mad-woman?

DRUMMLE. Of course; all jealous women are mad. (*He goes out with* AUBREY)

MRS. CORTELYON. (*Hesitatingly, to* PAULA) Good-bye, Mrs. Tanqueray.

(PAULA *inclines her head with the slightest possible movement, then resumes her former position.* ELLEAN *comes from the hall and takes* MRS. CORTELYON *out of the room. After a brief silence,* PAULA *turns with a fierce cry, and hurriedly takes off her coat and hat, and tosses them upon the settee.*)

PAULA. Who's that? Oh! Oh! Oh!

(*She drops into the chair as* AUBREY *returns; he stands looking at her*)

AUBREY. I—you have altered your mind about going out.

PAULA. Yes. Please to ring the bell.

AUBREY. (*Touching the bell*) You are angry about Mrs. Cortelyon and Ellean. Let me try to explain my reasons—

PAULA. Be careful what you say to me just now! I have never felt like this—except once —in my life. Be careful what you say to me!

(*A* Servant *enters*)

PAULA. (*Rising*) Is Watts at the door with the cart?

SERVANT. Yes, ma'am.

PAULA. Tell him to drive down to the post-office directly with this.

(*Picking up the letter which has been lying upon the table*)

AUBREY. With that?

PAULA. Yes. My letter to Lady Orreyed.

(*Giving the letter to the* Servant, *who goes out*)

AUBREY. Surely you don't wish me to countermand any order of yours to a servant. Call the man back—take the letter from him!

PAULA. I have not the slightest intention of doing so.

AUBREY. I must, then. (*Going to the door. She snatches up her hat and coat and follows him.*) What are you going to do?

PAULA. If you stop that letter, I walk out of the house.

(*He hesitates, then leaves the door*)

AUBREY. I am right in believing that to be the letter inviting George Orreyed and his wife to stay here, am I not?

PAULA. Oh, yes—quite right.

AUBREY. Let it go; I'll write to him by and by.

PAULA. (*Facing him*) You dare!

AUBREY. Hush, Paula!

PAULA. Insult me again and, upon my word, I'll go straight out of the house!

AUBREY. Insult you?

PAULA. Insult me! What else is it? My God! what else is it? What do you mean by taking Ellean from me?

AUBREY. Listen—!

PAULA. Listen to *me!* And how do you take her? You pack her off in the care of a woman who has deliberately held aloof from me, who's thrown mud at me! Yet this Cortelyon creature has only to put foot here once to be entrusted with the charge of the girl you know I dearly want to keep near me!

AUBREY. Paula dear! hear me—!

PAULA. Ah! of course, of course! I can't be so useful to your daughter as such people as this; and so I'm to be given the go-by for any town friend of yours who turns up and chooses to patronize us! Hah! Very well, at any rate, as you take Ellean from me you justify my looking for companions where I can most readily find 'em.

AUBREY. You wish me to fully appreciate your reason for sending that letter to Lady Orreyed?

PAULA. Precisely—I do.

AUBREY. And could you, after all, go back to associates of that order? It's not possible!

PAULA. (*Mockingly*) What, not after the refining influence of these intensely respectable surroundings? (*Going to the door*) We'll see!

AUBREY. Paula!

PAULA. (*Violently*) We'll see!

(*She goes out. He stands still looking after her.*)

Act III

The drawing-room at "Highercoombe." Facing the spectator are two large French windows, sheltered by a verandah, leading into the garden; on the right is a door opening into a small hall. The fireplace, with a large mirror above it, is on the left-hand side of the room, and higher up in the same wall are double doors recessed. The room is richly furnished, and everything betokens taste and luxury. The windows are open, and there is moonlight in the garden.

(LADY ORREYED, *a pretty, affected doll of a woman, with a mincing voice and flaxen hair, is sitting on the ottoman, her head resting against the drum, and her eyes closed.* PAULA, *looking pale, worn, and thoroughly unhappy, is sitting at a table. Both are in sumptuous dinner-gowns*)

LADY ORREYED. (*Opening her eyes*) Well, I never! I dropped off! (*Feeling her hair*) Just fancy! Where are the men?

PAULA. (*Icily*) Outside, smoking.

(*A* Servant *enters with coffee, which he hands to* LADY ORREYED. SIR GEORGE ORREYED *comes in by the window. He is a man of about thirty-five, with a low forehead, a receding chin, a vacuous expression, and an ominous redness about the nose.*)

LADY ORREYED. (*Taking coffee*) Here's Dodo.

SIR GEORGE. I say, the flies under the verandah make you swear. (*The* Servant *hands coffee to* PAULA, *who declines it, then to* SIR GEORGE, *who takes a cup*) Hi! wait a bit! (*He looks at the tray searchingly, then puts back his cup*) Never mind. (*Quietly to* LADY ORREYED) I say, they're dooced sparin' with their liqueur, ain't they?

(*The* Servant *goes out at window*)

PAULA. (*To* SIR GEORGE) Won't you take coffee, George?

SIR GEORGE. No, thanks. It's gettin' near time for a whiskey and potass. (*Approaching* PAULA, *regarding* LADY ORREYED *admiringly*) I say, Birdie looks rippin' to-night, don't she?

PAULA. Your wife?

SIR GEORGE. Yaas—Birdie.

PAULA. Rippin'?

SIR GEORGE. Yaas.

PAULA. Quite—quite rippin'.

(*He moves round to the settee.* PAULA *watches him with distaste, then rises and walks away.* SIR GEORGE *falls asleep on the settee.*)

LADY ORREYED. Paula love, I fancied you and Aubrey were a little more friendly at dinner. You haven't made it up, have you?

PAULA. We? Oh, no. We speak before others, that's all.

LADY ORREYED. And how long do you intend to carry on this game, dear?

PAULA. (*Turning away impatiently*) I really can't tell you.

LADY ORREYED. Sit down, old girl; don't be so fidgety. (*PAULA sits on the upper seat of the ottoman, with her back to* LADY ORREYED) Of course, it's my duty, as an old friend, to give you a good talking-to—(*PAULA glares at her suddenly and fiercely*)—but really I've found one gets so many smacks in the face through interfering in matrimonial squabbles that I've determined to drop it.

PAULA. I think you're wise.

LADY ORREYED. However, I must say that I do wish you'd look at marriage in a more solemn light—just as I do, in fact. It is such a beautiful thing—marriage, and if people in our position don't respect it, and set a good example by living happily with their husbands, what can you expect from the middle classes? When did this sad state of affairs between you and Aubrey actually begin?

PAULA. Actually, a fortnight and three days ago; I haven't calculated the minutes.

LADY ORREYED. A day or two before Dodo and I turned up—arrived.

PAULA. Yes. One always remembers one thing by another; we left off speaking to each other the morning I wrote asking you to visit us.

LADY ORREYED. Lucky for you I was able to pop down, wasn't it, dear?

PAULA. (*Glaring at her again*) Most fortunate.

LADY ORREYED. A serious split with your husband without a pal on the premises—I should say, without a friend in the house—would be most unpleasant.

PAULA. (*Turning to her abruptly*) This place must be horribly doleful for you and George just now. At least you ought to consider him before me. Why didn't you leave me to my difficulties?

LADY ORREYED. Oh, we're quite comfortable, dear, thank you—both of us. George and me are so wrapped up in each other, it doesn't matter where we are. I don't want to crow over you, old girl, but I've got a perfect husband.

(SIR GEORGE *is now fast asleep, his head thrown back and his mouth open, looking hideous*)

PAULA. (*Glancing at SIR GEORGE*) So you've given me to understand.

LADY ORREYED. Not that we don't have our little differences. Why, we fell out only this very morning. You remember the diamond and ruby tiara Charley Prestwick gave poor dear Connie Tirlemont years ago, don't you?

PAULA. No, I do not.

LADY ORREYED. No? Well, it's in the market. Benjamin of Piccadilly has got it in his shop window, and I've set my heart on it.

PAULA. You consider it quite necessary?

LADY ORREYED. Yes; because what I say to Dodo is this—a lady of my station must smother herself with hair ornaments. It's different with you, love—people don't look for so much blaze from you, but I've got rank to keep up; haven't I?

PAULA. Yes.

LADY ORREYED. Well, that was the cause of the little set-to between I and Dodo this morning. He broke two chairs, he was in such a rage. I forgot they're your chairs; do you mind?

PAULA. No.

LADY ORREYED. You know, poor Dodo can't lose his temper without smashing something; if it isn't a chair, it's a mirror; if it isn't that, it's china—a bit of Dresden for choice. Dear old pet! he loves a bit of Dresden when

he's furious. He doesn't really throw things *at* me, dear; he simply lifts them up and drops them, like a gentleman. I expect our room upstairs will look rather wrecky before I get that tiara.

PAULA. Excuse the suggestion; perhaps your husband can't afford it.

LADY ORREYED. Oh, how dreadfully changed you are, Paula! Dodo can always mortgage something, or borrow of his ma. What *is* coming to you!

PAULA. Ah!

(*She sits at the piano and touches the keys*)

LADY ORREYED. Oh, yes, do play! That's the one thing I envy you for.

PAULA. What shall I play?

LADY ORREYED. What was that heavenly piece you gave us last night, dear?

PAULA. A bit of Schubert. Would you like to hear it again?

LADY ORREYED. You don't know any comic songs, do you?

PAULA. I'm afraid not.

LADY ORREYED. I leave it to you.

(PAULA *plays.* AUBREY *and* CAYLEY DRUMMLE *appear outside the window; they look into the room*)

AUBREY. (*To* DRUMMLE) You can see her face in that mirror. Poor girl, how ill and wretched she looks.

DRUMMLE. When are the Orreyeds going?

AUBREY. (*Entering the room*) Heaven knows!

DRUMMLE. (*Following* AUBREY) But *you're* entertaining them; what's it to do with heaven?

AUBREY. Do you know, Cayley, that even the Orreyeds serve a useful purpose? My wife actually speaks to me before our guests—think of that! I've come to rejoice at the presence of the Orreyeds!

DRUMMLE. I dare say; we're taught that beetles are sent for a benign end.

AUBREY. Cayley, talk to Paula again tonight.

DRUMMLE. Certainly, if I get the chance.

AUBREY. Let's contrive it. George is asleep; perhaps I can get that doll out of the way. (*As they advance into the room,* PAULA *abruptly ceases playing and finds interest in a volume of music.* SIR GEORGE *is now nodding and snoring apoplectically*) Lady Orreyed, whenever you feel inclined for a game of billiards I'm at your service.

LADY ORREYED. (*Jumping up*) Charmed, I'm sure! I really thought you had forgotten poor little me. Oh, look at Dodo!

AUBREY. No, no, don't wake him; he's tired.

LADY ORREYED. I must, he looks so plain. (*Rousing* SIR GEORGE) Dodo! Dodo!

SIR GEORGE. (*Stupidly*) 'Ullo!

LADY ORREYED. Dodo dear, you were snoring.

SIR GEORGE. Oh, I say, you could 'a' told me that by and by.

AUBREY. You want a cigar, George; come into the billiard-room. (*Giving his arm to* LADY ORREYED) Cayley, bring Paula.

(AUBREY *and* LADY ORREYED *go out*)

SIR GEORGE. (*Rising*) Hey, what! Billiard-room! (*Looking at his watch*) How goes the —? Phew! 'Ullo, 'Ullo! Whiskey and potass!

(*He goes rapidly after* AUBREY *and* LADY ORREYED. PAULA *resumes playing.*)

PAULA. (*After a pause*) Don't moon about after me, Cayley; follow the others.

DRUMMLE. Thanks, by and by. (*Sitting*) That's pretty.

PAULA. (*After another pause, still playing*) I wish you wouldn't stare so.

DRUMMLE. Was I staring? I'm sorry. (*She plays a little longer, then stops suddenly, rises, and goes to the window, where she stands looking out.* DRUMMLE *moves from the ottoman to the settee.*) A lovely night.

PAULA. (*Startled*) Oh! (*Without turning to him*) Why do you hop about like a monkey?

DRUMMLE. Hot rooms play the deuce with the nerves. Now, it would have done you good to have walked in the garden with us after dinner and made merry. Why didn't you?

PAULA. You know why.

DRUMMLE. Ah, you're thinking of the—difference between you and Aubrey?

PAULA. Yes, I *am* thinking of it.

DRUMMLE. Well, so am I. How long—?

PAULA. Getting on for three weeks.

DRUMMLE. Bless me, it must be! And this would have been such a night to have healed it! Moonlight, the stars, the scent of flowers; and yet enough darkness to enable a kind woman to rest her hand for an instant on the arm of a good fellow who loves her. Ah, ha! It's a wonderful power, dear Mrs. Aubrey, the power of an offended woman! Only realize it! Just that one touch—the mere tips of her fingers—and, for herself and another, she changes the color of the whole world.

PAULA. (*Turning to him calmly*) Cayley, my dear man, you talk exactly like a very romantic old lady.

(*She leaves the window and sits playing with the knick-knacks on the table*)

DRUMMLE. (*To himself*) H'm, that hasn't done it! Well—ha, ha!—I accept the suggestion.—An old woman, eh?

PAULA. Oh, I didn't intend—

DRUMMLE. But why not? I've every qualification—well, almost. And I confess it would have given this withered bosom a throb of grandmotherly satisfaction if I could have seen you and Aubrey at peace before I take my leave to-morrow.

PAULA. To-morrow, Cayley!

DRUMMLE. I must.

PAULA. Oh, this house is becoming unendurable.

DRUMMLE. You're very kind. But you've got the Orreyeds.

PAULA. (*Fiercely*) The Orreyeds! I—I hate the Orreyeds! I lie awake at night, hating them!

DRUMMLE. Pardon me, I've understood that their visit is, in some degree, owing to —hem—your suggestion.

PAULA. Heavens! that doesn't make me like them better. Somehow or another, I—I've outgrown these people. This woman—I used to think her "jolly!"—sickens me. I can't breathe when she's near me: the whiff of her handkerchief turns me faint! And she patronizes me by the hour, until I—I feel my nails growing longer with every word she speaks!

DRUMMLE. My dear lady, why on earth don't you say all this to Aubrey?

PAULA. Oh, I've been such an utter fool, Cayley!

DRUMMLE. (*Soothingly*) Well, well, mention it to Aubrey!

PAULA. No, no, you don't understand. What do you think I've done?

DRUMMLE. Done! What, *since* you invited the Orreyeds?

PAULA. Yes; I must tell you—

DRUMMLE. Perhaps you'd better not.

PAULA. Look here! I've intercepted some letters from Mrs. Cortelyon and Ellean to—him. (*Producing three unopened letters from the bodice of her dress*) There are the accursed things! From Paris—two from the Cortelyon woman, the other from Ellean!

DRUMMLE. But why—why?

PAULA. I don't know. Yes, I do! I saw letters coming from Ellean to her father; not a line to me—not a line. And one morning it happened I was downstairs before he was, and I spied this one lying with his heap on the breakfast table, and I slipped it into my pocket—out of malice, Cayley, pure deviltry! And a day or two afterwards I met Elwes the postman at the Lodge, and took the letters from him, and found these others amongst 'em. I felt simply fiendish when I saw them —fiendish! (*Returning the letters to her bodice*) And now I carry them about with me, and they're scorching me like a mustard plaster!

DRUMMLE. Oh, this accounts for Aubrey not hearing from Paris lately!

PAULA. That's an ingenious conclusion to arrive at! Of course it does! (*With an hysterical laugh*) Ha, ha!

DRUMMLE. Well, well! (*Laughing*) Ha, ha, ha!

PAULA. (*Turning upon him*) I suppose it *is* amusing!

DRUMMLE. I beg pardon.

PAULA. Heaven knows I've little enough to brag about! I'm a bad lot, but not in mean tricks of this sort. In all my life this is the most caddish thing I've done. How am I to get rid of these letters—that's what I want to know? How am I to get rid of them?

DRUMMLE. If I were you I should take Aubrey aside and put them into his hands as soon as possible.

PAULA. What! and tell him to his face that I—! No, thank you. I suppose *you* wouldn't like to—

DRUMMLE. No, no; I won't touch 'em!

PAULA. And you call yourself my friend?

DRUMMLE. (*Good-humoredly*) No, I don't!

PAULA. Perhaps I'll tie them together and give them to his man in the morning.

DRUMMLE. That won't avoid an explanation.

PAULA. (*Recklessly*) Oh, then he must miss them—

DRUMMLE. And trace them.

PAULA. (*Throwing herself upon the ottoman*) I don't care!

DRUMMLE. I know you don't; but let me send him to you now, may I?

PAULA. Now! What do you think a woman's made of? I couldn't stand it, Cayley. I haven't slept for nights; and last night there was thunder, too! I believe I've got the horrors.

DRUMMLE. (*Taking the little hand-mirror from the table*) You'll sleep well enough when you deliver those letters. Come, come, Mrs. Aubrey—a good night's rest! (*Holding the mirror before her face*) It's quite time.

(*She looks at herself for a moment, then snatches the mirror from him*)

PAULA. You brute, Cayley, to show me that!

DRUMMLE. Then—may I? Be guided by a fr— a poor old woman! May I?

PAULA. You'll kill me, amongst you!

DRUMMLE. What do you say?

PAULA. (*After a pause*) Very well. (*He nods his head and goes out rapidly. She looks after him for a moment, and calls "Cayley! Cayley!" Then she again produces the letters, deliberately, one by one, fingering them with aversion. Suddenly she starts, turning her head towards the door.*) Ah!

(AUBREY *enters quickly*)

AUBREY. Paula!

PAULA. (*Handing him the letters, her face averted*) There! (*He examines the letters, puzzled, and looks at her enquiringly*) They are many days old. I stole them, I suppose to make you anxious and unhappy.

(*He looks at the letters again, then lays them aside on the table*)

AUBREY. (*Gently*) Paula, dear, it doesn't matter.

PAULA. (*After a short pause*) Why—why do you take it like this?

AUBREY. What did you expect?

PAULA. Oh, but I suppose silent reproaches are really the severest. And then, naturally, you are itching to open your letters. (*She crosses the room as if to go*)

AUBREY. Paula! (*She pauses*) Surely, surely, it's all over now?

PAULA. All over! (*Mockingly*) Has my step-daughter returned then? When did she arrive? I haven't heard of it!

AUBREY. You can be very cruel.

PAULA. That word's always on a man's lips; he uses it if his soup's cold. (*With another movement as if to go*) Need we—

AUBREY. I know I've wounded you, Paula. But isn't there any way out of this?

PAULA. When does Ellean return? To-morrow? Next week?

AUBREY. (*Wearily*) Oh! Why should we grudge Ellean the little pleasure she is likely to find in Paris and in London?

PAULA. I grudge her nothing, if that's a hit at me. But with that woman—?

AUBREY. It must be that woman or another. You know that at present we are unable to give Ellean the opportunity of—of—

PAULA. Of mixing with respectable people.

AUBREY. The opportunity of gaining friends, experience, ordinary knowledge of the world. If you are interested in Ellean, can't you see how useful Mrs. Cortelyon's good offices are?

PAULA. May I put one question? At the end of the London season, when Mrs. Cortelyon has done with Ellean, is it quite understood that the girl comes back to us? (*AUBREY is silent*) Is it? Is it?

AUBREY. Let us wait till the end of the season—

PAULA. Oh! I knew it. You're only fooling me; you put me off with any trash. I believe you've sent Ellean away, not for the reasons you give, but because you don't consider me a decent companion for her, because you're afraid she might get a little of her innocence rubbed off in my company? Come, isn't that the truth? Be honest! Isn't that it?

AUBREY. Yes.

(*There is a moment's silence, on both sides*)

PAULA. (*With uplifted hands as if to strike him*) Oh!

AUBREY. (*Taking her by the wrists*) Sit down. Sit down. (*He puts her into a chair; she shakes herself free with a cry*) Now listen to me. Fond as you are, Paula, of harking back to your past, there's one chapter of it you always let alone. I've never asked you to speak of it; you've never offered to speak of it. I mean the chapter that relates to the time when you were—like Ellean. (*She attempts to rise; he restrains her*) No, no.

PAULA. I don't choose to talk about that time. I won't satisfy your curiosity.

AUBREY. My dear Paula, I have no curiosity—I know what you were at Ellean's age. I'll tell you. You hadn't a thought that wasn't a wholesome one, you hadn't an impulse that didn't tend towards good, you never harbored a notion you couldn't have gossiped about to a parcel of children. (*She makes another effort to rise; he lays his hand lightly on her shoulder*) And this was a very few years back—there are days now when you look like a schoolgirl—but think of the difference between the two Paulas. You'll have to think hard, because after a cruel life, one's perceptions grow a thick skin. But, for God's sake, do think till you get these two images clearly in your mind, and then ask yourself what sort of a friend such a woman as you are to-day would have been for the girl of seven or eight years ago.

PAULA. (*Rising*) How dare you? I could be almost as good a friend to Ellean as her own mother would have been had she lived. I know what you mean. How dare you?

AUBREY. You say that; very likely you believe it. But you're blind, Paula; you're blind. You! Every belief that a young, pure-minded girl holds sacred—that you once held sacred—you now make a target for a jest, a sneer, a paltry cynicism. I tell you, you're not mistress any longer of your thoughts or your tongue. Why, how often, sitting between you and Ellean, have I seen her cheeks turn scarlet as you've rattled off some tale that belongs by right to the club or the smoking-room! Have you noticed the blush? If you have, has the cause of it ever struck you? And this is the girl you say you love, I admit that you *do* love, whose love you expect in return! Oh, Paula, I make the best, the only, excuse for you when I tell you you're blind!

PAULA. Ellean—Ellean blushes easily.

AUBREY. You blushed as easily a few years ago.

PAULA. (*After a short pause*) Well! have you finished your sermon?

AUBREY. (*With a gesture of despair*) Oh, Paula!

(*Going up to the window, and standing with his back to the room*)

PAULA. (*To herself*) A few—years ago! (*She walks slowly towards the door, then suddenly drops upon the ottoman in a paroxysm of weeping*) O God! A few years ago!

AUBREY. (*Going to her*) Paula!

PAULA. (*Sobbing*) Oh, don't touch me!

AUBREY. Paula!

PAULA. Oh, go away from me! (*He goes back a few steps, and after a little while she becomes calmer and rises unsteadily; then in an altered tone*) Look here—! (*He advances a step; she checks him with a quick gesture*) Look here! Get rid of these people—Mabel and her husband—as soon as possible! I—I've done with them!

AUBREY. (*In a whisper*) Paula!

PAULA. And then—then—when the time comes for Ellean to leave Mrs. Cortelyon, give me—give me another chance! (*He advances again, but she shrinks away*) No, no! (*She goes out by the door on the right. He sinks onto the settee, covering his eyes with his hands. There is a brief silence, then a* Servant *enters.*)

SERVANT. Mrs. Cortelyon, sir, with Miss Ellean.

(AUBREY *rises to meet* MRS. CORTELYON, *who enters, followed by* ELLEAN, *both being in travelling dresses. The* Servant *withdraws*)

MRS. CORTELYON. (*Shaking hands with* AUBREY) Oh, my dear Aubrey!

AUBREY. Mrs. Cortelyon! (*Kissing* ELLEAN) Ellean dear!

ELLEAN. Papa, is all well at home?

MRS. CORTELYON. We're shockingly anxious.

AUBREY. Yes, yes, all's well. This is quite unexpected. (*To* MRS. CORTELYON) You've found Paris insufferably hot?

MRS. CORTELYON. Insufferably hot! Paris is pleasant enough. We've had no letter from you!

AUBREY. I wrote to Ellean a week ago.

MRS. CORTELYON. Without alluding to the subject I had written to you upon.

AUBREY. (*Thinking*) Ah, of course—

MRS. CORTELYON. And since then we've both written, and you've been absolutely silent. Oh, it's too bad!

AUBREY. (*Picking up the letters from the table*) It isn't altogether my fault. Here are the letters—

ELLEAN. Papa!

MRS. CORTELYON. They're unopened.

AUBREY. An accident delayed their reaching me till this evening. I'm afraid this has upset you very much.

MRS. CORTELYON. Upset me!

ELLEAN. (*In an undertone to* MRS. CORTELYON) Never mind. Not now, dear—not to-night.

AUBREY. Eh?

MRS. CORTELYON. (*To* ELLEAN, *aloud*) Child, run away and take your things off. She doesn't look as if she'd journeyed from Paris to-day.

AUBREY. I've never seen her with such a color. (*Taking* ELLEAN'S *hands*)

ELLEAN. (*To* AUBREY, *in a faint voice*) Papa, Mrs. Cortelyon has been so very, very kind to me, but I—I have come home.

(*She goes out*)

AUBREY. Come home! (*To* MRS. CORTELYON) Ellean returns to us then?

MRS. CORTELYON. That's the very point I put to you in my letters, and you oblige me to travel from Paris to Willowmere on a warm day to settle it. I think perhaps it's right that Ellean should be with you just now, although I—My dear friend, circumstances are a little altered.

AUBREY. Alice, you're in some trouble.

MRS. CORTELYON. Well—yes, I *am* in trouble. You remember pretty little Mrs. Brereton who was once Caroline Ardale?

AUBREY. Quite well.

MRS. CORTELYON. She's a widow now, poor thing. She has the *entresol* of the house where we've been lodging in the Avenue de Friedland. Caroline's a dear chum of mine; she formed a great liking for Ellean.

AUBREY. I'm very glad.

MRS. CORTELYON. Yes, it's nice for her to meet her mother's friends. Er—that young Hugh Ardale the papers were full of some time ago—he's Caroline Brereton's brother, you know.

AUBREY. No, I didn't know. What did he do? I forget.

MRS. CORTELYON. Checked one of those

horrid mutinies at some far-away station in India. Marched down with a handful of his men and a few faithful natives, and held the place until he was relieved. They gave him his company and a V.C. for it.

AUBREY. And he's Mrs. Brereton's brother?

MRS. CORTELYON. Yes. He's with his sister—*was*, rather—in Paris. He's home—invalided. Good gracious, Aubrey, why don't you help me out? Can't you guess what has occurred?

AUBREY. Alice!

MRS. CORTELYON. Young Ardale—Ellean!

AUBREY. An attachment?

MRS. CORTELYON. Yes, Aubrey. (*After a little pause*) Well, I suppose I've got myself into sad disgrace. But really I didn't foresee anything of this kind. A serious, reserved child like Ellean, and a boyish, high-spirited soldier—it never struck me as being likely. (*AUBREY paces to and fro thoughtfully*) I did all I could directly Captain Ardale spoke —wrote to you at once. Why on earth don't you receive your letters promptly, and when you do get them why can't you open them? I endured the anxiety till last night, and then made up my mind—home! Of course, it has worried me terribly. My head's bursting. Are there any salts about? (*AUBREY fetches a bottle from the cabinet and hands it to her*) We've had one of those hateful smooth crossings that won't let you be properly indisposed.

AUBREY. My dear Alice, I assure you I've no thought of blaming you.

MRS. CORTELYON. That statement always precedes a quarrel.

AUBREY. I don't know whether this is the worst or the best luck. How will my wife regard it? Is Captain Ardale a good fellow?

MRS. CORTELYON. My dear Aubrey, you'd better read up the accounts of his wonderful heroism. Face to face with death for a whole week; always with a smile and a cheering word for the poor helpless souls depending on him! Of course it's that that has stirred the depths of your child's nature. I've watched her while we've been dragging the story out of him, and if angels look different from Ellean at that moment, I don't desire to meet any, that's all!

AUBREY. If you were in my position—? But you can't judge.

MRS. CORTELYON. Why, if I had a marriageable daughter of my own, and Captain Ardale proposed for her, naturally I should cry my eyes out all night—but I should thank Heaven in the morning.

AUBREY. You believe so thoroughly in him?

MRS. CORTELYON. Do you think I should have only a headache at this minute if I didn't! Look here, you've got to see me down the lane; that's the least you can do, my friend. Come into my house for a moment and shake hands with Hugh.

AUBREY. What, is he here?

MRS. CORTELYON. He came through with us, to present himself formally to-morrow. Where are my gloves? (*AUBREY fetches them from the ottoman*) Make my apologies to Mrs. Tanqueray, please. She's well, I hope? (*Going towards the door*) I can't feel sorry she hasn't seen me in this condition.

(ELLEAN *enters*)

ELLEAN. (*To Mrs. CORTELYON*) I've been waiting to wish you good-night. I was afraid I'd missed you.

MRS. CORTELYON. Good-night, Ellean.

ELLEAN. (*In a low voice, embracing Mrs. CORTELYON*) I can't thank you. Dear Mrs. Cortelyon!

MRS. CORTELYON. (*Her arms round ELLEAN, in a whisper to AUBREY*) Speak a word to her. (*MRS. CORTELYON goes out*)

AUBREY. (*To ELLEAN*) Ellean, I'm going to see Mrs. Cortelyon home. Tell Paula where I am; explain, dear.

(*Going to the door*)

ELLEAN. (*Her head drooping*) Yes. (*Quickly*) Father! You are angry with me—disappointed?

AUBREY. Angry? No.

ELLEAN. Disappointed?

AUBREY. (*Smiling and going to her and taking her hand*) If so, it's only because you've shaken my belief in my discernment. I thought you took after your poor mother a little, Ellean; but there's a look on your face to-night, dear, that I never saw on hers —never, never.

ELLEAN. (*Leaning her head on his shoul-*

der) Perhaps I ought not to have gone away.

AUBREY. Hush! You're quite happy?

ELLEAN. Yes.

AUBREY. That's right. Then, as you are quite happy, there is something I particularly want you to do for me, Ellean.

ELLEAN. What is that?

AUBREY. Be very gentle with Paula. Will you?

ELLEAN. You think I have been unkind.

AUBREY. (*Kissing her upon the forehead*) Be very gentle with Paula.

(*He goes out, and she stands looking after him; then, as she turns thoughtfully from the door, a rose is thrown through the window and falls at her feet. She picks up the flower wonderingly and goes to the window.*)

ELLEAN. (*Starting back*) Hugh!

(HUGH ARDALE, *a handsome young man of about seven-and-twenty, with a boyish face and manner, appears outside the window*)

HUGH. Nelly! Nelly dear!

ELLEAN. What's the matter?

HUGH. Hush! Nothing. It's only fun. (*Laughing*) Ha, ha, ha! I've found out that Mrs. Cortelyon's meadow runs up to your father's plantation; I've come through a gap in the hedge.

ELLEAN. Why, Hugh?

HUGH. I'm miserable at The Warren: it's so different from the Avenue de Friedland. Don't look like that! Upon my word I meant just to peep at your home and go back, but I saw figures moving about here, and came nearer, hoping to get a glimpse of you. Was that your father?

(*He enters the room*)

ELLEAN. Yes.

HUGH. Isn't this fun! A rabbit ran across my foot while I was hiding behind that old yew.

ELLEAN. You must go away; it's not right for you to be here like this.

HUGH. But it's only fun, I tell you. You take everything so seriously. Do wish me good-night.

ELLEAN. We have said good-night.

HUGH. In the hall at The Warren, before Mrs. Cortelyon and a man-servant. Oh, it's so different from the Avenue de Friedland!

ELLEAN. (*Giving him her hand hastily*) Good-night, Hugh!

HUGH. Is that all? We might be the merest acquaintances.

(*He momentarily embraces her, but she releases herself*)

ELLEAN. It's when you're like this that you make me feel utterly miserable. (*Throwing the rose from her angrily*) Oh!

HUGH. I've offended you now, I suppose?

ELLEAN. Yes.

HUGH. Forgive me, Nelly. Come into the garden for five minutes; we'll stroll down to the plantation.

ELLEAN. No, no.

HUGH. For two minutes—to tell me you forgive me.

ELLEAN. I forgive you.

HUGH. Evidently. I shan't sleep a wink to-night after this. What a fool I am! Come down to the plantation. Make it up with me.

ELLEAN. There is somebody coming into this room. Do you wish to be seen here?

HUGH. I shall wait for you behind that yew-tree. You must speak to me, Nelly!

(*He disappears.* PAULA *enters*)

PAULA. Ellean!

ELLEAN. You—you are very surprised to see me, Paula, of course.

PAULA. Why are you here? Why aren't you with—your friend?

ELLEAN. I've come home—if you'll have me. We left Paris this morning; Mrs. Cortelyon brought me back. She was here a minute or two ago; papa has gone with her to The Warren. He asked me to tell you.

PAULA. There are some people staying with us that I'd rather you didn't meet. It was hardly worth your while to return for a few hours.

ELLEAN. A few hours?

PAULA. Well, when do you go to London?

ELLEAN. I don't think I go to London, after all.

PAULA. (*Eagerly*) You—you've quarreled with her?

ELLEAN. No, no, no, not that; but—Paula! (*In an altered tone*) Paula!

PAULA. (*Startled*) Eh! (ELLEAN *goes de-*

liberately to PAULA *and kisses her*) Ellean!

ELLEAN. Kiss me.

PAULA. What—what's come to you?

ELLEAN. I want to behave differently to you in the future. Is it too late?

PAULA. Too—late! (*Impulsively kissing* ELLEAN *and crying*) No—no—no! No—no!

ELLEAN. Paula, don't cry.

PAULA. (*Wiping her eyes*) I'm a little shaky; I haven't been sleeping. It's all right,— talk to me.

ELLEAN. There is something I want to tell you—

PAULA. Is there—is there?

(*They sit together on the ottoman,* PAULA *taking* ELLEAN's *hand*)

ELLEAN. Paula, in our house in the Avenue de Friedland, on the floor below us, there was a Mrs. Brereton. She used to be a friend of my mother's. Mrs. Cortelyon and I spent a great deal of our time with her.

PAULA. (*Suspiciously*) Oh! (*Letting* EL- LEAN's *hand fall*) Is this lady going to take you up in place of Mrs. Cortelyon?

ELLEAN. No, no. Her brother is staying with her—*was* staying with her. Her brother—

(*Breaking off in confusion*)

PAULA. Well?

ELLEAN. (*Almost inaudibly*) Paula—

(*She rises and walks away,* PAULA *following her*)

PAULA. (*Taking hold of her*) You're not in love! (ELLEAN *looks at* PAULA *appealingly*) Oh, *you* in love! You! Oh, this is why you've come home! Of course, you can make friends with me now! You'll leave us for good soon, I suppose; so it doesn't much matter being civil to me for a little while!

ELLEAN. Oh, Paula!

PAULA. Why, how you have deceived us— all of us! We've taken you for a cold-blooded little saint. The fools you've made of us! Saint Ellean, Saint Ellean!

ELLEAN. Ah, I might have known you'd only mock me!

PAULA. (*Her tone changing*) Eh?

ELLEAN. I—I can't talk to you. (*Sitting on the settee*) You do nothing else but mock and sneer, nothing else.

PAULA. Ellean dear! Ellean! I didn't mean it. I'm so horribly jealous, it's a sort of curse on me. (*Kneeling beside* ELLEAN *and embracing her*) My tongue runs away with me.

I'm going to alter, I swear I am. I've made some good resolutions, and as God's above me, I'll keep them! If you are in love, if you do ever marry, that's no reason why we shouldn't be fond of each other. Come, you've kissed me of your own accord—you can't take it back. Now we're friends again, aren't we? Ellean, dear! I want to know everything, everything. Ellean, dear, Ellean!

ELLEAN. Paula, Hugh has done something that makes me very angry. He came with us from Paris to-day, to see papa. He is staying with Mrs. Cortelyon and—I ought to tell you—

PAULA. Yes, yes. What?

ELLEAN. He has found his way by The Warren meadow through the plantation up to this house. He is waiting to bid me good-night. (*Glancing towards the garden*) He is —out there.

PAULA. Oh!

ELLEAN. What shall I do?

PAULA. Bring him in to see me! Will you?

ELLEAN. No, no.

PAULA. But I'm dying to know him. Oh, yes, you must. I shall meet him before Aubrey does. (*Excitedly running her hands over her hair*) I'm so glad. (ELLEAN *goes out by the window*) The mirror—mirror. What a fright I must look! (*Not finding the hand-glass on the table, she jumps onto the settee, and surveys herself in the mirror over the mantelpiece, then sits quietly down and waits*) Ellean! Just fancy! Ellean!

(*After a pause* ELLEAN *enters by the window with* HUGH)

ELLEAN. Paula, this is Captain Ardale— Mrs. Tanqueray.

(PAULA *rises and turns, and she and* HUGH *stand staring blankly at each other for a moment or two; then* PAULA *advances and gives him her hand*)

PAULA. (*In a strange voice, but calmly*) How do you do?

HUGH. How do you do?

PAULA. (*To* ELLEAN) Mr. Ardale and I have met in London, Ellean. Er—Captain Ardale now?

HUGH. Yes.

ELLEAN. In London?

PAULA. They say the world's very small, don't they?

HUGH. Yes.

PAULA. Ellean, dear, I want to have a little talk about you to Mr. Ardale—Captain Ardale—alone. (*Putting her arms around EL-LEAN, and leading her to the door*) Come back in a little while. (ELLEAN *nods to* PAULA *with a smile and goes out, while* PAULA *stands watching her at the open door*) In a little while—in a little—(*Closing the door and then taking a seat facing* HUGH) Be quick! Mr. Tanqueray has only gone down to The Warren with Mrs. Cortelyon. What is to be done?

HUGH. (*Blankly*) Done?

PAULA. Done—done. Something must be done.

HUGH. I understood that Mr. Tanqueray had married a Mrs.—Mrs.—

PAULA. Jarman?

HUGH. Yes.

PAULA. I'd been going by that name. You didn't follow my doings after we separated.

HUGH. No.

PAULA. (*Sneeringly*) No.

HUGH. I went out to India.

PAULA. What's to be done?

HUGH. Damn this chance!

PAULA. Oh, my God!

HUGH. Your husband doesn't know, does he?

PAULA. That you and I—?

HUGH. Yes.

PAULA. No. He knows about others.

HUGH. Not about me. How long were we—?

PAULA. I don't remember, exactly.

HUGH. Do you—do you think it matters?

PAULA. His—his daughter. (*With a muttered exclamation he turns away, and sits with his head in his hands*) What's to be done?

HUGH. I wish I could think.

PAULA. Oh! Oh! What happened to that flat of ours in Ethelbert Street?

HUGH. I let it.

PAULA. All that pretty furniture?

HUGH. Sold it.

PAULA. I came across the key of the escritoire the other day in an old purse! (*Suddenly realizing the horror and hopelessness of her position, and starting to her feet with an hysterical cry of rage*) What am I maundering about?

HUGH. For God's sake, be quiet! Do let me think.

PAULA. This will send me mad! (*Suddenly turning and standing over him*) You—you beast, to crop up in my life again like this!

HUGH. I always treated you fairly.

PAULA. (*Weakly*) Oh! I beg your pardon—I know you did—I—

(*She sinks onto the settee crying hysterically*)

HUGH. Hush!

PAULA. She kissed me to-night! I'd won her over! I've had such a fight to make her love me! and now—just as she's beginning to love me, to bring this on her!

HUGH. Hush, hush! Don't break down!

PAULA. (*Sobbing*) You don't know! I—I haven't been getting on well in my marriage. It's been my fault. The life I used to lead spoilt me completely. But I'd made up my mind to turn over a new leaf from to-night. From to-night!

HUGH. Paula—

PAULA. Don't you call me that!

HUGH. Mrs. Tanqueray, there is no cause for you to despair in this way. It's all right, I tell you—it *shall* be all right.

PAULA. (*Shivering*) What are we to do?

HUGH. Hold our tongues.

PAULA. Eh?

(*Staring vacantly*)

HUGH. The chances are a hundred to one against any one ever turning up who knew us when we were together. Besides, no one would be such a brute as to split on us. If anybody did do such a thing we should have to lie! What are we upsetting ourselves like this for, when we've simply got to hold our tongues?

PAULA. You're as mad as I am.

HUGH. Can you think of a better plan?

PAULA. There's only one plan possible—let's come to our senses!—Mr. Tanqueray must be told.

HUGH. Your husband! What, and I lose Ellean! I lose Ellean!

PAULA. You've got to lose her.

HUGH. I won't lose her; I can't lose her!

PAULA. Didn't I read of your doing any number of brave things in India? Why, you seem to be an awful coward!

HUGH. That's another sort of pluck altogether; I haven't this sort of pluck.

PAULA. Oh, I don't ask *you* to tell Mr. Tanqueray. That's my job.

HUGH. (*Standing over her*) You—you—you'd better! You—

PAULA. (*Rising*) Don't bully me! I intend to.

HUGH. (*Taking hold of her; she wrenches herself free*) Look here, Paula. I never treated you badly—you've owned it. Why should you want to pay me out like this? You don't know how I love Ellean!

PAULA. Yes, that's just what I *do* know.

HUGH. I say you don't! She's as good as my own mother. I've been downright honest with her, too. I told her, in Paris, that I'd been a bit wild at one time, and, after a damned wretched day, she promised to forgive me because of what I'd done since in India. She's behaved like an angel to me! Surely I oughtn't to lose her, after all, just because I've been like other fellows! No; I haven't been half as rackety as a hundred men we could think of. Paula, don't pay me out for nothing; be fair to me, there's a good girl—be fair to me!

PAULA. Oh, I'm not considering you at all! I advise you not to stay here any longer: Mr. Tanqueray is sure to be back soon.

HUGH. (*Taking up his hat*) What's the understanding between us, then? What have we arranged to do?

PAULA. I don't know what you're going to do; I've got to tell Mr. Tanqueray.

HUGH. By God, you shall do nothing of the sort! (*Approaching her fiercely*)

PAULA. You shocking coward!

HUGH. If you dare! (*Going up to the window*) Mind! If you dare!

PAULA. (*Following him*) Why, what would you do?

HUGH. (*After a short pause, sullenly*) Nothing. I'd shoot myself—that's nothing. Good-night.

PAULA. Good-night.

(*He disappears. She walks unsteadily to the ottoman, and sits; and as she does so her hand falls upon the little silver mirror, which she takes up, staring at her own reflection*)

Act IV

The Drawing-room at "Highercoombe," the same evening.

(PAULA *is still seated on the ottoman, looking vacantly before her, with the little mirror in her hand.* LADY ORREYED *enters*)

LADY ORREYED. There you are! You never came into the billiard-room. Isn't it maddening—Cayley Drummle gives me sixty out of a hundred, and beats me. I must be out of form, because I know I play remarkably well for a lady. Only last month—(PAULA *rises*) Whatever is the matter with you, old girl?

PAULA. Why?

LADY ORREYED. (*Staring*) It's the light, I suppose. (PAULA *replaces the mirror on the table*) By Aubrey's bolting from the billiard-table in that fashion I thought perhaps—

PAULA. Yes; it's all right.

LADY ORREYED. You've patched it up? (PAULA *nods*) Oh, I am jolly glad—! I mean—

PAULA. Yes, I know what you mean. Thanks, Mabel.

LADY ORREYED. (*Kissing* PAULA) Now take my advice; for the future—

PAULA. Mabel, if I've been disagreeable to you while you've been staying here, I—I beg your pardon.

(*Walking away and sitting down*)

LADY ORREYED. You disagreeable, my dear? I haven't noticed it. Dodo and me both consider you make a first-class hostess; but then you've had such practice, haven't you? (*Dropping on the ottoman and gaping*) Oh, talk about being sleepy—

PAULA. Why don't you—!

LADY ORREYED. Why, dear, I must hang about for Dodo. You may as well know it; he's in one of his moods.

PAULA. (*Under her breath*) Oh—!

LADY ORREYED. Now, it's not his fault; it

was deadly dull for him while we were playing billiards. Cayley Drummle did ask him
to mark, but I stopped that; it's so easy to
make a gentleman look like a billiard-marker.
This is just how it always is; if poor old Dodo
has nothing to do, he loses count, as you may
say.

PAULA. Hark!

(SIR GEORGE ORREYED *enters, walking
slowly and deliberately; he looks pale and
watery-eyed*)

SIR GEORGE. (*With mournful indistinct-
ness*) I'm 'fraid we've lef' you a grea' deal to
yourself to-night, Mrs. Tanqueray. Attra'-
tions of billiards. I apol'gise. I say, where's
ol' Aubrey?

PAULA. My husband has been obliged to
go out to a neighbor's house.

SIR GEORGE. I want his advice on a rather
pressing matter connected with my family—
my family. (*Sitting*) To-morrow will do just
as well.

LADY ORREYED. (*To* PAULA) This is the
mood I hate so—driveling about his precious
family.

SIR GEORGE. The fact is, Mrs. Tanqueray,
I am not easy in my min' 'bout the way I am
treatin' my poor ol' mother.

LADY ORREYED. (*To* PAULA) Do you hear
that? That's *his* mother, but *my* mother he
won't so much as look at!

SIR GEORGE. I shall write to Bruton Street
firs' thing in the morning.

LADY ORREYED. (*To* PAULA) Mamma
has stuck to me through everything—well,
you know!

SIR GEORGE. I'll get ol' Aubrey to figure
out a letter. I'll drop line to Uncle Fitz too—
dooced shame of the ol' feller to chuck me
over in this manner. (*Wiping his eyes*) All
my family have chucked me over.

LADY ORREYED. (*Rising*) Dodo!

SIR GEORGE. Jus' because I've married beneath me, to be chucked over! Aunt Lydia,
the General, Hooky Whitgrave, Lady Sug-
nall—my own dear sister!—all turn their backs
on me. It's more than I can stan'!

LADY ORREYED. (*Approaching him with
dignity*) Sir George, wish Mrs. Tanqueray
good-night at once, and come upstairs. Do
you hear me?

SIR GEORGE. (*Rising angrily*) Wha—!

LADY ORREYED. Be quiet!

SIR GEORGE. You presoom to order me
about!

LADY ORREYED. You're making an exhibi-
tion of yourself!

SIR GEORGE. Look 'ere—!

LADY ORREYED. Come along, I tell you!

(*He hesitates, utters a few inarticulate
sounds, then snatches up a fragile ornament from the table and is about to dash
it on the ground.* LADY ORREYED *re-
treats, and* PAULA *goes to him*)

PAULA. George!
                 (*He replaces the ornament*)

SIR GEORGE. (*Shaking* PAULA'S *hand*)
Good ni', Mrs. Tanqueray.

LADY ORREYED. (*To* PAULA) Good-night,
darling. Wish Aubrey good-night for me.
Now, Dodo?   (*She goes out*)

SIR GEORGE. (*To* PAULA) I say, are you
goin' to sit up for ol' Aubrey?

PAULA. Yes.

SIR GEORGE. Shall I keep you comp'ny?

PAULA. No, thank you, George.

SIR GEORGE. Sure?

PAULA. Yes, sure.

SIR GEORGE. (*Shaking hands*) Good-night
again.

PAULA. Good-night.

(*She turns away. He goes out steadying himself carefully.* DRUMMLE *appears outside the window, smoking*)

DRUMMLE. (*Looking into the room and
seeing* PAULA) My last cigar. Where's Aubrey?

PAULA. Gone down to The Warren to see
Mrs. Cortelyon home.

DRUMMLE. (*Entering the room*) Eh? Did
you say Mrs. Cortelyon?

PAULA. Yes. She has brought Ellean back.

DRUMMLE. Bless my soul! Why?

PAULA. I—I'm too tired to tell you, Cayley.
If you stroll along the lane you'll meet Aubrey. Get the news from him.

DRUMMLE. (*Going up to the window*)
Yes, yes. (*Returning to* PAULA) I don't want
to bother you, only—the anxious old woman,
you know. Are you and Aubrey—?

PAULA. Good friends again?

DRUMMLE. (*Nodding*) Um.

PAULA. (*Giving him her hand*) Quite,
Cayley, quite.

DRUMMLE. (*Retaining her hand*) That's capital. As I'm off so early to-morrow morning, let me say now—thank you for your hospitality.

(*He bends over her hand gallantly, then goes out by the window*)

PAULA. (*To herself*) "Are you and Aubrey —?" "Good friends again?" "Yes." "Quite, Cayley, quite."

(*There is a brief pause, then* AUBREY *enters hurriedly, wearing a light overcoat and carrying a cap*)

AUBREY. Paula dear! Have you seen Ellean?

PAULA. I found her here when I came down.

AUBREY. She—she's told you?

PAULA. Yes, Aubrey.

AUBREY. It's extraordinary, isn't it! Not that somebody should fall in love with Ellean, or that Ellean herself should fall in love. All that's natural enough and was bound to happen, I suppose, sooner or later. But this young fellow! You know his history?

PAULA. His history?

AUBREY. You remember the papers were full of his name a few months ago?

PAULA. Oh, yes.

AUBREY. The man's as brave as a lion, there's no doubt about that; and, at the same time, he's like a big good-natured school-boy, Mrs. Cortelyon says. Have you ever pictured the kind of man Ellean would marry some day?

PAULA. I can't say that I have.

AUBREY. A grave, sedate fellow I've thought about—hah! She has fallen in love with the way in which Ardale practically laid down his life to save those poor people shut up in the Residency. (*Taking off his coat*) Well, I suppose if a man can do that sort of thing, one ought to be content. And yet— (*Throwing his coat on the settee*) I should have met him to-night, but he'd gone out. Paula dear, tell me how you look upon this business.

PAULA. Yes, I will—I must. To begin with, I—I've seen Mr. Ardale.

AUBREY. Captain Ardale?

PAULA. Captain Ardale.

AUBREY. Seen him?

PAULA. While you were away he came up here, through our grounds, to try to get a word with Ellean. I made her fetch him in and present him to me.

AUBREY. (*Frowning*) Doesn't Captain Ardale know there's a lodge and a front door to this place? Never mind! What is your impression of him?

PAULA. Aubrey, do you recollect my bringing you a letter—a letter giving you an account of myself—to the Albany late one night—the night before we got married?

AUBREY. A letter?

PAULA. You burnt it; don't you know?

AUBREY. Yes; I know.

PAULA. His name was in that letter.

AUBREY. (*Going back from her slowly, and staring at her*) I don't understand.

PAULA. Well—Ardale and I once kept house together. (*He remains silent, not moving*) Why don't you strike me? Hit me in the face—I'd rather you did! Hurt me! hurt me!

AUBREY. (*After a pause*) What did you— and this man—say to each other—just now?

PAULA. I—hardly—know.

AUBREY. Think!

PAULA. The end of it all was that I—I told him I must inform you of—what had happened . . . he didn't want me to do that . . . I declared that I would . . . he dared me to. (*Breaking down*) Let me alone!—oh!

AUBREY. Where was my daughter while this went on?

PAULA. I—I had sent her out of the room . . . that is all right.

AUBREY. Yes, yes—yes, yes.

(*He turns his head towards the door*)

PAULA. Who's that?

(*A* SERVANT *enters with a letter*)

SERVANT. The coachman has just run up with this from The Warren, sir. (AUBREY *takes the letter*) It's for Mrs. Tanqueray, sir; there's no answer.

(*The* SERVANT *withdraws.* AUBREY *goes to* PAULA *and drops the letter into her lap; she opens it with uncertain hands*)

PAULA. (*Reading it to herself*) It's from— him. He's going away—or gone—I think. (*Rising in a weak way*) What does it say? I never could make out his writing.

(*She gives the letter to* AUBREY, *and stands*

near him, looking at the letter over his shoulder as he reads)

AUBREY. (*Reading*) "I shall be in Paris by to-morrow evening. Shall wait there, at Meurice's, for a week, ready to receive any communication you or your husband may address to me. Please invent some explanation to Ellean. Mrs. Tanqueray, for God's sake, do what you can for me."

(PAULA *and* AUBREY *speak in low voices, both still looking at the letter)*

PAULA. Has he left The Warren, I wonder, already?

AUBREY. That doesn't matter.

PAULA. No; but I can picture him going quietly off. Very likely he's walking on to Bridgeford or Cottering to-night, to get the first train in the morning. A pleasant stroll for him.

AUBREY. We'll reckon he's gone, that's enough.

PAULA. That isn't to be answered in any way?

AUBREY. Silence will answer that.

PAULA. He'll soon recover his spirits, I know.

AUBREY. You know. (*Offering her the letter*) You don't want this, I suppose?

PAULA. No.

AUBREY. It's done with—done with.

(*He tears the letter into small pieces. She has dropped the envelope; she searches for it, finds it, and gives it to him.*)

PAULA. Here!

AUBREY. (*Looking at the remnants of the letter*) This is no good; I must burn it.

PAULA. Burn it in your room.

AUBREY. Yes.

PAULA. Put it in your pocket for now.

AUBREY. Yes.

(*He does so.* ELLEAN *enters, and they both turn, guiltily, and stare at her.*)

ELLEAN. (*After a short silence, wonderingly*) Papa—

AUBREY. What do you want, Ellean?

ELLEAN. I heard from Willis that you had come in; I only want to wish you good-night. (PAULA *steals away, without looking back*) What's the matter? Ah! Of course, Paula has told you about Captain Ardale?

AUBREY. Well?

ELLEAN. Have you and he met?

AUBREY. No.

ELLEAN. You are angry with him; so was I. But to-morrow when he calls and expresses his regret—to-morrow—

AUBREY. Ellean—Ellean!

ELLEAN. Yes, papa.

AUBREY. I—I can't let you see this man again. (*He walks away from her in a paroxysm of distress; then, after a moment or two, he returns to her and takes her to his arms*) Ellean! my child!

ELLEAN. (*Releasing herself*) What has happened, papa? What is it?

AUBREY. (*Thinking out his words deliberately*) Something has occurred, something has come to my knowledge, in relation to Captain Ardale, which puts any further acquaintanceship between you two out of the question.

ELLEAN. Any further acquaintanceship . . . out of the question?

AUBREY. Yes.

(*Advancing to her quickly, but she shrinks from him*)

ELLEAN. No, no—I am quite well. (*After a short pause*) It's not an hour ago since Mrs. Cortelyon left you and me together here; you had nothing to urge against Captain Ardale then.

AUBREY. No.

ELLEAN. You don't know each other; you haven't even seen him this evening, Father!

AUBREY. I have told you he and I have not met.

ELLEAN. Mrs. Cortelyon couldn't have spoken against him to you just now. No, no, no; she's too good a friend to both of us. Aren't you going to give me some explanation? You can't take this position towards me —towards Captain Ardale—without affording me the fullest explanation.

AUBREY. Ellean, there are circumstances connected with Captain Ardale's career which you had better remain ignorant of. It must be sufficient for you that I consider these circumstances render him unfit to be your husband.

ELLEAN. Father!

AUBREY. You must trust me, Ellean; you must try to understand the depth of my love for you and the—the agony it gives me to hurt you. You must trust me.

ELLEAN. I will, father; but you must trust

me a little too. Circumstances connected with Captain Ardale's career?

AUBREY. Yes.

ELLEAN. When he presents himself here to-morrow, of course you will see him and let him defend himself?

AUBREY. Captain Ardale will not be here to-morrow.

ELLEAN. Not! You have stopped his coming here?

AUBREY. Indirectly—yes.

ELLEAN. But just now he was talking to me at that window! Nothing had taken place then! And since then nothing can have—! Oh! Why—you have heard something against him from Paula.

AUBREY. From—Paula!

ELLEAN. She knows him.

AUBREY. She has told you so?

ELLEAN. When I introduced Captain Ardale to her she said she had met him in London. Of course! It is Paula who has done this!

AUBREY. (*In a hard voice*) I—I hope you —you'll refrain from rushing at conclusions. There's nothing to be gained by trying to avoid the main point, which is that you must drive Captain Ardale out of your thoughts. Understand that! You're able to obtain comfort from your religion, aren't you? I'm glad to think that's so. I talk to you in a harsh way, Ellean, but I feel your pain almost as acutely as you do. (*Going to the door*) I—I can't say anything more to you to-night.

ELLEAN. Father! (*He pauses at the door*) Father, I'm obliged to ask you this; there's no help for it—I've no mother to go to. Does what you have heard about Captain Ardale concern the time when he led a wild, a dissolute life in London?

AUBREY. (*Returning to her slowly and staring at her*) Explain yourself!

ELLEAN. He has been quite honest with me. One day—in Paris—he confessed to me —what a man's life is—what his life had been.

AUBREY. (*Under his breath*) Oh!

ELLEAN. He offered to go away, not to approach me again.

AUBREY. And you—you accepted his view of what a man's life is?

ELLEAN. As far as *I* could forgive him, I forgave him.

AUBREY. (*With a groan*) Why, when was it you left us? It hasn't taken you long to get your robe "just a little dusty at the hem!"

ELLEAN. What do you mean?

AUBREY. Hah! A few weeks ago my one great desire was to keep you ignorant of evil.

ELLEAN. Father, it is impossible to be ignorant of evil. Instinct, common instinct, teaches us what is good and bad. Surely I am none the worse for knowing what is wicked and detesting it!

AUBREY. Detesting it! Why, you love this fellow!

ELLEAN. Ah, you don't understand! I have simply judged Captain Ardale as we all pray to be judged. I have lived in imagination through that one week in India when he deliberately offered his life back to God to save those wretched, desperate people. In his whole career I see now nothing but that one week; those few hours bring him nearer the saints, I believe, than fifty uneventful years of mere blamelessness would have done! And so, father, if Paula has reported anything to Captain Ardale's discredit—

AUBREY. Paula—!

ELLEAN. It must be Paula; it can't be anybody else.

AUBREY. You—you'll please keep Paula out of the question. Finally, Ellean, understand me—I have made up my mind.

(*Again going to the door*)

ELLEAN. But wait—listen! I have made up my mind also.

AUBREY. Ah! I recognize your mother in you now!

ELLEAN. You need not speak against my mother because you are angry with me!

AUBREY. I—I hardly know what I'm saying to you. In the morning—in the morning—

(*He goes out. She remains standing, and turns her head to listen. Then, after a moment's hesitation she goes softly to the window, and looks out under the verandah.*)

ELLEAN. (*In a whisper*) Paula! Paula!

(PAULA *appears outside the window and steps into the room; her face is white and drawn, her hair is a little disordered*)

PAULA. (*Huskily*) Well?

ELLEAN. Have you been under the verandah all the while—listening?

PAULA. No—no.

ELLEAN. You *have* overheard us—I see you have. And it *is* you who have been speaking to my father against Captain Ardale. Isn't it? Paula, why don't you own it or deny it?

PAULA. Oh, I—I don't mind owning it; why should I?

ELLEAN. Ah! You seem to have been very, very eager to tell your tale.

PAULA. No, I wasn't eager, Ellean. I'd have given something not to have had to do it. I wasn't eager.

ELLEAN. Not! Oh, I think you might safely have spared us all for a little while.

PAULA. But, Ellean, you forget I—I am your stepmother. It was my—my duty—to tell your father what I—what I knew—

ELLEAN. What you knew! Why, after all, what can you know? You can only speak from gossip, report, hearsay! How is it possible that you—! (*She stops abruptly. The two women stand staring at each other for a moment; then* ELLEAN *backs away from* PAULA *slowly.*) Paula!

PAULA. What—what's the matter?

ELLEAN. You—you knew Captain Ardale in London!

PAULA. Why—what do you mean?

ELLEAN. Oh!

(*She makes for the door, but* PAULA *catches her by the wrist*)

PAULA. You shall tell me what you mean!

ELLEAN. Ah! (*Suddenly, looking fixedly into* PAULA's *face*) You know what I mean.

PAULA. You accuse me!

ELLEAN. It's in your face!

PAULA. (*Hoarsely*) You—you think I'm—that sort of creature, do you?

ELLEAN. Let me go!

PAULA. Answer me! You've always hated me! (*Shaking her*) Out with it!

ELLEAN. You hurt me!

PAULA. You've always hated me! You shall answer me!

ELLEAN. Well, then, I have always—always—

PAULA. What?

ELLEAN. I have always known what you were!

PAULA. Ah! Who—who told you?

ELLEAN. Nobody but yourself. From the first moment I saw you I knew you were altogether unlike the good women I'd left; directly I saw you I knew what my father had done. You've wondered why I've turned from you! There—that's the reason! Oh, but this is a horrible way for the truth to come home to every one! Oh!

PAULA. It's a lie! It's all a lie! (*Forcing* ELLEAN *down upon her knees*) You shall beg my pardon for it. (ELLEAN *utters a loud shriek of terror*) Ellean, I'm a good woman! I swear I am! I've always been a good woman! You dare to say I've ever been anything else! It's a lie!

(*Throwing her off violently*)

(AUBREY *reënters*)

AUBREY. Paula! (PAULA *staggers back as* AUBREY *advances. Raising* ELLEAN.) What's this? What's this?

ELLEAN. (*Faintly*) Nothing. It—it's my fault. Father, I—I don't wish to see Captain Ardale again.

(*She goes out,* AUBREY *slowly following her to the door*)

PAULA. Aubrey, she—she guesses.

AUBREY. Guesses?

PAULA. About me—and Ardale.

AUBREY. About you—and Ardale?

PAULA. She says she suspected my character from the beginning . . . that's why she's always kept me at a distance . . . and now she sees through—

(*She falters; he helps her to the ottoman, where she sits*)

AUBREY. (*Bending over her*) Paula, you must have said something—admitted something—

PAULA. I don't think so. It—it's in my face.

AUBREY. What?

PAULA. She tells me so. She's right! I'm tainted through and through; anybody can see it, anybody can find it out. You said much the same to me to-night.

AUBREY. If she has got this idea into her head we must drive it out, that's all. We must take steps to—What shall we do? We had better—better—What—what?

(*Sitting and staring before him*)

PAULA. Ellean! So meek, so demure! You've often said she reminded you of her mother. Yes, I know now what your first marriage was like.

AUBREY. We must drive this idea out of her head. We'll do something. What shall we do?

PAULA. She's a regular woman, too. She could forgive *him* easily enough—but *me!* That's just a woman!

AUBREY. What *can* we do?

PAULA. Why, nothing! She'd have no difficulty in following up her suspicions. Suspicions! You should have seen how she looked at me! (*He buries his head in his hands. There is silence for a time, then she rises slowly, and goes and sits beside him.*) Aubrey.

AUBREY. Yes.

PAULA. I'm very sorry.

(*Without meeting her eyes, he lays his hand on her arm for a moment*)

AUBREY. Well, we must look things straight in the face. (*Glancing around*) At any rate, we've done with this.

PAULA. I suppose so. (*After a brief pause*) Of course, she and I can't live under the same roof any more. You know she kissed me to-night, of her own accord.

AUBREY. I asked her to alter towards you.

PAULA. That was it, then.

AUBREY. I—I'm sorry I sent her away.

PAULA. It was my fault; I made it necessary.

AUBREY. Perhaps now she'll propose to return to the convent—well, she must.

PAULA. Would you like to keep her with you and—and leave me?

AUBREY. Paula—!

PAULA. You needn't be afraid I'd go back to—what I was. I couldn't.

AUBREY. S—sh, for God's sake! We—you and I—we'll get out of this place . . . what a fool I was to come here again!

PAULA. You lived here with your first wife!

AUBREY. We'll get out of this place and go abroad again, and begin afresh.

PAULA. Begin afresh?

AUBREY. There's no reason why the future shouldn't be happy for us—no reason that I can see—

PAULA. Aubrey!

AUBREY. Yes.

PAULA. You'll never forget this, you know.

AUBREY. This?

PAULA. To-night, and everything that's led up to it. Our coming here, Ellean, our quarrels—cat and dog!—Mrs. Cortelyon, the Orreyeds, this man! What an everlasting nightmare for you!

AUBREY. Oh, we can forget it, if we choose.

PAULA. That was always your cry. How *can* one do it!

AUBREY. We'll make our calculations solely for the future, talk about the future, think about the future.

PAULA. I believe the future is only the past again, entered through another gate.

AUBREY. That's an awful belief.

PAULA. To-night proves it. You must see now that, do what we will, go where we will, you'll be continually reminded of—what I was. I see it.

AUBREY. You're frightened to-night; meeting this man has frightened you. But that sort of thing isn't likely to recur. The world isn't quite so small as all that.

PAULA. Isn't it! The only great distances it contains are those we carry within ourselves—the distances that separate husbands and wives, for instance. And so it'll be with us. You'll do your best—oh, I know that—you're a good fellow. But circumstances will be too strong for you in the end, mark my words.

AUBREY. Paula—!

PAULA. Of course I'm pretty now—I'm pretty still—and a pretty woman, whatever else she may be, is always—well, endurable. But even now I notice that the lines of my face are getting deeper; so are the hollows about my eyes. Yes, my face is covered with little shadows that usen't to be there. Oh, I know I'm "going off." I hate paint and dye and those messes, but by and by, I shall drift the way of the others; I shan't be able to help myself. And then, some day—perhaps very suddenly, under a queer, fantastic light at night or in the glare of the morning—that horrid, irresistible truth that physical repulsion forces on men and women will come to you, and you'll sicken at me.

AUBREY. I—!

PAULA. You'll see me then, at last, with other people's eyes; you'll see me just as your daughter does now, as all wholesome folks see women like me. And I shall have no weapon to fight with—not one serviceable little bit of prettiness left me to defend myself with! A worn-out creature—broken up, very likely, some time before I ought to be—my hair bright, my eyes dull, my body too thin or too stout, my cheeks raddled and ruddled—a ghost, a wreck, a caricature, a candle that gutters, call such an end what you like! Oh, Aubrey, what shall I be able to say to you then? And this is the future you talk about! I know it—I know it! (*He is still sitting staring forward; she rocks herself to and fro as if in pain*) Oh, Aubrey! Oh! Oh!

AUBREY. Paula—!

(*Trying to comfort her*)

PAULA. Oh, and I wanted so much to sleep to-night! (*Laying her head upon his shoulder. From the distance, in the garden, there comes the sound of* DRUMMLE'S *voice; he is singing as he approaches the house.*) That's Cayley, coming back from The Warren. (*Starting up*) He doesn't know, evidently. I—I won't see him!

(*She goes out quickly.* DRUMMLE'S *voice comes nearer.* AUBREY *rouses himself and snatches up a book from a table, making a pretence of reading.*)

(*After a moment or two,* DRUMMLE *appears at the window and looks in*)

DRUMMLE. Aha! my dear chap!

AUBREY. Cayley?

DRUMMLE. (*Coming into the room*) I went down to The Warren after you.

AUBREY. Yes?

DRUMMLE. Missed you. Well—I've been gossiping with Mrs. Cortelyon. Confound you, I've heard the news!

AUBREY. What have you heard?

DRUMMLE. What have I heard! Why—Ellean and young Ardale! (*Looking at* AUBREY *keenly*) My dear Aubrey! Alice is under the impression that you are inclined to look on the affair favorably.

AUBREY. (*Rising and advancing to* DRUMMLE) You've not—met—Captain Ardale?

DRUMMLE. No. Why do you ask? By the by, I don't know that I need tell you—but it's rather strange. He's not at The Warren to-night.

AUBREY. No?

DRUMMLE. He left the house half an hour ago, to stroll about the lanes; just now a note came from him, a scribble in pencil simply telling Alice that she would receive a letter from him to-morrow. What's the matter? There's nothing very wrong, is there? My dear chap, pray forgive me, if I'm asking too much.

AUBREY. Cayley, you—you urged me to send her away!

DRUMMLE. Ellean! Yes, yes. But—but—by all accounts this is quite an eligible young fellow. Alice has been giving me the history—

AUBREY. Curse him! (*Hurling his book to the floor*) Curse him! Yes, I do curse him—him and his class! Perhaps I curse myself, too, in doing it. He has only led "a man's life"—just as I, how many of us have done! The misery he has brought on me and mine it's likely enough we, in our time, have helped to bring on others by this leading "a man's life"! But I do curse him for all that. My God, *I've* nothing more to fear—I've paid *my* fine! And so I can curse him in safety. Curse him! Curse him!

DRUMMLE. In Heaven's name, tell me what's happened?

AUBREY. (*Gripping* DRUMMLE'S *arm*) Paula! Paula!

DRUMMLE. What?

AUBREY. They met to-night here. They—they—they're not strangers to each other.

DRUMMLE. Aubrey!

AUBREY. Curse him! My poor, wretched wife! My poor, wretched wife!

(*The door opens and* ELLEAN *appears. The two men turn to her. There is a moment's silence.*)

ELLEAN. Father . . . father . . . !

AUBREY. Ellean?

ELLEAN. I—I want you. (*He goes to her*) Father . . . go to Paula! (*He looks into her face, startled*) Quickly—quickly! (*He passes her to go out; she seizes his arm, with a cry*) No, no; don't go!

(*He shakes her off and goes.* ELLEAN *staggers back towards* DRUMMLE.)

DRUMMLE. (*To* ELLEAN) What do you mean? What do you mean?

ELLEAN. I—I went to her room—to tell her I was sorry for something I had said to her. And I *was* sorry—I *was* sorry. I heard the fall. I—I've seen her. It's horrible.

DRUMMLE. She—she has—!

ELLEAN. Killed—herself? Yes—yes. So, everybody will say. But I know—I helped to kill her. If I'd only been merciful!

(*She faints upon the ottoman. He pauses for a moment irresolutely—then he goes to the door, opens it, and stands looking out.*)

Bibliography

Each of the following book lists is divided into two parts:
(A) standard works of reference; (B) books for the general reader.

I

BOOKS ON THE GENERAL DEVELOPMENT OF DRAMA

A

Mantzius, Karl, *A History of Theatrical Art*. 6 vols. Translated by L. von Cossel. London, 1903-21.

B

Baker, George Pierce, *Dramatic Technique*. Boston, 1919.
Cheney, Sheldon, *The Theatre: Three Thousand Years of Drama, Acting, and Stagecraft*. New York, 1929.
Clark, Barrett H., *European Theories of the Drama*. New York, 1929.
Gassner, John, *Masters of the Drama*. New York, 1940.
Millett, F. B., and Bentley, G. E., *The Art of the Drama*. New York, 1935.
Nicoll, Allardyce, *The Development of the Theatre*. London, 1937.
———, *The Theory of Drama*. London, 1931.
Simonson, Lee, *The Stage Is Set*. New York, 1932.

II

BOOKS ON THE DEVELOPMENT OF ENGLISH DRAMA

B

Downer, Alan S., *The British Drama: A Handbook and Brief Chronicle*. New York, 1950.
Nicoll, Allardyce, *British Drama: An Historical Survey*. New York, 1933.
———, *The English Theatre: A Short History*. London, 1936.
Thorndike, A. H., *English Comedy*. New York, 1929.
———, *Tragedy*. New York, Boston, 1908.

III

MEDIEVAL DRAMA

A

Chambers, E. K., *The English Folk-Play*. Oxford, 1933.
———, *The Mediæval Stage*. 2 vols. Oxford, 1903.
Young, Karl, *The Drama of the Medieval Church*. 2 vols. Oxford, 1933.

B

Bates, Katherine Lee, *The English Religious Drama*. New York, 1893.
Pollard, Alfred W., *English Miracle Plays, Moralities and Interludes*. Oxford, 1927.
Rossiter, A. P., *English Drama from Early Times to the Elizabethans*. London, 1950.

IV

RENAISSANCE DRAMA

A

Bentley, G. E., *The Jacobean and Caroline Stage*. 2 vols. Oxford, 1941-.
Chambers, E. K., *The Elizabethan Stage*. 4 vols. Oxford, 1923.
Greg, W. W., *A Bibliography of the English Printed Drama to the Restoration*. Vol. I (to 1616). London, 1939-.
Schelling, F. E., *Elizabethan Drama, 1556-1642*. 2 vols. Boston, 1908.

B

Boas, F. S., *An Introduction to Tudor Drama*. Oxford, 1933.
———, *An Introduction to Stuart Drama*. Oxford, 1946.
Bowers, F. T., *Elizabethan Revenge Tragedy, 1587-1642*. Princeton, 1940.
Brooke, C. F. Tucker, *The Tudor Drama*. Boston, 1911.
Ellis-Fermor, Una, *The Jacobean Drama: An Interpretation*. London, 1936.
Harrison, G. B., *The Story of Elizabethan Drama*. Cambridge, 1924.
Parrott, T. M., and Ball, R. H., *A Short View of Elizabethan Drama*. New York, 1943.

V

RESTORATION DRAMA

A

Nicoll, Allardyce, *A History of Restoration Drama, 1660-1700*. Cambridge, 1928.
Summers, Montague, *The Playhouse of Pepys*. London, 1935.
———, *The Restoration Theatre*. London, 1934.

B

Dobrée, Bonamy, *Restoration Comedy, 1660-1720*. Oxford, 1924.
———, *Restoration Tragedy, 1660-1720*. Oxford, 1929.
Krutch, Joseph Wood, *Comedy and Conscience after the Restoration*. New York, 1949.
Lynch, K. M., *The Social Mode of Restoration Comedy*. New York, 1926.

VI

EIGHTEENTH CENTURY DRAMA

A

Genest, John, *Some Account of the English Stage from the Restoration in 1660 to 1830*. 10 vols. Bath, 1832.
Nicoll, Allardyce, *A History of Early Eighteenth Century Drama, 1700-1750*. Cambridge, 2nd ed., 1929.
———, *A History of Late Eighteenth Century Drama, 1750-1800*. Cambridge, 1927.

B

Bateson, F. W., *English Comic Drama, 1700-1750*. Oxford, 1929.
Bernbaum, Ernest, *The Drama of Sensibility*. Boston, 1915.
Krutch, Joseph Wood, *Comedy and Conscience after the Restoration*. New York, 1949.
Nettleton, G. H., *English Drama of the Restoration and Eighteenth Century (1642-1780)*. New York, 1914.

VII

NINETEENTH CENTURY DRAMA

A

Nicoll, Allardyce, *A History of Early Nineteenth Century Drama, 1800-1850*. 2 vols. Cambridge, 1930.
———, *A History of Late Nineteenth Century Drama, 1850-1900*. 2 vols. Cambridge, 1946.

B

Jones, H. A., *The Renascence of the English Drama*. New York, 1895.
Reynolds, Ernest, *Early Victorian Drama (1830-1870)*. Cambridge, 1936.
Watson, Ernest Bradlee, *Sheridan to Robertson: A Study of the Nineteenth-Century London Stage*. Cambridge, Mass., 1926.

This book may be kept

FOURTEEN DAYS

A fine will be charged for each day the book is kept overtime.

APR 2			
3/10			
3/28·04			
GAYLORD 142			PRINTED IN U.S.A.